A HISTORY OF
CHINESE PHILOSOPHY

中國哲學史

馮友蘭

A HISTORY OF
CHINESE PHILOSOPHY

Vol. II

THE PERIOD OF CLASSICAL LEARNING
(FROM THE SECOND CENTURY B.C. TO THE TWENTIETH CENTURY A.D.)

BY

FUNG YU-LAN

Translated by
DERK BODDE

With introduction, notes, bibliography and index

PRINCETON
PRINCETON UNIVERSITY PRESS
1953

First published 1953

This second volume of Fung Yu-lan's
History was first published in Chinese by
the Commercial Press, Shanghai, in 1934.
This English translation is published by
arrangement with the author and with
Henri Vetch, Peking, the original publisher
of Derk Bodde's translation of Volume I.

Publication of this volume has been aided
by a grant from the Bollingen Foundation.

Fourth Printing 1966

PRINTED IN THE UNITED STATES OF AMERICA

TABLE OF CONTENTS

DIAGRAMS AND TABLES

TRANSLATOR'S PREFACE

This is a translation of the second and final volume of the *Chung-kuo Che-hsüeh Shih* 中國哲學史 (History of Chinese Philosophy), by Fung Yu-lan 馮友蘭, Professor of Philosophy, National Tsing Hua University, Peking (formerly Peiping). Following the publication of the original Chinese edition by the Commercial Press, Shanghai, in 1934, my translation of the first volume was published in Peiping by Henri Vetch in 1937. This volume, long almost unobtainable outside of China, is now being republished by the Princeton University Press, together with the present volume.

Whereas the period of Chinese philosophy covered by the earlier volume is comparatively well known to Western scholars, that of the present volume is largely terra incognita. Only a handful of its many thinkers have, in fact, previously been adequately studied in Western languages. This is particularly true of those discussed in the lengthy section on Buddhism. Thus the appearance of the present volume for the first time makes available to the Western world a really competent study of its subject. In English, the only previous work of similar scope is Fung Yu-lan's own *Short History of Chinese Philosophy*, [1] which, however, does not pretend to be more than a good, but brief and semi-popular, introduction. Alfred Forke's three-volume opus in German [2] falls into a different category. On the one hand, it discusses quite a few figures who are not even mentioned in the Fung *History*. On the other, however, its value is greatly diminished by its traditionalist approach to the dating of early texts, its almost total neglect of Chinese Buddhism, and the fact that it is primarily a repertory of scattered persons and ideas, rather than a true *history* of the evolution of Chinese thought.

In this, as in the previous volume, it will be noticed that Dr. Fung, to a large degree, uses the method of direct quotation from the original sources. This not only makes of his work a valuable source-book of Chinese philosophy, but is advantageous because

---

[1] Edited by myself and published by Macmillan in 1948.

[2] *Geschichte der alten chinesischen Philosophie, Geschichte der mittelalterlichen chinesischen Philosophie*, and *Geschichte der neueren chinesischen Philosophie* (Hamburg, 1927, 1934, 1938).

it allows the ancient texts to speak for themselves. For the Western reader, however, it involves the drawback that sometimes a quotation seems sufficiently clear in itself not to require further comment from the author. In this connection it would be well for the reader to keep in mind an important characteristic of the Chinese language: Most of the original quotations are written in a literary or classical style differing radically, both in vocabulary and syntax, from modern colloquial Chinese. Therefore, without Professor Fung's interpretive comments—themselves written in the modern colloquial—such quotations would often be unclear to present-day Chinese readers. In English translation, of course, the need for such interpretation diminishes, since such translation is itself already an interpretation.

My entire translation of Vol. II, as well as that of Vol. I, has been read and approved by Professor Fung, to whom I am much indebted for many valuable suggestions. In translating original quotations, I have tried to be as literal as is consistent with good English style. Classical Chinese, however, is a highly concise language, commonly implying more than it explicitly states. For this reason additional words and phrases, enclosed in parentheses, have often had to be inserted into the translation. Whenever convenient, use has been made of existing Western translations. Comparison with these, however, will show how frequently I have found it advisable to modify their wording—sometimes drastically—for reasons of consistency or greater accuracy.

When translating Professor Fung's own remarks I have exercised greater freedom, being careful, however, not to change his essential meaning. All major alterations have been indicated in the footnotes. Additional information, intended to help the Western reader, has either been inserted directly into the text or provided in the many new footnotes which are marked Tr. The occasional typographical errors found in the Chinese edition, both in its text and its page references, have been corrected in the translation wherever detected but in order to avoid increasing the number of notes no attempt has been made to list them.

This translation of Vol. II embodies major revisions in several of its chapters, especially written for it by Professor Fung in Chinese, as follows:

Chapter V: More than half of the chapter has been rewritten, beginning with p. 169, note 3, and extending through the second paragraph on p. 191. The final one and one-half pages of text in the original Chinese edition have also been omitted.

Chapter VI: The final section has been rewritten, beginning with p. 234 and extending to the end of the chapter. In its present form this now follows the corresponding text in Fung Yu-lan's *Spirit of Chinese Philosophy* (London, 1947), as translated by E. R. Hughes.

Chapter VII: What in the Chinese edition was sect. 1 has been omitted entirely, so that what was there sect. 2 now becomes sect. 1. In the present sect. 2, a lengthy closing quotation has been omitted. Most of present sect. 3 has been rewritten so as to follow the corresponding text in *The Spirit of Chinese Philosophy*.

Chapter IX: All of sect. 2, beginning with sub-sect. i, has been rewritten so as to conform with the same work.

Chapter XIII: The page of introduction preceding sect. 1 has been rewritten.

Aside from the foregoing, the present volume, like its predecessor, contains sections not found in the original Chinese edition. These include the Historical Introduction, Chronological Table, Bibliography, and Index. In the Bibliography will be found all works mentioned in the text, with indications of the editions used. The citation of page references has been simplified, as compared with Vol. I, so that what there, for example, might have been cited as *chüan* 1, p. 3, here becomes merely 1.3. The Chinese characters for all persons, titles, places, and terms will be found either in the Bibliography, in the Index, or in the text itself.

To translate philosophy from one Western language into another is no easy task, but the difficulties are increased manyfold when the languages involved differ from each other as widely as do Chinese and English. When, furthermore, the philosophy being translated happens to belong, not to one but to many schools, each having its own style and technical vocabulary, and covering a total span of more than two millennia, the difficulties sometimes become almost insuperable. [1] It would be presumptuous, therefore, to suppose that

---

[1] Buddhist Chinese, for example, uses a vocabulary and syntax so different from those of the usual literary style that even well educated Chinese can hardly read it intelligibly without special study. Another example is that of the discourses between teacher and disciples which appear in Chinese philosophy from the eleventh century onward, and which, being recorded in the colloquial idiom of their own day, differ both from the literary style and from modern colloquial Chinese, thus sometimes creating special difficulties.

I have always been able to achieve the triple goal of accuracy, consistency, and clarity. I have no doubt that other scholars can and will suggest various improvements, all of which will be welcomed.

In the present volume, to a greater extent than in its predecessor, I have tried to translate, rather than merely transliterate, the titles of books, officials, and the like. The major classics, in fact, are almost always referred to by English rather than Chinese title, as are many lesser known works, following their initial citation both in Chinese and in English. In the Bibliography, however, all works are listed under their Chinese titles, with cross references under the English equivalents, when necessary. As in Vol. I, the system of romanization followed is that of Wade-Giles, with one minor exception: all words which in Wade-Giles would be transcribed *i*, are in the present volume consistently transcribed *yi*, whereas in Vol. I this procedure has been followed only when this syllable occurs at the beginning of a proper name.

In the case of philosophical terms I have likewise tried, for the most part, to give some sort of English equivalent. I realize very well, however, that such equivalents can often be no more than suggestive, and that in many cases no real "translation" of a given term is possible. A typical case is that of the Confucian word *jen* 仁 , variously rendered by other scholars as "benevolence," "goodness," "perfect virtue," "humanity," etc., and for which in Vol. I I often used the coined term "human-heartedness." Because this term is somewhat bizarre and not too clear in meaning, I have in the present volume, following the suggestion of Professor H. H. Dubs, [1] decided in general to use the simpler word "love."

This, however, raises the possibility of confusion with the everyday Chinese word for love, which is *ai* 愛 . *Ai*, unlike *jen*, includes the idea of sexual love. *Jen* is often loosely used in the sense of general goodness, but more specifically it denotes the *graded* kind of love that should be practiced in the Confucian form of hierarchical society. Inasmuch as the context usually makes it clear that *jen* is the word being used, it is hoped that its new rendition as "love" will create no real ambiguity. It so happens that there are a few passages in which *jen* is actually specifically defined in terms of *ai*.

---

[1] Made in his review of Fung Yu-lan's *Short History of Chinese Philosophy*, in *Journal of the American Oriental Society*, vol. 71 (1951), 90-91.

In such cases I have tried to forestall possibility of confusion between the two by either: (1) translating *jen* as "perfect virtue," rather than "love"; (2) transliterating but not translating it; or (3) translating *ai* as "affection" instead of "love."

The appearance of the present volume has long been delayed, owing primarily to the lack of opportunity for personal contact with the author during the war years. Chapters I, X, and XIII were originally translated and published by me independently as separate articles. [1] Professor Fung's stay at the University of Pennsylvania in 1946-47 as Visiting Professor gave me the opportunity to prepare a few further chapters at that time. The bulk of the translation, however, was carried out during the year 1948-49 spent by me in Peiping as a Research Fellow under the Fulbright Program. Conditions for work were not always ideal, for this was the climactic year when the Chinese Communists came into power. Particularly do I remember the dark days of siege of December 1948 and January 1949, when, with shell explosions and machine-gun fire rattling the windows, I with my family sat during the evenings around a primitive oil lamp, where I tried to render into intelligible English the terms for the eight Buddhist forms of consciousness discussed in Chapter VIII. Meanwhile Professor Fung was working at his university a few miles outside the city upon the revisions mentioned above. It was only weeks later, after the surrender of the city, that we were able to meet once more. [2]

In conclusion, I am happy to express my deep gratitude to those many organizations and individuals who have facilitated the completion of this task. To the Rockefeller Foundation I am indebted for bringing Professor Fung to the United States in 1946-47; to the University of Pennsylvania, for granting the leave of absence which enabled me to resume work with him in China two years later; to my original publisher, Henri Vetch, for authorizing the publication of this volume in America, together with the republication of Vol. I; to the Committee on the Advancement of Research at my university, for its financial grant used for compiling the Index; to Dr. Shen-yu

---

[1] In the *Harvard Journal of Asiatic Studies*, vol. 7 (1942), 1-51 and 89-125; vol. 9 (1947), 195-201. These have been considerably revised before being included in the present volume.

[2] Readers interested in modern China as well as in Chinese philosophy will find an account of this year in my *Peking Diary, a Year of Revolution* (N.Y.: Henry Schuman, 1950).

Dai, for skillfully and painstakingly performing much of this weary task; to my colleague, W. Norman Brown, Professor of Sanskrit, for checking upon the spelling and use of Sanskrit names and terms; to Mr. Joseph En-pao Wang, of the Division of Orientalia, Library of Congress, for looking up certain bibliographical data; and to the printers, E. J. Brill, for their great care in handling a difficult manuscript.

Above all, however, my profound thanks are due to three organizations: the Fulbright Program, and especially its administrators in China, who under extraordinarily difficult political and military conditions enabled me to complete my year in China; the Princeton University Press, headed by its cooperative and imaginative director, Datus C. Smith, Jr.; the Bollingen Foundation, which, at a time when foundations are increasingly reluctant to support scholarly publication, has granted the very substantial subvention making possible the appearance of this volume.

February 19, 1953   DERK BODDE
Philadelphia, Pa.

HISTORICAL INTRODUCTION

BY THE TRANSLATOR

Chronology of Chinese History

See also the Chronological Table of the Period of Classical Learning on pp. 722-725. Dates prior to 841 B.C. are those traditionally given, and may be as much as a century in error.

Pre-dynastic

A series of legendary sage-rulers and culture heroes, variously enumerated in different sources, and sometimes collectively referred to as the Three Sovereigns (*san huang*) and Five Emperors (*wu ti*). Notable among them are Fu Hsi (Subduer of Animals), Shen Nung (the Divine Farmer), Huang-ti (the Yellow Emperor), Yao, and Shun.

Hsia dynasty (2205?-1766? B.C.)

Founded by the Great Yü, who really belongs with the foregoing sages, and who is famous for having saved China from a terrible flood which had ravaged it for nine years.

Shang or Yin dynasty (1765?-1123? B.C.)

The first dynasty the historicity of which has been confirmed by archaeological findings, including written records.

Chou dynasty (1122?-256 B.C.)

Founded and consolidated by Kings Wen and Wu and the Duke of Chou, all political heroes of Confucianism.

Ch'un Ch'iu or Spring and Autumn period (722-481)

With the decay of the Chou royal power, several of the leading feudal lords tried to maintain interstate order by assuming the title of *Pa* ("Lord-protector" or "Tyrant," in the Greek sense). Confucius (551-479)

Warring States period (403-221)

The golden age of early Chinese philosophy.

Ch'in dynasty (255-207 B.C.)

In 221 B.C. all China was first united into a non-feudal centralized empire. Burning of Books, 213 B.C.

Han dynasty (206 B.C.-A.D. 220)
> Former Han (206 B.C.-A.D. 24)
>> Wang Mang usurps throne, A.D. 9-23
> Later Han (A.D. 25-220)

Period of Disunity (A.D. 221-589)

> A modern coined term for a period of many short-lived dynasties and states, among which those most commonly mentioned in the present volume are

> Wei (220-265) and
> Chin (265-419)

Sui dynasty (590-617)

T'ang dynasty (618-906)

Five Dynasties (907-959)

Sung dynasty (960-1279)
> Northern Sung (960-1126)
> Southern Sung (1127-1279)

Yüan (Mongol) dynasty (1280-1367)

Ming dynasty (1368-1643)

Ch'ing (Manchu) dynasty (1644-1911)

Republic (1912-   )

The history of Chinese philosophy has been divided by Professor Fung into two main phases: that of the Period of the Philosophers (inaugurated by Confucius in the sixth century B.C. and ending ca. 100 B.C.), and that of the Period of Classical Learning (late second century B.C. to early twentieth century A.D.). As these dates indicate, there is a slight overlap between the two periods. Culturally, the major distinction between them is that the Period of the Philosophers was characterized by the existence of many rival schools of thought, none orthodox until Confucianism achieved this position at the very end of the period. The Period of Classical Learning, on the other hand, had but three major schools: those of Confucianism, Taoism, and Buddhism (themselves subdivided, to be sure, into many lesser divisions). This ideological distinction is a reflection of the political differences between the two periods: During most of the Period of the Philosophers, China was divided into many independent and mutually hostile states. In 221 B.C., however, the age of Chinese feudalism was brought to an end when the state of Ch'in conquered the last of its rivals and created a unified empire, governed by a centrally appointed bureaucracy in place of the former hereditary landed nobility. The political pattern thus instituted was to remain the ideal, if not always the actual practice, of all later dynasties.

Han dynasty (206 B.C.-A.D. 220)

For further details about the political background of the Period of the Philosophers, the reader should consult the Historical Introduction to Vol. I of the present work. Under the Han—one of the greatest of all Chinese dynasties—the political unification begun by the Ch'in was continued, and the boundaries of the empire were extended to embrace most of present China proper as well as Chinese Turkistan. This consolidation was maintained despite the temporary interregnum of Wang Mang's usurpation (A.D. 9-23), and the resulting division of the dynasty into the Former or Western Han (206 B.C.-A.D. 24) and the Later or Eastern Han (A.D. 25-220).

In the world of thought, Confucianism became the state orthodoxy—a Confucianism, however, radically changed from early Confucianism by its absorption of ideas from other schools of thought, notably the *Yin-yang* school. The resulting ideology, known as the New Text school, is best represented by Tung Chung-shu (179?-104? B.C.), who is the subject of Chapter II of the present volume. Somewhat more grotesque examples of the same syncretistic tendency are provided by the apocryphal writings and numerological speculations appearing during the first century B.C., which are described in Chapter III. Toward the end of the Former Han period, the excesses of the New Text school led to a rationalistic reaction— also Confucian—known as the Old Text school. This school, exemplified by Yang Hsiung (53 B.C.-A.D. 18) and Wang Ch'ung (A.D. 27-ca. 100), is discussed in Chapter IV.

Period of Disunity (A.D. 190/221-589)

Like the contemporary Roman Empire, the empire of Han finally collapsed, officially in 220, though in actual fact the year 190 marks the end of unified rule. During the next four centuries China was divided into a large number of short-lived states and dynasties, no one of which succeeded in more than momentarily imposing its power over the entire country. Among them, those most commonly mentioned in the present volume are the Wei (220-265) and Chin (265-419), but the period as a whole may most conveniently be referred to by its modern coined appellation, that of Period of Disunity. Beginning in the early fourth century, the North was ruled by a series of non-Chinese Tatar peoples who invaded China from the steppe lands, while a series of native Chinese dynasties held out in the South, usually with their capitals at Nanking. The period was one of great political and social instability, sharp economic decline, and intense suffering for large numbers of people. Yet though in some ways it represents a throwback to the pre-Ch'in epoch of Chinese feudalism, the concept and institutions of political unity instituted by the Ch'in and Han were never forgotten or wholly abandoned.

It is not surprising that this age witnessed the eclipse of Confucianism—which had by now become primarily the ideology of the ruling civilian bureaucracy—and that the best minds of the time turned first to Taoism (during the third century) and then to Buddhism (during the fourth and following centuries). The movement known as Neo-Taoism, headed by men like Wang Pi (226-249), Hsiang Hsiu (ca. 221-ca. 300), and Kuo Hsiang (died 312), is treated in Chapters V and VI. Buddhism (which had reached China from India early in the first century A.D.) is the subject of Chapter VII, where we are told about the philosophy of the monks Hui-yüan (334-416), Seng-chao (384-414), and Tao-sheng (ca. 360-434), as well as the first organized schools in Chinese Buddhism, known as the "Six Houses" and "Seven Schools."

Sui (590-617) and T'ang (618-906) dynasties

The long centuries of China's "dark ages" were brought to an end by the Sui and T'ang dynasties, which reconstituted a powerful centralized empire, and firmly established the famous Chinese examination system as the chief instrument for recruiting its ruling bureaucracy—the beginnings of which, however, go back to the Han. Under the T'ang, it is not improbable that China politically and economically, as well as in some ways culturally, was the leading country of the world. Chinese Buddhism reached its apogee during this dynasty, and in Chapters VIII and IX we are given an account of its major schools: the Three-Treatise school of Chi-tsang (549-623), the Mere Ideation school of Hsüan-tsang (596-664), the Hua-yen school of Fa-tsang (643-712), the T'ien-t'ai school of Chih-k'ai (538-597) and his followers, and the Ch'an (or Zen) school of Hui-neng (638-713) and his followers.

In the ninth century, however, intellectual interest began to move away from Buddhism and back to Confucianism, thus inaugurating the movement which by modern scholars is commonly termed Neo-Confucianism. The deep influence, both of Taoism and Buddhism, upon this new kind of Confucianism, made of it something profoundly different from the Confucianism of earlier times. The ways in which this influence operated, and the beginnings of the movement as exemplified by Han Yü (768-824) and Li Ao (died ca. 844), are discussed in Chapter X.

Sung dynasty (960-1279)

The Sung, which succeeded the T'ang after the fifty-year interlude of warlord rule known as the **Five Dynasties** (907-959), was politically far weaker than its predecessor. Much of its energy was devoted to a losing struggle against a series of northern non-Chinese invaders, among whom the Mongols were the last and most formidable. In 1127, as a result, the government was forced to abandon North China entirely and shift its capital to Hangchow in the south. This event marks the division between the Northern and Southern Sung periods.

Culturally, however, the Sung stands on a par with the Han and T'ang. In philosophy, the stage was dominated by the meteoric rise of Neo-Confucianism. Chapters XI and XII describe the earlier figures in this movement: Chou Tun-yi (1017-73), Shao Yung (1011-77), Chang Tsai (1020-77), and the Ch'eng brothers, Ch'eng Hao (1032-85) and Ch'eng Yi (1033-1108). Chapter XIII deals exclusively with Chu Hsi (1130-1200), the greatest synthesizer in the history of Chinese thought, whose particular brand of Neo-Confucianism, known as Rationalism, remained *the* major orthodoxy from his death until recent decades.

Yüan dynasty (1280-1367)

Under this dynasty all of China fell for the first time under alien rule, that of the Mongols. Though politically important, however, it produced little of philosophical interest.

Ming dynasty (1368-1643)

This dynasty succeeded in expelling the Mongols and restoring

China to Chinese rule. It was a prosperous and reasonably stable period, but culturally less creative than the major dynasties of the past. In the field of thought, the Rationalism of Chu Hsi remained dominant. Of chief interest, however, was the rise of a rival school within Neo-Confucianism—that of Idealism. This school, which had started in the Sung with Chu's contemporary, Lu Chiu-yüan (1139-93), reached its climax during the Ming with Wang Shou-jen (1472-1529). It is the subject of Chapter XIV.

Ch'ing dynasty (1644-1911)

Under the Ch'ing, all China fell once more under alien rule, this time that of the Manchus. The first half of the dynasty, nonetheless, saw China reach its peak of political and economic glory. Culturally, major advances were made in the field of humanistic scholarship, dominated by a movement known as the Han Learning. Philosophically, this movement took the form of a sharp reaction against the Sung and Ming Neo-Confucianism. Because, however, it continued to concentrate upon the problems which had been of central importance during these dynasties, Professor Fung prefers to regard it as a continuation of Neo-Confucianism rather than as an entirely new school. Its leaders, Yen Yüan (1635-1704), Li Kung (1659-1746), and Tai Chen (1723-77), are discussed in Chapter XV.

During the nineteenth century the Ch'ing dynasty rapidly declined under the twin forces of internal decay and of growing political and economic pressure from the West. The climax was reached in 1911, when revolution drove the Manchus from the throne and established the Chinese **Republic** (1912-   ). In the world of thought, this Western impact, combining with indigenous factors, brought about the first major break with Neo-Confucianism. This took the form of an attempt by several scholar-statesmen, themselves influenced by Western thought, to found a new state ideology which would strengthen China against the West and create a basis for social and political reform. Their efforts led to a revival in modified form of the New Text school version of Confucianism which had lain dormant ever since the Han dynasty. The leaders in this movement included K'ang Yu-wei (1858-1927), T'an Ssŭ-t'ung (1865-98), and Liao P'ing (1852-1932). Their philosophy is described in Chapter XVI.

Their failure demonstrated the growing impossibility of trying to absorb the ever-increasing flow of new ideas by merely superficially grafting them upon the traditional systems of Chinese thought. Thus Liao P'ing's death in 1932 marks the logical conclusion of the Period of Classical Learning—a period which, curiously enough, had opened with the New Text school in the second century B.C., and was to end with the revival of this same school some two thousand years later.

A HISTORY OF
CHINESE PHILOSOPHY

CHAPTER I

A GENERAL DISCUSSION OF THE PERIOD OF CLASSICAL LEARNING

Historians of Western philosophy usually divide their subject chronologically into the three periods of ancient, medieval, and modern. This is no mere arbitrary division, for the philosophies of these three periods have, in fact, each their own individual spirit and character. Chinese philosophy, similarly, if considered purely from the point of view of time, may be divided into the same three periods. Their names, indeed, have already been used in the present work. From another point of view, nevertheless, it may be said that China has actually had only an ancient and a medieval philosophy, but still lacks a modern one.

This does not mean that China in modern times has had no philosophy. It does point, however, to an important difference between China and the West. The medieval and modern philosophy of the West are distinguished, quite aside from their obvious temporal differences, by very evident differences in spirit and character. Thus the systems established by such men as Plato and Aristotle became the central core of the ancient philosophies, and even with the coming of medieval philosophy, many persons continued to center themselves around these old systems. At the same time, to be sure, new elements appeared, such as the Christian view of the universe and of man, coincident with which, the medieval philosophers inevitably advanced new views of their own. Despite their newness, however, these elements and views all continued to conform to the ancient philosophical systems, and to be expressed in the ancient philosophical terminology. The saying that new wine cannot be poured into old bottles is applicable here. Thus despite the fact that Western medieval philosophy did not wholly lack new wine, it nevertheless remained possible for this new wine, either because it was small in quantity, or because, after all, it was not very new, to continue to be poured into and successfully stored within the bottles of classical philosophy.

In modern times, on the other hand, man's thinking in the West has undergone a complete transformation, and modern philosophers, much more than before, have attempted to make direct observations of facts. Their philosophy, as a consequence, has stripped itself of the old supports, while their terminology is also, in large part, newly coined. In modern times, in other words, the new wine has become so abundant and so new that it can no longer be contained in the old bottles; the old bottles, as a consequence, have burst, and new bottles have taken their place. This is the reason why I say of Western medieval and modern philosophy that, quite aside from their temporal differences, they also display very evident differences in spirit.

In Volume I of the present work, the age extending from Confucius (551-479 B.C.) to the Prince of Huai-nan (died 122 B.C.) has been referred to as the Period of the Philosophers, whereas that from Tung Chung-shu (179?-104? B.C.) to K'ang Yu-wei (A.D. 1858-1927) has been described as the Period of Classical Learning. [1] In order to gain a hearing for their ideas, the philosophers of this later period, no matter whether these ideas were new or not, were all obliged to attach themselves nominally to one or another of the schools that had flourished during the Period of the Philosophers, and more particularly, to the school of Confucian classicism. Likewise, in order to express their views, they usually had to make use of the terminology belonging to this ancient Period of the Philosophers. [2]

Thus the wine brewed by the philosophers of the Period of Classical Learning, regardless of whether it was new or old, was poured into the old bottles of the ancient philosophy and, for the most part, of Confucian classicism. Only very recently, indeed, have

---

[1] See Vol. 1, p. 403. The Period of the Philosophers (*tzŭ-hsüeh shih-tai* 子 學 時 伐) is so named by the author because of the many thinkers who flourished simultaneously during this time with no one of them being deemed orthodox. The Period of Classical Learning (*ching-hsüeh shih-tai* 經 學 時 伐), which might also be called the Period of Scholasticism, is so named because, after Confucianism became orthodox around 100 B.C., most philosophical development, as we shall see, centered around the interpretation either of the Confucian classics, of the Taoist classics, or, in the case of Buddhism, of the Buddhist scriptures. — Tr.

[2] In both Occidental and Chinese medieval philosophy, to be sure, it was possible to continue using the ancient terminology, while, at the same time, attaching to it new concepts. The appearance of such new concepts in medieval philosophy, however, without the development of corresponding new terms to express them, is but another example of the new wine that continues to be poured into old bottles.

these old bottles been broken. From this point of view, therefore, it may be said of Chinese philosophy that the whole period from Tung Chung-shu to K'ang Yu-wei has been that of medieval philosophy, while a modern philosophy still remains only in its budding stage.

All human thought, of course, is affected by the limitations imposed by its material and spiritual environment. Thus in the case of China, the crumbling of feudalism during the "Spring and Autumn" (722-481 B.C.) and Warring States (403-221 B.C.) periods resulted in fundamental political, economic, and social changes. Later, however, with the political unification that took place under the Ch'in (255-207 B.C.) and Han (206 B.C.-A.D. 220) dynasties, a corresponding crystallization also occurred in the economic and social orders. From this time onward, despite the frequent change of dynasties, there were no fundamental changes in the political, economic, and social spheres. In all these fields past achievements were merely preserved, so that there was less opportunity than before for new developments in human environment and experience. And with this crystallization, a corresponding phenomenon occurred in the realm of thought which, in contrast to its broadness and diversity during the preceding period, inevitably tended from the Han dynasty onward to lean conservatively upon the past.

During this Period of Classical Learning, nevertheless, Chinese thought did receive a wholly new element from the outside: that of the alien faith of Buddhism. Yet this Buddhism, too, as preached in China, was essentially medieval in spirit. This was because the Chinese Buddhists, regardless of the originality of their ideas, all tended to depend upon earlier Buddhist doctrines for the expression of their views. In so doing, moreover, they generally made use of the technical terms that had already been employed in the Buddhist scriptures (*sūtras*). Chinese Buddhism, as a consequence, may also be termed a sort of "classical learning," even though the classics it depended upon were the Buddhist *sūtras* rather than the "Six Disciplines" of the Confucian school.

Buddhism, as developed in China, nevertheless supplied a definitely new element to Chinese thought, which the Neo-Confucianists of the Sung (960-1279) and Ming (1368-1643) dynasties even incorporated into their expositions of the Confucian classics. Therefore to say that China lacks a modern philosophy does not mean that in medieval and modern times new elements have been wholly lacking, nor that the philosophers of these periods have wholly lacked new vision. The course of history never permits men to continue living under completely unchanging conditions. Thus, from the Han dynasty onward, those men who have expounded the philosophies of Confucius, the *Lao-tzŭ*, Chuang Tzŭ, and the other ancient philosophers, have indubitably been clearer and more perspicacious in their lines of reasoning than were these philosophers themselves, and the data on which their reasoning has rested have been more abundant and rich. Many new interpretations, too, have been propounded. What was said in the first volume of this work (pp. 4-5), that history means progress, may still quite appropriately be applied here. The new views thus presented by these men became the new wine of the Han dynasty onward.

Because, however, this new wine was not overly abundant or was not, after all, very new, it continued to be successfully contained within the bottles of the ancient philosophy, and even, for the most part, of the study of the ancient classics. Moreover, being extremely elastic, these old bottles were able to expand when they became filled by so much new wine that they could no longer contain it within their original compass. Thus the Chinese classics, which had been six in number, gradually increased to thirteen. Similarly, the four little works known as the *Lun Yü* or *Analects*, the *Mencius*, the *Ta Hsüeh* or *Great Learning*, and the *Chung Yung* or *Doctrine of the Mean*, eventually, owing to the stress laid on them by the Sung Confucianists, became the established basis of Chinese education under the title of the "Four Books." As such they enjoyed a prestige greater even than that originally held by the "Six Disciplines" during the Han dynasty.

A similar phenomenon occurred in the case of Buddhism, in which, as expounded by the Chinese, many new ideas were developed. Thus the great material and spiritual differences between the Chinese and Hindu environments made it quite natural that the former, when they took over Buddhism, should organize it, select from it, and interpret it according to their own Chinese point of view. And in so doing they added new ideas of their own. This, then, is another instance of the brewing of a new wine. Yet because this new wine, too, was not overly abundant or very new, it could still be successfuly poured into the old bottles of Buddhism. Even in the case of the Ch'an or Zen school, which was the most revolutionary and purely Chinese development in Buddhism, its success depended upon its claim to be a separate "esoteric teaching," meaning by this that it pretended to go back to the true teaching of Buddha. Here again, therefore, it was a case of pouring new wine into old bottles. Hence Chinese Buddhism, like other philosophic developments of the time, remained essentially medieval in spirit while its learning was a sort of classical learning.

The philosophy of medieval and modern times in China, then, must for the most part be found within the scholarly studies made upon the early Confucian classics and the Buddhist *sūtras*. Differences in philosophy have arisen out of differences in the way the study of the classics has been conducted at various times. Conversely, these philosophical differences have resulted in differences of approach at various times toward the study of the classics.

A general characteristic of the several schools of the Han dynasty onward is that each has had its own particular age when it alone was dominant.[1] This phenomenon contrasts with that of the simultaneous flourishing of many schools of thought, characteristic of the Period of the Philosophers. It explains why the first volume of the present work covers only some four hundred-odd years, whereas the second covers over two thousand. Herein lies another difference between the two periods, and one stemming inevitably from their differing political conditions: China's ancient history was marked by the rivalry of many simultaneously active and politically separate feudal states, whereas from the Ch'in and Han dynasties onward a unified empire has been the more general rule.

China, until very recent times, regardless of how we view it, has remained essentially medieval, with the result that in many respects it has failed to keep pace with the West. A modern age, indeed, has been lacking in Chinese history, and philosophy is but one particular aspect of this general situation. We would do well to remember in this connection that what we regard as differences between eastern and western cultures are in many cases actually only differences between a medieval and a modern culture. In the case of China, however, this situation does not derive from any peculiar incapacity of the Chinese to move forward. Rather it results from the fact that changes in human thought and conduct usually conform to the necessities imposed by environment. Once a certain type of thinking has been developed, therefore, men quite naturally cling to it as long as it continues to respond adequately to these environmental necessities. Indeed, even if new ideas are developed from time to time,

[1] See the Chronological Table of the Period of Classical Learning on p. 722. — Tr.

they continue to be superimposed upon the ancient system; as long as the old bottles remain unbroken, the new wine continues to be poured into them. It is only when the environment undergoes great changes, so that the old ways of thought are no longer able to respond to the trends of the time, that new types of thought develop to the point where they can no longer be contained in the old bottles. Thereupon the old bottles are shattered and new bottles are set up to take their place.

Since the beginning of extensive contact between China and the West, just such fundamental changes have been taking place in Chinese government, society, and economics. During the late nineteenth century, however, when Western ideas first became really influential, such reformers as K'ang Yu-wei and his followers continued to superimpose these new ideas on the old system of classical learning, wishing thus to pour this entirely new wine into the old bottles. These, however, had by this time already stretched to their greatest extent, and the new wine was so abundant and new that they were finally shattered. It is only recently, therefore, with this shattering of the old bottles of classicism, that the Period of Classical Learning in Chinese philosophy has reached its conclusion.

CHAPTER II

TUNG CHUNG-SHU AND THE NEW TEXT SCHOOL

1—THE SCHOOL OF YIN AND YANG AND THE NEW TEXT SCHOOL

Translator's Note: The New Text school (*Chin Wen Chia* 今文家),
which was dominant throughout most of the Former Han dynasty (206
B.C.-A.D. 24), gained this name only later in apposition to that of the Old
Text school (*Ku* 古 *Wen Chia*). The latter, as we shall see in Chapter IV,
rose to prominence about the time of Christ and gradually gained pree-
minence during the Later Han dynasty (A.D. 25-220). Its name is derived
from the fact that it based its doctrines on versions of the classics which
supposedly, after centuries of concealment, had come to light in the
first century B.C.; these were therefore written in the archaic and obsolete
script of the Chou dynasty. The New Text school, on the contrary, based
itself on versions which, having been committed to writing during the
Former Han dynasty, were therefore written in the newer form of script
in use at that time. The relative authenticity of these varying versions has
ever since been one of the most hotly debated subjects of Chinese scholarship. The controversy between the two schools, however, was much more
than one of mere textual criticism, for it embraced wide ideological differences as well. Textually speaking, the New Text school's version of the
classics is generally considered more authentic than that of the Old Text
school. Ideologically speaking, however, the New Text school tended
toward various superstitious excesses (such as the belief that Confucius
was a supernatural being) which were shunned by the more rationalistic
and sober minded Old Text school.

In this and subsequent chapters frequent reference will be made to
the *yang* 陽 and *yin* 陰 and the Five Elements (*wu hsing* 五 行). The
yang and *yin* are conceived of as two mutually complementary principles
or forces, of which the *yang* represents masculinity, light, warmth, dryness,
hardness, activity, etc., while the *yin* represents femininity, darkness, cold,
moisture, softness, passivity, etc. All natural phenomena result from the
ceaseless interplay of these two forces. Also conspicuous in Chinese cosmology are the Five Elements, which are earth, wood, metal, fire and
water, and which are regarded as abstract forces rather than as the actual
embodiment of these substances. Each element is believed to follow its
preceding element in a fixed sequence, and hence each period of history
is regarded as having flourished under the aegis of some one particular
element. Extensive correlations are also made, as we shall see, of the
Five Elements with the five directions (four compass points plus the

center), four seasons, five primary colors, five tastes, five notes of the scale, etc.

During the fourth and third centuries B.C. the *Yin-yang* school and the School of Five Elements seem to have existed quite separately from one another (see vol. 1, pp. 159, 383), but during the Han dynasty, in accordance with the eclectic trend of the time, they coalesced. The resulting amalgam was in turn taken over by that particular brand of Confucianism represented by the New Text school.

In the first volume of this *History* it has been pointed out that among the "arts of divination" practiced in antiquity, those of astrology, the almanac and the Five Elements all laid emphasis upon the relationship believed to exist between *T'ien* 天 or "Heaven" (that is to say, the natural universe) and man; it was asserted that a mutual interaction exists between the "Way of Heaven" and human affairs. [1] Later on, in what came to be known as the School of *Yin* and *Yang*, this religious sort of thinking was further developed and given logical form. [2] The *Yin-yang* school, furthermore, at the time when it became a school, seems to have had a tendency to coalesce with a section of the Confucian school. Even Confucius, as a matter of fact, apparently believed in the traditionally transmitted arts of divination. At least we are told that he once lamented: "The phoenix comes not, the river gives forth no chart," after which he added: "It is all over with me!" [3] On another occasion, when threatened with violence by the people of a place called K'uang, he exclaimed: "Since Heaven has not yet destroyed this culture, what can the men of K'uang do to me?" (*Analects*, IX, 5). Thus Confucius seems to have paid serious heed to the relationship believed to exist between Heaven and man.

We also find Ssŭ-ma Ch'ien (ca. 145-ca. 86 B.C.) including Tsou Yen, the leader of the School of Five Elements, in the same 74th chapter of his *Shih Chi* (Historical Records) in which he places the biographies of the Confucian philosophers, Mencius and Hsün Tzŭ. Therein, having described Tsou Yen's doctrines, he comments: "Yet if we reduce them to fundamentals, they all rested on the

---

[1] See vol. 1, pp. 26-30. — Tr.

[2] See vol. 1, chap. 7, sect. 7, esp. pp. 162-166.

[3] *Analects*, VIII, 9. The "phoenix" (*feng-huang*) was a bird of auspicious omen. The "River Chart" (*Ho T'u* 河 圖) was a diagram supposed to have been borne out of the Yellow river on the back of a "dragon horse" during the reign of the legendary Fu Hsi. Some accounts say it contained the delineation of the "eight trigrams" of the *Book of Changes*, whereas according to others it merely contained the data from which Fu Hsi was able to construct them. — Tr.

(Confucian) virtues of love (*jen*), righteousness(*yi*), restraint, frugality, and the practice of the association of ruler with subject, superior with inferior, and the six relationships. It is only the beginning (of his doctrines) which is excessive." [1] This shows that Tsou Yen, though leader of a school which in the Han dynasty came to be known as that of the *yin* and *yang*, nevertheless preached the Confucian teachings. Likewise, the *Hsün-tzŭ* (chap. 6) says of Tzŭ-ssŭ (grandson of Confucius) and of Mencius: "Basing themselves on ancient traditions, they created theories which they called (those of) the Five Elements" (*Aids*, p. 37). This conflicts with the fact that in the present version of the *Mencius* there is nowhere any reference to these Five Elements. The seeming discrepancy would be explained, however, if we accepted the hypothesis that the doctrines of the *Yin-yang* school did not enter the school of Mencius until after Mencius himself had died. Certainly it is a fact that later on, during the Ch'in and Han dynasties, the *yin-yang* doctrines came to be almost completely amalgamated with Confucianism.

Note added by the Author for the English edition: I am now inclined to believe that Hsün Tzŭ's criticism of Tzŭ-ssŭ and Mencius is based on solid fact. Thus in the *Doctrine of the Mean*, a work traditionally ascribed to Tzŭ-ssŭ, we read: "When a nation or family is about to flourish, there are sure to be happy omens; when it is about to perish, there are sure to be unlucky omens" (p. 320). Likewise we read in the *Mencius* (IIb, 13): "In the course of five hundred years, it is inevitable that a (true) king should arise." These prognosticatory statements seem to foreshadow the bent for prognostication characteristic of the *Yin-yang* school during the Han dynasty. I am furthermore inclined to believe that the New Text school of the Han, of which Tung Chung-shu (179?-104? B.C.) was the chief representative, traced its primary descent from that school in Confucianism represented by Mencius. Thus Tung's theory about the *Ch'un Ch'iu* or *Spring and Autumn Annals* (see sect. 12 below) is that of Mencius in an exaggerated form. In the same way, I believe that the Old Text school traced its primary descent from that school in Confucianism represented by Hsün Tzŭ. It, for example, in accordance with Hsün Tzŭ's rationalistic tendencies, avoided giving to the *Ch'un Ch'iu* the emphasis put on that work by the New Text school. It also turned against the more extravagant developments of *yin-yang* ideology characteristic of the New Text school.

Thus during the Former Han dynasty we find the exponents of the Confucian classics all expounding these works in terms of the *yin-yang* ideology; this indeed is the peculiar characteristic of the New

---

[1] See vol. 1, p. 161. — Tr.

Text school of classical learning. So widespread did this ideology become that most men took for granted the idea of a close interrelationship between the "Way of Heaven" and human affairs. Indeed, it became common for Confucianists to interpret unusual natural phenomena in terms of celestial "visitations" and "prodigies," the appearance of which was enough to inspire the Han rulers with dread. [1]

Likewise we know from records of the time that the duties of the "Three Highest Ministers" included, in addition to their normal administrative work, that of "harmonizing the *yin* and *yang*." For example, the statesman Ch'en P'ing (died 179 B.C.) is recorded as once having remarked to Emperor Wen (179-157): "The duty of the prime minister is to assist the Son of Heaven above to regulate the *yin* and *yang*, to cause the four seasons to follow their proper course, and to accord with what is fitting in all things." [2] Again we read that Ping Chi (died 55 B.C.), an important statesman under Emperor Wu (140-87), once happened to encounter an ox on the road that was panting from the heat, whereupon he said: "The Three Highest Ministers act to harmonize the *yin* and *yang*. Just now it is spring, when the lesser *yang* is operative in affairs, so that there should not yet be any great heat. Nevertheless, the ox is panting because of a summer-like heat, which, I fear, means that the seasons are out of joint. There is harm in such a situation." [3]

Thus it was one of the duties of the Three Highest Ministers to watch over the transformations of things in the world of nature; and,

---

[1] The Confucian scholars pointed to such abnormal phenomena as comets, eclipses, fogs, flies, droughts, floods, earthquakes, etc., as celestial warnings to the emperor that something was wrong with his rule. Phenomena of this kind were recorded with particular frequency during the reign of Emperor Ch'eng (33-7 B.C.). See H. H. Dubs, transl., *History of the Former Han Dynasty*, II, 363-365. See also below, sect. 10. — Tr.

[2] See his biography in the *Shih Chi* (56.10). — Tr.

[3] The whole story goes as follows: Once when Ping was traveling, he encountered a crowd of brawlers, some of whom had wounded or killed one another. To the surprise of his entourage he passed them by without stopping. Soon afterward, however, he met a man leading an ox which was panting with protruding tongue. At once he stopped his horse and inquired of the man how many miles he had been traveling. On being criticized by some of his followers for this seeming triviality, he told them that the brawlers could be left to those officials whose particular business it was to deal with such matters; the harmonizing of the *yin* and *yang*, however, was a matter of concern to the highest officials. See his biography in the *Ch'ien Han Shu* (History of the Former Han Dynasty), 74.11-12. —Tr.

when visitations and prodigies occurred, they were held responsible for them. This, which seems a strange idea to us today, was taken for granted by most people of the Former Han dynasty. [1]

2—THE COSMOLOGICAL SYSTEM OF THE YIN-YANG SCHOOL

In order to understand the thought of the Former Han period, one must first have a general idea of the doctrines of the *Yin-yang* school, and especially of its system of cosmology. This system is based on correlations made between the Five Elements, the four compass points (plus the center as a fifth direction), the four seasons, the five notes of the scale, the twelve months, the twelve pitch-pipes, the ten "heavenly stems," the twelve "earthly branches," and various other numerical categories.

Translator's Note: The five notes (*wu yin* 五音) of the usual Chinese scale are those of *kung* 宮, *shang* 商, *chiao* 角, *chih* 徵, and *yü* 羽, corresponding to C, D, E, G and A respectively. Another scale, however, is that of the twelve pitch-pipes (*shih erh lü* 十二律), consisting of a progression of twelve fifths which total exactly one octave and thus comprise the twelve half tones of the untempered chromatic scale. This scale, which is identical with that of Pythagoras, first appeared in China in the third century B.C. and may well have been brought there as a result of the Asiatic conquests of Alexander the Great. See Chavannes, *Mém. hist.*, III, ii, Appen. 2, "Des rapports de la musique grecque avec la musique chinoise," pp. 630-645.

The ten "heavenly stems" (*t'ien kan* 天干) and twelve "earthly branches" (*ti chih* 地支) are as follows:

Stems		Branches	
1. *chia*	甲	1. *tzŭ*	子
2. *yi*	乙	2. *ch'ou*	丑
3. *ping*	丙	3. *yin*	寅
4. *ting*	丁	4. *mao*	卯
5. *wu*	戊	5. *ch'en*	辰
6. *chi*	巳	6. *ssŭ*	巳
7. *keng*	庚	7. *wu*	午

---

[1] Beginning with the words in the third preceding paragraph: "It became common for Confucianists ...," see, for further details, Chao Yi (1727-1814), *Nien-erh Shih Cha-chi* (Notes on Twenty-two Dynastic Histories), *chüan* 2.

	Stems		*Branches*
8. *hsin*	辛	8. *wei*	未
9. *jen*	壬	9. *shen*	申
10. *kuei*	癸	10. *yu*	酉
		11. *hsü*	戌
		12. *hai*	亥

The combination of these cyclical signs in pairs, beginning with *chia-tzŭ* (1 and 1 of each series), and continuing until each stem has been combined with each branch, yields a total of sixty different combinations before *chia-tzŭ*, the first pair, reappears. This cycle was used as early as the Shang dynasty (2nd millenium B.C.) for the dating of days; its use for dating years, however, does not seem to have come before the Han dynasty.

The *yin* and *yang* operate among these various categories, causing transformations to take place and thereby bringing all things of the physical universe into being. Such correlations seem already to have been current in the "arts of divination" as practiced during the Chou dynasty. For example, we have the following passage from the *Mo-tzŭ* (chap. 47):

"When Mo Tzŭ was going north to Ch'i, he met a fortune teller. The fortune teller told him: 'God (*ti* 帝) is today going to kill the black dragon of the north. Your complexion, sir, is black. (Therefore) you must not go north.'... Mo Tzŭ said: 'If, (as you say), southerners should not go north, then northerners should (likewise) not go south. For there are some whose complexions are dark and others whose complexions are fair. But why, for this reason, should they not all (be permitted to) proceed? Furthermore, God kills the green dragon of the east on (the cyclical days) *chia* and *yi*; he kills the red dragon of the south on (the days) *ping* and *ting*; he kills the white dragon of the west on (the days) *keng* and *hsin*; he kills the black dragon of the north on (the days) *jen* and *kuei*; and he kills the yellow dragon of the center on (the days) *wu* and *chi*. [1] If your words were to be followed, this would result in prohibiting all traveling through out the world' " [2] (pp. 228-229).

---

[1] The last clause about the dragon of the center is added by the commentator Pi Yüan (1730-97) from the quotation of this passage found in the *T'ai-p'ing Yü-lan* encyclopedia (completed A.D. 983).

[2] Though it is hardly probable that this passage dates back to Mo Tzŭ himself (ca. 479-ca. 381), it represents the ideas of his follower or followers who after his time inserted it into the work bearing his name. — Tr.

Here we find the following correlations made between the ten "heavenly stems," the five primary colors, and the four compass points (plus the center): *chia* and *yi* with green and east; *ping* and *ting* with red and south; *keng* and *hsin* with white and west; *jen* and *kuei* with black and north; *wu* and *chi* with yellow and the center. Such correlations, as first used among the diviners, did not necessarily form any organized cosmological system. It was on their basis, nevertheless, that the *Yin-yang* School later established its doctrines. Thus in the *Yüeh Ling* or *Monthly Commands* [1] we find correlations of this sort being used as a formal cosmological framework for the *Yin-yang* school.

In this work, as well as in the "Regulations for the Seasons," the title of the fifth chapter of the *Huai-nan-tzŭ* (second century B.C.), the following correlations occur between the Five Elements and four seasons: wood with spring, fire with summer, metal with autumn, water with winter. The difficulty here is that the fifth element, earth, has no corresponding season with which to be matched. The *Monthly Commands* sidesteps this problem by merely stating that earth corresponds to the center, without mentioning any season for it. The *Huai-nan-tzŭ*, however, designates the third month of summer as a special period belonging to the element earth. These two treatises further correlate the Five Elements with the four directions (plus the center), five colors, ten heavenly stems, and five notes of the scale, as follows:

	Element	Direction	Color	Stems			Note
1.	Wood	east	green	*chia*	and	*yi*	*chiao*
2.	Fire	south	red	*ping*	and	*ting*	*chih*
3.	Metal	west	white	*keng*	and	*hsin*	*shang*
4.	Water	north	black	*jen*	and	*kuei*	*yü*
5.	Earth	center	yellow	*wu*	and	*chi*	*kung*

They likewise correlate the twelve months with the twelve pitch-pipes:

1. *Spring*: first month, pitch-pipe *t'ai-ts'ou* 太 簇 ; second month, pitch-pipe *chia-chung* 夾 鐘 ; third month, pitch-pipe *ku-hsien* 姑 洗 .

2. *Summer*: first month, *chung-lü* 中 呂 ; second month, *jui-pin* 蕤 賓 ; third month, *lin-chung* 林 鐘 .

---

[1] Third century B.C. See vol. 1, pp. 163-165. — Tr.

3. *Autumn*: first month, *yi-tse* 夷則 ; second month, *nan-lü* 南呂 ; third month, *wu-yi* 無射.

4. *Winter*: first month, *ying-chung* 應鐘 ; second month, *huang-chung* 黃鐘 ; third month, *ta-lü* 大呂.

And finally, they correlate the Five Elements with the following numbers: wood, 8; fire, 7; earth, 5; metal, 9; water, 6.

Note: The reason why these correlations follow the sequence they do becomes apparent from pertinent passages in the *Hung Fan* or *Grand Norm* section of the *Book of History* and in the *Book of Changes* (Appen. II). The former treatise gives the sequence of the Five Elements as follows: "Of the Five Elements, the first is named water, the second fire, the third wood, the fourth metal, the fifth earth" (p. 140). In the *Book of Changes* (Appen. II, p. 365) we further find that Heaven (which is the concrete manifestation in the physical universe of the *yang*) and Earth (which is the concrete manifestation of the *yin*) are given the following numerical correlations: to Heaven belongs 1, to Earth 2, to Heaven 3, to Earth 4, to Heaven 5, to Earth 6, to Heaven 7, to Earth 8, to Heaven 9, and to Earth again 10. By combining the sequences given in these two passages, we find that Heaven, with its number 1, corresponds to the element water; Earth, with 2, to fire; Heaven, with 3, to wood; Earth, with 4, to metal; Heaven, with 5, to earth; Earth, with 6, again corresponds to water; Heaven, with 7, to fire; Earth, with 8, to wood; Heaven, with 9, to metal; and Earth, with 10, to earth.

In this correlation, the numbers 1, 2, 3, 4 and 5 are those with which the elements water, fire, wood, metal and earth respectively come into being; the numbers 6, 7, 8, 9 and 10 are those with which they respectively attain their completed form. Thus with 1, the number pertaining to Heaven, the element water is produced, and with 6, pertaining to Earth, it reaches full development. Likewise fire is produced with 2 (Earth) and completed with 7 (Heaven); wood is produced with 3 (Heaven) and completed with 8 (Earth); metal is produced with 4 (Earth) and completed with 9 (Heaven); and earth (as an element) is produced with 5 (Heaven) and completed with 10 (Earth). Through these matchings, the *yin* and *yang* (of which, as stated above, Earth and Heaven are the concrete manifestations) give birth and completion to each of the Five Elements in turn. [1]

Acceptance of this sequence, however, and the fitting into it of the four seasons, forces the latter to assume the following unnatural order: winter (water), summer (fire), spring (wood), and autumn (metal). Nowhere is it explained why the sequence of the Five Elements should thus fail to harmonize with the natural order of the seasons.

---

[1] This explanation follows the commentaries of Cheng Hsüan (127-200) and K'ung Ying-ta (574-648) on the *Monthly Commands*, as found in the *Book of Rites*.

In the *Monthly Commands,* no attempt is made to fit the twelve "earthly branches" into this cosmological framework, but elsewhere this correlation has commonly been accepted as *tzŭ* (the first branch) for the eleventh month, *ch'ou* for the twelfth, *yin* for the first, *mao* for the second, *ch'en* for the third, *ssŭ* for the fourth, *wu* for the fifth, *wei* for the sixth, *shen* for the seventh, *yu* for the eighth, *hsŭ* for the ninth, and *hai* for the tenth. This correlation is found, for example, in the third chapter of the *Huai-nan-tzŭ.*

All of the above correlations may be shown more clearly through the following diagram:

Yin-yang School's Correlations of Elements, Seasons, Directions, Colors, Notes, Numbers, and Pitch-Pipes

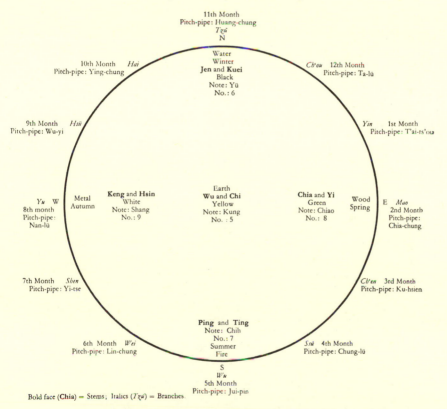

Bold face **(Chia)** = Stems; Italics *(Tzŭ)* = Branches.

It will be noted that the *Monthly Commands* fails to fit the eight trigrams of the *Book of Changes* into this cosmological framework. This is explained by the fact that, prior to the Ch'in dynasty, the theories of the Five Elements and those connected with the eight trigrams seem to have constituted two quite separate systems. [1] In our next chapter we shall see how the eight trigrams came to form a distinct cosmological system of their own. At present, however, we need only deal with the correlations between the *yin* and *yang* and the Five Elements, a clear understanding of which is basic for comprehending many of the theories developed by the thinkers of the Former Han dynasty.

3—TUNG CHUNG-SHU'S POSITION AMONG THE CONFUCIANISTS OF THE FORMER HAN DYNASTY

The spirit and ideology of the Former Han dynasty are well represented by the famous Confucian scholar, Tung Chung-shu 董 仲 舒 (179?-104? B.C.). [2] His biography in the *Ch'ien Han Shu* (History of the Former Han Dynasty) reads in part as follows:

"Tung Chung-shu was a native of Kuang-ch'uan. [3] In his youth he devoted himself to the *Spring and Autumn Annals*, and during the reign of (Emperor) Hsiao-ching (156-141) he became an erudit. [4] He expounded (his teachings) from behind a curtain, and these were transmitted by his disciples, one to another, to a remote distance, so that there were some who never saw his countenance. His spirit (of learning) is shown by the fact that (once) for three years he did not (even) look into his garden. In his conduct, bearing, and manner, there was nothing that did not conform to propriety. Scholars all

---

[1] See vol. 1, p. 383.

[2] These dates, which are not given in the biography of Tung cited below, are those suggested by Su Yü (died 1914), editor of the *Ch'un-ch'iu Fan-lu Yi-cheng*, the best edition of Tung's writings. [There are two important Western works dealing with Tung Chung-shu: Otto Franke's detailed but somewhat uncritical *Studien zur Geschichte des konfuzianischen Dogmas und der chinesischen Staatsreligion...* (Hamburg, 1920), and Woo Kang's more critical but less detailed *Trois théories politiques du Tch'ouen Ts'ieou ...* (Paris, 1932). See also Yao Shan-yu, "The Cosmological and Anthropological Philosophy of Tung Chung-shu," *Journal of the North China Branch of the Royal Asiatic Society*, vol. 73 (1948), 40-68. Franke, pp. 98-99, suggests dates for Tung Chung-shu of 170-90; Woo, pp. 25-28, suggests those of 175-105. — Tr.]

[3] About 10 miles east of the present Tsao-ch'iang 棗 强 hsien in the southern half of Hopei province. — Tr.

[4] *Po shih*, translated as "scholar of wide learning" in vol. 1, pp. 15-16, 404. The term erudit is here used in conformity with the terminology established by H. H. Dubs in his translation, *The History of the Former Han Dynasty*. — Tr.

regarded him as a teacher to be respected .... (Tung) Chung-shu's writings all served to elucidate the meaning of the classics. The items which he submitted to the emperor, together with his own instructions, totaled 123 sections. Moreover, his exposition of the good and bad points of the events (recorded) in the *Spring and Autumn Annals*, including such (writings) as his 'Exaltation of Tradition,' 'Jade Goblet,' 'Luxuriant Dew,' 'Pure Brightness,' and 'Bamboo Grove,' came to several additional tens of sections, amounting to more than 100,000 words. These were all transmitted to later generations" (chap. 56, pp. 1, 23).

Translator's Note: This is only a very brief extract from his lengthy biography. For detailed accounts of his life, see Franke, *op. cit.* pp. 91-98, and Woo, *op. cit.*, pp. 15-33. Tung never held a position of much political importance; part of his life was spent as minister at the courts of two provincial kings. Ideologically, however, his influence was enormous. In vol. 1, pp. 16-17 and 403 f., we have seen the part played by him in gaining official recognition for Confucianism by the Han government. Tung was a prolific writer, but much of what he wrote has been lost. His major surviving work is the *Ch'un-ch'iu Fan-lu* or *Luxuriant Dew of the Spring and Autumn Annals*. Of the compositions mentioned above, the "Jade Goblet" and "Bamboo Grove" are titles of chaps. 2 and 3 of this work; the words "Luxuriant Dew" are part of its own title. The other two titles are no longer extant. A translation of the "Bamboo Grove" has been made by Franke, *op. cit.*, pp. 276-308.

The *Ch'ien Han Shu* concludes its account with the following eulogy:

"Liu Hsiang [1] acclaimed Tung Chung-shu as one whose abilities were those of a minister of kings; even Yi and Lü would have nothing to add to them. [2] ... Hsiang's son, Hsin, regarded ... Chung-shu as one who, living during the Han — (an age) which

---

[1] 79-8 B.C. He was one of the most prominent of the Former Han scholars. Together with his son Hsin (mentioned immediately below; lived ca. 46 B.C.-A.D. 23), he collated the books in the imperial library and prepared an annotated catalogue which is the basis for the invaluable bibliography now contained in *Ch'ien Han Shu*, chap. 30. The dates here given for the two Lius, which differ somewhat from those given in vol. 1, are taken from Charles S. Gardner, *Chinese Traditional Historiography*, pp. 33-35, notes 37 and 38. — Tr.

[2] Yi Yin was the famous minister of the founder of the Shang dynasty; Lü Shang was the virtuous councillor of Kings Wen and Wu, founders of the Chou. — Tr.

had inherited the Ch'in extermination of learning, [1] and during which the Six Classics had become dispersed—put forth his energies from behind his curtain and concentratedly applied his mind to the great task, thus giving to later scholars something whereby they would be unified. He was the leader of all the literati" (*ibid.*, p. 23).

The *Ch'ien Han Shu* also says elsewhere:

"Of old, when the principles of Yin (i.e., the Shang dynasty) lost their hold, King Wen elaborated upon the *Chou Changes*; [2] when the principles of the Chou (dynasty) degenerated, Confucius (likewise) composed the *Spring and Autumn Annals*. [3] (In so doing) he patterned it upon the *yin* and *yang* of *ch'ien* and *k'un*, [4] and modeled it upon the prognostications in the *Grand Norm*. [5] Thus the ways of Heaven and of man were gloriously revealed. When the Han arose, it inherited the Ch'in extermination of learning. But in the days of (Emperors) Ching (156-141) and Wu (140-87), Tung Chung-shu directed himself to the *Kung-yang Ch'un-ch'iu* (Kung-yang's Spring and Autumn Annals), [6] and began to put forward the *yin-yang* (doctrines). He became the chief of the literati" (27a.2).

These passages indicate Tung Chung-shu's dominating position among the Confucian scholars of the Former Han period. The *Ch'un Ch'iu* or *Spring and Autumn Annals*, for example, though already highly regarded by earlier Confucianists, required Tung's

---

[1] The notorious Burning of the Books, carried out in 213 B.C. under the Ch'in dynasty. — Tr.

[2] This refers to the popular tradition that it was King Wen who combined the eight trigrams forming the original corpus of the *Book of Changes*, thus producing the sixty-four hexagrams. The alternate name of *Chou Changes* reflects the belief that this elaboration took place during the Chou dynasty. See vol. 1, pp. 379-380. — Tr.

[3] This tradition, though probably erroneous (see vol. 1, pp. 61-62), was widely accepted by Tung Chung-shu and other adherents of the New Text school, who believed that through the concise phraseology of this historical chronicle Confucius expressed, in veiled language, his moral judgments on the events it recorded. See below, sect. 12. — Tr.

[4] *Ch'ien* is the first and *k'un* the eighth of the eight trigrams. *Ch'ien*, which symbolizes Heaven, is also the graphic representation of the *yang* principle; *k'un*, which symbolizes Earth, also represents the *yin* principle. See vol. 1, pp. 382-383. — Tr.

[5] A section of the *Book of History*, already quoted on p. 14 above. — Tr.

[6] Better known as the *Kung-yang Chuan* (Kung-yang Commentary). It is one of several commentaries on the *Ch'un Ch'iu* which interpret it according to the "praise and blame" theory mentioned in note 3 above. Though perhaps composed earlier, it became prominent only during the Former Han dynasty, partially because of Tung Chung-shu's advocacy. — Tr.

embellishments and interpretations before its alleged "subtle language" and "great meaning" received a systematic exposition. Tung's writings on the *Ch'un Ch'iu*, indeed, are comparable in importance to the Appendices that were being added at about the same time to the original corpus of the *Book of Changes*.

4—Yüan, Heaven, the Yin and Yang, and the Five Elements

"Heaven," in the eyes of Tung Chung-shu, seems at times to be something materialistic, as in the phrase, "Heaven and Earth" (*t'ien ti* 天地), used to denote the physical universe. At other times, however, he seems to mean by it something somewhat akin to the Western concept of "Nature," yet at the same time something that possesses cognition and consciousness. Though these concepts would seem to be mutually exclusive, Tung Chung-shu's Heaven, while possessing cognition and consciousness, is definitely not an anthropomorphic deity. In his *Ch'un-ch'iu Fan-lu* (chap. 81), for example, he writes as follows:

"Heaven, Earth, the *yin and yang*, and wood, fire, earth, metal and water, make nine; together with man, they make ten. Heaven's number is with this made complete." [1]

In this statement, the Heaven of the first sentence is a limited and purely physical Heaven, standing in apposition to a physical Earth. That of the second sentence, on the contrary, is much broader in scope; it is a designation for the entire natural universe, with all its forces and attributes. [2]

Tung Chung-shu further asserts (chap. 4) that for all things in the universe there is that from which they derive their being. This first cause or point of beginning he describes as *Yüan* 元 or Origin:

"What is called the single *Yüan* (Origin) is the great beginning . . . . It is only the sage who is capable of relating the many to the one,

---

[1] See the edition edited by Su Yü, *Ch'un-ch'iu Fan-lu Yi-cheng* (Attested Meaning of the Ch'un-ch'iu Fan-lu), 17.6, to which all further citations in the present chapter refer, unless otherwise noted. [For the sake of simplicity, the numerous textual emendations suggested by Su Yü and adopted by Professor Fung will not be cited in this English translation, as they are easily found in Professor Fung's original Chinese text. — Tr.]

[2] There are some passages, however, in which Tung's Heaven seems to be conceived of semi-anthropomorphically. See, for example, his reference to the "mind" and "feelings" of Heaven at the very end of sect. 5 below. — Tr.

and thus linking them to *Yüan*. . . . This *Yüan* is like a source. [1] Its significance is that it permeates Heaven and Earth from beginning to end . . . . Therefore *Yüan* is the root of all things, and in it lies man's own origin. How does it exist? It exists before Heaven and Earth . . . ." (3.1-2).

Yüan or Origin thus exists before the physical Heaven designated by the phrase, "Heaven and Earth." Since it is also associated with man, this means that man's own origin likewise "exists before Heaven and Earth." Tung Chung-shu fails to indicate, however, whether *Yüan* also gives being to the other broader kind of Heaven of which he speaks — the Heaven which is Nature possessed of consciousness.

Concerning the *yin* and *yang*, Tung writes as follows (chap. 81):

"Within the universe exist the ethers (*ch'i* 氣) of the *yin* and *yang*. Men are constantly immersed in them, just as fish are constantly immersed in water. The difference between them and water is that the turbulence of the latter is visible, whereas that of the former is invisible. Man's existence in the universe, however, is like a fish's attachment to water. Everywhere these ethers are to be found, but they are less viscid than water. For water, compared with them, is like mud compared with water. Thus in the universe there seems to be a nothingness and yet there is substance. Men are constantly immersed in this eddying mass, with which, whether themselves orderly or disorderly, they are carried along in a common current" (17.7-8).

Here the *yin* and *yang* are regarded as two material ethers or fluids. As described by most followers of the *Yin-yang* school, however, as well as by Tung himself in many places, they are not conceived of so materialistically.

Concerning the Five Elements, Tung Chung-shu writes as follows (chap. 42):

"Heaven has Five Elements: the first is wood, the second fire, the third earth, the fourth metal, the fifth water. Wood is the starting point of (the cycle of) the Five Elements, water is its conclusion, and earth its center. Such is their heavenly sequence. Wood produces fire, fire earth, earth metal, metal water, and water wood. Such is

---

[1] There is a play of words here upon *Yüan* (Origin) and *yüan* 原 (source). — Tr.

their father-and-son (relationship). Wood occupies the left, metal the right, fire the van, water the rear, and earth the center. Such is their hierarchy as of father and sons, each receiving from and giving to the other . . . .

"Each of the Five Elements circulates according to its sequence; each of them exercises its own capacities in the performance of its official duties. Thus wood occupies the eastern quarter, where it rules over the forces (*ch'i* 氣) of spring; fire occupies the southern quarter, where it rules over the forces of summer; metal occupies the western quarter, where it rules over the forces of autumn; water occupies the northern quarter, where it rules over the forces of winter. For this reason wood rules over the production of life, while metal rules over its destruction; fire rules over heat, while water rules over cold . . . .

"Earth occupies the center, and is called the heavenly fructifier (*t'ien jun* 天潤). It is the assister of Heaven. Its power is abundant and good, and cannot be assigned to the affairs of a single season only. Therefore among the Five Elements and four seasons, earth embraces all. Although metal, wood, water, and fire each have their own particular duties, they could not stand were it not for earth. The case is like that of saltiness, sourness, acridness, and bitterness, which would be unable to be tastes were they not enriched by savoriness. Just as savoriness is the foundation of the five tastes, so earth is the ruler of the Five Elements. That the Five Elements have earth as their ruler is like the fact that the five tastes cannot but exist when savoriness is present" (11.3-5).

He also says (chap. 58):

"Collected together, the ethers (*ch'i*) of the universe constitute a unity; divided, they constitute the *yin* and *yang*; quartered, they constitute the four seasons; (still further) sundered, they constitute the Five Elements. These elements (*hsing*) represent movement (*hsing*). Their movements are not identical. Therefore they are referred to as the Five Movers. [1] These Five Movers constitute five

---

[1] *Wu hsing* 五行, the term ordinarily translated as Five Elements. It should always be remembered that when the Chinese speak of the Five Elements, they conceive of them as five active moving forces or agents; hence their use of the word *hsing* or "mover," elsewhere rendered for the sake of convenience as "element." — Tr.

officiating (powers). Each in turn gives birth to the next and is overcome by the next but one in turn" (13.7).

How the Five Elements produce each other has been described above. How they overcome or replace one another is outlined by Tung in chap. 59: "Metal overcomes wood .... Water overcomes fire .... Wood overcomes earth .... Fire overcomes metal .... Earth overcomes water" (13.11-13). The basic sequence of the Five Elements is wood, fire, earth, metal, and water, and each produces the next in that order. In the sequence in which each element is overcome by another, however, there is always an interval of one element between the one that is overcome and the one that does the overcoming. Thus metal overcomes wood, with water intervening; water overcomes fire, with wood intervening; wood overcomes earth, with fire intervening; fire overcomes metal, with earth intervening; and earth overcomes water, with metal intervening. This is the explanation of the statement that each element "is overcome by the next but one in turn."

Note: During the Later Han dynasty, in A.D. 79, a great meeting of Confucian scholars was held in the capital, at a place called the White Tiger Hall. At this meeting disputed passages in the classics were discussed, and a record was made of the results, which (with certain changes and omissions) has come down to us under the title, *Po Hu T'ung* (Comprehensive Discussions in the White Tiger Hall). This work (on which see Tjan Tjoe Som, *Po Hu T'ung*, 2 vols., Leiden, 1949 and 1952) represents the theories of the New Text school, and much of it agrees with the doctrines of Tung Chung-shu. Such is the case, for example, in what it says about the Five Elements producing and overcoming one another. Its statements on this point (chap. 9), however, are more detailed than those of Tung, and so may be quoted by way of further explanation:

"What are meant by the Five Elements? Metal, wood, water, fire, and earth are what are meant. They are spoken of as movers (*hsing*), it being wished in this way to express the idea that they are the moving forces of Heaven. Earth obeys Heaven as a wife serves her husband or a minister serves his ruler. Its position is lowly, and being lowly, it looks after matters by itself (without troubling Heaven about them). Therefore it identifies itself with one particular element (the element earth), in order to pay respect to Heaven" (II, 429).

Here the physical Earth (*ti*), spoken of as part of the universe in apposition to Heaven, is equated with the element earth (*t'u* 土). Since Earth cannot rank itself with Heaven, it identifies itself with the element earth, manifesting in this way its respect for Heaven.

The *Po Hu T'ung* says further in the same chapter: "Why do the Five Elements successively come to rule? Because they successively give birth to one another. Hence (each) has its end and beginning. Wood gives birth to fire, fire to earth, earth to metal, metal to water, and water to wood (again). .... The fact that they (may also) do harm to one another derives from the nature of the universe, according to which what is more abundant overcomes what is less abundant, and therefore water overcomes fire; what is etherial overcomes what is consolidated, and therefore fire overcomes metal; hardness overcomes softness, and therefore metal overcomes wood; what is concentrated overcomes what is diffused, and therefore wood overcomes earth; what is solid overcomes what is not solid, and therefore earth overcomes water" (II, 437-438).

Another passage in the same chapter of the *Po Hu T'ung*, no longer extant in the present text but cited in the commentary from a quotation in the *Wu-hsing Ta-yi* (Great Meaning of the Five Elements), [1] states further: "The reason why wood gives birth to fire is that the nature of wood is mild, and warmth lies concealed within it, which, when the drilling stick operates to create heat, comes to the outside. Therefore it gives birth to fire. The reason why fire gives birth to earth is that fire is hot, and so is able to burn wood. When wood is burned it becomes ashes, and these ashes are earth. Therefore fire gives birth to earth. The reason why earth gives birth to metal is that metal is found in the stones which rest on mountains, being a product of their fructification. Mountains are formed from the accumulation of earth, and such mountains always produce stones. Therefore earth gives birth to metal. The reason why metal gives birth to water is that the ether of the lesser *yin* moistens and fructifies. [2] And molten metal is also liquid; hence when mountains produce clouds, (they give their moisture to these clouds and) precipitation follows. Therefore metal gives birth to water. The reason why water gives birth to wood is that water moistens and is able to give life (to growing plants). Therefore water gives birth to wood (which comprises all plant life)."

In these passages we thus find rationalizations for the fact that the Five Elements give birth to and are overcome by one another in the way they do.

5—THE FOUR SEASONS

Wood, fire, metal, and water each preside over one of the four seasons, while earth, occupying the central position, gives assistance to all of them. The alternation of growth and decay as one season passes into another results in a yearly cycle of change. This alternation, furthermore, is caused by the operations of the *yin* and *yang*. Tung Chung-shu writes (chap. 51):

"The constant course of Heaven is that things in opposition to each other cannot both arise simultaneously. Therefore this (course

---

[1] Chap. 4, sect. 1, p. 24. It is the work of Hsiao Chi (died ca. A.D. 615). — Tr.

[2] The lesser *yin* is associated with autumn, the element of which is metal. See below, quotations on pp. 25 and 29. — Tr.

of Heaven) is spoken of as oneness. That it is single and not dual: such is the movement of Heaven. The *yin* and the *yang* are these mutually opposite things. Therefore when one of them expands outward, the other retracts inward; when the one is to the left, the other is to the right. In spring they both (move toward) the south, and in autumn (toward) the north. In summer they meet in the van, and in winter in the rear. They move parallel to each other, but not along the same road; they meet one another, and each in turn operates as the controller. Such is their pattern" (12.5).

He also writes (chap. 47): "The *yang* ether begins by emerging in the northeast and moves southward, so as to assume its position there. It (then) circles westward and retires in the north, there to hide itself for repose. The *yin* ether begins by emerging in the southeast and moves northward, so as also to assume its position there. It (then) circles westward and retires in the south, there to cover itself for concealment. Therefore the southern quarter is the proper position of the *yang*, while the northern quarter is its place of repose. The northern quarter is the proper position of the *yin*, while the southern quarter is its place of concealment. When the *yang* reaches its position there is great heat. When the *yin* reaches its position there is great cold" (11.15).

He says further (chap. 48): "When the course of Heaven has been completed, it begins again. Therefore the north is the quarter where Heaven begins and ends (its course), and where the *yin* and *yang* unite with and separate from (one another). After the winter solstice the *yin* holds itself low and retires in the west, while the *yang* raises itself up and emerges in the east. Their places of emerging and retiring are always directly opposite to one another, but there is always a mutual concord in the equable blending of their larger or smaller quantities. The quantity (of the one) may be more, yet there is no excess. That (of the other) may be less, yet there is no deficiency. In spring and summer the *yang* is more abundant and the *yin* less, while in autumn and winter the *yang* is less abundant and the *yin* more. These amounts do not remain constant, for there is never a time when one or the other is not being divided and dispersed. As they emerge or retire, they mutually diminish or increase, and as they become more or less abundant, they mutually fructify and enrich. As the more abundant becomes dominant, the less abundant goes into retirement at an increasing rate. The one that retires is diminished by one, while that which emerges is augmented by two.

Whichever of these is started by Heaven (on its course), as soon as it moves, thereupon becomes further increased (over its opposite in strength). It constantly holds a power opposed to, and moreover augmented over, that of the other. Thus, according to its own kind, it responds to the other. [1] In this way the ethers influence one another as they pass through transformations in the course of their mutual revolutions" (12.1).

And still again (chap. 46): "As to metal, wood, water, and fire, they each take that over which they are to preside, so as, in accordance with the (movements of the) *yin* and *yang*, to join forces with them in the performance of the common work. Thus the resulting achievements are not solely (due to) the *yin* and *yang*. Rather it is a case of the *yin* and *yang* basing themselves upon these (four elements), so as to supply assistance to them in those (seasonal tasks) over which (the elements) preside. In this way the lesser (*shao* 少) *yang* bases itself upon wood, thus assisting it in the germinating activities of spring. The greater (*t'ai* 太) *yang* bases itself upon fire, thus assisting it in the nourishing activities of summer. The lesser *yin* bases itself upon metal, thus assisting it in the maturing activities of autumn. And the greater *yin* bases itself upon water, thus assisting it in the storing-up activities of winter" (11.13).

The *yin* and *yang*, as here described, are two opposing forces which follow "the constant course of Heaven," but in so doing "cannot both arise at once." This means that when the *yang* emerges, the *yin* retires, and vice versa. The power of the one that retires is "diminished by one," while that of the one that emerges is "augmented by two." Thus the power of the emerging force becomes greatly increased over that of the retiring one. [2]

---

[1] The first half of this sentence is, in the opinion of the editor, Su Yü, corrupt. This and the preceding three sentences are hard to translate, primarily because we are not told the base figure from which the *yin* and *yang* move in such a way that, on retiring, they are "diminished by one," and, on emerging, are "augmented by two." As a result, it is impossible to determine what these phrases mean in absolute numerical terms. That is why the word *pei* 倍, ordinarily meaning "to double," is here translated more ambiguously as "at an increasing rate" and "increased." — Tr.

[2] Professor Fung originally wrote: "... becomes increased by two thirds over that of the retiring one." He now agrees, however, that in view of the ambiguity of the passage on which this statement is based (see preceding note), it is wiser not to try to interpret its meaning in exact numerical terms. — Tr.

In what he says here, Tung Chung-shu diverges from the usual theory. The *Huai-nan-tzŭ*, for example, says (14.7) that "the *yang* ether arises in the northeast and reaches its point of exhaustion in the southwest; the *yin* ether arises in the southwest and reaches its point of exhaustion in the northeast." This theory, which in later times became generally accepted, would, if adopted by Tung Chung-shu, demand radical changes in his own theory. For according to the *Huai-nan-tzŭ*, the *yang* arises in the northeast and moves southward, passing en route through the eastern quarter, where it encounters the presiding element of wood and helps it to flourish, thus producing spring. On arriving at the south, it encounters the presiding element of fire, which it likewise helps to flourish, thus producing summer. The *yin*, for its part, operates in a similar manner. Arising in the southwest and moving northward, it passes en route through the western quarter, where it encounters the presiding element of metal, which it helps to flourish, thus producing autumn. It then continues to the north, where it encounters the presiding element of water, which it likewise helps to flourish, thus producing winter. This theory may be graphically represented as follows:

Annual Revolution of the *Yin* and *Yang* as Described in the *Huai-nan-tzŭ*

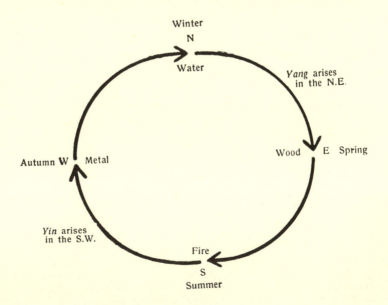

This provides a fairly simple explanation for the changing round of the seasons. Tung Chung-shu, however, maintains differently that "the *yang* ether begins by emerging in the northeast and moves southward," whereas "the *yin* ether begins by emerging in the southeast and moves northward." "In spring they both (move toward) the south, and in autumn (toward) the north. In summer they meet in the van, and in winter in the rear." Another passage (chap. 50) explains this idea in greater detail:

"When the course of Heaven first touches the great winter season, the *yin* and *yang* each come from their own quarter and transfer themselves to the rear. The *yin* comes westward from the east, and the *yang* comes eastward from the west. In the middle month of winter, they meet each other in the north, where they unite into one. This is called the (winter) solstice. [1] They then divide and move away from each other, the *yin* going toward the right and the *yang* toward the left. [2] ... When the winter months are completed, the *yin* and *yang* both return to the south. When the *yang* returns to the south, it emerges at *yin*, while when the *yin* returns to the south, it retires at *hsü*. [3] ... In the middle month of spring, the *yang* is precisely in the east while the *yin* is precisely in the west. This is called the spring equinox. At the spring equinox the *yin* and *yang* are evenly divided. Therefore day and night are the same (in length) and cold and heat are equal. The *yin* daily diminishes and weakens, while the *vang* daily increases and becomes mighty. Therefore there is (first) warmth and (then) heat.

"When the months of the great summer season are first reached, (the *yin* and *yang*) meet each other in the south, where they unite into

---

[1] According to the Chinese calendar, the winter and summer solstices mark the middle of winter and summer respectively, while the spring and autumn equinoxes mark the middle of spring and autumn respectively. — Tr.

[2] South, rather than north, is the primary direction for the Chinese. Hence Chinese maps are arranged so that south comes at the top of the page. This is why the *yang*, moving from west to east, is said to go toward the left, while the *yin*, moving in the opposite direction, is said to go toward the right. In the diagram given below these directions are reversed, since, in accordance with Western practice, it has been drawn with north at the top. — Tr.

[3] *Yin* and *hsü* are two of the twelve cyclical "earthly branches" (on which see beginning of sect. 2 above). These "branches" not only designate periods of time, but also, as will be seen from the diagram on p. 15, the points of the compass. What is meant here, therefore, is that as the *yang* moves from north to south on its circular orbit, it becomes prominent in the E.N.E. (*yin*), while as the *yin* moves from north to south on its corresponding orbit in the opposite direction, it goes into retirement in the W.N.W. (*hsü*). — Tr.

one. This is called the (summer) solstice. They then divide and move away from each other, the *yang* going toward the right and the *yin* toward the left.... When the summer months are completed, the *yin* and *yang* both return to the north. When the *yang* returns to the north, it retires at *shen* (W.S.W.), while when the *yin* returns to the north, it emerges at *ch'en* (E.S.E.).... In the middle month of autumn, the *yang* is precisely in the west while the *yin* is precisely in the east. This is called the autumn equinox. At the autumn equinox the *yin* and *yang* are evenly divided. Therefore day and night are the same (in length) and cold and heat are equal. The *yang* daily diminishes and weakens, while the *yin* daily increases and becomes mighty" (12.3-5).

These movements and relationships become clearer if we look at the following diagram:

Tung Chung-shu's Theory of Annual Movements of the *Yin* and *Yang*

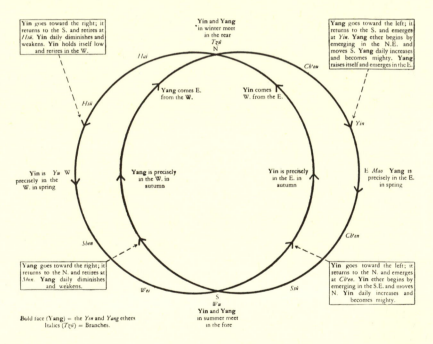

This theory is not only complicated, but raises a fundamental difficulty, namely: if, in autumn, the *yin* is in the east and not the west (as it is, according to the *Huai-nan-tzŭ* theory), how can it, from that distant point, assist the operations of the element metal, which presides over the west and over autumn? Tung Chung-shu resolves this difficulty as follows (chap. 48):

"When the autumn season arrives, the lesser *yin* arises, but it is not permitted, on behalf of autumn, to associate itself with metal (in the west), for such association would result in injury to the work accomplished by fire (during the summer season just preceding). Nevertheless, it appears in the east on behalf of autumn, where, holding itself low, it pursues its business in order to bring the year's work to completion. Is this not a case of proper adjustment? Thus the course of Heaven has its correct relationships, its natural order, and its proper adjustment" (12.2).

In the case of the *yang*, however, there is a somewhat different situation: "With the coming of spring, the lesser *yang* emerges in the east and proceeds to wood, with which it acts jointly as a generative force; with the coming of summer, the greater *yang* emerges in the south and proceeds to fire, with which it acts jointly to produce warmth" (*ibid.*, p. 1). Such is Heaven's "natural order." The lesser *yin*, on the contrary, emerges in the east, "where, holding itself low, it pursues its business." Thus it humbly brings the work of the year to completion. Such is Heaven's "proper adjustment." The reason why the *yin* is thus relegated to a lesser position is that Heaven "has trust in the *yang* but not in the *yin*; it likes beneficence but not chastisement" (chap. 47, 11.16). "For this reason Heaven, in its operation of the *yin* ether, takes only a small amount of it to give completion to autumn, while it assigns the remainder to winter" (chap. 49, 12.3).

Thus the transformations of the four seasons result from the waxing and waning movements of the *yin* and *yang*. When the *yang* is in the ascendancy, it assists wood and fire to form spring and summer, whereupon all things are born and grow. But when the *yin* is in the ascendancy, it assists metal and water to form autumn and winter, whereupon all things are stored up or go into hibernation. This is the reason why the *yang* (as stated below) constitutes "Heaven's beneficent power," whereas the *yin* constitutes its "chastising power." Thus Tung Chung-shu writes (chap. 49):

"The constant (principle) of Heaven and Earth is the succession of the *yin* and *yang*. The *yang* is Heaven's beneficent power, while the *yin* is Heaven's chastising power.... In Heaven's course, there are three seasons of formation and growth and one season of mourning and death. Death means the withering and decay of various creatures; mourning means the grief and sadness (engendered) by the *yin* ether. Heaven has its own feelings of joy or anger, and a mind (which experiences) sadness or pleasure, analogous to those of man. Thus if a grouping is made according to kind, Heaven and man are one" (12.2).

6—THE CORRELATION OF MAN WITH THE NUMERICAL CATEGORIES OF HEAVEN

That Heaven is the same in kind with man becomes still more evident in the field of human physiology. Tung writes (chap. 56):

"Nothing is more refined than the (*yin* and *yang*) ethers, richer than Earth, or more spiritual than Heaven. Of the creatures born from the refined essence (*ching* 精) of Heaven and Earth, none is more noble than man. Man receives the Decree (*ming*) of Heaven, and therefore is loftier (than other) creatures. (Other) creatures suffer troubles and distress and are unable to practice love (*jen*) and righteousness (*yi*); only man is capable of practicing them. (Other) creatures suffer trouble and distress and are unable to match themselves with Heaven and Earth; only man is capable of doing this.

"Man has 360 joints, which matches the number of Heaven. [1] His body, with its bones and flesh, matches the thickness of Earth. He has ears and eyes above, with their capacity for hearing and seeing, which correspond to the forms of the sun and moon. His body has its orifices and veins, which correspond to the forms of rivers and valleys. His heart has its sadness and pleasure, joy and anger, which are in a class with the spirit-like feelings (of Heaven). When we observe man's body, how much loftier is he (than other) creatures, and one, withal, the same in kind as Heaven! (Other) creatures derive their life from Heaven's *yin* and *yang* in a recumbent position, whereas man brilliantly bears its markings. Thus it is that among all (other) creatures, there are none that do not move about in a recumbent position; only man faces (Heaven) directly, with head erect and upright posture. [2] In this way, those who receive less from Heaven

---

[1] The comparison here (not very exact, because only a round number) is with the days of the year. This comparison appears earlier in the *Huai-nan-tzǔ*. See vol. 1, p. 399. In the text below the more accurate figure of 366 is given. Some of the other comparisons made below also appear in the *Huai-nan-tzǔ*. — Tr.

[2] This refers to the standing posture of man as contrasted with the recumbent one of other creatures. — Tr.

and Earth face them in a recumbent position, whereas he who receives more faces them directly. Herein may be seen man's distinction
from other creatures and how he is to be equated with Heaven and
Earth.

"In the physical form of man, for this reason, his head is large
and round, like Heaven's countenance. [1] His hair is like the stars
and constellations. His ears and eyes, with their brilliance, are like
the sun and moon. His nostrils and mouth, with their breathing, are
like the wind. The penetrating understanding that lies within his
breast is like the spiritual intelligence (of Heaven). His abdomen and
womb, now full and then empty, are like the hundred creatures. [2] ...
The symbols of Heaven and Earth, and the correspondences between
the *yin* and *yang*, are ever (found) established (also) in the (human)
body. The body is like Heaven, and its numerical (categories) correspond with those of the latter, so that its life is linked with the latter.
With the number (of days) that fills a year, Heaven gives form to
man's body. Thus the 366 lesser joints (of the body) correspond to
the number of days (in a year), and the twelve divisions of the larger
joints correspond to the number of months. Within (the body) there
are the five viscera, [3] which correspond in number to the Five Elements. Externally there are the four limbs, which correspond in
number to the four seasons. The alternating opening and closing
(of the eyes) corresponds to day and night. The alternation of hardness and softness corresponds to winter and summer. [4] The alternation of sadness and pleasure corresponds to the *yin* and *yang*. The
mind possesses the power of thinking, which corresponds to (Heaven's) power of deliberation and calculation. (Man's) conduct follows
the principles of proper relationship, which correspond to (the
relationship between) Heaven and Earth. ... In what may be numbered, there is a correspondence in number. In what may not be
numbered, there is a correspondence in kind. There is an identity in
both (cases) and a single correspondence (of man) with Heaven"
(13.2-4). Tung Chung-shu also writes (chap. 41):

---

[1] Heaven was believed by the Chinese to be round, while Earth was square.
— Tr.

[2] This comparison is not too clear. The passage following, omitted here,
states that the hundred creatures are the things that lie closest to Earth's surface,
and therefore that the portion (of the human body) lying below the waist corresponds to Earth. — Tr.

[3] Heart, liver, spleen, lungs, and kidneys. — Tr.

[4] What is meant by this hardness and softness is not clear. — Tr.

"What produces (man) cannot (itself) be man, for the creator of man is Heaven. The fact that men are men derives from Heaven. Heaven, indeed, is man's supreme ancestor. This is why man is to be classed with Heaven above. Man's physical body is given form through the transforming influence of the numerical (categories) of Heaven. Man's vigor is directed to love (*jen*) through the transforming influence of Heaven's will (*chih* 志). Man's virtuous conduct is expressed in righteousness (*yi*) through the transforming influence of Heaven's orderly principle (*li* 理). Man's likes and dislikes are influenced by Heaven's warmth and purity. Man's joy and anger are influenced by Heaven's cold and heat. ... The duplicate of Heaven lies in man, and man's feelings and nature derive from Heaven" (11.1).

With this identity between man and Heaven, a universe without man would be an incomplete universe; indeed, it would not be a universe at all. This is brought out in the following passage (chap. 19):

"Heaven, Earth, and man are the origin of all things. Heaven gives them birth, Earth nourishes them, and man perfects them. Heaven gives them birth by (instilling) filial piety and respect for elders; Earth nourishes them by (supplying) clothing and food; man perfects them by (creating) ritual (*li*) and music (*yüeh*). These three are to each other like the hands and feet, which, united, give the finished physical form, so that no one of them may be dispensed with. To do without filial piety and respect for elders would be to destroy that whereby they (all things) are born; to do without clothing and food would be to destroy that whereby they are nourished; to do without ritual and music would be to destroy that whereby they are perfected" (6.12-13).

These words reveal the lofty position which Tung Chung-shu assigns to man in the universe.

7—HUMAN NATURE AND THE FEELINGS

Human psychology embraces two aspects: that of man's nature (*hsing* 性) and that of his feelings or emotions (*ch'ing* 情). These are equated by Tung Chung-shu with the *yang* and *yin* respectively in the following passage (chap. 35):

"The (human) body has within it the nature (*hsing*) and the feelings (*ch'ing*), just as Heaven has the *yin* and the *yang*. To speak of man's 'basic stuff'[1] and exclude from this his feelings, is like speaking of Heaven's *yang* while excluding its *yin*" (10.11).

The outward manifestation of man's nature is to be found in the virtue of love or *jen* 仁, and that of his feelings in the quality of covetousness or *t'an* 貪. Tung says on this point (chap. 35):

"Truly, there exist in man (both) love and covetousness, each of which lies within his body. What is thus called the body is received from Heaven. Heaven has its dual manifestations of *yin* and *yang*, and the body likewise has the dual qualities of covetousness and love" (10.7-9).

The covetousness here spoken of is the outward expression of man's feelings, while love is the outward expression of his nature.

Note: When Tung Chung-shu speaks of the "nature" (*hsing*), he sometimes seems to conceive of it in a broader and sometimes in a narrower sense. The broader usage is exemplified when he says (chap. 35): "The material that is naturally produced (in man at birth) is called the nature. This nature constitutes man's 'basic stuff'" (10.6).[2] According to this definition, since the nature constitutes the "basic stuff" with which man is endowed at birth, it follows that the feelings are simply a particular element in this nature. Tung confirms this assumption when he writes in the same chapter: "What are called the nature (in the narrower sense) and the feelings are produced by Heaven and Earth. The feelings and the nature form a single unity. The feelings, too, are (part of) the nature (in the broader sense)" (10.10).

In the narrower sense, however, the nature stands distinct from and in opposition to the feelings; it constitutes the *yang* part of man's "basic stuff," whereas the feelings constitute that part which is *yin*. The *Shuo Wen* or *Explanation of Script*, a famous dictionary compiled by Hsü Shen about A.D. 100, reflects this idea when it states (10b.5, under characters *ch'ing* and *hsing*): "The feelings are that in man's *yin* ether which contains desire; the nature is that in man's *yang* ether which is by nature good." Likewise the *Lun Heng* or *Critical Essays* (by Wang Ch'ung, A.D. 27-ca. 100) says (chap. 13): "(Tung) Chung-shu, having scanned the writings of Mencius and Hsün Tzŭ, formulated a theory of the feelings and the nature, in which he said: 'The great principle of Heaven is that of the *yin* and *yang*; the great principle of man is that of the feelings and the nature. The nature is produced from the *yang* and the feelings from the *yin*. The *yin* ether is mean; the *yang* ether is benevolent (*jen*). He who says that the nature is good, is looking at the *yang*; he who says that it is evil, is looking

---

[1] The "basic stuff" (*chih* 質) is another term used by Tung Chung-shu to designate man's original nature in its totality. See below. — Tr.

[2] The term "basic stuff" (*chih*) had already been used by Confucius to designate man's inner, spontaneous nature. See vol. 1, pp. 66-69. — Tr.

at the *yin*' " (I, 388-389). Both these quotations follow Tung Chung-shu's narrower definition of the nature.

Inasmuch as man's "basic stuff" includes not only the nature (conceived in the narrower sense) but the feelings, and not only the virtue of love but also the undesirable quality of covetousness, it is impossible to say of it that it itself is wholly good. Tung Chung-shu comments (chap. 35):

"If one says that the nature is good, then what about the feelings?" (10.10).

Here he is speaking of the nature in its broader sense as equivalent to the "basic stuff." He writes again (chap. 36):

"Goodness is like a kernel of grain; the nature is like the growing stalk of that grain. Though the stalk produces the kernel, it cannot itself be called a kernel, and though the nature produces goodness, it cannot itself be called good. The kernel and goodness are both brought to completion through man's continuation of Heaven's (work), and are external (to the latter); they do not lie within (the scope of) what Heaven does itself. What Heaven does extends to a certain point and then stops. What lies within this stopping point pertains to Heaven; what lies outside pertains to the teachings of the (sage-)kings. The teachings of the (sage-)kings lie outside the nature. Yet, (when they are applied), the nature cannot but conform to them. Therefore I say that the nature possesses the stuff of goodness, but that it cannot by itself act for goodness. This is no mere rhetoric on my part, for it represents actual truth. What Heaven creates stops at the silk cocoon, the hemp plant or the stalk of grain. From the hemp plant cloth is produced, from the cocoon silk, and from the grain stalk kernels of grain. (Likewise) from the nature is produced goodness. These advances are all achieved by the sages by continuing (the work initiated by) Heaven. They could not be reached by the feelings and the nature in their raw state" (10.19).

In this passage the term "nature" is again used in its wider meaning to comprise all of man's "basic stuff." [1] Within this "basic stuff" there exists the narrower kind of nature (which, in opposition to the feelings, is good); hence it certainly possesses some degree of goodness. At the same time, however, the "basic stuff" also includes

---

[1] Except in the last sentence, in which the word is used in conjunction with the "feelings," but where it still obviously refers to the nature in its original uncultivated state. — Tr.

the feelings which, being bad, prevent the "basic stuff" itself from being wholly good. In order that a man may become good, therefore, human effort must be applied so as to check the feelings by means of the nature (narrowly defined). Tung Chung-shu writes further on this (chap. 35):

"That which confines the multitude of evil things within, and prevents them from appearing externally, is the mind. Therefore the mind is known as the confiner. ... Heaven has its restraints over the *yin* and *yang*, and the individual has his confiner of the feelings and desires; in this way he is at one with the course of Heaven. Thus the *yin* in its movements is not permitted to concern itself with spring and summer, and the moon when it is new is always obscured by the sun's light, sometimes completely and sometimes partially. Such is the way in which Heaven restrains the *yin*. [1] Why, then, should one not diminish one's desires and check one's feelings, in order thus to respond to Heaven? The body restrains that which Heaven (wishes) to be restrained, which is why it is said that (man's) body is like Heaven. Such restraint of what Heaven (wishes) to be restrained does not mean a restraint of Heaven itself. We must realize that if the nature (received by us) from Heaven does not undergo (further human) instruction, we shall unto the end be unable to confine it" (10.7-9).

By "instruction" (*chiao* 教), Tung Chung-shu thus means the process of restraining the feelings by means of the nature (taking this term now in its narrow sense). This educational or civilizing process is what he has in mind when he speaks of "man's continuation of Heaven's (work)," and is the way whereby man may model himself on Heaven.

From one point of view, Tung's theory of the nature may be said to be a combination of the views of Mencius and Hsün Tzŭ. [2] But though he agrees in part with Mencius by saying that man's "basic stuff" contains the beginnings of goodness, he also disagrees by saying that these *beginnings* are not, in themselves, sufficient cause

---

[1] Which, of course, is associated with the moon, just as the *yang* is associated with the sun. — Tr.

[2] Thus Tung agrees with Hsün Tzŭ in stressing "instruction" and "the teachings of the (sage-)kings" as essential instruments for improving the nature; likewise in referring to the mind (i.e., to a conscious and rational faculty) as the confiner of the feelings and desires. On Hsün Tzŭ's doctrine, cf. vol. 1, pp. 286-288. — Tr.

for us to regard the nature itself as actually good. This distinction clearly emerges in the following passage (chap. 35):

"It is said by some that since the nature contains the beginnings of goodness, and the mind contains the basic stuff of goodness, how can (the nature itself) not be good? But I reply that this is not so. For the silk cocoon contains silk fibers and yet is not itself silk, and the egg contains the chicken, yet is not itself a chicken. If we follow these analogies, what doubt can there be? Heaven has produced mankind in accordance with its great principle, and those who speak about the nature should not differ from each other. Nevertheless, there are some who say that the nature is good, and some who say it is not good. That is because when they thus speak of goodness, they each mean something different by it. Inasmuch as the nature contains within it the beginnings of goodness, the fact that a child's love for its parents is superior to that of the birds and beasts may be called goodness. Such is what Mencius means by goodness. But goodness may also be defined as conformity to the three bonds and five rules, [1] comprehension of the principles of the eight beginnings, [2] and the practice of loyalty, good faith, widespread love, generosity, and love of propriety (*li*). Such is what the sages meant by goodness. That is why Confucius has said: 'A good man it is not mine to see. Could I see a man of constant purpose I would be content' (*Analects*, VII, 25).

"Regarded in this way, what the sages called goodness is not easy to match. It is not the sort of goodness that is called such merely because it consists in being better than the birds and beasts. ... Indeed, to be better than the birds and beasts is no more to be considered goodness than is being wiser than the plants and trees to be called wisdom. ... If evaluated in comparison with the natures of birds and beasts, the natures of all men are indeed good. But if

---

[1] The three bonds are those linking ruler with subject, father with son, and husband with wife. See p. 42 below. Tung fails to define the five rules, but the *Po Hu T'ung* speaks of "six rules," which it defines as those governing the relationship between paternal uncles, elder and younger brothers, other relatives of the same surname, maternal uncles, the teacher, and friends. See p. 44 below. — Tr.

[2] *Pa tuan* 八 端 . What this refers to is unclear. Mencius speaks only of four beginnings—the feelings of commiseration, shame and dislike, modesty and yielding, and the sense of right and wrong—which, he says, are inherent in man's nature and, when developed, result in the virtues of love, righteousness, propriety and wisdom. See vol. 1, pp. 120-122. — Tr.

evaluated in comparison with the goodness of human morality
(*jen tao* 人道), men's natures fall short. I grant that the natures of
all men are better than those of birds and beasts, but not that they
have the goodness spoken of by the sages. My way of evaluating the
nature differs from that of Mencius. Mencius evaluates it in comparison with the doings of birds and beasts below, and therefore he
says that the nature itself is good. I evaluate it in comparison with
the doings of the sages above, and therefore I say that the nature is
not good. Goodness transcends the (ordinary) nature, (just as) the
sage transcends (ordinary) goodness" (10.14-15).

Tung is here speaking with special reference to the "basic stuff"
as found in the ordinary man. There are other men, however, who
diverge from the average: some who at birth possess more than the
mere beginnings of goodness, and others almost completely devoid
of such beginnings. Confucius once referred to them as "the wise
of the highest class" and "the stupid of the lowest class," [1] and Tung
Chung-shu no doubt has this statement in mind when he says (chap.
35):

"What I call the nature does not refer to that of the highest
or lowest class, but is that of the average (man)" (10.11). He further
says (chap. 36):

"The nature of the sage may not be called the nature, nor may
that of 'pecks and hampers' be called the nature. [2] What I call the
nature is that of the average man. The nature of the average man is
like a silk cocoon or an egg. An egg, after being incubated for
twenty days, can become a chicken. A silk cocoon, after being un-
ravelled in boiling water, can become silk thread. And the nature,
after being permeated with instruction and precept, can become good.
Thus goodness is the result of instruction and precept; it is not
something that can be reached by the 'basic stuff' in its raw state"
(10.19-20).

Thus Tung Chung-shu's theory of the nature seems to be an
attempt to harmonize those of Confucius, Mencius, and Hsün Tzǔ.

---

[1] *Analects*, XVIII, 3: "The Master said: 'It is only the wise of the highest
class and the stupid of the lowest class who never change.' " — Tr.

[2] See *Analects*, XIII, 20, where Confucius, on being asked his opinion about
the government officials of his day, replied: "Faugh! They are a set of pecks and
hampers, unworthy of being taken into consideration!" — Tr.

8—Individual and Social Ethics

In order to develop the beginnings of goodness in man's "basic stuff," thereby causing it to become wholly good, it is necessary to bring the various virtues into actual operation. In the field of individual ethics, two of the most important of these are love (*jen*) and righteousness (*yi*), of which Tung Chung-shu writes (chap. 3):

"Heaven, when it constituted man's nature, commanded him to practice love and righteousness, to be ashamed of what is shameful, and not to be concerned, like the birds and beasts, solely with existence and profit" (2.11).

Another passage further defines love and righteousness as follows (chap. 29):

"What the *Spring and Autumn Annals* regulates are others and the self. The instruments for thus regulating others and the self are love and righteousness. By love, others are put at peace; by righteousness, the self is rectified. Therefore love is spoken of with reference to others, while righteousness is spoken of with reference to the self. The distinction is apparent in the terms. [1] The fact that love applies to others and righteousness to the self cannot but be looked into. Yet men in general do not examine the matter; on the contrary, they take love to enrich themselves, while relegating righteousness to others. They violate the positions of these (two virtues) and run counter to their principles, so that it is rare that there is no disorder. Thus it is that men, while never desiring disorder, are ever commonly rushing into it, wholly because they are blind to the distinction between others and the self and have not looked into what love and righteousness consist of.

"For this reason the *Spring and Autumn Annals* has provided standards for love and righteousness. The standard for love lies in showing affection (*ai* 愛) to others, not to the self. That for righteousness lies in rectifying the self, not in rectifying others. Even though one is able to rectify others, this cannot be granted to be righteousness as long as one does not rectify the self. (In the same way) even though one has affection for oneself, this cannot be granted to be love as long as this affection is not applied to others. . . . The

---

[1] There is a play on words here between *jen* (love) and its homophone *jen* 人 (others); also between *yi* (righteousness) and *wo* 我 (self), the ideograph for which forms part of the ideograph for righteousness. — Tr.

further it extends, the finer it becomes, whereas the more it is confined, the meaner it becomes—such is affection. Therefore the affection of the (true) King extends to the outer barbarians, [1] whereas that of the Tyrant extends only to the feudal lords. [2] The affection of him who is secure extends to his feudal fief; that of him who is in danger to his immediate associates; that of the doomed to his own person. . . .

"Therefore I say that love consists in affection for others and not in affection for self. Such is its standard . . . . Righteousness and love differ from each other. Love refers to what moves away (from the self and is applied to others); righteousness refers to what approaches (the self and is applied to it). Love is important for what is distant; righteousness for what is near at hand. The application of affection to others is called love; the application of what is appropriate to the self is called righteousness. Love emphasizes others; righteousness emphasizes oneself. This, then, is what I mean when I say that love embraces other men, while righteousness embraces the self" (8.16-20).

In addition to love and righteousness, there is another essential quality, wisdom (*chih* 智), on which Tung Chung-shu writes as follows (chap. 30):

"Nothing is closer than love or more necessary than wisdom. . . . For love without wisdom means affection without discrimination, while wisdom without love means knowledge without the action (that this knowledge demands). Therefore love serves to show affection to mankind, while wisdom serves to extirpate its evils. . . . What is meant by wisdom? It is to speak first and afterward act accordingly. It is for a man first to measure with his wisdom any course of action for which he feels either desire or aversion, and only then to act. . . . The man of wisdom perceives calamity or good fortune when it is still remote, and understands what is beneficial or harmful when it is still early. When an object moves, he knows what changes will occur in it, and when an affair arises, he knows where it will lead. Seeing a beginning, he knows what its end will be. . . . His words are sparing yet sufficient, restrained yet illus-

---

[1] Lit., "the four barbarian (tribes)," who were conceived of as living in the four compass points beyond the pale of (Chinese) civilization. — Tr.

[2] On the feudal lords of the 7th and 6th centuries B.C. who held hegemony over the other lords and were known as *Pa* (Tyrant, in the ancient Greek sense), see vol. 1, p. 112, note 1 (where the title is rendered as Lord Protector). — Tr.

trative, terse yet penetrating, economical yet all-complete. When few, they may not be added to; when abundant, they may not be diminished. His acts are in accord with the proper relationships and his words in accord with practical affairs. Such is what is called wisdom" (8.22-24).

Thus, for Tung Chung-shu, love, righteousness, and wisdom constitute the three essential virtues, just as, in the *Doctrine of the Mean*, we find wisdom, love, and courage considered as the essential three.

Note: The relationship of the virtues and feelings to human psychology, physiology, etc., is explained in further detail in the thirtieth chapter of the *Po Hu T'ung* (II, 565-571): "What are meant by the nature and the feelings? The nature is a manifestation of the *yang*; the feelings are evolved out of the *yin*. Man is born endowed with the *yin* and *yang* ethers. Therefore he harbors within him five (aspects of the) nature and six (kinds of) feeling. The feelings mean passivity, while the nature means what is obtained at birth. [1] These (i.e., feelings and nature) are what man is endowed with by the six forces at birth. [2] ...

"What are the five (aspects of the) nature? They are love, righteousness, propriety, wisdom, and good faith. Love is the inability to bear (seeing the sufferings of others). [3] It is manifested in affection for others. Righteousness is what is proper. [4] It makes decisions in accordance with the mean. Propriety is to tread. [5] This means to tread the moral path (*tao*) and beautify it. Wisdom (*chih*) is to know (*chih* 知). It is a special vision and foresight. This means not to be deluded by things, and to know, when one sees the abstruse, what it will bring forth. Good faith (*hsin*) is sincerity (*ch'eng* 誠). It is unswerving singleness (of mind).

---

[1] There is a play on words here between *ch'ing* (feelings) and *ching* 靜 (passivity); also between *hsing* (the nature) and *sheng* 生 (what is obtained at birth). These pairs of words were pronounced identically, or almost identically, in ancient times. — Tr.

[2] The six forces (*liu ch'i* 六氣) are probably those of the six pitch-pipes, referred to in the second paragraph of p. 41 below. — Tr.

[3] There is a play on words here between *jen* (love) and *jen* 忍 (to bear). The passage is based on the *Mencius*, IIa, 6, which says: "All men have a mind which cannot bear (to see the sufferings of) others. The early kings, having this 'unbearing' mind, thereby had likewise an 'unbearing' government." — Tr.

[4] Here again there is a play on words between *yi* (righteousness) and *yi* 宜 (what is proper). This definition is also found in the *Book of Rites*, chaps. 21 and 37 (XXVIII, 227 and 312). — Tr.

[5] The play on words is here between *li* (propriety) and *li* 履 (to tread). See the *Book of Rites*, chap. 21 (XXVIII, 227). — Tr.

"Thus man, at birth, reacts to the forms of the eight trigrams (portrayed in the *Book of Changes*) and acquires the five forces as constant norms, these being love, righteousness, propriety, wisdom, and good faith.

"What is meant by the six feelings? They are defined as joy, anger, grief, pleasure, love, and hate, and serve to complement the five (aspects of the) nature. Why is it that there are five (aspects of the) nature and six feelings? It is because man is born endowed with the forces of the six pitch-pipes and those of the Five Elements. [1] Therefore within him there are the five viscera and six 'treasuries' (*fu* 府). It is from these that the feelings and the nature operate. ...

"What are the five viscera? They are the liver, heart, lungs, kidneys, and spleen. ... Of these five viscera, the liver corresponds to love, the lungs to righteousness, the heart to propriety, the kidneys to wisdom, and the spleen to good faith. How is it that the liver corresponds to love? The liver is the essence of (the element) wood, and love likes to be actively productive. The east is (the quarter of wood and of the actively productive) *yang*, and is where all things are first born. Therefore the liver resembles wood, being green in color and (shaped as if) having branches and leaves ....

"How is it that the lungs correspond to righteousness? The lungs are the essence of (the element) metal, and righteousness makes decisions. The west is also (the quarter of) metal, where all things, having reached maturity, are destroyed. Therefore the lungs resemble metal, being white in color. [2] ...

"How is it that the heart corresponds to propriety? The heart is the essence of (the element) fire. (The quarter of fire is) the south, where the exalted *yang* holds a superior position, while the lowly *yin* holds an inferior position. Propriety maintains (social differences between) the exalted and the lowly. Therefore the heart resembles fire, being red in color and pointed ....

"How is it that the kidneys correspond to wisdom? The kidneys are the essence of (the element) water, and wisdom proceeds unceasingly without any doubt or uncertainty. Water likewise moves forward without uncertainty. The north is (the quarter of) water (and has black as its corresponding color). Therefore the kidneys are black in color. Water is *yin*, and therefore the kidneys are two in number. [3] ...

"How is it that the spleen corresponds to good faith? The spleen is the essence of (the element) earth. The highest function of earth is to nourish all creatures so as to give them form. It produces creatures without

---

[1] The six pitch-pipes are part of the musical scale known as the twelve pitch-pipes, on which see p. 11 above. Half of these twelve, known as *lü* 律 , are correlated with the *yang* principle, and are the ones here spoken of; the other half, known as *lü* 呂 , are correlated with the *yin* principle. — Tr.

[2] Metal = west = autumn, which was the time when the government assizes were held, hence the time of "making decisions." — Tr.

[3] The duad is associated with the *yin*; the monad with the *yang*. — Tr.

partiality, which is the acme of good faith. Therefore the spleen resembles earth, being yellow in color. ...

"What is meant by the six 'treasuries'? They are the large and small intestine, the stomach, bladder, three openings, [1] and gall. 'Treasuries' means that they are the 'palace treasuries' (*kung* 宮 *fu*) for the five viscera. Therefore the *Evolutions of Rites* says: 'The six feelings serve to complement the five (aspects of the) nature.' [2] ...

"Joy lies in the west, anger in the east, liking in the north, hatred in the south, grief below, and pleasure above. Why is this? The west is where all things reach completion; therefore there is joy. The east is where all things are born; therefore there is anger. [3] The north is where the *yang* ether first begins to manifest itself; therefore there is liking. The south is where the *yin* ether first begins to arise; therefore there is hatred. Much pleasure lies above, while much grief lies below."

The correlation of the various virtues and feelings in this way with the bodily organs and physical phenomena is a natural extension of the concept of "the oneness of man with Heaven," i.e., with nature.

Concerning the ethics that underlie society as a whole, Tung Chung-shu propounds the doctrine (in his chap. 35, quoted above on p. 36) of the "three bonds" (*san kang* 三 綱) and "five rules" (*wu chi* 五 紀). The meaning of these "three bonds" is further explained by him as follows (chap. 53):

"In all things there must be correlates. Thus there are such correlates as upper and lower, left and right, external and internal, beauty and ugliness, obedience and disobedience, joy and anger, cold and heat, day and night. These are all correlates. The *yin* is the correlate of the *yang*, the wife of the husband, the son of the father, the subject of the ruler. There is nothing that does not have such correlates, and in each such correlation there is the *yin* and *yang*. ... Thus the relationships between ruler and subject, father and son, husband and wife, are all derived from the principles of the *yin* and *yang*. The ruler is *yang*, the subject *yin*; the father is *yang*, the son *yin*;

---

[1] *San chiao* 三 焦 , for which there are various interpretations, including entrance to the stomach, to the large intestine, and to the bladder. — Tr.

[2] *Li Yün*, the name of chap. 7 of the *Book of Rites*, which, however, today lacks this sentence. — Tr.

[3] There is probably an implied play on words here between *nu* 怒 (anger) and its homophone *nu* 努 (effort), referring to the effort (i.e., birth pangs) required to bring things into being. *Nu* (anger) was anciently sometimes used to mean *nu* (effort). [This explanation has been added by the author for this English edition. — Tr.]

the husband is *yang*, the wife *yin*. . . . The regulations for love, righteousness, and social institutions are wholly derived from Heaven.
Heaven acts as the ruler, who shelters and confers benefits (on the
subject). Earth acts as the subject, who assists and supports (the
ruler). The *yang* acts as the husband, who procreates (the son). The
yin acts as the wife, who gives assistance (to the husband). Spring
acts as the father, who procreates (the son). Summer acts as the son,
who supports (the father). Autumn acts as (the agent of) death, who
encoffins (living things). Winter acts as (the agent of) affliction, who
buries them. [1] The 'three bonds,' comprising the Way of the King
(*wang tao*), may be sought for in Heaven" (12.8-10).

Here, among the human relationships discussed by Confucius,
we find three—those of ruler and subject, father and son, husband
and wife—being singled out as the "three bonds." This doctrine has
enjoyed particular prestige in Chinese social thinking. Thus, from the
traditional point of view, loyalty and filial piety have been the chief
criteria for evaluating the individual. If in these major duties he
prove deficient, whatever remaining good qualities he may have are
hardly deemed worthy of notice. A wife, likewise, has traditionally
been judged almost entirely on whether or not she has been chaste;
in other words, on the basis of her relationship to her husband. The
Chinese have a saying on this point: "To die of starvation is a small
matter, but to lose one's chastity is a large matter." Once a wife loses
her chastity, therefore, there is nothing else worth saying about her.

Tung Chung-shu, by linking subject to ruler, son to father,
and wife to husband, makes subject, son, and wife secondary append-
ages of ruler, father, and husband. In so doing, he gives these
relationships metaphysical support by saying that they "are all
derived from the principles of the *yin* and *yang*." The same reasoning
is followed by the *Po Hu T'ung*. Thus we see the Han Confucianists
accepting the existing social relationships of ruler and subject, man
and woman, father and son, and applying them by analogy to their
discussions of the *yin*-and-*yang* relationship; conversely, this postulated
relationship gives them a basis for upholding these social relationships.

Note: Though Tung Chung-shu mentions the "three bonds" in
conjunction with what he calls the "five rules" (*wu chi*), he fails to elucidate

---

[1] These last four sentences about the seasons, which do not fit with what
precedes or follows, are probably interpolations of a later writer, according to
Su Yü.

the latter further. For them, therefore, we have to turn to the *Po Hu T'ung* (chap. 29), where, however, Tung's "five rules" are expanded to six:

"What is the meaning of the 'three bonds'? They refer to ruler and subject, father and son, husband and wife. As for the 'six rules,' they refer to (the relationships between) paternal uncles, elder and younger brothers, other relatives of the same surname, maternal uncles, teacher, and friends. Therefore the *Han-wen-chia* (Excellencies of Cherished Literature) says: [1] 'The ruler is the subject's bond, the father is the son's bond, and the husband is the wife's bond.' It says further: 'Respect for paternal uncles and elder brothers puts the six rules into operation. There are (also) proper duties among maternal uncles, a proper hierarchy among relatives of the same surname, feelings of affection among brothers, honor towards the teacher, and long intimacy among friends.'

"What is meant by these 'bonds' and 'rules'? A bond gives orderliness; a rule regulates. What is greater is the bond; what is smaller is the rule. They serve to order and regulate (the relations between) superiors and inferiors, and to arrange and adjust the way of mankind. Men all cherish within themselves the nature with its five constant (virtues), and possess hearts of affection and love. It is thus that the bonds and rules exercise their transforming influence, just as a net has its cords and bonds, whereby its myriad openings are given orderly arrangement. The *Book of Odes* says: 'Indefatigable is King Wen. He makes bonds and rules for the four quarters.' [2] Ruler and subject, father and son, husband and wife: these make six persons. How then are they called the 'three bonds'? 'One *yin* and one *yang* constitute the Way (*Tao*).' [3] The *yang* gains the *yin* and thus becomes complete; the *yin* gains the *yang* and thus assumes its proper sequence. There is a mutual correlation between what is hard and what is soft. That is why these six persons constitute the three bonds" (II, 559-560).

In another passage (chap. 9), the *Po Hu T'ung* describes the manner in which the Five Elements and their accompanying seasons provide models for all social institutions:

"What is the model for the succession of the son upon the death of his father? This is modeled upon the fact that when (the element) wood reaches its end, fire becomes king (in its place). What is the model for a younger brother to carry on after the death of his elder brother? It is the succession of summer after spring. What is the model whereby approbation of goodness is to be extended even unto sons and grandsons (of the person whose goodness is thus approved)? It is that the productive forces of spring wait for summer to bring about further growth. And what is the model whereby hatred of evil stops with the person (who is

---

[1] One of the Han apocrypha on the *Li* or *Rituals*, now lost, save for scattered fragments. On these apocrypha, see the next chapter. — Tr.

[2] Cf. *Shih Ching*, III, i, Ode 4, where, however, the wording somewhat differs, reading "our king," for example, instead of "King Wen." — Tr.

[3] A famous passage in the *Book of Changes*, p. 355. — Tr.

thus hated)? This is modeled on the fact that autumn acts as the executioner without waiting for winter. [1]

"What is the model for the ministers to take over the administration during the minority of a ruler? This is modeled on the fact that (the element) earth exercises jurisdiction over affairs during the time from the last (month of summer) to the first (month of autumn). What is the model for a son avenging (a crime committed against his father)? This is modeled on the overcoming of (the element) water by earth, and of fire by water. What is the model for the obedience of son to father, wife to husband, and subject to ruler? This is modeled on the obedience of Earth to Heaven. What is the model for the fact that a man (who gets married) does not leave (the home of) his parents? This is modeled on the fact that (the element) fire does not separate from (the element) wood. What is the model for the fact that a woman (who gets married) leaves (the home of) her parents? This is modeled on the fact that (the element) water flows away from (the element) metal. What is the model whereby (a man), when he takes a wife in marriage, goes in person (to her home) to receive her? This is modeled on the fact that when the sun sets, the *yang* descends into the *yin*. , .." (II, 442-443).

The same passage contains other similar analogies which need not be quoted here.

A man must conduct himself according to these various ethical principles before he can be said to have completely developed his nature, or can, in fact, truly be considered a man. Tung Chung-shu is quoted in his biography in the *Ch'ien Han Shu* (56.16) as saying:

"Man has received life from Heaven in a manner markedly different from that of the great mass of living creatures. Within (the home) he has the family relationships of father and son, elder and younger brother. Outside, he has the social relationships of ruler and subject, superior and inferior. In his social contacts there are for him ways of manifesting (the distinction between) the aged and the young. He possesses clearly marked patterns for his social intercourse and joyfully displays affection in his love toward others. It is thus that man is noble. The five grains have been produced to feed him, the mulberry tree and hemp to clothe him, and the six domestic animals to nourish him. He tames the ox, rides the horse, traps the panther, and pens the tiger. It is thus that he has gained a spirituality from Heaven greater than that of other creatures.

"Therefore Confucius has said: 'Of all (creatures with their

---

[1] This idea of the extension of approbation and withholding of hatred is derived from the *Kung-yang Chuan*, under the year 522 B.C. — Tr.

different) natures produced by Heaven and Earth, man is the noblest.' [1]
Understanding his heavenly nature, he knows himself to be nobler
than other creatures. Knowing himself to be nobler than other
creatures, he comes to know love and righteousness. [2] Knowing
love and righteousness, he comes to value propriety and its regulations. Valuing propriety and its regulations, he comes to dwell at
peace in goodness. Dwelling at peace in goodness, he joyfully comes
to conform to right principles. Joyfully conforming to right principles, he may be called the superior man (*chün tzŭ*). This is what
Confucius meant when he said: 'He who does not understand the
Decree (of Heaven) cannot become a superior man' (*Analects*,
XX, 2)."

Thus a man, unless possessed of the eternal ethical principles
underlying the human relationships, is in no way different from the
"great mass of living creatures," that is, the birds and beasts.

9—POLITICAL AND SOCIAL PHILOSOPHY

It is because men's natures are not wholly good in themselves,
that the instution of kingship is necessary. Such is the argument advanced by Tung Chung-shu in the following passage (chap. 35):

"Heaven has produced mankind with natures containing the
'basic stuff' of goodness but unable to be good (in themselves).
Therefore it has established kingship to make them good. This is
Heaven's purpose. The people receive from Heaven this nature which
is unable to be good (by itself) and, conversely, receive from the
king the instruction which gives completeness to their nature. The
king, following Heaven's purpose, accepts as his charge the task of
giving completeness to the people's nature" (10.12).

The king, being entrusted by Heaven in this way with the task of
ruling men, holds a lofty position and heavy responsibility. Tung
Chung-shu says (chap. 44):

"The ancients, when they invented writing, drew three (horizontal) lines which they connected through the center (by a vertical

---

[1] This saying is attributed to Confucius in the *Hsiao Ching* (Classic of Filial
Piety), chap. 9, p. 476. — Tr.

[2] *Yi* 誼, here and in the next sentence, is to be taken as equivalent to its
homophone *yi*, "righteousness." [This comment has been added by Professor
Fung for the English edition. — Tr.]

stroke), and then called this 'king.' [1] These three lines represent Heaven, Earth, and man, while the connecting of them through the center represents the (king's) penetration of their (interrelated) principles. Who, indeed, if not a (true) king, could take the central position between Heaven, Earth, and man, so as to act as the connecting link between them? Therefore the king models himself on Heaven. He takes its seasons as his model and gives them completeness. He models himself on its commands and circulates them among all men. He models himself on its numerical (categories) and uses them when initiating affairs. He models himself on its course and thereby brings his administration into operation. He models himself on its will and with it attaches himself to love (*jen*)" (11.9).

As to how the king thus "models himself on Heaven" and "takes its seasons as his model and gives them completeness," Tung Chung-shu continues (chap. 44):

"Thus the ruler's likes and dislikes, joy and anger, are equivalent to Heaven's spring, summer, autumn, and winter. Through the transformations it makes in their warmth, coolness, cold, and heat, it (Heaven) accomplishes its work. When Heaven brings forth these four (qualities) seasonably, the year is fine; when unseasonably, it is bad. (Likewise) when the ruler of men brings forth his four (qualities) in their correct relationship, the world is well ordered; when he fails to do this, it falls into disorder. Therefore a well-ordered world is the same in category as a good year, and a world in disorder is the same in category as a bad year. In this may be seen how the principles of man duplicate the course of Heaven. ...

"The ruler of men holds a position of life or death (over other men), and shares with Heaven its transforming power. There are no things that do not respond to Heaven's transforming influence; the transformations of Heaven and Earth are exemplified in the four seasons. (Hence) when (the ruler) manifests a liking for something, this acts like the warm atmosphere (of spring), and births take place in the human world. When he manifests a dislike for something, this acts like the cool atmosphere (of autumn), and deaths take place in the human world. His joy acts like the hot atmosphere (of summer),

---

[1] The character for "king," *wang* 王 , consists of three horizontal lines connected by a vertical one. This etymology, of course, is false. The original form of the character was a pictograph of a man, viewed from the front, who stood erect on the ground with outstretched arms and legs. — Tr.

and there is then nourishing and growth. His anger acts like the cold atmosphere (of winter), and there is then a cessation (to human activities). The ruler of men, with his likes and dislikes, joy and anger, transforms the habits and customs (of men), just as Heaven, with its warmth, coolness, cold and heat, exercises a transforming influence upon plants and trees. When the joy and anger (of the ruler) are seasonable and proper, the year is fine; when they are unseasonable and improper, it is bad. Heaven, Earth, and the ruler of men are one" (11.11-12). He also says (chap. 55):

"In Heaven's course, spring with its warmth germinates, summer with its heat nourishes, autumn with its coolness destroys, and winter with its cold stores up. Warmth, heat, coolness, and coldness are different forces but their work is identical, all being instruments whereby Heaven brings the year to completion. The sage, in his conduct of government, duplicates the movements of Heaven. Thus with his beneficence he duplicates warmth and accords with spring, with his conferring of rewards he duplicates heat and accords with summer, with his punishments he duplicates coolness and accords with autumn, and with his executions he duplicates coldness and accords with winter. His beneficence, rewards, punishments and executions are different in kind but their work is identical, all being instruments whereby the king completes his virtue. Beneficence, rewards, punishments, and executions match spring, summer, autumn, and winter respectively, like the fitting together (of the two parts) of a tally. Therefore I say that the king is co-equal with Heaven, meaning that Heaven in its course has its four seasons, while the king, in his, has his four ways of government. Such are what Heaven and man share in common" (13.1).

The ruler's joy, anger, grief, and pleasure, and his beneficence, rewards, punishments, and executions, are thus modeled on the four seasons. Let each operate in its proper degree, and then "the world is well ordered."

"Heaven, when it constituted man's nature, commanded him to practice love and righteousness and to be ashamed of what is shameful" (cf. p. 38 above). The king "models himself on its (Heaven's) commands and circulates them among all men" (cf. p. 47). He must, on behalf of Heaven, promulgate "the instruction which gives completeness to (men's) nature" (cf. p. 46), and "continue (the work initiated by) Heaven" (cf. p. 34), in order thus to complete the goodness of man. Tung's biography in the *Ch'ien Han Shu* (56.16) quotes him as saying:

"The commands of Heaven are called its Decree (*ming*), but this Decree will not operate except through the sage. The 'basic stuff' in its raw state is called the nature (*hsing*), but unless this nature be changed through instruction, it will not assume finished form. Man's desires are called the feelings (*ch'ing*), but unless they be regulated by (human) institutions, they will not be kept in proper check. Therefore the king respectfully carries forward the purpose of Heaven above, thus conforming to its Decree. He busies himself below with his perspicacious instruction so as to transform the people, thus giving finished form to their natures. He rectifies his laws and regulations according to what is appropriate, and differentiates upper and lower (social classes) according to their proper sequence, in order to keep (men's) desires in proper check. By practicing these three things he promotes the great fundamental basis (of society)."

This, then, is the way in which the king provides instruction for mankind and thus "carries forward the purpose of Heaven."

Concerning the statement (cf. p. 47) that the king "models himself on its (Heaven's) numerical (categories) and uses them when initiating affairs," Tung writes further (chap. 24):

"The king, in instituting his officials, has his three highest ministers (*san kung* 三 公), nine lower ministers (*chiu ch'ing* 九 卿), twenty-seven great officials (*ta fu* 大 夫), and eighty-one first-class officers (*yüan shih* 元 士), a total of 120 persons, with which his hierarchy of ministers is made complete. [1] I have heard that the model followed for this by the sage-kings is the great course of Heaven, which has three (monthly) starting points to make (one season), and four (seasonal) revolutions to complete (one year). Is not this the model for the similar arrangement of the officials? That three men constitute the first selection (of officials) is modeled on the fact that three months constitute one season. And that four such selections are made and no more, is modeled on the fact that with the four seasons (the year) is brought to its conclusion. [2] The three

---

[1] This is the official system as imagined by later scholars to have existed during the Chou dynasty. See *Book of Rites*, chap. 3 (XXVII, 213). — Tr.

[2] The meaning here is as follows: The ruler selects three men to be his three highest ministers; this is the first selection (*hsüan* 選) of officials. The three highest ministers then each select three men as assistants, or an aggregate of nine men, who are the nine lower ministers; this is the second selection. These in turn each select three assistants, or an aggregate of twenty-seven men, who are the

highest ministers are the men by whom the king supports himself. Heaven completes itself by three, [1] and the king supports himself by three. When this complete number is established and (the process of selection) is multiplied four times, there can be no error. The significance of arranging Heaven's numerical categories for partⁱicipation in (human) affairs is that the government should be conducted with careful attention to the course (of Heaven)....

"Does not the fact that there is one *yang* (for spring), but three spring (months covered by it), derive from the appropriateness of three? Heaven then multiplies this by four (the number of the seasons), the number (of months) being identical (for each season). Heaven has its four seasons and the seasons have their three months. (Likewise) the king has his four selections (of officials, in each of which) three ministers are selected. Thus it is the characteristic of each season that it has a first, second, and third month, just as it is the characteristic of each selection (of officials) that it comprises an upper, lower, and medium (class official). That three ministers constitute one selected group, and that the process of selecting is limited to four: herein lies the complete expression of the characteristics of man. Among men of superior endowment there indubitably exist four (categories used in) selection, just as among the seasons of Heaven there indubitably take place four (seasonal) changes. Sages (*sheng jen*) comprise the first selected group, superior men (*chün tzŭ*) the next, men of goodness (*shan jen* 善人) the next, and upright men (*cheng* 正 *jen*) the next. [2] Those below these last are unworthy to be selected.

"Each of these four selections proceeds according to regulation. Thus Heaven selects the four seasons, bringing them to completion with the twelve (months); in this way the transformations of Heaven are completely expressed. And it is only the sage who can (similarly) give complete expression to the changes of man and harmonize them

twenty-seven great officials; this is the third selection. And these again each select three assistants, or an aggregate of eighty-one men, who are the eighty-one first-class officers; this is the fourth and final selection. — Tr.

[1] A number explained by Su Yü as referring to the courses of Heaven, Earth, and man. — Tr.

[2] In other words, the three highest ministers (the first selected group) are supposed to be sages, the nine lower ministers (second group) to be superior men, the twenty-seven great officials (third group) to be "men of goodness," and the eighty-one first-class officers (fourth group) to be "upright men." See below. — Tr.

with those of Heaven. This is why it is he who institutes kingly affairs.... Hence within a year there are four seasons and within a season three spans (of time): such are the divisions of Heaven. Man is produced by Heaven and embodies these heavenly distinctions. Therefore in him too there are variations in greatness and pettiness, generosity and meanness: such are the characteristics of man. The former kings, adapting themselves to these human characteristics, distinguished between their variant forms, thus carrying out the four selections (of officials). For this reason, sages were selected for the positions of the three highest ministers; superior men for those of the three lower ministers (attached to each of the highest ministers); men of goodness for those of the three great officials (attached to each of the lower ministers); and upright and straightforward men for those of the three (first-class) officers (attached to each of the great officials).

"Thus, according to their variations, men were classed so as to constitute the four selected groups, in each of which there were established (subsidiary groups of) three ministers (each). This is similar to the way in which Heaven divides the year according to its variations, thus forming the four seasons, in each of which there are three (monthly) divisions. Heaven, harmonizing the groupings of the four seasons with those of the twelve (monthly) divisions, thus completes the year. (Likewise) the king smooths out the mutual relationship between the four ranks of selections and the twelve ministers (who fill them), thus attaining the height (of good conduct). [1] Good conduct must extend to its utmost limit. Only then can it gain (for mankind) Heaven's and Earth's beautiful (bounty)" (7.26-30).

Thus, according to Tung Chung-shu, the establishment of the official hierarchy cannot be made haphazardly, but must be carefully modeled on Heaven's numerical categories.

As to Tung's statement that the king "models himself on its (Heaven's) course and thereby brings his administration into

---

[1] The number twelve is somewhat arbitrarily arrived at by the following progression: (a) three highest ministers, (b) three lower ministers selected by each of the preceding as assistants, (c) three great officials selected by each of the preceding, (d) three first-class officers selected by each of the preceding. Logically speaking, of course, if the three highest ministers are accepted as the first unit in the series, then the progression should thereafter successively be nine (and not three) lower ministers, twenty-seven (and not three) great officials, and eighty-one (and not three) first-class officers. This, however, would destroy the desired analogy between the number of officials and the months of the year. — Tr.

operation" (cf. p. 47), he writes further as follows (chap. 45):

"The course of Heaven has its sequence and seasons, its regulations and controls. It undergoes changes, yet retains a constancy; it passes through opposite phases (of winter and summer, spring and autumn), which nevertheless assist one another. It is minute, yet extends to what is remote; it is distant, yet reaches unto the finest essence; it is single, yet collects into itself (all things). Spread out widely, it nevertheless has solid actuality; an empty void, it nevertheless is filled. The sage, when he acts, observes Heaven. Therefore he shows careful discrimination as to the occasion for (displaying) his likes or dislikes, joy or anger, wishing to harmonize these with Heaven's avoidance of unseasonable appearances of warmth, coolness, cold, and heat. [1] ... By his shame for shallow superficiality and empty surface glitter, and his esteem for solid genuineness and loyal good faith, he wishes to harmonize himself with Heaven, which remains silent and without speech, yet brings its task of virtue to a successful conclusion. By his refusal to assent to partisanship or selfishness, and his praise of comprehensive love and the common good, he wishes to harmonize himself with the way in which Heaven, by giving a minimum of frost and an abundance of dew, brings things to their completed growth" (11.12-13).

Thus does the ruler "model himself on Heaven's course," in order thereby to "bring his administration into operation."

As to how the king "models himself on its (Heaven's) will and with it attaches himself to love" (cf. p. 47), Tung writes further as follows (chap. 44):

"The beautiful expression of love (*jen*) lies in Heaven, for Heaven *is* love. Heaven protects and shelters all creatures, generates and produces them, nourishes and forms them. Its work is without end; when it reaches a conclusion, it returns again to its beginning. And everything that it produces it hands over to man for his service. If we examine the purpose of Heaven, (we see that) it is boundless and infinitely loving. Man, receiving his life from Heaven, (likewise) receives from it love and is thereby himself loving. Therefore man ... possesses the family relationships of father and elder brother, son and younger brother; his heart is one of loyalty, good faith, kindliness, incorruptibility, and humbleness; he makes decisions as to what is

---

[1] The following sentence is corrupt and so is left untranslated. In general idea it is parallel to the sentences below. — Tr.

right or wrong, improper or proper. His cultured principles are manifest and abundant, his knowledge broad and extensive. It is only man, indeed, who in his conduct can equate himself with Heaven. The purpose of Heaven is ever to love and confer benefit; its work is ever to nourish and create growth. Spring, autumn, winter, and summer are all its instruments for this. The king, likewise, ever takes as his purpose the loving and benefiting of all beneath Heaven, and as his work the giving of peace and contentment to the entire world. His likes, dislikes, joy, and anger are all his instruments for this" (11.9-10).

The point here made, that the purpose of Heaven is to love and benefit man, and that the king, by imitating Heaven, likewise takes as his purpose the loving and benefiting of man, resembles Mo Tzŭ's doctrine that men are to practice universal love because it is the Will of Heaven for them to do so. [1]

In his social philosophy, Tung Chung-shu stresses the need for equalizing riches and poverty and closing the paths to private aggrandizement. Thus he writes (chap. 27):

"Confucius has said: 'I am not concerned over poverty, but over the lack of equality.' [2] Therefore where there is accumulation and amassing (of goods), there is also emptiness and lack. Where there is great wealth there is arrogance, while where there is great poverty there is anxiety. Anxiety leads to brigandage, and arrogance to oppression. Such is the nature of the generality of men. The sage observes what it is in the nature of the generality of men that leads to disorder. Therefore in his governing of men he differentiates between upper and lower (classes), permitting the rich to have enough to display their noble position, but not to the point of arrogance, and the poor to have enough to support life, but not to reach the point of anxiety. If a harmonious balance is maintained according to this rule, there will then be no lack of material resources and upper and lower (classes) will be mutually at peace. Therefore good government will be conducted with ease.

"The present generation, however, has discarded this principle, so that people all pursue their own desires. Their desires have no

---

[1] Cf. vol. 1, pp. 96 f. — Tr.

[2] A variation of *Analects*, XVI, 1: "I have heard that the ruler of a kingdom, or the chief of a house, is not concerned about his people being few, but about their lack of equality; nor is he concerned over poverty, but over the presence of discontent." — Tr.

bounds and, with unlimited power, they vulgarly (strive to) gain dissipation for themselves. Prominent people are afflicted by insufficiency above, and the little people suffer want below. Thereupon the rich become ever more greedy for gain and are unwilling to practice righteousness, while the poor daily violate the prohibitions and cannot be made to stop. In this way the world becomes difficult to govern. ...

"Heaven does not bestow twice. Thus what has horns is not (in addition) permitted to have upper teeth. [1] Hence one who has already acquired the greater share is not additionally permitted to acquire the lesser share. Such is the rule of Heaven. And since Heaven cannot permit such a thing, how much more is this true of man! This is why the intelligent sage, patterning himself on the acts of Heaven, creates his governmental institutions in such a way that all who receive large incomes will not at the same time be permitted to annex lesser profits for themselves, thus contending with the (common) people for gain. For such is the principle of Heaven" (8.1-3).

Through such governmental institutions, based on "the principle of Heaven," undue aggrandizement is prevented.

As to the question of land distribution, Tung advocates a revival of the ancient "well-field" or *ching t'ien* system. [2] He writes (chap. 28):

"A square *li* (about one third of a mile) comprises one 'well' (square), and such a 'well' comprises 900 *mou* (Chinese acres), on which the population is settled. A square *li* contains eight families, each having 100 *mou*, whereby (at the minimum) it may feed five persons. But a superior farmer, by cultivating 100 *mou*, can feed nine persons; one of the next class, eight persons; one of the next, seven; one of the next, six; one of the next, five" (8.10). [3]

The collapse of feudalism at the end of the Chou dynasty had as its immediate effect the freeing of men from their old political and economic bonds. This freedom, however, merely paved the way

---

[1] This seems to have been a popular belief of the day, for the same statement appears in the *Lü-shih Ch'un Ch'iu*, XXIV, 5 (p. 427); the *Huai-nan-tzŭ*, 4,9; and the *Ta Tai Li Chi*, chap. 81 (p. 251). — Tr.

[2] Supposed, with no certain proof, to have existed during the early part of the Chou dynasty. See vol. 1, pp. 10-13. — Tr.

[3] This gradation is said in the commentary to refer to the different qualities of agricultural land rather than to the abilities of the cultivators themselves. — Tr.

for new struggles for economic power—struggles which, during the Ch'in and Han dynasties, led to the rise of many new families to positions of wealth, resulting in growing economic inequalities. This phenomenon was remarked on by many clear-sighted men of the time, among whom Tung Chung-shu, like others, seems earnestly to have desired to rectify the resulting abuses. [1]

10—Visitations and Prodigies

Tung Chung-shu, as we have seen, firmly believes that an intimate relationship exists between Heaven and man. Therefore, so he argues, the occurrence of unharmonious and abnormal events in the human world inevitably stirs Heaven to manifest corresponding abnormal phenomena in the natural world. Such phenomena are variously known as "visitations" (*tsai* 災) or "prodigies" (*yi* 異). [2] Thus he writes (chap. 30):

"According to a rough classification, when things in Heaven and Earth undergo abnormal changes, these are called 'prodigies'; lesser ones are called 'visitations.' Visitations always appear first and are then followed by prodigies. Visitations are the reprimands of Heaven; prodigies are its warnings. If (man), being thus reprimanded, still fails to understand, he is then made to feel awe through such warnings. When the *Odes* (IV, i, Ode 7) says: 'Stand in awe of Heaven's warnings,' it probably refers to this. The source of all such visitations and prodigies lies in faults that exist within the nation. Heaven sends forth fearful visitations in order to announce its reprimand. If, being thus reprimanded, (man) fails to understand (the reason for) these manifestations, strange prodigies then appear in order to strike him with terror. And if, being thus terrified, he still does not understand (the cause for) his fear, only then do misfortunes and calamities overtake him. From this may be seen the goodness of Heaven's purpose and its unwillingness to bring ruin upon man" (8. 24).

---

[1] It is evident, however, that Tung, like all other Confucianists, tacitly accepted the existing class system. His aim was not to destroy class differences, but merely to harmonize these differences by checking the abuses of extreme exploitation. At the same time he, like others, accepted the possibility that particular individuals might work their way from one social class to another. — Tr.

[2] This doctrine was politically important during the Han dynasty. See above, p. 10, note 1 — Tr.

As to the manner in which these visitations and prodigies appear in response to improper human behavior, Tung Chung-shu writes further (chap. 57):

"If now water be poured on level ground, it will avoid the parts that are dry and move toward those that are wet. Whereas if (two) identical pieces of firewood are exposed to fire, the latter will avoid the one that is wet and catch to that which is dry. [1] All things avoid that from which they differ and cleave to that to which they are similar. Thus forces that are similar meet each other, and tones that match respond to each other. Experience makes this evident. For suppose (two) lutes are played in alternation to each other. If the note of *kung* is struck on the one, that of *kung* will respond on the other, and if the note of *shang* is struck on the one, that of *shang* will respond on the other. Among the five notes, each one that matches sounds of itself. There is nothing supernatural in this. It is because of their numerical (harmonies). (Likewise) a thing that is beautiful will call to itself another beautiful thing the same in kind, whereas an ugly thing will call to itself another ugly thing the same in kind. For example, when a horse neighs, another horse will respond; when an ox lows, another ox will respond. In the same way, when an emperor or king is about to arise, auspicious omens first appear, whereas when he is about to be destroyed, evil auguries likewise first appear. Thus it is that things of the same kind call to one another. ...

"Heaven possesses the *yin* and *yang* and man also possesses the *yin* and *yang*. When the *yin* ether of the universe arises, man's *yin* ether likewise arises in response. And vice versa, when man's *yin* ether arises, the *yin* ether of the universe should arise in harmonious response. Their course is one. He who understands this, when he wishes to bring rain, activates the (human) *yin* in order to arouse the *yin* (of the universe); when he wishes to stop rain, activates the (human) *yang* in order to arouse the *yang* (of the universe). Therefore the bringing of rain is not a supernatural matter, though its principle, abstruse and wonderful, resembles the supernatural. It is not solely the *yin* and *yang* ethers which thus approach and withdraw according to their kind. The generation of inauspicious misfortune or of good fortune also proceeds in the same way. It is nothing but a case in which, when one begins something oneself, things act in response according to their kind" (13. 4-6).

---

[1] This metaphor is also found in the *Hsün-tzŭ*, chap. 27 (19.23). — Tr.

Tung's biography in the *Ch'ien Han Shu* (56. 5) also quotes him as saying:

"If corporal punishments are not administered correctly, an evil effluvium (*hsieh ch'i* 邪氣) is created. With the accumulation of this evil effluvium below, resentments and hatreds are nourished above. When superiors and inferiors are no longer in harmony, the *yin* and *yang* become twisted and perverse and evil auguries appear. This is the cause for the rise of visitations and prodigies." He further writes (chap. 81):

"Man causes the myriad things to grow below, and equates himself with Heaven and Earth above. Therefore, as a result of his good or disorderly government, the forces of activity or of calm, of compliance or of contrariness, act either to diminish or increase the transformations of the *yin* and *yang* and to agitate all within the four seas. Even in the case of things difficult to understand, such as the supernatural, it may not be said to be otherwise. Thus then, if (something) is thrown onto (hard) ground, it is (itself) injured and destroyed and causes no movement in the latter; if thrown into soft mire, it causes movement within a limited distance; if thrown into water, it causes movement over a greater distance. Thus we may see that the softer a thing is, the more readily does it undergo movement and agitation. The transforming ether is much softer than water (or the other things here mentioned); yet the ruler of men ever acts upon all of them without surcease. This is why the influences of government are constantly becoming maladjusted in respect to the transforming influences of Heaven and Earth, with the result that there is no good government.

"Therefore when the human world is well governed and the people are at peace, or when the will (of the ruler) is equable and his character is correct, then the transforming influences of Heaven and Earth operate in a state of perfection and among the myriad things only the finest are produced. But when the human world is in disorder and the people become perverse, or when the (ruler's) will is depraved and his character is rebellious, then the transforming influences of Heaven and Earth suffer injury, so that their (*yin* and *yang*) ethers generate visitations and harm arises" (17. 7).

Here we have the doctrine that improper human conduct produces a mechanical response on the part of the *yin* and *yang* ethers, resulting in the appearance of abnormal phenomena. This mechanistic interpretation differs from the other theory quoted at the beginning of this section, according to which such visitations and prodigies result from Heaven's conscious reprimands and warnings against improper human conduct. Tung Chung-shu fails to resolve this contradiction either by definitely stating which of the theories he thinks is correct, or by suggesting that possibly both are mutually operative. Already before Tung's time, as a matter of fact, this contradiction between a mechanistic and teleological point of view had appeared in the *Yin-yang* school's discussions on the alleged inter-relationship between Heaven and man. [1]

11—Philosophy of History

It is not surprising that Tung Chung-shu and other Han thinkers, believing as they did in the existence of a close interrelationship between Heaven and man, should also believe that a similar re-lationship links the course of human history with the laws of Heaven. On this point there were two main theories. One, associated with the Five Elements or Powers (*te*), had already been propounded in the late fourth century B.C. by Tsou Yen, of whom it was said: "Starting from the time of the separation of Heaven and Earth and coming down, he made citations of the revolutions and trans-mutations of the Five Powers, arranging them until each found its proper place (in history)." [2] The basic concept behind this theory, namely that each period or dynasty of human history lies under the influence of some one of the Five Elements, continued unchanged throughout the Han dynasty. The manner of its application to actual historical periods, however, differed from group to group. A hotly debated question of the time, for example, was whether the Han dynasty itself was dominated by water, or whether its real controlling element was earth or fire. Besides this Five Element theory, however, quite a different one also existed, which tried to explain history in terms of what it called the "Three Sequences" (*san t'ung* 三 統). These sequences, sometimes also known as the "Three Beginnings" (*san cheng* 正), consisted of blackness, whiteness and redness, and are described by Tung Chung-shu as follows (chap. 23):

"Among the Three Beginnings, the Black Sequence comes first.

---

[1] See vol. 1, pp. 164-165.
[2] See vol. 1, p. 160.

On the first day of its year, the sun and new moon stand in the constellation of the Barracks, [1] and the Big Dipper stands in *yin*. [2] Heaven's all-embracing ethers then first begin to permeate and generate things, from which buds of growth appear. Their color is black. Therefore the clothes worn at court on the first day of the month are black, as are the pendants on official caps, the imperial chariots, and their horses. The cords that carry the great seals (of the officials) are black, as are their headdresses, the flags, the great precious jades, and the animals used in the suburban sacrifices. The horns of these animals are egg-shaped. The ceremony of capping (that takes place when a youth comes of age) is performed at the eastern steps (before the main hall). In the marriage ceremony, (the groom) goes to meet (the bride) in the courtyard (of the ancestral temple of her home); in the funeral ceremony, the deceased is encoffined above the eastern steps (leading to the main hall). [3] ...

"In the White Sequence, the sun and new moon, on the first day of the year, stand in the Hollow, [4] and the Great Dipper stands in *ch'ou*. [5] Heaven's all-embracing ethers then first cause things to shed their coverings and be generated, and these things begin to bud. Their color is white. Therefore the clothes worn at court on the first day of the month are white, as are the pendants on official caps, the imperial chariots, and their horses. The cords that carry the great seals (of the officials) are white, as are their headdresses, the flags, the great precious jades, and the animals used in the suburban sacrifices. The horns of these animals are shaped like a silk cocoon. The ceremony of capping is performed at (the platform before) the main hall. In the marriage ceremony, (the groom) goes to meet (the bride) at (the platform before) the main hall (of the ancestral temple of her home); in the funeral ceremony, the deceased is encoffined between the columns (on the platform of the main hall). ...

"In the Red Sequence, the sun and new moon, on the first day

---

[1] *Ying shih* 營室, i.e., Pegasus. — Tr.

[2] Third of the twelve "earthly branches" (on which see p. 11 above), corresponding, among the compass points, to E.N.E. — Tr.

[3] For a detailed account of these ritualistic practices, as well as those associated with the White and Red Sequences which are described below, see Woo, *Trois théories politiques*, pp. 145-160. — Tr.

[4] *Hsü* 虛, a constellation situated in Aquarius and Pegasus. — Tr.

[5] Second of the twelve "branches," corresponding to N.N.E. — Tr.

of the year, stand in the Cowherd, [1] and the Great Dipper stands in *tzŭ*. [2] Heaven's all-embracing ethers then first come forth and generate things, and these things begin to move. Their color is red. Therefore the clothes worn at court on the first day of the month are red, as are the pendants on official caps, the imperial chariots, and their horses. The cords that carry the great seals (of the officials) are red, as are their headdresses, the flags, the great precious jades, and the animals used in the suburban sacrifices. The horns of these animals are shaped like a chestnut. The ceremony of capping is performed in the side chamber. In the marriage ceremony, (the groom) goes to meet (the bride) at the door (to the eastern side chamber of the ancestral temple of her home); in the funeral ceremony, the deceased is encoffined above the western steps (leading to the main hall). . . .

"The significance of these changes in Beginnings arose in (the king's) service to Heaven. The ancient kings, after receiving the (heavenly) Mandate that made them kings (of a new dynasty), changed the institutions, titles, and beginning of the year (which had been in force under the preceding dynasty). Having determined the color for clothing, they at the suburban sacrifices announced (the accession of their dynasty) to Heaven and Earth and the multitude of spirits. [3] They offered sacrifices to their distant and nearer ancestors, and then proclaimed (the accession of their dynasty) throughout the empire. This (proclamation) was received in their ancestral temples by the feudal lords, who then announced it to their spirits of the land and grain, to the ancestors, and to the spirits of mountains and streams. Thus there was a single rule (for all) to respond to. . . . This was the way in which Heaven's sequences were made clear.

"The reason why these sequences are known as the 'Three Beginnings' is that 'Beginning' means 'what is correct.' [4] (Heaven's) sequences bring the (*yin* and *yang*) ethers into operation, to which all things respond and are thus made correct, so that when the sequences are correct, everything else is correct. What is vital

---

[1] *Ch'ien niu* 牽牛, i.e., the stars alpha, beta, and gamma in Aquila. — Tr.

[2] First of the twelve "branches," corresponding to north. — Tr.

[3] These sacrifices were annually made by the ruler to Heaven in the southern suburb of the capital on the winter solstice, and to Earth in the northern suburb on the summer solstice. — Tr.

[4] *Cheng*, which usually means "what is correct," is also technically used to designate the "beginning" of the year. This is the meaning it has in the term "Three Beginnings," *san cheng*. — Tr.

for the entire year is (the starting point of) its first month. [1] The way to take what is correct as a model is to rectify what is fundamental, so that what is secondary will respond, and to rectify what is internal, so that what is external will respond. Then, as movements and activities are initiated or stopped, there will be nothing that does not follow (an orderly sequence) in its transformations. Such may be called taking what is correct as a model. ...

"Therefore for the kings (who found new dynasties), there are certain respects in which they should not change (their institutions from those of the preceding dynasty); certain respects in which they should revert (to those of a preceding dynasty) after (a cycle of) two (dynasties); certain respects in which they should revert after (a cycle of) three; certain respects in which they should revert after (a cycle of) four; certain respects in which they should revert after (a cycle of) five; and certain respects in which they should revert after (a cycle of) nine. [2] ...

"The institutions of these kings are those of Shang, Hsia, Simplicity (*chih* 質), and Refinement (*wen* 文). Those of Shang and those of Simplicity take Heaven as their guiding principle; those of Hsia and those of Refinement take Earth as their guiding principle; while (the reigns covered by) the *Spring and Autumn Annals* (722-481 B.C.) took man as their guiding principle" (7. 10-19).

Equated with actual history, the dynasty of Hsia (trad. 2205-1766 B.C.) constituted the Black Sequence; its year began with the *yin*, or first, month of the later calendar, and it took black as its primary color. The dynasty of Shang (trad. 1766-1123 B.C.) constituted the White Sequence; its year began with the *ch'ou*, or twelfth, month of the calendar, and it took white as its primary color. The dynasty of Chou (1122?-256 B.C.) constituted the Red Sequence; its year began with the *tzŭ*, or eleventh, month of the calendar, and it took red as its primary color. The dynasty following Chou would again be that of the Black Sequence, and this historical cycle would continue indefinitely. Concerning Tung's statement that "for the kings (who found new dynasties), there are certain respects in which they should

---

[1] In ancient China each dynasty began its year with a different month, the determination of which was the prerogative of the ruling house. There is a constant play on words here between *cheng*, "correct," and *cheng*, meaning (when applied to periods of time) "the beginning." Thus when coupled with the word month, it means "the first month." — Tr.

[2] These dynastic cycles are all explained below. — Tr.

not change (their institutions from those of the preceding dynasty),"
he writes elsewhere (chap. 1) as follows:

"What I now say, that a new king must change his institutions,
does not mean that he changes his (fundamental) course or alters his
(basic) principles. (It means that), having received a Mandate from
Heaven (to found a new dynasty), he rules under a surname different
(from those of the preceding kings), and does so as a new king rather
than as the direct successor of these preceding kings. For if he
uninterruptedly continued the former institutions and practiced the
old pursuits without making any changes, there would be no way to
distinguish him from the direct line of succession of the preceding
kings. When a ruler receives the Mandate of Heaven, this is a great
manifestation of Heaven's (favor). He who serves a father carries
out the latter's ideas, and he who serves a ruler exemplifies the latter's
will. The same is true of (a ruler's) service to Heaven. So now, if
Heaven makes a great manifestation (of its favor) to someone (by
conferring on him its Mandate), and yet things in the replacing
(dynasty) are perpetuated unchanged (from that preceding), then no
proper manifestation is made (of Heaven's Mandate), and such is not
in accordance with the will of Heaven.

"Therefore (the founder of a new dynasty) must shift his place
of residence, assume a new title, change the beginning of the year,
and alter the color of the clothing—all for no other reason than that
he dares not but obey the will of Heaven and make clear the manifestation (of the Mandate it has conferred) on him. But as to the great
bonds of human relationship, and as to morality, government,
instruction, customs, and the meanings of words: these remain
wholly as they were before. For why, indeed, should they be changed?
Therefore the king (of a new dynasty) has the reputation of changing
his institutions, but does not in actual fact alter his (basic) principles.
Confucius has said: 'Not to act and yet to give good government—
was not Shun such a person?' [1] He meant to say that he (Shun) did
nothing more than take the principles of (his predecessor) Yao as a
guide. Is this not the good result of avoiding an alteration (of fundamentals)?" (1. 11-13).

Tung's biography in the *Ch'ien Han Shu* (56. 18) also quotes
him as saying: "The great source of right principles (*tao*) derives

---

[1] *Analects*, XV, 4. "Not to act" is the Taoist phrase *wu wei*, and Shun, of
course, is the legendary sage-ruler. — Tr.

from Heaven; Heaven does not change, nor do these principles." This illustrates what Tung means here. As to his earlier statement about the founders of new dynasties that there are "certain respects in which they should revert (to the institutions of a preceding dynasty) after (a cycle of) two (dynasties)," what he has in mind is the dynastic interchange between "Refinement" or *wen* and "Simplicity" or *chih*. In this cycle the one periodically replaces the other in order to correct the abuses that would otherwise develop. (This is further explained in the *Note* immediately below.) And when he likewise says of dynastic founders that there are "certain respects in which they should revert (to the institutions of a preceding dynasty) after (a cycle of) three," he has in mind the cycle of the Three Sequences or Beginnings such as has already been described.

Note: Tung Chung-shu's concept of alternation between Refinement and Simplicity is further elaborated in the *Po Hu T'ung* (chap. 27) as follows:

"How is it that the kings (who found new dynasties) must alternate between Simplicity and Refinement? It is in order that they may carry out (the work of) Heaven and Earth, and accord with the *yin* and *yang*. When the course of the *yang* has reached its apogee, that of the *yin* takes over, and when the *yin*'s course has reached its apogee, that of the *yang* takes over. It is evident that there cannot be two *yin* and two *yang* each carrying on from the other. [1] The fact is simply that Simplicity is modeled on Heaven and Refinement on Earth. Thus Heaven creates (things in their basic) Simplicity, which, being taken over by Earth, are then transformed, nourished, and given completed form, so that there is thus created (an elaborated) Refinement. The *Shang-shu Ta-chuan* (Amplification of the Book of History) [2] says: 'The fact that the kings (who found new dynasties) alternate between Simplicity and Refinement is based upon the course of Heaven and Earth.' And the *San Cheng Chi* (Record of the Three Beginnings) of the *Rituals* [3] says: 'Simplicity is modeled on Heaven and Refinement on Earth.' When, upon the new arisal of emperors and kings, the first of them (follows) Simplicity and the next Refinement, this is done in order to accord with the course of Heaven and Earth, with the meaning of what is primary and what secondary, and with the sequence of what comes first and what afterward. For it is true of all things that they ori-

---

[1] I.e., the *yin* is invariably followed by the *yang* and vice versa; it is inconceivable that either *yin* or *yang* could immediately be followed by a second *yin* or *yang*. — Tr.

[2] A work now lost save for scattered fragments, attributed to Fu Sheng (died dur. 179-157 B.C.), noted specialist on the *Book of History*. — Tr.

[3] One of the Former Han treatises on the *Li* or *Rituals*, now known only through scattered fragments. — Tr.

ginally pertain to Simplicity by nature, and only afterward acquire the decorations of Refinement"[1] (II, 553-554).

The same chapter of this work also elaborates (II, 548-551) on Tung's concept of the Three Sequences or Beginnings:

"Why is it that a king, having received (Heaven's) Mandate (to found a new dynasty), must change the beginning of the year? It is to show that he belongs to a different family and is not simply perpetuating (the former ruling house). It is to show that he has received it (the Mandate) from Heaven and not from man (i.e., not from the preceding dynasty). Hence he transforms the minds of the people and provides changes for their ears and eyes, in order thus to facilitate the transforming influence (of his rule). Therefore the (Shang-shu) Ta-chuan says: 'When the king (of a new dynasty) first arises, he changes the beginning of the year, alters the color of clothing, assumes new titles, employs different tools and weapons, and differentiates his clothing.' ...

"How is it that there are three beginnings to the year? It derives from the fact that Heaven has its Three Sequences, these having reference to the three (differing) months of minute (beginnings for the year). Intelligent kings must conform to them and give them finished form. Therefore each, when he receives (Heaven's) Mandate, takes one of these Beginnings as his Sequence, thus showing his respect for what originates and his esteem for what is fundamental. The beginning of the year signifies revival and change. That is to say, all things undergo change and renewal at this time, which therefore marks a (new) Sequence. The San Cheng Chi of the Rituals says: 'There is a triple changing of the beginning of the year, while there is a dual alternation of Refinement and Simplicity.'

"What is meant by the three minute (beginnings)? (This means that) when the yang ether first begins to emanate from the 'Yellow Springs,' its activities are still minute and invisible.[2] During the eleventh month, when the yang ether first begins to nourish the roots of plants, down in the Yellow Springs all things are red.[3] This redness is that of the yang ether when it is in full flood. That is why the Chou (dynasty), having Heaven's Beginning for itself, assumed red as its primary color.[4] But in the twelfth month all things first begin to bud and are then white, and this whiteness

---

[1] I.e., all things tend to evolve from initial simplicity to growing complexity and elaboration. This natural law explains why the simple and severe institutions of one dynasty are supposed to give way to the more complex and sophisticated institutions of the next. — Tr.

[2] "Yellow Springs" is the name of the Chinese underworld, but here it simply means what is beneath the ground. The yang ether at first operates underground, there causing the seeds of plants to germinate; its above-ground operations become evident only later, as spring progresses and the young plants shoot up from the soil. — Tr.

[3] I.e., the underground roots of plants are supposed to be red. — Tr.

[4] The idea here is that the yang is associated with Heaven, just as yin is with Earth. Hence the Chou dynasty, as the follower of the Beginning or Sequence pertaining to Heaven, assumed red as its primary color and also started its year with what, during the Han dynasty, was actually the eleventh month. — Tr.

is that of the *yin* ether. [1] That is why the Yin (dynasty), [2] having Earth's Beginning for itself, assumed white as its primary color. [3] And in the thirteenth month, when all things first begin to burst from their enclosing husks and to emerge, they are then all black, and man is able to apply his work to them. [4] That is why the Hsia (dynasty), having Man's Beginning for itself, assumed black as its primary color. [5] The *Shang-shu Ta-chuan* says: 'The Hsia (dynasty) took the first month of spring as the beginning (of its year); that of Yin (i.e., Shang) took the last month of winter as its beginning; that of Chou took the second month of winter as its beginning.'

"The Hsia took the thirteenth month as its beginning, assumed black as its primary color, and started its year with dawn. The Yin (or Shang) took the twelfth month as its beginning, assumed white as its primary color, and started its year with the cock's crow. The Chou took the eleventh month as its beginning, assumed red as its primary color, and started its year with midnight. [6] The beginning (of the year) cannot be placed in the second month or later, because then the myriad creatures are no longer uniform (in their development) and none follow a standard sequence. Therefore it must be placed among the three (above-mentioned) months of minute (beginnings of growth). The mutual succession of these Three Beginnings continues in an endless cycle. Thus when Confucius fell heir to the abuses of the Chou, he put into operation the calendar of Hsia, knowing that he, as successor to (a dynasty that had used) the eleventh month as the (year's) beginning, must himself use the thirteenth month." [7]

As to Tung Chung-shu's statement (p. 61 above) about the founders of new dynasties, that there are "certain respects in which

---

[1] White is the color of the west, which is the quarter of the *yin*. This sentence no doubt refers to the spring rains (water being *yin*) which cause plants to bud above ground after the *yang* ether has earlier poured into their roots underground. — Tr.

[2] Another name for the Shang dynasty. Conceivably, though not necessarily, there is a play on words between the name Yin and the *yin* ether. — Tr.

[3] The Shang dynasty began its year with what, during the Han dynasty, was the twelfth month. — Tr.

[4] I.e., after plants have germinated and sprung up, man is able to assist their further growth through his agricultural labors. —Tr.

[5] The Hsia dynasty began its year with what, during the Han dynasty, would have been a thirteenth (i.e., actually the first) month. — Tr.

[6] Midnight, cock's crow, and dawn are, respectively, names of the first three of the twelve two-hour periods into which the Chinese day was formerly divided. — Tr.

[7] I.e., since the Hsia, Shang, and Chou calendars had already been successively used, the next phase in the cycle would be a return to the Hsia calendar. This has reference to the belief elaborated by Tung Chung-shu (see next sect.), according to which Confucius was an "uncrowned king" who by rights should have become founder of a new dynasty, even though, through force of circumstances, the Chou dynasty actually continued after his time for several centuries. We know from *Analects*, XV, 10, that Confucius did indeed advocate a return to the Hsia calendar. — Tr.

they should revert (to a preceding dynasty) after (a cycle of) four (dynasties)," what he means by this is the cyclical alternation of Shang, Hsia, Simplicity, and Refinement. (The terms Shang and Hsia, however, are purely abstract conceptions; Tung does not literally mean the historical dynasties of these names.) This cycle is described by him as follows (chap. 23):

"The course of him who reigns, taking Heaven as his guiding principle and modeling himself on Shang, is that of the *yang* in all its fullness. It emphasizes family relations and exalts love and honest simplicity. Therefore the succession (to the throne) passes to the son, while generosity is displayed toward those younger brothers (of the king) who are born of the same mother. (If the king has a concubine who bears him a son, that) concubine gains an honorable title because of her son. As regards the marriage and capping (i.e., coming of age) ceremonies: (at the latter), the son is given his new name (*tzǔ* 字) by the father; (at the former, the groom and bride at first) do not glance at each other, (but later) husband and wife sit opposite each other (on different mats) when eating (their first meal). At their funeral service they are buried separately, and when sacrifices are made to them, pork fat is the first thing that is offered. (In the ancestral temple, the tablets of the deceased) husband and wife occupy separate positions on the left (*chao* 昭) and right (*mu* 穆) sides. ...

"The course of him who reigns, taking Earth as his guiding principle and modeling himself on Hsia, is that of the growing *yin*. It emphasizes the honoring of superiors and exalts the regulations governing the proper relationships. Therefore the succession (to the throne) passes to the (king's) grandson, while generosity is displayed toward the (king's own) heir apparent. (If the king has a concubine who bears him a son, that) concubine does not gain an honorable title because of her son. As regards the marriage and capping ceremonies: (at the latter), the son is given his new name by the mother; (at the former, the groom and bride at first) do not glance at each other, (but later) husband and wife sit together (on the same mat) when eating (their first meal). At their funeral service they are buried together, and when sacrifices are made to them, cooked (food) is the first thing that is offered. (In the ancestral temple, the tablet of the deceased) wife follows that of the husband, (both) being arranged (together, either) on the left or right sides. ...

"The course of him who reigns, taking Heaven as his guiding principle and modeling himself on Simplicity, is that of the *yang* in all its fullness. It emphasizes family relations and exalts simplicity and affection. Therefore the succession (to the throne) goes to the son, while generosity is displayed toward those younger brothers (of the king) who are born of the same mother. (If the king has a concubine who bears him a son, that) concubine gains an honorable title because of her son. As regards the marriage and capping ceremonies: (at the latter), the son is given his new name by the father; (at the former, the groom and bride at first) do not glance at each other, (but later) husband and wife sit opposite each other (on different mats) when eating (their first meal). At their funeral service they are buried separately, and when sacrifices are made to them, grain is the first thing that is offered. (In the ancestral temple, the tablets of the deceased) husband and wife occupy separate positions on the left and right sides. . . .

"The course of him who reigns, taking Earth as his guiding principle and modeling himself on Refinement, is that of the growing *yin*. It emphasizes the honoring of superiors and exalts propriety and refinement. Therefore the succession (to the throne) passes to (the king's) grandson, while generosity is displayed toward the (king's own) heir apparent. (If the king has a concubine who bears him a son, that) concubine does not gain an honorable title because of her son. As regards the marriage and capping ceremonies: (at the latter), the son is given his name by the mother; (at the former, the groom and bride at first) do not glance at each other, (but later) husband and wife sit together (on the same mat) when eating (their first meal). At their funeral service they are buried together, and when sacrifices are made to them, liquor made from glutinous millet is the first thing that is offered. (In the ancestral temple, the tablet of the deceased) wife follows that of the husband, (both) being arranged (together, either) on the left or right sides. . . ." (7. 20-24).

These "four models" of Shang and Hsia, Simplicity and Refinement, are "like the four seasons. When (their cycle) is completed, it begins again; when it reaches its conclusion, it returns to its starting point" (*ibid.*, p. 25). Equating this system with actual history, Tung tells us that "when Shun (legendary pre-dynastic ruler) reigned, he took Heaven as his guiding principle and modeled himself on Shang; . . . when Yü (founder of the first dynasty, the Hsia) reigned, he took Earth as his guiding principle and modeled himself on

Hsia; ... when T'ang (founder of the second dynasty, the Shang) reigned, he took Heaven as his guiding principle and modeled himself on Simplicity; ... when King Wen (founder of the third dynasty, the Chou) reigned, he took Earth as his guiding principle and modeled himself on Refinement." With the completion of this cycle, the successor to the Chou dynasty should again "reign, taking Heaven as his guiding principle and modeling himself on Shang" (*ibid.*).

It will be remembered that Tung Chung-shu also speaks (p. 61 above) of "certain respects in which they (the founders of new dynasties) should revert (to the institutions of a preceding dynasty) after (a cycle of) five (dynasties)." He means by this that when a new dynasty is founded, its ruler should give feudal fiefs to the descendants of the two preceding dynasties, allowing them to retain their title of king, and "permitting them to wear their own (color of) clothing, practice their own ritual and music, and be treated as guests when they come to court," in order thus to "link together the Three Sequences" (*ibid.*, p. 15). At the same time he should confer the title of "emperor" (*ti* 帝) on those rulers, five in number, who antedated these two immediately preceding dynasties, and should enfeoff the descendants of each of these five emperors "with a small state, so as to enable them to offer sacrifices to their (forebears)" (*ibid.*).

In addition, he should confer the title of "sovereign" (*huang* 皇) to those rulers, nine in number, who lived prior to the "five emperors," and to their descendants should give somewhat smaller subsidiary fiefs known as *fu-yung* 附 庸 . This explains Tung Chung-shu's statement (p. 61 above) that there are "certain respects in which they (the founders of new dynasties) should revert (to the institutions of a preceding dynasty) after (a cycle of) nine (dynasties)." By way of summary he concludes that "those who are remote (in time) have more honorable titles but smaller territories; those who are nearer (in time) have lowlier titles but larger territories. Herein is (indicated) the significance of ties that are close and ones that are more remote" (*ibid.*, p. 17). [1]

---

[1] In Tung Chung-shu's day it was believed that the rulers of the three earliest dynasties (Hsia, Shang, Chou) had held the title of king or *wang*; that before them there had ruled "five emperors" (for names of which see vol. 1, p. xxxvi); and that still earlier there had been a series of brothers known as the "nine sovereigns," who had reigned a total of 45,600 years (see Chavannes, *Mém. hist.*,

Note: The reasons why the founder of a new dynasty should thus maintain fiefs for the descendants of the two preceding dynasties are explained as follows in the *Po Hu T'ung* (chap. 27): "Why should the king (of a new dynasty) preserve the descendants of the two (preceding dynasties') kings? It is in order to pay honor to these preceding kings and to link together the Three Sequences of the world. It is to show that the world is not the possession of a single family, and marks the height of attentive respect and humble deference. Therefore he gives them a fief of 100 *li* (about 30 miles) and permits them to wear clothing of their own proper color, to practice their own rituals and music, and to pay perpetual service to their first ancestors" (II, 552). The reasons for similarly preserving the titles of the still earlier "five emperors" and "nine sovereigns" would presumably be the same. [1]

Tung's biography in the *Ch'ien Han Shu* (56. 18) also reports him as advancing a doctrine known as that of the "three teachings" (*san chiao* 三 教):

"The Hsia exalted Faithfulness (*chung* 忠), the Yin (i.e., Shang) Respectfulness (*ching* 敬), and the Chou Refinement (*wen*). He who would follow these (dynasties), if he is to save himself (from preceding excesses), must (likewise) use these three (teachings). Confucius has said (*Analects*, II, 23): 'The Yin perpetuated the civilization of the Hsia; its modifications and accretions can be known. The Chou perpetuated the civilization of the Yin, and its modifications and accretions can (also) be known. Whatever others may succeed the Chou, their character, even a hundred ages hence, can be known.'

I, 19). Tung Chung-shu, however, does not equate his system with these specific legendary beings, because, according to his theory, the rulers of the existing and the two immediately preceding dynasties are always known as king or *wang*; those of the five regimes before that as emperors or *ti*; and those of the nine regimes again before that as sovereigns or *huang*. Hence as one dynasty follows another, a ruler who once was known as king subsequently becomes emperor and still later becomes sovereign. At the same time, however, the fiefs allotted to his descendants become progressively smaller. Cf. Woo, *Trois théories politiques*, pp. 114-116. — Tr.

[1] When the Chinese Republic supplanted the Ch'ing dynasty in 1912, it made an arrangement with the Ch'ing imperial family in many ways similar to what is described here: the former emperor was to retain his title and continue living in the Forbidden City in Peking, surrounded by a court at which the rituals of former days could be maintained; he was to be given an annual stipend of four million taels and to receive treatment equivalent to that accorded the sovereign of a foreign country. Other similarities appear in the Republic's institution of new official titles, substitution of the Western for the Chinese lunar calendar, and (in 1927) shift of the capital from Peking to Nanking. [This note has been added by Professor Fung for the English edition. — Tr.]

He means by this the (continued) practice of these three (teachings) by the kings of a hundred (succeeding generations)."

In other words, when Faithfulness has been so exalted that it develops abuses, it is replaced by Respectfulness, and when this too has been over-exalted, its place is taken by Refinement, which, in turn, must inevitably give way once more to Faithfulness. Thus the process continues in an unbroken cycle. Hence the dictum about future rulers that "their character, even a hundred ages hence, can be known."

Note: The *Po Hu T'ung* (chap. 28) further elaborates this doctrine as follows:

"Why is it that the kings (of each dynasty) have established the 'three teachings'? It is because they have each inherited the decay (of the preceding dynasty) and attempted to rectify its abuses, wishing their people to return to the proper course. Having certain faults (in their rule), the kings of the three (dynasties) have therefore established the 'three teachings' as guiding principles which might be received, one from another. The people of Hsia were taught by their kings to be faithful, but this resulted in the fault of rustic boorishness, to rectify which there is nothing better than Respectfulness. (Hence) the people of Yin were taught by their kings to be respectful, but this resulted in the fault of crafty deceit, to rectify which there is nothing better than Refinement. (Hence) the people of Chou were taught by their kings to be refined, but this resulted in the fault of superficiality, to rectify which there is nothing better than Faithfulness. (Likewise) the successor to the Chou exalts the institutions of the Black (Sequence), in this way being identical with the Hsia. Thus these three (teachings) follow one another in a continuous cycle which revolves until it reverts to its origin. ...

"Why is it that these teachings should be three in number? It is because they are patterned upon the inner Faithfulness, the outer Respectfulness, and the manifested Refinement, of Heaven, Earth, and man. Thus being three, they are all-complete. In what manner does each show itself as modeled on Heaven, Earth, and man? Faithfulness is modeled on man, Respectfulness on Earth, Refinement on Heaven. The way of man takes Faithfulness as its ruling principle, and this highest principle, being taught by man to man, results in the acme of Faithfulness. This Faithfulness, being thus used by man for his teaching, thereby constitutes the teaching of man. The way of Earth is to be humble and lowly, for what Heaven produces, Earth respectfully nourishes. Thus this Respectfulness constitutes the teaching of Earth"[1] (II, 555-556).

---

[1] It is pointed out in the commentary that the *Po Hu T'ung* must originally have contained a further statement on Refinement as the teaching of Heaven, which has now disappeared. [It is peculiar that Refinement is here associated with Heaven, whereas on p. 63 above we have seen that Simplicity is associated with Heaven and Refinement with Earth. — Tr.]

This concept of the interrelationship between man and the physical universe makes of history a "divine comedy." Utterly lacking though it be in historical reality, we must at least admit that it constitutes a systematic philosophy of history.

12—Significance of the Spring and Autumn Annals

We have already read in the first volume of this work (pp. 61-66) of the question of the relationship of Confucius with the *Ch'un Ch'iu* or *Spring and Autumn Annals*—that brief chronicle history of his native state of Lu which covers the years 722-481 B.C. After his death the work became increasingly favored by the Confucian school, which offered interpretations more and more elaborate of what it believed to be its hidden inner meaning. It was only with Tung Chung-shu, however, that this "esoteric meaning" received its most systematic treatment. Coincident with this development, we find the position of Confucius being advanced in the eyes of his followers from that of mere "teacher" to that of "king."

It is Tung's contention that Confucius, shortly before his death, received from Heaven its Mandate or Decree (*ming*) to correct the faults of the then decadent Chou dynasty and establish the institutions of a new king and dynasty. Tung furthermore interprets the famous incident with which the *Ch'un Ch'iu* concludes its chronicle as a concrete omen of Confucius' receiving of the Mandate. This incident revolves around the capture of a *lin*—the female of a fabulous creature of good omen commonly, though inexactly, translated into English as "unicorn." In 481 B.C., so the *Ch'un Ch'iu* tells us, such a creature was captured in the western part of Lu, where, according to tradition, it was then viewed by Confucius.[1] Tung Chung-shu comments on this event as follows (chap. 16):

"There are things that cannot be brought to pass through (human) effort, yet happen of themselves. Such was the hunt in the west which captured the *lin*—an omen of (Confucius') receiving of (Heaven's) Mandate. He then made use of the *Ch'un Ch'iu* to correct what was incorrect and reveal the meaning of the changing of (a dynasty's) institutions. In it he attempted to unify (the world) under a ruler, while expressing sorrow for the world's sorrows. He labored

---

[1] See the *Tso Chuan*, pp. 833-835, and the *Shih Chi*'s biography of Confucius (*Mém. hist.*, V, 415-417). — Tr.

to rid the world of its evils, wishing with (the *Ch'un Ch'iu*) to penetrate (the principles of) the 'five emperors' in early times and reach (those of) the kings of the three (dynasties) of later times. In this way he came to comprehend the principles of a hundred kings and to accord with Heaven's course from beginning to end. (In this chronicle) he embraced the results of gains and failings and investigated the operations of the manifestations of (Heaven's) Mandate. He plumbed the principles whereby the feelings and nature (of man) are given their completely proper expression, thus complying with Heaven's countenance" [1] (6. 4-5).

In chapter 23 Tung further elaborates on the way in which Confucius used the *Ch'un Ch'iu* to convey his ideas as to how a new ruler should establish his institutions:

"Heaven's Mandate is not unvarying. It rewards only virtue. [2] Therefore the *Ch'un Ch'iu*, in response to Heaven, did what a new king should do. In its calendar it took, as the beginning (of its year), that used in the Black Sequence. It entrusted (the function of) the (new) king to (the state of) Lu, took black as the primary color, pushed the Hsia (dynasty) further back, took (that of) Chou as its immediate predecessor, and (the state of) Sung as the descendant of its more remote predecessor. [3] In music it regarded the use of the Shao dances as fitting, so as thus to maintain a closer relationship with Yü. [4] In its ranks of nobility it regarded Shang as the suitable (cycle to follow), these ranks being those of earl, viscount, and baron, combined to form a single class" (7. 8-10).

Tung also writes: "When T'ang (founder of the Shang) received (Heaven's) Mandate and thus became king, he, in response to Heaven, changed the Hsia and created the title of Yin (i.e., Shang). He made his calendar start (its year) according to the White Sequence. ... In his ceremonials he instituted (the cycle of) Simplicity, in order thus to serve Heaven. And when King Wen (founder of the Chou) re-

---

[1] This is a classic expression of the belief (almost certainly unfounded) that Confucius himself composed the *Ch'un Ch'iu*, using its esoteric phraseology to convey his moral teachings. — Tr.

[2] I.e., Heaven does not permanently confer its Mandate on any one ruling house. — Tr.

[3] Sung, one of the feudal states of the Chou period, was ruled by descendants of the preceding Shang dynasty. — Tr.

[4] Another name for the sage-ruler Shun. Shao was the music of Shun and was renowned for its moral excellence. This passage is difficult and Su Yü suspects a corruption of the text. — Tr.

ceived (Heaven's) Mandate and thus became king, he, in response to Heaven, changed the Yin and created the title of Chou. He made his calendar start (its year) according to the Red Sequence. ... In his ceremonials he instituted (the cycle of) Refinement, in order thus to serve Heaven" (*ibid.*, p. 7). Since the Chou dynasty was thus linked with the Red Sequence, it is evident its successor should follow that of the Black. This explains why Tung, after stating that "the *Ch'un Ch'iu*, in response to Heaven, did what a new king should do," goes on to say that it entrusted the functioning of the new dynasty to the state of Lu, had its calendar start its year according to the Black Sequence, and assumed black as the primary color. This exemplifies the tripartite cycle referred to by him earlier (p. 61) when he says of the founders of new dynasties that there are "certain respects in which they should revert (to the institutions of a preceding dynasty) after (a cycle of) three (dynasties)."

Likewise, Tung's statement that the new dynasty should "push the Hsia (dynasty) further back, take (that of) Chou as its immediate predecessor, and (the state of) Sung as the descendant of its more remote predecessor," has reference to his doctrine (see p. 68 above) that a new king should give fiefs to the descendants of the two immediately preceding dynasties, permitting them to retain the title of "king," while at the same time maintaining looser relations with the descendants of still earlier dynasties and conferring on them the more grandiose title of "emperor." As applied to the new king envisioned by the *Ch'un Ch'iu*, this would mean that he would share his title of king with the descendants of the Chou rulers and with the rulers of the state of Sung (descended from the Shang dynasty), while the descendants of the earlier Hsia dynasty would be grouped among the "five emperors." The *Ch'un Ch'iu*'s new king, as the successor to the Chou, must, in Tung's words (p. 66 above), "reign, taking Heaven as his guiding principle and modeling himself on Shang." The sage ruler Shun, as we have seen (p. 67), also modeled himself on Shang. This explains Tung's statement that "in music it (the *Ch'un Ch'iu*) regarded the use of the Shao dances as fitting," for it was this music that was particularly associated with Shun.

As for the other dual cycle of Simplicity and Refinement, we have already read that the Chou founder, King Wen, "in his ceremonials instituted (the cycle of) Refinement, in order thus to serve Heaven." Here we have the reason why the *Ch'un Ch'iu* should exalt the succeeding cycle of Simplicity. Tung writes on this point (chap. 3):

"What is important in ceremonials is the mental attitude (of him who performs them). Let that attitude be one of respect and the proper order (of the ceremony) be completely carried out, and the superior man will acknowledge such a one as understanding ceremonials. Let the attitude (in playing music) aim at harmony and (the resulting musical sounds) be refined, and the superior man will acknowledge such a one as understanding music. Let the attitude (in performing the mourning ceremonies) be one of grief and the mode of life be ascetic, and the superior man will acknowledge such a one as understanding mourning.

"Therefore when it is said that (ceremonials) should not be emptily applied, this refers to the (proper) emphasis on the mental attitude. This attitude pertains to Simplicity, whereas the (external) objects (involved in the ceremonies) pertain to Refinement. Refinement finds its manifestation within Simplicity; thus if Simplicity holds no place for Refinement, how will Refinement give to that Simplicity (an adequate) display? Only when Simplicity and Refinement both exist complete can the ceremonials assume their finished form. For should either Simplicity or Refinement be excessive, one would be hard put to say which could (better) be dispensed with. [1] And yet, in a case in which it is impossible for both to be all-complete, so that there is an excess of the one, it is then better to have Simplicity and lack Refinement. For although such a person cannot be granted as competent in ceremonials, he may still win approval to some extent. ... Whereas if he possess only Refinement and lack Simplicity, not only can that approval not be given him, but he may suffer some degree of disapproval. ...

"Thus the sequence of the *Ch'un Ch'iu* is to place Simplicity first and Refinement afterward, and to give the right-hand (i.e., primary) position to the mental attitude and the left-hand (secondary) one to (external) objects. Hence (Confucius') statement: ' "Ceremonials!" they say, "Ceremonials!" Can mere gems and gowns be called ceremonials? "Music!" they say, "Music!" Can mere bells and drums be called music?' [2] For this reason, when Confucius instituted the conduct of a new king, he made it clear that the mental attitude is to be valued as a means for resisting profit-seeking, and that sincerity is to be cherished as a means for obliterating artificiality.

---

[1] Lit., "one could not make any distinction between 'you' and 'me,' " i.e., it would be impossible to say which is more important. — Tr.

[2] *Analects*, XVII, 11. — Tr.

It is because he (Confucius) succeeded to the abuses of the Chou (which had emphasized Refinement), that he (expressed himself) in this way" (1.18-19).

Here is a further exemplification of what Tung means when he says (p. 61 above): "There are certain respects in which they (the founders of new dynasties) should revert (to the institutions of a preceding dynasty) after (a cycle of) two (dynasties)."

Note: This theory is further elaborated by Ho Hsiu (129-182), in his commentary on the treatise on the *Ch'un Ch'iu* known as the *Kung-yang Chuan* or *Kung-yang Commentary*, under the 11th year of Duke Huan (701 B.C.):

"When the king (of a new dynasty) arises, the reason why he must change from Simplicity or from Refinement is that he is the inheritor of the decay and disorder (of the preceding period) and (wishes to) save men from their faults. Thus the way of Heaven is rooted in (concern for) what is below, and in it is expressed a cherishing of the family relationships, which are marked by Simplicity. But the way of Earth consists in respect toward what is above, and in it is expressed the honoring of superiors, which is marked by the elaboration of Refinement. Therefore when a (new) king arises, he, in governing the world, begins by basing himself upon the way of Heaven, which is one of Simplicity and of cherishing the family relationships. But when this degenerates, the fault lies in an (excess) cherishing of family relationships, without a (corresponding) honoring (of superiors). Therefore when a later king arises, he, in governing the world, models himself on the way of Earth, which is one of Refinement and of honoring superiors. But when this (too) degenerates, the fault lies in an (excess) honoring of superiors, without a (corresponding) cherishing (of family relationships). Therefore there is a reversion once more to Simplicity" (2.12).

The fact that Confucius wrote the *Ch'un Ch'iu* after having received the Mandate of Heaven gives this work, in Tung's eyes, a very special significance. Thus he writes (chap. 5):

"The *Ch'un Ch'iu*, as an object of study, describes the past so as to illumine the future. Its phrases, however, embody the inscrutableness of Heaven and therefore are difficult to understand. To him who is incapable of proper examination it seems as if they contain nothing. To him, however, who is capable of examining, there is nothing they do not contain. Thus he who concerns himself with the *Ch'un Ch'iu*, on finding one fact in it, links it to many others; on seeing one omission in it, broadly connects it (with others). In this way he gains complete (understanding) of the world" (3.22).

Thus the *Ch'un Ch'iu* is a divinely inspired text, whose phrases "embody the inscrutableness of Heaven." Included in its deep meaning, so Tung asserts, are what he calls the "Ten Guiding Principles," "Five Beginnings," and "Three Ages." Concerning the Ten Guiding Principles (*shih chih* 十指) he writes as follows (chap. 12):

"The *Ch'un Ch'iu* is a text covering 242 years, in which the great outline of the world and the broad changes of human events are all fully included. In summary, however, it may be reduced to Ten Guiding principles, with which (all) the events (it narrates) may be linked, and from which (all) the transforming influences (in the rule) of kings may be derived. To describe the changes in human events and show what is important in them is one guiding principle. To show what these changes lead to is another. To utilize that by which they are led and thus control them is another. To strengthen the trunk, weaken the branches, stress what is primary, and minimize what is secondary, is another. To discriminate among uncertainties and differentiate what (seemingly) belong to similar ca egories is another. To discuss the appropriate (utilization) of the good and talented, and differentiate them according to the abilities in which they are preeminent, is another. (To show how a ruler should) cherish persons who are close to him, induce those who are distant to come near, and identify himself with the desires of his people, is another. (To show how), having inherited the Refinement of Chou, he is to revert to Simplicity, is another. (To make clear that) Heaven's starting point lies in the fact that (the element) wood produces (the element) fire, which constitutes summer, is another. [1] And to analyze how those whom it criticizes are punished, and examine how prodigies are accordingly applied in (compliance with) Heaven's principle, is another.

"By thus describing the changes in human events and showing what is important in them, it brings peace to all the people. By showing what these changes in human events lead to, it discriminates between gains and faults. By utilizing that by which these events are led and thus controlling them, it rectifies them at their source. By strengthening the trunk, weakening the branches, stressing what is primary, and minimizing what is secondary, it makes clear the

---

[1] In other words, Heaven's yearly cycle begins with spring, which is equated with the element wood; the latter is followed by fire, which corresponds to summer. This is explained in greater detail later. — Tr.

distinctions between ruler and subject. By discriminating among uncertainties and differentiating what (seemingly) belong to similar categories, it makes manifest what is right and wrong. By discussing the appropriate (utilization) of the good and talented, and different-iating them according to the abilities in which they are preeminent, it provides an orderly sequence for the hierarchy of officials. (By showing how a new ruler), having inherited the Refinement of Chou, is to revert to Simplicity, it sets up the activities (that are to be fol-lowed) in the change (from one dynasty to another). (By showing how a ruler should) cherish persons who are close to him, induce those who are distant to come near, and identify himself with the wishes of his people, it gives full play to love and kindliness. (By showing that) wood produces fire and fire constitutes summer, it permits the *yin* and *yang* and the principles of the four seasons to take over from one another in an orderly sequence. And by analyzing how those whom it criticizes are punished, and examining how prodigies are accordingly applied, it gives free operation to the wishes of Heaven.

"By its knitting together and exemplification of these things, it causes love and righteousness to circulate, and virtue, in all its richness, to spread its tide unto (all within) the four seas. The *yin* and *yang* assume a harmonious balance, and each and every thing conforms to its own proper principle. Those who discuss the *Ch'un Ch'iu* all use these (Ten Guiding Principles), and it is in this that its existence as a model consists" (5.9-10).

The first of these principles, that of "describing the changes in human events and showing what is important in them," is touched on further by Tung in his third chapter:

"Such is the way in which the *Ch'un Ch'iu* respects the good and emphasizes the people. Thus although there are several hundred instances of warfare and aggression (in its 242 years of history), it records them all one by one, thereby to express sorrow at the heavy extent of their harm" (2.2).

In the same chapter Tung also comments on the fifth principle, that of "discriminating among uncertainties and differentiating what (seemingly) belong to similar categories":

"Feng Ch'ou-fu suffered death for himself in order to give life to his ruler. How is it then that it is not said of him (in the *Ch'un Ch'iu*) that he understood the proper adjustment (to circumstances)? [1]

---

[1] *Ch'üan* 權 . Feng is not mentioned at all in the *Ch'un Ch'iu*, but the in-

(It is because) Ch'ou-fu deceived (the state of) Chin. Chai Chung, (on the other hand), complied with (the demands of) Sung. [1] Thus both deviated from what was proper in order to preserve their rulers. [2] (Feng) Ch'ou-fu's deed, however, was more difficult than that of Chai Chung. How is it, then, that Chai Chung is shown as a good person, whereas Ch'ou-fu (is not mentioned at all and therefore) is considered a bad one?

"The answer is that this is a case where it is difficult to distinguish between right and wrong, there being (two) uncertain things which though seemingly similar are dissimilar in principle, and hence require (further) investigation. Thus (a ruler's) abdication in order to avoid (trouble with) his brother is an act highly esteemed by the superior man. [3] For him to be taken prisoner, however, and then to flee as a refugee, is an act that the superior man despises. Now Chai Chung, in order to save his ruler's life, placed him in that (above-mentioned) position which men esteem so highly. Hence the *Ch'un Ch'iu* rates him as a man who understood the proper adjustment (to circumstances), and therefore praises him. But (Feng) Ch'ou-fu, in order to save his ruler's life, placed him in a position which men deeply despise. For this reason the *Ch'un Ch'iu* rates him as a man who lacked understanding of this proper adjustment, and therefore fails to mention him. Both were alike in deviating from what was

---

cident is described at length in the *Tso Chuan* (pp. 345-346), under the year 589 B.C. Feng Ch'ou-fu was a lancer in the chariot of the Duke of Ch'i at a battle in which Ch'i was badly defeated by the state of Chin. Feng saved his master from capture by allowing himself to be captured by the Chin army in place of the Duke. His captors, however, instead of putting him to death, as Tung Chung-shu suggests, were, according to the *Tso Chuan*, so struck by his loyalty that they gave him his freedom. — Tr.

[1] This event is recorded briefly in the *Ch'un Ch'iu* under the year 701 B.C. with the words: "In the ninth month, the officials of Sung seized Chai Chung of (the state of) Cheng." The *Tso Chuan* (pp. 56-57) explains that through this seizure, Chai was compelled by a certain Sung official to establish the latter's grandson, who was a younger brother of the legitimate Duke of Cheng, as ruler of that state. However, in 697 B.C. (*Tso Chuan*, p. 64), Chai succeeded in expelling this usurper and reestablishing his former ruler. — Tr.

[2] According to the *Kung-yang Chuan* (2. 11-12), the state of Sung was so strong and Cheng so weak that Chai Chung could preserve his ruler's life only by complying with the Sung demand to put another in his place, meanwhile biding his time until he could succeed in restoring his own ruler to the throne. — Tr.

[3] This refers to the legitimate ruler of Cheng, who, following Chai Chung's forced compliance with the Sung demands, gave up his throne and allowed his younger brother, backed by Sung, to take it. — Tr.

proper in order to save their rulers. Nevertheless their principles differed in that the one thereby made his ruler glorious while the other made his ruler shameful. [1]

"Thus in all men's deeds, if their first act be wrong, yet later results in right conduct, they are then said to understand the proper adjustment (to circumstances); indeed, even if they be unsuccessful, the *Ch'un Ch'iu* praises them. This is the case with Duke Yin of Lu and Chai Chung of Cheng. [2] Whereas if they first do what is proper, but later deviate from it, this is called an evil course; indeed, even though it result in success, the *Ch'un Ch'iu* shows no liking for it. This is the case with Duke Ch'ing of Ch'i and Feng Ch'ou-fu" [3] (2.10-11).

Here then we have a case of two men, both of whom "deviated from what was proper in order to preserve their rulers," yet the one is approved by the *Ch'un Ch'iu* while the other is not. Such is the way in which this work "discriminates among uncertainties and differentiates what (seemingly) belong to similar categories."

The ninth of the *Ch'un Ch'iu*'s Ten Guiding Principles, it will be remembered, is to show how "Heaven's starting point lies in the fact that (the element) wood produces (the element) fire, which constitutes summer." This statement is based upon the correlation supposedly existing between wood and spring, and fire and summer, as well as upon the fact that spring, being the first season of the year, is therefore "Heaven's starting point." This last fact is, for Tung, expressed by the standard phraseology with which the *Ch'un Ch'iu* begins each year of its chronicle: "In spring, the first month. . . ." [4]

---

[1] This is typical of the sophistry used to explain the gaps and inadequacies of the *Ch'un Ch'iu* in terms of the "praise and blame" theory. The fact is that the *Tso Chuan*, which, unlike the *Kung-yang Chuan*, was not composed according to this theory, devotes even greater space to Feng Ch'ou-fu than it does to Chai Chung. — Tr.

[2] In 712 B.C. an evil courtier advised Duke Yin to put his younger brother to death in order to prevent him from taking the throne. Duke Yin refused, whereupon the courtier had Duke Yin assassinated, thus allowing the younger brother to come to the throne of Lu as Duke Huan. Cf. the *Tso Chuan*, p. 34. — Tr.

[3] The commentary claims that the text is corrupt when it mentions Duke Ch'ing of Ch'i at this point. [There seems, however, no valid reason for this assertion, as Duke Ch'ing (598-582) was the ruler who was saved by Feng Ch'ou-fu in the manner described above. — Tr.]

[4] For details, see below. Tung Chung-shu, in his eleventh chapter (5. 8-9), also expounds what he calls the "six rules" (*liu k'o* 六科) of the *Ch'un*

Besides the *Ch'un Ch'iu*'s Ten Guiding Principles, it also has, according to Tung, what he calls the Five Beginnings (*wu shih* 五始). Concerning these he writes (chap. 15):

"The Way of the *Ch'un Ch'iu* is, by means of the profundity of *Yüan* (Origin), to correct Heaven's starting point; by means of Heaven's starting point, to correct the government of the king; by means of the government of the king, to correct the accession of the feudal lords to their positions; and by means of the accession of the feudal lords to their positions, to correct the administration of their territories. When these five are all equally made correct, then the transforming influence (of universal good government) broadly operates" (6.4).

Here we have reference to that same *Yüan* or "Origin" which Tung has elsewhere described (see sect. 4 above) as a metaphysical first principle constituting "the root of all things" and "existing before Heaven and Earth." Now it happens quite by chance that this same word *yüan* occurs in the opening sentence of the *Ch'un Ch'iu*, where we read: "In the first (*yüan*) year (of the duke of Lu), in spring, the king's first month. ..." [1] For Tung, however, this occurrence is more than fortuitous, and the word *yüan* here signifies something more than its everyday meaning of "first" or "beginning." His reasoning runs as follows:

(1) In the phrase, "In the first (*yüan*) year, in spring," *yüan* is closely linked with "spring," which is "Heaven's starting point." The use of this phrase, therefore, is an example of how the *Ch'un Ch'iu*, "by means of the profundity of *Yüan*, corrects Heaven's starting point." [2] (2) Likewise in the phrase, "in spring, the king's first month," the two words "spring" and "king's" are closely linked, which exemplifies the way in which the *Ch'un Ch'iu*, "by means of Heaven's starting point, corrects the government of the king." (3) Finally, we have a correlation in this sentence between

---

Ch'iu. However, as these are roughly the same as his "Ten Guiding Principles," they need not be quoted here. [As to the latter, he treats in detail only the first, fifth and ninth, as just described. — Tr.]

[1] The "king" here referred to is that of the Chou ruling house. It is a characteristic of the *Ch'un Ch'iu* that, although it is a chronicle of the state of Lu, it always follows the calendar of the royal house of Chou. — Tr.

[2] Actually, of course, this interpretation is nonsensical, since, as we know, the use of the word *yüan* in the *Ch'un Ch'iu* is quite different from the metaphysical significance given it by Tung Chung-shu. — Tr.

the "first year" of the duke of Lu's reign and the "first month" of the royal calendar of the house of Chou. This exemplifies how the *Ch'un Ch'iu*, "by means of the government of the king, corrects the accession of the feudal lords to their positions." [1]

Tung further maintains that the 242 years of history covered by the *Ch'un Ch'iu* are to be grouped under what he calls the Three Ages (*san shih* 三 世). Thus he writes (chap. 1):

"The *Ch'un Ch'u* is divided into twelve generations, [2] which fall into three groups: those that were (personally) witnessed (by Confucius), those that he heard of (through the oral testimony of elder living contemporaries), and those that he heard of through transmitted records. [3] Three (of these twelve generations) were (personally) witnessed, four were heard of (through oral testimony), and five were heard of through transmitted records. Thus (the reigns of Dukes) Ai, Ting, and Chao were those that the superior man (Confucius) witnessed (personally); those of Hsiang, Ch'eng, Wen, and Hsüan were ones that he heard of (through oral testimony); and those of Hsi, Min, Chuang, Huan, and Yin were ones that he heard of through transmitted records. Those that were (personally) witnessed comprise 61 years (541-480 B.C.); that were heard of (through oral testimony), 85 years (626-542 B.C.); and that were heard of through transmitted records, 96 years (722-627 B.C.).

"Regarding what he (personally) witnessed, he uses concealing phraseology; regarding what he heard of (through oral testimony), he expresses sorrow for calamities; regarding what he heard of through transmitted records, he sets his compassion aside (and writes dispassionately). This is in accordance with the feelings (appropriate to each situation). [4]

---

[1] So that Tung actually interprets the word *yüan* as simultaneously having both a metaphysical and non-metaphysical significance. His flimsy line of reasoning seems to be based on the presumption that, if there were no esoteric meaning intended, the *Ch'un Ch'iu* would have used the word *yi* (one or first) instead of the word *yüan* in order to have expressed the idea of "first." (For the sake of clarity, I have in this paragraph somewhat expanded the author's original exposition). — Tr.

[2] Those of the twelve dukes of Lu whose reigns (extending from 722 to 481 B.C.) are recorded in the *Ch'un Ch'iu*. — Tr.

[3] *Yu chien* 有 見 , *yu wen* 聞 , and *yu ch'uan* 傳 *wen*. — Tr.

[4] The idea here is that Confucius, owing to his sense of loyalty to those dukes of Lu whom he had known personally, sometimes used concealing phraseology to record the discreditable events of the period which he had personally

"Thus when Chi was expelled (by a crowd of men in Lu), he says (only that a crowd assembled) to restore the ceremonial for obtaining rain, in this way using concealing phraseology. [1] And when Tzŭ-ch'ih was assassinated, he could not bear to record the day (of the event), in this way expressing his sorrow for the calamity. [2] But when Tzu-pan was assassinated, he recorded (the day as that of) *yi-wei*, in this way putting his compassion aside. [3]

"(Confucius') purpose, which is sometimes to be extensive and sometimes restricted, and his text, which is sometimes detailed and sometimes sketchy, both accord with these (principles). I thereby have come to understand the manner in which he treats what is near with close attention, what is remote with lesser attention, what is dear to him with affection, and what is less dear with lesser affection. I also understand how he values what is precious, belittles what is mean, attaches weight to what is weighty, and treats lightly what is less weighty. Likewise I understand how he treats substantially what is substantial, indifferently what is indifferent, praises what is good, and condemns what is bad. Furthermore I understand how he treats the *yang* as the *yang*, the *yin* as the *yin*, the white as the white, and the black as the black" (1.6-7).

At a somewhat later time the Kung-yang school of the *Ch'un Ch'iu* elaborated on the theory of the Three Ages by describing them

---

witnessed (541 until his death in 479). This was no longer necessary in the case of the earlier period of which he learned through oral testimony (626-542); nevertheless he felt and expressed sorrow for the calamities that then occurred. In the case of the most remote period (722-627), however, of which he learned only through transmitted records, he was able to set his compassion aside and write quite dispassionately. Cf. Franke, *Studien zur Geschichte des konfuzianischen Dogmas*, pp. 44-45, for a translation of this passage; also Woo, *Trois théories politiques*, pp. 97-99. — Tr.

[1] Cf. the *Ch'un Ch'iu* under the year 517 B.C., where this rain ceremony is recorded with no mention of Chi's expulsion. The expulsion appears in the *Kung-yang Chuan*, which explains its absence from the *Ch'un Ch'iu* in the same way as does Tung Chung-shu. Cf. Woo, *op. cit.*, p. 98, note 1. The *Tso Chuan* (p. 709), on the other hand, says nothing about the expulsion, but, like the *Ch'un Ch'iu*, mentions only the rain ceremony. — Tr.

[2] Tzŭ-ch'ih, son of Duke Wen of Lu, was assassinated in 609 B.C. Both the *Ch'un Ch'iu* and *Tso Chuan* (pp. 281-282) fail to record the day of the murder. Tung's interpretation here again agrees with that in the *Kung-yang Chuan*. Cf. Woo, *op. cit.*, p. 99, note 1. — Tr.

[3] Tzŭ-pan, son of Duke Chuang of Lu, was assassinated in 662 B.C. Cf. the *Tso Chuan* (pp. 121-122), where, however, the day is given as *chi-wei*, not *yi-wei*. The *Kung-yang Chuan* lacks this explanation, which therefore seems to be original with Tung. Cf. Woo, *op. cit.*, p. 99, note 3. — Tr.

as those of Disorder (*shuai luan* 據 亂), Approaching Peace (*sheng p'ing* 升 平), and Universal Peace (*t'ai p'ing* 太 平). Ho Hsiu (129-182), for example, writes in his commentary on the *Kung-yang Chuan* under the year 722 B.C.:

"In the age of which he heard through transmitted records, (Confucius) made visible (through his records) that there was an order arising amidst decay and disorder, and so directed his mind primarily toward the general (scheme of things). Therefore he considered his own state (of Lu) as the center and treated the rest of the Chinese hegemony (*chu hsia* 諸 夏) as something outside (his scheme). He gave his first detailed treatment to what was close at hand, and only then paid attention to what was farther away. He made a careful record of major (events), but only passing reference to lesser ones. And he recorded lesser villainies within (his own state), but not those that were outside. Thus great officials, when belonging to large states, (would be recorded as such), but in the case of one of a small state, he would merely use the less precise term, 'person.' (Likewise) in the case of an assembly that failed to reach any agreement, were it one within (his own state) he would record it, but were it outside, he would not do so.

"In the age of which he heard (through oral testimony), he made visible that there was an order arising of Approaching Peace. Therefore he considered the Chinese hegemony as the center and treated the outlying barbarian tribes as something outside (his scheme). Thus he recorded even those assemblies outside (his own state) which failed to reach any agreement, and the great officials of even small states. . . .

"Coming to the age which he (personally) witnessed, he made evident that there was an order arising of Universal Peace. Thus (at this time, as reported by the *Ch'un Ch'iu*), the barbarian tribes became part of the feudal hierarchy, and the whole world, far and near, large and small, was like one. Hence he applied his mind still more profoundly to make a detailed record (of events of this age), and therefore exalted (acts of) love and righteousness, while criticizing (the use of) double personal names. [1] . . .

---

[1] Two-character personal names were comparatively rare during the *Ch'un Ch'iu* period, and Ho Hsiu here suggests that Confucius objected to them. In the following omitted passage, he cites as illustration the cases of two statesmen with double personal names, Chung-sun Ho-chi and Wei Man-to. Under the

"The reason why there should be these Three Ages is that, according to the rites, the period of fasting and mourning for (the death of) the parents is three years; for that of the grandparents, one year; for that of the great grandparents, three months. Love begins with the immediate parents. Therefore (in similar fashion) the *Ch'un Ch'iu* bases itself on (the reign of Duke) Ai (494-468), while recording (as far back as Duke) Yin (722-712), thus including in its treatment the ancestors (of Duke Ai). The reason why its 242 years take (the reigns of) twelve dukes as their pattern is that the number of Heaven is thereby made complete. In this way it (the *Ch'un Ch'iu*) succeeds in standing as a pattern for good government." [1]

In this last statement we find the implied belief that the reason why the *Ch'un Ch'iu* restricts itself to the reigns of twelve and only twelve dukes of Lu is that it is thereby able to conform with Heaven's pattern of twelve months in a year. As pointed out by several modern

---

year 504 B.C. the *Ch'un Ch'iu* (p. 762) refers to the former simply as Chung-sun Chi, whereupon the *Kung-yang Chuan* (11. 6) comments as follows: "This refers to Chung-sun Ho-chi. Why then is he called Chung-sun Chi? It is as a criticism of double personal names, for such are violations of propriety (*li*)." Ho Hsiu further explains that this impropriety derives from the necessity, imposed upon a son until recent times in China, of avoiding, either in speech or writing, the character or characters occurring in the personal name of his father or preceding male ancestor. Hence double personal names are harmful, so Ho Hsiu argues, since they needlessly impose upon a son the duty of avoiding not one but two words.

This interpretation is invalidated, however, by the fact that the *Ch'un Ch'iu*, under the same year of 504 B.C. but in an earlier paragraph, refers again to Chung-sun Chi, this time, however, giving him his full name of Chung-sun Ho-chi. The *Kung-yang Chuan* makes no comment on this exception to its rule, nor does it do so for the numerous other places in which the full name Kung-sun Ho-chi appears in the *Ch'un Ch'iu*: those on pp. 740, 748, 768, 776, 780, 794, 798, 801, 809. It seems obvious that the single abbreviated citation is caused by nothing more than an inadvertent dropping out of the character *ho* from the original text.

A similar situation holds for Ho Hsiu's other illustration, that of Wei Man-to. Under the year 482 B.C., the *Kung-yang Chuan*'s version of the *Ch'un Ch'iu* (12.8) records this individual's name as Wei To, whereupon the *Kung-yang Chuan* makes a comment similar to that quoted above. In the *Tso Chuan*'s version of the *Ch'un Ch'iu* (p. 831), however, the same name appears as Wei Man-to, as it also does under the year 488 B.C. (p. 813), where, however, the *Kung-yang Chuan* makes no comment.

All this demonstrates the inconsistencies that constantly beset anyone trying to interpret the *Ch'un Ch'iu* according to the "praise and blame" theory. — Tr.

[1] Quoted as a commentary to the *Kung-yang Chuan* (1.6).

scholars, the theory of the Three Ages in certain ways resembles the political philosophy found in the little treatise known as the *Li Yün* or *Evolutions of Rites*. [1]

It is not surprising that Tung, believing as he does that the key to the *Ch'un Ch'iu* lies in the analysis of its phraseology, should also put much stress on the general importance of correct phraseology. Thus he writes (chap. 35):

"The basis for giving good government to the world lies in the analytical discrimination of what is important. And the basis for discrimination of what is important lies in the profound examination of names (*ming* 名) and appellations (*hao* 號). Names are the representative symbols of great principles. One records the meanings of these representative symbols in order thereby to spy out the things that lie within them. Thereupon right and wrong can be known, conformity and non-conformity (to Heaven) become self evident, and one comes close to penetrating (the meaning of) Heaven and Earth. The standards for right and wrong are derived from (those for) conformity and non-conformity. The standards for conformity and non-conformity are derived from names and appellations. The standards for names and appellations are derived from Heaven and Earth. Thus Heaven and Earth are the great standards for names and appellations.

"The ancient sages emitted ejaculations which mimicked (the sounds of) Heaven and Earth, and which were called appellations. When issuing orders, they uttered sounds which were called names. Thus names may be described as sounds uttered to give orders, while appellations may be described as ejaculations uttered in mimicry. Ejaculations emitted in mimicry of Heaven and Earth constitute appellations; sounds uttered to give orders constitute names. [2] Names and appellations are variously pronounced, but have the same origin in that all consist of sounds and ejaculations uttered to make known the meaning of Heaven. Heaven speaks not, yet it enables men to make evident its meaning. It acts not, yet it enables men to conduct themselves in accordance with the mean. Names, therefore,

---

[1] Described in vol. 1, pp. 377-378. It comprises chap. 7 of the *Book of Rites*. — Tr.

[2] There is a play on words here between *ming* (names), *ming* 鳴 (to utter sounds), and *ming* 命 (orders); also between *hao* (appellations), *hsiao* 譹 (to emit ejaculations), and *hsiao* 效 (to mimic). — Tr.

constitute Heaven's meaning as it has been discovered by the sages, and as such they should be deeply looked into.

"A ruler who has received (Heaven's) Mandate is a person to whom Heaven has conveyed its meaning. This is why he bears the appellation 'Son of Heaven' (*t'ien tzŭ* 天 子), in order fittingly to signify that Heaven is to him as a father and that he serves Heaven with filial piety. (Likewise) the appellation 'feudal lords' (*chu hou* 諸 侯) is given to such persons in order fittingly and carefully to signify that they wait upon and serve the Son of Heaven. [1] The appellation of 'great official' (*ta fu* 大 夫) is given to such persons to signify that they should be fittingly generous in their loyalty and good faith, sincere in following propriety and righteousness, and should accomplish greater goodness than does the common man, in this way making themselves worthy to act as transforming influences. [2] (The appellation of) 'lower officer' (*shih* 士) means 'affairs' (*shih* 事); that of 'people' (*min* 民) means 'blindness' (*ming* 瞑). [3] The lower officer does not act as a transforming influence; he may merely be employed to carry out the affairs (assigned to him) and to obey his superiors.

"These five appellations are each self-descriptive of a specific (social) division, but within these divisions each specific detail bears its own name. (The result is that) names are more numerous than appellations. An appellation applies to a general large category, while names are applied to the separate aspects (of this category). Appellations are general and summarizing; names are specific and detailed. Being specific, (names) make multiple discriminations among things; being general, (appellations) only present the large (general outline). Thus the one (general) appellation for the offerings to the spirits is 'sacrifice' (*chi* 祭). But the varying names for (specific kinds of) sacrifice are: that of spring, *tz'ǔ* 祠; that of summer, *yüeh* 礿; that of autumn, *ch'ang* 嘗; that of winter, *ch'eng* 烝. (Likewise) the

---

[1] There is a play on words here between *hou* (lords) and *hou* 候 (to wait upon). — Tr.

[2] Here there is another play on words. The words *ta*, "great" (in the phrase "greater goodness") and *fu*, "man" (in the phrase "common man"), combine to form the title *ta fu*, "great official" (here interpreted as an individual who is greater than the ordinary man). — Tr.

[3] This last etymology reflects the belief that the people are "blind" and hence require guidance from above. — Tr.

one (general) appellation for the pursuit of bird and beasts is 'hunt' (*t'ien* 田). But the varying names for (specific kinds of) hunting are: that of spring, *miao* 苗 ; that of autumn, *sou* 蒐 ; that of winter, *shou* 狩 ; that of summer, *hsien* 獮 . Among these there is not one that does not conform to Heaven's meaning. There is no single thing for which there is not a general appellation, and no single appellation for which there are not varying names, such as these.

"Each thing, therefore, conforms to its name; each name conforms to Heaven; and Heaven and man are thereby united to form one. They join to share a common principle; they act for each other's mutual benefit; they conform to and receive from one another. Such is called the course of virtue and is what is meant by the *Odes* when it says (II, iv, Ode 8, 6): 'They utter their appellations (*hao*), which have principles, have reason' " [1] (10. 1-4).

Here names and appellations are conceived of as symbols representative of the meaning of Heaven and imbued with mystic significance. According to Tung Chung-shu, therefore, we can, by studying their meanings, come to know how the things denoted by them ideally ought to be.

---

[1] This whole passage is an interesting continuation of the ancient Confucian doctrine of the Rectification of Names, begun by Confucius and greatly developed by Hsün Tzŭ. See vol. 1, pp. 59-63, 302-311. — Tr.

CHAPTER III

PROGNOSTIGATION TEXTS, APOCRYPHA, AND NUMEROLOGY DURING THE HAN DYNASTY

1—APOCRYPHA AND PROGNOSTICATION TEXTS

We have already seen in the preceding chapter that no attempt is made in the *Yüeh Ling* (Monthly Commands) to fit the eight trigrams into the cosmological system of the *Yin-yang* school. [1] The reason, no doubt, is that these trigrams could very well be used to form a cosmological system of their own, quite distinct from that of the Five Elements with which the *Monthly Commands* is associated. With the advent of the Former Han dynasty, however, we find the scholars of classical learning devoting much time to the interpretation of the classical Confucian texts in terms of the *yin-yang* ideology. Among these, the *Yi Ching* or *Book of Changes* had originally been used for fortune telling and had become one of the "arts of divination" (*shu shu* 術數). For this reason it was a peculiarly suitable vehicle for the numerological interpretations of the *Yin-yang* school which became so popular during this time. As for the so-called "apocrypha" (*wei* 緯) on the *Book of Changes*, these are simply texts of Han date written for the purpose of interpreting this classic in terms of the new ideology. Actually they are but part of a large body of apocryphal literature which, from the middle of the Former Han dynasty onward, was written on several other of the early classics as well as on the *Changes*.

The Chinese word for "apocrypha," *wei* 緯, literally means the "woof" of a fabric, in apposition to *ching* 經, "warp," a word which for the sake of convenience is commonly rendered as "classic"

---

[1] See pp. 15-16; also vol. 1, p. 383. The present chapter will refer constantly to the eight trigrams (each consisting of three divided or undivided lines) and the sixty-four hexagrams (each consisting of six divided or undivided lines, derived by combining the eight trigrams with one another). These trigrams and hexagrams, on which the *Book of Changes* is based, are treated in detail in vol. 1, chap. 15. — Tr.

when referring to literary texts. Used in apposition to each other as names of literary genres, the two terms metaphorically denote the latitudinal and longitudinal threads of knowledge which, woven together, were regarded by the Chinese as a unified fabric covering all human wisdom. [1]

Besides these apocrypha, however, the Han dynasty also saw the appearance of another kind of writing known as "prognostication texts" (*ch'an shu* 讖書). The chapter on literature in the *Sui Shu* (History of the Sui Dynasty) describes the relationship between these two types of writing as follows:

"There are those who also say that Confucius, having edited the six classics so as to illumine the way of Heaven and man, realized that later generations would be unable to grasp their meaning. Therefore he additionally created apocrypha and prognostication texts to bequeath to coming generations. These writings, which came to light during the Former Han (period), included the 'River Chart' in nine sections and the 'Lo Writing' in six sections; they were said to be original texts (of the sage-rulers), transmitted from the Yellow Emperor down through King Wen of Chou. [2] Furthermore there are thirty other sections which, so it is said, beginning with the first (of the sages) and extending down to Confucius, were additions made by the Nine Sages to expand the meaning of these (above-mentioned two works). [3] There are, in addition, apocrypha for seven of the classics, likewise said to have been written by Confucius. The total of all the preceding amounts to eighty-one sections. ... Their style, however, is shallow and ordinary, contradictory and fallacious, and they do not accord with the ideas of the sages. It is to be suspected that, as they have come down to us, they are the products of ordinary people or have perhaps in later times suffered additions and changes. Thus they are not genuine texts" (32.31-32).

These apocrypha and prognostication texts, though now commonly grouped together, originally formed separate categories.

---

[1] I have slightly expanded the author's explanation at this point. — Tr.

[2] On the "River Chart," see chap. 2, p. 8, note 3. The "Lo Writing" (*Lo Shu* 洛書) was a similarly mystic diagram, supposed to have been borne out of the Lo river on the back of a tortoise at the time when the legendary Yü was draining off the waters of the great flood. — Tr.

[3] The Nine Sages are not explained. Perhaps they are the mythological "five emperors" (*wu ti*), plus the founders of the three dynasties of Hsia, Shang, and Chou, plus Confucius himself. — Tr.

This is clearly pointed out in the great eighteenth century bibliography of Chinese literature, the *Ssŭ-k'u Ch'üan-shu Tsung-mu T'i-yao* (Critical Catalogue of Complete Writings in the Four Divisions):

"Scholars for the most part speak of the prognostication texts and apocrypha (together), but in actuality they each belong to themselves and do not form a single class. The prognostication texts cunningly make hidden statements, with which to determine good or bad fortune in advance. What is said in the sixth chapter of the *Shih Chi* (Historical Records) about Master Lu's presentation of the *Lu T'u* writing marks their beginning. [1]

"The apocrypha, (on the other hand), constitute transverse (threads) to the classics (*ching*), and develop the side meanings of the latter. Examples of them are to be found in chapter 130 of the *Historical Records*, when it quotes the *Book of Changes* as saying: 'A miss of a hair's breadth is like that of a thousand miles'; [2] or in chapter 77 of the *Han History*, when it quotes the *Book of Changes* as saying: 'For the Five Emperors, the world (belonged) to all; for the Three Kings, it (belonged) to their own family.' [3] Commentators all regard these passages as belonging to the apocrypha on the *Changes*.

"From the Ch'in and Han (dynasties) onward, scholars, it would seem, being far removed from the days of the Sage (Confucius), advanced various doctrines and each made books of their own which were originally quite distinct from the classics. Thus in the case of Fu Sheng's *Shang-shu Ta-chuan* (Great Amplification of the Book of History) and Tung Chung-shu's (writings on the) *Spring and Autumn Annals* and on the *yin* and *yang*, [4] if we examine their styles we see that they are (actually) apocrypha; but being so well-known in connection with their authors, they could not (like other apocrypha) be attributed to Confucius.

"However, in the case of other compositions that have been

---

[1] The *Lu T'u* 錄圖 was a text which a magician, Master Lu', presented in 215 B.C. to the superstitious First Emperor of the Ch'in dynasty, and which accurately foretold the destruction of this dynasty. See *Mém. hist.*, II, 167; also Bodde, *China's First Unifier*, pp. 179-180. — Tr.

[2] "A miss is as much as a mile." Cf. *Shih Chi*, 130.10. — Tr.

[3] *Ch'ien Han Shu*, 77.4. Neither this nor the preceding quotation is found in the present *Book of Changes*, which is why they are believed to derive from now lost apocrypha on that work. — Tr.

[4] On the *Shang-shu Ta-chuan* (2nd cent. B.C.), see chap. 2, p. 63, note 2. The *Ch'un-ch'iu Fan-lu*, undoubtedly the work by Tung here referred to, is treated in detail in chap. 2. — Tr.

privately transmitted, and have suffered gradual admixture with the doctrines of the 'arts of divination,' (it has been possible), inasmuch as their authors are unknown, to give them (high sounding) attributions, thus providing divine (inspiration) for their words. In the course of time, as they increasingly lost (their original purity) while being transmitted, false and heterodox passages were added to them, until they merged with the prognostication texts to become one" (6.14).

The *Hou Han Shu* (History of the Later Han Dynasty), in its biography of the noted writer, astronomer, and mathematician Chang Heng (75-135), quotes a memorial by him to the emperor in which he says: "(Writings in which) statements are made in advance as predictions of what is to come ... are called prognostication texts (*ch'an shu*). When these texts first appeared, it would seem that there were few who knew about them. ... They were first heard of only after the time of (Emperors) Ch'eng (37-7 B.C.) and Ai (6-1 B.C.). ... It would seem very probable that their material was (first) seized upon by an empty and false group of lowly people in order to attract the attention of the world" (89.12). This early statement makes it evident that the prognostication texts and apocrypha should not be lumped together. The latter, nonetheless, do contain obviously fabulous materials similar in nature to those in the prognostication texts. Both types of literature, it would seem, represented a common tendency of their time. [1]

2—NUMEROLOGY

Most of the apocrypha are no longer extant today, save as fragments collected from quotations in other works. Judging from the few examples that have survived, however, particularly those on the *Book of Changes*, it would seem that their subject matter was primarily concerned with what the Neo-Confucianists of the Sung dynasty (960-1279) later were to describe as the "study of emblems and numbers." [2] Already in the *Tso Chuan*, under the year 645 B.C., the following statement is made about such "emblems" and "num-

---

[1] For another account in English of the apocrypha, see Tjan Tjoe Som, *Po Hu T'ung* (Leiden, 1949), I, 100-120. — Tr.

[2] *Hsiang shu chih hsüeh* 象 數 之 學. For simplicity's sake this term is usually rendered in this chapter as "numerology." — Tr.

bers": "The tortoise-shell has its emblems (*hsiang*), the milfoil its numbers (*shu*). [1] Things having been produced, there are then emblems; these emblems go on to multiply; that multiplication having taken place, there are then numbers" (p. 169). This statement, that first there are physical objects, then the emblems or graphic representations of these objects, and finally various numerical categories based on these emblems, is not far from common sense. As already pointed out in Vol. I (pp. 384, 390, 393), the Appendices of the *Book of Changes* contain several references to such emblems. Thus in Appendix III we are told that "when the eight trigrams were in completed order, there were emblems in each" (p. 379), and again, that men should set highest value "on the emblems (of the *Changes*) for the making of utensils" (p. 368). The same Appendix also speaks of numbers (*shu*), as in the passage: "To Heaven belongs (the number) 1; to Earth, 2; to Heaven, 3; to Earth, 4; to Heaven, 5; to Earth, 6; to Heaven, 7; to Earth, 8; to Heaven, 9; and to Earth, 10" (p. 365).

The assumption in these passages is that emblems come into existence only after those physical objects which they symbolize. In the *Book of Changes*, for example, we are further told that the mythological ruler Fu Hsi first carefully observed the natural objects about him, that on the basis of these observations he then created the emblems known as the eight trigrams, and that only after that, when these emblems had thus become the common possession of mankind, were they used as models for the manufacture of man-made implements. [2] In other words, these emblems, though existing prior to the invention of man-made things, did not come into being until after the existence of their natural prototypes. In later commentaries on the *Book of Changes*, however, we find increasing stress being laid on the mystic significance of the eight trigrams themselves. The result is the gradual elaboration of a theory according to which numbers are what existed first in the universe, followed by emblems (i.e., the trigrams), and only then by actual physical objects. This theory, however, existed only in embryonic form during the Han dynasty, and did not become clearly formulated until the Sung, when the "study of emblems and numbers" reached its peak.

---

[1] On these two methods of divination, see vol. 1, pp. 27-28. — Tr.
[2] Cf. vol. 1, pp. 393-394. — Tr.

Though this "study of emblems and numbers" seems at first sight to be little more than a mass of superstition, its aim was a reasonable one: to give a systematic explanation of the cosmos and its movements. In its preoccupation with "numbers" and "emblems," it is not a little reminiscent of the Pythagorean school in Greek philosophy. Let us read, for example, what Aristotle has to say about the followers of Pythagoras: [1]

"It is evident that these thinkers ... consider number to be a first principle, both as the material of things and as constituting their properties and states. The elements of number, according to them, are the Even and the Odd. Of these the former is limited and the latter is unlimited; Unity consists of both (since it is both odd and even); number is derived from Unity; and numbers, as we have said, compose the whole sensible universe. Others of the same school hold that there are ten principles, which they enunciate in a series of corresponding pairs: (i) Limit and the Unlimited; (ii) Odd and Even; (iii) Unity and Plurality; (iv) Right and Left; (v) Male and Female; (vi) Rest and Motion; (vii) Straight and Crooked; (viii) Light and Darkness; (ix) Good and Evil; (x) Square and Oblong."

Diogenes Laërtius likewise quotes what Alexander records of the Pythagorean philosophy as follows: [2]

"The monad was the beginning of everything. From the monad proceeds an indefinite duad, which is subordinate to the monad as to its cause. ... From the monad and the indefinite duad proceed numbers. And from numbers signs. And from these last, signs of which plane figures consist. And from plane figures are derived solid bodies. And from solid bodies sensible bodies, of which last there are four elements: fire, water, earth, and air."

The modern writer Burnet furthermore states of Eurytos, a follower of Pythagoras: "We are told of him ... that he used to give the number of all sorts of things, such as horses and men, and that he demonstrated these by arranging pebbles in a certain way .... Aristotle compares his procedure to that of those who bring numbers into figures like the triangle and square." [3] He writes further: [4]

---

[1] *Metaphysics,* I, v, 5-6 (transl. of Hugh Tredenwick in Loeb Classical Library, p. 35).

[2] Diogenes Laertius, *Lives and Opinions of Eminent Philosophers*, Bk. 8 (transl. of C.D. Yonge, p. 348).

[3] John Burnet, *Early Greek Philosophy* (London, 2nd ed., 1908), pp. 110-111.

[4] *Op. cit.*, pp. 113-114.

"Tradition ... represents the great revelation made by Pythagoras to mankind as having been ... the *tetraktys*. ... In later times
there were many kinds of *tetraktys*, but the original one ... was the
'tetraktys of the dekad.' It was a figure like this —

●

●   ●

●   ●   ●

●   ●   ●   ●

and represented the number ten as the triangle of four. In other
words, it showed at a glance that $1 + 2 + 3 + 4 = 10$. Speusippos
tells us of several properties which the Pythagoreans discovered
in the dekad. It is, for instance, the first number that has in it
an equal number of prime and composite numbers. How much
of this goes back to Pythagoras himself, we cannot tell; but we
are probably justified in referring to him the conclusion that it is
'according to nature' that all Hellenes and barbarians count up to
ten and then begin over again. It is obvious that the *tetraktys*
may be indefinitely extended so as to exhibit the sums of the series
of successive numbers in a graphic form, and the sums are accordingly called 'triangular numbers.' For similar reasons, the sums of
the series of successive odd numbers are called 'square numbers,'
and those of successive even numbers 'oblong.' If odd numbers
are added to the unit in the form of *gnomens*, the result is always
a similar figure, namely a square, while, if even numbers are
added, we get a series of rectangles, as shown by the figure:

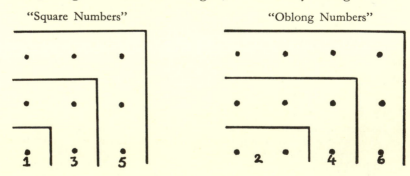

"Square Numbers"   "Oblong Numbers"

We know also that Pythagoras made studies in music which led to the discovery of the octave and the numerical relationship between different harmonic intervals. This seems to have brought him to the conclusion that all other things are likewise based on numbers. For "if musical sounds can be reduced to numbers, why should not everything else?" [1] The heavenly spheres, therefore, according to him, also constitute a harmony and a series of numbers.

Striking similarities emerge when we compare the doctrines of the Pythagoreans with the Chinese "study of emblems and numbers." Appendix III of the *Book of Changes*, for example, contains the famous passage: "In the *Changes* there is the Supreme Ultimate, which produced the two Forms" (p. 373). This is similar to the Pythagorean theorem that "from the monad proceeds the indefinite duad." Likewise, if we examine the series of ten pairs of antinomies enunciated by the Pythagoreans, such as Limit and the Unlimited, it is evident that what they call Limit corresponds fairly closely to what the exponents of the *Book of Changes* call the *yang*, while the Pythagorean Unlimited similarly corresponds to the Chinese *yin*. In Greek philosophy it has been generally maintained that the Unlimited constitutes matter, Limit constitutes form, and that physical things are the result of the imprint of form upon matter. In China, likewise, the exponents of the *Book of Changes* maintained that the *yang* is active and hence gives forth, whereas the *yin* is passive and hence receives. Indeed, among the ten above-mentioned pairs of antinomies, there are only two that differ markedly from the theories of the exponents of the *Changes*:

(1) The first is that which equates Limit (i.e., in Chinese terms, the *yang*) with the Square, and the Unlimited (i.e., in Chinese terms, the *yin*) with the Oblong. The exponents of the *Changes*, on the contrary, maintain that Heaven (which is the concrete manifestation of the *yang*) is round, while Earth (the concrete manifestation of the *yin*) is square. When, however, the Pythagoreans argue for this equation on the basis that odd numbers (which correspond to Limit) are "square numbers," and even numbers (which correspond to Limit) are "oblong numbers," this is a point on which the exponents of the *Changes* would agree. For the latter likewise maintain that the numbers of the *yang* are odd and those of the *yin* even.

(2) However, the Pythagorean equation of Limit with Rest and

---

[1] Burnet, *op. cit.*, p. 118.

of the Unlimited with Motion runs directly counter to the Chinese
point of view, inasmuch as the latter equate the *yang* with movement
and the *yin* with quiescence.

We have read above how the Pythagoreans correlated many
kinds of things with numbers and demonstrated these correlations
by arranging pebbles in a certain way, thus "bringing numbers
into figures." In China, too, the exponents of the *Book of Changes*
discoursed in a similar way about "emblems" and "numbers." And
finally, Pythagoras maintained that the heavenly spheres constitute
a harmony and that the effect of numbers can best be observed in
astronomy and music. In China, likewise, from the Han dynasty
onward, those who developed theories about the notes of the scale
and the arrangement of the calendar all did so on the basis of the
"numbers" found in the *Book of Changes*. Only general points of
similarity between the exponents of the *Changes* and the Pythagoreans
have here been indicated, but these are enough to arouse surprise.

3—The Numbers of the Yin and Yang

The Appendices of the *Book of Changes*, though composed during
the early years of the Han dynasty, clearly reveal in their important
ideas the influence of the *Lao-tzŭ* school in Taoism. This has already
been explained earlier (see vol. 1, pp. 383-385). It would thus seem
that when they were written the *Yin-yang* school's ideology had not
yet thoroughly permeated the study of the *Changes*. To be sure, the
statement in Appendix III that "the number of the Great Expansion
is 50" (p. 365) was later taken by the exponents of numerology as
their starting point. In its original context, however, it obviously
refers merely to the manipulating of the stalks of the milfoil plant
for divination purposes. Thus the same passage continues a few
sentences later: "(The heaps of milfoil stalks on both sides) are
manipulated by fours to represent the four seasons; then the re-
mainders are returned and placed (between) the two middle fingers
of the left hand to represent the intercalary month." The implication
is that in this method of divination, the idea was to manipulate the
stalks of the milfoil in such a way as to reproduce various astronomical and calendrical numerical categories. It was only in later times
that the exponents of numerology conceived of these categories as
being themselves actually patterned upon the combinations of the
milfoil. This distinction will become more evident below.

The *Yi-wei Ch'ien-tso-tu* says: [1] "Anciently the sages based themselves on the *yin* and *yang* to determine the waxing and waning (movements of the universe), and instituted *ch'ien* and *k'un* in order to encompass (the principles of) Heaven and Earth. [2] But the formal is the product of the formless. From what, then, were *ch'ien* and *k'un* produced? [3] It may be said in reply that there was (first) the Great Principle of Change (*t'ai yi* 太易), [4] (then) the Great Beginning (*t'ai ch'u* 初), (then) the Great Origin (*t'ai shih* 始), and (then) the Great Simplicity (*t'ai su* 素). During (the time of) the Great Principle of Change, there was no manifestation of the ether (*ch'i* 氣). The Great Beginning was the originator of the ether; the Great Origin was the originator of forms; the Great Simplicity was the originator of corporeal matter (*chih* 質). [5] (At the time of the Great Principle of Change), the ether, forms, and corporeal matter were intermingled and undifferentiated. Therefore this was called Chaos (*hun lun* 渾淪).

"This chaos meant that all things were then mixed together and had not yet separated from one another. It could neither be seen, heard, nor touched. That is the reason for the name, Principle of

---

[1] One of the Han apocrypha on the *Book of Changes*, hereafter referred to as *Ch'ien-tso-tu*. It has a commentary by Cheng Hsüan (127-200). The title may be roughly translated as *Apocryphal Treatise on the Changes: A Penetration of the Laws of Ch'ien*. Ch'ien, the first of the sixty-four hexagrams in the *Changes*, consists of six undivided lines (☰), and symbolizes Heaven and the *yang* principle. — Tr.

[2] *K'un*, the second of the sixty-four hexagrams, consists of six divided lines (☷), and symbolizes Earth and the *yin* principle. — Tr.

[3] Cheng Hsüan explains that the formal (*yu hsing* 有形) refers to Heaven and Earth, which emerged from the formless (*wu* 無 *hsing*). From what then, the text asks, did *ch'ien* and *k'un* likewise originate? — Tr.

[4] *Yi* is the same word as that used in the title of the *Book of Changes*, the *Yi Ching*, but it does not here refer to that work. — Tr.

[5] Centuries later *ch'i* and *chih* became key terms of Sung Neo-Confucianism: *ch'i* as a designation for matter in general, and more specifically for undifferentiated semi-gaseous matter before the evolution of an organized universe; *chih* as a designation for matter in its more tangible aspects, and especially for that denser and more solid matter that became concentrated in the terrestrial half of the universe following the end of the period of undifferentiated chaos. It is interesting that these definitions agree with Cheng Hsüan's interpretation of the passage here. *Ch'i*, he says, is matter before the existence of differentiated physical objects; "forms" (*hsing*) refer to the objects in Heaven (sun, moon, etc); *chih* to the objects on Earth. — Tr.

Change. In this Principle of Change there was no division into forms. But then the Principle of Change transmuted to form 1; 1 transmuted to become 7; and 7 transmuted to become 9. With this 9, the transmutations of the ether reached their limit, and so there was a transmutation back again to 1. [1] This 1 is the origin of the transmutation (of the ether) into forms, during which the purer and lighter parts (of the ether) ascended to form Heaven, while the coarser and heavier parts descended to form Earth. [2]

"Things have their beginning, time of maturity, and end. Therefore *ch'ien* is formed of three lines. [3] The *ch'ien* and *k'un* (trigrams) combine to produce the hexagrams, just as (physical) things (are produced through the combination of) the *yin* and *yang*. For this reason there is a doubling of these (three lines), resulting in six lines with which the hexagrams become formed. [4] ... The *yang* in operating advances; the *yin* in operating withdraws. Therefore the *yang* takes 7 and the *yin* takes 8 as (the numbers for) their unchanging lines. [5] The interchange of one *yin* and one *yang*, combining (their

---

[1] In 2.2, where the same passage is repeated, Cheng Hsüan comments that "1" is a mistake for "2," so that the text should read: ". . . and so there was a transmutation back again to 2." He further states that this should be followed by the words: "2 transmuted to become 6; and 6 transmuted to become 8." This emendation seems logical, because it gives a progression in even numbers (representative of the *k'un* hexagram, i.e., the *yin*) comparable to the foregoing progression of 1, 7, 9, which represents the *ch'ien* hexagram or *yang*.

[2] The entire passage to this point duplicates, with minor variations, that found in the *Lieh-tzŭ* (chap. 1, pp. 19-20). — Tr.

[3] The *ch'ien* trigram consists of three undivided lines, which, when doubled, result in the first of the sixty-four hexagrams, also known as *ch'ien*. — Tr.

[4] Just as the doubling of the *ch'ien* trigram results in the *ch'ien* hexagram, so the doubling of the *k'un* trigram (consisting of three divided lines) results in the *k'un* hexagram. — Tr.

[5] *T'uan* 彖 , ordinarily the name for the general descriptions of each of the hexagrams which, grouped together, form Appendix II of the *Book of Changes*. Cheng Hsüan explains that in the present context, however, *t'uan* is the name for "that line (in each of the hexagrams) which does not change or move"; hence I render the word as "unchanging line." Since *yang* = the *ch'ien* hexagram and *yin* = the *k'un* hexagram, the text here means that 7 and 8 are the numbers of the unchanging lines of *ch'ien* and *k'un* respectively. As we shall see below, 9 and 6 are the numbers of the unstable or changing lines of these same two hexagrams. This nomenclature derives from the system of divination with which the *Book of Changes* was anciently associated, in which stalks of the milfoil plant were shuffled to obtain various numerical combinations. When these shufflings resulted in the numbers 7 or 8, these were respectively regarded as symbolizing a *yang* (undivided) or *yin* (divided) line. When, however, they resulted in the numbers 9 or 6, these were respectively interpreted as symbolizing a shift from a *yin* to a

numbers) to make 15, is called the Way (*Tao*) (of the universe). [1] The *yang* changes from 7 to 9, while the *yin* changes from 8 to 6, both of which cases add up to 15, so that the numbers of the unchanging and changing lines (of their respective hexagrams) are the same. [2] The five notes, the six (*yang*) pitch-pipes, and the seven stellar mansions took their rise from these (numbers). [3] Therefore 'the number of the Great Expansion is 50,' [4] with which the (numerical) transformations are produced and spiritual (influences) are caused to operate. With the ten 'stems' correspond the five notes. [5] With the twelve periods of the day correspond the six (*yang*) pitch-pipes. [6] With the twenty-eight stellar constellations correspond the seven stellar mansions. [7] The total (number) of 50 (derived by adding these figures of 10, 12, and 28) is the great producer of (all physical) things. Confucius has said: 'The correct position of *yang* lies in 3, and of *yin* in 4' " [8] (1.4-6).

We have already quoted the passage in the *Changes*, Appendix III, which states: "To Heaven belongs (the number) 1; to Earth, 2; to Heaven, 3; to Earth, 4; to Heaven, 5; to Earth, 6; to Heaven, 7; to Earth, 8; to Heaven, 9; and to Earth, 10" (p. 365). This gives the *yang* (which corresponds to Heaven and to the *ch'ien* hexagram) a progression of odd numbers running from 1 to 9. Correlating this statement with what is said in the *Ch'ien-tso-tu*, we arrive at the following formulation: 1 is the number with which the *yang* first comes into being; 3 is its "correct position"; [9] 7 is the number

---

yang line, and from a *yang* to a *yin* line. Hence the numbers 7 and 8 symbolized the "unchanging" lines; those of 9 and 6, the "changing" lines. — Tr.

[1] An allusion to the *Book of Changes* (Appen. III, p. 355): "The alternation of the *yin* and *yang* is called *Tao*." — Tr.

[2] 7 plus 8 (the unchanging lines) and 9 plus 6 (the changing lines) both add up to 15. — Tr.

[3] For "seven stellar mansions" the text reads "seven transmutations"; this translation follows the wording of the same passage as repeated in 2.4. [The "seven stellar mansions" are probably the seven constellations covering the southern quadrant of the zodiac. On the five-note scale and the twelve pitch-pipes (six of which are equated with the *yang* and six with the *yin*), see chap. 2, p. 11; also sect. 7 below. — Tr.]

[4] This passage from the *Book of Changes* has already been quoted at the beginning of this section. — Tr.

[5] One note goes with each two stems. On these stems see pp. 11-12. — Tr.

[6] These twelve two-hour periods are named after the twelve "earthly branches," on which see *ibid*. — Tr.

[7] The seven mansions (see note 3) are the southern fourth of the twenty-eight constellations, which comprise the Chinese zodiac. — Tr.

[8] This, of course, is an apocryphal saying. — Tr.

[9] Cheng Hsüan explains the reason for this correlation by pointing out

of the unchanging line of *ch'ien*, that is of *yang*; 9 is the number of its changing line. A similar progression holds good for the *yin*: 2 is the number with which the *yin* first comes into being; 4 is its "correct position"; [1] 8 is the number of the unchanging line of *k'un*, that is, of *yin*; 6 is the number of its changing line. As stated above in the *Ch'ien-tso-tu*: "The *yang* in operating advances; the *yin* in operating withdraws." These words explain why the numerical progression of the *yang* is an advancing one, from 7 to 9, whereas that of the *yin* is a retrogressing one, from 8 to 6. They also explain why 9 and 6 are key numbers, so that, among the sixty-four hexagrams of the *Book of Changes*, the number 9 is assigned to all lines which are undivided or *yang* (——), whereas the number 6 is assigned to all which are divided or *yin* (— —). [2]

The *Ch'ien-tso-tu* furthermore seemingly establishes a correlation between the numbers 15 and 50 when it says of the numerical progressions of the *yin* and *yang* that they "both ... add up to 15," and then concludes that "therefore 'the number of the Great Expansion is 50.' " The reason seems to be that, in Chinese, the digits "5" and "10" are used to write the number "50" (*wu shih* 五 十), and, in reverse order, are also used to write "15" (*shih wu*). Cheng Hsüan comments: "5 represents the number of Heaven, which is odd; 10 represents the number of Earth, which is even. The combination of these numbers of Heaven and Earth is called the Way (*Tao*) (of the universe)." 15 and 50, therefore, are both "combinations" of 5 and 10, the numbers of Heaven and Earth.

In the above-quoted passage from the *Ch'ien-tso-tu* we also read that "the Principle of Change transmuted to form 1; 1 transmuted to become 7; and 7 transmuted to become 9 .... Therefore *ch'ien* is formed of three lines." The reasoning here is that all odd numbers (1, 3, 5, 7, 9) pertain to the *yang*; therefore the *ch'ien* trigram, since it symbolizes the *yang*, logically consists of three

---

that the diameter of a circle is to its circumference as (roughly) 1 to 3. [The *yang* is graphically represented by *ch'ien*, which also symbolizes Heaven, which is round. — Tr.]

[1] Cheng Hsüan explains this by pointing out that the one side of a square is to its four sides as 1 is to 4. [The *yin* = *k'un* = Earth, which is square. — Tr.]

[2] Thus the lowest line in a hexagram, if undivided, is called "first 9"; if divided, "first 6." The remaining lines, progressing upward, are called "9 (or 6) second," "9 (or 6) third," etc., until the topmost line is reached, which is called "upper 9 (or 6)." See Legge's note in his translation of the *Book of Changes*, pp. 58-59. — Tr.

undivided (i.e., unitary or odd) lines. Similarly, all even numbers (2, 4, 6, 8, 10) pertain to the *yin*; therefore the *k'un* trigram, since it symbolizes the *yin*, logically consists of three divided (i.e., double or even) lines. Finally we are told that *ch'ien* (and, by analogy, each of the other trigrams) is drawn with three and only three lines. In this way, according to the *Ch'ien-tso-tu*, the trigrams graphically symbolize the principle that "things have their beginning, time of maturity, and end." There is an evident similarity between these conceptions and the Pythagorean doctrine that "from the monad proceeds an indefinite duad. [1] ... From the monad and the indefinite duad proceed numbers. And from numbers signs."

The passage we have quoted from the *Ch'ien-tso-tu* is repeated in the second section of that work, save for a variant which reads as follows:

"The *yang* in operating advances, changing from 7 to 9 and thus symbolizing the waxing of its ether. The *yin* in operating withdraws, changing from 8 to 6 and thus symbolizing the waning of its ether. Therefore the Supreme One (*t'ai yi* 太 —) takes these (*yin* and *yang*) numbers as it circulates among the nine halls, (which include) the four main compass points and four intermediary compass points. (The numbers of the trigrams) in every case add up to 15" (2.3).

The statement about the Supreme One is not further explained in the remainder of the text. [2] In later times, however, the arrangement indicated by it was illustrated by a diagram, called the "River Chart" by an early Sung Taoist, Liu Mu, and the "Lo Writing" by the Neo-Confucianist Chu Hsi (1130-1200). [3] Diagrams of this sort

---

[1] The *Book of Changes* (p. 373) likewise states: "In the *Changes* there is the Supreme Ultimate, which produced the two Forms."

[2] We know, however, that an imperial cult was instituted ca. 123 B.C. to a new divinity, the Supreme One, for whom an octagonal altar was erected, having openings on each of its sides for the entry of spirits. Cf. *Mém. hist.*, III, ii, 466-467. The celestial residence of this divinity was said to be the pole star. Cf. *ibid.*, p. 339. Cheng Hsüan, commenting on the *Ch'ien-tso-tu*, explains that the eight trigrams occupy the eight compass points and that their places of residence, plus that of the Supreme One in the center, constitute the "nine halls" (*chiu kung* 九 宮).
He further states that the Supreme One paid regular visits from its central hall to its satellite divinities, which he defines as those of the eight trigrams. This explains why the altar erected to the Supreme One was octagonal, why it had openings on its sides as passageways for spirits, and who these spirits were. — Tr.

[3] On these two terms, see p. 89, note 2 above. On Liu Mu and the other Taoists whose charts gave Chou Tun-yi (1017-73) the inspiration for his famous "Diagram of the Supreme Ultimate," see chap. 11, sect. 1, i; also below, p. 118, note 1. — Tr.

remind us of how the Pythagoreans are said to have graphically represented numerical categories "by arranging pebbles in a certain way."

4—The Positions of the Eight Trigrams

Already in the *Book of Changes*, Appendix V, we find a cosmological system which is based on a correlation made between the eight trigrams, eight compass points, and four seasons. Thus we read:

"All things issue forth in *chen* (trigram no. 4), which is in the east. (The processes of their production) are brought into full and equal operation in *sun* (no. 5), which is in the southeast. This act of being brought into full and equal operation refers to the purity and equal arrangement of all things. *Li* (no. 3) gives the idea of brightness. All things are now made manifest. It is the trigram of the south.... *K'un* (no. 8) denotes Earth (and is placed in the southwest), where all things receive from it their fullest nourishment. Hence it is said: 'The greatest service is done in *k'un.*' *Tui* (no. 2) corresponds exactly (to the west and) to autumn, the season in which all things rejoice. Hence it is said: 'Rejoicing refers to *tui.*' There is struggle in *ch'ien* (no. 1), which is the trigram of the northwest. The idea is that there the *yin* and *yang* contend with one another. *K'an* (no. 6) denotes water. It is the trigram of the exact north, and of comfort and rest, around which all things rally. Hence it is said: 'Comfort and rest are found in *k'an.*' *Ken* (no. 7) is the trigram of the northeast. In it what has been accomplished by all things (during the past year) is brought to a close, and what is to be accomplished (during the coming year) is commenced. Hence it is said: 'Accomplishment refers to *ken*' " (pp. 425-426).

The *Book of Changes* itself fails to give any adequate explanation for these correlations, but in the *Ch'ien-tso-tu* they are elaborated as follows: "Confucius has said that the Principle of Change (*yi*) took its origin in the Supreme Ultimate (*t'ai chi*). The Supreme Ultimate divided to become two and thus produced Heaven and Earth. Heaven and Earth have the divisions of spring, autumn, winter, and summer, and thus produced the four seasons. The four seasons are divided according to the *yin* and the *yang*, the hard and the soft, and thus produced the eight trigrams. When the eight trigrams assumed their proper order, the course of Heaven and Earth was thereby established and the emblems (*hsiang*) for thunder, wind, water, fire, mountains, and marshes were made fixed. [1]

"As to the distribution of their operations: *chen* in the east produces things, and its position (in the year) is that of the second month; *sun* in the southeast gives them dissemination, and its position is that of the fourth month; *li* in the south gives them growth, and its position is that of the fifth month; *k'un* in the southwest nourishes them, and its position is that of the sixth month; *tui* in the west receives (i.e., harvests) them, and its position is that of the eighth month; *ch'ien* in the northwest puts them into good order, and its position is that of the tenth month; *k'an* in the north stores them up, and its position is that of the eleventh month; *ken* in the northeast marks their termination and beginning, and its position is that of the twelfth month.

"With the conclusion (of the cycle) of the eight trigrams, the divisions between the four primary and four secondary compass points are clearly delineated; the processes of production, growth, receiving (i.e., harvesting) and storing up are made complete; the forms of the *yin* and *yang* are defined; the beneficent power of spiritual intelligence is made to permeate; and all things are brought to completion, each according to its species. All this is what is included in the Principle of Change. Far reaching indeed is its power!

"Confucius has said that the year has 360 days, with which (the circulation of) Heaven's (*yin* and *yang*) ethers is complete. The operation of the eight trigrams over affairs amounts to forty-five days each, with which the year is brought to completion. ... Confucius has (also) said that *ch'ien* and *k'un* are the lords of the *yin* and *yang*. The *yang* commences its growth in *hai* (N.N.W.), and assumes form in *ch'ou* (N.N.E.). [2] *Ch'ien* holds a position in the northwest, where the *yang* bases itself when it is in the minute beginnings of its growth. The *yin* commences its growth in *ssŭ* (S.S.E.), and assumes

---

[1] Trigram *chen* symbolizes thunder, *sun* wind, *k'an* water, *li* fire, *ken* mountains, and *tui* marshes. *Ch'ien* and *k'un*, of course, symbolize Heaven and Earth. Cf. vol. 1, p. 382, where in line 3 of the second paragraph from the bottom "rain" is a misprint for "wind." — Tr.

[2] *Hai, ch'ou*, etc., are the names of the twelve "earthly branches" which have been mentioned frequently already. — Tr.

form in *wei* (S.S.W.). It must base itself upon its proper position. Therefore *k'un* holds a position in the southwest, which is that proper to the *yin*. [1] The way of the ruler is to promote and initiate, while that of the subject is to complete and make correct. This is the reason why *ch'ien*'s position lies in *hai* (N.N.W.), while that of *k'un* lies in *wei* (S.S.W.). In this manner the functions of the *yin* and *yang* are made evident, and the positions of ruler and subject are made definite" (1.2-3).

This correlation of the eight trigrams with the eight compass points and with the seasonal fluctuations of the *yin* and *yang* is of later date than that based on the Five Elements. Once promulgated, however, it had the advantage of being readily understandable, and therefore soon gained wide currency, even though the earlier correlation of the Five Elements with the phases of the year also enjoyed continued popularity.

The *Ch'ien-tso-tu* further correlates the eight trigrams with the Confucian "five constant virtues" or *wu ch'ang* 五常, namely love (*jen*), righteousness (*yi*), propriety (*li*), wisdom (*chih*), and good faith (*hsin*):

"Confucius has said that after the eight trigrams assumed their orderly position, the five forces (*wu ch'i* 氣) assumed visible form. Man, therefore, responds at birth to the forms of these eight trigrams by acquiring the five forces which constitute the five constant virtues, namely love, righteousness, propriety, wisdom, and good faith.

"Thus all things issue forth in *chen*, which is the trigram of the east. There the *yang* ether undergoes its first growth, thus denoting the process whereby physical form is acquired (by the individual). Therefore east is the direction of love. [2]

"They (all things) are brought to completed growth in *li*, which is the trigram of the south. There the *yang* gains its correct place above, while the *yin* gains its correct place below, so that the emblems for honorable and lowly position are made fixed. This

---

[1] Cheng Hsüan comments: "The *yin* ether commences its growth in *ssū* (S.S.E.), undergoes further growth in *wu* (S.), and assumes form in *wei* (S.S.W.). The way of *yin* is to be lowly and compliant, so that, when only in its place of commencement, it does not yet dare to stand erect. That is why it takes as its proper position that place in which it assumes form."

[2] Love is primary among the five virtues and is innate in man at birth. Therefore it fittingly belongs to east = spring = the beginning of life. — Tr.

denotes the orderly hierarchy of propriety. Therefore south is the direction of propriety. [1]

"They enter into *tui*, which is the trigram of the west. There the *yin* operates among affairs in such a way that all things gain what is their due, which is the principle of righteousness. Therefore west is the direction of righteousness. [2]

"They become submerged in *k'an*, which is the trigram of the north. There the *yin* ether burgeons into abundance, so that the *yang* ether is swallowed up by it, which makes this a case analogous to good faith. [3] Therefore the north is the direction of good faith.

"The meanings embodied in these four directions are all linked together by the central position. Therefore *ch'ien*, *k'un*, *ken*, and *sun* occupy the four intermediate quarters (between the four main compass points occupied by *chen*, *li*, *tui*, and *k'an*). There, through the judgments exercised by wisdom in the center, they are knitted together with the operations of (these four other trigrams in) the four main compass points. Therefore the center is the position of wisdom.

"Thus good conduct is promoted by love, established by propriety, made orderly by righteousness, made definite by good faith, and completed by wisdom. These five constitute the divisions of human morality and the links between Heaven and man. Through them the sage penetrates to Heaven's meaning, regulates human relationships, and comprehends the highest form of conduct" (1.4).

---

[1] South (= summer) is that position in which the *yang* reaches its apogee and the *yin* its lowest point. Hence it is that in which the difference between the two is greatest. Likewise in the human world sharp social differences occur, but the virtue of propriety (*li*) teaches each individual how to act in conformity with his particular social station. In the *li* trigram ($\equiv$) there are two dominant *yang* lines surrounding a subservient *yin* line, thus symbolizing these social distinctions. Perhaps there is also a play on words here between the name of the trigram, *li*, and that of propriety, *li*. — Tr.

[2] The *yin* becomes prominent in the west = autumn, and hence, though normally subservient to the *yang*, now comes to dominate affairs. The virtue of righteousness (*yi*) likewise emphasizes the subordination of one's own interests to those of other people. Perhaps this idea is symbolized in the trigram *tui* ($\equiv$) by the fact that in it a divided or *yin* line occupies the topmost or dominant position. — Tr.

[3] For the term "*yang* ether," the text reads "*yin-yang* ether(s)," which makes no sense, so that it is obvious that the word *yin* should be omitted. The *k'an* trigram ($\equiv$) consists of two *yin* lines surrounding a single *yang* line. This is a case in which good faith is needed if the *yang* is not to be entirely obliterated by the *yin*. — Tr.

All these foregoing correlations may be summarized as follows:

Cosmological Diagram of the Eight Trigrams

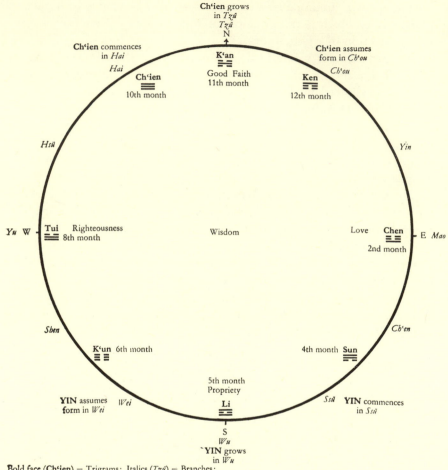

Bold face (**Ch'ien**) = Trigrams; Italics (*Tzŭ*) = Branches;
Capitals (**YIN**) = *Yin* and *Yang*.

5—THE HEXAGRAMS AND THE "BREATHS" OF THE YEAR

In another of the apocrypha on the *Book of Changes*, that known as the *Yi-wei Chi-lan-t'u* (Apocryphal Treatise on the Changes: Consultation Charts), we find an even more complex correlation built up between the sixty-four hexagrams and the divisions of a year. In this work the twelve "earthly branches," their corresponding months and directions, and the hexagrams, are equated as follows:

Months	Branches	Directions		Hexagrams
1	*yin*	E.N.E.	nos.	62, 4, 42, 53, 11
2	*mao*	E.	,,	5, 17, 35, 40, 34
3	*ch'en*	E.S.E.	,,	16, 6, 18, 49, 43
4	*ssŭ*	S.S.E.	,,	56, 7, 8, 9, 1
5	*wu*	S.	,,	14, 37, 48, 31, 44
6	*wei*	S.S.W.	,,	50, 55, 59, 30, 38
7	*shen*	W.S.W.	,,	32, 60, 13, 41, 12
8	*yu*	W.	,,	57, 45, 26, 22, 20
9	*hsü*	W.N.W.	,,	54, 25, 36, 47, 23
10	*hai*	N.N.W.	,,	52, 63, 21, 28, 2
11	*tzŭ*	N.	,,	64, 39, 27, 61, 24
12	*ch'ou*	N.N.E.	,,	3, 15, 38, 46, 19

This leaves four hexagrams unaccounted for, which are equated with the following numbers:

K'an (no. 29) with 6; *chen* (no. 51) with 8; *li* (no. 30) with 7; *tui* (no. 58) with 9.

It will be seen that aside from these primary hexagrams—described in the text as the four "emblems" or *hsiang*—the remaining sixty hexagrams are correlated in such a way that five of them go with each month. Each hexagram, furthermore, is stated to have a duration of six days and seven parts, so that the entire year has a duration of $365\frac{1}{4}$ days. [1]

The *Chi-lan-t'u* says further:

"According to the *Yi-wei Shih-lei-mou*, [2] there are, for each of the four primary hexagrams, six lines; each of these lines governs one of the (twenty-four) 'breaths.' [3] Each of the remaining sixty hexagrams governs six days plus seven parts out of an 80-part day. The total year consists of $365\frac{1}{4}$ days. Thus with the sixty (hexagrams) there is a single (year's) cycle" (2.18).

---

[1] *Chi-lan-t'u*, 2.1. [For the "seven parts," see below. This passage, quoted in extenso by the author, has here been paraphrased for reasons of simplicity; likewise the hexagrams have been designated by number instead of by name. — Tr.]

[2] *Apocryphal Treatise on the Changes: Classified Deliberations.* The statement here quoted does not appear in the present edition of this work. — Tr.

[3] *Ch'i* 氣 , a series of twenty-four divisions (based on solar reckoning) occurring at fifteen day intervals throughout the year, and still observed to some extent in China, especially by farmers. They are variously named Beginning of Spring, Rain Water, Waking of Insects, Spring Equinox, etc. — Tr.

The four primary hexagrams, *chen*, *li*, *tui*, and *k'an*, are further
said to be correlated with the compass points, the seasons, and with
certain numbers, as follows:

Hexagram	Direction	Season	Number
chen	east	spring	8
li	south	summer	7
tui	west	autumn	9
k'an	north	winter	6

These four hexagrams have a total of twenty-four lines, each of
which is said in the text to govern one of the twenty-four "breaths"
or solar periods of the year. The *Chi-lan-t'u* then explains further that
the first or lowest line, divided, of *k'an*, governs the Winter Solstice;
the first or lowest line, undivided, of *chen*, governs the Spring
Equinox; the first line, undivided, of *li*, the Summer Solstice; and
the first line, undivided, of *tui*, the Autumn Equinox. The reader
will find the correlations between the remaining twenty lines and
their "breaths" given in the table in sect. 6 below.

We have already seen that the remaining sixty hexagrams are
each said to have jurisdiction over six days of the year plus "seven
parts out of an 80-part day." The six days governed by each hexagram, multiplied by 60 (the number of hexagrams), yield a total
of 360 days, thus leaving a surplus period for the year of 5¼ days.
If we multiply 5¼ by 80 (the number of parts into which a single
day is said to be divided), we obtain a total of 420 parts. This figure,
divided by 60 (the number of the hexagrams), results in an allotment
of 7 parts of a day to each hexagram. This is the basis for the statement that each hexagram exercises jurisdiction over six days plus
seven parts. [1]

As stated earlier, each month is to be equated with five hexagrams. In a continuation of the preceding quotation, the *Chi-lan-t'u*
gives the following titles to the individual hexagrams within each
group of five: (1) Son of Heaven (*t'ien tzǔ* 天 子, i.e., ruler), (2)
Vassal Lord (*chu hou* 諸 侯), (3) Duke (*kung* 公), (4) Lower Minister
(*ch'ing* 卿), (5) Great Official (*ta fu* 大 夫). In the case of the first
month (designated by the cyclical character *yin*), this works out as

---

[1] Converted into western time reckoning, this means a duration for each
of 6 days, 2 hours, 6 minutes. — Tr.

follows: hexagram no. 11 is its "Son of Heaven," no. 62 its "Vassal Lord," no. 53 its "Duke," no. 42 its "Lower Minister," and no. 4 its "Great Official." For the twelve months as a whole (beginning with the eleventh, in which the *yang* principle is supposed to make its first growth following the winter cold), the hexagrams that are "Sons of Heaven" are respectively nos. 24, 19, 11, 34, 43, 1, 44, 33, 12, 20, 23, and 2. As rulers of the months to which they are attached, they are also described by the *Chi-lan-t'u* as *pi* 辟 or "sovereign" hexagrams.

The reason why these particular hexagrams should be selected as rulers becomes apparent when we examine them in sequence. Thus in the first six of the series, nos. 24 ䷗, 19 ䷒, 11 ䷊, 34 ䷡, 43 ䷪, and 1 ䷀, we see that the *yang* influence (symbolized by the single undivided line at the bottom of no. 24) steadily grows in succeeding hexagrams, until in the final one (*ch'ien*, no. 1) all lines are *yang*; at the same time there is a corresponding decrease in the *yin* influence (symbolized by the divided lines). The reverse is true, however, in the second series of six, nos. 44 ䷫, 33 ䷠, 12 ䷋, 20 ䷓, 23 ䷖, and 2 ䷁. Here the *yang* lines become fewer while the *yin* lines increase, until in the final hexagram (*k'un*, no. 2) all lines are *yin*. Now if we equate these twelve hexagrams with the months in such a way that the first in the series, no. 24, goes with the eleventh month (supposed to mark the beginning of the solar year), and the last, no. 2, with the tenth or final month of the solar year, we then see in the increase and diminution of the *yang* and *yin* lines a graphic representation of the corresponding fluctuations of the *yin* and *yang* throughout the year. The *Chi-lan-t'u* fails to provide any comparable explanation, however, as to why the remaining hexagrams should bear the titles they do.

6—Meng Hsi and Ching Fang

The names of two of the men who expounded the theory of correlations between the hexagrams and the "breaths" of the year are known to us. They are Meng Hsi 孟喜 and Ching Fang 京房, both of whom lived in the first century b.c. The *Ch'ien Han Shu* (History of the Former Han Dynasty) states in its biography of the latter:

"His doctrines specialized upon the explanation of (natural) visitations and anomalies. He allotted sixty of the hexagrams in such a way that each in turn had jurisdiction over the affairs of certain days. He regarded the wind, rain, cold, and heat (of the year) as manifestations, for each of which prognostic omens exist" (75.6).

Centuries later a Buddhist monk of the T'ang dynasty, Yi-hsing 一 行 (673-727), wrote as follows in his treatise known as the *Kua Yi* (Meaning of the Hexagrams): [1]

"(The correlations of) the hexagrams with the twelve months originated with the comments of Mr. Meng. In his explanation of the *Changes* he based himself on the 'breaths' (of the year), and then elucidated it further in the light of human affairs. Mr. Ching went on from this to equate the lines of the hexagrams with the days of the year."

Yi-hsing then writes further:

"According to Mr. Meng, *chung fu* (hexagram 61) dominates affairs beginning with the Winter Solstice. The numbers of a single month, 9 and 6 and 7 and 8, together make 30. [2] The hexagrams (operate) according to 6, which is the number of Earth. The 'periods of time' operate according to 5, which is the number of Heaven. [3] With the multiplication of 5 with 6, the evolutions (of a month) go through one revolution, and with twelve such revolutions, the year returns to its beginning. Each of the lines in the hexagrams *k'an*, *chen*, *li*, and *tui* successively governs (one of) the twenty-four 'breaths' (of the year). Their first (i.e., lowest lines) thus (govern) the two solstices and two equinoxes.

"In *k'an* (䷜) the (two) *yang* (lines) are surrounded by *yin* (lines). Hence (in this hexagram we see how), starting at the northern point (the Winter Solstice), the *yang* in its minute beginnings becomes

---

[1] Quoted in the *Hsin T'ang Shu* (New History of the T'ang Dynasty), 27a.13. [In the beginning of this same chapter we read that in 721, owing to the imperfections in the calendar then in use, Yi-hsing was asked by the government to prepare a new one, on which he labored until his death in 727. This calendar is recorded in *Hsin T'ang Shu*, chaps. 27a-b. — Tr.]

[2] The unchanging number of the *yang* is 7 and of the *yin* 8; their changing numbers are respectively 9 and 6. See above, p. 98, note 5. This is why, at the end of the quotation below, 7 and 8 are said to be associated with the less active phases of the *yang* and *yin* respectively, and 9 and 6 with their more active phases. — Tr.

[3] These "periods of time" (*hou* 候) are different from the twenty-four solar periods or "breaths" of the year, being seventy-two in number. See p. 113 below. — Tr.

active below. It rises upward but does not yet reach (the extreme top of the hexagram). Attaining its final limits in the second month, when the freezing (*yin*) ether melts, the cycle of *k'an* then comes to an end.

"The Spring Equinox appears in *chen* (☳), in which (the *yang*) begins to base itself upon the myriad creatures in their opening phase and acts as a ruler within (the hexagram). Consequently the several *yin* (lines) are affected by it and conform to it. Attaining its final limits with the southern point (the Summer Solstice), with which the evolutions of fertile growth reach their end, the work of *chen* is then concluded.

"In *li* (☲) the (two) *yin* (lines) are surrounded by *yang* (lines). Hence (in this hexagram we see how), starting at the southern point (the Summer Solstice), the *yin* in its minute beginnings generates beneath the ground. It accumulates but does not yet shine forth. Lasting until the eighth month, when the clearly manifested substance (of growing things) begins to decay, the cycle of *li* then comes to an end.

"In the middle of autumn (the Autumn Equinox), the *yin* assumes form in *tui* (☱), in which it begins to follow the myriad creatures in their final stage and acts as a ruler within (the hexagram). Consequently the several *yang* (lines) make their submission to it and acknowledge it as superior. Attaining its final limits with the northern point (the Winter Solstice), with which the dissemination of Heaven's fructifying forces comes to an end, the work of *tui* is then concluded.

"Thus the *yang*'s less active phase of 7 begins with *k'an*; its more active phase of 9 with *chen*. The *yin*'s less active phase of 8 begins with *li*; its more active phase of 6 with *tui*. In this way the transformations of the four emblems (the hexagrams) embrace the six lines of each, in which the responses to the divisions (of the year) are completely manifested" (*ibid.*, pp. 13-14).

The Meng and Ching mentioned here are Meng Hsi and Ching Fang, concerning whom the *Ch'ien Han Shu*, in its chapter on noted scholars, writes as follows:

"Meng Hsi, styled Ch'ang-ch'ing 長卿, was a native of Lan-ling in Tung-hai. [1] ... He received the writings of that school of

---

[1] Roughly 17 miles east of the present Yi 山崒 hsien in southern Shantung. — Tr.

the *Changes* which made prognostications about the visitations and anomalies caused by the *yin* and *yang*. ... Ching Fang received the *Changes* from Chiao Yen-shou, who was a native of Liang. [1] Yen-shou stated that he on occasion addressed questions about the *Changes* to Meng Hsi. On Hsi's death, (Ching) Fang maintained that Yen-shou's (version of the *Changes*) belonged to the Meng school. ... When, in the time of Emperor Ch'eng (32-7 B.C.), Liu Hsiang [2] made his collations of literature, he examined the expositions of the *Changes* and maintained that its various schools of exposition had all originated with T'ien Ho, Yang Shu, and General Ting, and were identical in their general ideas, save that of Ching Hsi, which belonged to a separate group. [3] Chiao Yen-shou alone gained a certain hermit's doctrines and associated them with Mr. Meng. They were not the same (as the other schools of interpretation). (Ching) Fang gained the favor of the emperor by elucidating (the meaning of) visitations and prodigies. He was executed as a result of the slander of Shih Hsien" [4] (88.8-11).

The *Ch'ien Han Shu* fails to give Meng Hsi's dates; its only clue is the statement that Shih Ch'ou, a member of the intellectual group to which Meng belonged, participated in the famous assembly of scholars held in 51 B.C. in the Shih-ch'ü Pavilion to discuss the meanings of the classics. [5] Of Ching Fang, however, we know that he suffered execution in 37 B.C.

We have seen that Meng Hsi, Chiao Yen-shou (i.e., Chiao Kan), and Ching Fang all expounded the *Book of Changes* in terms of its supposed connection with the natural visitations and anomalies produced by the *yin* and *yang*. Their doctrines are so fragmentary today, however, that it is impossible to know whether any minor differences existed between them. The only thing we can say with assurance is

---

[1] The commentator Yen Shih-ku (581-645) remarks that Yen-shou 延 壽 was Chiao's "style" (*tzŭ*), and that his personal name was Kan. [Liang was a kingdom south of the present Shang-ch'iu 商 邱 hsien in eastern Honan. — Tr.]

[2] 79-8 B.C. See on him chap. 2, p. 17, note 1. — Tr.

[3] T'ien Ho lived at the very beginning of the Han dynasty. The personal name of Yang Shu 叔 was Ho, and that of General Ting was K'uan. On the line of transmission of the *Book of Changes*, see also vol. 1, pp. 381-382. — Tr.

[4] A notorious eunuch who died 32 B.C. and had Ching Fang executed in 37 B.C. Cf. Dubs, *History of the Former Han Dynasty*, II, 297. — Tr.

[5] This assembly is described in Dubs, *op. cit.*, pp. 271-274, and Tjan Tjoe Som, *Po Hu T'ung*, I, 128-136. — Tr.

that all three men interpreted the *Book of Changes* in terms of the *Yin-yang* school's ideology. Nor is it possible, with regard to the theories described above in which the hexagrams are correlated with the divisions of the year, to determine whether: (1) these theories originated with Meng Hsi and Ching Fang, and were then borrowed by the writers of the apocrypha on the *Changes*; or (2) whether, conversely, Meng Hsi and Ching Fang derived them from these apocrypha; or (3) whether, finally, Meng, Ching, and their followers may not themselves have been the actual authors of these apocrypha.

According to Yi-hsing's much later account, quoted above, Meng Hsi agrees with the writers of the *Changes* apocrypha in correlating the hexagrams *k'an*, *chen*, *li*, and *tui* with the four compass points and seasons, and their twenty-four lines with the twenty-four "breaths" or divisions of the year. In the same passage, however, Yi-hsing also refers to "periods of time" (*hou*), which, he says, operate "according to 5, which is the number of Heaven." What he here has in mind are the "seventy-two periods" (*ch'i-shih-erh hou*), a sequence derived from the *Yüeh Ling* or *Monthly Commands* (now the fourth chapter of the *Book of Rites*), and one quite distinct from the twenty-four yearly "breaths."

Thus we read in the opening sentence of the *Monthly Commands*: "In the first month of spring ... the east wind dissipates the cold, the hibernating insects begin to move, the fish rise to the ice above, the otter (seems to) offer the fish in sacrifice, and the wild ducks return" (p. 251). Under which Cheng Hsüan comments: "These (phenomena) are all the records of a particular period (*hou*) of time." K'ung Ying-ta (574-648) likewise explains further: "The total (duration) of the twenty-four 'breaths,' when divided by three, gives seventy-two 'breaths,' each of which lasts for a little over five days. Therefore one year consists of seventy-two such periods." [1]

It is these seventy-two periods that Yi-hsing, quoting Meng Hsi, refers to when he says that "the periods of time operate according to 5, which is the number of Heaven." This statement is based on the fact that the numbers of Heaven (the concrete essence of the *yang*) are odd, and that therefore 5 is the medial number of Heaven, lying as it does midway in the sequence of odd numbers, 1, 3, 5, 7,

---

[1] Since the twenty-four "breaths" each last a fraction more than 15 days, a division of their total duration by three produces a series of seventy-two shorter ' 'breaths" or "periods," each lasting a trifle over five days. — Tr.

and 9. As for the statement that "the hexagrams (operate) according to 6, which is the number of Earth," this is based on the fact that each hexagram exercises jurisdiction over a period of slightly more than six days. Not only this, however, but the fact that the numbers of Earth (which is the concrete essence of the *yin*) are even means that 6 is the medial number of Earth, since it lies midway in the sequence of even numbers, 2, 4, 6, 8, and 10. The multiplication of these two base numbers of Heaven and Earth, 5 and 6, gives 30, which is the number of days in a month, and with which "the evolutions (of a month) go through one revolution." Meng Hsi, as quoted by Yi-hsing in the same passage, links together the numbers 9 and 7, and 6 and 8. As we have seen earlier (pp. 98-99), the former pair is especially associated with the *yang*, as the latter pair is with the *yin*. The addition of all four numbers results once more in 30, which is the number of days in a month.

Yi-hsing, following the ideas of Meng Hsi, has prepared a table which, reproduced below, gives a clearer picture of the correlations between the hexagrams and the periods of the year: [1]

TABLE OF HEXAGRAMS AND SEVENTY-TWO PERIODS OF THE YEAR [2]

24 Breaths	Month and Primary Hexagram	72 Periods (3 go with each Breath)		
		Period A and its Hexagram	Period B and its Hexagram	Period C and its Hexagram
1 Winter Solstice	11th month (middle) *K'an*: 1st line, divided	Earth-worms curl up. No. 61: Duke	Moose shed their horns. No. 24: Sovereign	Springs of water are in movement. No. 3: Marquis (inner part)

---

[1] *Hsin T'ang Shu*, 28a.2-5.

[2] The numbers appearing in this chart are those of the hexagrams. The phrases, "Earth-worms curl up," etc., are all taken from pertinent passages in the *Monthly Commands*. It will be noticed that every sixth hexagram is twice repeated, with the qualifying remark: "inner part" or "outer part." This is necessitated by the fact that the author was faced with the problem of equating sixty hexagrams with seventy-two periods of the year. It will also be noticed that the designation of every fifth hexagram is "Marquis" (*hou*), whereas in the *Yi-wei Chi-lan-t'u* (see end of last sect.) it is "Vassal Lord" (*chu hou*). "Marquis" certainly seems to fit better with "Duke" and the other titles here given, and it is not impossible that the word *chu* in the *Chi-lan-t'u* should be deleted. — Tr.

24 Breaths	Month and Primary Hexagram	72 Periods (3 go with each Breath)		
		Period A and its Hexagram	Period B and its Hexagram	Period C and its Hexagram
2 Slight Cold	12th month (beginning) *K'an*: 2nd line, undivided	Wild geese go north. No. 3: Marquis	Magpies begin to build nests. No. 15: Great Official	Pheasants begin to crow. No. 38: Lower Minister
3 Great Cold	12th month (middle) *K'an*: 3rd line, divided	Hens begin to hatch. No. 46: Duke	Birds of prey fly high and fast. No. 19: Sovereign	Rivers & lakes are frozen thick. No. 62: Marquis
4 Beginning of Spring	1st month (beginning) *K'an*: 4th line, divided	East winds dissipate cold. No. 62: Marquis	Hibernating creatures begin to move. No. 4: Great Official	Fish rise up to the ice. No. 42: Lower Minister
5 Rain Water	1st month (middle) *K'an*: 5th line, undivided	Otters sacrifice fish. No. 53: Duke	Wild geese appear. No. 11: Sovereign	Plants bud and grow. No. 5: Marquis (inner part)
6 Waking of Insects	2nd month (beginning) *K'an*: 6th line divided	Peach trees begin to blossom. No. 5: Marquis (outer part)	Orioles sing. No. 17: Great Official	Hawks are transformed into doves. No. 35: Lower Minister
7 Spring Equinox	2nd month (middle) *Chen*: 1st line, undivided	Swallows arrive. No. 40: Duke	Thunder utters its voice. No. 34: Sovereign	Lightning begins to be seen. No. 16: Marquis (inner part)
8 Pure Brightness	3rd month (beginning) *Chen*: 2nd line, divided	Elaeococco begins to flower. No. 16: Marquis (outer part)	Moles are transformed into quails. No. 6: Great Official	Rainbows begin to appear. No. 18: Lower Minister
9 Grain Rain	3rd month (middle) *Chen*: 3rd line, divided	Duckweed begins to grow. No. 49: Duke	Cooing doves clap their wings. No. 43: Sovereign	Crested birds light on mulberry trees. No. 56: Marquis (inner part)

24 Breaths	Month and Primary Hexagram	72 Periods (3 go with each Breath)		
		Period A and its Hexagram	Period B and its Hexagram	Period C and its Hexagram
10 Beginning of Summer	4th month (beginning) *Chen*: 4th line, undivided	Green frogs croak. No. 56: Marquis (outer part)	Earth-worms appear. No. 7: Great Official	Royal melons grow. No. 8: Lower Minister
11 Grain Full	4th month (middle) *Chen*: 5th line, divided	Sow-thistle is in seed. No. 9: Duke	Delicate herbs die. No. 1: Sovereign	Period of slight heat arrives. No. 14: Marquis (inner part)
12 Grain in the Ear	5th month (beginning) *Chen*: 6th line, divided	Praying mantis is born. No. 14: Marquis (outer part)	Shrikes begin to cry. No. 37: Great Official	Mockingbirds cease to sing. No. 48: Lower Minister
13 Summer Solstice	5th month (middle) *Li*: 1st line, divided	Deer shed their horns. No. 31: Duke	Cicadas begin to sing. No. 44: Sovereign	Midsummer herb grows. No. 50: Marquis (inner part)
14 Slight Heat	6th month (beginning) *Li*: 2nd line, divided	Warm winds come. No. 50: Marquis (outer part)	Crickets live in the walls. No. 55: Great Official	Young hawks learn to fly. No. 59: Lower Minister
15 Great Heat	6th month (middle) *Li*: 3rd line, undivided	Decaying grass becomes fire-flies. No. 10: Duke	Ground is humid and air is hot. No. 33: Sovereign	Great rains come frequently. No. 32: Marquis (inuer part)
16 Beginning of Autumn	7th month (beginning) *Li*: 4th line, undivided	Cool winds arrive. No. 32: Marquis (outer part)	White dew descends. No. 60: Great Official	Autumn cicadas chirp. No. 13: Lower Minister
17 Stopping of Heat	7th month (middle) *Li*: 5th line, divided	Hawks sacrifice birds. No. 41: Duke	Heaven and Earth begin to be severe. No. 12: Sovereign	Grain is presented. No. 57: Marquis (inner part)

24 Breaths	Month and Primary Hexagram	72 Periods (3 go with each Breath)		
		Period A and its Hexagram	Period B and its Hexagram	Period C and its Hexagram
18 White Dew	8th month (beginning) *Li*: 6th line, undivided	Wild geese arrive. No. 57: Marquis (outer part)	Swallows return. No. 45: Great Official	All birds store up provisions No. 26: Lower Minister
19 Autumn Equinox	8th month (middle) *Tui*: 1st line, undivided	Thunder restrains its voice. No. 22: Duke	Hibernating creatures stop up entrances to their burrows. No. 20: Sovereign	Waters begin to dry up. No. 54: Marquis (inner part)
20 Cold Dew	9th month (beginning) *Tui*: 2nd line, undivided	Wild geese come as guests. No. 54: Marquis (outer part)	Sparrows enter the sea and become mollusks. No. 25: Great Official	Chrysanthemums show yellow flowers. No. 36: Lower Minister
21 Frost's Descent	9th month (middle) *Tui*: 3rd line, divided	Wolves sacrifice large animals. No. 47: Duke	Leaves of plants become yellow and fall. No. 23: Sovereign	Hibernating creatures all push downward. No. 52: Marquis (inner part)
22 Beginning of Winter	10th month (beginning) *Tui*: 4th line, undivided	Water begins to freeze. No. 52: Marquis (outer part)	Ground begins to harden. No. 63: Great Official	Pheasants enter the water and become mollusks. No. 21: Lower Minister
23 Slight Snow	10th month (middle) *Tui*: 5th line, undivided	Rainbows hide and are invisible. No. 28: Duke	Heaven's ether ascends, Earth's ether descends. No. 2: Sovereign	All is closed up and winter is fully formed. No. 64: Marquis (inner part)
24 Great Snow	11th month (beginning) *Tui*: 6th line, divided	Yellow pheasants stop their cries. No. 64: Marquis (outer part)	Tigers begin to pair. No. 39: Great Official	Broom-sedge grows. No. 27: Lower Minister

Li Kai, who lived at the beginning of the Sung dynasty (tenth or early eleventh century), prepared a somewhat similar table of hexagrams and periods of the year, in which he correlated the twelve sovereign hexagrams with the twelve months, and their seventy-two lines with the seventy-two periods of the year. This chart was in turn incorporated by Chu Chen (1072-1138) into his *Han-shang Yi-chuan* (Commentary on the Changes from the Han River). [1]

7—THE HEXAGRAMS AND MUSIC

The twenty-third chapter of the *Ch'ien Han Shu*, entitled "Treatise on the Pitch-pipes and the Calendar," follows the theories of Liu Hsin in the correlations it makes between the twelve "pitch-pipes" and the months of the year. [2] It also correlates the months with the twelve lines of the *ch'ien* and *k'un* hexagrams (nos. 1 and 2), and furthermore singles out three of the pitch-pipes, those of *huang-chung* 黃鐘, *lin-chung* 林鐘, and *t'ai-ts'ou* 太簇, as representative of Heaven, Earth, and man respectively. All these correlations appear in the following passage:

"The Three Sequences are those of Heaven, with its emanating power, Earth, with its generating power, and man, with his affairs. [3] The eleventh month is that of the first line, undivided, of (the hexagram) *ch'ien*. In it the *yang* ether, lying hidden below the Earth, first begins to become manifest in its undivided unity, and the myriad things bud and grow. It acts upon the great *yin*. [4] Therefore *huang-chung* constitutes the Sequence of Heaven. Its pitch-pipe is 9 inches long. [5] It is through this number 9 that it reaches the highest point of central harmony, so that it marks the origin of the myriad crea-

---

[1] On Li Kai and his relationship to the famous "Diagram of the Supreme Ultimate" by Chou Tun-yi (1017-73), see chap. 11, sect. 1, i. Chu Chen's work incorporated not only this but other numerological charts of the Han dynasty onward. — Tr.

[2] On Liu Hsin (ca. 46 B.C.-A.D. 23), see chap. 2, p. 17, note 1. On the twelve pitch-pipes see chap. 2, p. 11. — Tr.

[3] It will be seen that these Three Sequences (*san t'ung*) are quite different from those of Tung Chung-shu, discussed in chap. 2, sect. 11. — Tr.

[4] *Chung* 鐘, "bell," is here used as an equivalent for *tung* 動, "to act upon." Cf. the *Po Hu T'ung* (II, 436): "*Chung* means 'to act upon' (*tung*)." — Tr.

[5] Nine is the number of *yang* = Heaven = *ch'ien*. — Tr.

tures. [1] The *Changes* (p. 423) says: 'The established Way of Heaven is that of the *yin* and *yang*.'

"The sixth month is that of the first line, divided, of (the hexagram) *k'un*. In it the *yin* ether, taking over the task from the great *yang*, continues to nourish and generate the tender myriad creatures, so that they grow into luxuriance during the sixth month, [2] thus causing them to multiply and become firm, strong, and large. Therefore *lin-chung* constitutes the Sequence of Earth. Its pitch-pipe is 6 inches long. [3] It is through this number 6 that it takes into itself the emanations of the *yang*, making them flourish within the six cardinal directions, [4] and giving embodiment to the strong and the weak. 'The established Way of Earth is that of the weak and strong.' [5]

" '*Ch'ien* (symbolizes Heaven, which) directs the great beginning (of things); *k'un* (symbolizes Earth, which) gives to these things their completion.' [6] The first month is that of the second line, undivided, of *ch'ien*. [7] The myriad creatures grow and assume manifest form during the first month, [8] when man takes over the task and gives them their completion. By love (*jen*) he nourishes them, and by righteousness (*yi*) he makes them operate, causing each affair and thing to accord with its own proper principle. The first month is that of (the element) wood, which corresponds to love. Its note is that of *shang*, which corresponds to righteousness. [9] Therefore *t'ai-ts'ou* constitutes the Sequence of Man. Its pitch-pipe is 8 inches long, in imitation of the eight trigrams. It is by means of it that Fu Hsi placed himself in accord with Heaven and Earth, 'comprehended the

---

[1] There is a play on words here between "nine" (*chiu* 九) and "reaches" (*chiu* 究). — Tr.

[2] Lit., "during *wei*," which is the cyclical designation of the sixth month. — Tr.

[3] Six is the number of *yin* = Earth = *k'un*. — Tr.

[4] The four compass points, the zenith, and the nadir. — Tr.

[5] *Book of Changes*, Appen. V, p. 423. — Tr.

[6] *Ibid.*, Appen. III, p. 349. — Tr.

[7] The text reads "third line," which, as pointed out in the commentary, is a mistake for "second line."

[8] Lit., "during *yin*," which is the cyclical designation of the first month. — Tr.

[9] Wood, the symbol of growing things, corresponds to east and to the first month of spring and of the year. *Shang* is the second note in the Chinese five-note scale, but in the *Monthly Commands* it is equated with the three autumn months (months 7-9), whereas the note of the first two spring months is that of *chiao*. — Tr.

spiritual intelligence, and classified the attributes of the myriad creatures.' 'The established Way of Man is that of love and righteousness.'[1]

" 'In Heaven the (celestial) bodies are created; on Earth the
(earthly) forms are created.' '(Then) the sovereign, through his
fashioning activities, gives completion to the course of Heaven and
Earth and assists the application of the adaptations furnished by them,
in order to benefit his people.' [2] This is the significance of the three
pitch-pipes and is what is meant by the Three Sequences" (21a. 5-6).

Later in the same chapter, the *Ch'ien Han Shu* says: "Nine and
six and the *yin* and *yang*: these constitute the relationship between
husband and wife, son and mother. The taking of a wife by the *yang*
pitch-pipe and the bearing of a son by the *yin* pitch-pipe: these constitute the nature of Heaven and Earth" (21a.20-21). [3]

This statement is to be explained as follows: The length of the
lin-chung pitch-pipe (which is *yin*) is 6 inches; that of the *huang-chung*
pitch-pipe (which is *yang*), 9 inches; that of the *t'ai-ts'ou* pitch-pipe,
8 inches. In other words, *lin-chung* is two thirds the length of *huang-
chung*, while *t'ai-ts'ou* is four thirds the length of *lin-chung*. Following
the same formula, the length of each of the remaining nine pitch-
pipes is derived from that of its predecessor by alternately multi-
plying by $\frac{2}{3}$ and then by $\frac{4}{3}$. *Huang-chung, lin-chung,* and *t'ai-ts'ou* are
the first three pitch-pipes in this progression, [4] a fact symbolized
in the text by its reference to "the taking of a wife by the *yang* pitch-
pipe" (meaning that *lin-chung* is the "wife" of *huang-chung*), and to
"the bearing of a son by the *yin* pitch-pipe" (meaning that *t'ai-ts'ou*
is born by *lin-chung* as the result of this "marriage"). Since Heaven,
Earth, and man are, in that sequence, the three main powers of the
universe, it naturally follows, if *huang-chung* represents the Sequence
of Heaven, that *lin-chung* must then represent the Sequence of Earth,
and *t'ai-ts'ou* the Sequence of Man.

In the same chapter of the *Ch'ien Han Shu*, as in the earlier
Monthly Commands, correlations are also made between the Chinese

---

[1] Cf. *Book of Changes*, Appen. III, pp. 382-383 (where it is further stated that
Fu Hsi invented the eight trigrams), and Appen. V, pp. 423-424. — Tr.

[2] *Ibid.*, Appen. III, p. 348, and Appen. II (comment on hexa. 11), p. 281.
— Tr.

[3] It has been pointed out earlier (p. 99, note 3) that six of the
twelve pitch-pipes are to be equated with the *yang* and six with the *yin*.
— Tr.

[4] This explanation has been added by the author for the English edition.
— Tr.

five-note scale (a scale quite different from that of the pitch-pipes), the Five Elements, and the four seasons. Whereas neither text explains the reason for these correlations, however, there is, in the case of the pitch-pipes, a plausible explanation based on musical criteria. Thus it is logical that *huang-chung*, as the longest and therefore lowest pitched of the pitch-pipes, should be placed first, followed by *ta-lü* 大呂, *t'ai-ts'ou*, etc., until the sequence ends with *ying-chung* 應鐘, the shortest and therefore highest in pitch. In the *Ch'ien Han Shu* this sequence is equated with the months as follows: *huang-chung* with the eleventh month (the month in which the *yang* first appears), *ta-lü* with the twelfth, *t'ai-ts'ou* with the first, and so through the sequence, ending with *ying-chung* and the tenth month. The difficulty here, however, is that the progression of pitch-pipes does not accurately mirror the alternating growth and decline of the *yin* and *yang* forces which actually occur during the year. Thus whereas the pitch-pipes are arranged in an unbroken sequence of ascending tones throughout the year, the *yang* and *yin* pass through a double cycle: during the first half of the year (eleventh through fifth month), the *yang* steadily increases while the *yin* correspondingly decreases; during the second half of the year (sixth through tenth month), the *yin* steadily increases while the *yang* correspondingly decreases.

The *Huai-nan-tzŭ* (second century B.C.) avoids this difficulty by offering a different correlation. Thus in its third chapter we find the following sequence of pitch-pipes and twenty-four yearly "breaths": "The Winter Solstice is to be equated with *ying-chung*, [1] from which there is a gradual progression to the lower notes. The Summer Solstice is to be equated with *huang-chung*, from which there is a gradual progression to the higher notes. Thereby the twelve pitch-pipes accord with the changing phases of the twenty-four (solar) periods" (3.22).

The same chapter also says that "the *yang* appears in the eleventh month, the *yin* in the fifth month" (p. 14). [2] It prefaces these words by stating that the Winter Solstice is to be equated with *ying-chung*, the shortest and highest of the pitch-pipes. [3] The next period after

---

[1] The text reads *lin-chung*, which, as pointed out in the commentary, is a mistake for *ying-chung*.

[2] Lit., "in *tzŭ*" and "in *wu*," the cyclical designations of these two months. — Tr.

[3] Since each of the twelve pitch-pipes must be correlated with two of the twenty-four solar periods, *ying-chung* is actually to be equated not only with the

the Winter Solstice is that of Slight Heat, which, in the same manner, is to be equated with *wu-yi* 無射, the pitch-pipe that, next to *ying-chung*, is the shortest and highest in tone. Thereafter, as the *yang* steadily increases and the *yin* correspondingly decreases, this fact is reflected in the correlation of subsequent solar periods with pitch-pipes that are progressively lower in tone. This continues until the Summer Solstice (thirteenth of the solar periods after the Winter Solstice) is reached, the correlate of which is *huang-chung*, the lowest-pitched and therefore the most intensely *yang* of all the pitch-pipes. [1]

Thereafter there is a similar progression, but this time in the opposite direction: as the *yang* diminishes and the *yin* increases, the remaining solar periods are equated with the same twelve pitch-pipes previously used, but now in a sequence moving from lower to higher pitch. Thus Slight Heat, the period immediately following the Summer Solstice, is equated with *ta-lü*, while Great Heat, the period following Slight Heat, goes with *t'ai-ts'ou*. [2] Thereafter the cycle continues until it reaches Slight Snow (period no. 23), the correlate of which is *wu-yi*, and Great Snow (period no. 24), the correlate of which is *ying-chung*. [3] In this manner the round of the year is brought to completion. [4] The *Huai-nan-tzŭ* thus gives a logical and well-rounded theory, in which the growths of the *yang* and *yin* are respectively equated with the descending and ascending tones of the pitch-pipes.

In the *Ch'ien Han Shu* passage quoted at the beginning of this section, it is stated that the first line, undivided, of the *ch'ien* hexagram goes with the eleventh month, and the first line, divided, of *k'un* with the sixth month. The explanation is to be found in the *Yi-wei*

Winter Solstice (solar period no. 1, at which time the *yang* is at its lowest ebb), but also with Great Snow (period 24, immediately preceding the Winter Solstice). — Tr.

[1] But for reasons explained in the preceding note, *huang-chung* must also be equated with Grain in Ear (the immediately preceding period no. 12), even though the *yang* has then not quite reached its apogee. — Tr.

[2] The sequence is as follows: *huang-chung* goes with Grain in Ear and with the Summer Solstice (periods 12 and 13); *ta-lü* with Grain Full (period 11) and with Slight Heat (period 14); *t'ai-ts'ou* with the Beginning of Summer (period 10) and with Great Heat (period 15), and so on. — Tr.

[3] At this end of the calendar, the sequence is as follows: *ying-chung* goes with Great Snow (period 24) and with the Winter Solstice (period 1); *wu-yi* with Slight Snow (period 23) and with Slight Cold (period 2), and so on. — Tr.

[4] Cf. *Huai-nan-tzŭ* (3.12-14), the original text of which contains certain errors, here corrected. [For greater clarity, I have somewhat expanded and modified the author's exposition of this passage. — Tr.]

Ch'ien-tso-tu when it says: "*Ch'ien* is *yang* and *k'un* is *yin*. They both exercise jurisdiction, but operate in alternation to one another. *Ch'ien's* proper place is in the eleventh month, *tzŭ*, from which (its six lines) move toward the left, the duration of the *yang* being six (months). *K'un's* proper place is in the sixth month, *wei*, from which (its six lines) move toward the right, the duration of the *yin* being six (months). Thus, in mutual accord, (the two hexagrams) bring the year to completion. When one year has reached its end, the next follows with (the hexagrams) *t'un* (no. 3) and *meng* (no. 4)" (2.5).

What this passage means is this: In the *ch'ien* hexagram, its first line dominates the eleventh month, its second line the first month, its third line the third, its fourth line the fifth, its fifth line the seventh, and its sixth line the ninth. This is the implication of the words: "*Ch'ien's* proper place is in the eleventh month, *tzŭ*, from which (its six lines) move toward the left, the duration of the *yang* being six (months)."

Similarly with *k'un*: its first line dominates the sixth month, its second line the eighth, its third line the tenth, its fourth line the twelfth, its fifth line the second, and its sixth line the fourth. This is the implication of the words: "*K'un's* proper place is in the sixth month, *wei*, from which (its six lines) move toward the right, the duration of the *yin* being six (months)." In this manner the *yin* and *yang*, symbolized by *k'un* and *ch'ien*, "both exercise jurisdiction, but operate in alternation to one another." [1]

After the completion of a year thus dominated by *ch'ien* and *k'un*, however, the next year falls under the domination of the two subsequent hexagrams, *t'un* and *meng* (nos. 3 and 4), the lines of which, like those of *ch'ien* and *k'un*, exercise alternate control over the months. This process continues until all sixty-four hexagrams, in pairs, have each jointly ruled one year, whereupon the thirty-two year cycle begins anew. This theory underlies the *Ch'ien Han Shu's* statement at the beginning of this section that the first line of *ch'ien* goes with the eleventh month, and the first line of *k'un* with the sixth month.

---

[1] It is natural that the odd months should go with *ch'ien* and the even numbers with *k'un*, since the numbers of *ch'ien* are odd and those of *k'un* even. The reason why the lines of *ch'ien* are said to "move toward the left" from the eleventh month, and those of *k'un* "toward the right" from the sixth month, instead of in the opposite directions, as we should expect, is that Chinese maps are oriented with south instead of north at the top of the page. See chap. 2, p. 27, note 2. — Tr.

8—OTHER APOCRYPHA

The remaining apocrypha on classics other than the *Book of Changes* are all alike in that they stress the "Way of Heaven and man," in other words, the mystic relationship believed to exist between man and the universe. This is exemplified in the following passage from the *Shang-shu-wei Hsüan-chi-ch'ien*: [1]

"In the title of the *Shang-shu*, *shang* 尚 means 'above' (*shang* 上), and *shu* 書 means 'to accord with' (*ju* 如). Heaven suspends its conspicuous emblems (sun and moon, etc.) above, and makes known its rules and regulations. The (*Book of History*'s) writings (*shu*) are made to accord with (*ju*) the operations of Heaven" (53.47).

Again:

"The writings (of the *Book of History*) speak about things in accordance with Heaven" (*ibid.*).

The *Book of Odes* has a similar purpose, according to the *Shih-wei Han-shen-wu* (Apocryphal Treatise on the Odes: The Spirit-filled Aura):

"The *Odes* comprise the mind of Heaven and Earth, the virtue of the ruler and family patriarch, and the source of all happiness; they provide the sounds (i.e., songs) for all things. They hold in themselves what is minute and at the same time regulate what is conspicuously manifest. Above they provide a link with the first sovereigns; [2] below they give an orderly sequence to the Four Beginnings and a systematic arrangement to the Five Periods" (54.5).

The *Ch'un-ch'iu-wei Shuo-t'i-tz'ŭ* (Apocryphal Treatise on the Spring and Autumn Annals: Discussion of Phraseology) says similarly:

"The *Odes* are the refined essence of the heavenly bodies and (indicate) the rules governing the stars and planets; they exercise control over the minds of men" (56.34).

The above-mentioned "Four Beginnings" (*ssŭ shih* 四 始) and

---

[1] *Shang-shu* is another name for *Shu Ching*, the *Book of History*; *hsüan* and *chi* are the names of two stars in the Great Dipper. Hence the title roughly means: *Apocryphal Treatise on the Book of History: The Linchpin Holding in Place the Great Dipper*. This and the other apocrypha cited in this section are all lost save for the fragments collected in Ma Kuo-han's (1794-1857) *Yü-han Shan-fang Chi-yi-shu*, to which the citations below refer. — Tr.

[2] Probably the "Three Sovereigns": Fu Hsi (Subduer of Animals), Shen Nung (the Divine Husbandman), and Huang-ti (the Yellow Emperor). — Tr.

"Five Periods" (*wu chi* 五 際) are explained in the following two passages from the *Shih-wei Fan-li-ch'u* (Apocryphal Treatise on the Odes: Pivot of the Extensive Calendar):

" 'Great Brilliance' stands in *hai*, which marks the beginning of water. [1] 'The Four Steeds' stands in *yin*, which marks the beginning of wood. [2] 'The Fish' stands in *ssŭ*, which marks the beginning of fire. [3] 'The Wild Geese' stands in *shen*, which marks the beginning of metal" [4] (54.2). Again:

"The period between *wu* (the fifth month) and *hai* (the tenth month) is that for changing (Heaven's) Decree. [5] The period between *mao* (the second month) and *yu* (the eighth month) is that for reforming and rectifying. *Ch'en* (the third month) lies in the Gate of Heaven, where, coming and going, it watches and listens. [6]

---

[1] This is the title of III, i, Ode 2 in the *Book of Odes*. *Hai* is the tenth month of the year and the first month of winter, the element for which is water. — Tr.

[2] This is II, i, Ode 2, and *yin* is the first month of the year and of spring, the element for which is wood. — Tr.

[3] This is the abbreviated title of II, ii, Ode 5, and *ssŭ* is the fourth month of the year and first month of summer, the element for which is fire. — Tr.

[4] This is II, iii, Ode 7, and *shen* is the seventh month of the year and the first month of autumn, the element for which is metal. Thus these odes symbolize the beginnings of the four seasons, which constitute the "Four Beginnings." — Tr.

[5] I.e., for establishing a new ruling dynasty. — Tr.

[6] This same passage is quoted in the *Hou Han Shu* (History of the Later Han Dynasty), 60b.10, where, however, it reads somewhat differently: "(The period between) *mao* (the second month) and *yu* (the eighth month) is that for making changes in the government. (The period between) *wu* (the fifth month) and *hai* (the tenth month) is that for changing (Heaven's) Decree. The Spirit lies in the Gate of Heaven, where, coming and going, it watches and listens. That is to say, the Spirit, lying (between) *hsü* (the ninth month) and *hai* (the tenth month), judges and watches the rise and decline, gains and failings, of emperors and kings. When these are good, they (the emperors and kings) prosper, but when evil, they are destroyed."

[This makes better sense than the passage as quoted above, where *ch'en* 辰 (third month) is evidently an error for *shen* 神 (Spirit). Sung Chün (ca. A.D. 10-76), as quoted in the *Hou Han Shu*'s commentary, explains "Spirit" and "Gate of Heaven" (*t'ien men* 天 門) as follows: "The Spirit is the ruling hexagram (*ch'ien*), which represents the *yang* ether. The Gate of Heaven is the juncture between *hsü* (the ninth month) and *hai* (the tenth month)." According to the Ch'in calendar which continued to be used during the Han prior to the reform of 104 B.C., the new year began with the tenth month; the "juncture between *hsü* and *hai*" would therefore in this calendar refer to the beginning of the new year. "Gate of Heaven" is also defined in the *Tz'ŭ-yüan* dictionary as a name for the north star, around which the universe revolves. It therefore has both a spatial and

"*Mao* (the second month) is that of 'The Protection of Heaven' (II, i, Ode 6); *wu* (the fifth month) is that of 'Plucking White Millet' (II, iii, Ode 4); *hai* (the tenth month) is that of 'Great Brilliance' (III, i, Ode 2).

"Thus *hai* is the time for changing (Heaven's) Decree. This is the first Period. The juncture between *hsü* (the ninth month) and *hai* [1] is furthermore the Gate of Heaven, where (the hexagram *ch'ien*), coming and going, watches and listens. This is the second Period. *Mao* (the second month) is the point at which the *yin* and *yang* meet each other. This is the third Period. *Wu* (the fifth month) is that in which the *yang* (begins to) decline and the *yin* to arise. This is the fourth Period. *Yu* (the eighth month) is that in which the *yin* becomes flourishing while the *yang* dwindles away. This is the fifth Period" (54.2).

Here we find various poems in the *Book of Odes* being given a place in the cosmological system of the *Yin-yang* school. These correlations should be compared with the other correlations of this school as presented in the diagrams in this and the preceding chapter.

In the *li* or rites or ceremonials is also to be found an expression of the relationship between man and the universe. The *Li-wei Chi-ming-cheng* (Apocryphal Treatise on Rites: Investigation of Omens) says:

"The movements of the rites accord with the (*yin* and *yang*) ethers of Heaven and Earth. When the four seasons are in mutual accord, when the *yin* and *yang* complement each other, when the sun and moon give forth their light, and when superiors and inferiors are in intimate harmony with one another, then persons and animals are in accord with their own natures" (54.2).

Likewise we read in the above-cited *Ch'un-ch'iu-wei Shuo-t'i-tz'ŭ*: "The rites serve to establish (standards of human) conduct and to illumine the forms of Heaven and Earth" (56.34). Again:

"The rites constitute an essential substance. Man possesses the feelings of grief and pleasure, just as the Five Elements have their

---

temporal significance: in space it is the north star, the pivot of the universe; in time it is the moment of transition from the old to the new year. In this central position rests the *ch'ien* hexagram, the embodiment of the *yang*, from which it watches the acts of human rulers, decreeing good or bad fortune for them according to their deeds. — Tr.]

[1] The text omits the words, "The juncture between *hsü* and," which, as pointed out in the commentary, should be added at this point. [The preceding note provides further support for this change. — Tr.]

(periods of) rise and decline. Therefore the rites have been established for the offering of food and drink to the aged, for marking the beginning and end of grief (in mourning), for following the proprieties in the marriage ceremony, and for making a proper display at the court audiences. Then the eminent and the humble maintain an orderly hierarchy, and superiors and inferiors have their proper substance. The king, by performing the rites, gains the central harmony of Heaven. When the rites are maintained, all things under Heaven gain their proper place, the *yin* and *yang* nourish and fertilize, all things are in accord with one another, and the four seasons operate in proper harmony. Whether active or non-active, one must constantly follow (the rules of ceremony); they may not be neglected for even an instant" (*ibid.*).

In music, too, we have an expression of the relationship between man and the universe. The *Yüeh-wei Tung-sheng-yi* (Apocryphal Treatise on Music: Meaning of Movements and Sounds) says:

"The sage-kings knew that when a period of highest prosperity has been reached, it is followed by decay; when heat attains its apogee, it is followed by cold; when joy reaches its height, it is followed by grief. This is why the sun, having climbed to its meridian, declines, and the moon, having become full, diminishes. The waxings and wanings of Heaven and Earth accord with the growth and decay of the seasons. The purpose of instituting rites and creating music is thereby to reform the popular manners, promote auspicious customs, cause the rains and dews to come at the proper time, and enable the people to obtain blessings from sovereign Heaven" (54.45).

The *Yüeh-wei Hsieh-t'u-cheng* (Apocryphal Treatise on Music: A Graphic Representation of its Harmonies) says similarly:

"When the sages created music, it was not something to serve their own amusement, but was used so that the results of gains and failings might be noted. Hence the sages did not take their music from one man alone (i.e., from themselves), but invariably conformed themselves to the eight skilled officers. In this way those who tapped the bells, beat the drums, struck the stone chimes, and strummed the lute, were all definitely versed in these instruments. Therefore of the eight skilled officers, some (through their music) harmonized the *yin* and *yang*, some the Five Elements, some the growth and decay (of the seasons), some the pitch-pipes and the calendar (equated with these pitch-pipes), and some the five notes (of the scale). [1] When they harmonized their virtue with the spiritual intelligence of Heaven and Earth, the Seven Beginnings and Eight Breaths each gained their proper place. [2] ... Always, at the Winter Solstice, the eight skilled officers gave completeness to Heaven's markings and, at the Summer Solstice, gave completeness to Earth's configurations. [3] In order to give completeness to the markings of Heaven, they played *yin* music; in order to give completeness to the configurations of Earth, they played *yang* music" [4] (54.54-56).

In the *Spring and Autumn Annals*, likewise, there is supposedly an expression of the relationship between man and the universe. The *Ch'un-ch'iu-wei Wu-ch'eng-t'u* (Apocryphal Treatise on the Spring and Autumn Annals: Chart of Complete Sincerity) says:

"Confucius made the *Ch'un Ch'iu* in order to set forth the division between Heaven and man, record prodigies, and investigate omens" (56.13).

We also read in the *Ch'un-ch'iu-wei Han-han-tzŭ* (Apocryphal Treatise on the Spring and Autumn Annals: Cherished Beginnings of Growth of the Han Dynasty):

"Confucius has said: 'I have examined the historical records, drawn upon ancient charts, and investigated and collected (cases of) natural anomalies, so as to institute laws for the emperors of the Han (dynasty), arranging charts and records for them in an orderly manner' " (56.3).

To the extent that these quotations all emphasize the "Way of Heaven and man," they stay within the ideological range of the New Text school. But in the statement that Confucius created the *Ch'un*

---

[1] Here only five instead of eight functions are listed for the eight skilled officers (*pa neng shih* 八 能 士). Other longer lists, all rather far-fetched, are given in the *Tz'ŭ-hai* dictionary under *pa neng*. — Tr.

[2] The Seven Beginnings (*ch'i shih* 七 始) are those of Heaven, Earth, man, and the four seasons, according to the *Tz'ŭ-hai*. The Eight Breaths are probably the more important ones among the twenty-four "breaths," namely, the two solstices, two equinoxes, and four Beginnings of Spring, Summer, Autumn, and Winter. — Tr.

[3] This perhaps refers to the music played during the ruler's annual sacrifices to Heaven at the Winter Solstice, and Earth at the Summer Solstice. — Tr.

[4] The idea here is perhaps that the *yin* and *yang* music (whatever that may have been) was played to Heaven and Earth respectively, in order to counteract their predominant *yang* and *yin* influences and thus restore balance to the natural forces of the universe. — Tr.

Ch'iu "so as to institute laws for the emperors of the Han (dynasty)," we meet a new and unexpected doctrine, variously enunciated in several of the apocrypha. Typical is the following passage from the *Ch'un-ch'iu-wei Yen-k'ung-t'u* (Apocryphal Treatise on the Spring and Autumn Annals: Expository Chart on Confucius):

"Confucius' mother, Cheng-tsai, once while taking a walk happened upon the mound of a large tomb, where she fell asleep and dreamed that she received an invitation from a Black Emperor. She went to him and in her dream had intercourse with him. He spoke to her, saying: 'Your confinement will take place within a hollow mulberry tree.' When she awoke she seemed to feel (pregnant) and (later) gave birth to Confucius within a hollow mulberry. [1] This is why he is called the First Sage. [2] He derived his personal name from the fact that his head resembled the Ni Hill. [3]

"On Confucius' breast there was writing which said: 'The act of instituting (a new dynasty) has been decided and the rule of the world has been transferred.' Confucius was ten feet high and nine spans in circumference. Sitting, he was like a crouching dragon, and standing, like the Cowherd. As one approached him he was like the Pleiades, and as one gazed upon him, like the Ladle. [4] Sages are not born for nothing; they must surely institute something, in order to reveal the mind of Heaven. Thus Confucius, as a wooden-tongued bell, instituted laws for the world. [5] ...

"After the unicorn was caught, [6] Heaven rained blood which

---

[1] This story is similar to, and may have been influenced by, that according to which the founder of the Han dynasty was born as the result of a union between his mother and a dragon. Cf. Dubs, *History of the Former Han Dynasty*, I, 28-29. Since the Chou dynasty is supposed to have ruled with red as its dominant color, and since the color of the following dynasty was to be black, the reference here to a "Black Emperor" is intended to convey the idea (widespread in the Han dynasty) that with Confucius the Chou dynasty had come to an end and a new regime had been inaugurated. See chap. 2, sect. 12. — Tr.

[2] *Yüan sheng* 元 聖, in commemoration of his unusual birth. — Tr.

[3] Ch'iu, the personal name of Confucius, means hill, while Confucius' "style" (*tzŭ*), Chung-ni, commemorates the Ni Hill, near which he was born. — Tr.

[4] The Cowherd, Pleiades, and Ladle are nos. 9, 18, and 8 of the twenty-eight constellations. — Tr.

[5] An allusion to *Analects*, III, 24, where it is said of him: "Heaven is going to use the Master as an arousing wooden-tongued bell." — Tr.

[6] On this event, which happened in 481 B.C. and was interpreted as a sign that Heaven had conferred its Mandate on Confucius to found a new dynasty, see chap. 2, p. 71. — Tr.

formed into writing on the main gate (of the capital) of Lu, and which said: 'Quickly prepare laws, for the Sage Confucius will die; the Chou (ruling house), Chi, will be destroyed; a comet will appear from the east. The government of the Ch'in (dynasty) will arise and will suddenly destroy the literary arts. [1] But though the written records will then be dispersed, (the teachings of) Confucius will not be interrupted.'

"(Confucius' disciple), Tzu-hsia, next day went to look at this, whereupon the writing of blood flew away as a red bird. This then changed itself into white writing, the composition of which is called the Yen-k'ung-t'u. [2] In it are delineated charts for instituting laws.

"While Confucius was discoursing on the classics, there was a bird which (came and) transformed itself into writing. Confucius accepted it and with it made an announcement to Heaven. A small red bird which settled on this writing became a piece of yellow jade, carved with an inscription which said: 'Confucius, holding (Heaven's) Mandate to act, has created these governmental institutions in accordance with the laws. A small red bird came and settled on them' " (56.50-51).

In this apotheosis of Confucius we have an example of the way in which ideas stemming from the prognostication texts filtered into the apocryphal writings. During his own lifetime and the centuries immediately following, Confucius seems to have been viewed by most people simply as a great teacher of his age. Then, in the school of interpretation of the Ch'un Ch'iu represented by the Kung-yang Chuan, his position was advanced, as we have seen in the last chapter, from that of teacher to one of king. And finally, in the prognostication texts and apocrypha of about the first century B.C., it was again advanced from king to supernatural being. Thus the changing status of Confucius reflects the shift in thinking from age to age.

The rise of such bizarre ideas during the latter decades of the Former Han dynasty coincides with the extensive spread of the prognostication literature. The latter's influence is revealed in the history of the time: when Wang Mang usurped the throne from A.D. 9 to 23, he was induced by magic portents to change the name of his dynasty from Han to Hsin; for similar reasons, when a scion of the

---

[1] An allusion to the notorious Burning of the Books carried out by Ch'in in 213 B.C. — Tr.

[2] "Expository Chart on Confucius," title of the work here being quoted. — Tr.

preceding imperial house overthrew him and ruled as Emperor Kuang-wu (25-56), the old name of Han was restored. Portents likewise played an important part in the rise and fall of some of the great statesmen of the period. Though there is little doubt that such ideas as these were originally alien to the *Yin-yang* school, it was yet possible for it, because of its emphasis upon "the Way of Heaven and man," to accept beliefs that led to such extravagances.

9—THE YIN-YANG SCHOOL AND SCIENCE

Though the *yin-yang* theories thus came to embrace many absurdities, they at the same time contained the beginnings of Chinese science. What I mean by this is that, underlying all the *yin-yang* thinking, was the fundamental aim of creating a truly inclusive system of thought—a system that would embrace and explain the phenomena of the entire universe. Granted that its methodology was faulty and its data inadequate, it was nevertheless scientific in spirit in its desire to organize and systematize universal phenomena, and to know their why and wherefore. In the environment of political unification of the Ch'in and Han dynasties it is not surprising that men were inspired to seek a corresponding ideological unification of the universe as well. This political unification, so unprecedented and so seemingly impossible, made them feel that everything else was possible as well. Their resulting attempt to give unity and system to all things may seem to us like brash foolhardiness. Viewed against their environment, however, its motivating spirit becomes understandable.

This chapter demonstrates how heavily, in such fields as astronomy and music, the Chinese have leaned on the doctrines of the *Yin-yang* school. The same is true of other fields, such as medicine and mathematics—exemplified, for instance, by such works as the *Huang-ti Nei-ching* (Classic of Internal Medicine of the Yellow Emperor) and the *Chou-pi Suan-ching* (Mathematical Classic on the Gnomen). [1] In all these fields, indeed, the influence of the *yin-yang* ideology has persisted until very recently. Up to the founding of the Chinese Republic in 1912, for example, the imperially-issued yearly almanacs

---

[1] Works probably dating from the Han dynasty, though traditionally ascribed to a much earlier time. — Tr.

continued to embody such features as the seventy-two solar "periods." [1] From this point of view, therefore, it seems correct to say that China, since the Han dynasty, has remained in the Middle Ages, and that only very recently has a modern age begun to show itself.

------

[1] Even at the present day, as a matter of fact, almanacs of this sort are still issued by private concerns. — Tr.

CHAPTER IV

THE OLD TEXT SCHOOL, AND YANG HSIUNG AND WANG CH'UNG

1—The "Old Learning" and Liu Hsin

During the Former Han dynasty there were already men who, dissatisfied with the exposition of the classics in terms of the prevalent *yin-yang* ideology, created an opposing school of their own. The *Sui Shu* (History of the Sui Dynasty) states in its chapter on literature:

"Wang Mang had a liking for omens, and Kuang-wu arose with the aid of charts and prognostications, which then became widely current in the world. [1] During the (Later) Han period, furthermore, an imperial mandate ordered Ts'ang, Prince of Tung-p'ing, to rectify the explanations by paragraphs and sentences of the five classics, all in conformity with (the theory of) prognostications. [2] As time went on, the vulgar literati increasingly practiced this sort of learning, and the number of chapters and books (devoted to it) became ever augmented. Those who discussed the five classics all relied upon prognostications for their theories. Only such scholars as K'ung An-kuo, the Messrs. Mao, Wang Huang, and Chia K'uei, objected to this, each in turn considering it as heretical and false, and as throwing disorder into the (classical) texts devoted to the middle way. [3] Therefore they based themselves upon the ancient texts

---

[1] Wang Mang brought the former Han dynasty to an end through his usurpation of the throne, A.D. 9-23. After his death a scion of the Han ruling house recovered the throne and founded the Later Han dynasty, reigning as Emperor Kuang-wu (25-56). — Tr.

[2] This prince, Liu Ts'ang (died A.D. 83), was the eighth son of Emperor Kuang-wu. We are told near the beginning of his biography in the *Hou Han Shu* (History of the Later Han Dynasty), chap. 72, that he loved the classics as a youth, and that in the year 59 he, with other officials, was called upon to discuss and determine the forms of ceremonial to be used in the state ritual. It also records a number of his memorials, in which his belief in prognostications appears. — Tr.

[3] These were all scholars of the Old Text school of classical learning. K'ung An-kuo (ca. 156-ca. 74 B.C.), a descendant in the eleventh generation of Confucius, was important for his recension of the Old Text version of the *Book of History*. Mao Heng and his son, Mao Ch'ang, prior to the middle of the second century

obtained during the (Former) Han by Prince Kung of Lu and Prince Hsien of Ho-chien. These they collated and examined, in order to formulate their ideas, designating them the 'old learning' " [1] (32.32).

This "old learning" (*ku hsüeh* 古 學) has reference to the study of the classics carried on by the Old Text school. In expounding these classics, this school rejected the doctrines found in the apocrypha, prognostication texts, and other writings of the *Yin-yang* school. It swept away the latter's supernatural and extravagant theories, in the process restoring Confucius from the position of supernatural being to that of a purely human "teacher." These were truly revolutionary developments, viewed against the prevailing ideology of the day.

Almost two thousand years later, in the last decades of the Ch'ing dynasty (1644-1911), a revival of the New Text school took place, as we shall see in the final chapter of this book. Its proponents maintained that the Old Text school's versions of the classics had all been forged by the noted scholar and statesman, Liu Hsin 劉 歆 (ca. 46 B.C.-A.D. 23), and that this wholesale forging had been done to provide Liu's patron, Wang Mang, with ideological justification

---

B.C., compiled and commented upon that version of the *Book of Odes* which has since become orthodox. Wang Huang (late first century B.C.) is said to have transmitted the Old Text versions of the *Book of Changes* and *Book of History*, as well as the Mao version of the *Odes*. Chia K'uei (A.D. 30-101) was an imperial historiographer who strongly favored the *Tso Chuan* in opposition to the *Kung-yang Chuan*, which had been favored by the New Text school. — Tr.

[1] Prince Hsien (died 130 B.C.), the son of Emperor Ching, was an ardent bibliophile whose agents scoured the country for copies of the classics and other works. These, we are told in the *Ch'ien Han Shu*, chap. 53, were all written in "ancient script," i.e., the form of script that had been current before the Burning of the Books of 213 B.C. Prince Kung (died 127 B.C.), the fifth son of Emperor Ching, is famed for the destruction of the home of Confucius which took place when he enlarged his own palace, in the course of which "old text" versions of the *Book of History, Book of Rites, Analects*, and *Classic of Filial Piety* were allegedly unearthed. They became the foundation for the Old Text school (*Ku Wen Chia* 古 文 家), in apposition to the New Text school, whose versions of the classics were written in the new form of script current during the Han dynasty.

There is strong evidence, however, that the story of the discovery of the classics in the wall of Confucius' house is nothing but a legend. Moreover, the Old Text version of the *Book of History* was itself lost in later times, and the version today bearing this name is a forgery probably belonging to the late third or early fourth century A.D. Cf. Paul Pelliot, "Le *Chou king* en caractères anciens et le *Chang chou che wen*," in *Mémoires concernant l'Asie orientale*, vol. 2 (Paris, 1916), 123-176. — Tr.

for the sweeping innovations introduced by him during his usurpation. [1]

Certainly there is no doubt that the texts and interpretations
of the Old Text school are later than those of the New Text school. If,
however, we are therefore to call them forgeries, we must then
in all fairness be ready also to admit that the New Text school's
versions of the classics are themselves far from being genuine products of early Confucianism, since they assumed their present form
only during the Han dynasty. In interpreting these classics, furthermore, the Old Text school is actually closer in spirit to early Confucianism than is the New Text school, whose superstitious and
supernatural beliefs would have been inconceivable to Confucius
himself. On these grounds, therefore, it is difficult to accept the New
Text doctrines as "genuine."

So numerous, furthermore, are the texts and interpretations
of the Old Text school, as virtually to preclude the possibility that
they could have been forged by any single individual. Only if Liu
Hsin be regarded as a superman is such a deed conceivable. Much
more logical is the hypothesis that a series of individuals, becoming
dissatisfied with the texts and doctrines of the orthodox school
of their time—the New Text school—began to stress other texts
and doctrines, which they maintained went back to Confucius himself,
and that out of the efforts of these men there eventually arose the
so-called "old learning." Such a major ideological revolution must
have required considerable time to gain headway, and therefore
can hardly be attributed to any single individual. [2]

Granted, however, that the "old learning" was thus not solely
created by Liu Hsin, it is undeniable that he was its most illustrious
protagonist. In its beginnings it received no official recognition,
but was a movement restricted to literati who lived among the
common people. Under Emperor Ch'eng (32-7 B.C.), however, "the

---

[1] Liu Hsin and his father, Hsiang (79-8 B.C.), were entrusted by the government with the compilation of a detailed catalogue of all literature extant in their
day. Their labors created the basis for the invaluable "Treatise on Literature"
which now forms the thirtieth chapter of the *Ch'ien Han Shu*. According to the
Ch'ing revivers of the New Text school, it was while Liu Hsin was engaged in
this work under Wang Mang that he himself forged the Old Text versions of the
classics. — Tr.

[2] For the possible connection of the New Text school with the group in
early Confucianism headed by Mencius, and of the Old Text school with that
headed by Hsün Tzŭ, see chap. 2, p. 9. — Tr.

Imperial Household Grandee, Liu Hsiang, (was ordered to) collate (the books) in the Imperial Library, and the Internuncio, Ch'en Nung, was sent as Messenger to seek in the empire for lost books." [1] It was presumably then that the Old Text versions and interpretations of the classics entered the Imperial Library, where they were listed as "lost writings." There they gained the favorable attention of Liu Hsin, who followed his father as cataloguer of the Imperial Library. The result was that during the reign of Emperor Ai (6-1 B.C.), he endeavored to gain official recognition for such works as the *Tso Chuan*, the Mao version of the *Book of Odes*, the *Yi Li* (Dispersed Rituals), and the *Ku-wen Shang-shu* (Book of History in Ancient Script). In so doing, however, he met violent opposition from the Erudits (*po shih*), with whom he debated the matter, but by whom he was ultimately defeated. Thus it is evident that Liu Hsin, more than anyone else, used all his official and scholarly prestige to gain a hearing for the "old learning"; he may, indeed, be justly regarded as its leading spirit.

In his own thinking, nonetheless, it is noteworthy that Liu remained an exponent of the Five Element ideology and of the closely allied belief in "visitations" and "prodigies." [2] In this respect, therefore, he was unable to free himself from the prevailing influence of the *Yin-yang* school, despite his interest in the "old learning." His *Ch'i Lüeh* or "Seven Summaries," on the other hand, which is the name of his descriptive catalogue of the Imperial Library, is noteworthy for the way in which it comprehensively traces the evolution of the various schools of literature from early times, adducing certain historical factors to explain the rise of each, and carefully excluding all supernatural or superstitious explanations. The rationalistic approach of this treatise, therefore, makes it admirably representative of the Old Text school's point of view, and a truly revolutionary work for its time. [3]

2—YANG HSIUNG

The Old Text school's major contribution was to sweep away

---

[1] Cf. *Ch'ien Han Shu*, chap. 10 (Dubs, *History of the Former Han Dynasty*, II, 386), where this event is dated in the year 26 B.C.

[2] Cf. The "Treatise on the Five Elements," which forms chaps. 27a-27e of the *Ch'ien Han Shu*, and is derived in good part from materials compiled by Liu Hsin and his father.

[3] It is the basis for the "Treatise on Literature" which constitutes the thirtieth chapter of the *Ch'ien Han Shu*. — Tr.

the more extravagant and superstitious excesses of the New Text school, and to divorce Confucianism from that marriage with the *Yin-yang* school from which the New Text doctrine had sprung. Its contribution, in other words, was more negative than positive.

Philosophically speaking, the best representatives of this new movement are Yang Hsiung (53 B.C.-A.D. 18) and Wang Ch'ung (A.D. 27-ca. 100). From a positive point of view, to be sure, their ideas are not startlingly new. Historically, however, they merit our attention as marking the final phase of Han thought and as opening the way for that of the Wei (220-265) and Chin (265-419) dynasties. Roughly speaking, we may say that whereas the thought of the Han was dominated by the amalgamation of Confucianism with the *Yin-yang* school, that of the Wei and Chin saw a new amalgamation take place between Confucianism and Taoism.

Yang Hsiung's biography in the *Ch'ien Han Shu* reads in part as follows:

"Yang Hsiung 楊雄, styled Tzŭ-yün 子雲, was a native of Ch'eng-tu in the Commandery of Shu.[1] ... While young he was fond of study and (when reading a text) did not confine himself to a word-for-word analysis but tried to penetrate to its meaning as a whole. He perused widely so as to overlook nothing. In his character he was simple and easy. Because of an impediment in his speech, he was unable to speak rapidly. He was not loquacious, but had a fondness for deep meditation, and was modest and unassertive, so that only rarely did he indulge his desires. He neither strained eagerly after wealth and honors, nor became vexed over poverty and mean position. He avoided any cultivation of incorruptibility merely with the idea of gaining a reputation in his generation. Though his household possessed no more than ten gold pieces and he himself had resources of but a few catties, he remained content. He maintained high standards for himself and had no liking for writings other than those of the sages and wise men. Nor would he do anything that did not accord with his own ideas, even though it might mean wealth and honors. ... Truly was he a lover of antiquity who delighted in the moral path (*Tao*), and his aim was through his writings to gain a reputation among later generations. He maintained that among the classics none is greater than the *Changes*; hence (in imitation) he composed the *T'ai Hsüan* (Great Mystery). Also that among the

---

[1] The present city of Chengtu in Szechwan province. — Tr.

commentaries none is greater than the *Analects*; hence (in imitation) he composed the *Fa Yen* (Model Sayings). ... At the age of seventy-one, in the fifth year of the T'ien-feng period (A.D. 18), he died" [1] (87a.1 and 87b.21).

The most philosophical of Yang's writings is the *T'ai Hsüan* or *Great Mystery*, modeled, as we have seen, on the *Book of Changes*. Inasmuch as the latter's Appendices themselves betray influence of the *Lao-tzŭ*, [2] it is not surprising that ideas from both these books should appear in Yang's own work. Such ideas, in fact, are strongly evident in another of his writings, the *T'ai Hsüan Fu* or "Prose-Poem on the Great Mystery," in which he says:

"I have observed the great *Change*'s waxings and its wanings, [3]
And have viewed the 'leanings and restings' of Mr. Lao. [4]
I have examined the common door to joy and sorrow,
And looked into good and bad fortune's mutual realm.
As brilliantly as sun and moon, thus shine (these principles).
Why then by vulgar 'sage's' murky lamp (are they not seen)?
Why, to covet favor, court disaster,
And then gnaw at one's navel for not succeeding?
For a hurricane never lasts beyond the morning,
Nor does a rainstorm endure the livelong day. [5]
Thunder, resounding, suddenly then ceases,
And fire which blazes fiercely then goes out.
Since things which have their waxing, then have waning,
So too for human affairs which reach a peak." [6]

This poem restates the concept, already prominent in the *Lao-tzŭ* and *Book of Changes*, that all things, having reached one extreme, must inevitably revert to the other. In this respect, it expresses nothing new. Considered in the context of its age, however, when

---

[1] From other portions of the biography we also learn that he accepted office under the usurper Wang Mang, for which he has been severely blamed by history. He is most famous, however, for his literary work, which includes, in addition to the titles just mentioned, a considerable amount of poetry and some philological treatises. — Tr.

[2] See vol. 1, pp. 383-385, 389, 391-392. — Tr.

[3] I.e., the waxings and wanings of the *yin* and *yang* forces. — Tr.

[4] An allusion to the *Lao-tzŭ*, chap. 58: "It is upon bad fortune that good fortune leans, and upon good fortune that bad fortune rests." — Tr.

[5] These two lines are taken almost unchanged from the *Lao-tzŭ*, chap. 23. — Tr.

[6] Contained in the *Ku Wen Yüan* (Park of Ancient Literature), 4.1.

the apocrypha and prognostication texts were at their height of popularity, this re-expression of the naturalistic world view of these two works assumes revolutionary significance. It is to them, therefore, that we should look for Yang's ideological basis when he composed the *Great Mystery*.

i. *The Great Mystery*

In the tenth chapter of his *Great Mystery*, Yang writes:

"What is to be esteemed in a writer is his conformity to and embodiment of spontaneity (*tzŭ jan* 自 然). When his conformity to it is great, then his embodiment is sturdy, but when his conformity is small, then his embodiment is feeble. (Likewise) when his conformity to it is straight, then his embodiment is complete, but when his conformity is crooked, then his embodiment is diffused. Therefore he neither discards what is possessed (by spontaneity), nor strains after what it lacks. The case is like that of the body: adding to it results in excrescence, while cutting away results in injury. [1] Thus what is primary and substantive lies in spontaneity; what is supplementary and decorative lies in human affairs. [2] Can the (latter), then, in any way add to or subtract from (the former)?" (7.17).

What Yang is here saying is that anyone who expresses himself in writing should aim at spontaneity. To the extent that he succeeds or fails in so doing, the ideas he expresses are correspondingly significant or insignificant. To make one's ideas the embodiment of spontaneity: this is of the essence. As for the words in which these ideas are clothed, they are merely "supplementary and decorative," and cannot in themselves add to or subtract from the central essence of spontaneity.

Regarding the *Hsüan* 玄 or Mystery, which gives Yang the title for his book, he writes as follows (chap. 9):

"The Mystery secretly permeates the myriad species (of crea-

---

[1] The thought here is reminiscent of that in the *Chuang-tzŭ*, chap. 8: "The duck's legs are short, but if we try to lengthen them, the duck will feel pain. The crane's legs are long, but if we try to cut off a portion of them, the crane will feel grief. Therefore we are not to amputate what is by nature long, nor to lengthen what is by nature short" (p. 101). — Tr.

[2] The words "human affairs" are repeated twice by mistake, so that their repetition should be deleted.

tures), yet its form is not visible. Does it, then, take sustenance from emptiness and nothingness, and thus produce life? (The reply is that) it manipulates the spiritual intelligence and so creates fixed forms. It links together past and present, so as thus to give free development to the various species (of things). It extends and sets forth the *yin* and *yang*, and gives free operation to their ethers. ... Gaze upward, and one will see it on high. Gaze downward, and one will spy it below. Stretch forward, and one will see it in advance. Cast it aside and neglect it, and it is still at one's rear. One may wish to avoid it, yet this is impossible. But by remaining silent one will reach its dwelling place. Such is the Mystery. ... The *yang* knows the *yang* but not the *yin*. The *yin* knows the *yin* but not the *yang*. But that which knows both the *yin* and the *yang*, both cessation and movement, both darkness and light—is it not the Mystery?" (7.5-9). Again (chap. 14):

"The Mystery constitutes the course (*Tao*) of Heaven, the course of Earth, and the course of man" (10.4).

Thus described, the Mystery is the supreme first principle of the universe; it is the moving force whereby all things in the universe are brought into being, and from which they receive their orderly arrangement. Yang writes further (chap. 1):

"Equable is the Mystery, as it moves endlessly on its vast course, precisely in the manner of Heaven. The *yin* and *yang* join with it so as to form a trinity. Through the single *yang*, it directs its entire sequence, and the myriad creatures thereby receive their form. In this way the *fang* 方, *chou* 州, *pu* 部, and *chia* 家 are distributed and brought to a state of completion in groups of threes. Being arranged in multiples of 9 times 9, there is production through these numbers. The *tsan* 贊 manifest their multitudinous principles, being grouped according to the designations (of their *shou*). And with the eighty-one *shou* 首, the affairs of a year are all made correct" (1.2-3). Again he writes (chap. 14):

"The Mystery has a single course, whereby it starts things in threes and creates things in threes. What are thus started in threes are the *fang*, *chou*, *pu*, and *chia*. What is thus created in threes is the *yang* ether, which, being triply divided, forms into a series of three, and from this extends to form nine halting places (*ying* 營). There is thus identity in origin, but separation in growth: this is the constant course of Heaven and Earth. And there is thus permeation laterally and upward and downward: thereby the myriad creatures are knitted together. The nine 'halting places' are distributed within the cycle (of a year), resulting in correctness from beginning to end. (This cycle, which) begins with the eleventh month and ends with the tenth month, consists of nine progressions, each lasting forty days" (10.4).

Here Yang means to say that the all-embracing first principle of the universe, called the Mystery, evolves to form three divisions which he calls *fang*. [1] Each of these then again becomes divided into three *chou* (continents), i.e., a total of nine *chou*, which in turn each undergo a further tripartite division, resulting in twenty-seven lesser parts called *pu* (sections). These, through yet another tripartite division, yield a total of eighty-one still lesser parts, called *chia* (clans). Such is what we should understand by his statements that "the *fang, chou, pu*, and *chia* are distributed and brought to a state of completion in groups of threes," and that the Mystery "starts things in threes." [2]

The eighty-one *chia* into which the Mystery ultimately evolves are also referred to in one of the passages quoted above as *shou* or "heads," which, in Yang's system, are apparently comparable to the sixty-four hexagrams of the *Book of Changes*. Concerning the group of three *chia* evolved out of the first *pu* of the first *chou* of the first *fang*, we are told that the first *chia* in this group is at the same time the "central" (*chung* 中) *shou*, and that the second *chia* is the "sur-

---

[1] Lit., "regions," but it and the terms following have a special metaphysical connotation for Yang which their literal meanings (given in parentheses below) fail to express. — Tr.

[2] The fact that Yang makes the process of tripartite division from the Mystery stop after four and only four stages is probably because of the belief, widespread in his day, that anciently the governmental hierarchy had likewise consisted of four major official ranks beneath the ruler himself. Thus he writes (chap. 10): "The *fang, chou, pu*, and eighty-one *chia* are (each) divided into inferior, medium, and superior (categories), thus representing (everything within) the four seas (i.e., the whole physical world). And the Mystery, with its arts, illumines them (all). (Likewise in the human world there are) one sovereign (*pi*), three highest ministers (*kung*), nine lower ministers (*ch'ing*), twenty-seven great officials (*ta fu*), and eighty-one first-class officers (*yüan shih*). In this way the few govern the many, and non-being (*wu*) governs being (*yu*). The Mystery, with its arts, illumines them (all)" (7.16). [The statement, "Non-being governs being," is an idea derived from the *Lao-tzŭ*, chap. 40: "Being is the product of non-being." — Tr.] Though Yang here maintains that the four official ranks are modeled upon the four stages of the evolution of the Mystery, there is every reason to suppose that in actual fact his concept of these four stages was inspired by the current belief in the four official ranks. [These ranks are also discussed by Tung Chung-shu. See chap. 2, pp. 49 f. — Tr.]

rounding" (*chou* 周) *shou*. [1] Each of the eighty-one *shou*, furthermore, is subdivided into nine *tsan* or "eulogies," just as each of the sixty-four hexagrams consists of six component lines. This is the meaning of Yang's statement that "the *tsan* manifest their multitudinous principles, being grouped according to the designations (of their *shou*)." There being eighty-one *shou*, each having nine *tsan*, it follows that the total number of *tsan* is 729. Yang is referring to these various numerical progressions when he says that "being arranged in multiples of 9 times 9, there is production through these numbers"; that "the *yang* ether, being triply divided, forms into a series of three, and from this extends to form nine halting places"; or that the Mystery "creates things in threes."

The reference here to the *yang* as being triply divided should be compared with Yang's other statements about the *yin* and *yang*: they "join with it (the Mystery) to form a trinity"; the Mystery "extends and sets forth the *yin* and *yang*, and gives free operation to their ethers"; it "knows both the *yin* and the *yang*." Despite these joint references to both principles, it is evident that the *yang* definitely holds primary place in Yang Hsiung's theory of the generative activities of the Mystery. This fact appears clearly in his statement that "through the single *yang* it (the Mystery) directs its entire sequence, and the myriad creatures thereby receive their form."

The Mystery, together with its three *fang*, nine *chou*, twenty-seven *pu*, eighty-one *chia* or *shou*, and 729 *tsan*, constitutes for Yang a cosmological framework within which all growth and change takes place. Hence his statement that "there is thus identity in origin, but separation in growth: this is the constant course of Heaven and Earth." It is this cosmological framework, too, that makes the existence of all things possible. Hence his following statement that "there is thus permeation laterally and upward and downward: thereby the myriad creatures are knitted together." The cycle of the seasons, too, falls into this system, which is why Yang says: "The nine 'halting places' are distributed within the cycle (of a year), resulting in correctness from beginning to end," or again that "with the eighty-one *shou*, the affairs of a year are all made correct."

We have seen in the preceding chapter how the writers of the *Book of Changes* apocrypha, notably Meng Hsi and Ching Fang, created elaborate correlations between the sixty-four hexagrams and

---

[1] Cf. the *Great Mystery*, chap. 1 (1.4 and 6). — Tr.

twenty-four "breaths" or solar periods of the year. Yang Hsiung makes a similar correlation with the year, substituting, however, the eighty-one *shou* for the sixty-four hexagrams. Among these *shou*, nine are of particular importance, namely the first *shou* of the first *chia* of the first *pu* of each of the nine *chou*. Because they are particularly associated with the major seasonal changes of the year, he gives them the distinctive designation of *T'ien* or "Heaven." In his eleventh chapter he describes these nine "Heavens" as follows:

"Among the nine Heavens, the first is the central (*chung* 中) Heaven, the second is the fructifying (*hsien* 羡) Heaven, the third is the assisting (*ts'ung* 從) Heaven, the fourth is the renewing (*keng* 更) Heaven, the fifth is the purifying (*sui* 睟) Heaven, the sixth is the extending (*k'uo* 廓) Heaven, the seventh is the diminishing (*chien* 減) Heaven, the eighth is the submerging (*ch'en* 沈) Heaven, and the ninth is the completing (*ch'eng* 成) Heaven" (8.15).

Each of these "Heavens" exercises jurisdiction over a period of forty days in the year, a fact alluded to in the statement that the year "begins with the eleventh month, ends with the tenth month, and consists of nine progressions (i.e., Heavens), each lasting forty days." Elsewhere Yang elaborates on this theory as follows (chap. 14):

"What is unmixed and held within is associated with the central (Heaven). What diffuses and goes forth is associated with the fructifying (Heaven). The coursing of clouds and dispersion of rain is associated with the assisting (Heaven). The changing of regulations and shifting of rules is associated with the renewing (Heaven). Beautiful brilliance and unblemished perfection is associated with the purifying (Heaven). Emptiness within and expansion without is associated with the diminishing (Heaven). Collapse and withdrawal into obscurity is associated with the submerging (Heaven). The termination of life is associated with the completing (Heaven). [1]

---

[1] The commentary by Fan Wang (third century A.D.) explains that the nine "Heavens" exercise jurisdiction over the following periods of the year:

1. Central Heaven: 11th month.
2. Fructifying Heaven: 12th month.
3. Assisting Heaven: 1st month through 2nd month.
4. Renewing Heaven: 1st decade of 3rd month through 1st decade of 4th month.
5. Purifying Heaven: 2nd decade of 4th month through 2nd decade of 5th month.

(see over)

"Therefore in the first to ninth (Heaven), the movements of the *yin* and *yang* are computed. Or, presenting the matter in another way, in *tzŭ* may be seen how the *yang* germinates during the eleventh month, and how the *yin* reaches the conclusion (of its dominant phase) during the tenth month; in *wu* may be seen how the *yin* germinates during the fifth month, and how the *yang* reaches the conclusion (of its dominant phase) during the fourth month. [1] For the growth of the *yang* there is nothing like *tzŭ*, and for the growth of the *yin* there is nothing like *wu*. In the northwest the beauty of *tzŭ* comes to an end, and in the southeast the beauty of *wu* reaches its final point" (10.5-6).

In other words, the *yang* first appears in *hai* (the tenth month), and begins to grow in *tzŭ* (the eleventh month), whereas the *yin* first appears in *ssŭ* (the fourth month) and begins to grow in *wu* (the fifth month). The (astronomical) year begins with the eleventh month, that of the central *shou* or central "Heaven." This is the time when growing things first come to life, but without yet having put forth shoots of visible growth. Hence Yang's statement that "what is unmixed and held within is associated with the central (Heaven)." Likewise, the year reaches its end with the tenth month, that of the completing *shou* or "Heaven." This is the time when all growing things have been harvested and stored away, or have dried up and died, which is why Yang says that "the termination of life is associated with the completing (Heaven)."

Not only does this process of growth, maturity and decay apply to the yearly cycle, however. It also characterizes the cycle of human life, in which Yang distinguishes nine comparable stages of evolution. Thus he writes (chap. 14):

"Therefore the appearance of thoughts in the mind represents the first (stage); the turning over (of these thoughts) represents the second; their formulation into definite ideas, the third; the

---

6. Extending Heaven: 3rd decade of 5th month through 3rd decade of 6th month.

7. Diminishing Heaven: 1st decade of 7th month through 1st decade of 8th month.

8. Submerging Heaven: 2nd decade of 8th month through 3rd decade of 9th month.

9. Completing Heaven: 10th month. — Tr.

[1] *Tzŭ* is the cyclical character for north and for the eleventh month; *wu* is that for south and for the fifth month. — Tr.

extension of these (into action), the fourth; their manifestation (in resulting achievements), the fifth; the attainment of greatest (achievement), the sixth; (subsequent) decline and loss, the seventh; disintegration and collapse, the eighth; destruction and annihilation, the ninth.

"The first (of these stages) is that of the birth of consciousness, than which there is nothing prior. The fifth is that of central harmony, than which there is nothing more perfect. The ninth is the seat of suffering, than which there is nothing more tormenting.

"The first is that of thought in its minute beginnings. The fourth is that of the richness of good fortune. The seventh is the stepping stone to calamity.

"The third is that of thought in its highest development. The sixth is the highest peak of good fortune. The ninth is the utmost depth of calamity.

"The second, fifth, and eighth are the three midway ones (between the above-mentioned first and third, fourth and sixth, and seventh and ninth stages)" (10.6).

This nine-stage cycle of human life rises and falls as follows: (1) the stage of the beginning of thought; (2) that of conscious reflection; (3) that in which there is a definite formulation of ideas; (4) that in which these ideas, through "extension," become operative in actual conduct; (5) that of their concrete "manifestion" in corresponding achievement, resulting in "good fortune"; (6) that of "the attainment of the greatest (achievement)," which means "the highest peak of good fortune." Thereafter there is a corresponding decline: (7) the stage of "decline and loss," which is "the stepping stone to calamity"; (8) that of "disintegration and collapse"; (9) the final stage of "destruction and annihilation," which marks the "utmost depth of calamity." Yang summarizes by saying (chap. 14):

"From the first to the third (stage), one suffers poverty and mean position and the heart is afflicted. From the fourth to the sixth, one enjoys wealth and noble position and is honored and esteemed. From the seventh to the ninth, one meets calamities and incurs disasters. Those below the fifth are ones of growth; those above the fifth ones of decay. Persons in the more advanced (stages) have (previously) experienced noble position, but are in actual fact suffering adversity. Those in the less advanced (stages) are experiencing meanness of position, but will in actual fact enjoy abundance. Growth and decay are interlinked; noble and mean position are interlocked" (10.7).

All this is simply an elaboration of the theory of rise and fall already found in the *Lao-tzŭ* and *Book of Changes*.

Yet Yang, in the final analysis, fails to free himself wholly from the *Yin-yang* school's ideology. The fourteenth chapter of his *Great Mystery*, for example, contains a passage which is pure numerology:

"One and 6 have a common origin (in the north); 2 and 7 have a common light (in the south); 3 and 8 form friends (in the east); 4 and 9 have an identical course (in the west); 5 and 5 mutually support each other (in the center)" [1] (10.8).

Here, as in the *Yin-yang* school, numbers are correlated with directions. There is, however, one slight difference: whereas the *Yin-yang* school correlates only those numbers which symbolize the Five Elements in their state of completed growth, Yang goes one step further by also enumerating those with which these Five Elements come into being. [2] The graphic portrayal of such numerology resulted in later times in those diagrams which Liu Mu (late 10th or early 11th century) called the "River Chart," and which Chu Hsi (1130-1200) called the "Lo Writing." [3]

ii. *The Model Sayings*

In the *Great Mystery*, Yang Hsiung shows obvious indebtedness to the ideas of the *Lao-tzŭ* and *Book of Changes*. Yet in his companion work, the *Fa Yen* or *Model Sayings*, we find him giving final allegiance to Confucius and Confucianism:

"Mountain paths are too numerous to be (all) walked over, and doors in walls are too numerous to be (all) entered. So it may be asked: 'By what is one to walk or enter?' I reply: 'By Confucius. Confucius is the door'" (2.2).

"Someone asks: 'Everyone approves of what he himself considers to be right and disapproves of what he himself considers to be wrong. Who, then, may serve to give a correct judgment?' I reply: 'Since the myriad things (of this world) are mixed and confused, let us depend on Heaven. Since the multitudinous statements (of the present day) are incoherent and disordered, let us take the (Confucian) Sage as the standard.' It may be asked: 'How may we see the Sage

---

[1] The directions given in parentheses are added from the commentary. — Tr.
[2] Cf. chap. 2, p. 14.
[3] See chap. 3, p. 101, and chap. 11, sect. 1, i. — Tr.

and thus take him as a standard?' I reply: 'If he be living, we take a man, but if he be dead, we take his writings. The standard is the same' " (2.3-4).

Regarding the *Lao-tzŭ*, Yang Hsiung writes as follows:

"I have taken something from what Lao Tzŭ says about the Way (*Tao*) and its Power (*Te*). But as for his attacks on love (*jen*) and righteousness (*yi*), and his abolition of the rituals (*li*) and learning, I refuse to accept this" (4.1-2).

As to other non-Confucian thinkers, he writes:

"Chuang (Tzŭ) and Yang (Chu) were unrestrained and did not conform to a standard; Mo (Tzŭ) and Yen (Ying) were miserly and did away with propriety (*li*); Shen (Pu-hai) and Han (Fei-tzŭ) were dangerous and lacked culture; Tsou Yen was fanciful and untrustworthy" [1] (8.4).

And here is what he has to say about the classics:

"For discussing Heaven, there is nothing more discerning than the *Book of Changes*. For discussing (human) affairs, there is nothing more discerning than the *Book of History*. For discussing the essential substance (of things), there is nothing more discerning than the *Book of Rites*. For discussing intentions, there is nothing more discerning than the *Book of Odes*. For discussing principles, there is nothing more discerning than the *Spring and Autumn Annals*" (7.1).

Practically all of these works, Yang maintains further, are connected in one way or another with Confucius:

"Someone asks: 'May the classics be subtracted from or added to?' I reply: 'The *Changes* originated with the eight trigrams, but with King Wen (these were increased to) sixty-four, so that his additions to it may be known. [2] As to the *Odes*, *History*, *Rites*, and *Spring and Autumn Annals*, some of these were (merely) utilized (by Confucius in his teaching); some were written (by him); but (all) were brought to perfection by Confucius, so that his additions to them may be known' " (5.1-2).

Yang's conclusion is that later thinkers should always take care to base themselves on the classics when formulating their own ideas:

"Books that do not follow the classics are no books. Words

---

[1] All these men are famous as Chou philosophers save Yen Ying (died 493 B.C.), a statesman noted for his thrift, who is mentioned incidentally in vol. 1, pp. 35-36. — Tr.

[2] For this and similar theories, see vol. 1, p. 379. The phrase, "his additions to it may be known," is derived from the *Analects*, II, 23. — Tr.

that do not follow the classics are no words. Words and books that do not follow the classics are all useless" (5.3).

The *Yin-yang* school's doctrines do not, however, in Yang's opinion, accord with the standards of the ancient sages:

"Someone asks: 'Did the sages (of antiquity) make divinations about Heaven?' I reply: 'They did.' 'If this be so, then how do the astrologers (of today) differ from them?' [1] I reply: 'These astrologers use Heaven to divine about men, whereas the sages used men to divine about Heaven' " (8.3). Again he writes:

"Someone asks: 'What about the cycle (starting) from Huang-ti (the Yellow Emperor)?' [2] I reply: 'Fictitious indeed! Anciently, Yü (is said to have) brought good order to the waters and lands; hence witches (of today) commonly perform the Pace of Yü. [3] Pien Ch'iao (is said to have) been a native of Lu; hence doctors (of today) commonly (call themselves natives) of Lu. [4] Wishing to expound what is false, one must always falsify the truth. So what (can be definitely said) about Yü, Lu, or the cycle (of the Yellow Emperor)?' " (10.1).

And yet again: "It may be said: 'How unreliable is the transmission of the written records (of antiquity)!' I reply: 'If it is unreliable, then indeed it is unreliable. But how much more so is the drum beating of the witches (of today)!' " (12.2).

Yang is equally skeptical about the Taoist magicians of his

----

[1] The word *shih* 史 , translated "astrologer," is usually rendered "historian," but during the Han dynasty it could also designate persons concerned with astrology and divination, and that is obviously the way it is used here. — Tr.

[2] A reference to the *yin-yang* theory that each period of history is dominated by one of the Five Elements. — Tr.

[3] This reflects the legend according to which Yü, founder of the Hsia dynasty, while laboring to control the flood that then ravaged China, contracted an illness which shriveled up his body and so affected his legs that he could not move one beyond the other. Based on this legend, there came into existence a magical dance known as the "Pace of Yü" (*yü pu* 禹 步), which, as practiced by witches and sorcerers, brought to them supernatural powers. See Marcel Granet, *Danses et légendes dans la Chine ancienne* (Paris, 1926), II, 549 f. In the present text, Yü's literal designation is "of the clan of Ssŭ 似 ," Ssŭ being the name of his reputed descendants during the Chou dynasty. — Tr.

[4] Pien Ch'iao was a famous doctor of the latter part of the Chou dynasty, many details of whose life, however, are obviously fictitious. Lu was southwest of the present Ch'ang-ch'ing 長 清 hsien in Shantung. — Tr.

day, with their popular doctrine that immortality may be gained through magical techniques:

"Someone asks: 'What about the many spirits in the time of Chao?' [1] I reply: 'As to the existence or non-existence of vague and uncertain supernatural prodigies, the sage does not discuss them' " [2] (10.1). Again:

"Someone asks: 'Are there immortals such as people talk about?' (I reply): 'Bah! Even of Fu Hsi, Shen Nung, Huang-ti, Yao, and Shun, I have heard that death and decay came to them all. (The same fate met) King Wen at Pi and Confucius north of the capital of Lu. So why should you, sir, be the only one concerned about death? It is something about which men can do nothing, and on which the immortals can certainly add nothing to your store (of knowledge).'

"Someone says: 'The sages do not learn from the immortals, their arts being different. The sage, vis-à-vis the world, feels shame for every object that he does not understand, whereas the immortal, via-à-vis the world, feels shame for every day that he does not live.' I reply: 'Life! Life! They call it life but it is really death.'

"Someone asks: 'But if then there are no immortals in the world, why is there this talk about them?' I reply: 'Is it not because of the tremendous hubbub raised by those who do the talking? By keeping up this hubbub they are able to cause the non-existent seemingly to exist.'

"Someone then asks: 'What is the actual truth about immortals?' I reply: 'There is nothing to be said about them. Their existence or non-existence is not something about which one should ask. What one should ask are questions about loyalty and filial piety. A loyal subject or filial son finds no leisure (for asking useless questions about immortals)' " (12.3-4).

Yet again: "Where there is life there must be death, and where there is a beginning there must be an end. Such is the natural course" (12.4).

This being so, it is absurd, Yang argues, to suppose that life can be prolonged through human means. In the China of his day, with its widespread belief in the powers of Taoist magicians, and in

---

[1] Presumably the state of this name of the late Chou dynasty, which was apparently known as a center for supernatural occurrences. — Tr.

[2] An echo of *Analects*, VII, 20: "The Master (Confucius) would not discuss prodigies, prowess, lawlessness, or the supernatural." — Tr.

the gross superstition that arose in the wake of the *yin-yang* ideology, such views must surely have had a salutary influence.

If we turn to another topic, that of the long debated question of human nature (*hsing*), we find that here too Yang holds an independent position for which he has won recognition in later times. Thus he writes: "In man's nature, good and evil are intermixed. If he cultivates the good elements, he becomes a good man, but if he cultivates the evil elements, he becomes an evil one" (3.1).

Here Yang borrows both from Mencius and Hsün Tzŭ, in the process trying to reconcile their divergent points of view.

Though only partially agreeing with Mencius on this point, however, Yang elsewhere singles him out for special praise: "Someone asks whether Mencius understood the essentials of words and the deep mystery that underlies virtue. I reply: 'He was not one who merely superficially understood these things. He was also one who truly practiced them.' Someone (further) asks: 'You, sir, belittle the various philosophers (except Confucius). But does not Mencius belong to these same philosophers?' I reply: '(I belittle) the various philosophers because their knowledge differs from Confucius, but as for Mencius, does he differ?'" (12.1).

Yang, in fact, in his role as a reviver of true Confucianism, even goes so far as to compare himself with Mencius:

"Anciently, when Yang (Chu) and Mo (Ti) blocked the path (of truth), Mencius through his words widely opened it once more. In later times there have also been those who have blocked this path, and I venture to compare myself with Mencius" (2.3).

Philosophically speaking, Yang obviously falls far short of Mencius in creative achievement. His chief merit, however, is that he, more systematically than most other members of the Old Text school, restored Confucianism from its intermingling with the *yin-yang* beliefs. Historically speaking, therefore, he has earned a secure niche for himself.

3—Wang Chung

Contemporary with Yang Hsiung, and, like him, an opponent of numerology and prognostication, there lived Huan T'an (died ca. A.D. 25). We read in his biography in the *Hou Han Shu* (History of the Later Han Dynasty): "He was a skilled writer, and one especially fond of the 'old learning.' With Liu Hsin and Yang Hsiung he frequently debated and analyzed doubts and differences. ... He wrote a book in twenty-one sections, called the *Hsin Lun* (New Discourses), in which he discussed the current affairs of his age" (58a.1 and 6). This work, however, has since been lost.

The first century A.D., which saw the prognostication literature and the apocrypha reach their highest popularity, also saw the beginnings of a revival of interest in Taoism. This school, more than any of the others of ancient China, had been far removed from the "arts of divination." Most conspicuous in its revival was the Later Han philosopher, Wang Ch'ung 王充 (A.D. 27-ca. 100), who in his large work, the *Lun Heng* or *Critical Essays*, used Taoist naturalism to attack the superstitions of his day. By so doing he undoubtedly did much to purge China of a great mass of popular superstition. Because, however, his ideas were primarily destructive rather than constructive, their intrinsic value is less than some recent scholars have supposed.

In Wang's autobiography, which forms the eighty-fifth and final chapter of his *Critical Essays*, we read:

"Wang Ch'ung was a native of Shang-yü in K'uei-chi. [1] He was styled Chung-jen 仲任, ... and was born in the third year of the Chien-wu period (A.D. 27). ... Though high in talent, he did not like doing things only for effect. Though eloquent in speech, he was not fond of argument. Unless he found the proper audience, he would not speak the entire day. What he had to say seemed strange in the beginning to the generality of men, but when they had heard it to the end, they would give it their approval. Such was also the case with the products of his pen. ... The study of the old texts was his debauchery, and strange stories his relish. In the current books and common sayings he found much to which he could not acquiesce. As a recluse living in solitary retirement, he tried to find out truth and falsehood" (I, 64-66).

Wang's biography in the *Hou Han Shu* (chap. 79) states that he died during the Yung-yüan period (98-104), which would place his death roughly around the year 100. [2] Let us turn now to the *Critical*

---

[1] The present Shao-hsing 紹興 in Chekiang province. — Tr.

[2] This biography is translated by Forke in the Introduction to his translation of the *Critical Essays*, I, 4-5. In it we learn further that Wang came of a poor family, that he lost his father as a boy, and that most of his life was spent in teaching, though he also held a few minor official posts, none higher than that of sub-prefect. Forke demonstrates elsewhere in his translation (II, 419) that the *Critical Essays* was probably completed during the years A.D. 82 and 83. — Tr.

Essays, written by him "as a recluse living in solitary retirement," to see how he thus "tried to find out truth and falsehood" among the "current books and common sayings" of his day.

i. *Naturalism*

In studying "current books and common sayings," Wang based himself primarily on Taoist naturalism. This concept is clearly described in the fifty-fourth chapter of the *Critical Essays*:

"By the fusion of the (*yin* and *yang*) ethers of Heaven and Earth, all things are spontaneously produced, just as by the union of the fluids of husband and wife, children are spontaneously produced. Among the myriad things thus produced, those with blood in their veins are sensitive to hunger and cold. Seeing that the five grains may be eaten, they use them as food, and seeing that silk and hemp may be worn, they use them as clothing. ... When Heaven moves, it does not desire to produce things thereby, but things are produced of their own accord: such is spontaneity (*tzŭ jan*). When it gives forth its ether, it does not desire to create things, but things are created of themselves: such is non-activity (*wu wei*). What is it of Heaven that is thus a spontaneous and non-acting principle? It is its ethers (*ch'i*), which are placid, tranquil, desire nothing, do nothing, and are concerned with nothing. ...

"Men who are perfect in virtue and untarnished in purity are those who are endowed with Heaven's ethers in abundance. For this reason they are able to pattern themselves on Heaven's spontaneity and non-activity. ... Among those of such unblemished worthiness there were Huang and Lao. This Huang was Huang-ti (the Yellow Emperor) and this Lao was Lao Tzŭ. Huang and Lao controlled their bodies in such a way that they maintained themselves in a state of quiescence and tranquillity. They governed others with non-activity and kept their own persons rectified, so that the *yin* and *yang* were of themselves harmonious with one another. They had no mind for action, but things evolved of themselves; they had no idea of creating, but things became formed of themselves.

"The *Changes* (p. 383) says: 'Huang-ti, Yao, and Shun allowed their robes to hang (undisturbedly) downward, and the world was well governed.' That they allowed their robes to hang (undisturbedly) downward means that they (simply) let them hang thus, folded their arms, and did nothing. ... The *Changes* (p. 308) says again: 'The great man harmonizes his virtue with Heaven and Earth.' Huang-ti, Yao, and Shun were such great men whose virtue harmonized with Heaven and Earth; therefore they understood non-activity.

"The Way of Heaven (*T'ien Tao*) is one of non-activity. Therefore in spring it does not act to germinate, in summer to cause growth, in autumn to give maturity, and in winter to store up. But the *yang* ether comes forth of itself (in spring and summer), and things of themselves germinate and grow; the *yin* ether arises of itself (in autumn and winter), and things of themselves reach maturity and are stored up.

"When we draw water from wells or drain ponds in order thus to irrigate fields and gardens, things do, to be sure, germinate and grow. It is when torrents of rain descend, however, that the stalks, leaves, and roots of these things become soaked in real abundance. Measured by the amount of moisture, how can the drawing of water from wells or the draining of ponds compare (with the rain)? Hence actionless activity is what gives the greatest (results). It does not inherently seek for achievement, yet for that very reason achievement is attained. It does not inherently seek for a good name, yet for that very reason a good name is created. Great indeed is the achievement and good name of the abundant rains, but Heaven and Earth do not work for them. It is simply that their (*yin* and *yang*) ethers unite and the rain gathers of itself" (I, 92-99).

Here we find stress on that same naturalistic principle of spontaneity which appears so prominently in Taoism.

ii. *Criticism of Contemporary Beliefs*

Basing himself on this concept, Wang Ch'ung in his *Critical Essays* presents a systematic critique of the "truth and falsehood" found in the "current books and common sayings" of his day. Thus he writes in the forty-first chapter:

"Those who talk about cold and heat say that when the ruler is joyful, there is warmth, and when he is angry, there is cold. How is this? (They say that) joy and anger develop within his bosom and afterward find their way to the outside, where they give form to rewards and punishments. There being these manifestations of his joy and anger, cold and heat consequently become widespread, and cause things to wither or do injury to men" (I, 279).

On this, a conspicuous doctrine of the *Yin-yang* school, Wang then comments as follows (chap. 41): "Now the Way of Heaven is that of spontaneity, and this spontaneity means non-activity. It may fortuitously happen that the two (*yin* and *yang*) principles coincide (with human events) in such a way that, when a human event occurs, these ethers of Heaven are already present. This, therefore, is called the Way (of Heaven). If, however, such an occurrence were to be regarded as a 'response' to the acts of government, this would be to deny its spontaneity" (I, 283).

Again Wang writes (chap. 42):

"With regard to visitations (*tsai*) and prodigies (*yi*), it is said that when ancient rulers departed from the right way in their government, Heaven used these visitations and prodigies to reprimand them. Such visitations and prodigies are not single, but are repeatedly manifested in the form of cold or heat. When, for example, the ruler's application of punishments comes at the improper time, there is then cold, and when his issuing of rewards violates the correct period, there is then warmth. The Spirit of Heaven (*T'ien Shen* 神) reprimands the ruler, just as the ruler shows reproving anger to his subjects below" (I, 118).

On this, another doctrine of the *Yin-yang* school, Wang comments as follows (chap. 42): "The Way of Heaven is that of spontaneity, which consists of non-activity. But if it were to reprimand men, that would constitute action and would not be spontaneous. The school of Huang and Lao, in its discussions on the Way of Heaven, has found the truth" (I, 120).

Again he writes (chap. 43): "Those who talk about visitations and prodigies have themselves already expressed doubt as to whether Heaven employs such visitations and prodigies to reprimand people. So in place of this they say that the coming of visitations and prodigies is, as it were, caused by the administrative activities of the sovereign, which operate upon Heaven in such a way that Heaven activates its ethers in response. The case is like that of beating a drum or striking a bell with a hammer. The drum is like Heaven, the hammer like the administrative activities, and the sound of the drum or bell like Heaven's response. When the ruler of men acts below, the ethers of Heaven come accordingly" (I, 109).

Concerning this belief of the *Yin-yang* school, Wang goes on to comment (chap. 43): "Man holds a place within the universe like that of a flea or louse under a jacket or robe, or of a cricket or ant within a hole or crevice. Can the flea, louse, cricket, or ant, by conducting themselves either properly or improperly, effect changes and movements in the ether that lies under the jacket and robe or in the hole or crevice? The flea, louse, cricket, and ant are incapable of this, and to suppose that man alone is so capable is to misconceive of the principles of things and of the ethers. ... Cold and warmth are dependent on Heaven and Earth and are linked with the *yin* and *yang*. How can human affairs or the administration of the country have any influence on them?" (I, 109-111).

Wang also writes (chap. 49): "The school of changes and reversions (*pien fu chih chia* 變復之家) says that the eating of grain by insects is caused by the officials of the various departments. Out of covetousness they make encroachments, and this results in the insects eating the grain. When these latter have black bodies and red heads, it is said to be the military officials (who are to blame), whereas when they have black heads and red bodies, then it is said to be the civil officials. When punishment is brought to those officials whom the insects resemble, these insects thereupon disappear and are no longer seen" (II, 363).

On this, yet another belief based on the *Yin-yang* school, Wang writes (chap. 49): "Among the three hundred naked 'insects,' man takes precedence. Consequently man is also an 'insect.' [1] Man eats the food of insects and insects likewise eat the food of man. Both being 'insects,' what wonder that they eat each other's food.

"Supposing insects had intelligence, they would scold man saying: 'You eat the produce of Heaven, and we eat it as well. You regard us as a plague, but are unaware that you yourself are a calamity to us.' Inasmuch as all creatures possessing breath relish the taste of certain things, their mouths and bellies do not differ from each other. Man relishes the five grains and detests the insects for eating them. Being himself born in the universe, he detests the coming forth of these insects. Supposing that insects could speak, they would scold man in this way and he would have nothing with which to castigate them in return. ...

---

[1] The word *ch'ung* 蟲 or insect can sometimes, as pointed out in the *Tz'ŭ-hai* dictionary, refer to animals in general, which is the way it is apparently intended by Wang here. As used in the sentences below, however, it is evident that it retains its more usual meaning of insect. — Tr.

"In the universe, all creatures produced by the *yin* and *yang*, such as scaly dragons, intestinal worms, or wriggling insects, are born endowed with breath, open their mouths to eat, and share in common likes for certain foods and dislikes for others. The strong and large devour those that are small and weak, and the intelligent and clever turn against the dull and stupid. If other creatures, small or big, eat one another, we do not regard this as a calamity. So, then, if we are solely to regard the eating of grain by insects as a response to governmental activities, this is to misunderstand true principles and to miscomprehend the nature of creatures and their ethers" (II, 365-367).

Such is the way Wang criticizes the beliefs of the *Yin-yang* school. In similar fashion he argues against other current superstitions. Among his arguments, those about the existence of the soul are of philosophical interest. Thus he writes (chap. 62):

"People of the world say that the dead become ghosts, are conscious, and can hurt people. Yet if we try to prove this by other sorts of creatures, (we find that) the dead do not become ghosts, have no consciousness, and are unable to hurt people. How shall we prove this? Let us do so by means of (other) creatures. Man is a creature, and (other) creatures are likewise creatures. These creatures do not become ghosts when they die. Why, then, should men alone become ghosts at death? If in this world it is possible to distinguish man from (other) creatures on grounds other than his ability to become a ghost, then it is difficult (on these grounds alone) to determine clearly whether or not man does become a ghost. [1] But if, on the contrary, it is impossible to distinguish (between man and other creatures), then too there is no way of knowing whether he can become a ghost.

"Man is brought into existence by means of the vital forces, and when he dies these vital forces are extinguished. It is the blood of the arteries that is able to make these vital forces (in man), and when man dies the blood of his arteries is exhausted. With this exhaustion, the vital forces are extinguished; with this extinction, his physical frame decays; and with this decay, he becomes ashes and earth. How, then, can he become a ghost? . . .

"Since a dead man cannot become a ghost, he also cannot have

---

[1] The text may be corrupt at this point, so that I am not confident that I have correctly expressed the meaning of this sentence — Tr.

any consciousness. How may we prove this? From the fact that man, before his birth, has no consciousness. Before his birth, he forms part of the primal ethers, and upon his death he reverts to these primal ethers. These primal ethers are widespread and indeterminate, and the human ethers form a part of them. Before birth man is devoid of consciousness, and after death he reverts to this original condition of unconsciousness. How, then, can he have consciousness?

"The reason why man is intelligent and sagacious, is that he has within him the ethers which form the five constant (virtues); the reason why the ethers of these five constants exist in man is that the five viscera lie within his body. [1] As long as the five viscera remain uninjured, man is intelligent and wise, but when they become diseased, then he becomes dim and confused, and this dimness and confusion lead to stupidity and dullness.

"At man's death his five viscera putrefy, and thereupon the five constants no longer have any basis for support. With the destruction of that which harbors intelligence, the exercise of this intelligence likewise disappears. The body requires the ethers in order to acquire form, and the ethers require the body in order to give consciousness. Nowhere in the world is there a fire that burns wholly from itself. How, then, could there be a vital essence in the world that is self-sustaining apart from the body? . . .

"Human death is like the extinction of fire. When a fire is extinguished, its light does not shine any more, and when a man dies, his intellect does not comprehend any more. The actuality of both is the same. So if people nevertheless say that the dead have consciousness, they are mistaken. For what is the difference between a sick man about to die and a light about to go out? When a flame is extinguished, its radiation is dispersed and only its candle remains, and when a man dies, his vital essence is gone and the body alone remains. To assert that a man after death is still conscious is like saying that an extinguished flame may again have light.

"During the months of deep winter, when the cold air reigns supreme, water freezes to become ice, but at the approach of spring the air becomes warm and the ice melts to water. Man's life within

---

[1] On the five constant virtues, see chap. 3, p. 104, and on the correlation between them and the five viscera, see chap. 2, p. 41. It is interesting that although Wang attacks the *Yin-yang* school on many points, he accepts from it this correlation. — Tr.

the universe is like ice. The *yin* and *yang* ethers crystallize to form man, but when his years are completed and his span of life is ended, he dies and reverts to those ethers. Since the water of spring cannot become ice again, how can the soul of a dead man become a body again?" (I, 191-196).

Here we find Wang Ch'ung applying his naturalistic view to the problem of life and death.

iii. *View of History*

Wang also holds a distinctive view of history. Most earlier thinkers had appealed to the past for support for their doctrines, with the result that men generally tended to idealize antiquity and to value the old simply because it was old. Wang Ch'ung vigorously attacks this attitude by saying (chap. 56):

"Those who in ancient times gave good government were sages, and those who in later times have given good government are likewise sages. The virtue of the sages then and now does not differ, and therefore their government, anciently and today, is likewise not different. The Heaven of antiquity was the Heaven of later ages. Heaven has not changed, and its ethers have not been altered. The people of early ages were the same as those of later ages. They have all been equally endowed with the primal ethers, and these primal ethers have remained unchanged in their purity and harmony from antiquity until today. Why then should beings endowed with bodies not be identical, one with another? Being imbued with the ethers to an equal degree, their natures are equal, and their natures being equal, their physical frames are alike. Their physical frames being alike, they must be ugly or handsome to an equal degree, and this being so, their length of life must be the same. One Heaven and one Earth jointly produce all beings. When these beings are produced, they all receive the same ether, and the scarcity or abundance of this ether has been the same for all ages. In every age emperors and kings have governed the world according to the same principles. ...

"Anciently there were unrighteous men, and today there are gentlemen of integrity and honor. Goodness and badness are mixed, so what age is devoid of either? Narrators of events like to exalt antiquity and disparage the present; they esteem what they know through hearsay and slight what they themselves see. Debators discourse on what is long ago, and men-of-letters write on what is far away. The curious things near at hand the debators do not mention, and the extraordinary events of our own time the writers do not record" (I, 471-476).

Not only, however, are people wrong in thus valuing antiquity above their own day. In actual fact, Wang goes on to say, the present age is even better than the past. Thus he writes (chap. 57):

"As far as the actual transformations effected by virtue are concerned, the Chou (dynasty) cannot equal the Han, whereas if we speak about fortunate omens and presages, the Han excels the Chou. And if we measure their extent of territory, that of Chou was more limited than that of Han. How then is the Han (dynasty) not equal to that of Chou? It may only be claimed that the Chou had many sages, whose government brought about universal peace. But the literati, in acclaiming the sages, go too far, placing them on such a pedestal that their actual traces are lost. In acclaiming their government they are also too fulsome, treating of universal peace as something that has been cut off and has had no continuation" (II, 200).

In other words, the sage-kings and their government, so talked about by the literati, are only idealizations of an uncertain past. To judge solely on the basis of such idealizations is to deny the title of sage-king to all save those shadowy beings whom we choose to place "on such a pedestal that their actual traces are lost." It is to make of the concept of universal peace "something that has been cut off and has had no continuation."

iv. *Methodology*

Wang Ch'ung writes (chap. 61): "Though the *Odes* number three hundred, one phrase can cover them all, namely, 'With undiverted thoughts.' [1] And though the chapters of my *Critical Essays* may be numbered in the tens, one phrase likewise covers them all, namely, 'Hatred of fictions and falsehoods' " (II, 280).

This dictum is constantly exemplified by Wang in his analysis of "current books and common sayings." Activated by his "hatred of fictions and falsehoods," he maintains that for every doctrine there must be a factual basis. Whenever he makes an assertion, consequently, he tries to support it by specific instances. As he

---

[1] A quotation from the *Analects*, II, 2. — Tr.

himself says (chap. 48): "I cite manifest instances, in order to make the factual proof certain" (II, 362). Or again (chap. 67): "In things there is nothing more clarifying than having an example, and in argument there is nothing more decisive than having evidence" (II, 370).

By "evidence," Wang means the factual basis of one's argument. Granted, however, that such a basis is helpful, we all know the frequent difficulty of determining whether the adduced "facts" in a given case are really facts or not. Mo Tzŭ, for example, had said that "any statement must have three tests," and that in order to establish such a statement, it must be "verified by the senses of hearing and sight of the common people." [1] Yet in applying this principle, he was content to cite numerous instances in which ghosts had reputedly been seen in earlier times. From these he then adduced the existence of ghosts as a proven fact. [2] Thus he apparently failed to realize that men's sensory impressions do not always accord with reality, and that they may therefore not always furnish an adequate basis for a given doctrine. This fact is discussed by Wang Ch'ung in the following passage (chap. 67):

"If in argument one does not exercise the purest and most undivided thought, but indiscriminately uses examples from the outside to establish the correctness or wrongness of things, trusting what one hears and sees from the outside, and not interpreting it by one's internal (intellect), this is to use the ears and eyes for argument, without exercising any judgment of the intellect. Now such use of the ears and eyes for argument results in the formulation of statements on the basis of empty semblances. And when such empty semblances serve as examples, this results in actual things passing for fictions.

"Therefore truth and falsehood do not depend upon the ear and eye, but require the exercise of intellect. The Mohists, in making judgments, did not use their minds to verify things, but indiscriminately believed what they heard and saw. Therefore although their proofs were clear, they failed to reach reality. Judgments which thus fail to reach reality are difficult to impart to others, for although they may gain the sympathies of stupid people, they will not harmonize with the minds of the learned. They lose (the reality of) things and are useless, thus being of no benefit to the world. This

---

[1] Cf. the *Mo-tzŭ*, chap. 35, p. 183 (cited in vol. 1, p. 85). — Tr.
[2] Cf. the *Mo-tzŭ*, chap. 31, "On Ghosts."

would seem to be the reason why the arts of the Mohists have failed to be propagated" (II, 370-371).

Thus sensory impressions that do not accord with actuality are nothing but "empty semblances." This means that, having been received, they must still, in order to be accepted as valid, be interpreted by the "intellect" (*hsin yi* 心 意). Those which the intellect then recognizes as according with actuality may be acknowledged as representing actual fact. The Mohists, however, maintained that a thing need merely be "verified by the senses of hearing and sight of the common people"; they "did not use their minds to verify things, but indiscriminately believed what they heard and saw." The result was that, in arguing about ghosts, "although their proofs were clear, they failed to reach reality." Such is Wang Ch'ung's methodology, and its scientific spirit makes one regret that it has found no later followers.

v. *Theory of Human Nature*

On the long debated problem of human nature (*hsing*), Wang expresses himself as follows (chap. 13):

"The feelings (*ch'ing*) and the nature (*hsing*) are the roots of human activity and the source from which spring ceremonials (*li*) and music. Hence ceremonial observances and music act as checks and restraints upon the excesses of the original nature and feelings. In the nature there exist the qualities of humbleness, modesty, and yielding; hence the ceremonials have been instituted in order to direct these along the proper channels. Among the feelings there are those of liking and disliking, joy and anger, grief and pleasure; hence music has been created in order to give a decorous expression to them all. It is thus the feelings and the nature for which ceremonials have been instituted and music created. The ancient literati and scholars who have written essays have all touched on this subject, but none have been able to reach a true statement. . . .

"From this point of view it may be said that the facts are easy to know, but their principle is difficult to explain. Style and diction may be ever so brilliant and flowery, and conceptions and arguments as sweet as honey, yet they need not necessarily reach the truth. The actual truth is that man's nature may be either good or bad, just as human talent may be either high or low. . . . I am decidedly of the opinion that what Mencius says of the goodness of human nature refers to people above the average, whereas what Hsün Tzŭ says of its badness refers to people below the average, and when Yang Hsiung says that in man's nature goodness and badness are mixed together, he refers to average people. Though violating the norm, (these theories to some extent) accord with truth, and so may constitute some teaching; as to the (real) principles of the nature, however, these they fail to exhaust" (I, 165-172).

Even the natures of evil men, however, may be made good if subjected to moral inculcation. Wang Ch'ung writes (chap. 4):

"If we speak of the natures of men, there are in truth some that are good and some that are bad. The good ones are definitely so of themselves, whereas the bad ones may be caused to become good by undergoing inculcation which leads them to exert themselves. All rulers or fathers, seeing that the natures of their subjects or sons are good, should thereupon support, encourage, and lead them on, not allowing them to come in contact with evil; but if these be bad, they should thereupon give assistance, should shield, and place prohibitions upon them, so as to enable them gradually to shift to goodness. It is through the gradual transition of goodness into evil, and the transformation of evil into goodness, that the activities of the nature assume their final form. . . . According to the Way of Heaven, there exists what is genuine and what is artificial. The genuine definitely accords with Heaven of itself, but if man applies his knowledge and astuteness to the artificial, that too will become in no wise distinguishable from the genuine" (I, 374-378).

Here Wang borrows both from the theories of Mencius and Hsün Tzŭ, and in so doing effects a compromise between them.

vi. *View of Fate*

Besides human nature, there exists an external factor known as Fate or Destiny (*ming* 命), on which Wang Ch'ung writes as follows (chap. 6):

"The nature (*hsing*) and Fate (*ming*) are distinct from one another, for there are persons whose natures are good and who yet meet an unlucky Fate, whereas there are others whose natures are bad and who yet meet a lucky Fate. The doing of good or bad depends upon one's nature, but calamity or good fortune and good or bad luck depend upon Fate. Some people perform good deeds and yet reap calamity; this is a case where the nature is good but Fate is unlucky. Others perform bad deeds and yet gain good fortune; this is a case where the nature is bad but Fate is lucky. The nature is either good or bad of itself; Fate is either lucky or unlucky of itself. Suppose it be a man who enjoys a lucky Fate, even though he do not practice goodness he will not lack good fortune; but if it be a man who suffers an unlucky Fate, even though he exert all his efforts he will not necessarily escape from calamity" (I, 139).

Wang develops this idea to refute the popular belief of his time that "goodness is requited with goodness, and evil with evil." The latter belief is described by him as follows (chap. 20):

"People of the world say that doers of good meet with good fortune, evil-doers are visited with misfortune, and that these responses of good or bad fortune all come from Heaven, so that as a man acts, Heaven responds accordingly. The deeds of such a man, when their goodness is clearly manifest, are rewarded by the ruler; his virtue, when it consists of less obviously manifested kindness, is requited by Heaven and Earth. There is nobody, noble or mean, worthy or stupid, who would disagree with this view" (I, 156).

Again (chap. 21):

"People of the world say that when a person enjoys good fortune and protection, these are the result of his good conduct. They also say that when a person suffers calamity and injury, these are incurred because of his wickedness. It is maintained, of those who possess hidden wickedness and concealed iniquity, that they are punished by Heaven and Earth and suffer retaliation from the spirits. These punishments of Heaven and Earth are applied (impartially), whether small or great; the retaliation of the spirits reaches (everywhere), whether far or near" (I, 164).

Wang's reply to such beliefs is as follows (chap. 5): "In conducting affairs men may be either talented or stupid, but when it comes to calamity or good fortune, there are some who are lucky and some unlucky. The things they do may be right or wrong, but whether they meet with reward or punishment depends on chance. If (several persons) simultaneously suffer an armed attack, those who find a hiding place are not wounded; if (several growing plants) suffer from frost on the same day, those under shelter receive no injury. These are not cases in which the wounded or injured are necessarily wicked, or in which the ones finding hiding or shelter are necessarily good. It is simply that the latter happen to be lucky and the former unlucky. There are many persons who wish to display their loyalty (to a ruler), yet he rewards some and punishes others; there are many who wish to do him benefit, yet he trusts some and mistrusts others. Those whom he rewards and trusts are not necessarily the true ones, nor are those whom he punishes and mistrusts necessarily the false. It is simply that the rewarded and trusted ones are lucky, while those who are punished and mistrusted are unlucky.

"Among the seventy and more disciples of Confucius, Yen Hui suffered premature death, upon which Confucius exclaimed: 'Unluckily his span was short, and so he died!' [1] Since a short span is unlucky, a long span is obviously a matter of luck and a short one of bad luck. . . .

When a man walks on ground where ants are creeping, those ants on which he steps instantly die, whereas those on which he does not step remain alive and unhurt. Or when wild grass catches fire through pressure of a chariot passing over it, ordinary folk are delighted about the unburned part, calling it the 'lucky grass.' Yet not to be stepped on by the foot or reached by the fire is no necessary sign of goodness, for the movements of the fire and the feet are matters of accident" (I, 151-152).

Thus good or bad conduct do not necessarily respectively result in fortune or misfortune, since the latter wholly depend upon whether a person happens to be lucky or unlucky. If he had stopped here, Wang would have remained consistent with his general naturalistic view of the universe, as well as in accord with actual fact. He goes on to say, however, that man's good or bad luck is wholly a matter of predestination. Thus he writes (chap. 3):

"The good fortune or harm encountered by men all comes from Fate. There is a Fate governing death and life, long or short existence, and also a Fate governing riches and honors, poverty and mean position. From princes and dukes down to common people, and from sages and worthies down to the stupid—for all who have heads and eyes and blood in their veins—each and every one possesses his own Fate. He for whom Fate has decreed poverty and mean position, though he be enriched and ennobled, will nevertheless (later) experience calamities and disasters. He for whom Fate has

---

[1] *Analects*, VI, 2. Yen was Confucius' favorite disciple. — Tr.

decreed riches and noble position, though he be impoverished and reduced to mean position, will nevertheless (later) encounter good fortune and bliss. Therefore he whose Fate it is to have noble rank will of himself attain to it from a mean position, whereas he whose Fate it is to have mean position will of himself fall into danger from a wealthy station. This is why the wealthy and noble seem to enjoy the help of the spirits, whereas the poor and mean seem to suffer calamities from demons. ...

"Hence wisdom or stupidity in overseeing matters, and purity or corruption in conducting affairs, are questions of one's own nature and talents, whereas noble or mean position in an official career, and poverty or wealth in business, depend upon Fate and time. This Fate may not be forced nor the time coerced" (I, 144-145).

Not only is individual success or failure decided by Fate, however, but there is even a Fate for the entire country, which determines its prosperity or decay, its good or bad government. Wang writes (chap. 6):

"(The states of) Sung, Wei, Ch'en, and Cheng all suffered a disaster on the same day. [1] Among the people of these four states, there must have been some whose prosperity was still at its height and who hence should not yet have entered into decline. Yet they all equally met disaster, being overcome by the calamity of the country. Hence a country's Fate is stronger than that of the individual, just as the Fate that determines one's length of life is stronger than that determining one's prosperity" (I, 137).

But by logical extension, if a country's fortune or misfortune and good or bad government all depend on its "national Fate," it then follows that such matters have nothing to do with the good or bad qualities of the ruler himself. Thus we read (chap. 53):

"Men all know that (an individual's) affluence, peace, and contentment, are consequences of a generous provision of Fate. What they ignore is that a country's peaceful government and its civilizing influence evolve from destined circumstances (shu 數). This means that the world's good government is not the work of worthies and sages, nor are decay and disorder the result of lack of moral principle. If a country be destined for decay and disorder,

---

[1] On a certain summer day of the year 524 B.C., according to the *Ch'un Ch'iu* and *Tso Chuan* (pp. 670-671), a fire simultaneously broke out in the capitals of these four states. It was believed to have been foreshadowed by a comet that had appeared in the winter of the preceding year. See *op. cit.*, p. 668. — Tr.

worthies and sages cannot make it prosper, nor when it is destined for good government, can evil men throw it into disorder. The world's order and disorder depend on the time and not on the government. A country's peace or danger depend on its destined circumstances and not on its (moral) teachings. Neither a wise nor an unwise ruler, neither an enlightened nor an unenlightened government, can in any way add to or subtract from this fact" (II, 11).

Elsewhere (chap. 6) we are told that there is a connection between human fate and celestial phenomena: "The host of stars lie in Heaven, which has its signs. When a man has a sign pointing to wealth and noble position, he receives such wealth and noble position, but when he has a sign pointing to poverty and mean position, he receives such poverty and mean position" (I, 138). Wang, in fact, even goes so far as to assert (in chap. 11, I, 304 f.) that a man's Fate can be read from the formation of the bones in his body.

Wang's conception of Fate, therefore, is quite unlike that of the earlier Confucian and Taoist schools. Thus we read in the *Mencius*: "That which happens without man's causing it to happen, is from Fate" (Va, 6). And in the *Hsün Tzǔ*: "What one meets with by chance is called Fate" (chap. 22, p. 282). Likewise the *Chuang-tzǔ* says: "Recognize the inevitable and quietly be at ease in it as the appointment of Fate." [1] Or again: "I have been thinking who could have brought me to this extremity, but have not succeeded. For my parents would surely not wish me to be poor! And Heaven covers all things without partiality, while Earth supports them all without partiality. How, then, could they single me out to make poor? I have been seeking to know who it is, but without success. Surely, then, what has brought me to this extremity must be Fate!" (chap. 6, p. 90). In other words, when a man encounters good or bad luck and is at a loss to explain its cause, he calls it Fate. It is something "one meets with by chance" and which "happens without man's causing it to happen."

Wang expresses a similar view in the passage from his fifth chapter which was cited on pp. 163-164. In subsequent quotations, however, he develops the more extreme view that each individual and country has its own pre-determined Fate, and that their good or bad fortune is simply a concrete expression of this Fate, over which human effort has no control. Such a concept well agrees

---

[1] Chap. 4, p. 46; repeated in chap. 5, p. 60.

with popular views on the subject, and certainly contains an element of superstition. On this point, therefore, Wang shows himself unable to escape from the popular beliefs of his day.

Furthermore, despite Wang's numerous attacks on the *Yin-yang* school's beliefs, he, like it, accepts the theory of omens. In his fifty-seventh chapter (II, 192 f.), for example, he cites, in a manner quite reminiscent of the *Yin-yang* school, a number of favorable omens alleged to have been manifested during the Han dynasty. All this he does despite his self-proclaimed "hatred of fictions and falsehoods," and his efforts to found his theories on factual proof. This demonstrates how powerful was the prevailing ideology of his age—so powerful, indeed, that even such an exceptional person as himself could sometimes hardly tear himself from its grasp.

CHAPTER V

NEO-TAOISM DURING THE PERIOD OF DISUNITY

(Part I)

1—The Mysterious Learning and Confucius

As we have seen in the third chapter, the middle of the Han dynasty (1st century B.C.-1st century A.D.) was the period in which the apocryphal and prognostication texts were most prevalent. With the rise of the Old Text school, however, this literature gradually fell into disfavor and the position of Confucius reverted from that of a semi-divine being back once more to that of "teacher." The next development was a revival of Taoism. This is hardly surprising, for Taoism, more than any of the other early schools, had stressed naturalism, and such naturalism was a prominent ingredient in the Old Text school. We have seen in the preceding chapter, for example, the part it plays in Wang Ch'ung's *Critical Essays*. After his death, therefore, Taoism became increasingly important during the Period of Disunity. [1]

In order to differentiate this revived Taoism from original Taoism, it is convenient for us today to use the name Neo-Taoism. Among its own contemporaries, however, it was known as the *Hsüan Hsüeh* 玄學 or "Mysterious Learning." [2] The expression appears, for example, in the *Chin Shu* (History of the Chin Dynasty), in its biography of Lu Yün (262-303). There (chap. 54) we are told of Lu that he was originally not conversant with the Mysterious Learning. One evening, however, having lost his way while travel-

---

[1] This term is here used to designate the period of political division lasting from the disintegration of the Han dynasty (officially in A.D. 220, though practically speaking in 190) until the reuniting of the empire under the Sui (590-617) and T'ang (618-906) dynasties. According to official chronology, the epoch is divided into: (1) the Period of the Three Kingdoms (221-280, among which the kingdom of Wei, 220-265, was most important); (2) the Chin dynasty (265-419); (3) the Northern and Southern Dynasties (420-589). — Tr.

[2] *Hsüan* also means dark. The term originates in the first chapter of the *Lao-tzŭ*: "This sameness (of being and non-being) we call the Mystery. It is the Mystery of Mysteries." — Tr.

ing, he came to a house where he asked to spend the night. There he met a youth with whom he fell into deep conversation on the *Lao-tzŭ*. It was only after arising the next morning that he discovered the house to be none other than that of the noted commentator on the *Lao-tzŭ*, Wang Pi (226-249). Following this episode, he is stated to have made extraordinary progress in the Mysterious Learning. [1]

Again we are told by the *Nan Shih* (History of the Southern Dynasties), in its twenty-second chapter, that under the Sung dynasty (420-478) the national educational system had fallen into decay, but that in 470 Emperor Ming created a Tsung-ming Kuan or Academy of General Learning, in which four divisions were established: those of Confucianism, "the Mystery," literature, and history, each staffed by ten scholars. We are also told, in the same work's chapter on the literati (chap. 71), that Fu Man-jung (421-502) was skilled in the *Lao-tzŭ* and *Book of Changes*, and that, when he retired from court, he used to discuss the principles of the Mystery with his friend Yüan Ts'an (420-477). Of Yen Chih-chih (457-508) we are likewise told that as a youth he was skilled in the *Lao-tzŭ* and *Chuang-tzŭ* and was an expert speaker on the Mystery; and of T'ai-shih Shu-ming (474-546), that as a youth he was skilled in the same two works and especially adept in the "Three Mysteries." The latter term is explained in Yen Chih-t'ui's (551-591 or later) *Yen-shih Chia-hsün* (Yen's Instructions for the Family) as referring to the *Lao-tzŭ*, *Chuang-tzŭ*, and *Book of Changes*. [2] From these references it would appear that after Wang Pi wrote his famed commentaries on the *Lao-tzŭ* and *Book of Changes*, these two works, though originally stemming from entirely different streams of thought, came to be generally regarded as forming a common category. [3]

Noteworthy is the fact that though all these men were adherents of Taoism, some nevertheless continued to regard Confucius as the greatest of all the sages, and maintained that between Confucianism and Taoism there lies no essential distinction. This is illustrated in the following passage from the *Chin Shu*:

---

[1] Wang is discussed in detail in sect. 3 below. Since Lu lived later, the implication of the story is that the young man who entertained him was the ghost of Wang Pi. — Tr.

[2] See Chap. 8 (1.30).

[3] Beginning here, and extending as far as the first five paragraphs of sect. 4 (p. 191 below), the text has been revised by the author from that in his original work. — Tr.

"When Juan Chan (died ca. 312) saw the Minister of Interior Wang Jung (234-305), the latter asked him: 'The Sage valued morals and institutions (*ming chiao* 名教), whereas Lao and Chuang (Lao Tzŭ and Chuang Tzŭ) threw light on the natural (*tzŭ jan*). Are they the same or different in their underlying meaning?' To which the reply was made: 'Can they be without similarity?' " [1] (49.5).

The "Sage" here mentioned is Confucius, and to "value morals and institutions" or "throw light on the natural" summed up, for most people of the time, the difference between Confucianism and Taoism. Therefore, when the questioner asked, "Are they the same or different in their underlying meaning?", he did so because he suspected that this difference was only superficial. And when his friend replied, "Can they be without similarity?" he meant to imply that they could neither be said to be wholly the same nor wholly different.

In what, then, lay the real distinction between the two schools? An answer is given in another passage from the *Contemporary Records* (chap. 4), which says of Wang Pi:

"In his young days he paid a visit to P'ei Hui, who asked him: 'Truly, non-being (*wu* 無) is the basis of all things. How is it then that the Sage (Confucius) was never willing to speak about it, whereas Lao Tzŭ dilated on it endlessly?' To which (Wang) Pi replied: 'The Sage, being identified with non-being, realized that it could not be made the subject of instruction and so felt bound to deal with being (*yu* 有). Lao and Chuang, however, not yet having completely escaped from the sphere of being, constantly spoke of that in which they were themselves deficient' " (1b.11).

Concerning the meaning of "non-being," we shall have something to say later on. At the moment it is only necessary to point out that it is quite impossible for anyone already "identified with non-being" to talk about some other kind of "non-being," external to that of his own; even the first "non-being," in fact, is fundamentally undiscussable. This explains why Confucius could only talk about

---

[1] In Liu Yi-ch'ing's (403-444) *Shih-shuo Hsin-yü* (Contemporary Records of New Discourses), chap. 4 (1b.14), this conversation is attributed to Juan Hsiu (270-311) and Wang Yen, the younger brother of Wang Jung. [The *Shih-shuo Hsin-yü*, which is a valuable source for our knowledge of thought during the third and fourth centuries, will hereafter be referred to as *Contemporary Records*. — Tr.]

"being." As for Lao Tzŭ and Chuang Tzŭ, the very fact that they constantly expatiated on "non-being" reveals that in their approach to it they were deficient. Chuang Tzŭ's axiom: "Those who know do not speak; those who speak do not know," [1] perfectly expresses Wang Pi's idea. In other words, what Wang Pi means to say is that in Lao Tzŭ's thinking an antithesis remains between "being" and "non-being." It is only from "being" that he gains a view of "non-being," with the result that he discusses it constantly as if it were something external to himself. In the thinking of Confucius, on the contrary, this antithesis is completely synthesized. Being already identified with "non-being," he speaks of "being" from the point of view of "non-being," and therefore is in a position really to speak about it.

Though Wang Pi is the best of all the commentators on Lao Tzŭ, it is noteworthy that he does not rank him as the equal of Confucius. Nor, similarly, does Kuo Hsiang (died 312), [2] though admittedly the best of all the commentators on Chuang Tzŭ, grant the latter such equality. This latter fact emerges in Kuo's Introduction to his *Chuang-tzŭ Commentary*. [3]

"Chuang Tzŭ may be said to have had knowledge of fundamentals, with the result that he never concealed the wildness of his statements. These did not meet (the general requirements of mankind), being merely solitary responses (to his own needs). If a statement responds (only to individual needs) but does not meet (men's general requirements), it follows that though it may be right, it is nevertheless useless. Similarly in the case of a statement which goes counter to events and things: it may be lofty but is not practical. There is certainly a gap between such a man and the man who is in a state of inward silence and quietude, from which something emerges without any volition on his part.

"Whereas the former may indeed be said to have knowledge about the mind in a state of inaction, he whose mind is (really) in a state of inaction then responds to any stimulus, and the response varies according to the time. Therefore he is cautious about speaking. The result is that he is identified (*t'i* 體) with (the world pro-

---

[1] *Chuang-tzŭ* (chap. 13, p. 170).

[2] Discussed in detail in chap. 6. — Tr.

[3] *Chuang-tzŭ Chu.* The next five paragraphs follow, with minor variations, the text in Fung Yu-lan, *The Spirit of Chinese Philosophy*, translated by E. R. Hughes (London, 1947), pp. 135-137. — Tr.

cess of) transformation, glides in conformity with all ages, and is undifferentiable from all things. How can such a one (as did Chuang Tzŭ) make dialogues which are conducted only with himself and lead him beyond the bounds (of the ordinary world)! This is why Chuang Tzŭ has not become a classic, though he is the highest of the philosophers. Yet though he failed to identify himself (with the process of world transformation), his words are perfect. They give an understanding of the structure of Heaven and Earth, lay open the order in the natures of all things, make intelligible the changing phases of life and death, and throw light on the way of sageliness within and kingliness without. Above he knows that there is no Being who creates other beings; below he knows that existing things are created of themselves."

Here we have a critique of Chuang Tzŭ which is divisible into two parts. The one is that Kuo Hsiang does not regard Chuang Tzŭ's level of spiritual development as equal to that of Confucius. Though Chuang Tzŭ admittedly possesses some knowledge of "fundamentals" and of "the mind in a state of inaction," he neverthe- less only "knows" these things; he does not succeed in "identifying himself" with them. That is why he "never conceals the wildness of his statements," but is satisfied to "make dialogues which are conducted only with himself," and which deal with matters outside the range of ordinary human needs. Kuo's point is that when the sage becomes "identified with (the world process of) transformation," he not merely has "knowledge about the mind in a state of inaction," but his mind itself is actually in that state. He is then ready to "respond to any stimulus." Such is what is meant by saying that he "is in a state of inward silence and quietude, from which something emerges without any volition on his part." In this state he allows himself to respond freely to the actual, his response varying according to the particular occasion. But he avoids going into elaborate discussion about the matter; in fact, he "is cautious about speaking."

In uttering this criticism, Kuo Hsiang completely agrees with Wang Pi. For just as Wang criticizes Lao and Chuang for "not yet having completely escaped from the sphere of being," so Kuo criticizes Chuang Tzŭ for only "knowing," but not himself entering into, the state of inaction of the mind.

In his second criticism, Kuo stigmatizes Chuang Tzŭ's state- ments as mere "solitary soliloquies," made to meet his own require- ments but not those of men in general. This is why, he says, however right they may be, they are yet of no use; however lofty, they are yet ineffectual. Though he has indeed expounded the "way of sageliness within and kingliness without," his emphasis has been too much on the sageliness and too little on the kingliness.

It is on these two counts that Kuo Hsiang asserts "there is indeed a difference" between Chuang Tzŭ and the real sage, meaning Confucius. That is why Chuang Tzŭ has failed to become a classic and is only the best of the non-classical philosophers. With this verdict in mind, we can understand more clearly the meaning of the reply, "Can they be without similarity?" made to the question as to whether or not a real difference exists between Lao and Chuang on the one hand and Confucius on the other. Their similarity is that they all, Confucius included, emphasized "non-being"; their difference is that Confucius had already identified himself with this "non-being," whereas Lao and Chuang were only able to "know" it. This difference, however, is only one of relative development; it does not mean that between Confucius and the two Taoists there exists a fundamental dissimilarity.

Historically speaking, this theory has one peculiar aspect, namely, that Wang Pi, Kuo Hsiang, and the other Neo-Taoists, though they acknowledged Confucius to be the greatest sage, nonetheless interpreted the meaning of "sage" in a Taoist rather than Confucianist way. They accepted from Confucianism the theory that Confucius is the one great sage, but at the same time used Taoist philosophy to reinterpret the sayings of Confucius. For example, in the *Analects* (XI, 18) Confucius is recorded as commenting about his favorite disciple, Yen Hui: "As for Hui, he was near (perfection), yet frequently was devoid (of wordly goods)." On which the noted scholar Ho Yen (died 249) writes: "One scholar says that 'frequently' here means 'very often,' and that 'devoid' (*k'ung* 空, lit., "empty") means 'in a state of vacuity' (*hsü chung* 虛中)." [1] This idea was expanded by later commentators, for example Ku Huan (420-483):

"Not even to have desire for the state of non-desire: this is the constant quality of the sage. To have desire for this state of non-

---

[1] Quoted in Huang K'an (488-545), *Lun-yü Chi-chieh Yi-su* (Exegesis of Collected Comments on the Analects), 6.10. [By using this Taoist term, Ho Yen means to say that Yen Hui was a constant practitioner of Taoist techniques of meditation. He thus denies the usual interpretation that Yen was "empty" in a literal and more matter-of-fact sense, i.e., devoid (of wordly goods). — Tr.]

desire: this is the distinguishing quality of the worthy.[1] By being equally lacking in both kinds of desire, [2] one becomes wholly 'empty' and thereby may be called a sage. By having one (kind of desire only) while lacking the other, one can very often enter a state of 'vacuity' and thereby be called a worthy. The worthy, from the point of view of 'having' something, does not have any desire for having desire; but from the point of 'not having,' he does have desire for not having desire. His 'vacuity' is not complete, so how can it be described otherwise than as something 'frequent' ? " (*ibid.*, p. 11).

T'ai-shih Shu-ming (474-546) also comments:

"Master Yen was a worthy of a superior order, of the same quality (as Confucius), though on a smaller scale. Therefore, there was for him no (temporary) advance and then falling back, so that it is according to principle that the term 'frequent' should be applied (to what he achieved). By seting aside love (*jen*) and righteousness (*yi*), forgetting the rituals (*li*) and music, abandoning his body and discarding his knowledge, he succeeded in 'sitting in forgetfulness' with the Infinite. [3] This is the principle of forgetting existence. His forgetting of existence was instantaneous and complete, so how can it be described by any other term than 'emptiness'? And yet if we examine it from the point of view of the sage, the sage forgets even the fact of his forgetting—something that even a great worthy (like Yen Hui) was unable to do. The latter was unable to forget his forgetfulness, so that he failed to extinguish completely the recurrent activity of his mind. Thus in one respect he did not fully attain, but in another he was 'empty.' That is the reason for the term 'frequently' (which is applied to what he did)" (*ibid.*).

Here are illustrations of how Confucius' words are interpreted in terms of Chuang Tzŭ's "fast of the mind" and "sitting in forgetfulness." [4]

That Wang Pi and Kuo Hsiang, as followers of the "Mysterious

---

[1] *Hsien* 賢 , the man who, though of remarkable attainments, has not progressed as far in his spiritual development as has the sage (*sheng* 聖). The sage has no desires and is not even aware that he has no desires. The worthy is anxious to be without desire, but through this very fact still retains desire. — Tr.

[2] The desire of the ordinary man for things, prestige, etc., and the desire of the Worthy to be without desire. — Tr.

[3] The story that Yen Hui was able to enter this mystic state goes back to the *Chuang-tzŭ* (chap. 6, p. 89), where the same phraseology is used. See vol. 1, p. 241. — Tr.

[4] See the *Chuang-tzŭ* (chap. 4, p. 43; chap. 6, p. 89).

Learning," should emphasize Taoist doctrines is scarcely surprising. The question arises, however, why, in that case, they should still honor Confucius as the greatest sage. Two possible explanations offer themselves, the one social, the other philosophical.

Socially speaking, ever since the unification of thought effected early in the Han dynasty, when Confucianism triumphed over the other schools, Confucius had traditionally been accepted as the one great sage. In the final chapter of the first volume of this book we have already pointed out that, from the Han dynasty onward, the position of Confucianism in Chinese thinking has been like that of a constitutional ruler. Though that ruler stands always as the "connecting link of a myriad generations," his governmental policy must as certainly ever change with the succession of his privy councillors. [1] In the thinking of such Neo-Taoists as Wang Pi and Kuo Hsiang, therefore, Confucius was like a ruler, whereas Lao Tzŭ and Chuang Tzŭ were like his councillors. This was in accord with social tradition, and resulted in a situation in which Confucius' position throughout this period remained ostensibly higher than that of Lao and Chuang, even though in actual fact the latter's ideology replaced that of the former.

Philosophically speaking, there is no doubt that the Taoism of Wang and Kuo came closer to Confucianism than did the earlier Taoism of Lao Tzŭ and Chuang Tzŭ. This is because Wang and Kuo were not only the expositors of Lao and Chuang; they were at the same time critics of them and modifiers of their ideas. We today are in the habit of using the name Neo-Confucianism to describe the movement known during the Sung and Ming dynasties as the *Tao Hsüeh* or "Learning of the Truth." It seems equally reasonable, therefore, to apply the name Neo-Taoism to the "Mysterious Learning" developed by Wang Pi, Kuo Hsiang, and their group. This point will become more evident as we read further.

2—NAME-PRINCIPLES [2]

A common subject of discussion among the thinkers of the Wei and Chin periods was what they called *ming li* 名理 or "name-principles." The *Contemporary Records* (chap. 4), for example, states

---

[1] See vol. 1, pp. 406-407.

[2] This section, with minor variations, is the same as what appears in Fung Yu-lan's *Spirit of Chinese Philosophy*, translated by E. R. Hughes, pp. 131-134. — Tr.

that a certain Chief Secretary Wang composed a discourse in several hundred words which he himself described as a "remarkable presentation of name-principles" (1b.21). Liu Hsün (462-521), in his commentary, quotes from the biography of Hsieh Hsüan (343-388), in which it is said: "Hsüan was able in philosophical discourse and skilled in name-principles." "Skilled in name-principles" means, to quote a phrase from Kuo Hsiang, "ability in distinguishing names (i.e., terms) and analyzing principles." [1] In the ninth chapter of the first volume of the present work we have examined the theories of the School of Names or Dialecticians, such as Kung-sun Lung's "a white horse is not a horse," and "the separateness of hardness and whiteness." These are examples of distinguishing names and analyzing their principles, i.e., of making a logical analysis of principles through a differentiation of terms, without regard for actual facts. This sort of activity had previously been criticized as "specializing in the definition of names while losing sight of human feelings." [2]

The *Contemporary Records* tells us: "The Minister Yüeh [3] was asked by a visitor about (the statement): 'A *chih* 旨 (concept) does not reach.' (Yüeh) Kuang did not analyze the sentence but immediately touched the table with the handle of a deer's-tail fly-whisk, saying: 'Does it reach or not?' The visitor answered: 'It does.' Yüeh then raised the fly-whisk and asked: 'If there was a reaching, how can it be removed?' " (*ibid.*, p. 13). The statement: "A *chih* does not reach," is a paradox emanating from Kung-sun Lung's group among the Dialecticians, preserved for us in the *Chuang-tzŭ* (chap. 33, p. 452). [4] When the fly-whisk is touched to the top of the table, it is ordinarily considered to have "reached" (*chih* 至) that table. But if the reaching is a true reaching, that is, if the act has truly taken place, then that reaching cannot be "removed" (*ch'ü* 去), in other words, the act cannot be wiped out. [5] If it could, the reaching

---

[1] See his commentary on the *Chuang-tzŭ*, chap. 33 (*Chuang-tzŭ Chu*, 10.56).

[2] A criticism made by Ssu-ma T'an (died 110 B.C.). See vol. 1, p. 194. — Tr.

[3] Yüeh Kuang (died 304). — Tr.

[4] Save that the word *chih*, "concept," is there written 指, "finger," or "that which is pointed to." Regardless of which graph is used, the word *chih* in Kung-sun Lung's philosophy seems to be roughly equivalent in meaning to the Western philosophical term "universal." See vol. 1, pp. 205-206. — Tr.

[5] As pointed out by E. R. Hughes (translation of *Spirit of Chinese Philosophy*, p. 132, note 1), there can be no return to the *status quo ante*. (The occurrence of the act, once it has taken place, is irrevocable.) — Tr.

would not have been a true reaching. Here by means of the term "reached" the principle underlying that term is analyzed, and by means of that principle criticism is made of a concrete and particular instance of reaching. This is an illustration of what is meant by "distinguishing names and analyzing principles."

Liu Hsün, commenting on this passage, says: "A boat concealed to view moves imperceptibly, and a man passed shoulder-to-shoulder is irrevocably passed. A moment of time can never be held up; in a flash someting has happened and something has ceased to happen. That is why the shadow of a flying bird is never seen to move and the wheel of a chariot does not touch the ground. Hence the removal (of the fly-whisk) was not a removal; how then could there have been a 'reaching'? Likewise, since the reaching did not reach, how could there have been a removal? Moreover, because there (seems to) be a similarity between a prior reaching and a later reaching, the term 'reaching' comes to be established. Because there (seems to) be a similarity between a prior removing and a later removing (which, however, is only a seeming similarity), the term 'removing' comes to be abolished. [1] Now in all the world there is thus no such thing as removing. So, then, is not this idea of removing false? And as it is false, how can the idea of reaching be true?"

We do not know if this comment represents Liu Hsün's own ideas or those of someone else. The statements about the shadow of the flying bird never being seen to move and the wheel of the chariot never touching the ground are two of the paradoxes of the Dialecticians as recorded in the *Chuang-tzŭ* (chap. 33, p. 452).

The main idea in Liu's comment is this: Things and events are ever in a process of change. Every moment is marked by a coming-into-being and a ceasing-to-be. Therefore the shadow of a flying bird at one particular moment of time is not the shadow of that bird at the moment before. The shadow of that preceding moment

---

[1] The premises in these two sentences are exactly the same. How then do they lead to two opposite conclusions? The only explanation is that the argument is presented elliptically and that the full statement would be something as follows: "Moreover, because there (seems to) be a similarity between a prior reaching and a later reaching, the term 'reaching' comes to be established. (Actually, however, because this similarity is only a seeming one, the term 'reaching' comes to be abolished.) Because there (seems to) be a similarity between a prior removing and a later removing, (the term 'removing' comes to be established.) (Actually, however, because this similarity is only a seeming one), the term 'removing' comes to be abolished." — Tr.

perished with the passing of that moment, and the shadow of the succeeding moment is one newly born with that moment. Therefore if we link the two moments together, we see movement, but if we take them individually, there is no movement. The same principle underlies the paradox that the wheel of a chariot never touches the ground.

Similarly, what we call removal is really nothing more than a large number of separate removals, each taking place in its own moment of time; it consists of a series of "prior removals and later removals," all linked together. In the same way, what we call reaching consists of many momentary reachings, linked together into one sequence. Because the earlier and later stages of the reaching *seem* to be alike, and there seems to be a single integrated act of reaching, therefore the term "reaching" is allowed to stand (though it is really incorrect). In the same way, the earlier and later stages of the removing are similar, but only seemingly similar, and hence what we call a single integrated removal is likewise only seemingly so. Consequently the term "removal" must in actual fact be abolished. Thus, then, by concentrating on the coming-to-be and ceasing-to-be of any single moment, it becomes evident that there is actually no such thing as "removal" and, by the same token, no such thing as "reaching."

Here, then, is an example of "distinguishing names and analyzing principles." Two of the other paradoxes of the Dialecticians, as recorded in the *Chuang-tzŭ* (chap. 33, pp. 451, 453), read: "If a rod one foot in length is cut short every day by one half of its length, it will still have something left even after ten thousand generations," and: "Connected rings can be separated." On them and the remaining paradoxes Kuo Hsiang comments: "These bear no relation to the functioning of the state; indeed, they may truly be called useless talk. But since young aristocrats must have some amusement when they are tired with the canonical writings, if they can distinguish names and analyze principles as an expression of their spirit and intellectual discipline, and if this serves to prevent dissipation in future generations, is it not better than gaming?" [1] Kuo Hsiang himself went further than the Dialecticians, for he reached the point where, in the words of Chuang Tzŭ, "having caught the fish, he could forget the fish-trap." [2] What this meant was that though he

---

[1] *Chuang-tzŭ Chu*, 10.56. — Tr.
[2] A phrase from the *Chuang-tzŭ* (chap. 26, p. 362). — Tr.

outwardly seemed to be opposed to distinguishing names and analyzing principles, he was actually not thus opposed. His real objection was to doing this and nothing more. He himself, in fact, was exceptionally skilled at distinguishing names and analyzing principles, and his *Chuang-tzŭ Commentary* is an outstanding model of that kind of work. In the following chapter we shall devote ourselves especially to that *Commentary*.

3—WANG PI [1]

Wang Pi 王弼 (226-249), like Kuo Hsiang, was "skilled in name-principles." This is why his and Kuo's interpretations of the *Lao-tzŭ* and *Chuang-tzŭ* differ so greatly from those of the Han dynasty, as found, for example, in the *Huai-nan-tzŭ*. Metaphysically speaking, the *Huai-nan-tzŭ*'s interpretation is cosmological, whereas that of Wang and Kuo is ontological. It is the character of cosmology that it makes positive assertions regarding actuality; of ontology, that it asserts very little in this way. Neo-Taoism of the Wei and Chin periods, as represented by men like Wang and Kuo, used the method of "distinguishing names and analyzing principles" to expound ontology; therefore it made very little assertion about actuality. From the point of view of common sense, what these men talked about must to ordinary people have sounded very much like "vacuous nothingness" or "mysterious vacuity."

Wang Pi, styled Fu-ssŭ 輔嗣, was undoubtedly one of the most precocious geniuses in the history of Chinese thought. His life was so short, however, that there is little of significance to be recorded. Tucked into another biography, that of Chung Hui (225-264), which is found in the *San Kuo Chih* (History of the Three Kingdoms), we merely read the following:

"Already as a youth, Hui, together with Wang Pi of Shan-yang, [2] gained a name for himself. Pi loved to talk about Confu-

---

[1] For another excellent study of Wang Pi, see T'ang Yung-t'ung, "Wang Pi's New Interpretation of the *I Ching* and *Lun-yü*," transl. by Walter Liebenthal, *Harvard Journal of Asiatic Studies*, vol. 10 (1947), 124-161. See also Arthur F. Wright, Review of A. A. Petrov, *Wang Pi (226-249): His Place in the History of Chinese Philosophy* (in Russian; Moscow, 1936), in *Harvard Journal of Asiatic Studies*, vol. 10 (1947), 75-88. — Tr.

[2] The present Huai-an 准安 hsien in Kiangsu. — Tr.

cianism and Taoism, his turn of phrase making him a superlative debater. He wrote commentaries on the *Changes* and *Lao-tzŭ*, and became a departmental secretary. When he was only a little over twenty he died" (28.37).

i. *"Non-Being"*

Wang Pi writes in his *Chou Yi Lüeh-li* (Outline of the System Used in the Chou Changes):

"The many cannot be governed by the many. It is the supremely solitary one (i.e., the sovereign) who governs the many. Activity cannot be controlled by activity. It is he who is stable and single who controls the world's activities. Therefore in order that the many may all be equally sustained, the ruler must to the highest degree maintain his oneness. In order that activities may all equally function, the originator of them must not be dual. That things are what they are is not willful. They must follow the principle proper to them. For integrating them there is a basis. For uniting them there is a head. Then, though complex, they are not disordered; though multiple, they cause no confusion. ... Therefore, if guided according to an integrated principle, we know that things, though multiple, may be kept under a single rule. If examined according to what is basic to them, we know that concepts, though broad, may be recorded under a single name." [1]

In this passage Wang Pi's aim is to explain the general concept underlying the statements made by the First Appendix on the separate hexagrams. He also writes: "What is the significance of the First Appendix? It provides an integrated discussion of the structure of any given hexagram, explaining what it is in each of them that holds the ruling position" (*ibid.*, p. 2). By this he means that among the six lines comprising any given hexagram, there is always one that acts as ruler over the others. That is why he begins his treatise with the general thesis that all multiplicity must be ruled by oneness, and all activity controlled by quiescence. This is the first of his metaphysical principles.

On the twenty-fourth hexagram, entitled *fu* 復 or "return,"

---

[1] Sect. on "Explaining the First Appendix." (See Wang's *Chou Yi* or *Chou Changes*, 10.2-3.) Appendix I of the *Book of Changes* explains the general meaning of each of the sixty-four hexagrams.

we read in Appendix I of the *Changes*: "In *fu* do we not see the mind of Heaven and Earth?" (p. 233). On this Wang comments:

"*Fu* signifies a reversion to the original state—a state constituting the mind of Heaven and Earth. The cessation of activity always means quiescence, but this quiescence is not something opposed to activity. The cessation of speech means silence, but this silence is not something opposed to speech. Thus though Heaven and Earth, in their greatness, are richly endowed with the myriad things; though their thunder moves and their winds circulate; though through their evolving operations the myriad transformations come to be—yet it is the silent and supreme non-being (*wu* 無) that is their origin. Therefore it is with the cessation of activity within Earth that the mind of Heaven and Earth becomes visible. For if it were being (*yu* 有) that constituted this mind, then the other various kinds (of being) would have no way of maintaining their common existence" (*Chou Yi*, 3.4).

When Wang speaks of the "myriad things" of Heaven and Earth and the "myriad transformations" resulting from their operations, what he means is *all* being and *all* transformation, that is, all phenomenal activity. But the *cause* of all transformation or activity must itself be unchanging and quiescent. Such quiescence, however, is not a something standing on the same level with activity and opposed to it; it is simply the root from which activity springs. That is why Wang says: "The cessation of activity always means quiescence, but this quiescence is not something opposed to activity. The cessation of speech means silence, but this silence is not something opposed to speech." The same is also true as regards being: the ruler or originator of all being is "the silent and supreme non-being." It cannot itself be being, for if it were, it would simply be one particular kind of being among all the many other kinds, and as such it could not be the origin of "all" being. That is why Wang says: "If it were being that constituted this mind, then the other various kinds (of being) would have no way of maintaining their common existence." The logical conclusion, expressed by Wang in his comment on the *Lao-tzŭ* (chap. 40), is that "non-being is the origin from which being originated."

Things of the world are extremely numerous, but the origin of this multiplicity is oneness. Appendix III of the *Book of Changes* has the passage: "The number of the Great Expansion is 50, but use is made only of 49" (p. 365). On this Wang Pi is quoted by Han Po (died ca. 385) as saying: [1]

"In the expansion of the numbers of Heaven and Earth, 50 is (the round number which is) taken as a basis. But use is made only of 49, so that 1 is not used. It is not used, but through it the use (of the other numbers) takes place; it is not a number (like other numbers), but through it the numbers are formed. Thus this (oneness) constitutes the super-ultimate of the process of change; [2] 49 constitutes the ultimate of numbers. [3] Non-being (*wu*) cannot be made manifest through non-being; this must be done by means of being (*yu*). Therefore through the ultimate of existing things, the origin from which these come (i.e., oneness or non-being) is always made manifest" (*Chou Yi*, 7.8).

The passage from Appendix III of the *Changes* on which this commentary is written was originally intended to explain the way in which, during the early Chou dynasty, divination was carried out by manipulating the odd and even stalks of the milfoil plant. In the process, one stalk out of the total of 50 was first put aside, leaving only 49 that were actually used. [4] As Wang Pi interprets the passage, however, the number 49 represents multiplicity, and thus symbolizes "the ultimate of existing things," whereas oneness is "the origin from which these come." The number 50 is the round total of the odd numbers 1, 3, 5, 7, and 9 = 25, plus the even numbers 2, 4, 6, 8, and 10 = 30 (more exactly totaling 55). Out of this round total, however, one is not used, leaving 49 as "the ultimate of numbers." Commenting on the *Lao-tzŭ* (chap. 39), Wang writes: "One is the beginning of numbers and the ultimate of things." Because one is the basis from which all other numbers are built up, it is said to be

---

[1] Wang's commentary on the *Changes* does not cover Appendices III and V-VII, on which Han Po therefore added commentaries of his own, wherein, however, he sometimes quoted from Wang. — Tr.

[2] I.e., it is the "Supreme Ultimate" (*T'ai Chi*) which is mentioned in the *Book of Changes* (Appen. III, p. 373), and which was to became the basis of Neo-Confucian cosmological speculations. See below, chap. 11. — Tr.

[3] "Numbers" = being; oneness = non-being. By using the terms "ultimate" and "super-ultimate," Wang means to say that numbers are finite, oneness is infinite. — Tr.

[4] Because, as explained by Legge in the note on his translation (p. 368), "50 divining slips or stalks, when divided, give either two odd numbers or two even; and therefore one was put on one side. The remaining 49, however divided, were sure to give two parcels of stalks, one containing an even number of stalks and the other an odd." — Tr.

"not a number (like other numbers), but through it the numbers are formed." And because it is "the origin from which these (i.e., all existing things) come," it is therefore also described as "the ultimate of things."

Wu or "non-being" is, in Wang's philosophy, equivalent to the "super-ultimate" or "Supreme Ultimate" (*T'ai Chi*) of the *Book of Changes*, or to the *Tao* of the *Lao-tzŭ*. Its functioning, however, can only be made manifest in the form of being (*yu*). That is why Wang says: "Non-being cannot be made manifest through non-being; this must be done by means of being." On the passage in Appendix III of the *Changes*: "The alternation of the *yin* and *yang* is called *Tao*" (p. 355), Han Po comments:

"What is meant by *Tao?* It is a term for non-being, which permeates all and from which all originates. The name *Tao* is especially used because it (non-being) is itself silent and without substance, and cannot make any tangible appearance. It is when the ultimate of the functioning of being is reached that the achievement of non-being is manifested" (7.3).

What Han Po says here agrees closely with Wang's ideas. It is the "functioning of being" that constitutes "the achievement of non-being." Non-being itself is invisible; only its "achievement" may be seen, and this achievement consists of "the functioning of being."

On the passage in the *Lao-tzŭ* (chap. 42): "*Tao* produced oneness," Wang Pi comments: "All things and shapes may be reduced to oneness, but from what derives this oneness? It derives from non-being."

Here oneness is merely the product of *Tao*, and therefore not the *Tao* itself. This therefore contradicts Wang's comment on the *Book of Changes*, in which the "one," being the "origin from which come" all "existing things," is therefore itself equivalent to *Tao*. In Lao Tzŭ's system it is obvious that since "*Tao* produced oneness," it is itself superior to the one. In Wang's system, however, the "one" stands in opposition to "multiplicity," for whereas "multiplicity" consists of all "existing things," the "one" is the "origin from which come" all these existing things. This means that oneness is itself the *Tao*. The explanation for this inconsistency would seem to be that in commenting on the forty-second chapter of the *Lao-tzŭ*, Wang is trying to explain Lao Tzŭ's original meaning, whereas in his *Book of Changes* commentary he is developing his own ideas.

ii. *Concepts and Principles*

In his *Chou Yi Lüeh-li* Wang writes: "Symbols [1] serve to express ideas. Words serve to explain symbols. For the complete expression of ideas there is nothing like symbols, and for the complete explanation of symbols there is nothing like words. The words are intended for the symbols. Hence by examining the words one may perceive the symbols. The symbols are intended for the ideas. Hence by examining the symbols one may perceive the ideas. The ideas are completely expressed by the symbols, and the symbols are explained by words. Therefore the purpose of words is to explain the symbols, but once the symbols have been grasped, the words may be forgotten. The purpose of symbols is to preserve the ideas, but once the ideas have been grasped, the symbols may be forgotten. ...

"Therefore he who clings to words does not get the symbols, and he who clings to symbols does not get the ideas. The symbols are intended for the ideas, but, if clung to, are no longer the symbols (of those ideas). The words are intended for the symbols, but if clung to, are no longer the words (of those symbols). Thus by forgetting the symbols one gets the ideas; by forgetting the words one gets the symbols. The acquisition of the ideas depends upon forgetting the symbols, and the acquisition of the symbols depends upon forgetting the words. Therefore the symbols are (initially) established in order completely to express the ideas, but the symbols themselves may then be forgotten. The lines (of the hexagrams) are (initially) multiplied in order completely to express the qualities (of things), but the lines themselves may then be forgotten. Therefore in keeping with the category, the symbol thereof may be made; in agreement with the concept, the graph thereof may be made. If the concept consists of firmness, what need for a horse (to explain its meaning)? If the category is one of compliance, what need for a cow (to explain it)? If a line expresses compliance, what need for *k'un* to be made into a cow? If the concept corresponds to firmness, what need for *ch'ien* to be made into a horse?" [2]

---

[1] *Hsiang* 象 , here meaning not only symbols in general, but more especially the hexagrams and their individual lines, each of which is supposed to symbolize a certain thing or situation. — Tr.

[2] Sect. on "Explaining the Second Appendix." See *Chou Yi*, 10.9-10. *Ch'ien*, the first hexagram, symbolizes masculinity, and therefore has firmness as its characteristic. *K'un*, the second hexagram, symbolizes femininity, and therefore

Several problems are raised by this passage. The first is connected with the theory—current among some people of Wang's age—that "words can completely express ideas." This theory runs counter to original Taoism, which maintained on the contrary that ideas can never be completely expressed in words. The saying in the *Chuang-tzŭ*: "Those who know do not speak; those who speak do not know," is a case in point. [1] The strength acquired during Wei and Chin times by the doctrine that words can on the contrary completely express ideas is attested by numerous references. We are told in the *Contemporary Records* (chap. 4), for example, about Wang Tao (267-330):

"After crossing to the south of the (Yangtze) river, [2] he spoke about nothing but three principles: that in music there is neither sorrow nor pleasure, about how to nourish life, and that words can completely express ideas. Nevertheless (these principles) are connected with one another, and there is nothing that they do not permeate" (1b.15).

Among the writings of Hsi K'ang (223-262), there was an essay on the subject that in music there is neither sorrow nor pleasure, and another one on the nourishment of life. We also know that Ou-yang Chien (died 300) wrote a treatise on the thesis that words can completely express ideas. A summary of this is given by Liu Hsün in his comment on the above passage from the *Contemporary Records*:

"Principles are apprehended by the mind, but without words they cannot be communicated. Things hold their position in relation to other (things), but without names they cannot be distinguished. Names shift in accordance with things, and words change in accordance with principles. (In neither case) can they be dual. [3] If this duality be avoided, there will be no case in which words do not completely express (the meaning)" (*ibid.*).

Wang Pi, however, as we have seen, maintains that "once the symbols have been grasped, the words may be forgotten. ... Once the ideas have been grasped, the symbols may be forgotten." In this

---

has compliance as its characteristic. Wang is here attacking the concretely minded Han commentators, who had the habit of comparing *ch'ien* to a horse (masculine) and *k'un* to a cow (feminine). — Tr.

[1] See above, p. 171. — Tr.

[2] This was in 317, when the Chin dynasty was forced by political troubles to shift its capital south to the present Nanking. — Tr.

[3] I.e., be divorced from the things and principles to which they pertain. — Tr.

he agrees with early Taoism. Yet when he also says: "For the complete expression of ideas there is nothing like symbols, and for the complete explanation of symbols there is nothing like words," he is obviously advocating the contrary thesis that "words can completely express ideas," and thus diverges from early Taoism. Not everybody of the Chin dynasty agreed with this doctrine. Yin Jung (flourished ca. 300), for example, is said to have composed an essay entitled "Symbols Cannot Completely Express Ideas." [1]

The second problem is that of the relationship between what Wang calls "ideas" (*yi* 意) and "concepts" (*yi* 義). He begins his statement, it will be remembered, by saying: "Symbols serve to express ideas." But in his commentary on the *Book of Changes* (Appen. IV, top line of hexagram 1) he says: "As to the engendering of the symbols, they are engendered from concepts" (1.3). It would thus appear that what he calls "ideas" and what he calls "concepts" are essentially the same.

Again, he says in his *Chou Yi Lüeh-li*: "That things are what they are is not willful. They must follow the principle (*li* 理) proper to them." [2] He also says in his commentary on Appendix IV (first hexagram): "By understanding the activities of things, we may know all the principles which make them what they are" (*op. cit.*, p. 4). Or again (commenting on second line of hexagram 16): "Therefore he has no improper pleasure, but distinguishes the necessary principles" (2.7). And yet again (commenting on Appen. IV, first line of hexagram 40): "A concept (*yi*) is the same as principle (*li*)" (4.11). In this last definition, Wang clearly equates "concept" with "principle." Both terms, therefore, would seem to be his designations for the primary principles which underly the phenomenal world, whereas by "ideas" he would seem to mean these same objective principles as they are mentally imprinted in men's minds.

The third problem in Wang's statement involves the word "category" (*lei* 類). "In keeping with the category (*lei*)," he says near the end, "the symbol thereof may be made; in agreement with the concept, the graph thereof may be made. If the concept consists of firmness, what need for a horse (to explain its meaning)? If the

---

[1] Referred to in the commentary on the *Contemporary Records* (*ibid.*, p. 31), where, however, it is not clearly explained.

[2] See above, p. 180. — Tr.

category is one of compliance, what need for a cow (to explain it)?"
This seems to imply that there are numerous different categories of
things and events in the universe, and that each of the hexagrams
in the *Book of Changes* represents one or several of these categories.
The first hexagram, *ch'ien*, for example, represents all those things
whose nature partakes of "firmness," while the second hexagram,
k'un, represents all those whose nature partakes of "compliance."
"Firmness" and "compliance" are the "concepts" or "principles"
of these respective categories of things, while the horse and cow
mentioned in the text are their respective "symbols." The verbal
explanations made of these "symbols" constitute "words." All
things whose nature partakes of "firmness," such as Heaven, the
ruler, the father, the husband, are represented by the hexagram
ch'ien; all those whose nature partakes of "compliance," such as
Earth, the minister, the son, the wife, are represented by *k'un*. The
horse and cow are no more than the "symbols" for *ch'ien* and *k'un*.
Hence having once comprehended the "concepts" which are symbolized by these "symbols," we may put the symbols aside and hold
these concepts as "ideas" within our mind. This is what Wang
apparently means when he says that "once the ideas have been
grasped, the symbols may be forgotten."

Wang's interpretation of the above three problems, if led to its
logical conclusions, would resemble in many ways the theories of
the Rationalistic school in Sung and Ming Neo-Confucianism. [1]
Wang himself, however, failed to draw these logical conclusions.
He likewise failed to explain the relationship between what he calls
"concept" or "principle" and *Tao*.

iii. *The Emotions of the Sage*

The several problems discussed above were absent from early
Taoism, and were raised for the first time only by Wang Pi. Another
point of departure from early Taoism was his doctrine regarding
the emotions (*ch'ing* 情) of the sage. P'ei Sung-chih (372-451),

---

[1] The major representative of whom, Chu Hsi (1130-1200), is treated at
length in chap. 13. Wang's *li*, here translated as "principle," is the same *li* which
holds such an important place in the philosophy of that school, in which context
its English equivalent is capitalized in the present work as "Principle." — Tr.

in his commentary on the *San Kuo Chih* (History of the Three King-doms), writes as follows:

"Ho Yen [1] maintained that the sage lacks either joy or anger, sorrow or pleasure. His discourse was extremely subtle, and Chung Hui [2] followed him. (Wang) Pi, however, differed on this. He main-tained that where the sage is vitally superior to other men is in his spirit-like intelligence, but where he is like other men is in having the five emotions. [3] Being superior in his spirit-like intelligence, he is able to identify himself with the harmonious whole, so that he is imbued with non-being (*wu*); but being like others in his five emotions, he cannot but react to things with emotion. The emotions of the sage are such that though he reacts to things, he is not en-snared by them. It is a great error, consequently, to say that because he is not ensnared by things, he therefore has no (emotional) reactions to them.

"When (Wang) Pi composed his commentary on the *Changes*, a certain man from Ying-ch'uan, named Hsün Jung, raised difficulties against Pi's explanation of the 'Great Expansion.' [4] Pi wrote a letter of reply, expressing his own ideas, in which he made fun of him, saying: 'Though one's understanding may be sufficient to investigate the furthest reaches of the dark and abstruse, one cannot get away from what is natural to one's nature. Master Yen was a man of such capacity that Confucius felt joy in his presence. Thus whenever he met him he could not but feel pleasure, and when he lost him he could not but feel grief. [5] I therefore often used to belittle this man (Confucius), maintaining that he was incapable of making his emotions follow reason. Now, however, I know that what is natural cannot be changed. Your capacities have already become crystallized within your breast. Why then are you thinking so much about me when we have been separated only for about a month? [6] Through this I know

---

[1] Died 249, the same year as Wang Pi. Noted both for his commentaries on Taoist writers and on the *Analects* (see above, p. 173). — Tr.

[2] 225-264. It is in the commentary on his biography that the present passage occurs. — Tr.

[3] Joy, anger, sorrow, pleasure, and hatred. — Tr.

[4] A reference to the passage in the *Book of Changes* stating that "the number of the Great Expansion is 50." Wang's comment on it has been quoted on p. 182. — Tr.

[5] When Yen Hui, the favorite disciple of Confucius, died, the latter ex-claimed: "Alas! Heaven has bereft me. Heaven has bereft me." Cf. *Analects*, XI, 8. — Tr.

[6] Wang means to say that Hsün himself has emotions. — Tr.

that in Confucius' attitude toward Master Yen there 'could not have been any great error' " [1] (28.37).

Chuang Tzŭ's philosophy teaches us to transform our emotions by means of reason, as when he says: "Those who are quiet at the proper occasion and follow the course of nature cannot be affected by sorrow or joy." [2] Ho Yen's thesis that "the sage lacks either joy or anger, sorrow or pleasure," represents this doctrine of Chuang Tzŭ—a doctrine also initially accepted by Wang Pi, as shown by the way in which he criticized Confucius for his inability to "make his emotions follow reason." This is based on the known fact that Confucius, when Yen Hui died, "bewailed him with exceeding grief." [3] From the standpoint of those who "follow the course of nature," and who look at such matters from the point of view of "reason," death is simply the natural conclusion of life, and therefore there is no reason for experiencing grief. Such is the theory of transforming the emotions by means of reason.

On the other hand, as Wang Pi later realized, it may also be argued that human emotion is something "natural to one's nature." This being so, one "cannot but react to things with emotion." From this point of view, therefore, it was natural and inevitable that Confucius should lament the death of Yen Hui. What is important about such a sage, however, is that "though he reacts to things" emotionally, he does not allow himself to be "ensnared" by such things. This is in line with the statement in the *Chuang-tzŭ* (chap. 7) that "the Perfect Man employs his mind as a mirror. It grasps nothing; it refuses nothing. It receives, but does not keep. Thus he can triumph over things, without injury to himself" (pp. 97-98). This method of dealing with the emotions was largely disregarded in Chuang Tzŭ's philosophy itself, whereas by Wang Pi it was developed into a general principle. As we shall see later, it also became the method used by the Sung Neo-Confucianists for dealing with this problem.

In discussing Wang Pi, we have stressed the points in which he differed from early Taoism. As to the manner in which he used his commentaries on the *Lao-tzŭ* and *Book of Changes* to elaborate theories already present in original Taoism, there is no need to discuss this here.

---

[1] An allusion to the *Analects*, VII, 16. — Tr.
[2] *Chuang-tzŭ* (chap. 6, p. 81). — Tr.
[3] *Analects*, XI, 9. — Tr.

4—Materialism and Mechanism in the Lieh-tzŭ

In the eyes of the Wei and Chin Neo-Taoists, the difference between Confucianism and Taoism is that the latter, unlike the former, advocates "transcending morals and institutions and following nature." [1] But what is meant by "following nature"? We read in the *Lao-tzŭ* (chap. 12): "The five colors blind the eye. The five sounds deafen the ear. The five tastes spoil the palate. Excess of hunting and chasing makes men's minds go mad. Products that are hard to get impede men's movements." All these things pertain to the conscious strivings of mankind, whereas by rights men should "have Unadornment to look upon and Unwrought Simplicity to hold. Let them have selflessness and fewness of desires" (chap. 19). Only then, according to this theory, can they really be said to "follow nature."

In rebuttal, however, it might be argued that the desires for the five colors, five sounds, etc., are really inherent and "natural" to all men, and since this is so, men can truly "follow nature" only when these desires have been fully satisfied. Such, at least, is the way many Wei and Chin thinkers interpreted the dictum to "follow nature." Their conduct, as a result, tended toward what people of their own day variously termed "abandonment" (*fang* 放), "understanding" (*t'ung* 通), or "comprehension" (*ta* 達). Thus the *Contemporary Records* (chap. 1) tells us: "Such men as Wang P'ing-tzŭ and Hu-mu Yen-kuo all achieved 'comprehension' by means of unrestrained abandonment" (1a.7). On which Liu Hsün comments:

At the end of the Wei, Juan Chi used to indulge himself in wine and wild abandonment. He would uncover his head, let loose his hair, take off his outer clothes, and lie sprawled on the ground. Later on the youth of the nobility, such as Juan Chan (died ca. 312), Wang Teng (i.e., Wang P'ing-tzŭ, 269-312), Hsien Kun (280-322), and Hu-mu Fu-chih (Hu-mu Yen-kuo), were all followers of his example. They said this was the way to attain the origin of the great *Tao*. Therefore they would get rid of their caps, pull off their clothes, and exhibit shameful behavior, as if they were birds and beasts. Doing this to an extreme degree was called 'understanding'; doing it to a lesser degree was called 'comprehension' " (*ibid.*).

---

[1] A saying by Hsi K'ang (223-262). Cf. his *Hsi Chung-shan Chi* (Collected Writings of Hsi K'ang), 6.1.

"Abandonment" means a refusal to accept the bonds of morals and social conventions. "Understanding" and "comprehension" describe the states of mind of those who, conscious of the uncertainties of human life, show corresponding disdain for good or bad fortune, success or failure. To men such as these of the Wei and Chin dynasties the term *feng-liu* was often applied.[1] They were persons completely opposed to the morals and institutions of the Confucian school.

The view of life of these men finds a comparatively systematic expression in the book known as the *Lieh-tzŭ* (including its seventh chapter, entitled "Yang Chu"). According to tradition, the *Lieh-tzŭ* as a whole is the work of Lieh Yü-k'ou 列禦寇, a Taoist who lived during the latter centuries of the Chou dynasty, while its "Yang Chu Chapter" expresses the philosophy of another Chou Taoist, Yang Chu, who has already been discussed in the first volume of this book. This tradition has been attacked by modern scholars, however, who for the most part regard the *Lieh-tzŭ* not as a Chou work, but as the product of some unknown Wei or Chin writer.[2] The ideas expressed in the "Yang Chu Chapter," too, differ from those of the historical Yang Chu, but agree well with the Wei and Chin emphasis on "abandonment" and "comprehension."

In the *Lieh-tzŭ* we find numerous expressions of a philosophy of materialism and mechanism, as for example in the sixth chapter:

"Effort (*li* 力) said to Destiny (*ming* 命): 'How can your achievements be compared with mine?' 'And what, then,' replied Destiny, 'are your achievements with things, that you wish to compare them with mine?' 'Why,' said Effort, 'the length of man's life, his measure of success, his rank and his wealth, are all things that I have the power to determine.'

---

[1] 風流, lit., "wind and stream." For this elusive term, the words "romantic" or "romanticism" seem to be the nearest English equivalent. See Fung Yu-lan, *A Short History of Chinese Philosophy*, edited by D. Bodde (New York, 1948), pp. 231-232. The twentieth chapter of this book gives a detailed study of the *feng liu* tradition of the Wei and Chin periods. — Tr.

[2] This view, held by most modern Chinese scholars, has been questioned by a number of Western sinologists. Though it seems not impossible that some parts of the *Lieh-tzŭ* may go back to the Chou dynasty, it could hardly have been compiled in its present form until a later time; much of it seems to be a patchwork of materials that were earlier current in other works, or to contain legends generally regarded as of Han or later date. — Tr.

"Replied Destiny: 'The wisdom of P'eng Tsu (an ancient worthy noted for his longevity) did not exceed that of (the legendary sages) Yao and Shun, yet he lived to an age of eight hundred. The ability of Yen Yüan (favorite disciple of Confucius) was not inferior to that of the generality of men, yet he died when only four times eight. The virtue of Confucius was not less than that of the feudal lords, yet he was reduced to straits between Ch'en and Ts'ai. [1] The conduct of Chou, (last tyrant ruler) of the Yin (Shang dynasty), did not exceed that of the Three Men of Virtue, [2] yet he held a ruler's position. Chi-cha lacked noble position in Wu, whereas T'ien Heng usurped the power in the state of Ch'i. [3] Yi and Ch'i starved at Shou-yang, whereas the Chi clan was richer than Ch'an Ch'in. [4] If these were all things brought about by your efforts, how is it that for one (P'eng Tsu) you allotted long life, and for another (Yen Yüan) an untimely death; for the Sage (Confucius) failure, and for the impious success; for the wise man mean position, and for the fool high honors; for the good poverty, and for the wicked wealth?'

" 'If,' said Effort, 'it is as you say, is it that I really have no control over things to make them as they are? And is it, then, all owing to your management?'

"Destiny replied: 'Once one speaks of it as Destiny, how can there be any such question of *management*? If a thing is to be straight, I push it straight along, but if it is to be crooked, I let it remain so. Old age or early death, failure or success, high rank or humble station, riches or poverty: all these come of themselves. For how could I have any conscious knowledge of them? Yes, how indeed could I have such knowledge?' " (pp. 97-99).

---

[1] For this incident, cf. his biography in the *Shih Chi*, chap. 47 (*Mém. hist.*, V, 364-371). — Tr.

[2] The Viscounts of Wei and Chi, together with Pi Kan, who were respectively exiled, imprisoned, and disemboweled by the tyrant Chou. — Tr.

[3] Chi-cha was offered the throne of Wu in 561 B.C., but voluntarily declined it, as by doing otherwise he would have usurped the rights of his elder brother. T'ien Heng was the minister of Duke Chien of Ch'i (484-481 B.C.), whom he murdered. By this act he gave his family a predominant position in Ch'i, culminating in its usurpation of the throne from 386 B.C. onward. — Tr.

[4] Yi and Ch'i are Po Yi and Shu Ch'i respectively, two worthies who, when the Shang dynasty was replaced by that of Chou, starved to death rather than shift their allegiance to the new dynasty. The Chi clan was for generations the most powerful family in the state of Lu, where it usurped many of the prerogatives of the legitimate ruling house. Ch'an Ch'in, better known as Liu-hsia Hui, was an official of the same state who lived prior to Confucius and was noted for his honesty. — Tr.

"Effort" here represents human effort, while "Destiny" re-presents the Mandate or Fate decreed by Heaven. The changing conditions of all things take place entirely of themselves, without either human effort or even the Fate of Heaven being able delib-erately to change their course. It is inevitable, moreover, that these changing conditions should take place the way they do. This is brought out in the following passages from the same chapter:

"Thus, then, it was not that Kuan Yi-wu (deliberately) slighted Pao Shu, but there was nothing he could do but slight him. Nor was it that he (deliberately) favored Hsi P'eng, but there was nothing he could do but favor him. [1] He who begins by favoring someone, may end up with slighting him, and he who begins by slighting someone, may likewise end up with favoring him. The manifestation or non-manifestation of such favoring or slighting does not depend upon the individual." [2]

Again: "Teng Hsi maintained theories that were open to op-posite interpretations, and instituted endless verbiage (in debate). While Tzŭ-ch'an held the government, he (Teng Hsi) created a penal code on bamboo (tablets) which was used by the state of Cheng. [3] He repeatedly made trouble for Tzŭ-ch'an's administration, so that Tzŭ-ch'an, being afflicted by him, seized and punished him, and suddenly executed him. Thus, then, it was not a question of Tzŭ-

---

[1] Kuan Yi-wu (died 645 B.C.), better known as Kuan Chung, was the famous adviser of Duke Huan of Ch'i (685-643), whose other advisers were Pao Shu and Hsi P'eng. According to a tradition preserved in the passage immediately preceding this one, Kuan Chung, on his deathbed, was asked by the Duke who should be appointed in his (Kuan Chung's) place. In reply he refused to endorse Pao Shu, despite the fact that Pao was his closest friend. This was because Pao was so morally strict himself that in his eagerness to force others to adopt equally high standards he would only create opposition. Kuan Chung therefore advised the Duke to select Hsi P'eng instead, as a man who would be more flexible in his dealings. — Tr.

[2] This passage is omitted by Giles from his translation, but it occurs in the Chinese text a few sentences before the paragraph in Giles, p. 99, that begins with the words: "Yang Chu had a friend. . . ."

[3] On Teng Hsi (died 501 B.C.), who was a "lawyer" of the state of Cheng, noted for his ability to argue on any side of a question, see vol. 1, pp. 193-195. His famous penal code replaced the earlier code of 536 B.C. prepared by Tzŭ-ch'an (died 522), noted prime minister of Cheng. The difference in date between the two men makes impossible the story that follows, according to which Teng Hsi was executed by Tzŭ-ch'an. The Tso Chuan (p. 772) tells us that the execution was done, not by Tzŭ-ch'an himself, but by Tzŭ-ch'an's successor. — Tr.

ch'an finding it possible to use the bamboo penal code, but there was nothing he could do but use it. [1] Nor was it a question of Teng Hsi being capable of afflicting Tzŭ-ch'an, but there was nothing he could do but afflict him. And so with Tzŭ-ch'an, it was not a question of being capable of executing Teng Hsi, but there was nothing else for him to do but execute him." [2]

In similar vein, the *Lieh-tzŭ* (chap. 8) says: "Mr. T'ien of Ch'i was holding an ancestral banquet in his hall, to which a thousand guests were invited, some of whom came forward with presents of fish and geese. Eying them, Mr. T'ien exclaimed: 'How generous is Heaven to man! It causes the five kinds of grain to grow, and creates fish and birds, especially for our use.' The multitude of guests applauded him to the echo, save for the twelve year old son of a Mr. Pao, who, regardless of seniority, came forward and said: 'It is not as you say, my lord. All the creatures in Heaven and Earth have been created in the same category as ourselves, and one is of no greater intrinsic value than another. It is only by reason of size, knowledge, or strength that some one of them gains the mastery, or that one preys upon another. None are produced in order to serve the needs of others. Man catches and eats those that are fit for food, yet can it be said that Heaven creates these expressly for man's use? Mosquitoes and gnats, moreover, bite his skin, and tigers and wolves devour his flesh, yet can it be said that Heaven creates man expressly for the benefit of mosquitoes and gnats, or to provide flesh for tigers and wolves?' " (pp. 119-120).

These are excellent illustrations of the dictum that "Heaven and Earth are not benevolent." [3] Natural changes and human activities are equally mechanistic in their operation, and there is no such thing as divine or human freedom, divine or human purpose. This doctrine, enunciated with such shattering finality, probably provided the basis for the hedonism so conspicuous in the seventh chapter of the *Lieh-tzŭ*, which is the subject of the next section.

---

[1] This accords with the statement in the *Tso Chuan* that although Teng Hsi was executed, his code continued in use. — Tr.

[2] This passage, omitted like the preceding from the translation of Giles, follows immediately after it.

[3] Cf. the *Lao-tzŭ*, chap. 5. Wang Pi, commenting on this same passage in the *Lao-tzŭ*, writes similarly: "Earth does not grow grass for the sake of animals, yet animals eat grass. Nor does it produce dogs for the sake of man, yet man eats dogs." — Tr.

5—HEDONISM IN THE "YANG CHU CHAPTER" OF THE LIEH-TZŬ

The seventh chapter of the *Lieh-tzŭ*, entitled "Yang Chu," purports to represent the doctrines of the Chou dynasty philosopher by this name; actually, however, it is a work of post-Han date. [1] Basic in it is the concept that human life is not only fleeting, but contains a great deal which, strictly speaking, is unworthy to be called "human life" at all. Thus we read:

"One hundred years is the limit of a long life. Not one in a thousand ever attains to it. Yet even supposing that there is such a one, helpless infancy and doddering old age take up about half of this time. The time that is obliterated while asleep during the night, and that which is wasted while awake during the day, again amounts to another half of the rest. And yet again, pain and sickness, sorrow and bitterness, destruction and loss, grief and fear, fill up about another half. Thus, then, there is only a space of some ten odd years which one really gets (for his own enjoyment), and even then there is not one hour which is not linked with anxiety" (pp. 38-39).

Though life is thus tragically fleeting, death is equally futile, for it leads only to complete annihilation:

"In life the myriad creatures all differ from each other; in death they are reduced to a single uniformity. In life they may be virtuous or degenerate, honorable or despicable: that is how they differ from each other. But in death they will stink and rot and decompose: that is how they are all equal to each other. However, virtuousness or degeneracy, honorableness or despicableness, can no more be controlled (by the individual) than can stinking, rotting, and decomposition. [2] Thus we cannot make life or death, virtue or degeneracy, honorableness or despicableness, what they are, for all creatures live and die equally, and are equally virtuous or degenerate, honorable or despicable. Perhaps it may be ten years or perhaps a hundred years; they will all nevertheless die. They may be virtuous and sage, or they may be evil and degenerate; quite regardless they will die. In life they may be (sage rulers like) Yao and Shun; in death they will only be rotting bones. In life they may be (tyrants like) Chieh and Chou; in death they too will be rotting bones. In being rotten bones they are all alike. Who, then, will be able to distinguish

---

[1] See vol. 1, p. 135. — Tr.

[2] This idea is analogous to that found in the *Lieh-tzŭ*, chap. 6, in the debate between Effort and Destiny, quoted above. — Tr.

their (former) differences? Let us hasten, therefore, to enjoy our life, for why should we worry about what comes after death!" (pp. 40-41).

This sums up the philosophy of life as found in the "Yang Chu Chapter." Only pleasure, it holds, gives value to human life, and it is solely in this that the purpose and aim of life consists. The more the desires are satisfied, therefore, the more pleasurable is life. Thus we read further:

"Yen P'ing-chung asked Kuan Yi-wu how to nourish life. [1] Kuan Yi-wu replied: 'It suffices to give it free course, neither checking nor obstructing it.' P'ing-chung asked: 'What about the details?'

"Kuan Yi-wu replied: 'Allow the ear to hear what it likes, the eye to see what it likes, the nose to smell what it likes, the mouth to say it likes, the body to enjoy the comforts it likes, and the mind to do what it likes. Now what the ear likes to hear are musical sounds, and its not being permitted to do so is what I call obstruction of listening. What the eye likes to see are beautiful colors, and its not being permitted to do so is what I call obstruction of sight. What the nose likes to smell are the pepper plant and orchid, and its not being permitted to do so is what I call obstruction to scent. What the mouth likes to talk about is right and wrong, and its not being permitted to do so is what I call obstruction of the understanding. The comforts liked by the body are finery and ease, and its not being permitted to follow these is what I call obstruction to what it finds agreeable. What the mind likes is to be free and at ease, and its not being permitted to operate thus is what I call obstruction to its nature. All these various obstructions are the causes of great distress. To rid oneself of these causes, and thus in a happy manner to await death for a day, a month, a year, or ten years, is what I call nourishing (life). But to cling to these causes, choosing and not discarding them, thus painfully dragging out one's life for a hundred, thousand, or ten thousand years, is not what I call nourishing it' " (pp. 43-44).

This, then, is the way to gain happiness. In thus seeking to satisfy the desires, however, there remains the difficulty that these desires are often contradictory to each other. It is impossible in this world of ours to satisfy all desires alike, and hence the first essential

---

[1] Yen P'ing-chung, more properly known as Yen Ying, was a noted statesman of the state of Ch'i, as was Kuan Yi-wu, on whom see p. 193, note 1, above. The fact that Yen died in 500 B.C., while Kuan died in 645, shows clearly the apocryphal nature of this conversation. — Tr.

is to make a selection of those whose satisfaction is most desirable. Though no such principle of selection seems to be followed in the passage just quoted, in actual fact there is one. For according to what it says, what should be sought for are ease and luxury, rather than long-term health, even though both objectives are desired by men. In the same way, we should seek only for the unhampered expression of our feelings and opinions, without regard for the resulting praise or blame of society, and this despite the fact that the individual normally desires not only free expression for himself, but also the approval of society. In short, the desires which the "Yang Chu Chapter" selects and regards as worthy of satisfaction are the ones that are immediate and more readily satisfiable. It disregards all those whose satisfaction requires time and laborious preparation. As a result, it lays chief stress on bodily pleasures, perhaps because these, above all others, may most readily be gratified. In the same way it selects immediate pleasures precisely in order to escape long-term pain and suffering.

Among the Cyrenaics of Greece it was maintained "that there was nothing naturally and intrinsically just, or honourable, or disgraceful; but that things were considered so because of law and fashion." According to Theodorus, furthermore, such law and fashion owe their existence "to the consent of fools." [1] For though law and custom admittedly do have their value, it is a value only with regard to a future and not an immediate benefit. Hence if one disregards the future and looks only at the immediate present, all laws and regulations become nothing more than "obstructions" to the desires. The "Yang Chu Chapter" seems to make a similar attack on laws and regulations when it says:

"What, then, is the object of human life? What makes it pleasant? Finery and ease, music and beauty. Yet we cannot always sate ourselves with finery and ease, or incessantly enjoy music and beauty. On the contrary, being warned and exhorted by punishments and rewards, urged forward or repelled by fame and laws, we anxiously strive for an hour of empty fame and plan for a glory that will survive our death. Carefully we reflect upon what our eyes and ears see and hear, and pay pitying regard to what is right or wrong for our bodies and minds. Thus we vainly lose the highest pleasures of the present

---

[1] See Diogenes Laertius, *The Lives and Opinions of Eminent Philosophers*, transl. of C. D. Yonge (London, 1915), pp. 91, 94.

year, being unable to give release to ourselves for even an hour. How, then, do we differ from an important criminal laden with manacles?

"The ancients knew that we come into life for but a brief moment, and that we depart equally speedily in death. Therefore they acted in accordance with their own hearts, and did not turn against what they naturally liked. They did not rid themselves of what gave their bodies pleasure, and therefore did not exhort themselves for sake of fame. They followed their own natures, without denying to themselves what all creatures like. They did not seek posthumous fame, and therefore avoided action for which they might be punished. As to whether fame and praise might come now or later, and whether their span of life might be much or little, to this they paid no heed" (pp. 39-40). Again:

"Po Yi was not desireless, for out of pride in his erroneous purity, he allowed himself to starve to death. [1] Ch'an Chi was not passionless, for out of pride in his erroneous chastity, he allowed himself to reduce his family. [2] Such is the erroneous 'goodness' that results from purity and chastity like this" (p. 41).

Real "goodness," to the writer of this treatise, means immediate pleasure.

Nevertheless, the "Yang Chu Chapter" is forced to admit that fame, too, is something desired by man. Therefore it says:

"Yü Tzŭ has said: 'He who renounces fame has no sorrow.' [3] And Lao Tzŭ has said: 'Fame is secondary to reality'. [4] Nonetheless, people frenziedly hasten after fame without ceasing, so that it seems that neither can (the desire for) fame be eliminated, nor fame be made secondary. This is because, in the present age, fame means honor and glory, while the lack of it means lowliness and disgrace. And with this honor and glory come ease and pleasure, while with lowliness and disgrace come grief and suffering. Grief and suffering are contrary to human nature, while ease and pleasure are in accord with it. This is where the connection with reality appears. So, then, how can (the desire for) fame be eliminated, or fame be made to take

---

[1] See p. 192, note 4. — Tr.

[2] On Ch'an Chi or Ch'an Ch'in, better known as Liu-hsia Hui, who was a man so chaste that he refused to procreate offspring, see the same note. — Tr.

[3] Yü Tzŭ, i.e., Yü Hsiung, is a semi-legendary writer on government supposed to have lived at the beginning of the Chou dynasty. — Tr.

[4] This saying does not occur in the present *Lao-tzŭ*. — Tr.

a secondary place? The only thing to dislike is a clinging to fame when this involves real (loss), for when this happens, one can no longer be saved from distressing danger or destruction. Thus it then becomes no longer merely a question of ease and pleasure on the one hand and grief and suffering on the other" (p. 64). [1]

According to this, fame is not to be belittled in itself; it becomes objectionable only when it is an empty fame bringing in its train a disastrous reality. Moreover, time is required to create a good name for oneself. Indeed, such a name commonly is achieved only in the distant future or sometimes not until after death itself. It is doubtful whether the gaining of such a fame, even during one's own life, is sufficient compensation for the resulting sacrifice of immediate pleasure. Certainly it cannot be when it comes only after death. The "Yang Chu Chapter" says:

"The praise of the world is all for Shun, Yü, (the Duke of) Chou, and Confucius, while its hate is all for Chieh and Chou. ... None of the former four sages, while alive, enjoyed a single day of pleasure, yet in death they gained a fame lasting ten thousand years. This fame, however, certainly cannot bring reality back to them. Although you now acclaim them, they are not conscious of it, and although you honor them, they are not aware of it. What is there to distinguish them from a block of wood or clod of earth? Those four sages, although they were the object of praise, nevertheless suffered miseries up to their very end, and then all equally passed on to death. Whereas the other two villains, though objects of hatred, enjoyed pleasures up to their very end, when they too all equally passed on to death" (pp. 54-57).

Again: "From Fu Hsi until now it is more than 300,000 years. Virtue and degeneracy, beauty and ugliness, success and failure, right and wrong: there is none of these that has not become effaced (in the course of this period). It is only a question of sooner or later. If anyone, being concerned about the blame or praise of one time, therefore tortures his spirit and body, wanting to gain a fame that will endure after death a few hundred years, how will this revive his dried bones or give them back the joy of living?" (pp. 59-60).

This being so, why should we discard immediate pleasure so as to gain a posthumous fame of which we will be unconscious?

---

[1] The last two sentences are omitted from the English translation by Forke here cited. — Tr.

Thus it is only immediate pleasures that the "Yang Chu Chapter" selects as worthwhile. If these are obtainable, it asserts, there is no need to bother about the ultimate results, whatever they may be:

"Tuan-mu Shu of Wei was a descendant of Tzŭ-kung. [1] Through the wealth of his ancestor his family had an accumulation of ten thousand (pieces of) gold. Quite indifferent to the activities of the world, he allowed his inclinations to go where they would. During his life he did everything that people like to do, and amused himself with everything that people like to amuse themselves with. ... The remains from what he spent he divided first among his clansmen. What they left was then divided among his fellow townspeople, and what was still left was distributed throughout the whole state.

"But when he reached the age of sixty and his spirit and frame began to decline, he abandoned his household affairs and completely distributed his accumulated stores, pearls and gems, carriages and dresses, concubines and female attendants, so that within a year they were completely disposed of and no fortune was left to his offspring. When he fell ill, he had no means to buy medicines or mineral drugs, and when he died, there was not even money for his funeral. The people of his whole state who had received his bounty, however, contributed money to bury him, and gave back the fortune to his descendants.

"When Ch'in Ku-li [2] heard of this, he said: 'Tuan-mu Shu was a madman who brought disgrace on his ancestor.' But when Tuan-kan Sheng [3] heard of it, he said: 'Tuan-mu Shu was a man of perspicuity, whose virtue surpassed that of his ancestor. The way he acted and behaved shocked common opinion, yet in truth it accorded with correct principle. The "superior men" of Wei for the most part merely adhered to the teachings of (conventional) propriety. They were certainly unworthy to attain to the mind of this man' " (pp. 49-51).

The worst thing that can happen is death, and the fear of it can, in fact, cause much worry, and thus prevent men from enjoying immediate pleasure. This is why all followers of Hedonism

---

[1] Tzŭ-kung, more properly known as Tuan-mu Tz'ŭ, was a disciple of Confucius. He succeeded in amassing a considerable fortune for himself and his family. — Tr.

[2] The chief disciple of Mo Tzŭ, but he seems also to have had some connection with the Confucian school. Cf. vol. 1, pp. 81, 106. — Tr.

[3] Not definitely identifiable. — Tr.

commonly stress the fact that death is really not something to be feared. As shown in the following passages, the "Yang Chu Chapter" is no exception:

"Kuan Yi-wu said: 'Now that I have told you how to nourish life, what about the way of burying the dead?' Yen P'ing-chung replied: 'There is not much to burying the dead. What can I say about it?' 'Nevertheless,' Kuan Yi-wu said, 'I should definitely like to hear about it.'

"P'ing-chung replied: 'Once I am dead, what has it to do with me? They may burn my body, cast it into water, inter it, leave it exposed, throw it wrapped in a mat into some ditch, or cover it with princely apparel and embroidered garments and rest it in a stone sarcophagus. All that depends on mere chance.'

"Kuan Yi-wu looked at Pao-shu Huang-tzŭ (unknown elsewhere) and said: 'We have both made some progress in the doctrine of life and death'" (pp. 44-45).

Again: "Meng-sun Yang (unknown elsewhere) asked Master Yang (i.e., Yang Chu), saying: 'There are men who so value life and love their bodies that they seek for immortality. Can this be done?'

"The reply was: 'According to (natural) principle, there is none who does not die.'

"'Yet what about seeking for a prolongation of life? Is that possible?'

"The reply was: 'According to (natural) principle, there is no such thing as a prolongation of life. Life is not something that can be preserved through attaching value to it, nor is the body something that can be benefited by being loved. Of what use, moreover, is a prolongation of life? The likes and dislikes of the five feelings were the same anciently as today. So were the safety or danger of the four limbs, the sufferings or pleasures of human affairs, and the shifting order and disorder of human government. Having seen, heard, and experienced these things one by one, a hundred years would be enough to make one wearied of them. How much more would the sufferings of a still greater prolongation of life!'

"Meng-sun Yang said: 'If, then, a speedy death is better than a prolonged life, the way to get what we desire is to step on a sharp sword or enter boiling water or fire.'

"'Not so,' replied Master Yang. 'Having come into life, leave it alone and give it free rein. Pay heed to its desires and thus await death. Likewise, when about to enter death, leave it alone and give it free rein. Pay heed to what it brings and thus float away into annihilation. If in both cases you leave everything alone and give everything free rein, how can you tremble lest (your life end) either sooner or later?' " (pp. 51-52).

This reminds us of Epicurus, who similarly maintained: "Accustom yourself to think death a matter with which we are not at all concerned, since all good and all evil is in sensation, and since death is only the privation of sensation. On which account, the correct knowledge of the fact that death is no concern of ours, makes the mortality of life pleasant to us, inasmuch as it sets forth no illimitable time, but relieves us from the longing of immortality. ... Therefore, the most formidable of all evils, death, is nothing to us, since when we exist, death is not present to us; and when death is present, then we have no existence." [1]

Since there is no need to fear death itself, there is likewise no need to fear anything else resulting from our conduct.

What we must seek for, then, is immediate pleasure, irrespective of any resulting future harm. In the same way, what we must avoid is immediate suffering, irrespective of any resulting future good. The "Yang Chu Chapter" says:

"Master Ch'in [2] asked Yang Chu, saying: 'If by plucking a single hair from your body, you could save the whole world, would you do it?' Master Yang replied: 'The world is certainly not to be saved by a single hair.' Master Ch'in said: 'But suppose it could be saved, would you do it?'

"Master Yang made no reply. Thereupon Master Ch'in went out and told it to Meng-sun Yang, who said:

" 'You have not grasped the Master's meaning. I beg to explain it to you. Supposing for tearing off a piece of your skin you were to get ten thousand (pieces of) gold, would you do it?'

"He replied: 'I would.'

"Meng-sun Yang continued: 'But supposing for cutting off one of your limbs you were to gain a whole kingdom, would you do it?'

"Master Ch'in was silent for a while, and Meng-sun Yang went on: 'It is evident that a hair is insignificant compared with the skin, and the skin is insignificant compared with a limb. Nevertheless,

[1] Diogenes Laertius, *The Lives and Opinions of Eminent Philosophers*, p. 469.
[2] Ch'in Ku-li, mentioned above. — Tr.

the accumulation of single hairs forms the skin, and the accumulation of skin forms a limb. Since a single hair is truly one out of the ten thousand parts that comprise the body, how can we regard it lightly?'

"Master Ch'in replied: 'I do not know how to answer you. And yet, though your words would be found correct if addressed to Lao Tan and Kuan Yin, my words would also be found correct if addressed to the great Yü and Mo Ti.'[1]

"Meng-sun Yang thereupon turned toward his disciples and spoke of other matters" (pp. 53-54).

This is an elaboration of the famous doctrine of the actual Yang Chu of the Chou dynasty, as reported by Mencius: "The principle of Master Yang is 'Each one for himself.' Though he might have benefited the whole world by plucking out a single hair, he would not have done it" (*Mencius*, VIIa, 26). For the plucking of a single hair entails immediate suffering, whereas the gaining of the world is only a future result. We should avoid all immediate suffering, regardless of what great benefit such suffering may ultimately bring. This doctrine, as expressed in the "Yang Chu Chapter," goes further than that of the original Yang Chu. For, so it says, not only should we not sacrifice a single hair to *benefit* the world, but we should not even do so in order to *gain* the whole world.

This doctrine, although extreme, is regarded by the "Yang Chu Chapter" as a way by which the world can actually be saved. For once it is assumed that everybody in the world seeks only his own immediate pleasure, this automatically eliminates the struggle for power and self-profit among men, since such power and profit can only be gained as the result of troublesome preparation and laborious effort. Granted, therefore, that people only seek immediate pleasure, this means that what they seek is limited, since it does not go beyond what they themselves can immediately enjoy. The *Chuang-tzŭ* (chap. 1) says in similar vein:

"The tit, building its nest in the mighty forest, occupies but a

---

[1] Lao Tan is the philosopher, Lao Tzŭ, and Kuan Yin is the official at the pass in West China to whom he is reputed to have handed the text of his *Tao Te Ching*, when leaving China for Central Asia. As Taoists, these men would naturally approve of the principle of non-interference in the affairs of others. Mo Tzŭ, however, with his famous altruistic regard for others, followed a policy that was the opposite of non-interference, and the same is true of the legendary Yü, who is reputed to have labored for nine years to save the world from a great flood. For the special affinity which Mo Tzŭ seems to have felt for Yü, see vol. 1, p. 80. — Tr.

single twig. The tapir, slaking its thirst from the river, drinks only enough to fill its belly. ... I have no need of the world" (p. 6).

When such is the case, the struggle for gain is automatically eliminated. Therefore the "Yang Chu Chapter" says:

"If the ancients, by injuring a single hair, could have benefited the world, they would not have done so; and if the entire world had been offered to a single person, he would not have accepted it. When all men refuse to injure a single hair or to benefit the world, the world is well ordered" (p. 53).

It would not seem that such a simple procedure would suffice to solve the many complicated problems of the world. Nevertheless, it is a fact that the disorders of the world originate in large part from men's struggles for power and personal profit, so that this doctrine admittedly has a certain measure of reason and logic. [1]

---

[1] The final page and a half of the original text of this chapter have been omitted from this revised version. — Tr.

CHAPTER VI

NEO-TAOISM DURING THE PERIOD OF DISUNITY

(Part II)

1—HSIANG HSIU AND KUO HSIANG

Wang Pi's commentaries on the *Lao-tzŭ* and *Book of Changes* are important products of Wei and Chin Neo-Taoism. Another equally valuable work is the *Chuang-tzŭ Commentary* or *Chuang-tzŭ Chu*, which, though bearing the name of Kuo Hsiang 郭象 (died 312), has by some been attributed to his contemporary, Hsiang Hsiu 向秀 (ca. 221-ca. 300). The *Chin Shu* (History of the Chin Dynasty) says in its biography of the latter:

"Hsiang Hsiu, styled Tzŭ-ch'i 子期, was a native of Huai in Ho-nei. [1] He was clear in understanding and far-reaching in knowledge. As a young man he became known to Shan T'ao. [2] He had an extraordinary liking for Lao and Chuang. Among the Taoist devotees of successive generations there had not been lacking those who had perused the several tens of 'inner' and 'outer' chapters composed by Chuang Chou. None, however, had adequately discussed their general meaning. Hence (Hsiang) Hsiu prepared an interpretation which revealed their secrets, explaining them with surpassing clarity and evoking the real spirit of Taoism. Readers of it, as a consequence, found their minds extraordinarily clarified by it, and there was nobody who did not enjoy the time given to it. Then during the period of Emperor Hui (290-306), Kuo Hsiang continued and enlarged it, with the result that the remaining traces of Confucianism and Mohism went into eclipse, and the doctrines of Taoism became flourishing" [3] (49.16).

---

[1] Southwest of the present Wu-chih 武陟 hsien, just north of the Yellow river in Honan. — Tr.

[2] Lived 205-283. He was noted as a statesman, but even more so as one of the Seven Worthies of the Bamboo Grove, a group of Taoistically minded men who used to meet in a bamboo grove for convivial and often bibulous conversation. Hsiang Hsiu himself also belonged to this group. — Tr.

[3] Little further is known of Hsiang Hsiu's life, save that for a while he held some official positions of minor importance. — Tr.

The *Chin Shu*'s biography of Kuo Hsiang, however, presents these events rather differently:

"Kuo Hsiang, styled Tzŭ-hsüan 子玄, already as a youth showed outstanding talent. He was fond of Lao and Chuang and an adept in 'pure talk.' [1] ... He died at the end of the Yung-chia period (A.D. 312). ... Before this time there had already been several tens of scholars who had made commentaries on the *Chuang-tzŭ*, but none had succeeded in completely reaching its meaning. Aside from these earlier commentaries, Hsiang Hsiu had prepared an interpretation which marvelously expanded on them and greatly extended the spirit of Taoism. He died, however, before finishing the two chapters, 'The Autumn Flood' and 'Perfect Happiness' (chaps. 17-18). Hsiu's son, while young, allowed his (father's) treatise to become scattered. It was preserved, however, in a number of other copies. Now (Kuo) Hsiang himself was a man of petty character, and on seeing that (Hsiang) Hsiu's treatise was not transmitted in the world, he plagiarized it and made it out to be his own commentary. He wrote a commentary of his own upon 'The Autumn Flood' and 'Perfect Happiness,' and made changes in the chapter on 'Horses' Hoofs' (chap. 9). As for the many other chapters, he seemingly did nothing more but establish the correctness of their text. Later on, however, the other copies of (Hsiang) Hsiu's treatise appeared, so that today there are two versions of the *Chuang-tzŭ* by Hsiang and Kuo. In substance, however, they are the same" [2] (50.8-9).

Thus in Hsiang Hsiu's biography we are told that Kuo "continued and enlarged" Hsiang's commentary, whereas in Kuo's own biography it is asserted that he actually "plagiarized it and made it out to be his own commentary," and that, aside from adding commentaries to chaps. 17-18 and making some changes in Hsiang's commentary to chap. 9, his own contribution seemingly consisted of nothing more than "establishing the correctness of the text." Chang Chan, [3] in his commentary on the *Lieh-tzŭ*, has occasion to

---

[1] *Ch'ing yen* 清言 (or *t'an* 談), the art of conversing about philosophy and abstract topics only, and avoiding all mundane matters. This type of conversation was very popular among the Neo-Taoists of the period. — Tr.

[2] From the biography we learn little more of Kuo Hsiang's life, save that he was a native of the present Loyang in Honan and at various times held a number of official posts. — Tr.

[3] Exact dates unknown. He lived during the Eastern Chin dynasty (317-419). — Tr.

expound a number of passages in which the *Lieh-tzŭ* quotes from the *Chuang-tzŭ*. In so doing he himself often quotes by name either from the Hsiang Hsiu or the Kuo Hsiang commentary. When he does the former, what he quotes usually agrees fairly well with the commentary which today passes under the name of Kuo Hsiang. Sometimes, however, he also quotes directly from what he calls the Kuo Hsiang commentary, without mentioning Hsiang Hsiu's name at all. When this happens, the probable reason is either that Hsiang Hsiu's commentary did not cover the particular passages of the *Chuang-tzŭ* being quoted by the *Lieh-tzŭ* and there commented on by Chang Chan, or that its exposition of them was inferior to that of Kuo Hsiang. It should be remembered that Chang's grandfather was the nephew of the cousin of Wang Pi (226-249), and that Chang himself lived very close in time to Kuo Hsiang. Thus he was in a position to have seen the Hsiang Hsiu commentary while it still circulated under Hsiang's name, which would explain why he so frequently refers to it as Hsiang Hsiu's work, and not that of Kuo Hsiang.

It is further noteworthy that none of the comments on the *Chuang-tzŭ* which Chang explicitly attributes to Kuo Hsiang deal with the three *Chuang-tzŭ* chapters entitled "The Autumn Flood," "Perfect Happiness," and "Horses' Hoofs." This indicates that the *Chin Shu* is unreliable when, in its biography of Kuo, it says that "he wrote a commentary of his own upon the 'Autumn Flood' and 'Perfect Happiness,' and made changes in the chapter on 'Horses' Hoofs.' As for the many other chapters, he seemingly did nothing more than establish the correctness of their text." On the other hand, the fact that what Chang Chan quotes from Hsiang Hsiu agrees so well with the commentary that today goes under Kuo Hsiang's name makes it obvious that Hsiang's earlier commentary must have been extensively utilized by Kuo when he prepared his own commentary. The conclusion that emerges, therefore, is that what is today known as the Kuo Hsiang commentary is really the joint product of Hsiang Hsiu and Kuo Hsiang, and hence that what the *Chin Shu* says in its biography of Hsiang Hsiu is close to the truth. This being so, we shall hereafter refer to it simply as the *Chuang-tzŭ Commentary*.

2—Self-Transformation

Wang Pi, as we have seen in the last chapter, refers to the Way or *Tao* as "non-being" (*wu*), without, however, explaining very clearly what he means by this term. But when we turn to the *Chuang-tzŭ Commentary*, it becomes apparent that "non-being" is there interpreted as actually signifying a state of nothingness. In other words, it is equivalent to what we would today describe as a mathematical zero. Hence *Tao*, since it is "non-being," cannot be regarded as the first cause or prime mover for things in the world of being. On the contrary, we are told that all things are the way they are simply because of an inherent natural tendency which causes them to be thus. For example, under the passage in the *Chuang-tzŭ* (chap. 6): "It (*Tao*) causes the gods to be divine and the world to be produced" (p. 76), we read in the *Commentary*:

"As it is non-being (*wu*), how can it (*Tao*) produce the gods? It does not cause the gods to be divine, but they are divine of themselves. Their divinity is thus an uncaused divinity. It does not produce the world, but the world is produced of itself. Its production is thus an uncaused production." [1]

On the passage in the same chapter: "It is above the zenith, but is not high..." (p. 76), the *Commentary* says:

"This means that *Tao* is everywhere. Therefore it is in the highest place, but is not high. It is in the lowest place, but is not low. It is in ancient times, but is not itself ancient. It is in old age, but is not itself old. It is everywhere, but everywhere it is nothing" (*ibid.*, p. 15).

Or again, on the passage in the *Chuang-tzŭ* (chap. 22): "Was what there was before the universe a thing?" (p. 291), the *Commentary* says:

"In existence, what is prior to things? We say that the *yin* and *yang* are prior to things. But the *yin* and *yang* are themselves things. What, then, is prior to the *yin* and *yang*? We may say that nature (*tzŭ jan* 自 然) is prior to them. But nature is simply the naturalness of things. Or we may say that the supreme *Tao* is prior to things. But this supreme *Tao* is supreme non-being (*wu*). Since it is non-being, how can it be prior? Thus what can it be that is prior to things? And yet things are continuously being produced. This shows that things are spontaneously what they are. There is nothing that causes them to be such" (7.78-79).

On the passage in the second chapter: "The winds as they blow differ in thousands of ways, yet all are self-produced" (p. 13), the

---

[1] 3.14. Many of the passages quoted below are also found in Fung Yu-lan, *Chuang Tzŭ, a new selected translation with an exposition of the philosophy of Kuo Hsiang* (Shanghai, 1933).

Commentary states: "Since non-being (*wu*) is non-being, it cannot produce being (*yu*). Yet before being itself has yet been produced, it cannot go on to produce (other things). What, then, produces things? They spontaneously produce themselves. Being spontaneously produced, it is not I who produces them. And just as I cannot produce things, things also cannot produce me. Hence I am spontaneously what I am. That everything is spontaneously what it is, is called natural. And to be natural means not to be made to be so. ... Therefore everything produces itself and does not issue from anything else. This is the Way of Heaven" (1.25).

According to these statements, what we call the Way or *Tao* is simply a designation for the principle that "everything produces itself and does not issue from anything else." By saying that "before being itself has yet been produced, it cannot go on to produce (other things)," the *Commentary* simply wants to make it fully evident that "everything spontaneously becomes what it is." For in actual fact, "being" as such eternally exists; hence strictly speaking it is impossible to speak of a time "before being has yet been produced." Only of individual things is it possible to speak in this way; one cannot thus speak of "being" itself, which is the sum total of these individual things. This is brought out apropos of the passage in the *Chuang-tzŭ* (chap. 22): "There is no past, no present, no beginning, no end" (p. 291), on which the *Commentary* states:

"Not only is it that non-being cannot become being, but being also cannot become non-being. Though being may change in thousands of ways, it can never change into non-being. This being so, there is no time when there is no being; being eternally exists" (7.78).

This sort of reasoning very much resembles that of Parmenides.

The reason why the *Commentary* emphasizes that "everything produces itself and does not issue from anything else," is that, no matter how far human knowledge may be enlarged, or how many times man may ask himself the question: "What is the origin of things?" he is always eventually confronted by the reply: "They spontaneously produce themselves." And then, faced by this inscrutable mystery, he is forced to use such terms as God, *Tao*, the atom, or the electron. This idea is expressed under the passage in the *Chuang-tzŭ* (chap. 14): "In Heaven there are the six supreme principles and five constants" (p. 174), on which the *Commentary* says:

"We may claim that we know the causes of certain things. But if we push our investigation of these causes to the furthest limit, (we reach) something which is self-produced without any cause. Being self-produced, we can no longer ask what is the cause of this something. We can only accept it as it is" (5.57).

Since in the final analysis things are "self-produced without any cause," the *Commentary* accepts as its first premise the fact that all things are as they are of themselves and do not depend upon anything else. This doctrine it terms that of "self-transformation." For example, under the passage in the second chapter: "Does that something upon which I depend still have to depend upon something else in order to be what it is?" (p. 32), the *Commentary* states:

"If we ask upon what it depends and from what it derives, then our asking will continue indefinitely until (we realize that) there is nothing upon which it depends. In this way the principle of 'self-transformation' (*tu hua* 獨 化) is made clear" (1.63).

And on the passage in the same chapter: "How can I tell why I am so, or why I am not otherwise?" (p. 32), we read:

"Some people say that the penumbra is dependent upon the shadow, the shadow upon bodily forms, and bodily forms upon a Creator. But I venture to ask whether the Creator is or is not? If He is not, how can He create things? If He is, then, (being one of these things), He is incapable of creating the mass of bodily forms. Hence only after we realize that the mass of bodily forms are things of themselves can we begin to talk about the creation of things. Therefore throughout the realm of things, there is nothing within the Mystery, even the penumbra, which is not 'self-transformed.' Hence the creating of things has no Lord; everything creates itself. Everything produces itself and does not depend on anything else. This is the normal way of the universe" (1.63).

"The creating of things has no Lord; everything creates itself": such is the "principle of self-transformation."

3—The Relationships of Things in the Universe

The statement: "Everything produces itself and does not depend on anything else," means merely that we cannot designate any particular thing as the cause of any other particular thing. It does not at all mean that there are no relationships between one thing and another. On the contrary, the *Commentary* maintains that such relationships do exist and are necessary. Thus under the passage in the *Chuang-tzŭ* (chap. 17): "If we look at things from the point of view of their function ..." (p. 206), it says:

"There are no things under Heaven which do not hold a relationship to one another as of the 'self' and the 'other.' Yet both the 'self' and the 'other' equally desire to act for themselves, thus being as opposed to each other as are east and west. On the other hand, the 'self' and the 'other' at the same time hold a relationship to one another as that of the lips and teeth. The lips and teeth never (deliberately) act for one another, yet 'when the lips are gone, the teeth feel cold.' [1] Therefore the action of the 'other' on its own behalf at the same time plays a great function in helping the 'self.' Thus, though mutually opposed, they at the same time are mutually indispensable" (6.26).

And on the passage in the sixth chapter: "Who can associate in non-association ... ?" (p. 83), we read:

"The hands and feet differ in their duties; the five internal organs differ in their functions. They never associate with one another, yet the hundred parts (of the body) are held together by them in a common unity. This is the way in which they associate through non-association. They never (deliberately) cooperate, and yet, both internally and externally, all complete one another. This is the way in which they cooperate through non-cooperation" (3.25).

Yet again, on the passage in the same chapter: "He who knows the work of man ..." (p. 68), the *Commentary* tells us: "When a man is born, though he be but seven feet tall, [2] he is always completely endowed with the five constants. [3] Therefore, however insignificant his body may be, he needs the whole universe to be the condition of his existence. Hence all things in the universe, all that exist, could not cease to exist for even one day without him also ceasing to exist. If even one thing were lacking, he would have no means of living. If one principle were violated, his life would be unable to conclude its natural span" (3.1-2).

The given condition of a certain individual depends upon the given condition of the entire universe. Strictly speaking, each and

---

[1] A proverbial saying. — Tr.

[2] I.e., very short and insignificant. The Chinese foot was shorter than the English one. — Tr.

[3] The five virtues of love, righteousness, propriety, wisdom and good faith. — Tr.

every thing in the universe has relationship with each and every other thing. Therefore the words: "However insignificant his body may be, he needs the whole universe to be the condition of his existence. Hence all things in the universe, all that exist, could not cease to exist for even one day without him also ceasing to exist."

In human affairs, likewise, the shifting phases of "order" and "disorder" are something natural and inevitable. On the passage in the sixth chapter: "How does one know that what one calls nature is not man? . . ." (p. 68), the *Commentary* states:

"The human sphere, too, is equally a part of the natural process. Thus, order and disorder, success and failure, what happens and what does not happen: none of these is caused by man; they are all natural" (1.2-3).

And on the statement in the fourteenth chapter: "Men constituted themselves into separate classes throughout the world" (p. 187), the *Commentary* reads:

"If there is no general uniformity of all things, then each and every individual differentiates himself from every other individual. This is (what the text means by saying that) 'men constituted themselves into separate classes.' The developments of a hundred past generations, combined with the changes of recent times, are responsible for the present crisis. It is not caused by Yü (or any other individual). Hence (the text) speaks of 'the world.' It is not the activity of the sages that disturbs the world, but the world itself inevitably becomes disorderly" (5.78).

"The developments of a hundred past generations," combined in their totality with "the changes of recent times" in their totality, lead inevitably to certain conditions. This is the principle of historical necessity. On the other hand, we cannot postulate with assurance that any one specific condition is the cause of any other specific condition. This is the principle of "self-transformation." This point of view is very similar to the materialistic concept of history. The Russian Revolution, for example, was, according to this concept, the inevitable result of the total objective environment of its time; it was not caused by Lenin or any other particular individual. The statement quoted earlier, that things, "though mutually opposed, at the same time are mutually indispensable," may also be interpreted as an illustration of Hegelian dialectic, if one likes to read it into the *Chuang-tzŭ Commentary.*

4—NATURAL AND SOCIAL CHANGE

It has already been pointed out that in some ways the ideas in the *Chuang-tzŭ Commentary* resemble those of Parmenides. In other ways, however, they seem equally close to Heraclitus; for example, in the thesis that all things in the universe constantly undergo change. Thus on the passage in the *Chuang-tzŭ* (chap. 6): "But at midnight a strong man may come and carry them away on his back" (p. 75), the *Commentary* remarks:

"Of the forces which are imperceptible forces, none is greater than that of change. It transports Heaven and Earth toward the new. It carries hills and mountains to quit the old. The old never stops for a minute, but suddenly has already become the new. Thus Heaven, Earth, and all things are ever in a state of change. The world is ever renewed, yet it regards itself as old. A boat daily undergoes change, yet it seems to us like the old one. A mountain daily undergoes renewal, yet it seems to us like the former one. We touch the arm (of some passerby) today and lose it. Everything imperceptibly passes away. Therefore the 'I' of the past is no longer the 'I' of today. We must go with what there is today, for how can we forever cling to what is past? Yet nobody in the world realizes this fact, but perversely says that we can attach ourselves to what we meet today and remain with it. How benighted this is!" (3.12).

Though the philosophies of Parmenides and Heraclitus are complete opposites, the *Chuang-tzŭ Commentary* resembles both. This is because when it asserts, on the one hand, that there is only being and that this being externally exists, it says this with reference to the universe as a whole. But when, on the other hand, it also asserts that things are in a constant flux, it says this with reference to the individual things which make up that universe. A great river like the Yangtze exemplifies this dual concept: its waters are ever changing, yet it itself as a whole remains ever what it was before.

Society, too, is subject to this same eternal law of change, so that the social institutions designed for one age are ever becoming nullified and outmoded by the changes of the times. In the *Chuang-tzŭ* (chap. 14) we read: "The social relationships were first of all created, but what about women today?" (p. 187), on which the *Commentary* states:

"The fact that today, when women become wives, they are unsubmissive to their superiors (i.e., husbands), is not because (the social relationships) which were first created were unreasonable, but because when the reason for them lost its adequacy, the present situation resulted" (5.78).

On the passage in the same chapter: "That woman saw the beauty of knitted brows, but she did not see wherein the beauty of those knitted brows lay ..." (p. 182), the *Commentary* says:

"Hsi Shih exemplifies one whose manners were suitable for the occasion; the ugly woman exemplifies one who failed to cast them aside even after the proper occasion for them had passed" [1] (*ibid.*, p. 70).

Again, on the passage in the same chapter: "When he (Confucius) was surrounded between Ch'en and Wei ..." (p. 180), we read:

"The institutions of the former kings were intended to meet the needs of the time. If they are not discarded after the time for them has passed, they become the bogy of the people and there thus appear the beginnings of artificiality" (*ibid.*, p. 68).

And on yet another passage: "The morals of the former kings are as temporary lodging places. You may stop in them for one night, but not for long, or you will incur reproach" (p. 183):

"Morals belong to human nature, but this nature changes in accordance with the differences between past and present. Hence if you temporarily stop in them (in the morals of the past) and then pass on, you retain your inconspicuousness. But if you allow yourself to be obstructed and tied to one spot, you then become conspicuous. By being conspicuous you develop artificiality, and with this artificiality you incur much reproach" (*ibid.*, p. 72).

Society constantly changes under the impact of inevitable forces, and with these changes its old procedures and institutions become "ugly" and the "bogy" of the people. By clinging to them despite the trends of the times, we show our inability to conform with the natural; the result is "the beginning of artificiality." On the passage in the tenth chapter: "Yet one morning T'ien Ch'eng Tzŭ slew the Prince of Ch'i and stole his kingdom" (p. 111), the *Commentary* says:

"Those who imitate the sages imitate what they have already

---

[1] Hsi Shih was a woman famed for her beauty. According to the story in the *Chuang-tzŭ*, on which this is the comment, her beauty was such that it remained intact even when, being distressed in mind, she would knit her brows. A certain ugly woman, noticing this, thought she could improve her own appearance by doing likewise. When people saw her knit her brows, however, her appearance was so horrible that they closed their doors to her. — Tr.

done. But what they have done is something already gone and therefore cannot meet the changes (of the present). Why then should we respect and cling to it? If we cling to the crystallized achievements (of the past) as a means for dealing with the amorphous (present), then the crystallized (past) acts as an obstruction to the amorphous (present)" (4.21).

New changes require new procedure and institutions. By instituting these when the need arises, the sage demonstrates his ability to conform with the natural. On the passage in the *Chuang-tzŭ* (chap. 17): "Be quiet, oh River Spirit . . ." (p. 208), the *Commentary* says:

"What is valued by the world sometimes becomes mean. What is large among things may be belittled by the world. Therefore there cannot but be variety in the ways in which one conforms to things. This explains the difference between the Five Emperors and Three Kings" (6.30).

And on the passage in the twelfth chapter: "If all the world had been equally well governed, would it have been necessary for Shun to govern it? . . ." (p. 152), we read: "This says that both these sages [1] set the world in order because there was disorder. However, the fact that one of them did so by peaceful methods, whereas the other used military force, was because of the differences of their times, and does not indicate any superiority or inferiority between them" (5.26).

The sages "conform to things" in accordance with the "differences of their times." Hence "there cannot but be variety" in the manner in which they thus conform. All of them are alike in that they do conform, however, and therefore, irrespective of their outward differences, there is no "superiority or inferiority between them." Thus it is clear that the *Chuang-tzŭ Commentary* (unlike the early Taoists) does not oppose moral institutions as such. It only opposes such as do not fit their own time.

5—"Non-Activity"

In order to meet the changes of the times, it is natural and inevitable that men should devise new procedures and institutions for themselves. By allowing free scope to what is thus done by these men themselves, it is possible to achieve that Taoist ideal of "non-

---

[1] Shun and King Wu, with whom Shun is here being compared. — Tr.

activity" (*wu wei*), whereby all things become accomplished. On the passage in the sixth chapter: "To consider knowledge as the requirement of the time means to follow the inevitable course of things" (p. 73), the *Commentary* says:

"When (water) runs down from a high place to a low one, the current is irresistible. When small things group with the small and large ones with the large, the tendency cannot be opposed. When a man is empty and without bias, everything will contribute its wisdom to him. What will he do, who is the leader of men facing all these hundred currents? He simply trusts the wisdom of the time, relies on the necessity of circumstances, and lets the world take care of itself" (3.9).

"What will he do?" Simply rely on non-activity. By thus relying on non-activity there will be nothing unaccomplished.

On the passage in the eleventh chapter: "Therefore for the superior man who is unavoidably summoned to power over the world, there is nothing like non-activity" (p. 122), the *Commentary* states:

" 'Non-activity' does not mean folding one's hands and remaining silent. It simply means allowing everything to follow what is natural to it, and then its nature will be satisfied. 'Unavoidably' does not mean coercing through strict punishments. It simply means embracing the *Tao*, cherishing Simplicity (*p'u* 朴), and giving free scope to the inevitable, and then the world will take care of itself" (4.36).

And on the passage in the thirteenth chapter: "Keep to this (non-activity) when coming forward to tranquillize the world ..." (p. 159), we read.

"Non-activity is great in its substance, for where in the world is there a place where it is not to be practiced? Thus if the ruler above does not interfere with the duties of the prime minister, then the prime minister is left in peace to conduct his administration. [1] If the prime minister does not interfere with the duties of the various officials under him, then these various officials are left in peace to carry out these duties. If the officials do not interfere with the activities of the people as a whole, then the people as a whole are left in peace to carry on their occupations. If the people do not

---

[1] For "prime minister," the text reads "Yi and Lü." Yi Yin was famous as the prime minister of T'ang, founder of the Shang dynasty, and Lü Shang as the prime minister of Kings Wen and Wu, founders of the Chou dynasty. — Tr.

interchange the capabilities properly belonging either to self or to others, then, throughout the world, what pertains to self or to others is peacefully and automatically determined. Hence from the Son of Heaven down to the common people, and including even the insect world still further below, who can hope to succeed through interference? Therefore the more one practices non-activity, the more one is honored" (5.36).

On another passage in the same chapter: "Therefore the men of old prized non-activity" (p. 160), we read:

"The artisan's non-activity consists in the carving of wood; his activity consists in the functioning of his axe. The ruler's non-activity consists in the management of affairs; his activity consists in the functioning of his ministers. It is the ministers who can manage affairs, but it is the ruler who can cause them to function. It is the axe that can carve the wood, but it is the artisan who can cause it to function. When each limits himself to what he himself is capable, then natural principles operate of themselves and there is no assertive activity .... Hence let everyone perform his own proper function, so that high and low both have their proper places. This is the perfection of the principle of non-activity" (*ibid.*, p. 39).

And on yet another passage in the same chapter: "The ruler must practice non-activity in order to utilize the world" (p. 161): "Therefore as regards superior and inferior, the ruler is quiescent while the minister is active. Comparing the ancient with the modern, Yao and Shun practiced non-activity, whereas T'ang and Wu were occupied with affairs. Yet each of them followed his own nature, thus mysteriously manifesting the functions of Heaven. Hence non-activity was the rule in the case of past and present, superior and inferior, alike. Who of them (really) practiced activity?" (*ibid.*, p. 40).

If we compare past with present, the affairs and activities of today are certainly more complex than those of former times, but this increased complexity is simply the inevitable and natural trend of the time. This being so, modern men, though more active than those of the past, are still "each following his own nature," and in so doing are still conforming to non-activity. The same is true with regard to the respective functions of superior and inferior: each should "limit himself to what he himself is capable." As for the completely negative kind of "non-activity" ordinarily thought of when people use the term, this is definitely opposed in the *Chuang-tzŭ Commentary.*

Thus on the passage in the *Chuang-tzǔ* (chap. 9): "And more than half of the horses died" (p. 106), it says:

"A good driver must let (his horses) exercise to the fullest extent of their ability. The way to do so is to give them freedom. Some people, however, cause them to gallop, using them to an extent beyond their ability. The result is that they are exhausted so that most of them die. But if we let them go slowly or quickly according to whether one of them is a broken-down jade or another a speedy courser, then though we travel with them to the outer wastes of the world, the nature of each horse will be preserved intact. But hearing that freedom should be given to the natures of the horses, some people think they should be let loose and not driven at all. Hearing of the theory of non-activity, they think that sleeping is better than walking. Why do such people go so far astray? Do they not go far beyond Chuang Tzǔ's real meaning?" (4.15).

On the passage in the first chapter: "You, sir, give good order to the world, and the world is already in good order" (p. 6), the *Commentary* reads:

"As regards order issuing from disorder and activity emanating from non-activity, Yao himself was adequate. So what need was there for him to borrow from Hsu Yu?[1] It is because some people say that non-activity is reached only by folding one's hands in silence amidst the mountains and forests, that the teachings of Lao and Chuang are rejected by men of affairs. This is why these men feel compelled to keep to the sphere of activity and do not revert (to non-activity)" (1.12).

What people ordinarily have in mind when they quote the exhortation in the *Lao-tzǔ* (chap. 28): "Let us return to Unwrought Simplicity (*p'u*)," is likewise opposed by the *Chuang-tzǔ Commentary*. Thus on the passage in the fifteenth chapter: "The state of Unadornment (*su* 素) is that in which there is nothing mixed" (p. 194), we read:

"If by primitivity (*tun* 純) we mean the undistorted, then even a man capable of a hundred kinds of action and prepared for a myriad

---

[1] The passage in the *Chuang-tzǔ* to which this comment refers records an imaginary conversation between the sage-ruler Yao and a hermit, Hsü Yu, in which the former wished to hand over the rule of the world to the latter. The text points out, however, that since each of them was already performing the functions natural to himself, there was no need for them to exchange their positions. — Tr.

kinds of change may be of the utmost primitivity. If by unadornment (*su*) we mean the unmixed, then the form of the dragon or features of the phoenix, though surpassing in their beauty, are of the utmost unadornment. On the other hand, even the skin of a dog or a goat cannot be simple or unadorned if its natural qualities are mixed with foreign elements" (6.8).

Thus the simplicity and unadornment of anything have no relation with its complexity or beauty, but depend only upon the extent to which the latter are its "natural qualities," and are not "mixed with foreign elements." It is the foreignness, not the complexity, that makes a thing unnatural.

6—SAGE WISDOM

In the *Lao-tzŭ* (chap. 19) we read: "Banish wisdom, discard knowledge, and the people will be benefited a hundredfold." From what has already been said, it is evident that the *Chuang-tzŭ Commentary* does not oppose sage wisdom as such, but only the imitation of such wisdom. Thus under the passage in the *Chuang-tzŭ*'s ninth chapter: "But with the coming of the sages..." (p. 108), we read:

"The term 'sage' (popularly) refers to people who have the appearance of having fulfilled their nature, rather than to what it is that makes this appearance (a reality). ... Whenever such an *appearance* of sageliness shows itself, love and righteousness straightway lose their genuineness, and propriety and music depart from the nature, leaving only their superficial semblance behind. Whenever there is such a 'sage,' these are the faults that he has. This is something that cannot be helped" (4.17).

And on the passage in the thirteenth chapter: "The men of old, together with what they were unable to transmit, are dead..." (pp. 171-172), we read:

"The events of antiquity have already perished with that antiquity. Though attemps may be made to transmit them, who can cause them to happen again in the present? The past is not the present, and what happened today is already changing. Therefore we should give up the study (of the past), act according to our nature, and change with the times. This is the way to perfection" (5.56).

Sage wisdom is really sage wisdom when it accords with what is natural; only then do its "dragon form and phoenix features" have "the utmost unadornment." By consciously trying to imitate it, we succeed only in acquiring its "superficial semblance." This "semblance" is that of something that has already passed away, and hence is useless for the present day. The moral is that it is wrong to try to imitate the sages.

On the passage in the *Chuang-tzŭ* (chap. 10): "Tseng, Shih, Mo, the music master K'uang, Kung Ch'ui, and Li Chu..." [1] (p. 116), the *Commentary* says:

"The endowments of these men were many-sided, for which reason they caused the whole world to leap to imitate them. But imitation leads to loss of individuality, and when individuality is lost through (imitation of) something else, that something else becomes the creator of disorder. The great disaster in the world is the loss of individuality" (4.29).

Again on the passage in the same chapter: "Confuse the six pitch-pipes..." (p. 115):

"For sounds and colors there were (the music master) K'uang and Li (Chu). They were esteemed by everyone having ears and eyes. But the nature of everything has its limit, and if one is led by what offers inducement to go beyond it, then this nature will be lost. One should disregard the inducement and live according to one's own self, not according to others. Then the senses will remain intact and each man will preserve what is genuine in him" (*ibid.*, p. 28).

And yet again on the passage (chap. 10): "Therefore it is said that great skill looks like clumsiness" (p. 115):

"Just as the spider and scarab, despite their humble surroundings, can spread their net or roll their ball without seeking the aid of any artisan, so for all creatures, each has that in which it is skilled. Although their skills differ, they themselves are alike in that they all practice these skills. This, then, is the kind of 'skill that looks like clumsiness.' Therefore the talented employer of men uses those who are skilled in squares to make squares, and those who are skilled in circles to make circles, allowing each to perform his particular skill, and thus to act in accordance with his nature. He does not demand from his people as a whole the skill of a Kung Ch'ui. That

---

[1] All men who were famed for special abilities of one kind or another. Tseng was the disciple of Confucius, Tseng Tzŭ. Shih was Shih Ch'iu, an historian of the state of Wei of the sixth century B.C., acclaimed by Confucius for his honesty. See *Analects*, XV, 6. Yang was Yang Chu and Mo was Mo Ti. The music master K'uang was noted as a musician of the sixth century B.C., Kung Ch'ui as an artisan who could draw a perfect circle with his unaided hand, and Li Chu (also known as Li Lou) for his extraordinary eyesight. — Tr.

is why, being different from one another, their multitude of separate skills seem like clumsiness. Yet because everyone in the world has his own particular skill, the result seems like great skill. By the use of these innate skills, the compass and measuring-square may be discarded and the fingers of the 'marvelous artisan' (Kung Ch'ui) may be cut off (dispensed with)" (*ibid.*).

Every man has his own particular nature and particular skill, and the essence of sage wisdom lies simply in following this nature and developing this skill. If, however, a man casts his own skill aside and foolishly tries to study how to be a wise sage, the result is to lose his own nature. The famous T'ang poet Li Po, for example, was born a Li Po and could not be otherwise. But if, lacking the "nature" of a Li Po, a man nevertheless strives to be one, he not only is sure to fail, but in the attempt must lose his own original abilities. The sole compensation will be that he becomes a second rate versifier. True wisdom consists simply in developing one's own ability. That is why the proper way to employ men is to "allow each to perform his particular skill." The one important principle to keep in mind is that those who lack the qualifications of the sage should not lose their individuality in straining to be one; they should simply follow their own nature. The statement in the *Commentary*: "The compass and measuring-square may be discarded and the fingers of the 'marvelous artisan' may be cut off," refers to the passage in the *Chuang-tzŭ* (chap. 10): "Discard the compass and measuring-square and throw away the fingers of Kung Ch'ui" (p. 115). It very definitely does not, however, mean that only persons other than Kung Ch'ui should be left free to follow their capabilities, and that Kung Ch'ui himself should be prevented from doing so.

On the passage in the *Chuang-tzŭ* (chap. 3): "There is a limit to our life, but to knowledge there is no limit" (p. 33), the *Commentary* reads:

"If, irrespective of whether we lift something heavy or hold something light, our spirit remains content, this is because (we realize that every) strength has its limits. But if, because of regard for fame and liking for supremacy, we redouble our efforts and yet remain dissatisfied, this is because our knowledge has no limits. That is why the term 'knowledge' is born out of failure to hold to what is suited to oneself. It disappears when one fully accepts one's limitations. To accept one's limitations means to conform freely to one's allotted capacity, without attempting anything beyond. In this way, though called upon to carry a load of a myriad stone, we still remain calmly oblivious to its weight as long as it conforms with our capabilities; though called upon to respond to a myriad stimuli, we still remain serenely unconscious of the impact of events upon ourselves. This, then, is the principle for nourishing life" (2.1).

And on the passage in the second chapter: "These five are round yet tend to become square" (p. 25), the *Commentary* says:

"These five all allowed what was proper to them to be injured by self-assertion. There are persons who can never remain content with their own nature, but always seek for something beyond. To seek outside oneself for what is unseekable is to be like a circle that essays to be a square, or a fish that hankers to be a bird. The one may hope to have the wings of a phoenix, or the other decide to be round like the sun or moon, yet the nearer they get to their goal, the farther off it is. The more knowledge they gain, the more nature they lose. Therefore the equality of things means the dispersion of the bonds of one-sidedness and over-emphasis" (1.49).

It may be seen that the *Commentary* does not insist that those capable of "carrying a load of a myriad stone" should carry only ten stone instead, or those capable of being phoenixes should change themselves into sparrows. The one essential is that phoenix and swallow alike should "remain content with their own nature," and not try to "seek for something beyond"; they should "conform freely to their allotted capacity," and not "attempt anything beyond." "The term 'knowledge' is born out of failure to hold to what is suited to oneself"; true wisdom always consists in staying within "one's allotted capacity." Geniuses act as they do because they cannot act otherwise; such action is in their case really nothing more than "non-activity." Knowledge naturally gained in this way, no matter how great, is different from "knowledge" in the popular sense of something acquired through effort. On the other hand, any knowledge derived through effort and deliberate self-assertion does constitute this inferior kind of so-called "knowledge," no matter how small it may be.

On the passage in the *Chuang-tzŭ* (chap. 4): "Happiness is lighter than a feather, but no one knows (how to carry it)..." (p. 55), we read in the *Commentary*:

"The feet can walk; let them walk. The hands can hold; let them hold. Hear what is heard by the ears; see what is seen by the eyes. Let your knowledge stop at what you do not know; let your ability stop at what you cannot do. Use what is naturally useful; do what you spontaneously can do. Act freely within the limit of your nature, but have nothing to do with what is beyond it. In this way the principle of non-activity becomes supremely easy. When you follow non-activity, your life cannot but be perfect. Perfection of life unaccompanied by happiness is unheard of. Happiness lies in what we thus call perfection. Aside from this it needs nothing else, not even the additional weight of a swan's feather.

"Act in accordance with one's nature and without exceeding one's own lot. This will be found to be the easiest thing under Heaven. Lift what one oneself should lift. Carry what one oneself should carry. Then it will be found to be the lightest thing under Heaven. ... Lift what is within one's nature, and though it be the burden of a myriad stone, its weight will not be felt. But assume anything additional, and though its weight be less than a hair, you will be unable to endure it. Happiness lies within, and therefore is extremely light. Calamity comes from without, and therefore is extremely heavy. To undergo the extreme weight of calamity without knowing how to avoid it: this is the great delusion of the world" (2.39).

To "act freely within the limit of your nature" is to practice non-activity, whereas to disregard the precept: "Have nothing to do with what lies beyond it," is to practice self-assertion. When the *Commentary* tells us: "The feet can walk; let them walk," etc., it is not opposing sage wisdom, for the abilities of the feet, hands, ears, eyes, and mind naturally differ from one individual to another. Sage wisdom is such of itself, and what the *Commentary* means to say is simply that individuals who lack the qualifications of the sage should not try to be an imitation of one. For by so doing they "lose the extremely easy principle of non-activity, and practice the extremely difficult one of self-assertion" (*ibid.*). The result is sure to be disastrous.

On the passage in the *Chuang-tzŭ* (chap. 5): "*Tao* gives him the appearance, and nature gives him the form" (p. 67), the *Commentary* tells us:

"Man's life does not result from his conscious desire to have it, nor is the knowledge gained by him in life the result of his conscious desire to know. Therefore those who consciously desire to be a Li (Chu) or a (music master) K'uang are unable to be so, whereas Li and K'uang themselves possess their special gifts without any conscious desire on their part. (Likewise) those who consciously desire to become worthies and sages are unable to be so, whereas the worthies and sages themselves are what they are without any conscious desire on their part. But it is not only the worthies and sages who are irrevocably remote, nor Li and K'uang to whom it is difficult to aspire. To be stupid, deaf, or blind, or to crow like a rooster or bark like a dog—even this will we find ourselves incapable of, if it is our conscious desire to be and do such" (2.62).

Man's life is not given to him because of a conscious desire to live, nor are his knowledge and abilities acquired through conscious study and practice. The ordinary man cannot try to be a genius any more than the genius can try to be an ordinary man. The case is like that of a dog and man: the dog cannot try to be a man, any more than a man can try to be a dog.

7—"THE HAPPY EXCURSION"

The sage is inevitably destined for greatness, just as the man-in-the-street is destined for ordinariness. The case is like that of the large *p'eng* bird and the young dove spoken of in "The Happy Excursion" (the name of the first chapter in the *Chuang-tzŭ*): they cannot be otherwise than large and small respectively. On the words near the beginning of this chapter: "When this bird moves itself in the sea, it is preparing to start for the Southern Ocean" (p. 1), we read in the *Commentary*:

"It (the *p'eng*) cannot move itself, unless in the ocean. The air cannot bear its wings, unless it reaches a height of 90,000 *li*. It does not do this out of any liking to be unusual, but simply because it is inevitable that large things are produced in large places, and equally inevitable that large places produce such large things. Reason makes it naturally thus. There need be no fear of mistake, nor is there room for conscious purpose" (1.2).

Again on the sentence in the same chapter: "Then it ascends on a whirlwind to a height of 90,000 *li*" (p. 1), we read:

"Since the wings are large, they are difficult to move. That is why it must mount upon a whirlwind in order to get up, and must rise 90,000 *li* in order to support itself. Having such wings, how could it suddenly get itself up and down within a space of only several tens of feet? This is a matter of necessity and not of its own pleasure" (*ibid.*).

Or again on the words: "What do these two creatures know?"

(pp. 2-3): " 'These two creatures' refers to the *p'eng* and cicada. [1] Their different inclinations result from the difference between large and small. But are these differing inclinations the result of conscious knowledge? In the case of both, they are naturally the way they are without being conscious of why they are thus. They are naturally so and do not try to be so. This is the general meaning of the 'happy excursion' " (*ibid.*, p. 5).

It is as inevitable that the movements of the great *p'eng* should be large, as that those of the little bird should be small. In each case "reason makes it naturally thus." This, indeed, is as true of the differences in the human world as in those of nature. It was equally inevitable, for example, that Alexander the Great should be a great conquerer as that Plato should write his *Dialogues*. In both cases these men were simply following their own natures.

Thus despite the differences between different things, all are happy if each but follow its own nature. On the passage in "The Happy Excursion": "Then it goes on a flight of six months' duration" (p. 1), the *Commentary* says:

"The large bird flies with a duration of half a year and stops at the Celestial Lake. The small bird flies with a duration of half a morning and stops after it reaches the trees. If we compare their ability, there is indeed a difference. But in both following their own natures, they are the same" (*ibid.*, p. 2).

Again on the passage: "If the water lacks sufficient depth..." (p. 2): "This all shows that the fact that the *p'eng* must fly at such a height is because of the largeness of its wings. What the small needs is not the great; what the great needs cannot be the small. Therefore reason has its fittest course; things have their proper limitation. Each thing is capable of doing something; they can all equally succeed. If we miss the fundamental principle of forgetting life, and struggle for what is beyond the most proper, neither acting in accordance with our natural strength nor moving in accordance with our genuine feeling, we will surely get into trouble, regardless of whether we have wings which becloud the sky, or simply make sudden bursts of flight" (*ibid.*, p. 3).

Again on the words: "A cicada and a young dove laughed at it (the *p'eng*), saying..." (p. 2): "If there be satisfaction for their nature,

---

[1] In the text the cicada is described as laughing at the *p'eng* for its exertions. — Tr.

the great *p'eng* has nothing to be proud of in comparison with the small bird, and the small bird has no desire for the Celestial Lake. There is more than enough to honor the desires of both. Therefore, though there be a difference between the great and the small, their happiness is the same" (*ibid.*, p. 4).

And finally on the passage: "P'eng Tsu (the Chinese Methuselah) was the one especially renowned until the present day for his long life" (p. 3), the *Commentary* says: "Such are the differences regarding age and knowledge. If there be anything to be regretted by people, this is certainly it. Yet the fact that they do not regret it is because the nature of each has its proper limitations. Once we know these limitations, and that beyond them there is nothing to be striven for, how can there be any cause for regret in the world? Things, when great, usually do not crave to be small, but, when small, almost surely long to be great. Therefore (Chuang Tzŭ) showed the proper limitations of the great and the small, and that they cannot be attained to by any mere longing or craving. In this way the bonds of longing and craving may be broken. Regret springs from these bonds; hence when the bonds are broken, the regret is dissipated. Never is there a case in which dissipation of this regret does not give peace to one's nature" (*ibid.*, p. 6).

In the natures of all things there is what is "most proper," to exceed which in longing and craving leads only to "bonds" and "regret." Such is the source of all human suffering.

8—"The Equality of Things"

Human misery, however, arises precisely because of men's inability to remain at peace with their own natures and cast off "the bonds of craving and longing." The small hopes to become great, the lowly to become eminent, the stupid to become wise. They "neither act in accordance with their natural strength nor move in accordance with their genuine feeling." This means that they are "sure to get into trouble, regardless of whether they have wings which becloud the sky, or simply make sudden bursts of flight." The best way to enable men to escape the "bonds of craving and longing" is to make them understand the meaning of what the *Chuang-tzŭ*, as the title of its second chapter, calls "The Equality of Things." On the passage in this chapter: "You may have heard the music of man, but not the music of earth ..." (p. 12), the *Commentary* says:

"The flutes and pipes may differ in length; their notes may belong to different scales. Hence their resulting sounds may differ in innumerable ways, some being short, some long, some high, some low. But despite these myriad differences, their endowment conforms in every case to a single standard, so that there is no question of superiority or inferiority between them" (1.23).

Again on the passage in the same chapter: "These come like music sounding from an empty tube, or mushrooms springing out of steamy warmth" (p. 14), we read in the *Commentary*:

"All things are what they are, without knowing why and how they are. Hence though different in their forms, they are the same in being what they are" (*ibid.*, p. 28).

This is true of the natural and human worlds alike, despite the infinite variations of things. Although a man and a dog admittedly differ from one another, they are the same in being man and dog respectively. Why, then, should we ascribe "superiority" to the one and "inferiority" to the other? Once we recognize this principle, such qualitative differences become equalized.

On the words in the same chapter: "This being so, are they all servants?" (p. 15), we read:

"Error arises when one has the qualities of a servant but is not satisfied to perform a servant's duties. Hence we may know that (the relative positions of) ruler and subject, superior and inferior, hand and foot, external and internal, conform to a natural principle of Heaven and are not really caused by man .... Let the servants simply accept their own lot and assist each other without dissatisfaction. Let them assist each other like the hand and foot, the ear and eye, the four limbs, and the hundred other parts of the body, each having its own particular duty and at the same time each acting on behalf of the others.... Let those whom the age accounts worthy be the rulers, and those whose talents do not meet the requirements of the world be the subjects, just as Heaven is naturally high, Earth naturally low, the head naturally rests above, and the feet naturally lie below.... Although there is no (conscious) arrangement of them according to what is proper, the result is inevitably proper" (*ibid.*, pp. 23-30).

That the more talented should be rulers and the less talented subjects is "a natural principle of Heaven." Though each "has its own particular duty," they at the same time function on behalf of one another. Once we recognize this principle, the differences between eminence and lowliness become equalized.

On the passage: "The universe is a finger; all things are a horse" (p. 19), we read: "To regard the self as right and the other as wrong is the constant tendency of the self and others. . . . But in order to show that there is no distinction between right and wrong, there is nothing better than illustrating one thing by another. In illustrating one thing by another, we see that others and the self all agree in considering themselves to be right and the others wrong. Since they all agree in considering the others wrong, there can be no right in the world. But since they all agree that they themselves are right, there can be no wrong in the world. How can it be shown that this is so? If the right is really right, there should be nothing in the world that considers it wrong. But if the wrong is really wrong, there should also be nothing in the world that considers it right. The fact that there is no fixed guide as to right and wrong, but only confusion between them, shows that these distinctions arise because of the partiality with which each believes in its own point of view, and that (behind these seeming differences) they are (really) in agreement. Whether we look high or low, this is true everywhere. That is why the Perfect Man, knowing that the universe is but a finger and all things are a horse, thus rests in great peace. The universe and all things in it function according to their nature. They all enjoy themselves. There is no such thing as right or wrong" (*ibid.*, p. 37).

Once we recognize this principle, the differences between right and wrong become equalized.

On the passage in the same chapter: "In all the world there is nothing greater than the tip of an autumn hair; Mount T'ai is small" (p. 23), we read:

"If we compare their forms, Mount T'ai is indeed larger than an autumn hair. But if things each conform to their own nature and fully accept their limitations, then even what is large has no superfluity and what is small suffers no inadequacy. Being satisfied with their natures, the autumn hair does not single out its own smallness as smallness, nor does Mount T'ai single out its own largeness as largeness. If adequacy in one's nature be called great, there is nothing more adequate in the world than the autumn hair. If adequacy in one's nature be not called great, even Mount T'ai may be accounted small.

This is why it is said: 'In all the world there is nothing greater than the tip of an autumn hair; Mount T'ai is small.'

"If Mount T'ai is small, there is nothing great under Heaven; if the autumn hair is large, there is nothing small under Heaven. There is no smallness, no greatness, no long life, no premature death. This is why the chrysalis does not hanker to be the great *ch'un* tree, but is joyously happy within itself; nor does the quail set value upon the Celestial Lake, but finds enough to satisfy its desires. [1] Once there is satisfaction with the natural, and a calm acceptance of one's nature, even Heaven and Earth cannot be considered as long lived, but came into being with me together; all things cannot be accounted different, but are one with myself. [2] How, then, should Heaven and Earth not be equal, or all things not one?" (*ibid.*, pp. 45-46).

Once we recognize this principle, then greatness and smallness, long life and premature death, become equalized.

Again on the passage: "The 'that' and the 'this' produce one another" (p. 18), we read: "The changes of life and death are like the sequence of the four seasons: spring and autumn, winter and summer. Therefore life and death, though different in aspect, are one inasmuch as each represents the calm acceptance of what occurs. What is alive considers life as life, but what is dead may consider life as death. Thus there is no such thing as 'life.' What is alive considers death as death, but what is dead may consider death as life. Thus there is no such thing as 'death.' There is no death, no life; nothing possible and nothing impossible..." (*ibid.*, p. 35).

And on the passage: "This is a case of what is called the transformation of things" (p. 32): "Time stops not even for a moment. What is here now cannot subsequently be preserved. Therefore yesterday's dream is already transformed today. But wherein do the changes of life and death differ from this? Why, then, should we torment our minds about them?" (*ibid.*, p. 65).

On the passage in the sixth chapter: "What incomparable bliss is this!" (p. 75), the *Commentary* says: "When what is not human becomes transformed into a man, it in so doing loses its original

---

[1] These are allusions to the *Chuang-tzŭ* (chap. 1, pp. 3-4), where the chrysalis which knows not the alternation of spring and autumn is compared with the great *ch'un* tree, each of whose springs and autumns has a duration of 8,000 years, and where the quail is compared with the great *p'eng* bird. — Tr.

[2] This sentence is an allusion to the statement in the *Chuang-tzŭ* (chap. 2, p. 23). — Tr.

state. Though it loses its original state, it is joyful—joyful with whatever it meets. Since the process of changs is inexhaustible, what is there that will not eventually be met with? To be happy with anything one meets: is this not the height of bliss?" (3.13).

Once we recognize this principle, life and death become equalized.

Again on the passage in the second chapter: "These three men are still living (primitively) among the mugwort and brushwood..." (p. 26), we read:

"That in which men find satisfaction is no longer sordid to them. Thus even mugwort and brushwood become marvelous habitations for these three men.... If one wishes to tear them away from their desire for the mugwort and brushwood, and to force them to follow one's own self, can this agree with the greatness of the supreme *Tao*? This is the reason why there is unhappiness. Let everything enjoy its own nature and have its own satisfaction. No matter whether far, near, or deeply hidden, leave them alone, each in its own proper sphere. Then they are all content and we too are happy" (1.51).

That in which all things "find satisfaction" is the enjoyment of following their own way. Once they enjoy this, their surroundings become "no longer sordid." Let the savage be content with his mugwort and brushwood, and these thereupon become his "marvelous habitation." Therefore the right thing to do is to "leave him alone," and not to "force him to follow one's own self." Once we recognize this principle, wisdom and stupidity, culture and barbarism, become equalized.

By understanding that all things are equal and that life and death belong to a single sequence, we free ourselves from self-assertion and egoism. On the passage in the second chapter: "Therefore what the sage aims at is the light out of darkness ..." (p. 22), the *Commentary* reads:

"The sage is one who has no ego. Therefore he aims to dwell in the light out of darkness. Greatness, wickedness, perverseness, and strangeness, he penetrates and unifies. He allows the host of diverse things each to have its own satisfaction, and the multitude of men not to lose that which each finds agreeable. He, as a result, is not used by things, but the uses of all things are fully employed. When all things function of themselves, who is right and who is wrong? Therefore though the changes may be widespread and the differences startling, if one circuitously complies with them and allows them to function of themselves, their functions, though myriad in their difference, will become clear of themselves in an ordinary way" (*ibid.*, p. 43).

And on the passage: "He blends together ten thousand years and stops at the one, the whole, the simple" (p. 29), we read: "It is only the great sage who does not assert himself, and hence is simple and straightforward in his conduct, making himself one with every change. Making himself one with every change, he makes excursion in the One. Therefore though he blends together a hundred thousand ages, a thousand distinctions, and ten thousand variations, yet 'the *Tao* evolves and achievements result,' and then there are achievements from antiquity to today; 'things have names and are what they are,' and then all things agree in being what they are. [1] That there is no thing that is not what it is, and no age that does not have achievements: this is what is meant by simplicity.... Extended to all ages, all ages agree in being what they are; extended to all things, all things agree in being what they are. Therefore he (the sage) neither knows what comes first and what afterward, as between life and death, nor what is superior and what inferior, as between the 'other' and the 'self' " (*ibid.*, p. 57).

In this way the sage forgets the distinctions between life and death, the self and others, right and wrong. In the *Chuang-tzŭ*'s second chapter we read: "Let us forget life. Let us forget moral distinctions. Let us find enjoyment in the realm of the infinite and stop there" (p. 31). To which the *Commentary* adds:

"By forgetting life we mysteriously equate life and death. By forgetting moral distinctions we link together right and wrong. The right and wrong, life and death, thus become one: this is the supreme principle. This supreme principle leads onward to what is without limits, and therefore he who rests in it can likewise never reach an end" (*ibid.*, p. 62).

By the time one reaches this stage, all distinctions are already forgotten, and one is no longer restricted to a mere "knowing" of the principle of "the equality of things."

9—"THE PERFECT MAN"

He who reaches this mystic state is known as the "Perfect Man" (*chih jen* 至 人), the sage, or the "man who depends on nothing

---

[1] These quotations are taken from the *Chuang-tzŭ* (chap. 2, p. 19). — Tr.

else." On the passage in the *Chuang-tzŭ* (chap. 1): "Small knowledge is not to be compared with great knowledge ..." (p. 3), the *Commentary* says:

"Everything has its own nature. Every nature has its own limitation. (Their differences) are all like those of age or knowledge, which cannot possibly be compared. From here onward, until he reaches Lieh Tzŭ, [1] (Chuang Tzŭ) cites successive examples of differences in age and knowledge, (showing how) each believes in its own sphere, yet none is really able to surpass the others. After that he finally concludes with the man who is completely independent of everything, [2] who forgets his own self and others alike, and who ignores all these multitudinous differences. They (i.e., things in general) enjoy themselves in different spheres, but he (the independent man) has neither achievement nor name.

"Therefore for him who unites the small with the great, there is no longer any distinction between small and great. But as long as this distinction remains, the great *p'eng* bird, as compared with the quail, or the minor official, as compared with him who rides the wind, are equally encumbered by things. For him, however, who equalizes life and death, there is no longer any distinction between life and death. As long as this distinction remains, even the great *ch'un* tree, as compared with the chrysalis, or P'eng Tsu, as compared with the morning mushroom, equally suffer an early death. Therefore he who makes excursion into the realm of non-distinction between small and great, is himself without limitation. He who ignores the distinctions between life and death, himself has no terminal. But those whose happiness is attached within the finite sphere, even when left free to roam as they will, still suffer from certain limitations. They are not able to be completely independent" (1.5-6).

A thing may be able to "conform to its own nature." [3] Even so, however, as long as it remains ignorant of the equality of all things, and thereby incapable of "mysteriously equating life and death" and "linking together right and wrong," [4] it will, while finding

---

[1] Who, in the text that follows in the *Chuang-tzŭ*, is described as being able to ride on the wind. — Tr.

[2] And who therefore transcends Lieh Tzŭ, for the latter, though he could ride on the wind, was still dependent on that wind for his movement, and therefore for his happiness. — Tr.

[3] See above, p. 228. — Tr.

[4] See above, p. 231. — Tr.

satisfaction with one thing, still remain dissatisfied with something else. Though it find happiness in life, it will not necessarily find happiness in death. Though it find peace in what it gains, it will not necessarily find peace in what it loses. This is what happens to "those whose happiness is attached within the finite sphere." Their happiness remains limited, because it is contingent on certain prerequisites, without which it cannot be fulfilled. That is why, "even when left free to roam as they will, they still suffer from certain limitations."

Such, however, is not the case with the "man who depends on nothing else." On the passage in the first chapter: "But suppose there is one who chariots upon the normality of the universe and rides upon the transformations of the six elements" (p. 5), the *Commentary* reads:

"The universe is the general name of all things. The universe has all things as its substance, and the norm of all things must be the natural. What is naturally so, and not made to be so, is the natural. Thus the capacity of the great *p'eng* to fly high, of the quail to fly low, of the *ch'un* tree to live long, and of the morning mushroom to live short, are all natural capacities and not consciously made. They are not made to be so, but are naturally so; thus they are normal. Therefore, 'to chariot upon the normality of the universe' is to follow the nature of all things. 'To ride upon the transformations of the six elements' is to make excursion along the road of change and evolution. By proceeding in this way, how can one ever reach the end? By charioting on whatever one meets, what will one still be dependent on? Such is the happiness of the Perfect Man who mysteriously equates all others with the self" (*ibid.*, p. 10).

Again, on the passage in the sixth chapter: "If you hide the universe in the universe, there will be no room for it to be lost" (p. 75), the *Commentary* says:

"He who has nothing to hide but allows all to take its free course, thereby becomes merged with all things and is one with all transformations. Therefore for him there is no longer the internal or external, life or death. He is identified with the universe and fused with its evolutions. Though he may search for a place in which to be lost, he will not find it. Such is the great quality of eternal existence; it is not a tortuous individualized kind of petty concept" (3.13).

The Perfect Man, by forgetting all distinctions and "becoming merged with all things," is thereby able to be "identified with the universe and fused with its evolutions." Since these evolutions continue inexhaustibly, he himself likewise continues inexhaustibly. [1]

To be such a Perfect Man, however, entails more than merely "folding one's hands in silence amidst the mountains and forests." [2] Herein the *Commentary* differs from the *Chuang-tzŭ*, in the first chapter of which, for example, such hermits as Hsü Yu are praised, while the sage-rulers Yao and Shun are deprecated. Thus when Yao is described as wanting to resign as ruler of the empire in favor of Hsü Yu, the latter is made to reply: "You, sir, return and be quiet. I have no need of the empire" (p. 6). Likewise it says: "Even the dust and refuse, the chaff and husks (of the spirit man), could form a Yao and Shun" (p. 8). Or again: "Yao ruled the people of the empire and maintained perfect government within the seas. But having paid a visit to the four wise men of the Miao-ku-yi mountain, he returned to the south of the Fen river and silently forgot his empire" (*ibid.*). Hsü Yu and the other hermits were men who wandered outside the world, whereas Yao and Shun were men who kept within it. On the third of these passages, however, the *Commentary* gives a new and completely opposite interpretation, in which it praises Yao and Shun and deprecates Hsü Yu:

"Those who live in accordance with themselves stand in contrast to things; those who accord with things do not stand in contrast to them. Therefore there was nothing in the empire with which Yao stood in contrast, whereas Hsü Yu was on a level with Chi and Hsieh (two ministers of that time). How do I come to say that this is so? In the case of those who are merged with things, the result is that all the different kinds of things cannot divorce themselves from them. Hence, with no deliberate mind they make a profound response to them; submitting themselves to the stimulus from them, they drift like an unmoored boat, floating hither and thither with no self-volition. Therefore there is nothing they do which is not in accord with the people, no place to which they go where they are not sovereign over all. Being sovereign in this way, they are of themselves as exalted as Heaven. This indeed is the virtue of the true sovereign. But suppose a man stands in solitude, above all others, on some high mountain peak. How can he make himself exclusive in this way unless it be to preserve the one-sided predi-

---

[1] From here to the end of the chapter the text has been revised so as to agree with what appears in Fung Yu-lan's *Spirit of Chinese Philosophy* (translated by E. R. Hughes), pp. 144-146. — Tr.

[2] See above, p. 218. — Tr.

lections of himself or of some one particular school? Such a man is certainly nothing more than just one thing among the ordinary ruck of things; he is merely one of Yao's outer ministers" (1.12).

In other words, the fact that each individual thing customarily holds to its own predilections means that each stands in contrast to all the others. Not so, however, with the man who conforms to things: he thereby "reaches the center of the circle," [1] wherein he no longer keeps any personal predilections. To say that he conforms to all things really means that he transcends them all, thereby reaching a position in which he no longer stands in contrast to things. In this way he is no longer a mere "thing among the ordinary ruck of things," nor does he stand in contrast to anything else in the world. To all the innumerable changes of each day, he responds without any deliberate mind. In short, "though he reacts to things, he is not ensnared by them." [2]

On the passage in the first chapter: "There lived a spirit man ... whose manner was elegant and graceful like that of a maiden" (p. 7), the *Commentary* reads:

"The sage, even when occupying the highest place at court, is mentally no different from the way he is when amidst the mountains and forests. How then can he be understood by the world? When it only sees him occupying the imperial chariot and wearing the imperial seal, it then says that this is enough to trammel his mind. When it sees him traversing mountains and rivers and participating in the affairs of the people, it then says that this is enough to weary his spirit. How can it know that the man who is perfect in perfection cannot suffer any loss?" (*ibid.*, p. 14).

He does not suffer any loss because he responds to the world, but is not trammeled by it; he responds to all things, but is not ensnared by things.

Though the sphere of the sage is so exalted, his actions may be completely ordinary. Apropos of the already quoted passage in which Yao visited the four holy men, the *Commentary* says: "He whose footsteps carry him furthest, by following them comes closer and closer (to men and things); he who reaches the highest point, reverts to what is below" (*ibid.*, p. 18). Again: "He who ardently reaches for a position of solitary eminence, and does not put himself on an

---

[1] *Chuang-tzŭ* (chap. 2, p. 18). — Tr.
[2] A doctrine of Wang Pi. See chap. 5, p. 188. — Tr.

equality with the ordinary run of men, is a hermit of the mountains and vales, but not one who is unconditioned" (*ibid.*). And we have already read the passage (at the end of sect. 5): "It is because some people say that non-activity (*wu wei*) is reached only by folding one's hands in silence amidst the mountains and forests, that the teachings of Lao and Chuang are rejected by men of affairs. This is why these men feel compelled to keep to the sphere of activity and do not revert (to non-activity)" (*ibid.*, p. 12).

According to this new interpretation, therefore, there is no longer any distinction, for the sage, between being outside or within the world. This idea is further developed in commenting on the words in the sixth chapter: "They travel outside the world; ... I travel within it" (p. 84):

"When principle is carried to its highest point, the without and the within become mutually merged. There is no one who, wandering in the without to the highest point of perfection, does not remain merged with what is within. Nor is there anyone who, able to remain merged with what is within, cannot wander in the without. Therefore the sage constantly wanders in the without in order to enlarge what is within. He voids himself of a deliberate mind in order to conform to all existence. Therefore though he works his body the livelong day, his essential spirit is not affected. Though he directs his gaze at every kind of activity, he himself equably remains just what he is" (3.27).

He who can really wander in the without must also merge himself with the within, and he who can really merge with the within must also wander in the without. The sage has no deliberate or assertive mind while conforming with all existence. Lacking such a mind, he becomes merged with the within; conforming with all existence, he therefore wanders in the without. This, we are told, is "the main idea in the writings" of Chuang Tzŭ. Let us but understand it, and "then the way of wandering in the without and extending the sphere of the within becomes self evident. Thus the purpose of Chuang Tzŭ's book is to teach us how to ferry over to the ordinary and encompass the existing world" (*ibid.*). In these words we see how Hsiang Hsiu and Kuo Hsiang strove to remake the philosophy of early Taoism, with its stress on the solitary and contemplative life, into a new philosophy of this world and of the ordinary beings in it. In this important aspect they come closer to Confucian doctrine than did the original Taoists.

CHAPTER VII

BUDDHISM AND ITS CRITICS DURING THE PERIOD OF DISUNITY

Translator's Note: With Buddhism, to which this and the two following chapters are devoted, we reach a world of ideas very different
from traditional Chinese thought, and one with a highly specialized
terminology. The following summary of some of its basic concepts may
be useful at this point:

(1) From traditional Hindu thought Buddhism accepts the theory
of reincarnation. The deeds or *karma* of each sentient being in successive
past existences determine what he is to be in existences still to come.
These rebirths take place on several different levels: that of the beings
in the various hells, of animals, of human beings, of the divine beings in
the various heavens, etc. In their totality they constitute the wheel of life
and death.

(2) There has been no single act of divine creation that has produced
the stream of existence. It simply is, and always has been, what it is. Even
the gods in the Buddhist heavens are attached to the wheel of life and
death and are not its creators. Thus the wheel is permanent and unchanging
in the sense that it goes on eternally. It is impermanent and changing,
however, in the sense that everything in it is in a state of flux. This means
that phenomenal "existence," as commonly perceived by the senses, is
illusory; it is not real inasmuch as, though it exists, its existence is not
permanent or absolute. Nothing belonging to it has an enduring entity or
"nature" of its own; everything is dependent upon a combination of
fluctuating conditions and factors for its seeming "existence" at any given
moment. This is the Buddhist theory of causation.

(3) It is a characteristic of human thinking that it abhors the impermanent and desires the permanent. Expressed in Buddhist terms, this
takes the form of escaping from the inexorable and ever-continuing wheel
of life and death, and gaining union with the ultimate unchanging reality
which lies behind phenomenal existence. "All life is suffering." Such escape,
however, can only be achieved by preventing the continued operation of
the effects of previous *karma*, that is, by breaking the chain of causation.
The resulting state of oneness with reality is that of *Nirvāṇa*, and the
Buddhas (lit., "enlightened ones") are those beings who belong to this
state. The historical Gautama Buddha is only one of many such enlightened
beings. The other Buddhas, as they came to be developed in the Buddhist
religion, represent personifications for the popular mind of various aspects
of reality. Thus the Buddhas are not gods or divine creators, for by transcending the wheel of life and death they also infinitely transcend the gods

of the Buddhist heavens who, though possessing supernatural powers, still belong to that wheel.

(4) Escape or salvation is to be gained through enlightenment. In part it consists in the acquisition of religious merit through good deeds, but more important is a transcendent understanding or perception which can peer through the veil of illusion and see the reality behind. When this perception arises, the ties of false sensory discrimination and of the passions (greed, envy, etc.) are broken, so that we are no longer carried along in the stream of phenomenal existence. Enlightenment, however, is more than a mere intellectual realization of the falseness of the universe as ordinarily perceived; to be genuine, it must consist of the intuitive experiencing of Truth with one's whole being—an act through which the experiencer becomes merged with that Truth.

These are some of the general tenets underlying Buddhism, in the elaboration of which, however, infinite variations exist within the individual schools. Among the latter, the two main groups are those of the Hīnayāna or "Lesser Vehicle" and the Mahāyāna or "Greater Vehicle." (These terms, of course, are of Mahāyānist and not Hīnayānist origin.) Hīnayāna Buddhism, which is closer to the tenets of original Buddhism, has to this day remained dominant among the Buddhist countries of Southeast Asia. Mahāyāna Buddhism, which is an enormously elaborated and sophisticated development of primitive Buddhism, received its chief growth in the countries north and northeast of India: Central Asia, China, and Japan, especially China. We shall see in the following chapters the complexity of its psychological and metaphysical doctrines, with their variations of the theory that the world as we see it is a product of the mind.

Among the many differences between the two groups, we need here cite only two: (1) In Hīnayāna Buddhism salvation is a personal matter; the individual concerned must work out his own salvation and can do little to help others to achieve theirs. In Mahāyāna Buddhism, on the contrary, the concept of the Bodhisattva is prominent. This is the being who seeks Buddhahood but seeks it altruistically; he wants enlightenment, but wants it to enlighten others; he willingly sacrifices himself for these others, and therefore, even after enlightenment, voluntarily remains within the wheel of life and death. (2) Because of this distinction, *Nirvāṇa*, for the Mahāyānist, loses its original meaning of extinction and simply designates the state of the enlightened being. Such a being continues to live in this world, where he works for the salvation of sentient beings but, because of his enlightenment, he has no attachments and therefore no *karma*. He is in the wheel of life and death, yet is immune to its effects. These distinctions between Mahāyāna and Hīnayāna doctrine perhaps in part reflect the differences between the "this-worldliness" of Chinese thought and "other-worldliness" of that of India.

To designate the realms of the phenomenal and the real, the Chinese use such terms as "being" or "existent" (*yu* 有), "non-being" or "non-existent" (*wu* 無), "voidness" or "void" (*hsü* 虛), "illusion" or "illusory" (*huan* 幻), "emptiness" or "empty" (*k'ung* 空), "reality" or "real" (*shih* 實), etc. Some of them are derived from Taoism. As we meet them in Buddhism, two points should be kept in mind:

(1) They often have differing implications in different contexts. Thus the world of phenomenal existence is commonly described as that of "being," but, because it is phenomenal and impermanent, may also be described as that of "non-being" or "emptiness." The world of reality, on the other hand, is commonly described as "non-being" or "emptiness," but may also be termed "being," meaning by this true or absolute being. In general, however, the terms "being" or "illusion" refer to phenomenal existence, and those of "non-being" or "emptiness" to permanent reality.

(2) These terms are not to be taken in their literal meaning. Thus the fact that the phenomenal world may be sometimes described as "non-being" does not mean that the objects in it do not exist. It simply indicates the fact that their existence is impermanent, and hence is otherwise than it seems to our mundane senses. Likewise, the fact that reality is spoken of as "emptiness" or "non-being" obviously does not mean that it does not exist at all, but simply that its existence is different from that of the mundane world, and is devoid of those phenomenal qualities which characterize the latter. — Tr.

The Period of Disunity (221-589) was marked by the appearance of a major new ingredient in Chinese thought: Buddhism. This religion and philosophy, which first entered China (via Central Asia) as early as the first century A.D., continued to acquire influence there during the remainder of the Han dynasty. It was only during the centuries of political turmoil following the collapse of the Han, however, that Buddhism really became a major force in China, and that the Chinese began to acquire a systematic understanding of its ideas. Its spread was helped by a steady flow into China of non-Chinese Buddhist missionaries from India and from the other Buddhist countries of Central and Southeast Asia, coupled with a counter flow of Chinese pilgrims toward India, where they studied and collected the sacred Buddhist texts or *sūtras*. Through the combined efforts of these men an enormous body of literature was gradually translated from Sanskrit into Chinese, and with it thousands of new terms were assimilated into the Chinese language. The resulting Chinese version of the Buddhist Canon or *Tripiṭaka* is greater than that in any other language, and preserves many texts of which the Sanskrit originals have been lost. Thus beginning in the fourth and fifth centuries, and continuing until the early part of the Sung dynasty (roughly around the year 1000), Buddhism absorbed the best energies

of most philosophically minded Chinese, while the native philosophies suffered comparative eclipse.

1—BUDDHISM AND TAOISM [1]

The early stages of the Period of Disunity, as we have seen
in the last two chapters, witnessed a major revival of Taoism. It is
characteristic of the thought of this time that many Neo-Taoists
failed to realize that there was any fundamental difference between
Lao Tzŭ and Chuang Tzŭ on the one hand and Buddhism on the
other. This fact appears, for example, in the following statement by
Liu Ch'iu (438-495): "From the K'un-lun mountains eastward the
term 'Great Oneness' is used. [2] From Kashmir westward the term
sambodhi is used. [3] Whether one looks longingly toward 'non-being'
(*wu*) or cultivates 'emptiness' (*k'ung*), the principle involved is the
same." [4] Fan Yeh (398-445) similarly writes of Buddhism in his
Hou Han Shu (History of the Later Han Dynasty): "If we examine
closely its teachings about purifying the mind and gaining release
from the ties (of life), and its emphasis upon casting aside both 'emptiness' and 'being,' (we see that) it belongs to the same current as do
the Taoist writings" (118.23).

Thus it was common to regard Taoist and Buddhist scholars
as belonging to a single intellectual trend. Sun Ch'o (ca. 301-ca.
380), for example, is known to have written a *Tao Hsien Lun* (Essay
on Buddhist Monks and Taoist Worthies), in which he compared

---

[1] This, in the author's original version, was sect. 2. The original sect. 1,
"Chinese Buddhism and Native Chinese Thought," has been omitted from this
revised English version and replaced by the foregoing *Translator's Note*. So has a
lengthy quotation which originally concluded the present section. — Tr.

[2] Great Oneness is a Taoist term. See vol. 1, pp. 384, 399. The K'un-lun
mountains form the boundary between Chinese Turkistan and Tibet, so that
"east" of them refers to China and its sphere of cultural influence. For K'un-lun,
the text literally reads Hsüan-p'u 玄 圃 , which was a semi-mythical place
supposed to be located on these mountains. — Tr.

[3] *Sambodhi* (*cheng-chüeh* 正 覺) means the wisdom or omniscience of a
Buddha. The region west of Kashmir refers to India and its sphere of cultural
influence. — Tr.

[4] This statement is preserved in *chüan* 9 of Seng-yu's (445-518) *Ch'u San-
tsang Chi-chi* (Excerpts from the Tripitaka), which is no. 2145 in the Taishō edition
of the *Tripiṭaka*. (See vol. 55, p. 68.) The latter edition will hereafter be referred
to as TT.

seven fourth-century Buddhist monks with the famous Seven Worthies of the Bamboo Grove of third century Taoism. [1]

It is not surprising, therefore, that many people of the time used Chuang Tzǔ's ideas to expound Buddhism. Hui-chiao (died 554), for example, writes as follows about Hui-yüan (334-416) in his *Kao Seng Chuan* or *Biographies of Eminent Buddhist Monks*: [2]

"The monk Hui-yüan was originally surnamed Chia 賈 and was a native of Lou-fan in Yen-men. [3] ... He had a wide grasp of the Six (Confucian) Classics, but was especially skilled in Lao and Chuang.... When he was in his twenty-first year, ... the monk Tao-an (312-385) established a monastery on Mount Heng in the T'ai-hang (range), [4] ... to which (Hui-)yüan retired.... In his twenty-fourth year he began to give lectures, the attendants of which, however, on one occasion raised objections against his theory of reality. Though the discussion continued for some time, they became increasingly doubtful and bewildered. Thereupon Yüan quoted ideas of Chuang Tzǔ that belonged to the same category, and in this way the skeptics came to understand."

Such use of Taoist terminology to explain Buddhist concepts was known at the time as *ko yi* 格義 or the "method of analogy" (lit., "extending the idea"). We are told about this method in the *Kao Seng Chuan*'s biography of the fourth-century monk Fa-ya:

"Fa-ya was a native of Ho-chien. [5] ... As a youth he was skilled in external (non-Buddhist) studies, but as he grew up he came to comprehend the concepts of Buddhism.... At this time his disciples were only versed in the non-Buddhist writings, but not in Buddhist principles. So Ya, with K'ang Fa-lang and others, equated the contents of the *sūtras* with the external writings, in order to establish examples

---

[1] The treatise has been lost, but is mentioned in the *Ch'u San-tsang Chi-chi*, 7.98. — Tr.

[2] TT no. 2059, *chüan* 6 (vol. 50, pp. 357-358). [Hui-chiao's compilation is the most important source for the monks before his time. On Hui-yüan, who will be frequently mentioned in this chapter, and who is famous as the founder of the Pure Land sect and the first Chinese monk to create a Buddhist community in China, see Walter Liebenthal, "Shih Hui-yüan's Buddhism as Set Forth in His Writings," *Journal of the American Oriental Society*, vol. 70 (1950), 243-259. Passages from his writings are quoted below, sect. 4, i, end, and sect. 5, near beginning. — Tr.]

[3] Near the present Yen-men-kuan 雁門關 in north central Shansi. — Tr.

[4] In northern Shansi. It is the northern of the five "sacred mountains." — Tr.

[5] The present *hsien* of the same name in central Hopei. — Tr.

that would create understanding. This was called the method of analogy (*ko yi*). Others, such as P'i-fou and Hsiang-t'an, also used this method in their arguments in order to instruct their disciples. Ya's manner was liberal and he was skilled in asking and answering questions. In this way external writings and Buddhist *sūtras* were alike transmitted, each being expounded in terms of the other" (4.347).

Among the "external writings" used in this way, the most suitable were undoubtedly those of Lao Tzŭ and Chuang Tzŭ. [1] Sometimes, however, the *Book of Changes* was also included. The monk Tao-an (312-385), for example, was among those who expounded the Buddhist *sūtras* in terms of the so-called "Three Mysteries." [2] This is illustrated in his Introduction to his Commentary on the *Ānāpāna Sūtra* (Sūtra on Breathing):

"*Ānāpāna* (breathing technique) refers to the exhalation and inhalation (of breath). As to the resting places of the Way (*Tao*) and the Power (*Te*), there is nowhere where they are not found. Therefore *ānāpāna* achieves integration by means of the breath; the four kinds of meditation (*dhyāna*) achieve concentration by means of the body. Use of the breath results in the six stages (leading to integration). Use of the body results in the four steps (leading to concentration). [3] These gradations by stages mean 'being subtracted and yet again subtracted, to the point of non-activity (*wu wei*),' and these divisions by steps mean 'forgetting and yet again forgetting, to the point of non-desire.' Through non-activity comes accord with all things; through non-desire comes agreement with all affairs. Being in accord with all things, one can 'open up things'; agreeing with all affairs, one can 'complete one's task.' By 'completing one's task' one causes all that exists to consider itself as the other. By 'opening up things' one causes the whole world equally to forget the self. To eliminate 'others' and 'self': this is to rest in single integration." [4]

Ānāpāna (an-pan 安 般), literally "exhalation and inhalation," has reference to the technique of counting the breaths for the purpose of mystical concentration. In the words of the text: "*Ānāpāna*

---

[1] For this explanation of the "method of analogy," I am indebted to Professor Ch'en Yin-k'o.

[2] The *Lao-tzŭ, Chuang-tzŭ*, and *Book of Changes*. See beginning of chap. 5. — Tr.

[3] These and the six stages constitute the phases (variously enumerated) of the road to Buddhist enlightenment. — Tr.

[4] See Seng-yu's *Ch'u San-tsang Chi-chi*, 6.43.

achieves integration by means of the breath." Another technique of self-cultivation is that of contemplation of the impurities of the body, which is what the text has in mind when it continues: "The four kinds of meditation achieve concentration by means of the body." The words: "Being subtracted and yet again subtracted, to the point of non-activity," are taken from the *Lao-tzŭ* (chap. 48). Those about "forgetting and yet again forgetting, to the point of non-desire," are reminiscent of Chuang Tzŭ's ideas. [1] The phrases, "open up things" and "complete one's task," are taken from the *Book of Changes* (Appen. III, p. 371). Thus in this quotation we have a good illustration of the use of the "Three Mysteries" to explain Buddhism.

2—THE "SIX HOUSES" AND "SEVEN SCHOOLS" [2]

As we have seen in the last two chapters, one of the problems to which the exponents of Lao Tzŭ and Chuang Tzŭ devoted major attention at this time was that of being or existence (*yu*) and non-being or non-existence (*wu*). This subject was also a prominent one among the Buddhists, who, however, often used the word "emptiness" (*k'ung*, Sanskrit *śūnyatā*) as a substitute for "non-being" (*wu*). This suggests the possibility either that the Taoists were influenced by the Buddhists, or that the Buddhists were influenced by the Taoists, or, most probably, that each school influenced the other. In any case there is no doubt that the problem of the relationship of "being" to "non-being" or "emptiness" was common both to Taoism and Buddhism, and that it was long to remain central for the latter.

On the Buddhist side, the exponents of this problem were, during the Period of Disunity, grouped under what were known as the "six houses" (*liu chia* 六家) and "seven schools" (*ch'i tsung* 七宗). The available information on these earliest divisions in Chinese Buddhism is scattered and obscure. Much of it consists of fragmentary quotations from now lost treatises, culled from two large works of considerably later date: the *Chung-kuan-lun Su* or *Commentary on the Mādhyamika Śāstra*, by Chi-tsang (549-623), [3] and the *Sub-*

---

[1] See vol. 1, pp. 241-242. — Tr.

[2] This subject is also treated in Walter Liebenthal, *The Book of Chao* (Peiping, 1948), Appen. I, "Note on the First Schools of Chinese Buddhism," pp. 146-166, where a number of the quotations appearing below have been translated. — Tr.

[3] TT no. 1824 (vol. 42, pp. 1-169). — Tr.

commentary on the same *śāstra*, known as the *Chung-lun Su-chi*, and written in 801-806 by the Japanese monk Anchō. [1] The latter tells us:

"The monk Pao-ch'ang of the Liang (dynasty, 502-556) composed an 'Essay on the Succession of the Truth' 續 法 論 , in which he says: 'The monk T'an-chi of the Sung (dynasty, 420-478), in his "Treatise on the Six Houses and Seven Schools" (*Liu-chia Ch'i-tsung Lun*), says that there are six houses, split into seven schools. The first (of the latter) is the School of Original Non-being, the second is the Variant School of Original Non-being, the third is the School of Matter as Such, the fourth is the School of Non-being of Mind, the fifth is the School of Stored Impressions, the sixth is the School of Phenomenal Illusion, and the seventh is the School of Causal Combination. What are now called the six houses consist of these seven schools, minus the Variant School of Original Non-being.' Some people, commenting on this statement, remark that it is not clear and that what ought to be said is that the six houses consist of the seven schools, minus the School of Original Non-being" (3b.93).

In the following pages we shall discuss these seven schools in the order here enumerated.

(1) *School of Original Non-being* or *Pen-wu* 本 無 *Tsung*:

Chi-tsang writes in his *Chung-kuan-lun Su*:

"Prior to the arrival in Ch'ang-an of the Buddhist Teacher Kumārajīva (343/344-413), three kinds of doctrine already existed. One of these was expounded by the monk Tao-an (312-385) as that of Original Non-being. He said that non-being (*wu*) lies prior to the myriad kinds of evolution, and that emptiness (*k'ung*) is at the beginning of the multitudinous shapes (of physical things). Man's impediment consists in being confined to the secondary (sphere of) being. If he would but rest his mind in original non-being, heterodox thoughts would then cease.... Examining this idea, (we see that) according to Tao-an's explanation of original non-being, all the different *dharmas* [2] are in their original nature void and empty. Hence the term 'original non-being.' Fundamentally, this differs in no way from what is said by the universalistic (i.e., semi-Mahāyānistic)

---

[1] TT no. 2225 (vol. 65, pp. 1-248). — Tr.

[2] *Fa* 法, one of the most important Buddhist terms, hereafter often translated as "things." The *dharmas* are the concrete objects, the abstract qualities and attributes, the elements and forces, etc., that make up the universe. — Tr.

sūtras, as well as by the monks Kumārajīva and Chao" [1] (2b.29).

Anchō comments in his *Chung-lun Su-chi*:

"The monk Tao-an says in his 'Treatise on Original Non-being': 'When the Tathāgata [2] arose in the world, he proclaimed the teaching of original non-being. That is why the many universalistic *sūtras* all make clear that the five *skandhas* [3] are originally non-existent. The doctrine of original non-being has had a long history. Its meaning is that non-being lies prior to the first evolution, and emptiness is the beginning of the multitudinous shapes (of physical things). Man's impediment is that of being confined to the secondary (sphere of) being. If he would but rest his mind in original non-being, heterodox thoughts would then cease' " (3b.92).

Kumārajīva, mentioned above, is the famous Indian monk who was brought as a captive to Ch'ang-an (the present Sian) at the beginning of the year 402, where he remained expounding and translating numerous Budhist texts until his death in 413. [4] Tao-an 道安 (312-385) was one of the most famous exponents of Buddhism in Ch'ang-an prior to Kumārajīva. [5] Before this he had lived in Hsiang-yang (the present city of the same name in northern Hupeh) but,

---

[1] I.e., Seng-chao (384-414), treated below in sect. 3. — Tr.

[2] *Ju-lai* 如來, variously defined as "the one who comes as do (all the Buddhas)," or "the absolute come one." It is a title for a Buddha. — Tr.

[3] *Yin* 陰, the five kinds of aggregates or components, both physical (matter) and mental (sensation, thought, etc.), out of which all sentient beings are constituted. — Tr.

[4] He was a native of Kucha (in north central Chinese Turkistan), where he was born in 343 or 344 of an Indian father and a mother who was related to the Kucha ruling clan. In his seventh year he began his Buddhist studies, and eventually became so famous that after Kucha was sacked by the kingdom of Liang (in modern Kansu) in 384, he was brought there as a captive. Later he was again captured by the ruler of the neighboring Ch'in kingdom, an ardent Buddhist, and brought to the Ch'in capital, Ch'ang-an, in 402 (officially 401, but the last lunar month of this year, when he arrived, corresponds to January or February, 402). Of all the early Indian monks who came to China, Kumārajīva is the most famous, and through his scholarly work and personality he did more than any other to consolidate the prestige of Buddhism. His biography is found in the *Kao Seng Chuan*, *chüan* 2. Seng-chao and Tao-sheng, both discussed below, were two of his most illustrious disciples. — Tr.

[5] He "read the Taoist world-view into the Buddhist system" and "was perhaps the first Chinese who took Buddhism as a religion seriously, which he felt it his duty to propagate. ... Of his scriptures only some Introductions are extant." Cf. Walter Liebenthal, *The Book of Chao*, p. 159. One of his Taoist interpretations has been quoted at the end of the preceding section. — Tr.

like Kumārajīva after him, he was captured and brought to Ch'ang-an in 379, where, however, he was treated with great respect by the Ch'in ruler. "An, being full of earnest love for the scriptures, set his will upon propagating the Buddhist faith. The foreign monks who were invited by him ... translated numerous *sūtras* totaling more than a million words." [1] The seventh century monk Yüan-k'ang, in the preface to his commentary on Seng-chao's *Book of Chao*, [2] says that Tao-an was the author of a *Hsing K'ung Lun* 性空論 or "Treatise on the Emptiness of the Natures (of Things)." Though this has been lost, its main idea, judging from what Chi-tsang says, would seem to be that "all the different *dharmas* are in their original nature void and empty." This, then, is the School of Original Non-being. Judging from Tao-an's other preserved statement that "non-being lies prior to the myriad kinds of evolution, and emptiness is at the beginning of the multitudinous shapes (of physical things)," there would seem to be no great difference between this school and the Variant School of Original Non-being, treated below. According to what Chi-tsang says, its doctrine would also seem to resemble Seng-chao's theory of the "emptiness of the unreal," to be discussed later. [3]

(2) *Variant School of Original Non-being* or *Pen-wu Yi* 異 *Tsung*: Chi-tsang continues in his *Chung-kuan-lun Su*:

"In the next place, it is said by the Buddhist Teacher Shen: [4] '(The meaning of) original non-being is that before there were yet material things, there was then non-being. Therefore being (*yu*) issues from non-being (*wu*). Since non-being is prior to being, and being is posterior to non-being, we have the term original non-being.' This exposition is demolished by Master Chao in his 'On the Emptiness of the Unreal.' [5] Likewise it is not mentioned in the scriptures" (2b.29). Anchō comments:

"In the treatise composed by him, he (Fa-shen) says: 'Non-being, what is it? An emptiness without shapes, yet out of which the myriad things are engendered. Though the existent is productive, the non-existent has the power to produce all

---

[1] *Kao Seng Chuan*, 5.354.

[2] TT no. 1859 (vol. 45, p. 262). — Tr.

[3] See sect. 3, ii. Seng-chao, however, criticized this school. See his *Book of Chao*, chap. 2, p. 59. — Tr.

[4] Fa-shen, i.e., Chu Tao-ch'ien (286-374), on whom see below. — Tr.

[5] Second chapter of the *Book of Chao*. — Tr.

things. [1] That is why the Buddha told the Brahmacārin [2] that the four great elements (earth, water, fire, air) arise from emptiness (*k'ung*).' And in the second part of the chapter on the double truth in the fifth book of the *Mysterious Meaning of the Monastery* [3] it is said: 'Again there is Chu Fa-shen who said that all *dharmas* are originally non-existent. The emptiness that is without shapes represents the highest truth; the myriad things produced from it constitute the worldly truth' " (3b.93).

Anchō remarks further: "This Buddhist Teacher Shen was Chu (Tao-)ch'ien 竺道潛 of the Chin (dynasty, who lived) on Mount Yang in eastern Yen. [4] He was styled Fa-shen 法深, his (lay) surname had been Wang 王, and he was a native of Lang-ya. [5] In his eighteenth year he left his family (to become a monk).... In his eighty-ninth year, which was the second year of the Ning-k'ang period of the Chin (374), he died in his mountain retreat. Some texts, when speaking of the Buddhist Teacher Shen, write his name Shen 琛" (*ibid.*). Chu Tao-ch'ien's biography is to be found in the fourth *chüan* of the *Kao Seng Chuan*.

Contemporary with him lived another Buddhist, Chu Fa-t'ai 竺法汰 (320-387), who also maintained a theory of original nonbeing. The *Kao Seng Chuan* says of him: "Chu Fa-t'ai was a native of Tung-kuan. [6] In his youth he was a fellow student of Tao-an, and though unequal to him in talent for debate, yet in attractiveness of manner he surpassed him.... In the twelfth year of the T'ai-yüan period of the Chin (387) he died, during his sixty-eighth year.... The commentaries composed by T'ai, as well as his correspondence with Ch'i Ch'ao about original non-being, are all current in the world" [7] (5.354-355).

---

[1] I.e., the existent produces individual things, but the totality of all things, that is, total being, is itself a product of non-being. — Tr.

[2] The disciple of a Brahman or a recluse. — Tr.

[3] *Shan-men Hsüan-yi* 山門玄義. On this now lost work, probably of the Ch'en dynasty (557-589), see Liebenthal, *op. cit.*, p. 148, note 646. — Tr.

[4] A little southwest of the present Sheng 嵊 hsien in eastern Chekiang. — Tr.

[5] On the coast of Shantung, south of the present Tsingtao. — Tr.

[6] The present Yi-shui 沂水 in central Shantung. — Tr.

[7] They are no longer extant. Ch'i Ch'ao was a Neo-Taoist and also a high official. — Tr.

The theory of original non-being singled out by Seng-chao
for attack in his second chapter, "On the Emptiness of the Unreal,"
is stated by his commentator, Yüan-k'ang, to be that of Chu Fa-t'ai.
It, with Chu Tao-ch'ien's theory, seemingly constitutes the Variant
School of Original Non-being. The essential thesis of this school
derives from the statement in the *Lao-tzŭ*: "Heaven and Earth and the
ten thousand things are produced from Being; Being is the product
of Non-being" (chap. 40). Thus it seems to be an attempt to expound
Buddhism in terms of Lao Tzŭ's teachings.

(3) *School of Matter As Such* or *Chi-se* 即色 *Tsung* : [1]

Chi-tsang continues in his *Chung-kuan-lun Su*:

"The second theory (following that of original non-being) is
that of matter as such, in which, however, there are two groups. The
first is the theory of matter as such (developed by a teacher) from
within the Pass. [2] This says that matter as such is empty, that is,
that (visible) matter lacks any (permanent) nature of its own. That is
why it says that matter as such is empty, but not that the original
nature underlying this matter is empty. This theory has been attacked
by Seng-chao, who says that while it understands that (visible) matter
is not matter of itself, it fails to accept (the further fact) that (all)
matter (whether visible or invisible) is (actually) not matter" [3]
(2b.29). Anchō's comment helps to clarify this passage:

"The theory of this teacher (from within the Pass) is: Through
the conglomeration of fine (i.e., invisible) matter, coarse (visible)
matter is formed. As regards emptiness, it is only the coarse matter
which is empty and not the fine matter. From the point of view of
fine matter, the coarse matter is not matter of itself. Thus in the same
way, from the point of view of black color, [4] when there is white
color, this white color is not color of itself. [5] That is why, when it

---

[1] *Rūpa* (*se*) means color, matter, the phenomenal world. — Tr.

[2] The region around Ch'ang-an, i.e., modern Sian. — Tr.

[3] See the *Book of Chao*, chap. 2, p. 59. — Tr.

[4] The word *se* or *rūpa*, as already pointed out, means both "matter" and
"color." — Tr.

[5] The text reads, "is not white color." On the analogy of the preceding
sentence, however, I believe that a corruption has crept into the text and that 白 ,
"white," should be emended to 自 , "of itself." White, for the Chinese, is not
a positive color in itself but simply the absence of color; its opposite, black, is
therefore the most basic or fundamental color. The meaning seems to be that
white does not exist in itself; it is simply derived from, or based upon, black.
— Tr.

is said that *rūpa* (matter, color) as such is empty, this does not mean that all *rūpa* is entirely non-existent. Thus matter which has determinant qualities must necessarily exist without being dependent on causation (for its manifestation). Similarly in the case of coarse matter: having determinant qualities, it would then necessarily be formed without causation from fine matter. This is the meaning of the theory that invisible (i.e., fine) matter is not empty" (2b.94).

We have no way of identifying the teacher from "within the Pass" who advanced this theory. The statement about the black and white color is not easy to interpret, [1] but the general underlying idea seems to be that coarse matter is "empty," whereas fine matter is not. This is because coarse matter lacks determinant qualities, that is to say, it changes and fluctuates and thus lacks any absolute or enduring entity. The point being made is that it is only matter as it appears to us that thus lacks stability; this is not to say that the "nature," i.e., the principle that lies within this outer appearance, is itself empty. This is the ground for Seng-chao's criticism of this school that "while it understands that (visible) matter is not matter of itself, it fails to accept (the further fact) that (all) matter (whether visible or invisible) is (actually) not matter." Anchō remarks further: "It only knows that matter is not of itself matter, being formed through causation. It does not know, however, that matter is itself fundamentally empty. Hence it clings to a seeming kind of existence" (*ibid.*).

This, then, is the theory of the first group in the School of Matter as Such. Its details remain obscure, but judging from the fragmentary remarks here quoted, its general concept of matter seems similar to that of modern science. Thus the atom, electron, etc., of science would correspond to the "fine" or invisible matter of this school, which, being stable and permanent, is therefore not "empty." The larger concrete objects formed through the agglomeration of these atoms and electrons would correspond to the "coarse" or visible matter of this school, which, being ever in a process of change, is therefore "empty."

As to the second group within the school, Chi-tsang continues: "The next is that of Chih Tao-lin (314-366), who composed a 'Treatise on Wandering in the Mystery Without Departing from Matter as Such' (*Chi-se Yu-hsüan Lun* 即色遊玄論). He says

---

[1] But see my preceding note. — Tr.

that matter as such is itself empty. That is why he speaks of wandering in the Mystery without departing from matter as such. In this, without destroying unreal phenomena, he speaks of reality. He thus does not differ from (the theory of) the Teacher An (i.e., Tao-an) about the emptiness of the original nature" (2b.29).

Of Chih Tao-lin 支道林, otherwise known as Chih-tun 遁, we read as follows in the *Kao Seng Chuan*:

"Chih-tun was styled Tao-lin. His original surname was Kuan 關, and he was a native of Ch'en-liu. [1] Some, however, say that he was a native of Lin-lü in Ho-tung. [2] ... For generations his family had been devotees of Buddhism, and he himself early came to realize the principle of impermanence.... In his twenty-fifth year he left his family (for Buddhism). Whenever expounding anything, he was skillful in indicating its general meaning, but in his word-for-word exposition he was sometimes negligent.... At the White Horse Temple he often talked with Liu Hsi-chih and others about the 'Chapter on the Happy Excursion' in the *Chuang-tzŭ*. [3] It was then once said: 'Happiness consists in everyone following his own nature.' To this Tun made denial, saying that the nature of (the tyrants) Chieh and Chou was to do destructive harm, so that, if achievement (of happiness simply) consists in following one's nature, they too enjoyed perfect happiness. Thereupon he withdrew and wrote a commentary on 'The Happy Excursion' which all the old-time scholars admired and followed.... In the first year of the T'ai-ho period of the Chin (366) ... he died in his residence, in his fifty-third year" (4.348-349). Anchō writes of him:

"The fifth book of the *Mysterious Meaning of the Monastery* says that the eighth was Chih Tao-lin, who composed a 'Treatise on Wandering in the Mystery without Departing from Matter as Such,' in which he says: 'As to the nature of matter, matter is not matter of itself. Not being so in itself, though (seemingly) matter, it is (really) empty. (In the same way), knowing does not know of itself. Though it (seemingly) knows, it remains ever tranquil.' His idea here is this: Matter and mind are both empty as to their natures: this is the

---

[1] Near the present Kaifeng in Honan. — Tr.

[2] The present Lin 林 hsien near the northern tip of Honan. — Tr.

[3] Title of the first chapter. The White Horse Temple is the famous Buddhist monastery at Loyang. Liu Hsi-chih is apparently unknown elsewhere. — Tr.

highest truth. Yet this 'empty' matter and mind are nowhere non-existent: this is worldly truth.

"The commentary [1] says that he (Chih-tun) composed a 'Treatise on Matter as Such' in which he says: 'I maintain that matter as such is empty, having no need to be destroyed in order to become so. What do I mean by this statement? As to the nature of matter, it does not exist as matter of itself. Since it does not exist of itself, though (seemingly) matter, it is (really) empty. (In the same way), knowing does not know of itself. Though it (seemingly) knows, it remains ever tranquil.' If we examine this idea, (we see that) it is identical with (that of Seng-chao) regarding the emptiness of the unreal. For matter, being subject to causation, exists only as the result of causation and not in itself. Hence it is termed empty—an emptiness that does not wait upon its destruction. This is the reason for saying that as to the nature of matter, it does not exist as matter of itself and, not existing of itself, though (seemingly) matter, it is (really) empty. However, this does not go to the biased extreme of saying that there is no such thing (as empty matter) itself. Therefore we may know that it is identical with (the theory of) the emptiness of the unreal" (3b.94).

Chih-tun's biography in the *Kao Seng Chuan* confirms his authorship of a "Treatise on Wandering in the Mystery without Departing from Matter as Such." In the fourth chapter of the *Shih-shuo Hsin-yü* or *Contemporary Records of New Discourses*, however, just as in the commentary quoted by Anchō, it is cited under the abbreviated title of "Treatise on Matter as Such." Liu Hsün (462-521) writes in his commentary on the *Contemporary Records*:

"Chih Tao-lin says in the 'Essay on Marvelous Insight' in his collected works: [2] 'As to the nature of matter, it does not exist as matter of itself. Since it does not exist of itself, even though (seemingly) matter, it is empty. Therefore I say that matter as such is empty, and yet that matter is otherwise than empty' " [3] (1b.19).

---

[1] A commentary by an unknown Japanese author, also on the *Mādhyamika Śāstra.* — Tr.

[2] *Miao-kuan Chang* 妙 觀 章 . It is now lost, like all of Chih-tun's philosophical writings. — Tr.

[3] Matter is "empty" inasmuch as it lacks any enduring nature of its own, yet it is otherwise than "empty" because, despite its lack of an enduring nature, it nevertheless has a mundane or temporal kind of existence. In other words, "emptiness" does not mean absolute annihilation. — Tr.

This is approximately the same as Chi-tsang's quotation. Its idea is that matter in any form is utterly devoid of an inner nature of its own. In other words, not only is the coarser or visible kind of matter empty, but the finer or invisible kind as well. This being so, it follows that matter as such (that is, matter considered in itself apart from any inner nature) is empty. By accepting this concept we can, in the words of the title of Chih-tun's treatise, "wander in the Mystery without departing from the realm of matter as such." This then is the theory of the second group in the School of Matter as such. As stated above, it seems to be in essential agreement with Seng-chao's theory of the emptiness of the unreal.

Chih-tun's biography in the *Kao Seng Chuan* also tells us that he composed an essay "On the Sage Not Arguing or Possessing Knowledge." [1] Its essential idea is probably expressed in Anchō's quotation: "Knowing does not know of itself. Though it (seemingly) knows, it remains ever tranquil." If so, it would seem to be in agreement with the third chapter in Seng-chao's *Book of Chao*, entitled "On *Prajñā* Not Being Knowledge." [2]

(4) *School of Non-being of Mind* or *Hsin-wu* 心 無 *Tsung*:

Chi-tsang says on this: "The third theory (after those of original non-being and matter as such) is that of non-being of mind as developed by the Buddhist Teacher Wen. This non-being of mind means that (the sage) lacks any (deliberate) mind toward the ten thousand things (of the external universe); it does not mean that these things themselves are ever non-existent. The explanation of this idea is this: The statement in the *sūtras* that all things (*dharmas*) are empty is intended to induce the essence of the mind to be void and free from its erroneous clinging (to things). It is thus that non-being is spoken of, but this does not make external objects empty, that is, it does not make the world of all things empty" (2b.29). Anchō comments:

"The fifth (book) of the *Mysterious Meaning of the Monastery* says that the first was the monk Wen, who composed a 'Treatise on the Double Truth of Non-being of Mind,' [3] in which he said: 'Being means the existence of shapes; non-being means the absence of forms. What has shapes cannot be non-existent, and what lacks

---

[1] *Sheng Pu-pien Chih Lun* 聖不辯知論.

[2] See below, sect. 3, iii. — Tr.

[3] *Hsin-wu Erh-ti Lun* 心無二諦論.

forms cannot be existent. So when the *sūtras* say that matter does not exist, it is only so as to stop (the activities of) the mind within, and does not make external matter empty.' ... The 'Essay on Seeking the Mystery through the Double Truth'[1] says of Chu Fa-wen of the Chin that he was a disciple of the monk Fa-shen. In his 'Treatise on the Non-being of Mind' he writes: 'Being means the existence of shapes; non-being means the absence of forms. Thus what possesses form cannot be called non-existent, and what lacks shape cannot be called existent.[2] Hence the existent really exists, and matter is genuinely matter. When the *sūtras* say that matter is empty, this is only so as to stop (the activities of) the mind within, and not let it be impeded by external matter. (Having reached the stage in which) external things are no longer present among the feelings within, how could this be described otherwise than by non-being? But how can the non-being of matter really mean a void absence of shapes?' " (3b.94).

Appended to the *Kao Seng Chuan*'s biography of Fa-shen[3] is an account of Chu Fa-yün 竺法蘊, who perhaps is the same as the Chu Fa-wen 溫 here mentioned.[4] The theory of non-being of mind presented in the first *chüan* of Chi-tsang's *Erh-ti Chang* or *Essay on the Double Truth* is roughly the same as that just described.[5] The latter is reminiscent of Chuang Tzŭ's ideas and thus would seem an attempt to expound Buddhism in terms of Chuang Tzŭ.

In the *Contemporary Records* (chap. 26), however, we are told of a variant of the theory of non-being of mind that was proposed by a certain Chih Min-tu 支愍度 :[6]

"When the religious mendicant Min-tu was about to cross the (Yangtze) river, he made friends with an indigent northern mendi-

---

[1] *Erh-ti Sou-hsüan Lun* 搜玄論, a now lost work by a certain "Buddhist Teacher T'ai 泰" of the Sui dynasty (590-617). There is speculation regarding his identity. See Liebenthal, *op. cit.*, p. 148, note 646. — Tr.

[2] The text reads "non-existent" by mistake.

[3] I.e., Chu Tao-ch'ien (286-374), on whom see above, p. 247. — Tr.

[4] The identification seems almost certain. See Liebenthal, *op. cit.*, p. 151. His dates, however, are not certain. — Tr.

[5] See below, chap. 8, sect. 1. — Tr.

[6] Dates uncertain. He fled south of the Yangtze to escape political disorders during the period of 326-342. See Liebenthal, *op. cit.*, p. 149, note 649. — Tr.

cant. [1] In the course of planning together they said: 'If we come to the Eastern Yangtze region with nothing to use but the old doctrine, it is to be feared we won't be able to contrive a living.' So together they set up (another) doctrine of the non-being of mind. It then happened that the other mendicant did not succeed in crossing, but Min-tu (did and) actually preached the doctrine there for several years. Eventually another indigent northerner arrived, carrying with him a message from the first which said: 'Tell Min-tu on my behalf that he must not propagate the doctrine of non-being (of mind). We invented the idea as an expedient to save us from hunger. Cease, lest it offend the Tathāgata!' " (3b.28).

Liu Hsün, in his commentary, explains the difference between the "old doctrine" and that devised by Chih Min-tu as follows: "The old doctrine maintains: With the achievement of Omniscience (sarvākārajñatā), perfect understanding becomes possible. The myriad ties (to life) are then ended; this is called the state of empty non-being. Yet there is then a state of eternal unchangingness; this is called the state of mysterious being (miao yu). The (other) doctrine of non-being (of mind) maintains, however: The state of Omniscience is that of a great open void. Yet though void, it permits the possibility of cognizing; though non-existent, it permits the possibility of reacting. (He who has achieved it) dwells at the root of things and attains the highest consummation, so is it not one of non-being?" (ibid.). It is uncertain whether this passage represents the original text of Chih Min-tu's theory of non-being of mind or not.

In the Kao Seng Chuan's biography of Chu Fa-t'ai [2] we are told of yet a third theory of non-being of mind as propounded by Tao-heng 道 恆 (died 417): [3]

"At that time the monk Tao-heng, an extremely gifted man, used to propagate the doctrine of non-being of mind in Ching. [4] T'ai said: 'This is a heresy that has to be refuted.' So he arranged a large meeting of famous monks and ordered his pupil T'an-yi to

---

[1] Ts'ang 傖 , "indigent," was a contemptuous term applied by the people of the lower Yangtze valley to the northerners who fled as political refugees south of the Yangtze at this time. In order to convey this idea I add "northern" to the translation. — Tr.

[2] 320-387. See above, p. 247. — Tr.

[3] On him see Liebenthal, op. cit., p. 150, note 654. — Tr.

[4] The central Yangtze valley in modern Hupeh. — Tr.

argue against him. [1] The latter put forth theories based on the *sūtras*, and the debate become more and more heated. Heng brandished his arguments, unwilling to accept defeat. When the day was drawing to a close (they separated), only to meet again the next morning. Hui-yüan, [2] who was also present, had repeatedly attacked, and the tempers grew hot. Heng himself felt that his chain of reasoning was faulty. He lost his mental poise, his fly-whisk beat the table, and he hesitated to give his answers. Yüan then said: 'If you are to make haste by not hurrying, what are you doing there with your weaving shuttle?' [3] The assembly broke into laughter, after which nothing more was heard of the theory of non-being of mind" (5.354).

Thus a theory bearing this name was advocated by three different men: Fa-wen or Chu Fa-yün, Chih Min-tu, and Tao-heng. Anchō writes: "The doctrine of non-being of mind, as held among eminent Buddhist monks by the monk Tao-heng, was merely borrowed from the teachings of Fa-wen; it was not a theory of his own creation. Later Chih Min-tu further pushed the study of (Fa-wen's) earlier theory" (3b.94). This statement, however, is inaccurate, because Chih Min-tu and Tao-heng both lived earlier then Fa-wen. [4] Moreover, judging from the foregoing quotations, there is a difference between the doctrines of Chih Min-tu and Tao-heng, and that of Fa-wen. Thus the latter stresses that external matter is not empty, whereas Chih Min-tu is interested in showing that the mind's essence is "a great open void." Tao-heng's ideas are not described, and the only conceivable clue to their meaning is Hui-yüan's attack, presumably made in allusion to Tao-heng's central thesis. The words Hui-yüan uses: "If you are to make haste by not hurrying, what are you doing there with your weaving shuttle?" are in part borrowed from the *Book of Changes*, where they describe the spirit-like operations of that work. As applied to Tao-heng, therefore, they suggest the possibility that he may have conceived of the mind as likewise spirit-like and super-mundane. In other words, they suggest that he may

---

[1] This meeting occurred in 365. See Liebenthal, p. 150, note 653. T'an-yi is otherwise unknown. — Tr.

[2] 334-416. See above, p. 241, note 2. — Tr.

[3] A sarcastic allusion to the *Book of Changes* (Appen. III, p. 370), where it is said of the *Changes*, apropos of its mysterious operations: "Being spirit-like, it makes haste by not hurrying, and reaches its destination by not moving." — Tr.

[4] See Ch'en Yin-k'o, "A Study of Chih Min-tu's Doctrines" (article in Chinese), *Studies Presented to Ts'ai Yuan P'ei on His Sixty-fifth Birthday* (Peiping, Pt. I, 1933), pp. 10-14.

have agreed with Chih Min-tu's thesis that the mind, "though void, permits the possibility of cognizing; though non-existent, permits the possibility of reacting."

(5) *School of Stored Impressions* or *Shih-han* 識含 *Tsung*:

Chi-tsang writes: "These four teachers [1] belong to the Chin period. Then, in the Sung (420-478), the Buddhist Teacher T'an-chi, of the Ta Chuang-yen Monastery, composed a 'Treatise on the Seven Schools,' [2] in which, having described these preceding four men in turn, he maintained that the fifth was Yü Fa-k'ai 于法開, who, following their four schools, established the theory of stored impressions. (Its tenets are): The Threefold World [3] is the abode of the Long Night (of our mundane existence), and the mind and consciousness are the source of the great dream (taking place during that night). All the (phenomena of) existence which we now perceive are the apparitions of that dream. When we awaken from it and the long night gives way to day, the consciousness which gives rise to illusion becomes extinguished and the Threefold World is all (seen to be) empty. At this time it (the mind) no longer has anything from which to be produced, yet there is nothing it cannot produce" (2b.29).

Anchō comments: "The fifth (book) of the *Mysterious Meaning of the Monastery* says that the fourth was Yü Fa-k'ai, who composed a 'Treatise on the Double Truth of the Illusory Consciousness,' [4] ... (in which he maintained that) what is seen through illusion represents worldly truth, whereas (the realization of) the emptiness of all things, which comes at the time of awakening, represents the highest truth" (3b.95). Regarding Yü Fa-k'ai, we are told by the *Kao Seng Chuan* that "his provenance is unknown. He was a disciple of Master Lan" (4.350). This "Master Lan" is Yü Fa-lan, whose biography appears in the fourth *chüan* of the same work. [5] This, then, is the School of Stored Impressions.

---

[1] Tao-an, Fa-shen, Chih-tun, and Fa-wen, proponents of the doctrines hitherto described.

[2] See p. 244 above. — Tr.

[3] *Trailokya* (*san chieh* 三界), consisting of the realms of desire, of form, and of spirit. The term means the whole phenomenal universe. — Tr.

[4] *Huo-shih Erh-ti Lun* 惑識二諦論.

[5] His dates are uncertain, as are those of Yü Fa-k'ai; the latter was an elder contemporary of Fa-shen and Chih-tun. See Liebenthal, p. 162, note 700. — Tr.

(6) *School of Phenomenal Illusion* or *Huan-hua* 幻化 *Tsung*:

Chi-tsang continues:

"The sixth is the Buddhist Teacher Yi, who says that the things (*dharmas*) of ordinary truth are all illusion (*māyā*). That is why the *sūtras* say that from the beginning onward there has never been any (real) being" (2b.29).

Anchō comments: "The *Mysterious Meaning* says that the first was the monk Tao-yi, who composed a 'Treatise on the Double Truth of the Spirit,' [1] in which he says: 'All the *dharmas* are equally illusory, and being so, constitute what pertains to ordinary truth. But the spirit (*shen*) of the mind is genuine and not empty, and as such pertains to the highest truth. For if this spirit were likewise empty, to whom could the (Buddhist) Doctrine be taught, and who would there be to cultivate its path, renounce the world, and become a Sage? Hence we know that the spirit is not empty" (3b.95).

The *Kao Seng Chuan* tells us that "Tao-yi 道壹, whose surname had been Lu 陸, was a native of Wu. [2] ... He received his teaching from Master T'ai (Chu Fa-t'ai).... During the Lung-an period of the Chin (397-401), he fell ill and died, in his seventy-first year" (6.357). This, then, is the School of Phenomenal Illusion.

(7) *School of Causal Combination* or *Yüan-hui* 緣會 *Tsung*:

Chi-tsang continues:

"The seventh is Yü Tao-sui, who said that being results from the combining of causes, and as such is called worldly truth. With the dissipation of these causes, however, non-being results, which constitutes the highest truth" (2b.29).

Anchō comments: "The *Mysterious Meaning* says that the seventh was Yü Tao-sui, who composed a 'Treatise on the Double Truth of Causal Combination,' [3] in which he said: 'Because of the combining of causes there is being, which is worldly truth. The disconnecting of them results in non-being, which is the highest truth. The case is like that of clay and wood which, put together, make a house. The house previously lacked any substance; it had a name but no reality. That is why the Buddha told Rādha [4] that with the destruction of material phenomena, nothing remains to be seen" (3b.95).

---

[1] *Shen* 神 *Erh-ti Lun.*

[2] The region around the lower Yangtze river. — Tr.

[3] *Yüan-hui Erh-ti Lun.*

[4] Identification uncertain, as Rādha is a common Indian name. — Tr.

We are told in the *Kao Seng Chuan* that "Yü Tao-sui 于道邃 was a native of Tun-huang.[1] ... In his sixteenth year he left his family and became a disciple of Master Lan (Yü Fa-lan)" (4.35). His exact dates are unknown. According to this school, all things or *dharmas* are the result of many combining causes, with the dissipation of which the things no longer exist, just as the existence of a house is dependent on the continuing combination of its constituent parts (clay, wood, etc.). This, then, is the School of Causal Combination.

3—SENG-CHAO [2]

In Buddhist thought there is the antithesis between the *Bhūtatathatā* or Absolute (*chen-ju* 眞如) on the one hand, and production-annihilation or the temporal on the other; between permanence and change; between *Nirvāṇa* (*nieh-p'an* 湼槃) and the cycle of life and death. Thinkers of the Period of Disunity regarded the first contrast as equivalent to the Taoist one between non-being (*wu*) and being (*yu*), the second as equivalent to the Taoist contrast between quiescence (*ching* 靜) and movement (*tung* 動), and the third as equivalent to the Taoist contrast between non-activity (*wu wei*) and having-activity (*yu wei*). Some Buddhist exponents, in fact, used all these Taoist concepts, for which reason their brand of "Buddhism" might really be described as a branch of the "Mysterious Learning," i.e., of Neo-Taoism. Despite a superficial resemblance in their technique to the method of "analogy" described at the beginning of this chapter, however, they were original thinkers who, not satisfied to remain bound to the literal meaning of words, succeeded in producing well rounded systems of thought of their own. Seng-chao 僧肇 (384-414), despite his short life, was one of the most gifted of these men, and his writings on such topics as the immutability of things, and the emptiness of the unreal, are outstanding

---

[1] The city at the western tip of Kansu which later became a famous Buddhist center. — Tr.

[2] This section has been revised, so that, save for the inclusion of Seng-chao's biography and the concluding *Note* on p. 269, it now in general follows Fung Yu-lan's *Spirit of Chinese Philosophy*, translated by E. R. Hughes (London, 1947), pp. 147-154. — Tr.

products of this branch of the "Mysterious Learning." The *Kao Seng Chuan* describes his life as follows: [1]

"The monk Seng-chao was a native of Ching-chao. [2] As his family was poor, he had to earn his living as a copyist. Thus in the course of his copying he gained an acquaintance with the classics and histories, and became thoroughly versed in the literary style of writing. His fondness was for the mystic, and he ever regarded Lao and Chuang as especially important as regards the mind. After he had read the *Lao-tzŭ*'s chapters on the Power (*Te*), he exclaimed: 'Beautiful it surely is, yet in its method for spiritually obliterating the ties (of mortality) it is not wholly good.' Later when he saw the old (translation of the) *Vimalakīrti Sūtra*, he was filled with joy and accepted it completely. Studying it over, he thoroughly enjoyed it and said: 'Now at last I know where I belong.' Because of this he left his family (to become a monk), and studied with special favor the universalistic (i.e., semi-Mahāyānistic) writings, but also became conversant with all of the *Tripiṭaka*....

"Later, when Kumārajīva came to Ku-tsang, [3] Chao went there from afar to be his disciple. Kumārajīva was boundless in his praise of him, and when he went to Ch'ang-an (in 402), Chao accompanied him. Yao Hsing [4] appointed Chao, with Seng-jui [5] and others, to stay in the Park of Perfect Happiness in order to help in the explaining and collating of the texts. Chao knew that because the Saints (who had composed the scriptures) were gone long ago, the meaning of the words was often confused, and that occasional mistakes had crept into the earlier commentaries. So when he visited Kumārajīva, he would consult with him and thus came to understand much more. Hence after they had issued (the translation of) the *Pañcaviṁśatikā* (in 403-404), Chao composed the 'Treatise on *Prajñā* Not Being Knowledge' totaling more than two thousand words. [6] When it was

---

[1] See 6.365-366. [It has been translated in Walter Liebenthal's *The Book of Chao* (Peiping, 1948), pp. 4-6, which is a complete translation of Seng-chao's writings. — Tr.]

[2] Administrative district which included Ch'ang-an (the modern Sian). — Tr.

[3] Capital of the Liang in Kansu. This happened in 384 or shortly afterward (see above, p. 245, note 4), so Seng-chao could not have come there until considerably later. — Tr.

[4] The ruler of the Later Ch'in, at whose orders Kumārajīva had been captured and brought to Ch'ang-an. — Tr.

[5] A disciple of Tao-an. — Tr.

[6] It is the third chapter in Seng-chao's works, and is discussed in sect. iii below. — Tr.

finished he presented it to Kumārajīva, who read it, praised it, and said to Chao: 'My understanding does not yield to yours, but my phrasing is inferior.'

"When the recluse Liu Yi-min of Mount Lu saw Chao's treatise, [1] he said emphatically: 'I never thought that among the clerics there could be another P'ing-shu.' [2] He therefore passed it on to Master Yüan (Hui-yüan), who was enthusiastic. 'Absolutely unique!' was his comment. Thereupon the entire community read and enjoyed it; it went from hand to hand and each one wanted to keep it longer . . . . In the tenth year of the Yi-hsi period of the Chin (414), (Seng-chao) died at Ch'ang-an in his thirty-first year."

Kumārajīva, as we have seen near the beginning of the preceding section, was among the first men who systematically introduced Hindu thought into China. Seng-chao was not only his personal disciple, but at the same time was an admirer of Lao Tzŭ and Chuang Tzŭ. Hence his writings, collected under the title of *Chao Lun* or *Book of Chao*, represent an interesting combination of Buddhism and Neo-Taoism.

i. *The Immutability of Things*

In the first chapter of the *Book of Chao*, entitled "On the Immutability of Things," [3] Seng-chao says: "What people mean by movement (*tung*) is that, because things of the past do not reach to the present, they are therefore said to move and not remain quiescent (*ching*). [4] But what I mean by quiescence is likewise that, because things of the past do not reach to the present, they may therefore be

---

[1] It was brought to him in 408. Liu Yi-min, i.e., Liu Ch'eng-chih (died 410), was a minor official who became a lay member of the religious community established by Hui-yüan on Mount Lu in norther Kiangsi. — Tr.

[2] I.e., Ho Yen, the noted Neo-Taoist, mentioned in chap. 5, pp. 173 and 188. — Tr.

[3] *Wu Pu-ch'ien Lun* 物 不 遷 論 . The *Chao Lun* or *Book of Chao* is TT no. 1858 (vol. 45, pp. 150-161). References below are to the translation of Liebenthal. — Tr.

[4] They do not reach to the present because, if they did, this would mean that the things of the past would be identical with those of today. Nevertheless, according to this view, a constant process of change does take place whereby the things of the past *evolve* to become those of today. Because all things are thus subject to this evolutionary process, they may therefore be said to be in movement. — Tr.

said to be quiescent and not in movement. [1] (People believe that) they move and are not quiescent, because they do not come down (to the present time). (I believe that) they are quiescent and do not move, because they do not depart (from their place in the past)" (pp. 47-48).

Again: "If we look for past things in the past, (we find that) they are never non-existent in that past. But if we demand that they move from the past into the present, (we find that) they never exist in that present. That they never exist in the present shows that they do not come (up to the present). That they are never non-existent in the past shows that they do not depart (from their place in the past). Let us now turn our attention to the present. The present, likewise, does not depart (from its relative position in time). It follows that past things are in the past and do not go there from the present, and that present things are in the present, and do not go there from the past" (pp. 48-49).

And yet again: "Thus it is clear that things cannot come and go (between one time period and another). Since there is no slightest sign of such coming and going, what movement can there be for anything? That is to say, the raging storm that uproots mountains (at the end of a Buddhist world period) is in fact ever quiescent. Rivers which compete with one another to inundate the land do not flow. The 'wandering air' [2] that blows about is not moving. The sun and moon, revolving in their orbits, do not turn round. What is there strange about this after (what I have said)?" (p. 49).

In the fifth chapter we have quoted Liu Hsün's comment on the *New Discourses* to the effect that in reaching there is a prior reaching and a later reaching, and that in removing there is a prior removing and a later removing. [3] Seng-chao's idea here is similar. The "prior reaching" and "prior removing" do not come down from the past to the present. The "later reaching" and "later removing" likewise do not recede from the present into the past. Any event or thing of any particular moment is only that particular event or thing of that particular moment, nothing more. The particular event or thing of any other moment is actually another thing

---

[1] A past thing, for Seng-chao, remains forever past; it undergoes no process of change whereby it evolves to become a thing of today. Inasmuch as it thus does not come down to us in the present, this means that it is quiescent and does not move. — Tr.

[2] An allusion to the *Chuang-tzŭ*, chap. 1, p. 1. — Tr.

[3] See p. 177, apropos of the paradox that "a *chih* does not reach." — Tr.

altogether, and not a continuation of the thing of the preceding moment. We read further:

"A Brahmacārin [1] left his family. White-haired he came home. Seeing him, the neighbors said: 'Is that man (whom we knew) in the past still living today?' The Brahmacārin replied: 'I look like that man of the past but I am not he' " (p. 51).

The later Brahmacārin was only seemingly the former Brahmacārin. The former Brahmacārin belonged to the past and did not come down from that past into the present. The later Brahmacārin belonged to the present and did not recede from that present into the past. Seng-chao continues:

"To say that (an age) has gone away does not mean that it has definitely gone away. Antiquity and the present both ever remain where they are, because they do not move (from their relative time positions). To say that (an age) has departed does not definitely mean that it has departed. It merely means that antiquity cannot be reached from the present, because it does not come (forward to the present). As there is no coming, there is no running to and fro between antiquity and the present. There being no movement, therefore each individual remains stationed in his own period of time" (pp. 52-53).

The events and things of the past are historical facts. And because they eternally remain, they have abiding effects. Thus we read further in the same chapter:

"That is why the good *karma* of the Tathāgata (the Buddha) eternally remains even after the course of ten thousand generations, and his teaching becomes increasingly firm after passing through a hundred aeons. A mound borrows its completion from the first basketful of earth. The finishing of a long journey depends on the first step taken. [2] The reason is that *karma* can never decay. It never decays, and therefore, though lying in the past, does not undergo change. It does not undergo change, and therefore is immutable. It is immutable, and therefore obviously remains as vigorous as ever" (p. 54).

The illustrations here are of men piling up a hill: each basketful of earth produces the *karma* of that basket; or of men taking a journey: each step produces the *karma* of that step. The final mass of the hill depends on the very first basketful of earth, and the final reaching

---

[1] A Brahmacārin may be a disciple of a Brahman or a recluse. — Tr.

[2] Sayings respectively reminiscent of the *Analects*, IX, 18, and *Lao-tzŭ*, chap. 64. — Tr.

of the destination depends on the very first step taken. The *karma* or effect of the first basket and first step remains in the past without ever undergoing change. Because it does not undergo change, it is evident that it is immutable.

According to the ordinary view, two assumptions about events and things are possible: (a) If they are assumed to be quiescent, it necessarily follows that the events and things of today must be regarded as actually identical with those of yesterday. (b) But if, on the contrary, they are assumed to be in movement, it necessarily follows that the events and things of yesterday, while not identical with those of today, have nevertheless undergone a process of change (i.e., of movement) whereby they have *evolved* so as to become those of today. In either case, "quiescence" and "movement" are regarded as mutually antithetical concepts. [1]

According to Seng-chao, however, neither of these formulations is actually correct, for in truth it is wrong to say either that the events and things of today are identical with those of yesterday, or that they have evolved out of those of yesterday. In his own words, movement is "movement (only) in appearance but quiescence (in actuality)"; departing is "departing (only) in appearance but lasting on (in actuality)" (pp. 49-50). Hence such seeming movement is not really antithetical to quiescence, nor is such seeming departing really antithetical to lasting on. We read again:

"In our search for immutability, we surely do not find quiescence by putting movement aside. We must seek for movement in the quiescent, just as we must seek for quiescence in movement. Therefore though (things) move, they are ever quiescent. Because we do not find quiescence by putting movement aside, therefore though (things) remain quiescent, they are ever in movement" (p. 46). Thus what are popularly spoken of as movement and quiescence do not basically involve an antithesis. The true aspect of things (*dharmas*) is that they are neither in movement nor quiescence. Or, to put the matter another way, they are both in movement and quiescence. To use the formulation of the Buddhist theory of the Middle Path: By saying that there is either movement or quiescence, we fall into one of the

---

[1] As indicated by the quotation at the beginning of this section, Seng-chao regards the latter concept as representing the prevailing popular view. In this and the following paragraph I have, for the sake of clarity, slightly changed and expanded Professor Fung's original wording. — Tr.

two "borders" or extremes. By saying that there is neither movement nor quiescence, we follow the Middle Path. [1]

ii. *Emptiness of the Unreal*

In the second chapter of the *Book of Chao*, entitled "On the Emptiness of the Unreal," [2] Seng-chao writes:

"All things are really in one way not existent and in another way not non-existent. Because of the former fact, though (seemingly) existent, they are not existent. Because of the latter fact, though (seemingly) non-existent, they are not non-existent" (p. 62).

This, Seng-chao continues, is because all things without exception are products of causation:

"If the being (of things) were absolute being, this being would be eternal in itself and surely not dependent on causation. By the same token, if the non-being (of things) were absolute non-being, this non-being would be eternal non-being and surely not dependent on causation. Since the existent is not existent in itself, but only becomes so as the result of causation, we may know that it does not have absolute existence. Since it does not have absolute existence, though it 'exists,' it cannot be called (real) existence. (The same applies to the term) 'not non-existent.' Non-existent implies being fixedly unmoving: this may be called non-existence. So if all things were non-existent, they could not arise, but since they do arise, they are not non-existent. Inasmuch as they arise as the result of causation, therefore they are not non-existent....

"Thus all *dharmas*, because actually in one way they are not existent, cannot be considered as existent; but because in another way they are not non-existent, they cannot be considered as non-existent. Why is this? If you wish to speak of their being, this being is not absolute being. If you wish to speak of their non-being, their manifestations have forms. These phenomenal forms do not con-

---

[1] Thus what Seng-chao calls "immutability" (*pu-ch'ien*) is a mystical concept that transcends both quiescence (*ching*) and movement (*tung*) as ordinarily conceived. According to his theory, each event and thing is forever fixed in the particular flash of time to which it belongs. Yet the succession of these flashes creates the illusion that a process of movement is taking place, just as the successive images on a strip of moving picture film give the illusion of movement, even though each of these images is in itself static and remains forever distinct from the other images. — Tr.

[2] *Pu-chen K'ung Lun* 不眞空論.

stitute non-being, yet, not having absolute reality, they also do not constitute real being. This, then, elucidates the theory of the emptiness of the unreal. Therefore the *Fang-kuang* says:[1] 'All the *dharmas* are false symbols, not real. They resemble a man produced by magic: this man is not non-existent, yet, being a product of magic, is not a real man' " (pp. 64-65).

All things come into existence through the combination of causes and perish again with the separation of these causes, like a man created through magical arts. In this respect they are all "in one way not existent." Yet the magic man, though not a real man, does exist as a magic man, and the same is true of all things generally: though they are constantly being either produced or destroyed, they nevertheless do exist as things undergoing these phases. From this point of view, therefore, the state of "emptiness" or unreality that is commonly attributed to them is on the one hand "empty," yet on the other hand not empty. Hence all things "are in another way not non-existent."

The popular view of "non-being" is that there is nothing there, and of "being," that there is really and truly something there. As a matter of fact, there *are* things there, but they are not real. They exist in one sense but not in another. In Seng-chao's words: "If 'being' does not mean that they are real, and 'non-being' does not mean that they are obliterated without trace, then 'being' and 'non-being,' though differing terms, express the same basic meaning" (p. 63).

Thus being and non-being do not involve an antithesis. The true aspect of things is that they neither exist nor non-exist, or, one may also say, they both exist and do not exist. Following again the formulation of the Buddhist theory of the Middle Path mentioned at the end of the preceding section: By saying that there is either being or non-being, we fall into one of the two extremes. By saying that there is neither being nor non-being, we follow the Middle Path.

iii. *Prajñā Is Not Knowledge*

Seng-chao defines the Sanskrit term *Prajñā* (Chinese *pan-jo* 槃若) as "sage wisdom."[2] "Knowledge," very broadly defined,

---

[1] The *Pañcaviṃśatisāhasrikā Prajñāpāramitā Sūtra*, chap. 27; TT no. 221 (vol. 8, p. 128). — Tr.

[2] *Sheng chih* 聖智. It is the perfect wisdom of the Bodhisattva (the being

may be granted as including sage wisdom among its categories. Such knowledge, however, is no longer the same as ordinary "knowledge," for the act of knowing necessarily entails having something which is known—a "something" which, in modern parlance, is designated as the object of that knowledge. The object of sage wisdom, however, is what the Buddhists call Absolute Truth or *paramārtha satya* (*chen ti* 眞諦), and Absolute Truth cannot possibly be made an object of knowledge. This is because knowledge entails the knowing of its object, but Absolute Truth has no "what" to be known, and therefore it is impossible that it should be an object of knowledge. In the third chapter of Seng-chao's book, "On *Prajñā* Not Being Knowledge," [1] he writes: "Because Wisdom (is assumed to) know what is to be known and to apprehend the qualities (of things), it is said to be knowledge. But since Absolute Truth inherently lacks any phenomenal qualities, how is it to be 'known'?" (p. 80). The qualities [2] of a thing are the answer to the question of what that thing is. To know what a thing is, is to apprehend the qualities of that thing. But since Absolute Truth is not a "thing," it lacks the qualities of such and hence cannot be known by ordinary knowledge.

From another point of view, knowing and what is known are complementary. To know necessarily entails something known, and for something to be known necessarily entails knowing. We read in the same chapter: "Knowing and what is known go together either in existing or not existing" (p. 79). Again: "What is known gives rise to knowledge, but knowledge also gives rise to what is known. Since what is known arises together (with knowledge), it is a conditional something. Being conditioned, it is not absolute, and not being absolute, it does not constitute Absolute Truth" (p. 80). An object of knowledge comes to be because it is known; knowing comes to be because there is something known. That is to say, the objects of knowledge are born of causation, and being so born, they are not absolute or real. But what is not real is not Absolute Truth. Hence Absolute Truth cannot be an object of knowledge.

Prajñā, on the other hand, is directly concerned with know-

---

who not only seeks for enlightenment for himself, but strives to help all other sentient beings to achieve enlightenment also). — Tr.

[1] *Pan-jo Wu-chih Lun* 槃若無知論.

[2] *Lakṣaṇa* (*hsiang* 相). — Tr.

ledge of Absolute Truth. This kind of knowledge takes as its object the very things which cannot be objects of knowledge in the ordinary sense. Hence it is not the same as what is ordinarily supposed to be knowledge. We read again: "Hence real knowledge, when it regards Absolute Truth, never apprehends what is known (as does ordinary knowledge). Since it does not do this, how can such Wisdom 'know'?" (*ibid.*). Thus *Prajñā*'s "knowledge" is really the absence of knowledge. "The sage, by means of the *Prajñā* which has no knowledge, illumines the Absolute Truth which has no phenomenal qualities" (p. 76). "Void and unmoving, it (*Prajñā*) has no knowledge, yet knows everything" (*ibid.*). To be without knowledge and yet know everything: this is to have the knowledge which is not knowledge.

Yet we should not suppose that what is called Absolute Truth exists in isolation from the sphere of events and things. It is, on the contrary, the actuality of those events and things. In Buddhist terminology it is "the real quality (*shih hsiang* 實 相) of all things." Since these all come into existence through causation, they are as illusory as the man conjured up through the tricks of a magician. What they are is illusion and their qualities are unreal; in other words, they are "non-existent." This fact of "non-existence" constitutes their actuality, and the knowledge of such actuality constitutes *Prajñā*. Anything whose qualities are "non-existent" cannot be taken as the object of ordinary knowledge, and therefore *Prajñā* is not such knowledge. In his letter to Liu Ch'eng-chih, [1] Seng-chao writes: "The development of knowledge reaches its apex within (the sphere of) qualities. But since the *dharmas* fundamentally do not (really) possess such qualities, [2] how can sage wisdom be knowledge?" (p. 106). Again, in his "On *Prajñā* Not Being Knowledge," he says that this sage wisdom is "knowledge of what is qualityless," and that the sage, having this kind of mind, has the "illuminating power of not-knowledge" (p. 70).

This "illuminating power of not-knowledge" is the power to reveal the real quality of all things. This means that sage wisdom is not actually divorced from things. To express this fact, Seng-chao uses such terms as *ying hui* 應 會 or *fu* 撫 *hui*, by which he means

---

[1] On whom see p. 260, note 1 above. The letter forms part of the third chapter of the *Book of Chao*. — Tr.

[2] I.e., since phenomenal qualities do not represent the actuality of things. — Tr.

the act of dealing with events and things. Of the sage who possesses the *Prajñā* which is not knowledge, he says that he "empties his mind." [1] As to such a sage's "illuminating power of not-knowledge," he says that it "illumines what is real" (p. 71). We read further:

"Though void, it (*Prajñā*) illumines; though it illumines, it is void" (p. 73).

"Wisdom knows not, yet it illumines the deepest profundity. Spirit (*shen* 神) calculates not, yet it responds to the necessities of the given moment (*ying hui*). Because it calculates not, spirit shines in lonely glory in what is beyond the world. Because it knows not, Wisdom illumines the Mystery (*hsüan*) beyond mundane affairs. Yet though Wisdom lies outside affairs, it never lacks them. Though Spirit lies beyond the world, it stays ever within it" (pp. 71-72).

"Hence it illumines the qualityless, yet never loses the power of dealing with things (*fu hui*). It observes phenomenal activity, yet does not turn away from the qualityless." [2]

"Hence the sage is like an empty hollow. He cherishes no knowledge. He dwells in the world of change and utility, yet holds himself to the realm of non-activity (*wu wei*). He rests within the walls of the nameable, yet lives in the open country of what transcends speech. He is silent and alone, void and open, where his state of being cannot be clothed in language. Nothing more can be said of him" (*ibid.*, p. 109).

That he "dwells in the world of change and utility" and "rests within the walls of the nameable," refers to the sage's sphere of activity. That he "holds himself to the realm of non-activity" and "lives in the open country of what transcends speech," refers to his sphere of being.

We read further in Seng-chao's "On *Prajñā* Not Being Knowledge":

"Therefore Ratnakūta says: [3] 'Without mentation, he yet acts.' And the *Fang-kuang* says: [4] 'He (the Buddha), in his state of motionless enlightenment, establishes all the *dharmas* in their places.' That is why the footprints of the sage, though a thousandfold, all lead to

---

[1] An allusion to the *Lao-tzŭ*, chap. 3. — Tr.

[2] Letter to Liu Ch'eng-chih, p. 107.

[3] Ratnakūta is the title of the Buddha as adorned with heaps of treasures, symbolizing his powers, truths, etc. On this quotation see Liebenthal, *op. cit.*, p. 73, note 275. — Tr.

[4] Chap. 20 (TT vol. 8, p. 140). On this work see p. 265, note 1 above. — Tr.

the same end; why *Prajñā*, though void, illumines; why Absolute Truth, though forgotten, can be known; why amid ten thousand movements there may be quiescence; and why the sage reacts with nothing, yet accomplishes. Thus he knows not, yet of his very nature knows. He acts not, yet of his very nature acts. Indeed, what further 'knowledge' or 'action' should he have?" (pp. 73-74).

The sage both acts and does not act, or, to express it another way, he neither acts nor does not act. Following the formulation of the Buddhist theory of the Middle Path: By speaking either of activity or non-activity, we fall into one of the two extremes. By saying that there is neither activity nor non-activity, we follow the Middle Path.

Note: Seng-chao, as we have seen in this section, compares the mind of the individual who has achieved self-cultivation to a brilliant mirror capable of illuminating all things. This is reminiscent of Chuang Tzŭ's statement (chap. 7, p. 97) that "the Perfect Man employs his mind as a mirror." As we shall see in later chapters, it became a common metaphor of the Sung and Ming Neo-Confucianists. Seng-chao, in his *Commentary to the Vimalakīrti-nirdeśa Sūtra*, [1] writes:

"For those who regard (only) what is the Way (*Tao*) as the Way, and what is not the Way as not the Way, [2] love and hatred both arise, and the defiling ties (of life) increasingly show themselves. How can they bring their minds to a comprehension of the mysterious meaning, and attain the (really) egalitarian Way? But for those who are capable of not regarding (only) what is the Way as the Way, and what is not the Way as not the Way, (the distinctions of) right and wrong are severed from the mind, and they can ride upon anything they encounter. This is the way to abide with the right, yet without feeling the right as right; to abide with the wrong, yet without feeling the wrong as wrong. Therefore they are able to equalize their views of beauty and ugliness, and always to enjoy good fortune even though suffering reverse. They blend glory with worldly trouble, so that the more obscure they may be, the more prominent they become. This may be called the state of all pervasiveness without obstruction, and the Buddhist Way of universal equality."

Among those who during the Period of Disunity expounded Buddhism in terms of Lao Tzŭ and Chuang Tzŭ, there were many who developed the themes of the equalization of being and non-being, the harmonization of movement and quiescence, and the unification of others with the self. Few, however, had much to say about Chuang Tzŭ's "linking together of right and wrong." [3] In this passage we see how this latter

---

[1] *Wei-mo Chieh Ching Chu, chüan* 7; TT no. 1775 (vol. 38, p. 390).

[2] I.e., who maintain an absolute distinction between right and wrong. — Tr.

[3] A phrase used by Kuo Hsiang in his commentary on the *Chuang-tzŭ*. See above, chap. 6, p. 231. — Tr.

concept, so prominent in Chuang Tzǔ's second chapter, is used by Seng-chao to expound the Buddhist *sūtras*.

4—TAO-SHENG

Contemporary with Seng-chao, and like him a student of Kumā-rajīva, there lived Tao-sheng, also known as Chu Tao-sheng 竺道 生 (ca. 360-434). His biography in the *Kao Seng Chuan* reads:

"Chu Tao-sheng, originally surnamed Wei 魏, was a native of Chü-lu, his home being located at P'eng-ch'eng. [1] ... As a boy he was of outstanding comprehension and divinely intelligent.... Later he came in contact with the monk Chu Fa-t'ai, [2] whereupon he turned away from his life as a layman, accepted the faith, humbled himself, and became a disciple.... Still later, together with Hui-jui and Hui-yen, he traveled to Ch'ang-an, where he became a pupil of Kumārajīva. [3] There his fellow monks of the region within the Pass all spoke of his divine understanding....

"After having deeply meditated for a long time, Sheng's understanding penetrated to what lies beyond words, whereupon he exclaimed: 'The purpose of symbols is to gain a complete understanding of ideas, but once the ideas have been gained, the symbols may be forgotten. [4] The purpose of words is to explain the Truth (*li* 理), but once Truth has been entered, words may be suspended. Ever since the transmission of the scriptures eastward (to China), their translators have encountered repeated obstacles, and many have been blocked by holding (too narrowly) to the text, with the result that few have been able to see the complete meaning. Let them forget the fish-trap and catch the fish. Then one may begin to talk with them about the Way (*Tao*).' [5] With this he made comparative study of the highest and worldly (truths), investigated causes and effects,

---

[1] The present Suchow, in northern Kiangsu, at the intersection of the Tientsin-Pukow and Lunghai railroads. — Tr.

[2] 320-387. See p. 247 above. — Tr.

[3] This happened in 406. Hui-jui died during the Yüan-chia period (424-453), probably in 439, in which case his dates would be 355-439; Hui-yen's dates are 363-443. — Tr.

[4] The Neo-Taoist Wang Pi expressed almost precisely the same idea. See chap. 5, p. 184. — Tr.

[5] The metaphor of the fish-trap comes from the *Chuang-tzǔ*, chap. 26, p. 362. — Tr.

and thus created (the doctrines that) 'a good deed entails no retribution,' and 'Buddhahood is achieved through instantaneous enlightenment.'

"Furthermore, when the six-book version of the *Nirvāṇa* [1] first reached the capital, Sheng analyzed the principles of the *sūtra* and entered deeply into its profound meaning. He then asserted that even all *icchantikas* [2] possess the possibility of achieving Buddhahood. At this time (the full text of) the *Great Nirvāṇa Sūtra* had not yet arrived in our land, and he with his single understanding was the first to develop this unique view, in opposition to that of most people.... Then when suddenly the *Great Nirvāṇa Sūtra* reached the capital, it was really found to say that all *icchantikas* possess the Buddha nature.... In the eleventh year of the Yüan-chia period of the Sung (434) ... he died" (7.366-367).

i. *Theory of Retribution*

The Japanese ninth-century monk Sō, in his *Yi-ch'eng Fo-hsing Hui-jih Ch'ao*, [3] quotes Tao-sheng's doctrine as follows: "Sheng says: 'All those who receive the two principles [4] have the right cause that may lead to *Nirvāṇa*, and (continued) endurance of life within the Threefold World is (simply) the result of delusion. Since the *icchantikas* fall within the class of beings who partake of life, why should they be the only ones to lack the Buddha nature?" (p. 173). Since the *icchantikas*, though Buddhist non-believers, are thus, according to Tao-sheng, endowed with the Buddha nature and capable of achieving Buddhahood, the logical conclusion is that there is no one to whom this goal is not open. Tao-sheng insists that the words of the scriptures are mere "traps" which must be forgotten once the fish are caught. Only then can one begin to talk about the Way or *Tao*, the understanding of which results in the immediate achievement of Buddhahood. The Ch'an school, as we shall see in the ninth

---

[1] I.e., the *Nirvāṇa Sūtra*. This incomplete version, which had been brought from India to China by the pilgrim Fa-hsien in 414, was the one generally current at this time. — Tr.

[2] Non-believers in Buddhism. — Tr.

[3] *Transcript of the Single-vehicle Buddha-nature Wisdom*. It is TT no. 2297 (vol. 70, pp. 173-194). The identity of its Japanese author is uncertain. By some he is identified with the monk Ensō, who died in 883. — Tr.

[4] The *yin* and *yang*. — Tr.

chapter, follows the same idea in its deprecation of the written word and stress on intuitive understanding.

We have no way of knowing the details of Tao-sheng's dictum that "a good deed entails no retribution," but a treatise by Hui-yüan, "On the Explanation of Retribution," [1] deals with the same subject and may well have been inspired by Tao-sheng's ideas. [2] In it he writes: [3]

"If we investigate the natures of the four major elements, [4] so as to understand the basis from which our physical forms are received, (we see that) they (each) depend on something else, and it is thus that they constitute one common whole. Physical life is no more than some thrown-away dust, and its rise and annihilation belong to a single span of transformation. This is (the truth) to which the insight of wisdom and sword of knowledge lead us. Through it we may ride the natural cycle of coming and departure, [5] so that despite the coalescence and dispersion (of physical bodies), it is no longer we (who undergo these changes). Inhabiting innumerable bodies during our Great Dream, [6] though we actually dwell in the midst of being, yet we identify ourselves with non-being. How, when this is so, can there be divisions in what come to us, or can we have any ties of greedy love?

"Suppose this Truth is acquired by our minds before others become conscious of it. Then, regretting the failure of our solitary goodness to achieve merit (for others), and being conscious of our duties as beings possessed of prior understanding, we straightway expound the great Way (Tao) in order to illustrate its teachings: herein consist the virtues of love (jen) and altruism. It is as if the I and the not-I are mutually joined, so that there is no antithesis in the mind between the two. Should we then encounter sword-play, we

---

[1] *Ming Pao-ying Lun.* On Hui-yüan (334-416), with whom Tao-sheng lived for a considerable time in the Mount Lu community, see above, pp. 241 and 255. — Tr.

[2] This has been suggested to me by Professor Ch'en Yin-k'o.

[3] It is preserved in the *Hung-ming Chi* (Collected Essays on Buddhism), a valuable compendium by Seng-yu (445-518), TT no. 2102 (vol. 52, pp. 1-96). See *chüan* 5, p. 33. [The following passage has already been translated by Walter Liebenthal, pp. 253-254 of his article on Hui-yüan cited above on p. 241, note 2. — Tr.]

[4] Earth, water, fire, and air, according to Hindu thought. — Tr.

[5] The cycle of life and death. — Tr.

[6] The Great Dream is the cycle of phenomenal existence. The innumerable bodies are our successive existences in that cycle. — Tr.

lose ourselves in mystic contemplation. Should we join in battle, we meet the situation as if encountering good friends. Should we wound somebody, not only can no harm to our spirit result, but there will not even be the killing of physical life. It was thus that Mañjuśrī, holding his sword, was rebellious in manner, yet conformed with the Way. Had he continued brandishing his lance and raising his sword to the end of time, it would still have been to no purpose. [1] Such a person as this may transform the whole world either by civil or military means. [2] No reward will be received for such great merits, but what punishment, on the other hand, will be entailed?

"By considering the opposite of this and examining its operation (in life), we can understand retribution. By pushing into affairs and seeking their underlying meaning, we can talk about punishment. Let me try to describe these. The effects of causation and products of change follow a definite course. Ignorance [3] is the source of the net of delusion. [4] Greedy love [5] is the storehouse for the various (mortal) ties (*lei* 累). The following of these two principles obscures the functioning of the spirit, and it is because of them that good and bad fortune, blame and calamity, operate. Because ignorance beclouds the understanding, feeling and thought become clamped to external objects. Because greedy love saturates the nature, the four elements cohere to form the body. By their cohering in the body, a boundary comes to be fixed between the I and the not-I. By the clamping of feeling, an agent of good and evil arises. If there be a

---

[1] This has reference to a legend according to which Mañjuśrī, the Bodhisattva of wisdom, in order to teach the assembled followers of the Buddha about the deeper mystery, deliberately seized a sword and attacked the Buddha. At this the Buddha called out: "You cannot harm me, for even if you try to do so, it will be beneficial harm." He then went on to explain that all things are illusory, including the distinction between the self and others, and therefore that it is impossible for one being to harm another. The followers then understood the meaning and acclaimed Mañjusri for his wise teaching. — Tr.

[2] Lit., "may, utilizing drum and dance, develop to the utmost the spirits (of sentient beings), and, exercising shield and halberd, give perfection to the metamorphoses (of sentient life)." The first clause uses phraseology borrowed from the *Book of Changes* (Appen. III, p. 377). — Tr.

[3] *Avidyā* (*wu ming* 無明). — Tr.

[4] *Huo wang* 惑網. *Huo* (*moha*) also means doubt, unbelief. — Tr.

[5] *Rāga* (*t'an-ai* 貪愛). — Tr.

boundary between the I and the not-I, the body is then regarded as belonging to the I, and thus cannot be forgotten. If there be an agent of good and evil, a greedy love for life results, so that life can no longer be sundered. In this way one becomes willing to sleep in the Great Dream and be blinded by delusion. Doubt is hugged to the breast during that Long Night and there is nothing but attachment. The result is that failure and success push after one another, and blessing and calamity follow on each other's heels. With the accumulation of evil, divine retribution comes of itself. With the committing of sin, hell metes out its punishment. This is the unavoidable fate without the shadow of a doubt....

"Thus the retributions of punishment or blessing depend upon what are stimulated by one's own (mental) activities. They are what they are according to these stimuli, for which reason I say that they are automatic. By automatic I mean that they result from our own influence. How then can they be the work of some other Mysterious Ruler?"

Here we find a combination of Taoist and Buddhist ideas. What we call retribution results from the activity of the mind. Our aim, therefore, should be to respond to external situations without interposing the mind, since such a course permits physical activity, yet involves no mental activation. This is the way to transcend the cycle of transmigration, so that our acts no longer entail any retribution.

ii. *Theory of Instantaneous Enlightenment* [1]

Regarding Tao-sheng's other famous dictum, that "Buddhahood is achieved through instantaneous enlightenment (*tun wu* 頓悟)," our main source of information is the *Pien Tsung Lun* or *Discussion of Essentials* by Hsieh Ling-yün (385-433). [2] In this we read:

"According to the doctrine of the Buddha, the Way of the sage, though remote, may be reached through the accumulation of learning. Only with the ending of the ties (of existence), and the

---

[1] The same subject is discussed in Liebenthal, *The Book of Chao*, Appen. III, "Notes on Instantaneous Illumination and Connected Problems," pp. 169-190, where some of the quotations given below have been translated. — Tr.

[2] Now contained in *chüan* 18 of Tao-hsüan's (596-667) *Kuang Hung-ming Chi* (Further Collection of Essays on Buddhism), TT no. 2103 (vol. 52, pp. 224-228). All further quotations in the present section are to this work unless otherwise indicated. — Tr.

shining forth of the mirror (of the mind), can there come the response of gradual (*chien* 漸) enlightenment. But according to the doctrine of Confucius, the Way of the sage is mysterious, even though Yen (Hui) almost reached it. One must become identified with non-being (*wu*) and mirror the whole, for Truth (*li*) is one and final" (pp. 224-225).

Here we have a curious comparison between the Buddha and Confucius. The Buddha, according to Hsieh Ling-yün, stressed the accumulation of learning as the proper way to free the mind from its ignorance, release it from the bonds of existence, and thus allow it to shine forth in its true aspect. This would imply a gradual process, requiring many rebirths to reach completion. Turning to Confucius, however, Hsieh then alludes to his famous statement about his disciple, Yen Hui: "As for Hui, he was near (perfection), and frequently was 'empty.' " [1] This, Hsieh apparently means to suggest, might superficially imply that Confucius, like the Buddha, believed in a process of gradual enlightenment. And yet, Hsieh argues, the reverse is true, for what Confucius actually preached was instantaneous enlightenment. As "proof," he attributes to Confucius—quite erroneously, of course—a belief in the mysterious Way of the sage, the need for identification with non-existence, and the fact that "Truth is one and final." Hsieh then goes on to say:

"There is a Buddhist with a new doctrine, according to which the state of mirror-like voidness (of *Nirvāṇa*) is abstruse and mysterious and does not admit of any stages (for its attainment). [2] But the accumulating of learning is an endless process, for how can it stop of itself? Now I would discard the Buddha's (doctrine of) gradual enlightenment, but accept his (belief in the) possibility of attaining (to Truth). I would discard Confucius' (statement about) almost reaching it, but accept his (view) that it is one and final. One and final means that it is different from gradual enlightenment, and being able to attain to it is not the same as almost reaching it. Thus what is to be discarded from Truth sets it apart from either Confucius or the Buddha, though it borrows from both. I claim that these two state-

---

[1] *Analects*, XI, 18. For the way in which the Neo-Taoists, like Hsieh Ling-yün, gave a mystic interpretation to this originally matter-of-fact statement, see chap. 5, pp. 173-174.

[2] According to the believers in gradual enlightenment, *Nirvāṇa* is achieved only after traversing several progressive stages (*bhūmi*) of spiritual cultivation (variously ennumerated as six, seven or ten). — Tr.

ments (of Confucius and the Buddha) are said simply with the intent of helping creatures, [1] but that it is the doctrine of this (other) Buddhist that (really) catches the idea. I venture to analyze among them and allow myself to say that the new doctrine is the correct one" (p. 225).

We know that this "Buddhist with a new doctrine" must have been Tao-sheng, because we are explicitly told by the scholar-official Lu Ch'eng (425-494) that Tao-sheng maintained the theory of instantaneous enlightenment, and that it was then recorded by Hsieh Ling-yün in his *Discussion of Essentials*. [2] While the first two sentences quoted above may represent Tao-sheng's actual words, the remainder of the passage, beginning: "Now I would discard the Buddha's...," seems to represent Hsieh's own comments. By accepting from the Buddha his alleged statement that the Way of the sage is attainable, while rejecting his views on "gradual enlightenment," and by accepting from Confucius his equally imaginary statement that "Truth is one and final," while rejecting his belief that it may nevertheless be "almost reached," a theory exclusively focussed on instantaneous enlightenment is reached.

Why should the Buddha and Confucius have respectively emphasized in this way the gradual accumulation of learning and instantaneous enlightenment? The *Discussion of Essentials* continues:

"The differences between the two teachings are manifestations of geography, resulting from the differences of the lands in which they have evolved. Roughly compared, they reflect the peoples (of these two lands). Thus the people of China have a facility for mirroring (i.e., intuitively comprehending) Truth, but difficulty in acquiring learning. Therefore they close themselves to the (idea of) accumulating learning, but open themselves to that of the one final ultimate. The foreigners (of India), on the other hand, have a facility for acquiring learning, but difficulty in mirroring Truth. Therefore they close themselves to (the idea of) instantaneous comprehension, but open themselves to that of gradual enlightenment. Though gradual enlightenment reaches (a certain point), it remains in the dark about the fact that Truth is to be instantaneously perceived. Though knowledge resides in the one final ultimate, it is unconnected

---

[1] They are a kind of pious propaganda. — Tr.
[2] This statement is quoted in Seng-yu's *Ch'u San-tsang Chi-chi*, *chüan* 12 (TT vol. 55, p. 84).

with the hopes aroused by the accumulation of learning. The Chinese are right (in saying) that the comprehension of Truth cannot be gradual, but wrong in asserting that the way toward it involves no learning. The foreigners are right (in saying) that the understanding of Truth embraces learning, but wrong in asserting that the way toward it is gradual. Thus while (the two peoples) have been alike in that they teach according to convenience, the way in which they have done so differs in each case" (*ibid.*).

Nevertheless, as we have seen, "the state of mirror-like voidness (of *Nirvāṇa*) is abstruse and mysterious and does not admit of any stages (for its attainment)." What is called *wu* or "non-being" represents this highest state—a state which, if it is to be achieved at all, can be achieved only *in toto*, and not in a gradual and piecemeal fashion. Hence the "accumulation of learning" can merely serve as preparatory work; as far as the final state of "non-being" is concerned, this can only be reached in a single flash of insight. Everything done previous to this final experience may be called learning, but it cannot be regarded as enlightenment itself. Strictly speaking, in fact, there is not even such a thing as "gradual enlightenment." The *Discussion of Essentials* records a number of arguments between Hsieh Ling-yün and others on this point, including the objections of a certain Seng-wei, the first of which is:

"According to the Buddhist Teacher who holds the new doctrine, the final goal is abstruse and mysterious, and so does not admit of any stages (for its attainment). Now let us suppose that the student, having exhausted the limits of being (in his studies, has gone on to study non-being). In that case he naturally merges with non-being, fitting into it exactly, so that there is no longer any need to talk about it. But (on the other hand), suppose that (before having yet exhausted the previous state of being), he utilizes (his study of) non-being in order to bring the state of being to an end. May this not be called (a process of) gradual enlightenment?" (*ibid.*).

In other words, once the student has exhausted the limits of being, he of himself become merged with non-being. Hence there is naturally no need for him at that point to devote any further "talk" to it, that is, any further study. Before having thus finished with being, however, he must "utilize (his study of) non-being in order to bring the state of being to an end." Can this not, therefore, be considered a process of gradual enlightenment by means of stages? Hsieh Ling-yün's reply is:

"As long as his ties (with being) have not yet been ended, non-being cannot be gained. Only with the ending of the last remnants of these ties can he achieve it. The ending of the ties results in non-being, into which he then truly fits exactly. Before throwing off these ties, one must rely on (the Buddha's) teaching, but as long as one remains within the sphere of being, one continues learning, but does not as yet (actually) experience enlightenment. For such enlightenment lies beyond the confines of being, even though one relies on learning in order to come toward it. The talk about stages is only a means of instructing simple folk. The theory of a single (flash of) enlightenment is the one that gains the truth" (*ibid.*).

Thus "non-being" cannot be achieved before the ties of being have been ended, and though learning is a requisite for the ending of these ties, it is in itself only a preparatory work and cannot represent enlightenment itself. On the other hand, such preparation is a necessary step before there can be any enlightenment.

Seng-wei counters with a second objection: "(Let us assume that) enlightenment lies beyond the confines of being and cannot be achieved gradually. But do you, or do you not, grant that those who study with the aim of reaching the goal can gain daily advance in understanding? If we suppose there can be no such daily advance, this amounts to the same as saying that there is no such thing as talk (i.e., instruction). But as long as there is such a thing as daily advancement in understanding, is this not a process of gradual enlightenment?" (*ibid.*). Hsieh's reply is:

"Understanding is not to be gradually reached, whereas faith arises (gradually) from instruction. What do I mean by this? The fact that faith arises from instruction (shows that) there is such a thing as the work of daily advancement. But since (final) understanding is not gradual, there can be no such thing as partial entry into illumination. However, with the turning of oneself toward the Way, good intentions arise; with the decrease of the harmful ties of life, contaminations are subdued. This subdual seems identical with non-being, and the good intentions seem to be the opposite of evil. But what is wrought in this way is not equivalent (to the true state of enlightenment), and is not the same as the mind's fundamental absence of ties. On the other hand, when the single enlightenment comes, all the myriad impediments are equally brought to an end" (*ibid.*).

This means that the effort devoted to learning can increase

one's faith, which can in turn diminish the mind's "ties" and subdue its "contaminations." The result "seems identical with non-being," but is actually not the same. The faith induced by instruction, therefore, though it helps the daily advance toward the goal, cannot itself induce that state in which the mind's ties are really non-existent. It must be climaxed by the "single enlightenment" in which "all the myriad impediments are equally brought to an end"—an enlightenment the experiencing of which is "instantaneous" and not "gradual." Seng-wei counters with a third objection:

"(Let us take the case of) one who pushes toward the goal, full of reverence for the teachings. Though he cannot make use of them forever, may he not, during the time when he is extending them, gain temporary union with non-being? And if we grant that this may be, is it not better than no union at all? What is it if it is not gradual?" (*ibid.*).

That is to say, even if the knowledge of being cannot be completely exhausted by means of learning, cannot the process of learning result in a temporary union with "non-being," and, if so, is this not a process of gradual enlightenment? Hsieh's reply is:

"What is temporary is false; what is genuine, permanent. Temporary knowledge has no permanence; permanent knowledge has no falseness. How, with the impermanence of false knowledge, can one invade the genuineness of permanent knowledge? As you truly say, temporary union is better than no union at all. Yet I have (a story) which throws light on this matter. [1] On the day when the minister Wu rebuked King Chuang (of Ch'u for wanting to take the courtesan Hsia into his harem), the things (of the external world) were thereby kept at a distance, and thus principle was placed ahead of feeling. But when he later took this courtesan Hsia for himself, he thereby involved himself in (external) things, and thus placed feeling above principle. In this way feeling and principle alternated like clouds, and there was a struggle between (external) things and the self; such is the usual case with persons of average understanding. If he, on that day when he rebuked (the king), had (really) possessed enlightenment, how would he ever have fallen into the error of taking (the courtesan Hsia) for himself?

"Let us suppose that the south is the residence of the sages, and the north that of ignorant beings. If someone turns his back on

---

[1] See the *Tso Chuan* under the year 589 B.C. (p. 347). — Tr.

the north and faces south, this means that he is not going to remain in the north. It does not mean, however, that he will reach the south. Yet by facing the south there is the possibility of reaching it, and by turning his back on the north he is not going to remain there. By not remaining in the north, he can get away from ignorance; by having the possibility of reaching the south, he has the possibility of gaining enlightenment" (*ibid.*).

When the minister Wu rebuked King Chuang, his own inclinations were not yet completely extinguished but only momentarily subdued; that is why he later took the courtesan Hsia for himself. Learning can only result in such temporary "subdual of the ties," whereas true enlightenment means their genuine and permanent elimination.

The *Discussion of Essentials* records a further debate along the same lines between Hsieh Ling-yün and a certain Hui-lin:

" 'Is the momentary union reached through false knowledge the same as that of genuine knowledge or not?' First reply: 'It is not the same.'

"Lin's second question: 'How does it differ?' Second reply: 'The sort of Truth that is reached through a subdual of the ties, when this is achieved through false knowledge, may temporarily function. But this functioning being only temporary, the knowledge it entails is impermanent. Truth reached through the state of illumined calm achieved by genuine knowledge, however, can permanently function. This functioning being permanent, the genuine knowledge it entails is eternal.'

"Lin's third question: 'Because the ties are not eliminated of themselves, Truth is sought to achieve their elimination. Now during the momentary union achieved by false knowledge, Truth really is present in the mind. Since despite its presence the ties are not eliminated, how is one going to eliminate them?' Third reply: 'The ties arise because of the mind, and the mind, through its contact (with them), forms (further) ties. He whose mind is in constant contact with these ties, suffers ever from confusion, whereas he whose mind utilizes the teachings, ever subdues them. This subduing of the ties, if protracted, leads to their final extinction. The moment of their extinction, however, is subsequent to the period of their subdual. The subdual of the ties and the extinction of the ties, though identical in appearance, are actually different and need to be closely examined. In the state of extinction of the ties, (external) things and the self are equally forgotten, and being and non-being are viewed in one and the same way. Whereas in the condition in which the ties have been subdued (but not extinguished), others and the self are differingly felt, and non-being and being are differently perceived. This differentiation between being and non-being, others and the self, leads inward to impediment, whereas the equating of non-being and being, others and the self, leads outward to illumination" (*ibid.*).

Here the thesis is reiterated that learning can achieve merely the subduing of the ties, but that their total extinction comes only with enlightenment. The statement that the subdual, if protracted, may lead up to the final extinction, but that the latter is necessarily subsequent to the former, follows the idea, already expressed (p. 278), that "enlightenment lies beyond the confines of being, even though one relies on learning in order to come toward it." For him who has achieved extinction, all the so-called distinctions between being and non-being, the self and others, are resolved into a single unity, whereas they remain for him who has merely succeeded in subduing the ties.

Let us return now to Hsieh's statement quoted earlier (p. 278): "Understanding is not to be gradually reached, whereas faith arises (gradually) from instruction.... The fact that faith arises from instruction (shows that) there is such a thing as the work of daily advancement. But since (final) understanding is not gradual, there can be no such thing as partial entry into illumination." This idea was criticized by a certain military officer, Wang Hung (379-432), as follows:

"If the faith derived from instruction gives not even partial entry into illumination, it is then merely a blind faith in the sages. In such a case, Truth will not be the concern of one's mind—a fact which may truly be called the height of blasphemy. How, then, can (faith such as this) act for daily advancement?" (p. 227).

In other words, faith without enlightenment is only a blind kind of faith unconnected with the genuine comprehension of Truth. If this be the sole result of Buddhist instruction, it not only means that this instruction brings no enlightenment, but that it cannot even aid the gradual advance toward Truth. Hsieh Ling-yün records Tao-sheng as having replied by letter to this argument as follows:

"Examining what Hsieh Yung-chia (Hsieh Ling-yün) says, I find myself in complete agreement. It seems to be wonderfully good, and I cannot but quote it with joy. The problem raised by you is vitally important and I hope you will understand (Hsieh's meaning) after thinking the matter over carefully. Now I myself should like to try to outline the ideas I have derived from his statements, in order thus to express my joyful feelings. He maintains that there cannot be faith without knowledge; in fact, the faith derived from instruction is itself knowledge. The Truth obtained through this knowledge, however, remains external to the self. Even so, by utilizing (such knowledge), it (Truth) may be approached by the self. Hence why should not (the knowledge in question) help to induce daily advancement? On the other hand, since such knowledge is not an integral part of ourselves, how can there through it be any partial entry into illumination? Since Truth is seen (even) in something external, this means that there is no complete darkness. But since the knowledge does not lie within us, this also means that it cannot yet produce illumination" (p. 228).

That is to say, though the Buddhist teachings can give us a knowledge of "Truth," the knowledge thus obtained remains only knowledge, and the "Truth" it reveals is something external to ourselves. Under these circumstances we can only "know" Truth, but not yet experience it. That is why instruction *per se* cannot give "any partial entry into illumination," even though the knowledge derived from it does provide a basis whereby we may hope to experience the final "Truth." As Tao-sheng himself says: "By utilizing (such knowledge), it (Truth) may be approached by the self. Hence why should not (the knowledge in question) help to induce daily advancement?" It is evident from Tao-sheng's letter that he wholly approved of Hsieh's views, and that, since he helped answer the objections to them, they in actual fact represent his own doctrine.

The *Discussion of Essentials* also records the attempt of a certain Hui-lin to compromise these disparate points of view: [1]

"When the Buddha said there is gradualness, it was because from the point of view of embodied beings there is such gradualness. Likewise Confucius' non-gradualness is non-gradualness from the point of view of the Way (*Tao*). How do I know this is so? To men (above) the average one may discourse on higher things; through prolonged practice human nature may be changed: such are the

---

[1] Not to be confused with the two T'ang monks of the same name who lived 737-820 and 750-832, nor with the Hui-lin mentioned on p. 280 above, the second syllable of whose name is written with a different character. — Tr.

teachings of Confucius. [1] The single union occurs in the (final) Place of Truth, and not in the gradations of the Ten Stages: this was what the Buddha preached. Such statements about gradualness and abruptness were rarely indulged in by the two sages, but does this mean that the foreigners (Indians) confine themselves only to (the theory of gradual) instruction, or that the Chinese cling only to that of (the instantaneous apprehension of) Truth? I am afraid the arguments made to discriminate (between the two sages) are conducted too much in favor of (Tao-sheng's) new doctrine" (p. 226).

Here we have the theory that the Buddha and Confucius both actually maintained two doctrines: those of sudden and of gradual enlightenment. This theory, as applied to the Buddha, was prevalent during this period. Several instances of it, for example, are recorded by Hui-yüan (523-592): [2]

"According to the statement of the Chin hermit of Mount Wu-tu, Liu Ch'iu, [3] what the Tathāgata (the Buddha) preached during his entire teaching never put forth (any distinction between) instantaneousness or gradualness.... Master Tan further says: [4] 'There are two Buddhist doctrines, the one gradual, the other instantaneous.' ... And Bodhiruci [5] says that the Buddha responds with a single teaching to all occasions, so that there is no distinction between gradualness or instantaneousness. This, however, is not so. For though the Tathāgata responds to everything with a single teaching, he does so in accordance with (the individual conditions of)

---

[1] See *Analects*, VI, 19, and XVII, 2: "To men above the average one may discourse on higher things; but to those who are below the average one may not discourse on higher things." "In their original natures men closely resemble each other. In their acquired practices they grow wide apart." These statements are here referred to to support the argument that Confucius, though stressing that the final experiencing of enlightenment is instantaneous, also acknowledged the need for a prior process of gradual cultivation. In the same way, the subsequent statement, attributed to the Buddha, is supposed to indicate his belief that though gradual cultivation is essential, the final enlightenment to which it leads is indeed instantaneous. — Tr.

[2] To be distinguished from the Hui-yüan (334-416) who has already been repeatedly referred to in this chapter. — Tr.

[3] 438-495. He has already been quoted on p. 240. Mount Wu-tu was north of Mien-chu 帛系竹 hsien, itself some distance north of Chengtu in Szechwan. — Tr.

[4] I.e., Hui-tan, who died at the beginning of the Chen-kuan period (627-649), when over seventy. — Tr.

[5] An Indian monk who died in 535 after more than thirty years in China. Not to be confused with a later Bodhiruci who died in 727. — Tr.

all sentient beings, and therefore does not fail to distinguish between gradualness and instantaneousness. Since there are some sentient beings whose resources are shallow and for whom the (final) step is still remote, he has therefore proclaimed the doctrine of gradualness. But since there are also those who are capable of making the one single leap to great understanding, he has therefore (also) proclaimed the doctrine of instantaneousness. How, then, can he have made no distinction between the two?" [1]

Here we have the theory of the so-called "classification of teachings" (*p'an chiao* 判 教)—a theory which came to be variously elaborated by the schools of Chinese Buddhism from this time onward· It was motivated by the need to resolve a basic contradiction: that between the theory that the Buddhist scriptures were all utterances of the Buddha himself, and therefore represented a single unified teaching; and the actual fact that, having really been written by many different persons at different times, they were therefore often quite inconsistent with one another. The Chinese solution was to develop the theory that the scriptures were indeed all utterances of the Buddha, but that he had often deliberately varied his teachings to suit the particular occasion and audience for which they were intended. In accordance with this theory, the Buddhist teachings came to be classified by the various Chinese schools into several groups, all of which, these schools maintained, expressed, despite their outward differences, the same underlying truth. Since theories of this kind have only slight philosophical interest, there is no need to discuss them further here.

5—CONTEMPORARY DEBATES ON THE IMMORTALITY OF THE SOUL

There were many persons during the Period of Disunity—usually Confucianists or Taoists—who strongly opposed the Buddhist theories. A number of the resulting polemics have been preserved in two compilations: the *Hung-ming Chi* or *Collected Essays on Buddhism*, by Seng-yu (445-518), and its continuation, the *Kuang Hung-ming Chi* or *Further Collection of Essays on Buddhism*, by Tao-hsüan (596-667). In general the objections of the opponents were of six sorts, which are enumerated as follows by Seng-yu in the postface to his *Hung-ming Chi*:

---

[1] Hui-yüan, *Ta-ch'eng Yi-chang* (Exposition of Mahāyāna), *chüan* 1 (TT no. 1851, vol. 44, pp. 465-466).

"If we closely examine the lay (i.e., non-Buddhist) teachings, they are all patterned on the Five Classics. They reverence only Heaven and take only the Sage (Confucius) as their exemplar, yet none of them have measured the shape of Heaven or peered into the mind of the Sage. Though they respect and believe in these, they themselves remain blind and uncomprehending. How much more should this be so when they come to the Buddha, who is more to be reverenced than Heaven, and to his doctrines, which are more marvelous than those of the Sage! Though the transforming influence (of Buddhism) lies within our own world, its Truth transcends the ties of existence. Chien Wu was once greatly startled by the River of the Milky Way. Why then should laymen not have doubts and excitement over the Sea of (Buddhist) Understanding—doubts certainly equal to any caused by the Milky Way? [1]

"The first of their doubts is that the doctrines of the *sūtras* are sweeping, wild, vast, and cannot be verified. The second is that when man dies, his soul perishes, so that there is no such thing as the three ages (of past, present and future). [2] The third is that no one has seen the genuine Buddha, and that the rule of the country derives from him no benefit. The fourth is that anciently there was no Buddhist teaching, and that it appeared only recently during the Han era. The fifth is that this teaching belongs to barbarian lands, and does not accord with our Chinese customs. The sixth is that the Buddhist doctrine was unimportant (in China) during the Han and Wei (dynasties), and bcame flourishing only with the Chin. Because of these six doubts, the mind of faith cannot be established" (14.95).

Among these objections, the second, concerning the immortality of the soul (*shen* 神), has philosophical interest and therefore merits discussion. We have already seen (pp. 273-274) the way in which Hui-yüan (334-416) expressed the popular Chinese interpretation of the Buddhist theory of reincarnation: the soul does not perish at death, for the very fact that man lives at all is due to his ignorance (*avidyā*) and greedy love (*rāga*), which lead him astray from his original nature. As long, therefore, as such ignorance and greedly love are

---

[1] Chien Wu is a fictitious personage mentioned in the *Chuang-tzŭ* (chap. 1, p. 7), where he is not actually said to have been startled by the Milky Way itself, but by another person's statements, which seemed to him "as boundless as the Milky Way."— Tr.

[2] I.e., no reincarnation, in the course of which one may pass from one time-sphere to another. — Tr.

not cut off, he must continue, after the death of one body, to receive another and thus be reborn. Such is the wheel of transmigration. [1]

The opponents of Buddhism criticized this doctrine by maintaining that man's soul is inseparable from his body, and that therefore when the body perishes, the soul does likewise. The prevalence of this theory during the Chin dynasty is attested by a tract of Hui-yüan, preserved in the *Hung-ming Chi*, in which he first cites it in order to demolish it with his own arguments:

"A questioner may say: ... The endowment of the vital force (*ch'i* 氣) is confined to a single life. With the termination of that life it melts away again so that there is nothing left but non-being. Thus soul (*shen*), though a mysterious thing, is a product of the evolutions of the *yin* and *yang*; evolving, they produce life, and again evolving, they produce death. With their coalescence there is a beginning, and with their dispersion an end. By extending this principle we may know that soul and body evolve together, so that from their origin onward they do not constitute separate sequences. What is fine and coarse both belong to the one vital force, and from beginning to end share the same dwelling. As long as the dwelling is intact, the vital force remains coalesced so that there is a spirit. Upon the disintegration of that dwelling, the vital force dissipates so that the intelligence is extinguished. With that dissipation, what has been received returns to the great origin. With that extinction, there is a reversion to nothingness. This return and reversion to the final end is a natural process. Who is there to make it thus?

"But suppose that they (body and soul) are originally different from one another. Then it is simply a case of different vital forces combining with one another, and having combined, of evolving together. In this way, too, the soul finds a place in the body, as fire does in wood. During life it can be sustained, but with the (final) disintegration it must perish. According to this principle, with the departure of the body the soul dissipates, no longer having a place in which to live, just as with the disintegration of the wood the fire

---

[1] Actually, this is a distortion of the true Buddhist view, which while affirming that the deeds or *karma* of one existence carry over into, and influence the following existence, denies the existence of an enduring entity (soul, ego or *ātman*) which is carried along with *karma* into that existence. This, however, is a difficult doctrine for the mind to grasp, so that it is not surprising that most Chinese interpreted the cycle of transmigration to mean that there is an enduring entity or soul which does not perish. — Tr.

becomes quiescent, no longer having anything on which to support itself.

"Even supposing that it is obscure and difficult to decide whether (body and soul) are (originally) the same or are separate from one another, (irrespective of which theory is correct), the doctrine of being and non-being can be sustained only on that of coalescence and dispersion. 'Coalescence and dispersion' is the inclusive term applied to the evolutions of the vital force and to its myriad fluctuations between birth and extinction. [1] Therefore Chuang Tzŭ says: 'The life of man results from the coalescence of the vital force. Its coalescence is life; its dispersion, death. If then life and death are but consecutive states, what have I to grieve about?' [2] The ancients who were skilled in talking about the course (of nature) have surely been able to arrive at the truth. If it is really as (I have described it), the highest principle is that of the concentration (of the vital force) within a single life. With the conclusion of this life there is no further evolution. This theory is possible to investigate." [3]

Here two alternative views are expressed: (1) "What is fine and coarse both belong to the one vital force," that is, body and soul are indivisible. As long as the body exists, the soul does also; when it perishes, the soul likewise perishes. (2) Body and soul are originally distinct, but during life the soul finds a place in the body, just as fire does in wood. When the wood fails, the fire no longer has anything on which to sustain itself; in the same way, when the body is gone, the soul no longer has a place in which to live. Though it may not be easy to determine precisely which theory is correct, there is no doubt that in either case "the doctrine of being and non-being can be sustained only on that of coalescence and dispersion." The coalescence of the vital force means existence; its dispersion means non-existence. Therefore man's existence is limited to a single lifetime. Hui-yüan counters these arguments as follows:

"In reply I say: What is the soul? It is a spiritual something of the finest essence. Being of the finest essence, it cannot be portrayed

---

[1] This theory reminds us of the similar one of Chang Tsai (1020-77) regarding the coalescence and dispersion of the *ch'i* (there translated as Ether). See chap. 12, sect. 1, i. — Tr.

[2] *Chuang-tzŭ*, chap. 22, p. 278. — Tr.

[3] *Hung-ming Chi*, 5.31. [This and the following quotation have already been translated by Walter Liebenthal, pp. 251-252 of article cited above on p. 241, note 2. — Tr.]

by the lines of the hexagrams (of the *Book of Changes*). That is why the sages 'speak of it as a marvelous something,' [1] whose aspect cannot be determined, nor its deep meaning plumbed, even by persons of superior wisdom. Yet those who (now) talk about it use ordinary knowledge to create doubts, causing everyone to become equally self-confused. The making of such false statements has already gone far....

"Chuang Tzŭ has uttered a profound statement on the great origin when he says: 'The Great Lump (the universe) toils me through my life and rests me in death.' [2] Again he says that life is man's halter, and death is a return to the real. [3] From these statements we may know that life is a great calamity, and its absence is a return to the origin. Wen Tzŭ has quoted the Yellow Emperor as saying: 'The body suffers destruction, but the soul undergoes no change. With its unchangingness it rides upon change and thus passes through endless transformation.' [4] While Chuang Tzŭ says further: 'To have attained to the human form is a source of joy. But, in the infinite evolution, there are thousands of other forms that are equally good.' [5] From these statements we may know that life is not something coming to an end with a single transformation and having no return as it pursues creatures (in various forms of existence). Although these two philosophers do not fully reach the truth in what they say, they have heard something of its partial meaning. In your discussion, without investigating the doctrine of the alternation of life and death, you have suspected that coalescence and dispersion are (restricted to) only the single evolution (of a single lifetime). Without thinking that the course of the soul is that of something marvelous and spiritual, you say that what is fine and coarse both come to an end together. Is this not deplorable?

"As for your comparison of the fire and wood, it originates from the writings of the sages. [6] However, you have lost its correct

---

[1] An abbreviated allusion to the *Book of Changes* (Appen. V, p. 427). — Tr.

[2] *Chuang-tzŭ* (chap. 6, p. 75; repeated on p. 82). The term, "great origin," appears in the title of this chapter. — Tr.

[3] A paraphrase of statements in *ibid.*, pp. 83 and 84. — Tr.

[4] In l. 21 of the work bearing the name of Wen Tzŭ (a shadowy figure reputedly a disciple of Lao Tzŭ), a close paraphrase of this quotation appears, which, however, is there attributed to Lao Tzŭ, not the Yellow Emperor. — Tr.

[5] *Op. cit.*, p. 75. — Tr.

[6] Specifically, from Chuang Tzŭ, as becomes clear below. — Tr.

outline and so have brought it forward unclearly without proper investigation. ... Let me explain and study it from the point of view of fact. The transmission of fire by fuel is like the transmission of the soul by the body, the fire being transmitted to another bundle of fuel just as the soul is transmitted to another body. The earlier bundle of fuel is not the same as the later bundle; from this we may understand the mystery of the manner in which 'the fingers come to an end.' [1] Nor is the earlier body the same as the later body; from this we may understand the profound way in which our spiritual faculties operate. Doubters, seeing that the body decays after a single lifetime, suppose that the soul perishes with it. This is like seeing how the fire comes to an end on one piece of wood, and then saying that it is completely extinguished for all time. Such is a distortion of what is said in 'The Cultivation of Life,' [2] and fails to probe deeply into its real character" (*ibid.*, pp. 31-32).

Here the passage in the *Chuang-tzŭ* about the transmission of fire from one pile of fuel to another is used to illustrate the Buddhist thesis that the body and soul are distinct from one another, so that when one body comes to an end, the soul is simply transmitted to another.

A major opponent of Buddhism during the Ch'i (479-501) and Liang (502-556) dynasties was the scholar and official, Fan Chen 范縝 (ca. 450-ca. 515), author of a famous *Essay on the Extinction of the Soul*. [3] Fan, who was styled Tzŭ-chen 子眞 and was a native of Wu-yin, [4] is said to have been "widely versed in the classics and histories, and especially expert on the three rituals." "At first, during the Ch'i era, (Fan) Chen served under Tzŭ-liang, King of

---

[1] An allusion to the *Chuang-tzŭ* (chap. 3, p. 37): "The fingers may come to an end in their supplying of the fuel. But the fire is transmitted, and we know not when it will come to an end." — Tr.

[2] Name of the chapter in the *Chuang-tzŭ* in which the foregoing quotation occurs. — Tr.

[3] *Shen Mieh Lun*. It is preserved in the *Hung-ming Chi* and in Fan's biography in the *Liang Shu* (History of the Liang Dynasty), chap. 48. For an account of Fan and a translation of his essay, see Stefan Balázs, "Der Philosoph Fan Dschen und sein Traktat gegen den Buddhismus," *Sinica*, vol. 7 (1932), pp. 220-234. The dates of Fan's life are not given in his *Liang Shu* biography. The ones offered here are those suggested by Balázs. — Tr.

[4] Twenty miles northwest of the present Pi-yang 沁陽 hsien in southern Honan (not to be confused with another Pi-yang-hsien, also in Honan, but north of the Yellow river). — Tr.

Ching-ling. [1] Tzŭ-liang was an ardent believer in Buddhism, whereas Chen widely proclaimed that there is no Buddha." [2] In his *Essay on the Extinction of the Soul* he writes:

"The body is the substance of the soul; the soul is the functioning of the body. ... The relationship of the soul to its substance is like that of sharpness to a knife, while the relationship of the body to its functioning is like that of a knife to sharpness. What is called sharpness is not the same as the knife, and what is called the knife is not the same as sharpness. Nevertheless, there can be no knife if the sharpness is discarded, nor sharpness if the knife is discarded. I have never heard of sharpness surviving if the knife is destroyed, so how can it be admitted that the soul can remain if the body is annihilated?" [3]

Fan Chen goes on by posing an objection from an imaginary opponent to the effect that man possesses a body and so does a tree. The difference, however, is that whereas man's body has consciousness, that of the tree has none. Is this not because man, besides his body, also has a soul? To this objection Fan replies as follows:

"Man's substance is substance which possesses consciousness. That of the tree is substance which lacks consciousness. Thus man's substance is not the substance of the tree, nor is the tree's substance the substance of the man. For how, in the case of a substance like that of a tree, could there be a consciousness which differentiates it from that tree?" (*ibid.*).

In other words, man's substance is substance inherently possessed of consciousness, whereas a tree's substance is substance inherently devoid of consciousness. This explains why man possesses consciousness, and a tree does not. To this argument Fan then raises another imaginary objection: Man's body, after death, no longer possesses consciousness. Hence it may be seen that the substance of man's body is, after all, inherently devoid of consciousness, and thus is actually the same as that of the tree. The logical deduction is that man does possess, in addition to his body, something else which distinguishes him from the tree. Is not this something else a soul? Fan's answer is:

"A dead person has a substance which is like that of a tree,

---

[1] Hsiao Tzŭ-liang (460-494) was the second son of Emperor Wu (483-494) of the Ch'i dynasty, and noted for the Buddhist and other scholars whom he gathered about him. Ching-ling was northwest of the present T'ien-men 天門 hsien, itself some distance west of Hankow in Hupeh. — Tr.

[2] *Liang Shu*, 48.5.

[3] *Hung-ming Chi*, 9.55.

but does not have a consciousness which differentiates him from the tree. A live person has a consciousness which differentiates him from a tree, but does not have a substance which is like that of the tree. [1] . . . The living body is not the same as the dead body, and vice versa, because the one has already changed from the other. How can an individual possess both the body of a living man and the corpse of a dead one?" (*ibid.*).

The body of the dead man, through the very fact of the intervention of death, is absolutely distinct from the living body. Hence it is incorrect to conclude, because the body of the dead man resembles that of the tree in its lack of consciousness, that therefore the body of the living man likewise shares this resemblance. This argument, however, leads to another self-imposed objection: If the dead corpse differs from the living body, "from where, then, does this corpse come?" Fan's answer is: "The case is one in which the body of the living man has become transformed into the corpse of the dead one" (*ibid.*). In other words, it is permissible to say that the living body *transforms* into the dead corpse, but not on that account to conclude that the latter is the same as the former.

Fan Chen asserts further that "the body *is* the soul." Therefore "the hands, etc.," are "all parts of the soul," which explains why "the hands, etc., are conscious of such things as pain or itching." As to the "mental discrimination of right and wrong," this "is determined by the instrument of the mind." This instrument Fan describes as "the visceral heart." [2]

The motivation for Fan's arguments emerges in the following statement: "Buddhism is injurious to government and its monks do harm to custom. . . . Its influence flows endlessly and its evils are unlimited. We should realize that creation is a gift of nature (*tzŭ jan*), the infinite patterns of which all evolve of themselves. [3] Impalpably there is being of itself, and imperceptibly there is no longer being. [4]

---

[1] The substance is not the same, because it is "substance-possessed-of-consciousness," and hence is different from the tree's "substance-devoid-of-consciousness." — Tr.

[2] Lit. "the heart of the five viscera." The word *hsin*, lit. "heart," is used by the Chinese to designate both the heart and the mind, because they anciently believed that the heart was the seat of understanding. By qualifying *hsin* as "the *hsin* of the five viscera," Fan means to say that *hsin* (heart, mind) is something purely physical, like any other part of the body. — Tr.

[3] *Tu hua*. Fan Chen is here following the language of Kuo Hsiang. See chap. 6, p. 210. — Tr.

[4] Here Fan uses the language of the *Lao-tzŭ*, chap. 21: "For the *Tao* is a thing impalpable, imperceptible." — Tr.

When we come it is not because we cause it to come, and when we go it is not because we drive it away. We but ride upon the principle of Heaven, and should each act in accordance with his own nature. [1] Lesser folk should find sweetness in their cultivated acres, and superior men should preserve their quiet simplicity. Let food be grown and it will not be exhausted. Let clothing be spun and it will not come to an end. Let inferiors present their surplus to their superiors, and superiors practice non-interference (*wu wei*) toward their inferiors. By the use of this principle there will be sufficiency for life and support for the parents; it will be possible to act for oneself and also for others; the country will remain in order and the ruler will be in his place" (*op. cit.*, p. 57).

Buddhism places major attention on the question of life and death, and regards the life-death cycle as suffering. Therefore it teaches men how, through self-cultivation, to break away from this cycle. If we would but realize that such a cycle does not actually exist, and that life and death are simply part of a natural process, then "lesser folk would find sweetness in their cultivated acres, and superior men would preserve their quiet simplicity." In this way what seems such a major problem to the Buddhists would really be no problem at all.

We read in Fan's biography in the *Liang Shu* that "when this essay appeared, in and outside of the court there arose a hubbub, and though Tzŭ-liang assembled Buddhist monks to argue against him, they were unable to make him give in" (48.10). The *Hung-ming Chi* (*chüan* 9) contains rebuttals composed by the well known official, Hsiao Ch'en (478-529), as well as by a certain Ts'ao Ssŭ-wen. It further contains (*chüan* 10) a decree issued by the ardent Buddhist, Emperor Wu (502-549), answering the arguments that the soul perishes; also a letter to Wu's courtiers from the monk Fa-yün (467-529), together with a reply signed by sixty-three of the latter, all upholding the emperor's position. The *Kuang Hung-ming Chi* (*chüan* 22) likewise contains a statement by the noted scholar Shen Yüeh (441-513) on the immortality of the soul, and another one replying to Fan Chen's arguments. All these indicate the intense interest aroused by this problem among people of the time. [2]

---

[1] Again the language of Kuo Hsiang. See chap. 6, pp. 220, 223 — Tr.

[2] Cf. also Kenneth Ch'en, "Anti-Buddhist Propaganda during the Nan-ch'ao," *Harvard Journal of Asiatic Studies*, vol. 15 (1952), 166-192; Walter Liebenthal, "The Immortality of the Soul in Chinese Thought," *Monumenta Nipponica*, vol. 8 (Tokyo, 1952), 327-396; Arthur F. Wright, "Fu I and the Rejection of Buddhism," *Journal of the History of Ideas*, vol. 12 (1951), 33-47. — Tr.

CHAPTER VIII

BUDDHISM DURING THE SUI AND T'ANG DYNASTIES

(Part I)

1—CHI-TSANG'S THEORY OF DOUBLE TRUTH

With the political unification achieved under the Sui (590-617) and T'ang (618-906) dynasties, Buddhism became, if anything, even more influential than during the Period of Disunity. One of the prominent Buddhists at the beginning of this new age was Chi-tsang 吉 藏 (549-623), about whom we read in the *Hsü Kao Seng Chuan* (Further Biographies of Eminent Buddhist Monks): [1]

"The monk Chi-tsang, whose lay surname was An 安, was by origin a native of An-hsi. [2] But his ancestors, in order to escape a vendetta, moved to the South Seas, where they subsequently established residence in the area between Chiao and Kuang. [3] Still later they moved to Chin-ling, [4] where Tsang was born. ... There, while attending the lectures of the Buddhist Teacher Tao-lang of the Hsing-huang Monastery, [5] he immediately comprehended what he heard, as if he had a natural understanding. On reaching his seventh year he entrusted himself to Lang and became a monk. He absorbed and marched forward into the Mystery, daily reaching new profundities. In all that he asked and talked about, he marvelously grasped the essential" (11.514).

Chi-tsang's literary activity, unparalleled for his age or before, includes commentaries on the *Mādhyamika Śāstra*, [6] the *Śata Śāstra*,

---

[1] By Tao-hsüan (596-667); TT no. 2060 (vol. 50, pp. 425-707). — Tr.

[2] A kingdom in present Russian Turkistan. — Tr.

[3] The present Hanoi and Canton respectively. — Tr.

[4] The present Nanking. — Tr.

[5] I.e., Fa-lang (507-581); to be distinguished from two other monks of this name, one of whom died during the period of 502-519, and the other at the end of the period of 605-617. — Tr.

[6] This commentary has been quoted frequently in chap. 7, sect. 2. — Tr.

and the *Dvādaśa-nikāya Śāstra*. Through these he contributed greatly to the development of the Three-Treatise school. [1] The ideas expressed in these works, however, are scholastic and of only slight philosophical interest. Hence we shall confine ourselves here to a discussion of his theory of double truth (*erh ti* 二 諦), as developed by him in his *Erh-ti Chang* or *Essay on the the Double Truth*. [2] In this he writes:

"The Teacher Jui says in his Introduction to the *Mādhyamika Śāstra*: [3] 'The *Śata Śāstra* deals with externals in order to restrain their evil. The present text eliminates what lies within in order to loosen (the mind's) impediments. The depths of the *Prajñāpāramitā-upadeśa Śāstra* [4] are profound. The fine points of the *Dvādaśa-nikāya Śāstra* are far reaching. ... By becoming versed in these four treatises, the principles of Buddhism may be comprehended.'

"Although these four treatises mentioned by the Teacher differ in name and content, their general purpose in every case is to develop the (theory of) double truth and clarify the way that avoids the two (extremes). Once the double truth is comprehended, the four treatises may be understood with brilliant clarity, but as long as it is not comprehended, they will remain obscure. This is the reason why it is necessary to become conversant with the double truth. Once it is comprehended, not only will the four treatises become clear, but all the many *sūtras* as well. How do I know this? Because it is said in the treatises that the Buddhas all rely on the double truth for expounding their teaching. ..." (1.78).

This double truth, Chi-tsang continues, exists in three different categories or levels:

"From the Patriarch of Hsing-huang [5] it has been transmitted among all the monasteries that the double truth is to be expounded under three categories. The first explains that to speak of being (*yu*) is mundane (*shih* 世) truth, but of non-being (*wu*) is Absolute (*chen* 真) Truth. The second explains that to speak either of being or non-

---

[1] *San-lun Tsung* 三 論 宗, a school based on the above three *śāstras* or treatises. The *Śata Śāstra* is TT no. 1827 (vol. 42, pp. 232-309); the *Dvādaśa-nikāya Śāstra* is TT no. 1825 (vol. 42, pp. 171-212). — Tr.

[2] TT no. 1854 (vol. 45, pp. 77-115). — Tr.

[3] Preserved in Seng-yu's *Ch'u San-tsang Chi-chi* (11.77). Jui, i.e., Seng-jui, was the disciple both of Tao-an and Kumārajīva. See chap. 7, p. 259, note 5. — Tr.

[4] TT no. 1509 (vol. 25, pp. 57-756). It, like the other *śāstras* here mentioned, was translated by Kumārajīva. — Tr.

[5] Chi-tsang's teacher, Fa-lang, of the Hsing-huang Monastery. — Tr.

being is to fall into the two (extremes), and so is mundane truth; to speak neither of being nor non-being is to avoid the two (extremes), and so is Absolute Truth. ... As to the third level in the theory of double truth: In this double truth (we have passed the second stage in which to speak of) either being or non-being is to fall into the two (extremes), and (to speak of) neither being nor non-being is to avoid these two (extremes). At this point, to say that there either are or are not two (extremes) is mundane truth; to say that there neither are nor are not two (extremes) is Absolute Truth. [1]

"Inasmuch as the double truth consists of these three categories, it is invariably relied on when expounding the Buddhist teaching. Anything expressed in words does not go beyond these three categories" (*ibid.*, p. 90).

Translator's Note: This statement may be schematized as follows:

Three Levels of Double Truth

Mundane	*Absolute*
1. Affirmation of being	1. Affirmation of non-being
2. Affirmation of either being or non-being	2. Denial of both being and non-being
3. Either affirmation or denial of both being and non-being	3. Neither affirmation nor denial of both being and non-being

Thus, in a manner curiously reminiscent of Hegelian dialectics, the highest level of truth is to be reached through a series of successive negations of negation, until nothing remains to be either affirmed or denied.

Chi-tsang explains the necessity for the three categories as follows:

"These three categories of double truth all consist of the idea of gradually renouncing (ordinary belief), like a framework which leads upward from the ground. Why? Ordinary people say that the true account of things (*dharmas*) is that they exist; they do not realize that there is no cause for them to exist. Hence the Buddhas propound the thesis that in the final analysis things are empty (*k'ung*), and have no cause to exist, and that when things are said to have being, it is only being in the ordinary sense, and as such is mundane or ordinary

---

[1] In other words, the mundane truth of the third level still maintains a duality, which the Absolute Truth avoids by its denial of all denials. Thus the Absolute Truth of the second level becomes the mundane truth of the third, just as the Absolute Truth of the first level becomes the mundane truth of the second. — Tr.

truth. Whereas according to the knowledge of the worthies and sages, things are by nature empty: this is the Absolute or Sage Truth. Therefore, in order to induce people to pass from the mundane into the real, and to renounce the ordinary state for one of sageliness, this first level of the double truth is propounded.

"Next comes the second category, which explains that (the belief in) being or non-being alike is mundane truth, while the denial of them both is Absolute Truth. It is now explained that being and non-being are two extremes: being is one extreme, but non-being is another. Likewise permanency and impermanency, or life-and-death and *Nirvāṇa*, equally belong to the two extremes. Acceptance of either the genuine or the mundane, and of either life-and-death or *Nirvāṇa*, means falling into the two extremes, and hence is mundane truth; whereas denial of both the genuine and the mundane, and of both life-and-death and *Nirvāna*, constitutes the middle path between the two, and thus becomes the Highest Truth.

"The next is the third category, in which (to affirm that) there either are or are not the two (extremes) is mundane truth, whereas to deny that there either are or are not the two (extremes) is the Highest Truth. Previous to this it has been explained that both the genuine and the mundane, and both life-and-death and *Nirvāṇa*, since they (equally) belong to the two extremes and are thus one-sided, therefore constitute mundane truth; whereas that the denial both of the genuine and the mundane, and both of life-and-death and *Nirvāṇa*, is the middle path between the two (extremes), which is the Highest Truth. Yet in this (assertion) there still lie two extremes. Why? (It has been said that) the two (extremes) are both one-sided, and that what belongs to neither of them is the middle path. (In actual fact, however), one-sidedness is one extreme, but centrality is another. Thus one-sidedness and centrality still result in two extremes, and this being so, (in the third stage, the belief in either one of them) is called mundane truth. But the denial both of one-sidedness and centrality constitutes the middle path which is the Highest Truth. All the teachings made by the Buddhas to cure the ills of sentient beings never go beyond these concepts. Therefore they expound the double truth according to these three categories" (*ibid.*, pp. 90-91).

Chi-tsang records an imaginary questioner as asking: "(To speak of) being and non-being has the purpose of showing that there is neither being nor non-being. But when we realize this, does it mean that (all statements about) being and non-being are to be discarded?" In other words, once the theory of double truth has given to men an understanding which enables them to avoid the two extremes, is the concept of double truth itself to be discarded? Chi-tsang's answer is:

"According to the exposition of the Teachers, it is both to be discarded and not discarded. As to discarding, what is connected with sentient beings must be discarded. Why? The state of being which you perceive is something that you erroneously think of (as real), and such objects as a vase or a suit of clothing are all things that sentient beings erroneously think of (as real) and mistakenly perceive as being. ... Therefore these must be discarded. For this purpose (the concept of) emptiness is employed to discard that of being.

"But then when one is attached to (the concept of) emptiness, this too must be discarded in turn. Why? Because this emptiness is itself originally derived from being. Hence if there is then no longer being, how can there be emptiness? [1] ... Emptiness and being of this sort both alike pertain to sentient beings, and therefore must both be discarded. ... For what reason? Because everything perceived by the senses is void and illusory, and so is to be discarded.

"However, it is not merely illusion that is to be discarded, for 'reality' too does not (actually) exist. The reason is that reality exists only because originally there is illusion (i.e., only as the antithesis of illusion). No illusion and therefore no reality: herein is manifested the pure and correct path. It is variously called the *Dharma-kāya*, [2] the Correct Path (*cheng tao* 正 道), or the Real State (*shih hsiang* 實 相). As such, however, it transcends what was (considered as such) hitherto. Why? Hitherto it was said that one must discard the practice of clinging to the passions as realities, or of activating retributions within the six modes of existence, [3] and that by discarding these six modes of existence, the *Nirvāṇa* of the Tathāgata (the Buddha) would be gained. But now it is made clear that whereas, when there is life and death, there may be *Nirvāṇa*, as soon as there is no life and death, there is then also no *Nirvāna*. No life and death

---

[1] I.e., the concept of emptiness exists only as the antithesis of that of being. — Tr.

[2] *Fa-shen* 法 身 , "embodiment of Truth." — Tr.

[3] *Liu tao* 六 道 , the six conditions of sentient existence: those of the hells, of hungry ghosts, of animals, of malevolent nature spirits, of human beings, and of gods. — Tr.

and hence no *Nirvāṇa*: (this means that) life and death and *Nirvāṇa* are equally illusory, whereas the denial both of life and death and of *Nirvāṇa* is called the Real State. Consistently up to this point reality has been discerned as the antithesis of illusion, which means that, unless there be illusion, there can also be no realness. . . .

"How, then, can we merely discard the first level of the double truth? For even as far as the third category, all must be descarded. Why so? They must be discarded because they all equally pertain to sentient existence" (*ibid.*, pp. 91-92).

From this point of view, therefore, all three categories of the double truth are to be discarded. Yet from another point of view, there is need for their retention. Chi-tsang continues:

"It is expedient [1] that the three be not discarded, that is, that the Real State of things be discussed without destroying unreal phenomena. 'He (the Buddha), in his state of motionless enlighten-ment, establishes all the *dharmas* in their places.' [2] . . . Since unreal phenomena are the same as the Real State, why should they be discarded? . . . When (we reach the stage in which) being becomes empty, and emptiness becomes being, so that what is dual is not dual, and what is not dual is dual, then, from side to side and top to bottom, no impediments remain. That is why the Teacher Chao says: 'If you wish to speak of their being, this being is not absolute being. If you wish to speak of their non-being, their manifestations have forms.' Or again: 'They resemble a man produced by magic: this man is not non-existent, yet, being a product of magic, is not a real man.' [3] . . . This is true of all things. Therefore they are not to be discarded" (*ibid.*, p. 92).

By quoting Seng-chao, Chi-tsang acknowledges the affinity between his own views and the latter's theory of the emptiness of the unreal. Chi-tsang's general emphasis, however, is that all three cate-gories of the double truth must eventually be discarded; in this emphasis he is expressing the ideology of those Mahāyāna schools that stress emptiness (*śūnyatā*). Although the metaphysical position of these schools differs from that of the Taoists, there is at least a superficial resemblance between their nihilistic approach to Reality and statements like that of Lao Tzŭ that *"Tao* is eternally nameless,"

---

[1] *Upāya* (*fang-pien* 方便).— Tr.

[2] On this quotation, see chap. 7, p. 268, note 4. — Tr.

[3] See Seng-chao's *Book of Chao* (chap. 2, p. 65); quoted above in chap. 7, pp. 264-265. — Tr.

or of Chuang Tzŭ that "those who know do not speak; those who speak do not know." [1] This fact helps to explain the popularity enjoyed by these Buddhist schools among one group of Chinese.

2—Hsüan-tsang's Completion of The Doctrine of Mere Ideation

The beginning of the T'ang dynasty saw the appearance of one of the greatest figures in the history of Chinese Buddhism, the pilgrim and translator Hsüan-tsang 玄奘 (596-664). [2] At the age of thirteen he entered the Buddhist church, and in 629, impelled by a burning desire to visit the sacred places of Buddhism in India, started alone on the pilgrimage which has made him world famous. After a hazardous journey through the deserts and mountains of Central Asia, during which he several times narrowly escaped death, he arrived safely in India in 633. There he spent the next ten years in travel and study before starting his journey home, again via Central Asia, this time carrying with him 657 Buddhist texts which he had collected. In 645 he arrived at the Chinese capital, Ch'ang-an, where he was received in triumph. [3] The remainder of his life was spent in translation work in the capital together with his disciples. By the time of his death in 664 he had completed the translation of no less than seventy-five works, which both in style and accuracy are recognized as among the finest of Chinese renderings from Sanskrit.

As a translator, Hsüan-tsang was primarily interested in introducing to China that particular form of Buddhism that had been developed by Vasubandhu (4th or 5th century) and Dharmapāla (5th or 6th century). His writings, consequently, are more Indian than Chinese in spirit, and provide an interesting contrast with the more purely Chinese reactions to Buddhism which we have hitherto been treating. Philosophically, however, they are of outstanding interest. For this reason we shall discuss below the most famous of

---

[1] See the *Lao-tzŭ* (chap. 32), and *Chuang-tzŭ* (chap. 13, p. 170). — Tr.

[2] Lay surname Ch'en 陳. He was a native of Kou-shih (south of the present Yen-shih 偃師 hsien in Honan, itself not far east of Loyang).

[3] His account of this pilgrimage is one or our most precious records of the India of that time, as well as of the countries lying between India and China. It has been translated by Thomas Watters, *On Yuan Chwang's Travels in India, 629-645* A.D. (London, 2 vols., 1904-05). — Tr.

them, the *Ch'eng Wei-shih Lun* or *Completion of the Doctrine of Mere Ideation*, as representative of the Mere Ideation school. [1]

i. *The Mere Ideation Theory of Equally Avoiding Being and Non-being*

According to the teachings of this school, all sentient beings suffer from two erroneous beliefs: that in the subjective existence of an ego or *ātman* (*wo* 我), and that in the objective existence of external things or *dharmas* (*fa* 法). The purpose of the Mere Ideation or Wei-shih 唯識 school is to destroy these two beliefs by showing that both are equally unreal (empty or *śūnya*). Thus the *Ch'eng Wei-shih Lun* maintains that what we call the "ego" and "things" have "only a false basis and lack any real nature of their own"; their manifestations are "all mental representations dependent upon the evolutions of consciousness." [2] The latter is further defined in the same passage as signifying "mental discrimination." [3] Thus it is something somewhat akin to what in Western philosophy is called mind, as opposed to matter. Both the seeming "ego" and the seeming "things" or *dharmas* of the external world are products of this consciousness, which acts as their evolving agent.

"Consciousness," furthermore, is a general term which actually comprises eight kinds of mental activity. These in turn may be grouped under three general categories. Thus Hsüan-tsang quotes Vasubandhu as saying: "This evolving agent is three-fold: the maturing consciousness, [4] that of intellection, [5] and that which

---

[1] Sanskrit title: *Vijñapti-mātratā-siddhi*. It is TT no. 1585 (vol. 31, pp. 1-60). References below are to the French rendering (often a paraphrase rather than a close translation) by Louis de La Vallée Poussin, *Vijñaptimātratāsiddhi, la Siddhi de Hiuan-Tsang* (Paris, 2 vols., 1928-29). Hsüan-tsang's work itself is more than a literal translation, for it consists of Vasubandhu's *Vijñapti-mātratā-siddhi ; Triṃśikā* (*Wei-shih San-shih Lun* or *Treatise in Thirty Stanzas on Mere Ideation*), with which Hsüan-tsang has synthesized the commentaries of Dharmapāla and nine other men. — Tr.

[2] *Vijñāna* or *shih* 識 . It is to be noted that "consciousness" is only an approximate translation of this term, since it in some cases includes an unconscious kind of "consciousness," i.e., what modern psychologists would describe as the subconscious. — Tr.

[3] *Ch'eng Wei-shih Lun*, 1.8. For this term, see next page, note 1. — Tr.

[4] Lit., "varyingly maturing consciousness," *vipāka-vijñāna* (*yi-shu shih* 異熟識), so named because, as we shall see, it is in this consciousness that the "seeds" of conduct and phenomena are "matured" at varying times. — Tr.

[5] *Manyanā* (*ssŭ-liang* 思量). On this unusual Sanskrit term, see transl. of Louis de la Vallée Poussin, *op. cit.*, note on p. 90.

discriminates ¹ (external) objects." ² The "maturing consciousness" is also known as the eighth kind of consciousness. That of intellection is the seventh. That which discriminates (i.e., perceives and distinguishes) external objects, itself has six divisions, namely, those of the five senses (sight, hearing, smell, taste, and touch), plus a sixth consciousness which coordinates these senses. ³

By realizing that the "ego" and "external things" are "all mental representations dependent upon the evolutions of consciousness," and that they "lack any real nature of their own," we attain comprehension of the two kinds of "emptiness" or unreality (that pertaining to the ego, and that pertaining to external things). At the same time, however, inasmuch as the consciousness upon which this ego and these things depend is itself real, we cannot very well say that the ego and things are absolutely "empty" or unreal. This is pointed out by K'uei-chi 窺 基 (632-682), in his commentary on the *Ch'eng Wei-shih Lun* known as the *Ch'eng Wei-shih Lun Shu-chi*: ⁴

"From this (it may be seen that) the inner consciousness is not, in its essential nature, non-existent, whereas the ego and things, considered as external to the mind, are not, in their essential nature, existent. In this way we exclude the heterodox doctrine which clings to the additional reality of objects aside from the mind; we also exclude the erroneous view which, because it wrongly believes in 'emptiness,' sets aside consciousness itself as non-existent, thus reducing (everything) to 'emptiness.' Equally to avoid (the dogmas of) 'emptiness' on the one hand and 'being' on the other: this is what the School of Mere Ideation teaches. (Belief in) the (objective) existence of things external to the mind results in (being bound to) the cycle of transmigration. But realization of the one mind leads to the eternal casting off of transmigration" (1a.243).

To say that there is a realm of existence external to the mind is to "cling to the additional reality of objects," that is, to add something to their actual state. But to say that even consciousness itself does not exist is to "reduce (everything) to 'emptiness,' " that is, to take away from their actual state. The *Ch'eng Wei-shih Lun*, for

¹ *Vijñapti (liao-pieh* 了 別), the perceptive consciousness. — Tr.
² *Ch'eng Wei-shih Lun*, 1.6. — Tr.
³ These will all be explained in detail below. — Tr.
⁴ *Transmitted Notes on the Ch'eng Wei-shih Lun*; TT no. 1830 (vol. 43, pp. 229-606). K'uei-chi was Hsüan-tsang's leading disciple, and his commentary is of great value for explaining the teachings of his master. — Tr.

its part, follows a middle path. It denies the existence of external things as such, but affirms that of consciousness. This is what K'uei-chi means when he says: "Equally to avoid (the dogmas of) 'emptiness' on the one hand and 'being' on the other: this is what the School of Mere Ideation teaches." Such, however, is only the most elementary teaching of this school, for in the final analysis even consciousness "depends upon something else." This will be explained in detail in section vi.

ii. *The Four Functional Divisions of Consciousness*

The *Ch'eng Wei-shih Lun* says: "Impure consciousness, when it is born, manifests itself under (two) seeming aspects: that of the object and that of the subject (of cognition). [1] This should likewise be understood of all the associated mental activities. As a seeming object, it is called the perceived division. [2] As a seeming subject, it is called the perceiving division. [3] . . . But there is a something upon which what is thus perceived and what perceives are dependent, and which is their essential substance. This is called the self-corroboratory division. [4] If this were lacking, there would be no way of remembering (the things evolved by) the mind and its activities. . . . But if we make a subtle analysis, . . . (we see that besides these three aspects of consciousness) there is also a fourth, which is that of 'corroborating the self-corroboratory division.' [5] For if this were lacking, by what would the third (division) be corroborated?" (2.125-126, 128, 132).

"Impure," in the term "impure consciousness," refers to the evil passions which are the causes of affliction. [6] Consciousness which carries with it these passions is "impure consciousness." As we have seen in the last section, one of the functions of consciousness is that

---

[1] *Ālambana* (*so yüan* 所緣), lit., "what is caused," and *sālambana* (*neng* 能 *yüan*), lit., "what can cause." — Tr.

[2] *Lakṣaṇa-bhāga* (*hsiang-fen* 相分). — Tr.

[3] *Darśana-bhāga* (*chien* 見 *-fen*). — Tr.

[4] *Svasaṃvitti-bhāga* (*tzŭ-cheng* 自證 *-fen*). — Tr.

[5] *Svasaṃvitti-saṃvitti-bhāga* (*cheng* 證 *-tzŭ-cheng-fen*). — Tr.

[6] *Kleśa* (*fan-nao* 煩惱). According to Buddhism, affliction is inherent in existence and is caused by the passions, which, according to the Mere Ideation school, arise out of the consciousness of the individual. — Tr.

of "mental discrimination," i.e., of perceiving and discriminating "external things." Therefore when consciousness is born, it manifests itself under two aspects: that of what discriminates, which is called "subject," or more literally "what can cause"; and that of what is thus discriminated, which is called "object," or more literally "what is caused." Because there is a subject which discriminates, there must also be an object of this act of discrimination. It is important to keep in mind that this "object" (i.e., the seemingly external world) is just as much a product of the evolutions of consciousness as is the "subject" which "mentally discriminates" it. The perceiver and the perceived are actually one.

However, in addition to the perceiving and perceived divisions or functional aspects, there is another division upon which these are dependent and which constitutes their "essential substance." It checks upon or corroborates the results obtained through the interaction of the other two divisions, and it is through it that what we call knowledge is obtained. It is called the self-corroboratory division because it is the realization by the consciousness of itself. Even here, however, the process does not stop, for there is still a fourth division which re-tests or re-corroborates what has been corroborated by the third division. This is called the division which "corroborates the self-corroborating division." [1]

The "ego" and the "things" or *dharmas* of the external world are all equally evolved by consciousness. "Evolution (*pien* 變) means that consciousness develops into what seem to be two divisions," namely those of perceiver and perceived, i.e., of subject and object. "It is in dependence upon these two divisions that the ego (*ātman*) and things (*dharmas*) are established." [2] These manifestations, however, are false, for as the *Ch'eng Wei-shih Lun* points out:

"These phenomena of the *ātman* and the *dharmas*, though within the consciousness, seem, because of (false) mental discrimination, to

---

[1] These four functional divisions of consciousness should not be confused with the eight different kinds of consciousness, enumerated earlier. The process is one in which there are: (1) the manifestations by consciousness of seemingly objective objects and phenomena, which are (2) perceived by a seemingly subjective consciousness. The resulting sensed images are (3) checked upon by the self-corroboratory division, resulting in the accumulation of organized knowledge. (4) A second corroboratory division further checks this knowledge to insure its correctness. — Tr.

[2] *Ch'eng Wei-shih Lun*, 1.8.

be manifested in the external world. That is why all sentient beings, from time without beginning, have believed in them as a real *ātman* and real *dharmas*. The case is like that of a man in a dream, who, under the force of this dream, in which his mind manifests what seem to be all kinds of external objects, believes that these really exist as external objects. What the ignorant thus imagine to be a 'real' *ātman* and 'real' *dharmas* are all absolutely devoid of (objective) existence. They are simply established in this way in accordance with these people's own mistaken beliefs. This is why we maintain that they are false. Thus the seeming *ātman* and seeming *dharmas* which are evolved within the consciousness, although (in one way) they do exist, nevertheless do not have the nature of a real *ātman* and real *dharmas*, despite their seeming appearance as such. [1] This, then, is the reason for saying that they are false. (In other words, what we believe to be) external objects are established thus in accordance with our (mistaken) beliefs, and do not 'exist' in the same way as does consciousness. But the inner consciousness, being the causation on which their appearance depends, is not 'non-existent' in the same way as are these (external) objects" (1.10-11).

This doctrine, that external objects do not "exist" in the same way as does consciousness, and that consciousness is not "non-existent" in the same way as are external objects, is that known as avoiding the two extremes and following the middle path. However, as we shall see later, it is only the first teaching in the theory of Mere Ideation.

iii. *The Eighth or Ālaya Consciousness*

The *Ch'eng Wei-shih Lun* says: "The primary evolving consciousness is, in the Mahāyāna and Hīnayāna teachings alike, termed that of *ālaya* 阿賴耶. (The name of) this consciousness has in it the idea of storing: it is both able to store and to be stored. In other words, it and the defiling elements condition one another, so that sentient beings take it to be their inner ego. [2] ... This (*ālaya* consci-

---

[1] I.e., being products of consciousness, they do exist, yet at the same time they do not really exist in the sense of possessing objective reality apart from consciousness. — Tr.

[2] The *ālaya-vijñāna* is the most primary or basic of the eight kinds of consciousness, a sort of "subconsciousness." From it there evolve what seem to us to be external phenomena, but at the same time these phenomena act upon (and

ousness), because it is able to induce the varyingly matured fruition of the good or evil acts [1] committed in the course of transmigration through the various realms of existence, is therefore called the maturing (consciousness). ... But because it is able to hold firmly all the 'seeds' of things, [2] without allowing them to be lost, it is therefore called the seed (consciousness)" (2.96-98).

The Sanskrit name of this eighth kind of consciousness, *ālaya-vijñāna*, means "storehouse consciousness" (*tsang shih* 藏識), because it "has in it the idea of storing: it is both able to store and to be stored." It is also called the "maturing consciousness," or literally, "varyingly maturing consciousness," [3] because the fruits or phenomena evolved from it mature at varying times and in varying categories. And finally, it is called the "seed consciousness" (*chung-tzŭ shih*), because within it are stored the "seeds" or germs of all things both within and outside of our existing world.

As regards these "seeds," one theory asserts that "they are all innately existent (from the beginning), and not engendered as the result of 'perfuming.' This perfuming influence can only induce their further growth (after they already exist)" (*ibid.*, p. 102). That is to say, the seeds from which spring the seeming manifestations of things in the outer world are all of them eternally innate in the *ālaya* consciousness. They are thus not engendered by the "perfuming influence" of the other seven kinds of consciousness, but only stimulated in their further growth by this influence. [4]

According to another theory, however, "all the seeds are engendered as the result of perfuming. However, both (the seeds them-

---

defile) the *ālaya* consciousness in a never ending cycle. It is the "storehouse" of the "seeds" which produce defilement (on which see below), and at the same time it is these "seeds" themselves (since they spring from the *ālaya*). That is why it both stores and is itself stored. — Tr.

[1] *Karma* (*yeh* 業). — Tr.

[2] *Bījas* (*chung-tzŭ* 種子). They are the "seeds" or causes of all phenomena, which are continuously being stored up in the *ālaya* consciousness and as continuously germinating to produce external phenomena. — Tr.

[3] For this term see above, p. 300, note 4. — Tr.

[4] By "perfuming" or *vāsanā* (*hsün-hsi* 熏習) is meant the flow of influence from the other seven kinds of consciousness which (according to different theories) either engenders the seeds in the *ālaya* consciousness, or stimulates their growth. Since this influence is itself originally derived from the *ālaya*, there is actually a continuing flow of cause and effect. — Tr.

selves and the perfuming of them) have existed from time without beginning. Hence there has never been a time when the seeds have not been engendered. 'Seeds' is simply another name for the repetitive influence which comes from the perfuming, just as the odor of the hemp plant is engendered by the perfumage of its flowers" (*ibid.*, p. 105). This metaphor refers to the fact that the hemp itself has no odor until it is perfumed by its flowers. The process of perfuming and being perfumed has always gone on as it does now, and therefore there has never been a time when the seeds of the *ālaya* consciousness have not been engendered.

Finally, there is a third theory which says that there are actually two kinds of seeds: "The first are those which have innately existed (from all time); the second are those whose existence has had a beginning" (*ibid.*, p. 107). Here we find an attempt to compromise between the two foregoing theories.

The seeds can further be classified into those with taint [1] and those without taint. The tainted seeds are the causes of all the (impure) *dharmas* which belong to our imperfect world; the untainted seeds are the causes of all the (pure) *dharmas* which belong to another transcendental world. Thus the *Ch'eng Wei-shih Lun* says:

"From this we must believe that sentient beings have from all time possessed untainted seeds, not derived from perfuming but naturally complete of themselves. Later, if (these beings) attain to excellence, (the seeds) are caused to grow as the result of perfuming. In this way is caused the rise of untainted *dharmas* (in such perfected beings). And with the rise of these untainted (*dharmas*), they in turn perfume and thus produce (new untainted seeds). The same is true, we must understand, of the seeds of the tainted *dharmas*" [2] (*ibid.*, p. 113).

This means that the seeds contained in the *ālaya* consciousness, being perfumed by the other seven forms of consciousness, are thus caused to grow, resulting in the appearance of things or *dharmas*. The *ālaya* consciousness (of which the seeds are a part) is what is perfumed; the other seven consciousnesses are the agents of the perfuming. We read further:

---

[1] *Āsvara* (*lou* 漏). — Tr.

[2] I.e., some of the tainted seeds, too, exist from the beginning. Their growth is facilitated by perfuming, as a result of which they produce tainted *dharmas*, and these in turn perfume and thus produce new tainted seeds. — Tr.

"The consciousnesses which perfume and the consciousness which is perfumed live and perish together; on this is established the concept of perfuming. In this way the seeds that lie within what is perfumed (i.e., within the *ālaya* consciousness) are engendered and caused to grow, just as the hemp plant is perfumed (by its flower). Hence the term perfuming. As soon as the seeds are engendered, the consciousnesses which perfume act in their turn as causes to perfume and mature the seeds. These three elements (the seed which is first born, the consciousnesses which then perfume, and the seeds which are either engendered or caused to grow by this perfuming) revolve in a cycle, simultaneously acting as cause and effect, just as a wick engenders flame and the flame engenders the incandescence of the wick. Or again they are like bundles of reeds (stacked side by side), each of which is supported by the other. It is according to unshakable reason that cause and effect should be simultaneous" (*ibid.*, p. 122).

This, then, is the way in which the perfumer and what is perfumed reciprocally act upon one another as cause and effect. The tainted seeds produce tainted *dharmas*, which in turn perfume tainted seeds, and the untainted seeds produce untainted *dharmas*, which in turn perfume untainted seeds. Because of the former, beings are kept bound to the wheel of transmigration; because of the latter, they are enabled to escape from this wheel. However—and this is an important doctrinal difference between the Mere Ideation and some of the other Mahāyāna schools—the untainted seeds are not universally possessed by all beings alike. This explains the differences in nature between different beings: some are wholly devoid of the untainted seeds, some possess seeds qualifying them only for the two lesser Vehicles of Buddhism, [1] and some possess the untainted seeds of Buddhahood itself. This is why, according to the Mere Ideation school, not all men possess the Buddha-nature or can achieve Buddhahood.

What we perceive as external phenomena, such as mountains, rivers, etc., are all evolved by the seeds within the *ālaya* consciousness. Thus the *Ch'eng Wei-shih Lun* says:

"As regards the (external) localization (of mental representations),

---

[1] Those of Hīnayāna (the Lesser Vehicle) and Madhyamayāna (the Middle Vehicle). The followers of the latter follow a middle course between Hīnayāna (which stresses individual salvation) and Mahāyāna (which stresses salvation for all living creatures). — Tr.

what is meant is that the maturing consciousness, through the 'maturing' influence of its 'universal' seeds, evolves the manifestations of the seeming matter, etc., of the receptacle-world, that is, the external major elements [1] and the matter formed upon them. Although what is evolved by sentient beings in this way is separate for each, the resulting appearances are each like the other, so that there is no differentiation in their (external) localization. The case is like that of the illuminations cast by many lamps, which though separate for each, seem to form a common whole" (*ibid.*, pp. 135-136).

This tells us that such objects as mountains, rivers, etc., are evolved out of the "universal" (*kung hsiang* 共 相) seeds which belong to all *ālaya* consciousnesses in common. Thus they are not simply the product of any single consciousness. We read further: "By whose maturing consciousnesses are these appearances evolved? . . . This world is evolved by the maturing consciousnesses of those beings who now live in it or who are going to be reborn in it. . . . Their deeds (*karma*) being the same, (their consciousnesses) thus evolve in a way common to one another" (*ibid.*, p. 136). In other words, the mountains, rivers, etc., of the world evolve out of the "universal" seeds which are contained in all the maturing consciousnesses alike of all those beings who now live or will at some future time be reborn in the world of which these mountains and rivers are a part. The maturing consciousness of each such sentient being individually evolves its own particular mountains, rivers, etc. But because this is done by means of the "universal" seeds which are common to the consciousnesses of all other beings, "the resulting appearances are each like the other," just as the separate illuminations from many lamps combine to make a seemingly single illumination.

The *Ch'eng Wei-shih Lun* continues: "As regards the sense faculties and their (supporting physical) body, what is meant is that the maturing consciousness, through the maturing influence of its non-universal (i.e., private) seeds, evolves what seem to be the sense faculties and the bodily basis for these faculties, [2] that is, the internal major elements and the matter formed from them. It (this consciousness), through the maturing influence of its universal seeds, also

---

[1] Earth, water, fire, and wind, which are the four major elements in the physical universe, according to Hindu thought. — Tr.

[2] The sense faculties are those of seeing, hearing, etc. Their bodily basis is the physical eye, ear, etc., which do the seeing and hearing. — Tr.

in the same way evolves the bodily basis (for the sense faculties) of others. For if it were not so, I would be unable to perceive (the physical sense organs of) those others. But at this point there are some who hold that (not only the physical sense organs of those other persons but) also their sense faculties are evolved (by one's own consciousness). [1] Thus according to what is said in the *Madhyānta-vibhāga*, [2] it (the *ālaya* consciousness) produces manifestations which seem to be those of the five sense faculties that pertain both to one's own and to other bodies (i.e., individuals). But against this it is held that it is only the seeming bodily basis (of the sense faculties of those other beings) which can be evolved (by our own consciousness), whereas their actual sense faculties are not useful to us (and hence not evolved by our consciousness). (In actual fact), what is said (in that work) is that the manifestations, seemingly those of the five sense faculties of oneself and of others, respectively evolve out of the individual consciousnesses of oneself and of those others. This is why, when someone is reborn in another stage [3] or has entered *Nirvāṇa*, the body which he leaves behind him continues to be visible (to our own consciousness)" (*ibid.*, pp. 138-139).

There are five sense faculties—themselves intangible and invisible—together with the "bodily basis" of these faculties, i.e., the physical organs of the eye, ear, etc., in which the faculties are lodged, and which, in their totality, constitute the body of the person concerned. In one's own case, these five faculties, together with their physical organs, are all evolved from the "non-universal" or private seeds that lie within one's own maturing consciousness. Similarly, the sense faculties and organs of other persons are, for those persons themselves, evolved from the "non-universal" seeds of their own particular consciousness. For us vis-à-vis those persons, however, the situation is different: their physically visible sense organs, which, for them, are evolved out of the "non-universal" seeds of their consciousness, are, for us, evolved out of the "universal" seeds that lie within our own consciousness. For if this were not so, how

---

[1] I.e., to take one example, that our own consciousness not only evolves the physical eye of another person (which is the reason why we are capable of perceiving that eye), but also the seeing faculty of that eye. — Tr.

[2] *Pien Chung-pien* (Discrimination between the Middle and the Extremes), a work by Hsüan-tsang based on a work by Vasubandhu. It is TT no. 1600 (vol. 31, pp. 464-477). — Tr.

[3] There are supposed to be ten stages (variously enumerated) through which it is necessary to pass before achieving Buddhahood. — Tr.

would we be able to perceive those sense organs of other persons?

At this point, however, the suggestion is made that our own consciousness evolves for us in this way not only the bodily sense organs of the other persons (which are visible to us), but also even the faculties of those organs (which are invisible). The *Madhyānta-vibhāga* is cited here in seeming support. There is another theory, however, which denies this thesis on the ground that the sense faculties of any given individual are perceptible and useful only to that individual; they "are not useful to us," that is, to persons other than the individual particularly concerned. What the *Madhyānta-vibhāga* really means to say, therefore, according to this second theory, is simply that the consciousness of each separate being individually evolves its own sense faculties.

Here, however, another question arises: How are we to know that the bodily sense organs of other beings really do evolve out of the "universal" seeds which are common to our own consciousness and to those of other beings? The answer is that when someone is reborn in a new stage of existence, or has entered *Nirvāṇa*, his body (including the physical sense organs, such as the eye, ear, etc.) should, if it were really the product of his own consciousness only, no longer be present. Nevertheless, it is a fact that "the body which he leaves behind him continues to be visible" to us. From this we can deduce that this body is a product of our own consciousness.

Still another difficulty arises, however, for on the one hand, according to what has been stated, the sense faculties of a given individual, together with the bodily basis for these faculties, are both evolved out of the "non-universal" seeds contained in that individual's own consciousness. At the same time, however, it is also stated that the bodily basis of the senses is perceptible to us who are outsiders, and that it is therefore evolved from the "universal" seeds of our own consciousness. But if this be so, how can what is thus evolved by the "non-universal" seeds of another individual's consciousness exactly coincide with what is evolved by the "universal" seeds of our own consciousness? To this major problem the *Ch'eng Wei-shih Lun* gives no answer.

Regarding the *ālaya* consciousness we read further in the same work:

"Is the *ālaya* consciousness permanent or impermanent?[1] It

---

[1] I.e., does it remain forever immutable or does it come to an end? The answer, as we shall see, is that it does neither. It continues; hence it is not im-

is neither permanent nor impermanent, for it is in perpetual revolution. By 'perpetual' is meant that this consciousness, from time without beginning, has constituted a homogeneous successive sequence, without interruption. For it is the basis of the manifestations of the transmigratory course through the (various) realms, and in its nature it is firm enough to hold the seeds without allowing them to be lost. By 'revolution' is meant that this consciousness, from time without beginning, is born and perishes again from moment to moment, ever successively changing. As cause it perishes and as fruit it is then born. Thus it never remains continuously single. Through the evolutions of the (other) consciousnesses it is perfumed and thus forms seeds. 'Perpetual' bars from it the idea of impermanence; 'revolution' indicates that it is not permanent.

"In (its sequence of) cause and effect it is like a violent torrent—a torrent which is never impermanent yet never permanent, and ever flows onward in sequence, (carrying with it) what sometimes floats, sometimes sinks. Thus too is this consciousness, in which, from time without beginning, there is a successive sequence of being born and perishing, so that it is neither permanent nor impermanent. It (carries along) sentient beings, sometimes floating, sometimes sinking, without allowing them to leave (the cycle of existence).

"Again it is like a violent torrent which, though beaten by the wind into waves, flows onward without interruption. So too is this consciousness, which though it encounters conditions arising from the visual and other kinds of consciousness, perpetually maintains its onward flux.

"Or yet again it is like a violent torrent, in whose waters fish are borne below and grasses above, without it itself abandoning its flow. So too is this consciousness, which perpetually follows its onward revolution, with its perfumed (seeds) which lie within, and sensory stimuli which lie without.

"These comparisons show that this consciousness, from time without beginning, has been both cause and effect, and so is neither impermanent nor permanent. They mean that from time eternal this consciousness is one in which from moment to moment effects are born and causes perish. Because these effects are born, it is not impermanent; because these causes perish, it is not permanent. To

---

permanent. But in so doing it ever undergoes change; hence it has no absolute permanence. — Tr.

be neither impermanent nor permanent: this is the principle of causation. That is why it is said that this consciousness is in perpetual revolution like a torrent" (3.156-157).

In this way, then, the *ālaya* consciousness perpetually rolls onward like a torrent, carrying with it all sentient beings, floating or submerged beneath its waters, and thus causing them to pass through the endless cycle of life and death.

iv. *The Seventh or Manas Consciousness and the Six Other Consciousnesses*

Of the eight kinds of consciousness, the seventh, known as the *manas* 末那 consciousness or consciousness of intellection, is described in the *Ch'eng Wei-shih Lun* as follows:

"Having first dealt with the evolving maturing consciousness, we must now explain the evolving consciousness of intellection. [1] In the sacred teachings this consciousness is given the alternate name of *manas*, because in its perpetual practice of intellection it surpasses the other kinds of consciousness" [2] (3.226).

This seventh or *manas* consciousness "perpetually thinks about the ego (*ātman*), to which it clings" (4.254). As a result, it has close relationship with the four fundamental *kleśas* or sources of affliction and delusion (defined below). We read further:

"This *manas*, which spontaneously and perpetually links itself with the *ālaya* consciousness, has a reciprocal relationship with the four fundamental sources of affliction. What are these four? They are ego-ignorance and ego-belief, together with self-conceit and self-love. [3] Ego-ignorance means lack of understanding. It is to be ignorant of the (true) nature of the ego, and deluded as to the principle that there is no ego. Therefore it is called ego-ignorance. Ego-belief means the clinging to (the principle of) ego. It wrongly imagines certain things to be an ego when they are not so. Therefore it is called ego-belief. Self-conceit means pride. Basing itself on the belief in an ego, it causes the mind to assume a high and mighty air. Therefore it

---

[1] See above, p. 300, note 5. — Tr.

[2] *Manas* means in Sanskrit mind, thought, intellection. This, above all others, is the thinking consciousness. — Tr.

[3] *Ātmamoha* (*wo-ch'ih* 我 癡), *ātmadṛṣṭi* (*wo-chien* 見), *ātmamāna* (*wo-man* 慢), and *ātmasneha* (*wo-ai* 愛). — Tr.

is called self-conceit. Self-love means a greedy desire for the self. Because of its belief in the ego it develops deep attachments for it. Therefore it is called self-love....

"These four, by their constant rise, disturb and pollute the innermost mind (the *ālaya* consciousness), and cause the outer (i.e., the remaining seven) operating consciousnesses perpetually to produce defiling elements. It is because of these (four) that sentient beings are bound to the cycle of transmigration without being able to escape. That is why they are called the afflictions (*kleśas*)" (4.255-256).

Besides the eighth or *ālaya* and seventh or *manas* consciousnesses, there remain six others, of which we are told:

"Having next dealt with the evolving consciousness of intellection, we must explain the evolving consciousness which discriminates (seemingly external) objects. [1] This consciousness is divided into a total of six categories, in accordance with the six sense organs and their respective spheres (of perception). They are known as the visual consciousness and so on down to that of the sense-center" [2] (5.289).

Thus the consciousnesses which sensually discriminate the objects of the external world are of six kinds: the five senses (sight, hearing, smell, taste, and touch), plus a sixth faculty, the sense-center, which, as we shall see, unifies and coordinates the ideas derived from the five senses. We read further:

"In dependence upon the basic (i.e., *ālaya*) consciousness, the five (sensory) kinds of consciousness manifest themselves in accordance with conditioning factors, sometimes together, sometimes separately, just as waves depend upon water. But the (sixth) sense-center manifests itself constantly, except for beings born into the 'Heaven without Thought,' [3] those in the two mindless meditations, and those who are torpid or unconscious" (7.398).

This is elaborated as follows: "The basic consciousness is the *ālaya* consciousness, [4] because it is basic for the birth of the other kinds of consciousness, both soiled and pure. 'In dependence upon'

---

[1] See above, p. 301, note 1. — Tr.

[2] *Mano-vijñāna* (*yi-shih* 意 識), lit., "thought consciousness." — Tr.

[3] The thirteenth of the eighteen Heavens, a Heaven in which thinking no longer takes place. — Tr.

[4] Lit., *ādāna* 阿 陀 那 consciousness, an alternate name for the *ālaya*, meaning "holding together," i.e., functioning as the basic nexus of the whole organism. — Tr.

means that the first six evolving kinds of consciousness take this basic consciousness as their common and immediate support. 'The five kinds of consciousness' refers to the first five evolving consciousnesses which, being similar in category, are spoken of together. The words, 'manifest themselves in accordance with conditioning factors,' indicate that this (manifestation) does not occur constantly. By 'conditioning factors' [1] are meant such factors as the mental activity (of the sixth or sense-center consciousness), the sense organs (whose attention is directed in accordance with this sense-center), and the (external) objects (toward which this attention is directed). This means that the five (sensory) kinds of consciousness are dependent internally upon the basic (*ālaya*) consciousness, and are coordinated externally with such conditioning factors as the mental activity (of the sense center), the five sense organs, the (external) objects (sensed by these organs), etc. Only then do they get to be manifested. For this reason they sometimes act together, sometimes separately, according to whether the combining of external factors occurs suddenly or gradually. Thus they are like the waves on water, which, in accordance with conditioning factors, are sometimes numerous, sometimes few. Further comparisons may be found in the *sūtras*.

"The operations of the (first) five kinds of consciousness are crude and unstable, and the conditioning factors on which they depend are often incomplete. Therefore they act only sometimes and often do not act at all. As to the sixth or sense-center consciousness, it too is crude and unstable. Nevertheless, the conditioning factors on which it depends are always present, so that it is only when adverse factors are present that it sometimes does not operate. In the case of the seventh and eighth kinds of consciousness, their operations are fine and subtle, and the conditioning factors on which they depend are at all times present. Therefore no adverse factor can ever prevent them from acting in toto" (*ibid.*, pp. 398-399).

Thus the seventh or *manas* and eighth or *ālaya* consciousnesses never fail to manifest their activities, whereas the first five consciousnesses, those of the senses, must wait upon the concatenation of numerous conditioning factors before they can do so. As for the sixth or sense-center consciousness (*mano-vijñāna*), the function of which is to coordinate and direct the preceding five, it is ever operative save under certain adverse factors. These, for example, are those

---

[1] *Pratyaya* (*yüan* 緣). — Tr.

of beings who have been reborn into the "Heaven without Thought," or who have escaped from thought by entering a state of meditation, or who are in a condition of torpor or unconsciousness.

Although the general term for all of the above eight kinds of consciousness is *vijñāna* or consciousness, this word especially applies to the first six of them, whose function is more particularly that of discriminating or perceiving external objects. The *Ch'eng Wei-shih Lun* says:

"That which accumulates and produces (all things) is called mind, [1] that which reasons is called intellection (*manas*), and that which discriminates is called consciousness (*vijñāna*). Although the three terms apply to all the eight kinds of consciousness, they respectively apply with particular appropriateness (to the three following categories): The eighth is called mind, because in it the seeds of all things are accumulated and from it all things arise. The seventh is called intellection because, being linked with the storehouse (i.e., the *ālaya*) consciousness, it through its perpetual intellection regards the latter as an ego (*ātman*), etc. And the remaining six are (more particularly) called consciousness because their operations are those of discriminating—even though crudely, unstably, and with interruptions—according to the six spheres (of their senses)" (5.275).

Thus although the general term for all eight *vijñānas* is consciousness, if we wish to define their functions more specifically, we say that the eighth is mind, the seventh intellection, and the remaining six are consciousness in particular.

What is popularly regarded as the "ego" or *ātman* (*wo*), together with the various *dharmas* (*fa*), i.e., all those things, phenomena and forces that are external to the seeming ego, are all alike evolved out of the primary or *ālaya* consciousness. This seeming ego and these seeming *dharmas* are then regarded by the remaining seven consciousnesses as having a real or objective existence. Belief in the realness of such an ego is called "ego-clinging"; that in the realness of such *dharmas* is called "*dharma*-clinging." [2] The *Ch'eng Wei-shih Lun* says on this:

"The ego-clingings are, generally speaking, of two kinds: (1) that which is innate, (2) that which results from mental discrimination. The ego-clinging which is innate is perpetually present in the

---

[1] *Citta* (*hsin* 心). — Tr.

[2] *Ātma-grāha* (*wo-chih* 我執) and *dharma-grāha* (*fa-chih*). — Tr.

individual, owing to the internal causal influence of a false perfuming which has been going on since beginningless time. Thus, without depending on (external) erroneous teachings or discriminations, it spontaneously operates. That is why it is called innate.

"This, however, is again subdivided into two kinds: The first is constant and continuous, and pertains to the seventh consciousness, which, directing itself to the eighth consciousness, produces from this an individualized mental image to which it clings as a real ego. The second kind is at times interrupted and pertains to the sixth consciousness, which, directing itself to the five tenacious aggregates [1] that are evolved from consciousness, sometimes in toto, sometimes separately, produces from them an individualized mental image to which it clings as a real ego. These two kinds of ego-clinging, being subtle, are difficult to cut off. It is only later, during the course of cultivation in which the eminent contemplation of unreality is repeatedly practiced, that these can finally be annihilated.

"As for the ego-clinging which results from mental discrimination, it derives from the force of external factors and so is not innate in the individual. It must wait for erroneous teachings or discriminations before it can arise. That is why the term 'mental discrimination' is applied to it. It pertains exclusively to the sixth sense-center consciousness" (1.16-18).

Another passage in the *Ch'eng Wei-shih Lun* (2.80-81) describes the *dharma*-clingings in virtually identical words. These too are of two sorts: that which is innate and that which results from mental discrimination. The former may again be subdivided into that which is continuous and pertains to the seventh consciousness, and that which is sometimes interrupted and pertains to the sixth. As for the *dharma*-clinging which results from mental discrimination, it, like its counterpart among the ego-clingings, is manifested as the result of erroneous teachings and discriminations, i.e., of external rather than internal factors, and it pertains to the sixth consciousness.

In summary, the seventh consciousness accepts the seemingly individualized mental images that arise from the eighth consciousness

---

[1] *Skandhas* (*yün* 蘊), the five aggregates of various factors which constitute the personality. They are form (body), perception, conception, volition, and consciousness (mind). The reason why they are described as "tenacious" (*upādāna* or *ch'ü* 取) is that they give rise to tenacious grasping or desire, which in turn produces the *skandhas*. — Tr.

and regards them as a true ego and true *dharmas*. In the same way, the sixth consciousness accepts the five *skandhas* or aggregates that are evolved by sensory consciousness and regards those of them which seemingly comprise the sensory faculties as being a true ego. Those which seemingly comprise the material things of the external world (mountains, rivers, etc.) it likewise regards as true *dharmas*. Thus the sixth and seventh kinds of consciousness are the originators of these two sorts of erroneous clinging.

The eight consciousnesses, furthermore, can neither be said to be separate units nor to form a single whole. That is, in the words of the *Ch'eng Wei-shih Lun*, they can neither be said to be "definitely different" nor "definitely one":

"The eight kinds of consciousness cannot, in their natures, be said to be definitely one. This is because their activities, the conditioning causes on which they depend, and their associated qualities, are different. It is also because one of them may perish without the others doing so, and because they differ in character inasmuch as some can perfume and the other is perfumed. [1]

"At the same time they are not definitely different, for as is said in the *sūtra*, the eight kinds of consciousness are like the waves which cannot be differentiated from the water. This is because, if they were definitely different, they could not be as cause and effect to one another. Thus they are like the tricks of a conjurer, for which no definite nature can be ascertained.

"As to what has been said previously regarding the varying characteristics of the different kinds of consciousness, this conforms to a wordly kind of reasoning; it is not the highest truth. In this highest truth (the various kinds of consciousness) can neither be thought nor spoken of. As is said in the hymn: The mind, intellection, and the (other) kinds of consciousness, eight in all, from a popular point of view have different characteristics, but from the point of view of truth they have no difference. For neither their own characteristics, nor those things to which they give characteristics, have any existence" (7.414).

v. *All Is Mere Ideation*

In order to destroy the two "clingings" just described, it is necessary to realize that neither the seemingly genuine ego nor the

---

[1] The eighth consciousness is perfumed; the other seven perfume. — Tr.

seemingly genuine external *dharmas* "really exist." The *Ch'eng Wei-shih Lun* says:

"What we have previously spoken of are the three evolving categories of consciousness and their mental qualities. The term 'evolving' is applied to them because they are all capable of evolving into two seeming aspects: that of the perceiving division and that of the perceived division. [1] The evolved perceiving division is termed 'discrimination,' [2] because it takes the perceived division (as the object of perception). The evolved perceived division is termed 'that which is discriminated,' because it is taken by the perceiving division (as the object of perception). According to this correct principle, there are definitely no 'real' ego or *dharmas* aside from what is thus evolved from consciousness. For apart from what thus 'takes' or 'is taken,' there exists nothing else; there are no 'real' things apart from these two aspects. Therefore everything phenomenal (*yu wei* 有爲) and noumenal (*wu wei*), everything seemingly 'real' and 'false' alike, is all inseparable from consciousness. The word 'mere' (in the term Mere Ideation) is used to deny that there are any 'real' things aside from consciousness, but not to deny that the mental functions, *dharmas*, etc., as inseparable from consciousness, do exist.

"(Use of the term) 'evolving' indicates that the internal consciousness evolves manifestations of what seem to be an ego and the *dharmas* of the external world. This evolutionary capacity is called 'discrimination.' Because of its nature, it falsely discriminates (things as being real), namely the minds and their mental functions pertaining to the Threefold World. [3] The objects to which it clings are termed 'that which is discriminated,' and consist of an ego and of *dharmas* which it falsely regards as real. In this way discrimination evolves what seem to be external objects, consisting of a false ego and *dharmas*. But the ego and *dharmas* thus discriminated as real all very definitely have no existence. We have already, by the use of quoted teachings and by reason, widely refuted this idea.

"Therefore everything is Mere Ideation. But as for false discrimination itself, it may definitely be accepted as an established fact.

---

[1] For these terms, see above, p. 302, notes 2-3. — Tr.

[2] *Vikalpa* (*fen-pieh* 分別). See also p. 301, note 1, for almost the same term. — Tr.

[3] I.e., the entire world of sentient beings. See chap. 7, p. 256, note 3. — Tr.

For 'mere' does not deny the *dharmas*, etc., as long as they are inseparable from consciousness, and in this sense 'open space' and so
forth do exist. In this way we avoid the two extremes of either adding
(something to consciousness) or reducing (consciousness to nothing).
The meaning of Mere Ideation is established, and so we are able to
keep to the middle path" (7.417-419).

Thus Mere Ideation means that nothing exists apart from consciousness. "The word 'mere' is used to deny that there are any
'real' things aside from consciousness"—things which in themselves
"all very definitely have no existence." On the other hand, "the
dharmas, etc., as inseparable from consciousness, do exist." By
maintaining these two points of view the Mere Ideation theory
"avoids the two extremes of either adding or reducing" and is thus
"able to keep to the middle path."

In his *Ch'eng Wei-shih Lun*, Hsüan-tsang has recorded numerous
possible objections to this theory, together with his own rebuttals.
Some of the philosophically more interesting ones will be quoted in
the following pages. The first is that of an imaginary opponent who
is represented as objecting:

"If what seem to be external objects are simply products of
the inner consciousness, why is it that the things which we see in the
world, both animate and inanimate, such as places, times, bodies, and
functions, are in some cases determinate, in some indeterminate?"

To which Hsüan-tsang answers: "This uncertainty may be
explained by comparison with the world of dreams" (*ibid.*, p. 425).

K'uei-chi adds in his commentary: "The outsider objects that
if there is only inner consciousness and no objects apart from mind,
why is it that, among things as we see them in the world, inanimate
ones, such as place and time, are both determinate, whereas animate
ones, such as bodies, as well as their functions, which are inanimate, are both indeterminate? The general idea in this statement is
that place, time, and function are inanimate things, whereas bodies
are animate things. Here we should rely on the reasoning presented
in the *Twenty Stanzas*, where these four points are all explained." [1]

The work here referred to is the *Wei-shih Erh-shih Lun* or *Treatise
in Twenty Stanzas on Mere Ideation*. [2] It is Hsüan-tsang's translation

---

[1] *Ch'eng Wei-shih Lun Shu-chi*, 7b.490.
[2] *Vijñapti-mātratā-siddhi*; *Viṃśatikā*; TT no. 1590 (vol. 31, pp. 74-77).
References below are to the English translation of Clarence Hamilton. — Tr.

of a short treatise in twenty stanzas by Vasubandhu, together with an accompanying commentary by Dharmapāla. Because it greatly expands the brief questions and answers recorded in the *Ch'eng Wei-shih Lun*, we should turn to it for an understanding of the four major objections to the Mere Ideation doctrine, and their refutation. These objections are first enumerated in the *Wei-shih Erh-shih Lun* as follows:

"Why does this consciousness arise in a certain place, not in all places? Why, in this place, does the consciousness arise at a certain time, not at all times? When many streams of consciousness [1] are together at one time and place, why is the representation not determined to arise according to some particular one of them; just as a person with defective eyes sees hairs and flies, while those with good eyesight do not have these representations arise? Again, why is it that the hairs, etc., seen by persons with defective eyes do not function as hairs, etc.? The drink, food, knives, cudgels, poisons, clothes, etc., which we get in a dream lack the functions of (real) drink, etc. A city of the Gandharvas [2] cannot be used as a city. But other hair, etc., is not without use. If they (i.e., dream and waking) are really the same in that in neither case are there (real) external objects, there being only an inner consciousness which produces these seeming external objects, then (1) their determination in space, (2) their determination in time, (3) the indetermination of the stream of consciousness (which does the perceiving in each case), and (4) the existence of functioning things, all cannot be established" (pp. 22-23).

The first of these objections is based on the fact that, according to common knowledge, a world external to the mind does actually exist. A mountain, when we look at it, for example, has real existence quite apart from our own consciousness of it. This fact explains why we are able to perceive it only when we ourselves actually go where it is; we cannot perceive it anywhere else, as might be expected were it merely a product of our own consciousness. This fact is termed "determination in space."

The second objection, like the first, is based on the commonly acknowledged fact that the mountain does have real existence apart

---

[1] *Saṃtāna (hsiang-hsü* 相 續), lit., "continuity." For the explanation of this term, see Hamilton's translation, p. 21, note 10; also below, note 1 on next page. — Tr.

[2] Heavenly musicians and actors who are able to produce a magic city in which to play. — Tr.

from our own consciousness. This is why we are able to see it only at that particular time when we go where it is, and not at other times, as again might be expected were it merely a product of our own consciousness. This fact is termed "determination in time."

The third objection runs as follows: Suppose a given individual [1] suffers from faulty eyesight, which causes him falsely to see hairs, flies, etc. These false hairs and flies do not belong to the real world which, according to the ordinary view, exists independently of consciousness. This is why they are perceived only by the person suffering from defective eyesight but not by other people having normal vision. According to the Mere Ideation doctrine, however, nothing whatsoever in the outside world really has any existence in itself; everything is simply a product of our own consciousness. Yet if this be so, why is it that all the things in it are seen by all persons alike? Why should not certain things be seen only by certain persons, just as the hairs and flies of the man with defective eyesight are seen only by him and not by everyone else?

The fourth objection is that the hairs, etc., seen by the man with defective eyesight, since they are imaginary, therefore cannot actually function. The same is true of the things seen in a dream, or of the imaginary city conjured up by the Gandharvas. In the case of the ordinary hairs and cities, however, as seen by all men generally, these can all actually function, the reason being that they all really exist as objects external to the mind. For if this were not so, would they not be as incapable of functioning as are the hairs and flies of the man with defective eyesight, or the cities of the Gandharvas?

The *Wei-shih Erh-shih Lun* refutes these four objections as follows:

"The case is like that of a dream, in which there are no real objects, and yet it is in a certain place that such things as a village, a garden, a man, or a woman are seen, not in all places; and in this place it is at a certain time that this village, garden, etc., are seen, not at all times. From this, though there are no real objects apart from consciousness, yet spatial and temporal determination can be established.

---

[1] Lit., "body." The term means the same as the "stream of consciousness" mentioned on the preceding page. K'uei-chi comments (*op. cit.*): " 'Stream of consciousness' (*hsiang-hsü*) is another name for a sentient being. The term 'stream of consciousness' has reference to the fact that (in the case of such a being) when the previous group of aggregates (*skandhas*, which link it to the wheel of existence) comes to an end, a succeeding group is immediately produced."

"The words (in the preceding text), 'as the ghosts,' have reference to hungry ghosts. [1] The river (there mentioned), because it is full of pus, is called the pus river, as we speak of a ghee-bottle, meaning that it is full of ghee (clarified butter). That is, the case is like that of hungry ghosts who, because of the 'different maturing' (in each of them) of the same kind of deeds, are assembled together and all in common see the pus river; it is not determined that in this (assembly) there be only one who sees. The 'etc.' (of the preceding text) signifies the other things seen (by the hungry ghosts), such as ordure, etc., and creatures holding swords and clubs, who ward them off and stand guard, so as not to allow them to get food. From this (we see that) though there are no real objects apart from consciousness, yet the principle of the indetermination of the many streams (of consciousness which do the perceiving) is explained. [2]

"Again as in a dream, although the objects are unreal, they yet have function, such as causing the loss of semen, blood, etc. From this, although there are no real objects apart from consciousness, yet the principle that unrealities can function is established. [3]

"Thus also, relying upon diverse examples, we make it evident that the four principles of spatial determination, etc., may be established" (p. 25).

Thus even in a dream, the objects in which admittedly possess no reality apart from the mind, a village or a garden are seen only at a certain time and place, not at all times and places. From this we may deduce that "though there are no real objects apart from consciousness, yet spatial and temporal determination can be established."

Again in the case of the horde of hungry ghosts, because their deeds or *karma* are the same, they therefore all equally see the river of pus which cannot be drunk; it is not the case that this river is seen by only one of them and not by all. From this we may deduce that "though there are no real objects apart from consciousness, yet

---

[1] Ghosts who through their paucity of merit are condemned to suffer extreme hunger and thirst. — Tr.

[2] The idea here is that the pus river, etc., beheld by the hungry ghosts who are in hell, is not real but is simply the fruition of the individual consciousness of each of the ghosts, for all of whom it appears the same because all have committed the same evil deeds. — Tr.

[3] Since even the unreal things in a dream may function, the fact that things in the outside world likewise function is no proof that they are not a product of consciousness. — Tr.

the principle of the indetermination of the many streams (of consciousness which do the perceiving) is explained."

And yet again, "when, for example, it is dreamed that there is sexual intercourse between two persons, although the objects (of this dream) are unreal, they yet function so that (the dreamer), if a man, loses semen, and if a woman, loses blood." [1] From this we may deduce that "although there are no real objects apart from consciousness, yet the principle that unrealities can function is established." In summary, therefore, "although there are no real objects apart from consciousness, yet the four principles of spatial determination, etc., are all established." [2]

Returning now to the *Ch'eng Wei-shih Lun*, we find there the following further objections and rebuttals:

Outsider: "If the various forms of matter sensed by the sense organs do indeed pertain in their nature to consciousness, why is it that the latter, when it thus manifests itself in the semblance of matter, evolves in a continuing series which is homogeneous, solid, and abiding?"

Reply: "Because (the various kinds of consciousness) are under the influence of names and concepts, and because they are the supporting basis both for the pure and impure *dharmas*. Without this (kind of influence) there could be no delusion. Hence there could be no defiling elements, any more than there could be *dharmas* that are pure. That is why consciousness manifests itself in the semblance of matter" (7.428).

The objector here asks: If the various kinds of matter or *rūpa* (*se*) sensed by the sense organs (i.e., what we would term the objective world) do pertain to consciousness, why then are they "homogeneous, solid and abiding," i.e., why are they not transient and unstable? K'uei-chi comments: " 'Homogeneous' conveys the idea of mutual similarity. It means a continuing homogeneity from first to last, without any evolving differences or interruptions. Hence the term 'solid and abiding.' Vasubandhu says: 'It is to remain abiding at all times, that is to say, it refers to an evolution (of consciousness) which continues uninterruptedly.' What is 'homogeneous,

---

[1] Cf. K'uei-chi's commentary, the *Wei-shih Erh-shih Lun Shu-chi, chüan* 1; TT no. 1830 (vol. 43, p. 986).

[2] K'uei-chi, *op. cit.*, supposedly quoting the original text of the *Wei-shih Erh-shih Lun*, which, however, slightly differs.

solid, and abiding' is an evolution which continues uninterruptedly." [1]
He further comments on the reply as follows:

"This means that within the individual, from time without
beginning, there is the perfuming influence of names and concepts.
Through the force of this influence the matter, etc. (of the seemingly
external world) arises and continues to be evolved in an endless
sequence.... Delusion arises simply because of the clinging to the
matter, etc., of this (external) world (as real). Hence if it were not
for this matter, etc., there would be no delusion. Delusion consists
of the erroneous clinging to the world of matter, which is the product
of consciousness. If there were no delusion thus produced by consciousness, there would be no defiling elements. These defiling
elements are engendered through the deeds of the evil passions
(kleśas); that is, delusion is in its essence produced through the deeds
of these passions. Hence were these absent, the barriers of defilement
would not exist. [2] And if the barriers of defilement did not exist,
then, there being no impurity, there would also be no (contrasting)
purity. There would be nothing (impure) needing to be cut off, and
therefore no (need for) the clean and pure" (ibid.).

Again the hypothetical outsider is represented as asking: "The
matter, etc., of external objects is clearly discriminated and corroborated (by the sense consciousnesses). Being thus cognized, how
can it be set aside as non-existent?"

To which the answer is given: "When cognizing (first) takes
place, (these objects) are not regarded as external. It is only later that
the sense-center (the sixth consciousness), through its discrimination,
falsely creates this notion of externalness. Hence the objects thus
cognized (by consciousness) become its 'perceived division.' Inasmuch as this is evolved from consciousness it, like (the perceiving
division of consciousness), may be said to exist. But inasmuch as it
is regarded by the sense-center consciousness as constituting external
and real matter, etc., and is thus falsely believed to exist, we therefore
say that (in this sense) it does not exist. This world of matter, etc.,
is not matter though it seems to be so; it is not external though it
seems to be so. It is like the product of a dream, which cannot be
regarded as real and external" (Ch'eng Wei-shih Lun, pp. 428-429).

---

[1] Ch'eng Wei-shih Lun Shu-chi, 7b.492.
[2] The two barriers (varaṇa or chang 障) are: (1) the passions which aid
rebirth and hinder entrance into Nirvāṇa, (2) mundane wisdom, i.e., accounting
the seeming as real. — Tr.

Here the outsider asks: If the physical matter, etc., of the external world is so clearly perceived by our senses, how can it be dismissed as non-existent? To which the answer is made: What is cognized in this way constitutes in itself pure experience, and so is not at the time regarded as external; it only later comes to be regarded as such owing to the analytical discrimination of the sixth or sense-center consciousness. In the sense that what is cognized is simply the objective or perceived aspect of consciousness, it may be said to "exist." In the sense, however, that the sixth consciousness regards it as something having "real" and "external" existence apart from consciousness, it cannot be said to exist.

The outsider objects further: "(You have said that) the things (seen) during one's waking state are all like the world of dreams and are inseparable from consciousness. But when awakening from a dream, we know that the latter is only mental. Why, then, when we are awake, do we not know that the world of matter (around us) is all Mere Ideation?"

The reply to this is: "Until we have awakened from the dream, we are incapable of realizing (that it is a dream). It is only after we have awakened that we can catch up in our understanding. The same is true of our knowledge regarding the material world of our waking period. Until we have truly awakened, we cannot ourselves know it. It is only when we reach the genuine Awakening that we can catch up in our understanding. Before this genuine Awakening is achieved, we perpetually remain as in a dream. It is because of the failure to comprehend that the material world is Mere Ideation, that the Buddha speaks of the long night of transmigration" (*ibid.*, p. 429).

Chuang Tzŭ remarks very similarly: "By and by comes the Great Awakening, and then we shall find out that life itself is as a great dream." [1] What he refers to, however, is simply an awakening to the emptiness of standards of right and wrong and other such distinctions, whereas Hsüan-tsang has in mind an awakening to the realization that everything whatsoever is empty and imaginary.

The outsider asks again: "If external matter really does not exist, it may be granted that it is not the object of the internal consciousness. [2] But since another person's mind does really exist, why

---

[1] *Chuang-tzŭ*, chap. 2, p. 30. — Tr.
[2] It is not the "object" of that consciousness, being only its external manifestation and therefore having no objective existence apart from it. — Tr.

then is it not made the object of one's own (consciousness)?" [1]

The reply is: "Who says that another person's mind is not the object of one's own consciousness? We only deny that it is made its immediate object. This means that when there is consciousness (of another person's mind), it (that other mind) has no real function (in this consciousness). Thus the case is different from that of the hands, etc., which directly grasp external things themselves, or the sun, etc., which directly spreads its light itself, thus shining upon external objects. (In its relationship to another person's mind, the consciousness) is only like a mirror, in which the semblances of external objects are manifested. It is then said to understand the mind of the other person, but this understanding cannot be done by it directly. What it does understand directly is (only) what it itself evolves. That is why the *sūtra* says that there is not the least thing that can 'take' (*ch'ü* 取, i.e., perceive) any other thing. [2] The only point is that when there is consciousness, it manifests a semblance of another thing, and is then said to 'take' that thing. In this way it makes another person's mind its object, as it does the physical matter, etc., (which is evolved out of that mind)" (*ibid.*, p. 430).

Here the objector, while granting that external matter has no real, i.e., objective, existence in itself, argues that this is not true as regards the mind of another person, for since that mind is not evolved out of our own consciousness, it does possess objective existence vis-à-vis our consciousness. If, therefore, our consciousness can take that other person's mind as its object, this means that it can perceive something externally distinct from itself.

To this the reply is that the mind of another being can in actual fact be made the object of our own consciousness. The point is, however, that it cannot be "made its immediate object" in the way that the hand directly grasps an external object or the sun directly shines upon its surroundings. Our consciousness is like a mirror, and the other person's mind is like an image in that mirror. In this situation the consciousness is said to "understand" or perceive that other mind, but it cannot do so directly. K'uei-chi comments: " 'Not

---

[1] The mind of another person, i.e., another person's consciousness and mental activities, "exists" in the sense that it lies outside of, and is not evolved from, one's own "stream of consciousness." Therefore why is it not accepted as an object and cognized as such by one's own consciousness? — Tr.

[2] I.e., no one stream of consciousness can take any other stream of consciousness as the immediate object of its perception. — Tr.

the least thing' means that not the least real thing (i.e., no consciousness) can 'take' (i.e., perceive) any other thing. 'Other' refers to those 'real' things which lie outside (one's own) mind. One's own real mind cannot 'take' another person's mind. It is only a case in which, there being consciousness, its mind manifests a semblance of that other mind and is then said to 'take' that mind.... The same is true when it takes as its object the physical matter which constitutes the objective division of that other (person's consciousness): the case is similar to that of the physical matter evolved by the separate senses belonging to a single individual." [1] Thus it is not only the mind of the other person which cannot be made the direct object of our own consciousness; the same is true of the "objective division" of that mind, that is, of its seemingly external phenomenal manifestations. The situation is like that existing between the sense faculties belonging to a single individual, no one of which can sense what the other senses sense. The ear, for example, cannot sense what the eye perceives, or vice versa.

The outsider then asks: "Since there thus exists an object distinct (from one's own consciousness), how can this be called Mere Ideation?"

The answer is: "What an extraordinarily opinionated view is this, aimed at producing doubts! For how does the teaching of Mere Ideation speak only of a single consciousness? ... If there were only a single consciousness, how in that case would the distinctions be (evolved) between all the holy honored ones and lowlier men, or between the causes and the fruits of the ten cardinal directions? Who (could then expound) the Buddhist Teaching, and for the sake of whom (would it be done)?" (*Ch'eng Wei-shih Lun*, pp. 430-431).

Here the questioner objects that if other consciousnesses exist external to and not evolved out of our own consciousness, this means that objects do exist independently of our consciousness. How can this fact be harmonized with the theory of Mere Ideation? The reply is that the Mere Ideation doctrine has never postulated a single consciousness only. It freely grants the existence of other consciousnesses external to our own. For if, indeed, there were only a single consciousness, how would the distinctions be evolved between the holy honored ones (the enlightened beings) and ordinary men? And if there were no enlightened beings, who would be available to

---

[1] *Ch'eng Wei-shih Lun Shu-chi*, 7b.494.

expound the Buddhist Teaching, while if there were no ordinary men, for whom would this expounding be done?

The outsider's next question is: "If only ideation exists, without any external causation, from what are generated the many forms of distinctions?"

The answer is: "The stanza says: 'From the consciousness which contains all seeds (the *ālaya* consciousness) such and such evolution takes place. Through the force of this process these various kinds of distinction are engendered.' The commentary says on this: ... The meaning of this stanza is that, though there is no external causation, yet because of the differing evolutions of all the seeds present in the primary (*ālaya*) consciousness, and because of the evolving influence of the eight kinds of consciousness in their manifested activity, such-and-such kinds of distinctions are produced. Why assume an external cause to explain their birth? The birth of the pure *dharmas* should be understood in the same manner. They are produced through the activity of the pure (seeds of the *ālaya* consciousness)" (*ibid.*, pp. 433-435).

The *ālaya* consciousness contains both pure and impure seeds. The pure seeds spontaneously produce pure *dharmas* or things, and the impure seeds impure *dharmas*. Thus out of the *ālaya* are produced all *dharmas*, pure and impure alike, and these in turn react to "perfume" the *ālaya*. This is why the *Ch'eng Wei-shih Lun* says: "The *ālaya* consciousness and the impure *dharmas* interact on one another as cause and effect, just as the wick and the flame (interact to) produce the incandescence (of a lamp), or bundles of reeds (stacked side by side) support one another. It is only through these two (the *ālaya* and the impure *dharmas*) that causality is established. There need be no other causality" (2.108). Precisely the same process of reciprocal causation also operates between the *ālaya* and the pure *dharmas*. Thus the *ālaya* is in itself both cause and effect, and in itself is capable of producing all things, both pure and impure. What need, then, to look for external causation? The fact that all sentient beings are bound to the perpetual flux of life and death "springs from internal causation, independent of external causes. Therefore there is only ideation." [1]

vi. *The Three Characters of Existence and Non-existence, and the Bhūtatathatā*

There are three aspects or characters (*san hsing* 三 性) of

---

[1] *Op. cit.*, 8.502.

existence or being, under which all things may be regarded, depending upon the degree of true understanding we ourselves possess of these things. They are called: (1) character of sole imagination, (2) character of dependency on others, (3) character of ultimate reality. [1] The *Ch'eng Wei-shih Lun* says:

"These three characters are all inseparable from the mind and its attributes. That is to say: (1) The mind and its attributes, together with the manifestations evolved by it, are engendered through numerous conditioning factors, and are thus like a conjurer's tricks which, not (really) existing even though they seem to exist, deceive the ignorant. All this is called the 'character of dependency on others.' (2) The ignorant thereupon perversely believe in them as an ego and as *dharmas* which exist or do not exist, are identical or different, are inclusive or exclusive, etc. But like 'flowers in the sky,' [2] they are non-existent both in (inner) nature and (external) aspect. All this is called the 'character of sole imagination.' (3) These things, which are thus dependent on others and are wrongly regarded as an ego and as *dharmas*, are all (really) empty (*śūnya*). The genuine nature of consciousness thus revealed by this 'emptiness' is called the 'character of ultimate reality.' Thus these three (characters of things) are all inseparable from mind, etc." (8.533).

All things, therefore, are (1) "manifestations falsely evolved by the mind and its attributes under the inducement of numerous conditioning factors. Like the tricks of a conjurer, heat mirages, the objects of a dream, images in a mirror, reflections of light, echoes in a valley, the moon's reflection in water, or transformations of magical beings, they are not, yet seem to be" (*ibid.*, p. 532). This kind of delusion pertains to their "character of dependency on others." (2) Through lack of understanding, however, ignorant people fail to recognize things as being merely falsely evolved manifestations, and therefore erroneously look upon them as constituting a real ego and real *dharmas*. This kind of delusion pertains to their "character of sole imagination." (3) If, however, we can but recognize that all things are merely the product of numerous causes, and that they therefore have no inner reality in themselves but are

---

[1] Respectively: (1) *parikalpita-svabhāva* (*pien-chi so-chih hsing* 遍計所執性), (2) *paratantra-svabhāva* (*yi-t'a-ch'i* 依他起 *hsing*), (3) *parinispanna-svabhāva* (*yüan-ch'eng-shih* 圓成實 *hsing*). — Tr.

[2] A metaphor for what is illusory, like spots before the eyes. — Tr.

merely falsely evolved manifestations, then they may be seen, either in their aspect as a seeming ego or as seeming *dharmas*, to be equally "empty." The true aspect of things and of consciousness which is revealed through these two kinds of "emptiness" pertains to their "character of ultimate reality."

Paralleling these three aspects or characters of existence, under which all things may be viewed, they have three corresponding characters of non-existence (*san wu hsing*), namely: (1) non-existent as regards characteristics, (2) non-existent as regards origination, (3) non-existent as regards the highest truth. [1] The *Ch'eng Wei-shih Lun* says:

"(1) In connection with the first '(character of) sole imagination,' the fact that (things) are 'non-existent as regards characteristics' may be established. (As viewed) in this way, they are absolutely non-existent, both in essence and appearance, like 'flowers in the sky.' (2) In connection with the second '(character of) dependency on others,' the fact that they are 'non-existent as regards origination' may be established. (As viewed) in this way, they are like a conjurer's tricks, which originate (i.e., take place) only because of various (unseen) causes. They do not, as is falsely supposed, have a nature (i.e., independent existence) of their own. But though we may allege that they are non-existent, they are not wholly non-existent. (3) In connection with the final '(character of) ultimate reality,' the fact that they are 'non-existent as regards the highest truth' may be established. The highest truth is far removed from the first 'character of sole imagination,' in which (things) are believed to be a (real) ego and *dharmas*. Therefore though we allege that it is 'non-existent,' it is not wholly non-existent" (9.559).

Of these three forms of non-existence, only the first is really so; as to the third (and the second as well), we merely "allege that it is non-existent." Thus we read again:

"The latter two characters are really not ones of (ordinary) non-existence. Ignorant people, however, impose upon things their own false belief that these really have a nature of their own as ego or as *dharmas*, and this is called belief in their '(character of) sole imagination.' In order to eradicate this belief, therefore, the revered Buddha

---

[1] Respectively: (1) *lakṣaṇa-niḥsvabhāva* (*hsiang wu hsing* 相 無 性), (2) *utpatti-niḥsvabhāva* (*sheng* 生 *wu hsing*), (3) *paramārtha-niḥsvabhāva* (*sheng-yi* 勝 義 *wu hsing*). — Tr.

has applied the term 'non-existence' both to what (really) exists (the so-called second and third forms of non-existence), and to what does not exist (the first form)" (*ibid.*, p. 558).

Thus the doctrine of the three characters of non-existence does not really express the ultimate truth. The *Ch'eng Wei-shih Lun* continues:

"The statement in the *sūtras* about the three characters of non-existence is not the highest revelation of truth, and those who are wise should not rely on it" (*ibid.*, p. 561).

As a matter of fact, we are told, even mind with its attributes pertains to the "character of dependency on others":

"Mind with its attributes, including its perceived and perceiving divisions, and its tainted and untainted (seeds), is engendered through numerous conditioning factors, so that it is entirely activated in dependence on other things. Yes, it becomes activated only in dependence on other multiple factors" (8.525-526). This means that:

"All minds with their attributes, being activated in dependence on other things, are like a conjurer's tricks, which have no genuine existence. In order to refute the false belief that external to the mind and its attributes there exist real objects, it is said that there is nothing but Mere Ideation. But to believe in the genuine existence of Mere Ideation is like believing in that of external objects; it too is a kind of *dharma*-clinging" (2.79-80).

Thus mind itself, like all things which are the product of mind, becomes activated only in dependence on other factors. Such is the true aspect, the true nature, of mind and things alike. By failing to comprehend this true nature, and by clinging to the false belief that these things have a true existence of their own, we fall into the error of accepting them in their "character of sole imagination." By comprehending this true nature, however, we can come to see them in their "character of ultimate reality."

This true nature of all things is known as *Bhūtatathatā*. [1] The *Ch'eng Wei-shih Lun* says: "*Chen* (genuine) means genuine and real. It indicates that it is not baseless and false. *Ju* (thusness) means constantly thus. It indicates that it does not evolve or change. The meaning is that this genuine reality remains, under all conditions, constantly thus in its nature. Therefore it is called *Chen-ju* (*Bhūta*-

---

[1] *Chen-ju* 眞 如 , lit., "Genuine Thusness." It is the Absolute Reality or Absolute Truth of Buddhism. — Tr.

tathatā), which conveys the idea that it is profoundly immovable, not baseless, and not false. The word 'also' (in the preceding text) indicates that it also has many other names, such as *Dharmadhātu* [1] or *Bhūtakoṭi*" [2] (9.560).

Again: "For the *Bhūtatathatā*, which is revealed by the 'emptiness' of the non-ego, there is neither 'being' nor 'non-being.' It is sundered both from the 'road of mind' and 'road of words.' It is neither identical with, nor different from, all the *dharmas*. As it is the genuine principle of the *dharmas*, it is called the *Dharma*-nature (*fa-hsing*) . . . . In order to refute the idea that it does not exist, it is said to exist. In order to refute the idea that it exists, it is said to be empty. Because one cannot say of it that it is baseless or illusory, it is said to be real. Because its principle is neither false nor perverted, it is called *Bhūtatathatā*. We are not like the other schools (according to which) a real eternal *dharma* exists, apart from matter, mind, etc., which is called the *Bhūtatathatā*" (2.75-78).

And yet again: "The seven aspects of *Bhūtatathatā* are: (1) The *Bhūtatathatā* of the flow of transmigration. This means the real nature of the phenomenal *dharmas* in their transmigratory flow. (2) The *Bhūtatathatā* of the two realities. This means the real nature as revealed in the two non-egos. [3] (3) The *Bhūtatathatā* of Mere Ideation. This means the real nature of the pure and impure *dharmas* which belong to Mere Ideation. (4) The *Bhūtatathatā* of steadfastness. This means the real nature of suffering. (5) The *Bhūtatathatā* of wrong conduct. This means the real nature of origination. (6) The *Bhūtatathatā* of untainted purity. This means the real nature of annihilation (i.e., *Nirvāṇa*). (7) The *Bhūtatathatā* of right conduct. This means the real nature of the Way" [4] (8.534-535).

Since the *Bhūtatathatā* comprises the real nature of all things or *dharmas*, it naturally includes that of the "flow of transmigration" and of the other "real natures" here enumerated.

---

[1] *Fa-chieh* 法界 or "*dharma*-element," the unifying underlying reality which is the ground or cause of all *dharmas* or things. — Tr.

[2] *Shih-chi* 實際, "realm of reality." — Tr.

[3] Namely: (1) no (permanent) human ego or soul; (2) no (permanent) individuality or independence of things. — Tr.

[4] *Mārga* (*Tao* 道). The Way to enlightenment or *Nirvāṇa*, described in the following section. — Tr.

vii. *The Transformation of Consciousness into Wisdom*

In the preceding section we have seen that to be ignorant of the real nature of things, and therefore to accept their seemingly independent existence as real, is to fall into the erroneous position of looking at them only in their "character of sole imagination." By understanding their true nature, however, we can achieve insight into their "character of ultimate reality." This achievement implies more than mere intellectual understanding, for even when the Mere Ideation of all things is intellectually admitted, it all too often happens that in actual fact we still cling *emotionally* to the belief that they possess real existence. That is to say, because the dual belief in a subjective ego and in objective things has been so strongly implanted in our minds, special cultivation is required for us emotionally, as well as intellectually, to "awaken to and enter Mere Ideation." How is such cultivation to proceed? According to the *Ch'eng Wei-shih Lun* it embodies five steps or stages:

"What are the five stages for awakening to and entering Mere Ideation? The first is that of 'moral provisioning.' [1] It means cultivation to the point where, in conformity with the Mahāyāna (teachings), one gains (intellectual) liberation (from delusion). The second is that of 'intensified effort.' [2] It means cultivation to the point where, in conformity with the Mahāyāna (teachings), one is able to decide and select. The third is that of 'unimpeded understanding.' [3] It means the position of insight into truth held by the Bodhisattvas. [4] The fourth is that of 'exercising cultivation.' [5] It means the position of the cultivation of truth held by the Bodhisattvas. The fifth is that of 'final attainment.' [6] It means abiding in the unsurpassed perfect Wisdom (*Bodhi*).

"It may be asked what is the gradual way of progression for thus awakening to and entering Mere Ideation. The meaning is that

---

[1] *Sambhāra (tzŭ-liang* 資糧). — Tr.

[2] *Prayoga (chia-hsing* 加行). — Tr.

[3] *Prativedha (t'ung-ta* 通達). — Tr.

[4] This is the first of the three stages of the Bodhisattva (the being who seeks enlightenment). The others are the two that follow. — Tr.

[5] *Bhāvanā (hsiu-hsi* 修習). — Tr.

[6] *Niṣṭhā (chiu-ching* 究竟). — Tr.

in the stage of moral provisioning (i.e., of acquiring right knowledge) as to the aspect and nature of consciousness, the Bodhisattva is able to acquire deep faith and understanding. In the stage of intensified effort, he is gradually able to suppress and eliminate (the belief in) 'what is taken' and 'what takes' (i.e., in an object and a subject), and to develop a genuine view (of things). In the stage of unimpeded understanding, he penetrates and comprehends reality. In that of exercising cultivation, he continually cultivates himself in accordance with the principles of insight which he has acquired, and sunders himself from the remaining barriers (to enlightenment). In the stage of final attainment, he emerges from these barriers into complete enlightenment and is able, until the end of future time, to strive for the conversion of all sentient beings, thus causing them too to awaken to and enter Mere Ideation" (9.562-563).

In the first stage of "moral provisioning," the novitiate is able to accept and understand the concept of Mere Ideation; nevertheless, this is only an intellectual acceptance, and in actual fact he remains as yet unable to divest himself of a lingering belief in the real existence of a subjective ego and an objective universe, i.e., of "what takes" and "what is taken." The *Ch'eng Wei-shih Lun* points out:

"The habit-influences (i.e., perfumings) arising from the two 'takings' are called 'attachment' and 'torpor.' [1] They are so called because they attach themselves to sentient beings and remain torpidly concealed in the storehouse (*ālaya*) consciousness; or, through their attachment, they increase the faults (of sentient beings). They are the same as the seeds of the (two) barriers: that of (wordly) knowledge and that of the delusions (*kleśas*).

"The barrier of the delusions means the belief in what is wholly imaginary as being a real ego; it gives precedence to the view that there is real individuality. [2] Its 128 primary delusions (*kleśas*), with the other accompanying delusions, all torment the bodies and minds of sentient beings and act as a barrier to *Nirvāṇa*. That is why these are all termed the barrier of the delusions.

The barrier of (wordly) knowledge means the belief in what is

---

[1] *Anu* (*sui* 隨) and *śaya* (*mien* 眠). — Tr.

[2] *Satkāya-dṛṣṭi* 薩迦耶见. — Tr.

wholly imaginary as being real *dharmas*; it too gives precedence to the view that there is realness of individuality. Its (false) view, together with doubt, ignorance, desire, hate, conceit, etc., obscures the true nature of the cognized world and acts as a barrier to perfect Wisdom (*Bodhi*). That is why these are all termed the barrier of (wordly) knowledge" (*ibid.*, pp. 565-567).

Thus the two barriers of the delusions and of worldly knowledge spring from the two "takings": "what takes" and "what is taken." Belief in the former, i.e., in what perceives, as being a real ego, results in the barrier of the delusions; belief in the latter, i.e., in what is perceived, as being real *dharmas*, results in the barrier of worldly knowledge.

In the second stage, that of "intensified effort," the novitiate devotes himself to the examination or study of the "names" and "essences" of things, together with their "natures" and "differences." In this way he discovers that all these "are only supposed to exist; as realities they do not exist"; they "all evolve from the mind and thereby are supposed to exist, but as realities do not exist." [1] From this he realizes that " 'what is taken' does not exist," and, advancing further, that "since no real objects exist apart from the consciousness which takes them, how can real consciousness itself exist apart from the objects which are taken by it? For what is taken and what takes are in mutual dependence, one on the other" [2] (*ibid.*, p. 579). For him at this point "there begins the superior knowledge of reality, by which the emptiness of the two takings is confirmed and the first wordly truth is established" (*ibid.*, pp. 580-581). This knowledge is knowledge regarding the true nature of all things; the "first worldly truth gives confirmation of the double emptiness" (*ibid.*, p. 581). The *Ch'eng Wei-shih Lun* continues:

"Throughout (the stage of intensified effort, the thought of the novitiate) remains attached to the (dual) aspects (of seeming being and non-being), and so is as yet unable to experience reality. That is why it is said that the Bodhisattva, during the four phases of this (stage), [3] still places something before him and con-

---

[1] *Ch'eng Wei-shih Lun* (*ibid.*, pp. 577-578).

[2] I.e., neither has absolute existence, for each "exists" only in relation to the other. — Tr.

[3] The four kinds of contemplation which, during this stage, he practices in order to examine the names, essences, natures, and differences mentioned at the beginning of the preceding paragraph. — Tr.

siders it to be the genuine and transcendent nature of Mere Ideation. This is because, the dual aspects of emptiness and being not yet having been eliminated for him, his mind of contemplation still remains attached to them and does not really peacefully abide in the genuine principle of Mere Ideation. Only with the obliteration of these aspects can he peacefully abide in reality" (*ibid.*).

This is why the "first wordly truth" remains only "wordly." The novitiate during this stage still clings to the dualism between what "exists" and what is "empty." That is why he is forced to "place something before him and consider it to be the genuine and transcendent nature of Mere Ideation." To use present day philosophical language, the distinction between subject and object still remains for him; hence one can only say that he intellectually "knows" the transcendent principle of Mere Ideation, but not that he "abides" in it.

As for the third stage, that of "unimpeded understanding," the *Ch'eng Wei-shih Lun* tells us:

"The undiscriminating wisdom of the Bodhisattva takes no hold upon the objective world, and accepts no kind of sophistry about its (seeming) appearance. He is now said really to abide in the genuine and transcendent nature of Mere Ideation, that is, he experiences the *Bhūtatathatā*. His wisdom [1] and the *Bhūtatathatā* are on the same plane, both being equally divorced from the aspects of subjects and object. The latter both constitute discrimination, being the sophistical manifestations of that mind which holds to something (as its object)" (*ibid.*, pp. 585-586).

In this stage, then, there is an "abiding" in Mere Ideation, for now at last the novitiate "experiences the *Bhūtatathatā*." The path of cultivation has virtually reached its goal; all that is needed is further practice.

Regarding the fourth stage, that of "exercising cultivation," we are told: "The Bodhisattva, from the time when he has achieved the preceding (stage of) insight into truth, now constantly cultivates the Wisdom of non-discrimination, in order to sunder the remaining barriers and achieve the experiencing of 'revulsion.' [2] This Wisdom,

---

[1] *Jñāna* (*chih* 智). — Tr.

[2] *Āsraya-parāvṛtti* (*chüan-yi* 轉 依). It is the final "revulsion" (lit., "turning over the base") which takes place at the base of consciousness, enabling the devotee to gain the innermost truth and achieve complete emancipation. — Tr.

being far removed from object and subject, is said to take nothing
and to be inconceivable. Or, being removed from all sophistry, it
is said to take nothing; being marvelous in its functioning and
difficult to fathom, it is termed inconceivable....

" 'Base' [1] means that which serves as a base. That is, it is the
base on which other things depend, because it is that on which
both the pure and impure *dharmas* are dependent. [2] 'Impure' refers to
what is falsely imagined to be true. 'Pure' refers to what truly pertains to ultimate reality. 'Turning over' [3] refers to the 'turning over'
process whereby these two groups (the impure and pure *dharmas*) are
respectively discarded and acquired. By the repeated cultivation of
the Wisdom of non-discrimination, the coarse dross of the two
barriers within the primary (*ālaya*) consciousness is cut away. Thus
through the process of 'turning over' (i.e., transformation) it is
possible to discard the product of the false imagination which over-
lies (i.e., is more superficial than) the principle of 'dependency on
others,' and to acquire the 'character of ultimate reality' which lies
behind this principle. By rolling (away) the delusions (*kleśas*), the
great *Nirvana* is gained; by rolling (away) the barrier of (wordly)
knowledge, the supreme Enlightenment [4] is experienced. The reason
for establishing the doctrine of Mere Ideation is so that sentient beings
may experience these two fruits resulting from this process of 'revulsion.'

"Or perhaps by 'base' should be understood the *Bhūtatathatā*
of Mere Ideation, [5] for this is the basis both for transmigration and
Nirvāna. The ignorant, being deluded through their errors about this
Bhūtatathatā, have therefore from time without beginning been subject to the sufferings of transmigration. But the holy ones, by divorcing themselves from error, awaken to this *Bhūtatathatā*, thus
achieving *Nirvāna* and final felicity" (*ibid.*, pp. 607, 610-611).

This, then, is the ultimate result of the course of self-cultivation.

Regarding the fifth stage of "final attainment" we also read:
"It should be understood that the 'revulsion' which is reached

---

[1] *Yi*, in the term *chüan-yi* or "turning over the base," i.e., "revulsion." — Tr.

[2] The reference here is to the *ālaya* consciousness. — Tr.

[3] *Chüan*, in the above mentioned term, "turning over the base," i.e., "revulsion." — Tr.

[4] *Bodhi* (*chüeh* 覺). — Tr.

[5] The third of the seven aspects of the *Bhūtatathatā*, on which see end of
preceding sect. — Tr.

during the preceding stage of exercising cultivation represents the stage of final attainment. This means that the two fruits resulting from the revulsion of this preceding (stage) are the untainted harvest of this storehouse-realm of final attainment. The term 'untainted' is used because the tainted elements are forever eliminated and have no place for further attachment, and because it (the storehouse-realm) is pure, perfect, and clear in nature. D*hātu* (storehouse-realm) here has the meaning of storing up, because the great merits contained in it are infinite and sublime. Or perhaps it has the idea of cause, [1] because it can produce the blessings and joys, both wordly and super-wordly, of the five vehicles" [2] (10.693-695).

At this time the eight kinds of consciousness are all "turned over" or transformed into *Jñāna* or true Wisdom, and become untainted, i.e., devoid of all tainted seeds. These taintless consciousnesses can, like any ordinary consciousness, evolve external manifestations. In their case these consist of the various Buddha-embodiments and Buddha-realms. [3] The *Ch'eng Wei-shih Lun* says:

"These embodiments and realms are manifested through the evolutions of taintless consciousness, in the same way as are the pure or unclean (*dharmas* evolved by ordinary consciousness). In common with their evolving consciousness, they are entirely good and without taint. For being produced by causes that are utterly good and untainted, they are the accumulated result of the Truth of the Right Path, [4] and not that of suffering" (*ibid.*, pp. 714-715).

Thus in consciousness there lie two kinds of seeds, the tainted and untainted, which respectively evolve pure and impure *dharmas*. The Buddha-embodiments and Buddha-realms stem from the untainted seeds, and belong to a universe lying outside that of ordinary sentient beings.

---

[1] *Hetu* (*yin* 因). — Tr.

[2] *Wu ch'eng* 五 乘, the five vehicles which convey one to *karma*-reward, the reward differing according to the vehicle. There are various enumerations, among them that of rebirth among men, among gods, among Śrāvakas (Buddhist saints), among Pratyeka-Buddhas (beings who seek enlightenment for themselves only), and among Bodhisattvas. — Tr.

[3] *Buddha-kāya* (*fo-shen* 佛身) and *Buddha-kṣetra* (*fo-t'u* 土). The former are the various aspects in which a Buddha is revealed. They are three in number, but each has various subdivisions. The latter are the realms corresponding to the Buddha-embodiments. — Tr.

[4] *Mārga-satya* (*Tao-ti* 諦). — Tr.

3—Fa-tsang's Essay on The Gold Lion

The preceding section makes it evident that the Mere Ideation theory, as introduced by Hsüan-tsang, runs sharply counter to the general tendency of Chinese thought. To assert that the outside world is the manifestation of our own consciousness, and then that even this consciousness has the "character of dependency on others," is to propound (as did Hume in the West) a theory of absolute subjective idealism completely contradictory to common sense. Seng-chao too, as we have seen in Chapter VII, asserted in his theory of the emptiness of the unreal that all things "resemble a man produced by magic." Yet while making this assertion, he at the same time was primarily interested in demonstrating that "this man is not (really) non-existent," so that he differed fundamentally from Hsüan-tsang, who, on the contrary, was primarily interested in proving that "this man, being a product of magic, is not a real man." [1] The underlying concepts of the two thinkers being different, it is natural that their points of emphasis should differ as well.

Hsüan-tsang, furthermore, though not denying the continued activity of the individual in the phenomenal world after he attains Buddhahood, pays but scant attention to this point. Moreover, he says that only certain men possess the untainted seeds of the Buddha, that is, that not all men possess the Buddha nature and can achieve Buddhahood. It might be argued that since consciousness is itself dependent upon something else, and since the "seeds" it contains are therefore likewise dependent, this means that even those who now lack the Buddha nature may acquire it later on. At the very least, however, Hsüan-tsang maintains that the potentialities for its achievement differ from individual to individual. Furthermore, by enumerating the various stages through which the novitiate must pass in order to reach the final goal, he in effect preaches a doctrine of gradual rather than instantaneous enlightenment. In all these respects, therefore, his ideas differ from those of the Buddhist thinkers whom we have hitherto been discussing.

Among the men of Hsüan-tsang's own day who disagreed with his views, the most notable is Fa-tsang 法藏 (643-712), also widely known under his "style" as Hsien-shou 賢首. He was

---

[1] For these quotations from Seng-chao's *Book of Chao*, see chap. 7, p. 265. — Tr.

born of a non-Chinese family, surnamed K'ang 康 and originally native to Sogdiana. [1] From there, however, his grandfather migrated to China, where the family became sinified. Fa-tsang himself was born in the capital, Ch'ang-an (the modern Sian), where, after becoming a monk, he assisted Hsüan-tsang for a time in the latter's work of translation. Subsequently, however, "differences in viewpoint caused him to leave the translation hall." [2] Thereafter he independently labored to develop the theories of the monks Tu-shun (557-640) and Chih-yen (602-668). [3] It was thus that the Hua-yen 華嚴 or "Wreath" school came to be established. [4] We read further in the *Sung Kao Seng Chuan*'s biography of Fa-tsang:

"Tsang expounded the new version of the *Avataṃsaka Sūtra* for Tse-t'ien, [5] but when he came to the theories of the ten mysteries of Indra's net, the *samādhi* of the ocean symbol, the harmonizing of the six qualities, and the realm of universal perception, the chapters on which all constitute general or special principles in the *Avataṃsaka*, the Emperor became puzzled and undecided. Then Tsang pointed to the golden lion guarding the palace hall by way of illustration. In this way he presented his theories so that they were explained quickly and easily. (In the resulting work written by him), called the *Essay on the Gold Lion*, [6] he enumerated ten principles, with their general or special qualities. Thereupon the Emperor came to understand his meaning" (*ibid.*)

In the following pages we too shall base ourselves on this essay for studying the Hua-yen philosophy as represented by Fa-tsang, supplementing it, however, with pertinent passages from two of his other works. [7]

---

[1] Near Samarkand, in modern Russian Turkistan. — Tr.

[2] See his biography in Tsan-ning's (919-1001) *Sung Kao Seng Chuan* (Sung Compilation of Biographies of Eminent Buddhist Monks), *chüan* 5; TT no. 2061 (vol. 50, 5.732).

[3] Not to be confused with a later Chih-yen who lived 737-818. — Tr.

[4] So called because it was based on the *Hua-yen Ching* or *Avataṃsaka Sūtra*, of which three Chinese recensions exist: TT nos. 278, 279, and 293 (vols. 9, pp. 395-788, and 10, pp. 1-144, 661-851). — Tr.

[5] The famous usurper, Empress Wu (ruled 684-705). She called herself "Emperor," which is why this title is used of her below. This lecture took place in 704. — Tr.

[6] *Chin Shih-tzŭ Chang*. It is TT no. 1880 (vol. 45, pp. 663-667). — Tr.

[7] These are: (1) *Hua-yen Ching Yi-hai Pai-men* (Hundred Theories in the Sea of Ideas of the Avataṃsaka Sūtra); TT no. 1875 (vol. 45, pp. 627-636). (2) *Hsiu Hua-yen Ao-chih Wang-chin Huan-yüan Kuan* (Cultivation of the Contemplation

i. *Understanding of Arisal through Causation*

The above-mentioned ten principles or theories (*men* 門) are enumerated in the *Essay on the Gold Lion* as follows: "The first is the understanding of arisal through causation, the second the discriminating of the emptiness of matter, the third the summarizing of the three characters, the fourth the revelation of the qualityless, the fifth the explaining of non-generation, the sixth the discussion of the five teachings, the seventh the mastering of the ten mysteries, the eighth the embracing of the six qualities, the ninth the achievement of *Bodhi*, the tenth the entry into *Nirvāṇa*" (p. 663).

Concerning the first of these, the understanding of arisal through causation, we read further:

"This means that the gold (metal of the lion) lacks any inherent nature of its own. It is because of the technical skill of the artisan that the aspect of the lion arises, and this arising is solely the result of causation. [1] Therefore this fact is called arising through causation" (*ibid.*).

Here and below the gold metal of the lion symbolizes the noumenon, whereas the figure of the lion into which the metal is cast symbolizes phenomenon. The noumenal world is described by Fa-tsang as the *li fa chieh* 理法界 or "realm of principle," in contrast to the phenomenal world, which he calls the *shih* 事 *fa chieh* or "realm of things." [2] He further describes the noumenon as "the substance which by its own nature is clear, pure, all-perfect, and brilliant." "It is the substance of the *dharma*-nature [3] which lies within the *Tathāgata-garbha*, [4] and from all time it is, through its own nature, self-complete and sufficient. It is neither stained by contact with defiling elements, nor purified by cultivation. That is why it is said to be by its own nature clear and pure. Its substance shines everywhere; there is no obscurity it does not illumine. That is why it is said to be all-perfect and brilliant." [5]

of the Mysterious Meaning of the Avatamsaka for Extinguishing False Thought and Returning to the Origin); TT no. 1876 (vol. 45, pp. 637-641). The latter is hereafter abbreviated as *Hua-yen Huan-yüan Kuan*. — Tr.

[1] *Pratyaya* (*yüan* 緣). — Tr.

[2] *Hua-yen Yi-hai Pai-men*, p. 627.

[3] *Dharmatā* (*fa-hsing*), the nature underlying all things. — Tr.

[4] *Ju-lai tsang* 如來藏, the storehouse of the *Tathāgata* or Absolute (on which see also chap. 7, p. 245, note 2). — Tr.

[5] *Hua-yen Huan-yüan Kuan*, p. 637.

This noumenon may be compared to water, and phenomenon
(meaning by this the events and things of the phenomenal world)
to the waves of that water. In the case of the lion, the gold itself is
the primary cause or factor that makes the production of the lion
possible; the work of the artisan who shapes the gold metal is its
secondary or contributing cause or factor. All events and things of
the phenomenal world arise only through the combination of such
primary and secondary causes. This is what is meant when it is said
that their arisal is due to causation.

ii. *Discriminating the Emptiness of Matter*

Regarding the second of the ten principles in the *Essay on the
Gold Lion*, that of "discriminating the emptiness of matter," we read
in that work:

"This means that the (outward) aspect of the lion is void,
and it is only the gold that is real. The fact that the lion is not (really)
existent, whereas its gold substance is not non-existent, is called
'the emptiness of matter.' [1] This emptiness, furthermore, lacks
any inherent quality of its own; it shows itself only within the limitations of matter. Yet it is not prevented thereby from having illusory
existence. This fact is called the emptiness of matter" (pp. 663-664).

Things of the phenomenal world are all manifestations of
illusion or *māyā* (*huan* 幻). This fact is termed "the emptiness of
matter." Such "emptiness" (*śūnyatā*), however, does not signify an
absolute vacuum or non-presence of things, for as pointed out in the
Hua-yen Huan-yüan Kuan:

"The meaning is that matter, [2] inasmuch as it has no inherent
nature of its own, is 'empty'; but inasmuch as it gives the illusion
of having seeming qualities, it is 'existent.' The best thing (to say)
is that illusory matter (*rūpa*), inasmuch as it lacks any inherent substance of its own, cannot be differentiated from emptiness; and that
genuine emptiness, being all perfect, penetrates to what lies beyond

---

[1] By matter (*rūpa* or *se*) is meant phenomenally apparent matter, and not
the noumenon described in the preceding section. Being phenomenal, it is
"empty," i.e., unreal in an absolute sense. — Tr.

[2] *Guṇa* (*ch'en* 塵). In Chinese, the term means matter as composed of
tiny particles or atoms. *Rūpa*, also translated "matter," has special reference to
the coloring and phenomenal appearance of the material, i.e., phenomenal,
world. — Tr.

existence. By viewing matter as empty we achieve Great Wisdom, [1] so that we do not abide in (the cycle of) life and death. By viewing emptiness as matter we achieve Great Pity, [2] so that we do not abide in *Nirvāṇa*. [3] Only by creating no dualism between matter and emptiness, and no differentiation between pity and wisdom, do we reach Truth. [4]

"The *Treatise on the Precious Nature* says: [5] 'The (prospective) Bodhisattva, before achieving the Way, has three doubts concerning this genuine emptiness and mysterious being. In the first place, suspecting that emptiness means the annihilation of matter, he holds to an emptiness that is completely annihilatory. Secondly, suspecting that emptiness is different from matter, he holds to an emptiness that is external to matter. Thirdly, suspecting that emptiness is itself a "thing," he holds to emptiness as constituting a state of being.'

"In elucidation of this I would now say: The fact that matter is illusory cannot create a barrier between it and emptiness, nor can the fact that emptiness is genuine create a barrier between it and matter. For emptiness separated from matter becomes complete annihilation, while matter separated from emptiness becomes something real" (p. 638).

Thus emptiness is not "completely annihilatory," i.e., utterly devoid of objects, nor is it "external to matter," nor, finally, is it a "thing," for if so it would itself constitute a state of "being." The *Essay on the Gold Lion* holds that what we call "being" is illusory, and it is in this sense that it applies the word empty to matter. That is why it says: "This emptiness, furthermore, lacks any inherent quality of its own; it shows itself only within the limitations of matter."

iii. *Summarizing the Three Characters*

Concerning this, the third principle, the *Essay on the Gold Lion* says:

---

[1] *Mahāmati* (*ta chih* 大智). — Tr.

[2] *Mahākaruṇā* (*ta pei* 悲), the compassion felt by the Buddhas and Bodhisattvas toward all sentient beings. — Tr.

[3] According to Mahāyāna Buddhism, the enlightened person renounces *Nirvāṇa* in order to rescue all sentient beings from their sufferings. — Tr.

[4] *Tattva* (*chen-shih* 眞實). — Tr.

[5] Apparently a reference to the *Mahāyānottaratantra Śāstra*, translated by the Indian Ratnamati (arrived in China in 508). It is TT no. 1611 (vol. 31, pp. 813-848). However, I have failed to find this quotation in that work. — Tr.

"The fact that, from (the point of view of) the senses, the lion exists, is called its (character of) sole imagination. The fact that (from a higher point of view) the lion only seemingly exists, is called its (character of) dependency on others. And the fact that the gold (of wich the lion is made) is immutable in its nature, is called (the character of) ultimate reality" (p. 664).

This means that the events and things of the phenomenal world all arise only as the result of causation. Though they give the illusion of having being, this being lacks any inherent nature of its own. Therefore it is said to have the character of dependency on other things, that is, on factors external to itself. The identical term is used in the same sense by the *Ch'eng Wei-shih Lun*. Again, the fact that the seeming state of being of these things is commonly but mistakenly regarded as constituting genuine being, is described as their character of sole imagination. Here too the term and usage are the same as those in the *Ch'eng Wei-shih Lun*. Underlying these false appearances,. however, there is the noumenon, which remains forever immutable. This fact constitutes the character of ultimate reality. But while the term here used is similar to that in the *Ch'eng Wei-shih Lun*, its meaning is somewhat different. [1] For in the *Ch'eng Weih-shih Lun* it is said that not only all things or *dharmas*, but even consciousness itself, is dependent on something else for its manifestation; this true fact is what constitutes the character of ultimate reality. In the *Essay on the Gold Lion*, on the other hand, ultimate reality is said to be the noumenon itself, stripped of outer phenomenon and remaining eternally immutable.

iv. *Revelation of the Qualityless*

Concerning this principle we read further:

"This means that the gold completely includes the lion, for apart from the gold, the lion itself has no qualities (*lakṣaṇa*) that may be seized. This fact is therefore called that of the qualityless" (p. 664).

The *Hua-yen Yi-hai Pai-men* tells us:

"To contemplate the qualityless is (to contemplate) the fact that the qualities of the tiniest particle of matter (*guṇa*) arise out

---

[1] On this and the preceding terms, as used in the *Ch'eng Wei-shih Lun*, see above, sect. 2, vi. — Tr.

of the evolutions of mind. Their position is false and has no reality, so that when seizing them one does not get them. From this we may know that the qualities of matter are void and non-existent, being products of mind and completely lacking any inherent nature of their own. This fact is called that of the qualityless" (p. 627).

Here we are told that all events and things of the phenomenal world are simply the illusory manifestations of mind. Being illusory, their state of "being" is not genuine being. Hence they may be said to be in actual fact without quality or qualityless.

v. *Explaining Non-generation*

Concerning this fifth principle the *Essay of the Gold Lion* tells us: "This means that when we see the lion as something that has been generated (*sheng* 生), it is only the gold that has generated it. External to the gold there is nothing else. Thus whereas the lion undergoes generation and destruction, the gold itself incurs neither increase nor decrease. This fact is therefore called that of non-generation" (p. 664).

The *Hua-yen Yi-hai Pai-men* says: "The meaning of non-generation is that matter (*guṇa*) is the contributing cause of mind, and mind is the primary cause of matter. Through the combination of these causes, illusory manifestations are generated. Being thus generated through causation, they cannot have any nature of their own. Why is this? Matter is not self-caused, but necessarily remains dependent on mind. Mind, however, does not derive from itself, but is likewise dependent on (phenomenal) causation. Because of this mutual dependency, what is generated through causation is indeterminate. It is this fact of indeterminateness that is called non-generation. We are not speaking of any kind of non-generation apart from causation" (p. 627).

"Matter is the manifestation of mind. But having been thus manifested, it becomes the contributing cause of mind. There must first be this causation before any 'mental things' (*hsin fa*) can arise" (*ibid.*).

According to these last two statements, mind must be faced with an external object for it to generate "mental things," i.e., thoughts and ideas. These "mental things" therefore arise as the result of the causation of "matter," that is, of external objects. Hence

matter acts as a causative agent upon mind. At the same time, however, "matter is the manifestation of mind," that is, mind is the cause
of matter. The events and things of the phenomenal world all depend
for their generation upon a combination of causes, and being thus
dependent, are indeterminate. This fact is described as "non-generation," meaning no absolutely fixed pattern of generation. What is
said earlier in the *Essay on the Gold Lion*, however, is slightly different,
for there it is stated that the things of the phenomenal world are
illusory, and, being illusory, their existence is not real existence.
By consequence their generation is likewise not real generation.

vi. *Discussing the Five Teachings*

Of these, the sixth principle, we read in the *Essay on the Gold
Lion*:

"The first is that though the lion is a product of causation,
and undergoes generation and destruction from moment to moment,
there is really no quality to the lion that may be grasped. This is
called the teaching for ignorant Śrāvakas. [1]

"The second is that all things, being the product of causation,
lack any nature of their own, and that in the final analysis there is
only emptiness. This is called the elementary teaching of Mahāyāna.

"The third is that although, in the final analysis, there is only
emptiness, this does not conflict with the illusory appearance of
being. Causation and hypothetical being are both to be retained. This
is called the final teaching of Mahāyāna.

"In the fourth, these two (emptiness and being) are mutually
annulled and thus both abolished, and the false impressions of the
senses are cast aside, so that neither of them (emptiness or being)
retains any influence. (The concepts of) emptiness and being are both
discarded, the road of words and speech is cut short, and the mind
rests in non-attachment. This is called the instantaneous teaching
of Mahāyāna.

"In the fifth, all things of the senses are revealed in their true
essence, and become merged into one great mass. Great functions
arise, every one of which represents the Absolute (*chen* 眞). The
myriad manifestations, despite their variety, harmonize and are not

---

[1] The followers of Hīnayāna Buddhism, who are regarded as standing on
a lower intellectual and moral level than the adherents of Mahāyāna. — Tr.

disparate. The all is the one, for all things equally have the nature of non-being. The one is the all, for cause and effect follow in an unbroken sequence. In their power and function, each implies the other and freely rolls up or spreads out. This is called the perfect teaching of the One Vehicle" [1] (pp. 664-665).

Here we have an example of the theory of the "classification of teachings." [2] As developed by the Hua-yen school, the aim is to arrange the various schools of Buddhism into an unbroken sequence in which each holds its proper place and represents some one aspect of the total truth. By the first teaching, that "for ignorant Śrāvakas," Fa-tsang has Hīnayāna Buddhism in mind. Thus in the *Hua-yen Huan-yüan Kuan* he writes further:

"Not to believe indiscriminately in the (external) appearance of matter: this is the Hīnayāna teaching. (To see that) the nature of matter undergoes neither production nor destruction by itself, its seeming existence being dependent on other things: this is the Mahāyāna teaching" (p. 638).

In terms of the theory of the "three characters" discussed above in section iii, the Hīnayāna school goes so far as to recognize that things, as ordinarily viewed, have the "character of sole imagination." Thus it points out that inasmuch as the lion is from moment to moment either being produced or destroyed, we should not believe in its true existence.

The Mahāyāna school goes a step further by recognizing the fact that things have the character of dependency on others. Thus it maintains that the lion, which from moment to moment undergoes either production or destruction, "lacks any nature of its own, and that in the final analysis there is only emptiness."

This, however, is only the elementary teaching of Mahāyāna. The next step is to cause people to understand that although the lion's existence is illusory, this should not interfere with our acceptance of its state of being as such. "Causation and hypothetical being are both to be retained." In other words, though we speak of emptiness on the one hand, this need not prevent our acceptance of the fact that there is nevertheless illusory being. This, then, is the final teaching of Mahāyāna.

---

[1] *Ekayāna* (*yi ch'eng* 一乘), a designation for the highest Buddhist truth. — Tr.

[2] On this term, see chap. 7, p. 284 — Tr.

Let it be granted, however, that the lion has being, even though of an illusory sort. If for this reason we are to stress the fact of its illusoriness, the result will be that the concept of being will be annulled by that of emptiness. Yet if, on the other hand, we are to stress the fact of its being, this again will result in the concept of emptiness being annulled by that of being. The next step, therefore, is one in which "the two are mutually annulled and thus both abolished, ... so that neither of them retains any influence. (The concepts of) emptiness and being are both discarded." The aim is to bring people to the stage in which they no longer remain conscious of either being or emptiness. At this point "the road of words and speech is cut short, and the mind rests in non-attachment." This, then, is the instantaneous teaching of Mahāyāna, in other words, that in which there is instantaneous enlightenment.

Yet at this point it is still necessary to realize that the myriad manifestations of the phenomenal world all pertain to the substance of mind—a mind that is absolute and all-embracing. This is the meaning of the passage: "The leaping waves (of the phenomenal world), boiling as in a cauldron, are the functioning of the complete and genuine substance. This substance is a mirror of pure and limpid water, which follows causation, yet remains ever still. It is like the diffused radiance of the sun, which, without deliberate purpose, illumines the ten directions. It is like the upright figure of a clear mirror, which, motionless itself, presents all forms." [1] In other words, each and every event and thing of the phenomenal world is a representation of this absolute mind in its totality. We read further:

"Moreover, when we see, for example, the height and width of a mountain, it is mind that manifests this largeness; there is no largeness apart (from mind). Or when we see the utter tinyness of a particle of matter (*guṇa*), here again it is mind that manifests this tinyness; there is no tinyness apart (from mind). Thus when we see this particle, it is the manifestation of that same mind which also sees the height and width of the mountain" (p. 630).

This explains the meaning of the earlier statements that "every one of them represents the Absolute," and that "the all is the one" and "the one is the all." By the latter phrases is meant that the one has the capacity to absorb the all, and the all has the capacity to absorb the one. We read further in the *Hua-yen Yi-hai Pai-men*:

---

[1] *Hua-yen Yi-hai Pai-men*, p. 630.

"To explain (the idea of) 'rolled up or spread out': [1] This means that a particle of matter, though it lack any nature of its own, yet embodies everything extending within the ten directions: such is what it is to be spread out. (Likewise) what lies within the ten directions, though it lack any essence of its own, may yet, in compliance with causation, be wholly manifested within a particle of matter: such is what it is to be rolled up. It is said in the *sūtra*: 'The one Buddha-realm fills the ten directions, and though the ten directions be compressed into the one (Buddha-realm), there is still no surplus.' Rolled up, all things are manifested within the single particle of matter. Spread out, the single particle of matter permeates everything. The spread-out is the rolled-up, because in the single particle is gathered the all. The rolled-up is the spread-out, because in the all is gathered the single particle. That is why (the Absolute) can freely be rolled up or spread out" (p. 631).

To enable men to understand this doctrine is the purpose of the fifth or perfect teaching of the One Vehicle.

vii. *Mastering the Ten Mysteries*

Concerning these, the seventh principle, the *Essay on the Gold Lion* says:

"The first is that the gold and the lion are simultaneously established, all-perfect, and complete. This is called the theory of simultaneous completeness.

"The second is that if the eyes of the lion are taken to include the whole lion, the all is the eyes. [2] But if the ears are taken to include the whole lion, the all is the ears. And if all the organs are simultaneously taken to include the whole lion, every one of them is the perfect whole. Thus they are each and every one of them both 'pure' and 'mixed,' thereby constituting a complete 'storehouse.' This is called the theory of the pure and mixed attributes of various storehouses.

"The third is that the gold and the lion are mutually compatible, and there is no interference between the one and the many. The noumenon and phenomenon differ, inasmuch as (the former) is the one and (the latter) is the many, so that each occupies its own position.

---

[1] See the end of the first quotation in this section. — Tr.

[2] Because the all is the one and the one is the all. — Tr.

This is called the theory of mutual compatibility between the dissimilarities of the one and the many.

"The fourth is that the various organs of the lion, down to each and every hair, all include the whole lion, in so far as they are all the gold. Thus each and every one of them permeates the eyes of the lion. The eyes are the ears, the ears are the nose, the nose is the tongue, and the tongue is the body. They each are freely established and do not impede one another. This is called the theory of mutual freedom among things.

"The fifth is that if we look at the lion as a lion only, without gold, then the lion is prominent while the gold becomes obscure. But if we look at the gold as gold only, without the lion, then the gold is prominent while the lion becomes obscure. Whereas if we consider both of them together, they are then both equally prominent and equally obscure. Obscure, they are hidden; prominent, they are displayed. This is called the theory of hidden-and-displayed corelation.

"The sixth is that the gold and the lion may be prominent or obscure, one or many, pure or mixed, potent or impotent. The one is the other. Leader and subordinate interchange their radiance. Noumenon and phenomenon equally manifest themselves. Being mutually compatible, they peacefully stand without interfering with one another. This is achieved even in the case of what is minute and abstruse, and is called the theory of peaceful compatability of the minute and abstruse.

"The seventh is that in the lion's eyes, ears, limbs, and every separate hair, the gold lion is present. The lion of all the hairs, taken together, is at the same time all found within a single hair. Thus these many hairs have an infinitude of lions, and this infinitude of lions of these many hairs is further contained within each single hair. In this way there is an endless doubling and redoubling, like the jewels of Indra's net. This is called the theory of the realm of Indra's net. [1]

"The eighth is to talk about the lion in order to make clear (the meaning of) ignorance (*avidyā*), and to discuss its golden substance in order to throw light on the (mind's) genuine substance. By jointly discussing noumenon and phenomenon, one reaches the highest consciousness (*ālaya-vijñāna*) and creates right understanding

---

[1] Indra, the sky god of Hinduism, was taken over by Buddhism to become its protective deity. The meaning of his net is described below. — Tr.

among sentient beings. This is called the theory of relying on phenomenal things in order to elucidate truth.

"The ninth is that the lion is something phenomenal, and as such undergoes production or destruction from instant to instant. Every instant of time consists of three parts: past, present, and future. But these three divisions each consist in turn of a past, present, and future, resulting in a total of three times three units. In this way there exist nine ages, bound together, however, to form a single sequence. Thus though there are nine ages, each different from the other, they yet stand in sequence, harmoniously interconnecting without mutual interference, and constituting in their totality only one instant of time. This is called the theory of the variable formation of the ten ages in sections.

"The tenth is that the gold and the lion may be obscure or prominent, one or many. They both lack a nature of their own, being derived according to the evolutions of mind. Whether we speak of phenomenon or noumenon, both are formed and stand in this way. This is called the theory of excellent achievement according to the evolutions of mind only" (pp. 665-666).

Let us now examine these ten theories in greater detail.

(1) Each event and thing of the phenomenal world represents the absolute mind in its totality. This is true of the lion as of everything else. Hence the statement: "The gold and the lion simultaneously stand, all-perfect and complete. This is called the theory of simultaneous completeness."

(2) "The one is the all" and "the all is the one." "Noumenon does not interfere with phenomenon, for what is pure is ever mixed. (Likewise) phenomenon ever comprises noumenon in its totality, for what is mixed is ever pure. Since noumenon and phenomenon each have their own course, there is no barrier between what is pure and what is mixed." [1] That is to say, everything of the phenomenal world is a manifestation of mind, in other words, constitutes the noumenon in its totality. Thus the eyes of the lion, inasmuch as they constitute this mind, thereby constitute the all, and as such are "mixed," that is, all-embracing. But inasmuch as "the all" also comprises the lion's eyes, these eyes are at the same time "pure," that is, have in them the noumenon. Hence "they are each and every one of them both 'pure' and 'mixed,' " in this way "constituting a com-

---

[1] *Hua-yen Yi-hai Pai-men*, p. 630.

plete 'storehouse.' This is called the theory of the pure and mixed attributes of various storehouses."

(3) Absolute mind is one; phenomena are many. From one point of view every phenomenon is the manifestation of this mind in its totality. Hence the one is the many, the many are the one. This is the idea intended by the words: "The one is the many, and only thus may be called the one. The many are the one, and only thus may be called the many. There is no separate one outside of the many, from which we may know that within the many lies the one. But there are also no separate many outside of the one, from which we may know that within the one lie the many. Not many, yet it can be one within the many. Not one, yet they can be many within the one." [1] From another point of view, however, phenomenon remains phenomenon, distinct from noumenon, so that the gold, which is noumenon, remains the one, whereas the lion, which is phenomenon, remains the many. "Each occupies its own position" and remains distinct, despite the fact that there is no incompatibility or barrier between the one and the many. "This is called the theory of mutual compatibility between the dissimilarities of the one and the many."

(4) From one point of view, all things of the phenomenal world are the manifestations of mind in its totality, that is, the one is the all and the all is the one. "The ears are the nose, the nose is the tongue." Yet from another point of view, each thing remains only that particular thing. The ears are only ears, the nose only a nose. "They each are freely established and do not impede one another." Therefore "this is called the theory of mutual freedom among things." It, like the preceding theory, stresses the fact that each thing has its own particular aspect. Whereas the preceding theory, however, deals with the difference between mind and phenomenon, the present theory restricts itself to the realm of phenomenon, and to the differences between individual things within this realm.

(5) If we direct our attention upon the things of the phenomenal world, these become displayed, whereas the noumenon remains hidden. But if we direct our attention upon the noumenon, this becomes displayed, whereas phenomenal things are no longer so. "This is called the theory of hidden-and-displayed co-relation."

(6) It is apparent from the foregoing that the noumenal and the phenomenal may be one or many, pure or mixed, potent or

---

[1] *Hua-yen Yi-hai Pai-men*, p. 630.

impotent, this or that, leader or subordinate. Regarding the latter two opposites, the *Hua-yen Huan-yüan Kuan* says: "This means to take the self as leader and regard others as subordinates. We may take one thing as leader and all the rest as subordinate, or we may take one body as leader and all the others as subordinate" (p. 640). For example, if we direct our attention upon the lion, the lion is leader and everything else is subordinate. Despite this differentiation, however, nothing impedes anything else. This "is called the theory of peaceful compatibility of the minute and abstruse."

(7) All things and events of the phenomenal world are manifestations of absolute mind in its totality or, to reverse the equation, mind embraces all things. This being so, it follows that within the phenomenal world, each individual thing embraces all other individual things. Not only this, however, but each individual thing also embraces everything else that is embraced by every one of those other individual things. And the same is true of what is thus embraced by those other things; each in turn itself embraces all things. This is what the *Essay on the Gold Lion* means when it says: "Thus these many hairs have an infinitude of lions, and this infinitude of lions of these many hairs is further contained within each single hair."

The *Sung Kao Seng Chuan* says of Fa-tsang that "because his students failed to understand, he then used a clever expedient. He took ten mirrors, arranging them, one each, at the eight compass points and above and below, in such a way that they were a little over ten feet apart from each other, all facing one another. He then placed a Buddhist figure in the center and illuminated it with a torch so that its image was reflected from one to another. His students thus came to understand the theory of passing from 'land and sea' (the finite world) into infinity" (5.731). In this way each mirror not only reflected the image of the other mirrors, but also all the images reflected in each of those other mirrors. This is like the net of Indra, mentioned as a metaphor in the *Essay on the Gold Lion*. Each loop of this net is decorated with a jewel, in such a way that each jewel not only reflects the image of every other jewel, but also all the multiple images reflected in each of those other jewels. In this way the doubling and redoubling of reflections continues without end. "This is called the theory of the realm of Indra's net."

(8) To speak of the lion as illustration of the phenomenal, is to approach one aspect of absolute mind—that of production and destruction. To speak of the gold of the lion as illustration of

the noumenal, is to approach its other aspect—that of reality. The absolute mind, failing to have a true awareness of itself, remains in a state of activity, the result of which is the cycle of production and destruction. To designate this lack of self awareness, the text uses the term *avidyā* or "ignorance." These two approaches, however, each represent only one aspect of mind, whereas the union of the two, that is, of "production and destruction" and of "non-production and non-destruction," results in the highest or *ālaya* consciousness. The use of examples like the lion in order to explain absolute truth along lines like these is "called the theory of relying on phenomenal things in order to elucidate truth."

(9) A single instant is the manifestation of the absolute mind in its totality, but so are the nine ages. Therefore a single instant is equivalent to the nine ages, and the nine ages to a single instant. The *Hua-yen Yi-hai Pai-men* says:

"As regards the harmonizing of an instant with an aeon: [1] . . . Since a single instant lacks any essential nature of its own, it becomes interchangeable with a great aeon, and since a great aeon also lacks any essential nature of its own, it belongs to a single instant. Since both lack any essential nature of their own, there is no differentiation between the long and the short. This reaches the point where realms both far and near, the Buddhas and sentient beings, and all things of the three ages (of past, present, and future), are all found manifested within a single instant. How is this? All phenomenal things depend upon mind to be manifested. Since there is no separating barrier between the (individual) instants, there is a corresponding blending among the things. Hence in a single instant all things of the three ages may clearly be seen. The *sūtra* says: 'A single instant may be a hundred or a thousand aeons; a hundred or a thousand aeons may be a single instant' " (p. 630).

This is what the *Essay on the Gold Lion* means when it says that the nine ages (the three ages of past, present, and future, each of which has its own past, present, and future) in their totality constitute a single instant. Yet even within this instant these nine ages still retain

---

[1] *Kṣaṇa* (*nien* 念) with *kalpa* (*chieh* 劫). A *kṣaṇa* is the shortest period of time. According to one definition, 60 *kṣaṇa* equal one finger-snap. A *kalpa* is of indefinite but enormous length. According to one definition, a small *kalpa* lasts 16,800,000 years, a *kalpa* 336,000,000 years, and a great *kalpa* (mentioned below) 1,334,000,000 years. — Tr.

their individual identity, so that, together with the instant itself, they actually constitute a total of ten ages. "This is called the theory of the variable formation of the ten ages in sections."

(10) In summary, all things whatsoever are manifestations of mind. All "lack a nature of their own, being derived according to the evolutions of mind." "This is called the theory of excellent achievement according to the evolutions of mind only."

viii. *Embracing the Six Qualities*

Concerning this eighth principle we read in the *Essay on the Gold Lion*:

"The lion (as a whole) has the quality of generalness. Its five organs, inasmuch as they each differ (from the lion as a whole), have the quality of speciality. However, inasmuch as they (together with the lion as a whole) all arise from a single cause, they have the quality of similarity. But the fact that the eyes, ears, etc., do not overlap (in their functions), gives them the quality of diversity. However, inasmuch as these various organs combine to make the lion, this is their quality of integration. But the fact that each of these organs occupies its own particular position, gives them the quality of disintegration" (p. 666).

Applying this principle to any object of the phenomenal world, we find that the object as a whole has the quality of generalness, whereas each of its parts has the quality of speciality. Inasmuch as the object as a whole, as well as its separate parts, are all products of causation, this is their quality of similarity. Yet inasmuch as each part remains distinct from the other parts, this is their quality of diversity. Inasmuch, however, as the combination of the parts results in the formation of the object as a whole, this is their quality of integration. But, as long as they do not combine, they remain only so many separate parts, with the result that the object as a whole cannot be formed. This is their quality of disintegration.

ix. *Achievement of Bodhi*

Concerning the ninth principle, the achievement of *Bodhi* or perfect Wisdom, the *Essay on the Gold Lion* says:

"*Bodhi* in our language signifies the Way (*Tao*) and enlightenment (*chüeh* 覺). This means that when we look at the lion, we should see that all phenomenal things, even before their (physical) integration, have from the beginning been in a state of calm extinction. By avoiding both attachment and renunciation, we gain the road to bring us into the sea of Omniscience. [1] This is therefore called the Way. Comprehension of the fact that from time without beginning all the illusions fundamentally have no reality, is called enlightenment. The final embodying of all wisdoms is called the achievement of *Bodhi*" (p. 666).

What is essential is to know that all phenomenal things, to which we formerly clung as real, are from the very beginning empty; or in the words of the text, that "even before their (physical) disintegration, they have from the beginning been in a state of calm extinction." Such knowledge is like the awakening from a dream, in which we realize for the first time that the objects of that dream have always been unreal. We read further in the *Hua-yen Yi-hai Pai-men*:

"(The metaphor of) comprehending a dream's illusion means that the physical manifestations which our deluded minds considered to exist are under examination seen to be as unreal as a man conjured up by magic. The case is indeed like awakening from a night dream to the realization that everything in it was non-existent. If we now understand what is void and non-existent, that means we have nothing to get. The appearance cannot be gotten; all things cannot be gotten. This is known as awakening from the world and comprehending that in emptiness there is nothing" (p. 633).

Again: "Delusion means that physical manifestations have a point of origination from which they undergo production and destruction. [2] Such is delusion. But if we now understand that these physical manifestations have no solid reality, this is enlightenment. Delusion comes from nowhere, nor does enlightenment go somewhere. How is this? It is because what the deluded mind takes as being, (actually) from the very beginning lacks any solid reality. It is like a snake made of rope, which (when it is believed to be a real snake) does not come from somewhere, nor (when it is seen to be only rope) go somewhere. [3] Why is this? Because this 'snake,' which

---

[1] *Sarvajña (sa-p'o-jo* 薩婆若). — Tr.

[2] I.e., they possess internal reality, even though they pass through phases of production and destruction. — Tr.

[3] The rope remains where it is all the time even though during one's state of delusion it is believed to be a snake, whereas during one's state of enlightenment it is seen to be only a rope. — Tr.

the deluded mind perversely imagines to exist, is from the very beginning lacking in any solid reality. If we imagine that it comes from somewhere (when we first think it is a snake), or goes somewhere (when we later realize it is only a rope), this is still to remain deluded. Enlightenment consists in understanding that it neither comes nor goes.

"However, enlightenment and delusion stand in mutual relationship, one to the other. It is not a case of the pure mind coming first and ignorance (*avidyā*) afterward. Not being two separate objects, they cannot be considered as such. Comprehension of (the sameness of) illusion and non-illusion: herein lies the pure mind. We should know that according to final truth there is no pure mind that comes first nor ignorance that comes afterward" (p. 636).

We are also told in the *Hua-yen Huan-yüan Kuan*: "It is like a man who, being deluded, says that east is west. After he has become enlightened, (what he formerly regarded as) west becomes east, so that no other east remains for him to turn toward. Sentient beings, because of their delusion, say that we should discard the illusory so as to enter the real. But once we have reached enlightenment, the illusory itself becomes the real, so that no other reality remains for us to enter" (p. 639).

The person in a dream holds to the objects of that dream as real. This is delusion. After awakening he realizes that these objects have never been real, and with this realization the delusion is stripped of its seeming reality. To know this means to "enter the real," apart from which, "no other reality remains for us to enter." To attain to this state is to achieve *Bodhi*. Only then does the "pure mind" first realize that everything previous was a state of ignorance or *avidyā*. This is why Fa-tsang says: "It is not a case of the pure mind coming first and ignorance afterward." According to this doctrine, the aim of spiritual cultivation is to reach a new state of being—a state, however, which is essentially the same as the old one. The only real difference between them is that of enlightenment and unenlightenment.

x. *Entry into Nirvāṇa*

Regarding this final step, the *Essay on the Gold Lion* says:

"(At this point), when we look at the lion and the gold, the qualities of both are completely extinguished for us, and the passions (*kleśas*) are no longer produced. Beauty and ugliness are both merely so many manifestations, and the mind is tranquil like the sea. Deluding thoughts are all extinguished, and there remain no compulsions. We cast off our bonds, emerge from our barriers, and eternally abandon the source of suffering. This is called entry into *Nirvāṇa*" (p. 666).

Having reached this highest state through cultivation, we no longer have any awareness of the phenomenal world, but neither are we conscious of the noumenal world. This is because the retention of such consciousness would mean retention of a false distinction between "what knows" and "what is known," in other words, between subject and object. In that case, even though we should no longer be conscious of phenomenal things, the noumenon would still remain as the object of our knowledge. Hence the highest stage is really reached only when it can be said of us that "when we look at the lion and the gold, the qualities of both are completely extinguished." On the other hand—and this is important—once we have reached this stage, this does not mean that we are then merely to dwell forever after in *Nirvāṇa*. Thus the *Hua-yen Yi-hai Pai-men* tells us:

"The experiencing of the Buddha-realm [1] means the emptiness of matter (*guṇa*), absence of personal ego (*ātman*), and absence of phenomenal quality (*lakṣaṇa*). ... However, having experienced entry into this realm, one may not dwell forever after in calm extinction, for this would be contrary to the teaching of the Buddhas. One should teach what is beneficial and joyous, and (for this purpose) should study the expedients [2] and wisdom of the Buddhas. It is in this realm that one should think about all these things" (p. 636).

This is because the Buddhas not only possess Great Wisdom (*mahāmati*) but also Great Pity (*mahākaruṇā*). This means that, having achieved Great Wisdom, they therefore do not dwell in the cycle of life and death; but having achieved Great Pity, they therefore also do not dwell in *Nirvāṇa*. [3]

xi. *Subjective and Objective Idealism*

The fourth patriarch of the Hua-yen school, Ch'eng-kuan, [4]

---

[1] For this term, see p. 338, note 3. — Tr.

[2] The different ways of teaching practiced by the Buddhas as expedient (*upāya*) to the time and occasion. — Tr.

[3] See p. 343 above. — Tr.

[4] A native of Shan-yin (near the present Shao-hsing 紹興 in Chekiang), originally surnamed Hsia-hou 夏侯. His dates are uncertain. According to

says that the *Hua-yen Ching* or *Avataṃsaka Sūtra* speaks of four kinds of *dharmadhātu* (*fa-chieh*) or realms of reality: those of phenomenon, of noumenon, of unimpededness between noumenon and phenomenon, and of unimpededness between phenomenon and noumenon. [1] The truth of this statement is evident from what has been said above. It is likewise evident that the central element in Fa-tsang's philosophy is a permanently immutable "mind" which is universal or absolute in its scope, and is the basis for all phenomenal manifestations. That is to say, his philosophy is a system of objective idealism. As such, it approaches realism more closely than does an idealism which is purely subjective. This is because, in a system of objective idealism, it is possible for the objective world to survive even when separated from a subject. Moreover, the fact that all things in such an objective world are manifestations of one all-embracing absolute mind, gives to them a degree of "reality" seemingly even greater than what they would have in a non-idealistic universe of ordinary common sense. From what has been said in the present chapter, it is clear that the "character of ultimate reality" as described by Hsüan-tsang differs from that of Fa-tsang. Thus "emptiness," for the latter, is less uncompromisingly "empty" than is Hsüan-tsang's "emptiness," whereas "phenomenon" is accepted as necessary to the scheme of the universe. In these respects Fa-tsang, to a greater extent than Hsüan-tsang, follows the general trend of Chinese thought.

---

the *Sung Kao Seng Chuan* (5.737), he died during the period 806-820, when in his seventies. [Other sources, however, variously give the following dates: 719-838, 736-837, 738-839. See Ch'en Yüan, *Shih-shih Yi-nien Lu* (Chronologies of Buddhist Monks), Peiping, 1939 (5.1). Ch'en himself favors the dates of 738-839. —Tr.]

[1] See his *Hua-yen Fa-chieh Hsüan-ching* (Mysterious Mirror of the Avataṃsaka Dharmadhātu), *chüan* 1; TT no. 1883 (vol. 45, p. 672).

CHAPTER IX

BUDDHISM DURING THE SUI AND T'ANG
DYNASTIES

(Part II)

1—THE T'IEN-T'AI SCHOOL'S MAHĀYĀNA METHOD OF CESSATION AND CONTEMPLATION

One of the most important Buddhists of the Ch'en (557-589) and Sui (590-617) dynasties was Chih-k'ai (538-597). [1] The T'ien-t'ai 天台 school, which he was primarily responsible for establishing, derives its name from the fact that he lived and taught in the T'ien-t'ai mountains. [2] Because it took the *Lotus Sūtra* [3] as its basic text, it is sometimes referred to as the Fa-hua 法華 or Lotus school. Chih-k'ai, who followed Hui-wen (550-577) and Hui-ssŭ (515-577) as its third patriarch, was a prolific writer. Most of his works, however, are primarily concerned with techniques of self-cultivation, so that for the more purely philosophical tenets of the school it is necessary to turn to another major work, the *Ta-ch'eng Chih-kuan Fa-men* or *Mahāyāna Method of Cessation and Contemplation*. [4] This, though traditionally ascribed to Hui-ssŭ, contains quotations from the *Awakening of Faith*, [5] a text not yet available in Hui-ssŭ's day. Moreover, it bears clear marks of influence from the Mere Ideation and Hua-yen schools, so that it could not have been written until after these schools had become widespread. [6] In the following

---

[1] Not 531-597, as often stated. See Ch'en Yüan, *Shih-shih Yi-nien Lu*, 3.1. — Tr.

[2] Near the eastern tip of Chekiang province.— Tr.

[3] *Saddharma-puṇḍarīka Sūtra*. Translated from the Chinese version in abbreviated form by William E. Soothill as *The Lotus of the Wonderful Law* (Oxford, 1930). — Tr.

[4] TT no. 1924 (vol. 46, pp. 641-664). — Tr.

[5] *Mahāyāna-śraddhotpāda Śāstra*. Translated by D. T. Suzuki as *Açvaghosha's Discourse on the Awakening of Faith in the Mahāyāna* (Chicago, 1900). — Tr.

[6] This has been pointed out to me by Professor Ch'en Yin-k'o. [Though the *Awakening of Faith* was supposedly translated into Chinese while Hui-ssŭ was still alive, several Chinese scholars have questioned the authenticity of this translation. — Tr.]

pages we shall discuss it as representative of the T'ien-t'ai philosophy as it developed during the T'ang dynasty.

i. *The Bhūtatathatā and Tathāgata-garbha*

The universe in its entirety is regarded by the T'ien-t'ai school as consisting of a single absolute mind, known as the *Bhūtatathatā* or the *Tathāgata-garbha*. *Bhūtatathatā* (*Chen-ju* 真 如) literally means "Genuine Thusness"; *Tathāgata-garbha* (*Ju-lai tsang* 如 來 藏) means "*Tathāgata*-storehouse," i.e., "Storehouse of the Thus Come." The significance of the former term is explained as follows in the *Ta-ch'eng Chih-kuan Fa-men*:

"Ali things (*dharmas*) depend upon this mind to have their being, and take mind as their substance. Regarded in themselves, they are all void and illusory, and their being is not (real) being. In contrast to these illusory things, it (mind) is said to be genuine. Furthermore, though really not existent, they, because of illusory causation, have the appearance of undergoing generation and destruction. Yet when these void things undergo generation, mind itself is not generated nor, when they undergo destruction, is it destroyed. Not being generated, it undergoes no increase; not being destroyed, it undergoes no diminution. Being neither increased nor diminished, it is therefore termed 'Genuine' (*chen*).

"The Buddhas of the three ages (past, present, and future), together with sentient beings, all equally have this one pure mind as their substance. All things, both ordinary and saintly, each have their own differences and diverse appearances, whereas this genuine mind is devoid of either diversity or appearance. That is why it is termed 'Thusness' (*ju*). [1]

"Further as to (the combined term) *chen-ju* or *Bhūtatathatā*: It is that of all things which, being genuinely and really thus, consists of the single mind only. This single mind is therefore called 'Genuinely Thus' (*Bhūtatathatā*). Anything external to it is neither genuine nor thus, but consists only of false and diverse appearances. That is why the *Awakening of Faith* says: [2] 'That in all things which for all time has been independent of speech, terms, and mental causation, and which in the final analysis is everywhere the same, under

---

[1] What remains eternally "thus" and not otherwise. — Tr.
[2] See TT vol. 46, p. 576. — Tr.

goes no change, and cannot be broken or destroyed: such is the one mind, which is therefore named the *Bhūtatathatā*.' This is another reason why this mind, which by its own nature is clear and pure, is called the *Bhūtatathatā*" (1.642).

As to the *Tathāgata-garbha*, we read in the same work:

"The *Tathāgata*-storehouse embraces the natures of all sentient beings, each of which differs from the others, thus constituting differences within what is without difference. Thus the natures of each and every one of these sentient beings, for all time, contain qualities that are immeasurable and boundless. This statement has reference to all the impure things of the mundane world, such as the six modes (of existence), [1] four kinds of birth, [2] suffering and happiness, beauty and ugliness, ignorance and wisdom; also to all the pure things that transcend the world, such as the causes and effects derived from the Three Vehicles. [3] All these endlessly differentiated qualities are contained within the natures of each and every sentient being, all-complete without the slightest diminution. For this reason the storehouse of the *Tathāgata* has originally and for all time contained the two natures, the one impure, the other pure. Because of its impure nature, it is capable of manifesting the impure things pertaining to all sentient beings. Hence its storehouse, being in this respect the *Dharmakāya* as it lies within the barriers, [4] is called the Buddha-nature. But because it also contains the pure nature, it is capable of manifesting the pure attributes of all the Buddhas. Hence its storehouse, being in this respect the *Dharmakāya* as it transcends the barriers, is also called the pure-in-nature *Dharmakāya* or pure-in-nature *Nirvāṇa*" (2.647).

This mind "embodies the functionings of the two natures, impure and pure, so that it is capable of generating both this-worldly and other-worldly things" (1.644). In other words, it has stored within it the natures of all things that are. Hence the term "storehouse" that is applied to it.

---

[1] Those of the beings in the hells, of hungry ghosts, of animals, of malevolent nature spirits, of human beings, and of heavenly beings. — Tr.

[2] Viparous (mammals), oviparous (birds), water-born (worms and fish), and metamorphic (such as moths emerging from the chrysalis). — Tr.

[3] The Hīnayāna and Mahāyāna teachings, and those which fall between the two. — Tr.

[4] I.e., within the phenomenal world. The *Dharmakāya* is the embodiment of Truth, the Absolute. The barriers (*varaṇas*) are the delusions, etc., that prevent enlightenment. — Tr.

"Because of its impure nature, it is capable of manifesting the impure things pertaining to all sentient beings." Here we should pay close attention to the distinction between "nature" (*hsing*) and "things" (*shih* 事). From the point of view of Buddhist terminology, "nature" is equivalent to *t'i* 體, i.e., the essence, inner body, or latent state of a thing. The external operations or applied activities of this *t'i* are called its *yung* 用 or functioning, and the phenomenal manifestations resulting from this functioning are termed *shih*, i.e., things and affairs. [1] Transposed into Western philosophical terminology, the *shih* are concrete events and things, that is, they pertain to actuality. The word *hsing* or "nature," on the other hand, refers to the potentiality of these things. Hence to say that *hsing* becomes manifest as *shih*, is equivalent to saying that potentiality becomes manifest as actuality. If we apply this explanation to the passages we have been reading, we arrive at the doctrine that there is potentially present in the mind not only all so-called goodness but all so-called evil as well. This concept is expressed, for example, in the statement: "The storehouse of the *Tathāgata* has originally and for all time contained the two natures, the one impure, the other pure." The mind, because it originally contains these two natures, therefore likewise contains all the innumerable things, both pure and impure, which are manifestations of these natures. This dualistic theory, as we shall see more clearly in section vii, is a special characteristic of the T'ien-t'ai school.

Mind thus "embraces two kinds of nature, impure and pure, and two categories of things, impure and pure." Yet these disparate elements, despite their multiplicity, "have no possibility of interfering with one another" (*ibid.*). From one point of view, as we shall see, mind may be said to be "empty" and undifferentiated. From another viewpoint, however, it is neither the one nor the other. Thus we read again in the *Ta-ch'eng Chih-kuan Fa-men*:

"The storehouse in its substance (*t'i*) is everywhere the same, and in actual fact is undifferentiated. In this respect it is the 'empty' *Tathāgata-garbha*. In its functioning (*yung*), on the other hand, it is unimaginably diverse, and therefore embodies the natures of all

---

[1] On *t'i* and *yung*, which are really untranslatable terms, though they are sometimes rendered as "substance" and "application," see Walter Liebenthal, *The Book of Chao* (Peiping, 1948), pp. 18-20. They are important concepts not only in Chinese Buddhism, but in other Chinese philosophy as well. — Tr.

things and is differentiated. In this respect it is the 'non-empty' *Tathāgata-garbha*. In this (seeming paradox) lies the fact of there being 'differences within what is without difference.'

"How can I say this? What I mean is that it is not like a lump of clay, made up of a large number of particles of earth. How so? Because this lump of clay, (regarded as an entity), is false; it is only its particles of earth that are real. Therefore, whereas each such particle has its own distinct substance, it is only through their combination that the lump of clay becomes formed, and thereby comes to contain all the distinctions of these many particles.

"Such, however, is not the case with the *Tathāgata-garbha*. How so? Because the *Tathāgata-garbha* is something genuine and real, a perfectly harmonious undivided whole. Hence the *Tathāgata-garbha* is, in its totality, the nature of a single hair-pore that belongs to a single sentient being; (at the same time) it is, in its totality, the natures of all the hair-pores of that sentient being. And as in the case of the nature of the hair-pore, so in that of the natures of each and every other thing that there is in the world. As in the case of the nature of a single sentient being, so in that of the natures of all sentient beings of this world, and likewise of all the Buddhas who transcend this world. They are (each and all of them) the *Tathāgata-garbha* in its totality" (2.648).

Thus there is a difference between the way in which the *Tathāgata-garbha* comprises the natures of all things, and, let us say, that in which a bundle of straw consists of a large number of separate straws. This is because, in the former case, the nature of each individual thing actually *is* in itself the *Tathāgata-garbha* in its totality. From this point of view, therefore, the latter's relationship to the natures embraced by it, both pure and impure, differs from that of an ordinary whole to its parts, for in its case each of these parts actually *is* the whole. This means that on the one hand the *Tathāgata-garbha*, though containing all natures, lacks the multiple differentiations that characterize these natures. In the words of the text: "The storehouse in its substance is everywhere the same and in actual fact undifferentiated. In this respect it is the 'empty' *Tathāgata-garbha*." Yet on the other hand the fact that it comprises all natures means that it is capable of manifesting all things. From this point of view, therefore, it does after all contain differences, for which reason it may be termed the " 'non-empty' *Tathāgata-garbha*."

ii. *The Three Characters*

As we have seen, the impure nature is inherent in absolute mind, and manifests itself in the form of "impure things"—by which we should understand the concrete events and things of the phenomenal world. On this process we are informed further in the *Ta-ch'eng Chih-kuan Fa-men*:

"This impure nature, being perfumed by impure deeds (*karma*), creates the condition of ignorance (*avidyā*) and the seeds of all impure things. [1] In accordance with these seeds, various kinds of retribution are manifested. This ignorance, together with these fruits of *karma*, constitute the things of impurity. This condition of ignorance, however, together with the retributions induced by the seeds, though manifested in various forms that are spoken of as (phenomenal) things, nevertheless all have the single mind as their substance and do not lie outside this mind. This is the reason why the mind is not (really) 'empty.' The case is like that of images reflected in a bright mirror. These have no substance other than the single mirror, yet this fact does not prevent them from being demarcated according to their differences, and these differing images, being all reflected in the mirror, the latter is therefore said not to be empty" (2.647).

The images thus reflected in the non-empty mirror are those of the phenomenal world.

In order to comprehend the way in which impure *karma* originates, it is necessary to grasp the theory of the "three characters" (*san hsing*), that is, the varying degrees of reality which all things possess according to the way in which they are viewed. These characters are those of reality (*chen-shih* 眞 實), of dependency on other things (*yi-t'a* 依 他), and of ordinary sensory perception or discrimination (*fen-pieh* 分 別). We are told about them:

"As to the three characters: The *Bhūtatathatā* as it transcends the barriers, and with it the pure Buddha-attributes, are all termed the character of reality. The *Bhūtatathatā* as it lies within the barriers, being combined there with impurity, is called the *ālaya* consciousness. This has the character of dependency. The erroneously imagined (sensory) discriminations of the six consciousnesses, together with the

---

[1] The terms and concepts of "perfuming" and "seeds" are derived from the Mere Ideation school, described in the preceding chapter. — Tr.

seventh, are all termed the character of discrimination" [1] (3.655).

The foregoing is "a summary exposition of the three characters." Concerning the *ālaya* consciousness, also known, among other things, as the primary or "basic" (*pen* 本) consciousness, we are told further:

"Primary consciousness, *ālaya* consciousness, harmonizing and combining consciousness, seed consciousness, and retributive consciousness: these are all varying names for the one identical substance. ... As to the points of similarity and difference between the *Bhūtatathatā* and the *ālaya*: ... Genuine mind (i.e., the *Bhūtatathatā*) constitutes the essential substance (*t'i*); the primary consciousness (the *ālaya*) is its manifested appearance (*lakṣaṇa*); the (first) six and the seventh consciousness are its functioning (*yung*). The case is like that of water, which is substance; the current (of the water) is its manifested appearance; the waves are its functioning. Through these comparisons we can come to understand. That is why the *śāstra* says: [2] 'What is neither generated nor destroyed, yet combines with what undergoes generation and destruction: this is called the *ālaya* consciousness.' It is also the primary consciousness, being so termed because it serves as the primary basis for (the cycle of) life and death. That is what is meant when the *śāstra* says: [3] 'Considered from the point of view of the seeds, it (primary consciousness) is the *ālaya* consciousness, because it acts as the fundamental seed for all things.'

"In a *sūtra* there is also mention of 'the mind which by its own nature is clear and pure.' Yet it says too that 'this mind is polluted by the passions (*kleśas*).' [4] This makes it clear that genuine mind, though on the one hand it embodies the pure nature, on the other also embodies the impure nature, for which reason it becomes polluted by the passions. From these discussions we may clearly understand that as substance, in which one aspect of its nature is emphasized, we term

---

[1] Here again the terminology is borrowed from the Mere Ideation school. The *ālaya* or eighth consciousness is the nexus of all the various consciousnesses. The seventh and the other six kinds of consciousness are respectively those of mentation and of sensory perception. Save for minor details, the classification here made in terms of the three characters is essentially the same as that of the Mere Ideation and Hua-yen schools. — Tr.

[2] See *The Awakening of Faith* (TT vol. 32, p. 576). — Tr.

[3] I have not found this quotation in *The Awakening of Faith*. — Tr.

[4] The former quotation, though attributed to a *sūtra*, occurs several times in *The Awakening of Faith*, which is a *śāstra*. See *op. cit.*, pp. 576, 577, 579. I have not identified the latter quotation. — Tr.

it pure mind; but as appearance, in which it diversely combines with impure things, we term it the primary consciousness" (3.653).

"Genuine mind, though on the one hand it embodies the pure nature, on the other also embodies the impure nature." Analysing the three characters further from this point of view, we learn that the character of reality "in its turn has two sub-divisions: in the first, the 'pure mind in its aspect of pollution' constitutes the character of reality; in the second, the 'pure mind in its aspect of non-pollution' constitutes that character. By 'pure mind in its aspect of pollution' is meant the substantive reality that pertains to all sentient beings, and the original nature that pertains to the things of pollution. . . . By 'pure mind in its aspect of non-pollution' is meant the substantive nature of the Buddhas, and the original reality of the attributes of purity" (*ibid.*, p. 656).

Thus the originally unitary genuine mind, in the aspect in which it "embodies the pure nature," is called the "pure mind in its aspect of non-pollution"; in that in which it "embodies the impure nature," it is called the "pure mind in its aspect of pollution." This genuine mind itself is neither generated nor destroyed. Nevertheless, "being unaware of itself, it is therefore active and thus produces the manifestations of illusory forms" (1.643). In this way the phenomena of generation and destruction result. These dual aspects of the genuine mind—that pertaining to generation and destruction and that which does not do so—are jointly known as the *ālaya* consciousness. The character of this consciousness is that of dependency, in other words, there is an interdependence between it and things. This character of dependency and the third character of sensory discrimination are, like the first character of reality, each subdivided into pure and impure aspects. We shall have more to say about their pure aspects in section vii. As to their impure aspects, we are told that it is from these that the phenomenal world takes its rise. Thus the *Ta-ch'eng Chih-kuan Fa-men* states:

"Within the character of dependency in its aspect of pollution, and amid its unreal forms, there are such things as seeming color, seeming consciousness, seeming matter, etc. Why are these all termed 'seeming'? Because they are all manifested by the single mind, in accordance with its perfuming. These manifestations of mind, however, are only seeming things without reality. That is the reason for the term seeming. At the moment when the seeming consciousnesses are manifested, there simultaneously arises the semblance of matter.

Therefore when this process of arising takes place, we fail to realize that the seeming matter, seeming color, etc., are merely products of mind, and are thereby false in appearance and without reality. Because of our failure to realize, we discriminate them erroneously and thereby take the false to be real. Because of our erroneous belief, the objects thus evolved from mind all become (to us like) real things. They it is that ordinary people of today look upon as 'things.' While clung to in this way, they from moment to moment perfume the mind, thus further reacting upon it to create in turn the character of dependency. On the basis of this further clinging, the character of discrimination is additionally created. In this way these false delusions from moment to moment engender one another.

"*Question*: 'Since the character of discrimination and that of dependency thus engender one another, what, in the final analysis, is the difference between them?' *Answer*: 'The fact that things have the character of dependency means that they arise from the mind's nature in accordance with its perfuming but, being solely manifestations of mind, are void of substance and lack reality. Whereas the fact that things have the character of discrimination means that, owing to ignorance, we fail to realize that things that are dependent on others are therefore void; the result is that we erroneously cling to them as real. For this reason, although there is no distinction in substance as to what are mutually produced (either through the character of dependency or that of discrimination), there is such a distinction as to the (way in which we then regard these things as either) real or unreal. That is why I speak of the character of discrimination (as distinct from the other character)' " (3.656).

The "seeming consciousnesses" mentioned near the beginning of this passage are the first six consciousnesses, plus the seventh. [1] The *Bhūtatathatā*, "being unaware of itself, is therefore active." This activity results in the manifestation of various illusory forms, among them the seeming consciousnesses which, failing to realize that all these illusory forms, including themselves, are products of mind, cling to them as real. The fact that these forms are void by origin constitutes the "character of dependency on others in its polluted aspect." And the fact that, despite this voidness, they are erroneously regarded as real constitutes the "character of discrimination in its

---

[1] See *op. cit.*, 1.642.

polluted aspect." The things thus erroneously discriminated as "real" are the objects of the phenomenal world.

What the T'ien-t'ai school thus terms the "character of discrimination in its polluted aspect" is equivalent to the Mere Ideation school's "character of sole imagination," and its "character of dependency on others" is likewise equivalent to the same term in the Mere Ideation school. The "character of reality" of the T'ien-t'ai school, however, differs somewhat from the "character of ultimate reality," as conceived by the Mere Ideation school, whereas it agrees with that of the Hua-yen school.

All things of the phenomenal world have the character of dependency on other things. Underlying this fact, however, is the further fact that they are also manifestations of the mind's character of reality in its polluted aspect. Thus we read:

"The genuine mind has the capacity of forming the substance of all things, both ordinary and saintly. This mind-substance embraces the natures of all *dharmas*. The formation of all things, whether this-worldly or other-worldly, in every case derives its principle from the mind's nature. Were anything to lack this principle, its formation could never take place" (2.652).

Thus all that there is is a manifestation of the character of reality. In other words, there is nothing external to mind.

iii. *Universal and Non-universal Consciousness*

If all things are the manifestations of a single mind, why is it that sentient beings of the phenomenal world differ among each other in what they perceive and enjoy? This problem is raised and answered in the following passage of the *Ta-ch'eng Chih-kuan Fa-men*:

"*Question*: 'Since all beings, both ordinary and saintly, have the single mind as their substance, why is it that sometimes they perceive things in common and sometimes not, sometimes they enjoy things in common and sometimes not?'

"*Answer*: 'When it is said that all beings, both ordinary and saintly, have the single mind as their substance, this statement is made with reference to the two aspects of mind: that as substance (*t'i*) and that as manifested appearance (*lakṣaṇa*). The first is that of the *Bhūtatathatā*, which is everywhere the same. This is its substance. . . . The second is that of the *ālaya* consciousness. This is its manifested appearance. . . . Thus there are combined in the mind two separate things: one is universal (*kung hsiang*) consciousness; [1] the other is non-universal consciousness. Why is this? Because within the substance of the *Bhūtatathatā* there are embodied the two natures of universal and non-universal consciousness. All beings, ordinary and saintly, by jointly creating identical deeds (*karma*), through which the universal nature is perfumed, thereby produce universal consciousness. But by individually creating differing deeds, through which the non-universal nature is perfumed, they thereby produce non-universal consciousnesses....

" 'However, the features of terrain (such as mountains, rivers, etc.) that are utilized in common (by sentient beings) are all nothing but mind in its aspect of manifested appearance. Hence the term universal consciousness that is applied to them. ... As to the term non-universal, this has reference to the individual retributions incurred by each and every ordinary or saintly being in his own person. When each such being creates differing *karma* of his own which perfumes the genuine mind, the non-universal nature of that mind, responding to these perfumings, manifests varying retributions which differ for each individual and separate him from the others. These differing retributions, however, are (also) simply mind in its aspect of manifested appearance. Hence the term non-universal consciousness that is applied to them' " (2.652).

Thus such phenomenal things as mountains, rivers, plains, etc., being manifestations produced by *karma* which is identical for all sentient beings alike, are consequently perceived and enjoyed by all these beings in common. Those particularized manifestations resulting from individually differing *karma*, however, such as an individual's own bodily organs, can only be utilized by that individual and by no one else. Each category of conduct induces the corresponding kind of nature in the absolute mind to manifest itself phenomenally; the more numerous the acts belonging to a certain category, the more profound the influence exerted upon the corresponding nature. Thus "each being," according to the way in which he "creates differing *karma* of his own," receives a correspondingly different kind of retribution.

iv. *The Integration of All Things*

All things and events of the phenomenal world, despite their

---

[1] A term borrowed from the Mere Ideation school. See chap. 8, p. 308. — Tr.

manifold variety, are in a state of harmonious integration (*she* 攝), one with another. The *Ta-ch'eng Chih-kuan Fa-men* says:

"If we consider even such a thing as a single hair-pore, it is integrated with all other things, both this-worldly and other-worldly. And as in the case of this hair-pore, thus integrated with all things, so in that of each and every existing thing, both this-wordly and other-wordly: there is an integration of them all, whether this-worldly or other-worldly. Why is this? Because all this-worldly and other-worldly things are embodiments of this-worldly and other-worldly natures. There being a harmonious integration among these natures, there is likewise a harmonious integration and absence of barrier among these things" (2.648).

Thus the fact that things are the embodiments of various natures, each of which is the *Tathāgata-garbha* in its totality, means that the things themselves are likewise manifestations of the *Tathāgata-garbha* in its totality. The manner of integration of things and natures is illustrated in the following conversation:

"The monk asked: 'If you close your eyes and mentally imagine a single small hair-pore on the body, can you see it or not?' The outsider, having thus imagined such a hair-pore, replied: 'I have come to see it.'

"The monk continued: 'Now if you close your eyes and mentally imagine a great city several tens of miles in extent, can you see it or not?' The outsider, having imagined such a city, replied: 'I see it in my mind.'

"The monk said: 'Do the hair-pore and city differ in size or not?' The outsider replied: 'They do.'

"The monk went on: 'The hair-pore and city which you imagine, are they or are they not simply the product of mind?' 'They are,' replied the outsider.

" 'Does this mean, then,' said the monk, 'that there is a (corresponding) largeness or smallness of your mind?' 'The mind has no shape,' replied the outsider, 'so how can it be either large or small?'

"The monk said: 'When you imagine the hair-pore, is it the mind reduced in size that does this, or is it the entire mind functioning as a whole?' The outsider replied: 'Since the mind has no shape, how can it be reduced in size when functioning? Hence, when I imagine the hair-pore, it is functioning in its entirety.'

"The monk continued: 'And when you imagine the great city, is it only you yourself who do the imagining, or does it also involve the mental activities of other people?' 'It is only my own mind that creates the city,' replied the outsider. 'There is no other person's mind involved.'

" 'Thus,' said the monk, 'it is only the single mind that in its totality produces the one small hair-pore, yet that also in its totality produces the great city. The mind, being single, has neither large-ness nor smallness. The hair-pore and the city both embody the single total mind as their substance. From this we should realize that the hair-pore and the city are integrated in substance and everywhere the same.'

"For this reason the small admits of the large; thus there is nothing large that is not small. The large integrates the small; thus there is nothing small that is not large. Because there is nothing small that is not large, the large may enter the small, yet is not diminished. Because there is nothing large that is not small, the small may con-tain the large, yet is not increased. Thus the small undergoes no untoward increase; hence the former substance of a mustard seed remains unchanged. The large undergoes no untoward diminution; hence the vast appearance of Mount Sumeru remains as before. [1] This is based on the principle of origination as due to causation. But if we look at it from the point of view of mind as substance that is everywhere the same, then the (phenomenal) appearances of largeness and smallness are both fundamentally non-existent. There is neither generation nor destruction, but only the single genuine mind" (2.650).

Thus Mount Sumeru might be placed within a mustard seed, yet "the former substance of the mustard seed would remain un-changed," and "the vast appearance of Mount Sumeru would remain as before." Here the argument is presented in terms of space. The same theory, but now from the point of view of time, is developed in the following conversation:

" 'I now ask you again, do you ever dream or not?' 'I do,' replied the outsider.

"The monk asked further: 'In your dream do you ever see things happening over a space of five or ten years?' The outsider replied: 'I have in fact seen the passage of many years or of a few days. There may be (the succession of) day and night, just as if I were awake.'

---

[1] An allusion to the Indian saying that Mount Sumeru (which stands in the center of the world, according to Hindu folklore) may be put inside a mustard seed. — Tr.

"The monk continued: 'After waking up, have you known how much time passed while you were asleep?' 'On awakening,' replied the outsider, 'I have asked other people, and they have told me that since I went to sleep there has elapsed only the space of a meal.'

" 'How strange!' exclaimed the monk, 'within the space of a meal to see the events of many years.'

"According to this idea, if, from the point of view of the wakeful state, we speak of a dream, what may be a lengthy period within that dream becomes unreal, whereas if, from the point of view of the dream, we speak of the wakeful state, the space of a meal during that state also becomes something false. Thus if we discuss wakefulness and dreaming from the point of view of the senses, then the statement, applied to either one of them, that it is long or short, is in each case maintained to be true. The result is a disharmony between them. If, however, we discuss wakefulness and dreaming from the point of view of Truth, their long or short durations become integrated. The long period becomes short and the short period long, without interfering with their distinctive differences as to length or shortness.

"Regarded in terms of the single mind, long and short duration are equally non-existent, for fundamentally there is only that single mind which is everywhere the same. It is precisely because of this uniformity of mind that there is neither long nor short duration. That is why the manifested appearances of length and shortness, arising from the mind's nature, lack the reality of such length or shortness and hence can be integrated. For if the long period and the short one were in their own substance long and short, and were not the products of the single mind, then there could be no integration of their length and shortness.

"Or again, even supposing they both did embody the single mind, if the long period were a product of mind in its complete functioning, whereas the short period were one only of mind as reduced in size, there could be no integration of their length and shortness. It is precisely because the mind in its totality produces both the long and the short period, that there can be integration between them. For this reason the sage, basing himself on this principle of uniformity, does not see the three ages as either long or short. Basing himself on the principle of origination as due to causation, he knows that a short or long period are harmonious by their substance and mutually integrated" (*ibid.*, pp. 650-651).

Thus in terms of space, the seemingly large and the seemingly small are in actual substance harmonious and integrated; in terms of time, the same principle applies to long and short duration. It is universally applicable, in fact, to all things of the senses. Thus we read further:

"Therefore a *sūtra* says: 'Each and every particle of matter is a manifestation of all the Buddha-realms of the ten directions.' Again: 'The three ages and, in fact, the totality of time, become, when understood, a single instant.' This is the point (we have been discussing). The *sūtra* also says: 'The past is the future, the future is the present.' This is the way in which the three ages are integrated. The fact that all other things, whether mutually opposed or not, such as purity and pollution, good and bad, height and lowness, this and that, brightness and darkness, sameness and diversity, tranquillity and disorder, being and non-being, etc., can all be integrated, is because, being manifestations, they have no reality in themselves, but must depend upon mind to arise. Because in the substance of mind there is an integration, therefore in its manifestations there is also no barrier" (*ibid.*, p. 650).

Every phenomenon is the manifestation of the genuine mind in its totality. This doctrine differs from that of certain non-Buddhists, which speaks of the diffusion of the genuine mind among all things. Thus we read:

"*Question*: '... What is the difference between this (doctrine), that the genuine mind permeates everywhere, and that imagined by non-Buddhists, that there is an an ego [1] that permeates everywhere?'

"*Answer*: 'The non-Buddhists believe that there are things external to mind which, whether large or small, far or near, the three ages or the six modes (of existence), [2] are all equally real. But they suppose that the ego, being minute and abstruse, yet extensive and vast, therefore permeates all places, just as does space, (which is everywhere). From this it may be seen that (for these non-Buddhists) the manifestations of those "real" things are different from the ego, and the manifestation of the ego is different from those "real" things. Now even supposing that they account the ego as being everything, so that the ego and things are one, nonetheless they still hold that these things are real (in themselves), so that there is no merging of the one (the ego) with the other (the things).

---

[1] *Ātman* (*shen wo* 神我), lit., "divine self." — Tr.

[2] See above, p. 362, note 1. — Tr.

" 'Such is not the case according to the Buddhist teaching. We know that all things are the product of mind. Because, however, they arise as the result of (diverse) causations derived from the mind's nature, they themselves are not lacking in diversity of appearance. Despite this diversity, however, they all have the single mind as their substance. Because this substance (*t'i*) has its functioning aspect (*yung*), it is said that reality reaches everywhere. This "reaching," however, does not mean that external to mind there are real things, among which the mind diffuses itself' " (2.650).

Thus nothing real exists outside of mind, and hence all phenomena are manifestations of that mind. This is not the same as merely saying that there is a mind that permeates all things. In this respect, therefore, the T'ien-t'ai theory differs from pantheism as ordinarily conceived.

v. *Cessation and Contemplation*

From the foregoing it may be seen that men's ordinary views of the universe and life are based on illusion. That is why they are eternally caught in the wheel of life and death and suffer from the afflictions or *kleśas*. In order to destroy this illusion and escape from the wheel, spiritual cultivation is needed which will enable the pure nature of our original mind to become manifested. For this purpose there are two methods, described in the *Ta-ch'eng Chih-kuan Fa-men* as those of "cessation" (*chih* 止) and "contemplation" (*kuan* 觀): [1]

"What is called cessation (*chih*) is the realization that all things (*dharmas*), from the very beginning, are devoid of any nature of their own and undergo neither production nor destruction. It is only because of the illusory effects of causation that, though non-existent, they (seem to) exist. Thus the 'being' of those things is not (real) being. They consist solely of the single mind, in whose substance there is no differentiation. By carrying out observation of this kind it is possible to stop the flow of erroneous thoughts. This is therefore termed 'cessation.'

"As to what is called contemplation (*kuan*), through it we know that (things), though neither originally generated nor now destroyed, nevertheless arise out of the causation of the mind's

---

[1] *Chih* or cessation is the silencing or putting to rest of one's active thoughts. *Kuan* or contemplation is a more positive technique of observing and examining the nature of things. — Tr.

nature and hence do not lack functioning of a void and mundane kind. Like the illusions of a dream, they have 'being,' though not (real) being. This is therefore called 'contemplation' " (1.642).

Again: "We should know that by means of contemplation it is possible to establish (the theory of) the three characters, and the fact that it is causation that produces (seeming) being. By means of cessation it is possible to eliminate the three characters and enter into the three non-characters. [1] This entry into the three non-characters means: (1) elimination of the character of discrimination, and entry into that of the absence of all qualities; (2) elimination of the character of dependency on others, and entry into that of the absence of all generation; (3) elimination of the character of reality, and entry into that of the absence of all the characters. . .

"Let us take as an example a handkerchief (made by a conjurer to look like a rabbit): (1) From the very beginning there is no rabbit. The same principle applies to a thing in its character of reality, which consists solely of the single pure mind, by its very nature devoid of all quality. (2) But through the effort of the conjurer the handkerchief assumes the appearance of the rabbit. The same principle applies to a thing in its character of dependency on others: the genuine nature, being perfumed by illusion, produces the manifestations of the six modes (of existence). (3) The stupid and ignorant, however, take this rabbit to be real. The same thing applies to a thing in its character of discrimination: because of mental delusion, what is void is clung to as something real. That is why the *sūtra* says: 'All things are like a conjurer's tricks.' This exemplifies the method of contemplation (*kuan*) as applied to the three characters.

"(Now as regards the three non-characters): (1) Suppose we realize that the rabbit depends upon the handkerchief for its seeming existence and is (in itself) only void and unreal. The same principle applies to the knowledge of the character of the absence of all qualities: it is the realization that all things depend upon mind for their seeming existence, and are only void forms, lacking any character of having real qualities. (2) Suppose we realize that the unreal appearance of the rabbit (really) consists only of a handkerchief; the 'existence' of the rabbit of that handkerchief is not (real) existence, and from the very beginning it has never been generated. The same principle applies to the knowledge of the character of the absence

---

[1] On the relationship of the theory of the three non-characters to that of the three characters, see chap. 8, sect. 2, vi. — Tr.

of all generation: it is the realization that the unreal appearances (of the phenomenal world) are only manifestations of the genuine mind; that, this being so, their 'existence' is not (real) existence; and that in their own nature they have no generation. (3) Suppose we realize that it is the handkerchief that originally exists, and do not take the non-existence of the rabbit to be the handkerchief. The same principle applies to the knowledge of the character of the absence of all the characters: it is the realization that the pure mind exists through its own innate nature, and that we should not take the (mere) absence of the two (other) characters as constituting the character of reality. This exemplifies the method of cessation (*chih*) as applied to the three non-characters" (3.658).

Thus what is called the elimination of "the character of reality" does not mean a complete nihilism. It does not mean, for example, that the *Bhūtatathatā* consists merely of the absence of the two characters of dependency and discrimination. This is why we are told further: "Merely eliminating from (our concept of) the genuine nature such perversely clung-to kinds of 'genuineness' as these, does not mean that we should utterly obliterate the substance of the *Bhūtatathatā* itself" (*ibid.*). Having reached this stage, "our thoughts come to an end of themselves, and this is called the experiencing of the *Bhūtatathatā*. It is not the experiencing of something else (outside the mind), but is simply like the cessation of the waves and their entry into their (underlying body of) water" (*ibid.*).

In this stage we come to rest in *Nirvāṇa*. The Buddhas, however, have the power of returning from this state to the phenomenal world, and reentering the wheel of life and death, solely in order to convert and save all sentient beings. To achieve *Nirvāṇa* is the function of cessation; to return thence to the ordinary world is that of contemplation. Thus we read:

"The functions of cessation and contemplation are these:

"(1) The achievement reached by cessation is that of embodying and experiencing the pure mind, becoming merged by means of Truth with the non-dual nature, and forming with all sentient beings a single perfect body. Thereupon the Three Precious Ones [1] become fused so that they are no longer three, and the Dual Divisions grow together so that they are no longer two. How unchanging the con-

---

[1] *Triratna* (*san pao* 三 寶), the Buddha, the Buddhist Law or *Dharma*, and the Buddhist Ecclesiastical Assembly or Order. — Tr.

gealed depthes of the placid pool! How calm the limpid purity of the inner silence! It functions without appearing to function, and acts without appearing to act. All things are originally everywhere the same, and so too is the nature of the mind. This then is the profound nature in its essential substance.

"(2) The achievement reached by contemplation is that of manifesting the essential substance of the mind so that it functions without interference within the world of physical things, and spontaneously emanates the potentialities of all things, both pure and impure. . . .

"Again, because of the achievement of cessation, since the mind is everywhere the same, one does not dwell within (the cycle of) life and death. Yet because of the achievement of contemplation, since its attributes function in response to causation, one does not enter *Nirvāṇa*. Or again, because of the achievement of cessation, one dwells within the great *Nirvāṇa*. Yet because of the achievement of contemplation, one stays within (the cycle of) life and death. Or yet again, because of the achievement of cessation, one is not polluted by the world. Yet because of the achievement of contemplation, one is not restricted to silent inactivity. Or finally, because of the achievement of cessation, one functions yet remains ever still. But because of the achievement of contemplation, one stays still yet remains ever functioning" (4.661).

This is the meaning of the words: "Only eliminate the ills but not the things. The ills consist in the sensory clingings, but not in the great functioning itself" (3.654). Or again: "Although we know that the 'existence' of things is not (real) existence, we also know that this does not prevent their non-existence from 'existing' " (4.661). As long as we void ourselves of our sensory clingings to the phenomenal world, we can remain within that world without that fact causing any impediment to ourselves.

vi. *The Impure Natures of the Buddhas*

Thus "the mind-substance of each and every Buddha, even while it creates *Nirvāṇa* in response to its perfuming, is not prevented thereby from having the functioning of the impure nature" (1.646).

We have read in the preceding section that "because of the achievement of cessation, one dwells within the great *Nirvāṇa*. Yet because of the achievement of contemplation, one stays within (the cycle of) life and death." "Functioning of the impure nature" is the technical designation for such continued stay within the world. The logical implications of this doctrine are somewhat startling, namely: not only ordinary sentient beings, but even the Buddhas, all possess the impure nature and, conversely, not only the Buddhas, but even ordinary sentient beings, all possess the pure nature (otherwise known as the Buddha-nature). The reason why the impure nature should thus be retained even after the achievement of Buddhahood is that the nature, whether pure or impure, remains fundamentally unchange-able; spiritual cultivation, therefore, can only check the outward manifestations of its impure aspect, but cannot eliminate or change the nature itself. Thus we read in the *Ta-ch'eng Chih-kuan Fa-men*:

"*Question*: 'Regarding the fact that the storehouse of the *Tathā-gata* embodies two kinds of nature, the one impure, the other pure: does this mean that these natures become formed as the result of habit, or do they remain (forever) unchangeable?'

"*Answer*: 'These natures, both as substance and function, are (forever) unchangeable and are not formed as the result of habit. That is why it is said that the Buddha-nature, the great ruler, is not something created. How then can it be formed as the result of habit? And since the Buddha-nature, that is, the pure nature, cannot be created, this means that the impure nature, which is identical in sub-stance though it belongs to the world of physical things, likewise cannot be formed as the result of habit" (2.648).

The fact that the pure and impure natures are thus both equally unchanging and not formed through habit means, in the case of ordinary beings, that though their impure nature manifests itself in the form of impure things, this has no destructive effect upon their pure nature. Conversely it means for the Buddhas that though their pure nature manifests itself in the form of pure things, this again does not destroy their impure nature. Thus we are told:

"The mind-substance of each and every sentient being, and of each and every Buddha, originally contains the two natures, without the slightest distinction for all. Throughout they are exactly of the same sort, and have remained indestructible from antiquity until the present. But with the perfuming of the impure nature by impure *karma* (the wheel of) life and death becomes manifested whereas, with the perfuming of the pure nature by pure *karma*, *Nirvāṇa* in its functioning aspect becomes manifested. ... In this way each and every sentient being and Buddha is equally endowed with the two natures, pure and impure; the world of physical things follows the same pattern, never being devoid of them. Nevertheless, according to the influence of perfuming, there may be a chronological difference in the activation of their functioning. Thus with the cessation of impure perfuming, a 'revulsion' may be experienced by ordinary beings. [1] And with the rise of pure *karma*, saintliness may be achieved. Yet the two natures of the mind-substance are in actual fact neither created nor destroyed thereby. ... That is why it is said in a *sūtra*: 'Among the pure *dharmas* there is no increase by even one.' That is to say, the pure nature's original endowment has been as it is without a beginning. (Or again): 'Among the passion *dharmas* there is no diminution by even one.' That is to say, the impure nature's original endowment cannot be destroyed" (1.646).

Thus as far as the original nature is concerned, no difference exists between ordinary sentient beings and the enlightened Buddhas, save this: sentient beings, as the result of the perfuming of their impure nature by impure *karma*, experience impure things such as the events of life and death, whereas the Buddhas, as the result of the perfuming of their pure nature by pure *karma*, experience pure things such as *Nirvāṇa*. Despite this fact, however, the pure nature of sentient beings remains ever undestroyed, so that the potentiality remains to them of creating pure *karma* and thereby perfuming their pure nature; and by the same token, the impure nature of the Buddhas is never destroyed by the fact that they dwell in purity, so that the potentiality likewise remains to them of entering the wheel of existence and there giving rise to impure activities.

vii. *Enlightenment and Unenlightenment*

If the pure and impure natures are both innate in the *Tathāgata-garbha*, why should the former be of greater value than the latter? In other words, what is the need for sentient beings to strive to perfect themselves in order to achieve Buddhahood? The reply is found in what the *Ta-ch'eng Chih-kuan Fa-men* calls "impure *karma* being opposed to mind," and "pure *karma* following mind." Thus we read:

"Although impure *karma* arises out of the mind's nature, it is perpetually opposed to mind, whereas pure *karma*, which also arises out of the mind's nature, perpetually follows mind. ... There is no

---

[1] On such "revulsion," see chap. 8, pp. 336-338. — Tr.

doubt that the impure things of ignorance (*avidyā*) take their rise from the mind-substance in its impure nature. But because of that ignorance it is not realized that the self, together with the objects of the external world, all arise from mind, nor is it realized that the pure mind embraces two kinds of nature, the pure and impure, between which there is no quality of distinction, and which are exactly the same in kind for all. It is because of failure to realize this principle that the term 'opposed' is used in this case.

"There is (also) no doubt that the pure things of wisdom [1] take their rise from the mind-substance in its pure nature. Because of that understanding it can be realized that the self, together with other things, are all products of mind, and further that the pure mind does embrace two kinds of nature, the pure and impure, between which there is no quality of distinction, and which are exactly the same in kind for all. It is because of the realization of this truth that the term 'following' is used in this case" (1.646-647).

From this it may be seen that the reason why the impure nature of sentient beings gives rise to impure *karma* is that these beings lack enlightenment or *bodhi* (*chüeh*); this lack of enlightenment is called *avidyā* or ignorance. However, through the pure *karma* that arises from the pure nature, men can gain this enlightenment, also known as *jñāna* or wisdom. This explains why the pure nature is of greater value than the impure one, and why sentient beings should strive to achieve Buddhahood. The distinction between Buddhas and ordinary beings is simply one of enlightenment as against unenlightenment. This means that though the Buddhas, like other beings, perform impure acts and enter the cycle of existence as the result of their impure nature, they remain enlightened while so doing. That is to say, even when surrounded by impurity, they remain conscious that "the self, together with other things, are all products of mind." Sentient beings, on the other hand, not only live amidst impurity, but at the same time are devoid of enlightenment Hence they can only be described as living in a dream and deserving of compassion.

The impure, i.e., mundane, things arising from the Buddhas are described as having the "character of dependency on others in its pure aspect," whereas the functioning of these things as instruments for teaching and conversion is described as the "character of discrim-

---

[1] *Jñāna (chih-hui* 智慧). — Tr.

ination in its pure aspect." [1] Thus we read in the *Ta-cheng Chih-kuan Fa-men*:

"*Question*: 'With the extinguishing of impure perfuming, the nature in its impure functioning no longer produces (the cycle of) life and death. Yet does this mean that after the achievement of Buddhahood the nature completely fails to function?'

"*Answer*: 'This nature, not being perfumed by pollution, no longer produces (the cycle of) life and death. And yet, as long as mind is motivated, it (the nature), being perfumed by the compassionate wish (of the Buddhas to save all beings), may still act as an instrument for conversion. It may thus, as a result of such perfuming, function for the instruction of non-conformers, and in this way may still become manifest. This refers to (the various means used by the Buddhas to save sentient beings, such as) the manifesting of themselves among the six modes (of existence), the instructing of those who cling to the three poisons, [2] their temporary acceptance of the retributions of suffering, their responses to death and destruction, etc. All these have the character of discrimination in its pure aspect. . . .'

"*Question*: 'What you have been speaking of are things having the character of dependency on others. Why then do you use the term, character of discrimination?'

"*Answer*: 'These virtues, inasmuch as they arise through the perfuming caused by the compassionate wish (to save all beings), have the character of dependency on others. But inasmuch as they are manifested for purposes of conversion, in response to circumstances, they are things said to have the character of discrimination' " (3.656).

The virtues here described, though they have both the character of dependency and that of discrimination, all lie within the sphere of *bodhi* or enlightenment. That is why they are still said to be pure. We are further told that the awareness which the Buddhas, as enlightened beings, possess of their pure mind, is actually a self-awareness by that mind of itself:

"*Question*: 'Is a Buddha termed such because, possessing wisdom, he is able thereby to be aware of his pure mind? Or is he so called because this pure mind of his has its own self-awareness?'

"*Answer*: 'Both statements apply. According to the one, he

---

[1] On the division into pure and impure aspects of the three characters of discrimination, dependency on others, and reality, see above, pp. 366-369. — Tr.

[2] Greed, hate, ignorance. — Tr.

has an awareness of his pure mind. According to the other, the pure mind has an awareness of itself. Although these are described as two separate ideas, in their essence there is no distinction between them' " (1.642).

This doctrine is similar to that of Hegel, according to whom, once theoretical reason and practical reason unite, the implicit nullity of the contrast of subject and object is at once explicitly realized. Reason knows that the subjective purpose is no longer subjective, and that the objective world is but its own truth and substantiality. It turns to itself and is now the Speculative or Absolute Idea. [1]

viii. *The T'ien-t'ai School Compared with the Mere Ideation and Hua-yen Schools*

From the foregoing, it is evident that the teachings of the T'ien-t'ai school, as expressed in the *Ta-ch'eng Chih-kuan Fa-men*, have been greatly influenced both by the Mere Ideation and Hua-yen schools. Thus according to the T'ien-t'ai philosophy, the *Tathāgata-garbha* contains the natures of all things, both pure and impure, which resembles the Mere Ideation theory that the "seeds" of all things are contained in the *ālaya* consciousness. There is, however, one important difference: According to the Mere Ideation school, the *ālaya* consciousness is itself dependent upon causal factors for its activity, which means that it is susceptible to mutation; hence its seeds are likewise causally dependent and mutable. The *Ta-ch'eng Chih-kuan Fa-men*, on the contrary, maintains that the natures of all things, both pure and impure, are forever immutable, and that the same is true of the various evils of the phenomenal world, since these pertain to the impure nature.

The *Ta-ch'eng Chih-kuan Fa-men* furthermore conceives of a genuine or absolute mind, itself ever constant, as the noumenon that lies behind the shifting panorama of the phenomenal world. In this it agrees with the Hua-yen school. In terms of the metaphor cited in section v, this genuine mind is symbolized by the handkerchief, whereas the things of phenomenon are the rabbit conjured up by the magician out of that handkerchief. "It is the handkerchief that originally exists. We should not take the non-existence of the rabbit to

---

[1] See *The Logic of Hegel*, translated by William Wallace (Oxford, 2nd ed., 1892), pp. 372, 373. This paragraph, save for the first eight words, has been added to the original text from my *Comparative Study of Life Ideals* (Shanghai, 1924), p. 235.

be the handkerchief." The Mere Ideation school, on the other hand, says nothing about a forever immutable genuine mind. In other words, it is precisely the non-existence of the rabbit that it considers as the handkerchief. This point of view not only differs from the *Ta-ch'eng Chih-kuan Fa-men*, but also from the Hua-yen school, both of which maintain that every event and thing is a manifestation of the absolute mind in its totality.

The *Ta-ch'eng Chih-kuan Fa-men*, however, goes still further by saying that the reason why such things "exist" is that their natures are all innate in the *Tathāgata-garbha*. Being thus innate, each such nature itself *is* the *Tathāgata-garbha* in its totality, and hence remains immutable. This means that, for the T'ien-t'ai school, these phenomenal things possess a greater degree of reality than the Hua-yen school would allow. Thus the *Ta-ch'eng Chih-kuan Fa-men*, in its approach to the Buddhist problem of "emptiness" and "being," shows a strong preference for the concept of "being."

As to the problem of the activity of beings who have reached the highest realm of enlightenment, the *Ta-ch'eng Chih-kuan Fa-men* expresses itself unequivocally. The Buddhas, it says, like ordinary sentient beings, possess the impure nature and therefore may, like them, be engaged in impure or mundane acts. The only difference between the two is one of enlightenment as against unenlightenment. On this problem, therefore, the *Ta-ch'eng Chih-kuan Fa-men* is again comparatively concrete in its interpretation of the statement, as regards the enlightened being, that he "functions yet remains ever still; . . . stays still, yet remains ever functioning." [1]

ix. *Chan-jan's Theory that "Even Inanimate Things Possess the Buddha-nature"'*

Logically developed, the theory that each and every thing is a manifestation of the genuine mind in its totality leads to the conclusion that "even inanimate things possess the Buddha-nature." [2] Such is the view expressed by the ninth patriarch of the T'ien-t'ai

---

[1] See above, p. 378. — Tr.

[2] *Wu ch'ing yu hsing* 無情有性, lit., "what lack feelings (also) possess the (Buddha) nature." — Tr.

school, Chan-jan 湛 然 (711-782), [1] in a work called the *Chin-kang Pi* (Diamond Stick). [2] There he writes:

"Therefore we may know that the single mind of a single particle of dust comprises the mind-nature of all sentient beings and Buddhas. ... All things (*dharmas*), being immutable, are the *Bhūta-tathatā*, and the *Bhūtatathatā*, responding to causation, is all things. ... Therefore when we speak of all things, why should exception be made in the case of the tiny particle of dust? Why should the substance of the *Bhūtatathatā* pertain exclusively to 'us' rather than to 'others'? Thus there is no water without waves; there are no waves without wetness. This wetness does not distinguish between the muddy and the limpid, yet the waves are of themselves either clear or turbid. Irrespective of their clarity or turbidity, there is for them only the one undifferentiated nature. And irrespective of what is primarily or secondarily created (by *karma*), according to ultimate Truth there is not the slightest distinction. If on the one hand we grant that what responds to causation remains itself immutable, yet on the other say that inanimate things lack (this immutable nature), do we not fall into a self-contradiction?" (p. 782).

By "primarily created," Chan-jan has in mind our own bodily organs; by "secondarily created," he means the mountains, rivers, etc., of the external world. Both the one and the other are the results of our previous *karma*. According to the Mere Ideation school, since these results, whether primary or secondary, are the products of our own consciousness, they exist only for our own enjoyment or use, and have no independent existence or value in themselves.

According to the Hua-yen and T'ien-t'ai schools, on the other hand, all things are manifestations of the one genuine or absolute mind in its totality. Hence they are like the waves of water which, though differing in clarity or turbidity, are all one in having wetness as their nature. In Chan-jan's own words: "Irrespective of their clarity or turbidity, there is for them only the one undifferentiated nature. And irrespective of what is primarily or secondarily created (by *karma*), according to ultimate Truth there is not the slightest distinction." Though the *Bhūtatathatā*, under the stimulus of varying

---

[1] Lay surname Ch'i 戚 . He was a native of Ch'ang-chou (the present Wu-chin 武進 hsien, southeast of Nanking, on the Shanghai-Nanking Railroad). For his biography, see the *Sung Kao Seng Chuan*, 6.739.

[2] TT no. 1932 (vol. 46, pp. 781-786). — Tr.

causation, manifests itself as various things, it nevertheless retains its eternal immutability within each of those things. "Why should the substance of the *Bhūtatathatā* pertain exclusively to 'us' rather than to 'others'?" This being so, each and every thing has its own personal existence, yet at the same time possesses the one Buddha-nature. Hence Chan-jan's conclusion: "If on the one hand we grant that what responds to causation remains itself immutable, yet on the other say that inanimate things lack (this immutable nature), do we not fall into a self-contradiction?"

According to this reasoning, the distinction ordinarily drawn between inanimate and animate things really no longer exists. Chan-jan continues:

"The man who is of all-round perfection, knows from beginning to end that Truth is not dual and that no objects exist apart from mind. Who, then, is 'animate,' and who 'inanimate'? Within the Assembly of the Lotus, all are present without division. In the case of grass, trees, and the soil (from which they grow), what difference is there between their four kinds of atoms? [1] Whether they (merely) lift their feet or (energetically) traverse the (long) path, they will all reach the Precious Island. [2] By snapping their fingers and joining their palms, they will all achieve the causation for Buddhahood. [3] Whether they agree with the One or the Three (Vehicles), they will none of them run counter to the original concept (of Buddhism). How can it still be said unto today that inanimate things are devoid (of the Buddha-nature)?" (p. 785).

The preceding chapters have demonstrated that logical premises existed for this universalistic theory. Hence Chan-jan's extension of Tao-sheng's thesis that the Buddha-nature is possessed even by the *icchantikas* or non-believers in Buddhism is no mere accident. There is no doubt, however, that in the history of Chinese Buddhism, Chan-jan represents the culmination of this particular trend of thought.

2—THE CH'AN SCHOOL [4]

Of all the schools of Chinese Buddhism, the most uniquely

---

[1] *Ssŭ wei* 四微, the four minutest components of things, respectively perceived by the senses of sight, smell, taste, and touch. — Tr.

[2] *Ratnadvīpa*, a poetic term for *Nirvāṇa*. — Tr.

[3] These are the gestures of Buddhist monks, signifying their joyous acceptance of the teaching. — Tr.

[4] Beginning with sub-section i below, this entire section has been revised

Chinese and probably the best known outside of China is that of Ch'an 禪. This name (better known to Westerners under its Japanese pronounciation of Zen, owing to the great vogue enjoyed by the school in Japan) is an abbreviation of *ch'an-na* 那, which is the Chinese phonetic rendering of the Sanskrit *dhyāna*, meaning meditation.

According to Ch'an tradition, the school originated with certain esoteric teachings allegedly expounded by the historical Buddha to a disciple, and thereafter transmitted through a series of Indian patriarchs of the school. "There was a transmission from mind to mind without the use of written texts."[1] Finally the twenty-eighth of these patriarchs, the famous Bodhidharma, came to China during the reign of Emperor Wu (502-549) of the Liang dynasty, thus becoming the first Ch'an patriarch in China. After his death the school was successively headed by his disciple Hui-k'o (487-593) as the second Chinese patriarch, by Seng-ts'an (died 606) as the third,[2] by Tao-hsin (580-636) as the fourth, and by Hung-jen (602-675) as the fifth. After Hung-jen's death, a schism split the school into a northern branch, headed by Shen-hsiu (ca. 600-706), and a southern one, headed by Hui-neng (638-713). Each of these men was regarded by his adherents as the legitimate sixth patriarch. In addition, several lesser schisms developed.

The special characteristic of the southern branch was its emphasis upon instantaneous enlightenment. Its founder, Hui-neng 慧能,[3] after having studied under Hung-jen in the north, returned south to teach at Shao-chou (in present northern Kwangtung). His disciple Shen-hui 神會 (686-760),[4] after studying under Hui-neng, went north with his master's teachings to attack the northern branch. As a result this branch became so weakened that it finally

---

so that it now follows Fung Yu-lan's *Spirit of Chinese Philosophy* (transl. of E. R. Hughes, pp. 157-174). — Tr.

[1] A statement traditionally said to have been made by Bodhidharma to his disciple, Hui-k'o.

[2] Not to be confused with another monk of the same name who lived 529-613. — Tr.

[3] Lay surname Lu 盧. Native of Hsin-hsing (southwest of Canton). Biography in the *Sung Kao Seng Chuan*, 8.754-755.

[4] Lay surname Kao 高. Native of Hsiang-yang (on the Han river in Hupeh). Not to be confused with another Shen-hui who lived 720-794. Biography in *ibid.*, pp. 756-757.

fell into oblivion, leaving the southern branch as the recognized orthodox transmitter of Ch'anism.

Such is the popular account of the early history of the Ch'an school. In actual fact, however, its development in India may safely be regarded as entirely imaginary, and even Bodhidharma, its alleged transmitter to China, looms uncertainly through the mists of tradition as a half legendary person. All that we can say with assurance is that in China itself, as early as the Period of Disunity, the theory of instantaneous enlightenment had been developed; that this theory gained wide currency during the T'ang dynasty; and that the split in the Ch'an school between Shen-hsiu and Hui-neng, arising from their differing attitudes toward this theory, is a historical fact. As for the history of the school prior to this schism, it is far from being as systematic and continuous as later accounts would have us believe. [1]

i. *Intellectual Basis of the Ch'an School*

Ideologically speaking, the origin of the Ch'an school goes back to Tao-sheng (ca. 360-434). In the seventh chapter we have discussed his two famous theses that "a good deed entails no retribution," and that "Buddhahood is achieved through instantaneous enlightenment." It is these that provide the theoretical basis for Ch'an philosophy.

In the same Buddhist community with Tao-sheng there lived the well known layman Liu Ch'eng-chih (died 410), who in his letter to Seng-chao wrote: "The sage's mind is dark and still. Through Truth (*li*) he reaches the ultimate aim and is identified with non-being (*wu*)." Or again: "Although his life is spent in the midst of the nameable, he is far away amid the unnameable." [2] And we read in Hsieh Ling-yün's (385-453) *Pien Tsung Lun* or *Discussion of Essentials*: "One must become identified with non-being and mirror the whole, for Truth is one and final." [3] In our discussion of Seng-chao we have seen that non-being or *wu* is without quality, and to be qualityless is the real quality of all things. It is the knowledge of that real quality

---

[1] On the unreliability of such accounts, see Hu Shih, "The Development of Zen Buddhism in China," *Chinese Social and Political Science Review*, vol. 15 (1931), pp. 475-505. For a detailed discussion of Ch'anist philosophy, with voluminous translations from Ch'an texts, see D. T. Suzuki, *Essays on Zen Buddhism*, first, second, and third series (London, 1927, 1933, 1934). — Tr.

[2] See Seng-chao's *Book of Chao*, chap. 3, p. 90.

[3] See above, chap. 7, p. 275.

that constitutes *Prajñā* or Wisdom. On the other hand, what is without quality cannot be an object of knowledge; hence *Prajñā* is knowledge which is not knowledge. In other words, to have the *Prajñā*-knowledge of the real quality of all things means in actual fact to become identified with that real quality. This is the implication of the two quotations just cited. The sage, being one with non-being, is all-complete in his enlightenment, and thereby has an all-embracing vision of all things. His state of identification is called *Nirvāṇa*, and *Prajñā* is simply the name for another aspect of that same state. *Nirvāṇa*, in short, is the sphere in which lives the man who has acquired *Prajñā*; *Prajñā* is the wisdom of the man who has gained *Nirvāṇa*. To obtain the one is to obtain the other, and vice versa.

Just as identification with non-being, once done is done, so with *Nirvāṇa* and *Prajñā*, once gained they are gained. It is impossible for the man engaged in spiritual cultivation to identify himself with one part of non-being today and another part tomorrow, for non-being cannot be divided into parts. His identification, therefore, can only mean complete identification, otherwise it is no identification at all. And with *Nirvāṇa* and *Prajñā* it is the same: either he has them *in toto* or not at all. This is the basis for the theory that "Buddhahood is achieved through instantaneous enlightenment." Instantaneous enlightenment means gaining *Prajñā*, and achieving Buddhahood means gaining *Nirvāṇa*. Hsieh Ling-yün remarks: "There is a Buddhist with a new doctrine, according to which the state of mirror-like voidness (of *Nirvāṇa*) is abstruse and mysterious and does not admit of any stages (for its attainment)." Again he says that "the talk about stages is only a means of instructing simple folk. The theory of a single (flash of) enlightenment is the one that gains the truth." [1] The Buddhist scholar here referred to is Tao-sheng.

What in the last resort is this *wu*, translated as "non-being"? Two interpretations exist. One is that it is nothing at all, an "ultimate emptiness," a nullity so final that it even nullifies its own nullity. Because it lacks all qualities whatsoever, it cannot be defined in terms of anything. That is why the sage's mind, being identified with this nullity, is commonly said to be like empty space. The other interpretation is that *wu* is another designation for the mind from which all things arise. Without mind there could be nothing at all. Hence when the mind is active, the various kinds of phenomenal

---

[1] See above, chap. 7, pp. 275, 278.

existence appear; when it is inactive, they fail to appear. The real quality of things is the "original mind" in all sentient beings, also sometimes called the "original nature" or "Buddha-nature." To have a vision of the real quality of things is equivalent to comprehending this mind and perceiving this nature in oneself. Tao-sheng expresses this as follows: "To turn one's back on delusion is to attain to the ultimate; to attain to the ultimate is to attain to the origin." [1]

Seng-chao accepted the first interpretation; Tao-sheng, with his theory of the Buddha-nature, seemingly the second. Later on, within the Ch'an school itself, two tendencies developed. One was in the direction of the first interpretation, with the slogan: "Not mind, not Buddha." The other was in the direction of the second, with the slogan: "Being mind, being Buddha." The second remains closer to the temporal world of phenomenon.

All Ch'anists, however, irrespective of which interpretation they accept, emphasize five main points: (1) the Highest Truth or First Principle is inexpressible; (2) "spiritual cultivation cannot be cultivated"; (3) in the last resort nothing is gained; (4) "there is nothing much in the Buddhist teaching"; (5) "in carrying water and chopping wood: therein lies the wonderful *Tao*."

ii. *The First Principle Is Inexpressible*

The Highest Truth or First Principle (*ti-yi yi* 第 一 義) is inexpressible because what it attempts to express is actually "beyond the realm of causation and the (conscious) mind." [2] According to Ch'an tradition, Shen-hsiu (ca. 600-706) wrote a hymn in which he said:

> "The body is like unto the *Bodhi*-tree,
> And the mind to a mirror bright.
> Carefully we cleanse them hour by hour
> Lest dust should fall upon them."

This was countered by Hui-neng (638-713) with another hymn which said:

---

[1] Quoted ·in the *Nieh-pan Ching Chi-chieh* or *Collected Commentaries on the Nirvāna Sūtra, chüan* 1. See *Tripiṭaka Supplement*, Pt. Ia, case 94, vol. 2, p. 109.

[2] A statement by Seng-chao in his reply to Liu Ch'eng-chih. See *Book of Chao*, chap. 3, p. 105.

"Originally there was no *Bodhi*-tree,
Nor was there any mirror.
Since originally there was nothing,
Whereon can the dust fall?" [1]

The first two lines of Shen-hsiu's hymn give affirmation of a sort about what the term "First Principle" is believed to express; they thus give quality to what is really without quality. His last two lines assert the need for spiritual cultivation in order to reach what is thus expressed. Hui-neng's first two lines, on the contrary, point out that what the "First Principle" expresses is really inexpressible, and his last two lines say that for reaching it there can be no spiritual cultivation. No cultivation does not really mean the absence of any kind of cultivation. What it signifies is a "cultivation by means of non-cultivation." These differences between Shen-hsiu and Hui-neng represent differences between the northern branch of Ch'anism (which later became discredited), and the southern branch. Thus it was asserted by most subsequent Ch'anists that the way to express the First Principle is not to say anything about it, that is, "to state through non-statement"; likewise they maintained that the way to cultivate spiritual cultivation is not to cultivate, that is, "to cultivate through non-cultivation."

A story is told of Hui-neng's famous disciple, Huai-jang (677-744), in the record of the latter's sayings: "Ma-tsu [2] lived in the Ch'uan-fa Monastery on the Southern Peak. [3] There he occupied a solitary hut in which all alone he practiced meditation (*ch'an*), paying no attention to those who came to visit him. ... One day (Huai-jang) kept grinding a brick in front of the hut, but Ma-tsu still paid no attention. This having continued for a long time, (Ma-tsu) finally asked: 'What are you doing?' The Teacher (Huai-jang) replied that he was grinding to make a mirror. 'How can a mirror be made by grinding bricks?' asked Ma-tsu. Replied the Teacher: 'If a mirror cannot be made by grinding bricks, how can a Buddha be made by

---

[1] For these hymns, see the *Liu-tsu T'an-ching* (Sūtra Spoken by the Sixth Patriarch), chap. 1, pp. 348 and 350. [Full title: *Liu-tsu Ta-shih Fa-pao T'an-ching* (Sūtra Spoken by the Sixth Patriarch, Teacher of the Buddha-Truth), compiled by Tsung-pao (preface dated 1290); TT no. 2008 (vol. 48, pp. 345-365). — Tr.]

[2] More properly known as Tao-yi (709-788). Not to be confused with another Tao-yi who lived 679-754. — Tr.

[3] The southern of the five "sacred mountains," north of Hengyang in Hunan. — Tr.

practicing meditation?' " [1] To say that a Buddha cannot be made by practicing meditation was as much as to say that spiritual cultivation cannot be cultivated.

Another statement is preserved in the record of Tao-yi's (i.e., Ma-tsu's) own sayings: "The question was asked how to cultivate spiritual cultivation. The Teacher (Tao-yi) replied: 'Spiritual culti- vation does not belong among those things that can be cultivated. If we say it can be obtained by cultivation then, once cultivated, it can again be lost, which is the case with the *śrāvakas* (adherents of Hīnayāna). But if we say it is not cultivatable at all, then we are in the state of ordinary people' " (*ibid.*, p. 80). The way to acquire spiritual cultivation is neither through cultivating nor not culti- vating; it consists in cultivation through non-cultivation.

To practice cultivation through cultivation is to act with con- scious mind, that is to say, to practice assertive activity. Such activity lies within the sphere of the things of life and death, and therefore is itself a thing subject to generation and destruction. As said by Hsi-yün: [2] "Suppose that through innumerable aeons a man has practiced the six *pāramitās* [3] and gained Buddha-wisdom, even this is not final. How so? Because all these acts pertain to causation. Hence with the exhaustion of their force he is brought back to the imper- manent." Again: "All deeds ultimately bring one back to the im- permanent, because their forces all have their final day. They are like a dart discharged through the air: when its strength is exhausted, it turns and falls to the ground. Thus do they all revert to the wheel of life and death. Hence to practice cultivation in this way is to mis- understand the Buddha's idea, and entails much fruitless suffering. How vastly wrong is this! " [4]

Cultivation with a deliberate purpose is assertive activity. Hence its gain is only a temporal thing among other temporal things, which it cannot transcend. The real way to transcend them is through what the Ch'an school describes as "ceasing to be linked with all

---

[1] *Ku-tsun-hsü Yü-lu* (Recorded Sayings of Ancient Worthies), 1.79-80. [Compiled by a not clearly identified "Master of the *Tripiṭaka* Tse" of the Sung dynasty, and contained in *Tripiṭaka Supplement*, Pt. Ib, case 23, vols. 2-4. Referred to below as *Sayings of Ancient Worthies*. — Tr.]

[2] Variously stated to have died in 848, 849, 850, and 855. See Ch'en Yüan, *Shih-shih Yi-nien Lu*, 5.9. — Tr.

[3] The six acts or things that ferry one beyond the sea of mortality to *Nir- vāṇa*: (1) charity or giving, (2) keeping the commandments, (3) patience under insult, (4) zeal and progress, (5) meditation, (6) *Prajñā*. — Tr.

[4] *Sayings of Ancient Worthies*, 3.93, 95.

things." Thus the lay Buddhist P'ang Yün is reported to have asked Tao-yi: "What kind of man is he who is not linked with all things?" To which Tao-yi replied: "Wait until at one gulp you can drink up all the water in the West river, and I will tell you" (*ibid.*, 1.80). Not to be linked with all things is an inexpressible state. It is inexpressible because, as soon as one tries to express it, what one expresses is itself a thing, which means that by so doing one remains in the state of being linked with things. By his answer, therefore, Tao-yi meant to say that he really could not answer. This in itself, however, was the real answer; it was an example of "statement through non-statement." If one wants to say what it means not to be linked with all things, such expressions must be used as will not express it. If one wants to obtain it, one must practice "cultivation through non-cultivation."

iii. *"Spiritual Cultivation Cannot Be Cultivated"*

Since the conscious practice of spiritual cultivation is a form of deliberate activity, the actions it entails, being bound to the wheel of life and death, operate as causes resulting in inescapable retribution. Hsi-yün points out:

"If you fail to comprehend how to be devoid of mind, your attachments to objects will all be those of devil-*karma*. Even if you do things with a view to the Pure Land of the Buddha, these too will produce a *karma* which is called the Buddha-hindrance because it hinders the mind. Thus you will be bound by cause and effect, and have no degree of freedom in your going and staying (i.e., dying and living). Actually there is no such thing as *Bodhi* or Wisdom. That the Tathāgata (the Buddha) talked about it was simply in order to educate men, just as yellow leaves may be taken as gold coins in order to stop the crying of children. Therefore there is really no such thing as absolute enlightenment (*anubodhi*). If you once understand this, what need to be driven hither and thither (in your search)? The only thing to be done is to rid yourself of your old *karma*, as opportunity offers, and not create more from which will flow new calamities." [1]

Thus to avoid creating new *karma* involves the non-practicing of spiritual cultivation. This non-practice, however, is itself a kind of cultivation, which means that it is "cultivation through non-cultivation." On the other hand, to avoid creating new *karma* does not

---

[1] *Sayings of Ancient Worthies*, 3.95.

mean to do nothing at all, but only to have no deliberate mind in whatever one does. Tao-yi says in two statements:

"The intrinsic nature (of man) is already enough. Not to be clamped either to good or evil is all that a man engaged in spiritual cultivation needs to do. To cleave to the good and eschew evil, to contemplate emptiness, and to enter the state of concentration: all these are deliberate activities. And it is worse still if you are feverishly active over externals. The more you do that, the further away you get" (*ibid.*, 1.80).

"In a *sūtra* there is the statement: 'It is only through the combination of various things that this body of ours is formed. When it appears, it is only those things that appear; when it fades away, it is only those things that fade away.' Do not say that this appearance of things is the appearance of a 'me,' or that their fading away is the fading away of that me. (When you see that) earlier thoughts, later thoughts, and those in between, are each independent of the other, and each fades away of itself, this is called the 'ocean symbol contemplation' "[1] (*ibid.*).

Not to be clamped either to good or evil is to have no deliberate mind. It is not to be attached or fixed, which means not to be tied to the feelings. In the record of the conversations of Huai-hai (720-814) we read:

"It was asked: 'How is it that when the feelings are present there is no Buddha-nature, but when they are absent there is the Buddha-nature?' The Teacher replied: 'To pass from being a man to being a Buddha is a "sagely" kind of clinging to the feelings. To pass from being a man to being in hell is a mortal kind of clinging to them. To have a polluting love for either the sagely or mortal spheres is to have feelings, and thereby to lack the Buddha-nature. But if, vis-à-vis these sagely and mortal spheres, including all things "existent" and "non-existent," you have no mind that selects or rejects; if, in fact, you do not even have the idea of selection or rejection—this is to lack feelings and thereby to possess the Buddha-nature. It is called lacking them simply because one is not tied to them. This is not the same as the absence of feeling of a tree, a stone, the empty air, a yellow flower, or the blue-green bamboo' " (*ibid.*, p. 86). Again:

"Having trod the ladder of the Buddha, one lacks feelings

---

[1] *Sāgara mudrā samādhi*, a state of contemplation which is all-embracing like the ocean. — Tr.

and so has the Buddha-nature. Not having trod that ladder, one has feelings and so lacks the Buddha-nature" (*ibid.*).

To be without deliberate mind is to have no thoughts. The *Sūtra Spoken by the Sixth Patriarch* (chap. 4, p. 353) has the following pertinent statements by Hui-neng. "In the teaching of our school from its founders down to today, we have established 'no thought' as the essential, 'no phenomenon' as the substance, and 'no abiding' as the basis. 'No phenomenon' means to be amid the phenomenal yet devoid of the phenomenal. 'No thought' means to be in thought yet devoid of thought. 'No abiding' means ... during the process of successive thoughts not to think of the objects before one." Again: "To think of all things without abiding in them: this is to be free of the bonds; it is to make 'no abiding' the basis." What is called here no thought does not mean "not to think of anything at all," nor does it mean "the complete expulsion of thought" (*ibid.*). For this would in itself be a case of being "bound by things."

Again, we are told by Hui-neng's disciple, Shen-hui: "The *śrāvaka* (adherent of Hīnayāna), cultivating and abiding in emptiness (*k'ung*), is bound by that emptiness; cultivating and abiding in intent meditation (*samādhi* or *ting* 定), is bound by that meditation; cultivating and abiding in quiescence (*ching*), is bound by that quiescence; cultivating and abiding in silence (*chi* 寂), is bound by that silence." [1] Thus "not to think of anything at all" is to "cultivate and abide in emptiness." To have "no thought," on the other hand, is "not to allow the mind to be contaminated by various objects," and to be "ever detached from these objects." [2] In other words it is, as stated above, "during the process of successive thoughts not to think of the objects before one." This is the meaning of "no abiding," or of being "amid the phenomenal yet devoid of the phenomenal." In other words, it is the meaning of "no phenomenon." Hence when the *Sūtra Spoken by the Sixth Patriarch* talks of "no thought," "no phenomenon," and "no abiding," it is really only saying "no thought." As it puts it (chap. 2, p. 350): "The prior moment of thinking, in which there is attachment to things, is that of affliction (*kleśa*); the next moment of thinking, in which there is separation from things, is that of perfect Wisdom (*Bodhi*)." This is what is meant

---

[1] *Shen-hui Ho-shang Yi-chi* (Preserved Writings of the Monk Shen-hui), edited by Hu Shih, "Conversations," 1.119.

[2] *Sūtra Spoken by the Sixth Patriarch,* chap. 4, p. 353.

by the slogans: "A good deed entails no retribution," and "Buddha-hood is achieved through instantaneous enlightenment."

Yi-hsüan (died 867) says in two passages: [1] "Students of today fail to achieve their ends. What is their fault? It lies in not having faith in themselves. By lack of faith you fall into a state of uncertainty, in which you conform to all the fluctuations in your surroundings, subjecting yourself to their myriad revolutions, so that you are unable to achieve freedom. If, however, you succeed in stopping the mind as it momentarily dashes hither and thither in its search, you then become indistinguishable from the Patriarchs and Buddhas. Do you want to know who are the Patriarchs and Buddhas? All of you listening to my teaching here before me are such."

"You followers of the Way, there is no need for you to devote effort to the Buddhist teaching. Only do the ordinary things with no special effort: relieve your bowels, pass water, wear your clothes, eat your food, and, when tired, lie down. The simple fellow will laugh at you, but the wise will understand."

The man engaged in cultivation need only have faith in himself and abandon all else. There is no need to exert oneself in special cultivation outside the daily round of living. The only thing is, in the midst of that round, to be unmindful of the phenomenal and have no thought. This, then, is striving through non-striving, and cultivation through non-cultivation.

Yi-hsüan says further: "There are times when the man is eliminated but not his surroundings, times when his surroundings are eliminated but not the man, times when both are eliminated, and times when neither are eliminated" (*ibid.*). "Man" is the subject which knows; "surroundings" are the objects of that knowledge. A Ch'an story describes how the Abbot Hui-ming (697-780) approached Hui-neng, the Sixth Patriarch, begging for the doctrine. The Patriarch said: "For the moment, concentrate your mind, not letting your thoughts dwell either on good or evil." After the Abbot said that he was thus prepared, the Patriarch continued: "Now that you are no longer thinking of either good or evil, recall the aspect of the Abbot Ming as he was before his parents had yet brought him to life." The Abbot, under the impact of these words, abruptly entered a state of silent identification. He then did obeisance and said: "It is like a man who drinks water. He knows in himself whether it is cold or warm." [2]

---

[1] *Sayings of Ancient Worthies*, 4.100, 101.
[2] *Sūtra Spoken by the Sixth Patriarch*, chap. 1, p. 349.

Prior to the birth of the Abbot Ming, there was no Abbot Ming as subject, nor were there any objects standing in contrast to him. Thus by telling him to recall his aspect as he was prior to birth, the Patriarch caused both subject and object to be eliminated for him. In this way he enabled him to enter the state of "silent identification" (*mo ch'i* 默契), in other words, to become identified with "non-being." Such a state does not merely mean the intellectual realization that there is non-being, but the entry into actual oneness with it.

Abrupt silent identification is another name for instantaneous enlightenment (*tun wu*), which is also what is referred to in the statement: "With a single thought accord (with Truth). Then one achieves the real enlightenment." [1] There is a difference between such enlightenment and what is ordinarily termed knowledge, for in the latter a contrast exists between the knower and the known, whereas in the former there can be no such contrast. Because enlightenment has no object, we may rightly say that it is not knowledge. On the other hand, it is not the same as the mere absence of knowledge. Actually it is neither the one nor the other; rather it is the "knowledge that is not knowledge."

In the record of sayings of Ts'ung-shen (778-897) we read: "The Teacher asked Nan-ch'üan: [2] 'What is the *Tao*?' Ch'üan replied: 'The ordinary mind is the *Tao*.' The Teacher then asked whether it could be something aimed for. 'By delineating it, you turn your back on it,' was the reply. The Teacher went on: 'But if you do not delineate it, how do you know it is the *Tao*?' The *Tao* is not classifiable as either knowledge or non-knowledge,' Ch'üan replied. 'Knowledge is illusory understanding; non-knowledge is blind lack of understanding. If you really comprehend the indubitable *Tao*, it is like a vast emptiness; so how can distinctions be forced in it between right and wrong?' " [3]

In the same work (32.288) we read:

"My late teacher [4] at thirty-five became a monk, and being then in Ch'eng-tu, listened there to the teachings of the Mere Ideation school. In the course of a lecture he heard it said: 'When a Bodhisattva enters into vision of the *Tao*, knowledge and Truth become

---

[1] *Shen-hui Ho-shang Yi-chi*, "Conversations," 1.130.

[2] I.e., P'u-yüan. Dates variously given as 745-831, 748-834, 749-835, and 752-838. See Ch'en Yüan, *Shih-shih Yi-nien Lu*, 5.5. — Tr.

[3] *Sayings of Ancient Worthies*, 13.153.

[4] I.e., Fa-yen, who died in 1104 when in his eighties. — Tr.

merged, and objects and spirit become united. Thus there ceases to be a distinction between the experiencer and the thing experienced. (Once long ago) a heretic objected that if there be no distinction between the experiencer and the thing experienced, how can there be anything that he experiences? At the time no one was able to reply. (The lecturers) no longer sounded the bell and drum (for classes), but went home and discarded their robes. Later, however, when Hsüan-tsang of the T'ang came to this point, he saved the doctrine by saying that at the time when knowledge and Truth are merged, and objects and spirit united, the situation is like that of a man drinking water: he knows in himself if it is cold or warm.'

"After (this lecture was over, Fa-yen) thought to himself that (the metaphor of) cold and warmth is quite right; the question is, however: what is it to know in one's self? Becoming deeply plunged in doubt, he asked the lecturer, saying that he could not understand the principle of knowing in oneself. The lecturer was unable to answer. . . .

"Still later, having come to Mount Fou-tu,[1] he there met Yüan-chien, who saw that he had penetrated close to the inner hall (of Truth), for everything that he himself said was relevant to the issues in (Fa-yen's) mind. So the latter remained for a year, and was instructed to consider the saying: 'The Tathāgata (the Buddha) had secret teachings, but (his disciple) Mahākāśyapa did not keep the secret.' One day (Yüan-chien) said: 'Why did you not come sooner? I am old. You can go to the monk Tuan of the White Cloud (Monastery).'

"My former teacher then went to the White Cloud. There one day, as he entered the discussion hall, he gained great enlightenment regarding (the statement) that the Tathāgata had secret teachings, but Mahākāśyapa did not keep the secret. 'Truly so, truly so,' (he exclaimed). 'The merging of knowledge and Truth, and uniting of objects and spirit, is like a man drinking water: he knows in himself if it is cold or warm. How true is this statement!' He then took the occasion to write a poem of praise:

'Before the mountain lies a patch of fallow land.
Hands folded in salute, I repeatedly asked the ancient Patriarch:
How many times have you sold and then rebought this land?
It was in pity for its wind-enticing pines and bamboos, he replied.'

---

[1] In south central Anhwei, near the Yangtze river. — Tr.

"The monk Tuan, after scanning it, nodded his head in assent."

Truth holds an objective position vis-à-vis knowledge, and external things vis-à-vis the spirit. Knowledge and spirit represent the knower; Truth and external things are what he seeks to know. The merging between these opposites, therefore, represents the merging between the knower and known, until no distinction remains. There is no distinction, and the person himself realizes that they are undifferentiable. This is the meaning of the metaphor of the man who, drinking water, knows in himself if it is cold or warm. As P'u-yüan said: "The *Tao* is not classifiable as either knowledge or non-knowledge." This is because, on the one hand, no distinction can apply to the *Tao* such as exists in the case of ordinary knowledge between the knower and what he knows; such ordinary knowledge, therefore, is merely "illusory understanding." On the other hand, however, the state of non-distinction between knower and known which comes through enlightenment is not an unwitting state, for if it were, it would be not different from the inchoate ignorance of primitive peoples—a state of non-knowledge which is simply a "blind lack of understanding." This means that the *Tao* is not "knowledge," ordinarily conceived, but neither is it non-knowledge.

The Ch'an school commonly describes enlightenment as "the bottom of a tub falling out": when that happens, all its contents are suddenly gone. So with the man who has gained enlightenment as to *Tao*: he finds all his problems suddenly solved. They are solved not in the sense that he gains positive solutions for them but in the sense that all his problems have ceased any longer to be problems. That is why the *Tao* thus reached is called "the indubitable *Tao*."

iv. *In the Last Resort Nothing Is Gained*

As we have just seen, what is gained through enlightenment is not any positive kind of knowledge. In the last resort, in fact, it is not gain of any *thing* at all. As remarked by Ch'ing-yüan (1067-1120): "If you now comprehend it, where is that which you did not comprehend before? What you were deluded about before is what you are now enlightened about, and what you are now enlightened about is what you were deluded about before." [1] In Ch'anism there is the common expression that "the mountain is the mountain, the river

---

[1] *Sayings of Ancient Worthies*, 32.289.

is the river." In one's state of delusion, one sees the mountain as the
mountain and the river as the river. But after enlightenment one still
sees the mountain as the mountain and the river as the river. In the
preceding section we have read the question about the patch of fallow
land before the mountain: "How many times have you sold and
then rebought this land?" What was sold and rebought was just that
patch of land, no more than what the monks had in the beginning.
If one wanted to get more out of the patch than what it was, that
would be a case of "riding an ass to search for the ass." And if, even
after having found the ass and realized it to be that on which one was
already riding, one were still to regard it as something quite new,
that would be a case of "riding an ass and being unwilling to dismount." Ch'ing-yüan says further:

"There are only two diseases: one is riding an ass to search
for the ass; the other is riding an ass and being unwilling to dismount. You say that riding an ass to search for the ass is silly, and that
he who does it should be punished. This is a very serious disease.
But I tell you, do not search for the ass at all. The intelligent man,
understanding my meaning, stops his error of searching for the ass,
and thus the deluded state of his mind ceases to exist.

"But if, having found the ass, one is unwilling to dismount,
this disease is most difficult to cure. I say to you, do not ride the
ass at all. You yourself are the ass. Mountains, rivers, and plains
are all the ass. Why do you ride on it? If you ride, you cannot cure
your disease. But if you do not ride, the universe in all directions
becomes one wide expanse. With these two diseases expelled, nothing
remains to affect your mind. This is spiritual cultivation. You need
do nothing more" (*ibid.*, 31.280).

Before enlightenment there is no spiritual cultivation that
can be deliberately practiced. After it, there is no Buddhahood to
be achieved. We read in the recorded conversations of Hsi-yün: "It
was asked where the Buddha is at the moment when one is enlightened. The Teacher said: 'Speech or silence, activity or inactivity,
every sight or sound: all these pertain to the Buddha. So where
should you go to find him? You cannot put another head above a
head, or another mouth above a mouth" (*ibid.*, 3.94). Not only is
there no Buddhahood to be achieved, but also no enlightenment to
be gained. As Tao-yi says: "We speak of enlightenment in contrast
to delusion. But since there is originally no delusion, enlightenment
also cannot stand" (*ibid.*, 1.80). This is what is known as "an ob-

taining which is not an obtaining," and also "in the last resort nothing gained."

Thus the life of the sage is no different from that of ordinary men. The ordinary man, as the Ch'anists never tire of saying, wears his clothes, eats his food, relieves his bowels, and passes water; but so does the sage. In the *Hsü Ch'uan-teng Lu* [1] we read of a conversation that occurred in 1171 between Hui-yüan (1103-76) and the Sung Emperor Hsiao-tsung (1163-89):

"The Teacher said: 'Formerly ... there was a certain disciple who stayed at the Square Pool Ch'an Monastery at Shih-fang in Han-chou. [2] There he made a poem which he displayed widely and which read:

> In the square pool there is a turtle-nosed serpent.
> Ridiculous indeed when you come to think of it!
> Who pulled out the serpent's head?'

"The Emperor said: 'Another line is needed.' 'It was only made with three lines,' replied the Teacher. 'Why only three lines?' asked the Emperor. The Teacher replied: 'His idea was to wait (for someone else to finish the poem). For two hundred years no one was able to add anything, but later an old monk of the Ta Sui (Monastery), named Yüan-ching, after reading over the first three lines, made a statement of his own which said: "In the square pool there is a turtle-nosed serpent" ' " (28.663).

After the serpent's head had been pulled out, there was still the same turtle-nosed serpent in the square pool. This illustrates the expression that "in the last resort nothing is gained."

v. *"There Is Nothing Much in the Buddhist Teaching"*

The basic tenets of the Ch'an school, once the veil of paradox is pierced, are really clear and simple. As Ch'ing-yüan remarks: "My late teacher used to say ... that the practice of Ch'an is to be described as the gold-and-ordure method. Before it is comprehended, it is all like gold; after it is comprehended, it is all like ordure." [3]

---

[1] *Supplement to the Transmission of the Lamp*, compiled by Chü-ting (died 1404); TT no. 2077 (vol. 51, pp. 469-714). It is a continuation of the *Ch'uan-teng Lu*, on which see the following page, note 1. — Tr.

[2] Near Chengtu in Szechwan. — Tr.

[3] *Sayings of Ancient Worthies*, 32.288.

In other words, once the veil of paradox is pierced, there is nothing fantastic or secret. That is why its teachers commonly say: "The Tathāgata had secret teachings, but Mahākāśyapa did not keep the secret." On which Tao-ying (died 901 or 902) comments: "As long as you do not understand, it remains a secret of the World-Honored One (the Buddha); but once you do understand, it becomes the unkept secret of Mahākāśyapa." [1] The only secret is that the mass of people do not understand. As Fo-kuo (died 1135) said: "That Ma-hākāśyapa did not keep the secret was the Tathāgata's real secret. What is not kept secret is a secret; what is kept secret is not a secret." [2] The secret that is not kept secret is what is called an open secret.

The cosmological and psychological theories of original Buddhism are regarded by the Ch'anists as "arguments which are the ordure of nonsense." [3] By Wei-yen (751-834) they are also termed "useless furniture." [4] Such nonsense arguments were for them only fit to be thrown away, just as unused furniture is really of no use. Once they have been cleared away, all that remains in the Buddhist teaching is a few open secrets. There is a story of how Yi-hsüan, when studying under Huang-po (another name for Hsi-yün), three times asked his teacher about the main tenets of Buddhism, and three times received a beating. Later, when studying with Ta-yü, he achieved great enlightenment and said: "At bottom there is nothing very much in Huang-po's Buddhism." [5] As a matter of fact, not merely did Huang-po's Buddhism not have much to it, but Buddhism itself does not have much. This appears in the *Transmission of the Lamp* (12.290), where there is a different version of Yi-hsüan's words, namely that there is not much to Buddhism.

vi. *"In Carrying Water and Chopping Wood: Therein Lies the Wonderful Tao"*

To pass from delusion to enlightenment means to leave one's mortal humanity behind and enter sagehood. The life of the sage,

---

[1] *Ch'uan-teng Lu* (Transmission of the Lamp), 17.235. [Full title: *Ching-te Ch'uan-teng Lu*. Compiled by Tao-yüan in 1004; TT no. 2076 (vol. 51, pp. 196-467). — Tr.]

[2] *Yüan-wu Fo-kuo Ch'an-shih Yü-lu* (Recorded Conversations of the Ch'an Teacher Yüan-wu Fo-kuo), 15.782. [Compiled by Shao-lung and others in 1134; TT no. 1997 (vol. 47, pp. 713-810). — Tr.]

[3] A phrase by Huai-hai (720-814). See *Sayings of Ancient Worthies*, 2.87.

[4] *Transmission of the Lamp*, 14.312.

[5] *Sayings of Ancient Worthies*, 5.108.

however, once this has happened, is no different from that of ordinary men, for "the ordinary mind is the *Tao*," [1] and the sage's mind is the ordinary mind. This latter fact is therefore described as leaving sagehood behind and entering once more into ordinary humanity. Though the term "falling into" is used to designate this reentry, it really is only a partial description of what happens, for from another point of view the process means a transcending of sagehood as well. [2] This latter idea is expressed through the common metaphor of "rising yet another step over the top of the hundred-foot bamboo." P'u-yüan makes the statement: "After coming to understand the other side, you come back and live on this side." [3] To go to the other side is to leave mortal humanity behind and enter sagehood; to come back and live on this side is to leave sagehood behind and reenter mortal humanity.

What the sage does is the same as ordinary men but because, when doing it, he has already left sagehood behind and returned to mortal humanity, his acts have a different significance from those of the ordinary man. Huai-hai says: "That which before enlightenment is called lustful anger, is after enlightenment called Buddha-wisdom. Therefore the man is no different from what he was before; it is only that what he does is different" [4] (*ibid.*, 1.84). And Hsi-yün says: "Simply void your entire mind: this is to have unpolluted wisdom. Daily go out, stay at home, sit, or sleep, but in every word you say, do not attach yourself to the things of purposeful activity. Then, whatever you say or wherever you look, all will be unpolluted" (*ibid.*, 2.82). Likewise in the hymn of the eighth century Buddhist layman P'ang Yün we read: "Spirit-like understanding and divine functioning lie in carrying water and chopping wood." [5] These tasks, when performed by ordinary people, remain merely the car-

---

[1] See above, p. 397. — Tr.

[2] See the statements by Pen-chi (840-901) in the *Fu-chou Ts'ao-shan Pen-chi Ch'an-shih Yü-lu* (Recorded Conversations of the Ch'an Teacher Ts'ao-shan Pen-chi of Fu-chou), 2.543. [Compiled by the Japanese monk Genkei in 1740; TT no. 1987B (vol. 47, pp. 535-544). — Tr.]

[3] *Sayings of Ancient Worthies*, 12.149. In the *Ts'ao Tung Erh-shih Lu* (TT no. 1987A, vol. 47, p. 534; compiled by the Japanese monk E-in in 1752), this statement is slightly modified to read: "Having first passed to the other side so as to know about being, you then come back to this side to carry on."

[4] As pointed out below, there is probably a textual error in this last sentence, and it should really read: "What the man does is no different from what he did before; it is only that the man himself is not the same as he was." — Tr.

[5] *Transmission of the Lamp*, 8.263.

rying of water and chopping of wood; performed by the sage, however, they become spirit-like understanding and divine functioning.

Because of this difference, the sage, even when performing the tasks of ordinary men, is not subject, like them, to the retributions incurred within the wheel of life and death. In Hsi-yün's recorded conversations we read the following statements:

"It was asked whether mowing grass, felling trees, digging into the earth, and plowing new soil, have the quality of sin or not. The Teacher replied: 'It cannot definitely be said that they are sinful or not sinful. Whether there is sin or not depends on the man. If he be greedy for all things, both "existent" and "non-existent"; if his mind be set on selecting and rejecting; and if he be unable to pass beyond the three phrases [1]—then it may be positively stated that this man has sin. But if he go beyond the three phrases, if his mind be like a void emptiness, and if he not even think about this void emptiness, then it may be positively stated that this man is without sin' " (ibid., 1.84-85).

"According to the transmitted teachings of the Ch'an school, the mind should be like a void emptiness. It should not be detained by a single thing, nor even have the qualities of the void emptiness. Then to what can sin have attachment?" (ibid., p. 85).

"To eat all day yet not swallow a grain of rice, to walk all day yet not tread an inch of ground, to have no distinction during that time between object and subject, and to be inseparable from things the livelong day, yet not deluded by them: this is to be the man who is at ease in himself" (ibid., 3.99).

Wen-yen (864-949) similarly speaks of "discussing things the whole day, without ever having anything pass across one's lips and teeth, or uttering a single word; eating rice and wearing clothes the whole day, without ever touching a grain of rice or supporting a thread of silk" (ibid., 15.168).

Again, there is the story of how Liang-chieh (807-869) was fording a river with a certain elder Teacher Mi. Liang-chieh asked Mi: "What kind of action is it to ford a river?" "One that does not wet the feet," replied Mi. "Most reverend sir, you have declared it," exclaimed Liang-chieh. Then Mi asked in turn: "And how would

---

[1] Namely: (1) "being," (2) "non-being," (3) "neither being nor non-being." — Tr.

you describe it?" "The feet are not made wet," replied Liang-chieh. [1] To ford a river without wetting the feet symbolizes the doing of things without being obstructed or bound by them. It is the sage who is thus liberated or at ease with himself.

Such is the outcome of "cultivation through non-cultivation." While this cultivation is in progress, it is necessary to prevent the thoughts from being attached to phenomenal things. In other words, one must "be amid the phenomenal yet devoid of the phenomenal." [2] After the completion of cultivation, however, one's thoughts continue to be detached from phenomenal things, and one still remains "amid the phenomenal yet devoid of the phenomenal." The difference is that whereas during the earlier period this state of mind was achieved only through conscious effort, during the period after cultivation has been stopped, it comes of itself without the need for any effort. Yet this does not mean that this effortlessness comes merely because the man who has been engaged in cultivation eventually develops a certain habit. What it does mean is that at the moment of completion he experiences instantaneous enlightenment and is thereby identified with non-being. That is why he then need exert no effort but is naturally as he is.

The sphere of the sage is one in which "neither the man nor his surroundings are eliminated." [3] In this sphere a mountain is still a mountain and a river a river, but the man is no longer the one who has left mortal humanity behind him and entered sagehood. Huai-hai, it will be remembered, said that "the man is no different from what he was before; it is only that what he does is different." [4] In the full context of Ch'an philosophy it seems likely that a textual corruption has crept into this sentence. What he ought to have said is that "what the man does is no different from what he did before; it is only that the man himself is not the same as he was." The first step of leaving mortal humanity behind and entering sagehood is that in which "both the man and his surroundings are eliminated," in other words, in which neither subject nor object longer exist for him.

---

[1] *Tung-shan Liang-chieh Ch'an-shih Yü-lu* (Recorded Conversations of the Ch'an Teacher Liang-chieh of Tung-shan), p. 521. [Compiled by Yüan-hsin (1571-1646) and Kuo Ning-chih (passed *chü-jen* exmination during period of 1621-27); TT no. 1986B (vol. 47, pp. 519-526). — Tr.]

[2] See above, p. 395. — Tr.

[3] See Yi-hsüan's statement on p. 396. — Tr.

[4] See p. 403 above. — Tr.

But the final step is that in which he returns from his sagehood and rejoins the world of mortal humanity, and by so doing reaches the final synthesis in which "neither the man nor his surroundings are eliminated."

In earlier chapters we have seen how Neo-Taoists and Buddhists alike maintain that the sage responds to the call of affairs, just as do other men, yet he is not handicapped by so doing. Seng-chao says, for example, that the sage "dwells in the world of change and utility, yet holds himself to the realm of non-activity," [1] by which he means that the one state is not incompatible with the other. To speak in this way, however, is to make the sage's mysterious aloofness a different course from his response to affairs and to this world; it fails to merge them into one. For the Ch'anists, on the contrary, the sage's response to affairs, and to the world, in itself constitutes the mysterious *Tao* or Way. To live in the world of active functioning is the same as to reside in that of non-activity; and to maintain this is to see that there are not two courses but only one.

Thus the Ch'an school took a further step in synthesizing the sublime with the common. Yet if carrying water and chopping wood are really of the nature of the mysterious *Tao*, why should it still be necessary for the man engaged in spiritual cultivation to abandon his family and become a monk? Why should not the mysterious *Tao* equally consist in performing the duties of father and sovereign? Here there was need for a further word, and it became the mission of the Neo-Confucianists of the Sung (960-1279) and Ming (1368-1643) dynasties to say that word.

CHAPTER X

THE RISE OF NEO-CONFUCIANISM AND ITS BORROWINGS FROM BUDDHISM AND TAOISM

The T'ang dynasty, during which Buddhism reached its apogee, also witnessed the beginnings of a notable revival of Confucianism—an intellectual movement which was to become dominant during the Sung (960-1279) and Ming (1368-1643) dynasties, and which, though today commonly referred to as Neo-Confucianism, has traditionally been known as the *Tao Hsüeh Chia* 道學家 or "School of the Study of the *Tao*" (the Way or Truth). This school will be the subject of most of the remaining chapters of this book.

Already prior to the T'ang dynasty, as a matter of fact, there lived a certain Confucian scholar, Wang T'ung 王通 (584-617), who, according to a contemporary, Tu Yen (died 628), is said to have had "more than a thousand men" as his disciples. Among them were such outstanding figures as Fang Hsüan-ling, Wei Cheng, Wen Ta-ya, and Ch'en Shu-ta, who were later to play leading parts in the founding of the T'ang dynasty. All these men, Tu Yen asserts, "placed themselves before him (Wang T'ung) to receive the principles for becoming 'helpers of kings.' " [1]

Tu writes further than when Wang died, "several hundred of his disciples held a discussion at which they said: 'What a perfect man was our Master! Since the time of Confucius there has been nobody like him. . . . He perpetuated the *Odes* and the *History*, rectified the *Rites* and music, compiled the *First Classic*, [2] and extolled the teachings in the *Changes*. [3] With him, the great principles of the sages, and 'all things that can be done in the world, have been brought to com-

---

[1] Cf. Tu Yen's biography of Wang T'ung, contained in Wang's *Chung-shuo* (Middle Sayings), 10.6.

[2] *Yüan Ching*, a chronicle history covering events from A.D. 290 to 589 (the year when China was reunited under the Sui dynasty), and written in imitation of the *Spring and Autumn Annals*. Although attributed to Wang T'ung, the work today bearing this title is probably a forgery by Juan Yi (11th century). — Tr.

[3] This entire sentence is written in imitation of the statements traditionally made about the literary activities of Confucius, among which the *Spring and Autumn Annals* is here replaced by Wang's *First Classic*. — Tr.

pletion.' ¹ 'Since Confucius is no longer alive, does not his culture rest with him (i.e., Wang T'ung)?' ² The *Changes* says (p. 269): 'The yellow lower garment indicates great good fortune. This is because its pattern (*wen*) occupies a central position (*chung*).' It is our wish, therefore, to confer on him the posthumous title of Wen-chung Tzŭ (Master Wen-chung)" (*ibid.*).

It is curious that despite this glowing account, the *Sui Shu* (History of the Sui Dynasty) does not even include Wang T'ung among its biographies, and that the *Chiu T'ang Shu* (Old History of the T'ang Dynasty) and *Hsin T'ang Shu* (New History of the T'ang Dynasty) mention him only incidentally in their chapters 163 and 196 respectively. There they merely say of him that he was a great Confucian scholar of the Sui dynasty. Thus it would seem that though Wang may have enjoyed a considerable scholarly reputation in his own day, what Tu Yen says of him is based on the elaborations of Wang's followers, and hence is unworthy of credence. ³ Certainly there is nothing very remarkable in the *Chung-shuo* or *Middle Sayings*, the work which today passes under Wang's name.

What is noteworthy, however, is that during the early seventh century, when Buddhism reached its height, there were nonetheless people ready to acclaim such a man as Wang T'ung as the true perpetuator of Confucius. Praise of this kind, though ostensibly directed to Wang T'ung, was actually indirect praise for Confucius himself. In this episode, therefore, we may see the beginnings of the movement which was to lead to the revival of Confucianism.

1—HAN YÜ

It is not until the second half of the T'ang dynasty, however, that we reach the man who may justly be regarded as the first real

---

¹ A quotation from the *Book of Changes*, p. 366. — Tr.

² A reference to a statement made by Confucius about himself: "Since King Wen is no longer alive, does not his culture (*wen*) rest with me?" Cf. *Analects*, IX, 5. — Tr.

³ It has been pointed out by some that P'i Jih-hsiu (died ca. 881), in his "Stele Inscription to Master Wen-chung" (i.e., Wang T'ung), points out that among Wang's disciples were such eminent men as Hsieh Shou, Li Ching, Wei Cheng, Li Chi, Tu Ju-hui, and Fang Hsüan-ling. See his *P'i-tzŭ Wen-shu* (Collected Writings of P'i Jih-hsiu), 4.50. Such a statement means little, however, in view of P'i's own admission that he lived "more than two hundred and fifty years" after Wang, a fact that leaves his remarks easily open to error.

protagonist of later Neo-Confucianism. This is the famous scholar and official Han Yü (768-824), who is best known as one of China's greatest masters of prose. His biography in the *Hsin T'ang Shu* reads in part as follows:

"Han Yü 韓愈, styled T'ui-chih 退之, was a native of Nan-yang in Teng-chou. [1] ... From the Chin through the Sui (dynasties), whereas Taoism and Buddhism were being conspicuously practiced, the Way of the Sages (i.e., of Confucianism) was perpetuated as by a thread, and Confucian scholars leaned upon the world's orthodox ideas (merely) to give support to the strange and the supernatural. (Han) Yü alone grievingly quoted the sages so as to combat the errors of the world and, though mocked by the stupid, met all rebuffs with renewed ardor. In the beginning nobody believed in him, but eventually he gained great renown in his age. Of old, Mencius, who was only two hundred years removed from Confucius, had refuted Yang (Chu) and Mo (Ti). (In the same way Han) Yü, though separated from Confucius by more than one thousand years, rejected the two schools (of Taoism and Buddhism). In his destroying of confusion and restoring of orthodoxy, he equals (Mencius) in merit and doubles him in energy, thus surpassing by not a little both K'uang and Hsiung. [2] Since his death, his words have gained wide currency, so that scholars now look up to him as if he were Mount T'ai or the Great Dipper" (76.15).

One of Han's most famous essays is that entitled *Yüan Tao* (On the Origin of the Truth), in which he writes:

"A love for everyone is called perfect virtue (*jen*). Conduct which proceeds in conformity with this is called righteousness (*yi*). What follows this course to its destination is called the Way (*Tao*). Sufficiency in oneself without dependence upon externals is called the Power (*Te*). *Jen* and *yi* are fixed terms, whereas *Tao* and *Te* hold indefinite positions. Therefore there is a *Tao* (Way) for the superior man or the petty man, and there is a *Te* (Power) that may be inauspicious or auspicious. ...

"The Book says: 'The ancients who wished clearly to exemplify illustrious virtue throughout the world, first ordered well their own states. Wishing well to order their states, they first regulated their families. Wishing to regulate their families, they first cultivated their

---

[1] Near the present Nan-yang-hsien in southern Honan. — Tr.
[2] Hsün Tzǔ and Yang Hsiung (on whom see chap. 4). — Tr.

own persons. Wishing to cultivate their persons, they first rectified their minds. Wishing to rectify their minds, they first sought for sincerity in their thoughts.' [1]

"Now what the ancients thus called the rectification of the mind and the search for sincerity in thought, was used by them in their actual conduct. Today, however, persons who wish to set their minds in order, thereby put themselves beyond the pale of the world and the country, thus destroying the natural constant (ties of mankind). Being sons, they do not treat their father like a father, and being subjects, they do not treat their ruler like a ruler. . . . They elevate the rules of the barbarians above the teachings of the early kings, thus becoming almost the same as barbarians themselves. [2]

"Now what were these teachings of the early kings? . . . Their texts are to be found in the *Odes*, the *History*, the *Changes*, and the *Spring and Autumn Annals*; their rules are to be found in the rites, music, penal laws, and government. . . .

"Now what is this *Tao* or Truth (that embodies these teachings)? I reply that what I call the *Tao* is not what has hitherto been so called by the Taoists and Buddhists. Yao transmitted it to Shun; Shun transmitted it to Yü; Yü transmitted it to T'ang; T'ang transmitted it to (Kings) Wen and Wu, and the Duke of Chou; Wen and Wu and the Duke of Chou transmitted it to Confucius; Confucius transmitted it to Mencius. After Mencius died, it was no longer transmitted. Hsün (Tzǔ) and Yang (Hsiung) selected from it, but without reaching its essential portion; they discussed it, but without sufficient clarity" (*Works*, 11.1-3).

Han Yü is more famous as a stylist than as a speculative thinker, and in the above quotation there is little of purely philosophical interest. Nevertheless, several points may be noted:

(1) He here pays high tribute to Mencius, placing him in the orthodox line of succession from Confucius. Though this became the generally accepted point of view from the Sung dynasty onward, such had not been the case in earlier times. During the Chou and

---

[1] A famous passage from the *Great Learning*, pp. 411-412. — Tr.

[2] This is a bitter attack upon the Chinese Buddhists, who follow an alien (and therefore "barbarian") faith, and who try to "set their minds in order" (i.e., gain enlightenment) by retiring from the human world to become monks, thereby destroying the human relationships so prized by Confucianism. In *Analects*, XII, 11, Confucius, being asked the way of good government, replies: "Let the ruler be ruler, the minister minister; let the father be father, and the son son." — Tr.

Ch'in dynasties, for example, Mencius had merely been regarded as the equal, not the superior, of his rival, Hsün Tzǔ. There was a time, indeed, during the subsequent Former Han dynasty, when the latter even outranked him. Only Yang Hsiung (53 B.C.-A.D. 18) had praised Mencius with anything like the warmth of Han Yü, and his example was imitated by no one until Han Yü himself. Following Han's advocacy, however, the supremacy of Mencius came to be generally accepted, and his book, the *Mencius*, became a basic text for the Sung and Ming Neo-Confucianists.

There are good reasons for this phenomenon. Thus the mystical tendency apparent in Mencius' philosophy; his discussions on mind and human nature; his statement that "all things are complete within us. There is no greater delight than to find sincerity when one examines oneself" (*Mencius*, VIIa, 4); his method of self-cultivation through "nourishing the mind" and "making fewer the desires" (*ibid.*, VIIb, 35): all these provided suitable answers to those same problems that were the center of Buddhist discussion in Han Yü's own day, and were regarded by his contemporaries as particularly significant. It is not surprising, therefore, that the book of Mencius should be selected from Confucian literature as the work which above all others was pertinent to these burning problems.

Han Yü, moreover, though in general opposed to Buddhism, shows himself in his writings not unmindful of its aims and practices. In a letter he states, for example: "During the time (when I was) at Ch'ao-chou, [1] there was an old Buddhist monk named Ta-tien, who was exceedingly intelligent and comprehending of philosophical principles. ... He was, in truth, able to transcend the bounds of the body, thereby conquering the self by means of reason, and not permitting himself to be invaded and thrown into confusion by material things. When I talked with him, although he could not completely understand, it must be admitted that within his breast there were no impediments (to his enlightenment)" (*Works*, 18.6). Elsewhere Han writes in similar vein: "Now the Buddhist Teacher Hsien [2] is one who has reduced life and death to a single plane, and has freed

---

[1] Near the present Swatow in northeastern Kwangtung. This was the time (819) when Han Yü was banished to this wild region for having protested against the honors with which the emperor proposed to receive an alleged bone of the Buddha. — Tr.

[2] Kao-hsien, a contemporary who had considerable reputation for his calligraphy. — Tr.

himself from external trammels. To be thus, his heart must be immobile, so that nothing can arouse it, and he must be indifferent to the world so that he tastes nothing of it" (*ibid.*, 21.3). In these passages Han shows himself not uninterested in those topics which, under the influence of Buddhism, were then the subject of widespread attention.

(2) We have seen how Han Yü quotes at some length an important passage from the *Great Learning*. This little treatise had previously been merely one of many chapters in the *Book of Rites*—one, moreover, that belonged to Hsün Tzŭ's rather than Mencius' school of Confucianism. Nobody since the Han dynasty seems to have paid it any particular attention. Han Yü, however, saw that certain of its phrases, such as the "exemplification of illustrious virtue," "rectification of the mind," and "sincerity in thought," could well be directed toward the problems that were of such burning interest in his own day. This explains why, after quoting in full the passage in which they occur, he commented: "What the ancients thus called the rectification of the mind and the search for sincerity in thought, was used by them in their actual conduct. Today, however, persons who wish to set their minds in order, thereby put themselves beyond the pale of the world and the country." Through this attack on Buddhism, Han wished to indicate that though the Confucianists, like the Buddhists, were anxious to "set their minds in order," they had different means for so doing, and therefore the results obtained by them must also differ. From this time onward the *Great Learning*, like the *Mencius*, became an extremely important text for Neo-Confucianism.

(3) Another characteristic of this essay is Han Yü's use of the word *Tao* (meaning Way, Truth or Teaching), and his theory of an orthodox transmission of this *Tao* or Truth through a line of early sage-rulers extending to Confucius, and finally to Mencius. This theory had already been sketchily outlined by Mencius [1] and, following Han's advocacy, it came to be generally accepted by the Sung and Ming Neo-Confucianists. From it, indeed, their school derived the name by which it is commonly known, that of the *Tao Hsüeh Chia*, i.e., School of the Learning of the *Tao* or Truth.

In all these three points, therefore, Han Yü may truly be said to be the first protagonist of Neo-Confucianism.

---

[1] See vol. 1, pp. 107-108. — Tr.

Another theory for which Han is well known concerns the problem of human nature, discussed in his essay, *Yüan Hsing* (On the Origin of the Nature). In this he maintains that "there are three grades of the nature: the superior, the medium, and the inferior. The superior is wholly good; the medium may be led to be either superior or inferior; the inferior is wholly evil." In the same essay he also defines as follows the difference between man's nature (*hsing*) and his feelings or emotions (*ch'ing*): "The nature comes into being coincident with birth; the feelings come into being as the consequence of contact with (external) objects." These feelings are of seven kinds: joy, anger, pity, fear, love, hate, and desire. Qualitatively they, like the nature, fall into the three grades of superior, medium, and inferior. The superior grade "holds to the mean (among the seven categories) in its operation. The medium grade either goes too far or is deficient in some of these seven; nevertheless, it attempts to hold to the mean among them. But the inferior grade is without exception either deficient or too extreme in its operation throughout all (seven kinds of) feelings" (*Works*, 11.3-5).

2—LI AO

Li Ao 李翱 (died ca. 844) was an important contemporary of Han Yü, and is said by some to have been his disciple. Thus we read in Li's biography in the *Hsin T'ang Shu*: "As a writer of essays, he was originally a follower of Han Yü of Ch'ang-li. [1] His literary style, which was extremely solid and rich, gained wide extension in his age. Therefore he was officially given the posthumous title of Wen (the Literary)" (177.11). Li himself, however, in two of his writings, [2] addresses Han Yü as "elder brother" (a polite term of address between friends), rather than as "teacher," which would have been the normal form had he actually been Han's disciple. The latter's relationship to him, therefore, would seem to lie somewhere between that of teacher and of friend.

Li's doctrines are best found in his *Fu-hsing Shu* (Essay on

---

[1] The ancestral home of Han Yü's family, in present Hopei, though Han himself was actually born in Honan. — Tr.

[2] "Reply Letter to Han Yü," and "Lament on Han Yü's Death," in his *Li Wen-kung Chi* (Collected Works of Li Ao), beginning of *chüan* 6 and 16 respectively. — Tr.

Returning to the Nature), a treatise containing the following three sections: (1) a general discussion on the nature (*hsing*), the feelings (*ch'ing*), and the sage (*sheng*); (2) the process of self-cultivation whereby one may become a sage; (3) the necessity for self-exertion in this process. In the first of these sections Li writes as follows:

"That whereby a man may become a sage is his nature (*hsing*). That whereby a man may betray his nature are the feelings (*ch'ing*). Joy, anger, pity, fear, love, hate, and desire: these seven are all the operations of the feelings. When the feelings cause obscurement, the nature is thereby drowned. This is not the fault of the nature, but is because, owing to the ceaseless revolutions and interminglings of these seven, the nature is unable to gain its fulfillment. When water is muddy, its flow will not be clear, and when a flame is smoky, its light will not be right. But this is not the fault of the water or flame in their (innate) clarity or brightness. For if the sediment is not muddy, the flow will be clear, and if the smoke is not dense, the light will be bright. (Likewise), when the feelings do not operate, the nature will gain its fulfillment. ... But when the movements of the feelings continue unceasingly, it becomes impossible to return to one's nature and to radiate the infinite light of Heaven and Earth" (*Works*, 2.5).

Though Li Ao, like Han Yü, here uses the terms *hsing* and *ch'ing*, he in doing so gives them an unmistakable Buddhist coloring. Thus what he calls the nature comes close to what the Buddhists call the "original mind" (*pen hsin*), while his concept of the feelings resembles what the Buddhists term the "passions" (*fan nao* or *kleśa*). A widespread Buddhist tenet, as we have seen in earlier chapters, is that not only the Buddhas themselves, but also ordinary sentient beings, are equally endured with the pure and wholly enlightened original mind; the only difference between them is that, for the latter, this mind is obscured by the unenlightened passions and so is unable to shine forth. Li expresses much the same idea when he says that though water may become muddied because of sediment, this fact does not change the fundamental purity of the water itself.

According to Buddhism, however, the unenlightened passions are not diametrically opposed to the original mind, for it is out of this very mind, in all its purity and enlightenment, that these same passions arise. Here again Li Ao expresses a similar point of view when he writes:

"The nature and the feelings cannot exist one without the

other. Thus without the nature, the feelings would have no source from which to come into being, because the feelings come forth out of the nature. The feelings are not of themselves feelings but become so from the nature. Likewise the nature is not of itself the nature, but its enlightenment derives from the feelings" (*ibid.*, p. 5).

This last sentence is further explained by him as follows:

"The sage is he among his fellows who is first in understanding. [1] With such understanding there comes enlightenment; without it there comes error which leads to darkness. Such enlightenment and darkness are known as contraries. Fundamentally, the nature is neither 'light' nor 'dark'; hence in it 'identities' and 'contraries' are equally absent. This is because enlightenment exists only in apposition to darkness, so that if this darkness be obliterated, enlightenment can also not exist" (*ibid.*, p. 6).

"Enlightenment (*ming* 明) exists only in apposition to darkness (*hun* 昏)"; in this apposition we find the reason why "the nature is not of itself the nature, but its enlightenment derives from the feelings."

In the earlier quotation it was said that "when the feelings do not operate, the nature will gain its fulfillment." The sage is the individual capable of developing himself toward this end, and this process is what Li calls "the return to the nature." There is a vital difference, however, between the final state thus reached, in which "the feelings do not operate," and the ordinary state of complete insensibility characteristic of a mere inanimate object. Thus Li tells us:

"How could the sage be utterly lacking in the feelings? The sage is silently immovable; he reaches his destination without traveling; he is divine without uttering a word; he glows without making any illumination. In his activities, he participates with Heaven and Earth; in his transformations, he harmonizes with the *yin* and the *yang*. He does possess the feelings, and yet has never had such feelings" (*ibid.*, p. 5).

This reminds us of the words in the Ch'an text, *Liu-tsu T'an-ching* or *Sūtra Spoken by the Sixth Patriarch*: "The formless lies in the formal, and yet is separate from the formal. The absence of thought lies in thought, and yet in it thought is absent" (chap. 4, p. 353). So too of the state described by Li Ao: it lies within the feelings,

---

[1] *Chüeh* or *bodhi*, a common Buddhist term for enlightenment. — Tr.

yet is one in which the feelings are absent. Although the sage, in such a state, participates in various activities and is subject to outer change, his "original mind" remains ever "silently immovable."

To describe the mental condition of the sage who has reached this state, Li Ao uses the Confucian term *ch'eng* 誠, "sincerity" or "utter sincerity." [1] Thus he writes:

"Therefore utter sincerity (*ch'eng*) means (the complete fulfillment of) the sage's nature. Silent is he and immovable, all embracing and purifying. He casts his light through Heaven and Earth, and, being acted on, penetrates to all phenomena under Heaven. [2] Whether in movement or at rest, speaking or silent, he holds always the topmost place. As to the return to the nature, this the worthy (*hsien*) pursues unceasingly; unceasingly, and so he is able to return to the Source. The *Changes* says (p. 417): 'The sage shares the attributes of Heaven and Earth, the radiance of the sun and moon, the orderly progression of the four seasons, the auspicious and inauspicious (faculties) of supernatural beings. He may precede Heaven, and Heaven will not act in opposition to him. He may follow Heaven, and will then act in accordance with the times of Heaven. Since Heaven will not act in opposition to him, how much less will men! How much less will supernatural beings!' All this is not to be gained from the outside. It consists simply in developing to the utmost one's own nature.

"Tzŭ-ssŭ says: [3] 'It is only he who has sincerity in utter perfection who can develop his nature to its utmost. Able to develop his nature to its utmost, he can do the same to the natures of other men. Able to develop the natures of other men to the utmost, he can do the same to the natures of things. Able to develop these to the utmost, he can assist the transforming and nourishing activities of Heaven and Earth. Capable of assisting in these transforming and nourishing activities, he can form a trinity with Heaven and Earth. Next to the above is he who cultivates to the utmost the shoots (of goodness in his nature), and who through this means succeeds in reaching utter sincerity. This sincerity will then gain embodiment;

---

[1] A famous term first elaborated in the *Great Learning* (see quotation on p. 410 above), and in the *Doctrine of the Mean* (quoted below). — Tr.

[2] Some of the phrases in these two sentences are based on the *Book of Changes*, p. 370. — Tr.

[3] The grandson of Confucius, and reputed author of the *Doctrine of the Mean*, a long passage from which (pp. 319-320) is here quoted. — Tr.

through this embodiment it will become manifested; manifested, it will become brilliant; being brilliant, it will move into action; moving into action, it will produce change; producing change, it will have a transforming influence. It is only he in the world who possesses sincerity in its utter perfection, who can exert a transforming influence in this way.'

"The sage knows that all men's natures are good, and that by following them, they (these men) may themselves become sages. Therefore he institutes the rules of propriety (*li*) to keep them under proper restraint, and creates music to keep them in harmony. Rest amidst the harmony of music is the foundation of music. Activity in accordance with propriety is the foundation of the rules of propriety.

"Therefore when he (the sage) is in his carriage, he listens to the harmonious sounds of the (carriage) bells, and when walking on foot, he listens to the tones of the pendant jades. [1] He does not abolish the music of the lute unless there be proper reason. In hearing, seeing, speech, and conduct, he acts ever in accordance with propriety. In this way he teaches men to forget indulgence and desire, and to return to the Way (*Tao*) of the nature and of Destiny (*Ming*).

"This Way is that of sincerity in its utter perfection. This sincerity, if uninterrupted, leads to 'vacuity' (*hsü*); vacuity, if uninterrupted, leads to enlightenment (*ming*); enlightenment, if uninterrupted, leads to an all-embracing illumination of Heaven and Earth. This, and nothing else, is the Way whereby to develop to the utmost one's nature and Destiny. Alas! All men are capable of reaching this state, yet, though no one stops them, they do not do so. Is this not indeed because of delusion?

"The ancient sages transmitted this teaching to Master Yen. . . . [2] Tzŭ-ssŭ, the grandson of Confucius, received the teaching of his grandfather and composed the *Doctrine of the Mean* in forty-seven sections, which he transmitted to Mencius. Mencius said: 'When I was forty I attained to a state of unperturbed mind.' [3] His disciples who understood this were Kung-sun Ch'ou and Wan Chang and they, it would seem, transmitted it onward. But when, under the Ch'in,

---

[1] In ancient China, according to such works as the *Book of Rites*, the officials wore small jade pendants which tinkled as they walked, and served to remind them that their conduct should be virtuous. — Tr.

[2] Yen Hui, the favorite disciple of Confucius. — Tr.

[3] *Mencius*, IIa, 2, para. 1. — Tr.

the books were destroyed (in 213 B.C.), only one section of the *Doctrine of the Mean* survived the burning, and thereupon this teaching became obscured and incomplete. ...

"Alas! Although writings dealing with the nature and with Destiny are still preserved, none of the scholars understand them, and therefore they all plunge into Taoism or Buddhism. Ignorant people say that the followers of the Master (Confucius) are incapable of investigating the teachings on the nature and Destiny, and everybody believes them. When someone once asked me about this, I taught him what I knew, and then wrote it down in this book, so as in this way to open the sources of sincerity and enlightenment. In this manner the interrupted, discarded, and unproclaimed *Tao* or Truth may perhaps be transmitted to my age" (*ibid.*, pp. 6-8).

He who has reached the state of *ch'eng* or "utter sincerity" is able to "share the attributes of Heaven and Earth," and "assist the transforming and nourishing activities of Heaven and Earth." In other words, he has gained union with the universe. Several points are worth noting in this lengthy quotation:

(1) The *Doctrine of the Mean*—originally only one of many sections in the *Book of Rites*—is here singled out for quotation by Li Ao, and from this time onward, like the *Great Learning*, became a key text for Neo-Confucianists; the same is true of the Appendices to the *Book of Changes*, also cited here by Li.

(2) According to early Confucian theories (see vol. 1, chap. 14), the purpose of the rites (*li*) and of music is to permit human desires and emotions to be expressed, yet not in a way that leads to excess. For Li Ao, however, their primary purpose is to "teach men to forget indulgence and desire, and to return to the Way of the nature and of Destiny." In other words, their significance in early Confucianism had been ethical, whereas for Li it is religious or even mystical. In early Confucianism ceremonies and music served to develop the completely virtuous personality; for Li they become an instrument for reaching the state of "utter sincerity."

(3) Li laments that "although writings dealing with the nature and with Destiny are still preserved, none of the scholars understand them, and therefore they all plunge into Taoism or Buddhism. Ignorant people say that the followers of the Master are incapable of investigating the teachings on the nature and Destiny, and everybody believes them." These words well exemplify the motivation underlying the propagation of the Neo-Confucian doctrines. It was

generally postulated by the Neo-Confucianists that the answers to all vital questions of their age could be found within the Confucian writings themselves. In using these writings, however, it was inevitable that these Confucianists should reinterpret them in the light of these problems. The concept of the sage, for example, as developed by Li Ao and later Neo-Confucianists, is no longer merely ethical, but religious or mystical as well. Thus whereas Mencius had described the sage as "the apogee of the human relationships," [1] for Li Ao and later Confucianists he is the being who develops these relationships and practices the ceremonies and music, not merely for ethical reasons, but in order to reach the highest state of self-cultivation—that of union between the individual and the universe. No doubt the reason for this shift lies in the burning interest felt by people of Li's time in the question of how to achieve Buddhahood. Li and later Neo-Confucianists were anxious to answer this question, but being Confucianists, they wanted to do so along Confucian lines. In other words, their aim was to induce men to follow a Confucian type of training which would make of them "Confucian Buddhas."

Of what should such training consist? Li's reply is as follows:

"Someone asked: Man's ignorance has been of long standing. If he is to return to his nature, it will have to be a gradual process. I venture to ask the method for doing this.

"I replied: Think not nor cogitate; then the feelings will not appear. When the feelings do not appear, thought becomes correct. The *Changes* (p. 389) says: 'Beneath Heaven, what is there of thinking or cogitation?' Again it says (p. 410): 'Guarding against depravity, he preserves his utter sincerity.' And the *Odes* (IV, ii, Ode 1, 4) say: 'Thoughts without depravity.'

"He asked: Is that all?

"I replied: No. This fasting and abstinence of the mind is inseparable from the state of quiescence. But when there is quiescence, it must be followed by movement, and when there is movement, it must be followed by quiescence. [2] This uninterrupted (sequence of) quiescence and movement constitutes the feelings. The *Changes*

---

[1] *Mencius*, IVa, 2. — Tr.

[2] This concept of the ceaseless alternation of quiescence (*ching* 靜) and movement (*tung* 動), which became basic in the Neo-Confucian system of cosmology, goes back to the *Book of Changes* (*passim*, esp. pp. 348 f.). The term "fast of the mind," however, was used by Chuang Tzŭ. See vol. 1, pp. 241-243. — Tr.

(p. 380) says: 'Good fortune and ill, occasion for repentance or regret, all arise from movement.' How, under such conditions, is one to return to one's nature?

"He asked me: What, then, is to be done?

"I replied: At the time of quiescence, to have a realization of the absence of thought in the mind: that is the state of 'fasting' and 'abstinence.' To realize that its original condition is that of the absence of thought; to be separated both from movement and quiescence; and to remain silently immovable: that is the state of sincerity in its utter perfection. The *Doctrine of the Mean* (p. 319) says: 'Given utter sincerity, there is enlightenment (*ming*).' And the *Changes* (p. 380) says: 'All movement beneath Heaven is subject to a single rule.'

"He asked me: During this time when there is no cogitation and no thought, if things intrude from without and the feelings respond to them from within, how is one then to halt (the feelings)? Is it possible to halt feeling by means of feeling?

"I replied: The feelings are the evil that is in the nature. By knowing that they are evil, this evil will not exist in the first place. If the mind remains silent and immovable, depraved thoughts will cease of themselves. As long as the nature clearly displays itself, how can evil appear? But if one were to stop feeling by means of feeling, this would result in increasing the feelings. For once the feelings are used to stop one another, there can be no end to the process. The *Changes* (pp. 392-393) says: 'The son of the Yen family, if he did anything that was not right, was always certain to be conscious of it. And being thus conscious, he never repeated the act.' It also says (p. 393): 'Returning from an error that has not led him far away, there is no occasion for repentance. There will be great good.'

"He asked: (You speak of) the original condition (of the mind) as that of absence of thought, and of separation from both movement and quiescence. But is one, then, not to hear the coming of sounds or to see the forms of objects?

"I replied: Not to see or to hear would mean no longer to be a man. And yet it is possible to have a clear kind of sight and hearing, which, however, do not disturb (the mind by their) seeing and hearing. To know everything; to do everything; to be immovable in mind and yet to illumine Heaven and Earth: this is the enlightenment that comes with utter sincerity. The *Great Learning* says: 'The extension of knowledge lies in the investigation of things.' [1] And the *Changes* (p. 370) says: 'The *Changes* does not think or act. It is silent and immovable; yet, when acted on, it penetrates forthwith to all phenomena beneath Heaven. If it were not the most divine thing beneath Heaven, how could it do this?'

"He asked: I should like to ask the meaning of the words, 'The extension of knowledge lies in the investigation of things.'

"I replied: 'Things' (*wu*) means 'all things' (*wan wu* 萬物). 'Investigation' (*ko* 格) means 'arriving' or 'coming.' When things come (before one), the mind should clearly understand and distinguish among them, yet at the same time should not be moved by them. Such is the 'extension of knowledge.' It is the bringing of knowledge to completion.

"Knowledge having been made complete, there is utter sincerity in thought. Thought being sincere, the mind is then rectified. The mind being rectified, the person becomes cultivated. The person being cultivated, the family is then regulated. The family being regulated, the state is then rightly governed. The state being rightly governed, the world is then put at peace. [2] It is in this way that one can form a trinity with Heaven and Earth.

"The *Changes* (pp. 354-355) says: 'He (the sage) resembles Heaven and Earth and therefore does not act in opposition to them. His knowledge embraces all things and his course extends itself to the entire world; therefore he falls into no error. He acts according to the exigency of circumstances without being carried away by their current. He rejoices in Heaven and understands its Decree (*ming*); hence he has no anxieties. He remains content in his position and cherishes perfect virtue (*jen*); hence he has the capacity to love. He holds in his scope the transformations of the entire universe, without any error; by an ever changing adaptation he brings completion to all things without omission; he penetrates to a knowledge of the course of day and night. Thus his spirituality is not limited to any single place, nor are the changes which he produces restricted to any form. The succession of the *yin* and *yang* is what constitutes the *Tao*.' Such is what I mean" (*ibid.*, middle sect., pp. 8-9).

The first step in the process of self-cultivation is to reach the

---

[1] *Op. cit.*, p. 412. This famous phrase became the basis for the process of self-cultivation developed by later Neo-Confucianists. — Tr.

[2] A quotation from the *Great Learning*, p. 412. — Tr.

"realization of the absence of thought in the mind." This mental state, however, represents only a relative kind of quiescence (*ching*); a quiescence that exists in apposition to movement (*tung*). In other words, it is a quiescence which, on reaching its inevitable conclusion, immediately gives way to movement or activity. The second step, however, leads to a further stage in which one realizes of the mind that "its original condition is that of the absence of thought." In this state one is "separated both from movement and quiescence," and remains "silently immovable." The quiescence now achieved is no longer one merely relative to movement, but an absolute quiescence that transcends both movement and quiescence as ordinarily conceived. The sage who has reached it, "being acted on, penetrates to all phenomena under Heaven." Nevertheless, in the innermost substance of his mind he remains "silently immovable." He possesses "a clear kind of sight and hearing, which, however, do not disturb (the mind by their) seeing and hearing." Being confronted by things, "his mind clearly understands and distinguishes among them, yet at the same time is not moved by them." Such is the final mystical state of *ch'eng* or utter sincerity, and *ming* or enlightenment is the name for the supra-mundane understanding that is achieved in this state. The one postulates the other, and vice versa.

It is to be noted that though Li Ao asserts the importance of the "realization of the absence of thought in the mind," he does not argue that coercive measures should be taken to *cause* the mind to be emptied of such thoughts. This is because the use of such coercion would mean "to halt feeling by means of feeling," and would entail an endless pitting of one feeling against another. [1] The feelings are evil, says Li, and once this fact is truly understood, they will disappear of themselves without the need for any coercive measures.

Finally, it should be noted that by quoting the famous sentence in the *Great Learning*, "The extension of knowledge lies in the investigation of things," Li inaugurates a subject that was to undergo constant discussion and innumerable interpretations at the hands of later Sung and Ming Neo-Confucianists.

3—Neo-Confucianism and Buddhism

The preceding sections show that, already in the T'ang dynasty, the foundations for Sung and Ming Neo-Confucianism had been laid

---

[1] See above, p. 420. It should be remembered that for Li Ao the feelings are a part of the mind. — Tr.

through the efforts of Han Yü and Li Ao. Of the two, Li made the greater countribution, and in him, too, Buddhist influence is particularly evident. The feelings, he maintained, are harmful, and can cause the nature to become darkened and to lose its calm. To "return to the nature," therefore, means to return to that quiescence and enlightenment which are inherent in the nature in its original state. This quiescence is more than the mere opposite of movement. It is an absolute kind of quiescence, transcending both movement and quiescence as ordinarily conceived, and is equivalent to what the *Doctrine of the Mean* calls *ch'eng* or utter sincerity. *Ch'eng* is automatically accompanied by *ming* or enlightenment, and vice versa. In formulating these ideas, Li Ao seems to have been influenced by the Buddhist theory of cessation (*chih*) and contemplation (*kuan*), which was developed by the T'ien-t'ai school. [1] In his *Chih-kuan T'ung-li* or *General Rules for Cessation and Contemplation*, for example, Liang Su (753-793) writes as follows: [2]

"What is meant by cessation and contemplation? They serve to guide the phenomena of multitudinous change in such a way as to bring them back to the Reality (*shih chi* 實際). What is this Reality? It is the original state of the nature (*hsing*). The failure of things to return to it is caused by darkness (*hun*) and movement (*tung*). The illuminating of this darkness is called enlightenment (*ming*), and the halting of this movement is called quiescence (*ching*). Such enlightenment and quiescence are (respectively) the substance of cessation and of concentration. Regarded as causative agents they are called cessation and contemplation. Regarded as end results they are called Wisdom (*chih* or *prajñā*) and Meditation (*ting* or *samādhi*)."

The terminology here used, and the apposition made between enlightenment and darkness, quiescence and movement, are in general suggestive of Li Ao's essay. There is one important difference, however, namely that Li applies these ideas toward the exposition, not of the Buddhist texts, but of such ancient Chinese works as the Appendices in the *Book of Changes*, the *Great Learning*, and the *Doctrine of the Mean*. We know from Liang Su himself that he derived his theory of cessation and contemplation from the T'ien-t'ai Patriarch Chan-jan, whose ideas we have discussed in the preceding chapter.

---

[1] See chap. 9, sect. 1, v. — Tr.

[2] The work is contained in TT no. 1915 (vol. 46, pp. 473-474). The passage here cited occurs on p. 473.

On the other hand, we also know that he expressed direct approval of Li Ao. [1] Thus it would seem that Li's *Essay on the Return to the Nature*, at least in part, was based on certain concepts of the T'ien-t'ai school, and more specifically on those of Liang Su. These concepts he elaborated in his own way, however, and applied, as we have seen, to the interpretation of the Confucian writings. Thus what had been a Buddhist doctrine became with Li a Confucian doctrine as well.

Nevertheless, Li remains a true Confucian in his emphasis upon the cultivation of self, regulation of the family, good government of the state, and pacification of the world. Like later Neo-Confucianists, he wished to lead men toward a Confucian type of "Buddhahood," which, for him, could be reached only through a process of self-cultivation lying within the range of ordinary human life and the social relationships. Thus it is true of him, as of later Neo-Confucianists, that though willing to accept certain Buddhist ideas, he remained in the last analysis opposed to Buddhism.

The flow of ideas between Buddhism and Confucianism was not always wholly one-sided. Thus during the Northern Sung dynasty (960-1126) there were not only Neo-Confucianists, but certain Buddhist monks as well, who were expounding Confucian works like the *Doctrine of the Mean*. We know of the monk Chih-yüan (976-1022), for example, that he gave himself the title of Chung-yung Tzŭ (Master Doctrine of the Mean), and wrote a work called by him the *Chung-yung-tzŭ Chuan* (Biography of Master Doctrine of the Mean). [2] Likewise, the monk Ch'i-sung (1007-72) wrote a *Chung-yung Chieh* (Explanation to the Doctrine of the Mean). [3] Thus by the eleventh century this type of text seems to have become common property of Confucianists and Buddhists alike.

4—One Stream of Thought in Religious Taoism

Neo-Confucianism, as we have seen, started through the combination of Confucianism with Buddhism. By the beginning of the Sung dynasty, i.e., around the year 1000, its development was further advanced through the addition of yet another stream of thought, taken by it from religious Taoism.

---

[1] See Li Ao's *Works*, 1.1. This has been pointed out to me by Professor Ch'en Yin-k'o.

[2] See his *Hsien-chü Pien* (Idle Essays), 18.55, in *Tripiṭaka Supplement*, Pt. Ib, case 6, vol. 1.

[3] See his *T'an-chin Wen-chi* (TT no. 2115; vol. 52, pp. 646-750), 4.666.

It is important at this point to distinguish between Taoism in its early form as a non-institutionalized philosophical school (*chia* 家), and, later, as an institutionalized cult or religion (*chiao* 教). The *Tao chiao* or Taoist religion originated in part as follows: During the second century B.C. the doctrines of the *Yin-yang* school entered Confucianism, resulting in the New Text school headed by Tung Chung-shu. Later, however, with the successive rise of the Old Text school and of Neo-Taoism, the *yin-yang* ideology went into eclipse. Yet while this was happening, the *Yin-yang* school itself took over certain Confucian texts, which it combined with some of the ideas stemming from early philosophical Taoism. The resulting amalgam became what is known as religious Taoism. Thus the same period witnessing the revival of philosophical Taoism in the movement known as Neo-Taoism, also saw the spread and popularization of religious Taoism. Between the two ideologies, however, there were not only important differences but often sharp antagonisms.

Offhand it may seem strange that the *Yin-yang* school's ideas could ever have become joined in this way to philosophical Taoism. The process was helped, however, by the terseness and ambiguity of the *Lao-tzŭ* itself, which made it possible for the religious Taoists to interpret it according to their own aims. Primary among these aims was that of acquiring long life or even permanent immortality, and it so happens that there are several paradoxical passages in the *Lao-tzŭ* that could readily be interpreted as esoteric allusions to this subject. Examples are: "He who has a true hold on life, when he walks on land does not encounter tigers or wild buffaloes" (chap. 50); "When one dies one is not lost: there is no other longevity" (chap. 33); "Make the roots penetrate deep and preserve the trunk: this is the way to maintain long life and protracted sight" (chap. 59). The seekers for immortality incorporated the *Yin-yang* school's cosmology into their own view of life, applied it to their techniques for gaining immortality, and produced a new ideological synthesis which became religious Taoism. By the end of the Han dynasty this cult had gained great prominence; during the Period of Disunity it developed a priesthood, a ritual, and an iconography; and during this period and the Sui and T'ang dynasties it was a rival of Buddhism, with which it alternated in popular favor.

One of the chief Confucian texts used by the religious Taoists was the *Book of Changes*—a fact hardly surprising when we remember that this work had originally been used for divination, and later became very important in the *Yin-yang* school. Many of the writings of the religious Taoists reveal through their very titles their connection with this book. Such is the case, for example, with one of the most famous, the *Ts'an-t'ung-ch'i* or *Akinness of the Trio*, the full title of which is *Chou Yi Ts'an-t'ung-ch'i* (Akinness of the Trio in the Chou Changes). This work is traditionally ascribed to Wei Po-yang, a Taoist said to have lived during the second century A.D. [1] Concerning his life, however, we have almost no fixed facts, and the *Ts'an-t'ung-ch'i* is not listed in the treatise on literature which comprises chaps. 32-35 of the *Sui Shu* (History of the Sui Dynasty). Hence it is uncertain whether or not it really does date from the second half of the Later Han dynasty.

In the *Ts'an-t'ung-ch'i* we find a correlation established between the eight trigrams, the ten cyclical signs or "stems," and the movements of the sun and moon, basically similar to that employed by the Han commentator on the *Book of Changes*, Yü Fan (164-233). [2] For example, on the passage in the *Changes* (p. 373): "The emblems suspended (in the sky) are brightly displayed; among them, none is greater than the sun and moon," Yü Fan comments as follows: [3]

"This means that the sun and moon, suspended in the sky, serve as emblems of the eight trigrams. On the evening of the third day (of the lunar month), it (the moon) comes forth in *keng* (stem 7) as the emblem of *chen* (trigram 4). On the eighth day, as the emblem of *tui* (trigram 2), it appears in *ting* (stem 4). On the fifteenth day, as the emblem of *ch'ien* (trigram 1), it is full in *chia* (stem 1). At dawn of the sixteenth day, as the emblem of *sun* (trigram 5), it withdraws from *hsin* (stem 8). On the twenty-third day, as the emblem of *ken* (trigram 7), it disappears in *ping* (stem 3). On the thirtieth day, as the emblem of *k'un* (trigram 8), it becomes obliterated in *yi* (stem 2). On the evening of the last day of the month and the dawn of the first day of the (following) month, as the emblem of *k'an* (trigram 6), it flows into *wu* (stem 5). In the center is the sun, which is *li* (trigram 3), and which accords with *chi* (stem 6). (The stems) *wu* and *chi* occupy the

---

[1] Wu Lu-ch'iang and Tenney L. Davis, in their translation of the *Ts'an-t'ung-ch'i*, state on p. 210 that it was "written by Wei Po-yang about 142 A.D.," and on p. 213 that "in the year 121 A.D. he [Wei] was summoned to Court." However, they give no source for these dates. — Tr.

[2] For a list of the ten stems, see chap. 2, pp. 11-12, and for correlations somewhat similar to those made here, see chap. 3, sect. 4. — Tr.

[3] Quoted in Li Ting-tso (fl. between 742 and 906), *Chou Yi Chi-chieh* (Collected Commentaries on the Chou Changes), 14.19-20.

position of earth; [1] hence the emblems (corresponding to them) appear in the center (at that time). Light comes as a product of the mutual meeting and withdrawal of the sun and moon (that occurs in the above-described never ending monthly cycle)."

Here we find six of the eight trigrams, those of *chen, tui, ch'ien, sun, ken,* and *k'un,* used to symbolize the fluctuations of the *yang* and *yin* (light and darkness) during the lunar month. At the same time eight of the ten stems (*chia, yi, ping, ting, wu, chi, keng,* and *hsin*)—each associated with one of the compass points—are used to indicate the varying positions in the heavens occupied by the sun and moon during the month. If we now turn to the *Ts'an-t'ung-ch'i,* we there find a practically identical correlation:

"Heaven's emblems (the sun and moon) advance and retreat, wane and wax, according to the season. Therefore the *Changes* sums up the Mind of Heaven; with its hexagram *fu* the first buds (of new growth) are established. [2] (In the *Changes*), the 'eldest son' [3] perpetuates the body of the 'father,' [4] and has his beginnings in the 'mother.' [5] The wanings and waxings (of the sun and moon) occur according to the (twelve) pitch-pipes. [6] Their risings and settings are pivoted upon the North Star.

"On the third day (of the month, the moon first) shows its light, and *chen* (trigram 8) receives *keng* (stem 7) in the west. On the eighth day, *tui* (trigram 2) receives *ting* (stem 4), and (the moon) is in its first quarter, level like a string. On the fifteenth, the form of *ch'ien* (trigram 1) comes forth, and (the moon) is full in *chia* (stem 1) in the east. Then are (to be seen) the toad and the hare, and the sun and moon are equally radiant. [7] This toad looks after the course of the trigrams, and the hare spits forth living light.

---

[1] Which holds a central position among the Five Elements. — Tr.

[2] *Fu,* hexagram 24, means "return," and consists of five divided or *yin* lines above one undivided or *yang* line, for which reason it is supposed to symbolize the return of light (shown by the bottom line), and of new growth following the winter solstice. The reference to "the Mind of Heaven" is an echo of what is said about *fu* in the *Book of Changes,* Appen. II, p. 233: "In *fu* do we not see the Mind of Heaven and Earth?" — Tr.

[3] I.e., *chen,* the fourth trigram. On the family relationships of the trigrams to one another, see vol. 1, p. 382. — Tr.

[4] *Ch'ien,* trigram 1. — Tr.

[5] *K'un,* trigram 8. — Tr.

[6] On the twelve pitch-pipes or notes of the scale, six of which are *yang,* the other six *yin,* see chap. 2, p. 11. — Tr.

[7] The moon is supposedly inhabited by a toad and a hare, both of which are fully visible only at full moon. — Tr.

"When the course of seven (plus) eight has reached its conclusion, [1] (the moon) declines and sets. When the sixteenth (day) rolls
in to carry on (the cycle), *sun* (trigram 5) appears in *hsin* (stem 8)
at dawn. When *ken* (trigram 7) is in line with *ping* (stem 3) in the south,
(the moon) is in its third quarter on the twenty-third (day). At *k'un*
(trigram 8) and *yi* (stem 2), on the thirtieth day, it loses its light in
the northeast. [2]

"When the divisions (forming one month) have come to their
end, they hand on (the cycle to the following month); thus the body
(of the 'father') is perpetuated, and the 'dragon' is reborn. [3] *Jen*
(stem 9) and *kuei* (stem 10) (respectively) match *chia* (stem 1) and *yi*
(stem 2); (the trigrams) *ch'ien* and *k'un* embrace the beginning and end
(of the entire cycle). [4] The number of seven and eight is fifteen; [5]
even so is nine and six. [6] These four (numbers) add up to thirty, [7]
with which the essence of the *yang* is brought to completion and
hidden away" (pp. 234-235).

According to this passage, the moon first becomes visible on
the third day of each lunar month. At this time it receives a very
limited amount of light from the sun, and is therefore symbolized
by the trigram *chen* ☳, consisting of a single *yang* (undivided) line
beneath two *yin* (divided) lines. In this form it appears at twilight in
the west, the direction of the stem *keng*. On the eighth day of the
month, the moon enters its first quarter and receives a growing

---

[1] I.e., when the moon has passed its period of fullness on the fifteenth day
of the month. — Tr.

[2] This is an echo of the passage describing *k'un* in the *Book of Changes*, p. 60.
Both the *Changes* and the *Ts'an-t'ung-ch'i* read 朋 (friends) instead of the graphically similarly 明 (light), but the latter reading has to be accepted here if the
Ts'an-t'ung-ch'i passage is to make any sense, and such a play on words accords well
with Wei Po-yang's general fondness for veiled allusion and ambiguity. — Tr.

[3] The dragon is *ch'ien*, trigram 1, also known as the "father." These words
have reference to the statement made earlier: "The 'eldest son' perpetuates the
body of the 'father,' and has his beginnings in the 'mother.' " They simply
mean that one lunar cycle has come to its close and is then repeated in the cycle
of the following month. — Tr.

[4] *Ch'ien*, as explained above, symbolizes the full moon of the fifteenth of the
month, while *k'un* symbolizes the new moon of the thirtieth day. — Tr.

[5] This has reference to the words in the preceding paragraph: "When the
course of seven (plus) eight has reached its conclusion, (the moon) declines and
sets." — Tr.

[6] The number symbolizing the undivided (*yang*) lines in the trigrams is 9;
that symbolizing the divided (*yin*) lines is 6. — Tr.

[7] Which is the last day in the cycle of a lunar month. — Tr.

amount of light from the sun, symbolized by the trigram *tui* ⚌
(two *yang* lines beneath one *yin* line). It then appears at twilight in the
south, the direction of *ting*. On the fifteenth day the moon is full and
receives the complete light of the sun. Therefore it is then symbolized
by the trigram *ch'ien* ☰ (three *yang* lines), and appears at twilight in
the east, the direction of *chia*. On the sixteenth day the moon has
passed its fullness, and its brilliance begins to be obscured from
below by a single *yin* line. Hence it is then symbolized by the trigram
sun ☴, and it disappears (i.e., sets) at dawn in the west, the direction
of *hsin*. On the twenty-third day, as the moon enters its final quarter,
it is obscured by a second *yin* line, so that it belongs to the trigram
ken ☶. On that day it disappears at dawn in the south, the direction
of *ping*. On the thirtieth day the moon is completely obscured by three
yin lines, and belongs to the trigram *k'un* ☷. It then lies hidden
in the northeast. And with the arrival of the following month it
repeats the same cycle, beginning once more with the trigram *chen*. [1]

This still leaves two of the trigrams, *k'an* (no. 6) and *li* (no. 3),
unaccounted for. They are explained in an earlier passage of the
Ts'an-t'ung-ch'i as follows:

"(The trigram) *k'an* and (the stem) *wu* are the essence of the
moon. (The trigram) *li* and (the stem) *chi* are the radiance of the
sun. The sun and moon are (the concrete representations of) the
Changes, the hardness (of the one) and softness (of the other) respectively standing for (the *yang* and *yin* lines in the trigrams). Earth
operates throughout the four seasons, knitting them together from
beginning to end, while green, red, black, and white each occupy one
of the cardinal directions. [2] From the Central Palace (*chung kung* 中
宮) they all receive the directing activities of *wu* and *chi*" (p. 233).

Here we have a correlation of trigram *k'an* with stem *wu*, and
trigram *li* with stem *chi*, all four of which occupy a position in the
center of the system. *Li* represents the radiance of the sun, which
inherently belongs to the center, whereas *k'an* represents the essence

---

[1] In this paragraph I follow the interpretation given by Chu Hsi (1130-1200),
in his commentary on the *Ts'an-t'ung-ch'i* entitled *Chou Yi Ts'an-t'ung-ch'i K'ao-yi*,
pp. 6-7.

[2] Here the Five Elements are introduced into the system. Green = E. = wood;
red = S. = fire; black = N. = water; white = W. = metal. Earth, the fifth
and central element, operates impartially throughout the four seasons. See vol.
1, p. 166. — Tr.

of the moon, which "on the evening of the last day of the month and the dawn of the first day of the (following) month" likewise "flows" into this position. In this correlation two of the ten stems, *jen* and *kuei* (nos. 9 and 10), are still unaccounted for. It is evident, however, that they should be equated with trigrams *ch'ien* and *k'un* respectively, for the *Ts'an-t'ung-ch'i* has already told us that *ch'ien* goes with the *chia* stem, and *k'un* with the *yi* stem, and then that "*jen* and *kuei* (respectively) match *chia* and *yi*." The whole series of correlations may be portrayed more clearly through the following diagram: [1]

Correlations of Eight Trigrams, Ten Stems, and Monthly Movements of Sun and Moon, as Described in the *Ts'an-t'ung-ch'i*

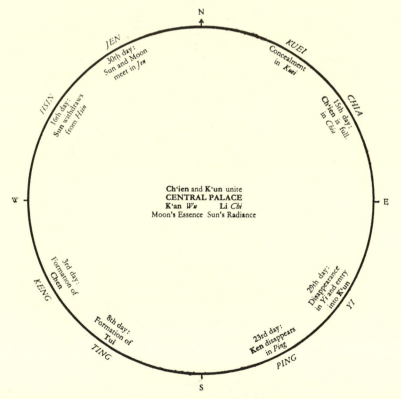

Bold face (Ch'ien) = Trigrams; Italics (*Chia*) = Stems.

---

[1] This diagram is taken from Hui Tung (1697-1758), *Yi Han-hsüeh* (Changes Lore during the Han Dynasty), *chüan* 3.

Such are the fluctuations of the *yin* and *yang* forces in the universe, as represented in the writings of religious Taoism. In order to acquire immortality, say the Taoists, we should wait until the *yang* reaches its apogee and the *yin* is weak. At this propitious moment we should, in the words of a recluse quoted in the following section, "seize for ourselves the secret forces of Heaven and Earth," in order thus to develop the "spiritual essence" (*ching* 精), the "vital force" (*ch'i* 氣), or the "spirit" (*shen* 神) that lies within us. This process is known as *lien tan* 鍊丹, "compounding the elixir," of which there are two kinds: an "inner elixir" (*nei* 內 *tan*), and an "outer elixir" (*wai* 外 *tan*). The "outer elixir" consists of various drugs, the swallowing of which will confer immortality. Such was the elixir of the immortals such as was so eagerly sought for by the First Emperor of the Ch'in (246-210 B.C.) dynasty, and by Emperor Wu of the Han (146-86 B.C.). The "inner elixir," on the other hand, does not depend on external means, but on the development of our own "spiritual essence," "vital force," or "spirit." [1] In this latter system, the human body is conceived of as a microcosm, within which the *yin* and *yang* and the eight trigrams exist, just as they exist in the universe as a whole. The means to immortality, therefore, can wholly be found within oneself. We shall see in the next chapter how the cosmology of the Taoist searchers for immortality influenced the thinking of the Sung Neo-Confucianists.

5—THE SCIENTIFIC SPIRIT OF RELIGIOUS TAOISM

Besides the group in religious Taoism which sought, either externally or internally, for an elixir of immortality, there was another group which likewise wished to prolong life, but hoped to do so through magical charms used to expel evil spirits and drive away disease. What is noteworthy is that both groups in religious Taoism, despite their superstitious excesses, contained at least some men who consciously aimed at the conquest of man over nature. The attempt

---

[1] There is a considerable literature on Chinese alchemy. For a study of its beginnings and possible influence on Western alchemy, see H. H. Dubs, "The Beginnings of Alchemy," *Isis*, vol. 38 (1947), 62-86. For the physical and breathing exercises, meditation techniques, etc., used for the "inner elixir," see Henri Maspero, "Les procédés de 'nourrir le principe vital' dans la religion taoiste ancienne," *Journal Asiatique* (1937), pp. 178-252, 353-430. — Tr.

to gain immortality, for example, ran directly counter to the natural and inevitable processes of life and death, and the same was true of the charms used against disease and evil spirits. This attitude toward nature is well exemplified by the famous Taoist, Ko Hung (ca. 250-ca. 330), in his *Pao-p'u-tzŭ* (The Master Who Embraces Simplicity): [1]

"In forming and fashioning the transforming power (of nature), there is none more spiritual than man. Therefore he who penetrates to its shallower (aspects) can put all things to his service, while he who penetrates to its deeper (aspects) can enjoy eternal life" (3.1).

The thirteenth century recluse and student of the *Ts'an-t'ung-ch'i*, Yü Yen, writes in similar vein: [2]

"I would say that man as he exists in the universe is merely a thing in that universe. Yet because his spirituality is greater than that of other creatures, he is given the special name of 'man.' How, then, can he stand co-equal with Heaven and Earth? If he seize for himself the secret forces of Heaven and Earth, in order thereby to compound for himself the great elixir of the golden fluid, [3] he will then exist coeval with Heaven and Earth from beginning to end. Such a one is called the True Man." [4] Again:

"Each time that Heaven unites itself with Earth, seize for yourself the secret springs of the creative activities of the *yin* and *yang*" (*ibid.*, 5.4).

Here we are urged to "seize for ourselves the secret forces of Heaven and Earth" and the "secret springs of the creative activities of the *yin* and *yang*," in order thus to "put all things to our service." In other words, we are to obtain our end through gaining control over the forces of nature. The stress here upon power is essentially scientific in spirit.

Science is commonly said to have two aspects. One is emphasis upon exactness and verification; for by obtaining precise and verified knowledge about things, we may gain the power to control them. The other is the emphasis upon power. Religious Taoism aimed at the second of these two goals, but unfortunately failed to acquire the body

---

[1] It is worth noting that this desire to conquer nature contradicts the aim of philosophical Taoism, which is to place man in harmony with nature. — Tr.

[2] In his *Chou Yi Ts'an-t'ung-ch'i Fa-hui* (Explanations on the Chou Yi Ts'an-t'ung-ch'i), 3.18-19.

[3] A reference to the making of artificial gold, which was an important ingredient in the elixir of immortality. — Tr.

[4] *Chen jen*, one of the terms used by Chuang Tzŭ to designate the Taoist adept. See vol. 1, pp. 239, 242. — Tr.

of verified knowledge needed to make such power possible (even though it itself claimed to possess this knowledge). Despite its stress on power, therefore, its interpretation of the universe remains mythological, and its method of gaining control over natural forces is a magical one.

Magic, nevertheless, has often proved the parent of science, as, for example, in the case of alchemy. In this connection, Santayana has observed that the difference between science and myth is not merely one of relative value, nor of the greater intellectual resources demanded by the former. The essential distinction, as he points out, lies in the fact that myth is based upon concepts that transcend the realm of human experience, whereas science is based upon laws that may be proved to be true within the field of human experience. [1] We have seen in Chapter IV how Wang Ch'ung (A.D. 27-ca. 100) similarly maintained that knowledge can be true only when it can be proved within our own experience, which is why he is said to be scientific in spirit. In this respect his philosophy runs directly counter to that of the *Yin-yang* school. Yet this does not prevent us from granting that not only he, but also the *Yin-yang* school, is scientific in spirit, though in a different way: the one emphasized the verification and precision that must go with science; the other emphasized its desire for power.

From the present chapter it may be seen that by the beginning of the Sung dynasty, i.e., by around the year 1000, the major existing schools of thought had all reached roughly comparable stages of development, in the course of which a considerable intermingling of ideas had occurred. All that was lacking was the series of great men who were presently to appear, and were to organize and unify all that had gone before into one great system. We shall deal with these in the following chapters.

---

[1] George Santayana, *Reason in Science* (in *Works*, N.Y., 1936, vol. 5, pp. 8-9).

CHAPTER XI

CHOU TUN-YI AND SHAO YUNG

1—CHOU TUN-YI

Among the Neo-Confucianists of the Sung dynasty (960-1279), the most conspicuous borrowers from religious Taoism were Chou Tun-yi (1017-73) and Shao Yung (1011-77). The biography of the former in the *Sung Shih* (History of the Sung Dynasty) reads in part as follows:

"Chou Tun-yi 周敦頤, styled Mao-shu 茂叔, was a native of Ying-tao in Tao-chou.[1] His original personal name was Tun-shih 實, but this was changed (to Tun-yi) because of the taboo on (the personal name of Emperor) Ying-tsung.[2] Through his uncle, Cheng Hsiang, who was a Scholar of the Dragon Chart Pavilion,[3] he became Assistant Prefect of Fen-ning.[4] ... Because of illness he requested to be transferred to Nan-k'ang-chün, and consequently established his household below the Lotus Peak in the Lu mountains.[5] In front (of the house) was a stream which flowed into the P'en river, and which he named the 'Stream of Waterfalls' after the

---

[1] The present Tao-hsien in the extreme southern end of Hunan province. — Tr.

[2] It was disrespectful in China to use the words occurring in the personal names of one's father, or of the emperors of the dynasty under which one lived. The personal name of Emperor Ying-tsung had been Tsung-shih. Hence when this emperor came to the throne (actually in 1063, though his reign is officially dated as beginning in 1064), Chou was compelled to change his personal name from Tun-shih to Tun-yi. Cf. Werner Eichhorn, "Chou Tun-i, ein chinesisches Gelehrtenleben aus dem 11. Jahrhundert," *Abhandlungen für die Kunde des Morgenlandes*, vol. 21, no. 5 (Leipzig, 1936), pp. 17 and 36. — Tr.

[3] A bureau that served as a repository for important government documents. The title of Scholar was the highest of the several ranks of officials attached to it. — Tr.

[4] The present Hsiu-shui 修水 hsien in northern Kiangsi. This event occurred in 1040. Cf. Eichhorn, *op. cit.*, p. 21. — Tr.

[5] Nan-k'ang-chün is the present Hsing-tzŭ 星子 hsien at the edge of Poyang lake in northern Kiangsi, and the Lu mountains are a few miles to the northwest. Chou's transfer here occurred very shortly before his death in 1073. Cf. Eichhorn, *op. cit.*, p. 45. — Tr.

stream of that name in Ying-tao where he had lived. [1] He died in his
fifty-seventh year. ... Huang T'ing-chien [2] acclaimed him as a man
of exceedingly high character, whose feelings were as free and un-
forced as a balmy breeze in a cloudless sky. ... He composed the
T'ai-chi T'u 太 極 圖 (Diagram of the Supreme Ultimate), in which
he elucidated the origins of 'Heavenly Principle' and probed into
the beginning and end of all things" [3] (427.3).

i. *Diagram of the Supreme Ultimate Explained*

Chou Tun-yi's most important contribution to Neo-Confucianism
is undoubtedly the above-mentioned *T'ai-chi T'u* or "Diagram of the
Supreme Ultimate," and its accompanying commentary. For the
"Diagram" itself see page 436.

Accompanying this "Diagram," Chou composed an explanatory text which, together with the "Diagram" itself, is known as the
T'ai-chi T'u-shuo (Diagram of the Supreme Ultimate Explained). This
text (hereafter referred to as the *Diagram Explained*) reads as follows:

"The Ultimateless (*wu chi* 無 極)! And yet also the Supreme
Ultimate (*t'ai chi*)!

"The Supreme Ultimate through movement (*tung*) produces
the *yang*. This movement, having reached its limit, is followed by
quiescence (*ching*), and by this quiescence it produces the *yin*. When
quiescence has reached its limit, there is a return to movement.
Thus movement and quiescence, in alternation, become each the

---

[1] Chou also named his house after this stream, Lien-hsi. It is because of this
that he himself came to be commonly referred to as Lien-hsi. — Tr.

[2] 1045-1104. One of the great men-of-letters of the Sung dynasty. — Tr.

[3] For an excellent detailed study of Chou Tun-yi's life, cf. Eichhorn, *op. cit.*,
and for a briefer account, cf. J. Percy Bruce, *Chu Hsi and His Masters* (London,
1923), pp. 18-30. From these we learn that Chou came from a family that had
long enjoyed a reputation for learning, and that his father, whom he lost while
yet a boy, had been a successful official. Chou himself spent most of his rather
short life in a succession of official posts (such as district Prefect), largely in
present Kiangsi and Kwangtung provinces. Though none of them was of great
importance, he earned an outstanding reputation for honesty and ability. Much
of his great personal influence seems to have lain in his attractive personality,
which was simple, straightforward, and warm-hearted. Another marked trait
was his strong love of nature; indeed, tradition has it that "he refused to allow
the grass in front of his window to be cut, because in its instinctive love of life
he recognized its kinship with himself" (Bruce, *op. cit.*, p. 29). — Tr.

Diagram of the Supreme Ultimate

The Ultimateless!
Yet also the Supreme Ultimate!

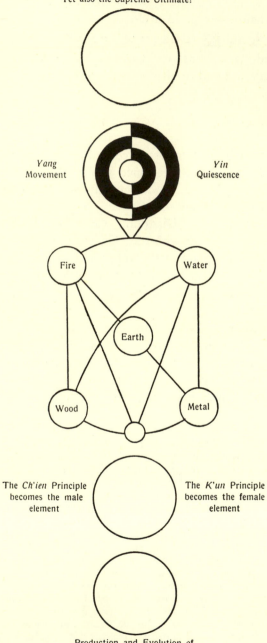

Yang
Movement

Yin
Quiescence

Fire

Water

Earth

Wood

Metal

The *Ch'ien* Principle
becomes the male
element

The *K'un* Principle
becomes the female
element

Production and Evolution of
All Things

source of the other. The distinction between the *yin* and *yang* is determined, and their Two Forms (*liang yi* 兩 儀) stand revealed.

"By the transformations of the *yang*, and the union therewith of the *yin*, water, fire, wood, metal, and earth are produced. These five ethers (*ch'i* 氣, i.e., elements) become diffused in harmonious order, and the four seasons proceed in their course.

"The Five Elements are the one *yin* and *yang*; the *yin* and *yang* are the one Supreme Ultimate; and the Supreme Ultimate is fundamentally the Ultimateless. The Five Elements come into being each having its own particular nature (*hsing*).

"The true substance of the Ultimateless, and the essences of the Two (Forms) and Five (Elements), unite in mysterious union, so that consolidation ensues. The *ch'ien* principle becomes the male element, and the *k'un* principle becomes the female element. [1] The two ethers (i.e., the *yin* and *yang*) by their interaction operate to produce all things, and these in their turn produce and reproduce, so that transformation and change continue without end.

"It is man alone, however, who receives all these in their highest excellence, and hence is the most intelligent (of all beings). His bodily form thereupon is produced, and his spirit develops consciousness. The five principles of his nature [2] react (to external phenomena), so that the distinction between good and evil emerges and the myriad phenomena of conduct appear.

"The sage regulates himself according to the mean, correctness, love, and righteousness, [3] and takes quiescence as the essential, [4] thus establishing the highest standard for mankind. Hence the sage's 'virtue is one with that of Heaven and Earth; his brilliance is equal to that of the sun and moon; his course is in harmony with that of the four seasons; and in his relation to good or bad fortune he is in harmony with the spirits.' [5] The superior man, by cultivating these (sagely virtues), enjoys good fortune, while the petty man, by violating them, incurs bad fortune.

---

[1] *Ch'ien* and *k'un* have already been repeatedly named in this book as the two primary trigrams and hexagrams of the *Book of Changes.* — Tr.

[2] The Confucian virtues of love (*jen*), righteousness (*yi*), propriety (*li*), wisdom (*chih*), and good faith (*hsin*). — Tr.

[3] Chou Tun-yi himself comments on this: "The Way of the sage is nothing else but that of love, righteousness, the mean, and correctness."

[4] Chou comments on this: "Having no desire, he is therefore in a state of quiescence."

[5] See *Book of Changes* (Appen. IV, p. 417). — Tr.

"Therefore it is said: 'The Way (*Tao*) of Heaven is established by the *yin* and *yang*; the Way of Earth is established by softness (*jou* 柔) and hardness (*kang* 剛); the Way of man is established by love (*jen*) and righteousness (*yi*).' [1] And again: 'By tracing things to their beginning and back again to their final issue, (the *Book of Changes*) comes to know the meaning of life and death.' [2] Great indeed is the *Changes*. Herein has been expressed its fullest (meaning)" (pp. 128-131).

Chou's first few sentences, describing the Supreme Ultimate, are obviously inspired by the passage in the *Book of Changes* (Appen. III, p. 373): "In the *Changes* there is the Supreme Ultimate, which produced the Two Forms. These Two Forms produced the four emblems (*hsiang* 象), and these four emblems produced the eight trigrams. The eight trigrams serve to determine good and bad fortune (for human affairs), and from this good and bad fortune spring the great activities (of human life)." In similar fashion, Chou begins by describing how the Two Forms, i.e., the *yin* and *yang*, are evolved from the Supreme Ultimate. Then, however, he diverges by speaking about the Five Elements instead of the eight trigrams. Thus despite the enthusiastic invocation of the *Changes* in his last sentence, it is evident that his "Diagram" is not wholly based upon that work.

For this reason, the problem of the origin of Chou's "Diagram" well merits our attention. A possible clue is to be found in one of the works of religious Taoism contained in the *Taoist Canon*. This work, dealing with techniques for acquiring immortality, bears the lengthy title of *Shang-fang Ta-tung Chen-yüan Miao-ching T'u* (Diagrams of the Truly First and Mysterious Classic of the Transcendent Great Cave). Among its several diagrams is that reproduced by us on p. 439, entitled "Diagram of the Supreme Ultimate that Antedates Heaven." [3]

The similarities between this and Chou's diagram are striking. Though its authorship is unknown, the treatise in which it appears has a preface by Emperor Hsüan-tsung (712-755) of the T'ang dynasty, so that it antedates Chou Tun-yi by several centuries. Thus it seems not unlikely that it was from it that Chou gained inspiration for his own "Diagram."

---

[1] *Ibid.* (Appen. V, p. 423). — Tr.

[2] *Ibid.* (Appen. III, p. 353). — Tr.

[3] *T'ai-chi Hsien-T'ien chih T'u* 先天之圖. See *op. cit.*, p. 3, in *Taoist Canon*, vol. 196.

Diagram of the Supreme Ultimate that Antedates Heaven

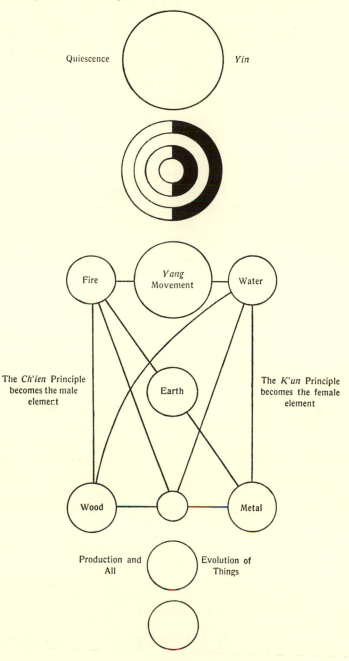

Quiescence

Yin

Fire

Yang
Movement

Water

The *Ch'ien* Principle
becomes the male
element

Earth

The *K'un* Principle
becomes the female
element

Wood

Metal

Production and
All

Evolution of
Things

Such a hypothesis is strengthened by what the *Sung Shih* says in its biography of Chu Chen (1072-1138):

"Chen's classical scholarship was deep and excellent. In his *Han-shang Yi-chuan* (Commentary on the Changes from the Han River), he says that Ch'en T'uan (ca. 906-989) transmitted the 'Diagram of What Antedates Heaven' (*Hsien-T'ien T'u*) to Ch'ung Fang (died 1014); Fang transmitted it to Mu Hsiu (979-1032); Mu Hsiu transmitted it to Li Chih-ts'ai (died 1045); Chih-ts'ai transmitted it to Shao Yung (1011-77). (He also says that Ch'ung) Fang transmitted the 'River Chart' and 'Lo Writing' to Li Kai (dates uncertain); Kai transmitted them to Hsü Chien (fl. dur. 976-984); Hsü Chien transmitted them to Fan O-ch'ang (dates uncertain); O-ch'ang transmitted them to Liu Mu (1011-64). (Likewise he says that) Mu Hsiu transmitted the 'Diagram of the Supreme Ultimate' to Chou Tun-yi" [1] (435.4).

From this it would appear that the early Sung practioners of the so-called "numerology" all traced their origin back to Ch'en T'uan, who himself, as we know, was a famous exponent of Taoist techniques for acquiring immortality. [2]

Significance also attaches to the remarks of the Ch'ing scholar, Mao Ch'i-ling (1623-1716), in his *T'ai-chi T'u-shuo Yi-yi* (Supplementary Discussion on the Diagram of the Supreme Ultimate Explained). There he asserts that the Taoist work known as the *Ts'an-t'ung-ch'i* or *Akinness of the Trio* (discussed by us in the last chapter) originally contained certain diagrams, which, however, were deleted from it after Chu Hsi (1130-1200) wrote his commentary on that text. Among them, Mao says, were two, at one time contained in the P'eng Hsiao edition of the *Ts'an-t'ung-ch'i*, that were entitled "Diagram of the Outline of (the Forces of) Water and Fire," and "Dia-

---

[1] On the "River Chart" (*Ho T'u*) and "Lo Writing" (*Lo Shu*), which were graphic representations of numerological theories of cosmology, based on the *Book of Changes*, see chap. 2, p. 8, note 3, and chap. 3, p. 89, note 2. The statement about the transmission of the "River Chart," here attributed to the *Han-shang Yi-chuan*, is confirmed in that work (appended sect. on diagrams, 1.2), which, however, does not give the similar details, here attributed to it, concerning the "Diagram of What Antedates Heaven," "Lo Writing," and "Diagram of the Supreme Ultimate." In the *Sung Shih* passage just quoted, this work is cited, not as *Han-shang Yi-chuan*, but as *Han-shang Yi-chieh* (Interpretation of the Changes from the Han River). — Tr.

[2] Cf. his biography in the *Sung Shih*, chap. 457. [On this numerology, see pp. 451-452 below, and chap. 3, sect. 2. — Tr.]

gram of the Three and Five Supreme Essences." [1] He then asserts of Chou's "Diagram of the Supreme Ultimate," that its second circle from the top, representing the interactions of the *yin* and *yang*, was derived from the foregoing "Diagram of the Outline of (the Forces of) Water and Fire," [2] and that its central portion, representing the interplay of the Five Elements, was likewise derived from the "Diagram of the Three and Five Supreme Essences." [3]

Further suggestive remarks come from Huang Tsung-yen (1616-86) and Chu Yi-tsun (1629-1709). Both scholars assert that Chou's "Diagram of the Supreme Ultimate" was originally known as the "Diagram of the Ultimateless" (*Wu-chi T'u*), and that Ch'en T'uan, while living on the famous "sacred mountain" of Hua Shan in Shensi, had a diagram bearing this same name carved on the face of a cliff. This, they say, consisted of several successive tiers arranged as follows: (1) At the bottom a circle labeled "Doorway of the Mysterious Female." [4] (2) Above this another circle, inscribed: "Transmuting the Essence so as to Transform It into the Vital Force; Transmuting the Vital Force so as to Transform It into the Spirit." [5] (3) The next and central portion represented the elements wood and fire on the left side, metal and water on the right, and earth in the center, all interconnected by lines. It bore the title: "The Five Forces Assembled at the Source." (4) Above this was a circle (or probably several concentric circles), made up of interlocking black and white bands, and entitled: "Taking from *K'an* to Supplement *Li*." [6] (5) A topmost circle with the inscription: "Transmuting the Spirit so that It May Revert to Vacuity; Reversion and Return to the Ultimateless." [7]

---

[1] P'eng Hsiao lived during the Five Dynasties period (907-959). It should be noted, however, that these diagrams are no longer extant in his edition of the *Ts'an-t'ung-ch'i*, as now found in the *Taoist Canon*, vol. 623.

[2] This diagram represented two of the eight trigrams: on the one side *k'an*, and on the other *li* (respectively symbolic of fire and water; see vol. 1, p. 382). — Tr.

[3] It will be remembered that Chou uses similar phraseology when he speaks of "the essences of the Two (Forms) and Five (Elements)." See above, p. 437. — Tr.

[4] This phraseology is derived from the *Lao-tzŭ*, chap. 6: "The Doorway of the Mysterious Female is the base from which Heaven and Earth sprang." — Tr.

[5] This, of course, is Taoist terminology descriptive of the techniques for gaining immortality. — Tr.

[6] It will be remembered that the *k'an* and *li* trigrams symbolize water and fire respectively. — Tr.

[7] Cf. Huang Tsung-yen, *T'ai-chi T'u-pien* (Discussion on the Diagram of

Huang states further that "when Master Chou acquired this diagram, he reversed its sequence, changed its name, linked it with the great *Changes*, and maintained that it had been secretly transmitted by the Confucianists. The fact is that the arts of the Taoist practitioners (*fang shih* 方 士) consist of creating the elixir (of immortality) through opposition (to Nature); hence (their diagram) was orientated from below upward. [1] But Master Chou's idea was (to show) how man is produced through conformity (to the course of natural evolution). Hence his (diagram) was orientated from above downward." [2] Unfortunately we do not know where Huang and Chu found the evidence for these assertions. But in any case there seems no doubt that Chou Tun-yi's "Diagram of the Supreme Ultimate" is closely connected with religious Taoism.

In borrowing from the Taoists, however, Chou reinterpreted what he took. His resulting "Diagram," together with its exposition (the *Diagram Explained*), became the first systematic product of Sung and Ming Neo-Confucianism. Its great importance lies in the fact that it came to be accepted by virtually all later Neo-Confucianists as the basis for their own cosmological speculations. In the following section we shall discuss it in conjunction with Chou Tun-yi's other major philosophical work, the *T'ung-shu* (Explanatory Text). The fact that the latter treatise was originally known as the *Yi T'ung* (Explanation of the Changes) shows that in it, as in his discussion of the Supreme Ultimate, Chou was writing with the *Book of Changes* very much in mind. [3]

---

the Supreme Ultimate), quoted in the *Sung-Yüan Hsüeh-an* (Writings of Sung and Yüan Philosophers), 12.20 ff.; also Chu Yi-tsun, *T'ai-chi T'u Shou-shou K'ao* (Study of the Transmission of the Diagram of the Supreme Ultimate), in his *P'u-shu-t'ing Chi, chüan* 58.

[1] In other words, it was intended to show the various stages through which man, by the conquest of Nature, must rise in order to become an immortal. This, as we have seen in the last chapter, is a typical concept of religious Taoism. — Tr.

[2] I.e., it was intended to show how the process of creation begins with the Supreme Ultimate, as the first cause, and passes thence through the *yin* and *yang* to the Five Elements, and finally to all created things, including man. — Tr.

[3] I am now inclined to believe that the *Yi T'ung* originally comprised all of Chou's philosophical writings, including the *Diagram Explained*, and that only later did the latter come to be known under a separate title. This would explain why, in later times, it has sometimes been argued that the *Diagram Explained* is not actually by Chou Tun-yi at all. See chap. 14, p. 589. [This note has been added by the author for the English edition. — Tr.]

ii. *Diagram of the Supreme Ultimate Explained* and the *Explanatory Text*

It will be remembered that the *Diagram Explained*, after invoking the name of the Supreme Ultimate, begins its exposition with the words: "The Supreme Ultimate through movement produces the *yang*. This movement, having reached its limit, is followed by quiescence, and by this quiescence it produces the *yin*. When quiescence has reached its limit, there is a return to movement. Thus movement and quiescence, in alternation, become each the source of the other. The distinction between the *yin* and *yang* is determined, and their Two Forms stand revealed." Though he thus speaks of the alternation of movement and quiescence, Chou also maintains that it is possible for both these phases to be concurrently present in the Supreme Ultimate. Thus he says in his *Explanatory Text* (chap. 16):

"When moving, they lack quiescence, and when quiescent, they lack movement: such are things (*wu* 物). When moving, it yet lacks movement, and when quiescent, it yet lacks quiescence: such is spirit (*shen* 神). But movement which thus lacks movement, and quiescence which thus lacks quiescence, do not mean non-movement or non-quiescence. For whereas things do not interpenetrate one another, spirit is the most mysterious of all things" (pp. 73-75).

That is to say, it is impossible for particularized physical objects, when in movement, simultaneously to be quiescent, or vice versa. For it is precisely their concrete particularity that prevents them from being otherwise than as they actually are; in Chou's own words: "Things do not interpenetrate one another." In the case of the universal first cause known as the Supreme Ultimate, however, such distinctions no longer apply. To say of it that when in movement it lacks movement, and when in quiescence it lacks quiescence, means that even as it moves, there is in it something of quiescence, and even as it remains quiescent, there is in it something of movement. Hence in its *yin* principle there is something of the *yang*, and in its *yang* principle there is something of the *yin*. This mysterious fact is expressed by Chou in the words: "Spirit is the most mysterious of all things."

The *Diagram Explained* states further: "By the transformations of the *yang*, and the union therewith of the *yin*, water, fire, wood, metal, and earth are produced. These five ethers become diffused in harmonious order, and the four seasons proceed in their course. The Five Elements are the one *yin* and *yang*; the *yin* and *yang* are the one

Supreme Ultimate; and the Supreme Ultimate is fundamentally the Ultimateless." From this passage it may be deduced not only that the *yin* and *yang* and Five Elements are derived from the Supreme Ultimate, but that the Supreme Ultimate in actual fact lies *within* the *yin* and *yang* and Five Elements. The *Explanatory Text* states similarly (chap. 22):

"The two ethers (the *yin* and *yang*) and Five Elements evolve to create all things. The five (latter tend toward) differentiation; the two (former toward) a (single) reality, their duality being rooted in oneness. Thus the myriad-fold constitutes a oneness, and the single reality divides to be a myriad-fold. The myriad and the one are equally correct; the small and the great equally have their fixed place" (p. 97).

It will be noted that here the *yin* and *yang* are termed the "two ethers," whereas in the *Diagram Explained* the Five Elements are likewise termed the "five ethers." This means that in Chou's thinking, both the *yin* and *yang* and the Five Elements pertain to what he calls the *ch'i* 氣 . This term was to become of key importance in later Neo-Confucianism, in which it is equivalent to what Westerners would call "ether" or "matter."

Opposed to *ch'i* is another key concept, that of *li* 理 or "principle." The word occurs in the title of the chapter from which this passage in the *Explanatory Text* is quoted: the *Li Hsing Ming Chang* or "Chapter on Principle, the Nature, and Destiny." As used in Neo-Confucianism, *li* is a designation for the immaterial and metaphysical principle or principles that underlie, yet transcend, the physical universe; in view of its great philosophical importance, its English equivalent will in this and the following chapters be capitalized as "Principle" or "Principles."[1] Often it is used as a

---

[1] This rendition is adopted in the present volume as preferable to that of "Law" or "Laws," which has been previously used by Bruce and others. The reason for this change is that, as pointed out by Needham in an important article, "such laws as these were not the statutes of a celestial lawgiver analogous to an earthly prince." On the contrary, *li* may be defined as "the 'principle of organization' in the universe." It represents "the order and pattern in Nature, not formulated Law. ... It is dynamic pattern as embodied in all living things, and in human relationships and in the highest human values." See Joseph Needham, "Human Laws and Laws of Nature in China and the West," *Journal of the History of Ideas*, vol. 12 (1951), pp. 218 and 209 respectively. His entire discussion is well worth reading. See esp. pp. 208-210, 216-222. The word *li* originally referred to the veins or markings in a block of jade. Its philosophical use in Neo-Con-

synonym for the Supreme Ultimate. Hence when Chou Tun-yi speaks in this chapter of "oneness," referring thereby to the Supreme Ultimate, it would seem that he also has in mind *li* or Principle; whereas when he speaks of the *yin* and *yang*, he has in mind forces which, for him, pertain to *ch'i* or matter. [1]

This apposition between *li* and *ch'i*, so important in later Neo-Confucianism, thus seemingly begins with Chou Tun-yi. It was not until Chu Hsi, however, that it was to become fully elaborated. In this passage from the *Explanatory Text*, we see that all things of the physical universe are derived from a "oneness," which is the Supreme Ultimate; the latter, therefore, though a transcendent principle, is at the same time regarded as actually being *within* all material things. In Chou's own words: "The myriad-fold constitutes a oneness, and the single reality divides to be a myriadfold."

The *Diagram Explained* goes on to say that, through the interaction of the *yin* and *yang*, all things (lit., "the ten thousand things") come into being. Being physical, these things are therefore limited and relative, and "do not interpenetrate one another." In other words, "The myriad and the one are equally correct; the small and the great equally have their fixed place."

The *Diagram Explained* continues: "It is man alone, however, who receives all these in their highest excellence, and hence is the most intelligent (of all beings). His bodily form thereupon is produced, and his spirit develops consciousness. The five principles of his nature react (to external phenomena), so that the distinction between good and evil emerges and the myriad phenomena of conduct appear." What this seems to indicate is that man is imbued both with the metaphysical *li* or Principle of the Supreme Ultimate, and with the essence of the physical Five Elements; as such he is the most spiritual of all creatures. To borrow a phrase from the quotation that follows, the Principle of the Supreme Ultimate is "unmixed and supremely good"; for this reason man's nature (*hsing*) is also fundamentally good. To denote this goodness, Chou uses a word which we

---

fucianism derives from several passages in the Appendices of the *Book of Changes*. See, for example, Appen. V, p. 422: "They plumbed *li* to its depths and completely penetrated the nature, thereby reaching to (an understanding of) Destiny." The Neo-Taoist Wang Pi also spoke of *li* in a manner which, if further developed, might have led to the Neo-Confucian concept. See chap. 5, sect. 3, ii, especially pp. 186-187. — Tr.

[1] In these two paragraphs I have, for the sake of clarity, somewhat expanded the author's original exposition. — Tr.

have already encountered in our discussion of Li Ao: that of *ch'eng*, "sincerity" or "utter sincerity." [1] Thus he writes in the *Explanatory Text* (chap. 1):

"Sincerity (*ch'eng*) is the foundation of the sage. 'Great indeed is the originating (power) of *ch'ien*! All things owe to it their beginning.' [2] This refers to the source of sincerity. 'The way of *ch'ien* is to change and transform, so that everything is correct in its nature and Destiny.' [3] In this way sincerity is established, unmixed and supremely good. Therefore it is said: 'The alternation of the *yin* and *yang* is called the Way (*Tao*). The perpetuation of it (in man) is good, and the formation of it (in him) constitutes his nature.' [4] Originating and penetrating is sincerity in its pervasiveness; fitting and correct is sincerity in its return (to its source). [5] Great indeed is the *Changes*, the source of (our concepts of) the nature and Destiny" (pp. 1-10).

The Way or *Tao* here mentioned is for Chou another designation for the Supreme Ultimate.

Regarding the origin of evil, Chou writes in his *Explanatory Text* (chap. 3): "Sincerity lies in the state of non-activity (*wu wei*); with the stirrings of activity come (both) goodness and evil" (pp. 19-20). By such "stirrings" (*chi* 幾) he means activity in its almost imperceptible beginnings. Thus the word is defined as follows in his fourth chapter: "Movement (*tung*) which has not yet acquired form and lies midway between being (*yu*) and non-being (*wu*): such is *chi*" (p. 26). Chou's theory is that though man's nature is originally good, its manifestations in actual conduct do not always accord with the mean; conduct of this sort we then call evil. In the *Explanatory Text* he develops this idea further (chap. 7):

"In the nature, there are hardness and softness, (which may result in) goodness or evil. All (is right) when there is the mean

---

[1] See chap. 10, sect. 2, where Li's derivation of it from the *Great Learning* and *Doctrine of the Mean* is traced. As used in Neo-Confucianism, it often means the complete and single embodiment by the individual of Principle (*li*) or the Supreme Ultimate, in all its perfection and goodness. We should remember that its metaphysical and mystical overtones can only weakly be expressed by "sincerity," the word by which it is usually translated. By E. R. Hughes it is rendered as "realness" in his *Great Learning and the Mean-in-Action* (New York, 1943). — Tr.

[2] Cf. *Book of Changes* (Appen. II, p. 213), commenting on the hexagram *ch'ien*. — Tr.

[3] *Ibid.* — Tr.

[4] *Op. cit.* (Appen. III, pp. 355-356). — Tr.

[5] These are the four qualities attributed to *ch'ien* in the *Book of Changes*, p. 57. — Tr.

(*chung*). (This explanation) not being understood, (Chou) continued: The goodness that results from hardness consists of righteousness (*yi*), straightforwardness (*chih* 直), decisiveness, strictness, firmness, determination, and steadfastness. [1] The evil resulting from it consists of ruthlessness, intolerance, force, and violence. The goodness that results from softness consists of compliance and docility. The evil resulting from it consists of weakness of will, indecisiveness, and underhanded sycophancy. The mean (*chung*) signifies harmony and proper proportion. This alone is the highest Way (*Tao*) of the world, and the concern of the sage. Hence the sage emphasizes those teachings which will cause men to reform their evils of themselves, proceed of themselves to the mean, and there stop" (pp. 35-39).

The *yang* principle is hard; the *yin* is soft. Because man is imbued with both these ethers, his nature likewise contains some qualities that are "hard" and others that are "soft." Sometimes, however, these lose their conformity to what is right; as Chou expresses it, "the five principles of (man's) nature react" to external phenomena in such a way that they no longer accord with the mean (see above, p. 437). The result is what we know as evil. According to this theory, evil is not to be conceived as an active force in itself. For whereas goodness is something positive, evil is simply a negative deflection from the mean. Chou goes on to warn us that "with the stirrings of activity come (both) goodness and evil," for which reason "the superior man is cautious in his movements" (chap. 5, p. 31).

The *Diagram Explained* continues: "The sage regulates himself according to the mean, correctness, love, and righteousness, and takes quiescence as the essential, thus establishing the highest stand-ard for mankind." This passage is paralleled by the statement in the *Explanatory Text* (chap. 6): "The Way of the sage consists of nothing else but love, righteousness, the mean, and correctness" (p. 32). The importance of the mean has already been explained. As to the reason for supplementing it with love and righteousness, we read in the *Explanatory Text* (chap. 11):

"Heaven gives birth to all things by means of the *yang*, and gives completion to all things by means of the *yin*. The act of giving

---

[1] Of these qualities, righteousness is one of the traditional Confucian vir-tues, while straightforwardness (meaning by this the truthful expression of one's inner nature) was much emphasized by Confucius, but less so by later thinkers. See vol. 1, pp. 66-69. The other qualities are not essentially Confucian. — Tr.

birth is one of love, and that of giving completion is one of righteousness. Therefore the sage, from his station on high, uses love to rear all things, and righteousness to rectify all people" (pp. 57-58).

The *Diagram Explained* continues by quoting a passage from the *Book of Changes*: "The Way of Heaven is established by the *yin* and *yang*; the Way of Earth is established by softness and hardness; the Way of man is established by love and righteousness." Assembling the various quotations that have been cited, we may summarize them as meaning that the individual should regulate himself in accordance with the mean and correctness; should govern others according to love and righteousness; and should "take quiescence as the essential" in order to make himself a sage. On this last point we have already quoted Chou's own comment: "Having no desire, he is therefore in a state of quiescence." In the *Explanatory Text* (chap. 20) this idea is developed further as follows:

"(It was asked:) 'May sageliness be acquired through study?' I replied: 'It may.'

"It was asked: 'Is there an important principle for this?' I replied: "There is.'

"On further inquiry, I replied: 'The important thing is singleness. This singleness means the absence of desire (*wu yü* 無欲). Such absence of desire results in vacuity (*hsü* 虛) when in quiescence, and straightforwardness (*chih*) when in movement. Vacuity in quiescence leads to enlightenment (*ming*), and enlightenment leads to comprehension (*t'ung* 通). (Likewise) straightforwardness in movement leads to impartiality (*kung* 公), and impartiality leads to universality (*p'u* 溥). One is well nigh (a sage when one has) such enlightenment, comprehension, impartiality, and universality!' " (p. 90).

This passage becomes clearer through comparison with the well known anecdote in the *Mencius* (IIa, 6): "If today men suddenly see a child about to fall into a well, they will without exception experience a feeling of alarm and distress. This will not be as a way whereby to gain the favor of the child's parents, nor whereby they may seek the praise of their neighbors and friends, nor that they are so because they dislike the reputation (of being unvirtuous)." This anecdote was to become a very popular one among the Sung and Ming Neo-Confucianists. It means that anyone, seeing a child about to fall into a well, will instinctively experience feelings of alarm and distress which, being straightforward reactions, will, if immediately translated into conduct, result in straightforward conduct. Feelings and conduct of this sort, in which no account is taken of personal gain or loss, are therefore impartial. This is the idea underlying Chou's assertion that "straightforwardness in movement leads to impartiality."

Let us suppose, however, that, instead of immediately acting, the person concerned pauses to think about the matter. There may then arise in him such thoughts as "gaining the favor of the child's parents," or "the praise of neighbors and friends." These thoughts, being no longer straightforward reactions, are therefore selfish; hence the conduct resulting from them is likewise selfish. Thoughts and conduct of this sort, based on considerations of personal advantage, are what the Neo-Confucianists describe as "selfish desires" (*ssŭ yü* 私 欲). As the Chinese saying has it: "Initial thoughts are those of sages and worthies; second thoughts are those of birds and beasts."

Thus our mind, when it lacks all desire and is in a state of quiescence, may be compared to a shining mirror. As long as it remains free from external stimuli, it is quiescent and "vacuous"; when, however, such stimuli appear, it responds to them with straightforward action. The *Explanatory Text* says (chap. 4): " 'To remain silently immovable': this is sincerity. 'To become activated and thereupon penetrate everywhere': this is spirituality (*shen*)" [1] (p. 26). The first phrase refers to the vacuity characteristic of the mind in its state of quiescence; the second to the straightforward conduct that springs out of this quiescence whenever activity is called for. This theme became a popular one among later Neo-Confucianists. Chou himself, however, refers only in passing to "desire," without trying to elucidate its position in metaphysics and ethics, or its relationship to *li* or "Principle."

The phrase in the *Explanatory Text*, "Enlightenment leads to comprehension," means that when our mind lacks desire and is in a state of quiescence, it becomes like a shining mirror which, though immovable itself, can reflect all things. [2] For explanation of the

---

[1] The quotations are from the *Book of Changes* (Appen. III, p. 370). — Tr.

[2] This metaphor of the mirror, which became a common one in Neo-Confucianism, had already been used in Buddhism and Neo-Taoism, and goes back to the *Chuang-tzŭ* (chap. 7, p. 97): "The Perfect Man uses his mind like a mirror." — Tr.

following phrase, "Impartiality leads to universality," we should turn to another passage in the *Explanatory Text* (chap. 37):

"The Way of the sage is nothing else but that of highest impartiality (*kung*). If someone ask: 'What does this mean?', I would reply: 'Heaven and Earth have nothing but the highest impartiality' " (pp. 144-145).

Chou here has in mind the fact that there is nothing in the world that Heaven and Earth do not "cover" or "support" respectively. Such is their "highest impartiality," for unless they were thus impartial, they would cover or support only certain things at the expense of others. "The Way of the sage," remarks Chou, "is nothing else but that of highest impartiality." Therefore, he exclaims: "One is well nigh (a sage when one has) such enlightenment, comprehension, impartiality, and universality!"

Concerning the final state in which, "lacking desire, one is quiescent," we are told further in the *Explanatory Text* (chap. 9):

"It is stated in the *Grand Norm*: [1] 'Of thought, let it be profound. . . . Profundity produces sageliness.' The absence of thought is the root, and the penetrating activity of thought is its application. With the stirrings of movement over there, his sincerity moves (in response) here; his thoughts are absent, yet penetrate everywhere: such is the sage. Were he not to think, he would be unable to penetrate the abstruse; were (his thoughts) not profound, they could not penetrate everywhere. Thus their universal penetration springs from the penetration of the abstruse. This penetration of the abstruse springs from the exercise of thought. Hence thought is basic in the work of the sage, and is the motive force leading to good or bad fortune" (pp. 46-51).

The mind, in its highest state of perfection, has two aspects, the one quiescent, the other active. "Absence of thought" (*wu ssŭ* 無 思) describes it in its quiescent aspect, in which it is "silently immovable." "The penetrating activity of thought" describes it in its aspect of awakened response to external stimuli, in which, "becoming activated, it thereupon penetrates everywhere." The synthesis of the two is expressed in the words: "One's thoughts are absent, yet penetrate everywhere." To reach this final state, however, it is obvious that some kind of preparatory intellectual activity is necessary. What this is, Chou Tun-yi does not tell us, but we may

---

[1] *Hung Fan,* one of the sections in the *Book of History*, p. 141. — Tr.

hazard the guess that it probably consists of a constant concentration upon one's inner condition of mind, such as Mencius refers to when he says (IIa, 2, para. 16): "There must be the (constant) exercise (of the mind)."

Toward the end of the *Diagram Explained*, we are told of the sage that "his virtue is one with that of Heaven and Earth, his brilliance is equal to that of the sun and moon," etc. The *Explanatory Text* (chap. 2) says somewhat less grandiloquently:

"The sage has nothing but sincerity. This sincerity is the root of the five constant (virtues), and the source of all conduct" (pp. 11-12).

By this Chou means to say that *ch'eng* or sincerity is the original condition of man's nature, and that the sage is a sage precisely because he has succeeded in returning his nature to this original condition. This doctrine, as we have seen in the preceeding chapter, had already been enunciated two centuries earlier by Li Ao. Beginning with Chou Tun-yi, it was generally accepted by all the Neo-Confucianists.

2—SHAO YUNG

We have previously seen how the Han dynasty apocrypha (*wei shu*) developed theories about the *Book of Changes* that were later perpetuated by being incorporated into religious Taoism. [1] With the coming of the Sung dynasty, this *Changes* lore was again transferred, this time from religious Taoism into Neo-Confucianism, where it became known as "the study of emblems and numbers." [2] Liu Mu, in the Preface to his *Yi-shu Kou-yin T'u* (Diagram Giving Secret Entry to the Numbers of the Changes), explains the meaning of "emblems" and "numbers" as follows:

"The term 'Changes' (*yi*) refers to the interaction between the *yin* and *yang* ethers. ... The trigrams (of the *Changes*) were instituted by the sages through their observation of emblems (*hsiang*). These emblems were the higher archetypes of physical forms (*hsing* 形). [3]

---

[1] See chap. 3, sect. 2, and chap. 10, sect. 4. — Tr.

[2] *Hsiang shu chih hsüeh*. This term, used frequently in chap. 3 (see esp. p. 91, note 2), has there, for the sake of convenience, usually been translated as "numerology." — Tr.

[3] In the *Book of Changes* the word "emblem" seems to be used in two different senses: (1) as a designation for the hexagrams, which are stated to have been

If we trace them to their source, (we find that) forms are the product of emblems, and the emblems have been instituted out of numbers (*shu*). Were these numbers to be set aside, there would then be no means of seeing the origin from which the four emblems have originated" [1] (p. 1).

By "forms," Liu Mu here has in mind all the manifold objects of the physical universe. According to his theory, before our universe had its present form, there was a time when there were only numbers and the combinations of these numbers. From these numbers there then evolved various archetypal images, called by him "emblems." Finally, modeled on these generalized "emblems," there came into being the particularized "forms" or physical objects of our existing universe. This theory, though implied in the Han apocrypha, was not expressed so explicitly until the Sung dynasty.

Chou Tun-Yi's "Diagram of the Supreme Ultimate" is an example of "emblemology" rather than numerology, since it depicts the process of universal creation solely in terms of symbols without recourse to numbers. In the philosophy of Shao Yung (1011-77), however, we find "emblemology" and numerology combined into a single cosmological system. His biography in the *Sung Shih* reads in part as follows:

"Shao Yung 邵雍 was styled Yao-fu 堯夫. His forebears had been natives of Fan-yang. [2] But his father, Ku 古, moved to Heng-chang, and then again to Kung-ch'eng. [3] Thus Yung, when in his thirteenth year, traveled to Ho-nan, where he buried his parents on the Yi river, subsequently becoming a native of Ho-nan. [4] ...

---

composed by the sages as graphic symbols representative of various natural phenomena; (2) as a designation for the various natural objects (especially those in Heaven, such as the sun, moon, and stars) which were observed by the sages when formulating these hexagrams. Cf. vol. 1, p. 390. — Tr.

[1] This reference to the "four emblems" goes back to the passage in the *Changes* (Appen. III, p. 373) which is quoted near the end of this section, shortly before sub-sect. i below. — Tr.

[2] Just south of the present Peking. — Tr.

[3] Heng-chang was another name for the small Chang river in the extreme northern tip of Honan province. Kung-ch'eng was equivalent to the present Hui 輝 hsien in northern Honan. — Tr.

[4] Not the present province of Honan, but its capital, the present Loyang. The Yi river flows from the south into the Yellow river, not far east of Loyang. — Tr.

"Li Chih-ts'ai, of Pei-hai, [1] became Acting Prefect of Kung-ch'eng. He heard that Yung was a lover of learning, and once went to his cottage, where he said to him: 'Have you, too, heard about the learning of the Principles (*li*) of things, and the nature and Destiny (of man)?' Yung replied: 'I should be happy to receive your teaching.' Thereupon he became a follower of Chih-ts'ai, receiving from him the diagrams and emblems of the 'River Chart,' 'Lo Writing,' eight trigrams of Fu Hsi, and sixty-four hexagrams. Chih-ts'ai's transmission of these came from remote beginnings. As for Yung, he delved into what was strange and hidden, thus in a wonderful manner coming to comprehend divine mysteries. Broadly and deeply he probed into dark secrets, so that there was much that he gained for himself. ... He died in the tenth year of the Hsi-ning period (1077), in his sixty-seventh year. ... During the Yüan-yu period (1086-94) he was conferred the posthumous title of K'ang-chieh" [2] (427.17-19).

The derivation of Shao Yung's "emblemology" and numerology from Li Chih-ts'ai is confirmed by the Neo-Confucian, Ch'eng Hao (1032-85), in his "Epitaph to Shao Yung." [3] And Li, as we have seen on p. 440 above, received his ideas through a line of thinkers that goes back to the Taoist, Ch'en T'uan (ca. 906-989). This is what the *Sung Shih* means when it says that "Chih-ts'ai's transmission of these· came from remote beginnings."

In Appendix III of the *Book of Changes* there appears the famous passage: "In the *Changes* there is the Supreme Ultimate, which produced the Two Forms. These Two Forms produced the four emblems, and these four emblems produced the eight trigrams. The eight trigrams serve to determine good and bad fortune (for human affairs),

---

[1] The present Wei 濰 hsien on the Tsingtao-Tsinan railroad in eastern Shantung. — Tr.

[2] 康節, the name by which he is best known in China. For a more detailed biography, see Bruce, *Chu Hsi and His Masters*, pp. 30-38. From this we learn that Shao was born of humble parents; that he himself never held a government position, though his reputation as a teacher made him the friend of many leading statesmen of the day, including some of the major opponents of the famous radical reformer, Wang An-shih (1021-88); and that most of his life was spent in a small cottage near Loyang, where he lived a simple existence. "His biographer tells us, perhaps somewhat hyperbolically, that 'He neither lit a fire in winter, nor used a fan in summer; he neither stretched himself on a·mat, nor reclined his head on a pillow' " (Bruce, *op. cit.*,.p. 31). — Tr.

[3] Cf. the *Ming-tao Wen-chi* (Collected Writings of Ch'eng Hao), 4.1-2. — Tr.

and from this good and bad fortune spring the great activities (of human life)" (p. 373). In a general way it may be said that all of Shao Yung's cosmology is an amplication of this passage, graphically illustrated by means of diagrams. Shao himself says of the latter: "Although my diagrams have no writing, I can discourse the livelong day without departing from them. For in them the principles of Heaven, Earth, and all things are completely embodied." [1]

Unfortunately, these diagrams are no longer contained in the present edition of Shao's major philosophical work, the *Huang-chi Ching-shih* (Cosmological Chronology). Several are preserved, however, in the large compendium entitled *Sung-Yüan Hsüeh-an* (Writings of Sung and Yüan Philosophers), the tenth *chüan* of which is devoted to Shao Yung and his group. These for the most part are taken from the *Yi-hsüeh Ch'i-meng* (Explanation of the Changes for Beginners). [2] Among them, however, is one, illustrating the sequence of the eight trigrams, in which the "Two Forms" of the *Changes* are equated with the *yin* and *yang*, and its "four emblems" with the greater and lesser *yin* and *yang*. This disagrees with statements in Shao's own *Kuan-wu P'ien* or *Treatise on the Observation of Things*, an important section in his *Huang-chi Ching-shih* or *Cosmological Chronology*. In the following pages, therefore, we shall disregard this particular diagram and refer instead to the corresponding one preserved in the *Ching-shih Chih-yao* (Important Principles in the Cosmological Chronology), an exposition of that work by Ts'ai Ch'en (1167-1230). By combining this last diagram with the others found in the *Sung-Yüan Hsüeh-an*, and studying all these in conjunction with what Shao Yung himself writes in his *Observation of Things*, we may hope to elucidate his philosophy.

i. *The Supreme Ultimate and the Eight Trigrams*

In Ts'ai Ch'en's *Ching-shih Chih-yao* there appears the following diagram, in which the divided and undivided lines of the trigrams of the *Book of Changes* are used to symbolize the process of cosmic evolution: [3]

---

[1] Cf. his *Kuan-wu P'ien* (described immediately below), Pt. IIa (12a.35). — Tr.

[2] A work by Chu Hsi (1130-1200), in which the *Book of Changes* is expounded according to Shao Yung's theories. — Tr.

[3] Cf. the *Hsing-li Ta-ch'üan* (Great Compendium of Neo-Confucianism), completed in 1415 under the editorship of Hu Kuang (1370-1418), 8.1, where Ts'ai's treatise, containing this diagram, appears.

Diagram of Cosmic Evolution in Terms of the Eight Trigrams

In this diagram, the second or middle tier should be studied in conjunction with the first or lower one. Thus combination of the undivided line beneath "*yang*" in the central tier, with the similarly undivided line beneath "movement" in the lower tier, results in two undivided lines, ▬▬, which gives us the symbol or "emblem" (*hsiang*) of the *yang* principle. Likewise combination of the divided line beneath "*yin*" in the central tier, with the undivided line beneath "movement" in the lower tier, results in one divided and one undivided line, ▬ ▬, which is the "emblem" of the *yin* principle.

In the same manner, the third or highest tier should be studied in conjunction with the middle and lower ones combined. Thus by combining the undivided line beneath "greater *yang*" in the upper tier, with the similarly undivided lines beneath "*yang*" and "movement" in the middle and lower tiers, we obtain a group of three undivided lines, ▬▬, which is *ch'ien*, the first of the eight trigrams. *Ch'ien* is the "emblem" of the "greater *yang*" (being composed entirely of undivided or *yang* lines). Likewise by combining the divided line beneath "greater *yin*" in the upper tier, with the undivided lines beneath "*yang*" and "movement" in the middle and lower tiers, we obtain a group of three lines, ▬▬, which is the *tui* trigram. *Tui* is the "emblem" of the "greater *yin*" (being composed of one divided or *yin* line above two undivided or *yang* lines). Still again, by combining the undivided line beneath the "lesser *yang*" in the upper tier, with the divided line beneath "*yin*" in the middle tier and the undivided line beneath "movement" in the lower tier, we obtain ▬▬, which is the *li* trigram, and is the "emblem" of the "lesser *yang*" (being composed of two undivided or *yang* lines surrounding one divided or *yin* line). By continuing the same process through the other combinations, we obtain the entire eight trigrams in the following sequence: *ch'ien* ☰, *tui* ☱, *li* ☲, *chen* ☳, *sun* ☴, *k'an* ☵, *ken* ☶, and *k'un* ☷. These respectively symbolize the greater *yang*, greater *yin*, lesser *yang*, lesser *yin*, lesser hardness, lesser softness, greater hardness, and greater softness.

This process should be compared with the following passage in Shao's *Kuan-wu P'ien* or *Observation of Things* (Pt. I):

"Heaven is produced from movement and Earth from quiescence. Through the alternating interplay of movement and quiescence, the course of Heaven and Earth is completely actualized. With the first appearance of movement, the *yang* is produced, and this movement having reached its apogee, the *yin* is then produced. Through the alternating interplay of the *yin* and *yang*, the functionings of Heaven are completely actualized. With the first appearance of quiescence, softness is produced, and this quiescence having reached its apogee, hardness is then produced. Through the alternating interplay of hardness and softness, the functionings of Earth are completely actualized.

"Movement in its major phase is called the greater *yang*; in its minor phase it is called the lesser *yang*. Quiescence in its major phase is called the greater *yin*; in its minor phase it is called the lesser *yin*. The greater *yang* constitutes the sun, the greater *yin* the moon, the lesser *yang* the stars, and the lesser *yin* the zodiacal spaces. [1] Through the interplay of sun, moon, stars, and zodiacal spaces, the bodily substance of Heaven is completely actualized.

"The greater softness constitutes water, the greater hardness fire, the lesser softness soil, and the lesser hardness stone. Through the interplay of water, fire, soil, and stone, the bodily substance of Earth is completely actualized" (11a.1).

Here we are told of the origins of the greater and lesser *yang* and *yin*, but not of the corresponding origins of the greater and lesser hardness and softness. Through logical extension, however, Shao's reasoning would probably be as follows: The emblems of "movement," of "*yang*," and of "hardness" are an undivided line; those of

---

[1] The "zodiacal spaces" are the *ch'en* 辰 , of which there are twelve. They are the spaces or divisions of the sky at which the sun and moon come into conjunction, and thus are somewhat analogous to our signs of the zodiac. — Tr.

"quiescence," of "*yin*," and of "softness" are a divided one. If we look once more at the first two tiers of Shao's diagram, we see that the right side, though dominated by movement below, also has a single divided line in its middle tier; in other words, there is a graphic representation here of the idea (already expressed by Chou Tun-yi, as we have seen on p. 443) that even when movement is dominant, there is in it something of quiescence. Hence it is possible for the upper tier, though dominated by movement below, to contain both the "greater *yin*" (described as "quiescence in its major phase") and the "lesser *yin*" (described as "quiescence in its minor phase"). The same reasoning would apply to the left half of the diagram which, though dominated by quiescence below, is conceived of as also having in it something of movement. This would mean, though Shao does not actually say so himself, that greater hardness is but another name for movement in its major phase, lesser hardness for movement in its minor phase, greater softness for quiescence in its major phase, and lesser softness for quiescence in its minor phase. This would be in harmony with the parallel statements he actually does make about the relation of quiescence and movement to the greater and lesser *yin* and *yang*.

In his *Observation of Things* (Pt. IIa) Shao also discusses the Supreme Ultimate, as when he says: "*Tao* (the Way) constitutes the Supreme Ultimate" (12a.36); or again: "Mind constitutes the Supreme Ultimate" (*ibid.*). He writes further (Pt. IIa):

"The Supreme Ultimate having divided, the Two Forms thereupon stand (revealed). Through the intercourse of the *yang* with the *yin* below, and the intercourse of the *yin* with the *yang* above, the four emblems are produced. Thus through the intercourse of the *yang* with the *yin*, and the *yin* with the *yang*, the four emblems of Heaven are produced. (Similarly) through the intercourse of hardness with softness, and softness with hardness, the four emblems of Earth are produced. In this way the eight trigrams assume finished form. [1] The intermingling of the eight trigrams with one another results in the production of all things.

"Therefore the one divides to make 2, 2 divides to make 4, 4 to make 8, 8 to make 16, 16 to make 32, and 32 to make 64. [2] Hence

---

[1] This passage shows that by "emblems" Shao means the eight trigrams, four of which he regards as pertaining to Heaven, and the other four to Earth. — Tr.

[2] Which is the total number of the hexagrams. — Tr.

it is said: 'With the division of the *yin* and *yang*, and the alternate
operation of softness and hardness, the six positions (of the lines
of each hexagram) in the *Changes* are given complete manifestation.' [1]
Ten divides to become 100, 100 to become 1,000, and 1,000 to become
10,000. It is like the fact that a root has a trunk, a trunk has branches,
and branches have leaves. The larger they are, the fewer they are; the
finer they are, the more numerous they are. Being brought together,
they become one; being extended, they become 10,000. Hence (the
trigram) *ch'ien* acts to divide them, *k'un* to assemble them, *chen* to
enlarge them, and *sun* to diminish them. Enlargement is followed by
division, division by diminution, and diminution by assemblage"
(12a.21).

Again in the same work (Pt. IIb): "The Supreme Ultimate is a
unity which does not move. It produces a duality, and this duality is
spirit (*shen*). ... Spirit produces numbers, the numbers produce
emblems, and the emblems produce implements (*ch'i* 器)" (12b.23).

And yet again: "The Supreme Ultimate, being unmoving, is the
essence (that underlies reality). Becoming manifest, it is spirit. Spirit
leads to numbers, numbers to emblems, and emblems to implements.
These implements, through transformation, are brought back once
more to spirit" (*ibid.*).

In other words, the Supreme Ultimate, being one and unmoving,
is the inner nature or essence of all things. It manifests itself, however,
under the two modes of movement and quiescence, which, being
supra-mundane and not concrete, are known as "spirit." The groups
of divided and undivided lines symbolic of the Two Forms (⎯⎯ and
⎯ ⎯), the four emblems (☲, ☳, etc.), and the eight trigrams (☷,
☶, etc.), are known as "emblems." The digits 1, 2, 4, 8, etc., are
"numbers." The concrete objects of the physical universe (Heaven,
Earth, sun, moon, soil, stone, etc.) are "implements." Shao writes
further (Pt. IIb):

"Spirit is not fixed in space, nor does the *Changes* have
any bodily substance. What is confined to one place, so that meta-
morphosis cannot take place, is not spirit. And what is fixed in its
substance, so that interpenetration (with other things) cannot take
place, does not belong to the *Changes*. Although the *Changes* may
(seem to) have substance, this substance (really) consists of emblems.

---

[1] *Book of Changes* (Appen. V, p. 424). — Tr.

These emblems serve as representations of substance, but they themselves lack all substance" (12b.19).

"Implements," as pointed out above, are the concrete, particularized objects of the physical universe, and therefore cannot be the same as spirit. They are "confined to one place" and "fixed in their substance." In apposition to them there is the *Changes* (by which Shao here means the abstract principles contained in that work, rather than its actual physical text). The name *Changes* denotes only the non-particularized "emblems" which "serve as representations of substances." In other words, these emblems are universal archetypes in accordance with which the growth and evolution of all individualized physical objects take place. All of Shao's diagrams are intended as graphic portrayals of these archetypes.

ii. *"Diagram of What Antedates Heaven" and Other Diagrams*

We have been told that "the one divides to make 2, 2 divides to make 4, 4 to make 8, 8 to make 16, 16 to make 32, and 32 to make 64." This is an example of Shao Yung's numerology. The emblems produced through the evolution of 1 to 8 have already been illustrated in the diagram of the preceding section. Those produced through the continuation of this evolution from 8 to 64 (the total number of hexagrams) are portrayed below: [1]

Diagram of Cosmic Evolution in Terms of the Sixty-four Hexagrams

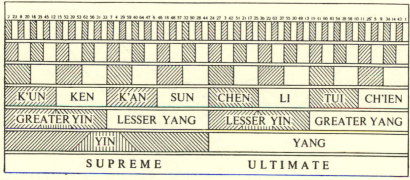

Numbers at top are those of Sixty-four Hexagrams
Names in middle are those of Eight Trigrams

---

[1] See the *Sung-Yüan Hsüeh-an*, 10.4. [To simplify matters, the hexagrams in this English edition, instead of being designated by name, are numbered according to their original sequence in the *Book of Changes*. — Tr.]

Let us turn now for a moment to the diagram illustrated at the beginning of the preceding section. It will be remembered that by variously combining the divided and undivided lines in its three tiers, the eight trigrams are obtained in the following sequence: *ch'ien, tui, li, chen, sun, k'an, ken, k'un.* Now let us take these same trigrams, arranging them in a circle in such a manner that the first four trigrams occupy the left side of the circle, running from top to bottom, and the remaining four occupy the right side, also from top to bottom. This results in what Shao calls the "Diagram of What Antedates Heaven" (*Hsien-T'ien T'u* 先天圖): [1]

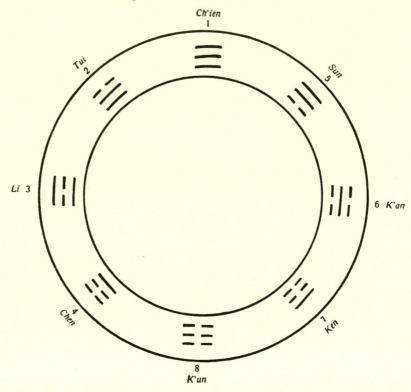

Diagram of What Antedates Heaven

"Antedating Heaven" is a term derived from the *Book of Changes* (Appen. IV, p. 417), when it says of the great man: "He may antedate

---

[1] *Ibid.*, p. 3. [It should be noted that all trigrams are oriented so as to face the center of the circle. — Tr.]

Heaven (*hsien T'ien*), and Heaven will not act in opposition to him; he may follow Heaven, and then will accord with it in its timeliness." As used by Shao Yung, however, the term designates the sequence of trigrams supposedly existing in the time of the legendary Fu Hsi (Subduer of Animals), in contradistinction to the later sequence allegedly given them by King Wen, founder of the Chou dynasty. [1] By applying the term to his diagram, therefore, Shao means to indicate that its arrangement of trigrams is the Fu Hsi sequence, not that of King Wen.

Now let us look at the diagram of the sixty-four hexagrams given at the beginning of the present section. If we arrange its hexagrams into a circle, in such a way that the first thirty-two (beginning with hexagram 1 on the extreme right) occupy the left side of the circle, running from top to bottom, and the remaining thirty-two (beginning with no. 44) occupy the right side, also from top to bottom, we then obtain the arrangement as shown in the diagram on p. 462. [2]

This circular diagram is an elaboration, carried out in terms of the sixty-four hexagrams, of the preceding circular diagram of the eight trigrams; as such it is intended to represent the growth and evolution of all things in the universe. Let us see, for example, how it applies to the seasonal changes of the year. For this purpose we should first turn to hexagram 24, located on the lower (i.e., north) side of the diagram. [3] This hexagram consists of a single divided or *yang* line below, surmounted by five divided or *yin* lines. In terms of time, it corresponds to midnight of the winter solstice, at which time its single *yang* line symbolizes the rebirth of the *yang*, following the apogee of the *yin*. In terms of the calendar, it symbolizes the eleventh lunar month (traditionally the beginning of the Chinese astronomical year). In direction, it symbolizes the north. Thereafter the course of the year is conceived of as traveling clockwise through the left (i.e., east) side of the circle toward the south; as it progresses, the *yang* becomes more and more prominent. Thus hexagram 19 (having two *yang* lines

---

[1] The King Wen sequence is that found in the *Changes*, Appen. V, the pertinent passage from which has been quoted in chap. 3, beginning of sect. 4. This explanation has been added to the author's original text for the benefit of Western readers. — Tr.

[2] See *Sung-Yüan Hsüeh-an*, 10.6. [Numbers in the diagram given below are those of the particular hexagrams mentioned in the following discussion. Here again all hexagrams are oriented so as to face the center of the circle. — Tr.]

[3] In accordance with Chinese ideas of orientation, the circle is arranged so that north is at the bottom and south at the top of the diagram. — Tr.

below) symbolizes the twelfth month; hexagram 11 (with three *yang* lines) the first month; hexagram 34 (with four *yang* lines) the second month; hexagram 43 (with five *yang* lines) the third month. The extreme southern (i.e., top) side of the orbit is occupied by hexagram 1, the six undivided lines of which symbolize the *yang* at its apogee in summer. Immediately next to it, however, comes hexagram 44, consisting of a single divided or *yin* line beneath five *yang* lines. This therefore symbolizes the rebirth of the *yin* that takes place after midnight of the summer solstice (the fifth month). Thereafter we see a continuing growth of the *yin* through hexagrams 33 (sixth month),

Circular Diagram of the Sixty-four Hexagrams

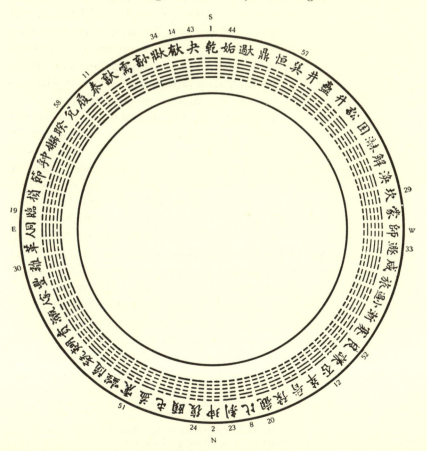

12 (seventh month), 20 (eighth month), and 23 (ninth month), until hexagram 2 (tenth month) in the north is reached, the six *yin* lines of

which symbolize the apogee of the *yin* just before midnight of the winter solstice Then the cycle commences again with the first appearance of the reborn *yang* in hexagram 24. [1]

The same symbolism applies to the growth and decay of individual things. Thus if we take a flower by way of illustration, hexagram 24 symbolizes that flower when it first begins to open, in hexagram 1 it is in full bloom, with hexagram 44 it first begins to drop its petals, and in hexagram 2 it has completely faded. This is the pattern of growth and decay that underlies all things in the universe.

It should be noted that Shao's use of the hexagrams to symbolize the changes of the year is nothing more than a restatement of the correlation made in Han times between the hexagrams and the twenty-four "breaths" (*ch'i*) or solar divisions of the year, with twelve of the hexagrams, known as *pi* or "sovereign" hexagrams, being singled out as exercising jurisdiction over the twelve months. [2] Comparison shows that these "sovereign" hexagrams of the Han correlation are the same as those holding the key positions in Shao Yung's system.

As arranged in Shao's diagram, however, these key hexagrams provoke the question as to why they should be spaced so unequally. Thus between hexagrams 24 (the eleventh month) and 19 (the twelfth month) there is an interval of sixteen hexagrams; between nos. 19 and 11 (the first month) of eight; between nos. 11 and 34 (the second month) of four; between nos. 34 and 43 (the third month) of only two; and finally, between nos. 43 and 1 (the fourth month) of none at all. A similarly diminishing progression holds good for the other half of the cycle. Nowhere does Shao himself explain the reason for this fact. In a later work, however, we find a disciple questioning his teacher, Chu Hsi, about it as follows:

"(In Shao's diagram), after the *yin* and *yang* first appear, they each pass through sixteen hexagrams in order to reach the next month, and then again pass through eight hexagrams in order to reach the month following. Whereas when the *yin* and *yang* approach their point of culmination, they only pass through four hexagrams to cover one month, and then only pass through a single hexagram. After that there is a bunching together of three hexagrams in succession (for the

---

[1] For purposes of clarity, I have somewhat enlarged upon the author's exposition in this paragraph, as well as in the second paragraph below. — Tr.

[2] See chap. 3, sect. 5.

remaining months). Thus in the beginning (of their growth) there is a wide spacing, while at the end there is a close crowding. Is this a proper principle for the expansion and contraction of the *yin* and *yang*?" [1]

To this question Chu Hsi is reported to have replied as follows:

"In observing the detailed manner in which, in (the diagram of) 'what antedates Heaven,' the hexagrams (governing) the 'breaths' (of the year) expand and contract, I too have thought about it in the same manner, but have not succeeded in explaining it. When the *yin* and *yang* first appear, their ethers are congealed and sluggish. Nevertheless, there should not be such a wide spacing as this, nor should there later be such a violent crowding together. In general, this diagram is established in such a manner that everything proceeds in a natural way. [2] Thus it is impossible that no explanation exists, and we should reflect on this matter further" (*ibid.*).

Although other attempts at explanation have not been lacking, none have succeeded in being very "natural." [3]

iii. *Creation of Individual Things*

The way in which the sun, moon, stars, zodiacal spaces, water, wood, soil, and stone of the universe come into existence has already been described on p. 456. These are the fundamental constituents of the concrete universe, from which all other things are derived in turn. Shao Yung writes in his *Observation of Things* (Pt. I):

"The sun constitutes heat, the moon cold, the stars day, and the zodiacal spaces night. Through the interaction of heat, cold, day, and night, the transformations of Heaven are made complete. Water constitutes rain, fire wind, soil dew, and stones thunder. Through the interaction of rain, wind, thunder, and dew, the evolutions of Earth are made complete. The transforming activities of heat result in the natures (*hsing*) of creatures; those of cold in their feelings

---

[1] Quoted in Hu Fang-p'ing (thirteenth century), *Yi-hsüeh Ch'i-meng T'ung-shih* (Interpretation of the Yi-hsüeh Ch'i-meng), 1.30-31. [I have omitted the first part of this question, because it simply repeats in detailed form what has already been stated by Professor Fung. — Tr.]

[2] Chu Hsi means to say that the spacing between the hexagrams, though difficult to explain, nevertheless follows a regularly diminishing progression of 16, 8, 4, 2, 1. — Tr.

[3] For such attempts, cf. Hu Fang-p'ing, *op. cit.*

(*ch'ing*); those of day in their physical forms; those of night in their physical substance. Through the interaction of the nature, feelings, form, and substance, the reacting movements of animals and plants are made complete. The evolutionary activities of rain result in walking creatures; those of wind in flying creatures; those of dew in grassy creatures; and those of thunder in tree-like creatures. Through the interaction of walking, flying, grassy, and tree-like (creatures), the responding movements of animals and plants are made complete" (11a.1-2).

Thus, for Shao Yung, the two main categories of living creatures are animals and plants. The former are in turn divided into those that walk and those that fly; the latter into grassy plants (which, for the Chinese, mean all annual plants), and tree-like plants (which include the perennials). Every living creature, furthermore, has its own nature, feelings, form or shape, and the physical substance or matter that constitutes this form. These various categories and qualities arise in response to the "transforming" and "evolutionary" activities of Heaven and Earth.

iv. *Men and the Sage*

Of all living creatures, man is the most intelligent, and among men, he of most perfect goodness is the sage (*sheng*). Shao writes in his *Observation of Things* (Pt. I):

"Man, too, is a creature (like other creatures), and the sage, too, is a man (like other men). ... But man is the most perfect of creatures, and the sage is the most perfect of men. ... How is this? It means that he (the sage) is a person able by means of his own single mind to observe a myriad other minds, by means of his own single body to observe a myriad other bodies, by means of a single (external) object to observe a myriad other objects, and by means of a single generation to observe a myriad other generations. It also means that he is one able with his mind to represent the meaning of Heaven, with his mouth to represent the words of Heaven, with his hands to represent the labors of Heaven, and with his body to represent the functions of Heaven. It means too that he is one able to possess knowledge of the seasons of Heaven above, to have a complete grasp of the principles of Earth below and, between these, to have a complete grasp of the qualities of things, and to comprehend clearly the affairs of men. In addition, it means that he is one able to supplement and carry onward (the activities of) Heaven and Earth, to come and go with creative and transforming influence, to pass to and fro between past and present, and to reach the inner and outer aspects of current affairs" (11a.4).

The sage is able to do all this because of his capacity to "observe things in terms of those things." Shao writes again (Pt. I):

"What I mean by the observation of things does not mean observing them with the eye. No, it is not observation with the eye, but observation with the mind. Nor is it observation with the mind, but observation of them in the light of their own Principles. [1] There is no creature in the world that does not have its own Principle (*li*), nature (*hsing*), and Destiny (*ming*). What I mean by Principle is something that can be known only after it has been plumbed to its depths. What I mean by nature is something that can be known only after it has been completely penetrated. What I mean by Destiny is something that can be known only after (our minds) have reached it. [2] These three kinds of knowledge are the real knowledge of the world, and even the sage cannot go beyond them. Anyone who tries to go beyond them is not what I call a sage. . . .

"The sage's ability thus to synthesize the qualities of all things lies in his ability to observe objectively. [3] By such objective observation I mean an observation of things not made in terms of self, by which I mean the observation of things in terms of those things themselves. When one is thus able to observe things in terms of those things, how can the self then be interposed between them? Thus I know that I, too, am like other men, that other men, too, are like me, and that I and other men are all equally creatures.

"In this way one acquires the ability to use the eyes of the entire world as one's own eyes, with which eyes there is nothing that is not observed; to use the ears of the entire world as one's own ears, with which ears there is nothing that is not heard; to use the mouths of the entire world as one's own mouth, with which mouth there is

---

[1] *Li*, the metaphysical principles that, according to Neo-Confucianism‘ underlie all physical things of the universe. See above, p. 444. — Tr.

[2] These three sentences are reminiscent of the *Book of Changes* (Appen. V, p. 422): "They plumbed Principle to its depths and completely penetrated the nature, thereby reaching to (an understanding of) Destiny." — Tr.

[3] Lit., "to observe in a reversed manner" (*fan kuan* 反 觀), i.e., as pointed out below, not to observe from the usual standpoint of self, but from that of other creatures. — Tr.

nothing that is not spoken; to use the minds of the entire world as one's own mind, with which mind there is nothing that is not deliberated upon.

"Is not such world-wide observation broad in perception? Is not such world-wide listening far-reaching in hearing? Is not such world-wide speech lofty in discussion? And is not such world-wide deliberation great in bringing happiness? He whose perception is so broad, hearing so far-reaching, discussion so lofty, and capacity to bring happiness so great; who is able to accomplish such broad, far-reaching, lofty, and great things, without interposing a single forced action in their midst—can he not be said to have the utmost spirituality and to be the highest sage?" (11b.16-17).

Thus the sage, by denying the ego and giving free play to other creatures, is able to reach a position in which, to quote the *Lao-tzŭ* (chap. 48), he "does nothing, yet there is nothing that is not done" (*wu wei erh wu pu wei*). Here we find Shao expressing a doctrine that goes back to early Taoism.

This denial of ego and giving free play to other creatures should also be practiced by the ordinary individual who wishes to cultivate his moral nature. We read in the following passages (Pt. IIb):

"To observe things in terms of those things: this is to follow one's nature (*hsing*). But to observe things in terms of the self: this is to follow one's feelings (*ch'ing*). The nature is impartial and enlightened; the feelings are partial and blind" (12b.3).

"To give free play to the self leads to the feelings; these feelings lead to obscuring; such obscuring leads to benightedness. But to accord oneself with other beings leads to the nature; this nature leads to spirituality; such spirituality leads to enlightenment" (*ibid.*, p. 2).

"When the mind is single and undivided, it can then respond undeviatingly to the myriad kinds of phenomena.[1] This is why the superior man causes his mind to be 'vacuous' (*hsü*) and unmoving" (*ibid.*, p. 5).

"To rejoice at things from the viewpoint of those things, and to grieve for things from the viewpoint of those things: these are manifestations that conform to the mean" (*ibid.*, p. 1).

---

[1] The words, "myriad kinds of phenomena" (*wan pien* 萬 變), are added from the reading found in other editions of the *Observation of Things*, which, however, lack the term "undeviatingly" (*fu wei* 弗 違) found here. — Tr.

"When practicing study so as to nurture the mind, the calamity lies in not following the straightforward Way, nor ridding oneself of desire for profit. If one follows the straightforward Way, giving free play to sincerity (*ch'eng*), one will then come to comprehend all things. The Way of Heaven and Earth is nothing else but that of straightforwardness, and must be sought for through such straightforwardness. But if one uses a knowledge which calculates (the personal profit of a course of action), and follows (circuitous) bypaths to seek for it, this results in a forcible twisting of (the Way of) Heaven and Earth, and the giving in to human desires. Is it not distressing?" (*ibid.*, p. 17).

These passages help to explain what is meant by "observing things in terms of those things." It means that we should feel joy or sorrow toward those things that are fitting objects of such joy or sorrow respectively; that our nature, when activated in conduct, should be allowed to express itself in the quality of straightforwardness (*chih*); and that our mind should become "vacuous" and unmoving. Chou Tun-yi expresses the same idea when he says (see above, p. 448): "Absence of desire results in vacuity when in quiescence, and straightforwardness when in movement."

Yet mankind, unfortunately, does not consist of sages only, for evil men, too, necessarily exist. Shao Yung writes (Pt. I):

"Heaven and man are to each other as the inner and outer sides (of a garment). In Heaven there are the *yin* and *yang*, and among men there are the correct and the depraved. As to whether such correctness and depravity are to come into being, this depends on the likes of the ruler. When the ruler likes virtue, the people conduct themselves correctly, but when the ruler likes speciousness, the people conduct themselves depravedly. This is the source of correctness and depravity. Even when there is a sage-ruler above, however, there cannot but be a few mean men. Nevertheless, it is then more difficult for them to act as mean men. Also even when there is a mediocre ruler above, there cannot but be a few superior men. Nevertheless, it is then more difficult for them to act as superior men.

"Since antiquity, there has never been an age like that of Yao for sagely rule. How many, indeed, were the superior men then! It was not an age in which mean men were completely lacking, but one in which they found it difficult to act as mean men. Hence its superior men were numerous. Although, therefore, there were then also the

'four miscreants,' they found it impossible to diffuse their evil. [1]
Also since antiquity there has never been an age like that of Chou
of the Shang for mediocre rule. How many, indeed, were the mean
men then! It was not an age in which superior men were completely
lacking, but one in which they found it difficult to act as superior
men. Hence its mean men were numerous. Although, therefore,
there were then also the 'three men of perfect virtue,' they found it
impossible to make their goodness effective" [2] (11b.1-2).

Thus though evil men cannot be completely eliminated from
the world, they can, under a sage-ruler, at least be kept out of influential positions and thus rendered comparatively ineffective.

v. *Cosmological Chronology*

Shao writes in his *Observation of Things* (Pt. IIb):

"When the numbers of the *Changes* reach the end (of their evolution), Heaven and Earth complete a cycle. It may be asked: 'Do
Heaven and Earth, then, also pass through a cycle (like other things)?'
I reply: 'Since growth and decay exist (for all things), why should
they not have such a cycle? Although Heaven and Earth are large,
they too consist of form and matter (*ch'i*), and thus constitute two
objects' " (12b.18).

We have seen earlier how all things of the universe undergo the
selfsame cycle of growth and decay, following the pattern laid down
in Shao's circular diagram of the sixty-four hexagrams. And since
Heaven and Earth, despite their greater size, are but physical objects
like any other, they too must conform to this pattern. The greater
part of Shao's *Huang-chi Ching-shih* or *Cosmological Chronology* consists
of a chronological table illustrative of the resulting cycle through
which the world must pass. In it, periods of time are expressed in
terms of what he calls *yüan* 元 (Cycles), *hui* 會 (Epochs), *yün* 運
(Revolutions), and *shih* 世 (Generations). Shao writes in his *Ob-*

---

[1] These "four miscreants" (*ssŭ hsiung* 四 凶) were evildoers of the age
of Yao, variously enumerated in different texts, around whom a considerable
amount of mythology has gathered. — Tr.

[2] These "three men of perfect virtue" (*san jen* 三 仁) were nobles and
statesmen who lived under the rule of Chou, tyrannical last king of the Shang
dynasty, and who valiantly, but vainly, attempted to turn him from his de-
bauches. — Tr.

servation of Things (Pt. I): "The course of the sun constitutes Heaven's Cycle (*yüan*); that of the moon constitutes Heaven's Epoch (*hui*); that of the stars constitutes Heaven's Revolution (*yün*); that of the zodiacal spaces constitutes Heaven's Generation (*shih*)" (11b.8). Thus these periods of time seem to be regarded as in some manner associated with the various heavenly bodies. [1]

The relationship of the periods to one another is as follows: 12 Generations = 1 Revolution; 30 Revolutions = 1 Epoch; 12 Epochs = 1 Cycle. For the explanation of these ratios, we must turn to a statement by Shao's son, Shao Po-wen (1057-1134), who writes: "In the great evolutionary flux, one Cycle is like a year." [2] Extending this correlation, it is evident that the twelve Epochs in a Cycle are analogous to the twelve months of a year, the thirty Revolutions in an Epoch to the thirty days of a month, and the twelve Generations in a Revolution to the twelve two-hour periods into which the Chinese have traditionally divided their day. By Cycle, Shao Yung means the space of time required for the physical universe to pass through one complete revolution of growth and decay. To the smallest of his time units, the Generation, he assigns a duration, in ordinary time, of thirty years. Taking this correlation as a basis, we arrive at the following formula: 1 Cycle = 12 Epochs = 360 Revolutions = 4,320 Generations = 129,600 years.

By equating his Generation with a span of thirty years in the ordinary time scale, it is possible for Shao to maintain, throughout the smaller time units, the alternation between the numbers 12 and 30 established by him in the case of the Epoch, Revolution, etc. Thus as the complete sequence we have: 1 Cycle = 12 Epochs; 1 Epoch = 30 Revolutions; 1 Revolution = 12 Generations; 1 Generation = 30 years; 1 year = 12 months; 1 month = 30 days; 1 day = 12 two-hour periods. [3]

---

[1] It should be noted, however, that this association is entirely arbitrary, since the duration of Shao's Cycles, Epochs, etc., has absolutely nothing to do with the actual duration of the revolutions of the sun, moon, etc. On the "zodiacal spaces," see above, p. 456, note 1. — Tr.

[2] Quoted in the *Hsing-li Ta-ch'üan*, 8.13. The sentence occurs in Shao Po-wen's commentary, immediately following the chronological chart which is reproduced below in the present work.

[3] It may be added that a Chinese *shih* or "generation" has traditionally been regarded as consisting of 30 years. The ideograph *shih* 卅, in fact, consists of the ideograph for "ten," *shih* 十, thrice repeated and combined into a single character. — Tr.

If we now coordinate Shao's Cycle with the pattern of evolution portrayed in his circular diagram of the sixty-four hexagrams, we find that he conceives of the world as coming into being with hexagram 24, and reaching its end with hexagram 2. Because of the length and complexity of the original table (contained in his *Cosmological Chronology*), we must content ourselves with the simplified version prepared by his son, Shao Po-wen: [1]

Table of Cosmic Chronology

Sun Cycle	Moon Epoch	Star Revolutions	Zodiacal Generations	Years	Hexagram	Events
1st (*Chia*)	1st (*Tzŭ*)	1- 30	1- 360	1- 10,800	24	
	2nd (*Ch'ou*)	31- 60	361- 720	10,801- 21,600	19	
	3rd (*Yin*)	61- 90	721- 1,080	21,601- 32,400	11	Star Revolution 76 (*Chi*): Beginning of creatures
	4th (*Mao*)	91- 120	1,081- 1,440	32,401- 43,200	34	
	5th (*Ch'en*)	121- 150	1,441- 1,800	43,201- 54,000	43	
	6th (*Ssŭ*)	151- 180	1,801- 2,160	54,001- 64,800	1	Star Revolution 180 (*Kuei*); Zodiacal Generation 2,157: Rule of Yao
	7th (*Wu*)	181- 210	2,161- 2,520	64,801- 75,600	44	Dynasties of Hsia, Yin, Chou, Ch'in, Two Han, Two Chin, Three Kingdoms, N. & S. Dynasties, Sui, T'ang, Five Dynasties, Sung
	8th (*Wei*)	211- 240	2,521- 2,280	75,601- 86,400	33	

[1] Contained in the *Hsing-li Ta-ch'üan*, 8.12.

Sun Cycle	Moon Epoch	Star Revo- lutions	Zodiacal Gener- ation	Years	Hexa- gram	Events
	9th (*Shen*)	241- 270	2,881- 3,240	86,401- 97,200	12 ䷋	
	10th (*Yu*)	271- 300	3,241- 3,600	97,201- 108,000	20 ䷓	
	11th (*Hsü*)	301- 330	3,601- 3,960	108,001- 118,800	23 ䷖	Star Revolution 315 (*Wu*): Ending of Creatures
	12th (*Hai*)	331- 360	3,961- 4,320	118,801- 129,600	2 ䷁	

Chia, the designation of the Sun Cycle, is the first of the ten "heavenly stems," traditionally used for chronological purposes (and also, in the column labelled "Events," used to designate the Star Revolutions). In the same way, the twelve "earthly branches," *tzŭ, ch'ou, yin*, etc., are used to designate the Moon Epochs (and also, though not in the table itself, the Zodiacal Generations). Chu Hsi, interpreting the table, explains that "Heaven came into being in *tzŭ* (Epoch 1), Earth came into being in *ch'ou* (Epoch 2), and man was born in *yin* (Epoch 3)." [1] Epoch 1 is that in which the *yang* principle first begins to appear in the universe, as symbolized by the single undivided *yang* line at the bottom of hexagram 24. We have already seen (p. 461) that in terms of the cycle of the year, this hexagram represents the *tzŭ* or eleventh month (marking the beginning of the astronomical year). In terms of a daily cycle, it would correspond to the two-hour period 11 p.m.-1 a.m.

In the second Epoch, with which Earth first comes into being, a further growth of the *yang* is symbolized by the two undivided lines at the bottom of hexagram 19. In terms of the year it corresponds to the *ch'ou* or twelfth month, and in terms of the day to the two-hour period of 1-3 a.m.

The third Epoch (designated by the cyclical character *yin*) is that of "the beginning of creatures," including man; this is why

---

[1] Cf. his commentary, quoted in the *Hsing-li Ta-ch'üan, loc. cit.* — Tr.

Chu Hsi says that "man was born in *yin*." In this Epoch there is a further growth of the *yang*, symbolized by hexagram 11 (with three *yang* lines below). The corresponding times in the year and day are those of the *yin* or first month, and the two-hour period of 3-5 a.m.

Continuing the same process, we come to the sixth Epoch, in which the *yang*, as symbolized by hexagram 1 (six *yang* lines), reaches its apogee. It is also the golden age of mankind, marked by the rule of the legendary Yao, which occurred in the 2,157th Generation of the 180th Revolution, counting from the beginning of the table.

With the following Epochs, however, a gradual decline sets in, marked by the decrease of the *yang* and appearance of the *yin*, as symbolized by the single divided *yin* line at the bottom of hexagram 44 in Epoch 7. Equated with human history, the fifteenth year of the 2,270th Generation of the 190th Revolution in this Epoch corresponds to the first year of Emperor Shen-tsung of the Sung dynasty (A.D. 1068), the reign during which Shao Yung compiled his table. Using this year as a base figure, the year 1931 (during which the present book is being written) would belong to the 2,299th Generation of the 192nd Revolution in this same Epoch. In terms of the year, the Epoch would correspond to the fifth month, and in terms of the day to a little more than 11:20 a.m.

In the following Epochs the *yin* continues to grow and the *yang* to diminish, until with the eleventh Epoch there is only one *yang* line remaining at the top of hexagram 23. It is during the 315th Revolution of this Epoch that the "ending of creatures" takes place; in other words, all life in the world comes to an end. Finally, the twelfth Epoch sees the *yin* reign supreme, as symbolized by hexagram 2 (consisting of six *yin* lines). At this time the entire present world will come to an end. It will then be replaced by a new one, which, after passing through an identical cycle, will be followed by still others. [1]

The idea that the world will some day be destroyed, thereafter to be replaced by a new world, is quite alien to traditional Chinese

---

[1] Equated with Western chronology, Shao's table begins in 67,017 B.C.; the 76th Revolution, when living creatures came into existence, lasted 40,017-39,657 B.C.; the 2,157th Generation, in which the rule of Yao occurred, lasted 2337-2307 B.C. (Yao's traditional dates are 2357-2256); the 315th Revolution, when living creatures are to come to an end, will be that of A.D. 46,023-46,383; the entire world will come to an end in A.D. 62,583. In the paragraphs discussing Shao's table, I have somewhat modified and abbreviated the author's original text. — Tr.

thought. In Buddhism, however, there is a theory—common also to other schools of Indian philosophy—that the world is ever passing through a recurring sequence of four *kalpas* or world-periods: those of formation, existence, destruction, and non-existence. This concept came to exert a marked influence upon all Neo-Confucian theories of cosmic evolution—most conspicuously so in the case of Shao Yung. In him, however, it is given a Confucian touch by being expounded in terms of the growth and decay of the *yin* and *yang*, as represented by the sixty-four hexagrams of the *Book of Changes*.

vi. *Political Philosophy*

From the preceding remarks it is evident that the present world, though far from its ultimate destruction, has nevertheless already passed through its most glorious epoch. As it exists today, it is like a fully opened flower, still magnificent, yet bearing signs of coming decay. This, moreover, not only applies to the physical world, but that of human government as well. Such government is classified by Shao Yung into four main categories: that of the Sovereign (*huang* 皇), of the Emperor (*ti* 帝), of the King (*wang* 王), and of the Tyrant (in the Greek sense) or Lord-Protector (*pa* 霸 or *po* 伯). [1] Thus he writes in his *Observation of Things* (Pt. IIb):

"He who (in his government) employs the principle of non-activity (*wu wei*) is a Sovereign; who employs kindliness and good faith is an Emperor; who employs justice and correctness is a King; who employs scheming and force is a Tyrant. (Government) below that of the Tyrant is one of barbarians, and that below the barbarians is one of beasts" (12b.13). Again (Pt. I):

"Confucius interpreted the *Changes*, which began with Hsi and Hsien. [2] He put in order the *Book of History*, which began with Yao

---

[1] This classification is based on the traditional account of Chinese history, according to which China was first ruled by the Three Sovereigns (variously enumerated), then by the Five Emperors (for one list, see vol. I, p. xxxvi), and then by the Three Kings (founders of the first three dynasties, Hsia, Shang, and Chou). Finally, with the decay of Chou royal power during the Spring and Autumn Period (722-481 B.C.), certain of the feudal lords (traditionally five) took for themselves the title of *Pa*, "Tyrant" or "Lord-Protector," in a vain attempt to maintain order. See vol. 1, p. 112, note 1. — Tr.

[2] I.e., Fu Hsi (Subduer of Animals) and Huang-ti (the Yellow Emperor). Hsien is an abbreviation for Hsien-yüan, reputedly the name of the hill where the Yellow Emperor lived, and therefore sometimes used as his appellation.

and Shun. He revised the *Odes*, which began with (Kings) Wen and Wu. He corrected the *Spring and Autumn Annals*, which began with (Dukes) Huan and Wen. [1]

"He began (the *Changes*) with Hsi and Hsien because he regarded the Three Sovereigns as 'grandfathers.' He began (the *Book of History*) with Yao and Shun because he regarded the Five Emperors as 'fathers.' He began (the *Odes*) with Wen and Wu because he regarded the Three Kings as 'sons.' He began (the *Spring and Autumn Annals*) with Huan and Wen because he regarded the Five Tyrants as 'grandsons' " [2] (11a.14). And yet again (Pt. I):

"The Three Sovereigns correspond to spring, the Five Emperors to summer, the Three Kings to autumn, and the Five Tyrants to winter. The Seven States correspond to the coldest continuation of that winter. [3] The (rulers of the) Han (dynasty) were in the category of Kings, but fell somewhat short (of the original Kings); those of the Chin were in the category of Tyrants, but were somewhat superior (to the original Tyrants); those of the Three Kingdoms were the more able of the Tyrants; those of the Sixteen States were the more petty of the Tyrants; [4] those of the Southern Five Dynasties were mere borrowers of the chariots of the Tyrants; those of the Northern Five Dynasties were mere sojourners in the dwellings of the Tyrants. [5] Those of the Sui were the 'sons' of those of the Chin, and those of the T'ang were the 'younger brothers' of those of the Han. The Tyrants of the commanderies of the end of the Sui were the last feeble waves of the Yangtze or Han rivers; those of the military posts of the end of the T'ang were the last expiring gleams of the sun or moon; those of the Five Dynasties were the lingering stars before sunrise. [6]

"From Emperor Yao until today there have been more than

---

[1] Dukes Huan of Ch'i (685-643) and Wen of Chin (635-628) were the two chief *Pa* or Tyrants of the Spring and Autumn period. — Tr.

[2] The terms "grandfather," "father," etc., are intended to indicate the diminishing respect with which Confucius regarded these various groups of rulers. — Tr.

[3] These were the seven leading feudal states of the Warring States period (403-221 B.C.). — Tr.

[4] The Sixteen States were a series of short-lived dynasties ruled by non-Chinese peoples who invaded North China during the Chin dynasty (A.D. 265-419). — Tr.

[5] The Northern and Southern Five Dynasties were those of the fifth and sixth centuries, ruled by non-Chinese and Chinese houses in North and South China respectively. — Tr.

[6] "Sunrise" here refers to the coming of Shao's own dynasty, the Sung. — Tr.

3,000 years, covering, from beginning to end, more than one hundred generations, for which clear records are provided by transmitted writings. During this time, within the four seas and among (China's) nine domains, there has sometimes been unity and sometimes division, sometimes good order and sometimes disorder, sometimes strictness and sometimes laxity, sometimes leadership and sometimes a mere following of others. But never yet has there been anyone who could give a (real) unity to its manners and customs for a period of more than one generation" (11b.10-11).

Thus of all the rulers from the Han dynasty onward, even the best have been nothing more than "Kings who fell somewhat short." It is evident that for Shao Yung the world's golden age has already long since passed away.

CHAPTER XII

CHANG TSAI AND THE CH'ENG BROTHERS

1—CHANG TSAI

Almost contemporary with, though slightly later than, Chou Tun-yi and Shao Yung, there lived another group of noted Neo-Confucianists, consisting of Chang Tsai (1020-77) and the Ch'eng brothers: Ch'eng Hao (1032-85) and Ch'eng Yi (1033-1108). Chang's biography in the *Sung Shih* reads in part as follows:

"Chang Tsai 張載, styled Tzŭ-hou 子厚, was a native of Ch'ang-an. [1] As a youth he delighted in discussing military matters.... When in his twenty-first year, he introduced himself through a letter to Fan Chung-yen, who as soon as he saw him realized that he had uncommon ability. [2] By way of warning, (Fan) then said to him: 'Since the scholar has morals and institutions in which to find his pleasure, why should he concern himself with military matters?' [3] And with this he encouraged him to read the *Doctrine of the Mean*. (Chang) Tsai read this book, yet found it not wholly satisfactory. So he turned his attention to Buddhism and Taoism, into whose doctrines he delved for several successive years. Yet here too he failed to acquire the (desired) understanding, so again he turned from them to the Six Classics (of Confucianism).... Having discoursed with the two Ch'engs about the important principles of Neo-Confucianism, [4] he came to acquire self-confidence and said: 'This Truth of ours is self-sufficient. What need, then, to search elsewhere?' And with this he completely discarded his heterodox learning and accepted orthodoxy.... (Chang) Tsai studied antiquity and vigorously practiced it, becoming the leading teacher among the scholars 'within the

---

[1] The present city of Sian in Shensi. Actually, however, he was born in the Sung capital, the present Kaifeng in Honan, though he left it when very young. See Eichhorn (work cited on p. 478, note 2, below), p. 2, note 4. — Tr.

[2] Fan Chung-yen (989-1052) was a prominent official and scholar. — Tr.

[3] On "morals and institutions" (*ming chiao*) as a synonym for Confucianism, see chap. 5, p. 170. — Tr.

[4] Lit., *Tao Hsüeh*, "Study of the Truth." — Tr.

pass.' [1] By the people of his generation he was referred to as Master Heng-ch'ü" [2] (427.14-16).

From Lü Ta-lin (died ca. 1090) we learn that Chang died in the tenth year of the Hsi-ning period (1077), and that he was the author of three important works: the *Cheng Meng* or *Correct Discipline for Beginners* (hereafter cited as *Discipline for Beginners*), the *Ching-hsüeh Li-k'u* (Assembled Principles of Classical Learning), and the *Yi Shuo* (Comments on the Book of Changes). Concerning the first and philosophically most significant of these, Lü writes: "In the autumn of the ninth year of the Hsi-ning period (1076), the Master (Chang Tsai) experienced a strange dream and hastily wrote to his students to tell them about it. He then compiled what he had said, and the result was called the *Correct Discipline for Beginners*. Showing it to his students, he said: 'This writing is the product of my applied thought over many years. Its doctrines, it may be hoped, are in accord with those of the former sages.' " [3] Thus this work, produced in the year before Chang's death, is the crystallization of his entire lifetime of philosophic thought.

i. *The Ether*

Chang Tsai's philosophy, like that of Chou Tun-yi and Shao Yung, takes as its point of departure certain ideas in the *Book of Changes*. Thus on the famous passage in that work (Appen. III, p. 373): "In the *Changes* there is the Supreme Ultimate (*t'ai chi*), which produced the Two Forms (the *yin* and *yang*)," he comments in his *Discipline for Beginners* (chap. 1):

---

[1] A designation for the present Shensi province. — Tr.

[2] 橫 渠 , name of a place some seventeen miles east of the present Mei 眉阝 hsien in Shensi, where Chang spent his later years. For more details about his life, see J. Percy Bruce, *Chu Hsi and His Masters* (London, 1923), pp. 50-55, and especially Werner Eichhorn, "Die Westinschrift der Chang Tsai," *Abhandlungen für die Kunde des Morgenlandes*, vol. 22, no. 7 (Leipzig, 1937), pp. 1-9. From these we learn that most of his life was spent in teaching, though he also held several positions in the government, one of which was abruptly terminated when he came in conflict with the noted reformer statesman, Wang An-shih (1021-86). He was an uncle of the Ch'eng brothers, and a turning point in his life was his meeting with them in 1056, alluded to in the *Sung Shih* passage just quoted, as a result of which he was converted to their point of view. At his death he was so poor that his disciples had to defray the cost of his coffin. — Tr.

[3] Cited in the *Yi-lo Yüan-yüan Lu* (Record of Origins from Yi-lo), 6.53-57. [This work, completed in 1173 under Chu Hsi's direction, is a major source for Neo-Confucianism prior to Chu Hsi. — Tr.]

"If the two are not established, the one cannot become visible, and if the one cannot become visible, the functions of the two come to an end. The (Supreme Ultimate's) embodiments are those of vacuity (*hsü*) and solidity (*shih* 實), of movement (*tung*) and quiescence (*ching*), of condensation (*chü* 聚) and dispersion (*san* 散), of purity (*ch'ing* 清) and turbidness (*cho* 濁). But in the final analysis they may be reduced to one" (2.9).

By this "one" Chang means the Supreme Ultimate, i.e., the transcendent first cause through which all things come to be. Thus he writes in his *Yi Shuo*:

"When there are the two, there is the one, which is the Supreme Ultimate. . . . Though single itself, it yet has dual embodiment. Is this not the Supreme Ultimate?" (3.11).

Sometimes Chang describes this "one" as the "Great Harmony" (*t'ai ho* 太和). In the first chapter of the *Discipline for Beginners*, he speaks of the "Great Harmony" as the equivalent of the *Tao* or Way, which is itself a common Neo-Confucian synonym for the Supreme Ultimate:

"The Great Harmony is known as the *Tao*. Because in it there are the interacting qualities of floating and sinking, rising and falling, movement and quiescence, therefore there are engendered in it the beginnings of the emanating forces which agitate one another, overcome or are overcome by one another, and contract or expand, one with relation to the other. . . . What does not have these emanations of 'wandering air' cannot be called the Great Harmony. Those who speak about the *Tao*, can only after knowing this be said to know the *Tao*, and those who study the *Changes*, can only after seeing this be said to see the *Changes*" (2.2-3).

"Wandering air" [1] is a term derived from the *Chuang-tzŭ* (chap. 1): "There is the wandering air (*yeh ma*); there are the motes; there are living things that blow one against another with their breath" (p. 1). Ssŭ-ma Piao (died A.D. 306) explains in his commentary on this: " 'Wandering air' means the drifting ether which forms in springtime in the midst of marshes."

Here we have a reference to that same *ch'i* 氣 or "ether" (lit., "gas") which has already been repeatedly mentioned in this book,

---

[1] *Yeh ma* 野馬, lit., "wild horses," but, as will be seen directly, the words have an entirely different meaning here. — Tr.

and which is a key concept in Chang's philosophy. The term "Great Harmony," as used by him, seems to be a generalized designation for this Ether in all its aspects. [1] Sometimes, however, it is dispersed and uncondensed, and is then invisible to the human eye. To describe it in this state, therefore, Chang uses another special term, "Great Void" (*t'ai hsü* 太 虛). For example, he writes: "The Great Void in which no shapes exist: such is the Ether in its original essence" (*ibid.*, p. 3). Or again:

"The (visible) Ether's condensation from and dispersion into the Great Void is like ice's freezing from and melting into water. Once we realize that the Great Void is the same as the (visible) Ether, (we may then realize that) there is no non-existence (*wu*)" (*ibid.*, pp. 6-7).

What Chang means by this is that the "Great Void," though seemingly completely empty, is not in actual fact utterly devoid of substance, for an absolute vacuum is inconceivable in the universe. As Chang himself puts it: "There is no non-existence." The term "Great Void," therefore, is used simply to describe the Ether when, being dispersed and uncondensed, it is therefore imperceptible, even though still existent.

When Chang says of the Ether that "in it there are the interacting qualities of floating and sinking, rising and falling, movement and quiescence," he has in mind the two modes of the *yin* and *yang*. The existence of these two modes within the single Ether causes him to write as follows in the *Discipline for Beginners* (chap. 2):

"What constitutes a single object, yet has two embodiments, is the Ether. Being single, it has spirituality (*shen*); being dual, it has transforming force (*hua* 化)" (2.11).

In its state of undifferentiated singleness the Ether "is pure, all-pervasive, and has no image, so that it has spirituality" (*ibid.*, pp. 1-2). Yet because the two modes of the *yin* and *yang* are also present, "therefore there are engendered in it the beginnings of the emanating forces which agitate one another, overcome or are overcome by one another, and contract or expand, one with relation to

---

[1] The philosophical use of the word *ch'i*, "ether," goes back to Mencius, who speaks about the *hao jan chih ch'i* or "all-embracing force." See vol. 1, p. 131. As used in Neo-Confucianism, *ch'i* is a designation for: (a) the undifferentiated ether or matter from which the universe is formed; (b) this same matter as differentiated in individual objects after the formation of an organized universe. Because of its great importance in Neo-Confucianism, the word Ether will hereafter be capitalized. — Tr.

the other." It is these emanations and interactions of the *yin* and *yang* which cause the Ether to condense and thus form the concrete objects of the physical universe. This is the reason for Chang's statement that "being dual, it has transforming force." He writes further:

"Vast and unseeable is the Ether as the Great Void. (Yet) it rises and falls and spreads about, never stopping for a moment. Is not this what the *Changes* speaks of as 'emanation'?[1] Or what Chuang Tzŭ describes as the 'wandering air' which living creatures blow one against another with their breath? Herein lie the pivots of vacuity and solidity, movement and quiescence, and the beginnings of the *yin* and *yang*, and of hardness and softness. The pure elements of the *yang* rise upward, while the turbid elements of the *yin* sink downward. Their interaction, condensation, and dispersion result in wind, rain, snow, and frost. Whether it be the myriad categories (of things) in their changing configurations, or the mountains and streams in their fixed forms, the dregs of wine, or the ashes of fire, there is nothing that does not (conform to) these principles" (*ibid.*, p. 5).

Because the interacting *yin* and *yang* modes are always potentially present, the Ether cannot remain permanently inert as the Great Void. There must be a time when it "rises and falls and spreads about, never stopping for a moment," and when its "emanating forces agitate one another," sometimes overcoming and sometimes being overcome, one by the other; sometimes expanding and sometimes contracting. The condensation of the Ether results in the formation of objects that are visible to the human eye; its dispersion results in their disappearance. Chang writes:

"When the Ether condenses, its visibility becomes apparent so that there are then the shapes (of individual things). But when it does not condense, its visibility is no longer apparent so that there are then no shapes. At the time of its condensation, can one say otherwise than that this is but temporary? But at the time of its dispersion, can one hastily say that it is then non-existent? Hence the sage, as he gazes aloft or looks below, only says that he understands the causes of visibility and invisibility.[2] He does not say that he understands the causes of being and non-being" (*ibid.*, p. 6).

---

[1] Cf. Appen. III, p. 393: "Heaven and Earth have their emanations." — Tr.

[2] An echo of what the *Book of Changes* (Appen. III, p. 353) says about the sage: "Gazing aloft..., he contemplates the brilliant phenomena of Heaven, and looking down, examines the markings on Earth. Thus he knows the causes of visibility and invisibility." — Tr.

In other words, the condensation of the Ether results in the appearance of visible shapes; with its dispersion, these shapes disappear. Because these phases of condensation and dispersion are fluctuating and unstable, the physical shapes resulting from them are likewise "temporary." That is why Chang says further: "The Great Void in which no shapes exist: such is the Ether in its original essence. But as it (momentarily) condenses and (momentarily) disperses, this results in the changing evolutions of temporary shapes" (*ibid.*, p. 3).

ii. *Orderly Sequence of Things in the Universe*

The formation of physical things through the condensation of the Ether proceeds according to a fixed pattern, which the *Discipline for Beginners* (chap. 5) describes as follows:

"In the process of production, some (things) come first and some afterward. This is Heaven's sequence. In the interrelationship and assumption of shape (by those things), some are small and some large, some lofty and some lowly. This is Heaven's orderliness. The production of things by Heaven has its sequence; the assumption of shape by these things has its orderliness" (3.2).

Again (chap. 1):

"Though the condensation and dispersion of the Ether of the universe pushes forward along a hundred different roads, its Principle (*li*) (for so doing) is orderly and real" (2.3).

Thus all things coming into being as the result of the "condensation and dispersion of the ether," do so, despite their infinite variety, according to a fixed sequence or pattern—described by Chang in one passage as "Heaven's sequence" or "Heaven's orderliness," but in the other identified more specifically as *li* or Principle. It is this *li* that prevents the creative process from proceeding haphazardly. What Chang seems to be implying here, though he does not say so explicitly, is that in order to have an organized universe, not only must the *ch'i* or Ether be present, but also something which he calls *li* or Principle. Formulated in Greek philosophical terminology, *ch'i* is matter, *li* is form, and the imposition of form upon matter is what makes possible the coming to be of concrete particular objects. *Li*, commonly translated in the present work as "Principle," was to become one of the most important terms in Neo-Confucianism. Its full significance, however, was developed only by Chu Hsi, and by Chang Tsai it was touched on only sketchily.

iii. *Some Universal Phenomena*

Once we accept the thesis that the condensation and dispersion of the Ether is not arbitrary but follows a definite pattern, it becomes possible, despite the seeming diversity of the universe, to detect in it certain types of phenomena which are universal and fixed. We read in the *Discipline for Beginners* (chap. 1):

"In its original state of vacuity, the Ether is tranquil and shapeless. But when it becomes activated and productive, it condenses to form semblances (*hsiang* 象). When there is such a semblance, there must also be its opposite; each of these always acts counter to what is done (by the other). This counter-action results in antagonism, but the antagonism always leads to harmonization and dissipation (of the antagonism). Thus the feelings of love and hate are both equally products of the Great Void, and eventually form part of the material desires. Abruptly they appear, and as suddenly they reach their conclusion, without the lapse of even a moment. How spirit-like this is!" (2.10).

Through the interaction of the *yin* and *yang*, the Ether becomes activated and condenses to form "semblances," i.e., concrete objects. For each such object, however, there always exists another to which it is diametrically opposed. The opposition between the two results in antagonism. But though mutually opposed, such objects also serve to complement or balance one another, and with the dispersion of the Ether, the opposed objects themselves revert to the Great Void— a phenomenon described by Chang as "harmonization and dissipation." The mutual opposition of two things results in hatred; their mutual complementing in love. Such hatred and love, etc.—called by Chang the "material desires" (*wu yü* 物 欲)—are, whether good or bad, all equally products of the Great Void, to which they must eventually return. Here is one of the universal phenomena of the world.

Chang writes further (chap. 5): "It is a Principle that nothing can exist independently in itself. Anything, unless it displays itself by resembling or differing (from other things), by contracting or expanding, or by passing through a beginning and an end, is not (really) a thing, even though it (seem to) be one. To attain completion, (a thing) must have a beginning and end. Unless it undergoes modifications caused by its similarity to and difference from (other things), and by (its seeming phases of) being and non-being, it cannot attain this state of completion. And unless it can attain completion, it is not (really) a thing, even though it (seem to) be one. Hence the statement: 'It is by the interaction of contraction and expansion that advantage is produced' " [1] (3.2).

Thus the existence of any given object requires the existence of an opposite. Indeed, the very fact that a thing is a thing, and can thereby "display itself," depends, in part, upon its relationship with other things. Another universal law of phenomenon, therefore, is that no one thing can exist in absolute isolation from other things.

Chang also writes (chap. 1): "Among created things, there is no one exactly alike. From this it may be known that despite the numerousness of all things, there is actually no one of them in which the *yin* and *yang* are not present. And from this we may understand that the transforming activities of Heaven and Earth lie in these two principles and nothing else" (2.10).

Here we find the formulation of another universal principle: "Among created things, there is no one exactly alike." Chang comments further: "The drifting Ether, in its multitudinous activities, unites to form concrete things, thus producing men and objects in infinite variety. The ceaseless circulation through them of its two *yin* and *yang* principles is the great basic fact of Heaven and Earth" (*ibid.*, p. 9). Since the *yin* and *yang* are inherent in the Ether, it is not surprising that they should also be present in all things produced through the condensation of that Ether. As to why, however, no one of these is ever exactly like another, Chang gives us no ready explanation.

He writes again:

"The Great Void cannot but consist of Ether; this Ether cannot but condense to form all things; and these things cannot but become dispersed so as to form (once more) the Great Void. The perpetuation of these movements in a cycle is inevitably thus" (*ibid.*).

Thus the condensation of the Ether into concrete objects, followed by its re-dispersion causing the physical dissolution of these objects, is a process that continues in an unending cycle. Here again is a general phenomenon of the universe.

iv. *Celestial and Terrestrial Phenomena*

In his *Discipline for Beginners*, Chang presents a number of theories regarding celestial and terrestrial phenomena, some of which we shall

---

[1] *Book of Changes* (Appen. III, p. 389). — Tr.

now describe as examples of the scope of that work. In its second chapter he writes:

"Earth consists of the unmixed *yin*, which is solidly condensed in the center (of the universe). Heaven consists of the buoyant *yang*, which revolves around the outside. These are the constant substances of Heaven and Earth. The fixed stars do not themselves move, but are all attached to Heaven, where they revolve endlessly with the buoyant *yang*. The fact that the sun, moon, and five planets move in a direction opposite to that of Heaven is because they are linked to and embraced by Earth" (2.10).

Translator's Note: Chang's theory becomes clearer if we supplement what is said here with the unquoted remainder of the passage, plus the commentaries on it by Chu Hsi and others. From these we can restate the theory as follows: The *yang* is active, the *yin* inactive. Therefore Earth, being *yin*, remains stationary at the center of the cosmos, whereas Heaven, being *yang*, rotates around it. The daily movements of the heavenly bodies around Earth are explained by the fact that these bodies are carried along by Heaven in its rotary motion. In these movements the fixed stars always hold relatively their same positions, one to another, whereas the rising and setting of the sun, moon, and five planets (Venus, Jupiter, Mercury, Mars, and Saturn) constantly vary. This is because the fixed stars are nearest to the outer part of Heaven, and are therefore carried along freely by it in its rotation. Though the other bodies also move with Heaven, they do so at a slower rate, owing to their closer position to Earth in the center which, being stationary, tends to impede their forward movement. The net result is that relatively, though not absolutely, their movement is opposite to that of Heaven and of the fixed stars. The degree to which their rotation is thus retarded by Earth, however, is not uniform for all. Thus the moon, being itself *yin*, is more affected by the *yin* of Earth than are the other bodies; hence its rotation is comparatively slow. The sun, on the contrary, being itself *yang*, is less affected; hence its rotation is comparatively rapid. Each of the five planets consists of one of the Five Elements, which in turn consist of the *yin* and *yang* in varying proportions. As a consequence, their movements are correspondingly faster or slower.

Again: "Earth rises and falls, and the day has a longer or shorter duration. Although Earth is a solidly condensed and undispersed body, the two Ethers (of the *yin* and *yang*) rise and fall within it, incessantly following one another. [1] When the *yang* daily ascends higher, and Earth daily sinks lower, this results in the waning (of the *yang*). But when the *yang* daily sinks lower, and Earth daily advances

---

[1] By mistake, Professor Fung's text reads "one Ether" instead of "two Ethers." — Tr.

upward, this results in its waxing. In this way there occur the cold and hot periods of a year.

"As for the fact that there is (also) a waxing and waning (of the *yang*), and a rise and fall (of Earth), taking place each day and night, this can be proved through observation of the morning and evening tides of the sea. The fact that between them there is lesser or greater difference (in their movements), is connected with the fact that, at new or full moon, the (*yang* and *yin*) essences of the sun and moon interfere with one another" (*ibid.*, p. 14).

Here are some of Chang's cosmological speculations. The hot season of the year is caused by the descent of the *yang* (i.e., the sun), and the rise of Earth to meet it, resulting in a greater amount of the *yang* then being near the earth's surface. In the same way, the cold season of the year is caused by the rise of the *yang*, and the descent from it of Earth, resulting in a smaller amount of the *yang* then being near the earth's surface. Not only, however, does this rise and fall of Earth follow the course of the year, but a similar movement takes place day and night. This is evidenced by the flow of the tides: when Earth rises, the ocean (which is supposed to surround the earth) falls; when Earth falls, the ocean correspondingly rises. [1]

Chang writes again (chap. 2): "The nature of the *yin* is to solidify and condense; that of the *yang* is to issue forth and disperse. Condensation caused by the *yin* must be followed by dispersion caused by the *yang*; the forces involved are equal. When the dispersing *yang* is laid hold of by the *yin*, they cling to each other and descend as rain. But when the *yin* is seized by the *yang*, they float about and rise as clouds. Hence clouds scattered through the Great Void consist of *yin* (Ether) which, being driven by the wind, remains condensed and undispersed. Whenever the *yin* Ether, being solidified and condensed, has within it *yang* (Ether) which is unable to break forth, there is then struggle, resulting in thunder. But when the *yang* lies outside (the *yin*) and is unable to gain entry, there is then ceaseless revolution (of the *yang* around the *yin*), resulting in wind. The condensation (of the *yin*) may be extreme or slight, substantial or unsubstantial; hence the (resulting) thunder and wind may be small or large, fierce or gentle.

---

[1] The fantasy of this sort of theorizing is sufficiently indicated by Chang's failure to explain realistically the fluctuating discrepancy between the movement of the tides and the supposed rise and fall of Earth. The best he can say is that this discrepancy is caused by an interaction between the *yang* and *yin* essences of sun and moon respectively, which supposedly occurs at new and full moon. — Tr.

If the dispersion (of the *yin* and *yang*) follows their harmonious union, this results in frost, snow, rain, and dew. But if their dispersion follows their unharmonious union, this results in abnormality of the Ethers and violent dust storms. Whenever the *yin* disperses in a gentle manner, and while so doing receives contact from the *yang*, wind and rain are then evenly proportioned, and cold and heat are equable" (2.19).

Again (chap. 5): "Sound results from the impact of solids or gases, one upon the other. (The impact of) two gases results in such sounds as echoing or thunder. That of two solids results in such as the beating of a drumstick upon a drum. The impact of solids upon gases results in such as those of a feather fan or a flying arrow. The impact of gases upon solids results in such as those of the human voice or the reed organ. These all represent the marvelous capacities of the interaction of one thing upon another. With them all men are familiar, yet they do not (trouble to) examine them!" (3.3).

Here are what may be called Chang Tsai's concepts of physics.

Chang writes elsewhere in the same chapter: "Animals derive their being from Heaven. Their progression through the stages of growth and decay depends upon their inhalation and exhalation of breath. Plants derive their being from Earth. Their progression through the stages of growth and decay depends upon the rising and falling movements of the *yin* and *yang*. When a creature is first born, the Ether day by day enters (into it) and increases there. But after the life of that creature has passed maturity, the Ether day by day reverts (from that creature) and becomes dispersed. Its entering is called spirit-like, because it is then expanding; its reversion is called ghost-like, because it then returns (to its source)" [1] (*ibid.*, p. 1).

Again: "That which possesses breath derives its being from Heaven; that which lacks breath derives its being from Earth. That which derives its being from Heaven is unimpeded in its movements; that which derives its being from Earth is confined to a single position. Herein lies the distinction between animals and plants" [2] (*ibid.*).

---

[1] There is a play on words here between spirit-like (*shen* 神) and expanding (*shen* 伸), and between ghost-like (*kuei* 鬼) and returning (*kuei* 歸). The association between the two former words is already found in the *Shuo-wen* dictionary (ca. A.D. 100), 14b. 8. For the latter two words, see the *Book of Rites*, chap. 21: "All living creatures must die, and when they die they must return (*kuei*) to the soil. This is the meaning of 'ghost' (*kuei*)" (XXVIII, 220). — Tr.

[2] The idea here no doubt is that Heaven is *yang*, hence active; Earth is *yin*,

Here are what may be called Chang Tsai's biological views.

v. *Theory of the Nature*

Chang writes in his *Discipline for Beginners* (chap. 5): "Man's inhalation and exhalation of breath is the manifestation of the mutual touchings of the hard upon the soft, and of the opening and closing movements of *ch'ien* and *k'un*. [1] In the state of consciousness, one's physical form lies open (to the outside world), and one's mental attention maintains contact with external things. In the dreaming state, one's physical form is closed (to the outside world), and the Ether remains concentrated within. The conscious state is one in which a knowledge of new things is derived (from without) by means of the ear and eye. The dreaming state is one in which contacts are established with the past by means of the exercise of the mind along already familiar lines" (3.3).

Again (chap. 1): "From the Great Void is derived the term 'Heaven.' From the evolutions of the Ether is derived the term 'Way' (*Tao*). From the combination of the Void with the Ether is derived the term 'nature' (*hsing*). From the combination of the nature with the intellective and perceptive faculties is derived the term 'mind' (*hsin*)" (2.7).

And yet again (chap. 6): "When shapes exist, there then exists the physical nature. The conquest of it by goodness leads to the preservation of the nature of Heaven and Earth. Therefore in the physical nature there is that which the superior man denies to be his nature" [2] (3.8).

Chu Hsi comments on this passage: "The theory regarding the physical element began with Chang and the Ch'eng (brothers). I regard them as having enormously helped the School of the Sages, and as having done great service to the scholars who have come

---

hence passive. That is why animals, which take their breath from the atmosphere of Heaven, are able to move freely, whereas plants, which take their sustenance from Earth, are rooted to a single spot. — Tr.

[1] See the *Book of Changes* (Appen. III, p. 372): "Shutting a door is like *k'un*; opening a door is like *ch'ien*." — Tr.

[2] In this passage the phrase, "when shapes exist," refers to the existence of individual things. The "nature of Heaven and Earth" refers to the nature in its transcendent uncorrupted state; the "physical nature" (*ch'i chih chih hsing* 氣 質 之 性) is this same nature after it is found embodied in existing creatures, and has thus become corrupted by the environment of the Ether. — Tr.

after. ... Before their time, there was no one who had touched on this point. ... If, therefore, the doctrines of Chang and the Ch'engs are admitted, those of the other philosophers go into discard." [1] Chu Hsi's cosmology is based upon a dualism between *li* (Principle) and *ch'i* (Ether or matter). This explains why in his psychology and ethics it is possible for him to agree with Chang that man possesses two kinds of nature: the "nature of Heaven and Earth," which retains its transcendent purity, and the "physical nature," which has been corrupted by its contact with the Ether or matter. Thus he says: "Those who speak about the nature of Heaven and Earth, do so with exclusive reference to Principle (*li*); those who speak about the physical nature, do so with reference to Principle as it is found mixed with the Ether (*ch'i*)." [2]

Chang Tsai himself says very little about Principle or *li*. However, his just quoted statement that "from the combination of the Void with the Ether is derived the term 'nature,'" should be compared with another passage in which he tells us (see above, p.480): "The Great Void in which no shapes exist: such is the Ether in its original essence." This proves that, for Chang, the Void or Great Void is the same as the Ether; hence for him to speak of "the combination of the Void with the Ether" is a tautology, equivalent to speaking of "the combination of the Ether with the Ether." The situation is further complicated by another passage:

"The nature pertaining to Heaven utterly permeates the Way (*Tao*), and cannot be affected by the Ether, regardless of whether the latter be dark or clear" (*ibid.*, p. 5).

By asserting, as he does earlier, that "from the Great Void is derived the term 'Heaven,'" Chang Tsai seems to imply that Heaven and the Great Void are identical. Furthermore, we have just seen that the Great Void is another name for the Ether in its original state. Yet now, in this last quotation, Chang tries to distinguish between this Ether and "the nature pertaining to Heaven." This leads us into an impasse: How can what pertains to Heaven be differentiated from the Ether when this Heaven is at the same time to be equated with the Great Void, which is itself the Ether? The answer would seem to be that Chang's cosmological system is essentially a monism,

---

[1] Cf. next chapter, pp. 554-555, where this statement is quoted. — Tr.

[2] See J. Percy Bruce, transl., *The Philosophy of Human Nature, by Chu Hsi* (London, 1922), p. 83. — Tr.

yet that when he comes to discuss the question of the nature, he at times unwittingly lapses into a dualism. Consequently his theory of the "physical nature," though accepted by later philosophers, seems difficult to reconcile with other aspects of his own system.

From another point of view, however, it is possible to argue that there is no real contradiction. Let us first consider the following passage in the *Discipline for Beginners* (chap. 17):

"All that has shape pertains to being (*yu*); all being consists of semblances (*hsiang*); and all semblances consist of Ether. The nature pertaining to the Ether is fundamentally vacuous and spiritual. Hence spirituality and the nature both definitely exist in the Ether" (4.23).

According to this, the Ether has a nature of its own, and it would follow that when the Ether condenses to form individual human beings, a portion of this nature thereby passes to these same human beings. Chang writes again (chap. 6):

"The nature pertaining to Heaven exists in man precisely as the nature of water exists in ice. Although freezing and melting are different (states), the substance (thus frozen or melted) remains one and the same" (3.6).

The "nature pertaining to Heaven" in this passage is the same as the previously mentioned "nature pertaining to the Ether," since, as we have seen, Heaven and the Great Void are identical, and the latter is equivalent to the Ether. With this equation in mind, let us look at the following passages:

"Heaven's capacity for goodness is fundamentally our own capacity for goodness. The only thing is that we have destroyed it" (*ibid.*, p. 6).

"Tranquillity and oneness characterize the Ether in its original aspect; aggressiveness and acquisitiveness characterize it in its aspect of desire. The concentration of the mouth and belly upon drinking and eating, and of the nose and tongue upon smelling and tasting: such is the aggressive and acquisitive kind of nature. He who understands virtue allows (his body) to have a sufficiency of these and no more. He neither enchains his mind with sensual desire, injures the great with what is small, nor destroys the root with what is peripheral" (*ibid.*, p. 7).

The purport of these statements is that the average human individual, because of his concern with self as opposed to non-self, ends by setting himself apart from Heaven, in other words, from that very Ether the condensation of which has given him being. As a result, he concentrates wholly on his own physical desires. Such action pertains to what Chang here terms "the aggressive and acquisitive kind of nature," but which he elsewhere characterizes as the "physical nature" (meaning by this the nature as found in the condensed Ether). Such an interpretation of his words, if correct, would seemingly make it possible to harmonize his theory of the "physical nature" with the remainder of his system. One question, however, still remains: Since not only men, but all other creatures as well, are formed through the condensation of the Ether, why is it that these creatures are not the same in nature as men? To this question Chang gives us no reply.

vi. *Unity of Man with Heaven*

The foregoing explanation of Chang Tsai's concept of the "physical nature" remains admittedly problematical. There is no doubt, however, that in his ethics and method of spiritual cultivation he heavily stresses the need for obliterating all distinction between the ego and the non-ego, in order thus to bring the individual into oneness with the universe. For example, he writes in his *Discipline for Beginners* (chap. 7):

"By expanding one's mind one is able to embody the things of the whole world. If things are not thus all embodied, there will be something that remains external to the mind. The minds of ordinary men are confined within the limits of hearing and seeing, whereas the sage, by completely developing his nature, prevents his mind from being restricted to hearing and seeing. As he views the world, there is in it no one thing that is not his own self. This is what Mencius means when he says that through the complete development of the mind one may come to know one's nature and know Heaven. [1] So vast is Heaven that for it there is nothing external. Therefore a mind which externalizes things is incapable of uniting itself with the mind of Heaven. Visual and auditory knowledge is knowledge derived through the (mind's) contact with things. Such is not the knowledge that is apprehended by the virtuous nature, for the virtuous nature's kind of knowledge does not spring from seeing and hearing" (3.11).

---

[1] *Mencius*, VIIa, 1: "He who has completely developed his mind, knows his nature. Knowing his nature, he knows Heaven." — Tr.

To regard the individual self as the only true ego, while externalizing all else, is to confine the mind to "the limits of hearing and seeing." The sage, on the contrary, destroys these sensory bonds, so that he may regard the entire world as one with himself. He "is able to embody the things of the whole world" in such a way that "as he views the world, there is in it no one thing that is not his own self." In this way he reaches a stage in which the entire universe is regarded by him as simply one supremely great ego. "So vast is Heaven (by which Chang here means the universe) that for it there is nothing external." If, through spiritual cultivation, man can but realize this fact, he can then gain the state of union with Heaven. Chang writes again (chap. 6):

"The nature is the one source of all things, and is not the private possession of one's own ego. It is only the great man who is able to exhaust its principles. Therefore his establishment must be an all-inclusive establishment, his knowledge must be an all-embracing knowledge, his love must be a universal love, [1] and his achievements must not be solitary achievements. As for him who so deludes himself that he knows not how to follow this principle of mine, there is indeed nothing that can be done" (3.4).

Here we find the "work of love" (to use Schopenhauer's expression) being cited as the means for destroying the delusions of the ego and thus attaining union with the universe. Essentially, what Chang is here doing is to develop further the mystical tendency that is apparent in the philosophy of Mencius. [2]

Epistemologically speaking, the only true knowledge is that possessed by the man who has reached this goal. Such knowledge is not "confined within the limits of hearing and seeing," nor does it merely "derive from the contact (of the mind) with things." Chang writes in the same chapter:

"The knowledge that comes from sincerity and enlightenment is Heaven's virtuous 'good knowledge'; it is not merely the petty knowledge of hearing and seeing" [3] (ibid., p. 3).

---

[1] It is interesting to note that Chang here uses the term *chien ai*, "universal love," which was so emphasized by Mo Tzŭ. See vol. 1, pp. 91-96, esp. p. 94. The question of whether or not Chang's concept is comparable with that of Mo Tzŭ is discussed below. — Tr.

[2] Cf. vol. 1, pp. 129-131.

[3] This "good knowledge" (*liang chih*) is the same as the "intuitive knowledge" which, as we shall see in Chapter XIV, was to be so emphasized by Wang Shoujen (1473-1529). The term originates from the *Mencius*, VIIa. 15: "The knowledge

These qualities of "sincerity" (*ch'eng*) and "enlightenment" (*ming*) are further described as follows:

"A state of functioning in which differentiation is made between Heaven and man cannot adequately be said to be 'sincerity.' A state of knowledge in which differentiation is made between Heaven and man cannot be considered as the utmost 'enlightenment.' What I call sincerity and enlightenment is a condition in which there is no perceptible distinction between the small and the great, that is, between one's own nature and the Way of Heaven" (*ibid.*).

From this it would appear that "sincerity" describes the state of mystical union between Heaven (the universe) and man, and that "enlightenment" describes the knowledge possessed in this state. Such is the genuine knowledge; it is not "the petty knowledge of hearing and seeing."

One of Chang's most famous writings is the brief essay popularly known as the *Hsi Ming* or *Western Inscription*, though originally it was but a part of the seventeenth chapter of the *Discipline for Beginners*. [1] It reads as follows:

"*Ch'ien* is called the father and *k'un* the mother. [2] We, these tiny beings, are commingled in the midst of them. I, therefore, am the substance that lies within the confines of Heaven and Earth, and my nature is that of the (two) Commanders, Heaven and Earth. (All) people are my blood brothers, and (all) creatures are my companions. The Great Ruler is the lineal descendant of my own father and mother, and his great ministers are the household retainers of that lineal descendant. By honoring those who are advanced in years, I carry out the respect for age which should be paid to *their* aged, and by evincing kindness toward the solitary and weak, I carry out the tender care for the young which should be paid to *their* young. [3]

---

possessed by men without the exercise of thought is their 'good' (i.e., intuitive) knowledge." — Tr.

[1] It gained its name from the fact that it was inscribed on the western wall of Chang's library. For a detailed account of the essay and its importance in Neo-Confucianism, see Werner Eichhorn, "Die Westinschrift des Chang Tsai" (Leipzig, 1937), pp. 9-29, which also (pp. 36-66) translates the text. — Tr.

[2] This statement is based upon a passage in the *Book of Changes* (Appen. V, p. 429): "*Ch'ien* is Heaven, and hence is called father. *K'un* is Earth, and hence is called mother." Thus these two primary trigrams are here invoked as personifications of Heaven and Earth, in other words, of the universe. — Tr.

[3] The words "their" refer to *ch'ien* and *k'un*, the personifications of Heaven and Earth, i.e., the universe. In other words, the aged and young who are to be treated with respect and kindness are not only to be taken as belonging to human society, but as members of the entire universe. — Tr.

The sage is one who merges his virtue with them (*ch'ien* and *k'un*), and the worthy is one who represents their fine essence. All persons in the world who are exhausted, decrepit, worn out, or ill, or who are brotherless, childless, widowers, or widowed, are my own brothers who have become helpless and have none to whom they can appeal. To maintain (our awe of Heaven) at the proper time is to show the respect of a son; to feel joy (in Heaven's Destiny), without regret, is to exemplify filial piety in all its purity.

"Deviation from such as this is called perversion of virtue; injury to love (*jen*) is called plundering. He who assists the wicked is an unworthy son, whereas he who fulfills his bodily design (by doing good) is a worthy one. To understand the evolutionary changes (of the universe) means to carry forward skillfully the activities (of *ch'ien* and *k'un*). To plumb the spiritual to its depths means to perpetuate skillfully the purpose (of *ch'ien* and *k'un*). He who even in the recessess of his house does nothing shameful, will bring no shame to anyone. He who preserves (his purity of mind) and nourishes his nature, will not become negligent.

"Through his dislike for fine wine, the Earl of Ch'ung's son showed his regard for the care (bestowed on him by his parents). [1] Through his development of the fine talents (of others), the frontier guardian at Ying extended (his filial piety) to (other members of his) kind. [2] It was the merit of Shun that without making a display of his exhausting labors, he caused (his father) to find delight (in what was good). [3] It was the veneration of Shen-sheng that caused him to await death without attempting to flee. [4] Shen was one who, having

---

[1] This son of the Earl of Ch'ung is none other than Yü, legendary founder of the Hsia dynasty. The phrase about the fine wine is taken from the *Mencius*, IVb, 20, and is intended to show how Yü, by carefully preserving the body that had been bequeathed to him by his parents, was setting an example of filial piety. — Tr.

[2] This is an allusion to the *Tso Chuan*, 722 B.C. (p. 6), where we read how Duke Chuang of Cheng, having quarreled with his mother, swore that he would never see her again in this world and had her confined at a place called Ying. There, however, the guardian of Ying showed the Duke such a touching example of filial love that he induced the latter to become reconciled with his own mother. — Tr.

[3] Cf. the *Mencius*, IVa, 28, which describes how the legendary Shun, through painstaking service to his physically and morally blind father, induced the latter at last to reform. — Tr.

[4] Lit., "to await death through boiling," which is merely a figurative way of saying that he was about to suffer the death penalty. Shen-sheng, heir presumptive of the state of Chin, was accused by his mother-in-law of having attempt-

received his body (from his parents), returned it intact (at death). [1]
And Po-ch'i fearlessly obeyed and conformed to the commands (of
his parents). [2]

"Wealth, honor, good fortune, and abundance have as their
aim the enrichment of our lives. But poverty, meanness, grief, and
sorrow serve to discipline us so as to make us complete. In life I shall
serve (*ch'ien* and *k'un*) unresistingly, and when death comes, I shall
be at peace." (pp. 36-66). [3]

Here we are clearly told the attitude that we should take toward
the universe and the creatures in it. Our own body is that of the universe, and our individual nature is identical with that of the universe.
We should regard the universe (personified as two universal parents,
ch'ien and *k'un*) as we do our own parents, and serve it in the same
manner as we do them. We should furthermore regard all men of
the world as our own brothers, and all creatures in it as our own kind.

Somewhat later a disciple of the Ch'eng brothers objected to
Chang's formulation on the grounds that it was identical with Mo
Tzŭ's discredited doctrine of "universal love" (*chien ai*). To this the
Ch'engs replied: "The *Western Inscription* makes it clear that though
Principle (*li*) is unitary, it is nevertheless manifest in its distinctions. For
Mo Tzŭ, on the other hand, (love) has a dual basis, and (therefore)
lacks all distinctions." [4] This argument was subsequently enlarged
upon by Chu Hsi as follows:

---

ed to poison his father, Duke Hsien of Chin. Rather than expose his mother-
in-law's wickedness and thus give unhappiness to his father, he committed
suicide. Cf. the *Tso Chuan*, 656 B.C. (pp. 141-142). — Tr.

[1] Shen is the personal name of Tseng Tzŭ, the disciple of Confucius who,
more than anyone else in early Confucianism, was responsible for the growing
emphasis upon filial piety. We have seen in vol. 1, pp. 357-361, that a mjor tenet
of filial piety is to preserve intact the body that has been bequeathed us by our
parents. — Tr.

[2] Yin Po-ch'i was the son of a general of King Hsüan (827-782 B.C.) of the
Chou dynasty, and, because of a wicked mother-in-law, was turned from his
home and forced to become a wanderer in the mountains. — Tr.

[3] The highly ornate and condensed prose of this passage is studded with
allusions to the classics, too numerous to be conveniently listed here. They will
be found in the translation of Eichhorn, *op. cit.*, from which the present version
differs, however, in a number of places. — Tr.

[4] Cf. commentary translated in Eichhorn, *op. cit.*, p. 74. The second sentence,
which differs somewhat from that as printed in Professor Fung's Chinese text,
is an illusion to the *Mencius*, IIIa, 5. There Mencius criticizes the Mohists for
assuming that love has a dual basis, i.e., is indiscriminate. The result, he says,
is that they fail to distinguish between the peculiar affection naturally felt by a
person toward his parents, and the less intense love felt toward other people
in general. — Tr.

"When *ch'ien* is regarded as the father, *k'un* as the mother, and this applies to all classes of living beings without exception, such is the meaning of the statement that Principle (*li*) is unitary. Yet when among men and all other living beings with blood in their veins, each loves his own parents as parents and treats his own son as a son, how can (Principle) not then be manifold in its distinctions? Once there is this unity which yet leads to a myriad distinctions, then even though the whole world is a single family and China is a single person, we do not drift into the error of 'universal love.' And once there are these myriad distinctions which may yet be reduced to a single unity, then even though the feelings expressed toward those close to us and those remote from us may differ, and even though class distinctions may exist between those of honorable and those of humble station, nevertheless we are not shackled by the selfishness of 'each one for himself.' [1]

"Such is the general meaning of the *Western Inscription*. We may observe how in it the rich love that is to be paid to the parents is expanded to lead to the impartiality of non-egoism, and how the sincerity that lies in service to the parents is utilized to lead to an understanding of the way to serve Heaven. In it there is nothing that does not conform to the statement that, though multiplicity exists, it may yet be reduced to the singleness of Principle." [2]

The argument here is based upon the difference between the Confucian concept of a graded love, and the Mohist concept of a love that is equal and undiscriminating for all. As we have already seen, however, Chang Tsai's doctrines are a development of the mystical tendency in Mencius. As such, their difference from Mo Tzŭ's doctrine of universal love, based on utilitarianism, goes much further than Chu Hsi indicates.

vii. *Criticism of Buddhism and Taoism*

The final statement in the *Western Inscription*: "In life I shall serve unresistingly, and when death comes, I shall be at peace," well repre-

---

[1] This last was the doctrine of Yang Chu, just as universal love was of Mo Tzŭ. Chu Hsi here follows Mencius, who attacked both extremes and attempted to chart a middle course of all-embracing yet graded love, based upon the natural human relationships. Cf. vol. 1, p. 125. — Tr.

[2] Cf. Chu Hsi's commentary to the *Western Inscription*, quoted in Eichhorn, *op. cit.*, pp. 69-70.

sents the general Neo-Confucian attitude toward life and death. Its divergence from the views of Buddhism and religious Taoism is clearly expressed in the following passage of the *Discipline for Beginners* (chap. 1):

"The Great Void cannot but consist of Ether; this Ether cannot but condense to form all things; and these things cannot but become dispersed so as to form (once more) the Great Void. The perpetuation of these movements in a cycle is inevitable thus. Hence the sage is one who completely understands the course that lies within (this cycle), who embodies it in himself without thereby giving it any encumbrance, and who to the highest degree preserves its spirituality. As for those who speak about *Nirvāṇa*, they mean by this a departure (from the universe) which leads to no return. And as for those who seek for life and cling to existence, they mean by this a (continued) existence as a being who yet undergoes no transformation. Although there is a gap between these two (viewpoints), they may equally be said to diverge from the (true) Way. ... Condensed, (the Ether) forms my body; dispersed, it still forms my body. With him who understands that death does not mean destruction, it is possible to talk about the nature" (2.3-4).

Again (chap. 6):

"Only after a person has completely developed his nature can he understand that life does not entail gain nor death loss" (3.4).

Buddhism seeks to break the chain of causation and thus bring life to an end—an aim criticized by Chang in the words: "As for those who speak about *Nirvāṇa*, they mean by this a departure (from the universe) which leads to no return." Religious Taoism, on the contrary, seeks for the indefinite prolongation of life—an aim equally criticized in the words: "As for those who seek for life and cling to existence, they mean by this a (continued) existence as a being who yet undergoes no transformation." Once, however, we realize that "condensed, (the Ether) forms my body; dispersed, it still forms my body," we then arrive at the natural corollary that "life does not entail gain nor death loss." Why, then, should we seek either to destroy or prolong existence? Our real aim should be simply to perform each day the duties belonging to that day, serene in the consciousness that the coming of death merely means our return to that Great Void from which we came. Such is the thought behind Chang's statement: "In life I shall serve unresistingly, and when death comes, I shall be at peace." It sums up, indeed, the general

Confucian attitude toward life and death—an attitude that remained unchanged in Neo-Confucianism. This is why the Neo-Confucianists, despite their obvious indebtedness to Buddhism and religious Taoism, consistently attacked both schools alike, always insisting that they themselves were nothing but Confucianists.

2—Ch'eng Hao and Ch'eng Yi

Although Chou Tun-yi, Shao Yung, and Chang Tsai all contributed important elements to the development of Neo-Confucianism, its real establishment as an organized school began with the Ch'eng brothers, Ch'eng Hao 程顥 (1032-85) and Ch'eng Yi 頤 (1033-1108). [1] The *Sung Shih* states in its chapter on Neo-Confucianism:

"When (Chou Tun-yi) held office at Nan-an, [2] Ch'eng Hsiang, who was an assistant sub-prefect in charge of military affairs, observed that his manner and countenance were not those of ordinary men. [3] On talking with him, he realized that he was one who, through study, had come to know the Truth (*Tao*). Therefore he became friends with him and sent his two sons, Hao and Yi, to study under him. Tun-yi would constantly tell them to find out wherein lay the happiness of Confucius and Yen, [4] and what it was that they found enjoyable. It was in this way that the learning of the two Ch'engs had its start" (427.4).

Concerning Ch'eng Hao, the *Sung Shih* tells us: "Cheng Hao was styled Po-ch'un 伯淳. His family had resided in Chung-shan, [5]

---

[1] For Ch'eng Hao's dates, see the biography by his brother in the *Yi-ch'uan Wen-chi* (Collected Writings of Ch'eng Yi), 7.8; for those of Ch'eng Yi, see the *Yi-lo Yüan-yüan Lu*, 4.35. [Professor Fung's original text, through a misprint, gives the year of Ch'eng Hao's death as 1086, not 1085. Most sources place Ch'eng Yi's death in the first year of the Ta-kuan period, i.e., 1107, not 1108. The *Yi-lo Yüan-yüan Lu* date of 1108 is preferable, however, since this is the earliest source available. — Tr.]

[2] The present Ta-yü 大庾 hsien, near the southern end of Kiangsi province. He was a military commander there from 1041 or slightly thereafter to 1048. Cf. Werner Eichhorn, "Chou Tun-i, ein chinesisches Gelehrtenleben aus dem 11. Jahrhundert," pp. 22-25. — Tr.

[3] Ch'eng Hsiang (1006-90) was father of the Ch'eng brothers, and a native of the present city of Loyang. — Tr.

[4] On the happiness of Confucius and Yen Hui, his favorite disciple, see *Analects*, VI, 9, and VII, 15. — Tr.

[5] The present Ting 定 hsien in Hopei. — Tr.

but later moved to K'ai-feng and then to Ho-nan. [1] ... Hao's spiritual endowment surpassed that of other men. His character of unblemished harmony permeated his countenance to his very back. [2] ... From the time when he was fifteen or sixteen, he, together with his younger brother, Yi, listened to Chou Tun-yi of Ju-nan discourse upon learning, and, becoming tired of preparing for the civil service examinations, enthusiastically set his mind upon the search for Truth (*Tao*). Yet for almost a decade he drifted among the various schools (of thought), and fluctuated between Taoism and Buddhism, before he reverted to the Six (Confucian) Classics for his search, where finally he found it (the Truth). ... At Hao's death, gentry and officials, both those acquainted with him and those who were not, all equally mourned him. Wen Yen-po, [3] having gathered the opinions of a great many people about him, inscribed his epitaph with (the posthumous title), Master Ming-tao" [4] (*ibid.*, pp. 4-9).

Again the *Sung Shih* says of Ch'eng Yi: "Cheng Yi was styled Cheng-shu 正 叔 . ... He was an omnivorous reader whose learning was rooted in sincerity (*ch'eng*). He took the *Great Learning, Analects, Mencius,* and *Doctrine of the Mean* as his guide, and delved into the Six Classics. Whether active or still, speaking or silent, he always took the Sage (Confucius) as his teacher, and refused to remain idle as long as he failed to attain to him. Thereupon he composed commentaries on the *Changes* and *Spring and Autumn Annals,* which he transmitted to the world. ... By the world he is referred to as the Master of Yi-ch'uan" [5] (*ibid.*, pp. 9-14).

---

[1] The present Kaifeng and Loyang respectively. — Tr.

[2] A figure of speech from the *Mencius*, VIIa, 21. — Tr.

[3] 1006-97; a well known official of the time. — Tr.

[4] 明 道, "Understander of the Truth." For further biographical details, see J. Percy Bruce, *Chu Hsi and His Masters,* pp. 41-45, where we learn that Ch'eng Hao distinguished himself in a number of government positions, becoming a Censor in 1069. At court, however, he soon came into collision with Wang An-shih, whom he fearlessly criticized, so that he was forced to resign. A series of provincial appointments followed, from which, too, he was finally dismissed. — Tr.

[5] 伊 川, the name by which he is most generally known. For further biographical details, see Bruce, *op. cit.,* pp. 45-47. Ch'eng Yi, unlike his brother, spent most of his life in retirement, though recommended for government office by high ministers on a number of occasions. Bruce says of him that he combined the straightforwardness of his brother with a certain bluntness and perhaps a little haughtiness which sometimes created for him enemies. — Tr.

The close relationship of the Ch'engs to their Neo-Confucian contemporaries is shown by the fact that they had Chou Tun-yi as their teacher, Shao Yung as their friend, [1] and Chang Tsai as their uncle. [2] Traditionally, their doctrines have commonly been regarded as forming a single school. This belief is reflected in the fact that the section of their works entitled "Recorded Conversations" contains many utterances loosely attributed to both brothers, with no effort made to distinguish between the two. Today, however, it has become increasingly clear that the ideas of the brothers, far from being wholly identical, contain the seeds of that difference which was later to divide Neo-Confucianism into two major schools. These are:

(1) The Ch'eng-Chu school, so named from its forerunner, Ch'eng Yi, and its major exponent, Chu Hsi (1130-1200). It is also commonly known as the *Li Hsüeh* 理 學 school or "School of the Study of Principle." For the sake of convenience, however, it will hereafter often be referred to as the Rationalistic school—a not wholly accurate rendering based on the fact that *Li*, "Principle," is also sometimes translated by Western scholars as "Reason."

(2) The Lu-Wang school, of which the elder Ch'eng, Ch'eng Hao, was the forerunner. It derives its name, however, from Chu Hsi's major philosophical rival, Lu Chiu-yüan (1139-93), who was its real founder, and from its chief exponent, Wang Shou-jen (1472-1528). It is also commonly known as the *Hsin Hsüeh* 心 學 school or "School of the Study of Mind," and will hereafter often be referred to as the Idealistic school. [3]

Though their ideology differed, however, the problems discussed by the Ch'engs were for the most part the same for both. In the following pages, therefore, we shall present these problems successively, comparing under each the answers given to them by the two brothers.

i. *Heavenly Principle*

The importance in Neo-Confucianism of the concepts of *li* (Principle) and *ch'i* (Ether, matter) has already been several times alluded

---

[1] Cf. Bruce, *op. cit*, p. 32. — Tr.

[2] Cf. above, p. 478, note 2. — Tr.

[3] I have somewhat expanded the author's exposition at this point. On the relationship of these schools to the two Ch'engs, see also end of next sub-section. — Tr.

to. Of the two, *ch'i*, owing largely to Chang Tsai, had by the time of the Ch'eng brothers become firmly established in Neo-Confucian thinking. *Li* or Principle, however, had been treated only sketchily. Chou Tun-yi, for example, barely mentions it in the twenty-second chapter of his *Explanatory Text*; Shao Yung merely says in his *Observation of Things* that for each individual creature (or thing) in the world there is *li*; and Chang Tsai in his *Discipline for Beginners* simply states that "though the condensation and dispersion of the Ether of the universe pushes forward along a hundred different roads, its Principle (*li*) (for so doing) is orderly and real." [1] It thus remained for the Ch'engs to give real prominence to *li* in Neo-Confucian ideology. Yet even they, as we shall see, though they frequently talked about "Principle" or "Heavenly Principle" (*t'ien li*), failed to define these terms with the clarity later given them by Chu Hsi. This becomes apparent as we read the following passages from the "Recorded Conversations" of the Ch'engs:

"As regards Heavenly Principle, where is its limit? It did not survive because of (the sage) Yao, nor did it disappear because of (the tyrant) Chieh. Being possessed by man, 'it is not increased by his great deeds, nor diminished by his dwelling in adversity.' [2] How then can one postulate of it either existence or non-existence, addition or reduction? In it there can fundamentally never be deficiency; all Principles are complete in themselves." [3]

" 'Unless one is able to examine oneself, the Heavenly Principles (that lie within) become extinguished.' [4] As regards these Heavenly Principles, they are all of them complete in themselves; in them there can never be deficiency. That is why, by examining oneself, one reaches the state of sincerity (*ch'eng*)" (*ibid.*, p. 20).

" 'All things are complete within us.' [5] This applies not only

---

[1] See chap. 11, pp. 444 and 466, and the present chap., p. 482. — Tr.

[2] See the *Mencius*, VIIa, 21. — Tr.

[3] *Erh-Ch'eng Yi-shu* (Literary Remains of the Two Ch'engs), 2a.18. [All further quotations in the present chapter are to this work, unless otherwise stated. It should be noted that since every category of objects in the physical universe has its own particular Principle, the *li* may sometimes be spoken of in the plural, as in the final sentence. Often, however, *li* is conceived of as a single collective metaphysical principle, standing in apposition to the physical *ch'i* or matter. In such cases it is better translated in the singular, as in the preceding sentences. As a synonym for *li*, the Neo-Confucianists also sometimes use the word *Tao* or Way. On *Tao* in this sense, see below, p. 510, note 1. — Tr.]

[4] See *Book of Rites*, chap. 17 (XXVIII, 96). — Tr.

[5] See the *Mencius*, VIIa, 4. — Tr.

to man but to all other beings; they all act in accordance with this (Principle). The only thing is that whereas these other beings are incapable of developing it further, man possesses this capability. Even when thus capable, however, does this mean that it (Principle) then becomes even slightly increased? Or when incapable, does this mean that it then becomes even slightly diminished? All the Principles are pervasively present. Can one say that the Way (*Tao*) of rulership was more when Yao exemplified it as a ruler, or that the Way of sonship was more when Shun exemplified it as a son? For (the Principles themselves) always remain what they are" (*ibid.*, p. 22).

"As for Principle, throughout the whole world it is but one. Therefore, though extending to (all within) the four seas, it remains the same. 'Being brought before Heaven and Earth, or examined in comparison with the Three Kings,' it ever remains an unchanging Principle" [1] (*ibid.*, p. 26).

"As to this Principle, 'the loving see it and call it love (*jen*). The wise see it and call it wisdom. The common people use it daily, yet without realizing it. This is why the Way of the Superior Man is seen by few.' [2] It itself, however, is neither diminished nor preserved; the fact simply is that men fail to perceive it" (*ibid.*, p. 31).

" 'To be silently immovable but, becoming activated, thereupon to penetrate everywhere.' [3] Such is Heavenly Principle, which is all-complete and in which there is fundamentally no deficiency. It did not survive because of Yao, nor did it disappear because of Chieh. (The relationships of) father and son, ruler and subject, are constant Principles which remain unchanging. How, then, can they be moved (by external forces)? It is because they are unmoving that they are spoken of as silent. Yet though unmoving, they may become activated so as to penetrate everywhere. This activation, however, does not come from without" (*ibid.*).

These statements are all jointly attributed to both the Ch'engs. Those that follow, on the other hand, are specifically attributed to Ch'eng Yi:

" 'To be silently immovable but, becoming activated, thereupon

---

[1] A close paraphrase of the *Doctrine of the Mean*, p. 325. The Three Kings are the founders of the Hsia, Shang, and Chou dynasties. — Tr.

[2] A close paraphrase of the *Book of Changes* (Appen. III, p. 356). — Tr.

[3] *Ibid.*, p. 370. — Tr.

to penetrate everywhere.' This already refers to matters in the human sphere. But as for *Tao* (the Way), its myriad Principles are complete in themselves. One cannot, then, say that they either do or do not become activated" (15.19).

"All things in the world may be understood through Principle. There being a thing, there must also be a pattern for it. Each individual thing must have its individual Principle" (18.12).

"Empty, vast, and without divisions, yet within it (i.e., Principle) the myriad phenomena (of the universe) are all contained. The time prior to its activation did not come first, nor did the time subsequent to its activation come afterward. It is like a hundred-foot tree, all of which, from roots and stem to branches and leaves, forms a single sequence. One cannot say that the things belonging to its upper portion are formless and invisible, and that they await man's orderly arrangement of them in order to become incorporated in the (proper) path. For there being such a path, it is the one and only path" (15.11).

"When anything exists, there must be a pattern for it. For a father, this consists of paternal affection; for a son, of filial piety; for a ruler, of benevolent love; for a subject, of respectfulness. There is no single thing or affair that does not have its own place. Gaining this place, there is peace; losing it, there is disorder. The sage's ability to give orderly coordination to all things does not derive from an ability to create the patterns for these things. It lies simply in the fact that to each he gives its proper place." [1]

These statements tell us, first, that Principle subsists eternally, without undergoing either addition or diminution. There it is, irrespective of whether men know of it or not. The sage Yao, for instance, by exemplifying the Way or *Tao* of rulership, gave the world a concrete example of how to be a ruler, yet the Principle of rulership was not thereby augmented. Even had there been no Yao, indeed, Principle itself would not have suffered the slightest diminution thereby; for this would merely have been a case in which "men fail to perceive it." Hence the statement: "All the Principles are pervasively present."

The second characteristic of Principle is that it remains ever unchanging: "As for Principle, throughout the world it is but one. Therefore, though extending to (all within) the four seas, it remains

---

[1] Ch'eng Yi, *Yi-chuan* (Commentary on the Book of Changes), 4.27, comment on hexagram 52. A considerably abbreviated version appears in the *Erh-Ch'eng Yi-shu*, 11.5, where, however, it is ascribed to Ch'eng Hao.

the same." This is true, for example, both of the Way of rulership, as exemplified by Yao, and of that of sonship, as exemplified by Shun.

The third point is that the Principles governing the many phenomena and things of the external world are at the same time all self-contained within our own mind. "They are all of them complete in themselves; in them there can never be deficiency. That is why, by examining oneself, one reaches the state of sincerity." In the words quoted from Mencius: "All things are complete within us." It is not only man, moreover, who is endowed with these Principles, but other beings as well, though they lack man's ability to develop the Principles further.

The fact that Principle neither increases nor diminishes, neither changes nor undergoes movement, is summed up in the phrase: "To be silently immovable." And the further fact that the many Principles of things are all contained in man's own mind, thereby enabling it to react to external phenomena, is expressed in the subsequent phrase: "To be silently immovable but, becoming activated, thereupon to penetrate everywhere." This phrase, however, only "refers to things in the human sphere." As to the general universe, we are told that the period before its many Principles were concretely exemplified did not come first, nor did the period subsequent to their exemplification come afterward. Indeed, the relationship between a Principle and its concrete exemplification is "like a hundred-foot tree, all of which, from roots and stem to branches and leaves, forms a single sequence. One cannot say that the things belonging to its upper portion are formless and invisible, and that they await man's orderly arrangement of them, in order to become incorporated in the (proper) path." It is because Principle is thus wholly independent of all human manipulation that it is further designated as "Heavenly Principle."

Finally, it would seem that the Principles of things represent what those things *ideally* ought to be. The sage does not create these Principles. He is simply one who "to each (thing) gives its proper place." In other words, he enables all things to be what they ought to be.

Such appears to be Ch'eng Yi's concept of Principle, as shown by the fact that, among the foregoing quotations, all those explicitly attributed to him may be consistently interpreted as I have done. Whether Ch'eng Hao held similar views is impossible to determine on the evidence so far, since, aside from those foregoing passages that are explicitly attributed to Ch'eng Yi, the remainder are simply said to derive from both Ch'engs jointly. That they too, however, actually originated from Ch'eng Yi, becomes probable when we compare them with those other passages in the *Erh-Ch'eng Yi-shu* for which Ch'eng Hao's authorship is definitely attested. The differences between these statements of Ch'eng Hao and those of his younger brother appear clearly in the following selections:

"Of the Principles of Heaven, Earth, and all things, there is not one that does not have its complement; they are all naturally the way they are and do not conform to any (artificial) arrangement. As I think of this each night, 'unconsciously my hands begin to move and my feet to dance' " [1] (11.4).

"The *Odes* say: 'Heaven produced the multitude of people, having bodies, having rules.' [2] ... For all things there is a Principle, conformity to which results in ease, and violation of which in difficulty. If each follows it own Principle, what burden will be imposed upon its labors?" (*ibid.*, p. 6).

"In Heaven's production of creatures, there is that which is long and that which is short, that which is great and that which is small. The superior man has gained what is great, so how can what is small also (hope to) become great? Such is the Principle of Heaven. How can it be violated?" (*ibid.*, p. 8).

"The 'yoking of oxen (to carts) and harnessing of horses (to carriages)' [3] are both acts performed in accordance with the natures of these (creatures). For why, indeed, might not oxen be harnessed (to carriages) and horses yoked (to carts)? It is because their Principles do not permit this" (*ibid.*, p. 10).

From these passages it would appear that when Ch'eng Hao speaks of Principle, he simply has in mind the natural or spontaneous tendency of any thing or things in the universe. This idea is further expressed by Hsieh Liang-tso (1050-1103), a disciple of the Ch'engs, when he says:

"In what is called the investigation of things and the exhaustive study of their Principles, one must first be able to recognize Heavenly Principle. [4] What is called Heavenly Principle is a natural

---

[1] A quotation from the *Mencius*, IVa, 27, expressive of uncontrollable joy. — Tr.

[2] *Book of Odes*, III, iii, Ode 6. — Tr.

[3] See *Book of Changes* (Appen. III, p. 384). — Tr.

[4] On the "investigation of things" (a famous phrase from the *Great Learning*, p. 412), see below, p. 529 f., where its importance in Ch'eng Yi's method of spiritual cultivation is described. — Tr.

Principle (*tao-li*), devoid of even the slightest hint of artificiality. If today men suddenly see a child about to fall into a well, they will without exception experience a feeling of alarm and distress. This feeling of fear, experienced at the moment when they see this happening, is what is called Heavenly Principle. But when there are (secondary considerations, such as) a desire to seek the praise of their neighbors and friends, or to gain the favor of the child's parents, or to act thus because they dislike the reputation (of being unvirtuous), these represent human desire (*jen yü* 人 欲). [1] . . .

"To base one's ideas on selfishness or pursue affairs in an artificial manner: this is what is known as the incitement of human desire. . . . What is called Heaven is simply Principle and nothing else. It consists simply of such (spontaneous acts) as seeing, hearing, and acting: all these pertain to Heaven. 'Heaven determines the virtuous: for them there are the five forms of clothing and five distinguishing marks. And Heaven punishes the guilty: for them there are the five punishments and five types of (penal) service.' [2] In all this there is nothing done artificially. The student only need understand that Heavenly Principle is a natural Principle, which cannot be changed. . . . Ming-tao (i.e., Cheng Hao) has said: 'Although in my learning there are things I have received from others, the two words, Heavenly Prin- Heavenly Principle, I have picked up myself.' " [3]

Heavenly Principle, as here described, simply signifies a natural tendency or force, the words Heaven or Heavenly being understood in the sense of Nature or the natural. The fact that Hsieh Liang-tso closes his remarks with a quotation from Ch'eng Hao suggests that his statement as a whole is based on the latter's concept. Its general tenor, indeed, agrees well with Ch'eng Hao's previously cited utterances. More particularly, we shall see that the sentence: "To base one's ideas on selfishness or pursue matters in an artificial manner: this is what is known as the incitement of human desire," is close in spirit to Ch'eng Hao's "Letter on the Composure of the Nature," discussed in sect. vii below.

A passage specifically attributed to Ch'eng Hao in the *Erh-*

---

[1] This famous anecdote comes from the *Mencius*, IIa, 6. — Tr.
[2] *Book of History*, II, iii, p. 56. — Tr.
[3] Hsieh Liang-tso, *Shang-ts'ai Hsien-sheng Yü-lu* (Recorded Conversations of Hsieh Liang-tso), 1.5.

Ch'eng Yi-shu makes the equation: "Heaven (i.e., Nature) is Principle" (11.14). In another undesignated passage we are told:

"All things are simply one Heavenly Principle. What, then, is the use of the intervention of the ego? As to the statement: 'Heaven determines the virtuous: for them there are the five forms of clothing and five distinguishing marks. And Heaven punishes the guilty: for them there are the five punishments and five types of (penal) service'—all this is simply the natural operation of Heavenly Principle, to which, if man sometimes adds something, such addition is that of his own selfish ideas. Both goodness and evil exist (in the world). According to Principle, goodness is a cause for happiness. Hence, by means of the five forms of clothing, a graded sequence (for evaluating goodness) is automatically provided, whereby they (virtuous people) may be distinguished. Also, according to Principle, evil is a cause for anger, and so it is because those other (evil people) cut themselves off from Principle, that there are the five punishments and five forms of (penal) service. But how can these involve any (personal) feelings of happiness or anger?" (2a.17-18).

Though the authorship of this statement is uncertain, its central idea agrees well with what Hsieh Liang-tso says, as well as with Ch'eng Hao's above-mentioned "Letter on the Composure of the Nature." Hence it seems probable that it too derives from Ch'eng Hao.

One thing, at least, can be stated with some assurance: Among the passages in the *Erh-Ch'eng Yi-shu* in which Principle or Heavenly Principle is discussed, those explicitly attributed to Ch'eng Hao do not speak of it as independently subsisting apart from actual things, whereas this concept is stressed in those definitely known to come from Ch'eng Yi. Principle, as conceived by the latter, seems, indeed, to be somewhat similar to the "idea" or "form" of the ancient Greeks.

There may, in fact, even be a parallel between the evolution of the Greek and Chinese concepts. Thus in Greek philosophy, as we know, Plato was influenced by the numerology of Pythagoras when he elaborated his own theory of Platonic ideas. Basic in this influence seems to have been the fact that numbers, being abstractions, can therefore be conceived of in complete independence of concrete objects. It is from these abstractions, apparently, that Plato arrived at his theory of ideas as self-sufficient entities that eternally subsist, irrespective of time and space, in a world of ideas outside of our own concrete world.

In China, similarly, the "study of emblems and numbers" by the Neo-Confucianists may have led some of them—known later as followers of the Rationalistic school—to the formulation of their theory of Principle—a theory based on the sharp demarcation between the world of *li* or Principle and that of the *ch'i* or Ether. As pointed out earlier in this chapter, this demarcation is similar to the one in Western philosophy between form and matter. Matter exists within the limits of time and space, where it forms the raw stuff from which concrete objects are made; it is susceptible to change, and hence undergoes both integration and disintegration. Form, on the contrary, transcends time and space and subsists eternally. In Neo-Confucian terminology, *ch'i* and the concrete objects made from it pertain to "what is within shapes" (*hsing erh hsia* 形 而 下, literally, "what is below shapes"), i.e., to what is physical. *Li*, on the contrary, pertains to "what is above shapes" (*hsing erh shang* 上), i.e., to what is metaphysical. [1]

If we turn to Ch'eng Hao's concept of Principle or Heavenly Principle, however, we find quite a different situation. Principle, for him, is nothing more than the natural tendency or force inherent in any concrete object, and as such does not subsist apart from such an object. This theory in later times came to be generally accepted by the Idealistic school, and its difference from that of Ch'eng Yi is my prime reason for asserting that in these two men we have the respective forerunners of the Idealistic and Rationalistic schools. Certainly it is rare to find an instance in the history of philosophy, as here, of two brothers establishing two major schools of thought—schools that were to remain dominant during the next several centuries.

ii. *Criticism of Buddhism*

Having comprehended Heavenly Principle, we should conform to it in our conduct. Thus speak the Ch'engs. Yet this, they continue, is precisely what the Buddhists fail to do, for the latter, instead of conforming to a universal standard in this way, insist on acting according to private standards of their own. Ch'eng Hao tells us, for example:

"The sage develops his mind of impartiality to the utmost,

---

[1] These terms are derived from the *Book of Changes*. See sect. iii. below. — Tr.

and exhausts the Principles of Heaven, Earth, and all things, so that each may gain its proper place. But Buddhism does everything for its own selfishness, so how can it agree (with the sage)? The sage conforms to Principle; therefore (what he does) is even and straight, and easy to carry out. But the activities of the other (non-Confucian) schools, whether great or small, require great effort, so that they lose naturalness. Therefore their departure (from the sage) is wide" (14.2).

Ch'eng Yi states similarly: "The doctrines of the Buddhists cannot indeed be said to lack wisdom, for they have pressed far into what is lofty and profound. And yet, in the final analysis, they fall into the pattern of egotism and self-seeking. Why do I say this? Within the universe, where there is life there is death, and where there is joy there is sorrow. But wherever Buddhism is, there we must look for unreasonableness. In its talk of escaping from life and death, and of gaining surcease from suffering, it reverts in the end to egotism" (15.10).

Again:

"The Buddhists wish to reject the affairs (of this world) without inquiring into them. But are these affairs in conformity with existence, or are they not in conformity? If they are, how can they be rejected? But if they are not, then naturally they do not exist at all, so what is there to reject? Yet those (Buddhist) recluses push their steps far into the depths of mountains and forests, in order there to strive designingly for tranquillity. This is because they do not understand Principle" (18.14).

In short, because the Buddhists fail to understand "Principle," their teachings are likewise violations of this "Principle."

iii. *The Physical and the Metaphysical*

The divergence between the Ch'engs, apparent in their attitudes toward Principle, crops up again in what they have to say about "what is above shapes" (*hsing erh shang*), i.e., the metaphysical, and "what is within shapes" (*hsing erh hsia*), i.e., the physical. In Ch'eng Hao's eyes, as we have seen, there is no Principle apart from actual things; it is natural, therefore, that he should make but little distinction between the spheres of the physical and of the metaphysical. Thus he says:

"Appendix III (of the *Changes*) says: 'What is above shapes is called *Tao* (the Way); what is within shapes is called instrument.' [1] Again it says: 'The *Tao* of Heaven is established by softness and hardness; the *Tao* of man is established by love and righteousness.' [2] And yet again: 'The alternation of the *yin* and *yang* is called *Tao*.' [3] The *yin* and *yang*, too, pertain to what is within shapes, yet they are said to be *Tao*. This statement speaks clearly of what is above (shapes), and what is within them. Fundamentally, however, these (*yin* and *yang* principles) are themselves nothing but the *Tao*. This fact should be silently reflected on and understood by men" (11.2). Another passage in the *Erh-Ch'eng Yi-shu* reads:

" 'The operations of supreme Heaven proceed without sound, without smell.' [4] Its essential character is said to be 'change' (*yi*); its Principle (*li*) is said to be the Way (*Tao*); its functioning is said to be 'spirituality' (*shen*); what it allots to man is said to be his 'nature' (*hsing*); the following of this nature is said to be the Way (of man); cultivation of this Way is said to be (moral) 'instruction' (*chiao* 教). Among all these, Mencius has furthermore expounded on the 'all-embracing force,' regarding which nothing more can be said. [5] That is why it is said that spirituality 'is, as it were, above one, and to one's left and right.' [6] There are many affairs, great and small,

---

[1] *Op. cit.*, p. 377. "Instrument" or *ch'i* 器 is an important technical term of Neo-Confucianism, derived from this single passage in the *Book of Changes*, and to be distinguished from the more frequently mentioned *ch'i* 氣 (Ether or matter). *Ch'i* or Ether is primarily a designation for the raw matter out of which all things in the physical universe are formed, whereas *ch'i* or instrument designates this same matter after it has become differentiated into separate objects (both natural and man-made). The underlying concept is that these objects are "instruments," each with its own specific functions to be performed in the universe as a whole. When the Neo-Confucianists speak of *ch'i*, "instrument," they commonly do so in apposition to *Tao* (the Way), owing to the apposition between the two in this *Book of Changes* quotation. As pointed out earlier (p. 501, note 3), *Tao* is often equated in Neo-Confucianism with *li* or Principle. — Tr.

[2] *Op. cit.* (Appen. V, pp. 423-424). — Tr.

[3] *Op. cit.* (Appen. III, p. 355). — Tr.

[4] The final sentence in the *Doctrine of the Mean*, p. 329, which in turn quotes it from the *Book of Odes*, III, i, Ode 1. — Tr.

[5] This mystic "all-embracing force" (*hao jan chih ch'i*) is described in the *Mencius*, IIa, 2, paras. 11-15. See vol. 1, p. 131, where, however, *hao* 浩 is by mistake read *huo* 活' so that the term is incorrectly translated as "the moving force." — Tr.

[6] See *Doctrine of the Mean*, p. 308, where, however, the phrase refers to personalized divine spirits, rather than to spirituality, conceived of in abstract terms. — Tr.

yet it is merely said that 'such is the impossibility of repressing the outgoings of sincerity (*ch'eng*).'[1] Penetrating high and low, there is nothing more than this. In 'what is above shapes,' it is *Tao*; in 'what is within shapes,' it is instrument (*ch'i*). Though we are forced to express ourselves in this way, instrument is (really) also *Tao*, and *Tao* is also instrument. Once we grant *Tao* to be present, it may then no longer be (specifically) associated with the present or the future, the self or the non-self" (1.5).

Though we are not told which of the Ch'engs uttered this statement, its purport is so similar to the preceding that it too probably comes from Ch'eng Hao. The *yin* and *yang*, being physical Ethers (*ch'i*), ever growing or decaying, expanding or contracting, therefore belong to "what is within shapes." And yet, as Ch'eng Hao says: "Fundamentally, . . . these are themselves nothing but the *Tao*." Or again: "In 'what is above shapes,' it is *Tao*; in 'what is within shapes,' it is instrument. . . . We are forced to express ourselves in this way." In other words, this is merely a convenient way of speaking, for in actual fact "instrument is also *Tao*, and *Tao* is also instrument." In later times, as we shall see, the Idealistic school, in contrast to the Rationalistic school, made no distinction at all between "what is above shapes" and "what is within shapes."

If we turn to Ch'eng Yi, however, we find such a distinction already apparent, as in the following passages:

"(As to the statement that) 'the alternation of the *yin* and *yang* is called *Tao*': this *Tao* is not itself the *yin* and *yang*, but it is that whereby the alternation of the *yin* and *yang* is caused" (3.8).

"If it were not for the *yin* and *yang*, there would be no (manifestation of) *Tao*; for *Tao* is that whereby there exists the *yin* and *yang*. The *yin* and *yang* are the Ether (*ch'i*), and this Ether belongs to what is within shapes. *Tao*, however, belongs to what is above shapes, and what is above shapes remains hidden" (15.20).

The expressions, "what is above shapes" and "what is within shapes," are derived, as we have seen, from a solitary passage in the third Appendix of the *Book of Changes*. According to the Rationalistic school, the "instruments" or *ch'i* mentioned in the *Changes* as lying "within shapes," are the concrete individualized objects that exist within time and space. On the other hand, the Way or *Tao*, stated as being "above shapes," is another name for that abstract Principle

---

[1] *Ibid.*, p. 308. — Tr.

or *li* that subsists eternally beyond the confines of time and space. This metaphysical Principle, however, manifests itself only when it finds embodiment in "what is within shapes." In other words, its manifestation depends upon those physical objects which we term "instruments." To quote Ch'eng Yi himself: "If it were not for the *yin* and *yang*, there would be no (manifestation of) *Tao*." As for this *Tao* itself, it is only "that whereby the alternation of the *yin* and *yang* is caused," but "is not itself the *yin* and *yang*." This clear distinction between the spheres of the physical and the metaphysical was generally maintained in the later Rationalistic school, though its implications were not fully developed until Chu Hsi.

Another passage in the *Erh-Ch'eng Yi-shu* tells us:

"Today you must yourself understand Principle, and then you will commit no error. 'What is above shapes' and 'what is within shapes' must also be more clearly distinguished" (2a.25).

Although we are not informed which of the Ch'engs made this statement it, like the preceding, probably comes from Ch'eng Yi.

iv. *The Ether*

Though Ch'eng Hao says little about the *ch'i* or Ether, Ch'eng Yi discusses it frequently. In so doing he advances the theory that the first members of each species of creature originated through what he terms the "evolutions of the Ether" (*ch'i hua* 化), in other words, what we would call spontaneous generation. Thus he says:

"A meteor has no (genetic) propagation, but is propagated from the Ether (*ch'i*). A unicorn (*lin*) likewise has no (genetic) propagation, but is also evolved from the Ether. The same is true of men when they first came into existence. When, for example, a sandbank rises from the sea, various sorts of animals and plants then appear on it, where they come into existence without any (genetic) propagation. ... Ever since mankind first came into existence, however, there has been no further case of men being evolved from the Ether" (15.19).

Chang Tsai, it will be rememberd, maintains that the formation and disintegration of concrete things results from the condensations and dispersions of the Ether. On this point he would seem to have influenced Ch'eng Yi, though the latter makes no explicit acknowledgment. A difference between the two, however, is that Ch'eng, unlike Chang, maintains that the Ether, once dispersed, reverts to nothingness and cannot condense again to form new objects. Such objects, he asserts, take shape only from newly produced Ether, quite unrelated to that already dispersed. This theory appears in the following passages:

"As to the opinion that Ether which has already reverted (to nothingness) may then again become (newly) expanding Ether, and that such (expansion) necessarily depends on this (old Ether): such (a theory) definitely does not correspond to the evolutionary process of the universe. For this process consists of spontaneous production and reproduction without end. How, then, can it depend for its work of creation on forms that are already dead, or on Ether that has already reverted? Let us take (as an example) what is near at hand in our own body. The fluctuating evolutions (of the universe) may be seen in the breathing of the nostrils. There is no need to inhale (already exhaled breath) a second time for making our (next) exhalation. For the Ether is produced of itself. Man's breath or Ether is produced from the True Source (*chen yüan* 眞 元),[1] and Heaven's Ether is likewise spontaneously produced from itself without end" (15.6).

"When anything disintegrates, its Ether comes to an end and there is no Principle by which it can revert to its original source. The universe is like a vast furnace in which even living things are smelted and fused until they reach their end. All the more so, then, in the case of the already dispersed Ether! How can it exist a second time? How can the universe use this already dispersed Ether a second time for its creative activities? These activities simply produce (new) Ether of themselves" (*ibid.*, p. 21).

The "True Source" in the first of these quotations is the name for a particular kind of Ether, as shown in the following statement by Ch'eng Yi:

"The Ether of the True Source is that from which the Ether (which man exhales) is produced. It does not mingle with the external Ether (around us), but is simply supported and nourished by this external Ether. ... Man dwells in the Ether of the universe precisely as does a fish in water"[2] (*ibid.*, p. 24).

---

[1] *Ch'i* literally means "gas, vapor, breath," so that the term "man's Ether" also means "man's breath." — Tr.

[2] This last statement is curiously similar to that made by Tung Chung-shu more than a millennium earlier: "Within the universe exist the ethers (*ch'i*) of the *yin* and *yang*. Men are constantly immersed in them, just as fish are constantly immersed in water." See chap. 2, p. 20. — Tr.

Ch'eng Yi here means to say that man, enveloped by the Ether of the universe, breaths in this Ether, called by Ch'eng the "external Ether." The Ether or breath which man exhales, however, is not the same as this external Ether, but is independently and newly produced from the True Source that lies within. Unfortunately Ch'eng Yi says nothing further about the Ether thus produced from this True Source.

v. The Nature

About the natures (hsing) of men and other creatures, as about the Ether, Ch'eng Hao says but little. Among his few utterances are the following:

"What is spontaneous in Heaven is called the Way (Tao) of Heaven. Heaven's allotment of this to all creatures is called the Decree (ming) of Heaven" (11.8).

"(In the statement that) 'the alternation of the yin and yang is called Tao,' this Tao is something spontaneous. 'The perpetuation of it (in man) is good.' [1] (That is to say), functioning results when Tao becomes manifest, for 'what is great and originating becomes (in man) the first and chief (quality of goodness).' [2] It is solely 'the formation of it (in man) that constitutes the nature (hsing).' [3] (That is to say), it is the duty of each person individually to rectify the nature that has been allotted to him" (12.1).

Here we have the theory that man derives his nature from the Way or Tao of Heaven. From the point of view that it is conferred on man by Heaven, it is known as the ming or Decree of Heaven; from the point of view that it is received by man from Heaven and thereby makes possible his existence, it is known as man's hsing or nature.

Another lengthy passage in the Erh-Ch'eng Yi-shu reads as follows:

" 'That which at birth is so is called the nature.' [4] The fact that the nature is the same as the Ether, and the Ether is the same as the nature, is what is meant by 'that which at birth is so.' In the Ether

---

[1] For these quotations, see the Book of Changes (Appen. III, pp. 355-356). — Tr.

[2] Ibid. (Appen. IV, p. 408). — Tr.

[3] Ibid. (Appen. III, p. 356). — Tr.

[4] A famous sentence from the Mencius, VIa, 3. — Tr.

with which man is endowed at birth, there is, according to Principle, some that is good and some that is bad. However, this does not mean that these two opposites are originally present in the nature itself at birth. There are cases in which goodness exists from infancy, and cases in which evil exists from infancy. These are the results of the endowment of the Ether. Goodness, to be sure, certainly belongs to the nature. Yet evil cannot be said not to belong also to that nature (as found in man after his birth), because 'that which at birth is so is called the nature.' As to what there is prior to the moment when 'man, at birth, is quiescent,' we cannot say anything. [1] For when we speak about the nature, it is then already no longer the (original) nature. What people in general speak of as the nature is only that referred to (in the phrase), 'the perpetuation of it (in man) is good,' and it is this that Mencius means when he says that man's nature is good.

"To say that 'the perpetuation of it (in man) is good,' is like (saying that) water, when it flows, tends to flow downward. All of it is the same water. Sometimes, however, it flows straight to the sea without ever becoming stagnant, and when this is so, what demands does it make upon human effort? Yet there are also cases when it already gradually becomes turbid before having flowed very far. Or again there are cases when it goes very far indeed before becoming turbid. Thus it is sometimes more and sometimes less turbid, and yet, though it may thus differ in turbidness, one cannot take that turbidness as meaning that it is then not water. This being so, man should certainly apply effort to it to make it limpid. For when that effort is applied promptly and persistently, it quickly becomes clear, whereas when the effort is applied indolently and sluggishly, it becomes clear only slowly. Once having become clear, however, it is then in no way different from the water as it was originally. Here, then, there is involved neither a case of replacing what is turbid with what is clear, nor of removing what is turbid and putting it away in some corner" (1.10-11).

Though the text itself says nothing about the authorship of

---

[1] See the *Book of Rites*, chap. 17 (XXVII, 96): "Man, at birth, is quiescent: this is his Heavenly nature. But, being (then) acted upon by external things, he becomes active: this represents the desires of the nature." The meaning here is that when we speak of man's nature, we ordinarily have in mind the nature as it exists in man following the moment of his birth, i.e., following the time when "man, at birth, is quiescent"; we do not mean the nature as it is prior to man's birth, i.e., as it is in the world of "what is above shapes." — Tr.

this statement, external evidence indicates that it probably comes from Ch'eng Hao. [1] Its meaning may be paraphrased as follows: Man, like any other creature, is a concrete entity; hence his coming into being is impossible without the Ether, which, as individualized in him at birth, is known as man's endowment of the Ether. At the same time, however, man receives from *Tao* (i.e., Principle) something else which is known as his *hsing* or nature. It is this nature as already found combined with the Ether following the moment of birth, that people are really talking about when they use the word *hsing*. They are not talking about it as it is *per se* prior to its combination with the Ether. This fact is the basis for Ch'eng's assertion that "the nature is the same as the Ether, and the Ether is the same as the nature." Ontologically speaking, it is no doubt true that the nature in its unmixed form is wholly good. Nevertheless we human beings, as concrete entities limited in our experience to that concrete universe in which we live, are really in no position to make any valid statement about it other than as it is found combined with the Ether. That is why Ch'eng tells us: "As to what there is prior to the moment when 'man, at birth, is quiescent,' we cannot say anything. For when we speak about the nature, it is then already no longer the (original) nature."

From here the quotation goes on to point out that, according to Principle, the Ether with which man is endowed may have in it either goodness or evil, just as water may be either clear or turbid. Only with the exertion of human effort, therefore, can the nature be restored to the state of original purity presumably possessed by it prior to the moment of birth. [2]

Turning now from Ch'eng Hao to Ch'eng Yi, we find the latter's views on the nature expressed in the following passages:

"As it pertains to Heaven, it is the Decree (*ming*); as it pertains to righteousness, it is Principle (*li*); as it pertains to man, it is the nature (*hsing*); as ruler of the body, it is the mind (*hsin*). These, in actuality, are all one. The mind itself is basically good, but the mental activity which is its manifestation is sometimes good, sometimes evil. What is thus manifested may be spoken of as feeling (*ch'ing*); it cannot be spoken of as mind" (18.24).

---

[1] This is the attribution made by Chu Hsi in his *Chu Wen-kung Wen-chi* (Collected Writings of Chu Hsi), 67.18, sect. entitled "Discussion of Ch'eng Hao's Theory of the Nature."

[2] In these two paragraphs I have, for added clarity, somewhat modified the author's exposition. — Tr.

"Mencius is right when he says that the nature is good; neither Hsün nor Yang knew anything about it. [1] It is because of his ability to understand the nature that Mencius has gained his unique position, exceeding that of the other literati. There is nothing in the nature itself that is not good; anything that is not good pertains to 'capacity' (*ts'ai* 才). The nature is the same as Principle (*li*), which is uniform from Yao and Shun down to the man of little intelligence. But 'capacity' means the endowment of the Ether, some of which is clear and some turbid. Persons endowed with its clear elements are the worthies, while those endowed with its turbid elements are the stupid people" (*ibid.*, pp. 24-25).

"The nature derives from Heaven, while 'capacity' derives from the Ether. If the Ether is clear, 'capacity' is also clear, but if the Ether is turbid, 'capacity' is also turbid. ... The case is like that of a tree: its (innate) crookedness or straightness is its nature, but its possibility of being made into the wheels or shafts of a carriage, or into the beams or pillars, clap-boards or rafters, of a house, is its 'capacity.' 'Capacity' may be either good or not good, but in the nature itself there is nothing that is not good" (19.6).

For Ch'eng Yi, as these passages show, the nature is what man receives from Principle, in which, of course, there is nothing that is not good. The concrete human individual, however, precisely because he is concrete and individual, requires the Ether, too, as a condition for existence, and this Ether may vary in its purity or turbidness. It is these differences that explain the corresponding moral and intellectual inequalities among human individuals, to designate which Ch'eng Yi uses the word *ts'ai* or "capacity." In later Neo-Confucianism this was to become an important technical term, and it still appears today in the everyday term *ts'ai-liao* 料, meaning "stuff" or "material."

The external manifestations of the nature in the form of the emotions or desires are called *ch'ing* or feeling. For example, the virtue *jen* is part of the nature itself. But "the feeling of distress, which is linked to love (*ai*), represents feeling (*ch'ing*) and not the nature. Because a person has a mind which experiences feelings of distress, one may deduce that he (innately also) possesses the quality of *jen*" (15.27). That is to say, the nature *per se* is not externally visible; what we see as its external manifestations are simply the feelings or emo-

---

[1] I.e., Hsün Tzǔ and Yang Hsiung, on whose theories see vol. 1, chap. 12, sect 4, and vol. 2, chap. 4, sect. 2, ii. — Tr.

tions. This is a point that was later to be considerably elaborated by Chu Hsi.

vi. *Fluctuations of the Yin and Yang and of Good and Evil*

Though saying little about the endowment of the Ether, Ch'eng Hao speaks as follows about the origin of evil:

"The goodness and evil of the world are both equally Heavenly Principle. To say that something is evil does not mean that it is inherently so. It is so merely because it either goes too far or does not go far enough. This is exemplified in such cases as those of Yang and Mo" [1] (2a.2).

For both the Ch'engs, the existence of evil is inevitable. Ch'eng Hao says:

"That some things are good and some evil is all equally a result of Heavenly Principle. For in Heavenly Principle it is inevitable that some things be beautiful and some ugly. That is, it is the characteristic of things that they have inequalities. What is necessary is for us to examine ourselves, lest we plunge ourselves into evil, and thereby become one of those things (subject to inequality)" (*ibid.*, p. 4).

Again:

"Among all things, there is none that does not have its opposite. Thus for the *yin* there is the *yang*, and for goodness there is evil. When the *yang* waxes, the *yin* wanes, and when goodness increases, evil diminishes. This is their Principle, and how far, indeed, it can be extended! What is vital is simply that it be understood by man" (11.6).

Ch'eng Yi says likewise:

"Within the universe, all things have their opposite: when there is the *yin*, there is the *yang*; when there is goodness, there is evil. The Ether of the superior man and that of the petty man are in a constant state of balance, so that not all of it can go to produce superior men. Sixty per cent of it for superior men, however, results in good government, whereas sixty per cent for petty men results in disorder. Seventy per cent of it for superior men results in exceeding good government, whereas seventy per cent for petty men results in

---

[1] The concept of evil as simply a negative deflection from the central mean is a common one in Confucianism. See, for example, chap. 11, p. 447. On Yang Chu and Mo Tzŭ as deviators from the mean, see p. 496 above. — Tr.

exceeding disorder. ... Thus even in the age of Yao and Shun there was, in their household, a perverse and wicked Ether which simultaneously produced Chu and Chün. [1] In their court, too, there were the four miscreants, who for a long time did not go away" [2] (15.20).

In the case of all concrete things, growth is followed by decline and integration by disintegration, and it is Principle that determines these changes. The *Erh-Ch'eng Yi-shu* says:

"As for the theory of the Principle of growth and decay, what does it have to do with the Buddhist doctrine of *kalpas*? [3] ... The latter speak of (these *kalpas* as constituting stages of) formative growth, static existence, decay, and utter annihilation. To speak of formative growth or destruction is permissible, but not of static existence or annihilation. For example, as soon as a child is born, it grows day by day. Thus it cannot have any kind of static existence. Fundamentally there is only the Principle of decline and growth, waxing and waning. Besides this there is nothing else" (2a.23). [4]

Ch'eng Yi also says: "As for successive historical epochs, those of the Two Emperors and Three Kings were ones of growth, and later ages were ones of decay. [5] As for a single epoch, (the reigns of) Wen, Wu, Ch'eng, and K'ang were a time of growth, and those of Yu, Li, P'ing, and Huan were one of decay. [6] As for a single ruler, the K'ai-yüan period was one of growth, and the T'ien-pao period one of decay. [7] As for a single year, spring and summer are its time of growth, and autumn and winter its time of decay. As for a single month, its first ten-day period is one of growth, and its last ten-day period one of decay. As for a single day, the hours of *yin* and *mao* are

---

[1] Tan-chu and Shang-chün were the degenerate sons of the sage-rulers Yao and Shun, respectively. — Tr.

[2] For the four miscreants, see chap. 11, p. 469, note 1. — Tr.

[3] On the *kalpas* or "world periods" of Buddhist cosmology, see chap. 11, p. 474. — Tr.

[4] It is not stated which of the Ch'engs made this utterance.

[5] The Two Emperors are Yao and Shun. The Three Kings are the founders of the first three dynasties, Hsia, Shang, and Chou. — Tr.

[6] The first group of names is that of the first four rulers of the Chou dynasty. The second group is that of the four kings (9th-8th centuries B.C.) under whom the dynasty rapidly declined. — Tr.

[7] These two periods (respectively 713-741 and 742-755) cover the reign of the famous emperor, Hsüan-tsung, whose early years saw the T'ang dynasty reach its height of glory, but who in later years suffered disasters which led to the decline of his dynasty. — Tr.

ones of growth, and those of *hsü* and *hai* ones of decay. [1] The same is true of a single (life-)time. Suppose a man live 100 years: the period before fifty is one of growth, and that after fifty is one of decay. There may be some cases in which decay is followed by (momentary) renewed growth, as well as others in which such revival does not take place.... Generally speaking, however, if we consider the great revolutions of the universe, their Principle is one of steady decay and decline (following a peak)" (18.19).

This theory is very similar to that of Shao Yung, from whom the Ch'engs may well have borrowed it. [2]

vii. *Ch'eng Hao's Theory of Spiritual Cultivation*

According to Ch'eng Hao, man's original state is that of union with the universe which, however, becomes lost through the assertion of the individual ego. Hence the aim of spiritual cultivation is to destroy the barriers created by the ego, and return to the state of universal oneness. He says:

" 'The great attribute of Heaven and Earth is the giving and maintaining of life.' [3] 'There is an intermingling of the genial influences of Heaven and Earth, and the transformation of all things proceeds abundantly.' [4] 'That which at birth is so is called the nature.' [5] The tendency toward life of all things is what is most worthy of our observation. 'What is great and originating becomes (in man) the first and chief (quality of goodness).' [6] This quality is known as love (*jen*). [7] Love is something that makes for oneness with Heaven and Earth. Why, then, does man especially belittle it?" (11.4).

Again: "In medical writings, paralysis of the hand or foot is described as 'non-love.' [8] This is a very good statement of the con-

---

[1] *Yin* and *mao* cover the period from 3 to 7 a.m.; *hsü* and *hai* that from 7 to 11. p.m. — Tr.

[2] See preceding chapter, sect. 2, v.

[3] *Book of Changes* (Appen. III, p. 381). — Tr.

[4] *Ibid.*, p. 393. — Tr.

[5] *Mencius*, VIa, 3. — Tr.

[6] *Book of Changes* (Appen. IV, p. 408). — Tr.

[7] This famous term is here obviously used by Ch'eng Hao in a far broader sense than it had in early Confucianism. For Ch'eng it becomes a deep feeling of sensitivity which not only binds man to his fellow men, but to all other things as well, and thus makes possible the state of mystic union of the individual with the universe. — Tr.

[8] *Pu jen.* Such is the curious term used in Chinese medicine. — Tr.

dition. The man of love takes Heaven, Earth, and all things as one with himself. To him there is nothing that is not himself. Recognizing them in himself, where will he then not reach? But lacking this recognition, it naturally follows that there will be no link between them and himself. Thus if the hand or foot lack love, the vital force (*ch'i*) will fail to circulate through them, and thus things will not be integrated with the self. This is why the function of the sage is that of extending widespread aid to the masses" (2a.2-3).

Thus the universe, for Ch'eng Hao, is one great stream of life, and one great love (*jen*); therefore it is the men imbued with this love who are capable of achieving oneness with the universe. As to how to reach this oneness, Ch'eng Hao says:

"The student must first comprehend love (*jen*). The man of love is undifferentiably one with other things. Righteousness (*yi*), propriety (*li*), wisdom (*chih*), and good faith (*hsin*): all these are love. Get to comprehend this truth and cultivate it with sincerity (*ch'eng*) and earnestness (*ching* 敬); that is all. There is no need to impose any other rules or pursue any further search. Confining rules exist when the mind is negligent, but unless it be negligent, why have such rules? Further search is necessary when the truth has not yet been grasped, but having become self-evident through prolonged cultivation, what need for such search?

"This Way or *Tao* has no counterpart among things; even the word 'great' is inadequate to express it. [1] The functions of Heaven and Earth are all my own functions. Mencius has said (VIIa, 4): 'All things are complete within us. There is no greater delight than to find sincerity (*ch'eng*) when one examines oneself.' But if, on examining oneself, this sincerity be found lacking, it is like having mutually opposed objects. Never, (under such circumstances), will it be possible to unite the self with the other (non-self). How, in that case, can any delight still be found? The concept in the *Correcting of the Ignorant* [2] is a perfect statement of this essential point. If we but follow this concept in cultivating ourselves, what more is there to do? 'We must do something, and never stop and never forget,

---

[1] An echo of the *Lao-tzŭ* (chap. 25): "There is a thing, formless yet complete. Before Heaven and Earth it existed. ... We do not know its name, but we term it *Tao*. Forced to give an appellation to it, I should say it was Great." — Tr.

[2] An alternate name for Chang Tsai's *Hsi Ming* or "Western Inscription," translated earlier in this chapter.

yet never help to grow.' [1] Never exert the tiniest bit of forced effort. Such is the way of cultivation. Let there be cultivation, and something must be gained, for the 'intuitive knowledge' and 'intuitive ability' are never destroyed. [2] It is because the habits of the past are not removed that it is necessary to cultivate the mind. If this be done for a long time, the old habits can be torn away. This truth is extremely simple; the only fear is lest one fail to cultivate it. Once having experienced the delight of being able to embody it, there will be no fear of being unable to cultivate it" (2a.4).

Again: "The student need not seek afar. Let him take what is near his own person, and only (realize that the essential is to) understand Heavenly Principle and earnestness (*ching*). Then it is simple enough. ... Therefore Heaven and man are one in that they both have the *Tao* and Principle; there is no further distinction between them. The 'all-embracing force' is my own force, which, 'being nourished without sustaining injury, fills up Heaven and Earth.' [3] 'Be uncorrupted in thought,' and 'in nothing not earnest': if one but practice these two phrases, how can there be error? [4] Error always springs from the absence of earnestness and correctness" (2a.7).

Thus all that is necessary is to realize that we are originally one with all things, and, having "comprehended this truth," to remember it unceasingly. Our every act should be motivated by this one thought. Such is what Ch'eng Hao means when he urges us to "cultivate it with sincerity and earnestness," or quotes the exhortation of Mencius that "we must do something." By continued persistence in this course we will naturally and easily attain the state of union. No other rules or further search are necessary. Such rules, indeed, are

---

[1] *Mencius*, IIa, 2, para. 16. For the mystical significance of these words, see vol. 1, p. 131 (where the quotation is translated slightly differently). The admonition: "Never help to grow," has allusion to the anecdote about a stupid man who, feeling grieved that his grain was not growing faster, decided to help it by pulling it up. With great self-satisfaction he returned home and said: "I am tired today. I have been helping the grain to grow long." Thereupon his son ran out, only to find that the grain had already all withered. The moral is that the process of spiritual cultivation should not be artificially forced. — Tr.

[2] Lit., "good knowledge" (*liang chih*) and "good ability" (*liang neng*), terms derived from the *Mencius*, VIIa, 15. On the former term, see above, p. 492, note 3. — Tr.

[3] A close paraphrase of the *Mencius*, IIa, 2, para. 13. On the "all-embracing force," see above, p. 510, note 5. — Tr.

[4] The first phrase comes from the *Book of Odes*, IV, ii, Ode 1, 4, and the second from the *Book of Rites*, chap. 1 (XXVII, 61). — Tr.

only part of that forced "helping to grow," against which Mencius warns. Another passage in the *Erh-Ch'eng Yu-shu* tells us:

"The student must preserve this mind with earnestness; he may not impatiently lay force upon it. He should cultivate and nurture it deeply and thoroughly, and immerse himself in it. Then it will be acquired of itself. But if he seek for it with impatient force, it will only be the selfish ego (that does this seeking), and he will never succeed in attaining to *Tao*" (2a.2).

In other words, the mind which seeks for speedy results is still the selfish mind and must be eliminated. "We must do something," neither being forgetful of our purpose, nor yet trying deliberately and artificially to "help to grow." Other than this, there should not be the least bit of forced effort. In this way, if this procedure be prolonged, the individual will of himself attain the state of union. "Extremely simple," indeed, is such a method. Though the quotation just cited is not explicitly attributed to Ch'eng Hao, it is of the sort that he might very well have made.

By allowing ourselves to accord freely with Heavenly Principle in all its naturalness, without interposing our own selfish thoughts, we enable our minds to become "empty" like a brilliant mirror, which, though reflecting with accuracy any object that confronts it, itself remains ever impassive and immovable. This idea is developed in a famous letter from Ch'eng Hao to Chang Tsai, now known as the "Letter on the Composure of the Nature" (*Ting-hsing Shu*). There we read:

"I have received your letter in which you say that you have not yet succeeded in bringing the composure of your nature to the point where it is (wholly) inactive, and that it seems to be still encumbered by external things. This (statement) is indeed the ripened thought of a worthy, so what further words can you expect from my humble self? Nevertheless, having thought about the matter, I venture to submit my theory to you.

"What is termed composure (*ting* 定) is something that persists irrespective of whether there be activity (*tung*) or quiescence (*ching*). It does not associate itself with anything, nor is there for it anything either internal or external. Now suppose that, because of our assumption that external objects are (actually) external, we therefore induce ourselves to pursue them. The result is to make a (false) distinction in the nature between what is internal and external. Or suppose again that we regard our nature as being (unduly) concerned with externals.

Then, while it is dealing with these externals, what will remain for it within? This would be a case of setting our minds upon cutting ourselves off from external allurement, while failing to realize that for the nature itself there is (actually) nothing either internal or external. As long as we regard internal and external as two separate principles, how, in the same breath, can we still speak about composure?

"The normality of Heaven and Earth is that their mind permeates all things, yet (of themselves) they have no mind. The normality of the sage is that his emotions accord with (the nature of) all things, yet (of himself) he has no emotion. Therefore, in the learning of the superior man, there is nothing better than an empty impartiality with which, when things appear, he reacts accordingly. The *Changes* says: 'Firm correctness will lead to good fortune, and there will be no cause for regret. But if one be unsettled in one's movements, (only) one's friends will follow one's purpose.'[1] As long as one sets oneself toward eradicating external allurement, what appears to be destroyed in the east springs up again in the west. The eradication fails not only because one's days are not enough, but because the roots (of what is to be eradicated) come to be viewed as interminable. Every man is, in fact, blinded in one way or another. Hence he is unable to accord with *Tao*. Generally speaking, the trouble with man is that he is selfish and mentally calculating. Being selfish, he cannot take action as a (spontaneous) response, and being mentally calculating, he cannot take intuition as his natural guide. Now to dislike the mind's concern with externals, and so seek for a position in which it has nothing at all on which to reflect, is to reverse the mirror (of one's mind), while yet seeking for its reflection.

"The *Changes* says: 'Determinedly turning one's back toward him, one does not gain possession of his person; advancing into his courtyard, one does not see the man there.'[2] Mencius also says (IVb, 26): 'What I dislike in your wise men is their (forcible) boring out (of conclusions).' Rather than deny the external and affirm the internal, it is far better to forget that there is either internal or external. Forgetting both, one reaches a limpid state in which one is disturbed by nothing. This state of non-disturbance results in composure; com-

---

[1] *Book of Changes*, p. 123 (comment under hexagram 31). — Tr.

[2] *Ibid.*, pp. 175-176 (comment under hexagram 52). Such independent conduct is regarded favorably, for the text continues: "There will then be no error." — Tr.

posure results in enlightenment; and being enlightened, how can one's reactions to things be regarded as encumbrances imposed by them?

"The sage expresses joy at things which properly call for joy, and anger at things which properly call for anger. Therefore the joy and anger of the sage are not connected with his mind, but with things. Why, then, should he not respond to things? How can one, believing that the pursuit of the external is wrong, still believe that the search for the internal is right? If from the selfish and mentally calculating kind of joy and anger, we turn to the correct joy and anger of the sage, which is better? Of the human feelings, the easiest to express and hardest to control is anger. Suppose, when one is angry, one succeeds in quickly forgetting the anger and observing the right and wrong of it according to Principle. Then one will also discover that external allurements are no sufficient cause for hatred, and can indeed think that one has reached more than half way to *Tao*." [1]

With this letter of Ch'eng Hao should be compared the similar statement by Ch'eng Yi, apropos of Confucius' remark in the *Analects* (VI, 2) about his disciple, Yen Hui, that Yen "never transferred his anger to another." Ch'eng Yi's comment on this is:

"We must understand why it is that he did not transfer his anger. When Shun, for example, punished the 'four miscreants,' his anger was directed toward them, but in what way did he participate in it himself? He was angry simply because these men had done something deserving of anger. The mind of the sage fundamentally lacks any anger itself. It is like a shining mirror in which a beautiful object produces a beautiful reflection, and an ugly object an ugly one. But the mirror itself has no likes or dislikes. Ordinary people, to be sure, being offended in their home, discharge their anger in the street. ... In the case of the sage, however, his anger operates only in accordance with (the nature of) things, and never exists within himself. ... The superior man is the master of things; the petty man is their slave. Now suppose a man, seeing something to be happy or angry about, allows himself to become the least bit identified with these (emotions). This is indeed to burden himself. But the mind of the sage is like still water" (18.31).

---

[1] *Ming-tao Wen-chi* (Collected Writings of Ch'eng Hao), 3.1. [This letter has also been translated by C. P. Hsu, *Ethical Realism in Neo-Confucian Thought* (Peiping, 1933), Appen., pp. xiii-xv, which also contains translations of several other short but famous Neo-Confucian writings. — Tr.]

Chuang Tzŭ states very similarly (chap. 7, pp. 97-98): "The Perfect Man employs his mind as a mirror. It does not move with things, nor does it anticipate them. It responds to things, but does not retain them. Therefore it is able to deal successfully with things, but is not affected by them." The Neo-Confucianists agree that we should "employ our mind" in this manner. Nevertheless, there is a difference between them and the Taoists, for whom the emotions are themselves included among the things with which the mind has to cope, and whose method of dealing with these emotions, therefore, is to transform them by means of reason in such a way that they are eliminated entirely. [1]

The Neo-Confucianists, on the contrary, argue that there is nothing wrong with the emotions *per se*; what is important is simply that they should not be a permanent part of the person who sometimes expresses them. The sage, for example, when confronted by something that properly calls for joy or anger on his part, expresses such feelings like anyone else. These feelings, however, are not inherent in his mind, but are simply his natural responses to the objects which have evoked them. With the disappearance of these objects, therefore, the emotions called forth by them disappear as well. This is quite different from the ordinary man, whose anger, being a part of him, is only incidentally connected with the external objects that are its ostensible cause. Hence it still remains after those objects have passed away, or may even be expressed against other objects not deserving of anger at all.

As Ch'eng Hao says: "The normality of the sage is that his emotions accord with (the nature of) all things, yet (of himself) he has no emotion." This is like Shao Yung, who urges us to "rejoice at things from the viewpoint of those things, and grieve for things from the viewpoint of those things." [2] This state of mind can be reached only through the elimination of selfishness and calculating thought. Avoidance of the former leads to that "empty impartiality" of which Ch'eng Hao speaks, while elimination of the latter enables one, "when things appear, to react accordingly." In its resulting state, the mind always illumines things, though it itself remains immovable; it always remains immovable, though it itself illumines things.

---

[1] Cf. vol. 1, p. 237.
[2] See chap. 11, p. 467. — Tr.

By spiritually cultivating ourselves to the point where we achieve union with all things, our nature reaches its highest development. To describe this process, Ch'eng Hao borrows a term from the *Book of Changes*, "the complete development of the nature" (*chin hsing* 盡 性):

" 'By the exhaustive study of Principle and complete development of the nature, one attains to (Heavenly) Decree (*ming*).' [1] These three are all reached at the same time; fundamentally, there is no sequence in them. The exhaustive study of Principle is not to be regarded as something pertaining only to knowledge. If one really succeeds in studying Principle exhaustively, then the Decree and the nature will also be gained" (2a.3).

This last sentence should be read in conjunction with Ch'eng Hao's earlier quoted statement: "The student must first comprehend love"; also his admonition: "Get to comprehend this truth and cultivate it with sincerity and earnestness; that is all." By ceaselessly doing this, the state of union with all things will be reached. This is the goal meant by the "exhaustive study of Principle," "complete development of the nature," and "attainment to (Heavenly) Decree," and it is because all three are fundamentally aspects of one and the same thing, that he concludes: "If one really succeeds in studying Principle exhaustively, then the Decree and the nature will also be gained." This too is the reason for his statement that "the exhaustive study of Principle is not to be regarded as something pertaining only to knowledge."

viii. *Ch'eng Yi's Theory of Spiritual Cultivation*

Though Ch'eng Yi, like Ch'eng Hao, emphasizes the exhaustive study of Principle as the way to practice spiritual cultivation, he interprets it in such a manner that for him it comes close to being that "something pertaining only to knowledge" to which his brother objects. Thus he says:

"(Spiritual) nurture requires the application of earnestness (*ching*); the advancement of learning lies in the extension of knowledge" [2] (18.7).

---

[1] *Book of Changes* (Appen. V, p. 422). — Tr.

[2] On this "extension of knowledge," which is a famous term from the *Great Learning*, see p. 529, note 2. — Tr.

The results achieved through earnestness are described as follows:

"Earnestness serves to rectify what is within. With this inner mastery, there results a state of 'vacuity' (*hsü*) in which the mind is naturally devoid of depraved thought. For when this is the case, how can there be aught but vacuity? But 'we must do something,'[1] and earnestness must be employed as the instrument for this doing. Such a procedure is extremely simple and easy, and furthermore saves effort. Although, in stating it, I come close to what is said by ordinary people, yet the holding to it for long must result in a difference" (15.7).

Again, on being asked how to avoid confusion in thought, Ch'eng Yi replied:

"This results only when the mind lacks a primary emphasis. But if it lay its emphasis on earnestness, naturally there will be no confusion. The case is like that of a pot of water cast into a body of water. If that pot be already full, even the water of a river or lake will be unable to enter it" (18.10).

"Earnestness" results in a mental state in which the mind, though "vacuous," may yet at the same time be said to be "full." "Earnestness," in short, sums up for Ch'eng Yi that work of spiritual cultivation to which Mencius alludes when he says: "We must do something."

It is noteworthy that the Ch'engs, by mutually stressing earnestness, differ sharply from Chou Tun-yi, for whom, as we have seen in the preceding chapter (sect. 1, ii), the key term is not the *ching* that means "earnestness," but the quite different *ching* meaning "quiescence." The distinction between the two concepts is emphasized by Ch'eng Yi in the following passages:

"Earnestness (*ching*) naturally results in vacuity and quiescence (*ching*), but vacuity and quiescence cannot be called earnestness" (15.15).

"By speaking of quiescence one immediately falls into Buddhist doctrine. Not 'quiescence' but only 'earnestness' is the word that should be used. For as soon as one speaks of quiescence, the result is that 'forgetting' (of which Mencius speaks). Mencius says: 'We must do something, and never stop and never forget, yet never help to grow.' When there is this doing of something, then we do not

---

[1] A phrase from the *Mencius*, IIa, 2, para. 16, also stressed by Ch'eng Hao (see p. 522, note 1). — Tr.

forget, and when there is no stopping, then there is no (forcible) helping to grow" (18.8).

Ch'eng Hao, as we have seen in his "Letter on the Composure of the Nature," likewise stresses composure (*ting*) rather than quiescence. For, as he points out, quiescence by itself is one-sided; composure, however, is all-inclusive, because it embraces not only quiescence but also activity. [1]

Another aspect of Ch'eng Yi's method for self cultivation centers around two famous terms in the *Great Learning*: the "extension of knowledge" and the "investigation of things": [2]

"(Someone asked what should come first in spiritual cultivation. Ch'eng Yi replied): There is nothing more primary than rectifying the mind and making the thoughts sincere (*ch'eng*). The making of the thoughts sincere lies in the extension of knowledge, and the extension of knowledge lies in the investigation of things. This 'investigation' (*ko*) means a 'reaching' into (*chih* 至). It is like the *ko* in the expression, 'the ancestors arrive (*ko*).' [3] Each individual thing has its own Principle, which we should exhaustively study. There are many ways for so doing: one may read books and expound their meaning; one may discourse on personages of the past and present, discriminating the right and the wrong in them; or one may take a proper stand in one's reactions to and contacts with (present day) affairs and personages. All these are ways of studying Principle exhaustively.

"It was asked whether the investigation of things required an investigation of them one by one, or whether one might simply investigate a single thing, and thereby come to a complete under-

---

[1] See above, p. 523: "Composure is something that persists irrespective of whether there be activity or quiescence." By thus rejecting quiescence, the Ch'eng brothers show themselves, in this respect at least, to be further removed from Buddhist influence than was Chou Tun-yi. — Tr.

[2] *Chih chih* 致知 and *ko wu* 格物 . See the *Great Learning*, pp. 411-412: "The ancients who wished clearly to exemplify illustrious virtue throughout the world, first ordered well their own states. Wishing to order well their states, they first regulated their families. Wishing to regulate their families, they first cultivated their own persons. Wishing to cultivate their persons, they first rectified their minds. Wishing to rectify their minds, they first sought for sincerity (*ch'eng*) in their thoughts. Wishing for sincerity in their thoughts, they first extended their knowledge. This extension of knowledge lay in the investigation of things." Beginning with Ch'eng Yi, this passage assumed tremendous importance for the Rationalistic school. It also became important for the Idealistic school, by which, however, it was differently interpreted. — Tr.

[3] See the *Book of History*, II, iv, p. 61. — Tr.

standing of the Principles of all? The reply was: How can one expect
to comprehend them all at once? Not even Master Yen [1] would have
dared to claim that by merely investigating a single thing one could
comprehend the Principles of all. What is necessary is today to investigate one thing, and tomorrow to investigate another. Only
after this has been practiced over a long period can one reach a
free and automatic comprehension of all" (18.7).

Thus the investigation of things has as its aim the gaining of
true knowledge about the *li* or Principles of those things. Once this
knowledge has been achieved, it can then be carried into action.
Ch'eng Yi says:

"A true knowledge of Principle means a true perception of right
and wrong. Whenever such true knowledge of Principle is possessed,
it naturally leads to a differentiation of one's mind (from that of other
people). What is heard with the ear or spoken with the mouth, however, does not represent the mind's true perception. Once this
perception exists, it will refuse to find satisfaction where there is no
satisfaction. ... To tread on water or fire is something men universally avoid. This is a case of true perception. One must needs have
a mind for which the sight of evil is like the touch of scalding
water; then one naturally becomes different (from other men). The
case is like that of someone who has once been wounded by a tiger.
When other people talk about the tiger, everyone, even small children,
know that it is to be feared. Yet never will their fear be like the
terror-filled countenance of the man who has actually been wounded
(by the tiger), and who fears it to his utmost depths. This is a case
of true perception" (15.4-5).

Thus the investigation of things aims at giving us a perception
of the true Principles of those things. Ch'eng Yi says further:

"When there is knowledge to be reached, we should reach it;
when there is knowledge to be made complete, we should complete it.
What is necessary is to take knowledge as the basic thing. When
knowledge is deep, conduct will surely go far. For there is no man
who has (true) knowledge, yet cannot carry it out. If he has knowledge, yet cannot carry it out, it is because it is merely a shallow kind
of knowledge. Though hungry, one does not eat (poisonous) aconite,
nor will any man tread on water or fire. This is simply the result of

---

[1] Yen Hui, the disciple of Confucius mentioned on p. 525 as one who
"did not transfer his anger." — Tr.

knowledge. Likewise if a man do something that is not good, this again is simply because he does not know" (*ibid.*, p. 23).

Here we find Ch'eng Yi advancing a theory that was later to become famous as that of the "unity of knowledge and conduct." [1]

The reason why the investigation of things, if long continued, results finally in the "free and automatic comprehension of all," is that the Principles for seemingly external things are yet actually at the same time all contained within our own mind. The exhaustive study of Principle, therefore, means not only the study of the Principles of external things but, through that very act, of the Principles within our mind. This theory emerges in Ch'eng Yi's answer to a questioner who asks whether, when observing external things, we should not at the same time also search within ourselves for the Principles of the external things thus being observed. Ch'eng's retort to this is:

"It need not be as you say. For there is only one Principle for other things and the self. As soon as you understand the one, you will comprehend the other. This is the way to unite the internal with the external" (18.12).

Since this is so, the man who can press the study of Principle to its furthest extent can thereby arrive at a comprehensive understanding of his own mind in its entirety. The reason is simply that the individual mind is nothing else than the mind of the universe. Ch'eng Yi says:

"The mind of a single person is the mind of Heaven and Earth; the Principle of a single thing is the Principle of all things; the cycle of a single day is the cycle of a whole year" (2a.1).

Therefore he also says: "The exhaustive study of Principle, complete development of the nature, and attainment to (Heavenly) Decree, are all no more than a single act. With the exhaustive study of Principle, one completely develops one's nature; with the complete development of one's nature, one attains to (Heavenly) Decree" (18.12).

Superficially, this statement seems indistinguishable from that of Ch'eng Hao (see beginning of preceding section). Its inner content, however, is very different, inasmuch as what Ch'eng Yi means by the exhaustive study of Principle is quite dissimilar from his brother's interpretation.

---

[1] *Chih hsing ho yi.* For its elaboration by Wang Shou-jen (1473-1529), see chap. 14, sect. 6, ii. — Tr.

It becomes evident from the foregoing, therefore, that in their theories of spiritual cultivation, as in other aspects of their thought, the Ch'eng brothers are the divergent forerunners of the Rationalistic and Idealistic schools. Both agree that earnestness or *ching* is essential for the process of self-nurture. Ch'eng Hao, however, asserts that the first thing needed is to "comprehend this truth," and that only then should we go on to "cultivate it with sincerity and earnestness." Here he is outlining the process later described by the Idealistic school as that of "establishing first what is more important." Ch'eng Yi's methodology, on the other hand, embraces two aspects. One is the exercise of earnestness for self-nurture, starting from the very beginning, so as to prevent the appearance of depraved thoughts in the mind. The other is the extension of knowledge through the continuing investigation of things, day by day, in order finally to gain a "free and automatic comprehension of all." This theory, as we shall see in the next chapter, was later further elaborated by Chu Hsi.

CHAPTER XIII

CHU HSI

In preceding chapters we have seen the growth of Neo-Confucianism through the efforts of Chou Tun-yi, Shao Yung, Chang Tsai, and the Ch'eng brothers. In studying the Ch'engs, we have also seen how their ideological differences paved the way for the emergence within Neo-Confucianism of two major schools: those of Rationalism (*Li Hsüeh* or "Study of Principle") and of Idealism (*Hsin Hsüeh* or "Study of Mind"). With Chu Hsi (1130-1200) we now reach the man who synthesized the ideas of all these predecessors into one all-embracing system and who, indeed, is probably the greatest synthesizer in the history of Chinese thought. Through his prolific writings and his commentaries on the classics, he brought the Rationalistic school to full maturity, and in the process created a version of Confucianism that was to remain orthodox until the twentieth century.

Chu Hsi 朱熹, styled Yüan-hui 元晦, was born into a literary family originally native to Wu-yüan 婺源, at the southern tip of Anhwei. His own birthplace, however, was Yu-hsi 尤溪, in central Fukien, where his father was then stationed as district magistrate. Though born more than two decades after the death of Ch'eng Yi, he is ideologically linked with the latter by a succession of men, including Yang Shih (1053-1135), who was a disciple of both the Ch'engs, and at the same time the teacher of Lo Ts'ung-yen (1072-1135), who in turn taught Li Tung (1088-1158), who, finally, was Chu Hsi's own teacher.

A story typical of Chu's precocity tells how, when only four, he asked his surprised father: "What is there beyond Heaven?" During his early years he studied both Buddhism and Taoism, and it was only when he was about thirty that, under Li Tung's influence, he finally renounced them in favor of Confucianism. Already at nineteen he had passed the government examination, and thereafter spent most of his life in a succession of official posts. Some were active positions which allowed scope for administrative ability. Others, however, were sinecures which permitted him to follow his extensive philosophic

and literary pursuits, and at the same time to instruct the considerable
number of disciples who gradually gathered about him. After suffering from momentary undeserved disgrace during the years 1197-99,
owing to court intrigue, he died of dysentery in 1200. He was post-
humously ennobled as Duke, and in 1241 had his tablet placed in the
Confucian temple. [1]

1—Principle and the Supreme Ultimate

Chu Hsi's metaphysical system is primarily based upon the
cosmogony expounded by Chou Tun-yi in his *Diagram of the Supreme
Ultimate Explained*. With this it combines Shao Yung's numerological
theories; Chang Tsai's theory of the Ether or *ch'i*; and the distinction
established by the two Ch'engs between "what is above shapes"
(*hsing erh shang*) and "what is within shapes" (*hsing erh hsia*), as well as
between Principle (*li*) and the Ether (*ch'i*), and between the Way (*Tao*)
and "instrument" or "instruments" (*ch'i* 器, a different word from
the foregoing, and one having reference to matter as found in individually differentiated physical objects). Thus Chu's philosophy may
be said to be a summation of the Neo-Confucian school before his time.

Regarding the last-named distinction between the Way or *Tao*
that subsists "above shapes," and the instruments or *ch'i* existing
"within shapes," Chu writes as follows:

"Everything that has shape and form is instrument (*ch'i*). That
which constitutes the Principle (*li*) of this instrument is the Way
(*Tao*)." [2]

The *Tao* here spoken of is an abstract first principle or concept,
whereas *ch'i* (instrument) is a designation for the concrete individual
objects of the world of matter. Thus Chu Hsi says:

"What is 'above shapes' (*hsing erh shang*) and has no shape or
shadow, is Principle (*li*). What is 'within shapes' (*hsing erh hsia*) and
does have actuality and shape, is instrument (*ch'i*)." [3]

---

[1] See his biography in the *Sung Shih*, chap. 429, and, for a detailed account
in English, J. Percy Bruce, *Chu Hsi and His Masters* (London, 1923), chap. 4.
The foregoing paragraphs replace, and to some degree enlarge upon, the corresponding section in the author's original text. — Tr.

[2] *Chu Wen-kung Wen-chi* (Collected Writings of Chu Hsi), 36.14. [Hereafter
referred to as *Writings*. The apposition between *Tao* and "instrument" or *ch'i*
is based upon a passage in the *Book of Changes* (Appen. III, p. 377). — Tr.]

[3] *Chu-tzŭ Yü-lei* (Classified Conversations of Chu Hsi), 95.6 (hereafter
referred to as *Conversations*).

He says further:

" 'The Ultimateless! And yet also the Supreme Ultimate!' [1] (These words) do not mean that it (the Supreme Ultimate) is a physical something glittering in a glorious manner somewhere. They only mean that in the beginning, when no single physical object yet existed, there was then nothing but Principle (*li*). ... And because this Principle is multiple, therefore physical objects (in the existing universe) are also multiple" (*Conversations*, 94.21-22).

Put into modern philosophical language, what Chu Hsi refers to as "above shapes" is whatever transcends time and space and *subsists*; what he refers to as "within shapes" is whatever lies within the bounds of time and space and *exists*. What transcends time and space in this way cannot have any visible shape or form. That is why he says of the Supreme Ultimate (*t'ai chi*) that it is not "a physical something glittering in a glorious manner somewhere." Hence also the words quoted by him from Chou Tun-yi's *Diagram of the Supreme Ultimate Explained*, on which he comments further: "(The words:) 'The Ultimateless! And yet also the Supreme Ultimate!' merely mean that it lacks shape but contains Principle" (*ibid.*, 94.1).

"Because this Principle is multiple, therefore physical objects are also multiple." This means that without a given Principle or *li*, no given object can exist, for as Chu remarks:

"When a certain thing is made, there is in it a particular Principle (*li*). For all things created in the universe, there is in each a particular Principle" (*ibid.*, 101.26).

This is not only true of natural objects, but of man-made things as well, as we see from the following passage in the *Conversations* (4.6):

"*Question*: 'How is it that dried up withered things also possess the nature (*hsing*)?'

"*Answer*: 'For them there has been from the beginning such a Principle (*li*). [2] Therefore it is said that in the universe there is no single thing that lies beyond the nature (*hsing*).' As he walked on the steps, (the Master then) said: 'The bricks of these steps have within them the Principle (*li*) that pertains to bricks.' And sitting down, he

---

[1] These are the opening words in Chou Tun-yi's *Diagram of the Supreme Ultimate Explained*, for which see chap. 11, beginning of sect. 1, i. They mean that the Supreme Ultimate is the final cause for all things, beyond which nothing further can be conceived. — Tr.

[2] Here the nature (*hsing*) is clearly equated with Principle (*li*). — Tr.

said: 'This bamboo chair has within it the Principle pertaining to bamboo chairs.' "

Again:

"*Question*: 'Principle is received from Heaven by both men and other creatures alike. But do inanimate things also possess Principle?'

"*Answer*: 'Certainly they possess Principle. For example, (the Principle of) a boat is that it can move only on water; of a cart, that it can move only on land" (*ibid.*).

Thus all things in the universe, whether natural or man-made, have their own Principle or *li* which causes them to be what they are. Before the thing itself can exist, moreover, there must first be its Principle. Thus Chu writes:

"Looking from the point of view of Principle, although a certain object may not yet exist, the Principle for that object is already there. Thus there is already the Principle itself, even when its object does not yet actually exist" (*Writings*, 46.26).

That is to say, before the boat or cart yet exists, the *li* or concept of that boat or cart is already there. In other words, what we call the invention of a boat or cart is nothing more than the discovery by man of the Principle that pertains to boats or carts, and the conforming to this Principle in order to create an actual boat or cart. The latter is thus only the physical embodiment of the already subsisting concept. For every potentially existent object, therefore, whether natural or man-made, there must first be a Principle—a Principle lying within a world "above shapes" that consists entirely of such Principle, and is in itself all-perfect and all-complete. The *Conversations* (1.3) states:

"*Question*: 'At the time before Heaven and Earth had yet separated, [1] were all the multitude of things of later times already in existence?'

"*Answer*: 'There were then only the Principles for all these things. As for the things themselves created in Heaven and Earth over thousands and tens of thousands of years, they from antiquity to today have never been more than simply so many things.' "

The "multitude of things of later times" are the many potentially existent things of the universe. Although "at the time before Heaven and Earth had yet separated," these things themselves were not actually in existence, the Principle for each of them was already there.

---

[1] I.e., before the physical universe as we know it had been formed. — Tr.

"As for the things themselves created in Heaven and Earth over thousands and tens of thousands of years, they from antiquity to today have never been more than simply so many things." This means that only with the presence of Principle can a thing conceivably exist; without such Principle no such a thing is possible. [1]

The Principle or *li* of a thing is the all-perfect form or supreme archetype of that thing. This is the meaning of the word "ultimate," [2] as used in the following passage from the *Conversations* (94.11):

"For every thing or object there is an Ultimate, which is the normative Principle (of that thing or object) in its highest ultimate form.

"Chiang Yüan-chin remarked: 'The benevolence of the ruler and the reverence of the subject are, then, such Ultimates?'

"The Master replied: 'These are the Ultimates of a single thing or a single object. But the Principles (*li*) of *all* the myriad things within the universe, brought into one whole, constitute the Supreme Ultimate (*t'ai chi*). The Supreme Ultimate did not originally have this name. It is simple an appellation applied to it.' "

The Supreme Ultimate, therefore, consists of the Principles or *li* of all things in the universe, brought together into a single whole. This being the case, it stands as the highest archetype of all things. Chu Hsi says on this:

"The Supreme Ultimate is simply an utterly excellent and supremely good normative Principle. ... What Master Chou (Chou Tun-yi) calls the Supreme Ultimate, is an appellation for all that is good in Heaven and Earth, and among men and things" (*ibid.*, 94.7).

Spoken of in this way, the Supreme Ultimate is very much like what Plato called the Idea of the Good, or what Aristotle called God.

That the Supreme Ultimate is thus made up of the Principles for all things in the universe, as brought together into a single whole, means that all Principles are complete within it. Chu Hsi says:

"The Supreme Ultimate possesses all the Principles governing the Five Elements and the *yin* and *yang*, and so is not something

---

[1] Another passage in the *Conversations* (94.8), however, reads as follows: "*Question*: 'What was the time like when no single object yet existed?' *Answer*: 'There was then a Principle common to the entire world, but there were not as yet Principles which had become embodied in any individual object.' " This differs somewhat from what has just been said.

[2] *Chi* 極, the same word used in the term *t'ai chi*. — Tr.

'empty' (*k'ung*). For if it were thus 'empty,' it would resemble the 'nature' (*hsing*) as termed by the Buddhists.

"He said further: The Buddhists see only the external shell, and do not see the many normative Principles that lie within. As to the (relationships between) ruler and subject and father and son, these they consider to be illusion and untruth" (*ibid.*, 94.2).

Again: "There was a certain Li Po-wen here, who had formerly studied Buddhism, and who thinking that he had gained something through his learning, year after year kept up his arguments, without being willing to yield in the slightest. Recently he made me a visit during which he reverted to an exposition of his former doctrines. I therefore asked him about (the words): 'What Heaven has conferred is called the nature.' [1] Does this sentence mean that it (the nature) is 'empty' and contains no single entity? [2] Or does it mean that within it all the multitudinous Principles (*li*) are complete? If it is something 'empty,' then Buddhism wins the argument. But if it actually contains (Principle), then Confucianism is correct. This matter can surely be decided without further argument" (*Writings*, 31.2).

Again: "The Supreme Ultimate is the Way (*Tao*) that stands 'above shapes' (*hsing erh shang*). The *yin* and the *yang* are the 'instruments' (*ch'i*) that exist 'within shapes' (*hsing erh hsia*). Hence, if it (the Supreme Ultimate) is considered in its visible aspects, (we find that) movement (*tung*) and quiescence (*ching*) do not co-exist in time, nor do the *yin* and the *yang* co-exist in space; whereas the Supreme Ultimate itself, on the contrary, is to be found everywhere. But if it is considered in its invisible aspects, (we find that the Supreme Ultimate) is something profound, mysterious, and imperceptible; yet within it are fully contained the Principles governing (the visible manifestations of) movement and quiescence, the *yin* and the *yang*." [3]

"Considered in its visible aspects" refers to the Supreme Ultimate as found embodied in concrete objects; "considered in its invisible aspects" refers to it as it is itself. The Supreme Ultimate lacks shape or form, yet all Principles are complete within it; hence the description of it as "profound, mysterious, and imperceptible; yet within it are fully embodied the Principles governing movement and quiescence,

---

[1] A famous sentence from the *Doctrine of the Mean*, p. 300. — Tr.

[2] *Fa*, the *dharma* of the Buddhists, meaning an ordered something, a thing, or a matter. — Tr.

[3] Commentary by Chu Hsi on Chou Tun-yi's *Diagram of the Supreme Ultimate Explained*.

the *yin* and the *yang*." Here Chu Hsi points to a difference between the Neo-Confucian and Buddhist points of view which we shall discuss in detail in section 7 below.

The Supreme Ultimate, furthermore, subsists eternally. Chu Hsi writes:

"There is Principle (*li*) before there can be the Ether (*ch'i*). But it is only when there is the Ether, that Principle has a place in which to rest. This fact applies to the coming into existence of all (things), whether as large as Heaven and Earth, or as tiny as the cricket or ant. ... If we are to pin down the word Principle, neither 'existence' (*yu*) nor 'non-existence' (*wu*) may be attributed to it. For before Heaven and Earth 'existed,' it already was as it is" (*Writings*, 58.11).

For anything, "whether as large as Heaven and Earth, or as tiny as the cricket or ant," there must first be Principle before the thing itself as a concrete object can come into being. As regards this Principle, "neither 'existence' nor 'non-existence' may be attributed to it," the reason being that Principle is eternal, and hence transcends ordinary existence or non-existence. In Chu's own words, "before Heaven and Earth 'existed,' it already was as it is." And since this is true of Principle, it is also true of the Supreme Ultimate, which is the sum total of all Principle.

This Supreme Ultimate, moreover, does not lie within the confines of space. Chu says:

"The Supreme Ultimate holds no determined place; it has no shape or body; there is no definite spot where it may be placed" (*Conversations*, 94.5).

Likewise, neither movement (*tung*) nor quiescence (*ching*) may be postulated of the Supreme Ultimate. A passage in the *Writings* (56.36) discusses this point:

"*Question*: In the *Diagram of the Supreme Ultimate* (*Explained*) it is stated: '... The Supreme Ultimate through movement produces the *yang*. This movement, having reached its limit, is followed by quiescence, and by this quiescence it produces the *yin*.' But the Supreme Ultimate is Principle, and how can Principle be in a state of movement or quiescence? What has shape may have such movement and quiescence. But the Supreme Ultimate has no shape, and therefore it seems as if one should not speak of it in terms of movement and quiescence. Yet Nan-hsien [1] says that the Supreme

---

[1] The "style" of Chang Ch'ih (1133-80), a friend of Chu Hsi, but at the same time a rival who belonged to another Neo-Confucian group. — Tr.

Ultimate cannot but have such movement and quiescence. I do not understand his meaning.

"*Answer*: It is only because there are Principles governing movement and governing quiescence, that the Ether (*ch'i*) thus has movement and quiescence. For if there were no Principles of movement or quiescence, how could the Ether in itself have such movement and quiescence?"

The *Conversations* (94.9) also states: "Once there is a Principle governing movement, there can then exist this movement to produce the *yang*. Once there is a Principle governing quiescence, there can then exist this quiescence to produce the *yin*. When there is movement, there is Principle within this movement. When there is quiescence, there is Principle within this quiescence.

"*Question*: Movement and quiescence pertain to the Ether. Is it then correct to say that it is because there is this Principle which is lord over the Ether, that the Ether can therefore operate in this manner?

"*Answer*: It is."

"Movement and quiescence pertain to the Ether." The Ether undergoes actual phases of movement and quiescence, however, only because there are implanted in it the Principles governing this movement and quiescence, which themselves pertain to the Supreme Ultimate. That part of the Ether which moves then constitutes the *yang*, while that part of it which remains quiescent constitutes the *yin*. The *yang* and *yin* both pertain to "what is within shapes," i.e., to the concrete and physical realm of the Ether or matter, [1] whereas the Principles that govern movement and quiescence are "above shapes," and hence incapable in themselves of undergoing either movement or quiescence. Therefore "one should not speak ... in terms of movement and quiescence" about them.

In every separate object not only is there a specific Principle or *li* which makes that object what it is; within it there is also the Supreme Ultimate in its entirety. Chu Hsi says:

"Every separate man possesses the one Supreme Ultimate; every separate thing possesses the one Supreme Ultimate" (*ibid.*, 94.7).

Again (94.41): " 'The myriad and the one are equally correct;

---

[1] Chu says: "As soon as you speak of the Ether, this is to speak of a physical thing. ... This is what is meant by 'what is within shapes' " (*Conversations*, 94.26).

the small and the great equally have their fixed place.' [1] That is to say, the myriad are the one, and the one is the myriad. In their sum total they constitute the Supreme Ultimate, yet each separate object also contains the Supreme Ultimate."

A continuation of the same passage reads:

"*Question*: The Commentary to the 'Chapter on Principle, the Nature, and Destiny' [2] states: '(For everything), from the most fundamental to the least essential, the reality of the one Principle gains (physical) embodiment by being shared among the myriad things (*wan wu*). Therefore each of the myriad things has the one Supreme Ultimate.' If this is so, does it mean that the Supreme Ultimate is split up into parts?

"*Answer*: Originally there is only one Supreme Ultimate; yet each of the myriad things partakes of it, so that each in itself contains the Supreme Ultimate in its entirety. This is like the moon, of which there is but one in the sky, and yet, by scattering (its reflection) upon rivers and lakes, it is to be seen everywhere. But one cannot say from this that the moon itself has been divided."

According to these statements, every object, in addition to its own particular Principle which makes it what it is, also holds within itself the Supreme Ultimate, i.e., the totality of all Principles. This Supreme Ultimate, though thus present within all things, "is not cut up into pieces. It is merely like the moon reflecting itself in ten thousand streams" (*ibid.*). This idea is similar to that of the Hua-yen school, with its metaphor of "the realm of Indra's net." [3] It also resembles the doctrine of the T'ien-t'ai school, which maintains that each and every thing is the *Tathāgata-garbha* or "Storehouse of the Absolute" in its totality, and has within itself the natures pertaining to all other things. [4] On this point, therefore, Chu Hsi may well have been influenced by these two Buddhist schools.

A certain difference remains, however, inasmuch as the Hua-yen school, when it speaks of "the realm of Indra's net," means by this that within any given individual concrete object, all other concrete objects are actually present. Likewise the T'ien-t'ai school, when it

---

[1] A passage from Chou Tun-yi's *T'ung-shu* or *Explanatory Text*, chap. 22 (quoted in chap. 11 above, p. 444). — Tr.

[2] Title of chap. 22 of Chou Tun-yi's *Explanatory Text*. The Commentary is that of Chu Hsi. — Tr.

[3] See chap. 8, p. 353. — Tr.

[4] See chap. 9, sect. 1, i. — Tr.

speaks of all things as being present in each individual thing, means by this that in each individual thing all other things exist *in potentia*. Chu Hsi, on the other hand, states somewhat differently that each concrete object has within it the Supreme Ultimate, that is, that it contains the *Principles* of all things. He does not state that these Principles are equivalent to the actual physical things themselves, or even to the existence *in potentia* of these things.

As to the problem of how the Principle governing a certain class of objects can be manifested simultaneously in all the individual objects belonging to that class, Chu Hsi fails to speak clearly. But following his preceding train of reasoning, this too would probably be explained by him in terms of his metaphor of "the moon reflecting itself in ten thousand streams."

2—The Ether

There is only *li* or Principle in the metaphysical world that is "above shapes." Besides this metaphysical world, however, there is another concrete world "within shapes," the formation of which is dependent upon the *ch'i* or Ether. *Li* is similar to what Greek philosophy called form; *ch'i* to what it called matter. Chu Hsi writes:

"Within the universe there are *li* and *ch'i*. *Li* constitutes the *Tao* that is 'above shapes'; it is the source from which things are produced. *Ch'i* constitutes the 'instruments' (*ch'i* 器) that are 'within shapes'; it is the (material) means whereby things are produced. Hence men or things, at the moment of their production, must receive this *li* in order that they may have a nature (*hsing*) of their own; they must receive this *ch'i* in order that they may have form" (*Writings*, 58.5). He says again:

"It would seem that the Ether is dependent upon Principle for its operation. Thus when there is a condensation of such Ether, Principle is also present within it. It is the Ether that has the capacity to condense and thus create, whereas Principle lacks volition or plan, and has no creative power. Yet the fact simply is that wherever the Ether condenses into one spot, Principle is present within it.

"Moreover, in the case of all human beings, plants, trees, birds, and beasts of the universe, not one can be produced save through (genetic) propagation. It is certain that without such propagation not a single creature could come into being. This all pertains to the Ether. Principle, on the other hand, constitutes only a pure, empty, and vast world, utterly shapeless and hence incapable of producing anything, whereas the Ether has the capacity to ferment and condense and in this way bring things into being. And yet, wherever this Ether exists, Principle is to be found within it" (*Conversations*, 1.3).

Thus the world of Principle is "pure, empty, ... vast," and "utterly shapeless," and the Principle within it "lacks volition or plan, and has no creative power." It is in this way that Principle transcends time and space and is eternal. Our concrete physical world, on the other hand, is a product of the Ether or matter. Nevertheless, the creative process of that Ether cannot take place without Principle. The case is like that involved in building a house. Though bricks, tiles, wood, stone, etc., are essential as building materials, there must also be an architectural plan or form in order that these materials may be used in construction. The materials are the "instruments" (*ch'i*, i.e., matter in its functional aspects) used for building the house, whereas its form or plan is the *li* or Principle which provides the "source" from which the house is constructed. Moreover, after that house has been built, its Principle, i.e., its plan or form, still inheres in it.

Although Principle, logically speaking, constitutes a separate world of its own, in actual fact, as has been indicated, it is also to be found within concrete things and objects. We are told further in a passage of the *Conversations* (1.3):

"*Question*: 'In what way is Principle displayed in the Ether?'

"*Answer*: 'For example, in the fact that the *yin* and *yang* and Five Elements, when they intermingle with one another, nevertheless do not lose their proper order and succession: this is due to Principle. But if the Ether did not form agglomerations (of separate objects), Principle would have no place to which to attach itself.'" Again (94.10):

"Principle holds itself upon the *yin* and *yang* just as a man sits astride a horse."

Did the inchoate Ether not condense to form separate things, Principle would have no point to which to attach itself; in other words, Principle would have no means of manifesting itself in concrete things. Such manifestation, moreover, gives to these concrete things the precise orderly arrangement which they have in the world.

As to whether there is a priority between Principle and the Ether, Chu Hsi tells us in the following passages of the *Conversations*:

"Before the thing exists, there is first its Principle. For example, there is the Principle governing (the relationship between) ruler and subject before there is any ruler and subject; there is the Principle governing (the relationship between) father and son before there is any father and son. It cannot be that originally there was no such Principle, and that it is only when ruler and subject, father and son, finally came into existence, that the normative Principle for them was implanted in them" (95.21).

"The Supreme Ultimate is merely the Principles of Heaven, Earth, and all the myriad things. As to Heaven and Earth, within this Heaven and Earth there is the Supreme Ultimate. And as to the myriad things, within each and every one of them there is also the Supreme Ultimate. Before Heaven and Earth yet existed, already then there was Principle" (1.1).

"Before Heaven and Earth existed, there was only Principle. There being this Principle, this Heaven and Earth then came to exist. If there were no Principle, there would also be no Heaven and Earth, no human beings, and no things. None of these would have any place on which to stand. There being Principle, there is then the Ether, which flows into movement to produce the myriad things" (*ibid.*).

"*Question*: 'Does Principle come first or does the Ether come first?'

"*Answer*: 'Principle is never separable from the Ether. Nevertheless, Principle pertains to what is above shapes (*hsing erh shang*), whereas the Ether pertains to what is within shapes (*hsing erh hsia*). Hence if we speak from the point of view of what is above and what is within shapes, how can there not be priority and posteriority?' " (1.2).

"Someone asked: 'How would it be to say that there must first be Principle before there can be the Ether?'

"*Answer*: 'Fundamentally, one cannot say of these that they have either priority or posteriority. Nevertheless, if one must push into the question of their origins, one is forced to admit that Principle has priority' " (*ibid.*).

According to Chu's system, there must be the Principle for any given thing before the concrete instance of that thing can exist. Nevertheless, as to the question of the priority between Principle and the Ether (the latter regarded as a whole, rather than as differentiated to form separate objects), this can be discussed from two angles.

From the matter of fact point of view, it may be said that, as soon as there is Principle, there is also the Ether. This is the implication of the words: "Movement (*tung*) and quiescence (*ching*) have no starting point; the *yin* and the *yang* have no beginning." [1] From a strictly logical point of view, however, "one is forced to admit that Principle has priority," the reason being that Principle transcends time and space and is ever unchanging, whereas the Ether exists within time and space and does undergo change.

The Supreme Ultimate, as we have seen, is simply all the many Principles brought together into a single whole. On the opening words in Chou Tun-yi's *Diagram of the Supreme Ultimate Explained*: "The Ultimateless! And yet also the Supreme Ultimate!" Chu Hsi comments as follows:

"The fact that Master Chou refers to it as the Ultimateless (*wu chi*) is precisely because it occupies no position, has no shape or appearance, and because he maintains that it was prior to physical things, yet has never ceased to stand after there were such physical things. He maintains that it lies beyond the *yin* and the *yang*, and yet that it never fails to operate within them. He maintains that it permeates all form and is everywhere contained, and yet that in the beginning there was no sound, smell, reflection, or resonance that could be ascribed to it" (*Writings*, 36.10).

This statement reminds us of the language often used by Taoist thinkers to describe their universal Way or *Tao*. Nevertheless, in the light of what has been described above, we may see how much added significance Chu has put into it.

Note: Chou continues in his *Diagram of the Supreme Ultimate Explained:* "The Supreme Ultimate through movement produces the *yang*. This movement, having reached its limit, is followed by quiescence, and by this quiescence it produces the *yin*." This statement does not harmonize with Chu's system, according to which we cannot say that the Supreme Ultimate itself undergoes either movement or quiescence, but only that it *contains* the Principles governing these two phases, through which the Ether is respectively activated or stilled, in this way generating *yang* or *yin* matter. Thus from the point of view of Chu's system, we cannot but admit that the Supreme Ultimate, as conceived by Chou, really belongs to the realm of "what is within shapes"; hence his description of it as "The Ultimateless! And yet also the Supreme Ultimate!" is actually close in spirit to the statement in the *Lao-tzŭ* (chap. 40) that "Heaven and Earth

---

[1] A saying of one of the Ch'eng brothers, quoted by Chu on p. 549 below. — Tr.

and the ten thousand things are produced out of being (*yu*); being is the
product of non-being (*wu*)." This fact was early pointed out by Chu's
major philosophical rival, Lu Chiu-yüan (1139-93). See the *Hsiang-shan
Hsien-sheng Ch'üan-chi* (Complete Works of Lu Chiu-yüan), 2.11; also below,
chap. 14, sect. 3. It shows that though Chu uses Chou Tun-yi's actual
phraseology, his interpretation of it differs considerably from Chou's
original meaning.

3—COSMOGONY

The Supreme Ultimate, as we have seen, contains the Principles
governing movement and quiescence, and because of these Principles,
the *ch'i* or Ether undergoes phases of movement and quiescence, in
the course of which it operates actively to become *yang* Ether, or
congeals to become *yin* Ether. Chu follows the cosmogony and some
of the phraseology in Chou's *Diagram of the Supreme Ultimate Explained* to describe this process as follows:

"Movement and quiescence, in their alternation, are each the
root of the other. There is movement and then quiescence; quiescence
and then movement. They open and close, come and go, succeeding
each other without pause. There is a division into the *yin* and the *yang*,
and the Two Forms (*liang yi*) are thus established. These Two Forms
are Heaven and Earth, and are different in meaning from the Two
Forms associated with the pictured trigrams. [1] ... When they
(Heaven and Earth) were yet in a state of chaos and not differentiated
from each other, the *yin* Ether and *yang* Ether were mingled together
and obscure. Upon their separation, a broad dispersion and illumination came about, and the Two Forms were then established.

"K'ang-chieh maintains that 129,600 years constitute one Cycle
(*yüan*). [2] This means that at the beginning of (each Cycle of) 129,600
years, such a great 'opening and closing' occurs, [3] while before
that again there is likewise the same process. [4] Throughout (successive

---

[1] The derivation of the Two Forms from the Supreme Ultimate, and their
further division into the four emblems and eight trigrams, is described in the
Book of Changes (Appen. III, p. 373), where, however, the Two Forms seem to
represent the two kinds of lines, one divided, the other undivided, the combinations of which form the trigrams and hexagrams. — Tr.

[2] K'ang-chieh is the posthumous title of Shao Yung. On his theory of
successive world Cycles, see chap. 11, sect. 2, v. — Tr.

[3] I.e., an alternation of movement and quiescence, as described above,
resulting in the creation of a new universe. — Tr.

[4] I.e., there is a never ending succession of Cycles, with which one universe
comes to an end only to be replaced by another. — Tr.

Cycles) there has been only this (alternation of) 'movement and quiescence, which have no starting point; the *yin* and the *yang*, which have no beginning.' [1] (In this eternal process), the small is but the reflection of the great, as may be seen simply in (the alternation of) day and night. ...

"The transformations of the *yang* and congealings of the *yin* thus produce water, fire, wood, metal, and earth. The *yin* and *yang*, which are Ether, in this way produce the Five Elements, which are 'corporeal matter' (*chih* 質). Among the created things of Heaven and Earth, the Five Elements come first. Terrestrial Earth is composed of (the element) earth, with which there is also incorporated a good deal pertaining to (the elements) metal and wood. What is there in the universe, then, that does not pertain to (one or several of) the Five Elements? These seven—the Five Elements and the *yin* and *yang*—as they boil forth and combine with one another, form the material from which objects are created. The Five Elements being distributed in harmonious sequence, the four seasons follow their proper course. Thus metal, wood, water, and fire respectively attach themselves to spring, summer, autumn, and winter, while (the element) earth operates throughout all four seasons" (*Conversations*, 94.3).

Here we find a distinction between the *yin* and *yang*, regarded as belonging to the primary Ether or *ch'i*, and the Five Elements, described as *chih* or "corporeal matter." Chu says further on this point:

"The *yin* and *yang* are Ether; the Five Elements are corporeal matter. There being this corporeal matter, (individual) things and objects thereby appear" (*ibid.*, 1.8).

"The pure part of the Ether remains ether; its more turbid part becomes corporeal matter" (*ibid.*, 3.4).

Ch'i or Ether, in these passages, is the basic material from which concrete things are produced, and to which *li* or Principle supplies the pattern or form. This "material" is equivalent to what Plato and Aristotle term matter, whereas *chih* (corporeal matter) is this same "material" when it appears in more solid and tangible form. Chu says:

"When Heaven and Earth first separated, there was only *yin*

---

[1] This saying of one of the Ch'eng brothers, already quoted in the preceding section, is discussed on p. 549 below. — Tr.

Ether and *yang* Ether. This Ether underwent rotary movements, being ground around and around. This movement went on at such a speed that finally a great deal of sediment was pressed out, which, being inside (the revolving mass), had no place to go, and so consolidated to form the Earth at the center. The purer part of the Ether, however, formed Heaven (the sky), with its sun, moon, and stars. It is only there, at the outside, that the revolving movement still perpetually goes on, whereas Earth lies in the center, where it does not move; it does not lie at the bottom (of the cosmos)" (*ibid.*, 1.5).

It is evident that the "sediment" here spoken of is the same as the *chih* or "corporeal matter" of the earlier passages.

Of this sediment, the first to be squeezed out was comparatively fine and volatile, whereas what emerged later was more coarse. Chu says:

"Generally speaking, in the creation of things of the universe, what is light and pure came first, followed by what is heavier and more turbid. First, in Heaven, water was produced, and then, on Earth, fire was produced. [1] These two are the lightest and purest among the Five Elements. Metal and wood came next to fire and water in weight, while earth is still heavier than metal and wood" (*ibid.*, 94.17).

Again:

"In the beginning of Heaven and Earth, when they were still in a state of undifferentiated chaos, I believe that there existed only water and fire. The sediment from water then formed the terrestrial Earth, so that today if one climbs to a high spot, all the mountains will be seen to be shaped like waves, owing to the fact that the water drifted in this way. Thus in the beginning everything was exceedingly soft, whereas later a solidification took place, though we cannot know just when this solidification occurred.

"*Question*: 'Do you think that this process was similar to the way in which the flow of the tide heaps up sand?'

"*Answer*: 'Just so. The most turbid part of water became the Earth, while the purest part of fire became such things as the wind, thunder, lightning, sun, and stars" (*ibid.*, 1.6).

Here we see that water and fire were the first of the Five Elements to appear, and that the element earth, which formed the terrestrial

---

[1] For these correlations, as carried out by the *Yin-yang* school, see chap. 2, p. 14. — Tr.

Earth, came last. Thus did our physical world come into existence.

Translator's Note: In these quotations, there seems to be an inconsistency between: (a) the last quotation, which says: "The sediment from water (i.e., the watery sediment which became the element earth) then formed the terrestrial Earth"; (b) the quotation just preceding, which says: "First, in Heaven, water was produced, and then, on Earth, fire was produced"; (c) the first quotation in the present section, which says: "Terrestrial Earth is composed of (the element) earth." This inconsistency, however, may be resolved if we assume that the Heaven and Earth of quotation (b) represent a comparatively early phase of creation, in which the process of differentiation of the originally inchoate Ether was only beginning, whereas the Heaven and Earth of quotations (a) and (c) belong to a later phase, characterized by the emergence of a more clearly differentiated universe immediately antecedent to that of today. This assumption of successive creative phases unfortunately does not seem to be directly confirmed by Chu Hsi's other available statements on the subject. Support for it, however, may be found in the *Yin-yang* school's speculations, which give Chu Hsi his basis for statement (b). Thus if we turn to chap. 2, p. 14, we are there told that "with 1, the number pertaining to Heaven, the element water is produced, and with 6, pertaining to Earth, it reaches full development. Likewise fire is produced with 2 (Earth) and completed with 7 (Heaven); ... and earth (as an element) is produced with 5 (Heaven) and completed with 10 (Earth)." This indicates that the elements assume their completed state only as the result of a two-stage evolutionary process that fluctuates between Heaven and Earth.

Being concrete, this physical world, like all other concrete things, must undergo both creation and ultimate destruction. The *Conversations* (94.4) tells us:

"Before the Supreme Ultimate, there must have been another world, just as the night of yesterday passes into the day of today. In the same way (the ceaseless alternation of) the *yin* and the *yang* constitutes a great 'closing and opening.'[1]

"*Question*: If one may deduce that this was the case before the Supreme Ultimate, must not the same be true for the future?

"*Answer*: Quite so. What Master Ch'eng says, 'Movement and quiescence have no starting point; the *yin* and the *yang* have no beginning,' illustrates this very clearly."

Again (94.12):

"*Question*: (What is the meaning of the words), 'Movement and quiescence have no starting point; the *yin* and the *yang* have no beginning'?

---

[1] A phrase based on the *Book of Changes* (Appen. III, p. 372). — Tr.

"*Answer*: This means that one cannot speak of (the alternation of the *yin* and *yang* as) having a beginning. For previous to that 'beginning' there ultimately is something else. It is in this manner that the whole universe, once having been created, is thereafter destroyed, and then again in the same manner re-created. And what end is there to all this?"

The curious phrase, "before the Supreme Ultimate," can here refer only to a time prior to that of the existing physical world. At that time an earlier world existed, just as, after our own world meets its end, it will be followed by yet another world. In this way the cycle of creation and destruction continues eternally. [1]

Within the present physical world, the first human beings, according to Chu Hsi, were produced through spontaneous generation (*tzŭ-jan pien-hua* 自然變化):

"In the beginning of the universe, how indeed can the existence of a human race be postulated? But then the steamy Ether consolidated to form two human beings, . . . each like the lice which today exist on men's bodies, where they come into being through spontaneous generation" (*ibid.*, 94.15).

To describe this process of spontaneous generation, Chu also uses another term, *ch'i hua*, lit., "evolutions of the Ether." [2] This he contrasts as follows with the more usual process of genetic propagation (*hsing sheng* 形生, lit., "propagation in the [same] image"):

" 'Evolutions of the Ether' occurred when, in the beginning, individual human beings were spontaneously produced without having any progenitors. 'Propagation in the (same) image' occurred when, there being these individual human beings, propagation thereafter took place from one to another without end" (*ibid.*).

Since human beings are said to have come into being in this way,

---

[1] Another passage in the *Conversations* (1.7), however, reads as follows: "*Question*: 'From the beginning (of the present universe) until today is less than 10,000 years. I do not know what things may have been like before then.' *Answer*: 'Before then there must also have been clarity and light as we have today.' *Question*: 'Can the universe ever be destroyed?' *Answer*: 'It itself cannot, but a time will come when, mankind having completely lost all moral principle (*tao*), everything will be reduced to a state of chaos. Men and creatures will then be entirely wiped out, but afterward there will again come a new beginning.' " This statement, that the universe itself is never destroyed, but that a time will come when the men and creatures in it will be utterly annihilated, differs from what has just been said.

[2] A term borrowed from Ch'eng Yi. See chap. 12, beginning of sect. 2, iv. — Tr.

it is reasonable to suppose that, for Chu, other creatures orginated similarly.

4—THE NATURE IN MEN AND OTHER CREATURES

Chu Hsi says:

"The creation of man depends simply upon the union of Principle with the Ether. Heavenly Principle (*t'ien li*) is, surely, vast and inexhaustible. Without the Ether, nevertheless, even though there be Principle, the latter will have no place to which to attach itself. Therefore the two Ethers (the *yin* and *yang*) must interact upon one another, condense, and thus create. Only then will Principle have something to which to adhere. All men's capacity to speak, move, think, and act, is entirely (a product of) the Ether; and yet within this (Ether) Principle inheres" (*Conversations*, 4.10).

Principle that is thus contained within the Ether to form an individual human being, is then known as the nature or *hsing*. This nature, however, is not restricted to human beings alone, for other creatures also have their own *hsing* or nature. We have seen how four centuries earlier the T'ien-t'ai monk Chan-jan (711-782) had proclaimed that "even inanimate things possess the (Buddha-)nature." [1] On this point it is conceivable that Chu Hsi may have been influenced by Chan-jan, for he himself says:

"There is no single thing in the world which does not have the nature. That is to say, when there is a thing, there must be its nature; when there is no thing, there is then no nature" (*Conversations*, 4.1).

That a thing's nature is the same as that thing's Principle or *li* is clearly indicated in the following passage:

"*Question*: 'How is it that dried up withered things also possess the nature?'

"*Answer*: 'For them there has from the beginning been such a Principle' " (*ibid.*, 4.6).

We read further: "*Question*: 'I have seen how in your reply-letter to Yü Fang-shu you maintain that even a dried up withered thing has Principle. But I do not understand how such dried up things as a tile or a pebble should have this Principle.'

"*Answer*: '(There is Principle) even for rhubarb or aconite. These

---

[1] See chap. 9, sect. 1, ix. — Tr.

too are dried up things, and yet rhubarb cannot act as aconite, nor can aconite act as rhubarb' " [1] (*ibid.*).

It has been stated earlier that every individual object contains the Supreme Ultimate in its entirety. It should be noted, however, that, for any individual thing, it is only that thing's own particular Principle that is able to manifest itself. As to the Supreme Ultimate as a whole, this, though also present, remains concealed. The reason lies in the fact that it is obscured by the physical Ether or *ch'i*, with which the object in question is also endowed. This is explained in the following passage from the *Conversations* (4.2):

"*Question*: 'Men and other creatures are all endowed with the Principle of the universe to give them their nature; they all receive the Ether of the universe to give them their shape. ... In the case of these other creatures, are they as they are because they have been incompletely endowed with Principle, or is this rather due to the opacity and cloudiness of the associated Ether which they also receive?'

"*Answer*: 'It is simply that the Ether received by them being limited, their Principle is also correspondingly limited. In the case of dogs and horses, for example, their physical constitution being what it is, the functions of which they are capable are correspondingly limited.'

"*Further question*: 'Since each individual thing possesses the entire Supreme Ultimate, does this not mean that Principle is everywhere complete?'

"*Answer*: 'You may speak of it either as complete or partial. As Principle it cannot be other than complete, yet from the point of view of the Ether it is necessarily partial. ' "

Again (*ibid.*, 4.10):

"From the point of view of the oneness of the Ether, all men and other creatures come into being by receiving this one Ether. But from the point of view of its varying degrees of fineness, the Ether received by man is perfect and free from obstruction, whereas that received by other creatures is imperfect and impeding. In the case of man, because he receives it in its perfection, Principle permeates it without anywhere being impeded. But in the case of other creatures, because they receive it in its imperfection, the Principle in

---

[1] I.e., each can follow only its own specialized function. The dried leaves and stems of these plants are used in China for medicine. — Tr.

them is impeded and fails to give them intelligence. ... Even among those creatures which do possess intelligence, it runs in one direction only. Examples are the crow's understanding of filial piety, and the otter's understanding of how to offer sacrifice. [1] Similarly, the dog can do no more than keep guard, and the ox no more than plough."

Thus Principle, with which all things are endowed, is fundamentally always complete. Owing to the imperfections and impediments of the Ether with which these things are also endowed, however, it is unable to manifest itself in its entirety, and so has the appearance of incompleteness. "In the case of dogs and horses, for example, their physical constitution being what it is, the functions of which they are capable are correspondingly limited." That is to say, it is only that particular Principle in them that causes them to be dogs and horses respectively, that succeeds in being manifested. When Chu says that "the Ether received by them being limited, their Principle is also correspondingly limited," what he really means, in the light of his general system, is that Principle can become manifested only to the extent that it is permitted to do so by the limitations imposed by the Ether.

The above supplies the clue to Chu's theory of the origin of evil. We read in two passages of the *Conversations* (4.13):

"*Question*: 'Since Principle is everywhere good, how is it that the Ether is differentiated into the pure and the turbid?'

"*Answer*: 'Because, as soon as one speaks of the Ether, there is then some that of itself is cold and some that is hot, some fragrant and some bad smelling.' "

Again: "In the beginning, how could the two (*yin* and *yang*) Ethers and the Five Elements have been anything but perfect? It is simply because they have since been swished and rolled to and fro, that they are no longer perfect."

Thus Principle, though wholly good in itself, loses its perfection as soon as it becomes actualized in the Ether, owing to the impediments imposed by the latter. The case is like that of a circle which,

---

[1] Because the crow is able to disgorge its food, there is a folk belief in China that it offers food to its parents. As to the sacrificing by the otter, we are told in the *Yüeh Ling* (Monthly Commands), p. 251, under the first month of spring: "The fish then rise to the ice and the otter offers them in sacrifice." Kao Yu (fl. 205-212) comments on this statement: "The otter is a water animal. It seizes carp which it places on the side of the stream, laying them out in all directions. It is commonly said of this that it sacrifices the fish." — Tr.

as an idea, is of course perfectly round, but, when actualized in a concrete object, is never absolutely circular. In the same way all the imperfections of the existing world result from the impediments of the Ether.

Since this is generally true of physical things, it logically follows that among human beings, too, there should be some who receive the Ether in its purer aspects, and some in its less pure. Chu says:

"As regards men's (physical) endowment, there are differences in it according to its opaqueness or clarity, purity or turbidness" (*ibid.*).

Persons who receive the Ether in its purity are sages (*sheng*); those who receive it in its impurity are evil men. Through such a theory, Chu believes, we may consistently solve that problem of the goodness or evilness of human nature that had been so hotly debated in Confucianism ever since the time of Mencius and Hsün Tzŭ.

A lengthy passage in the *Conversations* (4.15) states further:

"*Question*: 'With whom originated the theory regarding the physical element?' [1]

"*Answer*: 'It began with Chang (Tsai) and the Ch'eng (brothers). I regard them as having enormously helped the School of the Sages, and as having done great service to the scholars who have come after. A reading of them fills one with a strong realization that, before their time, no one had touched on this point. Han Yü, for example, in his *On the Origin of the Nature*, propounded the theory of the three grades (of the nature). Yet though what he said is true, he failed to state clearly that what he was speaking about is only the nature as found in the physical element. For how, in the nature (as originally constituted), could there be these "three grades" ? [2]

" 'When Mencius says that the nature is good, he speaks of it only with respect to its origin, and says nothing about it as found in the physical element. Thus he, too, fails to make a clear distinction. Other philosophers have asserted that the nature is evil, or that in it both good and evil are intermingled. [3] But if the doctrines of Chang and the Ch'engs had appeared earlier, there would have been no need for all this discussion and controversy. If, therefore, the doctrines

---

[1] The words *ch'i* (Ether or matter) and *chih* (corporeal matter) are here combined into a single term, translated as "physical element." — Tr.

[2] On Han Yü's theory, see chap. 10, end of sect. 1. — Tr.

[3] For theories of this sort, cf. vol. 1, pp. 147-148. — Tr.

of Chang and the Ch'engs are admitted, those of the other philosophers go into discard.'

"(The Master) then quoted Heng-ch'ü: [1] 'When shapes exist,
there then exists the physical nature. The conquest of it by goodness
leads to the preservation of the nature of Heaven and Earth. Therefore in the physical nature there is that which the superior man denies
to be his nature.'

"(The Master) further quoted the words of Ming-tao: [2] 'A discussion of the nature without the physical element is incomplete. A
discussion of the physical element without the nature leads to obscurity. To differentiate these into two separate entities is wrong.'

" 'Moreover,' (the Master continued), 'if we are to say that love,
righteousness, propriety, and wisdom alone constitute the nature,
how is it that there are some people born evil in the world? [3] It is only
owing to the physical endowment that this is so. If one does not take
this physical element into account, the theory will not be well rounded,
and therefore will be incomplete. But if, on the contrary, one takes
only the physical endowment into account, some of which may be
good and some bad, while disregarding the fact that in the first place
there were only these normative Principles, then one will fall into
obscurity.

" 'Since the time when Confucius, Master Tseng, Tzŭ-ssŭ, and
Mencius understood these ideas, no one has propounded them (until
Chang and the Ch'engs).'

"Ch'ien-chih [4] asked: 'According to the varying degrees of
opacity or clarity in the Ether of the universe, is Principle also
correspondingly opaque or clear?'

"*Answer*: 'Principle in itself never varies. It is only the Ether
that varies in this way.' "

---

[1] The literary name of Chang Tsai. The quotation is from Chang's *Correct
Discipline for Beginners*, and has already been cited in chap. 12, p. 488. There Chu's
comment is also cited, to the effect that the phrase, "the nature of Heaven and
Earth," has reference to Principle, i.e., to the nature before it is combined with
the Ether. — Tr.

[2] The posthumous name of the elder of the Ch'engs, Ch'eng Hao. The
quotation that follows is elsewhere, however, attributed by Chu to the younger
Ch'eng, Ch'eng Yi. See J. Percy Bruce, transl., *The Philosophy of Human Nature*,
by Chu Hsi (London, 1922), p. 74, note 2.— Tr.

[3] Lit., "born without any form" (*wu chuang* 無 狀), meaning here, "without any manifestation (of goodness)," but actually having a stronger connotation
of evil than these words literally indicate. — Tr.

[4] The "style" of Lin Kuang-ch'ao (1114-78), a Neo-Confucianist. — Tr.

Although Chu here merely claims to follow the doctrines of Chang Tsai and the Ch'eng brothers, his theory is actually based upon his own philosophical system as a whole, and represents a considerable advance over the statements of these three predecessors.

At the beginning of this section we have already read Chu's statement: "All men's capacity to speak, move, think, and act, is entirely (a product of) the Ether." Two passages in the *Conversations* (5.3) expand this idea:

"*Question*: 'Is (man's) intellectual faculty (*ling ch'u* 靈處) the mind (*hsin*) or is it the nature (*hsing*)?'

"*Answer*: 'The intellectual faculty is the mind alone and not the nature. For the nature is nothing but Principle.' "

Again:

"*Question*: 'As regards consciousness, is it the mind's intellectual faculty that makes it thus, or is it a product of the Ether?'

"*Answer*: 'It is not the Ether alone, because before (the Ether existed) there was already the Principle governing consciousness. But this Principle itself cannot exercise consciousness. There can be consciousness only when the Ether has condensed to form physical shapes, and Principle has united with the Ether. The case is like that of the flame of this candle. It is because the latter receives this rich fat that we have so much light.' "

In other words, consciousness, like every other thing, has its own particular Principle. In itself, however, this Principle is Principle and nothing else, which means that there can be no concrete exemplification of consciousness until after its Principle has united with the Ether. Chu stresses the fact that consciousness, otherwise known as the "intellectual faculty," is "mind alone and not the nature. For the nature is nothing but Principle." In other words, consciousness pertains to the concrete and physical world. Hence it manifests itself only as the result of the union of form with matter, just as the light of a candle depends upon the fat of that candle in order to manifest itself. The point at issue here is that Chu regards mind as concrete and as able to have concrete activity, whereas such is not the case with Principle.

Chu Hsi not only discusses the relationship between mind and nature, but also between them and another major category in Chinese psychology, that of the *ch'ing*, i.e., feelings or emotions:

"As to mind, nature, and the feelings, Mencius has given the best explanation. Love (*jen*) pertains to the nature, whereas commiseration pertains to the feelings, and so necessarily proceeds from the mind. [1] Mind is the unifying agent between the nature and the feelings. But as to the nature, it is simply what a thing ought to be. It is nothing but Principle, and is not a physical thing. For were it a physical thing, it would necessarily have evil as well as goodness. Not being a physical thing, however, but only Principle, it is therefore entirely good" (*Conversations*, 5.11).

Thus Chu distinguishes sharply between the nature, which is non-concrete and therefore wholly good, and the feelings, which pertain to the concrete world, and hence have the concrete mind as their point of emanation. Though the nature itself consists of Principle, however, it is that Principle only as found within the physical Ether. Therefore, though different from the feelings, it, like them, is contained within the mind. That is why Chu Hsi describes the mind as "the unifying agent between the nature and the feelings."

Chu goes on to discuss the relationship between mind, nature, the feelings, and another factor which he calls *ts'ai* 才, i.e., "capacity" or "ability":

"The nature is the mind's Principle; the feelings are the mind's movements; capacity (*ts'ai*) is that whereby the feelings are able to act in a certain way. The feelings and capacity are in fact very close to each other. But the feelings appear consequent to their encounter with (external) things, and their courses (of action) curve and twist (in accordance with these external stimuli). Capacity is that whereby they are able to act in this way. Though pressed along no matter how many complications and ramifications, [2] they invariably issue from the mind" (*ibid.*, 5.15).

Again: "Capacity (*ts'ai*) is the power of the mind, which has the energy to carry on activities. The mind is the controller and ruler; it is in this that its greatness consists. The mind may be likened to water. The nature is the Principle of that water and, standing motionless, represents that water when it is quiescent, whereas the feelings, in their activities, represent the water when it is in movement. Desire (*yü* 欲) is the pouring forth of that water until it overflows, and

---

[1] Mencius maintained that love, righteousness, propriety, and wisdom are innate virtues of human nature, which are manifested in objective conduct in the following feelings or senses: commiseration for others, shame and dislike for dishonorable conduct, modesty and yielding to others, and the sense of right and wrong. See vol. 1, pp. 119 f. — Tr.

[2] Lit., "a thousand heights and ten thousand courses (of events)." — Tr.

capacity is the water's physical force which enables it thus to pour forth. Its pouring forth may be sometimes rapid, sometimes slow, depending upon the differences in its capacity. This is what Yi-ch'uan means when he says that the nature is the endowment of Heaven, whereas capacity is the endowment of the Ether. [1] The nature alone remains constant, whereas the feelings, the mind, and capacity all conform (in their variations) to the Ether" (*ibid.*, 5.14-15).

Since the Principle with which men are endowed is ever the same, it follows that their "nature alone remains constant." Human inequalities, on the other hand, derive from inequalities in the purity of the Ether with which men are also endowed. As for desire, it is an excess compared to "the pouring forth of the water until it overflows." The sharp apposition established by Chu Hsi and the Rationalistic school generally between desire and Principle (often respectively termed "human desire" and "Heavenly Principle") will be explained in detail below.

5—Ethics and Theory of Spiritual Cultivation

Among the objective Principles or *li*, there are those governing the primary human virtues. Since man's nature is the summation of all Principles, it must necessarily contain the Principles for these specific virtues as well, namely *jen* or love, *yi* or righteousness, *li* or propriety, and *chih* or wisdom (meaning especially moral understanding). Chu Hsi speaks of them as follows:

"Love, righteousness, propriety, and wisdom constitute the nature. This nature has no shape that may be touched; it consists solely of Principle. The feelings, on the other hand, are susceptible to perception. They consist of commiseration (for others), shame and dislike (of anything dishonorable), modesty and yielding, and a sense of right and wrong" (*Conversations*, 6.9).

Again: "(Chu Hsi remarked:) 'The fact that the mind is able to do so much is, I would say, because it has within it many normative Principles.' He said further: 'How may we see that it possesses these four (virtues)? (The answer is that) because of its (feeling of) commiseration, we may know that it possesses love; because of its (feeling of) shame and dislike, we may know that it possesses righteousness' " (*ibid.*, 6.10).

---

[1] On this theory, as expressed by Ch'eng Yi (whose literary name was Yi-ch'uan), see chap. 12, p. 516. — Tr.

Principle is metaphysical and abstract, and therefore cannot itself be physically perceived. Nevertheless, because all men possess the feeling of commiseration for others, it may be deduced that within our natures there must be the Principle governing this feeling of commiseration, to which we give the name of *jen* or love. So too for the feeling of shame and of dislike, from the existence of which may be deduced the Principle of this feeling, called *yi* or righteousness. In the same way, from the feeling of modesty and yielding may be deduced the Principle which is called propriety, and from the sense of right and wrong may be deduced the Principle which is called wisdom, i.e., moral understanding. For every single thing there must be a Principle, without which the thing itself could not exist.

Within our natures, however, there are not only the four above-mentioned virtues, but also the Supreme Ultimate in its entirety. This, however, fails to be completely manifested, owing to the impediments of the physical Ether. The sage is he who is able to rid himself of these impediments, and thus permit the Supreme Ultimate to shine forth in its entirety. Chu says:

"Once there is Principle, the existence of the Ether follows. Likewise, once the Ether exists, there must be Principle. He who receives the Ether in its purity is a sage (*sheng*) or a worthy (*hsien*). He is like a precious pearl lying in clear cold water. But he who receives the Ether in its impurity is obtuse and degenerate. He is like a pearl lying in turbid water. What is called 'the exemplification of illustrious virtue' [1] is this process of cleansing the pearl from its surrounding turbid water. Other creatures also possess this Principle, which is then like the pearl dropped into the filthiest of muddy places" (*ibid.*, 4.17).

He says again (12.8):

"Confucius spoke of 'the conquest of self and return to propriety.' [2] The *Doctrine of the Mean* says: 'Advance toward equilibrium and harmony' (p. 300); or again: 'Prize the virtuous nature and pursue the path of inquiry and study' (p. 323). The *Great Learning* speaks of 'the exemplification of illustrious virtue.' And the *Book of History* says: 'The mind of the body is unstable; the mind of the spirit is but small. Be discriminating, be undivided, that you may

---

[1] A famous phrase from the *Great Learning*, p. 411. — Tr.
[2] *Analects*, XII, 1. — Tr.

sincerely hold fast to the mean.' [1] The teachings of the sage, whether they be a thousand or ten thousand words, are only that man should preserve Heavenly Principle (*t'ien li*) and extinguish human desire (*jen yü*). . . .

"Man's nature is originally clear, but it is like a pearl immersed in impure water, where its luster cannot be seen. Being removed from the dirty water, however, it becomes lustrous of itself as before. If each person could himself realize that it is human desire that causes this obscuring, this would bring enlightenment (*ming*). It is on this point alone that all one's efforts must be concentrated.

"At the same time, however, one should pursue the 'investigation of things.' [2] Today investigate one thing, and tomorrow investigate another. Then, just as when mobile troops storm a besieged city or capture a fortified spot, human desire will automatically be dissolved away.

"Therefore when the Ch'eng Masters speak of earnestness (*ching*), [3] they only mean that we ourselves have a luminous something here within us. And if, with this earnestness, we ward off the enemy, ever maintaining earnestness here within, then automatically human desire will be foiled. The Master (Confucius) said: 'Has love (*jen*) its source in oneself, or is it forsooth derived from others?' [4] The important point is just here within."

Man derives his nature from Principle, and his physical frame from the Ether. This nature is the "Heavenly Principle" mentioned above; it is the "mind of the spirit" of the *Book of History*. Man's feelings, on the other hand, arise from his physical frame, and are equivalent to the "mind of the body" also mentioned in the *Book of History*. When they go to excess, they become "human desire," another term for which, often used by Chu Hsi and other Neo-Confucianists, is "selfish desire" (*ssŭ yü* 私 欲). The former term

---

[1] *Book of History*, I, ii, p. 50. "Mind of the body" is the rendering for *jen hsin*, lit., "human mind," and "mind of the spirit" is that for *tao hsin*, lit., "mind of Tao." — Tr.

[2] The "investigation of things" (*ko wu*), and its correlate, the "extension of knowledge" (*chih chih*), are famous phrases from the *Great Learning*, pp. 411-412. On Ch'eng Yi's interpretation of them, which greatly influenced Chu's own interpretation, see preceding chapter, pp. 529 f. — Tr.

[3] Absolute seriousness of purpose and attentiveness to conduct. The word was stressed by both the Ch'engs, but especially by the younger brother, Ch'eng Yi. See preceding chapter, sect 2, vii-viii. — Tr.

[4] *Analects*, XII, 1. — Tr.

has reference to the fact that this desire results from the overflow or excess of feelings which are held in common by the whole human race. The latter term is used because these feelings more specifically tend to separate the individual from other individuals.

"Heavenly Principle," when obscured by this "human desire," is like the pearl lying in muddy water. It can never be wholly obliterated, however, as shown by the very fact that man is potentially capable of realizing that desire acts in this way. "All one's efforts must be concentrated" toward acquiring this realization, and this can best be done through what Ch'eng Yi calls the exercise of earnestness (*ching*), and the "extension of knowledge" (*chih chih*). As pointed out by Chu, the former simply means that within each and every one of us there exists a luminous spiritual something, and that in our every act we should keep the realization of this fact within our minds. As to the other line of procedure, that of the "extension of knowledge," Chu writes as follows:

"The words, 'the extension of knowledge lies in the investigation of things,' mean that we should apply ourselves to things so as to gain an exhaustive knowledge of their Principle. This is because there is no human intelligence (utterly) devoid of knowledge, and no single thing in the world without Principle. But because (the knowledge of) these Principles is not exhaustive, this knowledge is consequently in some ways incomplete. This is why the first instruction of the *Great Learning* is that the student must, for all the separate things in the world, proceed, by means of the Principles already known to him, to gain a further exhaustive knowledge of those others (with which he is as yet unfamiliar), in this way seeking to extend (his knowledge) to the furthest point. When one has exerted oneself for a long time, finally a morning will come when complete understanding will open before one. Thereupon there will be thorough comprehension of all the multitude of things, external or internal, fine or coarse, and every exercise of the mind will be marked by complete enlightenment." [1]

This theory was, as we shall see in the next chapter, to be hotly attacked by the Idealistic school of Lu Chiu-yüan and Wang Shou-jen. Effort of this kind, they maintained, is dissipating and irrelevant. From the point of view of Chu's own system, however,

---

[1] From Chu's *Ta Hsüeh Chang-chü* (Commentary on the Great Learning), sect. on "the investigation of things."

the theory is quite reasonable. For, according to this system, not only does each individual thing in the universe have its own Principle, but all these Principles are at the same time present within the nature contained within our own mind. To acquire exhaustive knowledge of the Principles of these innumerable external objects, therefore, is the way to gain an understanding of this inner nature. Hence the acquisition of such knowledge, if sufficiently continued, finally leads to a moment of sudden enlightenment, in which the Principles of the myriad things of the universe are visible to us within our own nature. This is what Chu means when he says (see p. 535 above): "In the universe there is no single thing that lies beyond the nature."

When we have at last reached this point, "there will be thorough comprehension of all the multitude of things, external or internal, fine or coarse, and every exercise of the mind will be marked by complete enlightenment." The question whether such a procedure will, in actual fact, achieve this result, is, of course, quite another matter. The fact remains that once Chu's general system is accepted, such a theory becomes quite plausible. [1]

6—POLITICAL PHILOSOPHY

Since for every individual thing there must be a Principle, it is inevitable that the organization of the state and society must also have its own Principle. The ruler's accordance with this Principle will therefore result in good government, whereas failure to do so will lead to political disorder. Thus this Principle becomes equivalent to that Way or moral order (*Tao*), so stressed in early Confucianism as the means for bringing good government to the state and peace to the world. This *Tao*, as conceived by Chu Hsi, has an eternal objectivity, as shown in the following passage:

"During (the past) fifteen hundred years, ... the *Tao* that had (previously) been transmitted by (the sage rulers) Yao and Shun,

---

[1] When Chu speaks of the investigation of things, he really has in mind only s system of moral self cultivation, and his aim is solely to reach an understanding of the workings of our own minds. Likewise, when Lu Chiu-yüan and Wang Shou-jen criticize him on this doctrine, they do so entirely from this same point of view of self cultivation. It is a mistake, therefore, to regard Chu as here displaying a truly scientific spirit, or to consider him as seeking only for pure knowledge. [Knowledge, for him as for other Confucian thinkers, remains simply a means to a moral end. — Tr.]

the Three Kings (who founded the first three dynasties), the Duke of Chou, and Confucius, has never for one day been permitted to operate in the world. As regards the eternity of *Tao*, it is completely beyond human interference. It simply is what it is, a thing that has been from antiquity through modern times, without ever ceasing to be. Hence despite the violence men have done to it during (the past) fifteen hundred years, unto the end they will never be able to bring it to destruction" (*Writings*, 36.22).

Again: "One might say that it is not the *Tao* that has ever ceased, but men themselves who have desisted from following it. This is why it is said that (at the end of the Western Chou) it was not the *Tao* that perished, but simply Yu and Li who did not follow it" [1] (*ibid.*, p. 27).

The *Tao* or Way for governing the state and bringing peace to the world has always been as it is since earliest antiquity, and will always remain such, even though its external actualization in the physical world depends wholly upon whether men follow it or not. All men, therefore, who make any kind of achievement in government or society, do so only because their conduct conforms to this *Tao*. Even they, however, as pointed out by Chu, cannot understand it completely and hence cannot wholly succeed in practicing it:

"I have ever maintained that throughout antiquity and modern times there has been only the one Principle (for government), and that those who accord with it attain success, whereas those who flout it go to disaster. Certainly it is not at all true that it was only the sages and worthies of antiquity of whom this is so. Among the so-called 'bravos' and 'heroes' of later ages also, there have never been any who, having abandoned this Principle, were capable of constructive accomplishment. The fact simply is that, from the foundation upward, these sages and worthies of antiquity bent their energies toward being discriminating and undivided, so that they might thereby hold to the mean. [2] Thus from top to bottom, everything (they did) was entirely good.

"The so-called 'heroes' of later ages, on the other hand, never exerted this effort, but only bobbed their heads up and down in the realm of profit and desire. Those of them who were of somewhat

---

[1] Yu (781-771 B.C.) and Li (878-842 B.C.) were two wicked kings under whom the Western Chou dynasty became greatly weakened and finally met its end. — Tr.

[2] An allusion to the passage from the *Book of History* which is quoted below (p. 565, note 1), and has already been quoted in the preceding section. — Tr.

greater talent succeeded in coming into an unwitting agreement (with this Principle), each making accomplishment according to his own degree. Regardless of whether they were sometimes correct or not, however, they were all equally unable to reach complete goodness. Herein lies the explanation for what your letter says, that the Three Dynasties (Hsia, Shang, Chou) succeeded in reaching complete agreement, whereas the Han and T'ang failed to do so.

"You, however, have only spoken about this completeness or incompleteness as a fact, without explaining *why* it is that they were thus complete or incomplete. Go, then, to the realm of profit and desire, and there compare (what you see) with the deeds of the sage, noticing where there are seeming similarities. Then you will admit that the manner of the sage depends on nothing more than this. Herein lies the meaning of the saying that a trifling error leads to a mistake of a thousand miles" [1] (*ibid.*, p. 29).

In order to build a house, it is necessary to follow that Principle or *li* that underlies the building of all houses. This Principle has been as it is now through all eternity, irrespective of whether or not it has always been known or practiced by human beings. When followed by the architect, it becomes physically realized in a house that is firm and enduring. This fact applies, however, not only to the house built by an architect, for any other would-be house-builder must also conform to the Principle for building houses if he is to reach success. Such a man, however, probably has only an imperfect understanding of this Principle. Therefore he can do little more than come into an "unwitting agreement" with it, resulting in a structure which will only partially conform to the general Principle for house building. Thus the quality of the house depends wholly upon the extent to which it agrees with the Principle for houses, and at best this agreement can never be complete. The same factor distinguishes the government of the sage or worthy (true "architects" of the state) from that of the "bravo" or "hero" (would-be architects). Rule by the latter can at most provide only a petty kind of peace and prosperity, whereas rule by the former will be that of the true King, this term being taken in the Confucian sense.

"From the foundation upward, these sages and worthies of antiquities bent their energies toward being discriminating and

---

[1] A saying reminiscent of an apocryphal quotation from the *Book of Changes*. See chap. 3, p. 90. — Tr.

undivided, so that they might thereby hold to the mean. Thus from top to bottom, everything (they did) was entirely good." This statement points to a process of self cultivation on the part of the true King, which Chu Hsi further explains as follows:

"It is said: 'The mind of the body is unstable; the mind of the spirit is but small. Be discriminating, be undivided, that you may sincerely hold fast to the mean.' [1] This is the esoteric doctrine that was handed down, one to another, by Yao, Shun, and Yü. Because man, from the time when he is born, is fettered by the selfishness of the body, he therefore cannot but have the 'mind of the body.' And yet, because he surely has been endowed with something of the perfection of Heaven and Earth, he therefore cannot but have the 'mind of the spirit.' During the day's activities, these two are both in operation, each in turn overcoming or being overcome by the other. With this (struggle) are linked the individual's right or wrong conduct, gains or failings, as well as the entire world's good or disordered government, peace or peril. One should, therefore, aim to discriminate minutely, and not permit the mind of the body to mingle with the mind of the spirit. One should aim at preserving the latter in its oneness, and not permit Heavenly Principle to be dissipated into human desire. Then in all one does one will never fail to hit the mean, and throughout the world and country one will ever be correct" (*ibid.*, p. 25).

This reminds us of Plato's philosopher-king, who must first undergo an intense process of self cultivation so that he may transcend the phenomenal world and enter the world of pure and perfect ideas. Only then can he become the ruler of the masses of humanity. So too, says Chu Hsi, must the sage-king free his nature from the impediments of its surrounding Ether, so that all the Principles that lie within may become manifest. "Then in all one does one will never fail to hit the mean," in other words, one will in every act conform to the Principle governing that act. In this way, "throughout the world and country one will ever be correct." The ruler of the so-called "bravo" or "hero" type, however, lacks this fundamental self cultivation, and hence his actions constantly impinge upon the realm of human desire and selfishness. Government by such a man can at best be only an "unwitting agreement" with Heavenly Principle, and will often

---

[1] For this quotation from the *Book of History*, and the terms, "mind of body" and "mind of the spirit," see p. 560, note 1. — Tr.

fail to be even this. At the most, therefore, it can lead only to a petty kind of peace and prosperity.

All the passages here quoted are taken from Chu's letter to another Neo-Confucianist, Ch'en Liang, who, for his part, had maintained that there is no fundamental qualitative difference between the kingly government of the ancient Three Dynasties, and the inferior government of the Han and T'ang dynasties. The only distinction, he said, was one of degree: the Three Dynasties had succeeded in reaching "complete agreement" in their government, whereas the Han and T'ang had fallen short of this aim. In so saying, he was expressing the views of the Yung-k'ang school in Neo-Confucianism. [1] Chu Hsi, on the contrary, maintains that merely to speak of "the completeness or incompleteness" of these dynasties' achievements is not enough; one must further explain "*why* it is that they were thus complete or incomplete." For herein precisely lies the difference between the true King of the Confucian type, and the ordinary ruler who governs through force.

7—CRITICISM OF BUDDHISM

For Chu Hsi, as we have seen earlier (pp. 538—539), a prime difference between Buddhism and Confucianism is that the former considers the nature (*hsing*) to be "empty" (*k'ung*, Sanskrit *śūnya*), whereas the latter maintains that it contains actual Principle. Many of Chu's criticisms of Buddhism are based on this point. Thus we read in the *Conversations* (126.6):

"Ch'ien-chih [2] asked: Everyone today says that the doctrine of the Buddhists is one of 'non-existence' (*wu*), whereas that of the Taoists is one of 'emptiness' (*k'ung*). What is the difference between this 'non-existence' and 'emptiness'?

"*Answer*: 'Emptiness' is a term embracing both existence and non-existence. The Taoists say that there is a division into a half that is existent and a half that is non-existent. Everything of the past is (today) non-existent, while everything that lies beneath our eyes at the present time is existent. Therefore (this doctrine) is called one of 'emptiness.' [3]

---

[1] This school derived its name from a district of the same name in Chekiang. — Tr.

[2] See above, p. 555, note 4. — Tr.

[3] This does not seem to be very consistent, inasmuch as Chu elsewhere attributes the doctrine of "emptiness" to the Buddhists and not to the Taoists. — Tr.

"But according to the doctrines of the Buddhists, *everything* is 'non-existent.' What has gone by is non-existent, and what today lies beneath our eyes is also non-existent. Phenomenal matter (*rūpa*) is the same as 'emptiness,' and 'emptiness' is the same as 'phenomenal matter.' Everything alike, from the myriad affairs and things on the one hand, down to the 'hundred bones and nine apertures' (of the human body) on the other, all pertains to the non-existent. One may eat rice the livelong day, and they (the Buddhists) will say that one has not chewed a single grain. One may wear clothes the livelong day, and they will say that one has not put on a single piece of fabric."

The Buddhists regard all things as *māyā* or illusion; in their eyes "phenomenal matter is the same as emptiness." The Hua-yen school, for example, maintains that there is a complete identity between the noumenal and the phenomenal—meaning by the latter the concrete things and objects of the physical world, which, it says, are an actual part of the *Bhūtatathatā* or Absolute.[1] At first sight, therefore, it would seem that this school does not regard the Absolute as truly "empty" or unreal. From the point of view, therefore, that the Absolute, in the eyes of this school, embraces these concrete things, it itself may not be said to be "empty" or unreal. But from the point of view that these things, being finite, therefore have no permanence and are ever in a state of change, it may be said that the Absolute, in which they are included, is on the contrary itself "empty" or unreal.

The Supreme Ultimate of Neo-Confucianism, on the other hand, is conceived quite differently. The infinitude of individual Principles contained within it transcend time and space and eternally subsist. Though their concrete manifestations in the physical world are constantly undergoing either creation or destruction, they themselves never experience these changes. It follows, therefore, that the Supreme Ultimate, like the Principles comprising it, cannot be something "empty" or unreal. This is the point emphasized by Chu Hsi in his critique of Buddhism. Our nature, he maintains, is identical with the Supreme Ultimate in all its completeness, and like the latter, contains all separate Principles; therefore it, no more than the world of Principle, can be "empty" or unreal. This argument he expresses as follows:

"When the Buddhists speak of 'emptiness,' this does not mean

---

[1] See chap. 8, sect. 3, esp. pp. 351-352. — Tr.

that they are (entirely) incorrect. And yet for there to be this 'emptiness,' there must first be within it some kind of normative Principle. [1] For what use can there be in merely saying that we are 'empty,' without understanding that there is a genuine Principle (lying behind this 'emptiness')? The case is like that of a pool of clear water, the clear coldness of which extends to the very bottom. When first seen, it appears to have no water at all, and a person will then say that it is only 'empty.' Unless he stretches his hand to feel whether there is coldness or warmth, he will not know that there is water within. But such, precisely, is the viewpoint of the Buddhists. This fact should particularly be kept in mind by those students who lay stress upon 'the extension of knowledge through the investigation of things' " (*ibid.*, 126.9).

The world of Principle is one that is "pure, empty, and vast." It "holds no determined place; it has no shape or body." [2] Nevertheless, it would be incorrect to say that it is therefore "empty" and non-existent in the Buddhist sense. For though the Buddhists may have a certain justification for their doctrine of "emptiness," thus obliging Chu to admit that "this does not mean that they are (entirely) incorrect," the fact remains that Principle, according to Neo-Confucianism, remains ever what it is, so that it is a mistake to say that everything whatsoever is "empty" or unreal. Chu comments further on this:

"Those (the Buddhists) take the view that mind is 'empty' and has no Principle. These (the Confucianists) hold the view that although mind itself may be 'empty,' all the myriad different Principles are complete within it" [3] (*ibid.*).

"The Confucianists maintain that Principle undergoes neither creation nor destruction. The Buddhists maintain that consciousness (*shen shih* 神識) undergoes neither creation nor destruction" (*ibid.*, p. 8).

Since our nature or *hsing* is equivalent to the entire Supreme Ultimate, it follows that "all the myriad different Principles are com-

---

[1] I.e., there can be "emptiness" only in contrast to some sort of underlying reality. — Tr.

[2] See above, pp. 542-543 and 539 respectively. — Tr.

[3] I.e., mind pertains to "what is within shapes," and so is "empty" in an absolute sense. Nevertheless, it is the lodging place in man of all different Principles, which pertain to "what is above shapes," and hence are eternal and "real."

plete within it." These Principles, furthermore, "undergo neither creation nor destruction." This means that even persons who deny that there is such a thing as Principle at all, remain in their conduct unwittingly subject to the unchanging Principles present in their own nature. Chu points this out as follows:

"Beneath Heaven, it is only this normative Principle that unto the end we cannot but follow. The Buddhists and Taoists, for example, even though they would destroy the social relationships, [1] are nevertheless quite unable to escape from them. Thus, lacking (the relationship of) father and son, they nevertheless on the one hand pay respect to their own preceptors (as if they were fathers), and on the other treat their acolytes as sons. The elder among them become elder brother preceptors, while the younger become younger brother preceptors. They are thereby clinging to something false, whereas it is the (Confucian) sages and worthies who have preserved the reality" (*ibid.*).

The organization of society can proceed only according to a certain Principle. The devotees of Buddhism, though they wish to cut themselves off from ordinary human society, create for this purpose their own form of monkish organization, which is itself a type of society. Thus they, like all other human beings, unwittingly conform to the universal Principle that underlies all human society. Here, says Chu, is an evident instance of the fact that "beneath Heaven, it is only this normative Principle that unto the end we cannot but follow."

Chu further maintains that the Buddhists, by maintaining that there is only a "consciousness" which exists for all time, fail to understand the true character of the *hsing* or nature. As a result they wrongly equate the mind with the nature. We read in the *Conversations* (126.13):

"Hsü Tzǔ-jung [2] engaged in a discussion as to whether a dried up withered thing has or has not the nature. The Master (Chu Hsi) commented on this: The nature is only Principle. Once a certain thing exists, there is a Principle for it. The error of Tzǔ-jung lies in the fact that he takes mind as being the nature, thereby being just like the Buddhists. The Buddhists only grind and rub this mind away down to its finest essence, as if it were a lump of something. Having scraped off one layer of skin, they then scrape off another,

---

[1] By becoming monks and thus cutting themselves off from the world. — Tr.
[2] I.e., Hsü Chao-jan, a disciple of Chu Hsi. — Tr.

until they have scraped to a place where they can no longer scrape. And when they have thus ground away until they have reached the mind's innermost essence, they then hold this to be the nature. They certainly fail to realize that this nature of theirs is exactly what the (Confucian) sage calls the mind. Therefore Shang-ts'ai [1] says: 'What the Buddhists call the nature is exactly what the (Confucian) sage calls mind, and what the Buddhists call mind is exactly what the sage calls thinking.' Mind itself merely serves to contain Principle, but the Buddhists from the beginning have failed to recognize this Principle, and throughout recognize the activities of consciousness as constituting the nature.

"Thus as to sight, hearing, speech, and facial expression, the sage knows that for sight there is a Principle, for hearing there is a Principle, for speech there is a Principle, for conduct there is a Principle, and for thinking there is a Principle. These are what the Viscount of Chi described as clearness of sight, distinctness of hearing, compliance (of speech to reason), respectfulness (in conduct), and perspicaciousness (in thought). [2]

"The Buddhists, on the contrary, merely recognize the (physical) *ability* (and not the Principle itself) of seeing, hearing, speaking, thinking, and acting, as constituting the nature. Whether this (physical process of) seeing results in clear perception or not, whether the (process of) hearing results in keen audition or not, whether the (process of) speaking results in compliance or not, or whether the thinking is perspicacious or not—all this they do not bother about. Higgledly-piggledly, they recognize it all as belonging to the nature. What they dread most is that someone will mention this word Principle, which they are all anxious to do away with. This is precisely the doctrine of Kao Tzŭ, that 'that which at birth is so, is what is called the nature.' " [3]

Chu's argument here is that even a dried up withered thing, though lacking in consciousness, nevertheless remains a thing, for which there must therefore be a particular Principle. This Principle

---

[1] The literary name of Hsieh Liang-tso (1050-1103), a disciple of the Ch'eng brothers. — Tr.

[2] See the *Hung Fan* (Grand Norm), p. 141, a section of the *Book of History* ascribed traditionally, but almost surely erroneously, to the Viscount of Chi, a virtuous noble who lived at the end of the Shang dynasty. — Tr.

[3] On Kao Tzŭ, a philosophical opponent of Mencius, and on his theory that man's nature is indifferent to either good or evil, see vol. 1, pp. 145-147. — Tr.

is called its *hsing* or nature. Consciousness, on the other hand, pertains solely to mind, which is quite distinct from Principle. By saying, therefore, that because a thing lacks consciousness it hence lacks a nature of its own, we thereby fall into the error of identifying mind with nature. The activities of consciousness derive from mind. Hence when the Buddhists try to recognize the nature in such activities, what they are really recognizing is mind. This mind has concrete existence and pertains to "what is within shapes," whereas Principle subsists only and pertains to "what is above shapes."'

From what has been said, it is evident that Chu Hsi's philosophy differs from what is ordinarily termed idealism and, in fact, comes closer to modern neo-realism. Unfortunately, however, there has been but little development of logic in Chinese philosophy, and Chu has likewise paid little attention to this aspect. Therefore what he calls Principle, which might otherwise be a wholly logical concept, has for him ethical qualities as well. The Principle for vision, for example, if conceived merely as that by which the act of vision is possible, is a logical concept. If, however, it is conceived as that by which clarity (i.e., excellence) of vision results, it then becomes an ethical concept. These two aspects, the logical and the ethical, are combined in Chu Hsi, for he maintains that the Principle of a thing not only makes that thing what it is but at the same time makes it what it *ought* (morally) to be. The reason is that Chu Hsi's interest is primarily ethical rather than logical. The same is also true of Plato, though to a lesser extent. It is likewise true of Chinese philosophy as a whole, which has always tended to place its primary emphasis upon ethics. [1]

---

[1] For an article which further discusses some of the points touched on in this section, see D. Bodde, "The Chinese View of Immortality: Its Expression by Chu Hsi and its Relationship to Buddhist Thought," *Review of Religion*, vol. 6 (1942), 369-383. — Tr.

CHAPTER XIV

LU CHIU-YÜAN, WANG SHOU-JEN, AND MING IDEALISM

1—Lu Chiu-yüan

Contemporary with Chu Hsi, the greatest figure in the Rationalistic (*Li Hsüeh*) school of Neo-Confucianism, there lived another thinker who is important as the real founder of the rival Idealistic (*Hsin Hsüeh* 心 學) school. This is Lu Chiu-yüan 陸 九 淵 (1139-93), better known under his literary name as Lu Hsiang-shan 象 山.[1] Yang Chien (1140-1225), in his biography of Lu contained in Lu's *Complete Works*, writes as follows:

"The Master's surname was Lu, his personal name was Chiu-yüan, and he was styled Tzǔ-ching 子 靜. . . . He was born with an exceptional endowment, being upright, firm, and unassuming. . . . When, as a boy, he heard people intone the words of Yi-ch'uan, he felt as though wounded by them.[2] Thus he once remarked to others: 'Why is it that Yi-ch'uan's words do not agree with those of Confucius and Mencius?' And when he first read the *Analects*, he suspected Master Yu's words of being involved and complicated.[3] Another day, in his reading of ancient books, he encountered the words *yü* 宇 and *chou* 宙, on which the commentary stated: 'The

---

[1] For these dates, see Siu-chi Huang, *Lu Hsiang-shan, a twelfth century Chinese idealist philosopher* (New Haven, 1944), p. 9, note 2, which, however, is incorrect in saying that Professor Fung gives the date of death as 1192. For a more detailed account of Lu's life than that given below, see *ibid.*, pp. 12-17, from which we learn that Lu was the youngest of six brothers in a well-to-do family; that he passed the highest of the government examinations, that of *chin-shih*, in 1172; that he then held a series of official positions; but that he was less interested in politics than in teaching, and devoted much of his life to the expounding of his philosophical ideas to a large number of students. — Tr.

[2] Since Yi-ch'uan, i.e., Ch'eng Yi (1033-1108), was the forerunner of the Rationalistic school which culminated with Chu Hsi, it is natural that Lu should feel less sympathetic to him than to his elder brother, Ch'eng Hao (1032-85), who was the forerunner of the Lu-Wang Idealism. — Tr.

[3] Master Yu, i.e., Yu Jo, was a disciple of Confucius. He is quoted in *Analects*, I, 2, 12-13, and XII, 9. — Tr.

four directions, together with what is above and what is below, are called *yü*; the bygone past and the coming future are called *chou*.' Then, with a sudden onrush of great insight, he said: 'Those affairs which are within the universe [1] are those which fall within my duty; those affairs which fall within my duty are those which are within the universe.'

"Again he once remarked: 'The universe (*yü chou*) is my mind, and my mind is the universe. [2] If in the Eastern Sea there were to appear a sage, he would have this same mind and this same Principle (*li*). If in the Western Sea there were to appear a sage, he would have this same mind and this same Principle. If in the Southern or Northern Seas there were to appear sages, they (too) would have this same mind and this same Principle. If a hundred or a thousand generations ago, or a hundred or a thousand generations hence, sages were to appear, they (likewise) would have this same mind and this same Principle.' " [3]

We are further told that Lu Chiu-yüan was a native of Chin-ch'i, in Fu-chou (the present Lin-ch'uan 臨川 hsien in Kiangsi province), and that he lived 1139-93.

We have seen that when, as a boy, Lu heard the words of Ch'eng Yi, he "felt as though wounded by them." This antipathy toward the younger Ch'eng contrasts with his corresponding predilection for the elder brother, Ch'eng Hao. The latter, for example, maintained that the student's first need in self-cultivation is to comprehend love (*jen*), and that once he comprehends this truth and cultivates it with sincerity (*ch'eng*) and earnestness (*ching*), there is no need for anything further. [4] Essentially the same idea is expressed by Lu Chiu-yüan when he remarks:

"Recently there was someone who criticized me, saying: 'Aside from the one sentence, Let a man first firmly establish the nobler part of his constitution, [5] he has no other tricks.' Hearing it, I replied: 'True indeed!' " (34.8).

---

[1] Lit., "within *yü* and *chou*." — Tr.

[2] This sentence, which does not occur in Yang Chien's account of this incident, is added from the corresponding passage in the chronology of Lu's life contained in the *Hsiang-shan Hsien-sheng Ch'üan-chi* (Complete Works of Lu Chiu-yüan), 36.5.

[3] See Lu's *Ch'üan-chi* or *Complete Works* (to which all further quotations in this section refer, unless otherwise stated), 33.4. [Many of the passages quoted below have also been translated by Huang, *op. cit.* — Tr.]

[4] See chap. 12, p. 521. — Tr.

[5] A quotation from the *Mencius*, VIa, 15. — Tr.

"Let a man first firmly establish the nobler part of his constitution" means, as far as Lu is concerned: Let him first understand that Truth or *Tao* is nothing other than the mind, and the mind is nothing other than Truth. For, as he explains in a passage quoted below: "Beyond the Truth, no thing exists; outside of things, no Truth exists." Lu's underlying theory here is similar to that of Ch'eng Hao when the latter exhorts the student first to comprehend *jen* or love. This becomes clearer when we read Lu's following statements:

"The ten thousand things are profusely contained within a square inch of space (i.e., the mind). Filling the mind and, pouring forth, filling the entire universe (*yü chou*), there is nothing that is not this Principle (*li*)" (34.38).

"Mencius said: 'He who has developed completely his mind knows his nature. Knowing his nature, he knows Heaven.' [1] Mind is only one mind. My own mind, or that of my friend, or that of a sage of a thousand generations ago, or again, that of a sage of a thousand generations hence—their minds are all only (one) like this. The extent of the mind is very great. If I can develop completely my mind, I thereby become identified with Heaven. Study consists of nothing more than to apprehend this" (35.18).

"This Principle permeates the universe. This is what is meant by saying that beyond the Truth (*Tao*), no thing exists; outside of things, no Truth exists. If, disregarding this, you take on other plans, aims, schemes, appearances, behavior, and achievement, you then have no concern with Truth, and the situation becomes merely one of heterodox views and desire for profit. This is known as sinking and drowning. It is known as (retiring into one's) old burrow. One's speech will then be depraved speech; one's view will be a depraved view" (15.56).

"The Truth permeates all under Heaven; there is not even the smallest space (where it does not reach). The four beginnings [2] and ten thousand virtues are all conferred upon us by Heaven. They do not impose upon man the burden of adding any further adornment. It is only men themselves who have vices, and therefore separate themselves from these (virtues)" (*ibid.*, p. 23).

---

[1] *Mencius*, VIIa, 1. — Tr.

[2] The four natural principles regarded by Mencius as innate in all men, through the development of which any man can be led to perfect goodness. Cf. vol. 1, p. 121. — Tr.

Our mind is fundamentally one with the universe. In the case of most men, however, this oneness becomes obscured by various factors. Thus Lu writes:

"The Way (*Tao*) fills the universe, nowhere being concealed. It is, in Heaven, called the *yin* and *yang*; in Earth it is called softness and hardness; in man it is called love (*jen*) and righteousness (*yi*). [1] Thus, then, love and righteousness are man's original mind. ... The foolish and unworthy are deficient, because they are blinded by material desire and thus lose their original mind. And the worthy and intelligent go too far because they too are blinded by their (dogmatic) views and lose their original mind" (1.12).

In short: "The universe has never limited and separated itself from man, but it is man who limits and separates himself from the universe" (36.6).

The purpose of study is to rid the mind of all those things by which it is blinded, in this way enabling it to return to its original condition. Lu says:

"How can this Principle, which lies within the universe, ever suffer impediment in any way? It is you yourself who have sunk and buried yourself, obscured and blinded yourself. Lying deep down within a dark pit, one knows nothing of what is called the high and distant. You must tear yourself out of that pit and look for a way to break your bonds" (35.28).

Only this kind of endeavor constitutes real study; nothing else counts. Lu says again:

"In the *Analects* there are many statements that suffer from the lack of a context. Thus, in such a saying as 'one may attain to it with knowledge and yet be unable to preserve it with love,' [2] one does not know what 'it' is that is thus to be attained to and preserved. Or again, (in the saying), 'to learn is to practice constantly,' [3] one does not know what it is that is to be practiced constantly. Unless one has ability for study, it is not easy to read. But if one does have ability for study, then one will know that what is to be attained is to attain to this (mind); that what is to be preserved is to preserve it; and that what is to be practiced constantly is to practice it. (In other words), to talk is to talk about it, and to rejoice is to rejoice in it.

---

[1] This sentence is derived from the *Book of Changes* (Appen. III, pp. 423-424). — Tr.

[2] *Analects*, XV, 32. — Tr.

[3] *Ibid.*, I, 1. — Tr.

It is like water (pouring down) from the gutter on top of a high house. [1] If in studying we know what is fundamental, the Six Classics will all serve as commentaries (on our mind)" (34.1).

"To investigate things (*ko wu*) is to investigate this (mind). Fu Hsi looked up to (contemplate the brilliant) forms (exhibited in Heaven), and looked down to (survey) the patterns (shown on Earth). [2] He was, indeed, the first to exert his efforts in (thus apprehending) this (mind). If it were not so, what is called the 'investigation of things' would be an insignificant matter" (35.60).

Granted that "to learn is to practice constantly," one must first know what it is that is thus to be practiced—in the words of Mencius, that man must "first firmly establish the nobler part of his constitution." This means to "know what is fundamental," and then, with all one's energies, to practice it, preserve it, and rejoice in it.

Once a man knows his mind, he need but allow it to act spontaneously, and it will of itself respond appropriately to whatever confronts it. This is brought out in two further passages:

"Let us concentrate our spirit, and act as masters of ourselves. For since 'all things are complete within us,' [3] what deficiency can there be? Then when it is time for compassion, we shall spontaneously display compassion; when it is time for shame and dislike, we shall spontaneously display shame and dislike; when it is time for leniency and softness, we shall spontaneously display leniency and softness; when it is time for strength and firmness, we shall spontaneously display strength and firmness" (35.32).

"The *Odes* (III, i, Ode 7, 7) say of King Wen: 'Unconsciously, unknowingly, he accorded with the pattern of God.' The song to Yao at K'ang-ch'ü, too, expressed nothing more than this. [4] And the *Analects* (VIII, 18) says of Shun and Yü: 'How sublime the way Shun and Yü undertook the empire, yet without any assertion and

---

[1] I.e., it is as smooth and easy as the downward flow of such water. — Tr.

[2] Cf. *Book of Changes* (Appen. III, p. 382), which describes how the legendary Fu Hsi, through his observation of natural phenomena, came to devise the eight trigrams. — Tr.

[3] A famous quotation from the *Mencius*, VIIa, 4. — Tr.

[4] This is an allusion to a Taoist story in the *Lieh-tzŭ* (chap. 4, end), according to which the sage Yao, after fifty years of rule, asked those about him whether his rule had been effective or not. On failing to receive an adequate answer, he traveled to K'ang-ch'ü, where he heard a small boy singing: "You have caused the multitude of people all to conform to your standard; and you, unconsciously, unknowingly, have accorded with the pattern of God." Delighted by this answer, Yao returned to his palace and there abdicated in favor of the sage Shun. — Tr.

interference.' If man can but realize the fault of such assertion and interference, and void himself of the vice of 'consciousness' and 'knowing,' his mind will become illumined and Principle (*li*) will become broadly extended; each thing will be in accord with other things, '(ever) seeking for this perfect excellence, (ever) turning to this perfect excellence.'[1] 'Wherever he (the superior man) passes, transformation follows; wherever he abides, there is a spiritualizing influence. This flows abroad above and below together with Heaven and Earth. How can it be said that he mends society but in a small way!'"[2] (1.12).

Here Lu Chiu-yüan seeks to explain his criticism (see p. 575 above) of persons who "go too far because they are blinded by their (dogmatic) views, and lose their original mind." He would agree with Ch'eng Hao's admonition against being "selfish and mentally calculating." Also the latter's assertion that, by avoiding these faults, we may achieve the state of "empty impartiality, with which, when things appear, to react accordingly."[3] What Lu describes as "the fault of assertion" corresponds to Ch'eng's "selfshness"; his "vice of consciousness and knowing" to Ch'eng's "mental calculation"; and when he asserts that the "mind will become illumined and Principle will become broadly extended," he is referring to that same state of "empty impartiality" of which Ch'eng Hao speaks.

The fault of the Buddhists, in Lu's eyes, is precisely their inability to achieve this state. He writes:

"I use these two words, righteousness (*yi*) and profit (*li* 利), to distinguish between Confucianism and Buddhism. They are also referred to as unselfishness and selfishness, though they are, in actual fact, righteousness and profit. According to the Confucianists, man, living betwixt Heaven and Earth, is of all things the most spiritual, of all beings the most noble, and so, together with Heaven and Earth, constitutes one of the Three Standards (*san chi* 三 極). For Heaven, there is the Way of Heaven; for Earth, there is the Way of Earth; and for man, there is the Way of man. Thus if man does not completely develop the Way of man, he cannot be equated with Heaven and Earth. Man has five senses, and each sense has its own proper

---

[1] Cf. *Book of History* (V, iv, p. 144). — Tr.

[2] Cf. the *Mencius*, VIIa, 13. — Tr.

[3] Cf. Ch'eng Hao, "Letter on the Composure of the Nature," quoted in chap. 12, pp. 523-525.

function. It is because of this that he has (perception of) right and wrong, gains and failings. Because of this, again, there are the teaching and learning (of right and wrong). The doctrines (of Confucianism) are established in accordance with this (concept). This is why it (Confucianism) is spoken of as being righteous and unselfish.

"But for the Buddhists, man, who lives betwixt Heaven and Earth, undergoes life and death, the wheel of transmigration, and sorrow and vexation. (For this reason), they consider (the life of man) to be extremely painful, and so seek to escape from it. ... Therefore they say: 'Life and death are a great matter.' ... The teachings (of Buddhism) are established in accordance with this (concept). This is why it (Buddhism) is spoken of as profit-seeking and selfish.

"Being righteous and unselfish, the one (Confucianism) deals with the world; being profit-seeking and selfish, the other (Buddhism) withdraws from the world. The Confucianists, even when they reach into what is without sound, without smell, without direction, and without substance, always base themselves on the idea of dealing with the world. The Buddhists, even when they strive to ferry (all beings across the sea of suffering) to a future realm, always base themselves on the idea of withdrawing from the world." (2.1-2).

Here we find the readiness to deal with the world being made the touchstone for distinguishing between Confucianism and Buddhism. To deal with the world means to follow what is natural to our minds; to withdraw from it means to follow selfishness and calculation.

In Lu Chiu-yüan's own eyes, there is also a difference between his technique for spiritual cultivation and that of Chu Hsi. Thus a passage in his "Conversations" reads:

"Speaking about Ting-fu's [1] (statement) that though old habits are not easy to eradicate, yet by eradicating them in one place one can eradicate them in all, I [2] said that such eradication cannot be achieved through Hui-an's (i.e., Chu Hsi's) method of dealing with affairs. To this the Master (Lu Chiu-yüan) replied: 'One cannot compare this (statement of Ting-fu) with that (of Chu Hsi). The latter's (method) is to add' " [3] (35.24).

---

[1] Liu Ting-fu, one of Lu's disciples. — Tr.

[2] The speaker here is another of Lu's disciples who recorded this particular conversation. — Tr.

[3] By "adding," Lu means to say that Chu Hsi's method of spiritual cultivation depends upon the "investigation of things," i.e., the increase of knowledge. Therefore it fundamentally differs from Lu's method, which consists simply in the intuitive restoration of, or return to, one's "original mind." — Tr.

Again Lu says:

"The words of the sages are self-evident, as, for example: 'When a youth is at home let him be filial; when abroad, respectful to his elders.' [1] This clearly states that when at home, you are to be filial, and when abroad, to be respectful to elders. What need, then, for any commentary? For the student to exhaust his energies over this is simply to make his burden heavier for himself. But when he comes to me, I simply try to make his burden lighter. Herein is all that is (meant by) 'the investigation of things' " (35.13).

In the *Lao-tzŭ* we read: "As the practice of learning daily increases, the practice of the *Tao* daily diminishes" (chap. 48). The idea here expressed is apparently taken by Lu as his point of departure from Chu Hsi. In 1175, for example, following the famous debate between the two held at the Goose Lake Temple, Lu wrote a poem in which he said (*Works*, 36.44):

"Work easy and simple is in the end lasting and great;
Activities involved and complicated are in the end aimless and
inconclusive." [2]

By "involved and complicated," Lu points to Chu Hsi's doctrines; by "easy and simple" he has in mind his own.

2—Yang Chien

Lu Chiu-yüan's basic theories are expressed with greater clarity by his chief follower, Yang Chien 楊簡 (1140-1226). Ch'ien Shih (fl. ca. 1200), one of Yang's fellow students, writes of Yang as follows:

"The Master's personal name was Chien, he was styled Ching-chung 敬仲, and his surname was Yang. ... In the fifth year of the Ch'ien-tao period (1169) he became Deputy Assistant Prefect of Fu-yang [3] ... When the Duke of Wen-an [4] had newly arrived at

---

[1] *Analects*, I, 6. — Tr.

[2] Lit., "float and sink," i.e., are as uncertain in their course as a bit of floating driftwood. For this meeting and the poem, cf. Huang, *op. cit.*, pp. 14-15. — Tr.

[3] The present *hsien* of the same name, on the Ch'ien-t'ang river in Chekiang, not far above the city of Hangchow. — Tr.

[4] The posthumous title of respect given to Lu Chiu-yüan.

Fu-yang, [1] ... an assembly met one evening in the Hall of Double
Enlightenment, at which (Lu) several times mentioned the two words,
'original mind' (*pen hsin*). Thereupon (Yang) asked in a measured
manner: 'What is meant by the original mind?'

"It so happened that early that morning he (Yang Chien) had
heard the lawsuit of a fan (vendor). So now the Duke (i.e., Lu Chiu-
yüan) replied loudly: 'In the case of that fan (vendor), there must
have been one (of the disputants) who was right and one who was
wrong. Since you were able to see who was right and who wrong,
and then to pronounce judgment that so-and-so was right and so-
and-so was wrong, what is this if not (knowledge that comes from)
the original mind?' On hearing this, the Master (Yang Chien) suddenly realized the pure clarity of his mind. 'Is that all?' he immediately
pressed. The Duke again replied loudly: 'What else can there be?'
The Master lingered for no further words, but saluted and retired.
He sat respectfully until the sun rose, and in its early radiance turned
his face to the north and prostrated himself (before Lu). For the rest
of his life he respected Lu as his teacher, and always spoke of his
gratitude to Master Lu, especially for the second answer. If (Lu) had
said anything further, it would have been merely involved and
complicated." [2]

Ch'ien Shih further states that Yang was a native of Tz'ŭ-hsi, [3]
and that he died in 1226 in his eighty-sixth year. Elsewhere Yang
himself elaborates upon the way in which he came to realize the
significance of the original mind:

"One evening, when I asked about the original mind, the Master
(Lu Chiu-yüan) mentioned by way of reply the right and wrong
involved in that day's case of the fan (vendor). I then suddenly came
to realize the pure and clear quality of our mind. I suddenly realized
that this mind has no beginning or end, and that it penetrates everywhere" (5.9).

This, then, is the starting point of Yang's philosophy. In his
treatise entitled *Chi Yi* or *The Self and the Book of Changes*, he
writes:

---

[1] This was in 1172. — Tr.

[2] *Tz'ŭ-hu Yi-shu* (Preserved Writings of Yang Chien), 18.2. [All other citations in the present section refer to this work, unless otherwise stated. For a
slightly more detailed version of this episode, see Huang, *op. cit.*, pp. 44. — Tr.]

[3] The present Tz'ŭ-hsi 慈 谿, slightly northwest of the city of Ningpo
in Chekiang. — Tr.

"The process of change [1] is the self and none other. It is not right to regard it simply as a book and not as the self. Nor is it right to regard it as the transformation of the cosmos and not of the self. The cosmos (lit., "Heaven and Earth") is my own cosmos, and its transformation is my own transformation; they are in no way external (to the self). Selfishness sunders it (the self) from (the cosmos), and results in diminution of the self. ... The constituents of the self are something more than mere blood, breath, and physical form. My nature is limpid and pure, and not a mere physical thing. It is penetrating and limitless, and not a mere physical quantity. Heaven is a symbol that lies within my own nature; Earth is a shape that lies within my own nature. That is why it is said: 'In Heaven there are the (different) symbols there completed, and on Earth there are the (different) shapes there formed.' [2] All are equally produced by me. Undifferentiably intertwined, they are neither internal nor external (to the self); all permeate one another, without distinction or difference. By observation of a single line (in the hexagrams of the *Book of Changes*), the meaning (of the self) becomes brilliantly apparent. ...

"From the fact that we are capable of experiencing the true mind through its feeling of distress when a child is about to fall into a well, (it is evident that) its marvelous quality of 'no thinking, no planning' [3] is originally possessed by everyone, and that its essence of pure realness and utter clarity, and its substance of illimitable broadness, are originally possessed by everyone. In times of ordinary eating and drinking this mind constantly manifests itself, as it also does in times of hurry and uncertainty; the only thing is that men themselves are not conscious of it. ...

"This mind is fundamentally one and not dual; it is never sundered and then afterward renewed. Never is there a time when it is at first not like this, and then again like this, or at first like this, and then again not like this. Day and night it remains one; from antiquity until today it has remained one. It is neither stronger in youth nor weaker in old age. ... By according with this original mind of mine in my movements, I can fly, remain hidden, be circumspect, or cautious. [4] ... Whether I accept office or retire from it,

---

[1] *Yi*, the same word as that used in the title of the *Book of Changes*. — Tr.

[2] *Book of Changes* (Appen. III, p. 348). — Tr.

[3] An allusion to the *Book of Changes* (Appen. III, p. 389). — Tr.

[4] An allusion to the symbolism of certain lines in the first hexagram of the *Book of Changes*, pp. 57-58. — Tr.

remain in it for long or speedily withdraw, I can in every case accord with what is proper. [1] Whether I circle or zigzag, I can in every case accord with what is right. It is not through labor and effort that this is accomplished, for my own mind itself has the correct standards for ten, a hundred, a thousand, or even a myriad widely scattered cases. The 'three hundred rules of ceremony and three thousand rules of demeanor' [2] are none of them external to my own mind. Therefore it is said: 'The virtue of the nature is the road which unifies the external with the internal, and hence the timely practice of it results in what is right.' [3] This refers to a rightness that is spontaneously so, and not one that is deliberately sought after" (7.1-10).

Thus everything within the universe also lies within the individual mind, and is one with the self. Yang Chien refers to the famous statement of Mencius (IIa,6): "If today men suddenly see a child about to fall into a well, they will without exception experience a feeling of alarm and distress," and uses it to argue that that child is fundamentally one with the self. If through this example we can come to understand our original mind, we may then realize that in our every act, all that is required is to rely upon the spontaneous promptings of this mind in order to do the right thing. Ch'eng Hao states that "the trouble with man is that he is selfish and mentally calculating," [4] meaning by this that such selfishness and calculation prevent our real minds from functioning freely. The same point is emphasized by Yang Chien in his *Chüeh-ssǔ Chi* or *Essay on the Four Abstentions*: [5]

"Man's mind is in itself understanding, and in itself spiritual. It is only when preconception arises, egoism becomes established, and predetermination and obduracy block the road, that this understanding and spirituality become lost. In the daily questions and answers between Confucius and his disciples, the faults from which he constantly warned them to abstain were, generally speaking, four in number: preconception, predetermination, obduracy, and egoism. If a disciple had any one of these, the sage (Confucius) invariably

---

[1] An allusion to what is said of Confucius in the *Mencius*, IIa, 2, para. 22; see also *ibid.*, Vb, 1. — Tr.

[2] A phrase from the *Doctrine of the Mean*, p. 323. — Tr.

[3] Cf. *ibid.*, p. 321. — Tr.

[4] See chap. 12, p. 524. — Tr.

[5] A title derived from the statement in the *Analects* (IX, 4) about Confucius: "The Master abstained from four things: he had no preconception, no predetermination, no obduracy, and no egoism." — Tr.

laid a prohibition against it. . . . For he realized that all men equally possess a nature that is utterly understanding, utterly spiritual, and broad and sagely in its wisdom. It need not be externally sought for or gained, but is inherent and innate, being spirit-like in itself and understanding in itself. When, however, the seeds of preconception appear, it becomes obscured; when predetermination exists, it becomes obscured; when obduracy exists, it becomes obscured; when egoism exists, it becomes obscured. All the beginnings of obscurity stem from these things. Therefore whenever one of these evils assumed form, he would give warning against it, saying: 'Be not like this, be not like this.' The sage is unable to impart the Truth (*Tao*) to men, but he is able to dispel their becloudings. [1] The case is like that of the sky's great expanse which, originally clear and bright, becomes obscured when clouds appear. As soon as these clouds are dispersed, however, it again becomes clear and bright. . . .

"What is meant by 'preconception' (*yi* 意)? The slightest stirrings (of the mind) mean preconception, but the slightest interruptions (of these stirrings) also mean preconception. The manifestations of preconception are innumerable. They may result in profit or harm, right or wrong, advancement or withdrawal. . . . Whether we expend the energy of a day or a year, and whether we speak up and down or back and forth, extensively or intensively, we shall never be able to exhaust all the instances of this sort. How, then, are we to distinguish between the (true) mind and such preconception? The two are originally not divided. It is only through the process of beclouding that they come to be so. What is unitary is the mind; what is dual is preconception. The mind is straightforward; preconception is involved. The one passes freely; the other becomes blocked. The straightforward mind functions straightforwardly; it is unconscious and unknowing. Despite the shifting flux of words and activities, it remains undivergent and unscattered. It simply reacts (to stimuli), and continues endlessly along its course, without (conscious) thought or action. Mencius made clear (the nature of) the mind, while Confucius placed a prohibition on preconception. With the prohibition of such preconception, this mind is made manifest. . . .

---

[1] The meaning here is that Truth is already innate in all men; hence it is not something that can be imparted by the sage. This Truth, however, can easily become obscured, and then it becomes the duty of the sage to remove the causes of the obscuring. — Tr.

"What is meant by 'predetermination' (*pi* 必)? This predetermination is the predetermination that results from preconception. It is a predetermination in favor of one thing, but not of another. It is a predetermination that desires the one, but not the other. However, the great Truth (*Tao*) does not lie in any particular corner, so how can it be thus absolutely defined? If we maintain that it lies in one thing, does this mean that it does not also lie in something else? Or, if it lies in something else, does this mean that it does not also lie in this? 'To be always certain of the truth (of one's words) and the efficacy (of one's acts)' [1] is indeed not right. Such assuredness and certainty lead only to self-dissipation and loss.

"What is meant by 'obduracy' (*ku* 固)? Such obduracy likewise results from preconception. To cling obdurately and pass no further onward: this is a path leading to nothing. To cling obdurately and not allow oneself to be changed: this is a path leading downward. Confucius has said: 'I am different from such. With me there is no inflexible *may* or *may not*.' And again: 'Am I indeed a man with knowledge? I have no such knowledge.' [2] Thus, then, lacking even a 'may' or 'may not,' should there still be obduracy? Or, lacking even 'knowledge,' should there still be obduracy?

"And what is meant by 'egoism' (*wo* 我)? Such egoism, too, is the egoism that results from preconception. With the birth of preconception, egoism arises; without that preconception, it too would not arise. In babyhood (the egoistic person) speaks of the milk suckled by him as 'my' milk; as he grows older, he speaks of the food eaten by him as 'my' food; his clothing he calls 'my' clothing; his actions 'my' actions; his repose 'my' repose; his studies 'my' studies; his official career 'my' official career; his fame 'my' fame; his trade 'my' trade. The steely hardness (of such egoism) is inferior to (the softness of) a lump of clay, of the air, or even an empty void. People are ignorant of that state of profundity and silence which antedates the rise of preconception and thought; a state in which there is not yet even 'non-being,' let alone the ego" (2.7-9).

"The mind is straightforward, preconception is involved." Referring again to Mencius' famous story of the child about to fall into a well, the first reaction of any spectator is one of instinctive alarm

---

[1] An allusion to the *Mencius*, IVb, 11. See also *Analects*, XIII, 20. — Tr.
[2] *Analects*, XVIII, 8; IX, 7. — Tr.

and distress, which, if immediately acted on, leads to an attempt to save the child. Such feeling represents our true "mind," and it and our resulting action are both "straightforward." Suppose, however, that we pause a moment to reflect upon the matter, and then either decide to rescue the child, hoping in this way to gain the favor of its parents, or, on the other hand, not to rescue it at all, because we happen to dislike them. In either case these secondary reflections are "involved" rationalizations, and as such entirely different from the straight-forward feeling and action springing directly from the true mind. Chou Tun yi writes: "Absence of desire results in vacuity when in quiescence, and straightforwardness when in movement." [1] And Ch'eng Hao says likewise: "Being selfish, one cannot take action as a (spontaneous) response. Being mentally calculating, one cannot take intuition as his natural guide." [2] In Yang Chien's essay we see how he further developed these ideas of his predecessors.

3—CHU HSI AND LU CHIU-YÜAN COMPARED

A popular way of contrasting Chu Hsi with Lu Chiu-yüan is to say that the former emphasizes the importance of study, whereas the latter emphasizes the "prizing of one's virtuous nature." Such a distinction, in fact, was already drawn between them in their own time. What it overlooks, however, is that the final goal of Chu Hsi, no less than of all the other Neo-Confucianists, is to explain the nature and functioning of our inner self. Hence, while we may no doubt accurately say that Lu does not greatly emphasize study as such, it does not equally follow that Chu fails to emphasize the "prizing of one's virtuous nature." Such a differentiation, moreover, relates merely to their respective methodologies, and hence leaves unanswered the question of whether, in the final analysis, the differences between them are more than methodological.

At the end of the last chapter we have pointed out that Chu Hsi's philosophy is not idealism in the ordinary sense, but comes closer to what in modern times has been termed neo-realism. With this point in mind, it becomes apparent that the difference between him and Lu involves considerably more than mere methodology. It is a difference, in fact, that goes back to the Ch'eng brothers, of

---

[1] See chap. 11, p. 448. — Tr.
[2] See chap. 12, p. 524. — Tr.

whom Ch'eng Yi started one trend culminating with Chu Hsi, whereas Ch'eng Hao started another which, after being further developed by Lu Chiu-yüan and Yang Chien, finally culminated with Wang Shou-jen (1472-1529). If we wish to sum up the difference between the two groups in a word, we may say that Chu's school emphasizes the "Learning of Principle" (*Li Hsüeh*, commonly rendered in this volume as "Rationalism"), whereas that of Lu emphasizes the "Learning of the Mind" (*Hsin Hsüeh*, commonly rendered as "Idealism"). The latter term, in fact, appears in the very first sentence of Wang Shou-jen's preface to Lu's *Complete Works*, in which Wang writes: "The Learning of the Sages is the Learning of the Mind." [1] Its use here fittingly symbolizes the difference between the Lu-Wang school and that of Chu Hsi.

For Chu, as we have seen, the nature (*hsing*) is equivalent to Principle (*li*). By Lu, on the other hand, it is explicitly stated that mind (*hsin*), and not the nature, is what should thus be equated with Principle. [2] Although these formulations differ by but a single word, that difference is truly fundamental. Thus according to Chu's argument, mind is simply a concrete object, which comes into being as the result of the combination of Principle with the Ether. As such it pertains to a realm wholly different from that of abstract Principle *per se*. This is in contradistinction to the *hsing* or nature, which is a designation for Principle as contained within the concrete mind. The conclusion is that though mind is the container of Principle, it cannot itself be identified as Principle; in other words, the equation of the nature with Principle is correct, but not that of the mind with Principle.

Lu Chiu-yüan, on the other hand, asserts precisely that the distinction between mind and nature (and therefore between mind and Principle) is unessential. This appears in the following record of his reply to a question posed him by his disciple, Li Po-min:

"Po-min asked: 'What is the distinction between nature (*hsing*), capacity (*ts'ai*), mind (*hsin*), and feeling (*ch'ing*)?' The Master replied: 'This question, my friend, is beside the point, but this is not my friend's fault; it derives from the world's ignorance. Present day scholars, when they study books, only explain their words; they do

---

[1] Cf. Frederick Goodrich Henke, transl., *The Philosophy of Wang Yang-ming* (London & Chicago, 1916), p. 481. — Tr.

[2] Cf. Lu's *Complete Works*, 11.10.

not seek into their flesh and blood. As to feeling, nature, mind, and capacity, these are all simply things belonging to a common category; the differences between them are immaterial ones of verbiage. ... If, however, one feels compelled to talk about these things, then what pertains to Heaven is the nature, whereas what pertains to man is the mind. I reply in this way in order to comply with you, my friend, but in actual fact there need be no (distinction made) like this' " (*Works*, 35.18).

There is no doubt that in Chu Hsi's eyes the distinction between nature and mind is a genuine one involving far more than the mere "explaining of words." Lu Chiu-yüan, by denying this distinction, thereby reveals the difference between his concept of reality and that of his rival. Thus for Chu Hsi, reality comprises two distinct realms, the one lying within the limits of time and space, the other transcending these limits. For Lu, however, reality comprises only a single realm, wholly confined to time and space; hence it and our own mind constitute an undifferentiated unity. This is why he says (p. 573 above): "The universe is my mind, and my mind is the universe," and is also why the term, "Learning of the Mind," should properly be applied only to his school of Neo-Confucianism.

At this point, however, a problem arises, namely: does Lu, when he speaks of "mind," really mean by it the same as Chu Hsi does? As long as this remains unsettled, we may reasonably question whether Lu's assertion that the mind is Principle significantly differs from Chu's that the nature is Principle. Closer examination, however, shows clearly that what the two men are talking about is really the same. For example, we have the following statement by Lu:

"Men are not trees or stones; how, then, can they be without mind? Mind is the noblest and greatest among the five senses. It is said in the *Grand Norm* (p. 141) that '(the virtue of) thinking is perspicacity, which becomes manifest in sagacity.' Mencius also said: 'To the mind belongs the office of thinking. By thinking it gets the right view of things; by neglecting to think, it fails to do this.' ... The 'four beginnings' constitute this mind. And 'what Heaven has conferred on us' also constitutes this mind. [1] All men possess this mind, and their minds all possess this Principle; thus mind is equivalent to Principle" (*Works*, 11.9-10).

---

[1] See the *Mencius*, VIa, 15. On the "four beginnings," see p. 574, note 2, and esp. vol. 1, p. 121. — Tr.

Turning to Chu Hsi, we find that for him "there is no single thing in the world which does not have the nature." [1] By this he means that everything which assumes physical form does so because it has within it its own particular *li* or Principle—a Principle thus constituting its nature. Therefore even trees and stones, though devoid of consciousness or mind, nevertheless possess a particular nature of their own. This agrees with Lu Chiu-yüan, who, as we have just seen, similarly denies by implication the possession of mind to trees and stones.

Furthermore, according to Lu's statement, the mind is characterized by the power of thought and reflection, which in turn agrees well with Chu's remark that "the intellectual faculty is the mind alone and not the nature." Elsewhere Chu also observes that "love (*jen*) pertains to the nature, whereas commiseration pertains to the feelings, and so necessarily proceeds from the mind. Mind is the unifying agent between the nature and the feelings." [2] The implication here is that the feeling or emotion (*ch'ing*) of commiseration is simply the concrete expression in our physical world of "the Principle or *li* of love," and as such belongs to "what lies within shapes" (*hsing erh hsia*), i.e., to the concrete and physical world. Hence his remark that it "necessarily proceeds from the mind." This again agrees with Lu, who, as we have seen, states that "the 'four beginnings' [3] constitute this mind." Thus we here have additional proof that he and Chu Hsi, when speaking of mind, are both referring to the same thing. So too is Yang Chien, when he maintains (p. 582 above) that "man's mind is in itself understanding, and in itself spiritual." There is no doubt, therefore, that the mind spoken of by the Lu school is identical with that of Chu Hsi, and hence that when the Lu school equates this mind with Principle, it is advancing a doctrine at variance with that of Chu Hsi.

This fundamental difference may be further demonstrated by examining the question from another angle. We have seen that Lu, while admitting for convenience's sake the propriety of saying that "what pertains to Heaven is the nature, whereas what pertains to man is the mind," nevertheless maintains that mind and nature alike are "simply things belonging to a common category." What is

---

[1] See chap. 13, p. 551.

[2] For these statements, see chap. 13, pp. 556-557.

[3] Among which the feeling of commiseration is one. — Tr.

important to remember is that, from Lu's point of view, "Heaven" and "man" both belong to a single realm. This makes him unwilling to accept the Chu Hsi school's differentiation between what it calls "Heavenly Principle" and "human desire." For as he himself re marks:

"What is said about (the difference between) Heavenly Principle and human desire is not the best doctrine. For if Heaven (alone) is (possessed of) Principle, while man is (possessed only of) desire, then Heaven and man are different in category. ... It is said in the *Book of History* (p. 50): 'The mind of the body is unstable; the mind of the spirit is but a spark.' Interpreters have frequently explained the 'mind of the body' as here being equivalent to human desire, and the 'mind of the spirit' as being equivalent to Heavenly Principle. This explanation is incorrect, for mind is one; how, then, can man have two minds?" (*Works*, 34.1).

Here Lu definitely denies the distinction between Heaven and man which is affirmed in Chu Hsi's system.

Chou Tun-yi writes in the opening sentence of his famous *Diagram of the Supreme Ultimate Explained*: "The Ultimateless! And yet also the Supreme Ultimate!" According to Chu Hsi, Chou's purpose in so writing was to indicate that the Supreme Ultimate (*t'ai chi*) lacks physical shape and pertains solely to Principle or *li*. Lu Chiu-yüan, however, points out that in Appendix III of the *Book of Changes*, where the Supreme Ultimate is first mentioned, only this term and none other is used. Hence, he argues, the appellation, "Ultimateless" (*wu chi*), should not be added to it. To quote his conclusion: "The *Diagram of the Supreme Ultimate Explained* is different in character from (Chou's) *Explanatory Text*, and may be suspected as not having been written by Master Chou himself. If this be not so (i.e., if it really be Chou's own work), it was perhaps written in his earlier days when his learning had not yet matured. Or, if this too be not so, it may have undergone interpolations from other men, which later men have failed to distinguish." [1] The debate between Lu and Chu Hsi that resulted from this assertion was famous in their day. At the heart of it lay the fact, evident from what has just been said, that Lu's philosophy acknowledges only a single realm, lying within the confines of time and space, and hence cannot possibly recognize anything as "lacking shape but containing Principle." [2]

---

[1] See Lu's first letter to Chu Hsi, in his *Works*, 2.9.
[2] A phrase of Chu Hsi quoted in chap. 13, p. 535. — Tr.

Thus it is evident that this debate was undertaken in no mere spirit of idle controversy.

Another point requiring elucidation arises in connection with the following statement by Lu Chiu-yüan:

"When speaking of 'what is above shapes,' we call this the Way (*Tao*); when speaking of 'what is within shapes,' we call this 'instrument' (*ch'i*). Heaven and Earth are both such 'instruments,' but in order that their generating and nurturing of physical things may take place, it is necessary that there be Principle" (*Works*, 35.57).

This statement, in itself, would seem to reveal no fundamental difference between Lu's philosophy and that of Chu Hsi. A different picture emerges, however, if we turn to Lu's first letter to Chu, in which he argues about the *Diagram of the Supreme Ultimate Explained*:

"In the 'Great Appendix' of the *Book of Changes* it is said: 'That which is above shapes is called the Way'; and again: 'The alternation of the *yin* and *yang* is called the Way.' [1] Thus if the *yin* and *yang* already pertain to what is above shapes, how much more does the Supreme Ultimate!" (*Works*, 2.11).

Inasmuch as Lu here places the *yin* and *yang* in the realm of "what is above shapes," it is evident that what he means by this term must differ from Chu Hsi's concept. A corresponding difference, in fact, already appears in the comments of the Ch'eng brothers on this same passage. Thus Ch'eng Hao says: "The *yin* and *yang*, too, pertain to 'what is within shapes,' yet they are said to be the Way. ... Fundamentally, these (principles) are themselves nothing but the Way. This fact should be silently reflected on and understood by men." Whereas Ch'eng Yi says: "(As to the statement that) 'the alternation of the *yin* and *yang* is called the Way': this Way is not itself the *yin* and *yang*, but it is that whereby the alternation of the *yin* and *yang* is caused." [2] The difference between these two statements represents the difference between Lu and Chu respectively, for if, in the former's philosophy, the *yin* and *yang* are said to pertain to "what is above shapes," this can only mean that, for him, whatever else belongs to "what is within shapes" must, like the *yin* and *yang*, also lie within the confines of time and space, and have a concrete existence of its own. Hence "what is above shapes" and "what is within shapes" really constitute a single common realm.

---

[1] *Book of Changes* (Appen. III, pp. 355 and 377). — Tr.

[2] For these two statements, see chap. 12, pp. 510 and 511.

Thus, for Lu, there is only a single realm of being, and this despite the fact that he continues, in a somewhat confusing way, to employ the old terms, "above shapes" and "within shapes." When we come to Yang Chien, however, we find this distinction denied entirely, as in the following passage:

"Again it is said (in the *Book of Changes*): 'That which is above shapes is called the Way; that which is within shapes is called instrument.' When the Way and instrument are thus separated from one another, does this mean that instrument is something external to the Way? If even the author of the 'Great Appendix' (in the *Changes*) falls into such an error, what hope can be held for later scholars?" (*Preserved Writings*, 9.45).

In actual fact the terms "above shapes" and "within shapes" assume significance only if we adopt Chu Hsi's theory that the concrete "instruments" of the physical world occupy a realm of being quite different from that of the abstract Way or *Tao*. This dualism, however, the Lu school was unable to accept. Hence it is hardly surprising that it finally denied entirely the authenticity of the reference in the *Book of Changes* to what is "above shapes" and "within shapes," asserting that these terms could not represent "the words of Confucius." [1]

This fundamental difference between the Chu and Lu philosophies is also alluded to by Chu Hsi himself in a general way. One of his criticisms of Buddhism, for example, is that the Buddhist doctrine of the nature "is precisely the doctrine of Kao Tzŭ, that 'that which at birth is so, is what is called the nature.' " [2] This criticism is based on the fact that, according to the Buddhists, the mind is to be equated with the nature, whereas, according to Chu, it belongs to "what is within shapes," and hence, unlike the abstract and metaphysical nature, can only exist when the concrete physical world comes into being. This Buddhist doctrine, Chu maintains, is therefore essentially the same as Kao Tzŭ's that the nature is simply man's natural constitution. Chu, moreover, further maintains that Lu Chiu-yüan falls into the same error. Thus we are told that when Lu died, Chu "led his disciples to the temple and there mourned for him. After a long time he remarked: 'Alas! Here has died a Kao Tzŭ.' " [3] The reason for this comparison is that Lu, in Chu's eyes, was equally guilty

---

[1] Yang Chien, *op. cit.*, 7.6.
[2] See chap. 13, p. 570, and, for Kao Tzŭ, what is there said under note 3.
[3] Chu Hsi, *Conversations*, 124.12.

with the Buddhists of promulgating the doctrine that the mind is equivalent to the nature.

The same comparison with Kao Tzŭ is made by later adherents of the Chu school, as, for example, by Ch'en Shun (1153-1217), one of Chu's disciples:

"The Buddhists regard the functioning (of the mind) as the nature. . . . They recognize nothing more than the Ether (*ch'i*), and say nothing about Principle (*li*). . . . Recently there have been some people who indulge in fabrications, and love to discourse loftily about the nature and (Heavenly) Decree. In general they whole-heartedly follow the Buddhist idea that (mental) functioning constitutes the nature, while glossing this over with sayings from the (Confucian) sages. . . . In actual fact (what they say) is nothing more than Kao Tzŭ's doctrine that 'that which at birth is so, is what is called the nature.' " [1]

On this particular point there is no doubt that Lu Chiu-yüan comes closer to Buddhism than does Chu Hsi.

From the preceding remarks it is evident that a very real difference separates the two men—a difference quite sufficient to explain the resulting bifurcation that took place in Neo-Confucianism. Lu and Yang Chien, however, merely built the foundations for what later came to be known as the "Learning of the Mind," and it was only with Wang Shou-jen (1473-1529) that this school reached its culmination. Thus the real rival of Chu Hsi is neither Lu nor Yang, but their illustrious follower, Wang Shou-jen, who lived two and a half centuries later.

4—RATIONALISM AFTER CHU HSI

During the two hundred and fifty years following Chu Hsi, the scope and clarity of his philosophy enabled it to acquire enormous prestige. Though Lu Chiu-yüan continued to be regarded as his chief rival, and though his methodology for spiritual cultivation enjoyed the advantage of greater simplicity and directness, his philosophy suffered from its failure to provide a really adequate interpretion of the universe as a whole. As a result, its popularity failed to equal that of the Chu school. This phenomenon is reflected, for example, in the way in which the *Sung Shih* or *History of the Sung*

---

[1] *Pei-hsi Tzŭ-yi* (Ch'en's Analysis of Philosophical Terms), 1.12.

Dynasty treats the two schools. Thus we find in this history not only the customary section on Confucian scholars (chaps. 431-438), but also an entirely new treatise devoted specifically to Neo-Confucianism (chaps. 427-430). The latter's purpose, we are told, is to record the names of those scholars regarded as having revived "the teachings which had remained untransmitted since the sages and worthies" of antiquity. [1] Significantly enough, Chu Hsi is given the central position in this new line of transmission, whereas Lu Chiu-yüan and Yang Chien do not appear in it at all, but are relegated instead to the other traditional section on Confucian scholars. Similarly indicative of bias is the way in which the growth of the Chu school down to the middle of the Ming dynasty (1368-1643) is described in the *Ming Shih* (History of the Ming Dynasty), in its treatise on Confucianism:

"The *Sung History* makes a distinction between Neo-Confucianism (*Tao Hsüeh*) and the (other) Confucian scholars (*ju lin* 儒林), in order to indicate that the origins of Yi and Lo stem back to the Shu and Ssŭ. [2] Nothing could be more correct than this (indication of the) line of transmission of Confucianism. ... In the beginning, the Confucian scholars of the early part of the Ming dynasty all belonged to various groups stemming from the various disciples of Master Chu, so that their line of transmission went back to the teacher (i.e., Chu Hsi) in an orderly progression. (At this time) Ts'ao Tuan (1376-1434) and Hu Chü-jen (1434-84), faithful in their conduct, carefully followed the moral rules and preserved the true teaching of the earlier Confucianists, without daring to make any changes. The division of doctrine began with Ch'en Hsien-chang and Wang Shou-jen. [3] The school which sprang from Hsien-chang was called the Chiang-men teaching. [4] It was a solitary and isolated movement, so that its transmission did not continue for long. The school which sprang from Shou-jen was called the Yao-chiang

---

[1] See *Sung Shih*, chap. 427, beginning.

[2] The Lo is a river which flows into the Yellow river near Loyang, and the Yi is its tributary. Their names therefore symbolize: (a) the Loyang region; (b) the Ch'eng brothers, who lived in this region; (c) through extension, as here, Neo-Confucianism in general. In the same way, the Ssŭ is a small river in Shantung, near the birthplace of Confucius, and the Shu is its tributary; hence these two names are used here to symbolize early Confucianism. — Tr.

[3] Discussed in the next two sections. — Tr.

[4] Chiang-men is near the mouth of the West river in Kwangtung. It was Ch'en Hsien-chang's birthplace. — Tr.

teaching. ¹ The concept underlying this unorthodox school obviously ran directly counter to that of Master Chu. Its followers
filled the world, and it continued to be transmitted for more than a
century. But as its teachings spread, its abuses ever became more
extreme" (282.1-2).

5—CH'EN HSIEN-CHANG AND CHAN JO-SHUI

Ch'en Hsien-chang 陳獻章 (1428-1500) was a native of Pai-
sha village, in the district of Hsin-hui, Kwangtung province. ² For
this reason he was popularly known as the Master of Pai-sha. Though
at one time a student of Wu Yü-pi (1391-1469), who had been a
follower of the Ch'eng-Chu school, his doctrines ultimately became
something very different from those of his teacher, as we may see
from his own account of himself:

"Because (I felt) my ability did not equal that of others, I ardently began to study in my twenty-seventh year under Mr. Wu. . . .
However, I failed to experience any final result. Hence on returning
to Pai-sha, I kept in seclusion and exclusively devoted myself to the
search for the right method of employing one's efforts. . . . Thereupon I cast aside the complexities of his (Wu's method), and sought
for a simple one of my own, entirely through 'quiet sitting.' ³ After
a long time I finally came to perceive the very structure of my mind,
which mysteriously became visible to me, ever as if it were a concrete
object. Throughout the varied reactions involved in my daily activities, I could follow whatever I desired, just like a horse that is
guided by the bit and bridle. . . . Thereupon I came clearly to have
trust in myself and said: 'Does not the effort of being a sage consist
in this?' And to those who came to study with me, I exclusively
taught quiet sitting." ⁴

Thus Ch'en Hsien-chang, beginning with the Chu philosophy,
finally acquired, through his own efforts, that of the Lu school. He
writes further:

---

¹ The Yao-chiang is a river in Chekiang, not far south of Hangchow bay,
which flows by Wang Shou-jen's native city. — Tr.

² N.N.W. of Macao and S.S.W. of Canton, being almost equidistant from
the two. — Tr.

³ *Ching tso* 靜 坐 , i.e., *dhyāna*, the Buddhist technique of contemplative
sitting. — Tr.

⁴ *Pai-sha-tzŭ Ch'üan-chi* (Complete Works of Ch'en Hsien-chang), 3.22.

"The effects of the activities of Principle (*li*) are extremely widespread. There is, for it, nothing internal or external, no beginning or end, no place to which it does not reach, and no moment when it does not operate. Comprehending this, I find that Heaven and Earth are established by me, their myriad transmutations issue forth from me, and the whole universe lies within myself. Having once taken this source of power into my hands, what need is there to do more? Past and present, the four points of the compass, the zenith and the nadir, can then all alike be strung upon one cord and piled into one heap. Whatever the time or wherever the place, there is nothing which this (Principle) does not permeate. Since you can trust everything to this original state, why should you toil your feet and tire your hands (in search of something further)?" (*ibid.*, 4.12).

Here we find an echo of Ch'eng Hao's statement: "Get to comprehend this Principle and cultivate it with sincerity and earnestness; that is all. ... Never exert the tiniest bit of forced effort." [1] Or again, it expresses the idea originally uttered by Mencius and approvingly repeated by Lu Chiu-yüan: "Let a man first firmly establish the nobler part of his constitution." [2] For Ch'en, as for Lu, Principle is conceived of as ceaselessly operating, and permeating all things at all times and all places. It thus differs completely from Chu Hsi's concept, according to which Principle is "above shapes," and therefore can neither be said to "operate" like a physical thing, nor to permeate all things. In short, Principle, for Ch'en, is equivalent to that mind which mysteriously came to be revealed to him. This concept emerges even more clearly in the writings of Ch'en's disciple, Chan Jo-shui.

Chan Jo-shui 湛若水 (1466-1560), styled Kan-ch'üan 甘泉, was a native of Tseng-ch'eng in Kwangtung province. [3] After studying under Ch'en Hsien-chang, he wrote a treatise called the *Hsin-hsing T'u-shuo* or *Explanation of the Diagram of the Mind and the Nature*, in which he says:

"The mind embraces and thus goes even beyond Heaven, Earth, and all things; yet (at the same time) it permeates what is within Heaven, Earth, and all things. What thus lie within and without are not to be differentiated. For Heaven and Earth there is nothing

---

[1] See chap. 12, pp. 521-522. — Tr.

[2] See above, p. 573. — Tr.

[3] About 30 miles E.N.E. of Canton. — Tr.

internal or external, and for the mind there is likewise nothing internal or external. (Such terms) are merely forced ways of speaking. Therefore those who say that only what lies within constitutes the original mind, and who consider that Heaven, Earth, and all things are external to it, reduce the mind, in their conception of it, to something extremely petty." [1]

Chan here speaks of mind in precisely the same terms as Ch'en speaks of Principle.

When Ch'en died in 1500, Wang Shou-jen was already in his twenties, and as for Chan, Wang is known to have debated with him on several occasions. Thus Wang's philosophy, though no doubt largely arrived at independently, must almost surely also have received some influence from these two men. Huang Tsung-hsi (1610-95), in his biography of Ch'en, indicates as much when he writes: "Among the Ming Confucianists, there were some who did not depart from the right course. But the 'work of being a sage' was first made clear with the Master (i.e., Ch'en Hsien-chang), and first became widespread with Wen-ch'eng (i.e., Wang Shou-jen)." [2] Thus just as Chu Hsi was the culminator of the Rationalistic wing in Neo-Confucianism, so Wang Shou-jen was the culminator of its Idealistic wing. Chronologically speaking, therefore, we may say that the former school reached its apogee during the Sung and Yüan dynasties, whereas the latter became most flourishing only during the Ming.

6—WANG SHOU-JEN

Wang Shou-jen 王守仁 (1472-1529), styled Po-an 伯安, but best known under the name given to him by his students, that of the Master of Yang-ming 陽明, was a native of Yü-yao in Chekiang province. [3] In his eighteenth year (1489), so we read in the biography contained in his collected works, he "was passing through Kuang-hsin, [4] where he visited (a famous scholar) Lou Liang, who talked to him about the 'investigation of things.' Much pleased, the Master

---

[1] *Kan-ch'üan Hsien-sheng Wen-chi* (Collected Writings of Chan Jo-shui), 21.1.

[2] Cf. his *Ming-ju Hsüeh-an* (Writings of Ming Confucianists), 5.4.

[3] South of Hangchow bay and not far west of Ningpo. Wang died on the twenty-ninth of the eleventh month of the seventh year of the Chia-ching period, which is equivalent to January 10, 1529, though the year as a whole corresponds to 1528. — Tr.

[4] The present Shang-jao 上饒 in Kiangsi. — Tr.

then asserted that it was definitely possible to become a sage through study. Later, after reading the transmitted writings of K'ao-t'ing (i.e., Chu Hsi), the thought occurred to him that according to the Confucianists, all things, external or internal, fine or coarse, and including each and every grass or tree, have embodied within them the supreme Principle (*li*). Hence, on seeing a bamboo, he took and began to investigate it. But though he pondered diligently, he had no success, and finally fell ill." [1] We read further that in his twenty-seventh year (1498), Wang "regretted that hitherto, notwithstanding great effort, he had failed to gain results, owing to over-anxiousness. Hence he began to study in a methodical way, yet unto the end the Principles of things and his own mind remained for him as two separate things. After being troubled for a long time, he suffered a recurrence of his former illness. Hearing a Taoist priest talk about the principle of 'nourishing life' (*yang sheng* 養生), however, he (again) became happy" (p. 8). Some ten years later he fell into disfavor at court and was exiled to a petty post at Lung-ch'ang, a small place in northern Kweichow, then a wild and thinly populated province. It was in his thirty-seventh year (1508), while living in these primitive surroundings, that he finally gained enlightenment through the realization of the basic principle which was to guide him through the remainder of his life. "Suddenly, in the middle of the night," we are told in the biography, "the meaning of 'the extension of knowledge through the investigation of things' dawned upon him. Without knowing what he was doing, he called out, got up, and danced about, so that his servants all became alarmed. Now for the first time he realized that for the Truth (*Tao*) of the sages, one's own nature is self-sufficient, and that it is wrong to seek for Principle (*li*) outside of it in affairs and things" (p. 13). This realization was further crystallized in his forty-third year (1514), when "he first began exclusively to teach his students about the extension of the 'intuitive

---

[1] See the *Yang-ming Chi-yao* (Important Selections from Wang Shou-jen), as translated by Frederick Goodrich Henke, *The Philosophy of Wang Yang-ming* (London & Chicago, 1916), p. 7. Elsewhere Wang himself describes in greater detail the failure of this attempt to make a practical test of Chu Hsi's theory of "the investigation of things." At first, so he tells us, a friend attempted to study the *li* or Principle of bamboo, but after three days he fell ill and was forced to desist. Then Wang himself assumed the task, but likewise became ill after seven days. Cf. Henke, *op. cit.*, pp. 177-178. — Tr.

knowledge' (*liang chih*)" (p. 15). This teaching he continued until his death in 1529. [1]

i. *Questions on the Great Learning*

The leading concept in Wang Shou-jen's philosophy appears in his treatise known as the *Ta Hsüeh Wen* or *Questions on the Great Learning*. Wang's disciple, Ch'ien Te-hung (1496-1574), in a comment appended to this treatise, [2] writes: "The *Questions on the Great Learning* is the textbook used by the students of the Teacher. When students first came to him, they were always initially given the ideas (in this treatise). ... (Before its formal compilation, however), when some students requested to record it in writing, he said: 'This (teaching) has to be transmitted verbally by you gentlemen. For if it were set down in writing, then people would consider it simply as some kind of literary document, and it would be of no benefit.' In the eighth month of the *ting-hai* year of Chia-ching (1527), however, when the Teacher was about to start forth on his Ssŭ-t'ien campaign, [3] the students renewed their request and the Teacher gave his consent."

---

[1] Wang's life is unusually interesting as that of a man whose striking contributions to philosophy were matched by a remarkably fruitful military and political career. Though born of a family long known for its scholarship, he failed in his first attempt (1493) to pass the highest of the three sets of civil service examinations. Six years later, however, he made up for this by passing second on the list, and thereafter held a variety of official positions. In 1506, because he had the temerity to memorialize the Emperor against the imprisonment of censors who had revealed the corruption of a certain notorious eunuch, he himself was punished with forty blows of the bamboo pole, under which he fainted. Thereafter he was exiled to Kweichow. It was during his stay among the aborigines of that distant province that he gained enlightenment. In 1510, however, he was recalled to Peking, and subsequently, despite vicious intrigues, became one of the most important officials in the empire. His positions included high civil and military duties in various southern provinces (Kiangsi, Fukien, Kwangtung), in the course of which he once suppressed within three months banditry that had been rife for decades, and on another occasion put down a serious rebellion. For his life, cf. Henke, *op. cit.*, pp. 3-44, and especially the excellent study by Chang Yü-chüan, "Wang Shou-jen as a Statesman," *Chinese Social and Political Science Review*, vol. 23 (1939-40), pp. 30-99, 155-252, 319-375, 473-517. For a detailed analysis of Wang's philosophy, see Wang Tch'ang-tche, *La philosophie morale de Wang Yang-ming* (Shanghai, 1936). — Tr.

[2] It is not included in Henke's translation (*op. cit.*, pp. 204-217), but, if included, would follow the end of the text on p. 217. — Tr.

[3] I.e., the campaign in the Ssŭ-en and T'ien-chou regions in northern Kwangsi, in the course of which Wang obtained the bloodless submission of certain aboriginal chiefs, and then restored to them their traditional system of tribal rule. — Tr.

This was hardly more than a year before Wang's death. Hence what is recorded in the *Questions on the Great Learning* may truly be said to represent his final views.

This treatise reads in part as follows:

"The (title of the) *Great Learning* has been regarded by former scholars as indicating that (this text) is designed for learning how to become a great man. But one may venture to ask why such learning should consist of the 'manifestation of the illustrious virtue'? [1]

"My reply is this: The great man is an all-pervading unity with Heaven, Earth, and all things. He regards all beneath Heaven as one family, and the Middle Kingdom as one man. Those who emphasize the distinction of bodily shapes, and thus make cleavage between the self and others, are the small men. The reason that the great man is able to be one with Heaven, Earth, and all things, is not that he is thus for some purpose, but because the love (*jen*) of his mind is naturally so and thus makes possible this union. But why should this apply only to the great man? The mind of the small man is exactly the same, only he himself makes it small. For this reason when he sees a child about to fall into a well, he too will certainly experience a feeling of alarm and distress. This is because in his love he is one with the child. The child, like him, belongs to the same species. When he hears the pitiful cry or sees the frightened appearance of a bird or beast, he will certainly find it unbearable to himself. [2] This is because in his love he is one with birds and beasts. The birds and beasts, like him, possess consciousness and feelings. When he sees plants and trees being torn and broken, he will certainly experience a feeling of sympathy and compassion. This is because in his love he is one with the plants and trees. The plants and trees, like him, possess life. And when he sees tiles and stones being smashed and destroyed, he will certainly experience a feeling of concern and regret. This is because in his love he is one (even) with tiles and stones.

"Thus this unifying quality of love is as surely possessed by the small man (as by the great one). It is rooted in his heavenly nature, where its spontaneous light cannot be obscured. This is why it is called the 'illustrious virtue.' . . . Thus when there is no obscuring caused by selfish desires, even the mind of the small man has this

---

[1] *Ming ming te* 明 明 德 . Cf. the opening sentence of the *Great Learning*, p. 411. — Tr.

[2] This and the famous foregoing example are both taken from the *Mencius*, IIa, 6, and Ia, 7 respectively. — Tr.

love for the whole, just as does the great man. But once there is this
obscuring, even the mind of the great man becomes divided and
hampered, just like that of the small man. Therefore the learning to
be a great man serves simply to clear away the obscuring caused by
selfish desires, so as thus to manifest in oneself the illustrious virtue,
and to return to the original state of union with Heaven, Earth, and
all things. It is not possible to add anything beyond this original
state. . . .

"It may then be asked how (the learning to be a great man)
consists in 'loving people.' ¹

"My reply is that 'to manifest the illustrious virtue' is to establish
one's state of unity with Heaven, Earth, and all things, and that 'to
love people' is to exercise the function of that same unity. Therefore
the manifestation of the illustrious virtue necessarily consists in
loving people, and loving people is the way to manifest the illustrious
virtue. . . . (Beginning with the relationships of) ruler and subject,
husband and wife, friend and friend, and reaching to mountains
and rivers, spirits and gods, birds and beasts, plants and trees, all
these should receive our affection, in order thus to extend our unifying love (*jen*). In this way there is nothing that is not manifested
in our illustrious virtue, so that we may truly succeed in becoming
one with Heaven, Earth, and all things. . . . This is what is meant
by the utmost development of one's nature.

"It may then be asked in what way (the learning to be a great
man) consists in the individual's 'resting in the highest good.' ²

"My reply is that the highest good is the supreme standard for
the manifesting of the illustrious virtue and loving people. Our
heavenly conferred nature is purely and utterly good. What cannot
be obscured in it is the manifestation of the highest good, and constitutes the illustrious virtue in its original state, which is also what
I call intuitive knowledge. When the highest good is manifested,
right is right and wrong is wrong. To things trifling or important,
significant or petty, it responds and reacts with unceasing transformation, yet in everything attaining to the natural mean. This,
then, is the supreme standard for man and things, to which nothing

---

¹ This is the second step enunciated in the opening sentence of the *Great
Learning*, following the "manifestation of the illustrious virtue." The word for
"love" in this phrase is not *jen* but *ch'in* 親 . — Tr.

² The third step enunciated in the opening sentence of the *Great Learning*.
— Tr.

can be added and from which nothing can be taken away. If there is the slightest addition or reduction, that means selfishness and a petty kind of 'knowledge,' and is not the highest good. ...

"Among former individuals there were some who certainly wished to manifest their illustrious virtue; only they did not know how to rest in the highest good. Instead they indulged their selfish minds by trying to do something more than the highest (state of personal perfection). In so doing they fell into the error of vacuous and empty meditation, and failed to do anything for family, nation, or the world. Such are the devotees of the two teachings (of Buddhism and Taoism).

"Certainly there were likewise some who wished to love people; only they too did not know how to rest in the highest good. Instead they drowned their selfish minds in base and trifling things. In so doing they fell into the error of calculated scheming and wise cunning, and of lacking the sincerity of love and pity. Such are the profit-striving followers of the five Tyrants. [1] In both cases the fault lies in ignorance of how to rest in the highest good" (pp. 204-208).

Here, presented with greater clarity and precision, we have essentially the same idea as that expressed in Ch'eng Hao's exposition of love or *jen*. [2] Lu Chiu-yüan says likewise: "The universe has never limited and separated itself from man, but it is man who limits and separates himself from the universe." [3] The distinction between the great and small man is that the former does not allow himself to be thus limited and separated. Even in the small man, however, there exists an original mind which possesses the "unifying quality of love." The "four beginnings" postulated by Mencius, such as the feeling of commiseration, the sense of right and wrong, etc., are simply the external manifestations of this original mind, which, by Wang, is also termed the "intuitive knowledge." [4] To develop and bring this intuitive knowledge into actual operation is called by him "extending the intuitive knowledge." Thus he writes:

"The mind of man constitutes Heaven in all its profundity,

---

[1] On these five feudal lords of the Chou dynasty, see chap. 11, p. 474, note 1. — Tr.

[2] See chap. 12, pp. 521-522. — Tr.

[3] See above, p. 575. — Tr.

[4] *Liang chih* 良知, lit., "good knowledge," a term derived from the *Mencius*, VIIa, 15: "The knowledge possessed without the exercise of thought is the 'good knowledge.' " — Tr.

within which there is nothing not included. Originally there was nothing but this single Heaven, but because of the barriers caused by selfish desire, we have lost this original state of Heaven. If now we concentrate our thoughts upon extending the intuitive knowledge, so as to sweep away all the barriers and obstructions, the original state will then again be restored, and we will again become part of the profundity of Heaven." [1]

"The illustrious virtue in its original state," Wang writes elsewhere, "is what is known as the intuitive knowledge." Hence manifesting the illustrious virtue and loving people are, for Wang, both ways of extending the intuitive knowledge, the latter process being understood as equivalent to the *Great Learning*'s "extension of knowledge." "If, however," he continues, "one wishes to extend one's intuitive knowledge, does this mean that one should stupefy oneself with shadows and echoes, and suspend oneself in empty unreality? [2] It is necessary to accept the reality of (external) affairs. Hence the 'extension of knowledge' necessarily consists in the 'investigation of things.' Here the word 'things' (*wu* 物) is to be interpreted as 'affairs' (*shih* 事)." [3] Again Wang says: "The activity of the mind is called 'thought' (*yi* 意), . . . and the objects toward which thought is directed are called 'things' (*wu*). For instance, when one's thought is directed toward the serving of the parents, this serving of the parents is then one of these 'things.' . . . When it is directed toward being benevolent to people and kind to creatures, this benevolence and kindness then becomes one of these 'things.' And when one's thought is directed toward seeing, hearing, speaking, and acting, each of these acts thereupon becomes one of these 'things.'" [4] As to the word *ko* 格 (the term linked with *wu*, "things," in the phrase *ko wu*, "investigation of things"), Wang comments as follows: "*Ko* means *cheng* 正 (rectifying). It means to rectify what is unrectified in order to restore it to a state of rectitude. To rectify what is unrectified means to get rid of evil. To restore it to rectitude means to practice goodness." [5]

---

[1] *Ch'uan-hsi Lu* or *Record of Instructions*, p. 154.

[2] Here Wang is attacking the meditative techniques of the Buddhists and Taoists.

[3] *Questions on the Great Learning*, p. 213.

[4] *Record of Instructions*, p. 59.

[5] *Questions on the Great Learning*, pp. 213-214.

As for the "intuitive knowledge," this is defined by Wang as "the nature which Heaven has conferred on us, the original state of our mind, which is spontaneously intelligent and keenly conscious. Any ideas which arise are without fail automatically comprehended by this 'intuitive knowledge' of our mind. If they be good, the intuitive knowledge in our mind automatically comprehends this. But if they be evil, this too the intuitive knowledge automatically comprehends" (*ibid.*, pp. 212-213). Therefore, Wang urges, "whatever the intuitive knowledge recognizes as either good or evil," we must then strive "sincerely to love or hate. In this way we will not deceive our intuitive knowledge, but will succeed in 'making our thoughts sincere' " [1] (*ibid.*, p. 213). By avoiding such deception, we can bring to realization the *Great Learning*'s "investigation of things," "extension of knowledge," "making our thoughts sincere," and "rectifying our minds." By the same token we can actualize the "manifesting of the illustrious virtue." By pursuing this process for a long time, we can completely eradicate the "barriers caused by selfish desire," and thus enable the "illustrious virtue" to restore us to the state of original oneness with Heaven, Earth, and all things. All these steps in their totality represent, for Wang, "the correct teaching of Yao and Shun," and "the true doctrine of Confucius" (*ibid.*, p. 215).

ii. *Unity of Knowledge and Conduct*

The initutive knowledge is itself something mental, but the act of "extending" it falls into the field of concrete conduct. Only through this extension or translation of the intuitive knowledge into conduct, can that knowledge be made complete. This is the principle underlying Wang Shou-jen's doctrine of the "unity of knowledge and conduct" (*chih hsing ho yi* 知行合一). The following conversation occurs in his *Record of Instructions*:

"It was asked: 'People of today all know that filial piety is due the father, and respect is due the elder brother; nevertheless, they are unable to practice such filial piety and respect. This indicates that knowledge and conduct are two separate things.'

"The Master replied: 'This is owing to the separation caused by selfish desires, and does not represent knowledge and conduct in their

---

[1] Another of the famous steps of moral cultivation prescribed by the *Great Learning*. See vol. 1, p. 362. — Tr.

original state. There is no such thing as knowledge which cannot be carried into practice, for such knowledge is really no knowledge at all. When the sages and worthies taught men about knowledge and conduct, it was precisely with the intention of restoring them to their original state, and not merely done in the manner you have just indicated. ... I have said that knowledge is the guide of conduct, and conduct is the work carried out by knowledge. Knowledge is the beginning of conduct; conduct is the completion of knowledge. At the moment of comprehension, though one may then speak solely of knowledge, conduct is already automatically included therein; or though one may then speak solely of conduct, knowledge is already automatically included therein" (pp. 53-55).

The mind in its original state is unobscured by selfishness. It is a mind in which knowledge and conduct are one and the same. Thus, to turn again to Mencius' familiar parable of the child about to fall in the well, any bystander, if he complies with the feeling of alarm which then spontaneously arises in him, will instantly rush forward to save the child. This act is thus the automatic projection of his feeling of alarm, and so is not something separate in itself. Such is what Wang means when he says that "knowledge is the beginning of conduct; conduct is the completion of knowledge." Suppose, however, that the bystander pauses to reflect on the situation, and then decides not to rescue the child, perhaps because of fear for the danger involved, or perhaps because of dislike for the child's parents. We then have a case in which there is knowledge without ensuing conduct. This situation, however, no longer represents knowledge and conduct in their original state.

The same is true of filial piety: when a man, knowing that he ought to be filial to his father, allows himself to follow the natural expression of this knowledge, his resulting conduct is bound to be filial. When, on the other hand, such conduct is lacking, the reason is that the mind has been obscured by selfishness. However, the fact that some people's minds are obscured in this way does not mean that their minds are innately devoid of the intuitive knowledge. All it means is that, in their case, this intuitive knowledge has been unable to find its free expression. This is why Wang says: "Conduct is the completion of knowledge."

Psychologically speaking, this theory is well based. For example, when a man flees from something which he realizes to be dangerous to himself, this is a manifestation of "knowledge and conduct in their original state." Therefore the fact that under certain circumstances he may refuse to flee from it must be attributed to supplementary inhibiting factors, either psychological or biological. It no longer represents "knowledge and conduct in their original state." Though this theory of the unity of knowledge and conduct is psychologically sound, however, "knowledge," for Wang, usually means the "intuitive knowledge," and whether such a knowledge actually exists is something which psychology has as yet failed to determine.

iii. *Chu Hsi and Wang Shou-jen Compared*

In his Preface to the *Doctrines Reached by the Master Chu in Later Life*, [1] Wang Shou-jen writes:

"Early in life I devoted my energies to the work of passing the state examinations, and sank my purpose into the practice of writing essays. Having gained some knowledge of what is meant by devoting oneself to true learning, I deplored the confusing and fatiguing effect caused by the multiplicity of different doctrines, resulting in a vagueness which I could not penetrate. For this reason I searched into Taoism and Buddhism, in which I was pleased to find a mental affinity, and which, therefore, I believed contained the learning of the sages. Yet when I tried to adjust them to the teachings of Confucius, and to arrange them for daily use, they were constantly deficient and without effect. Relying on them and then disregarding them, departing from them and then returning to them, I both believed and mistrusted them.

"Later, as an exiled official, I lived in distress among the barbarians at Lung-ch'ang (in Kweichow). In this way my mind was stimulated and my nature hardened. Then I underwent a brilliant mental enlightenment. Thereafter, during the change from winter to summer and back again, I sought and investigated, and confirmed my thought by the Five Classics and Four Philosophers. [2] I found that they all agree like a river which bursts its banks and flows into the sea. ... Only in the doctrines of Master Chu did I find disagreement—a fact which constantly distressed my mind."

Here we are told the various mental stages by which Wang

---

[1] *Chu-tzŭ Wan-nien Ting-lun*, pp. 492-493.
[2] I.e., the Four Books of Confucianism: *Analects, Mencius, Great Learning,* and *Doctrine of the Mean.* — Tr.

reached his final position of opposition to Chu Hsi. The passages quoted earlier from his *Questions on the Great Learning* make it apparent that the whole range of Wang's philosophy may be summed up in the phrase, "the extension of intuitive knowledge." In his biography we have already seen how, beginning in his forty-third year, he concentrated his teachings on this point. Such a doctrine was indeed simple and direct, and its interpretation of the *Great Learning*'s "extension of knowledge through the investigation of things" certainly differed fundamentally from that of Chu Hsi. As a matter of fact, the general difference between the two philosophies is essentially that already described by us in section 3, when comparing the school of the "Learning of Principle" with that of the "Learning of Mind."

Wang Shou-jen also sometimes touches upon the relationship between *li* or Principle and *ch'i* or the Ether, as in the following passage: [1]

"Principle (*li*) is the orderly Principle of the Ether (*ch'i*), while the Ether is the functioning of Principle. Without this orderly Principle there would be no functioning, and without this functioning there would likewise be no means whereby what we call orderly Principle could become visible."

Were we solely dependent on this one statement, we would have to admit that no great gap separates Wang from Chu Hsi. Elsewhere, however, Wang specifically points out the respects in which he and Chu Hsi differ:

"When the Master Chu speaks of the 'investigation of things,' he describes it as meaning that we should apply ourselves to things so as to gain an exhaustive knowledge of their Principle. [2] Such exhaustive knowledge of the Principle of things means that for each and every affair and thing we should seek for what he regards as its own fixed Principle. But by thus using our mind to seek out the Principles lying within each affair and thing, we cause a distinction to be made between mind and Principle. . . .

"When I speak about the extension of knowledge through the investigation of things, I mean by this an extension of our mind's *intuitive knowledge* to affairs and things. This intuitive knowledge of

---

[1] See Wang's *Shu* or *Letters*, p. 235. [An introductory sentence of philological definition has, for simplicity's sake, been omitted from this translation. — Tr.]

[2] This is Chu's definition as found in his commentary on the *Great Learning*. See above, chap. 13, p. 561. — Tr.

our mind is what is known as Heavenly Principle (*t'ien li*). If I extend
the Heavenly Principle of my mind's intuitive knowledge to affairs
and things, then each such affair and thing will thereby partake of
this Principle. That extension of my mind's intuitive knowledge is
(what the *Great Learning* means by) the extension of knowledge,
and the partaking of this Principle by each affair and thing is (what
it means by) the investigation of things. In this way mind and Principle are made one" (*Letters*, pp. 303-305).

Chu Hsi maintains that the one Supreme Ultimate is embodied in
each and every person and thing. Since this Supreme Ultimate is simply
the aggregate of all the multitudinous Principles of things, it follows
that the mind of man likewise "has within it the multitudinous
Principles, with which it responds to all different things." [1] Hence
to gain an exhaustive knowledge of the Principles of external things
means to gain a similar knowledge of the Principles which lie within
our own mind and form part of our nature. From this point of view
Wang's accusation that Chu splits mind from Principle is not entirely
justified. Nevertheless, according to Chu's system, the mind can only
exist through the combination of Principle with the Ether or *ch'i*.
This in turn means that even when the mind is physically non-
existent, Principle itself eternally subsists. Although, therefore,
there can practically speaking be no Principle without the Ether,
logically speaking there can be Principle without mind. From this
point of view, then, it is permissible to accuse Chu of divorcing mind
from Principle. According to Wang's system, on the other hand,
the fact that "I extend the Heavenly Law of my mind's intuitive
knowledge to affairs and things," is the reason why "each such
affair and thing will thereby partake of this Principle." It follows
that unless there be mind, there will be no Principle. Wang says
elsewhere:

"The mind itself is Principle. So in the world can there yet be
any thing or any Principle outside of the mind?" (*Record of Instructions*,
p. 50).

Another passage reads: "With regard to the statement that the
mind itself is Principle, it was further asked about the meaning of this
statement, inasmuch as Master Ch'eng says: 'What lies in things is
Principle.' [2] To this the Master replied: 'In the statement, "What lies

---

[1] This also is from Chu's commentary on the *Great Learning*, first sentence. — Tr.

[2] Probably only a paraphrase of Ch'eng's precise words. — Tr.

in things is Principle," before the term "what lies in" there should be added the single word "mind." This mind that lies in things is what constitutes Principle'" (*ibid.*, p. 180).

Wang writes further: "The substance of the mind is the nature, and the nature is Principle. Therefore, since there is the mind of filial love, it follows that there is the Principle of filial love. If there were no such a mind, there would be no such a Principle. And since there is the mind of loyalty to the sovereign, it follows that there is the Principle of loyalty. If there were no such a mind, there would be no such a Principle. How can these Principles be outside our mind? Hui-an (i.e., Chu Hsi) has said that what men call the objects of study are simply mind and Principle. Although the mind (in one sense merely) governs the individual body, it (at the same time in this way) actually controls all the Principles under Heaven. Though these Principles lie scattered through all things, they in truth are not external to man's single mind. Because they are thus divided from one another and yet at the same time united, he (Chu Hsi) has not escaped the error of suggesting to his students that mind and Principle are dual" (*Letters*, p. 298).

According to Chu Hsi's system, one can only say that the nature is Principle, but not that the mind is Principle. Similarly one can only say that there is the Principle of filial piety and the Principle of loyalty, and hence that there is a mind which experiences these feelings. One cannot reverse the statement by saying that because there is a mind that experiences filial piety, there is therefore a Principle of filial piety, and that without such a mind there would then be no such a Principle. In short, it is entirely possible for Principle to subsist quite independently of the mind, even though in physical reality this is not what actually happens. According to Wang, on the other hand, there can be no Principle, either in actual fact or logically speaking, unless there be mind. Herein lies a fundamental distinction between the Rationalistic and Idealistic schools. In Wang's philosophy no distinction is made between "what is above shapes" and "what is within shapes," and hence these terms, so frequently used by Chu Hsi, do not occur at all in Wang's conversations or writings.

Wang says further: "The intuitive knowledge of man is the intuitive knowledge of plants and trees, tiles and stones. If plants, trees, tiles, and stones lacked this intuitive knowledge of man, they would be unable to be plants, trees, tiles, and stones. But is this true of them only? If Heaven and Earth lacked man's intuitive knowledge, they too would be unable to be Heaven and Earth. The fact is that Heaven, Earth, and all things originally form a single unity with man, the most refined manifestation of which consists of that tiny bit of spirituality and intelligence comprising man's mind" (*Record of Instructions*, pp. 168-169).

We are further told in the next passage: "While the Master was taking recreation at Nan-chen (in Chekiang), one of our friends, pointing at the flowers and trees on a cliff, said: 'You say there is nothing under Heaven external to the mind. What relation, then, do these high mountain flowers and trees, which blossom and drop of themselves, have to my mind?' The Master replied: 'When you do not see these flowers, they and your mind both become quiescent. But when you look at them, their color at once becomes clear. From this fact you know that these flowers are not external to your mind' " (*ibid.*, p. 169).

Again we read: "The Master asked: 'According to you, what is the mind of Heaven and Earth?' I replied: 'I have often heard that man is the mind of Heaven and Earth.' He asked: 'And what is it in man that is called his mind?' I replied: 'It is simply the spirituality or consciousness.'

" 'From this' (he replied), 'we know that in Heaven and Earth there is only this spirituality or consciousness. But because of his bodily form, man has separated himself from the whole. My spirituality or consciousness is the ruler of Heaven, Earth, and spirits. ... If Heaven, Earth, spirits, and things are separated from my spirituality or consciousness, they cease to be. And if my spirituality or consciousness is separated from them, it ceases to be also. Thus they are all permeated with a single force, so how can we be separated from them?'

"I asked further: 'Since Heaven, Earth, spirits, and things have for a thousand ages of antiquity been seen to exist, how can it be that when my spirituality or consciousness becomes extinct, they should all cease to be?' He replied: 'Let us take the case of a dead man. Since his spirituality or consciousness has become dispersed, where can Heaven, Earth, and things still exist for him?' " (*ibid.*, pp. 184-185).

We have seen that for Chu Hsi the nature is Principle, whereas for Wang Shou-jen the mind is Principle. The question still arises, however, whether what Wang speaks of as mind may not actually be the same as what Chu speaks of as nature. If so, the whole preceding argument falls to the ground. Wang's description of the mind, however, as "simply the spirituality or consciousness" (*ling ming* 靈明), harmonizes well with Chu Hsi's statement that man possesses an intellectual faculty or consciousness (*ling ch'u*), which is the mind and not the nature. [1] This rules out the possibility that Wang and Chu are merely using different terms to refer to the same thing. Chu maintains that our mind holds within itself the Supreme Ultimate in its entirety, and that it therefore also contains all the various Principles of things. According to his system, however, it is only these Principles that are thus contained, and not the actual concrete things governed by these Principles. Wang, on the contrary, maintains that Heaven, Earth, and all things are themselves all actually present within our mind. Thus his philosophy represents an idealism with which Chu Hsi could never agree.

iv. *Criticism of Buddhism and Taoism*

The differences between Wang Shou-jen and Chu Hsi appear again in their respective criticisms of Buddhism and Taoism. Chu, for example, when speaking of the nature, emphasizes the fact that it embraces all Principles, and is therefore real. It is on this ground that he attacks the Buddhists for regarding it as "empty" or unreal (*k'ung*). [2] Wang, on the other hand, compares the mind's quality of love or *jen* to an ever-burning light, [3] the manifestation of which is the intuitive knowledge. All we need do, he urges, is to act according to this intuitive knowledge, avoiding "the slightest addition or reduction." [4] Otherwise we shall be guilty of being what Ch'eng Hao calls "selfish and mentally calculating." [5] Such is his basis for criticizing the Taoists and Buddhists. We read, for example, in his *Record of Instructions*:

"The Master often said that (the claim of) the Buddhists not to have attachment to phenomena (shows how) in reality they do have attachment to them, whereas we Confucianists, by (admitting that we) do have attachment to phenomena, in reality have no such attachment. I asked for an explanation and he continued: 'The

---

[1] See chap. 13, p. 556.
[2] See chap. 13, p. 567. — Tr.
[3] See above, p. 599. — Tr.
[4] See above, p. 601. — Tr.
[5] See chap. 12, p. 524. — Tr.

Buddhists, being afraid of the troubles involved in the relationships between father and son, ruler and subject, and husband and wife, therefore escape from these relationships. They are forced to escape because they are already attached to the phenomena of these relationships. But as for us Confucianists, there being the relationship of father and son, we respond to it with love. There being that between ruler and subject, we respond to it with righteousness. And there being that between husband and wife, we respond to it with mutual respect. How then can (it be said that) we are unduly attached to the phenomena of the relationships between father and son, ruler and subject, and husband and wife?' " (pp. 159-160).

Again he says: "When those who seek immortality (i.e., the religious Taoists) speak of 'the void' (*hsü*), can the (Confucian) sage add to it a hair of 'fullness' (*shih* 實)? And when the Buddhists speak of 'non-being' (*wu*), can the sage add to it a hair of 'being' (*yu*)? But when these seekers after immortality speak of the void, their motive is to preserve life, whereas when the Buddhists speak of non-being, their motive is to escape the sea of suffering of life and death. When they add these ideas to the original nature (of the mind), the original meaning of 'the void' and 'non-being' (as held by that mind) is no longer there, and thereby obstructions are raised around the (mind's) original nature. The (Confucian) sage, however, simply restores the intuitive knowledge to its original condition, and adds to it no idea whatsoever. The 'void' of the intuitive knowledge is the 'void' of Heaven, and the 'non-being' of the intuitive knowledge is the absence of shape of the 'Great Void.' [1] Sun, moon, wind, thunder, mountains, rivers, people, and things—in fact everything that has form and shape—all function and have their activity within this shapeless Great Void, and never become obstructions to Heaven. The sage merely conforms to the functioning of his intuitive knowledge, and Heaven, Earth, and all things all lie within the function and activity of our intuitive knowledge. How, then, can there be anything outside the intuitive knowledge, to hinder or obstruct it?" (*ibid.*, pp. 167-168).

The Buddhists consciously try "not to have attachment to phenomena," and seek for "non-being," but the result is merely to attach them to those phenomena and cause them to lose the state of non-being. Only by following the spontaneous promptings of the

---

[1] *T'ai hsü*, a term already used by Chang Tsai. See chap. 12, p. 480. — Tr.

intuitive knowledge, without interposing any conscious motivation
or calculation, can we achieve a state in which our "activity" becomes "non-activity." The "non-being" sought for in this state then
becomes genuine "non-being."

v. *The Gradations of Love*

In the eyes of the man of true love, Heaven, Earth, and all things
form one body with himself. Yet in actual fact it sometimes happens
that a man is forced to sacrifice something else in order to preserve
his own life. This is why Schopenhauer has said that man's life is a
great contradiction. Even the Buddhist, for example, though because of his compassion for sentient beings he eats no meat, is
nevertheless obliged to eat grain in order to sustain life. How, then,
is one to meet this dilemma? Wang's reply is found in the following
passage from the *Record of Instructions*:

"It was asked: 'If the great man has a common unity with other
things, why is it that the *Great Learning* refers to what is "more
important" and "less important"?' [1]

"The Master replied: 'It is a natural principle that there should
be things of greater and lesser importance. The body, for example,
is a unity, but if we use the hands and feet to defend the head and
eyes, does that mean that we belittle the importance of the hands and
feet? It simply means to accord with this natural principle. Thus
though animals and plants are both to be loved, we nevertheless
endure the fact that we make use of plants to nourish the animals.
And though men and animals are both to be loved, our minds
nevertheless endure the fact that we butcher animals to feed our
parents in life, to sacrifice to them after death, and to entertain guests.
(In the same way) love is to shown both to our close relatives and to
the passersby on the road. Yet suppose there be but a single dish of
food or bowl of soup, and that life or death depend upon whether
they be gained or not. When it thus becomes impossible to fulfill
(our love) in both cases, we then prefer to save our close relatives
rather than the passersby. Our mind endures this, moreover, because,
according to natural principle, it is proper that we should act in this
way. Only when we come to the question of the relationship between
us ourselves and our closest relatives, are we no longer able to

---

[1] *Great Learning*, p. 412. — Tr.

maintain this distinction between what is more or less important. This is because herein lies the source from which springs both our love (*jen*) toward men and our affection (*ai*) toward other things. Hence once we can endure (the necessity of choosing) in this case, we can endure everything else as well. What the *Great Learning* says about the more important and less important is a natural principle within our intuitive knowledge, and may not be transgressed. This then, is called righteousness (*yi*). Our compliance with it is called propriety (*li*), our knowledge of it is called wisdom (*chih*), and our belief in it from beginning to end is called good faith (*hsin*)' " (pp. 187-188).

Here Wang maintains that the intuitive knowledge does sanction partiality under certain circumstances, for of itself it knows what we should treat as more important and what as less. As he says elsewhere: "When the highest good is manifested, .. then to things trifling or important, significant or petty, it (the intuitive knowledge) responds and reacts with unceasing transformation, yet in everything attaining to the natural mean." [1] Therefore, by following this intuitive knowledge in our conduct, we can "extend the intuitive knowledge" and thus come to rest in the highest good.

Herein, Wang Shou-jen maintains, lies the real distinction between the Confucian concept of love, which it calls *jen*, and Mo Tzǔ's famous concept of impartial or "universal love" (*chien ai*). The *Record of Instructions* reports:

"It was asked: Master Ch'eng has said that the person of *jen* regards Heaven, Earth, and all things as one body. [2] Why, then, can the 'universal love' of Mo Tzǔ not be regarded as such *jen*?'

"The Master replied: 'It is very hard to give an adequate answer. You, sirs, will have to come to a self-realization of it in order to understand. *Jen* is the Principle (*li*) of unceasing creation and growth which, though boundless in extent and everywhere present, nevertheless operates and manifests itself only gradually in order to produce this unceasing growth. ... It is like a tree, which, when it begins to put forth a shoot, thereby gives its first manifestation of the start of its growth. ... The affection (*ai*) between father and son or elder and younger brother is the first manifestation of growth of the human mind, just like the tree's putting forth of a shoot. And the

---

[1] *Questions on the Great Learning*, p. 207.
[2] This statement comes from Ch'eng Hao. See chap. 12, p. 521. — Tr.

subsequent feelings of love (*jen*) toward men, and affection (*ai*) toward other creatures, are the development of (that tree's) trunk and the growth of its branches and leaves. But Mo Tzŭ's universal love has no gradations. It regards the father and son, elder and younger brother, of one's own family in the same light as it does a passerby, thereby destroying its own starting point. If no shoot is first put forth, we know that there can be no trunk, and hence no process of unceasing growth. How, then, can this be called *jen?*' " (pp. 106-108).

What the Confucianists mean by *jen* is the development of an innate feeling of sympathy and commiseration, initially manifested in the love for one's parents. As such, it differs from the universal love of the Mohists, which is based on utilitarian considerations. [1] What Wang stresses is the naturalness of the Confucian concept, and the fact that in its growth and selective operation it conforms to "a natural principle within our intuitive knowledge."

vi. *Origin of Evil*

"There is nothing under Heaven external to the mind"—this mind, for Wang, being "simply the spirituality or consciousness." [2] This being so, the origin of evil becomes a serious problem in his philosophy. In the *Record of Instructions* we read:

"I asked: 'The Master has said that good and evil are a single thing; yet good and evil are poles as mutually opposed to each other as ice and burning coals. How, then, can they be said to be only a single thing? The Master replied: 'The highest good is the mind's original substance. Whatever goes beyond this original substance is evil. It is not a case of there being something good, and then of there being something evil standing in opposition to it. Thus good and evil are only a single thing.'

"When I had heard this statement by the Master, I understood the saying of Master Ch'eng that 'goodness, to be sure, certainly belongs to the nature, yet evil cannot be said not to belong also to that nature.' [3] (The Master) continued: 'Good and evil are both Heavenly Principle. What we call evil is not original evil, but results either from transgressing or falling short of our original nature.' This statement of his is not to be doubted" (pp. 156-157).

---

[1] See vol. 1, p. 94. — Tr.
[2] See above, p. 609.
[3] See chap. 12, p. 515. — Tr.

Thus what we call evil results from the failure of our feelings and desires to conform with what is proper, which means that as long as they do conform, there is nothing wrong in them *per se*. Another passage in the *Record of Instructions* tells us:

"It was asked: 'Knowledge is like the sun, and desire like the clouds. Though the clouds can obscure the sun, they, like it, are inherent in the sky's atmosphere. Is not desire similarly inherent in man's mind?'

"The Master replied: 'Joy, anger, grief, fear, love, hate, and desire are known as the seven feelings, and these seven are all equally inherent in the human mind. The one vital thing, however, is that we should clearly recognize the intuitive knowledge. This is like the light of the sun, which cannot be pointed out as belonging to any one particular spot, because wherever a crack is found admitting light, there too the light of the sun is to be found. Even when the mist of the clouds closes in from all sides, the appearance of the Great Void (of Heaven) still remains distinguishable, it being the place where the light of the sun still remains unextinguished. Simply because clouds can obscure the sun, one should not on that account instruct Heaven to desist from producing clouds. When the seven feelings follow their natural course, they are all functions of the intuitive knowledge, and cannot be divided into good or evil. But at the same time one should not allow them to have any attachment (to things), because such attachment on the part of any one of them constitutes desire and obscures the intuitive knowledge. Whenever attachment exists, however, the intuitive knowledge is able to become conscious thereof, and being thus conscious, the obscuring is dispelled, so that its (original) condition is restored' " (pp. 171-172).

In connection with the phrase, "one should not allow them to have any attachment," there is another pertinent passage in the *Record of Instructions*:

"Inquiry was made about the section on 'being under the influence of passion.' [1] The Master replied: 'How can man's mind avoid the influence of passion? One may only (say) that we ought not to have it. Whenever a man is under the influence of passion, and his conscious thinking has caused him to suffer attachment (to the thing which stirs passion), his anger then exceeds what is proper, and he is no longer in his (original) state of empty impartiality. Hence

---

[1] See the *Great Learning*, p. 416. — Tr.

if passion be attached to the thing that causes it, it then no longer accords with what is proper. But if, whenever something happens to provoke passion, one simply responds to whatever comes, without injecting the least bit of mental calculation, one's mind will then be vast and all-embracing in its impartiality, and will keep to its correct original state. For example, if on going outside one happens to see men fighting, one's mind will feel anger at what is not right, but despite this anger, the mind itself will retain its vast broadness and not be stirred by the least bit of temper. So if one is to feel anger against somebody, it must be in this way, for only so will it be correct.' " [1]

The idea here expressed, that the seven feelings, if attached to things, will not conform to what is proper, is similar to that found in the Ch'an treatise, *Liu-tsu T'an-ching* (Sūtra Spoken by the Sixth Patriarch), when it says: "The prior moment of thinking, in which there is attachment to things, is that of affliction (*kleśa*); the next moment of thinking, in which there is separation from things, is that of perfect Wisdom (*Bodhi*)." [2] And Ch'eng Hao writes similarly: "The sage expresses joy at things which properly call for joy, and anger at things which properly call for anger." Yet he himself does not "have" either the joy or anger, for his mind, like a clear mirror, ever retains its "empty impartiality, with which, when things appear, he reacts accordingly." [3]

So far we have been discussing the problem of moral evil. There still remains, however, the question of whether there can be material evil, i.e., whether or not physical objects or phenomena can in themselves be either good or bad. Wang argues that such so-called "evil" depends entirely on our own likes and dislikes, rather than on the objects themselves. Thus we read in the *Record of Instructions*:

"While pulling out weeds from among the flowers, I asked: 'Why is it so difficult to cultivate the good in the universe and to get rid of its evil?' The Master replied: '... This way of looking at good and evil entirely from the point of view of the individual self is incorrect. In the plan of growth of the universe, flowers and weeds belong to a single category. How, then, can they be differentiated as good or evil? Wishing to have flowers to look at, you then consider

---

[1] This passage is not translated in Henke, *op. cit*. It occurs in the Chinese text between two of the passages which appear in Henke, p. 159. — Tr.

[2] Quoted above in chap. 9, p. 395.

[3] For these quotations, see chap. 12, pp. 525 and 524 respectively.

them good and the weeds evil. But should you wish to use the weeds, you would then on the contrary consider them good. Thus such good and evil spring from the likes and dislikes of your own mind, so that I know them to be erroneous.'

"I asked: 'Does this mean that there is neither good nor evil?' He replied: 'In the state of quiescence, which is that of reason, there is neither good nor evil. In the state of agitation, which is that of passion, both good and evil are present. As long as one remains unmoved by passion, there will be neither good nor evil, and this is the state of the highest good.'

"I asked: 'Buddhism, too, makes no discrimination between good and evil, so how does it differ (from what you say)?' He replied: 'The Buddhist attaches himself to a state in which neither good nor evil exists, but then disregards everything else, so that he is unable to deal with the (everyday) world. Whereas in the case of the (Confucian) sage, the absence of good and evil simply means that he neither acts because of (personal) likes nor because of (personal) dislikes. He remains unmoved by his passions. Nevertheless he accords with the Way of the (sage-)kings, and being able to carry this out to the highest degree, naturally comes to conform with Heavenly Principle, so that he can assist in its creative activities.'

"I said: 'Since the weeds are not evil, it would seem that they should not be pulled out.' He replied: 'This is the Taoist and Buddhist point of view. (But in your case), if they are a hindrance, what prevents you from removing them?'

"I said: 'In that case one is again acting according to one's (own personal) likes and dislikes.' He replied: 'Not to act according to one's likes and dislikes does not mean to be wholly lacking in likes and dislikes, for this would be the same as being wholly lacking in consciousness. To say of someone that he does not act (according to his likes and dislikes) means simply that in his likes and dislikes he wholly conforms to Principle, and that, aside from this, he does not attach himself to any mental calculating. To be like this is the same as not having likes or dislikes at all.'

"I said: 'How can weeding be construed as conformity to Principle without the slightest mental calculation?' He replied: 'If the weeds are a hindrance, according to Principle it is proper to uproot them, but nothing more should be involved than this uprooting. Suppose, for example, that by some chance they are not uprooted, this should not (be allowed to) disturb the mind. But if one attaches oneself to the least bit of mental calculation, the mind's (original) condition will become affected by it, and there will be a great deal of stirring of the passions' " (pp. 114-116).

Thus external things are neither good nor evil in themselves; their seeming goodness or badness derives simply from the way in which we, with our personal likes and dislikes, happen to regard them. However, our objective realization that they are neither good nor bad does not mean that we should suppress our own likes and dislikes. What is necessary is, while responding to them, to take care that we do not thereby become attached to external things. By avoiding such attachment we may preserve our mind in its original state of unperturbedness. Thus since our likes and dislikes are both inherent in the mind, our method should be that of the sage, whose "emotions accord with all things, yet (of himself) he has no emotion." [1]

vii. *Unity of Activity and Quiescence*

By saying that we should "wholly conform to Principle," Wang Shou-jen means that we should wholly conform to the natural promptings of the intuitive knowledge. He writes:

"The effort of the sage to extend his knowledge is characterized by utter sincerity and unceasingness. His intuitive knowledge is as brilliant as a clear mirror, unflecked by the slightest film. When beautiful or ugly objects come before it, their forms are reflected accordingly, without any stain being left behind on the mirror itself. This is the meaning of the saying that 'his emotions accord with all things, yet (of himself) he has no emotion.' It has been said by the Buddhists—and not incorrectly—that 'something springs from the mind, yet without having any attachment (to external things).' When the clear mirror's response to objects is such that beauty appears in it as beauty, and ugliness as ugliness, so that through its single reflecting power everything is shown in its true aspect, this is what is meant by 'something springing from the mind.' And when beauty appears in it as beauty, ugliness as ugliness, and nothing is left behind (on the mirror itself) after the disappearance of these things, this is what is meant by 'not having any attachment' " (*Letters*, p. 255).

"If the weeds are a hindrance, according to Principle it is proper

---

[1] A statement by Ch'eng Hao. See chap. 12, p. 524. It is repeated in the quotation immediately below. — Tr.

to uproot them." In this statement we have an example of a feeling which "springs from the mind." But "suppose, for example, that by some chance they are not uprooted, this should not (be allowed to) disturb the mind." In this further statement we have an example of a feeling "not having any attachment." By following these precepts, we can throughout our lives "perform action" externally, while at the same time preserving a state of "non-action" within our own minds. This combined achievement may be summed up as the unity of movement or activity (*tung*) and of quiescence (*ching*). Wang writes:

"The mind may neither be said to be active nor quiescent. Its 'quiescence' has reference to its (internal) substance (*t'i* 體), whereas its 'activity' has reference to its (external) functioning (*yung* 用). For this reason the learning of the superior man places no distinction between activity and quiescence. In his state of quiescence he remains ever perceptive, never (permanently) absent, and therefore always ready to respond (to whatever may arise). In his state of activity he remains ever composed, never (permanently) present, and therefore always ready to retire. By being ever ready to respond and equally ready to retire, his activity and quiescence both have their proper function. This is what is meant by 'the accumulation of righteous deeds.' [1]

"Having accumulated righteous deeds, he is therefore able to avoid any occasion for regret. This is what is known as being composed in activity, and also composed in quiescence. The mind is single and nothing more. Since quiescence refers to its inherent substance, to seek beyond this for yet a further basis of quiescence is to pervert this original substance. And since activity is its functioning, to be fearful of its becoming too readily active is to nullify its functioning. Therefore the very act of seeking for the quiescent mind implies activity, whereas mere dislike for the active mind does not imply quiescence. That is to say, in its state of activity it (the mind) is active, but in its state of quiescence it is also active. (These two modes) rise and fall as they anticipate things; they follow one another without end. Therefore we speak of conformity to Principle as quiescence, and giving in to desire as activity. Such desire does not necessarily pertain only to the external allurements of sound, color, and material benefits, for selfish thoughts arising in the mind equally constitute

---

[1] A phrase from the *Mencius*, IIa, para. 15. Cf. vol. 1, p. 131. — Tr.

desire. Hence once we conform to Principle, then despite our responses to all the manifold vicissitudes of life, we still remain always quiescent. This is what Lien-hsi (Chou Tun-yi) means when he talks about taking quiescence as the essential and being without desire.[1] It is what is meant by the accumulation of righteous deeds. But once we give in to desire, then despite (such techniques as) the 'fast of the mind' and 'sitting in forgetfulness,' we still remain always active.[2] These are Kao Tzŭ's compulsory measures for forcing growth; they form an external kind of righteousness' "[3] (*Letters*, pp. 387-388).

The harmonious unity of activity and quiescence results in genuine and absolute quiescence; its unswerving composure, displayed both in activity and quiescence, is a genuine and absolute composure. We have seen how the same idea has already been expressed by Ch'eng Hao in his famous "Letter on the Composure of the Nature."[4]

In the man who can follow this course, "the Heavenly Principle is eternally preserved, and his original state of brilliant perceptiveness is never diminished or obscured, never led astray or confused. He has no fear or distress; no fond regard or intemperate passion; no preconception, predetermination, obduracy, or egoism;[5] no discontent, insufficiency, shame, or remorse. Gently and harmoniously, brilliantly and pervadingly, he penetrates everywhere in his movements. His acts and demeanor are widely displayed, yet always they accord with propriety. He may follow what his mind desires without making any transgression"[6] (*Letters*, p. 260).

viii. *Reactions against Wang's Idealism*

With Wang Shou-jen, the "Learning of the Mind" reached its highest development. To bolster his position, he wrote a treatise

---

[1] A statement found in his *Diagram of the Supreme Ultimate Explained*, p. 131. — Tr.

[2] These terms, referring to yoga-like meditative practices for gaining enlightenment, go back to the *Chuang-tzŭ*. See vol. 1, p. 241. — Tr.

[3] This is the criticism made by Mencius of the artificial and forced techniques for self-development practiced by his opponent, Kao Tzŭ. Cf. the *Mencius*, IIa, 2, paras. 15-16, and vol. 1, p. 131. — Tr.

[4] Quoted in chap. 12, pp. 523-525. — Tr.

[5] The four faults against which Confucius warned. See above, p. 582. — Tr.

[6] This is the stage to which Confucius said that he had attained at the age of seventy. See *Analects*, II, 4. — Tr.

called *Doctrines Reached by the Philosopher Chu in Later Life*, [1] in which he maintained that Chu Hsi, though in early life differing from Lu Chiu-yüan, had in his later years regretted his errors and modified his views to accord with Lu's. When this theory appeared, it aroused much debate among the followers of the Chu school, some of whom wrote rebuttals to prove that the Chu and Lu teachings were really not the same. An example is the *K'un Chih Chi* (Remarks Reached after Hard Study), written by Wang's contemporary, Lo Ch'in-shun (1465-1547), in which Lo says:

"Master Ch'eng (Ch'eng Yi) has said that the nature is Principle (*li*), whereas Hsiang-shan (Lu Chiu-yüan) has said that the mind is Principle. Here there can only be one who is correct, not two. If the former is right, the latter is wrong; if the latter is right, the former is wrong. Why, then, can we not make a clear distinction?" (2.6).

Lo Ch'in-shun himself defines the difference between the mind and the nature as follows:

"The mind is the spirit-like intelligence of man; the nature is the Principle (*li*) with which he is born. That in which Principle rests is called the mind, and that which the mind possesses is called the nature. Thus these cannot be lumped together as one" (*op. cit.*, 1.1).

Since mind is distinct from nature, it follows that the statements, "The mind is Principle," and "The nature is Principle," likewise differ. Lo criticizes Wang Shou-jen on this point by saying:

"The *Record of Instructions* contains the statement: 'This intuitive knowledge of our mind is what is known as Heavenly Principle.' [2] ... It also has a question (about the following statement): 'The person of love regards Heaven, Earth, and all things as one body.' To which the reply is given: 'If man can but preserve a little of this tendency for growth, he is then able to become one with Heaven, Earth, and all things.' [3] It is then again asked: 'Does the growth of which you speak have in it (merely) the idea of life and activity? Or does it also include the capacity to know and be conscious?' (Wang's) reply to this is: 'Yes.' To which he then adds: 'The nature constitutes the

---

[1] See above, p. 605. Wang's preface to this treatise is translated in Henke, *op. cit.*, pp. 491-494. — Tr.

[2] See above, pp. 606-607. — Tr.

[3] The dialogue here quoted seems to be based on, though it is not wholly identical with, the passage that was quoted above on p. 613. It will be remembered that there, in reply to the identical statement (originally made by Ch'eng Hao), Wang defines love or *jen* as "the Principle (*li*) of unceasing creation and growth." — Tr.

tendency for growth in man.' These (statements) all clearly show that (for Wang) knowing and consciousness are what constitute the nature" (*op. cit.*, 3.1).

To say that "knowing and consciousness are what constitute the nature" is equivalent to saying that the mind constitutes Principle or *li*. Lo continues: "What the Buddhists call the nature consists of consciousness and nothing more" (*ibid.*). By this he means to imply that Wang's doctrine—"Knowing and consciousness are what constitute the nature"—is really a Buddhist one.

Another of Wang's contemporaries, Ch'en Chien (1497-1567), [1] wrote a work called *Hsüeh-p'ou T'ung-pien* (Analysis of the Prejudices of Philosophy), in which he maintains that in early life Chu Hsi and Lu Chiu-yüan really had agreed, and that only later did they come to differ. [2] Thus he reverses the theory advanced by Wang Shou-jen in his *Doctrines Reached by the Master Chu in Later Life*—a theory, incidentally, which had already been propounded before Wang's time by Ch'eng Min-cheng (ca. 1445-ca. 1500) in his *Tao-yi Pien* (Treatise on the Oneness of the Truth). In his rebuttal, Ch'en Chien further accuses the Lu school of Ch'anist tendencies when it defines the nature as simply being the faculty of knowing and consciousness. Thus he writes:

"Spirituality and consciousness have by Lao Tzŭ, Chuang Tzŭ, Ch'anism, and Lu (Chiu-yüan), all been regarded as belonging to Principle (*li*) in its most marvelous perfection. Master Chu, on the contrary, says in his *Conversations* that this spirituality pertains only to 'what is within shapes.' In the 'Discussion on Buddhism' in his *Collected Writings* he says: 'What they (the Buddhists) refer to as the intelligent mind and perceptive nature really amounts to the same thing as spirit (*ching shen* 精神) or soul (*hun po* 魂魄), and pertains to what we Confucianists call "what is within shapes." ' [3] Why should this be? It is because it pertains to the Ether (*ch'i*). Spirit and consciousness both belong to the Ether in its most marvelous functioning aspect, and, since they belong to it, have, as it were, shape and appearance. Hence the Lu philosophy speaks of (them metaphorically as like) a mirror, in which flowers may be seen

---

[1] Styled Ch'ing-lan 清瀾. He was a native of Tung-kuan 東莞, not far east of Canton.

[2] See *op. cit.*, 1.7. — Tr.

[3] See the *Chu-tzŭ Wen-chi Ta-ch'üan Lei-pien* (Classified Compilation of the Collected Writings of Chu Hsi), 9.10. — Tr.

or all phenomena (reflected). Having such shape and appearance, they are certainly visible, and the phenomena reflected in them certainly become manifest thereby. Thus (from the point of view of the Lu philosophy) it is quite fitting that they should be relegated to 'what is within shapes' " (10.7-8).

In this respect we must indeed agree that the Lu-Wang school approaches Ch'anism more closely than does that of Chu Hsi. This fact, indeed, has already been stressed by the Ch'ing scholar, Lu Lung-ch'i (1630-93). [1] There is no doubt, therefore, that the followers of Chu Hsi fully recognized the distinction between their own school's formula that "the nature is Principle," and the Idealistic school's formula that "the mind is Principle." What they failed to point out with equal clarity, however, is that these formulas spring from a basic metaphysical difference: the Rationalistic school postulates two realms of being, whereas the Idealistic school postulates only one.

7—WANG CHI AND WANG KEN

Among Wang Shou-jen's disciples there were two—Wang Chi and Wang Ken—in whom the trend toward Ch'anism is particularly apparent. Huang Tsung-hsi (1610-95), in his great compendium, the *Ming-ju Hsüeh-an* (Writings of Ming Confucianists), writes:

"Among the students of the Master of Yang-ming (Wang Shou-jen), there were T'ai-chou (i.e., Wang Ken) and Lung-hsi (i.e., Wang Chi), who spread (the Wang philosophy) throughout the empire. Yet because of them (its true teachings) also gradually failed to be further transmitted, (owing to the fact that) T'ai-chou and Lung-hsi, being frequently dissatisfied with their teacher's doctrines, supplemented them with the secret meaning of Buddhism, which they thereupon attributed to their own teacher. Thus they reduced Yang-ming's (teachings) to Ch'anism" (32.1).

Lung-hsi 龍溪 is the "style" of Wang Chi 王畿 (1498-1583), whose alternate name is Ju-chung 汝中, and who came from the same district and clan as Wang Shou-jen himself. [2] T'ai-chou 泰州

---

[1] See the *Hsüeh-shu Pien* (Analysis of Schools of Thought), in his *San-yü-t'ang Wen-chi*, *chüan* 2.

[2] See the biography and epitaph appended to his *Lung-hsi Ch'üan-chi* (Complete Works of Wang Chi).

is the name applied to Wang Ken 王艮 (1483-1540), [1] being so used because Wang's native town of An-feng-ch'ang was in T'ai-chou. [2]

One of the doctrines for which Wang Chi is known is that of the "four forms of non-existence" (ssǔ wu 四無), so named because it is a modification of four maxims often propounded by Wang Shou-jen to his students, which read: "The absence of good and evil characterizes the original substance of the mind. The presence of good and evil characterizes its exercise of thought. The knowledge of good and evil characterizes its intuitive knowledge. The doing of good and ridding of evil characterizes its correction of things."

Objecting to this formulation, Wang Chi therefore rewords it as follows: "The mind, its thinking, its knowledge, and the things (it is to correct) are all only one. Once it is realized that the mind is devoid of either good or evil, then its thinking, its knowledge, and the things (it corrects) all likewise become devoid of either goodness or evil." The reason, he continues, is that "the nature conferred by Heaven is so purely and utterly good that the motivation for its mental activities and responses is spontaneous and cannot be helped; hence 'goodness' (in the ordinary meaning of the word) cannot be ascribed to it. For it, evil is certainly originally absent, but goodness, too, cannot be held to exist." By "mental activities and responses," Wang means the mind's reception of external stimuli, together with its spontaneous responses to these stimuli. The mind, he says, should follow a "spontaneous flow of action," without "having any attachment to existence." In this way it becomes "a mind without a mind": its thinking becomes "thinking without thinking"; its knowledge becomes the "knowledge that is without knowledge"; and the external things which it corrects become "things without things." For a mind like this, "evil is certainly originally absent, but goodness, too, cannot be held to exist." This, then, is Wang's doctrine of the four forms of non-existence. [3]

Wang's statement that the mind should not have any attachment to existence, i.e., that it should follow its own spontaneous flow of

---

[1] Alternate name Ju-chih 汝止; styled Hsin-chai 心齋.

[2] See his biography in the *Wang Hsin-chai Hsien-sheng Yi-chi* (Preserved Writings of Wang Ken). [An-feng-ch'ang 安豐場 is on the Grand Canal, north of the Yangtze river in Kiangsu. — Tr.]

[3] See his *Complete Works*, 1.1.

action, uninfluenced by external things, resembles Wang Shou-jen's description of the sage (quoted in the last section): "His intuitive knowledge is as brilliant as a clear mirror, unflecked by the slightest film. When beautiful or ugly objects come before it, their forms are reflected accordingly, without any stain being left behind on the mirror itself." If Wang Chi had said only this, his words would certainly have gained Wang Shou-jen's hearty approval. He goes on, however, to quote from Ch'anism in support of his ideas:

"As to (the saying), 'What thinking or cogitation should there be?', [1] this does not mean that there should be no thinking or cogitation at all. Let thinking and cogitation be equally spontaneous, and equally devoid of any ulterior thought or cogitation. Why should there be any interference with my mind? It is like the light of sun and moon, which come and go of themselves, so that all things receive their radiance. Why should there be any interference with the sun and moon? ... Hui-neng has said: [2] 'Think not of good or evil, but neither interrupt your many thoughts.' Such is the Mahāyāna learning; it is the indivisible gateway to Buddhist truth" (op. cit., 3.15).

Again: "One clear and steadfast thought: this is the sage's learning. One thought means no thought; it means thought in which there is no thought. Therefore the superior man's course of study takes the absence of thought as its basic aim" (ibid., 15.37).

By self-cultivation of this sort, Wang asserts, one can escape from the endless wheel of life and death:

"The fact that there is the wheel of life and death for man is because of the trouble which comes with thought and consciousness. The act of thinking fluctuates, for it represents the functioning of two kinds of mind, one of them good, the other evil. From the variable fluctuations (of these two minds) germinate the seeds of the cycle of transmigration. (Likewise) consciousness involves the making of distinctions, and thus leads to the faculty of knowing, which suddenly appears and as suddenly disappears. This ceaseless appearance and disappearance acts as the causation of life and death. This principle has held good from antiquity until today, and at the present time is an actual fact. Confucianists, however, by maintaining that such teachings are heterodox and should be avoided and undiscussed,

---

[1] *Book of Changes* (Appen. III, p. 389). — Tr.
[2] On Hui-neng (638-713), famous Ch'an patriarch, see chap. 9, sect. 2. — Tr.

thereby reveal their self-delusion. Thought has its root in the mind. Hence it becomes void when men lack mind, so that then there is automatically no longer any wheel of transmigration. Consciousness evolves into knowledge. Hence it becomes void when men lack knowledge, so that then there is automatically no longer any life and death" (*ibid.*, 7.22).

As to the distinction between consciousness (*shih* 識) and knowledge (*chih* 知), Wang Chi comments as follows:

"Knowledge has no beginning or end, whereas consciousness has its subject and object. Knowledge is not limited to any fixed place, whereas consciousness has its discriminations and distinctions. Let us compare the situation to a bright mirror's reflection of things. The mirror itself is fundamentally empty, and so when things beautiful or ugly, black or white, come and go before this empty form, they do not increase or diminish it. But suppose these various things were to remain undissipated in a single spot, then the mirror would become obscured by them. The (original) emptiness of the mirror, to which nothing is added and from which nothing is taken away, represents the state in which both life and death are absent, and is what is known as the intuitive knowledge. When consciousness is transmuted into knowledge, it then becomes the functioning instrument of knowledge. But when it is regarded as itself being knowledge, it then becomes the thief of knowledge" (*ibid.*, 3.13).

As thus defined, consciousness would seem to be a term for that sort of knowledge or cognition that arises as the result of one's attachment to external things. By avoiding such attachment, a higher state is reached, previously described by Wang as that of the "knowledge that is without knowledge." In other words, it is a state in which consciousness has become transmuted into genuine knowledge.

Wang Chi's method of self-cultivation, as here described, agrees in good part both with Ch'eng Hao's "Letter on the Composure of the Nature," and with Wang Shou-jen's doctrine of the unity of activity and quiescence. His further claim, however, that one may thereby escape from the wheel of life and death, goes beyond anything stated by these other two thinkers. Wang Shou-jen, indeed, says quite explicitly (p. 611 above) that "when the Buddhists speak of non-being, their motive is to escape the sea of suffering of life and death. When they add these ideas to the original nature (of the mind), the original meaning of 'the void' and 'non-being' (as held by that mind) is no longer there." Here we have a fundamental distinction between Neo-Confucianism and Buddhism, the obliteration of which by Wang Chi not merely brings him close to Ch'anism, but would seem to make him an actual Ch'anist. We should not be surprised, therefore, to find him further asserting that there is really no fundamental difference at all between Confucianism, Buddhism, and Taoism:

"The teachings of these three schools have a common origin. Taoism speaks of 'vacuity' (*hsü*), but the doctrines of the (Confucian) sage also refer to 'vacuity.' Buddhism speaks of 'tranquillity' (*chi* 寂), but the doctrines of the (Confucian) sage also refer to 'tranquillity.' Who, then, is going to distinguish between them? Present day Confucianists, however, not having ascertained the origins of these (three philosophies), usually consider the two others as heterodox, thereby showing their inability to judge correctly" (*ibid.*, 17.8).

These words destroy one of the most important foundations of Neo-Confucianism, and represent a reversion to the eclectic attitude so prevalent during the third and fourth centuries A.D.

The foregoing passages show that Huang Tsung-hsi is not unjustified in accusing Wang Chi of Ch'anist bias. His similar criticism of Wang Chi's fellow student, Wang Ken, however, seems less well founded, and would appear to apply more appropriately to Yen Chün, a member of Wang Ken's group whose doctrines Huang describes as follow:

"Yen Chün 顔鈞, styled Shan-nung 山農, was a native of Chi-an. [1] ... In his teachings he maintained that man's mind is the most wonderful of all things and cannot be measured, and that his nature is a shining pearl, originally untainted by dust or dirt. Why, then, examine and listen to it? What need to be cautious and apprehensive about it? [2] In ordinary times we need only follow this nature in our conduct, wholly relying upon its spontaneity. This, then, is what is called the Way (*Tao*). Only when we allow ourselves to stray beyond (this course), need we work cautiously, carefully, and fearfully to cultivate it. All the knowledge of former scholars,

---

[1] At the present place of the same name in the southern half of Kiangsi. Yen's exact dates are uncertain. — Tr.

[2] An allusion to the *Doctrine of the Mean*, p. 300: "The superior man does not wait till he sees things, to be cautious, nor till he hears things, to be apprehensive." — Tr.

and all their doctrines and formulas, only suffice to obstruct the (true) Way." [1]

Such a viewpoint was never reached by Wang Ken himself, whose interpretation of the phrase *ko wu*, "investigation of things," was commonly known in his time as the Huai-nan doctrine. [2] As he himself explains, "*Ko* means a standard or pattern (*ko shih* 格式), and is equivalent to the 'measuring square' (spoken of) in the latter part (of the *Great Learning*). [3] Our own self is the measuring-square, and the world or the nation are the squares (which it is to measure). When we apply our measuring-square, we may know that the incorrectness of these squares means the incorrectness of our own measuring-square. The one necessity, therefore, is to correct that measuring-square, rather than to seek for such correctness in the (external) squares (measured by it). Once our own measuring square is correct, then the squares (to which it is applied) will also become correct, and once these squares have become correct, then the task of applying the pattern (*ko*) will have been completed." [4]

According to this interpretation, *ko wu* (usually rendered as "investigation of things") really means to apply the correct measure of one's own self to such external "things" as the world and nation, thereby making them also correct. With such a point of view, it is not surprising that Wang Ken greatly stresses the importance of correct conduct as concretely exemplified in the individual. Furthermore, in his *Wang Tao Lun* or *Treatise on the Kingly Way*—an essay modeled on the ancient *Chou Li* or *Chou Rituals*—he advances specific and down-to-earth suggestions for achieving universal peace. [5] This concreteness and practicality not only distinguishes him from Ch'anism, but also makes him a forerunner of Yen Yüan (1635-1704), to be discussed in the next chapter. The particular trend of thought it represents seems in the first instance to go back to Wang Shou-jen's doctrine of the unity of knowledge and conduct. Thus Huang Tsung-hsi writes:

"By *ko wu*, the Master (Wang Shou-jen) meant the extension of the intuitive knowledge of our own mind to each and every affair

---

[1] Introduction to the T'ai-chou school, in *Ming-ju Hsüeh-an*, 32.1.

[2] So named because Wang Ken was a native of the Kiangsu region known as Huai-nan. — Tr.

[3] See *Great Learning*, p. 419. — Tr.

[4] *Preserved Writings of Wang Ken*, 1.16.

[5] See *op. cit.*, p. 17.

and thing, so that these affairs and things would all conform to their proper principle. The instruction imparted by the sage to other men is simply an act of conduct, just as 'extensive study,' 'accurate inquiry,' 'careful reflection,' and 'clear discrimination' are all acts of conduct. [1] The 'earnest practice' of them means the practice of these several things unceasingly, and when the Master (speaks of) extending (the intuitive knowledge) to affairs and things, he by this 'extending' means 'practicing.' In this way he rectifies the fault of pursuing a hollow investigation of empty Principles (*li*), confined in its understanding wholly to the mental sphere." [2]

By being reduced to this simple interpretation, Wang Shou-jen's philosophy is brought close to the ideas later advocated by Yen Yüan and his followers. For to them, too, the question of concrete conduct was of paramount importance, so that they, like Wang, were inevitably opposed to a "hollow investigation of empty Principles, confined in its understanding wholly to the mental sphere."

---

[1] These terms and that in the following sentence are all taken from the *Doctrine of the Mean*, p. 318. — Tr.

[2] Huang Tsung-hsi, introduction to the section on the Yao-chiang school, in *Ming-ju Hsüeh-an*, 10.1.

CHAPTER XV

THE CH'ING CONTINUATION OF
NEO-CONFUCIANISM

1—THE HAN LEARNING AND THE SUNG LEARNING

With the advent of the Ch'ing dynasty (1644-1911), a shift in thinking led to the rise of what came to be known as the Han Learning (*Han Hsüeh* 漢 學). It was the contention of the followers of this movement that the Sung and Ming Neo-Confucianists, in their interpretations of the classics, had been corrupted by Buddhist and Taoist ideas, and that therefore, in order to understand the true teachings of Confucius and Mencius, it was necessary to go back to the classical commentaries of the Han dynasty. Juan Yüan (1764-1849) expresses this point of view when he writes: "The reason why it is necessary to follow the Classical Learning of the two Han epochs (the Former and Later Han) is that it was extremely close in time to the sages and worthies (of the Chou dynasty, i.e., Confucius and Mencius), whereas the doctrines of the two other schools (Buddhism and religious Taoism) had not yet appeared." [1] The Ch'ing scholars who thus went back to the Han for inspiration applied the term, Sung Learning (*Sung Hsüeh* 宋 學), to the Neo-Confucianism of the Sung and Ming dynasties, in order to distinguish it from their own self-termed Han Learning.

Though the Neo-Confucian schools of Rationalism and Idealism continued to find followers during the Ch'ing dynasty, they produced very little that was new. Hence it is to the Han Learning that we should turn for the creative developments of that dynasty. Even in this school, however, or rather that part of it particularly concerned with philosophy, [2] the topics that were discussed, such as Principle,

---

[1] See his Preface to Chiang Fan's (1761-1831) *Kuo-ch'ao Han-hsüeh Shih-ch'eng Chi* (Biographies of Leaders of the Han Learning of the Present Dynasty).

[2] It should be noted that only certain members of the Han Learning were directly interested in philosophy. Much of the energy of the movement turned to the development of new scholarly techniques in such fields as history, textual criticism, philology, epigraphy, geography, etc., in the course of which what were regarded as the subjective interpretations of the Sung scholars were rejected,

the Ether, the nature, Heavenly Decree, etc., and the classical texts that were used, such as the *Analects, Mencius, Great Learning,* and *Doctrine of the Mean,* remained the same as those of the Sung and Ming Neo-Confucianists. From this point of view, therefore, the Han Learning of the Ch'ing was a continuation of Sung and Ming Neo-Confucianism, the major contribution of which lay in its new answers and interpretations to the latter's traditional problems and texts. This new approach, moreover, had already been foreshadowed by certain tendencies taking place within Neo-Confucianism itself during the latter decades of the Ming and early part of the Ch'ing. Hence those adherents of the Han Learning who concentrated on philosophy should, despite their outward opposition to Neo-Confucianism, properly be regarded as its perpetuators and developers, rather than as the founders of a completely new school.

2—Yen Yüan, Li Kung, and One Group in Neo-Confucianism

Already before the Sung and Han Learning became formally established as separate schools, a new philosophical movement, known as the Yen-Li school, was arising in North China. Its name derives from those of its founders, Yen Yüan 顏元 (1635-1704) [1] and his disciple, Li Kung 李塨 (1659-1746). [2] Both men opposed

---

and a virtual reappraisal of Chinese civilization was made. This was the most fruitful movement in Chinese scholarship prior to the twentieth century, at which time the introduction of Western methods of scholarship led to a new wave of scholarly activity, represented, for example, by the present volume. — Tr.

[1] Alternate name Hun-jan 渾然, but best known under his "style" as Yen Hsi-chai 習齋. He was born in Li-hsien in present Hopei, but after 1763 took residence in his ancestral district of Po-yeh-hsien, immediately west of Li-hsien. Both places are located not far east of Ting 定 hsien, on the Peiping-Hankow Railroad.

[2] Alternate name Kang-chu 剛主, and styled Shu-ku 恕谷. He too was a native of Li-hsien. [For the biographies of these two men, see Arthur W. Hummel, ed., *Eminent Chinese of the Ch'ing Period* (Washington, 1943-44), vol. 2, pp. 912-915, and vol. 1, pp. 475-479, respectively; also Mansfield Freeman, "Yen Hsi Chai, a 17th Century Philosopher," *Journal of the North China Branch of the Royal Asiatic Society,* vol. 57 (1926), pp. 70-91. Yen's life, outwardly uneventful, was spent in study, teaching, and writing, for he never passed the government examinations and hence never became an official. Almost all of it was lived in his native district, aside from a year in Manchuria devoted to a vain search for his father (who had been kidnapped by marauding Manchu soldiers when he himself was only three years old), as well as a few lesser trips. Li Kung, Yen's chief

the Sung and Ming Neo-Confucianism, in place of which they propounded new doctrines claimed by them to represent the true teachings of Confucius and Mencius. Yen Yüan himself describes the significance of these doctrines as follows:

"From the Han and Chin (dynasties) onward there has been a flood of commentaries, with no realization that these commentaries are simply the means for transmitting the principles of the sages and worthies, but do not themselves constitute these principles. Likewise there has been a diligent emphasis upon 'pure conversation,' [1] with no realization that this 'pure conversation' is simply the means for explaining the teachings of the sages and worthies, but does not itself constitute these teachings. Because of this, empty superficiality has daily increased, and the universe has seen the virtual disappearance of the principles of Yao and Shun regarding the 'six treasures' and 'three tasks,' as well as of the teachings of the Duke of Chou and Confucius regarding the 'six virtues,' 'six patterns of conduct,' and 'six liberal arts'—all intended to give true support to Heaven and Earth, and a true nurture to all creatures. [2] With the flowering of Buddhism and Taoism, there were some who treated Heaven, Earth, and all things as completely empty, and therefore withdrew into a state of calm extinction, while others treated Heaven, Earth, and all things as non-existent, and therefore withdrew into a state of lofty escape. . . .

"The various persons who, during the cycle of the House of Chao, were promoted to the Temple of Confucius, [3] were all gentlemen whose collected commentaries continued to be word-for-word analyses; they were all individuals whose lofty discourses continued to be 'pure conversation.' When they talked about how to inculcate

---

follower, likewise spent most of his life as a private tutor. He was much less retiring than Yen, however, and lived for considerable periods in Peking, where he became acquainted with many notable scholars and officials. In this way he succeeded in propagating Yen's ideas, which otherwise might not have become so widely known. — Tr.]

[1] *Ch'ing t'an*, much practiced by the third century Neo-Taoists, who, alarmed and frustrated by the political disorders of the day, withdrew from practical affairs and discoursed on abstract topics and pure philosophy. See p. 206, note 1. — Tr.

[2] The "six treasures," "three tasks," etc., are explained at the end of this quotation. — Tr.

[3] I.e., who were canonized as great Confucian scholars by having their names admitted to the Temple of Confucius. The House of Chao was the ruling house of the Sung dynasty. — Tr.

filial piety, respect for elders, loyalty, and good faith, and maintained that evil is innate in (man's) physical endowment, what difference was there between them and the Taoists, who maintain that propriety and righteousness are the violators of (true) loyalty and good faith? Or between them and the Buddhists, who maintain that the ears, eyes, mouth, and nose are the six robbers (of true understanding)? Therefore, in my humble opinion, while it is correct to say that the Sung Confucianists are the great culminators of the Han and Chin Buddhists and Taoists, it is not correct to say that they are the true followers of Yao, Shun, the Duke of Chou, and Confucius....

"Alarmed by this, I have written the *Preservation of Learning* (*Ts'un-hsüeh*), in order to explain the principles of the three tasks, six treasures, six virtues, and six liberal arts of Yao, Shun, the Duke of Chou, and Confucius. My general purpose has been to show that these principles do not consist merely in a word-by-word analysis of the (ancient) poems and prose writings, nor does learning consist merely in quick comprehension in reciting and reading. My ambition would be, like the followers of Confucius, to be broadened by culture, restrained by propriety, [1] and in my own person really to study and practice this, [2] and throughout my life not to be negligent of it.

"I have also written the *Preservation of the Nature* (*Ts'un-hsing*), with the general purpose of showing that Principle and the Ether are both part of the Way of Heaven (*T'ien Tao*), and that the nature and the body are both conferred by Heaven. The nature received by man and his physical endowment, though differing for various individuals, equally pertain to a single goodness. For his physical endowment is simply the functioning instrument of his (heavenly) conferred nature, and as such cannot be said to be evil. That in him which is called evil results from the evil influence of enticement, delusion, habit, and contagion. I hope to cause men to realize that even the slightest act of evil smudges the brilliant luster of our (nature's) original state, and that full attainment to the goodness of the divine sages results only from the complete development of our existing physical bodies." [3]

Yen Yüan's mention here of the "six treasures" (*liu fu* 六府)

---

[1] This is what one of the disciples claims was achieved for him through the teaching of Confucius. See *Analects,* IX, 10; also VI, 25. — Tr.

[2] An echo of the *Analects,* I, 1. — Tr.

[3] *Ts'un-hsüeh Pien* (Treatise on the Preservation of Learning), 1.11-13.

and "three tasks" (*san shih* 三 事) is based on a passage in the *Book of History* where the former are defined as water, fire, metal, wood, earth, and grain, and the latter as the rectification (by the ruler) of the people's virtue, his utilization (of resources) for their benefit, and his abundant provision for their livelihood. [1] Likewise his reference to the "six virtues" (*liu te* 六 德), "six patterns of conduct" (*liu hsing* 行), and "six liberal arts" (*liu yi* 藝) is based on a passage in the *Chou Li* (Chou Rituals), in which it is stated that in ancient times the people were instructed in: (1) the six virtues, defined as wisdom, love, sageliness, righteousness, loyalty, and harmoniousness; (2) the six patterns of conduct, defined as filial piety, devotion to brothers, affection toward one's associates, marital constancy, forebearance, and compassion; and (3) the six liberal arts, defined as rituals, music, archery, charioteering, writing, and mathematics. [2]

Yen Yüan and Li Kung maintain that what the ancient sages taught was simply how in concrete terms to possess the six virtues, practice the six patterns of conduct, become proficient in the six liberal arts, and gain experience in the handling of the six treasures. As to the *Great Learning*'s famous phrase, *ko wu*, this, Li asserts, means nothing more than the concrete practicing of such activities. It does not mean, as interpreted by Chu Hsi, the "investigation of things." Thus the word *ko* (lit., "to reach into") means, in Li's own words, "to practice a thing with one's own hand," while the word *wu* (things) has reference to such matters as "the exemplification of the illustrious virtue, loving of people, (making) one's thoughts (sincere), (rectifying) the mind, (cultivating) the self, (regulating) the family, (giving good government to) the state, and (bringing peace to) the world. That these (acts) are referred to (in the *Great Learning*) as 'things' is because the acts of making sincere (the thoughts), rectifying (the mind), cultivating (the self), regulating (the family), giving good government (to the state), and bringing peace (to the world), are all tasks, for the learning of which certain 'things' (*wu*) are necessary. These, namely, are the rituals, music, etc., which in the *Chou Rituals* are spoken of as 'things.' " [3]

---

[1] *Shu Ching*, I, ii, pp. 47-48.

[2] *Chou Li*, Bk. IX (Biot's transl., vol. 1, pp. 213-214).

[3] Li Kung, *Ta-hsüeh Pien-yeh* (Analysis of the Great Learning), 2.8. [An unessential introductory sentence has been omitted from the translation. The point

Yen Yüan is no doubt historically correct when he maintains that the Sung Confucianists are "the great culminators of the Han and Chin Buddhists and Taoists," rather than "the true followers of Yao, Shun, the Duke of Chou, and Confucius." He goes astray, however, when he therefore concludes that their doctrines must be inherently wrong.

Though the term "Han Learning" was not yet used in Yen Yüan's day, so that he himself cannot strictly speaking be called a member of that school, the passage we have quoted indicates that his reasons for opposing Sung and Ming Neo-Confucianism are the same as those later advanced by the Han Learning itself. What is noteworthy, however, is that a very similar point of view was being expressed about this same time by certain of Yen's contemporaries who were regarded as orthodox Neo-Confucianists. An example is Lu Shih-yi 陸世儀 (1611-72), [1] who writes:

"The age is a decadent one in which there is no one in the world whose profession it is to preach his doctrines. However, it is an equally decadent one when everyone acts as preacher. In the era of the Three Dynasties, when rulers were (really) rulers and subjects subjects, and fathers were (really) fathers and sons sons, [2] every individual personally busied himself with his own affairs, and sincerely performed his own duties. Within the schools each simply recited the *Odes* and *History*, practiced the rituals and music, and that was all. Never did they exercise their mouths and tongues in controversy, simply for the sake of seeing who might win." [3]

Again: "When the moderns preach their doctrines, they mostly do so in the manner of the 'pure conversation' of the men of the

---

of the argument here is that the word *wu*, as ordinarily used, denotes static or concrete things or objects. In the *Great Learning*, however, it occurs in conjunction with a series of activities (rectifying the mind, etc.) which would ordinarily be referred to as *shih* (affairs, tasks), rather than "things." Li attempts to reconcile this difficulty by pointing out that though the rectification of the mind, etc., are properly "tasks," the adequate performance of these tasks requires a knowledge of "things" (*wu*, i.e., subjects) such as rituals, music, etc. In short, *ko wu* for him, means the personal practice by the individual of "things" of this kind — Tr.]

[1] Styled Tao-wei 道威 and also known as Lu Fu-t'ing 桴亭. He was a native of T'ai-ts'ang in southern Kiangsu. On him see Hummel, *Eminent Chinese*, vol. 1, pp. 548-549.

[2] An allusion to Confucius' famous doctrine of the Rectification of Names. See *Analects*, XII, 11, and vol. 1, pp. 59-62. — Tr.

[3] *Ssǔ-pien Lu* (Thoughts on Various Topics), 1.10.

Chin (dynasty), and great indeed is the (resulting) damage to affairs. The followers of Confucius, however, never made a single utterance without instructing people how to carry it out in actual practice" (*ibid.*).

In his just quoted *Ssŭ-pien Lu* or *Thoughts on Various Topics*, Lu Shih-yi, like Yen Yüan, devotes considerable attention to what he regards as practically important matters, such as warfare, agriculture, rituals, music, and political institutions. Conversely, we find that Yen Yüan agrees with Lu in stressing the importance of the *Great Learning*'s "rectification of the mind" and "making the thoughts sincere." Thus it would appear that Yen, despite his opposition to the Neo-Confucianists, was really the perpetuator and developer of one group among them.

i. *Principle and the Ether*

Much of Yen Yüan's teaching has to do with education and self-nurture. Of greater philosophical interest are his remarks in the *Ts'un-hsing Pien* or *Treatise on the Preservation of the Nature* on such topics as *li* or Principle, *ch'i* or the Ether, *hsing* or the nature, and *hsing* 形 or physical form. We are told in this treatise: "I have humbly presented seven diagrams in order to explain the basic ideas of Mencius" (2.2). The last of these diagrams, which is a summary of the preceding six, is reproduced on the opposite page.

Yen Yüan goes on to explain the diagram as follows:

"The large circle represents the Way of Heaven in its entirety. God (*Shang Ti*) presides over its center and cannot be portrayed. The left half is the *yang*, and the right half the *yin*, between which, because they unite with one another, there is no border. The operations of the *yin* and *yang* result in the creation of the four powers: *yüan* 元 (originating growth), *heng* 亨 (prosperous development), *li* 利 (advantageous gain), and *cheng* 貞 (correct firmness). [1] The

---

[1] Yen himself comments on this: "These four powers were by the early Confucianists correlated with spring, summer, autumn, and winter respectively, and are what the *Analects* (XVII, 19) refers to when it speaks of 'the courses of the four seasons.'" [*Yüan, heng, li,* and *cheng* are the attributes of the first hexagram in the *Book of Changes* (p. 57), and are enumerated as the four "powers" or "virtues" (*te*) in Appen. IV of that work (p. 408). There they are conceived of as dynamic forces rather than as static conditions, which is why I render *te* as "power" rather than "virtue." In Yen's cosmology they seem to take the place usually held in Chinese cosmology by the Five Elements. — Tr.]

Yen Yüan's Diagram of Cosmology

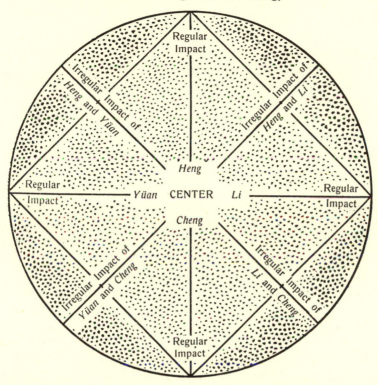

horizontal and vertical lines represent the Ether and the Principle of these four powers in their regular impact, while the four transverse lines represent them in their irregular impact. The lines intersecting these transverse lines represent their interpenetration with one another, and the small dots filling the entire face (of the diagram) represent the evolutionary growth of all things. Thus there is nothing that does not interpenetrate everything else, and nothing that does not undergo evolutionary growth. Nowhere is there anything which is not the Ether and Principle. Once it is understood that Principle and the Ether are amalgamated into a single continuum, then it may be understood that the two *yin* and *yang* forces constitute the original potentiality of the Way of Heaven; the four powers of *yüan, heng, li,* and *cheng* constitute the original potentiality of the two *yin* and *yang* forces; and the evolutionary growth of all things constitutes the original potentiality of the four powers, *yüan, heng, li,* and *cheng.* Once one understands that the two forces of the Way of Heaven, the four powers of the two forces, and the production of all things by the four powers, all constitute this original potentiality (*liang neng* 良 能), then one can examine this diagram (with proper understanding)" (*ibid.*, p. 3).

Nothing further is said about "God" or *Shang Ti* in the following text, and this concept would seem to be superfluous in Yen Yüan's cosmology. For him, therefore, the process of cosmic evolution begins with the *yin* and *yang* forces, which constitute "the original potentiality of the Way of Heaven," and whose operations "result in the creation of the four powers," *yüan, heng, li,* and *cheng.* Thereafter the process becomes increasingly complicated, for he continues: "The two forces and four powers conform, oppose, combine, and penetrate one another; they mingle, interweave, influence, warm, transform, change, arouse, stimulate, condense, disperse, roll, and unroll" (*ibid.*, p. 6). These activities constitute "the sixteen kinds of transformation of the four powers. Though the powers are but four in number, their transformations number sixteen. These sixteen transformations are inexhaustible (in their variations); their operation continues without pause" (*ibid.*). Thus all things in the universe come into existence as a result of these unceasing changes and interactions.

However, the statement about the inexhaustibility of the sixteen transformations refers only to their ultimate results. Initially they operate to produce thirty-two specific tendencies or governing conditions, which Yen describes as those of being "central or peripheral, straight or crooked, square or round, level or sloping, blunt or sharp, separate or combined, far or near, diverging or converging, large or small, thick or thin, clear or turbid, strong or weak, high or low, long or short, rapid or slow, complete or incomplete" (*ibid.*, p. 7). "These thirty-two categories," he continues, "are the further transformations resulting from the sixteen kinds of transformation. The transformations which they in turn produce are inexhaustible. Yet despite their inexhaustibility, (these later transformations) do not lie outside the range of the thirty-two categories; the thirty-two categories do not lie outside the range of the sixteen kinds of transformation; the sixteen kinds of transformation do not lie outside the range of the four powers; the four powers do not lie outside the range of the two forces; the two forces do not lie outside the range of the Way of Heaven" (*ibid.*, p. 9).

Thus all things, as they come into existence, are imbued with the two forces and four powers; at the same time, however, this initial endowment becomes varyingly modified in individual objects along the lines of one or another of the thirty-two categories enumerated above. This explains the differences between such objects with respect to their intelligence or stupidity, strength or weakness, longevity or short life, etc. (*ibid.*). Despite these later differentiations, however, there are no things that in their essential endowment "lie outside the range of the Way of Heaven." Yen tells us further:

"The nature of each thing results from the endowment of Principle, and its physical endowment results from the consolidation of the Ether. What is undeviating pertains to this Principle and this Ether, but what deviates also pertains to them; what is lofty and bright pertains to this Principle and this Ether, but what is lowly and dark also pertains to them; what is pure and sturdy pertains to this Principle and this Ether, but what is impure and slight also pertains to them. . . .

"Man is of all things the most pure, which is why he is said to be born holding a central position between Heaven and Earth. As to the two forces and four powers, they are man as he is before they have yet become consolidated; as to man, he is these two forces and four powers as they are after that consolidation has taken place. *Yüan, heng, li,* and *cheng,* when inhering (in man), constitute love, righteousness, propriety, and wisdom; the term 'nature' (*hsing*) is then used to designate them as thus internally present. When externally manifested, however, they become commiseration, shame and dislike, modesty and yielding, and (the sense of) right and wrong; the term 'feeling' (*ch'ing*) is then used to designate them as thus impinging on (external) things. 'Capacity' (*ts'ai*) is (the designation for) the nature's activation whereby it becomes feeling; it is the dynamic energy of *yüan, heng, li,* and *cheng*" (*ibid.*, pp. 3-4).

Despite Yen's references here to Principle, there is little doubt that the Ether is the primary factor in his cosmology. We have seen earlier, for example, how he speaks of Principle as being amalgamated with the Ether "into a single continuum (*yi p'ien* 一 片)." Herein appears a marked divergence between him and the Rationalistic school.

A similar theory of the oneness of Principle and the Ether had already been expressed, however, by certain earlier Neo-Confucianists, for example Liu Tsung-chou 劉宗周 (1578-1645):[1]

---

[1] Styled Nien-t'ai 念台, but best known as Liu Chi-shan 蕺山. He was a native of Shan-yin (the present Shao-hsing 紹興) in Chekiang. With the collapse of the Ming dynasty, he deliberately starved to death rather than

"Everything in the universe is filled by a single Ether (*ch'i*). This Ether is the same as Principle (*li*). Heaven, by obtaining it, thereby becomes Heaven; Earth, by obtaining it, thereby becomes Earth; men and creatures, by obtaining it, thereby become men and creatures. For one and all of them it is the same." [1] Again:

"Some say that the Ether is generated out of the Void (*hsü*), but since the Void is itself the Ether, how can it produce it in this way? Pushing backward, (we see that) there has never been a time when there has not been the Ether, and turning forward, that there will also never be a time when it is not here. Being contracted, it then passes from 'non-being' (*wu*) to 'being' (*yu*), but this 'being' does not result in (permanent) being; being expanded, it then passes from 'being' to 'non-being,' but this 'non-being' does not result in (permanent) non-being. What transcends being and non-being alike, yet is itself both being and non-being: this is the Great Void (*t'ai hsü*), which we also distinguish and honor by calling the Supreme Ultimate (*t'ai chi*)" (*ibid.*).

Here the Ether's state of contraction is regarded as one of "non-being," i.e., one in which no organized universe exists. This contraction, however, is invariably followed by expansion, resulting in a transition from "non-being" to "being," i.e., to a state in which an organized universe comes to exist. Thereafter as the Ether again contracts, "being" is in turn replaced by "non-being." Here we find the same doctrine as had originally been promulgated by Chang Tsai several centuries previously. [2]

A similar view of Principle and the Ether is expressed by Liu Tsung-chou's follower, Huang Tsung-hsi 黄宗羲 (1610-95): [3]

"In the great process of evolutionary change there is only the single Ether, which circulates everywhere without interruption. When, at the proper season, it produces mildness, this is spring. This mildness, generating warmth, results in summer. As the warmth declines, giving way to coolness, there is autumn. And with the rise of coolness until it becomes coldness, there is winter. After this the

---

serve under the Manchu conquerors. See Hummel, *op. cit.*, vol. 1, pp. 532-533.

[1] *Liu-tzǔ Ch'üan-shu* (Complete Works of Liu Tsung-chou), 11.3.

[2] See chap. 12, sect. 1, i. — Tr.

[3] Alternate name T'ai-ch'ung 太冲, but best known as Huang Li-chou 黎洲. He was a native of Yü-yao in eastern Chekiang, and is probably most famous for his great compilations on Neo-Confucianism, the *Sung-Yüan Hsüeh-an* and *Ming-ju Hsüeh-an*. See on him Hummel, *op. cit.*, vol. 1, pp. 351-354.

cold declines, giving way once more to mildness, and so it continues in an endless cycle. This is what is meant by 'production and reproduction constituting (the process of) change.' [1] The sage, because this process of rise and fall never loses its sequence and order, refers to it as Principle." [2]

Here, as with Liu Tsung-chou, the Ether is regarded as basic. In this connection it should be remembered that a fundamental difference between the Rationalistic and Idealistic schools is the former's necessity to postulate two spheres of being, whereas in the latter's metaphysics only one is necessary. The impetus given to Idealism by Wang Shou-jen, therefore, meant a corresponding impetus to a monistic philosophy; yet he himself said but little about the relationship between Principle and the Ether. Given this situation, it is not surprising that other men, anxious to retain the monism of the Idealists, yet confronted by the necessity of answering the problem of Principle and the Ether posed by the Rationalists, were led into the position of saying that the two "are amalgamated into a single continuum."

Contemporary with Huang Tsung-hsi there lived Wang Fu-chih 王 夫 之 (1619-93), [3] who, despite the lack of a teacher to help him in his studies, arrived at conclusions regarding Principle and the Ether essentially the same as those of Liu Tsung-chou. Thus he writes:

"Within the universe there are only Principle and the Ether. The Ether is the vehicle of Principle, through which it derives its orderliness." [4]

Thus Principle, for Wang, becomes merely the orderly pattern of the Ether, which, as a consequence, assumes a predominant position. Wang writes further:

"When speaking of mind, nature, Heaven, or Principle, it must in every case be on the basis of the Ether. If there were no Ether, none of them would exist. Master Chang (Chang Tsai) has said: 'From the evolutions of the Ether is derived the term 'Way' (Tao).' [5]

---

[1] *Book of Changes* (Appen. III, p. 356). — Tr.

[2] *Nan-lei Wen-an* (Prose Anthology of Huang Tsung-hsi), 3.6.

[3] Best known as Wang Ch'uan-shan 船 山 . He was a native of Hengyang, Hunan, and noted as an ardent patriot who refused to hold office under the conquering Manchus. See Hummel, *op. cit.*, vol. 2, pp. 817-819.

[4] *Tu Ssŭ-shu Ta-ch'üan-shuo* (Remarks on Reading the Four Books), 3.32.

[5] See chap. 12, p. 488. — Tr.

And Master Chu (Chu Hsi) has explained this, saying: '(The statement that) the alternation of the *yin* and *yang* is called the Way refers to the evolutions of the Ether.' [1] ... Likewise Master Ch'eng, by saying that Heaven is Principle, [2] that is, by speaking of Heaven in terms of Principle, also equates the two. Yet the fact that the Heaven which he thus equates with Principle is described in this way, does not mean that it is something separate from the Ether. This being so, the idea that Heaven is equivalent to Principle originated only from the fact that this Principle itself is nothing more than the Principle of the Ether" (*ibid.*, 10.58).

As to the relationship between Heaven, the *yin* and *yang* and Five Elements, Wang writes:

"Split apart, we call them the *yin* and *yang* and Five Elements, inasmuch as they consist of two (major) divisions and five (lesser) parts. But in their totality we call them all Heaven. The case is like that of the hands, feet, ears, eyes, and mental activities, which in their totality constitute man. For it is inconceivable that external to these ears, eyes, hands, feet, and mental activities, there can be other ears, eyes, hands, feet, and mental activities to operate them. In the same way, how can there be, external to the *yin* and *yang* and Five Elements, some other *yin* and *yang* and Five Elements to operate them?" (*ibid.*, 2.10).

In short, "Heaven" (i.e., Nature) is the general designation for the *yin* and *yang* and Five Elements in their totality, which means that since these all pertain to the Ether, Heaven's Principle is therefore nothing more than the Principle of that Ether. As to the relationship between "what is above shapes" (*hsing erh shang*) and "what is within shapes" (*hsing erh hsia*), in other words, between the Way (*Tao*) and "instrument" (*ch'i*), Wang also gives a clear exposition:

"Beneath Heaven there is nothing but 'instrument.' *Tao* is the *Tao* of instrument, but instrument cannot be said to be the instrument of *Tao*. To be sure, men are capable of saying that without *Tao* there would be no instrument. Yet on the other hand, if there be instrument, how can we then be afraid of there being no *Tao*? ... Few men are capable of saying that without instrument there would be no *Tao*, yet this is truly so. In the time of primeval wilderness, there was no *Tao* governing the practice of bowing and giving precedence to

---

[1] This is the well known quotation from the *Book of Changes* (Appen. III, p. 355). — Tr.

[2] This is Ch'eng Hao's statement. See chap. 12, p. 507. — Tr.

others; in that of Yao and Shun there was none governing the offering of consolation (to sufferers), or the inflicting of chastisement (on wrong-doers); in that of the Han and T'ang the *Tao* of the present time was not yet here; and at the present time a great many *Tao* of other days are absent. Before bows and arrows existed, there was no *Tao* for archery; before chariots and horses existed, there was no *Tao* for driving. ... Thus there are many cases when it might be possible to have certain *Tao*, yet we do not have them. Hence the statement that without instrument there is no *Tao* is a true one, only men have failed to look into it. ...

" 'Above' and 'below' are terms between which there is no fixed line of demarcation. 'What is above shapes' does not refer to an absence of shapes, but to the fact that there must first be shapes before there can be 'what is above shapes.' If we probe into Heaven or Earth, man or other creatures, never, from antiquity until today, throughout all the myriad evolutions, has there ever been an 'absence of shapes above.' " [1]

This concept of the relationship of *Tao* and instrument, so contrary to that of Chu Hsi, derives logically from Wang's own views of Principle and the Ether. Yet he firmly asserts that he is a true Neo-Confucianist, and that in giving primacy to the Ether he is merely following Chang Tsai. Thus in his self-composed epitaph he writes: "I have cherished the solid loyalty of Liu Yüeh-shih, [2] yet (unlike him) have had no opportunity to offer my life. I have striven for the true doctrines of Chang Heng-ch'ü, [3] yet my strength has not permitted me to attain to them. Fortunate though I am to rest unmolested within this grassy mound, I feel saddened for all eternity (by my failure)." [4] The fact that Wang Fu-chih, despite his lack of a teacher, arrived at views regarding Principle and the Ether substantially agreeing with those of Liu Tsung-chou, Huang Tsung-hsi, and Yen Yüan, indicates that all these men were following a common tendency of their time.

---

[1] *Chou-yi Wai-chuan* (Supplementary Commentary on the Chou Changes), 5.45.

[2] I.e., Liu Kun (270-317), a patriot noted for his devotion to the Chin dynasty during the troubles of that time. Wang Fu-chih's own loyalty to the Ming dynasty has been referred to in note 3 on p. 641 above. — Tr.

[3] I.e., Chang Tsai. — Tr.

[4] See Wang's biography in his *Ch'uan-shan Yi-shu* (Preserved Writings of Wang Fu-chih).

ii. *The Nature and the Physical Form*

Basing himself on the foregoing metaphysical position, Yen Yüan attacks the validity of Chu Hsi's distinction between the physical nature (i.e., the nature as combined with the physical Ether) and the moral nature (i.e., the nature subsisting independently of the Ether). [1] Between him and Chu there is no great difference when he says: "The nature of each thing results from the endowment of Principle, and its physical endowment results from the consolidation of the Ether." [2] The divergence begins, however, when in his next sentence he states that "what is pure and sturdy pertains (both) to this Principle and this Ether"—a statement made possible by his contention that "Principle and the Ether are amalgamated into a single continuum." In the case of Chu Hsi, such descriptive and therefore limiting terms as "pure," "sturdy," etc., cannot conceivably be applied to Principle, since this Principle subsists eternally and unchangingly. Hence they can apply only to the Ether, which is physical and temporal. For Yen Yüan, on the other hand, with his theory of the single continuum, the so-called moral nature becomes the same as the physical nature. It therefore follows that the latter cannot be adduced as the originator of evil. Thus he remarks in the continuation of the passage just quoted:

"To say that the feelings (*ch'ing*) contain evil is to say that *yüan, heng, li,* and *cheng,* once they are (externally) manifested, are no longer these *yüan, heng, li,* and *cheng* as they are prior to that manifestation. To say that capacity (*ts'ai*) contains evil is to say that what is potential is *yüan, heng, li,* and *cheng,* but what is capable of activity is no longer (the original) *yüan, heng, li,* and *cheng.* And to say that the physical endowment contains evil is to say of *yüan, heng, li,* and *cheng,* that their Principles may be called the Way of Heaven, but that their Ether may not be so called. Forsooth, is there beneath Heaven any Ether without Principle, or any Principle without the Ether? Or are there any Principle and Ether external to the two forces and four powers?" (*Preservation of the Nature,* 2.4).

In short, since the universe consists of but a single continuum, man therefore possesses but a single nature. Yen illustrates this point as follows:

"The Ether is the Ether of Principle, and Principle is the Principle

---

[1] On this distinction, see chap. 13, sect. 4. — Tr.

[2] See above, p. 639. — Tr.

of the Ether. How then can it be said that Principle is uniform and single in its goodness, whereas the physical endowment deviates toward evil? Let us take the eye as an example. Its socket, lid, and ball are its physical endowment, whereas its power of vision, with which it is able to perceive things, is its nature. Is one then to say that it is exclusively this Principle of vision that looks at what is proper, whereas it is the socket, lid, and ball that look at what is improper? I maintain that though the Principle of vision is certainly the gift of Heaven, the socket, lid, and ball all likewise constitute that gift. Therefore there is no further need to distinguish between the nature conferred by Heaven, and the nature pertaining to the physical endowment. It is only proper to say that the nature (i.e., makeup) of the eye has been conferred on man by Heaven; that its power of vision represents the goodness of the eye's nature; that the act of seeing represents the goodness of its feeling (*ch'ing*); [1] and that the distinctness or indistinctness, farness or nearness, with which this seeing operates, represents the strength or weakness of its capacity (*ts'ai*). None of these can be spoken of as evil. ... It is only when its vision is led astray by improper things, or blocked or beclouded by them, that its view of things becomes wrong, so that evil can first be spoken of. Yet when it is thus led astray, can this be solely blamed either to its nature or to its physical endowment? If the blame is to be put on its physical endowment, this forces us to the conclusion that the nature of the eye can be perfect only when the eye itself does not exist" (*ibid.*, 1.1).

The socket, lid, and ball of the eye are its physical constituents; its power of vision is its "nature." Each is inseparable from the other, for both are equally "the gift of Heaven." The leading purpose in Yen's *Treatise on the Preservation of the Nature* is to refute Chu Hsi's theory that the physical nature is the originator of evil. Such evil, Yen argues, is really caused by "enticement, delusion, habit, and contagion." Thus he continues:

"Evil results from enticement, delusion, habit, and contagion. Let us but imitate Confucius' search for love (*jen*) or Mencius' preservation of the mind and nourishment of the nature. Then can we make the goodness of our nature shine forth, and our ears, eyes, mouth, and nose all perform their functions properly. ... What is

---

[1] It will be remembered that feeling is the external manifestation of the innate nature. — Tr.

proper to look at let us look at, and what is proper to listen to let us listen to, but what is improper let us not do. Once our physical constituents are all made to conform to Heaven's correct pattern, it naturally follows that no corrupting colors or immoral sounds will be able to entice or delude us. Then how can we be fearful of becoming habituated to evil, or suffering contagion from evil? ...

"The six patterns of conduct are instituted in my nature; the six liberal arts are its instruments; the nine demeanors are its (external) manifestations; the nine virtues are its completed achievements. [1] The instituting of rituals, performing of music, harmonizing of the *yin* and *yang*, and regulating of Heaven and Earth: these are my nature's expansive activities. The bringing of all things into equable conformity, tranquillizing Earth, giving completion to Heaven, and bringing great harmony to the entire universe: these are my nature's final results. Therefore it is permissible to say that the (good) evolutionary changes wrought in the physical element are the efficacious result of the development of our natures, as for example when 'virtue adorns the body,' or when 'a mild harmony is imparted to the countenance and a rich fullness to the back, which spreads out to the four limbs.' [2] But it is not permissible to say that these evolutionary changes consist in transforming the evil of the physical element, or restoring (the goodness of) the nature, (for this is like) blaming the policeman for the offense (of the criminal), or blaming a piece of silk for the fact that it has been dyed" (*ibid.*, 1.2).

Yen's aim in this passage is to destroy the Rationalistic school's distinction between its so-called Heavenly-conferred nature and physical nature, or in other words, between the nature as such and the physical element. Nevertheless, if we look closely at his statement, it would seem that such a distinction still remains. For example, we have the passage: "What is proper to look at let us look at, and what is proper to listen to let us listen to, but what is improper let us not

---

[1] On the six patterns of conduct and six liberal arts, see above, p. 634. The nine virtues are defined in the *Book of History* (II, iii, p. 54) as "affability combined with dignity, mildness combined with firmness, honesty combined with respectfulness, aptness for government combined with reverent caution, docility combined with boldness, straightforwardness combined with gentleness, easy negligence combined with discrimination, boldness combined with sincerity, and courage combined with righteousness." Neither Professor Fung nor myself have been able to identify the "nine demeanors" (*chiu jung* 九 容). — Tr.

[2] The first quotation is from the *Great Learning*, p. 413, and the second from the *Mencius*, VIIa, 21. — Tr.

do. Once our physical constituents are all made to conform to Heaven's correct pattern, it naturally follows that no corrupting colors or immoral sounds will be able to entice or delude us." What Yen here calls "Heaven's correct pattern" [1] would seem to be hardly different from what the Rationalistic school either terms Principle or the nature. For this passage holds meaning only if we assume a distinction between "Heaven's correct pattern" and the physical ellement. And such a distinction is unavoidable, inasmuch as the physical element is said to "conform" to "Heaven's correct pattern," and, unlike this pattern, can be enticed by colors and sounds. In short, we have here a statement scarcely different from the Rationalistic doctrine that evil originates from the physical element. Furthermore, when Yen goes on to state that "the six patterns of conduct are instituted in my nature," etc., what he is saying is almost the same as Chu Hsi's theory that all the innumerable Principles of things are contained within our own mind. Yen does differ, however, in his contention that the desired goal is to be achieved through the exertions of our physical bodies, rather than through reliance on some kind of metaphysical principle. This appears, for example, in his statement that "full attainment to the goodness of the divine sages results only from the complete development of our existing physical bodies." [2]

In the above theory, as in his cosmology, Yen has been anticipated by Liu Tsung-chou and others. Liu writes, for example:

"Principle is the Principle of the Ether, and is certainly neither prior nor external to the Ether. Once we understand this, we can understand that the 'mind of the spirit' is the original mind of the 'mind of the body,' [3] and that the moral nature is the original nature of the physical element" (*Works*, 11.5).

Again: "As to mind, there is only the mind of the body; the mind of the spirit is that by which this physical (mind) can be the mind. As to the nature, there is only the physical nature; the moral nature is that by which the physical (nature) can be the nature" (*ibid.*, 13.31).

And yet again: "Former men, when explaining the mind of the body and mind of the spirit, (have said that) the mind of the spirit is dominant, and its commands are to be obeyed by the mind of the

---

[1] *T'ien tse chih cheng* 天 則 之 正.
[2] See above, p. 633. — Tr.
[3] On these terms (*tao hsin* and *jen hsin*), see chap. 13, p. 560, note 1. — Tr.

body. But such a theory would mean that two minds exist within the single body, whereas, aside from the mind of the body, there is no such thing as the mind of the spirit. To think of dressing when cold, and eating when hungry: this is the mind in its active state. To dress when it is proper to dress, and eat when it is proper to eat: this is the mind in its quiescent state. Nevertheless, whenever one thinks of dressing or eating (because of cold or hunger), at that very moment a decision must likewise be made on moral grounds as to whether it is then proper to dress or eat. It is incorrect to say that after having thought of dressing and eating, another thought arises as to whether it is then proper to dress and eat" (*ibid.*, p. 37).

Our previous criticism of Yen Yüan applies equally well to Liu Tsung-chou. For what Liu variously terms "the original mind of the mind of the body," or "that by which this physical (mind) can be the mind," can surely not itself be equated with the mind of the body; nor can what he terms either "the original nature of the physical element," or "that by which the physical (nature) can be the nature," be equated with the physical element itself. This is why, despite Liu's insistence that only one mind exists, he is forced to subdivide it into an active and a quiescent state.

Turning to Huang Tsung-hsi, we find a similar point of view:

"The feelings in man of commiseration, shame and dislike, modesty and yielding, and right and wrong, are all equally the single Ether. The sage takes the fixed and unchanging pattern (in these), which he then terms the nature. Hence Principle is nature which is manifested, [1] while the nature is Principle which is unmanifested. The statement of former Confucianists that 'the nature is Principle' has been consecrated by a thousand sages, yet in actual fact both of them (the nature and Principle) are themselves products of the single Ether" (*Prose Anthology*, 3.6).

Thus, though Huang grants the equation of the nature with Principle, he closes by giving the Ether definite primacy over both of them.

Wang Fu-chih's views on the same problem are expressed as follows:

"The doctrine originated by Master Ch'eng about the physical nature is extraordinarily striking. [2] ... Beginners, failing to com-

---

[1] Huang himself comments: "It is manifested in (external) things."
[2] This theory was developed by Ch'eng Hao. See chap. 12, pp. 514 ff. —Tr.

prehend it, suspect (it to mean) that two kinds of nature are present in man. So now I have no alternative but to try to clarify it. When one speaks of the physical nature, this is like saying that the nature lies within the physical element. This physical element is man's physical form, within the confines of which Principle is manifestly apparent. Lying as it does within the physical element, it there permeates the Ether. Between Heaven and Earth, whether within or outside the human body, there is nothing which is not the Ether, and therefore also nothing which is not Principle. Principle operates within the Ether, where it controls and apportions the Ether. Thus the physical substance (of individual objects) embodies the Ether, and the Ether embodies Principle. It is because this physical substance embodies the Ether that a given individual possesses life, and it is because the Ether embodies Principle that this same individual possesses a nature. For this reason, before this embodiment yet takes place, there can only be the Principle and Ether of the universe, but not any human individual. [1] Whenever, however, physical substance is occupied by the Ether, this Ether invariably possesses Principle. As far as man is concerned, the life and nature of an individual both pertain to the operations of Heaven. Having been initially (implanted) in him, they are thereby separated (from Heaven), nor will they (after death) fail to revert to what belongs to Heaven. Hence the nature, as found within the physical element, is still the original nature" (*Remarks on the Four Books*, 7.16).

By thus interpreting the term "physical nature" simply to mean the nature as this nature is found within the physical element, Wang is really equating it with Principle as this Principle is found within the physical element, which in turn is nothing other than what Chu Hsi calls the "moral nature." Wang continues:

"Sometimes it happens that some of the Ether in Heaven loses its equilibrium, and, being received by man, results in his birth. [2] Thereupon, because of this Ether's loss (of equilibrium), (man's) physical element is no longer correct" (*ibid.*).

This idea is analogous to Chu Hsi's theory of the physical nature.

---

[1] Wang himself comments: "This does not mean that prior to human beings there is a state of chaos, but only that supposing a certain Mr. X be born in a certain year, then in the preceding year, when there is as yet no Mr. X, Mr. X's allotment of Principle and Ether at that time still pertains to Heaven."

[2] Wang himself comments: "It is the Ether which comprises (man's) physical element."

Summarizing what has been quoted, it is evident that what the Rationalistic school terms Principle continues to hold a place in the system of Yen Yüan and the other thinkers. The major difference, however, is that for these men Principle does not transcend the Ether, nor does the nature transcend the physical element. This point is further clarified by Li Kung as follows:

"What operates through Heaven and man alike is called *Tao*. As to *li*, this word appears very rarely in the sacred classics. The 'patterned principle' (*wen li* 文理) of the *Doctrine of the Mean* (p. 326), and the 'orderly principle' (*t'iao li* 條理) of the *Mencius* (VIb, 1) both have reference to the fact that *Tao* has an orderly sequence, just as jade has its veins and markings, and the earth its dividing contours. The *Book of Changes* (Appen. V, p. 422) says: 'By the exhaustive study of Principle (*li*) and complete development of the nature, one attains to (Heavenly) Decree.' The manifestation of Principle in (external) things, the embodiment of the nature in the mind, and the issuing of the Decree from Heaven, all have in them this idea of an 'orderly principle' (*t'iao li*)." [1] Again:

"The 'orderly principle' of affairs is called their Principle (*li*), and is immanent in these affairs. But today there are those who say that Principle is transcendent to affairs, and who thus set it up as something separate in itself. With respect to Heavenly affairs we speak of Heavenly Principle, with respect to human affairs we speak of human Principle, and with respect to the affairs of other things we speak of the Principle of those other things. The *Odes* (III, iii, Ode 6) says: 'Heaven produced the multitude of people, having bodies, having rules.' Apart from affairs and things, how can there be anything called Principle?" (*ibid.*, p. 26).

Principle as described in these passages does not greatly differ from the Principle of the Rationalists. The distinction lies in Li Kung's contention that for the Rationalists Principle "is transcendent to affairs," whereas according to his own view it "is immanent in these affairs." The same point was later to be raised by Tai Chen in his refutation of the Rationalistic school. In this respect, therefore, Tai, as well as Yen Yüan and Li Kung, may rightly be regarded as a follower of Liu Tsung-chou, Huang Tsung-hsi, Wang Fu-chih, and their group.

---

[1] *Chuan-chu Wen* (Commentary on the Four Books), sect. on the *Analects*, p. 3.

3—TAI CHEN

Tai Chen 戴震 (1723-77), better known under his "style" as Tai Tung-yüan 東原, was a native of Hsiu-ning on the southern border of Anhwei. [1] His most important philosophical works are the *Yüan Shan* (On the Nature of Goodness), and his commentary on the *Mencius* entitled *Meng-tzŭ Tzŭ-yi Su-cheng* (General Survey of the Meaning of the Mencius). In the preface to the latter (hereafter referred to as *Meaning of Mencius*) he writes:

"Mencius debated against Yang (Chu) and Mo (Ti). But later men, accustomed to hearing the words of Yang, Mo, Lao Tzŭ, Chuang Tzŭ, and the Buddha, have used them to confuse the words of Mencius. For this reason I, who follow Mencius still later, have no alternative (but to dispute these erroneous doctrines)." [2] Again he writes:

"Before the Sung (dynasty), Confucius and Mencius on the one hand, and Lao Tzŭ and Buddha on the other, were quite distinct. Those who discussed Lao Tzŭ and Buddha made their words lofty and abstruse, and did not depend upon Confucius and Mencius. But from the Sung onward the writings of Confucius and Mencius have completely lost their (correct) interpretation, and scholars have plagarized the words of Lao Tzŭ and Buddha in order to interpret them." [3]

Thus Tai Chen, in the belief that the Sung and Ming Neo-Confucian interpretations of the classics were tinctured by Taoism and Buddhism, took it upon himself to refute their errors, just as, long before, Mencius had taken it upon himself to attack the doctrines of Yang Chu and Mo Ti.

---

[1] Though the son of a comparatively poor cloth merchant, he became one of the most famous scholars of his age, despite the fact that he failed no less than five times to pass the highest civil service examination, that of *chin shih*, and consequently did not become a government official. Most of his life (much of it spent in Peking) was devoted to scholarly pursuits. Aside from his position as one of the notable philosophers of the Ch'ing period, he made important contributions in such fields as mathematics, geography, and phonology. See Hummel, *Eminent Chinese*, vol. 2, pp. 695-699; also Mansfield Freeman, "The Philosophy of Tai Tung-yüan," *Journal of the North China Branch of the Royal Asiatic Society*, vol. 64 (1933), pp. 50-71. — Tr.

[2] Contained in Hu Shih, *Tai Tung-yüan ti Che-hsüeh* (The Philosophy of Tai Tung-yüan), Appen., p. 37.

[3] *Tai Tung-yüan Chi* (Collected Writings of Tai Chen), 8.13 (hereafter referred to as *Writings*).

i. *Tao and Principle*

Yen Yüan and Li Kung, as we have seen, accuse the Rationalistic school of believing that "Principle is transcendent to affairs." Tai Chen makes the same charge and attributes the error to the influence of Taoism and Buddhism. Thus he writes:

"According to the Taoists and Buddhists, as far as the individual self is concerned, it may be divided into a physical body and a spiritual intelligence, the latter being primary. Extending this idea upward, they regard this spiritual intelligence as the primary factor in Heaven and Earth, from which they go on to seek for whatever lacks shape and form, regarding it as genuine existence, whereas whatever possesses shape and form they look upon as illusory.

"As for the Sung Confucianists, they regard the physical body and spiritual intelligence as equally personal and private, whereas Principle, for them, is derived from Heaven. Extending this idea upward, they make a clearcut distinction between Principle and the Ether, regarding Principle as the shapeless and formless something which really exists, whereas whatever possesses shape and form they look upon as grossly impure. Extending and transposing the words of those others (the Buddhists and Taoists), they (the Neo-Confucianists) look at the Ether and call it the 'empty' (i.e., illusory) Ether; they look at the mind and call it the container of the nature.

"Thus the former (the Buddhists and Taoists) establish a dualism between body and spirit, (saying) that the spirituality of Heaven and Earth occupies this 'empty' Ether, and the spirituality of man occupies this container. The latter (the Neo-Confucianists), on the other hand, establish a dualism between Principle and the Ether, (saying) that the Principle of Heaven occupies this 'empty' Ether, and the Principle of man occupies this container" (*Meaning of Mencius*, 2.78).

To the statement, "The latter establish a dualism between Principle and the Ether," Tai appends a footnote: "Master Chu says: 'Within the universe there are Principle and the Ether. Principle constitutes the *Tao* that is above shapes; it is the source from which things are produced. The Ether constitutes the instruments (*ch'i*) that are within shapes; it is the means whereby things are produced.' "[1] Here Tai outlines the Rationalistic theory that Principle is transcendent to

---

[1] For this quotation from Chu Hsi, see chap. 13, beginning of sect. 2. — Tr.

and separate from the Ether. Then, to combat it, he advances his own thesis: that the *yin* and *yang* and Five Elements (which Chu Hsi's school relegates to the Ether) really pertain to *Tao*. Thus he writes:

"*Tao* is like 'movement' (*hsing* 行). The evolutionary operations of the Ether produce and reproduce without pause. That is why this process is called the *Tao*. The *Changes* (Appen. III, p. 355) says: ''The alternation of the *yin* and *yang* is called *Tao*.' And the *Grand Norm* (says) regarding the Five Elements: [1] 'The first is named water, the second fire, the third wood, the fourth metal, the fifth earth.' Here too the word *hsing* (movement, mover, i.e., element) is a general designation for *Tao*. The mentioning of the *yin* and *yang* implies the Five Elements, for the Five Elements are embodied both in the *yin* and the *yang*. And the mentioning of the Five Elements implies the *yin* and *yang*, for the *yin* and *yang* are possessed by each of the Five Elements" (*ibid.*, p. 73).

Tai then continues: "The *yin* and *yang* and Five Elements constitute the true substance of the *Tao*." Thus he clearly equates *Tao* with the Ether and not with an abstract Principle transcending time and space. In so doing he agrees with Yen Yüan, for whom, as we have seen, the Way or *Tao* of Heaven consists of the two forces (the *yin* and *yang*), together with the four powers (*yüan, heng, li,* and *cheng*). [2] It is interesting, however, that Tai replaces Yen's four "powers" or "virtues" (*te* 德) by the Five Elements, probably because the word *te* carries with it moral connotations which seem to him too suggestive of the implications carried by the word *li* or Principle.

As to the distinction between "what is above shapes" (*hsing erh shang*) and "what is within shapes" (*hsing erh hsia*), Tai writes:

"In the relationship of the evolutions of the Ether to individualized objects, there lies the distinction between what is above and what is within shapes. 'Shape' is a designation for the individualized objects (produced through the evolutions of the Ether), but not for these evolutions of the Ether themselves. ... It is a designation for what has already assumed shape and substance. (To speak of) 'what is above shapes' is like speaking of 'what is prior to shapes'; to speak of 'what is within shapes' is like speaking of 'what is posterior to shapes.' It is obvious that the *yin* and *yang*, not yet having assumed

---

[1] Lit., "Five Movers," *wu hsing*, See the *Hung Fan*, in *Book of History* (V, iv, pp. 140-141). — Tr.

[2] See above, pp. 636-638. — Tr.

shape and substance, should therefore be referred to as 'what is above shapes,' and not as 'what is within shapes.' As for 'instrument' (*ch'i*), this refers to what has assumed a state of completion and no longer undergoes change, whereas *Tao* refers to what infuses things and cannot be lost. Not only is it the case that the *yin* and *yang* do not lie within shapes, but the same is true of the Five Elements. For whereas water, fire, wood, metal, and earth, as substantive and visible entities, definitely do pertain to what is within shapes and so do not constitute instrument, nevertheless the *Ether* of these Five Elements, with which men and things are all equally endowed, pertains to what is above shapes" (*ibid.*, pp. 74-75).

Thus the Ether of the *yin* and *yang* and of the Five Elements lacks shape or concreteness, and as such constitutes the *Tao* that is above shapes. Men and things, however, "are all equally endowed" with this Ether, and it is with their formation that it assumes definite shape and substance. This process is known as that of the "evolutions of the Ether" (*ch'i hua* 化), while the concrete objects produced thereby constitute the particularized "instruments" that lie within shapes. The Five Elements, for example, are, as abstract forces, different from the particularized water, fire, wood, metal, and earth which are visible to us as concrete entities.

Inasmuch as the generation of men and things is thus attributed entirely to the "evolutions of the Ether," there would seem to be no need in Tai's system for the Principle or *li* of the Rationalists. Yet here we are faced with the question: Does this mean that these "evolutions" take place haphazardly without any order or sequence? Tai's reply is in the negative, for he writes:

"The unceasing evolutions of the universe constitute the *Tao*. Does not the alternation of the *yin* and *yang* result in production and reproduction? And does not this production and reproduction follow an orderly pattern? ... The process of production and reproduction is that of love (*jen*), [1] and never occurs except according to an orderly pattern. In the orderly unfolding of this pattern we find the highest manifestation of propriety (*li*). And in the distinctions that are laid down in the course of this orderly pattern we find the highest manifestation of righteousness (*yi*)." [2] Again:

---

[1] This idea was also expressed by Wang Shou-jen. See chap. 14, sect. 6, v. — Tr.

[2] *Writings*, 9.9 (sect. in which the nature is discussed in connection with Appen. III of the *Book of Changes*).

"With respect to Heaven, Earth, men, things, events, and activities, I have never heard of any of these to which the word Principle (*li*) may not be applied. This is why the *Odes* (III, iii, Ode 6) speaks of 'there being things, there being rules.' 'Things' is the term used to denote them as actual objects or events; 'rules' is that used to speak of their unmixed purity and central correctness. These actual objects or events are in themselves nothing but the natural. Yet it is in accordance with the necessary that they acquire the Principles governing them as Heaven, Earth, men, things, events or activities. Irrespective of how vast Heaven and Earth may be, how numerous men and things may be, or how complex and varied events and activities may be, as soon as each (category of these things) acquires its own particular Principle—such as that something straight accords with the plumb-line, something level with the water-level, something round with the compass, and something square with the measuring-square—then it remains standard for them, though applied to all under Heaven throughout a myriad generations. The *Changes* (Appen. IV, p. 417) says: 'He may precede Heaven and Heaven does not oppose him; he may follow Heaven and then conforms to Heaven's seasons. If Heaven does not act in opposition, how much less will men! How much less will the spirits!' ... To be like this is to acquire Principle and gain the general approval of men's minds. ...

"To exalt Principle by saying that Heaven and Earth, or the *yin* and *yang*, are unworthy to be equated with it, inevitably means to deny that there can be a Principle for Heaven and Earth, or the *yin* and *yang*. ... If, however, in the case of Heaven and Earth, men and things, events and activities, we seek that in them which is inevitable and unchangeable, their Principle then becomes very evident. There are persons, however, who go on to exalt this (Principle) still further by speaking not only about a Principle for Heaven, Earth, men, things, events, and activities but also, through a shift in speech, by saying that there is nowhere where there is not this Principle. Thus they look upon it as if it were a (physical) thing, despite the fact that even if scholars were to search for such a thing until their hair became white and they became utterly confused, they would still be unable to find it" (*Meaning of Mencius*, 1.60-61).

Tai thus acknowledges that there is a particular Principle for Heaven, Earth, men, things, events, and activities. The concrete actuality of all these is what is "natural" in them, whereas their "oughtness" and "necessity" is their Principle. This Principle "is inevitable and unchangeable," and "remains standard for them, though applied to all under Heaven throughout a myriad generations."

Tai says further: "Production and reproduction take place only because of this orderly Principle; were it to be lost, the pattern of production and reproduction would be cut short" (*ibid.*, 3.118). In this and the preceding statements he, like the Rationalists, acknowledges that there is such a thing as an objective Principle, that it is not to be identified with the concrete actualities of our physical world, but that it is nevertheless that upon which these actualities depend. His difference from the Rationalists is, verbally speaking, that they term this Principle the *Tao* or Way, whereas he does not. Conceptually speaking, it is that they say (according to him) that Principle transcends, i.e., is prior to, the Ether, whereas he himself maintains that it is immanent in the Ether. This is like the distinction made by Li Kung when he says that the Rationalists regard Principle as transcendent to affairs, whereas he himself regards it as immanent in affairs. [1]

Tai's verbal difference from the Rationalists may be dismissed as of no great consequence. As for his conceptual difference, it should be remarked that when the Rationalists assert the priority of Principle to the Ether, it is only from the point of view of logic that they do so. From the point of view of actuality, even they recognize that "there is no Ether without Principle, and no Principle without the Ether." [2] Hence for them, as for Tai, Principle, as actually experienced, lies within the Ether. Thus the only basis for difference remains in their assertion of the theoretical priority of Principle.

Tai also has the Rationalists in mind when he states: "To exalt Principle by saying that Heaven and Earth, or the *yin* and *yang*, are unworthy to be equated with it, inevitably means to deny that there can be a Principle for Heaven and Earth, or the *yin* and *yang*." Since these are all physical actualities Tai is quite right in saying that they cannot possibly be equated by the Rationalists with Principle. It does not at all follow, however, as he apparently supposes, that for this reason these things must be regarded by the Rationalists as actually devoid of Principle. On the contrary, the Rationalists state quite explicitly that Principle is everywhere, precisely on the ground

---

[1] See end of preceding section. — Tr.
[2] Chu Hsi, *Conversations*, 1.1. — Tr.

that each and every thing in the universe possesses its own Principle.

Tai says further: "For each individual thing there is an orderly Principle; for each individual act there is what there ought to be" (*Nature of Goodness*, 3.23). Why, then, we must ask, does he not also say, like the Rationalists, that Principle is everywhere present? Moreover, when he claims that some people look upon Principle as if it were a physical thing, he is asserting something that was never asserted by any of the Rationalists. Indeed, their very relegation of Principle to "what is above shapes" proves conclusively that it cannot, in their eyes, be a physical thing.

Thus there is no doubt that Tai's statements are open to criticism. His basis for making them, however, is clear. It is that the Rationalists, in his opinion, regard Principle as superior, or in other words, prior, to the Ether, whereas he himself regards it as lying within the Ether. To use the terminology of Western philosophy, Principle, for the Rationalists, is transcendental, whereas for Tai it is immanent. In reaching this conclusion, Tai is not only expressing his own views, but also those of his predecessors, Liu Tsung-chou, Huang Tsung-hsi, Wang Fu-chih, Yen Yüan, and Li Kung.

ii. *The Nature and Capacity*

A further difference between Tai Chen and the Rationalists centers around the latter's contention that each and every individual possesses the Supreme Ultimate; that this Supreme Ultimate constitutes the nature contained within his mind; and that, since the Supreme Ultimate is the aggregate of all the myriad Principles of things, therefore man's individual nature also contains all these many Principles. This thesis is opposed by Tai as follows:

"The *Book of Rites of the Elder Tai* [1] says: 'What is divided from *Tao* is called what is conferred. What is manifested in individual things is called the nature.' This means that men and creatures exist because of the allotment made to them from the *yin* and *yang* and Five Elements, and that their natures are formed in accordance with the fact that each man and creature is limited in what he is thus allotted. The *yin* and *yang* and Five Elements are the concrete substance of *Tao*, and the blood, breath, and mental faculty are the concrete substance of the nature. Because there is this concrete substance, it is possible

---

[1] *Ta Tai Li Chi*, chap. 80 (Wilhelm's transl., chap. 23, p. 244). — Tr.

to divide it, but because of this act of division, the result is not equal
for all" (*Meaning of Mencius*, 2.73).

By enumerating "blood, breath, and the mental faculty" as
"the concrete substance of the nature," Tai agrees with Yen Yüan
when the latter says: "The nature and the body are both conferred by
Heaven." [1] Tai continues:

"The nature is what is divided from the *yin* and *yang* and Five
Elements, thereby forming blood, breath, and the mental faculty,
which, for different categories of creatures, are not the same. The
activities, potentialities, and qualities possessed by each thing, subsequent to its birth, always depend upon this fact. That is why the
Changes (Appen. III, p. 356) says: 'What gives completion (to things)
is their nature.' Men and creatures are brought into existence as a
result of the evolutions of the Ether, but thereafter each continues
further growth according to its own particular species. For a thousand ages the differences between different species have remained
constant, simply following their original patterns. . . . As far as the
question of allotment is concerned, the limitations initially imposed
thereby result in inequalities with respect to incompleteness or completeness, thickness or thinness, purity or impurity, stupidity or
intelligence; each of these (qualities) assumes form in the individual
according to his own allotment, thus constituting his nature. But
despite these inequalities among (individual) natures, the major
distinctions are those of the different species" (*ibid.*, p. 80).

Tai's theory that each individual is produced through the
evolutions of the Ether, but that the different species to which individual creatures belong remain ever constant, leads him unwittingly
into a doctrine of unchanging universals similar to that of the Rationalists. For while granting the existence of individual differences
depending on one's individual endowment of the Ether, he subordinates these to the major differences between different species,
which remain ever constant, irrespective of lesser individual differences. In this way he explains why, for example, the natures of a cow
and a man, or of a man and a dog, are not comparable.

Tai also analyzes the distinction between the nature (*hsing*) and
capacity (*ts'ai*) as follows:

"Men and creatures are brought into being as a result of the
evolutions of the Ether. From the point of view that this process

---

[2] See above, p. 633. — Tr.

results in limitations for them according to their allotment (of the Ether), the term 'conferment' (*ming* 命) is used. From the point of view that it produces the basic beginning of men and creatures, the term 'nature' is used. And from the point of view of the physical element involved, the term 'capacity' is used. Because they each differ in their completed natures, therefore they each likewise differ in their physical capacities. The physical capacity is the means by which the nature displays itself (to the outside world). Were it put aside, how could we perceive what we call the nature? ... As examples, let us take the natures of a peach or an apricot: When wholly contained within the whiteness of their kernels, the shapes, colors, smells, and flavors (of the future peach or apricot) all lie innate, with no possibility of being seen. But when the budding sprouts burst forth, followed by stems, branches, and leaves, then the peach and apricot assume their individual differences. Thereafter they produce flowers and fruit, the shapes, colors, smells, and flavors of which are in each case clearly differentiated. Although it was their natures which made them thus, it is their capacities which cause these (differences) to become manifest" (*ibid.*, 3.102-103).

According to this formulation, the nature of a thing constitutes the potentiality of that thing, whereas its capacity is what serves to actualize that potentiality. Such potentiality, itself invisible, thus becomes manifest only as the result of this actualization. Conceived of in this way, the nature is something concrete, and as such differs from the nature as conceived by the Rationalistic school.

Note: Tai was anticipated in this theory by Ch'en Ch'üeh 陳確 (1604-77; native of Hai-ning 海寧, Chekiang), who, with Huang Tsung-hsi, was a fellow student under Liu Tsung-chou. In the epitaph written by Huang for Ch'en, Huang states that "of our teacher's doctrines, he (Ch'en) obtained forty or fifty per cent." (See Huang's *Prose Anthology*, 8.13.) In a letter to Ch'en, Huang also describes Ch'en's theory about the goodness of the nature as follows: "In the statement, 'He who has developed his mind to the utmost, knows his nature,' Mencius (VIIa, 1) expresses his fundamental idea of the goodness of the nature. That is to say, men's natures are always good, but this becomes apparent only as a result of the expansion and development of their capacities (*ts'ai*). It is like the case of the natures of the various grains. Unless they are planted, weeded, and hoed, how can the excellence of their seeds be known? ... This means that the nature of the good grain becomes fully actualized only after frequent and careful weeding. Certainly it does not follow that, because one's own remissness or diligence results in differing harvests, the nature of the grain is therefore either good or bad. (In the same way) the nature of the superior man becomes fully actualized only after being cultivated and developed. Certainly it does not follow that the natures given to people at birth are either good or bad, simply because their diligent respectfulness or their lack of restraint result in differing achievements" (*ibid.*).

This theory of Ch'en's was at first criticized by Huang as follows: "The goodness of the nature remains so from the beginning down to its very depths, being in no way added to by the expansion and development of capacity. Likewise it is in no way diminished even if this expansion and development be not applied" (*op. cit.*, 3.11). His idea here is precisely that of Chu Hsi, when the latter compares the nature to a bright pearl lying in turbid water. (See chap. 13, p. 559.) Later on, however, he wrote somewhat differently: "The mind of itself lacks any 'original state' (*pen t'i* 本 體). Its 'original state' consists of whatever its efforts lead it to." (See Huang's Introduction to his *Ming-ju Hsüeh-an* or *Writings of Ming Confucianists*.) In expressing this revised point of view, it is possible that Huang was influenced by Ch'en Ch'üeh. (For this point I am indebted to Professor Ch'ien Mu.)

As far as man is concerned, his nature, which consists of blood, breath, and the mental faculty, is itself divided into three particular aspects: those of the feelings (*ch'ing*), desires (*yü*), and knowledge (*chih*). Tai writes:

"Man, having been born, possesses feelings, desires, and knowledge. These three are spontaneous in his blood, breath, and mental faculty. Because the desires are given satisfaction by means of sounds, colors, smells, and tastes, one therefore has (an awareness of) love or fear. Because the feelings are expressed as joy, anger, sorrow, or pleasure, one therefore has (an awareness of) depression or exhilaration. Because knowledge discriminates between beauty and ugliness, right and wrong, one therefore has (an awareness of) likes and dislikes. The desire for sounds, colors, smells, and tastes helps to enrich one's life. The feelings of joy, anger, sorrow, and pleasure respond to and bring one into contact with (external) things. The knowledge of beauty and ugliness, or right and wrong, when developed to the utmost, enables one to penetrate (the mysteries of) Heaven, Earth, and the divine spirits. ... Only when the desires and feelings are supplemented by knowledge, do these desires gain fulfillment, and these feelings gain expression. All activities in the world should consist of nothing more than insuring this fulfillment of (human) desires, and expression of (human) feelings" (*Meaning of Mencius*, 3.105).

Such knowledge, Tai argues further, is essential for an understanding of the Principles of Heaven, Earth, and all things:

"Love (*jen*) consists of the unceasing production and reproduction brought about by the evolutionary operations of the Ether. This process of production and reproduction proceeds according to an orderly Principle of its own making. By observing the fixed sequence followed by this orderly Principle, one may get to know propriety. And by observing the unshakable distinctions laid down by this orderly Principle, one may get to know righteousness" (*ibid.*, p. 118).

Because of his knowledge, man can understand Principle, and thereby can, from what is natural (*tzŭ jan* 自 然), achieve an understanding of what is morally necessary (*pi jan* 必 然):

"The ear is able to discriminate between the world's sounds, the eye between the world's colors, the nose between the world's smells, the mouth between the world's flavors, and the mind between the world's ethical principles. ... Other creatures, however, are incapable of comprehending the correct standards of the universe, for which reason they lack internal restraints and simply follow what is natural to them. But man, because he possesses knowledge of the Heavenly virtues, is able to follow these correct standards. Through what is natural to him, he cooperates in the smooth operations of Heaven and Earth; through what is morally necessary, he cooperates in their constant norms. Neither of these is 'unnatural' to him, whereas the 'naturalness' of other creatures is unworthy to be mentioned in this connection. Mencius, when he says that the nature is good, is looking at the natural restraints present in man's raw capabilities, and it is these he calls goodness." [1]

Thus the difference between man and animals is that whereas the latter act only according to nature, man, through his possession of knowledge, is capable of understanding moral necessity. Conduct performed in accordance with this knowledge results in practice of the various virtues. Tai writes:

"Moral principles are that which man's mental faculty, by its thinking, immediately comprehends, leaving no possible uncertainty as to what should be practiced. ... Man's mental faculty, being daily employed upon the human relationships, can sense the least hints, wherever they may appear, of commiseration, shame and dislike, modesty and yielding, and right and wrong. This is the

---

[1] *Writings*, 8.11-12 (sect. on Mencius' discussion of human nature).

meaning of the statement that the nature is good. As soon as it senses commiseration, the enlargement and development of this feeling leads to the utmost expression of love (*jen*). As soon as it senses shame and dislike, the enlargement and development of this feeling leads to the utmost expression of righteousness (*yi*). As soon as it senses modesty and yielding, the enlargement and development of this feeling leads to the utmost expression of propriety (*li*). And as soon as it senses right and wrong, the enlargement and development of this feeling leads to the utmost expression of wisdom (*chih*). Love, righteousness, propriety, and wisdom are primary among the eminent virtues.

"Mencius has said (IIa, 6) that if today men suddenly see a child about to fall into a well, they will without exception experience a feeling of alarm and commiserating distress. What is called commiseration and what is called love, however, do not lie external to the mental faculty, as if they were some kind of (physical) object. They are stored within the mind. It is because one oneself is conscious of a love of life and fear of death, that one feels alarm over the danger to the child and commiseration over his death. For if this love of life and fear of death were absent from the mind, how could the latter then experience these feelings of alarm and commiseration? Through extension the same principle applies to the feelings of shame and dislike, modesty and yielding, and right and wrong" (*Meaning of Mencius*, 2.86). Again:

"Man's knowledge is in its lesser aspects able to encompass the widest ranges of beauty and ugliness, and in its greater aspects the widest ranges of right and wrong. It is because this is so that he is able not only to fulfill his own desires but, through their extension, the desires of others as well; not only his own feelings but, through their extension, the feelings of others as well. The highest morality consists of nothing more than insuring that the desires of all men reach fulfillment, and their feelings reach expression" (*ibid.*, 3.105).

Thus all morality is a product of knowledge. In other words, knowledge becomes equivalent to morality. It is because man possesses a knowledge denied to other creatures that he is able to comprehend Principle and moral necessity, and to conform to them in conduct. He is able to understand that fellow beings share common feelings and desires, and therefore to place himself in the position of other men. This is the reason why human nature is good.

Through the utmost development of knowledge, is conduct

brought into closest harmony with what is morally necessary, thus permitting the innate potentialities of the nature to be most nearly realized. Tai writes:

"Goodness is what is morally necessary, whereas the nature itself is something natural. To cause it (the nature) to conform to moral necessity, thereby giving a finished perfection to its naturalness: this is what is known as developing the natural to its highest point. In this manner the Way of Heaven, Earth, man, and creatures is given utmost expression" (*ibid.*, p. 111).

"Hsün Tzŭ knew that propriety and righteousness result from the teachings of the sages, but not that they also derive from the nature. He knew that they consist in the manifestation of what is morally necessary, but not that this moral necessity represents the highest ultimate pattern of the natural, to which it gives final perfection" (*ibid.*, 2.92).

Moral necessity is thus the highest development of the natural. In other words, it gives to the natural its most perfect development, which is then, says Tai, the highest excellence of the universe:

"For this reason man is the manifestation of the highest excellence of the universe, and it is only the sage who completely develops this excellence" (*Nature of Goodness*, 2.13).

The foregoing reveals the difference between Tai Chen and the Rationalists. He, like them, acknowledges that there is an objective Principle. Unlike them, however, he denies that this Principle can at the same time be present within man's own nature. Human nature, for him, consists simply of man's blood, breath, and mental faculty; in other words, it is what the Sung Neo-Confucianists would call the physical nature. This physical nature does not itself actually contain the multitudinous Principles of all things. Nevertheless, Tai says, it can, because of its faculty of knowledge, come to comprehend them. This explains why man, starting from what is purely natural to him, can elevate himself to what is morally necessary. "The Sung Confucianists," Tai says, "regard Principle as if it were a (physical) thing which, being obtained from Heaven, becomes embodied in the mind" (*Meaning of Mencius*, 1.61). Unlike Yen Yüan and Li Kung, who did not wholly succeed in overthrowing this doctrine, Tai successfully rejects it in favor of what we have just described. Even he, however, as we shall see, fails to develop his own theory to its full logical implications.

iii. *Methodology for Seeking Principle*

Man, as the possessor of knowledge, can achieve an understanding of objective Principle. As to how he is to do this, Tai writes as follows:

"Principle consists of those feelings which do not err (in their expression). No one can accord with Principle unless he succeeds in (giving correct expression to) the feelings. . . . Principle is manifested when the measure of the self is extended to others. Those who talk about Heavenly Principle mean by this the Principle of natural allotment. An example is when I measure the feelings of others in terms of my own feelings, in such a way that equal balance is given to them all . . . . It may be asked: (You say that) the measurement of feelings in terms of feelings, done without error, truly leads, when carried into practice, to the apprehension of Principle. But in that case what is the difference between the terms 'feeling' and 'Principle'? My reply would be: The term feeling applies to whatever pertains both to the self and others. But when a feeling neither goes too far nor falls short, it is then called Principle" (*Meaning of Mencius*, 1. 41-43).

Here is outlined the methodology for seeking the Principle pertaining to human affairs. "The measurement of feelings in terms of feelings" is equivalent to Confucius' principles of "conscientiousness to others" and "altruism," or to the *Great Learning*'s "principle of regulating by the measuring-square." [1] Human feelings and desires, unless manifested within the framework of certain fixed limits, result in harm to other people. These fixed limits constitute the "Principle of natural allotment," which, however, it is easy for the feelings either to exceed or fall short of. Only when there is no such exceeding or falling short is Principle itself attained.

We are still left with the problem of how to discover the Principles of things other than those within the sphere of human affairs. Tai remarks: "It is necessary to analyze these things with the utmost minuteness, and then their Principles will be obtained" (*ibid.*, 3.128). But how is this to be done, and how are we to know that the "Principles" discovered in this way are really what they seem to be? Tai says:

"Only what minds generally agree upon can be called Principle and called righteousness. What does not meet general agreement,

---

[1] See vol. 1, pp. 71-72, and 366 respectively. — Tr.

but is merely a single man's opinion, is neither Principle nor right-eousness. General agreement exists when every individual maintains that a thing is so, and throughout the world all generations say it is something unchangeable.... Every category (of things) has certain unchanging patterns, which are called Principles, while what is proper to them is called righteousness" (*ibid.*, 1.44).

Principle is objective and unchanging. Therefore, having analyzed something in order to discover its Principle, it is still necessary to subject the result to further observation in order to determine whether it really represents more than what we ourselves or a small group of individuals happen to hold as true. For unless it does, it is not real Principle at all, but only our own personal opinion. If, on the other hand, its permanent validity receives confirmation from many generations throughout the world, we may feel confident that what we have discovered is really Principle.

Here Tai Chen establishes a distinction between Principle, which is objective and universal, and opinion (*yi chien* 意見), which is subjective and private. The Sung Confucianists, he holds further, by their insistence that Principle is to be found within each individual mind, have often wrongly interpreted as Principle something that in reality is nothing more than personal opinion. Thus he says:

"The Sung Confucianists, too, have understood that Principle is to be sought in things, but because of their prior immersion in Buddhism, they have adapted the latter's concept of spiritual intelli-gence (the mind), and used it to designate their own Principle. This is why they look at Principle as if it were a (separate physical) object, so that not only do they talk about the Principle of things, but they also say that (a single) Principle lies scattered through these things. As to the Principles of things, it is necessary to analyze the things themselves with the utmost minuteness, and then their Principles will be obtained. (But the Sung Confucianists say that a single) Principle lies scattered through things; then, by mental concen-tration, they try to seek for this Principle. They say that there is a single root (i.e., Principle), but a myriad distinctions (i.e., things). They say that (this Principle), when released, extends to the six cardinal directions, but when rolled up, may be stored within a single mystery. Verily they arrive at this conclusion through a course analogous to that of the Buddhists, who say that the entire phenomenal world seen around us lies stored within a single particle of dust . . . . Because they regard Principle as if it were a (physical) object, they are obliged to reduce it to a unitary Principle, whereas (in actual fact separate) things must have their own Principles, differing for each. Therefore they further say that the (individual) mind contains all these many Principles, with which it reacts to all things. What is thus contained in the (individual) mind and issues forth from it: what else could it be except (personal) opinion?" (*ibid.*, 3.128-129).

This is a just criticism of one weakness in Sung Neo-Confucianism. All Neo-Confucianists were influenced to some extent by Buddhism: the Rationalists when they said that even though all things have their own Principle, these many Principles are at the same time contained within our own mind; the Idealists when they went on to the point of actually identifying mind with Principle. The result, for both groups, was the ever present danger that what they talked about as Principle might really be nothing more than their own subjective opinion.

iv. *Origin of Evil*

Human feelings, desires, and knowledge, Tai maintains, are all subject to certain failings:

"The failing in desire is selfishness, the sequel to which is the evil of greed. The failing in feeling is one-sidedness, the sequel to which is the sin of perverse unreasonableness. The failing in knowledge is delusion, the sequel to which is the error of fallaciousness. Freed from selfishness, the desires all correspond to love, propriety, and righteousness. Freed from one-sidedness, the feelings are inevitably mild and easy, even and altruistic. Freed from delusion, knowledge becomes what is known as (true) intelligence and sagely wisdom" (*Meaning of Mencius*, 3.105).

Thus evil arises from certain defects in the feelings, desires, and knowledge. Among these, selfishness (*ssŭ* 私) and delusion (*pi* 蔽) are the most notable:

"A man's failure to make utmost use of his capacities leads to two calamities, those of selfishness and delusion . . . . The best way to get rid of selfishness is to strengthen altruism. The best way to disperse delusion is to study" (*Nature of Goodness*, 3.22).

The way to strengthen altruism (*shu* 恕), according to

Tai, is to measure other men's desires in terms of one's own. Selfishness arises when the individual concentrates solely upon his own desires, while ignoring those of other people. As for knowledge, its relationship to the objects of knowledge is comparable to that of a light to the objects it illumines: Just as the light, if obscured, can no longer adequately illumine these objects, so knowledge, if deluded, can no longer gain correct comprehension of the objects of knowledge. [1] Thus, for Tai, knowledge is the equivalent of morality, and its deluding results in the rise of evil.

Tai also strongly attacks the Neo-Confucian distinction between Heavenly Principle and human desire:

"*Question*: 'From the Sung (dynasty) onward those who have talked about Principle have asserted that what does not issue from Principle issues from desire, and vice versa. Thus they have discriminated between the spheres of Principle and desire, maintaining that herein lies the distinction between the superior man and petty man. Now, however, you take Principle to be those feelings that do not err (in their expression), thus implying that Principle is inherent in the desires. Does this mean, however, that the complete absence of desire is something wrong?'

"*Answer*: 'When Mencius says that for nourishing the mind there is nothing better than making the desires few, [2] he clearly does not mean that the desires should be wholly obliterated, but merely that they should be made fewer. In the life of man there is nothing more distressing than to lack the wherewithal to live out that life. To desire to live, but at the same time to allow other people to live as well: this is love (*jen*). When, however, this desire to live reaches the point of disregarding the injury caused thereby to the lives of others, it becomes the violator of love. Here this violation undoubtedly arises because of the desire to live, so that were such desire absent, there would surely be no violation of love. Suppose, however, that this desire were (really universally) absent. This would mean that people would look at the resulting extinction of all human life with nothing more than cool indifference. In actual fact it is alien to the feelings to permit others to live, while not insisting on living oneself. Thus while it may be permissible to say that what does not issue from correctness issues from perverseness, and vice versa, it is not

---

[1] See the *Meaning of Mencius*, 1.48.
[2] *Mencius*, VIIb, 35. — Tr.

permissible to say that what does not issue from Principle issues from desire, and vice versa' " (*ibid.*, p. 54).

If this argument is to carry weight, we should first understand what the Sung Neo-Confucianists mean when they speak of human desire. Such basic desires as those for food and sex are not, by them, regarded as inherently evil, but become so only when they lose their "correctness" (*cheng* 正), in other words, when they go to excess. Chu Hsi, for example, compares desire to the pouring forth of water until it overflows, but he does not apply this comparison to the water that does not overflow. [1] Thus whenever the Sung Neo-Confucianists wish to indicate that a certain desire is evil in their eyes, they commonly do not use the single word "desire" to describe it, but add qualifying adjectives such as "human desire" or "selfish desire." In this way they make it clear that they are not stigmatizing the desires as a whole, but only those of which they disapprove. And this, precisely, is what Tai Chen seems to do when he uses the epithet "selfish" to designate those desires that seem to him improper. Furthermore, his dichotomy between what is correct and what is perverse does not appear, on close examination, to differ materially from that of the Sung Confucianists between Principle and desire. Indeed, this dichotomy, in the final analysis, seems to be based on a standard which by them would be called Principle, even though he himself chooses to call it moral necessity.

Note: Here again Tai has been anticipated by Ch'en Ch'üeh, when the latter says: "Master Chou's (Chou Tun-yi's) teaching of the absence of desire seems to be non-Ch'anist, yet is (really) Ch'anist. We Confucianists, however, speak only of making the desires fewer. What we call Heavenly Principle is originally absent from the human mind, and gains visibility only in the form of human desires, which, when they happen to hit the right mark, are then Heavenly Principle." (Recorded in Huang Tsung-hsi's first letter to Ch'en Ch'üeh; see Huang's *Prose Anthology*, 3.12.)

In his reply, Huang criticizes this statement as follows: "This statement of yours, my old friend, is derived from that of our elder teacher, when he said: 'The mind of the spirit is the original mind of the mind of the body; the moral nature is the original nature of the physical element. Apart from the physical element, there is nothing that may be called the nature.' [See p. 647 above, where the first part of this statement by Liu Tsung-chou has already been quoted. — Tr.] But while we may properly use (this statement) when talking about the physical element and the mind of the body, we may not thus use it when talking about human desire.

---

[1] See chap. 13, end of sect. 4. — Tr.

The physical element and the mind of the body both pertain to the whole, which is common to everything. But human desire is something that settles in a particular spot; it is the selfishness of a single person" (*ibid.*). By this Huang means to say that human desire, in the strict sense of the term, is always selfish and hence can never "happen to hit the right mark"; therefore it is entirely evil.

v. *Tai Chen and Hsün Tzǔ*

"The failing in knowledge is delusion," but "the best way to disperse delusion is to study." These words might well have been uttered by Hsün Tzǔ, who, it will be remembered, laid great emphasis on learning. A similar emphasis appears in the following statements by Tai:

"It is man's blood, breath, and mental faculty, originating from the *yin* and *yang* and Five Elements, that make up his nature. This blood and breath depend for nourishment upon food and drink, which, once having been metamorphosed into blood and breath, are no longer what they were when drunk and eaten. The same is true of the way in which the mental faculty depends upon the pursuit of learning in order to assimilate the latter to itself. As far as blood and breath are concerned, they start by being weak and later become strong: this means that they are then gaining their proper nourishment. In the case of the mental faculty, it starts by being narrow and small, dark and dull, and later becomes broad and large, bright and discerning: this (also) means that it is then gaining its proper nourishment. That is why it is said: 'Though stupid, he is sure to become intelligent' "[1] (*Meaning of Mencius*, 1.52).

"The body is at first immature and small, but in the end it becomes mature and large. Likewise the virtuous nature is at first dull and dark, but in the end it becomes sage and wise. The maturing and growth of the body depend upon its nourishment by food and drink, with which it increases its growth day by day until it becomes quite different from what it was in the beginning. (In the same way) the virtuous nature depends upon the pursuit of learning, through which it progresses until it becomes sage and wise, when it too, obviously, is no longer the same as what it was in the beginning" (*ibid.*, pp. 64-65).

Tai Chen, as we have seen, denies that the many Principles of

---

[1] *Doctrine of the Mean*, p. 318. — Tr.

things are themselves contained in the mind. For him, as for Hsün Tzŭ, the mind is simply "a physical substance capable of knowing." [1] Hence the Principles of things can be comprehended and actualized in personal conduct only through the study made of them by this physical mind. The perfection of our moral state, Tai argues, depends on the enrichment of our knowledge, and its fullest development is achieved only when what is natural to us comes into complete conformity with moral necessity. The resulting condition is one quite different from that of the beginning. In this theory there is a great similarity between him and Hsün Tzŭ. [2]

The difference between the two thinkers, however, is that in Hsün Tzŭ's cosmology no such thing as an objective Principle is postulated. Hence rites, standards of justice, and morality generally are simply conceived of as man-made artifacts designed to serve human existence. Tai Chen, on the other hand, acknowledges the presence of an objective Principle, and hence regards moral standards as the concrete manifestations of this Principle. In so doing he is, quite naturally, influenced by the Rationalistic school.

In the case of Hsün Tzŭ, moreover, the mind consists of three faculties only: those of knowing, of feeling, and of desire. What he calls the knowing faculty, furthermore, can initially merely comprehend the difference between what is beneficial and harmful, but not that between moral goodness and evil. Only through experience does it see that goodness often results in benefit and evil in harm, so that in this way it gradually comes to understand the nature of good and evil themselves. Tai Chen, too, clearly states that the mind consists of the knowing faculty, of feeling, and of desire. Yet from his further remarks it would seem that the mind, for him, quite aside from its possession of knowledge, is also capable of a direct moral apprehension of the nature of good and evil as such. This appears in the following statements:

"Tastes, sounds, and colors lie in (external) objects, not in ourselves, but when they come in contact with our blood and breath, we are able to discriminate between them and take pleasure in them. Those we find pleasurable are sure to be the ones that are particularly excellent. (In the same way) moral principles lie in the scattered

---

[1] *Hsün-tzŭ*, chap. 23, p. 313. — Tr.

[2] See vol. 1, chap. 12, sect. 5, esp. p. 293, where Hsün Tzŭ describes the superior man who is imbued with sincerity as "ever changing without returning to his original state."

strands of (external) affairs and circumstances, but when they come in contact with our mental faculty, we are able to discriminate between them and take pleasure in them. Those we find pleasurable are sure to be the ones that are supremely right" (*ibid.*, p. 47).

"Mencius has said (VIIa, 7) that 'moral principles are agreeable to our minds just as the flesh of grass-fed and grain-fed animals is agreeable to our mouths.' This is not merely a figure of speech, for whenever man does some act which accords with moral principle, his mind invariably happily enjoys it, whereas whenever he violates this moral principle, his mind invariably feels sadly depressed. From this it may be seen that the mind's reaction to moral principle, like the reactions of the blood and breath to what they relish, is equally brought about by the nature" (*ibid.*, p. 51).

Thus our mind is not only able to comprehend moral principles, but even to "take pleasure" in them. When our behavior agrees with these moral principles, we have a feeling of exhilaration, but when it fails to agree, we are saddened and depressed. This shows that our mind, in addition to what we ordinarily term knowledge, possesses something else analogous to what the Idealistic school would call the "intuitive knowledge." Tai says further:

"Hsün Tzŭ, when he emphasizes learning, (says that) there is no (foundation) for it within (the self), and that it is to be taken from what lies without. But Mencius, when he emphasizes learning, (says that a foundation for it already) does exist within, and that this is then to be further supported by what lies without. Now in the case of the food and drink utilized to nourish the body's blood and breath, the Ether thus utilized for this purpose is, like the Ether originally received by the body itself (at birth), derived from the universe. Thus they are not two separate things. This is the reason why what is thus utilized, though external (to the body), can be metamorphosed into blood and breath, thereby supplementing what (already) lies within. Were the original endowment of the Ether lacking, it would never be possible, having made contact with what is external, to utilize that (Ether) alone (for building up the body). The same principle applies to the (external) pursuit of learning in its relationship to the virtuous nature (which lies within)" (*op. cit.*, 2.92-93).

Pushing this statement to its logical conclusion, does it not mean that our ability to comprehend the many Principles of external things derives from the fact that we initially possess these Principles within ourselves? Or that the nature of the human individual is identical with the universe? Tai says:

"Man's capacity derives from the total potentiality of the universe, and interpenetrates the total virtue of the universe" (*Nature of Goodness*, 2.15).

Is this not precisely the doctrine of the Rationalistic school?

From the foregoing it is evident that despite the genuine points of difference between Tai Chen and the Sung Neo-Confucianists, he is unable fully to exploit and develop these differences, with the result that he fails to create a fully rounded system. For this reason his philosophy cannot be placed on a par with that of such men as Chu Hsi or Wang Shou-jen.

Although Yen Yüan, Li Kung, and Tai Chen all oppose the Sung Learning, it is noteworthy that they concentrate their attacks upon the Rationalists, while only rarely criticizing the Idealists. In part, perhaps, this is because of their feeling that the Idealistic school's resemblance to Ch'an Buddhism was so self-evident as to be sufficiently damning in itself, whereas the Rationalistic school, because of its orthodoxy and deceptive reasonableness, seemed to present much greater danger, and therefore to require more active opposition. Another factor, however, perhaps more evident to us today than it was at the time, is that the views of Yen, Li, and Tai regarding Principle, the Ether, the nature, the body, etc., actually agreed in certain ways with those of Liu Tsung-chou and Huang Tsung-hsi, who were themselves followers of the Idealistic school. In this respect, therefore, there seems to have been a certain affinity between the Idealists and the Yen-Li-Tai group.

CHAPTER XVI

THE NEW TEXT SCHOOL OF THE CH'ING DYNASTY

1—The Religious and Reform Movement at the End of the Ch'ing

The first real break with Neo-Contucianism came only toward the end of the Ch'ing dynasty, with the revival of interest in the New Text school (*Chin Wen Chia*). This school, as we have seen in Chapter II, had been dominant during the earlier half of the Han dynasty. With the rise of the Old Text school during the latter part of that dynasty, however, it suffered an eclipse from which it failed to emerge during the next seventeen or eighteen centuries. Only with the Ch'ing dynasty did this situation change, in part as the result of the great wave of scholarly activity which at that time raised Chinese techniques of textual criticism to hitherto unachieved levels of excellence. Most of the scholars who thus devoted themselves to the editing and collating of China's ancient writings began, naturally enough, with those texts that had been most emphasized from the T'ang dynasty onward. By the middle of the Ch'ing, however, the work on these had largely been completed, so that some scholars then turned to those other texts which, once popular under the Han dynasty, had since been largely neglected. The result was a gradual revival of interest in the *Spring and Autumn Annals*, the commentary on this known as the *Kung-yang Chuan*, and various other works of central importance in the New Text school. Through the study of these texts, philosophically minded Ch'ing scholars were brought face to face with intellectual problems vastly different from those stressed in Neo-Confucianism.

The rise of this new movement coincided with the appearance of other new intellectual influences, generated out of the growing impact of the West on China during the second half of the Ch'ing. At first this impact was largely confined to the proselytizing activities of Christian missionaries, but during the nineteenth century it expanded to include many other closely interrelated military, political, and economic pressures. These pressures created something like a crisis in the Chinese mind, and forced it to ask itself numerous searching questions, among them two of fundamental importance:

(1) Why is it that Westerners belong to organized churches, whereas the Chinese do not? Why, in other words, does China not have an institutionalized state religion?

(2) China, despite her size and population, is subject to all kinds of pressures from the West. Does this not point to the need for self reform on her part?

The attempts of thinking Chinese to answer these questions resulted in a new intellectual movement which sought to strengthen China internally by: (1) establishing an organized state church, and (2) instituting political reform. These attempts were made, however, at a time when the old bottles of Classical Learning had not yet reached their breaking point; as a result, anyone who wished to gain a hearing for his new views was still obliged to express them within the context of this Classical Learning. [1] In the eyes of the nineteenth century reformers, the New Text School of the Former Han dynasty seemed the most suitable vehicle for this task. An important reason lay in the commanding position held by Confucius in this school—a position which under its influence had successively risen from "teacher" to "king," and from king to supernatural being. We have seen in Chapter III, for example, how the Han apocrypha portrayed Confucius as a semi-divine religious leader. This meant that those Ch'ing reformers who wished to institute a Chinese state religion, found one ready for the taking in the New Text school's brand of Confucianism.

A second reason for the choice of the New Text school lay in its political appeal: the fact that it portrayed Confucius not only as a religious leader, but a political reformer as well—a reformer whose theory of the "Three Ages" and their accompanying political institutions had been established as a standard for all time. [2] Thus the doctrines of Confucius, as represented by this school, provided its Ch'ing revivers with sanctified models for the political and social reforms they themselves wished to institute. This trend of thinking is clearly reflected, for example, in the following description of Confucius by K'ang Yu-wei (1858-1927), one of the Ch'ing leaders of reform:

---

[1] See the present volume, chap. 1.
[2] On these "Three Ages," see below, and chap. 2, pp. 81 ff. — Tr.

"Heaven, having pity for the many afflictions suffered by the men who live on this great earth, (caused) the Black Emperor to send down his semen so as to create a being who would rescue the people from their troubles—a being of divine intelligence, who would be a sage-king, a teacher for his age, a bulwark for all men, and a religious leader for the whole world. [1] Born as he was in the Age of Disorder, he proceeded, on the basis of this disorder, to establish the pattern of the Three Ages, progressing with increasing refinement until they arrive at Universal Peace. He established the institutions of these Three Ages, basing himself (initially) on those of his native state (of Lu), but stressing the idea of the one great unity that would (ultimately) bind together all parts of the great earth, far and near, large and small." [2]

In K'ang Yu-wei's time there certainly seemed need for a Confucius like this, and only in the writings of the New Text school could it be met. This fact has curious consequences for the history of Chinese philosophy, for it means that the Period of Classical Learning, inaugurated by the New Text school in the second century B.C., was brought to an end some two thousand years later by a revival of that same school. The probable explanation is that fantastic and extreme ideas most easily take root in times of major environmental change, and that the New Text school, with its many borrowings from the *Yin-yang* school, was ideally suited to supply such ideas. In ancient China, the greatest period of such change had been that from the latter part of the Chou dynasty through the early part of the Han, when China suddenly emerged from a coterie of feudal states into a highly centralized empire. Equally abrupt, however, were the environmental and ideological changes occurring during the last hundred years of the Ch'ing dynasty, for it was then that the Chinese were forced by their growing contacts with the outside world to accept the fact that their country was neither the whole nor the center of that world, but simply one among many different nations.

---

[1] K'ang Yu-wei here has in mind a legend contained in one of the Han apocrypha, according to which Confucius was conceived as the result of a meeting between his mother and a "Black Emperor" in a dream. See chap. 3, p. 129. — Tr.

[2] See K'ang's Introduction to his *K'ung-tzŭ Kai-chih K'ao* (Study of Confucius as a Reformer), published in his magazine *Pu-jen Tsa-chih*, no. 1 (1913). This work is hereafter referred to as *Confucius as a Reformer*.

2—K'ang Yu-wei

i. *Confucius as a Religious Leader and Political Reformer*

In the religious and reform movement we have just been outlining, K'ang Yu-wei 康有爲 (1858-1927) [1] played a commanding part. [2] In his philosophical writings he on the one hand attacked the Old Text school's versions of the classics, maintaining that they had all been forged by Liu Hsin (ca. 46 B.C.-A.D. 23); on the other he espoused the theory that Confucius had been an active political reformer, and maintained that the New Text school's versions of the classics were genuine products of Confucius' own hand. For this purpose K'ang in 1891 completed his famous *Hsin-hsüeh Wei-ching K'ao* (Study of the Classics Forged during the Hsin Period). Central in this work is the theory that the Old Text versions of the classics, sponsored by Liu Hsin while serving under the usurper Wang Mang, had really been forged by Liu himself for political purposes, and hence are not products of the Chou dynasty, but of Wang Mang's own Hsin period. [3] K'ang himself states his case as follows:

---

[1] Styled Kuang-hsia 廣廈 ; alternate name Ch'ang-su 長素 . He was a native of Nan-hai 南海 , slightly southwest of Canton.

[2] K'ang is equally famed as political propagandist and reformer. Distressed by China's growing weakness (evidenced especially by her defeat in the first Sino-Japanese War of 1894-95, followed by numerous political and economic concessions wrung from her by the foreign powers), K'ang conceived of a sweeping reform program which, while adopting the military and industrial techniques of the West, would retain and revitalize China's ancient spiritual heritage (Confucianism). For this program, whose instrument was to be constitutional monarchy rather than republicanism, K'ang in 1898 succeeded in gaining the ear of the young Kuang-hsü Emperor. The result was the famous "Hundred Days of Reform" (June 11-September 20, 1898), during which the Emperor issued a series of sweeping decrees that, if duly carried out, would have radically changed China's political life. For the most part, however, they succeeded only in arousing the intense opposition of conservative court circles. In the end the movement was crushed when the Empress Dowager, through a coup d'état, resumed her former position as regent, imprisoned the Emperor, and executed six of the reformers. K'ang, however, succeeded in escaping to Japan, and in later years lived to see his views on constitutional monarchy—espoused by him to the end—ridiculed as hopelessly old fashioned by the revolutionaries who created the Chinese Republic in 1912. See Arthur W. Hummel, ed., *Eminent Chinese of the Ch'ing Period*, vol. 2, pp. 702-704; also Wolfgang Franke, *Die staatspolitischen Reformversuche K'ang Yu-weis und seiner Schule* (Berlin, 1935). — Tr.

[3] On Liu Hsin's relationship to the Old Text classics, and to Wang Mang, who usurped the throne A.D. 9-23, see chap. 4, sect. 1. K'ang's theory is today generally discredited. — Tr.

"Inasmuch as (Liu) Hsin glossed over the classics to assist in usurpation, and personally served the Hsin (dynasty) as its minister, these classics are therefore a product of the Hsin learning. Who can deny that this is a correct interpretation of them? In later times the adherents of the Han and Sung (schools of learning) have wrangled with one another (over the classics) as if they were water and fire. Thus regarded, what all later generations have pointed to as the Han Learning, including all the work of Chia, Ma, Hsü, and Cheng, is Hsin and not Han Learning; [1] the classics honored and expounded by the Sung scholars are for the most part forged and not those of Confucius" (1.2).

Thus K'ang sweepingly invalidates most of the work done on the classics from the Later Han period onward, contending that these do not go back to Confucius himself. It is only the New Text scholars, he argues further, who have expounded the genuine classics of Confucius and transmitted his esoteric teachings. As for Confucius himself, K'ang maintains that he was China's first great intellectual leader, the supremacy of whose teachings was never in doubt, even during the height of philosophical activity of the last centuries of the Chou. Thus K'ang writes:

"In all things, the accumulation of what is coarse eventually results in the birth of what is fine, the accumulation of what is mean in the birth of what is noble, and the accumulation of what is stupid in the birth of what is wise. Thus plants and trees spring from the accumulation of earth and stones, and birds and beasts evolve from the accumulation of insects and reptiles. Man, as the most spiritual of all creatures, was the latest to come into being. A vast flood covered the entire earth, only after which did the different races of man begin to exist. Thus the propagation of the many peoples of the earth began in the time of Yü of the Hsia. [2]

"Through the accumulation of population and wisdom during the next two thousand years, circumstances finally all became propitious, so that an irresistable outburst of surpassingly wonderful

---

[1] Chia K'uei (A.D. 30-101), Ma Yung (76-166), Hsü Shen (1st-2nd century), and Cheng Hsüan (127-200), were among the most famous classical commentators of the Later Han dynasty. Their work, however, dealt primarily with the Old Text versions, which is why K'ang regards it as "Hsin" and not "Han" Learning. — Tr.

[2] Legendary culture hero who saved China from a mighty flood, and founded the first dynasty, the Hsia. It is not impossible that K'ang Yu-wei also has the somewhat analogous story of Noah in mind here. — Tr.

wisdom occurred. [1] Every thinker, according to his natural endowment and social environment, established doctrines for himself,
collected disciples, reformed the institutions, and set up his own
standards, thinking thus to transform the world. But because of the
varying physical endowment (received by each) from the *yin* and
yang, their doctrines for the most part suffered from the defect of
one-sidedness. Thus each was able to comprehend only one idea,
just as the ears, eyes, mouth, and nose are unable to communicate
with one another. All of them, notwithstanding, resolutely carried
out their own will with firm and independent effort, and with abstruse
and cherished doctrines, thinking thus to establish teachings that
would embrace the whole world . . . .

"But there was one in whom was concentrated the excellence
of all the other philosophers, and whose surpassing god-like sageness
was such that all men rallied around him, so that he bound them
into one great unity, in this way becoming the model for a myriad
ages. How just, therefore, that the *Critical Essays* acclaims Confucius
as chief of all the philosophers. [2] After the world had rallied around
Confucius, the Great Way was thereby unified. That is why from
the Han onward there have been no other philosophers" (*Confucius
as a Reformer*, 2.1-2).

Among the most important of Confucius' teachings, according
to K'ang, are those of the "Three Sequences" and "Three Ages": [3]

"Vast indeed is the Way of Confucius. In its greatness it imitates
Heaven, and its operations are everywhere to be found . . . . Initially,
however, it was corrupted by the bigoted meanness of Hsün Tzŭ's
philosophy, later it was further confused by Liu Hsin's forgeries and
falsehoods, and finally it was damaged by Master Chu's (Chu Hsi's)
partiality. In this manner the Great Way of the 'uncrowned king' [4]
was darkened so that it could not shine forth, and stifled so that it
could not be manifested . . . .

"I have studied the teaching of Confucius comprehensively and
reverently. At first I followed the beaten track of the Sung scholars,

---

[1] This refers to the philosophical activity of the latter centuries of the
Chou. — Tr.

[2] See Wang Ch'ung, *Lun Heng*, chap. 13 (I, 384). — Tr.

[3] *San t'ung* and *san shih*. See on them chap. 2, pp. 58 ff. and 81 ff. — Tr.

[4] *Su wang* 素王. Confucius, the New Text school argued, was such a
great sage that by rights he should have become king, though he was prevented
by circumstances from doing so. — Tr.

where I eagerly thought that I had found it; then, however, I realized that Confucius could not have been so bigoted and narrow as that. So I pressed further along the path of the Han scholars, at every moment thinking that I was now treading on it; but then I realized that it could not be so fragmentary and confused as that. For if it stopped only there, Confucius would be a sage but not a divine being . . . .

"Thereupon I rejected the Old Text forgeries entirely, and sought for it (the Way of Confucius) in the New Text scholarship. This includes the Ch'i, Lu, and Han (versions of the) *Odes*; the Ou-yang and elder and younger Hsia-hou (versions of the) *Book of History*; the Meng, Chiao, and Ching (versions of the) *Changes*; the elder and younger Tai (versions of the) *Rites*; and the Kung-yang and Ku-liang (versions of the) *Spring and Autumn Annals*. [1] In this way I came to understand the transformations of the *yin* and *yang* (as portrayed) in the *Changes*, and the meaning of the Three Ages in the *Spring and Autumn Annals*.

"(At this point) I said that the Way of Confucius, though so great that it cannot be wholly seen, may at least be spied in its outlines. Alas, however, this Great Way is so deep and boundless that it cannot be summed up in a few words only. After this I completely discarded the commentaries and sought for it in the texts of the classics themselves. When I came to read the *Evolutions of Rites*, [2] I was greatly moved and exclaimed: 'Herein are to be found the successive changes of the Three Ages of Confucius, and the real truth of his Great Way.' . . . This text represents the esoteric words and true teaching of Confucius. It is a precious record without superior in any country, and a divine recipe for resurrecting all sentient beings throughout the world." [3]

K'ang Yu-wei further maintains that "the Way of Confucius

---

[1] The Ch'i, Lu, and Han versions of the *Odes* have largely been lost. Versions of the *Book of History* were transmitted for several generations by the Ou-yang family, as well as by the Hsia-hou family (uncle and nephew). On the transmission of the *Book of Changes* by Meng Hsi, Chiao Yen-shou, and Ching Fang, see chap. 3, p. 112. On that of the *Book of Rites*, as compiled by the elder and younger Tai (uncle and nephew), see vol. 1, p. 337. The Kung-yang and Ku-liang versions of the *Spring and Autumn Annals* are, of course, the *Kung-yang Chuan* and *Ku-liang Chuan*. — Tr.

[2] *Li Yün*. On this text, which comprises the seventh chapter of the *Book of Rites*, see vol. 1, pp. 377-378. — Tr.

[3] See K'ang's Introduction to his *Li-yün Chu* (Commentary on the Evolutions of Rites), contained in the *Pu-jen Tsa-chih*, no. 5 (1913).

embraces the evolutions of the Three Ages, Three Sequences, and
Five Powers (i.e., Elements). Love, righteousness, propriety, wisdom
and good faith operate in (successive) cycles in response to the
seasons. [1] The cycle of love constitutes the Way of Great Unity;
that of propriety constitutes the Way of Small Tranquillity." [2]
Likewise he maintains that the "Great Way" mentioned in the
Evolutions of Rites is that of "the Age of Universal Peace and Great
Unity, when human principles have reached their highest univer-
sality." Also its mention of the "Sages of the Three Dynasties"
(Hsia, Shang, Chou) is a reference to "the Way of Approaching
Peace and Small Tranquillity" (*ibid.*). In this way he seeks to correlate
the "Three Ages," as described in the *Kung-yang Chuan* (those of
Disorder or *luan shih*, Approaching Peace or *sheng p'ing shih*, and
Universal Peace or *t'ai p'ing shih*), with the Small Tranquillity and
Great Unity that are described in the *Evolutions of Rites*. [3] He goes even
further, however, to maintain that in the *Analects* itself these same
"Three Ages" are referred to by implication:

"The course of humanity always progresses according to a fixed
sequence. From the institution of the clan comes that of the tribe,
followed by that of the nation. And from the nation the Great
Unification comes to be formulated. (In the political sphere), from
the individual man the instituting of tribal chieftains gradually
becomes established, from which the relationship between ruler and
subject is gradually defined. The ruler-and-subject relationship
gradually leads to constitutionalism, and constitutionalism gradually
leads to republicanism. (Likewise in the social sphere), from the
individual man the relationship between husband and wife gradually
comes to exist, from which the relationship between father and son

---

[1] According to the New Text school, love is to be correlated with the east
(= spring), righteousness with the west (= autumn), propriety with the south
(= summer), wisdom with the north (= winter), and good faith with the center
(which does not go with any season, but assists them all in their operation). See
chap. 2, pp. 41-42. — Tr.

[2] *Li-yün Chu*, contained in *Pu-jen Tsa-chih*, no. 6 (1913). [The terms Great
Unity (*ta t'ung*) and Small Tranquillity (*hsiao k'ang*) occur in the *Evolutions of Rites*.
See vol. 1, p. 378. — Tr.]

[3] On the passage in the *Kung-yang Chuan* where they are mentioned, see chap.
2, pp. 82-84. In his eagerness to equate the statements in the *Kung-yang Chuan* and
the *Evolutions of Rites*, K'ang disregards the fact that the sequence in the former
work is evolutionary (Disorder, Approaching Peace, Universal Peace), whereas
that in the latter work is devolutionary (Great Unity degenerating into Small
Tranquillity). — Tr.

is gradually defined. This father-and-son relationship leads to the loving of the entire human race, which in turn leads gradually to the Great Unity, in which there is a reversion to individuality. [1]

"Thus there is an evolution from Disorder to Approaching Peace, and from Approaching Peace to Universal Peace. This evolution proceeds gradually in accordance with the changes which influence it. No matter in what country one looks, the process is the same. By observing the child, one can know the adult and old man; by observing the shoot, one can know (the future tree) when it becomes an arm-span (in circumference) and finally reaches to the sky. (In the same way) by observing the modifications and accretions of the three successive eras, Hsia, Shang, and Chou, one can through extension (know) the changes in a hundred generations to come.

"When Confucius prepared the *Spring and Autumn Annals*, he extended it to embrace the Three Ages. During the Age of Disorder he considered his own state (of Lu) as the center, treating the rest of the Chinese hegemony as something outside (his scheme). In the Age of Approaching Peace he considered the Chinese hegemony as the center, while treating the outlying barbarian tribes as something outside (his scheme). And in the Age of Universal Peace he considered everything, far or near, large or small, as if it were one. In doing this he was applying the principles of evolution.

"Confucius himself was born in the Age of Disorder. But at the present time communications extend throughout the great earth, and Europe and America, through their vast changes, are evolving toward the Age of Approaching Peace. There will be a day when everything throughout the earth, large or small, far or near, will be like one. There will no longer be any nations, no racial distinctions, and customs will be everywhere the same. With this uniformity will come (the Age of) Universal Peace. Confucius understood all this beforehand." [2]

K'ang Yu-wei writes these words with reference to the passage in the *Analects* (II, 23) in which Confucius says: "The Yin (i.e., Shang) perpetuated the civilization of the Hsia; its modifications and accretions can be known. The Chou perpetuated the civilization of the Yin, and its modifications and accretions can be known. Whatever others may succeed the Chou, their character, even a

---

[1] As we shall see below (near end of next section), K'ang's Utopia is one in which even the bonds of the family are obliterated. — Tr.

[2] *Lun-yü Chu* (Commentary on the Analects), 2.10.

hundred generations hence, can be known." In this statement, so K'ang believes, lies a veiled reference to the theory of the Three Ages.

In the *Doctrine of the Mean* (p. 324) there is also an ambiguous passage which may be rendered: "The rule of the world passes through three successive phases. (If due attention is paid to this fact), there will be few errors." On which K'ang comments: "*Ch'ung* 重 (successive phase) here means *fu* 復 (recurrence)." He then goes on to say: "The 'three successive phases' refer to the sequence of the Three Ages." [1] Thereafter he continues:

"Confucius' institutions were all founded on actual fact. For example, *tzŭ* was established as the first month (of the year) for the White Sequence, [2] and the color white was exalted, so that the clothes worn at court and the (official) caps were all white. [3] At the present time all the countries of Europe and America follow the same practice. [4] (In another sequence) *ch'ou* was established (as the first month of the year), and this too is the practice in the case of Russia and Islam. [5]

"Likewise according to the regulations for the 'Hall of Light,' this was to have thirty-six windows and seventy-two doors, and its structure was to be built high, steep, round, and large, and to be either an oval or a square, or round above and square below. [6]

---

[1] See his *Chung-yung Chu* (Commentary on the Doctrine of the Mean), p. 36.

[2] *Tzŭ*, the eleventh month, is that with which the year was made to begin during the Chou dynasty. During the Hsia and Shang dynasties the official calendar began with other months. — Tr.

[3] K'ang seems to have made a mistake here, for the White Sequence (in the Three Sequences of the New Text school) was, equated with actual history, the Shang dynasty. But, as we have just seen, *tzŭ* was the month which marked the beginning of the Chou calendar. See chap. 2, p. 61. — Tr.

[4] By this K'ang means to say that the Western New Year Day falls usually within the *tzŭ* (eleventh) month of the Chinese lunar calendar, since the Chinese New Year always occurs sometime between January 21 and February 20 of the Western calendar. — Tr.

[5] *Ch'ou*, the twelfth month, is that with which the year began during the Shang dynasty. By attributing the same practice to Russia, K'ang refers to the fact that the Russian calendar lagged (during the nineteenth century) twelve days behind the Gregorian one, and hence that the Russian New Year then began in what was usually the *ch'ou* month of the Chinese lunar calendar. Why he attributes the same practice to the Islamic world, however, is not clear, inasmuch as the Islamic New Year is not fixed, but in the course of centuries gradually revolves through all twelve months of the solar year. In 1900, when K'ang wrote this work, it fell on May 1. — Tr.

[6] The "Hall of Light" (*ming t'ang* 明堂) was the building in which important religious and ceremonial functions took place during the Chou

And this practice is followed in the case of the large buildings of Europe and America. In the case of clothing, this was to be long and have tails behind, which too is followed in the case of the formal costume of every country of Europe. The division of the day was to come either at midnight, cock's crow, or dawn, whereas in the West the division of the day comes at noon, which is a further extension of these three successive phases. [1] ...

"Men's feelings become blinded by what they themselves are accustomed to. They are so satisfied with the institutions of their own particular government and age that when they see other institutions, they become alarmed and suspicious. This is the cause for much error. If we but understood the meaning of Confucius' three successive phases, might we not avoid this sad and confused view of things?" (*ibid.*, pp. 37-38).

By propounding this theory of the Three Ages, K'ang Yu-wei wished to bring the new knowledge and conditions of his day within the scope of traditional Chinese thought. In other words, he was trying to pour new wine into old bottles. At the same time he obviously hoped to establish a basis for his own political reforms, for he writes further:

"The (spirit of the) regulations of Confucius is that they must be employed according to the proper period. If, in the Age of dark Disorder, before the influences of civilization had spread themselves, one were to practice the institutions of Universal Peace, this would certainly result in great harm. But if, in the Age of Approaching Peace, one were to continue to cling to (the institutions of the Age of) Disorder, this too would result in great harm. The present time, for example, is the Age of Approaching Peace. It is therefore necessary to promulgate the doctrines of self-rule and independence, and the actualities of parliamentary and constitutional rule. For if the laws are not reformed great disorder will result" (*ibid.*, p. 36).

In other words, the Age of Approaching Peace requires the institutions appropriate for that age. K'ang Yu-wei obviously regards his own political reforms as in accord with those that had been outlined by Confucius for this Age.

---

dynasty. This description is derived from the *Ta Tai Li Chi*, chap. 66 (not translated by Wilhelm; it should follow the passage appearing in his chap. 18, p. 212). By "round above and square below," K'ang probably has in mind the Western style dome. — Tr.

[1] According to the New Text school, the Hsia dynasty had its day begin with dawn, the Shang dynasty with cock's crow, and the Chou dynasty with midnight. See chap. 2, p. 65 — Tr.

ii. *Book of the Great Unity*

Though Confucius, according to the New Text school, had propounded the theory of the Three Ages, he had said extremely little about the third of them, that of Universal Peace (*t'ai p'ing* 太平) and the Great Unity (*ta t'ung* 大同). K'ang Yu-wei explains the reason for this silence as follows:

"Confucius developed many institutions for (the Ages of) Disorder and Small Tranquillity, but few for that of Universal Peace and the Great Unity. This is because the process of emerging from Disorder is a complex one which must proceed in accordance with the times. In the age of Confucius the world was still young and immature. It was like a child which in the course of its upbringing cannot be abruptly made into an adult simply by suddenly stripping it of its swaddling clothes. As to the institutions suitable for Disorder, therefore, Confucius had no alternative (but to make them himself). But as to the regulations for Universal Peace and the principles of the Great Unity, though he certainly intended to make them brilliantly evident, he was unable to achieve his purpose because he was not born at the proper time.

"The process of evolution follows an inevitable course which cannot be transgressed. When the proper time arrives, the changes suited to it take place of themselves. That is the reason for the individual differences among the regulations for the Three Ages and the principles for the Three Sequences. It is quite evident that (Confucius') sole intention was to save the (people of each) age. He knew that three thousand years after him another sage would arise, who would proclaim the teachings for the Great Unity. Such a one would surely not transgress the track leading from Approaching Peace to Universal Peace, nor would he consider the track leading from Disorder to Small Tranquillity as wrong." [1]

K'ang Yu-wei here has in mind Confucius' previously quoted statement in the *Analects* (II, 23): "Whatever others may succeed the Chou, their character, even a hundred generations hence, can be known." On which K'ang comments: "Since thirty years make one generation, one hundred generations amount to three thousand (years)" (*ibid.*). Here is the basis for his belief that some three thousand years after Confucius another sage would arise to promulgate the

---

[1] *Commentary on the Doctrine of the Mean*, p. 39.

teachings of the Great Unity. Quite obviously, K'ang regarded this sage as none other but himself, and it was to proclaim these new teachings that he wrote his famous treatise, the *Ta T'ung Shu* or *Book of the Great Unity*.[1] In the introductory chapter of this work he speaks as follows:

"Vast is the primal energy, the creator of Heaven and Earth.[2] Heaven is a single spiritual substance, and man too is a single spiritual substance. Though different in size, they both share the vast energy derived from the Great Origin (*t'ai yüan* 太 元),[3] just as if both were scooping up drops from the great sea. Confucius has said: 'Earth contains the spiritual energy, which (produces) the wind and thunder-clap. By the wind and thunder-clap the (seeds of) forms are carried along, and the multitude of creatures show the appearance of life.'[4] This spiritual thing is electricity, possessed of consciousness. As electric light, it can be transmitted everywhere. As spiritual energy, it can activate everything. It instills supernaturalness in the spirits and gods, and gives existence to Heaven and Earth. In its entirety it is the Origin; divided, it is man. Strange and supernatural is its power to strike. There are no creatures who are devoid of this electricity, this spirit. It is a conscious energy, a supernatural consciousness, an ethereal luminary, a spiritual intelligence, a brilliant virtue. Though these several names differ, the actuality to which they refer is the same. To whoever possesses consciousness it gives the power of attraction, like that of the lodestone, but how much more so in the case of man! The inability to endure (seeing the sufferings of others) is a manifestation of this power of attraction. This is why both love (*jen*) and wisdom are stored (within the mind), where wisdom holds precedence; it is why both love and wisdom are exercised (in external conduct), where love is more noble" (Pt. I, p. 6).

---

[1] First conceived of by K'ang in 1884, but probably not written down in its present form until 1901-02. On the dating of this and other writings by K'ang, which is not always easy to determine, see Ch'ien Mu, "A Critical Study on the Philosophy of K'ang Yu-wei" (article in Chinese), *Ch'ing-hua Hsüeh-pao* (Tsinghua Journal), vol. 11 (1936), pp. 583-658, esp. 644 ff. — Tr.

[2] This is an allusion to the "vast force" or energy of Mencius, on which see vol. 1, p. 131. — Tr.

[3] *Yüan* or Origin also appears in Tung Chung-shu's philosophy as a metaphysical concept. See chap. 2, sect. 4. — Tr.

[4] See *Book of Rites*, chap. 26 (XXVIII, 282), where this apocryphal statement is attributed to Confucius. — Tr.

This is essentially a restatement of the dictum, first enunciated by Ch'eng Hao and echoed in almost the same words by Wang Shou-jen, that "the man of love (*jen*) takes Heaven, Earth, and all things as one with himself." [1] It is supplemented, however, with new ideas drawn by K'ang from what he has heard of Western physics. Such eclectic borrowing from past and present was inevitable in the age in which he lived. Basically, however, his idea is that all men possess a mind which cannot bear to see the suffering of others, and that it is the existence of this mind that makes the teachings of the Great Unity possible.

Since man possesses consciousness, he is therefore subject both to pleasure and pain. K'ang writes:

"The consciousness possessed by living creatures derives from the fact that their brains have intelligence. The contacts (of the brain) with (external) objects, being sometimes favorable, sometimes unfavorable, result in what seem to it either appropriate or inappropriate, suitable or unsuitable. What is suitable and appropriate to the brain is then taken by the soul to be pleasure, while what is unsuitable and inappropriate is taken to be pain. In man, above all, the brain is especially intelligent, and the soul especially pure and clear. Hence the favorable and unfavorable reactions of the body to (external) things are in his case especially complex, subtle, and rapid, so that what is suitable or unsuitable is perceived with particular clarity. The suitable and appropriate is accepted; the unsuitable and inappropriate rejected. Therefore the life of man consists only of what is appropriate or inappropriate. What it finds inappropriate constitutes pain; what it finds appropriate and yet again appropriate, constitutes pleasure. Therefore the course taken by human life depends upon the way in which the individual (reacts to things), and is one consisting of nothing but either pain or pleasure. Therefore any planning made for humanity should seek only to get rid of pain in order thereby to gain pleasure. There is no other course" (*ibid.*, p. 9). Again:

"Therefore the path taken by all living creatures in the world is solely one of seeking pleasure and avoiding pain. There is no other course. Even persons who take a roundabout way, borrow another road, zig-zag in their course, or (choose to) endure pain without complaint, do so only with the idea of gaining (ultimate)

---

[1] See chap. 12, p. 521, and chap. 14, p. 599. — Tr.

pleasure. Despite the differences in nature of individual men, we can unhesitatingly assert that the way of mankind never consists in the search for pain and rejection of pleasure. The goodness of all goodness is reached when institutions are established, and religion promulgated, such as will cause men to enjoy (only) pleasure and no pain. Incomplete goodness is reached when they cause men to have much pleasure and little pain. The negation of goodness is reached when they cause men to have much pain and little pleasure" (*ibid.*, p. 11).

Acceptance of this standard means that the institutions and religion of "the Way of the Great Unity and Universal Peace" must necessarily be those enabling mankind to reach the highest state of felicity. K'ang continues:

"Even if we look everywhere at the institutions of the world, we shall find no means for saving living men from their sufferings, or for seeking their great pleasure, other than through the Way of the Great Unity. This Way of the Great Unity is the acme of fairness, justice, love, and good government. Even the best of all other ways cannot supersede it" (*ibid.*, p. 13).

Because Confucius, "the divinely intelligent sage-king," realized this fact, he "established institutions for the Three Sequences and Three Ages, with which to change Disorder into Approaching Peace, and then into Universal Peace, and with which to advance from the Small Tranquillity to the Great Unity" (*ibid.*).

"The sufferings of human life," K'ang maintains, "are so numerous as to be unimaginable." Nevertheless, "if we make a rough enumeration of the major ones which are more readily apparent," we find the following:

"The sufferings associated with man's (physical) life are seven: (1) being implanted in the womb, (2) suffering premature death, (3) suffering loss of a limb, (4) being a barbarian, (5) living outside (China), (6) being a slave, (7) being a woman.

"The sufferings associated with natural disasters are eight: (1) famine resulting from flood or drought, (2) epidemic, (3) conflagration, (4) flood, (5) volcanic eruptions, (6) collapse of buildings, (7) shipwreck, (8) locust plagues.

"The sufferings associated with the human relationships are five: (1) to be a widower or widow, (2) to be orphaned or childless, (3) to be ill and have no one to provide medical care, (4) to suffer poverty, (5) to have a low and mean station in life.

"The sufferings associated with human institutions are seven: (1) corporal punishment and imprisonment, (2) unjust taxation, (3) military conscription, (4) social stratifications, (5) oppressive institutions, (6) the existence of the state, (7) the existence of the family.

"The human feelings which cause suffering are six: (1) brutish stupidity, (2) hatred, (3) fatigue, (4) lust, (5) attachment (to things), (6) desire.

"The things which cause suffering because of the esteem in which they are held by men are five: (1) wealth, (2) eminent position, (3) longevity, (4) being a ruler, (5) being a god, sage, immortal, or Buddha"[1] (*ibid.*, pp. 13-17).

The elimination of these sufferings requires a knowledge of how they originate. In his sixth chapter K'ang writes:

"All these many things are the sufferings of mankind alone, without speaking of those endured by the feathered, furred, and scaly animals. Yet if we make an over-all survey of the sorrows of life, we find that in general they all spring from the nine kinds of sphere (*chiu chieh* 九 界). What are these nine spheres? The first is that of the nation: the political divisions between lands and peoples. The second is that of class: the distinction between those who are noble or humble, illustrious or insignificant. The third is that of race: the division between the yellows, whites, browns, and blacks. The fourth is that of physical distinction: the division between male and female. The fifth is that of the family: the distinctive relationships between father, son, husband, and wife. The sixth is that of occupation: the division between farmers, laborers, and merchants. The seventh is that of political disorder: the existence of institutions that are unequal, non-universal, non-uniform, and unjust. The eighth is that of species: the demarcation between men, birds, beasts, insects, and fish. The ninth is that of suffering itself: the fact that this suffering begets further suffering, and is thus transmitted endlessly in a way beyond all imagining" (*ibid.*, pp. 82-83).

Since all suffering originates in one or another of these nine spheres, its elimination can be achieved only through the elimination of these spheres. K'ang continues:

"How are these sufferings to be remedied? The knowledge of the disease is itself the cure. Let us eliminate the spheres and cast

---

[1] To illustrate this fifth point, K'ang (in Pt. I, chap. 6, near end) cites the sufferings of Confucius, Jesus, Socrates, the Buddha, and Mohammed. — Tr.

off their bondage. [1] Let us soar aloft until we touch Heaven itself and penetrate its innermost recesses. While remaining majestically free in spirit, let us reach afar to the highest happiness, to the realm of Universal Peace and the Great Unity, where we shall enjoy long life and eternal enlightenment. My method of curing our sufferings consists only of eliminating the nine spheres.

"First, let us eliminate the national sphere and unify the great world. Second, let us eliminate the class sphere and bring equality to all men. Third, let us eliminate the racial sphere and amalgamate the different races of mankind. Fourth, let us eliminate the sphere of physical division and maintain independence (for women as well as for men). Fifth, let us eliminate the sphere of the family and become 'citizens of Heaven.' [2] Sixth, let us eliminate the occupational sphere and foster means of livelihood common to all. Seventh, let us eliminate the sphere of political disorder and institute a government of Universal Peace. Eighth, let us eliminate the sphere of species and extend our love to all sentient beings. Ninth, let us eliminate the sphere of suffering and push on to the highest happiness" [3] (ibid., pp. 83-84).

Thus will mankind achieve the Age of Universal Peace and realm of highest happiness. Sublime though this realm may be, however, it is still limited by human institutions, whereas above it lies yet another limitless realm of Heaven itself. Concerning this, K'ang writes as follows in his *Chung-yung Chu* or *Commentary on the Doctrine of the Mean*:

"What Tzŭ-ssŭ [4] means to say is that the teachings perpetuated in the Six Classics, and the regulations established for the three successive phases (the Three Ages), are all connected with the insignificant and temporary regulations established through human authority, so that they do not represent the (highest) concept of Confucius' divine intelligence. For above (these human institutions)

---

[1] Here, as well as three times below, the word "eliminate" has been left blank in the edition of the *Book of the Great Unity* cited by Professor Fung. The same is true of the words "maintain independence" under the fourth sphere in the following paragraph. The blanks have been filled in from the readings given in the Chung Hua Book Co. edition of 1935. — Tr.

[2] A phrase from the *Mencius*, VIIa, 19. — Tr.

[3] The terminology used here is Buddhist. Thus "sentient beings" and "suffering" are both Buddhist terms, as is "highest happiness" (*chi lo* 極 樂, Sanskrit *Sukhāvatī*), which is a designation for the Western Paradise of Buddhism. See also next page, note 1. — Tr.

[4] Grandson of Confucius and reputed author of the *Doctrine of the Mean*. — Tr.

there still exists Heaven, [1] the origin of all origins, timeless, spaceless, without color, without smell, without sound, without substance. And there is a separate realm created by Heaven, unimaginable in thought and indescribable in words. Here roam the divine sages, whose desire it is to give to all living creatures the possibility to be, like them, transformed in the Heaven of Heavens. This is (the aim of) the highest Way of Confucius. This unspeakable and unimaginable realm, the creation of Heaven, is surely what was hinted at in the esoteric words heard by Tzŭ-ssŭ, and esoterically expressed by him at the end of his treatise, in order to convey its boundless mystery" (p. 46).

This passage has reference to the closing sentence in the *Doctrine of the Mean* (p. 329), itself a quotation from the *Book of Odes* (III, i, Ode 1, 7), in which we read: "The operations of high Heaven proceed without sound, without smell." This, for K'ang, is an allusion to that "realm created by Heaven" of which he speaks—a lofty realm transcending all human institutions.

Translator's Note: The above gives only a bare indication of the rich content of K'ang Yu-wei's *Book of the Great Unity*, the remaining nine parts of which describe in detail how the nine spheres of suffering will be eliminated and what the world will then be like. The whole work is remarkable as a mixture of Chinese and Western Utopian thinking. It combines idealism, radicalism, and keen prophetic insight, with a curiously naive confidence in technological progress as the key to human happiness, which in this respect makes it quite un-Chinese and typical of Western nineteenth century optimism.

The future world state, K'ang believes, will emerge within two or three centuries as the final result of a gradual process of political amalgamation, stimulated both by wars and by disarmament conferences. With the final achievement of unity, the very word "nation" will be deleted from the vocabulary, and the entire habitable globe will be divided into 3,000 administrative squares, each bounded by degrees of latitude and longitude. The world commonwealth will have a universal language, calendar, and system of weights and measures, and will be governed by a people's world assembly, elected through universal suffrage. Migration and intermarriage will gradually merge the existing races into a single uniform world race, and class distinctions will likewise disappear. Women will enjoy the same rights, perform the same tasks, and wear the same clothes as men. Marriage

---

[1] Here again K'ang uses a Buddhist term, *chu t'ien* 諸 天 , lit. "all the heavens," which is both a designation for the many heavens of Buddhism and for the deities (Sanskrit *devas*) pertaining to these heavens. For the sake of simplicity and consistency with the following sentences, where K'ang reverts to the ordinary non-Buddhist word *t'ien*, I here render *chu t'ien* in the singular as "Heaven." — Tr.

contracts will be valid for one year only, renewable after that time according to the wishes of the partners. The family will vanish, its functions being performed by state-operated nurseries, schools, hospitals, old-age homes, and similar institutions. There will be no private ownership of agricultural, industrial or commercial enterprise, all of which will be communized. (K'ang's phrase here, *kung ch'an* 共產 or "common production," is the same as that which today appears in the Chinese word for Communism.)

Machinery will be abundant in the new society. People will live in huge air-conditioned public apartments. They will eat in common dining halls seating thousands of persons. Great airships will transport them rapidly to all parts of the globe, being propelled either by electricity or by power produced through "the refining of some new substance" (*lien hsin chih* 錬新質; this seems like a prophetic allusion either to gasoline or to something like atomic energy).

The weightiest authority in the Age of Universal Peace will lie not with the officials but the doctors. This is because, with the elimination of the causes of human strife, the most important task will be the maintenance of high standards of hygiene. All persons will undergo daily medical examination, and in this way their life-spans will gradually be extended to several centuries or even a thousand years. Those having incurable illness, however, will be released from suffering by mercy killings (electrocutions). As part of his program for eliminating the eighth sphere of suffering, that of differences between species, K'ang proposes vegetarianism, but also asserts that synthetic foods will be developed. All animal life will be preserved as much as possible, though it will be necessary to confine dangerous animals to zoos, and to use chemicals to check the spread of harmful insects.

Inasmuch as love will be taken for granted in the Great Unity, religions like Christianity and Islam will no longer be needed, and hence will gradually wither away. More remarkable for a Confucianist like K'ang Yu-wei is his statement that Confucianism itself will by then have completed its historic mission, so that men's minds will turn to the (Taoist) arts of the immortals and to Buddhism. "After the Great Unity," he concludes his book by saying, "there will first come the study of the immortals and then that of Buddhism. Lesser wisdom will devote itself to the immortals, and higher wisdom to Buddhism. The study of Buddhism, however, will itself be followed by that of 'roaming in Heaven.'"

3—T'AN SSŬ-T'UNG

Another participant in the religious and reform movement at the end of the Ch'ing dynasty, and one whose thought deserves individual consideration, is T'an Ssŭ-t'ung 譚嗣同 (1865-98). [1] He, like K'ang, was a leading spirit in the "Hundred Days of Reform"

---

[1] Styled Fu-sheng 復生. He was a native of Liu-yang 瀏陽, almost due east of Changsha in Hunan.

of the summer of 1898, but, unlike the latter, disdained flight when
that movement collapsed. As a result, he became one of the "six
martyrs" who were executed at the orders of the Manchu Empress
Dowager on September 28 of that year. [1] Although less of a classical
scholar than K'ang, T'an shows himself more precise as a thinker.
His major philosophical work is the *Jen Hsüeh* or *Science of Love*
(written in 1896-98), in which he expounds his concept of the Great
Unity. In this he writes:

"All who would make a study of love should, among Buddhist
works, become conversant with the writings of the Hua-yen, Mind
(i.e., Ch'an), and the Idealistic (i.e., Mere Ideation) schools. Among
Western works they should become conversant with the *New
Testament*, as well as with the various writings on mathematics,
science, and the social sciences. Among Chinese works they should
become conversant with the *Changes*, the *Spring and Autumn Annals*,
Kung-yang Commentary, *Analects*, *Book of Rites*, *Mencius*, *Chuang-tzŭ*,
Mo-tzŭ, and *Shih Chi* (Historical Records), as well as with the
writings of T'ao Yüan-ming, [2] Chou Mao-shu (Chou Tun-yi), Chang
Heng-ch'ü (Chang Tsai), Lu Tzŭ-ching (Lu Chiu-yüan), Wang Yang-
ming (Wang Shou-jen), Wang Ch'uan-shan (Wang Fu-chih), and
Huang Li-chou (Huang Tsung-hsi)." [3]

This passage well illustrates the eclecticism with which T'an
Ssŭ-t'ung drew upon many disparate elements. Though the results
were not always consistent, he remains an eminent representative
of the thought of his age.

i. *Love and the "Ether"*

In his exposition of love (*jen*), T'an, like K'ang, adopts the
dictum of Ch'eng Hao and Wang Shou-jen that "the man of love
takes Heaven, Earth, and all things as one with himself." Also like

---

[1] For further details, see Hummel, *Eminent Chinese of the Ch'ing Period*,
vol. 2, pp. 702-705. Though the son of a conservative father, T'an early showed
the independence of thinking which caused him to gravitate into the reform
movement. During his short lifetime he traveled widely both in China proper
and in Chinese Turkistan. His readings included, in addition to those customary
for a Confucian scholar, books on Western science (read in Chinese translation),
and on Buddhism. He was active in the reform movement of his native Hunan
before being summoned to Peking by the Emperor in 1898. — Tr.

[2] A poet (372-427) noted for his Taoist inclinations. — Tr.

[3] *Jen Hsüeh* (to which all further citations in the present section refer, unless
otherwise noted), p. 2.

K'ang, however, he bolsters this basic thesis with ideas drawn from Western science. For example, he writes:

"Throughout the realms of physical phenomena, empty space, and sentient beings, [1] there is something supremely great and supremely subtle, which adheres everywhere, penetrates everywhere, and connects everything, so that all is permeated by it. The eye cannot see its color, the ear cannot hear its sound, nor can the mouth and nose taste or smell its flavor and fragrance. It has no name, but we call it the 'ether.' [2] As made manifest in action, Confucius variously referred to it as love (*jen*), as the 'power of originating growth,' [3] or as the nature (*hsing*). Mo Tzŭ referred to it as universal love (*chien ai*). The Buddha referred to it as the Buddha-nature, [4] and as compassion and mercy (*tzŭ pei* 慈悲). Jesus referred to it as spirit (*ling hun* 靈魂), and as loving others as oneself and regarding one's enemies as if they were friends. The scientists refer to it as the power of love and attraction. It is all these different things, and through it the realm of physical phenomena comes to be, that of empty space is established, and that of sentient beings issues forth" (p. 3).

This "ether" is the "element of elements," [5] and that whereby it is possible for an individual to be an individual, an organization an organization, and for one thing to communicate with another. T'an continues:

"The ether functions in its most spiritual and subtle aspect when it constitutes the brain in the human body.... It is the electricity in the atmosphere, but this electricity is not confined to the atmos-

---

[1] These are Buddhist terms: respectively *dharma-dhātu*, *ākāśa-dhātu*, and *sattva-dhātu*. For Buddhist influence on K'ang Yu-wei, see preceding section, final paragraph, and pp. 689-690, notes 3 and 1 respectively. — Tr.

[2] *Yi-t'ai* 以太, a Chinese phonetic transcription of the Western term. It is thus quite distinct from the Ether or *ch'i* of the Neo-Confucians, and will therefore be left uncapitalized. This and the preceding sentence are reminiscent of the description of the *Tao* given in the *Lao-tzŭ*, chap. 25, as quoted in vol. 1, p. 177. — Tr.

[3] *Yüan*, the first of the four attributes of the first hexagram in the *Book of Changes*, p. 57. — Tr.

[4] *Hsing-hai* 性海, lit., "sea of the nature," a figure of speech used in Buddhism to designate the reality which underlies all things. — Tr.

[5] *Yüan-chih chih yüan-chih* 原質之原質. See below, p. 695.

phere, for there is no object which it does not permeate. The brain is one of the places in which electricity assumes shape and substance. Since the brain is electricity which has shape and substance, it follows that electricity must be brain which lacks shape and substance. Just as men realize that it is the power of the brain that unites the five senses and the various bones (of the body) into a single organism, so should they realize that it is the power of electricity that unites Heaven, Earth, the myriad creatures, the self, and other men, into a single organism" (*ibid.*).

What Confucius called *jen* or love is nothing other than the functioning of the ether. T'an elaborates this point by saying:

"The presence or absence of love depends upon the degree to which it is pervasive or obstructed, for these qualities basically determine whether one is loving or not. When pervasive, it is like the wires of electricity which, stretching in all directions, no matter how far, thus bind together different regions as if they were a single body. This is why the *Changes* (p. 57), after first speaking of 'originating growth' (*yüan*), then goes on to speak of 'prosperous development' (*heng*). This 'originating growth' is love, while 'prosperous development' is its quality of pervasiveness. There being love, there must be pervasiveness. Likewise, only through pervasiveness can the strength of love be completely developed. Hence (the man of love) goes further and, through what represents 'advantageous gain' (*li*) for himself, gives 'advantageous gain' to others. In this way he establishes permanent stability through 'correct firmness' (*cheng*)" (p. 4).

Here we find T'an expressing an idea somewhat akin to that of Ch'eng Hao when he wrote: "In medical writings, paralysis of the hand or foot is described as 'non-love.' This is a very good statement of the condition." [1] At the same time T'an uses his theory of the functioning of the ether to interpret the opening statement in the *Book of Changes* (p. 57), which says of *ch'ien*, the first of the hexagrams: "*Ch'ien* represents originating growth (*yüan*), prosperous development (*heng*), advantageous gain (*li*), and correct firmness (*cheng*)."

ii. *Being and Non-being, Production and Destruction*

T'an Ssŭ-t'ung further maintains that all things are simply

---

[1] See chap. 12, p. 520.

the result of the combination of various chemical elements, and that therefore no individual thing possesses an enduring entity or nature of its own. Thus he writes:

"Do the differences in the natures of various animals and plants mean that these natures are innate, or do they derive from the fact that the arrangements and proportions of their physical constituents differ, one from another? Their physical constituents ate limited to seventy-three different elements. Hence the combination of one element with another results in the formation of a certain thing's nature, while their splitting apart and chemical recombination with other elements, either through the addition or subtraction of a certain element, results in the formation of another thing's nature. Even when the number of elements in chemical combination is the same, a minor change in their relative amount or dominancy results in the separate formation of the nature of yet another thing. The various transformations resulting in this way are too numerous to be recorded . . . . However, as to the elements themselves, they remain always as they are in the beginning, without undergoing either increment or diminution" (p. 10).

The original substance of which these elements are composed is the ether. T'an writes:

"Yet though there are seventy-three different elements, the 'element of elements' is nothing else but the single ether. Being single, it is neither produced (from something else) nor destroyed. Since it is not produced, one cannot say that it (sometimes) 'exists,' and since it is not destroyed, one cannot say that it (sometimes) does 'not exist' " [1] (*ibid.*).

From this statement it would appear that the ether, besides having the qualities attributed to it previously, is, to use Aristotle's terminology, the material cause of all things. As to its indestructibility, T'an writes:

"Is there evidence to show that it is neither produced nor destroyed? The reply is that as far as the eye can see, everything constitutes such evidence. Thus the principles of chemistry discussed above, if studied to the fullest extent, consist simply of the fact that the various elements may either be split apart from one another,

---

[1] I.e., the ether of which all things are made is eternal, regardless of the phases of "being" or "non-being" through which the individual things themselves may pass. — Tr.

or combined with one another. By utilizing what is already and necessarily so, there results, according to the favorable or unfavorable timing (of this operation), as well as according to the varying proportions of the compound, what is then called such-and-such a thing or such-and-such another thing. That is all there is to it. But how can any one element be itself ever ground away to nothing, or any one element manufactured?" (*ibid.*).

Since the ether *per se* can neither be produced nor destroyed, and its constituent elements can neither be added to nor subtracted from, it follows that the universe as a whole, though undergoing changing phases of existence, can never be said to come to an end. T'an continues:

"(So-called) 'being' or 'non-being' result from condensation and dispersion, but do not mean production or destruction.... Wang Ch'uan-shan, when he speaks of the *Changes*, says that each of its hexagrams consists of twelve lines, half invisible and the other half visible. Hence the great *Changes* does not speak of (alternating) being and non-being, but only of (alternating) invisibility and visibility" [1] (p. 11).

This is identical with Chang Tsai's statement that "when the Ether (*ch'i*) condenses, its visibility becomes apparent so that there are then the shapes (of individual things). But when it does not condense, the visibility is no longer apparent so that there are then no shapes." [2] Here T'an would seem to have borrowed Chang Tsai's concept, while illustrating it with ideas derived from Western chemistry.

Although the ether itself is neither produced nor destroyed, there is in it what T'an calls the "minute process of production and destruction." By this he means that though the ether as a whole never changes, the individual objects of which it consists are ever in a state of flux, and therefore, as separate entities, constantly do undergo production and destruction. T'an writes:

"If we look at the past, the process of production and destruction has never had a beginning. If we look at the future, the process will never come to an end. And if we look at the present, it is constantly going on.... Chuang Tzŭ has said: 'A boat may be hidden in a creek, ... where it may be said to be safe enough. But at midnight

---

[1] See Wang Fu-chih, *Chou-yi Nei-chuan* (Inner Commentary on the Chou Changes), 5a.5. — Tr.

[2] See chap. 12, p. 481.

a strong man may come and carry it away on his back.' [1] I would add that when he does this he will also carry the creek itself away on his back. Again it is said: 'Even the swan, after it has been soaring at a height of ten thousand cubits, comes down again to look for the marsh.' [2] I would add that it is the marsh, too, that has been soaring .... Once when Confucius was standing by a stream he observed: 'All is transient, like this! Unceasing day and night!' [3] The (change of) day and night is the principle of that stream, and the stream is the physical shape of the (change of) day and night ....

"There is neither singleness nor duality, neither interruption nor continuity. The cycle of production is followed by that of destruction; as soon as there is this destruction, it gives way to production. The alternations between production and destruction become minute and still more minute, until they can be made no further minute; they become hidden and still more hidden, until they can be made no further hidden. In this way they merge into a oneness in which there is neither production nor destruction. But though there is this state, that which causes the minute process of production and destruction certainly cannot be easily concealed" (pp. 14-15).

The fact that all things are thus ever fluctuating between production and destruction means that they are being ever renewed. T'an continues:

"Observing the other aspect of movement, we may call it that of daily renewal. Confucius has said: '*Ko* casts off the old; *ting* takes on the new.' [4] And again: 'The process of daily renewal is what is meant by the abundance of virtue.' [5] The height of goodness is marked by this process of daily renewal; the height of evil is marked by its absence .... All people admit that renewal is the fitting accompaniment of virtue. Why, then, is it only when we come to the present age that people cling to the old worthless ways of life,

---

[1] *Chuang-tzŭ*, chap. 6, p. 75. — Tr.

[2] This passage does not occur in the *Chuang-tzŭ*, but almost the identical wording appears in an essay by the poet Ssŭ-ma Hsiang-ju (mentioned below in sect. 4, iv). See his biography in the *Shih Chi*, 117.32-33, and in the *Ch'ien Han Shu*, 57b.8. — Tr.

[3] *Analects*, IX, 16. — Tr.

[4] *Book of Changes* (Appen. VII, p. 443). *Ko* and *ting* are hexagrams nos. 49 and 50. — Tr.

[5] *Ibid.* (Appen. III, p. 356). Neither of these statements, of course, was actually made by Confucius. — Tr.

and obstinately say that there is no need for changing the institutions?" (p. 18).

Here we find T'an's philosophical justification for the political reform movement of his own day.

iii. *Government in the Great Unity*

As an advocate of the idea that "the man of love takes Heaven, Earth, and all things as one with himself," T'an Ssŭ-t'ung takes upon himself the task of expounding K'ang Yu-wei's "religion of the Great Unity." Thus he writes:

"Global government is that in which only the world exists but no nations. Chuang Tzŭ has said: 'I have heard of letting the world alone, but not of governing the world (with success).'[1] 'Governing' implies the existence of nations; 'letting alone' implies their non-existence. When he speaks of 'letting alone,' he probably derives its idea through phonetic change from that of 'freedom.'[2] In order that every man enjoy freedom, it is necessary that they be citizens without a country. As soon as countries no longer exist, then national boundaries melt away, wars cease, envy is cut short, power plotting is dissipated, the distinction between others and the self is obliterated, and equality is manifested, so that although there still exists the world, it is as if there were no world at all. With the wiping out of the distinction between ruler and subject, there is a leveling of status between those who are noble and those who are mean. With the manifestation of the principle of equitableness, poverty and wealth are equalized. Within a thousand or a myriad miles it is as if there were but a single family or single individual. Everyone looks upon his own home as if it were a public hostel, and upon another individual as if he were his own brother. There is no longer need for a father to display parental tenderness,[3] nor for a son to display filial piety. Brothers forget their (special) friendship and respect for one another, and husbands and wives forget their respective positions

---

[1] *Chuang-tzŭ*, chap. 11, p. 119. — Tr.

[2] *Tsai yu* 在宥 (letting alone) sounds a little like *tzŭ yu* 自由 (freedom). T'an means to say that the idea of "letting alone" was suggested to Chuang Tzŭ by its phonetic similarity to the term for "freedom." This theory, of course, is devoid of scientific foundation. — Tr.

[3] Since everyone, both within and without the family, is treated with equal affection. — Tr.

of leadership and subordination. It is like the Millennium spoken of in Western books, or the Great Unity found in the *Evolutions of Rites*" (p. 49).

This Utopia, T'an further maintains, is alluded to in the *Book of Changes* and *Spring and Autumn Annals*:

"What I say about the (coming) changes in the world is not what I myself say, but what is said in the *Changes*. The *Changes* embraces within itself all the principles within the world. Therefore it is of the utmost profundity and may not be despised. I have heard X X speak about the *ch'ien* hexagram, and the way in which it harmonizes with the Three Ages of the *Spring and Autumn Annals*. [1] The *Changes* embraces the Three Powers and doubles them. [2] Therefore in it there is a doubling of the Three Ages. The inner trigram is that in which (the Three Ages) follow a contrary sequence, while the outer trigram is that in which they follow a normal sequence. [3]

[1] The name of the expositor is left blank in the text. Perhaps T'an is here referring to K'ang Yu-wei? *Ch'ien* is the first hexagram in the *Book of Changes*. — Tr.

[2] The Three Powers are Heaven, Earth, and man. This is an allusion to the statement in the *Book of Changes* (Appen. III, p. 402): "The *Changes* is a book of wide comprehension and great scope, embracing everything. There are in it the Way of Heaven, Way of man, and Way of Earth. It takes (the lines representing) these Three Powers, and doubles them (till they amount to six). What these six lines show is simply this: the Way of the Three Powers." This passage is an attempt to explain how the sixty-four hexagrams originated through a doubling of each of the eight primary trigrams. — Tr.

[3] Here and below T'an is speaking with exclusive reference to the first hexagram, *ch'ien*, made up of six undivided lines. The lower three of these are its "inner trigram"; the upper three its "outer trigram." As will be seen from what T'an says below, each of these six lines (running in the usual sequence from bottom to top) supposedly symbolizes one of the Three Ages, as follows:

	Lines	Sequence of Three Ages	Absolute Time Sequence
Outer Trigram	6	Age of Universal Peace	Distant future
	5	,, ,, Approaching Peace	Near future
	4	,, ,, Disorder	Confucius until today
Inner Trigram	3	,, ,, Disorder	Hsia dynasty until Confucius
	2	,, ,, Approaching Peace	Three Sovereigns and Five Emperors
	1	,, ,, Universal Peace	Prehistoric

From this schematized presentation it will be seen that, according to T'an, world history consists of two main phases: (1) a gradual deterioration from a prehistoric Age of Universal Peace down to the Age of Disorder of Confucius' day; (2) a gradual regeneration from Confucius' day, destined at some future date to culminate in a recurrence of the Age of Universal Peace. These contrary

" 'In the first (or lowest) line, undivided, (we see its subject as) the dragon lying hid (in the deep). It is not the time for active doing.' [1] This is the Age of Universal Peace and of the Primal Sequence (*Yüan T'ung* 元 統). There were then no religious leaders nor political rulers. It was, in time, that of the undifferentiated primitivity of greatest antiquity, when the people were simple and unsophisticated, and simply acknowledged one among them as their leader. (In the life of) an individual it would (correspond to) the time just after birth. (The phrase), 'It is not the time for active doing,' means that at that time nothing needed to be done.

" 'In the second line, undivided, (we see its subject as) the dragon appearing in the field. It will be advantageous to meet with the great man.' This is the Age of Approaching Peace and the Sequence of Heaven (*T'ien T'ung* 天 統). During this time there gradually came to be religious leaders and political rulers, but they were still not far removed from their people. That is why (the text) speaks of (the dragon) as 'appearing in the field.' [2] It was, in time, that of the Three Sovereigns and Five Emperors, [3] and for an individual would be that of infancy.

" 'In the third line, undivided, (we see its subject as) the superior man active and vigilant all the day, and in the evening still careful and apprehensive. (The position is) dangerous, but there will be no mistake.' This is the Age of Disorder and the Sequence of Rulers (*Chün T'ung* 君 統). At this time political rulers began to make an evil display of themselves, and so religious leaders had no alter-

cycles are what T'an means when he says that in the inner trigram the Three Ages go in counter sequence, whereas in the outer trigram they follow the normal sequence.

Incidentally, the whole theory of the Three Ages, and especially T'an's version of it, is interesting because, by promising a future golden age, it runs counter to the more prevalent Chinese concept of history as a process of steady deterioration from a golden age of antiquity. In his readiness to accept the new viewpoint, T'an may conceivably have been influenced to some extent by what he read about the theory of evolution in Western scientific literature, as well as about a coming millennium in Western theological literature. — Tr.

[1] This and the five quotations following are the expositions in the *Book of Changes* (pp. 57-58) of the six lines of the *ch'ien* hexagram. — Tr.

[2] Where, in an agrarian civilization like China's, most of the common people do their work. The dragon here symbolizes the leader, whether religious or political. — Tr.

[3] Variously identified in various texts. They antedate the first Chinese dynasty, the Hsia. — Tr.

native but to push themselves forward in order to restore the equilibrium. Therefore the expressions of sorrow and anxiety were numerous. It was, in time, that of the Three Dynasties (Hsia, Shang, Chou), and for an individual would be that when he comes of age. The above are the Three Ages of the 'inner trigram' running in reverse sequence.

" 'In the fourth line, undivided, (we see its subject as the dragon looking) as if he were exercising himself in the depths. There will be no mistake.' This is the Age of Disorder and the Sequence of Rulers, which lies neither in Heaven above nor the field below. [1] The phrase 'as if' is indicative of attempted action. For it is Confucius who 'knew he could not succeed, yet kept on trying to do so.' [2] It was, in time, the entire period from Confucius to the present day, and for an individual would be that of adulthood onward.

" 'In the fifth line, undivided, (we see its subject as) the dragon on the wing in the sky. It will be advantageous to meet with the great man.' This is the Age of Approaching Peace and the Sequence of Heaven, when all the many religious teachings throughout the globe will become unified by a single religious leader, and all the many nations throughout the world will become unified by a single political ruler. It is, in time, that of the single great unification, and for an individual would be that in which he 'understands the Will of Heaven.' [3]

" 'In the sixth (or topmost) line, undivided, (we see its subject as) the dragon exceeding the proper limits. There will be occasion for repentance.' This is the Age of Universal Peace and of the Primal Sequence, in which the entire globe is already under a single religious leader and a single political ruler. Being single, they are alone; being alone, they exceed the proper limits; exceeding the proper limits, there comes occasion for repentance. Because of this repentance, each and every individual becomes capable of acquiring the virtue of the religious leader, with the result that this leader himself is no longer needed; each and every individual becomes capable of

---

[1] An allusion to the Heaven (or sky) mentioned below in the fifth line, and to the field already mentioned in the second. This age, in other words, was one which failed to make contact either with the divine forces above or the everyday life of the people below. — Tr.

[2] *Analects*, XIV, 41. I.e., it is Confucius to whom the comment on the fourth line of the hexagram *ch'ien* refers. — Tr.

[3] I.e., in which he has passed the age of fifty. Confucius, as quoted in the *Analects* (II, 4), said: "At fifty I understood the Will of Heaven." — Tr.

acquiring the power of the political ruler, with the result that this ruler himself is no longer needed. It will be, in time, that when throughout the world the people themselves will rule, and for an individual would be that in which, through the maturing of his work of cultivation, it would be possible for him to say that he could 'follow the desires of the heart without transgressing the right.' [1] The above are the Three Ages of the 'outer trigram' running in normal sequence.

"Yet at that time there will still be some remaining traces (of what has gone before). So let us turn to (the following statements): 'As to the use of the undivided lines (in this hexagram), if the host of dragons who are thereby indicated were to divest themselves of a head (a leader), there would be good fortune.' 'Heaven's virtue cannot serve as the head.' Or again: 'Then the world is well governed.' [2] These refer to (a time following that of the Three Ages), in which all sentient beings will have attained Buddhahood. Not only will there then be no religious leader, but not even a religion itself. Not only will there be no political ruler, but even the people themselves will no longer rule. Not only will there be a single unified globe, but even that globe itself will no longer exist. Only when this stage has been reached will there be perfection and completion, with nothing more to be added" (p. 51).

The anonymous exponent of the *Book of Changes* mentioned at the beginning of this passage (p. 699, note 1) may well be K'ang Yu-wei himself. In any case, it seems undeniable that the highest realm here described, in which the "host of dragons (meaning human leaders) divest themselves of a head," can refer to none other than that "unspeakable and unimaginable" realm of which K'ang spoke, wherein "roam the divine sages."

iv. *Regarding Religious Leaders*

T'an Ssŭ-t'ung poses for himself an objection from an imaginary critic: "The ideas propounded by you, sir, are lofty indeed. But suppose they cannot be carried out and are just a flow of empty words. Then what is their good?" To which T'an replies:

---

[1] This was what Confucius was finally able to say of himself at the age of seventy. See *Analects*, II, 4. — Tr.

[2] All comments on the hexagram *ch'ien*, the first occurring in the main text of the *Changes*, p. 58, the second in Appen. II, p. 267, and the third in Appen. IV, p. 413. — Tr.

"I value knowledge rather than action, because knowledge is something of the spirit, whereas action is only of the body. Confucius has said: 'When you know a thing to know that you know it, and when you do not know it, to recognize that you do not know it: this is knowledge.' [1] Thus to know something is knowledge, but not to know it is also knowledge. This means that though action may have limits, knowledge has no such limits, and though action may be exhaustible, knowledge is inexhaustible . . . . Religion is the means of seeking for knowledge. Hence the work of all religious leaders and their followers consists in bequeathing 'empty words' to the world, even should they fail to carry them out themselves, and irrespective of whether they be reviled or disgraced by later generations. Jesus was executed, and all his twelve disciples suffered the same fate. Confucius was able to save only his own self, and there were few of his seventy disciples who gained (political) success. Buddha and his disciples all suffered from hunger and begged for their food. Unto the end they led lives of suffering. Thus all of these negated their own lives in order, through their prior knowledge, to enlighten those possessed of later knowledge, and through their earlier understanding, to give the same understanding to those possessed of later understanding. Why, then, should we idly ask whether or not they were successful in action? It was only Moses and Mohammed who possessed the authority necessary to carry out their teachings, and as a result they were nothing more than political rulers. Why should they deserve to be regarded as religious leaders?" (p. 50).

Thus the work of religious leaders is simply to impart their knowledge to others; this knowledge, if it be true knowledge, will ultimately prevail of itself.

Though the "three religions" of Jesus, Confucius, and Buddha "differ from one another, they are all the same in that they favor change. Though in the (manner of their) change they differ from one another, they are all the same in that they favor equality" (p. 28). This is because the highest ideal of all three religions is to attain that lofty realm described in the preceding section. The seeming differences between the words of their founders are therefore simply the result of the differing periods in which they lived. T'an writes:

"If measurement be made in terms of the Three Ages described

---

[1] *Analects*, II, 17. — Tr.

in the *Kung-yang Chuan*, Confucius was the most unfortunate. For in the time of Confucius the institutions of political rulership had already become extremely minute and numerous, and the so-called mores governing the social relationships, with all their confining bonds and gagging regulations, had already saturated men's minds, making it impossible to carry out any sudden changes. Living as he did in this Age of Disorder, Confucius was hard put to it. For his great esoteric ideas, he was forced to resort to veiled language and to pursue his course in a tortuous mysterious way. Such was the way in which he expressed his meaning. As to what appears in his ordinary (i.e., exoteric) discourses, he could not but continue to conform to the old institutions of political rulership, and to confine himself to the regulations of the Age of Disorder. This Age of Disorder was the Sequence of Rulers . . . .

"Jesus was next in misfortune. His age too was one of perverse political rulership. Nevertheless the (social) distinctions laid down in its mores were less than those of China, and there were in it certain manifestations of Approaching Peace. Hence Jesus succeeded in giving expression to his teachings on Heavenly government in the Age of Approaching Peace, and thus instituted the Sequence of Heaven . . . .

"The Buddha, however, was the only one who was really fortunate. From the very beginning his country had lacked the successive so-called 'divine-sage' leaders (of other countries)—such men as Moses, John, Yü, T'ang, Wen, Wu, and the Duke of Chou, who ground away the people's natural innocence and dissipated their pure simplicity. Furthermore, the Buddha regarded himself as a man who, having gone outside the human world and left the family, no longer felt need to conform to the world. Therefore he succeeded in giving full expression to his teachings on the Great Unity in the Age of Universal Peace, and thus instituted the Primal Sequence.

"As to the government of the Great Unity, it is not merely one in which a father is treated as a father or a son as a son, [1] for the father-and-son (relationship) is then no longer in existence, let alone that of ruler and subject. (In this age) all those gagging institutions and confining bonds which make autocrats of the rulers, and robbers of the people, are no longer allowed to be applied. The fact that

---

[1] An allusion to the *Evolutions of Rites*, p. 365. —. Tr.

the Buddha was thus able to assume a position of solitary eminence above the other religions was the inevitable result of his time and circumstances. All this, however, has nothing to do with the absolute reality [1] which underlies the religious leaders, for this is one and only one for all of them. X X X X (has said): 'The founders of the three religions are all one. When I bow to one, I bow to them all.' [2] I personally accept this statement" (pp. 28-29).

Here T'an pays high tribute indeed to Buddhism. His reason for so doing, however, is that it is in harmony with the loftiest teaching of Confucius. Hence this praise for Buddhism really amounts to praise for Confucius himself.

4—LIAO P'ING

Yet another exponent of the Ch'ing New Text school, and one whose thinking influenced K'ang Yu-wei, was Liao P'ing 廖平 (1852-1932). From the biography accompanying his published writings we learn that he was a native of Ching-yen 井研 in Szechwan (not far east of Kiating), that he was styled Chi-p'ing 季平, and that during successive periods of his life he adopted the literary names of Ssŭ-yi 四益, Wu-yi 五譯, and Liu-yi 六譯. [3]

i. *Interpretation of the Classics: First Phase*

Liao P'ing's interpretation of the classics passed through six successive phases, which explains the soubriquet he gave himself

---

[1] *Dharma-kāya* or *Dharma*-body, a Buddhist term. — Tr.

[2] The four-character name of the person making this statement has been left blank in the text. Though hardly what one would expect from a Christian missionary, could it conceivably be that of the Rev. Timothy Richard 李提摩太 (1845-1919), a far-sighted missionary who had intimate contacts with K'ang Yu-wei, T'an Ssŭ-t'ung, and other reformists? See Hummel, *op. cit.*, vol. 2, pp. 703-704. — Tr.

[3] After passing the highest of the governmental examinations, that of *chin shih*, Liao went to Kwangtung, which was then (during the years 1884 to 1889) governed by the "reformist" viceroy, Chang Chih-tung (1837-1909). There, through Chang, he met K'ang Yu-wei, whom he is said to have considerably influenced through his writings. Most of his life, however, was spent in scholarly retirement in his native Szechwan, where he produced a large number of philosophical, scholarly, and literary works. — Tr.

late in life of Liu-yi or "Six Interpretations." The earliest phase, beginning in 1883, was that of the "New and Old (Text schools)." [1] His argument during this phase is that the texts "taken as basic, either by the New or Old (Text) schools, all, for the most part, equally derive from Confucius, representing doctrines advanced by him either in his early or late years, while he was promoting his reforms patterned on antiquity" (*ibid.*, p. 2). In his *Chin-ku Hsüeh-k'ao* or *Study of the New and Old Learning* (completed in 1886), Liao outlines the differences between the texts used by the two schools, and then maintains that the split between them goes back not only to the late Chou dynasty but, in actual fact, to Confucius himself. Thus he writes:

"(Confucius says in) the *Analects* (III, 14): 'Chou had the advantage of surveying the two preceding dynasties. How replete was its culture! I follow Chou.' This statement was made by Confucius early in life, and is the origin of the Old Learning. (Again he says): [2] 'Adopt the calendar of Hsia. Ride in the state carriage of Yin (i.e., Shang). Wear the cap of Chou. In music adopt the Shao dances.' This statement was made by Confucius late in life, and is the origin of the New Learning. Yet again he says that the borrowings and changes made in (the civilization of) the Hsia and Yin (dynasties) by those who were to follow the Chou might be known, even a hundred generations hence. [3] Now it is in the *Royal Regulations* [4] that (we find the institutions described of) those kings whom he thus said would follow the Chou" (2.5).

According to Liao, Confucius in his early years had simply "honored the commands of the king and stood in awe of the great man." [5] In other words, he had then been merely a loyal follower of the House of Chou, without any revolutionary intentions. "In his late years," however, "he lamented that his principles made no progress," [6] and so, as an expression of what he would like to see happen, "wrote them (his hopes) into the *Royal Regulations*, and put them into the *Spring and Autumn Annals*" (*ibid.*, p. 3). What Liao means to say is that the chapter in the *Book of Rites* entitled *Royal*

---

[1] See Liao P'ing, *Ching-hsüeh Ssŭ-pien Chi* (Record of the Fourth Phase of Study of the Classics), p. 1 (hereafter referred to as *Fourth Phase of Study*).

[2] *Ibid.*, XV, 10. — Tr.

[3] *Ibid.*, II, 23. — Tr.

[4] *Wang Chih*, title of the third chapter in the *Book of Rites*. — Tr.

[5] An allusion to *Analects*, XIII, 20, and XVI, 8. — Tr.

[6] See *ibid.*, IX, 8. — Tr.

Regulations comes from the hand of Confucius himself, its name being derived from the fact that in it Confucius describes what he believes should be the institutions of those who would follow the Chou dynasty. In short, it represents Confucius' thinking in later life, after he had acquired revolutionary inclinations. As such, Liao goes on to argue, it stands in apposition to the *Chou Li* or *Chou Rituals*, which describes those institutions of the Chou dynasty itself such as Confucius in early life had wished to follow. But, Liao further maintains, Confucius was not the only man of his time who advocated reform, for "during the Spring and Autumn period all determined men were anxious to reform the Chou civilization, just as, among those who talk about government today, there is not one who does not wish to 'change his bowstring and renew his bow' " (*ibid.*, p. 24). It is not improbable that K'ang Yu-wei was inspired by this passage to express his own theory regarding the reforming activity of the Chou philosophers. [1]

The fact, however, that Confucius developed these differing conceptions at different times of life, led some people after his death, Liao believes, to champion the doctrines of his early years. These thus became the founders of the Old Text school, whereas other men who championed his later teachings became the founders of the New Text school. Liao writes:

"(The state of) Lu became the orthodox center of the New Learning, whereas (those of) Yen and Chao became the orthodox centers of the Old Learning . . . . Lu being Confucius' native state, his disciples there were numerous, and these students accepted the statements made by him late in life as his crystallized teachings . . . . Those disciples who belonged to Yen and Chao, on the other hand, had already left him and returned to their homes before he had yet set the *Spring and Autumn Annals* in order. Thus they only heard Confucius speak about following the Chou, and were no longer in personal contact with him when he later propounded his theories of reform. Therefore, because these ran counter to his earlier teachings, they suspected that they had been forged by the Lu disciples, and (then falsely) attributed by them to Confucius. Hence they themselves sincerely clung to the earlier teachings, with the result that arguments arose between them and (the adherents of) the Lu doctrines" (*ibid.*, p. 9).

---

[1] See above, pp. 677-678. — Tr.

Though in later times there has been unceasing controversy between the New and Old Text schools, their only real difference, Liao believes, lies in the institutional field. Thus he writes:

"(What) the *Analects* (says) about the modifications and accretions (made from one dynasty to another) relates only to the institutions (of these dynasties). As to their moral principles for governing the social relationships, these 'even a hundred generations hence can be known.'[1] Therefore the distinction between the Old and New (schools) consists wholly in the institutions (advocated by them), and not in their moral principles. With regard to moral principles, they are the same" (*ibid.*, p. 8).

Even with regard to institutions, in fact, "the truth of the matter is that what the New Learning has changed is slight, whereas what it has left unchanged is much, and in what it thus leaves unchanged it naturally follows the Old (Learning). Hence all who interpret the classics, if they find places where the New Learning is inadequate, may quite properly supplement them with the Old Learning" (*ibid.*). In short, the New and Old Text schools "may be compared to water and fire or the *yin* and *yang*," which, though "opposed to one another," at the same time "supplement one another" (*ibid.*, p. 1).[2]

ii. *Interpretation of the Classics: Second Phase*

The second phase in Liao P'ing's thinking, which began in 1888, consists of "exalting the New (Text school) and belittling the Old." Liao writes of this phase:

"At this time, through my investigations into the origin of the Old Text school, I saw that it emanated wholly from the false compilations of Hsü and Cheng[3] and their followers, and that the doctrines of the leaders of this school all emanated from the elaborations of Liu Hsin and his followers, based upon the *Chou Rituals* and *Tso Chuan*. I also investigated the Western (Former) Han and what preceded it, and saw that those who then discoursed upon the study of the classics all took Confucius as their leader, while making

---

[1] They can be known because they, unlike the outward institutions, remain unchanged. Again an allusion to *Analects*, II, 23. — Tr.

[2] This attempt to reconcile the differences between the Old and New Text schools is reminiscent of the Buddhist effort to reconcile the inconsistencies in various *sūtras*, all traditionally ascribed to the Buddha. See chap. 7, end of sect. 4, ii. — Tr.

[3] Hsü Shen and Cheng Hsüan. See above, p. 677, note 1. — Tr.

no mention of the Duke of Chou. The Six Disciplines are all new classics, not ancient records. [1] Thereupon, in order to exalt the New (Learning), I composed a *Chih Sheng P'ien* (Treatise on Comprehending the Sage), and, in order to refute the Old, a *P'i Liu P'ien* (Treatise on Refuting Liu Hsin)" [2] (*Fourth Phase of Study*, p. 3).

Thus during this period Liao P'ing accepted the New Text versions of the classics as the work of Confucius himself. "Emperors and Kings make themselves manifest in actual deeds, but Confucius could only resort to abstract words. The Six Disciplines are his recorded statutes, like the statutes of the Six Boards of today" [3] (*On Comprehending the Sage*, 1.2). As to the theories of the Old Text school, they stem from the forgeries of such men as Liu Hsin—stigmatized by Liao as "the Cho or Ts'ao among the followers of the Sage." [4] The fact that this thesis is similar to that found in K'ang Yu-wei's *Study of Confucius as a Reformer* and *Study of the Classics Forged during the Hsin Period*, gives Liao his apparent basis for claiming that these works were respectively modeled upon his own *Treatise on Comprehending the Sage* and *Treatise on Refuting Liu Hsin*.

Liao further asserts that Confucius was the first figure in Chinese history who really advocated reform. Thus he writes:

"Some [5] maintain that the various (Chou) philosophers all wished to transmit their writings, were all thinking of reform, and

---

[1] On the Six Disciplines, see vol. 1, p. 17, note 1; also below, note 3. The point to keep in mind here is that, according to the New Text school, most of the classics were composed by Confucius himself, so that they could not go back to the Duke of Chou, whereas the opinion of the Old Text school (accepted today by virtually all scholars) is that these classics antedate Confucius, and were, at the most, simply edited by him for teaching purposes. — Tr.

[2] Liao himself comments: "(K'ang Yu-wei's) *Study of Confucius as a Reformer*, which the outside (world) respects so much, was modelled after my *Treatise on Comprehending the Sage*, and his *Study of the Classics Forged during the Hsin Period* was modeled after my *Treatise on Refuting Liu Hsin*, but in the process he frequently fell short of their original meaning."

[3] The Six Boards or Ministries of the Ch'ing dynasty (which under varying names go back to earlier periods) were those of Civil Office, Revenue, Ceremonies, War, Punishment, and Works. Just how Liao wanted to correlate their statutes with the Six Disciplines or Classics (*Spring and Autumn Annals, Changes, Odes, History, Rites*, and music) is not clear. — Tr.

[4] *Ku-hsüeh K'ao* (Investigation of the Old Learning), p. 20. [Tung Cho (died 192) and Ts'ao Ts'ao (155-220) were warlords notorious for the way in which they disregarded legitimacy to put themselves in power. Their machinations and the accompanying political disorders caused the downfall of the Later Han dynasty. — Tr.]

[5] Here Liao has K'ang Yu-wei in mind. — Tr.

that in this way they set an example for Confucius. This is a great
error. For if we study the writings of these philosophers, (we see
that) they (really) stem from the 'four divisions' subsequent to the
Spring and Autumn (period), even though they have been (falsely)
attributed to earlier men. [1] Thus the practice of preaching one's
own teachings began with Confucius, and prior to the Spring and
Autumn (period) the only existing writings were those dealing with
arts and divination. All the philosophic schools arose after Confucius,
starting then with the 'four divisions,' from which they further
divided into the 'nine groups.' [2] Although all (their works) have been
attributed to famous ancient men, they are not really ancient writings"
(*On Comprehending the Sage*, 1.27-28).

It is this fact that makes of Confucius the one great Sage.

iii. *Interpretation of the Classics: Third Phase*

The third phase in Liao P'ing's thought, beginning in 1898,
is based on what he calls "the lesser and the greater." In it he follows
Shao Yung's classification of government according to four categories of descending quality: that of the Sovereign (*huang*), of the
Emperor (*ti*), of the King (*wang*), and of the Lord-Protector or
Tyrant (*po* or *pa*). [3] Liao further maintains that the *Royal Regulations*
and *Spring and Autumn Annals* were both written by Confucius to
illustrate the institutions required for the type of government
conducted either by the King or Tyrant. Such government was
regarded by Confucius as being applicable to China itself. Because,
however, Confucius was not a "sage of limited vision," he further
conceived of a higher form of government by the Sovereign or
Emperor, to describe which he used the *Chou Rituals* as his basic text,
supplemented by the *Book of History* to give a historical account of
its operation. These two works thus hold the same relation to one
another with respect to the government of the Sovereign or Emperor
as do the *Royal Regulations* and *Spring and Autumn Annals* with respect

---

[1] In *Analects*, XI, 2, Confucius classifies certain of his disciples as noted for
"moral character," "gifts of speech," administrative ability," and "literature
and learning." This is the origin of the term "four divisions." — Tr.

[2] The "nine groups" were the nine main schools of the late Chou dynasty:
Confucian, Taoist, *Yin-yang*, Legalist, Names, Mohist, Diplomatist, Eclectic,
and Agrarian. See Fung Yu-lan, *A Short History of Chinese Philosophy*, edited by
D. Bodde (New York, 1948), pp. 30-34. — Tr.

[3] See chap. 11, sect. 2, vi. — Tr.

to that of the King or Tyrant. It is in this way, Liao says, that Confucius "extended his planning to the entire globe," and "this is what the *Doctrine of the Mean* (p. 327) refers to when it speaks of someone whose fame 'overspreads the Middle Kingdom and extends to all barbarous tribes,' so that 'all who have blood and breath unfeignedly honor and love him,' or when the *Evolutions of Rites* propounds its doctrine of the Great Unity." [1]

As proof that the *Royal Regulations* and *Spring and Autumn Annals* contain Confucius' institutions for China only, whereas the *Book of History* and *Chou Rituals* contain those for his system of world government, Liao cites the fact that the geographic areas covered by the two sets of works are not the same. Thus we read in the *Huang-ti Chiang-yü T'u* (Geographical Charts for Sovereigns and Emperors): [2]

"The *Royal Regulations* speaks of (the area treated in) the *Spring and Autumn Annals* as 3,000 *li*, which constitutes the lesser plan. [3] The *Chou Rituals* speaks of (that treated in) the *Book of History* as ten times this amount, or a square of 30,000 *li*, and this constitutes the greater plan. [4] All human affairs lying within the six cardinal directions are completely embraced by this (latter area). The large 'nine continents' (*chiu chou* 九 州) spoken of in Tsou Yen's biography consist of 9 × 9, i.e., 81 squares, each square being 3,000 *li*, whereas the 'Nine Provinces' (*chiu chou*) of the scholars comprise only one of these eighty-one parts. Thus the 'Nine Provinces' spoken of by the scholars only refer to (the area covered by) the *Royal Regulations* and *Spring and Autumn Annals*" [5] (Chart 1, p. 1).

---

[1] *Fourth Phase of Study*, p. 4.

[2] Compiled by Liao's follower, Huang Jung 黃 鎔 , on the basis of Liao's statements.

[3] See *Book of Rites* (XXVII, 245): "All within the four seas, taking the length with the breadth, made up a space 3,000 *li* square." Three *li* = 1 English mile. — Tr.

[4] How Liao arrives at this figure is unclear. The *Chou Rituals* several times enumerates the various zones into which the world is allegedly divided, with their measurements. See Bks. XXIX, XXXIII, XXXVII (Biot, vol. 2, pp. 167-168, 276-277, 404-406). No matter how these figures are juggled, however, they fail to total 30,000. According to one calculation, the zones have a total area of 49 million *li*, but according to another, they constitute one large square measuring 3,000 *li* on each side (which agrees with the *Book of Rites* statement), and thus make up a total area of 9 million square *li*. See *op. cit.*, p. 277, note 4. — Tr.

[5] For Tsou's biography, see vol. 1, pp. 160-161, where it is stated that China (consisting of "Nine Provinces") is 1/81 the size of the entire world. Since, according

Thus, according to Liao, Tsou Yen's large "nine continents" (*chiu chou*) are not the same as the "Nine Provinces" (also *chiu chou*) of which scholars speak, and which cover only the area of China proper, as referred to in the *Royal Regulations* and the *Spring and Autumn Annals*. They are, on the other hand, the same as the much larger "Nine Provinces" (*chiu chou*) of which there is mention in the *Chou Rituals* and *Book of History*, [1] which means that they cover the entire extent of the known world today. We read further in the *Geographic Charts*:

"The evolution of the world is, culturally, from barbarism to civilization and, geographically, from the lesser to the greater. During the Spring and Autumn period the Nine Provinces totaled only a square of 3,000 *li* and, going back to the time of Shun and the Hsia (dynasty), conditions were then even more primitive and dark. When Confucius wisely edited the writings (of his time), he attributed the institutions promulgated therein to antiquity, and therefore secretly inserted the term 'province' (*chou*), current in his own day, into his charts for Sovereigns and Emperors, in which, however, he looked ahead to what would become current in later times. Stored up, (his regulations) are like Mount Sumeru contained within the mustard seed; spread out, they extend to everything within the four seas. [2] Yet in each case they remain equally applicable. How, then, could they have been designed merely to enable the state of Lu to rule over the other feudal states?" (Chart 8, p. 22).

Thus Confucius' teachings really supply a unified political and social plan for the entire world, and are essential to the world's future progress. Outwardly they seem merely to describe the governmental institutions of antiquity, beginning with those of Sovereign or Emperor, and retrogressing to those of King or Tyrant. In actual fact, however, Confucius' intention was "to set up an inverted image which, while showing retrogression, would, by telling men about the past, thereby inform them of the future, and in this way

---

to the *Royal Regulations*, China has a total area of 3,000 square *li*, this means, following Liao's interpretation, that the area of the entire world must be 81 × 3,000 = 243,000 *li*. This figure, however, far transcends that of 30,000 *li*, which Liao has just asserted is the one indicated in the *Chou Rituals*. — Tr.

[1] *Chou Rituals*, Bks. XXXIII, XXXVIII (Biot, vol, pp. 264-276, 406); *Book of History* (III, i, pp. 64-72). — Tr.

[2] Sumeru is the "world mountain" of Indian folklore, lying at the center of the universe. For this metaphor, see also chap. 9, p. 372. — Tr.

would induce them to return to him their (three) angles." [1] As a graphic portrayal of this concept, Liao P'ing has prepared the table shown on p. 714. [2]

According to this table, therefore, the classics merely represent theory, whereas history represents actual fact. Beginning with the Ch'in and Han dynasties, however, the theories contained in the *Spring and Autumn Annals* and *Royal Regulations* gradually came to be actualized as historical fact. Yet since Westerners have still not received the teachings of the Confucian classics, they remain even today in a stage roughly corresponding to that of the Chinese during the Spring and Autumn period. What is now needed, therefore, is propagation of the theories contained in the *Chou Rituals* and *Book of History*, until the entire world is converted by them into the Great Unity.

Liao further maintains that the so-called distinction between the New and Old Text schools is really simply one between the institutions devised by Confucius for the government of China, and those he devised for world government:

"Therefore I have changed the terms 'New' and 'Old' into those of 'lesser' and 'greater' .... The *Royal Regulations* serves to govern what lies within (a single country, i.e., China), and to establish a single authority .... But the Three Great Books and Five Canons of the Three Sovereigns and Five Emperors, wherein the entire overseas world (is dealt with), are all to be grouped under the *Chou Rituals* .... [3] This and the *Royal Regulations* respectively pertain to the greater and the lesser, the external and the internal. They are mutually opposed yet at the same time mutually complementary, each having its own proper place .... It is thus that Confucius becomes the divine Sage for the entire globe, and his Six Classics become the common doctrines of the universe" (*Fourth Phase of Study*, p. 5).

---

[1] *Ta-ch'eng-chieh Chiang-yi* (Lecture Delivered on the Birthday of Confucius), p. 24. [The mention here of the "three angles" has reference to Confucius' statement in the *Analects* (VII, 8): "When I have demonstrated one angle, and he (the student) cannot bring me back the other three, I do not repeat my lesson." — Tr.]

[2] *Ibid.*, p. 27.

[3] The Three Great Books (*san fen* 三 墳) and Five Canons (*wu tien* 五 典) are mentioned as such in the *Tso Chuan* under the year 530 B.C. (p. 641), but there is no unanimity among commentators as to what the terms really mean. The best guess is that they are simply the "names of old books," supposedly relating to the legendary Three Sovereigns and Five Emperors respectively. — Tr.

Table of Progress and Retrogression as Found in the Sacred Classics and in World History

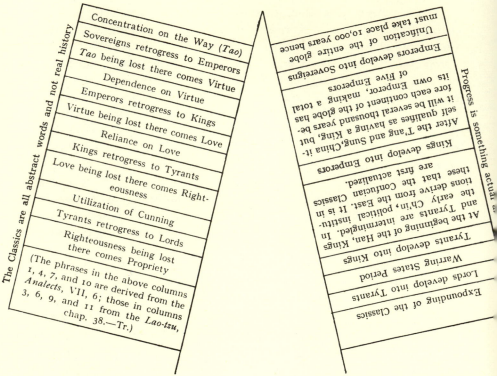

Confucius utilized the principle of retrogression (here shown) in order to establish his teachings. However, from retrogression one may understand progress. If we were exclusively to accept this retrogression (as an actual fact), it would mean that from Yao and Shun to the Spring and Autumn (period), there had been a successive decline through four stages, and that during the two thousand years from the Ch'in and Han until today there has been a further decline of four stages.[1] Extending this onward, there would be no men at all living a few thousands or tens of thousands of years hence. (According to this Table), when the retrogression has gone beyond the stage of Lord rule, China will revert to primitivity and darkness, and will arrive at the condition in which it was before the Warring States.

---

[1] By "stages," Liao means the shift in rule through Sovereign, Emperor, King, Tyrant, and Lord.—Tr.

The classics are in themselves only abstr words, and the actualizing of their instituti began only in the Warring States with (Marq Wen of Wei (403-387 B.C.) and (Kings) We Ch'i (357-320) and Chao of Yen (311-279). Be the Warring States, the condition of China's ru and people was roughly the same as that of West today. While Easterners (like to) talk, West acts. But the First Emperor of Ch'in (Emperor) Wu of the Han were creators, s as did not exist in (Chinese) antiquity. The tr sition (of institutions) from their exposition in classics until they became historical actuali occurred after the Warring States. The doctr of progress advocated by Westerners, as exem fied in the development of communications tween the five great continents, represent modern archievement, for it is not true that sea barriers had already been pierced prior Yao, Shun, and the Duke of Chou. Thus e after (Kings) Yu (781-771) and Li (893-8. (China) was still confined to 3,000 li.

Thus, for Liao, the classics of Confucius furnish models for the institutions of the entire world, and he and they thereby attain the highest position of eminence.

iv. *Interpretation of the Classics: Fourth Phase*

The foregoing is still not enough for Liao P'ing, for he continues:

"These, however, are no more than the Six Disciplines for the study of man, exclusively dealing with what lies within the six cardinal directions (the human universe). Hence if one only concerns oneself with the *Spring and Autumn Annals*, the *Book of History*, and the *Rites*, one gains only half (of the truth), inasmuch as the *Odes*, *Changes*, and *Music*, which deal with the study of Heaven, are not included in the above" (*Fourth Phase of Study*, p. 5).

Beginning in 1902, Liao's philosophy entered its fourth phase, that concerned with the spheres of "Heaven and man." He writes:

"At first I correlated the *Spring and Autumn Annals*, *Book of History*, *Odes*, and the *Changes*, with the *Tao* (Way), *Te* (Power), love, and righteousness of the Sovereign, Emperor, King, and Tyrant respectively . . . . But in the course of time I gradually realized that these four classics are, in their organization, intended to delimit Heaven from man, the study of man being confined to what lies within the six cardinal points, and the study of Heaven to what lies outside of them.

"When the *Spring and Autumn Annals* speaks of Tyrants, it thereby includes Kings, and when the *Book of History* speaks of Emperors, it thereby includes Sovereigns. The *Chou Rituals*, in what it says about the Three Sovereigns and Five Emperors, confines itself exclusively to (the period covered by) the *Book of History*; the *Royal Regulations*, in what it says about Kings and Tyrants, confines itself exclusively to (that covered by) the *Spring and Autumn Annals*. Hence the institutions pertaining to Sovereigns and Emperors, or Kings and Tyrants, are (respectively) to be found in the *Chou Rituals* and *Royal Regulations*; the (respective) classics dealing with them are the *Book of History* and *Spring and Autumn Annals*. (Of these latter two works), the one is lesser and the other greater. Together they constitute the two classics for the study of man . . . . This study is confined to what lies within the six cardinal points—a fact referred to in the statement about the 'ending of communications between Heaven and Earth,' such as had (once) 'reached to (Heaven) above and (Earth) below.' [1] It is man and not Heaven (that this study relates to). Hence (this reference to) separation of man and the spirits.

"As for the *Odes* and *Changes*, however, their great pattern is to move majestically above, there to float on what lies below. This is the ultimate realm referred to by the *Doctrine of the Mean* (p. 305) when it speaks of 'the kite flying up to Heaven, and the fish leaping in its pool, [2] thus giving insight into what is above and below.' To roam amid the six cardinal points and yet, as in a dream, have one's soul fly away from one's body, is indeed, judged by present day conditions, something of which our powers are incapable. Yet if, from the point of view of people of today, we look at the primeval darkness existing only a few thousands or tens of thousands of years ago, (we see that) our morality, customs, souls, and bodies cannot be compared with those of the past. Therefore if we add several thousand years of improvement and reform, as well as the enlightenment to be achieved through continued progress of the sciences, we may certainly reckon upon a further development to the point where what we call 'long life,' 'the swallowing of the vital force,' and 'no need for clothing and food,' will certainly be achieved" [3] (*ibid.*, p. 7).

Liao asserts that "once (the distinction between) the study of Heaven and of man has been clearly comprehended, then those works which scholars have hitherto referred to as strange and non-canonical will all receive their proper interpretation" (*ibid.*). Among these he lists such texts as the *Ling Ch'u* (Spiritual Pivot), [4] *Su Wen* (Plain Questions), [5] *Ch'u Tz'ŭ* (Elegies of Ch'u), [6] *Shan-hai Ching* (Classic of Mountains and Seas), [7] and *Mu T'ien-tzŭ Chuan* (Chronicle

---

[1] *Book of History*, V, xxvii, p. 257, and I, i, p. 32, respectively. — Tr.

[2] See also *Book of Odes*, III, i, Ode 5. — Tr.

[3] These phrases refer to the aims and techniques of the religious Taoists who sought for immortality. "Swallowing the vital force" or *fu ch'i* 服 氣 is a term for the breathing exercises which constituted one of these techniques. — Tr.

[4] A Han medical work on needling. It forms part of the *Huang-ti Nei-ching* (Classic of Internal Medicine of the Yellow Emperor), on which see p. 131, note 1. — Tr.

[5] Another Han medical treatise, also forming part of the *Huang-ti Nei-ching*. — Tr.

[6] A collection of imaginative poems of the third and second century B.C., on which see vol. 1, p. 416. — Tr.

[7] A "geographical" work, filled with fantastic stories and folklore about the

of Mu Son of Heaven). ¹ All these, for Liao, are fantastic non-canonical works which, because they deal with a realm beyond the ordinary world of human beings, therefore pertain to the study of Heaven. Of the *Ta-jen Fu* or "Prose-poem on the Great Man," a famous poem by Ssŭ-ma Hsiang-ju (ca. 179-117 B.C.), Liao likewise maintains that it "lies outside our existing world." The Buddhist *sūtras*, too, are linked by him to the study of Heaven, as in the following passage:

"The progress of the future world will lead all sentient beings to the point where they achieve Buddhahood, and where each and every human being will have no further need for food, but will fly away from his body to become 'devoid of anxiety.' ² This has been clearly described by recent persons. What they do not realize, however, is that the Buddha was a product of Taoism, being the first to undergo the process of the conversion of the barbarians. ³ What is said (in the Buddhist *sūtras*) will some day become an actual fact, and will constitute the final fruit of the study of Heaven. If a single man were to achieve it, it would be something extraordinary, but when the entire world becomes capable of it, it will be an ordinary matter" (*ibid.*, p. 10).

Thus Buddhism is a mere offshoot of Taoism, but since Taoism itself, in Liao's eyes, is derived from Confucianism, this gives to the Confucian classics a still greater scope.

v. *Interpretation of the Classics: Fifth Phase*

Liao P'ing's disciple, Huang Jung, comments as follows at the beginning of his master's *Ching-hsüeh Wu-pien Chi* (Record of the Fifth Phase of Study of the Classics): "In the year *wu-wu* (1918) he (Liao) abolished the terms 'New' and 'Old' and reduced them to those of 'lesser' and 'greater,' specifically allotting (each of) the Six

---

regions of China and surrounding areas. Much of it is probably of Han date, though some parts may go back to the late Chou. — Tr.

¹ An account of the miraculous journey of King Mu (1001-947 B.C.) to the countries west of China. It was allegedly recovered from a tomb in A.D. 281, but the present version is quite possibly a forgery. — Tr.

² A phrase from the *Chuang-tzŭ*, chap. 22, p. 277. — Tr.

³ An allusion to the story, invented by the Taoists in the early centuries A.D. as an antidote to the growing influence of Buddhism, that after Lao Tzŭ, late in life, left China through the western pass, he traveled to India and was there reincarnated as the Buddha. In this guise he "converted the barbarians," so that Buddhism is simply a foreign offshoot of Taoism. — Tr.

Classics to the greater and lesser divisions pertaining to Heaven or to man." This classification, as we shall see, differs from that of Liao's fourth phase, in which the *Spring and Autumn Annals* and *Book of History* respectively represented the lesser and greater phases of the study of man, whereas the *Odes* and *Changes* both represented the study of Heaven. In the new phase Liao now divides the Six Classics into six categories: three for the study of man, and another three for the study of Heaven. The first of the three categories pertaining to man is that of the lesser treatises on the rituals (*li*):

"Among the Six Disciplines there are first the lesser rituals [1] and lesser music. [2] These are the ritual classics for cultivating the person and regulating the family. They thus provide the basis for peaceful government. The cultivation of the person is the root, and this root consists in these rituals" (*Fifth Phase of Study*, 1.1).

Thus the lesser rituals and music have as their prime purpose the cultivation of the self, and thereby constitute the first of the three groups of classics connected with the study of man. As to the second group, we are told that the *Spring and Autumn Annals* "teaches how to give good government to the state, how to be a King or Tyrant, and how to practice love and righteousness. The *Royal Regulations* serves as its commentary." This and the preceding category comprise "the lesser plan for the study of man, having been accepted as basic by the Confucianists, Mohists, and the School of Names." As to the third group of classics, we are told that the *Book of History* "teaches how to give peace to the world, how to be a Sovereign or Emperor, and how to practice the Way (*Tao*) and its Power (*Te*). The *Chou Rituals* serves as its commentary." Together, those two works comprise "the greater plan for the study of man, having been accepted as basic by the Taoist and *Yin-yang* schools" (*ibid.*, pp. 4-11).

As to those other three categories of classics belonging to the study of Heaven, the first of these includes the works on music and the greater rituals. Regarding the former, Liao writes:

---

[1] Huang comments: "Such as the 'Summary of the Rules of Propriety' (*Book of Rites*, chap. 1), 'Lesser Rules of Demeanor' (chap. 15), 'Pattern for the Family' (chap. 10), 'Classic of Deportment' (chap. 39 of Chia Yi's *Hsin Shu*), and 'Duties of Youth' (*Kuan-tzŭ*, chap. 59)."

[2] Huang comments: "The *shao* which was danced at thirteen, and the *hsiang* which was danced as a full-grown lad." [See *Book of Rites*, chap. 10 (XXVII, 478), where these dances are mentioned as part of the curriculum for youth. Their exact nature is unknown today. — Tr.]

"The music of Kings and Tyrants has to some extent existed in China, but the epoch for the music of Sovereigns and Emperors is as yet there lacking, since the musicians for it have not yet been born. Hence I reserve what I have to say about it until they appear" (*ibid.*, 2.13).

On the greater rituals Liao likewise says little, perhaps for the same reason. These and music jointly comprise the first of the three groups of classics for the study of Heaven. Regarding the second group, we are told that the *Book of Odes* "teaches how to wander into the realm of the supernatural . . . . An example is the way in which the seekers for immortality transmute their soul to be like that of an infant, thus enabling their spirit to depart and leave their body behind. During the daytime, however, they are unable to shed their physical frame in this way and fly aloft. [1] This is why the *Odes* speaks only of the world of dreams, [2] in which, like a fish or a bird, one may rise aloft or descend below. [3] The (*Huang-ti*) *Nei-ching*, *Ling Ch'u*, *Su Wen*, *Shan-hai Ching*, *Lieh-tzŭ*, *Ch'u Tz'ŭ*, and the ancient prose-poems and poems of the wandering immortals: all these serve as commentaries on it (the *Odes*)" (*ibid.*, p. 15).

K'ang Yu-wei and T'an Ssŭ-t'ung both agree that above the government of the Great Unity there exists yet another "realm created by Heaven," and it is this that Liao has in mind when he speaks of the study of Heaven. In his exposition, however, he is somewhat more explicit than the other two men. [4]

5—CONCLUSION OF THE PERIOD OF CLASSICAL LEARNING

Liao P'ing's ideology, whether judged historically or philosophically, is equally devoid of value. As marking the conclusion of

---

[1] Huang comments: "But through the *Book of Changes* one is able thus to roam about in one's own physical body."

[2] Huang comments: "It resorts to these dreamland roamings in order to make clear the principles of reality."

[3] Huang comments: "Chuang Tzŭ dreamed that he was a bird soaring to Heaven; he dreamed that he was a fish swimming in the depths." [See the *Chuang-tzŭ*, chap. 6, p. 87, where, however, this statement is put in the mouth of Confucius. — Tr.]

[4] The third of the three categories of classics dealing with the study of Heaven should properly be that of the *Book of Changes*. Liao fails, however, to discuss it in the remainder of his treatise, and the edition seen by me evidently contains textual errors. We know, furthermore, that the fifth phase in his thinking was followed by a sixth phase, but inasmuch as no printed description of it has been available to me, I am unable to say wherein it differs from the fifth phase.

the Period of Classical Learning, however, it secures for him a certain importance in the history of Chinese philosophy. In the first chapter of the present volume I have pointed out that the entire two thousand years from Tung Chung-shu down to the present century has belonged to the Period of Classical Learning, and that all its philosophers, irrespective of their own originality or non-originality, could gain a hearing for their ideas only by attaching themselves to one or another of the philosophic schools of antiquity—which, for most of them, meant the Confucian classics. This process I have described as that of filling old bottles with new wine. It is not surprising, therefore, that when, in the nineteenth century, China was shaken by the political, social, economic, and ideological changes resulting from the impact of the West, the first reaction of her thinkers was simply to try to fit these new external elements into the existing framework of Classical Learning—in other words, to continue pouring this radically new wine into the old bottles. The three men treated in the present chapter are representative of this effort.

Of the three, Liao was the last to die. The fifth phase of his approach to the classics, in fact, began only in 1918, seven years after the founding of the Republic. By this time the Classical Learning had been stretched to its farthest limits, so that it is scarcely surprising that what was forced into it contained much that was ridiculous. This very fact, indeed, was a definite indication that the old bottles had reached their final breaking point. Thus from the point of view of chronology and content alike, Liao's ideology truly marks the conclusion of that Learning.

The changes wrought by history, however, can rarely be assigned with mathematical exactness to any precise hour or day, for it usually happens that the close of one age overlaps the opening of the next. This, at least, is true in the present instance, for already before Liao's death in 1932—in fact, even before he inaugurated his fifth phase in 1918—there were other Chinese who were beginning to cast aside the Classical Learning in order to express their own new thinking. That is to say, before the Period of Classical Learning had yet ended, the modern age of Chinese philosophy was already beginning. Among these new thinkers, however, none was as yet strikingly successful in achieving a well rounded system. Hence, as the present book goes to press (1934), this modern age still remains in its formative stage. This is why, rather than try to discuss these new developments, I close my account with the ending of the Period of Classical Learning. [1]

---

[1] Since 1934, however, Professor Fung has himself written a series of five significant works developing his own philosophical system. Though in these he in part follows the Rationalistic school of Neo-Confucianism, he at the same time, in his own words, avoids its "element of authoritarianism and conservatism," and applies the fruits of his study of Western philosophy. One of these works has been translated by E. R. Hughes as *The Spirit of Chinese Philosophy* (London, 1947). For a brief account by Professor Fung himself of his philosophy, see his *Short History of Chinese Philosophy*, chap. 28. Still more recently, of course, Marxism has become a major intellectual force in China. — Tr.

WESTERN THOUGHT	CHINESE DYNASTIES	CONFUCIANISM
		Confucianism *Yin-yang* School
		↘ ↙
	Former Han (206 B.C.-A.D. 24)	NEW TEXT SCHOOL
Lucretius (94-54 B.C.)		Tung Chung-shu (179?-104? B.C.) OLD TEXT SCHOO
		Apocrypha, Prognostica- Yang Hsiung
	HAN	tion Texts, and Numerology (53 B.C.-A.D. 18)
Philo (30 B.C.-A.D. 50)	Wang Mang (A.D. 6-23)	Meng Hsi and Ching Liu Hsin
		Fang (died 37 B.C.) (ca. 46 B.C.-A.D. 2
Epictetus (1st century A.D.)	DYNASTY (206 B.C.-A.D. 220)	Huan T'an (died A.D. 56)
		Po Hu T'ung Wang Ch'ung
	Later Han (A.D. 25-220)	(compiled after A.D. 79) (A.D. 27-ca. 100)
Marcus Aurelius (121-180)		Ho Hsiu (129-182)
		(commentator on
Plotinus (204-269)	Wei (220-265)	*Kung-yang Chuan*)
	Chin (265-419)	
	PERIOD OF	
Augustine (353-430)		
	DISUNITY (221-589)	
	Northern and Southern Dynasties (420-589)	
		Precursors of
	SUI (590-617)	*Neo-Confucianism*
		Wang T'ung (584-617)
	T'ANG (618-906)	
		Han Yü (768-824)
Scotus Erigena (810-877)		Li Ao (died ca. 844)

Left margin time scale: 200, 100, B.C. 0 A.D., 100, 200, 300, 400, 500, 600, 700, 800

TAOISM	BUDDHISM	
		— 200
		—
		— 100
		—
		B.C.
	Entry of Buddhism into China (early 1st century A.D.)	0
		A.D.
		— 100
RELIGIOUS TAOISM		—
O-TAOISM Wei Po-yang's		
ng Pi *Ts'an-t'ung-ch'i*		— 200
5-249) (ca. 142)		
ang Hsiu Yü Fan	"SEVEN SCHOOLS" (4th-5th century)	
221-ca. 300) (164-233)	1. Original Non- 4. Non-being of Mind	— 300
Hsiang Ko Hung (ca. 250-ca. 330)	being	
d 312)	Hui-yüan 2. Variant School 5. Stored Impressions	
ǒ-tzŭ (?)	(334-416) of Original Non- 6. Phenomenal	
	Seng-chao being Illusion	— 400
	(384-414) 3. Matter as Such 7. Causal Combination	
Huan (420-483)	Tao-sheng (ca. 360-434) ⎰ Instantaneous	
	Hsieh Ling-yün (385-433) ⎱ Enlightenment	
i-shih Shu-ming (474-546)	*Debators on Immortality of Soul*	— 500
	Seng-yu (445-518) and (non-Buddhist) Fan Chen	
	(ca. 450-ca. 515)	
	THREE- T'IEN-TAI CH'AN (Zen)	
	TREATISE Chih-k'ai Shen-hsiu	
	Chi-tsang (538-597) (ca. 600-706)	— 600
	(549-623) *Ta-ch'eng* Hui-neng	
	MERE HUA-YEN *Chih-kuan* (638-713)	
	IDEATION Fa-tsang *Fa-men* Huai-jang	— 700
	Hsüan-tsang (643-712) (677-744)	
	(596-664) Chan-jan Shen-hui	
	K'uei-chi (711-782) (686-760)	
	(632-682) Liang Su Tao-yi	— 800
	Ch'eng-kuan (753-793) (709- 788)	
	(738?-839?) (and many	
	others)	

	WESTERN THOUGHT	CHINESE DYNASTIES	CONFUCIANISM
900 —		FIVE DYNASTIES (907-959)	
		Northern Sung (960-1126)	NEO-CONFUCIANISM
1000 —			Chou Tun-yi (1017-73) Shao Yung (1011-77) Chang Tsa (1020-77)
		SUNG	*Rationalists* *Idealists*
1100 —	Abelard (1079-1142)		Ch'eng Yi (1033-1108) Ch'eng Hao (1032-85
		DYNASTY (960-1279)	
		Southern Sung (1127-1279)	Chu Hsi (1130-1200) Lu Chiu-yüan (1139-9 Yang Chien (1140-12:
1200 —	Acquinas (1225/27-74) Duns Scotus (ca. 1265-1308)	YÜAN (Mongol) (1280-1367)	
1300 —			
1400 —			
	Machiavelli (1469-1527) Bruno (1548-1600) Bacon (1561-1626) Descartes (1596-1650)	MING (1368-1643)	Ch'en Hsien-chang (1428-1 Chan Jo-shui (1466-1560) Lo Ch'in Wang Shou-jen (1472-1529 (1465-1547) Wang Ken (1483-1540) Ch'en Chien Wang Chi (1498-1583) (1497-1567) Yen Chün (16th century)
1500 —			
1600 —	Hobbes (1588-1679) Spinoza (1632-77) Locke (1632-1704) Leibniz (1646-1716) Berkeley (1685-1753) Hume (1711-76) Kant (1724-1804) Hegel (1770-1831) Schopenhauer (1788-1860) Mill (1806-73) Marx (1818-83) James (1842-1910) Bergson (1859-1941)	CH'ING (Manchu) (1644-1911)	*Ch'ing Continuators of Neo-Confucianism* Liu Tsung-chou (1578-1645) Lu Shih-yi (1611-72) Huang Tsung-hsi (161(Ch'en Ch'üeh (1604-77) Wang Fu-chih (1619-9 Yen Yüan (1635-1704) Li Kung (1659-1746) Tai Chen (1723-77)
1700 —			
1800 —			CH'ING REVIVAL OF NEW TEXT SCHO T'an Ssŭ-t'ung (1865-98) K'ang Yu-wei (1858-1927) Liao P'ing (1852-1932)
1900 —		REPUBLIC (1912-)	

TAOISM	BUDDHISM	
		—— 900
		——
		—— 1000
		—
		—— 1100
		——
Yü Yen (13th century)		—— 1200
		——
		—— 1300
		——
		—— 1400
		——
		—— 1500
		——
		—— 1600
		——
		—— 1700
		——
		—— 1800
		——
		—— 1900
		——

BIBLIOGRAPHY

This bibliography includes only those items that are mentioned or quoted in the body of this volume. It thus does not pretend to be a complete bibliography of its subject, nor does it list the numerous dictionaries and similar research tools used in the preparation of the translation, unless they have been actually cited by name in the text. Likewise it omits titles of a few works there mentioned which are, however, no longer extant today, or are preserved only through inclusion in other works.

Numbers at the end of each item are those of the pages in the present volume in which the item in question appears. Asterisks indicate items that have already been listed in the Bibliography of Vol. I. Information about specific editions has been omitted in the case of works cited in the text merely by title, without reference to specific pagination.

Arrangement is by author, save in the case of works whose authorship is uncertain, or of large compilations and certain other works better known by their titles than by their authors. In the body of this volume, many works are referred to by English rather than Chinese title. The reverse is true in this bibliography, however, where the Chinese title is always primary, though cross references under the English equivalents have been supplied in many cases. Cross references are also given for authors and translators who are associated with several scattered items. Chinese characters for words appearing more than once, either within a single item, or in several successive related items, have, when convenient, been omitted, following their first appearance.

I—ABBREVIATIONS

ch. and chap.: *chüan* and chapter respectively. A Chinese *chüan* or book often contains more than one chapter, though sometimes the two are identical.

comm., comms.: commentary or commentator (commentaries or commentators)

comp.: compilation, compilor, or compiled

CYTCS: *Cheng-yi-t'ang Ch'üan-shu* 正誼堂全書. Comp. by Chang Po-hsing 張伯行 (1652-1725), and subsequently amplified. Foochow ed. of 1866

ed.: edition, editor, or edited

Legge, *Chin. Clas.*: Legge, James, *The Chinese Classics*. 5 vols. (vols. 3-5 in 2 pts. each). Oxford: Clarendon Press, 2nd ed., 1893

Legge, SBE: Legge, James, translations of certain classics in *Sacred Books of the East*. F. Max Müller, ed. Vols. 3, 16, 27-28. Oxford: Clarendon Press, 2nd ed., 1899

ref., refs.: reference or references

SPTK: *Ssŭ-pu Ts'ung-k'an* 四部叢刊. Shanghai: Commercial Press, 1st, 2nd, and 3rd series, 1929-36.

Taoist Canon: Tao Tsang 道藏. 1,120 vols. Shanghai: Commercial Press, 1924-26

TCTCC: *T'ung-chih-t'ang Ching-chieh* 通志堂經解. Comp. by Hsü Ch'ien-hsüeh 徐乾學 (1631-94). Ed. of 1872

transl.: translation, translator, or translated

Tripiṭaka Supplement: *Hsü Tsang-ching* 續藏經. 720 vols. Shanghai: Han-fen-lou 涵芬樓 lithographic ed., 1923-25

TSCC: *Ts'ung-shu Chi-ch'eng* 叢書集成. Shanghai: Commercial Press, 1936-39

TT: Taishō ed. of the Chinese version of the *Tripiṭaka* or Buddhist sacred canon (*Taishō Shinshū Daizōkyō* 大正新修大藏經). 85 vols. Tokyo, 1922-33. (Such a citation as 65.1-248, within parentheses, indicates that the work in question occurs in vol. 65 of this ed., pp. 1-248.)

TW: T'ung Wen 同文 ed. of the dynastic histories, 1903

WYT: *Wu-ying-tien Chü-chen-pan Ts'ung-shu* 武英殿聚珍版叢書. Kuang-ya 廣雅 Book Co. reprint of ca. 1899

YHSFCYS: *Yü-han Shan-fang Chi-yi-shu* 玉函山房輯佚書. Comp. by Ma Kuo-han 馬國翰 (1794-1857). Changsha ed. of 1883

II—Works Cited

Aids to the Study of Chinese Philosophy, see under *Hsün-tzŭ*

Analects, see *Lun Yü*

Ānāpāna Sūtra, see Tao-an

Anchō 安澄 (Japanese Buddhist monk), comp., *Chung-lun Su-chi* 中論疏記 (Subcommentary on the Mādhyamika Śāstra). Comp. in 801-806 in 8 ch. TT no. 2225 (65.1-248): 244-253, 256-7

Aristotle, *Metaphysics*. Transl. of Hugh Tredenwick. London & New York: Loeb Classical Library, 1933: 93

Avataṃsaka Sūtra (*Hua-yen Ching* 華嚴經). Three Chinese recensions in 60, 80, and 40 ch. TT nos. 278, 279, 293 (9.395-788; 10.1-144 and 661-685). See also under Ch'eng-kuan; Fa-tsang: 340, 359

Awakening of Faith, see *Mahāyāna-śraddhotpāda Śāstra*

Balázs, Stefan, "Der Philosoph Fan Tschen und sein Traktat gegen den Buddhismus." *Sinica*, vol. 7 (Frankfurt, 1932), 220-234. See also Fan Chen: 289

Bodde, Derk, *China's First Unifier, a study of the Ch'in dynasty as seen in the life of Li Ssŭ (280?-208 B.C.).* Leiden: E. J. Brill, 1938: 90

——, "The Chinese View of Immortality: Its Expression by Chu Hsi and its Relationship to Buddhist Thought." *Review of Religion*, vol. 6 (1942), 369-383: 571
See also under Fung Yu-lan

Bruce, J. Percy, *Chu Hsi and His Masters, an introduction to Chu Hsi and the Sung School of Chinese philosophy.* London: Probsthain, 1923. See also under Chou Tun-yi; Chu Hsi, *Chu Wen-kung Wen-chi*: 435, 453, 478, 499-500, 534

Burnet, John, *Early Greek Philosophy.* London: Adam & Charles Black, 2nd ed., 1908: 93-95

Chan-jan 湛 然 (711-782), *Chin-kang Pi* 金 剛 錍 (The Diamond Stick). 1 ch. TT no. 1932 (46.781-786): 385-6

Chan Jo-shui 湛 若 水 (1466-1560), *Hsin-hsing T'u-shuo* 心 性 圖 說 (Explanation of the Diagram of the Mind and the Nature). Contained in *Kan-ch'üan Hsien-sheng Wen-chi* 甘 泉 先 生 文 集 (Collected Writings of Chan Jo-shui). 32 ch. Ed. of 1866: 595-6

Chang Tsai 張 載 (1020-77), *Cheng Meng* 正 蒙 (Correct Discipline for Beginners). 17 chaps. Cited as *Discipline for Beginners*. Contained in *Chang Heng-ch'ü Ch'üan-chi* 橫 渠 全 集 (Complete Works of Chang Tsai), ch. 2-4. CYTCS ed.: 478-493, 497, 501, 555

——, *Ching-hsüeh Li-k'u* 經 學 理 窟 (Assembled Principles of Classical Learning). 5 ch.: 478

——, *Hsi Ming* 西 銘 (Western Inscription). Also known as *Ting Wan* 訂 頑 (The Correcting of the Ignorant). Formerly a portion of his *Cheng Meng*, chap. 17, from which it was later separated. Refs. to Werner Eichhorn, transl., "Die Westinschrift des Chang Tsai, ein Beitrag zur Geistesgeschichte der Nördlichen Sung." *Abhandlungen für die Kunde des Morgenlandes*, vol. 22 (Leipzig, 1937), 1-85. This also contains the comms. of Chu Hsi (whom see), and others: 477-8, 493-6, 521

——, *Yi Shuo* 易 說 (Comments on the Book of Changes). 3 ch. TCTCC ed.: 478-9

Chang Yü-chüan, "Wang Shou-jen as a Statesman." *Chinese Social and Political Science Review*, vol. 23 (Peiping, 1939-40), 30-99, 155-252, 319-375, 473-517. See also Wang Shou-jen: 598

Changes, Book of, see *Yi Ching*

Chao Yi 趙 翼 (1727-1814), *Nien-erh Shih Cha-chi* 廿 二 史 札 記 (Notes on Twenty-two Dynastic Histories). 36 ch.: 11

Chavannes, Édouard, *Les mémoires historiques de Se-ma Ts'ien*, see under *Shih Chi*

Ch'en Chien 陳建 (1497-1567), *Hsüeh-p'ou T'ung-pien* 學蔀通辯 (Analysis of the Prejudices of Philosophy). 12 ch. CYTCS ed.: 622-3

Ch'en Hsien-chang 陳獻章 (1428-1500), *Pai-sha-tzǔ Ch'üan-chi* 白沙子全集 (Complete Works of Ch'en Hsien-chang). 8 plus 1 supplementary ch. Ed. of Wan-li period (1573-1620): 594-5

Ch'en, Kenneth, "Anti-Buddhist Propaganda during the Nan-ch'ao," *Harvard Journal of Asiatic Studies*, vol. 15 (1952), 166-192: 292

Ch'en Shun 陳淳 (1153-1217), *Pei-hsi Tzǔ-yi* 北溪字義 (Ch'en's Analysis of Philosophical Terms). 2 ch. Appended to *Pei-hsi Ta-ch'üan-chi* 大全集 (Complete Works of Ch'en Shun). 50 ch. Ed. of 1783: 592

Ch'en Yin-k'o 陳寅恪 (1889-   ), "A Study of Chih Min-tu's Doctrines" (article in Chinese). *Studies Presented to Ts'ai Yuan P'ei on His Sixty-fifth Birthday* 慶祝蔡元培先生六十五歲論文集. Peiping: Academia Sinica, Pt. I (1933), 1-18: 255

Ch'en Yüan 陳垣 (1879-   ), *Shih-shih Yi-nien Lu* 釋氏疑年錄 (Chronologies of Buddhist Monks). 12 ch. Peiping: Catholic University of Peking, 1939: 359, 392, 397

Ch'eng Hao 程顥 (1032-85), *Ming-tao Wen-chi* 明道文集 (Collected Writings of Ch'eng Hao). 5 ch. Contained in *Erh-Ch'eng Ch'üan-shu* 二程全書 (Complete Works of the Two Ch'engs), 164 ch. Pao-kao-t'ang 寶誥堂 ed. of K'ang-hsi period (1662-1722): 453, 525

——, *Ting-hsing Shu* 定性書 (Letter on the Composure of the Nature). Letter to Chang Tsai (whom see), contained in *Ming-tao Wen-chi*, 3.1. Also transl. in C. P. Hsu, *Ethical Realism in Neo-Confucian Thought* (Peiping: Yenching University, 1933), Appen., pp. xiii-xv: 506, 523-5, 529, 577, 620, 626

——, and Ch'eng Yi (whom see), *Erh-Ch'eng Yi-shu* 遺書 (Literary Remains of the Two Ch'engs). 25 ch. (of which ch. 2, 21, and 22 are divided into 2 pts.). Contained in *Erh-Ch'eng Ch'üan-shu* (see above): 501-3, 505-523, 525, 527-531

Cheng Hsüan, see under *Yi-wei Chi-lan-t'u*

Ch'eng-kuan 澄觀 (738?-839?), *Hua-yen Fa-chieh Hsüan-ching* 華嚴法界玄鏡 (The Mysterious Mirror of the Avatamsaka Dharmadhātu). 2 ch. TT no. 1883 (45.672-683): 359

Ch'eng Min-cheng 程敏政 (ca. 1445-ca. 1500), *Tao-yi Pien* 道一編 (Treatise on the Oneness of the Truth). 6 ch.: 622

Ch'eng Yi 程頤 (1033-1108), *Yi-chuan* 易傳 (Commentary on the

Chiu T'ang Shu 舊唐書 (Old History of the T'ang Dynasty). Comp. in 941-945 by Liu'Hsü 劉昫 (887-946) and others in 200 ch. TW ed.: 408

Chou Li 周禮 (Chou Rituals). 6 pts. Highly idealized late Chou or early Han Confucian comp. Refs. to Eduard Biot, transl., *Le Tcheou-li ou Rites des Tcheou.* 2 vols. Paris: Imprimerie Nationale, 1851: 628, 634, 707-8, 710-3, 715, 718

Chou-pi Suan-ching 周髀算經 (Mathematical Classic on the Gnomen). 2 ch. A Han dynasty work, though traditionally ascribed to much earlier date: 131

Chou Rituals, see *Chou Li*

Chou Tun-yi 周敦頤 (1017-73), *T'ai-chi T'u-shuo* 太極圖說 (Diagram of the Supreme Ultimate Explained). 1 ch. Cited as *Diagram Explained*. Refs. to transl. in J. Percy Bruce, *Chu Hsi and His Masters* (which see under Bruce), pp. 128-131. Cf. also transl. of Georg Von Der Gabelentz, *Thai-Kih-Thu, des Tscheu-Tsï Tafel des Urprinzipes ...* (Dresden, 1876): 435-8, 442-8, 450-1, 534-5, 538-9, 545-6, 589-590, 620

——, *T'ung-shu* 通書 (Explanatory Text [on the Book of Changes]). Also known as *Yi T'ung* (Explanation of the Changes). 40 chaps. Refs. to *Ein Beitrag zur Kenntnis der chinesischen Philosophie, T'ūng-šǔ des Čeǔ-tsï, mit Čū-Hī's Commentar, nach dem Sing-li Tsing-i.* Chaps. 1-20 transl. by Wilhelm Grube; chaps. 21-40 by Werner Eichhorn. Leipzig: Verlag Asia Major, 1932: 442-451, 501, 541, 589
See also under Eichhorn, Werner

Chou Yi Ts'an-t'ung-ch'i 周易參同契 (Akinness of the Trio in the Chou Changes). Commonly known as *Ts'an-t'ung-ch'i.* 1 ch. Attributed to Wei Po-yang 魏伯陽 , and said to have been written ca. A.D. 142. Refs. to transl. of Wu Lu-ch'iang and Tenney L. Davis, "An Ancient Chinese Treatise on Alchemy Entitled Ts'an T'ung Ch'i." *Isis*, vol. 18 (1932), 210-289: 426-430, 432, 440-1

Chou Yi Ts'an-t'ung-ch'i Fa-hui 發揮 (Explanations on the Chou Yi Ts'an-t'ung-ch'i). Comp. by Yü Yen 俞琰 (13th century) in 9 ch. *Taoist Canon* ed., vol. 625: 432

Chou Yi Ts'an-t'ung-ch'i K'ao-yi 考異 (Study of Variants in the Chou Yi Ts'an-t'ung-ch'i). Comp. by Chu Hsi (whom see) in 1 ch. TSCC ed., vol. 550: 429

Chu Chen 朱震 (1072-1138), *Han-shang Yi-chuan* 漢上易傳 (Commentary on the Changes from the Han River). 11 ch. of text, plus 3 ch. of diagrams and 1 supplementary ch. Refs. to TCTCC ed.: 118, 440

Chu Hsi 朱熹 (1130-1200), *Chu-tzǔ Wen-chi Ta-ch'üan Lei-pien* 子文

集大全類編 (Classified Compilation of the Collected Writings of Chu Hsi). 21 ch. Ed. of Yung-cheng period (1723-35): 622

——, *Chu-tzŭ Yü-lei* 語類 (Classified Conversations of Chu Hsi). Referred to as *Conversations*. 140 ch. Comp. by Chu's disciples and 1st published in 1270. Ying-yüan Shu-yüan 應元書阮 ed. of T'ung-chih period (1862-74): 534-544, 546-560, 566-570, 591, 622, 656

——, *Chu Wen-kung Wen-chi* 文公文集 (Collected Writings of Chu Hsi). Referred to as *Writings*. 100 plus 21 supplementary ch. Preface dated 1532. SPTK ed. [Excerpts from this and the preceding work are contained in the *Chu-tzŭ Ch'üan-shu* 全書 (Complete Works of Chu Hsi), 1st published in 1714 in 66 ch. Of this, ch. 42-48 are transl. in J. Percy Bruce, *The Philosophy of Human Nature, by Chu Hsi* (London: Probsthain, 1922), and ch. 49 in Stanislas Le Gall, *Le philosophe Tchou Hi, sa doctrine, son influence* (Shanghai: Variétés sinologiques no. 6, 2nd ed., 1923)]: 489, 516, 534, 536, 538-9, 542, 545, 555, 562-5

——, *Ta Hsüeh Chang-chü* 大學章句 (Commentary on the Great Learning). 1 ch.: 561, 606-7

——, *Yi-hsüeh Ch'i-meng* 易學啟蒙 (Explanation of the Changes for Beginners). 2 ch. See also Hu Fang-p'ing: 454

——, ed., *Yi-lo Yüan-yüan Lu* 伊洛淵源錄 (Record of Origins from Yi-lo). Completed in 1173 in 14 ch. Important source on Neo-Confucian school up to Chu Hsi. Ch. 6 contains an account of Chang Tsai (whom see) by Lü Ta-lin 呂大臨 (died ca. 1090). TSCC ed., vol. 3340: 478, 498

See also Bodde, Derk; Bruce, J. Percy; Chang Tsai, *Hsi Ming*; Chou Tun-yi; *Chou Yi Ts'an-t'ung-ch'i K'ao-yi*

Ch'u San-tsang Chi-chi, see under Seng-yu

Chu Yi-tsun 朱彝尊 (1629-1709), *T'ai-chi T'u Shou-shou K'ao* 太極圖授受考 (Study of the Transmission of the Diagram of the Supreme Ultimate). Contained in ch. 58 of Chu's *P'u-shu-t'ing Chi* 曝書亭集 (1st printed in 1714 in 80 ch.). See also under Chou Tun-yi: 442

*Ch'u Tzŭ 楚辭 (Elegies of Ch'u). Collection of imaginative poems of 3rd and 2nd centuries B.C.: 716, 719

Ch'uan-teng Lu 傳燈錄 (Record of the Transmission of the Lamp). Full title: *Ching-te* 景德 *Ch'uan-teng Lu*. Comp. by Tao-yüan 道原 in 1004 in 30 ch. An important source on Ch'an Buddhism. TT no. 2076 (51.196-467). See also *Hsü Ch'uan-teng Lu*: 401-4

*_Chuang-tzŭ_ 莊子. 10 ch. with 33 chaps. Represents philosophy of the Taoist Chuang Tzŭ (369?-286? B.C.). Refs. to H. A. Giles, transl., _Chuang Tzŭ_ (Shanghai: Kelly & Walsh, 2nd ed., 1926): 139, 166, 171, 174, 176-9, 185, 189, 203-235, 242, 250, 261, 269-270, 285, 288-9, 299, 325, 449, 526, 620, 692, 697-8, 717, 719

Chuang-tzŭ Commentary, see under Kuo Hsiang

*_Ch'un Ch'iu_ 春秋 and _Tso Chuan_ 左傳. The former is a brief historical chronicle of the state of Lu, 722-481 B.C.; the latter a much more extended "commentary" covering the same period and probably comp. in 4th century B.C. Refs. to transl. of Legge, _Chin. Class._, vol. 5. See also _Ku-liang Chuan_; _Kung-yang Chuan_; and index under _Ch'un Ch'iu_: 9, 16-19, 38, 61, 71-85, 90-92, 128, 130, 134, 136, 147, 165, 193-4, 279, 407, 410, 475, 494-5, 499, 673, 679, 681, 692, 699, 706-713, 715, 718

Ch'un-ch'iu Fan-lu, see Tung Chung-shu

Ch'un-ch'iu-wei Han-han-tzŭ 春秋緯漢含孳 (Apocryphal Treatise on the Spring and Autumn Annals: Cherished Beginnings of Growth of the Han Dynasty). This and three following works were probably written in 1st century B.C., but are now preserved only in re-collected fragments. Contained in YHSFCYS, 56.1-6: 128

Ch'un-ch'iu-wei Shuo-t'i-tz'ŭ 說題辭 (Apocryphal Treatise on the Spring and Autumn Annals: Discussion of Phraseology). YHSFCYS, 56.33-46: 124, 126-7

Ch'un-ch'iu-wei Wu-ch'eng-t'u 握誠圖 (Apocryphal Treatise on the Spring and Autumn Annals: Chart of Complete Sincerity). YHSFCYS, 56.13-17: 128

Ch'un-ch'iu-wei Yen-k'ung-t'u 演孔圖 (Apocryphal Treatise on the Spring and Autumn Annals: Expository Chart on Confucius). YHSFCYS, 56.47-58: 129-130

*_Chung Yung_ 中庸 (Doctrine of the Mean). Small Confucian work, traditionally but uncertainly ascribed to grandson of Confucius. Now contained in _Li Chi_, chap. 28. Refs. to transl. of Legge in SBE, vol. 28, pp. 301-329. See also Hughes, E.R.: 4, 9, 40, 416-8, 420, 423-4, 446, 477, 499, 502, 510-1, 559, 582, 605, 627, 629, 631, 650, 669, 682, 689-690, 711, 716

Classic of Filial Piety, see _Hsiao Ching_

Contemporary Records, see _Shih-shuo Hsin-yü_

Dharmapāla, see under Hsüan-tsang

*Diogenes Laertius, _Lives and Opinions of Eminent Philosophers_. Transl. of C. D. Yonge. London: G. Bell & Sons, 1915: 93, 197, 202

Doctrine of the Mean, see _Chung Yung_

Dubs, H. H., "The Beginnings of Alchemy," _Isis_, vol. 38 (1947), 62-86: 431

——, _History of the Former Han Dynasty_, see _Ch'ien Han Shu_

——, Review of Fung Yu-lan, *A Short History of Chinese Philosophy*, in *Journal of the American Oriental Society*, vol. 71 (1951), 90-91: xvi
See also under *Hsün-tzu*

Dvādaśa-nikāya Śāstra, see under Chi-tsang

Eichhorn, Werner, "Chou Tun-i, ein chinesisches Gelehrtenleben aus dem 11. Jahrhundert." *Abhandlungen für die Kunde des Morgenlandes*, vol. 21 (Leipzig, 1936), 1-66. See also under Chang Tsai; Chou Tun-yi: 434-5, 498

Evolutions of Rites, see *Li Yün*

Fa-tsang 法藏 (643-712), *Chin Shih-tzŭ Chang* 金師子章 (Essay on the Gold Lion). 1 ch. TT no. 1880 (45.663-667): 339-347, 349-351, 353-7

——, *Hsiu Hua-yen Ao-chih Wang-chin Huan-yüan Kuan* 修華嚴奧旨妄盡還源觀 (Cultivation of the Contemplation of the Mysterious Meaning of the Avatamsaka for Extinguishing False Thought and Returning to the Origin). Referred to as *Hua-yen Huan-yüan Kuan*. 1 ch. TT no. 1876 (45.637-641): 340-3, 347, 353, 357

——, *Hua-yen Ching Yi-hai Pai-men* 華嚴經義海百門 (The Hundred Theories in the Sea of Ideas of the Avatamsaka Sūtra). 1 ch. TT no. 1875 (45.627-636): 340-1, 344-5, 348-9, 351-2, 354, 356-8

Fan Chen 范縝 (ca. 450-ca. 515), *Shen Mieh Lun* 神滅論 (Essay on the Extinction of the Soul). Preserved in *Hung-ming Chi*, ch. 9 (which see under Seng-yu), and *Liang Shu*, ch. 48 (which see). See also Balázs, Stefan: 289-292

Fang-kuang 放光. Abbreviated Chinese title of *Pañcaviṃśatisāhasrikā Prajñāpāramitā Sūtra*. 20 ch. TT no. 221 (8.1-146): 259, 265, 268

Feng Yu-lan, see Fung Yu-lan

Forke, Alfred, *Geschichte der alten chinesischen Philosophie; Geschichte der mittelalterlichen chinesischen Philosophie; Geschichte der neueren chinesischen Philosophie*. Hamburg: 1927, 1934, 1938. See also under Wang Ch'ung: xiii

Franke, Otto, *Studien zur Geschichte des konfuzianischen Dogmas und der chinesischen Staatsreligion: das Problem des Tsch'un-Ts'iu und Tung Tschung-schu's Tsch'un-Ts'iu Fan Lu*. Hamburg: L. Friederichsen, 1920. See also Tung Chung-shu: 16-17, 82

Franke, Wolfgang, *Die staatspolitischen Reformversuche K'ang Yu-weis und seiner Schule*. Berlin: Mitteilungen des Seminars für Orientalische Sprachen, Pt. I, Ostasiatische Studien, 1935. See also under K'ang Yu-wei: 676

Freeman, Mansfield, "The Philosophy of Tai Tung-yüan." *Journal of the North China Branch of the Royal Asiatic Society*, vol. 64 (Shanghai, 1933), 50-71: 651

——, "Yen Hsi Chai, a 17th Century Chinese Philosopher." *Ibid.*, vol. 57 (1926), 70-91: 631

Fu-chou Ts'ao-shan Pen-chi Ch'an-shih Yü-lu 撫州曹山本寂禪
師語錄 (Recorded Conversations of the Ch'an Teacher Ts'ao-
shan Pen-chi of Fu-chou). Comp. by Japanese Buddhist monk Genkei
玄契 in 1740 in 2 ch. TT no. 1987B (47.535-544): 403

Fung [Feng] Yu-lan 馮友蘭 (1895-   ), *A Comparative Study of Life
Ideals*. Shanghai: Commercial Press, 1924: 383

——, *A Short History of Chinese Philosophy*. Ed. by Derk Bodde. New
York: Macmillan, 1948: xiii, xvi, 191, 710, 721

——, *The Spirit of Chinese Philosophy*. Transl. by E. R. Hughes. London:
Kegan Paul, 1947: xv, 171, 175-6, 234, 258, 387, 721
See also under Kuo Hsiang

Gardner, Charles S., *Chinese Traditional Historiography*. Cambridge: Harvard University Press, 1938: 17

Grand Norm, see *Hung Fan*

Granet, Marcel, *Danses et légendes de la Chine ancienne*. 2 vols. Paris: Félix
Alcan, 1926: 148

Great Learning, see *Ta Hsüeh*

Great Nirvāṇa Sūtra, see *Nieh-pan Ching Chi-chieh*

Han Po, see Wang Pi, *Chou Yi*

Han Shu, see *Ch'ien Han Shu*

Han-wen-chia, see *Li-wei Han-wen-chia*

Han Yü 韓愈 (768-824), *Ch'ang-li Hsien-sheng Chi* 昌黎先生集
(Collected Works of Han Yü). Referred to as *Works*. 40 ch. SPTK ed.:
441-2

——, *Yüan Hsing* 原性 (On the Origin of the Nature). Contained in
ibid., 11.3-5: 413, 554

——, *Yüan Tao* 道 (On the Origin of the Truth). Contained in *ibid.*,
11.1-3: 409-410

Hegel, Georg Wilhelm, *The Logic of Hegel*. Transl. of William Wallace.
Oxford: Clarendon Press, 2nd ed., 1892: 383

History, Book of, see *Shu Ching*

Ho Hsiu, see under *Kung-yang Chuan*

Hou Han Shu 後漢書 (History of the Later Han Dynasty). Comp. by
Fan Yeh 范曄 (398-445) in 120 ch. TW ed.: 91, 125, 133, 150-1, 240

Hsi K'ang 嵇康 (223-262), *Hsi Chung-san Chi* 中散集 (Collected
Writings of Hsi K'ang). 10 ch. SPTK ed.: 190

Hsiang Hsiu, see under Kuo Hsiang

Hsiao Ching 孝經 (Classic of Filial Piety). 18 chaps. A Confucian work
of the Ch'in or Han dynasty. Refs. to transl. of Legge in SBE, vol. 3,
pp. 465-488: 46, 134

Hsieh Liang-tso 謝良佐 (1050-1103), *Shang-ts'ai Hsien-cheng Yü-lu*

上蔡先生語錄 (Recorded Conversations of Hsieh Liang-tso). 2 ch. CYTCS ed.: 505-6

Hsieh Ling-yün 謝靈運 (385-433), *Pien Tsung Lun* 辯宗論 (Discussion of Essentials). Preserved in ch. 18 of *Kuang Hung-ming Chi* (which see under Tao-hsüan). TT no. 2103 (52.224-228): 274-283, 388-9

Hsin T'ang Shu 新唐書 (New History of the T'ang Dynasty). Comp. by Ou-yang Hsiu 歐陽修 (1007-72), Sung Ch'i 宋祁 (998-1061), and others in 225 ch. TW ed. See also under Yi-hsing: 110-111, 114-7, 408-9, 413

Hsing-li Ta-ch'üan 性理大全 (Great Compendium of Neo-Confucianism). Completed by Hu Kuang 胡廣 (1370-1418) in 1415 in 70 ch. San-wei-t'ang 三畏堂 ed. of 1711. See also under Shao Yung; Ts'ai Ch'eng: 454, 470-2

Hsu, P. C., *Ethical Realism in Neo-Confucian Thought*, see under Ch'eng Hao

Hsü Ch'uan-teng Lu 續傳燈錄 (Supplement to the Transmission of the Lamp). Comp. by Chü-ting 居頂 (died 1404) in 36 ch. TT no. 2077 (51.469-714). See also *Ch'uan-teng Lu:* 401

Hsü Kao Seng Chuan, see under Tao-hsüan

Hsüan-tsang 玄奘 (596-664), *Ch'eng Wei-shih Lun* 成唯識論 (Completion of the Doctrine of Mere Ideation). Sanskrit title: *Vijñapti-mātratā-siddhi*. 10 ch. A synthetic transl. from the Sanskrit of a comm. by Dharmapāla on a treatise by Vasubandhu, together with nine other main comms. TT no. 1585 (31.1-60). Refs. to Louis de la Vallée Poussin, transl., *Vijñaptimātratāsiddhi, la Siddhi de Hiuan-Tsang.* 2 vols. Paris: Paul Geuthner, 1928-29: 300-320, 324-338, 344

——, *Pien Chung-pien* 辯中邊 (Discrimination between the Middle and the Extremes). Sanskrit title: *Madhyānta-vibhāga.* 3 ch. Work based on a treatise in Sanskrit by Vasubandhu. TT no. 1600 (31. 464-477): 309-310

——, *Wei-shih Erh-shih Lun* 唯識二十論 (Treatise in Twenty Stanzas on Representation Only). Sanskrit title: *Vijñapti-mātratā-siddhi*; *Viṃśatikā.* 1 ch. Transl. of a Sanskrit work by Vasubandhu and the accompanying comm. by Dharmapāla. TT no. 1590 (31.74-77). Refs. to Clarence H. Hamilton, transl., *Wei Shih Er Shih Lun, or the Treatise in Twenty Stanzas on Representation-Only.* New Haven: American Oriental Society, 1938: 319-323

For this and *Ch'eng Wei-shih Lun*, see also under K'uei-chi. For Hsüan-tsang, see also under Watters, Thomas

*Hsün-tzŭ 荀子. 20 ch. with 32 chaps. The greater part probably by the Confucian Hsün Tzŭ (ca. 298-ca. 238 B.C.). Refs.:

(a) For the greater part of the work, to H. H. Dubs, transl., *The Works of Hsüntze*. London: Probsthain, 1928: 166, 670

(b) For a portion of chap. 6, to L. C. Porter, comp., *Aids to the Study of Chinese Philosophy* (Peiping: Yenching University, 1934). Cited as *Aids*: 9

(c) For untranslated portions, to SPTK ed.: 56

Hu Fang-p'ing 胡方平 (13th century), *Yi-hsüeh Ch'i-meng T'ung-shih* 易學啟蒙通釋 (Interpretation of the Yi-hsüeh Ch'i-meng). 2 ch. TCTCC ed. See also Chu Hsi, *Yi-hsüeh Ch'i-meng*: 463-4

Hu Shih 胡適 (1891-), "The Development of Zen Buddhism in China." *Chinese Social and Political Science Review*, vol. 15 (Peiping, 1931), 475-505. See also under *Shen-hui Ho-shang Yi-chi*; *Tai Chen*: 388

Hua-yen Ching, see *Avataṃsaka Sūtra*

*Huai-nan-tzŭ 淮南子. 21 ch. Eclectic work comp. under auspices of Prince of Huai-nan (died 122 B.C.). Refs. to Liu Wen-tien 劉文典, ed., *Huai-nan Hung-lieh Chi-chieh* 鴻烈集解. Shanghai: Commercial Press, 1933: 13, 15, 26, 28, 54, 121-2, 179

Huang Jung, see Liao P'ing, *Huang-ti Chiang-yü T'u*

Huang K'an 皇侃 (488-545), *Lun-yü Chi-chieh Yi-su* 論語集解義疏 (Exegesis of Collected Comments on the Analects). 10 ch. *Chih-pu-tsu Chai Ts'ung-shu* 知不足齋叢書 ed., comp. by Pao T'ing-po 鮑廷博 (1728-1814) and his son between 1776 and 1824: 173-4

Huang Siu-chi, *Lu Hsiang-shan, a twelfth century Chinese idealist philosopher*. New Haven: American Oriental Society, 1944. See also Lu Chiu-yüan: 572-3, 579-80

Huang-ti Nei-ching 黃帝內經 (Classic of Internal Medicine of the Yellow Emperor). 36 ch. A Han dynasty work, traditionally ascribed to a much earlier period. English transl. of first 34 chaps. by Ilza Veith, *Huang Ti Nei Ching Su Wen, the Yellow Emperor's Classic of Internal Medicine* (Baltimore: Williams and Wilkins Co., 1949). See also *Ling Ch'u; Su Wen*: 131, 716, 719

Huang Tsung-hsi 黃宗羲 (1610-95), comp., *Ming-ju Hsüeh-an* 明儒學案 (Writings of Ming Confucianists). 62 ch. Nanchang ed. of 1888: 596, 623, 627-9, 640, 660

——, *Nan-lei Wen-an* 南雷文案 (Prose Anthology of Huang Tsung-hsi). Referred to as *Prose Anthology*. 10 plus 1 supplementary ch. SPTK ed.: 640-1, 648, 659-660, 668-9

*——, comp., *Sung-Yüan Hsüeh-an* 宋元學案 (Writings of Sung and Yüan Philosophers). 100 ch. Supplemented by Ch'üan Tsu-wang

1 ch. Said to have been written in 1884, but probably actually written sometime during the period 1898-1902. Published in K'ang's magazine, *Pu-jen Tsa-chih* 不忍雜志, nos. 5-6 (1913): 678-680

——, *Lun-yü Chu* 論語注 (Commentary on the Analects). Written in 1 ch. in 1902. Contained in *Wan-mu-ts'ao-t'ang Ts'ung-shu* (see above): 680-1

——, *Ta T'ung Shu* 大同書 (Book of the Great Unity). First conceived of by K'ang in 1884, but probably not written down in its present form until 1901-02, and 1st partially published only in 1913. Shanghai: Ch'ang-hsing 長興 Book Co. movable type ed.: 684-691 See also Ch'ien Mu; Franke, Wolfgang

Kao Seng Chuan 高僧傳 (Biographies of Eminent Buddhist Monks). Comp. by Hui-chiao 慧皎 (died 554) in 14 ch. in 519. TT no. 2059 (50.322-423). See also *Sung Kao Seng Chuan*, and under Tao-hsüan: 241-2, 245-7, 250-5, 257-260, 270-1

Ko Hung 葛洪 (ca. 250-ca. 330), *Pao-p'u-tzŭ* 抱朴子 (The Master Who Embraces Simplicity). Divided into an "inner" sect. (4 ch. with 20 chaps.) and an "outer" sect. (4 ch. with 52 chaps). Two partial Western translations of the "inner" sect.: (a) Of chaps. 1-4 and 11, by Eugene Feifel, "Pao-p'u Tzu Nei-p'ien," *Monumenta Serica*, Peiping, vols. 6 (1941), 113-211; 9 (1944), 1-33; 11 (1946), 1-32. (b) Of chaps. 4 and 16, by Wu Lu-ch'iang and Tenney L. Davis, "An Ancient Chinese Alchemical Classic," *Proceedings of the American Academy of Arts and Sciences*, vol. 70 (1935), 221-284. Refs. to SPTK ed.: 432

Kramers, R. P., *K'ung Tzŭ Chia Yü*, see under *Ta Tai Li Chi*

Ku-liang Chuan 穀梁傳 (Ku-liang Commentary). A comm. on the *Ch'un Ch'iu*, traditionally, but doubtfully, attributed to Ku-liang Ch'ih 赤, said to be a disciple of Tzŭ-hsia (himself a disciple of Confucius). Like the *Kung-yang Chuan* (which see), it attaches an esoteric meaning to the *Ch'un Ch'iu*: 679

Ku-tsun-hsü Yü-lu 古尊宿語錄 (Recorded Sayings of Ancient Worthies). 48 ch. Stated to be written by a certain "Tripiṭaka Master" named Tse 賾 of the Sung dynasty (960-1279), whose exact identity is uncertain. *Tripiṭaka Supplement*, Pt. Ib, case 23; vols. 2-4. Cited as *Sayings of Ancient Worthies*: 392-403

Ku-wen Shang-shu 古文尚書 (Book of History in Ancient Script). 46 ch. A Han dynasty recension of the *Shu Ching* (which see): 136

*Kuan-tzŭ 管子. 24 ch. with 86 chaps. Electic work attributed to Kuan Chung 仲 (died 645 B.C.), but obviously much later, possibly 3rd century B.C. SPTK ed.: 718

Kuang Hung-ming Chi, see under Tao-hsüan

K'uei-chi 窺基 (632-682), *Ch'eng Wei-shih Lun Shu-chi* 成唯識論述記 (Transmitted Notes on the Ch'eng Wei-shih Lun). 20 ch. TT no. 1830 (43.229-606): 301, 319, 321, 323-4, 327

——, *Wei-shih Erh-shih Lun Shu-chi* 唯識二十論述記 (Transmitted Notes on the Wei-shih Erh-shih Lun). 2 ch. TT no. 1834 (43.978-1009): 323
For this and the preceding work, see also under Hsüan-tsang

Kung-yang Chuan 公羊傳 (Kung-yang Commentary). A comm. on the Ch'un Ch'iu attributed to Kung-yang Kao 高, said to be a disciple of Tzŭ-hsia (himself a disciple of Confucius). Like the *Ku-liang Chuan* (which see), it attaches an esoteric meaning to the *Ch'un Ch'iu*. Also known as the *Kung-yang Ch'un-ch'iu* or *Ch'un-ch'iu Kung-yang Chuan*. Has a commentary by Ho Hsiu 何休 (129-182). SPTK ed. See also Woo, Kang: 18, 45, 75, 78-79, 82-84, 130, 134, 673, 679-680, 692, 704

Kuo Hsiang 郭象 (died A.D. 312), *Chuang-tzŭ Chu* 莊子注 (Chuang-tzŭ Commentary). 10 ch. Though commonly attributed to Kuo Hsiang, it is actually the joint work of him and Hsiang Hsiu 向秀 (ca. 221-ca. 300). Refs. to *Chuang-tzŭ Chu-su* 疏 ed. in the *Ku-yi Ts'ung-shu* 古逸叢書, comp. by Li Shu-ch'ang 黎庶昌 (Tokyo, 1882-84). Many passages are also given in Fung Yu-lan, *Chuang Tzŭ, a new selected translation with an exposition of the philosophy of Kuo Hsiang* (Shanghai: Commercial Press, 1933): 171-2, 176, 178-9, 205-236, 269

Lao-tzŭ 老子. 81 chaps. Taoist work also known as *Tao Te Ching* 道德經. Probably 4th or 3rd century B.C. Good transl. by Arthur Waley, *The Way and Its Power* (London: Allen & Unwin, 1934). Refs. by chap. numbers. See also under Wang Pi: 4, 96, 138, 141, 146-7, 168-9, 179, 180-3, 189-190, 194, 198, 203, 205, 218-9, 242-3, 248, 259, 262, 268, 291, 299, 425, 441, 467, 521, 545, 579, 693, 714

Li Ao 李翱 (died ca. 844), *Fu-hsing Shu* 復性書 (Essay on Returning to the Nature). Short treatise in 2.5-9 of the *Li Wen-kung Chi* (which see): 413-421, 424

——, *Li Wen-kung Chi* 文公集 (Collected Works of Li Ao), 18 ch. Cited as *Works*. SPTK ed.: 413, 424

Li Chi 禮記 (Book of Rites). 46 chaps. A Confucian comp., embracing earlier materials, made during the Han dynasty. Refs. to transl. of Legge in SBE, vols. 27-28. See also *Li Yün*; *Ta Tai Li Chi*; *Wang*

Chih; *Yüeh Ling*: 14, 40, 49, 85, 113, 134, 147, 407, 412, 417-8, 487, 501, 514, 522, 679, 685, 692, 706, 709, 711, 715, 718

Li Kung 李塨 (1659-1733), *Chuan-chu Wen* 傳註問 (Commentary on the Four Books). 1 ch. Ssǔ-ts'un Hsüeh-hui 四存學會 movable type ed.: 650

——, *Ta-hsüeh Pien-yeh* 大學辯業 (Analysis of the Great Learning). 4 ch. Contained in *Chi-fu Ts'ung-shu* (which see under Yen Yüan): 634

Li Ting-tso 李鼎祚 (fl. between 742 and 906), *Chou Yi Chi-chieh* 周易集解 (Collected Commentaries on the Chou Changes). 17 ch. Contains comm. by Yü Fan 虞翻 (164-233). *Chin-tai Pi-shu* 津逮祕書 ed. of 1630-ca. 1642: 426-7

Li-wei Chi-ming-cheng 禮緯稽命徵 (Apocryphal Treatise on Rites: Investigation of Omens). This and the following work were probably written in 1st century B.C., but are now preserved only in re-collected fragments. Contained in YHSFCYS, 54.24-30: 126

Li-wei Han-wen-chia 含文嘉 (Apocryphal Treatise on Rites: Excellencies of Cherished Literature). YHSFCYS, 54.12-23: 44

*Li Yün 禮運 (Evolutions of Rites). Treatise now constituting chap. 7 of the *Li Chi* (which see). Refs. to transl. of Legge in SBE, vol 27, pp. 364-393: 42, 85, 679-680, 699, 704

Liang Shu 梁書 (History of the Liang Dynasty). Comp. by Yao Ch'a 姚察 (533-606) and his son Yao Ssǔ-lien 思廉 (died 637) in 56 ch. TW ed.: 289-290, 292

Liang Su 梁肅 (753-793), *Chih-kuan T'ung-li* 止觀統例 (General Rules for Cessation and Contemplation). Small treatise contained in TT no. 1915 (46.473-474): 423

Liao P'ing 廖平 (1852-1932), *Chih Sheng P'ien* 知聖篇 (Treatise on Comprehending the Sage). 2 ch. Contained in *Liu-yi-kuan Ts'ung-shu* 六譯館叢書. Chengtu: Ts'un-ku 存古 Book Co., 1925 (in which all the following works by Liao are also contained): 709-710

——, *Chin-ku Hsüeh-k'ao* 今古學考 (Study of the New and Old Learning). Completed in 1886 in 2 ch.: 706-708

——, *Ching-hsüeh Ssǔ-pien Chi* 經學四變記 (Record of the Fourth Phase of Study of the Classics). 1 ch. Referred to as *Fourth Phase of Study*: 706, 708-9, 711, 713, 715-7

——, *Ching-hsüeh Wu-pien Chi* 五變記 (Record of the Fifth Phase of Study of the Classics). 2 ch. Referred to as *Fifth Phase of Study*: 717-9

——, *Huang-ti Chiang-yü T'u* 皇帝疆域圖 (Geographical Charts for Sovereigns and Emperors). Comp. in 1 ch. by Liao's disciple, Huang Jung 黃鎔: 711-4

——, *Ku-hsüeh K'ao* 古學考 (Study of the Old Learning). 1 ch.: 709

——, *P'i Liu P'ien* 闢劉篇 (Treatise on Refuting Liu Hsin). 1 ch.: 709

——, *Ta-ch'eng-chieh Chiang-yi* 大成節講義 (Lecture Delivered on the Birthday of Confucius). Contained in sect. of same ed. entitled *Liu-yi-kuan tsa-chu* 雜著: 713

Liebenthal, Walter, *The Book of Chao*. Monumenta Serica, Monograph XIII. Peiping: Catholic University of Peking, 1948. See also under Seng-chao: 243, 245, 247, 253-6, 274, 363

——, "The Immortality of the Soul in Chinese Thought," *Monumenta Nipponica*, vol. 8 (Tokyo, 1952), 327-396: 292

——, "Shih Hui-yüan's Buddhism as Set Forth in His Writings," *Journal of the American Oriental Society*, vol. 70 (1950), 243-259. See also under Hui-yüan: 241, 272, 287

See also under T'ang Yung-t'ung

*Lieh-tzŭ 列子. 8 chaps. Chinese opinion regards it as a "forgery" (perhaps incorporating some earlier materials) of the 3rd or 4th century A.D. Western scholars are more inclined to accept a good part of it as possibly 3rd century B.C. Refs.:

(a) For chaps. 1-6 and 8, to Lionel Giles, transl., *Taoist Teachings from the Book of Lieh Tzŭ*. London: John Murray, 1925. This transl. omits some passages. For a complete transl., see Richard Wilhelm, *Liä Dsï, das wahre Buch vom quellenden Urgrund* (Jena: E. Diederichs, 1930): 98, 190-195, 206-207, 208, 576, 719

(b) For chap. 7, entitled "Yang Chu" 楊朱, to Anton Forke, transl., *Yang Chu's Garden of Pleasure*. London: John Murray, 1912: 191, 195-204

Ling Ch'u 靈樞 (Spiritual Pivot). 12 ch. Part of the Han medical work, *Huang-ti Nei-ching* (which see): 716, 719

Liu Hsün, see under *Shih-shuo Hsin-yü*

Liu Mu 劉牧 (1011-64), *Yi-shu Kou-yin T'u* 易數鈎隱圖 (Diagram Giving Secret Entry to the Numbers of the Changes). 3 ch. TCTCC ed.: 451-2

Liu-tsu Ta-shih Fa-pao T'an-ching 六祖大師法寶壇經 (Sūtra Spoken by the Sixth Patriarch, Teacher of the Buddha-Truth). Referred to as *Sūtra Spoken by the Sixth Patriarch*. Comp. in 1 ch. with 10 chaps. by Tsung-pao 宗寶. Preface dated 1290. Refs. to TT no. 2008 (48.345-365). There are also Western translations: (a) Of chaps. 1-6 only, by Erwin Rousselle, "Das Sūtra des sechsten Patriarchen,"

Sinica, Frankfurt, vol. 5 (1930), 177-191; vol. 6 (1931), 26-34; vol. 11 (1936), 131-137, 202-210. (b) Defective transl. by Wong Mou-lam, *The Sutra of Wei Lang (or Hui Neng)*. New ed. by Christmas Humphreys. London: Luzac & Co., 1947: 391, 395-6, 415, 616

Liu Tsung-chou 劉宗周 (1578-1645), *Liu-tzŭ Ch'üan-shu* 子全書 (Complete Works of Liu Tsung-chou). Referred to as *Works*. 40 ch. Wang-shih Chiao-k'an 王氏校刊 ed. of 1824: 640, 647-8

Lo Ch'in-shun 羅欽順 (1465-1547), *K'un Chih Chi* 困知記 (Remarks Reached after Hard Study). 2 plus 2 supplementary ch. CYTCS ed.: 621-2

Lotus Sūtra, see *Saddharma-puṇḍarīka Sūtra*

Lu Chiu-yüan 陸九淵 (1139-93), *Hsiang-shan Hsien-sheng Ch'üan-chi* 象山先生全集 (Complete Works of Lu Chiu-yüan). 36 ch., with a biography by Yang Chien (whom see). SPTK ed. See also Huang Siu-chi: 546, 572-9, 586-7, 589-90

Lu Lung-ch'i 陸隴其 (1630-93), *Hsüeh-shu Pien* 學術辨 (Analysis of Schools of Thought). Ch. 2 of his *San-yü-t'ang Wen-chi* 三魚堂文集, 1st printed in 1701 in 18 ch.: 623

*Lü-shih Ch'un Ch'iu 呂氏春秋 (Spring and Autumn of Mr. Lü). 26 ch. Eclectic work comp. under auspices of Lü Pu-wei 不韋 (died 235 B.C.). Refs. to Richard Wilhelm, transl., *Frühling und Herbst des Lü Bu We*. Jena: E. Diederichs, 1928. See also *Yüeh Ling*: 54

Lu Shih-yi 陸世儀 (1611-72), *Ssŭ-pien Lu* 思辨錄 (Thoughts on Various Topics). 22 ch. CYTCS ed.: 635-6

Lü Ta-lin, see under Chu Hsi, *Yi-lo Yüan-yüan Lu*

Lun Heng, see Wang Ch'ung

*Lun Yü 論語 (Analects). Sayings of Confucius and some of his disciples in 20 ch. Translations of Legge, *Chin. Clas.*, vol. 1; William E. Soothill, *The Analects of Confucius* (Yokohama, 1910); Arthur Waley, *The Analects of Confucius* (London: Allen & Unwin, 2nd ed., 1945). Refs. to ch. and sect. numbers: 4, 8, 36-37, 46, 53, 62, 65, 69, 74, 129, 134, 147, 149, 159, 164, 173, 188-9, 220, 262, 275, 283, 408, 410, 498-9, 525, 559-560, 572, 575-6, 579, 582, 584, 605, 620, 631, 633, 635-6, 650, 680-1, 684, 692, 697, 701-3, 706, 708, 710, 713-4

Mādhyamika Śāstra, see under Anchō; Chi-tsang

Madhyānta-vibhāga, see under Hsüan-tsang

Mahāyānottaratantra Śāstra. Transl. from Sanskrit into Chinese by Ratnamati 勒那摩提 (arrived in China in 508) in 4 ch. TT no. 1611 (31.813-848): 343

Mahāyāna-śraddhotpāda Śāstra. Transl. from Sanskrit into Chinese in 1 ch.

by Paramārtha 眞諦 of the Liang dynasty (502-556). TT no. 1666 (32.575-583). See also transl. of D. T. Suzuki, *Açvaghosha's Discourse on the Awakening of Faith in the Mahāyāna*. Chicago: Open Court Publishing Co., 1900: 360-1, 366

Mao Ch'i-ling 毛奇齡 (1623-1716), *T'ai-chi T'u-shuo Yi-yi* 太極圖 說遺議 (Supplementary Discussion on the Diagram of the Supreme Ultimate Explained). 1 ch. Contained in *Hsi-ho Ho-chi* 西河合集 (Collected Works of Mao Ch'i-ling), 189 ch. 1st printed ca. 1699. See also under Chou Tun-yi: 440

Maspero, Henri, "Les procédés de 'nourrir le principe vital' dans la religion taoiste ancienne." *Journal Asiatique* (Paris, 1937), pp. 178-252, 353-430: 431

*_Mencius_ 孟子. 7 ch. A collection of sayings of Meng Tzǔ or Mencius (372?-289? B.C.). Transl. of Legge in *Chin. Clas.*, vol. 2 Refs. to ch. and sect. numbers: 4, 9, 40, 166, 203, 411-2, 417, 419, 448, 451, 491-2, 494-5, 499, 501, 505-6, 510, 514, 520, 522-4, 528, 573-4, 576-7, 582, 584, 587, 599, 601, 605, 619-620, 631, 646, 650-1, 659, 662, 667, 671, 689, 692

Ming-ju Hsüeh-an, see under Huang Tsung-hsi

Ming Shih 明史 (History of the Ming Dynasty). Comp. by Chang T'ing-yü 張廷玉 (1672-1755) and others in 366 ch. TW ed.: 593-4

*_Mo-tzǔ_ 墨子. 15 ch. with 71 chaps. A collection of writings of the Mohist school. Refs. to Y. P. Mei, transl., *The Ethical and Political Works of Motse*. London: Probsthain, 1929: 12, 160, 692

Monthly Commands, see *Yüeh Ling*

Mu T'ien-tzǔ Chuan 穆天子傳 (Chronicle of Mu Son of Heaven). 6 ch. Account of a miraculous journey of King Mu (1001-947 B.C.) to the regions west of China, allegedly recovered from a tomb in A.D. 281, but quite possible a forgery: 716

Nan Shih 南史 (History of the Southern Dynasties). Comp. by Li Yen-shou 李延壽 (ca. 600-ca. 680) in 80 ch. TW ed.: 169

Needham, Joseph, "Human Laws and Laws of Nature in China and the West," *Journal of the History of Ideas*, vol. 12 (1951), 3-30, 194-230: 444

Nieh-pan Ching Chi-chieh 涅槃經集解 (Collected Commentaries on the Nirvāṇa Sūtra). Comp. by Pao-liang 寶亮 (444-509) in 71 ch. *Tripiṭaka Supplement*, Pt. Ia, case 94, vols. 2-4: 271, 390

Nirvāṇa Sūtra, see preceding item

Odes, Book of, see *Shih Ching*

Pañcaviṃśatisāhasrikā Prajñāpāramitā Sūtra, or *Pañcaviṃśatikā*, see *Fang Kuang*

P'ei Sung-chih, see under *San Kuo Chih*

Pelliot, Paul, "Le *Chou king* en caractères anciens et le *Chang chou che wen*." *Mémoires Concernant l'Asie Orientale*, vol. 2 (Paris, 1916), 123-176. See also *Shu Ching*: 134

Petrov, A. A., see under Wright, Arthur F.

P'i Jih-hsiu 皮日休 (died ca. 881), *P'i-tzŭ Wen-shu* 子文藪 (Collected Writings of P'i Jih-hsiu). 10 ch. SPTK ed.: 408

Po Hu T'ung 白虎通 (Comprehensive Discussions in the White Tiger Hall). Also known as *Po Hu T'ung-yi* 義 . 4 ch. with 44 chaps. Based upon the discussion on the classics held by scholars in A.D. 79, though contains interpolations. Traditionally, though uncertainly, ascribed to Pan Ku (whom see under *Ch'ien Han Shu*). Refs. to Tjan, Tjoe Som, transl., *Po Hu T'ung, the Comprehensive Discussions in the White Tiger Hall*. 2 vols. Leiden: E. J. Brill, 1949 and 1952: 22-23, 36, 40-45, 63-65, 69-70, 91, 112, 118

Prajñāpāramitā-upadeśa Śāstra. 100 ch. TT no. 1854 (45.77-115): 294

Rites, Book of, see *Li Chi*

Royal Regulations, see *Wang Chih*

Saddharma-puṇḍarīka Sūtra. 27 ch. Abbreviated transl. by William E. Soothill, *The Lotus of the Wonderful Law*. Oxford: Clarendon Press, 1930: 360

San Cheng Chi 三正記 (Record of the Three Beginnings). A now lost Han dynasty treatise on the *Li* or *Rites*: 63-4

San Kuo Chih 三國志 (History of the Three Kingdoms). Comp. by Ch'en Shou 陳壽 (233-297) in 65 ch., with a comm. by P'ei Sung-chih 裴松之 (372-451). TW ed.: 179-180, 188-9

Santayana, George, *Reason in Science*. Vol. 5 of his *Works*. New York: Triton ed., 1936: 433

Śata Śāstra, see under Chi-tsang

Sayings of Ancient Worthies, see *Ku-tsun-hsü Yü-lu*

Seng-chao 僧肇 (384-414), *Chao Lun* 肇論 (Book of Chao). 1 ch. with 4 chaps. TT no. 1858 (45.150-161). Refs. to transl. of Walter Liebenthal (which also see), *The Book of Chao*. Monumenta Serica, Monograph XIII. Peiping: Catholic University of Peking, 1948: 246, 248, 252, 259-269, 298, 339, 388, 390

——, *Wei-mo Chieh Ching Chu* 維摩詰經注 (Commentary to the Vimalakīrti-nirdeśa Sūtra). 10 ch. TT no. 1775 (38.327-420): 259, 269

Seng-yu 僧祐 (445-518), *Ch'u San-tsang Chi-chi* 出三藏記集 (Excerpts from the Tripiṭaka). 15 ch. TT no. 2145 (45.1-114): 240-2, 276, 294

*Shih Ching 詩經 (Book of Odes). Early Chou collection of 305 court poems and folksongs. Translations of Arthur Waley, *The Book of Odes* (London: Allen & Unwin, 1937), and Bernhard Karlgren, *The Book of Songs* (Stockholm: Museum of Far Eastern Antiquities, 1950). Refs. to odes as numbered in transl. of Legge, *Chin. Clas.*, vol. 4: 44, 55, 87, 124-6, 134, 136, 147, 159, 407, 410, 419, 475, 505, 510, 522, 576, 635, 655, 679, 690, 709, 715-6, 718-9

Shih-shuo Hsin-yü 世說新語 (Contemporary Records of New Discourses). Comp. in 3 ch. with 36 chaps. by Liu Yi-ch'ing 劉義慶 (403-444). With a comm. by Liu Hsün 劉峻 (426-521). Valuable source on Neo-Taoist thinkers, referred to as *Contemporary Records*. SPTK ed.: 170, 175-7, 185-6, 190, 251, 253-4, 261

Shih-wei Fan-li-ch'u 詩緯汜歷樞 (Apocryphal Treatise on the Book of Odes: Pivot of the Extensive Calendar). This and the next item were probably written in 1st century B.C., but are now preserved only in re-collected fragments. Contained in YHSFCYS, 54.2-4: 125-6

Shih-wei Han-shen-wu 含神霧 (Apocryphal Treatise on the Book of Odes: The Spirit-filled Aura). YHSFCYS, 54.5-11: 124

*Shu Ching 書經 (Book of History). Also known as *Shang-shu* 尚書. A collection of official speeches and documents, some from 1st millennium B.C., others later forgeries. New transl. of Bernhard Karlgren, "The Book of Documents," *Bulletin of the Museum of Far Eastern Antiquities*, No. 22 (Stockholm, 1950), pp. 1-81. Refs. to transl. of Legge in SBE, vol. 3. See also *Hung Fan*; *Ku-wen Shang-shu*; Pelliot, Paul; *Shang-shu Ta-chuan*: 14, 18, 63, 124, 133-4, 147, 407, 410, 450, 474-5, 506, 529, 559-560, 563, 565, 570, 577, 589, 634-5, 646, 653, 679, 709-713, 715-6, 718

*Shuo-wen Chieh-tzŭ 說文解字 (Explanation of Script and Elucidation of Characters). Dictionary comp. ca. A.D. 100 by Hsü Shen 許慎 in 15 sects., each divided into 2 pts. SPTK ed.: 33, 487

Spring and Autumn Annals, see Ch'un Ch'iu

Ssŭ-k'u Ch'üan-shu Tsung-mu T'i-yao 四庫全書總目提要 (Critical Catalogue of Complete Writings in the Four Divisions). The best annotated bibliography of Chinese writings, comp. in 200 ch. by a large group of scholars and completed in 1782 under imperial auspices. Shanghai: Ta Tung 大東 Book Co., 1930: 90-91

Ssŭ-ma Hsiang-ju 司馬相如 (ca. 179-117 B.C.), *Ta-jen Fu* 大人賦 (Prose-poem on the Great Man): 717

Su Wen 素問 (Plain Questions). 24 ch. Portion of the Han medical work, *Huang-ti Nei-ching* (which see): 716, 719

Su Yü, see under Tung Chung-shu

Sui Shu 隋書 (History of the Sui Dynasty). Comp. by Wei Cheng 魏徵 (580-643) and others in 85 ch. TW ed.: 89, 133-4, 408, 426

Sung Kao Seng Chuan 宋高僧傳 (Sung Compilation of Biographies of Eminent Buddhist Monks). Comp. by Tsan-ning 贊寧 (919-1001) in 30 ch. TT no. 2061 (50. 709-900). See also *Kao Seng Chuan*, and under Tao-hsüan: 340, 353, 385, 387

Sung Shih 宋史 (History of the Sung Dynasty). Comp. (traditionally) by T'o-t'o 脫脫 (1313-55) and others in 496 ch. TW ed.: 434-5, 440, 452-3, 477-8, 498-9, 534, 592-3

Sung-Yüan Hsüeh-an, see under Huang Tsung-hsi

Sūtra Spoken by the Sixth Patriarch, see *Liu-tsu Ta-shih Fa-pao T'an-ching*

Suzuki, D.T., *Essays on Zen Buddhism*. 1st, 2nd and 3rd series. London: Luzac & Co., 1927, 1933, 1934. See also under *Mahāyāna-śraddhotpāda Śāstra*: 388

Ta-ch'eng Chih-kuan Fa-men 大乘止觀法門 (Mahāyāna Method of Cessation and Contemplation). 4 ch. Attributed to Hui-ssŭ 慧思 (515-577), but actually later. TT no. 1924 (46.641-664): 360-384

*Ta Hsüeh 大學 (Great Learning). Short Confucian work showing affinities with the thought of Hsün Tzŭ (whom see), and now constituting chap. 39 of the *Li Chi* (which see). Refs. to transl. of Legge in SBE, vol. 28, pp. 411-424. See also Hughes, E.R.: 4, 410, 412, 416, 418, 420-3, 446, 499, 505, 527, 529, 538, 559-561, 599-600, 602-3, 605-7, 612-3, 615, 628, 631, 634-6, 646, 664

*Ta Tai Li Chi 大戴禮記 (Book of Rites of the Elder Tai). Traditionally said to have been comp. in 85 chaps. by the elder Tai, Tai Te 德 (1st century B.C.), and then reduced by his nephew, Tai Sheng 聖, to the work in 46 chaps. now known as the *Li Chi* (which see). On the authorship and dating of these two comps. see R.P. Kramers, *K'ung Tzŭ Chia Yü, the School Sayings of Confucius* (Leiden: E. J. Brill, 1950), pp. 130 ff. Refs. to Richard Wilhelm, transl., *Li Gi, das Buch der Sitte des älteren und jüngeren Dai*. Jena: E. Diederichs, 1930: 54, 657, 983

*Tai Chen 戴震 (1723-77), *Meng-tzŭ Tzŭ-yi Su-cheng* 孟子字義疏證 (General Survey of the Meaning of the Mencius). Referred to as *Meaning of Mencius*. 3 ch. Printed as a supplement in Hu Shih (whom see), *Tai Tung-yüan ti Che-hsüeh* 東原的哲學 (The Philosophy of Tai Tung-yüan). Shanghai: Commercial Press, 1927: 651-671

——, *Tai Tung-yüan Chi* 集 (Collected Writings of Tai Chen). Referred to as *Writings*. 12 ch. SPTK ed.: 651, 654, 661

——, *Yüan Shan* 原善 (On the Nature of Goodness). Referred to as *Nature of Goodness*. 3 ch. Printed in Hu Shih, *op. cit.*: 651, 657, 663, 666, 672

See also under Freeman, Mansfield

T'ai-p'ing Yü-lan 太平御覽. Encyclopedia completed in 977 by Li Fang 李昉 and others in 1000 ch.: 12

T'an Ssŭ-t'ung 譚嗣同 (1865-98), *Jen Hsüeh* 仁學 (Science of Love). 2 ch. Japanese movable type ed. of 1902: 692-705

T'ang Yung-t'ung, "Wang Pi's New Interpretation of the *I Ching* and *Lun-yü*," transl. by Walter Liebenthal, *Harvard Journal of Asiatic Studies*, vol. 10 (1947), pp. 124-161. See also Liebenthal, Walter; Wang Pi: 179

Tao-an 道安 (312-385), Introduction to his Commentary on the *Ānāpāna Sūtra* (Sūtra on Breathing) 安般經注序. Preserved in *Ch'u San-tsang Chi-chi* (which see under Seng-yu), 6.43: 242

Tao-hsüan 道宣 (596-667), *Hsü Kao Seng Chuan* 續高僧傳 (Further Biographies of Eminent Buddhist Monks). 30 ch. TT no. 2060 (50.425-707). See also *Kao Seng Chuan*; *Sung Kao Seng Chuan*: 293

——, *Kuang Hung-ming Chi* 廣弘明集 (Further Collection of Essays on Buddhism). 30 ch. TT no. 2103 (52.97-361). See also under Seng-yu: 274, 284, 292

Tao Te Ching, see *Lao-tzŭ*

Ts'ai Ch'en 蔡沈 (1167-1230), *Ching-shih Chih-yao* 經世指要 (Important Principles in the Cosmological Chronology). A study of Shao Yung's *Huang-chi Ching-shih* (which see under Shao Yung). Contained in *Hsing-li Ta-ch'üan*, 8.1 (which see): 454

Ts'an-t'ung-ch'i, see *Chou Yi Ts'an-t'ung-ch'i*

Ts'ao Tung Erh-shih Lu 曹洞二師錄 (Records of the Two Teachers Ts'ao and Tung). Comp. in 1752 in 1 ch. by Japanese Buddhist monk E-in 慧印 (died 1764). TT no. 1987A (47.526-536): 403

Tso Chuan, see *Ch'un Ch'iu*

Tu Yen, "Biography of Wang T'ung," see under Wang T'ung

*Tung Chung-shu 董仲舒 (179?-104? B.C.), *Ch'un-ch'iu Fan-lu* 春秋繁露 (Luxuriant Dew of the Spring and Autumn Annals). 17 ch. with 82 chaps. Refs. to Su Yü 蘇輿 (died 1914), ed., *Ch'un-ch'iu Fan-lu Yi-cheng* 義證. Dated 1910 inside title page, but contains preface by Wang Hsien-ch'ien 王先謙 (1842-1917) dated 1914.

See also Franke, Otto; Woo, Kang; Yao, Shan-yu: 16-17, 19-25, 27-40, 42-43, 46-56, 58-62, 66-68, 71-82, 85-87, 90

Tung-shan Liang-chieh Ch'an-shih Yü-lu 洞山良价禪師語錄 (Recorded Conversations of the Ch'an Teacher Liang-chieh of Tung-shan). Comp. in 1 ch. by Yüan-hsin 圓信 (1571-1646) and Kuo Ning-chih 郭凝之 (became *chü-jen* in period of 1621-27). TT no. 1986B (47.519-526): 404-5

Tz'u-hai 辭海 (Sea of Phrases). Dictionary in 2 vols. Shanghai: Chung-hua 中華 Book Co., 1937: 128, 155

Tz'u-yüan 源 (Origin of Phrases). Dictionary in 3 vols. Shanghai: Commercial Press, 1915-31: 125

Vasubandhu, see under Hsüan-tsang

Vijñapti-mātratā-siddhi, see under Hsüan-tsang; K'uei-chi

Wang Chi 王畿 (1498-1583), *Lung-hsi Ch'üan-chi* 龍溪全集 (Complete Works of Wang Chi). 22 ch. Ed. of Wan-li period (1573-1620): 623-7

Wang Chih 王制 (Royal Regulations). Treatise now constituting chap. 3 of the *Li Chi* (which see). Refs. to transl. of Legge in SBE, vol. 27, pp. 209-248: 706, 710-3, 715, 718

*Wang Ch'ung 王充 (A.D. 27-ca. 100), *Lun Heng* 論衡 (Critical Essays). Completed probably in A.D. 82 or 83 in 30 ch. with 85 chaps. Refs. to Engl. transl. of Alfred Forke, *Lun Heng*. 2 vols. London: Luzac & Co., 1907; Berlin: Georg Reimer, 1911. Chaps., however, are cited according to their original numbering, rather than as re-arranged by Forke: 33, 151-168, 678

Wang Fu-chih 王夫之 (1619-92), *Chou-yi Nei-chuan* 周易內傳 (Inner Commentary on the Chou Changes). 6 ch. Contained in *Ch'üan-shan Yi-shu* 船山遺書 (Preserved Writings of Wang Fu-chih). 150 ch. Ed. of 1865: 696

——, *Chou-yi Wai-chuan* 外傳 (Supplementary Commentary on the Chou Changes). 7 ch. Contained in *ibid.*: 642-3

——, *Tu Ssu-shu Ta-ch'üan-shuo* 讀四書大全說 (Remarks on Reading the Four Books). Referred to as *Remarks on the Four Books*. 10 ch. Contained in *ibid.*: 641-2, 648-9

Wang Ken 王艮 (1483-1540), *Wang Hsin-chai Hsien-sheng Yi-chi* 王心齋先生遺集 (Preserved Writings of Wang Ken). 5 ch. Tung-t'ai Yüan-shih 東臺袁氏 movable type edition of 1912: 624, 628

——, *Wang Tao Lun* 王道論 (Treatise on the Kingly Way). Contained in *ibid.*, ch. 1: 628

Wang Pi 王弼 (226-249), *Chou Yi* 周易 (Chou Changes). Wang's ed. of the *Yi Ching* (which see), with his own comm. and further comm. by Han Po 韓伯 (died ca. 385), in 10 ch. SPTK ed.: 180-184, 205

——, *Chou Yi Lüeh-li* 略例 (Outline of the System Used in the Chou Changes). Contained in his *Chou Yi*, ch. 10: 180, 184, 186

——, *Lao-tzŭ*. Wang's ed. of the *Lao-tzŭ* (which see), with his own comm., in 2 ch. WYT ed.: 181-3, 189, 194, 205
See also T'ang Yung-t'ung; Wright, Arthur F.

Wang Shou-jen 王守仁 (1472-1529), *Chu-tzŭ Wan-nien Ting-lun* 朱子晚年定論 (Doctrines Reached by the Master Chu in Later Life). Contained in *Wang Wen-ch'eng Kung Ch'üan-shu* 文成公全書 (Complete Works of Wang Shou-jen). 38 ch. Refs. to Frederick Goodrich Henke, transl., *The Philosophy of Wang Yang-ming*. Chicago & London: Open Court Publishing Co., 1916: 605, 621-2

——, *Ch'uan-hsi Lu* 傳習錄 (Record of Instructions). 3 ch. Contained in *ibid.* Refs. to Henke, *op. cit.*: 602-4, 607-618, 621

——, *Shu* 書 (Letters). 3 ch. Contained in *ibid.* Refs. to Henke, *op. cit.*: 586, 606-8, 618-620

——, *Ta Hsüeh Wen* 大學問 (Questions on the Great Learning). Contained in *ibid.* Refs. to Henke, *op. cit.*: 598-603, 606, 613

——, *Yang-ming Chi-yao* 陽明集要 (Important Selections from Wang Shou-jen). 15 ch. Refs. to Henke, *op. cit.*: 596-8
See also under Chang Yü-chüan; Wang Tch'ang-tche

Wang Tch'ang-tche, *La philosophie morale de Wang Yang-ming*. Shanghai: Variétés sinologiques no. 63, 1936. See also Wang Shou-jen: 598

Wang T'ung 王通 (584-617), *Chung-shuo* 中說 (Middle Sayings). 10 ch. Though attributed to Wang, this work was probably comp. by his followers. It contains a biography of Wang by Tu Yen 杜淹 (died 628). SPTK ed.: 407-8

——, *Yüan Ching* 元經 (First Classic). 10 ch. A chronicle history written in imitation of the *Ch'un Ch'iu* (which see), and covering the period A.D. 290-589. Though attributed to Wang, the work today bearing this name is probably a forgery by Juan Yi 阮逸 (11th century): 407

Watters, Thomas, *On Yuan Chwang's Travels in India, 629-645 A.D.* London: Oriental Translation Fund, new series, vols. XIV-XV, 1904-05. See also Hsüan-tsang: 299

Wen-tzŭ 文子. 2 ch. Attributed to a follower of Lao Tzŭ, but probably written considerably later Refs. to *Ssŭ-pu Pei-yao* 四部備要 ed. (Shanghai, Chung Hua 中華 Book Co.): 288

Woo, Kang, *Les trois théories politiques du Tch'ouen Ts'ieou, interprétées par Tong Tchong-chou d'après les principes de l'école de Kong-yang.* Paris: E. Leroux, 1932. See also *Kung-yang Chuan*; Tung Chung-shu: 16-17, 59, 69, 82

Wright, Arthur F., "Fu I and the Rejection of Buddhism," *Journal of the History of Ideas*, vol. 12 (1951), 33-47: 292

——, Review of A. A. Petrov, *Wang Pi (226-249): His Place in the History of Chinese Philosophy* (in Russian; Moscow, 1936), in *Harvard Journal of Asiatic Studies*, vol. 10 (1947), 75-80: 179

Wu-hsing Ta-yi 五行大義 (Great Meaning of the Five Elements). Written by Hsiao Chi 蕭吉 (died ca. 615) in 5 ch. TSCC ed., vols. 695-696: 23

Yang Chien 楊簡 (1140-1226), *Chi Yi* 己易 (The Self and the Book of Changes). Contained in *Tz'ŭ-hu Yi-shu* 慈湖遺書 (Preserved Writings of Yang Chien). 18 plus 2 supplementary ch. Ta-yu Shan-fang 大酉山房 ed. of Kuang-hsü period (1875-1907): 580-2

——, *Chüeh-ssŭ Chi* 絶四記 (Essay on the Four Abstentions). Contained in *ibid.*: 582-4

——, *Tz'ŭ-hu Yi-shu* (see above): 579-580, 591
   See also under Lu Chiu-yüan

"Yang Chu Chapter," see under *Lieh-tzŭ*

Yang Hsiung 楊雄 (53 B.C.-A.D. 18), *Fa Yen* 法言 (Model Sayings). 13 ch. SPTK ed. German transl. of Erwin von Zach, *Sinologische Beiträge IV, Yang Hsiung's Fa Yen* (Batavia: Drukkerij Lux, 1939), not available for consultation: 138, 146-150

——, *T'ai Hsüan* 太玄 (Great Mystery). 10 ch. with 15 chaps. SPTK ed.: 137-146

——, *T'ai Hsüan Fu* 賦 (Prose-poem on the Great Mystery). Contained in ch. 4 of the *Ku Wen Yüan* 古文苑 (Park of Ancient Literature), anonymously comp. anthology of poetry and prose covering 1st 5 centuries A.D. SPTK ed.: 138

Yao, Shan-yu, "The Cosmological and Anthropological Philosophy of Tung Chung-shu," *Journal of the North China Branch of the Royal Asiatic Society*, vol. 73 (Shanghai, 1948), 40-68: 16

Yen Chih-t'ui 顔之推 (531-591 or later), *Yen-shih Chia-hsün* 氏家訓 (Yen's Instructions for the Family). 2 ch. with 20 chaps. SPTK ed.: 169

Yen Yüan 顏元 (1635-1704), *Ts'un-hsing Pien* 存性編 (Treatise on the Preservation of the Nature). 2 ch. Contained in *Chi-fu Ts'ung-shu* 畿輔叢書, comp. by Wang Hao 王灝 and printed in 1879: 633, 636-9, 644-6

———, *Ts'un-hsüeh Pien* 學編 (Treatise on the Preservation of Learning). 4 ch. Contained in *ibid.*: 632-3
See also under Freeman, Mansfield

Yi-ch'eng Fo-hsing Hui-jih Ch'ao 一乘佛性慧日抄 (Transcript of the Single-vehicle Buddha-nature Wisdom). 1 ch. Identity of its Japanese author uncertain. The text gives the name only as Sō, which may be an abreviation for Ensō 圓宗, a monk who died in 883. TT no. 2297 (70.173-194): 271

Yi Ching 易經 (Book of Changes). Also known as *Chou Yi* (Chou [Dynasty] Changes). Consists of an original divination text, dealing with 64 hexagrams and probably dating from early Chou dynasty, followed by series of philosophical appendices, probably composed in early years of Han dynasty. Refs. to transl. of Legge in SBE, vol. 16. Appendices cited according to Legge's numbering. Also German transl. of Richard Wilhelm, rendered into English by Cary F. Baynes under title: *The I Ching or Book of Changes*. 2 vols. New York: Bollingen Series XIX, Pantheon Books, 1950: 8, 14-15, 18-19, 41, 44, 88, 90-92, 95-102, 106, 112-3, 119-120, 124, 134, 137-8, 141-2, 146-7, 152-3, 169, 180-3, 186-9, 205, 242-3, 255, 273, 288, 407-8, 410, 416, 418-421, 423, 425-9, 437-8, 440, 442, 445-6, 448-9, 451-4, 458-461, 466, 469, 474-5, 478-9, 481, 484, 488, 493, 499, 502, 505, 508-511, 514, 520, 524, 527, 534, 546, 549, 564, 575-6, 581, 589-591, 625, 636, 641-2, 650, 654-5, 658, 679, 692-4, 696-7, 699-700, 702, 709, 715-6, 718-9

Yi-hsing 一行 (673-727), *Kua Yi* 卦義 (Meaning of the Hexagrams). Contained in *Hsin T'ang Shu*, ch. 27a (which see): 110-1, 114-7

Yi Li 逸禮 (Dispersed Rituals). A series of "ancient text" treatises in 39 sects. on the *Li* or *Rites*, purportedly recovered during the Han dynasty: 136

Yi-lo Yüan-yüan Lu, see under Chu Hsi

Yi-wei Chi-lan-t'u 易緯稽覽圖 (Apocryphal Treatise on the Changes: Consultation Charts). Referred to as *Chi-lan-t'u*. 2 ch. This and the next two items were probably written in 1st century B.C., and have comms. by Cheng Hsüan 鄭玄 (127-200). WYT ed.: 106-109, 114

Yi-wei Ch'ien-tso-tu 乾鑿度 (Apocryphal Treatise on the Changes: A Penetration of the Laws of Ch'ien). Referred to as *Ch'ien-tso-tu*. 2 ch. WYT ed.: 97-105, 122-3

Yi-wei Shih-lei-mou 是類謀 (Apocryphal Treatise on the Changes: Classified Deliberations). 1 ch. WYT ed.: 107

Yü Fan, see under Li Ting-tso

Yüan-wu Fo-kuo Ch'an-shih Yü-lu 圓悟佛果禪師語錄. (Recorded Conversations of the Ch'an Teacher Yüan-wu Fo-kuo). Comp. in 1134 by Shao-lung 紹隆 and others in 20 ch. TT no. 1997 (47.713-810): 402

*Yüeh Ling 月令 (Monthly Commands). 3rd century B.C. almanac comprising sect. 1 of ch. 1-12 of *Lü-shih Ch'un Ch'iu* (which see), and chap. 4 of *Li Chi* (which see). Refs. to transl. of Legge in SBE, vol. 27, pp. 249-310: 13-15, 88, 113-4, 119-20, 533

Yüeh-wei Hsieh-t'u-cheng 樂緯叶圖徵 (Apocryphal Treatise on Music: A Graphic Representation of its Harmonies). This and the next item were probably written in 1st century B.C., but are now preserved only in re-collected fragments. Contained in YHSFCYS, 54.53-61: 127-8

Yüeh-wei Tung-sheng-yi 動聲儀 (Apocryphal Treatise on Music: Meaning of Movements and Sounds). YHSFCYS, 54.41-48: 127

INDEX

For almost all of the books and articles cited in the main text, see the Bibliography. Those few works listed here are very largely ones that are no longer extant today, or are preserved only through fragmentary quotations in other works.

In order to reduce as much as possible the number of Chinese characters required in this Index for Chinese names and terms, they have been omitted in the following cases:

(a) When the characters have already been given in the main text, in which case an asterisk (*), appearing before a page number in this Index, indicates the specific place in the main text where they will be found.

(b) When the characters have already appeared in the Index of Vol. I, in which case this fact is indicated in the present Index by the annotation "(I)," appended to the entry in question.

(c) When the characters are those for dynasties and states, or for their rulers, in which case, being readily available in other works of reference, they have been omitted here.

(d) When two or more successive entries begin with the same Chinese syllable, in which case the character for this syllable is not repeated under the second entry. For example, under the two consecutive entries Chang Chan and Chang Ch'ih, the character for Chang appears only under Chang Chan, but is omitted under Chang Ch'ih, where only the character for Ch'ih is given.